LITERATURE, CLASS, AND CULTURE

AN ANTHOLOGY

Paul Lauter
Trinity College

Ann Fitzgerald
American Museum of Natural History

THE LONGMAN LITERATURE AND CULTURE SERIES

General Editor: Charles I. Schuster, University of Wisconsin—Milwaukee

New York   San Francisco   Boston
London   Toronto   Sydney   Tokyo   Singapore   Madrid
Mexico City   Munich   Paris   Cape Town   Hong Kong   Montreal

Acquisitions Editor: Liza Rudneva
Marketing Manager: Carlise Paulson
Cover Design: John Callahan
Cover Photo: PhotoDisc
Text Design: David Munger, The Davidson Group
Electronic Page Makeup: Dianne Hall
Senior Manufacturing Buyer: Dennis J. Para
Printer and Binder: The Maple-Vail Book Manufacturing Group
Cover Printer: Coral Graphic Services, Inc.

Library of Congress Cataloging-in-Publication Data

Literature, class, and culture : an anthology / Paul Lauter, Ann Fitzgerald.
    p. cm. -- (Longman literature and culture series)
  Includes bibliographical references and index.
  ISBN 0-321-01163-5
    1. Social classes--United States--Literary collections. 2. American literature.
  I. Lauter, Paul. II. Fitzgerald, Ann, 1947- III. Series

  PS509.S46 L58 2001
  810.9'335--dc21

                                                                    00-038992

Please visit our website at http://www.awl.com

ISBN 0-321-01163-5

12345678910—MA—03020100

For Constance Coiner (1948–1996),

Our Comrade

Contents

II CLOTHES MAKE THE WOMAN: THE SOCIAL DIMENSIONS OF CLASS 179

III "BETWEEN THE WORKERS AND THE OWNERS": CLASS CONFLICT 469

CONTENTS BY GENRE

POEMS

Stories

NOVEL EXCERPTS

Essays

AUTOBIOGRAPHIES

SPEECH

SONG

FOREWORD

*If an answer does not give rise
to a new question from itself,
it falls out of the dialogue.*
—Mikhail Bakhtin

The Longman Literature and Culture Series, of which this volume is a part, presents thoughtful and diverse approaches to the teaching of literature. Each is devoted to a special topic and designed for classes ranging from composition courses with a literature emphasis to introductory courses in literature to literature courses that focus on special topics, American studies, and cultural studies courses. Although the selections in each volume can be considered in terms of their formal literary properties, the power of these works also derives from their ability to induce students to read, re-read, think, sort out ideas, and connect personal views to the explicit and implicit values expressed in the literary works. In this way, the Longman Literature and Culture Series teaches critical analysis and critical thinking, abilities that will serve all students well, regardless of their majors.

Popular Fiction focuses on prose fiction through the exploration of many types of fiction not ordinarily studied in the college classroom. *Literature and the Environment; Literature, Class, and Culture; Literature, Race, and Ethnicity;* and *Literature and Gender* are all multigenre, with thematic clusters of readings exploring the central topic of the individual anthologies. These thematic clusters create series of links, allusions, and inflections among a wide variety of texts, and in this way, invite students to read actively and think critically. Meaningful contexts for the readings are provided by an introduction to each volume as well as chapter introductions and headnotes for every selection. An Instructor's Manual is also available for each anthology. These anthologies can be used in combination with each other, individually, and with other texts to suit the focus of the course.

- *Popular Fiction: An Anthology*, by Gary Hoppenstand (Michigan State University), is a collection of historical and contemporary works of prose fiction, including such authors as Edgar Allan Poe, Janet Dailey, Tony Hillerman, Walter Mosely, Stephen King, and Octavia Butler, and representing five popular genres: detective, romance, adventure, horror, and science fiction.

- *Literature and the Environment: A Reader on Nature and Culture*, by Lorraine Anderson, Scott Slovic (University of Nevada, Reno), and John P. O'Grady (Boise State University), is a thematic multigenre anthology that explores our relationship to nature and the role literature can play in shaping a culture responsive to environmental realities. It includes early writers such as John Muir, Henry David Thoreau, and Mary Austin, alongside contemporary voices such as Gary Snyder and Terry Tempest Williams.

- *Literature, Class, and Culture: An Anthology*, by Paul Lauter (Trinity College) and Ann Fitzgerald (American Museum of Natural History), is a consideration of class in "classless" America, including such authors as Edith Wharton, F. Scott Fitzgerald, Woody Guthrie, Alice Childress, Jimmy Santiago Baca, and Dorothy Allison. The selections allow students to better understand their own economic, political, and psychological contexts through learning about the ways in which social class and "class consciousness" have been experienced and changed over time in America.

- *Literature, Race, and Ethnicity: Contested American Identities*, by Joseph Skerrett (University of Massachusetts, Amherst), invites students to examine the history, depth, and persistence of the complex cultural attitudes toward race and ethnicity in America. The selections span from the late 1700s to the present, including a variety of genres from poems and letters to fiction and autobiography, essays, speeches, advertisements, and historical documents, with works by such writers as Thomas Jefferson, Frederick Douglass, Jacob Riis, Henry James, Langston Hughes, Maxine Hong Kingston, Constantine Panunzio, Lorna Dee Cervantes, Lawson Inada, and Louise Erdrich.

- *Literature and Gender: Thinking Critically Through Fiction, Poetry, and Drama*, by Robyn Wiegman (University of California, Irvine) and Elena Glasberg (California State University, Los Angeles), assembles a provocative array of literary texts by such writers as Charlotte Perkins Gilman, Ernest Hemingway, Adrienne Rich, Tobias Wolff, Sherman Alexie, and Rita Dove, which explore the links between cultural beliefs, social institutions, sexual roles, and personal identity.

Although no single anthology, or series for that matter, can address the full complexity of literary expression, these anthologies do hope to engage students in the critical process of analysis by connecting literary texts to current social and cultural debates. In addition, these anthologies frame literature in pedagogically innovative ways, ways that will enable those students who find literature difficult to read, who think meaning is somehow locked inside a text, to critically engage with issues of interpretation, biography, and context. In this way, students begin to see that literature is a cultural expression that emerges from a complex consideration of and response to the world they share with the writers they read.

    Very often, literary texts invite discussion in the classroom of explosive issues, provoking students to argue about the sexism of a short story or the racism expressed by a character. These anthologies, however, encourage students to take a step backward so that they can interrogate the cultural contexts of diverse works of literature. This shift away from the personal and toward the cultural should invite thoughtful and considered classroom discussion. Once students perceive this cultural frame, they will be better able to engage with texts, to see them as both profound expressions of the ordinary and eloquent achievements written by real people living in real time.

In addition, no set of anthologies can hope to resolve completely what is intended by the two central terms that anchor this discussion: "literature" and "culture." One of the most exciting contemporary discussions in English departments today centers on the very definition of literature: what it is, what it excludes, and what makes it work. If figuring out what we mean by "the literary" is difficult, determining the definition of "culture" is probably impossible. Like "nature," a term that John Stuart Mill analyzed over a hundred years ago, "culture" seems to designate everything or nothing at all. Is it something we make or does it make us? Is culture a neutral term designating human social activity, or something akin to class and status, a quality that marks you as either refined or vulgar, well-bred or common?

Not that we presume to have the correct answers or even all the appropriate questions. We realize that both the questions and the answers will be tentative and exploratory. Literature, it seems to all of us involved in this series, demands a willingness to maintain uncertainty, to probe multiple possibilities. It invites analysis and demands interpretation. It provokes conversations. This is the intention of the Longman Literature and Culture Series: to invite readings and rereadings of texts and contexts, of literature within the cultural and culture within the literary. Rather than answers, these anthologies pose questions and invitations.

Crafted to the vision of the individual editors, *Popular Fiction; Literature and the Environment; Literature, Class, and Culture; Literature, Race, and Ethnicity;* and *Literature and Gender* present an extraordinary range of material in such a way as to unsettle previous readings and provoke new ones. We hope the Longman Literature and Culture Series provides a welcoming invitation to all students to see that literature is deeply reflective of the fabric of everyday life.

CHARLES I. SCHUSTER
General Editor
University of Wisconsin, Milwaukee

ACKNOWLEDGMENTS

The editors would like to thank the reviewers of the manuscript and a number of other colleagues who contributed substantially to creating this book. They include Constance Coiner of SUNY Binghamton—to whom this book is dedicated; Renny Christopher, California State University-Stanislaus; Joanne Ferreira, SUNY New Paltz; Peggy Gifford; Donna F. Grover, Bard College; Laura Hapke, Pace University; Mike Hill, Marymount Manhattan College; Sherry Linkon, Youngstown State University; Geraldine A. Murphy, City College, CUNY; Eric Shocket, Hampshire College; Seth Clark Silberman, Maryland College of Art and Design; Carolyn E. Whitson, Metropolitan State University; and Janet Zandy, Rochester Institute of Technology. The groundbreaking work of Nicholas Coles and Peter Oresick was a source of instruction and knowledge for us. We also wish to thank our patient and helpful editors, including Katharine Glynn, Ruth Halikman, Lisa Moore, and Liza Rudneva. Anyone who works in the intellectual and social space with which this book is concerned owes an enormous debt to Jack and Tillie Olsen, without whose writing and inspiration this book would not exist.

INTRODUCTION

Most Americans have been taught to disbelieve in class. We like to say that no such thing as real class divisions exist—at least here in the U.S.A. Elsewhere, they may, like in the old (European or Asian) worlds. But here, almost everybody is, or should be, "middle class," and ideas about class differences, much less class conflict, smack of . . . well, communism or something equally alien and passé. That, at least, is where many discussions about "class" begin and end.

It's odd, though—even our airplanes and trains have what they call different "classes" of service, and life in the "first-class" cabin is surely different from that back in "economy," much less on the Greyhound bus. People do live in enormously different circumstances in America: the trailer park outside Birmingham bears little resemblance to the homes of Grosse Pointe outside Detroit. The children from those communities attend quite different schools with vastly different facilities. Most go to different colleges—assuming those from the trailer park get to college at all. And they are likely to get very different kinds of jobs that produce significantly different incomes. For some, eating at Burger King is a treat and Red Lobster an occasion; for others, Ruth Chris is a standard, and The Four Seasons an available pleasure. Seats in the end zone of the Texas Stadium for a Cowboys' game are far away indeed from the sky boxes. You could easily construct lists to characterize the lives of inhabitants of areas like Grosse Pointe, Palos Verde, or Trump Tower in New York, on the one hand, or on the other, the South Bronx, Atlantic City away from the casinos, or the mining "hollers" of Harlan County, U.S.A.

To be sure, some people from that latter group of places will get into top-notch colleges, obtain excellent, high-paying jobs, buy the 15-room, six-bath house in Westport, join the country club, and otherwise travel up the class ladder. A few. And it's true that class alone does not entirely explain the vast differences we have been pointing to: after all, race and gender and ethnicity figure heavily into matters such as educational opportunity, income, and living circumstances. But when all is said and done, one has to acknowledge that very significant distinctions of what has to be called "class" mark American society. But what, then, explains or determines class? And why has denial of class been such a defining feature of American life and ways of thinking, a feature that helps distinguish the United States from Indonesia, India, Argentina, Great Britain, or any other country in which class divisions are acknowledged and often rigidly enforced?

These questions have taken on some urgency in recent years as the gap between the haves and have nots, or even the have-somes, has daily widened, and as the possibility of a good, stable job has for many come to seem a picture from days gone by. A 1999 study by the Center on Budget and Policy Priorities, "The Widening Income Gulf," showed that, as a New York *Times* story (September 5, 1999) put it, "the richest 2.7 million Americans, the top 1 percent, will have as many after-tax dollars to spend as the bottom 100 million." As the impact of the global economy on American workplaces has registered, many people have found themselves—even in the midst of economic expansion—facing "downsizing," lower-level jobs in service industries, part-time or temporary employment, or, in some recent years, a long search for any job. In fact, the bottom fifth of Americans in terms of income had less to spend in 1999 than they did in 1977. On the other hand, according to the CBPP report, "the top 20 percent of households" have secured an "average after-tax income gain of 43 percent between 1977 and 1999." As a result, in 1999, these households had "slightly more income than the other 80 percent of households combined." Translated into dollars, according to the report, "the top 1 percent of the population will have average . . . after-tax income of $516,000," the top fifth $102,300, as compared with $8,800 for the lowest fifth of the population. And, the report goes on, "wealth is much more concentrated than income, with the wealthiest 1 percent of households owning nearly 40 percent of the nation's wealth in 1995. The bottom 80 percent of households owned just 16 percent of the nation's wealth. . . ." Such data suggest that to think about the future, about what shapes or even limits our academic and work choices, it is useful, indeed necessary, to grasp the ways in which social class and "class consciousness" are produced and experienced and how they change over time. Understanding class provides a fuller perspective on the economic, political, and psychological realities that frame all of our life experiences.

Still, we have found that class remains the unaddressed member of that now-famous trio, "race, gender, class." Over the last two decades, there has been far more widespread acknowledgment and open discussion of race and gender, and indeed, sexuality, in classrooms, in the media, even in corporate boardrooms, while class has generally remained the silenced subject. To raise the specter of class, we are told, engenders class conflict—surely un-American. Besides, to the extent that class is addressed, it has been portrayed as an attribute specifically of the working class, a species viewed through a lens pointed down, or toward the past. Often, we have learned to associate the "working class" with a time gone by, the nineteenth century or the Great Depression of the 1930s. Likewise, many people identify working-class activism, like job actions, as an historical phenomenon and therefore, as Constance Coiner put it, don't consider strikes or other collective mobilizations as activities "in which they themselves might engage." So class realities are denied, deflected, mystified.

Even in classrooms, many people seem afraid to talk about class, whatever their own might be; such conversation often raises awkward and embarrassed silences. It is one thing, as the movements of the 1960s and 1970s emphasized, to be "black and be proud" or to proclaim "women's liberation," to assert self-respect in being female, or in one's sexual orientation. But to articulate, much less celebrate, one's class identity seems somehow inappropriate. To acknowledge economic difference and economic privilege with their entourage of conflicting social and cultural forms is said to be "just too personal" or too conflicted. Does a person really want others to know that one's mom works as a "nanny" for an Alzheimer's patient on Chicago's Lake Shore Drive? Or how much money one's father, an internist at the Cleveland Clinic, pays as alimony after a heavily contested divorce? Or even that you rode a taxi back and forth to your high school every day? Being working class in particular seems troublesome for many—even people whose objective circumstances might mark them as "working class" like to think of themselves as "middle class." Worse, for some, to be working class has amounted to an admission of failure. For, they think, in America one's class depends on what an individual accomplishes rather than from whom one is descended or what one inherits (is that true? are one's origins irrelevant?), and working people's lives are often tough and marked by constraints.

"Too personal," or of no great consequence? In America, the messages are dizzying. In "polite society," you don't discuss money or ask how much something costs. On the other hand, Wall Street brokers brag about their killings and celebrate publicly by treating colleagues to $1,000 bottles of wine. When is an expensive car a flashy expression of newly gotten and probably temporary wealth, and when is it a casual display of established status? At what point did jeans become a way of "dressing down" rather than the only affordable way of dressing? The study of class requires looking beyond, or through, external markers such as dress or cars or cell phones toward a consciousness and examination of the assumptions that people make about such items when they purchase or observe them.

Yet we need to start with such externals because they provide the specificity necessary to make sense of what are otherwise large generalities about class consciousness and class status. Class is in the first instance an economic and social phenomenon. It cannot be understood without examining discrepancies in living conditions, life chances, and outlook generated by real, material differences in peoples' economic standing. But class is not *only* a matter of money and power. It also cannot be understood without examining the differences in ways people think and feel. It is sometimes said that we all "have" class. A formula like "having" class or race or gender is shaped—like many notions about identity in America—on the pattern of commodities, things one possesses, like dark skin, or breasts, or Mexican ancestors. Of course, these attributes, unlike commodities, are hard to be rid of; but like commodities, they seem to play a significant role for most Americans in identifying themselves and others. Thus, dark skin identifies "African American," breasts identify female, Mexican ancestors identify Chicano or Chicana. Imitating this pattern, class comes to be seen as primarily a matter of things one possesses: a ranch in Arizona or a shack in L.A., a Mercedes-Benz or a bus token, a Versace gown or K-mart jeans. Such objects may help to describe matters of wealth and perhaps status. But class involves a more complicated set of relationships, relationships expressed not just in possessions or even in more personal attributes—like patterns of speech and dress—but mainly in ways of feeling, thinking, and understanding. To say it another way, class involves not just what you "have" or even what you "are," but what Raymond Williams calls "a structure of feeling": how you look at the world, what you see there, how you experience what you perceive—and how all of that differs from what other groups of people look at, see, and experience. Class is not, then, a thing, but a set of relationships that change over time and in different historical circumstances. But class is also more than a matter of outlook, of "consciousness"; as we have said, it is rooted in, but not equivalent to, the material conditions of our lives.

Perhaps an analogy with gender can be helpful: unlike males, females can bear and nurse children. That is a real, material distinction between the sexes. What is or should be made of that distinction is another matter altogether. It does not necessarily follow from this difference between male and female bodies that women are, for example, more "nurturing." "Gender" is the name given to the forms of behavior and the attitudes—dress, body language, other forms of expression, assumptions about propriety, and the like—generally associated with what a society names as "men" and "women." Similarly, material conditions such as jobs, income, wealth, what we own and do, situate people economically. But class consciousness—the ideas, feelings, attitudes—and the behaviors associated with one or another class are not absolutely determined, though they may be heavily influenced by, material factors. Just as the meanings of gender—being a woman, say—are not constituted entirely by the ability of females to birth and nurse children, so the meanings of class—being bourgeois, say—are not constituted entirely by one's position in the economic hierarchy.

To begin, then, with certain material factors and ideas about them, it can be helpful to see where consistency and where differences emerge in people's answers to questions such as these:

—Does your family live in a house or an apartment? Do they own or rent? Do you have your own bedroom? How do you feel about having or not having "a room of one's own"?

—Do you eat meals as a family? What do you eat, and where? Who prepares the food? Do you have responsibilities connected to meals?

—Are there many books? What books or magazines do family members read? Do family members read for entertainment or news, watch TV, or both? What TV programs are usually on in your family?

—On what does your family spend significant amounts of its money? Vacation? Car? Rent? Food?

—If your family takes vacations, to where do you go? At what kind of place do you stay?

—Do you and your friends play games or sports?

—What clothes do you and others wear around the house? What about when you get "dressed up"?

—What work do your family members and friends do? Do they (you?) own stocks or businesses?

—Where do your family members shop? For what? How do you pay for purchases?

—Was there one particular moment when you were intensely made aware of your own social class?

—What questions would you add to this list? In what order of importance would you organize it to clarify features of class difference?

Constructing such lists is not merely an exercise; it can, we believe, be quite revealing of assumptions and of "consciousness"—that is, our awareness of where we stand in today's class structure and our attitudes toward that position.

Still, such a list is only a starting point. Besides, possessions can be quite misleading. Not only do they, in countries like the United States, tend to uniformity (e.g., many people from vastly different classes wear Ralph Lauren), but the meaning of items can change sharply over time. That can be illustrated by consulting the list of living room objects compiled by Paul Fussell in his book *Class*: some objects, like Venetian blinds or aquariums, have taken on somewhat different valences over time, thus suggesting a certain instability in such supposed markers of class. Styles and fashions fluctuate, often depending less on class than upon what's "cool" or fashionable at a particular time, or upon other factors like ethnicity.

More important, construction of a list is only a beginning because the problem of understanding class does not lie in cataloguing items of consumption supposedly characteristic of different class positions. The value of making such a list depends less on what items appear on it, but in analyzing our assumptions about what is "normal" for a particular group of people in the way of a place to live, a job, and foodways and folkways. The issue, in other words, is what premises about the "normal" things of everyday life for different classes of people we all carry around, how class produces these different beliefs, and why. What is involved is what we sometimes grasp at through the vague term "lifestyle." That probably means the full repertoire of social and family relations, manners of expression, forms of talking and dressing, and the psychological and cultural phenomena, including artistic productions, that constitute everyday life.

But generally, what's really being referred to is what people consume. It is, of course, what we consume (and why) that presents one of the greatest complications in understanding class. It has been the genius of consumer capitalism to encourage us to define ourselves by what we buy and possess. The imperatives toward consumption in every area of life tend to overwhelm other definers of class consciousness. Because of the homogenization of American culture, particularly youth culture (e.g., in music, clothes, even food), the more subtle but powerful and meaningful aspects of class are masked. To own the latest pair of athletic shoes is to be in the shoes, for however fleeting a moment, of Michael Jordan or some other sports or movie idol who models them—or even the prep school son of the man who is said to "manufacture" them. Still, it's complicated. Some middle-class kids appropriate working-class styles of dress and speech to appear hip or rebellious or to provide themselves with modes of self-expression. External attributes, including commodities, can be turned to purposes different from what their producers intended.

Just what, then, is the relationship between what you own or buy and your class? Some people, following the sociologist Max Weber, would argue that what primarily marks class in a society dominated by consumer capitalism, and what shapes class consciousness, is precisely status and wealth—signaled by possessing commodities, including education and places to live—by occupation, and by access to power in the marketplace. In contradistinction, Marx and Marxists have held that class is largely determined by one's relationship to the means of production and distribution, and that factors like education and possessions are the results, not the determinants, of class position. The argument against Marx is that he had in mind a simpler model of production (we'll come back to that later) and control in which the "bourgeoisie" owned the machines the "proletariat" used to produce the world's goods. But now, it is said, the means of production and distribution are so varied and diffuse that it is difficult to define precisely one's "relationship" to them or even just who owns what, given new forms like mutual funds and stock-invested pension plans. Far easier and clearer, the argument continues, to note what people possess, and on that basis to mark them as "upper," "middle" or "lower" class. Others respond that our life in the marketplace mostly produces forms of "false consciousness"—that is, self-deluded understandings of one's class position and its consequences. Since so many items of consumption can be purchased, or at least seem to be available to people at many different levels of society, we are misled, they say, into wrongly perceiving ourselves to be situated at class levels considerably above reality and thus into identifying our interests with those "above" us in the class hierarchy. Thus, for example, many supposedly "middle-income" Americans in the $30,000–$40,000 per year range support changes in the tax laws that, in practice, favor mainly the very well heeled, those earning $300,000–$400,000 annually and more; so such middle-class folks help actually widen the gap between themselves and those far above them economically. The debate is not, therefore, an abstract one held in some library among academic social scientists. It has profound consequences in terms of government policies (as for example, with respect to tax cuts), which groups of people a particular policy benefits, what and who we vote for—or if we vote at all. How class is understood affects who pays taxes and how much, who can go to college and how much debt we accumulate in that process, and how wages are balanced against the bottom lines of businesses.

Here's another turn the debate takes: is our life as consumers in the marketplace to be seen as producing simply forms of "false consciousness"? Carolyn Steedman, whose writing is included in this book, argues that class consciousness must be understood, first, "not only as a structure of feeling that arises from the relationship of people to other people within particular modes of production"—which is a version of the traditional Marxist formula. She maintains that working-class consciousness also involves what she describes as a "proper envy of those who possess what one has been denied." She argues that "by allowing this envy entry into political understanding, the proper struggles of people in a state of dispossession to gain their inheritance might be seen not as sordid and mindless greed for the things of the marketplace, but attempts to alter a world that has produced in them states of unfulfilled desire." This is surely a powerful argument for the significance of possessions in defining class. Moreover, the potent role desire for commodities played in pulling down the Berlin Wall, not to speak of shaping everyday life (as in a story by Helena Viramontes reprinted later, "Miss Clairol"), testifies to the power of advertising, of the media, of the satellite in our backyards and the antennae on the roof of our bungalow, in helping produce such desires.

Yet the underlying metaphor of the marketplace as a single site may be misleading. The usual way of regarding consumer transactions is that we come into the marketplace differently enabled by financial standing, culture, and cleverness. Seen in this perspective, what differentiates people, as consumers, is only the weight of their pocketbooks and the shrewdness of their intellects. In fact, however, there is no single marketplace in which all people compete for goods. Rather, there are many marketplaces, to which we have in reality very different access. In America, we foster the illusion that anyone can, if he or she so wishes, shop in FAO Schwarz (as in Toni Cade Bambara's "The Lesson"), just as anyone can choose to sleep under the bridge, as Anatole France put it. Elsewhere, the lines are more forcefully drawn. Can those who work in the tanneries of Marrakech even enter its fancy leather-goods stores? Are the hard-currency shops open to most citizens of Ukraine (who not only may not have enough money but also not have access to the right kind of money)? The relative fluidity of consumer venues in the United States hides the fact that the very meanings of "the" marketplace vary widely by virtue of class.

Another part of the difficulty in talking about class derives from the fact that too often we only "study down" (to use anthropologist Laura Nader's formulation) instead of "studying up" as well. It's too easy—and misleading—to romanticize, to mock, or to mourn working-class life, as movies such as *Good Will Hunting* or *Titanic* illustrate. In selecting the texts contained in this book, we have looked not just at expressions of working-class experience and consciousness, such as those in stories by Tillie Olsen, Harvey Swados, or Junot Díaz, but also at upper-class life, as chronicled, for example, in Mary McCarthy's *The Group* and Edith Wharton's *The House of Mirth*. And also at ambiguous texts such as F. Scott Fitzgerald's "The Diamond as Big as the Ritz" and Rube Goldberg's "Art for Heart's Sake." For, just as "race" is not an attribute only of so-called "minorities," and just as "gender" is not a construction pertinent only to women or to homosexuals, so class experience and outlook is not a factor only in working-class life. Indeed, one could argue that the bourgeoisie are more explicitly class conscious than most others—read, for example, Andrew Carnegie's "The Gospel of Wealth" (in Section 3). We are all, in short, "classed."

We use that awkward formulation to call into question the idea that class can be seen primarily as a category of identity. To be sure, class deeply affects how we see ourselves and others, and it has a complex relationship to the usual markers of identity, like gender, race, ethnicity, and sexual orientation. What are the pictures we maintain in our heads of working-class or upper-class people? Do they carry gender and ethnic specificity? Traditionally in the United States, many working men have seen themselves primarily as "white" rather than as working class. Thus they have been inclined to make common cause with others seen as "white" rather than with those with whom, objectively, they share class position. In other words, "race" has marked a fracturing of class solidarity. Differently: can the pleasures of upper-middle-class American culture—the cafes, bookstores, galleries, collectible shoppes, veggie and Asian-fusion restaurants, B&B's—be perceived as somehow effete or, more dangerously, as unmanly? Can class divisions resonate along erotic lines? With what consequenses?

Again, in the late twentieth century, a larger and larger proportion of working-class people—indeed, a majority of union members—are white women and minorities. Does that fact incline some white men to avoid thinking of themselves as "working class," just as in the past the traditional image of the trade-unionist as white and male kept some women from seeing themselves as workers—and kept them and many minority people out of unions as well? Class is, in fact, heavily inflected by gender as well as by ethnicity. In her book *Landscapes for a Good Woman,* Steedman offers one explanation of why women do not fit comfortably into the traditional narrative of "wage-labour and capital," the narrative of the "exploiter and exploited, capital and proletariat" (p. 14). She writes that in a certain sense, "women are without class, because the cut and fall of a skirt and good leather shoes can take you across the river and to the other side: the fairy-tales tell you that goose-girls may marry kings" (pp. 15–16).

Then, too, class position may not survive movement across international borders: For example, many immigrants to the United States discover a wrenching contradiction between their original class training, their education, credentials, associations, and the jobs and status available to them in this country, as is dramatized in Gish Jen's "In the American Society." The linguist from China who works as a taxi driver or the nurse from Lithuania who works as a shop clerk may be caught between "old world" and "new world" determinants of class, disparities that can produce anger and despair as well as forms of self-assertion.

If, then, one's class position cannot be understood without reference to categories of identity—race, gender, nationality, sexual orientation, and the like—to what extent is class itself a category of identity? This, too, is quite a vexed question, argued over by scholars and activists. Some say that, consciously or not, class position over-whelmingly determines whatever we mean by the term "identity." Others respond that thinking about class in terms of identity is altogether misleading—and dangerous. For it would put those who identify primarily as working class, for instance, into compe-tition with those who identify primarily as black or Latino, female or gay. In fact, there is some reason to be apprehensive, lest "working-class" become the identity of last resort for those, mainly white men, left out of other identity categories. But in fact, significant numbers at least of working-class people see their identities as, in part, constituted by their class origins (see, for example, writings by Dorothy Allison and Liz Faue in this book). They argue that the culture of working-class life can be distin-guished by its bonds of loyalty to one's community, by its anger at privilege, by a lack of what many middle-class people display—that is, a sense of entitlement.

The British theorist Raymond Williams has formulated such distinctions in his book *Culture and Society* (a section of which is included in this collection). A central passage is the following:

> The crucial distinguishing element in English life since the Industrial Rev-olution is not language, not dress, not leisure—for these indeed will tend to uniformity. The crucial distinction is between alternative ideas of the nature of social relationships.
>
> "Bourgeois" is a significant term because it marks that version of social relationship which we usually call individualism: that is to say, an idea of society as a neutral area within which each individual is free to pursue his own development and his own advantage as a natural right. . . . [T]he indi-vidualist idea can be sharply contrasted with the idea that we properly asso-ciate with the working class: an idea which, whether it is called communism, socialism or cooperation, regards society neither as neutral nor as protective, but as the positive means for all kinds of development, including individual development. Development and advantage are not individually but com-monly interpreted. The provision of the means of life will, alike in produc-tion and distribution, be collective and mutual. Improvement is sought, not in the opportunity to escape from one's class, or to make a career, but in the general and controlled advance of all. The human fund is regarded as in all respects common, and freedom of access to it a right constituted by one's humanity; yet such access, in whatever kind, is common or it is nothing. Not the individual, but the whole society, will move. (pp. 325, 326)

Williams's somewhat schematic account of bourgeois and working-class culture may better fit Britain than the United States. Moreover, like most such binaries, this one—bourgeois/working-class—somewhat hides its preference for working-class culture. Moreover, it essentializes class categories, and it does so in forms drawn from mid-century British history, thus submerging the intersections of class with gender, race, ethnicity, and sexuality that we have discussed. It thus offers an overly stabilized idea of class just at a moment in which class structures are being reconstituted on a global basis. For class, like race and gender, is always being recast in changing historical circumstances, and needs to be seen as constantly in formation.

Still, Williams is useful because his formulation of the central distinction between working-class culture and identity and bourgeois culture and identity is suggestive. He offers an insight critical to opening an understanding of what one might call the ethics of class: that individualism and the market ideology it underwrites are not the only sources of value and judgment. That is especially important in a nation like the United States, where collectivity has been in low repute at least since 1623, when the Pilgrims gave up what William Bradford referred to as the "Common Course and Condition" and moved to individual, private plots of land. Williams helps us understand why so many Americans in the past—including such writers represented in this book as John Reed, Meridel LeSueur, and Langston Hughes—rejected the lures of individual advancement and committed themselves to collective projects for social change. Williams's formulation is even more useful in this post–Cold War moment, in which alternatives to consumer capitalism, like virtually all ideas about social cooperation, are in such low repute.

To be sure, it is easy to translate Williams's ideas into a formula for political defeat. To elevate collectivity over individualism, for example, is to insure that most Americans will simply reject the former. Similarly, Williams's ideas can be taken to imply a denial of the real pleasures of commodity culture, an idea criticized by Steedman. To understand the dynamics of class and culture, one must see that individuality and consumption are by no means demons, any more than they are gods. The reason a thinker like Williams is helpful, finally, is that he offers theoretical access to the ways of seeing, feeling, and thinking that he has coded as "working-class," ways of comprehending the world that are not wholly determined by the dominant ideologies of individualism and commodification central to most Americans' lives. He gives a certain content to the word "solidarity," which in the United States has come to represent working-class values and organizations, like unions; it is no accident that the song "Solidarity Forever" has come to be the unofficial anthem of American labor.

So far we have outlined some of the arguments related to class as a matter of *consumption* and as a matter of *identity*. But as we said at the outset, class cannot be understood apart from the question of *work*. And here, traditional Marxist categories of class become more useful. These have to do, basically, with one's relationship to the means of production and distribution. Are you an owner, a manager, a worker, someone who sells your labor for a wage, or—differently—your product for a price? Are you one of those "faceless" beings in the army of the unemployed or, like many working in college or for UPS, the part-time underemployed? Are you a creator of machines and their codes, a buyer or user of them, one entrusted with their care and feeding? Are you a painter in a municipal workforce, salaried at $20/hour, or a workfare recipient, doing the same job but getting only welfare checks amounting at best to $8,000 or $10,000 a year? Or are you among those who in various ways profit from how the city is "saving" so much money by undermining its unions and shifting its labor to a casual (as it is called), temporary, but permanently exploited class?

Class categories and conflicts are clear enough if we compare like those of Anzia Yezierska and Andrew Carnegie: they may speak to similar audiences, but what they say and the assumptions from which they work are strongly marked by their class positions. The implications of class are similarly easy to observe in stories such as

Lloyd Zimpel's *Foundry Foreman, Foundrymen*: the foreman, Prokop, exists in that conflicted space between the owner and the workers, and the drama of his life is how he can maintain that unsteady perch, given the boss's demands and the workers' injuries and defensive stalling. It's no surprise that the position of the "man in the middle" is unstable. For the labor many of us perform to earn a living is neither pleasant nor creative, and the less of it we can manage to do, the better. But not all work is "alienated," nor is selling our labor for a wage always and only destructive; many of us find satisfaction in our work, even if we are being terribly exploited.

Demarcations of class in terms of occupation have in fact become increasingly complicated, even unstable. First, the definitions of what constitutes "production"—as well as what is produced—and "distribution" have changed radically over the past 150 years. More and more Americans—some 30 million in 1996—work in part-time or temporary positions, especially in service or retail jobs. More and more, wealth is created by electronic exchanges rather than by the operations of machine tools. More and more, capital flows across borders while workers are stuck in dying cities like Flint or Youngstown. Terms like "working class," "middle class" and "upper class," inherently difficult, become ever more slippery to define. Managerial and professional work is now often performed by people who, in terms of salary, outlook, and self-identification, are working class, as a close look at the situations of branch bank "officers" or McDonald's shift "managers" will show. The workers on the electronic production line involved with stock transfers, bank exchanges, currency transactions, and the like are not, in any traditional sense, blue-collar employees, but while their bodies are not on the line, they perform analogous tasks in producing wealth for others. What defines their class position?

The vast expansion of part-time work, dramatized during the UPS strike in 1997, has added another confusing dimension to the problem of how work determines class identification. Are the part-time UPS drivers and freight handlers "working class"—as opposed to their full-time peers? And what of the part-time college faculty member, the "freeway flyer," who teaches as many as five classes at two or three different institutions as an "adjunct"? Such people usually have no benefits, no seniority or job security, and because they get paid as little as $1,200 per course, they can earn under $15,000 a year. College "professors" are usually thought of as "middle" or "upper middle" class, especially in terms of cultural and social attributes, but does such a categorization fit the itinerant adjunct? Or other part-time and temporary professional or managerial employees?

The study of class necessarily immerses us in a much richer understanding of work, not to speak of unemployment, hierarchy, and other aspects of industrial and post-industrial labor. As Sheryl Berg wrote in a post to the electronic discussion list of the Center for Working Class Studies, "Why should I (or anyone) care what the public may or may not think about me via my job? I do, though, even though I'm still the same person, whether I work as a college professor or as a maid, and I suspect that the rest of my culture does, too" (March 26, 1998). That is why this collection begins with a section devoted to work in its manifold forms.

We have said that what people understand about class is learned. What are the roles of educational institutions in teaching these lessons? First of all, it is important to see that colleges and universities are, like individuals, "classed." Americans pride ourselves on the idea that virtually everyone can go to college. But under what circumstances and to which colleges? While Trinity and Hartford Tech are both colleges, and located less than a mile from one another, they bear about as much resemblance as Palm Beach and Port-Au-Prince. In fact, while we continue to speak of "the university," the higher education system has increasingly been differentiated by roles, constituencies, facilities, available funds, and the like. A Harvard degree will surely provide more advantages than one from Hartford Tech. This is not meant as a put-down of community or technical colleges. It is to say that the marketplaces for which Trinity or Vassar or Harvard (think of the young women of *The Group*) are gateways are meaningfully different from the marketplaces to which Hartford Tech and Borough of Manhattan Community College open out. It is called "role differentiation" in current policy papers; an older name for it is "tracking"; a still older phrase, more accurate perhaps, is "class stratification." Still, because class borders in America are to some degree permeable, some people who begin in community colleges or without college at all do move up . . . and others—from Harvard and elsewhere—down.

At a still deeper level, every educational system teaches those it processes certain values important to the society in which schools are embedded. In the United States, schools teach the values of individualism and competition. In *Culture Against Man*, a book of 1963, Jules Henry reported his anthropologist's appraisal of elementary school training. He enters a classroom and the teacher asks "which of you nice little boys and girls would like to hang up Mr. H's coat?" Of course, all of the children eagerly begin waving their hands, whereupon the teacher must call on one to do the required task, which she could have done in the first place. But as Henry points out, a critical lesson is being reenforced in the episode, which can be seen by imagining what would happen if a child did not respond to the teacher's request: he or she would be seen as uncooperative, even deviant. By framing her question thus instead of calling on one student initially, the teacher is imposing a lesson in conformity and competition, a lesson the students absorb as what Henry terms the "noise" of the classroom. How central that lesson is may be suggested by the fact that one of the editors of this book was fired from his teaching job some years ago because he gave students in a course the option of writing a group exam and thus receiving a "collective" grade; this option was seen as antithetical to the virtues of individualism and competition, which it was his job to instill in his students. One might compare the "lessons" about class explored in Pat Dobler's poem "Field Trip to the Rolling Mill, 1950."

One further problem inhibits the study of class. Consider where, if at all, you would encounter it in the curriculum. Colleges in the United States have generally offered an attenuated approach to its study, largely restricting it to economics departments, which are primarily devoted to making businesses tick. Political economy, wherein one looks at the class-inflected intersections of political structures and economic power, remains rather an orphan in American universities. In fact, at many colleges, not a single course description in economics so much as mentions the word "class," including courses with such titles as "Poverty in America," "Labor Economics," "Industrial Organization and Public Policy," or "Urban Economics," though women and even race are occasionally referred to. While virtually every university will offer a variety of courses devoted to race and racism, to gender and sexuality, as well as to the social movements that have worked for change in such areas of life, in few does one find a course called, for example, "Class in America." To be sure, social scientists and historians, mainly those influenced by Marxism, have often provided opportunities to study class issues by tucking the subject into courses on inequality, immigration, ethnicity, social stratification, and the like. But it has often been difficult to determine where, in the American academy, one ought to study writers such as many of those in this volume, who emphasize class differences. Discussions of class rarely emerge in literature courses, even when a text as direct about the subject as Edith Wharton's *The House of Mirth* or Agnes Smedley's *Daughter of Earth* is included. And while there are programs and departments focused on women or on minorities, only within the last few years has a Center for Working Class Studies emerged, appropriately at Youngstown State University, located in a once-thriving blue-collar city.

The educational system has, then, placed certain barriers in the way of studying class. The media, a second major "teacher" in the United States, offer a related though somewhat different problem. The difficulty here arises from the largely stereotypical portraits, particularly of working-class characters, presented in the media, and especially in American movies. You might wish to try this exercise: construct images of typical class-defined men and women as they are portrayed in the media. What constitutes the characteristic portrait of a working-class man or woman? Of the very wealthy person? Are there features associated with gender, ethnicity, religion, or nationality used to define persons of a particular class? Is television different from film? In what respects? How do such portraits change over time? And do different audiences prefer different class narratives? How, for example, do video store favorites differ between South San Francisco and Russian Hill, the Central Bronx and the Upper East Side of Manhattan, Myrtle Beach and Nantucket? Are some films and some television shows aimed to capture particular class-defined segments of their markets? Answers to such questions can be based on informed speculation about the impact and meaning of media representations, on empirical data gathered from surveys, sales and rental figures, or on ethnographies and the like. The point, however, is that we can usefully construct snapshots of the media at its work constructing our ideas of class.

The media are powerful in their ability to project resonant images—that is why political candidates are so intent upon accumulating enough money to project the images they prefer, especially through television. Literary texts can, of course, embody stereotypes and clichés. But literary and other cultural texts can also provide us with opportunities to get beyond (and perhaps better understand) the sound-bite and the stereotype. Moreover, they enable us to reach through the limiting and often silencing effects of statistics to the human realities that inform quantitative descriptions. Thus, these texts enable us to situate ourselves, and our complex identities, in the world of real people. Besides, like the rest of us, writers struggle—not always successfully—to understand class dynamics; those struggles are themselves most revealing. For example, the narrators of Melville's "The Tartarus of Maids," Davis's "Life in the Iron-Mills," and Markham's "The Man with the Hoe" are all middle-class people observing aspects of working-class lives. Such narratives allow us to ask about what the speakers understand and also fail to see, whether they impose their own class perspectives on others' realities, and how their perceptions differ from those working-class people might have about their own lives. Moreover, the act of becoming a writer to some extent distances a person of working-class origins from heritage, kin, and perhaps from one's initial self. Such tensions provide much of the wonder, sadness, and humor, of works such as Steve Turner's "Night Shift in a Pickle Factory" or Kenneth Patchen's "The Orange Bears." Then, too, it is often in song and poem that the jumbled feelings associated with class conflict—rage, uncertainty, hope, envy, despair, triumph—are given shape and voice. We have ourselves found that some of these texts, to quote Frederick Douglass, give "tongue to interesting thoughts of my own soul, which had frequently flashed through my mind, and died away for want of utterance"—perhaps that will be our readers' experience, too.

At any rate, this book is intended to foster the study and discussion of class in courses primarily devoted to literature, culture, and writing. Our introduction has therefore emphasized certain cultural elements of class rather than economic considerations. We have selected a variety of texts, primarily stories, poems, songs, and some essays that embody class differences and conflicts in dramatic situations and in vivid language rather than in abstractions. But we do not want to suggest that "class" can be understood wholly as a cultural phenomenon. On the contrary, what we have been trying to suggest here, and what most of the texts that follow will in one way or another illustrate, is that class is constituted by a complex interaction of material and cultural factors, social and psychological phenomena. No single intellectual domain offers all the answers to the puzzles and tensions of class. In fact, studying class demands that we bring to bear an interdisciplinary perspective, some understanding of economics as well as of poetic discourse, a handle on social dynamics as well as on narrative. It is precisely because class remains such a protean, sometimes elusive, always conflicted concept that studying it can be so challenging, and thus rewarding.

A Note on Organization

This book is divided into four sections. The first looks at the ways in which work shapes—and is shaped by—class. Section II looks at the many ways in which daily life is fashioned by class. Here we are particularly concerned with consumption, exhibition, vacation, and social relationships of many kinds and characters. Section III focuses primarily on class conflict. Conflict is, of course, part of everyday life, occasioned sometimes by issues of personality, or religious, political, and sexual disposition. But it also derives from what we see as the fundamentally differing outlooks on the world generated by class position, as well as by the distinct interests that help to motivate people of contrasting class status. The last section of this book concerns the question of whether, or how, art is itself shaped by differences in class. In a sense, this final section concerns the relationships among the terms of the book's title, "literature," "class," and "culture."

Within each of these sections, we have tried to organize the works in two ways. Generally, they are arranged chronologically, not so much by composition as by the time period with which they deal. But we have also tried to place texts in dialogue with one another, bringing them together because they concern similar experiences—e.g., migrant labor, parents interacting with children, or contemporaneous but contrasting views of work or wealth or culture. In addition, we have placed at the beginning of each section one or two texts that exemplify some of the critical issues or themes to which the section is devoted. Our intention in these arrangements is *not* to trap readers into our frameworks, but to offer suggestive ways of enabling texts and authors to "talk" together—and to their audiences as well.

BREAD, LAND, AND STATION: WORK AND CLASS

This first section of *Literature, Class, and Culture* looks at the ways in which work shapes—and is shaped by—class. While the focus of this section is work, no section, indeed not even the largest book, could illustrate the varieties of work in which people engage. In the writings collected here, some of the workplaces—an office, a gas station, a kitchen—will be familiar to readers; others—a foundry, a brothel, a rolling mill—may not. Some of these narratives and poems reflect earlier forms of work in fields and factories; others are as contemporary as Burger King. But all involve the human interactions and the conditions of labor that make places of work also places of hope, conflict, possibility, fear, accomplishment, loss. We think the range of these texts will extend virtually any reader's experience of forms of work and of workplace relationships. A number of these texts, such as London's "The Apostate," also speak to rejecting the imperative to sell one's labor for a wage, an experience more dreamed about than enacted in most of our lives.

Our interest here, however, is not in illustrating many kinds of work, but rather in the ways in which work and class interact. Class origins can and do shape the kinds of job one can, or even might wish to, obtain. Class helps define, though it obviously does not limit, the horizons of job opportunity, even in a relatively fluid society such as that of the United States. To be sure, the relationships between one's class and the kinds of work one does—and vice versa—are less fixed than they once were, especially for new immigrants (as in Gish Jen's "In the American Society"). Moreover, race and gender critically shape not only job opportunities for most people, but ways of thinking about work and, as Eisenberg's "Hanging in Solo" suggests, the human relationships rooted in workplaces. Besides, in America nearly everyone holds as an article of faith that whatever your job, you belong to that great undifferentiated group called the "middle class."

Nevertheless, as these poems and narratives variously illustrate, what one does for a living critically affects—if it does not wholly determine—class consciousness. The experiences of class on the job, as stories such as "Foundry Foreman, Foundrymen" show, largely shape how one looks at one's fellow workers, as well as those differently situated; how, as "The Circuit" illustrates, one experiences a nation, a neighborhood, a household, even one's self. One's life on—and off—the job (even if the job is at home) is certainly not the same as one's life apart from it, but the two can hardly be pried apart, any more than mind and body.

Finally, then, these are not so much narratives or analyses of work. Rather, the diverse experiences of work presented here amount to a series of mirrors, differently configured, within which we see reflected the whole shape of human life.

SARAH N. CLEGHORN
(1876-1959)

We begin this book with a simple four-line poem by Sarah Northcliffe Cleghorn. The poem expresses two different class worlds, and it suggests in a subtle way how thinking about class requires that we consider play as well as work, the lessons of childhood as well as the status of adults, the daily routines as well as the special moments of life. In a number of ways, the poem illustrates how a "class analysis" can inform richer readings of literary and cultural texts.

Sarah Cleghorn spent much of her life in Vermont, where she was directly active in campaigns for prison reform, educational innovation, and against capital punishment. She wrote poetry and prose on behalf of pacifism, equal justice for minorities, and a democratic form of socialism. Some of the works in Cleghorn's Poems of Peace and Freedom *(1945) celebrate activists such as Harriet Tubman and Eugene Victor Debs. Her autobiography,* Threescore *(1936), discusses how she moved from her earlier sentimental and vaguely inspirational writing toward more direct and political expression of her deeply held feelings about racial and economic justice.*

THE GOLF LINKS

The golf links lie so near the mill
That almost every day
The laboring children can look out
And see the men at play.

WORKSONGS

Many of the earliest "operatives" in American factories were white women. At first, in the 1820s, they were often Yankee farm girls, who came to cities like Lawrence and Lowell to gain some experience and earn some money before they returned home to marry. That, at least, was the theory, a notion promoted by some of the mill owners, who tried to reassure the women themselves as well as their parents by housing them in regulated dormitories and offering them cultural events, lectures, and sermons to occupy their slight leisure time. In fact, however, factory work was never a paradise: twelve to fourteen hours or more a day, six days a week, in primitive conditions tending more and more looms. With the depression of 1837, working conditions worsened sharply, as owners increased hours, sped up the looms and spindles, and reduced wages in often hopeless efforts to stay in business. Moreover, with the advent of large numbers of poverty-stricken immigrant workers, desperate to sell their only resource, their labor, the nature of the industrial workforce changed. There emerged what contemporary commentators called, disapprovingly, a "permanent factory population." The potato famine in Ireland of the 1840s, together with land policies that forced large numbers of Irish and Scottish peasants out of their traditional villages, produced a flood of men, women, and children into the factories both of the English Midlands and of the "new world." A pattern was established that would persist well into the twentieth century in the United States: new waves of immigrants, attracted by hope for a better life and often driven by the misery of their existence in the "old" worlds of Europe and Asia, or in the segregated South, arrived—were often recruited—to work in the expanding Northern factories of what would in a few generations become the world's greatest industrial machine. In the United States, these immigrants, like native-born workers before them, faced difficult and often dangerous working conditions, an unrelenting fight for decent wages and opportunities to organize, and degraded living conditions in the slums of industrial cities and towns.

Nevertheless, they persisted. And while many industrial and farm workers were not, at least initially, literate, they produced a range of narratives and songs expressing their hopes and desires, the struggles in which they were engaged, and the many kinds of work they did. In fact, if one wishes to hear the voices of nineteenth-century people at work, one must for the most part turn to such narratives and songs, for few people who thought of themselves as writers—exceptions such as Melville and Rebecca Harding Davis come to mind—dealt very much with actual work, especially manual labor. One discovers such voices in descriptions of work, or strikes, and in a widely circulated song, "The Factory Girl." The voice in "Life Is a Toil" is somewhat more ironic and self-aware, reflecting on the saying that "women's work is never done." The song, which appeared in a number of nineteenth-century collections, appears to date from the ante-bellum period.

A different kind of labor is the focus of "The Farmer Is the Man." The song emerged after the Civil War among farmers in the west; it had great popularity in the social and political movements organized by such farmers, including the National Grange of the Patrons of Husbandry, and later the Greenback Party of the 1880s and the Populists of the 1890s. All these movements, and the songs associated with them, reflect growing discrepancies in wealth between farmers of the great midwest of America and those—the railroads, merchants, and banks—they saw as the forces bleeding them dry. But a song like "The Farmer Is the Man" also evokes a historical moment in which what had been a largely rural America, where the work of the farmer was a touchstone of value, was being replaced by an urban nation.

THE FACTORY GIRL

Yonder stande that spinning room boss
He looks so short and stout,
I'm going to marry a country boy
Before this year goes out.

Chorus:
Pity me all day, pity me I pray,
Pity me my darling, and take me far away.

I'll bid you factory girls farewell
Come see me if you can,
I'm gonna quit this factory work
And marry me a fine young man. (Chorus)

No more I'll hear that whistle blow,
The sound of it I hate,
No more I'll hear that boss man say,
'Young girl, you are too late.' (Chorus)

No more I'll hear that roaring,
That roaring over my head,
While you poor girls are hard at work,
And I'm at home in bed. (Chorus)

THE FARMER IS THE MAN

Oh, the farmer comes to town
With his wagon broken down,
But the farmer is the man who feeds them all.
If you'll only look and see,
I think you will agree
That the farmer is the man who feeds them all.

The farmer is the man, the farmer is the man,
Lives on credit till the fall,
Then they take him by the hand and they lead him from the land,
And the merchant is the man who gets it all.

When the lawyer hangs around
While the butcher cuts a pound,
Oh, the farmer is the man who feeds them all,
When the preacher and the cook
Go a-strolling by the brook,
Oh, the farmer is the man who feeds them all,

When the banker says he's broke
And the merchant's up in smoke,
They forget that it's the farmer feeds them all.
It would put them to the test
If the farmer took a rest;
Then they'd know that it's the farmer feeds them all.

LAST CHORUS:
The farmer is the man,
The farmer is the man,
Lives on credit till the fall—
With the interest rate so high
It's a wonder he don't die,
For the mortgage man's the one who get it all.

NARRATIVES OF JAMES CURRY AND ISRAEL CAMPBELL

In the South, slaves created a distinctive culture, one manifestation of which was songs, often called "spirituals." Few spirituals dealt directly with work, though on occasion they reflected the harsh everyday life of plantation slaves, as in "Many Thousand Go":

1. *No more peck o' corn for me,*

    No more, no more;

    No more peck o' corn for me,

    Many thousand go.

2. *No more driver's lash for me.*

3. *No more pint o' salt for me.*

4. *No more hundred lash for me.*

5. *No more mistress' call for me.*

The everyday life of slaves emerges much more directly in slave narratives, many of which took the form of "told to" stories, speeches, and other forms of "testimony." Such narratives, in part because they were composed during the ante-bellum agitation to abolish slavery, often emphasized the more brutal aspects of the slave system and the most degrading kinds of work. Brutality and degradation were, indeed, in plentiful supply in the system of slave labor, but it is also true that enslaved Africans and African Americans provided much of the skilled labor as carpenters, blacksmiths, coopers, shoemakers, and the like. Another difficulty in reading these narratives, in particular the speeches, is that they were often transcribed as given before live audiences. We do not, therefore, have the nuances of interaction between speaker and audience, nor can we be certain that the transcriptions are absolutely accurate. Nevertheless, the record they provide of slave labor offers a searing insight into that "peculiar institution" for extorting labor.

James Curry's narrative was delivered as a speech and transcribed for the January 10, 1840, issue of the abolitionist magazine The Liberator.

Curry had been brought up in Person County, North Carolina. His mother, as he writes, "was the daughter of a white man and a slave woman." In June of 1839 Curry and his two brothers fled the plantation on which they had been enslaved and headed north; en route, they were separated, and Curry never saw them again, nor was he able to be reunited with his wife, though he sought out his family after spending 27 years in Massachusetts and Canada.

Israel Campbell's narrative, which he published himself in Philadelphia in 1861, was entitled: Bond and Free, an Autobiography; or, Yearnings for Freedom from My Green Brier House: Being the Story of My Life in Bondage, and My Life in Freedom. *Campbell had initially been enslaved by a Nashville, Tennessee, tavern owner; subsequently he was forced to work in the cotton fields of Mississippi. He tried a number of times to escape, finally succeeding by crossing the Ohio River into Illinois and thence into Canada. Later in life, he continued the calling as a preacher he had established while in slavery.*

SPEECH OF JANUARY, 1840

From my childhood until I was sixteen years old, I was brought up a domestic servant. I played with my master's children, and we loved one another like brothers. This is often the case in childhood, but when the young masters and misses get older, they are generally sent away from home to school, and they soon learn that slaves are not companions for them. When they return, the love of power is cultivated in their hearts by their parents, the whip is put into their hands, and they soon regard the negro in no other light than as a slave. My master's oldest son was six months older than I. He went to a day school, and as I had a great desire to learn to read, I prevailed on him to teach me. My mother procured me a spelling-book. (Before Nat Turner's insurrection, a slave in our neighborhood might buy a spelling or hymn-book, but now he cannot.) I got so I could read a little, when my master found it out, and forbad his son to teach me any more. As I had got the start, however, I kept on reading and studying, and from that time till I came away, I always had a book somewhere about me, and if I got an opportunity, I would be reading in it. Indeed, I have a book now, which I brought all the way from North Carolina. I borrowed a hymn-book, and learned the hymns by heart. My uncle had a Bible, which he lent me, and I studied the Scriptures. When my master's family were all gone away on the Sabbath, I used to go into the house and get down the great Bible, and lie down in the piazza, and read, taking care, however, to put it back before they returned. There I learned that it was contrary to the revealed will of God, that one man should hold another as a slave. I had always heard it talked among the slaves, that we ought not to be held as slaves; that our forefathers and mothers were stolen from Africa, where they were free men and free women. But in the Bible I learned that 'God hath made of one blood all nations of men to dwell on all the face of the earth.' While I worked in the house and waited upon my mistress, she always treated me kindly, but to other slaves, who were as faithful as I was, she was very cruel. At one time, there was a comb found broken in a cupboard, which was worth about twenty-five or thirty-seven and a half cents. She suspected a little girl, 9 or 10 years old, who served in the house, of having broken it. She took her in the morning, before sunrise, into a room, and calling me to wait upon her, had all the doors shut. She tied her hands, and then took her frock up over her head, and gathered it up in her left hand, and with her right commenced beating her naked body with bunches of willow twigs. She would beat her until her arm was tired, and then thrash her on the floor, and stamp on her with her foot, and kick her, and choke her to stop her screams. Oh! it was awful! and I was obliged to stand there and see it, and to go and bring her the sticks. She continued this torture until ten o'clock, the family waiting breakfast meanwhile. She then left whipping her; and that night, she herself was so lame that one of her daughters was obliged to undress her. The poor child never recovered. A white swelling came from the bruises on one of her legs, of which she died in two or three years. And my mistress was soon after called by her great Master to give her account. . .

Before her death, my mistress used to clothe her people with coarse, common clothing. She had been dead eleven years when I came away. She died in October, and in the following spring, my master bought about one hundred yards of coarse tow and cotton, which he distributed among the slaves. After this, he provided no clothing for any of his slaves, except that I have known him in a few instances to give a pair of thoroughly worn-out pantaloons to one. They worked in the night upon their little patches of ground, raising tobacco and food for hogs, which they were allowed to keep, and thus obtained clothes for themselves. These patches of ground were little spots, they were allowed to clear in the woods, or cultivate upon the barrens, and after they got them nicely cleared, and under good cultivation, the master took them away, and the next year they must take other uncultivated spots for themselves. There were on this plantation nine men and eight out of this nine were always as decently clad as any slaves in that part of the country; and each had a better suit for Sunday. The ninth was a young fellow, who had not been taught by his mother to take care of himself, but he was fast improving when I came away. It was to him that my master gave the worn-out pantaloons. My step-father felled trees in the woods, and built for his family a commodious log-house. With my mother's assistance, it was furnished with two comfortable beds, chairs, and some other articles of furniture. His children were always comfortably and decently clothed. I knew him, at one time, to purchase for my mother a cloak, and a gown, a frock for each of my two sisters, two coats for two brothers younger than myself, and each of them a hat, all new and good, and all with money earned in the time allowed him for sleep. My mother was cook in the house for about twenty-two years. She cooked for from twenty-five to thirty-five, taking the family and the slaves together. The slaves ate in the kitchen. After my mistress's death, my mother was the only woman kept in the house. She took care of my master's children, some of whom were then quite small, and brought them up. One of the most trying scenes I ever passed through, when I would have laid down my life to protect her if I had dared, was this: after she had raised my master's children, one of his daughters, a young girl, came into the kitchen one day, and for some trifle about the dinner, she struck my mother, who pushed her away, and she fell on the floor. Her father was not at home. When he came, which was while the slaves were eating in the kitchen, she told him about it. He came down, called my mother out, and, with a hickory rod, he beat her fifteen or twenty strokes, and then called his daughter and told her to take her satisfaction of her, and she did beat her until she was satisfied. Oh! it was dreadful, to see the girl whom my poor mother had taken care of from her childhood, thus beating her, and

I must stand there, and did not dare to crook my finger in her defence. My mother's labor was very hard. She would go to the house in the morning, take her pail upon her head, and go away to the cow-pen, and milk fourteen cows. She then put on the bread for the family breakfast, and got the cream ready for churning, and set a little child to churn it, she having the care of from ten to fifteen children, whose mothers worked in the field. After clearing away the family breakfast, she got breakfast for the slaves; which consisted of warm corn bread and buttermilk, and was taken at twelve o'clock. In the meantime, she had beds to make, rooms to sweep, &c. Then she cooked the family dinner, which was simply plain meat, vegetables, and bread. Then the slaves' dinner was to be ready at from eight to nine o'clock in the evening. It consisted of corn bread, or potatoes, and the meat which remained of the master's dinner, or one herring apiece. At night she had the cows to milk again. There was little ceremony about the master's supper, unless there was company. This was her work day by day. Then in the course of the week, she had the washing and ironing to do for her master's family, (who, however, were clothed very simply,) and for her husband, seven children and herself.

She would not get through to go to her log cabin until nine or ten o'clock at night. She would then be so tired, that she could scarcely stand; but she would find one boy with his knee out, and another with his elbow out, a patch wanting here, and a stitch there, and she would sit down by her lightwood fire, and sew and sleep alternately, often till the light began to streak in the east; and then lying down, she would catch a nap, and hasten to the toil of the day. Among the slave children, were three little orphans, whose mothers, at their death, committed them to the care of my mother. One of them was a babe. She took them and treated them as her own. The master took no care about them. She always took a share of the cloth she had provided for her own children, to cover these little friendless ones. She would sometimes ask the master to procure them some clothes, but he would curse them and refuse to do it. We would sometimes tell her, that we would let the master clothe them, for she had enough to do for her own children. She replied, 'their master will not clothe them, and I cannot see them go naked; *I* have children and I do not know where their lot may be cast; I may die and leave them, and I desire to do by these little orphans, as I should wish mine to be done by.'

After I was sixteen, I was put into the field to work in the spring and summer, and in the autumn and winter, I worked in the hatter's shop with my uncle. We raised on the plantation, principally, tobacco, some cotton, and some grain. We commenced work as soon as we could see in the morning, and worked from that time until 12 o'clock before breakfast, and then until dark, when we had our dinner, and hastened to our night work for ourselves. We were not driven as field slaves generally are, and yet when I hear people here say they work as hard as slaves, I can tell them from experience, they know nothing about it. And even if they did work as hard, there is one striking difference. When they go home at night, they carry to their families the wages of their daily labor; and then they have the night for rest and sleep. Whereas, the slave carries to his family at night, only a weary body and a sick mind, and all he can do for them is done during the hours allowed him for sleep. A slave, who was hired during one summer by Thomas Maguhee, a rich slaveholder in our neighborhood, soon after his return, passed with me, one day, near a field on his plantation. Pointing to it, he said, 'I never saw blood flow any where as I've seen it flow in that field. It flows there like water. When I went there to work, I was *a man,* but now, I am *a boy.* I could then carry several bushels on my shoulder, but now I cannot lift one to it.' So very hard had he been worked. When arranging the slaves for hoeing in the field, the overseer takes them, one at a time, and tries their speed, and places them accordingly in the row, the swiftest first, and so on. Then they commence, and all must keep up with the foremost. This Thomas Maguhee used to walk into his field, with his hat close down on his head, and holding his cane over his shoulder. When he came up to the poor slaves, as they were tugging at their hoes, he would call out, 'boys!' Then they must all raise their hats and reply simultaneously, 'Sir.' 'Move your hoes.' They would spring forward and strive to increase their speed to the utmost; but presently he would call out, 'boys!' Again the hats were raised as they answered, 'Sir.' 'I told you to move your hoes, and you hav'nt moved them yet. I have twice to threat and once to fall.' (That is, if you do not move faster, I shall knock you down.) Now the poor creatures must make their last effort, and when he saw that their every power was exerted, he would set his hat on the top of his head, taking down his cane, set his arms akimbo and strut through the field.

FROM BOND AND FREE

The next day after my whipping, Mr. Crookesty came to me in the field where I was working and said, "Israel, I tell you what I will do; I have bought you, and you have caused me to give you a severe whipping for running away; this I do not wish to have to do any more. Now, if you will be a good boy and not run away any more, I will take you to wait on the house and let you be hostler at the stable; then you can have a chance of making some money, and I will give you enough to eat and wear."

"Sir," I replied, "I will do the very best I can."

So he took me to the house, and all of us had plenty to eat and wear, and never did he have occasion to whip me again. The place where he lived was an old town, about one hundred and ten miles from Nashville and twenty-five miles from the mouth of the Cumberland River, by the name of Centreville, and master was said to keep the best tavern in that part of Kentucky. After I had lived here a little over two years, master took a notion to go to Mississippi. He advertised and sold everything except his slaves. He then purchased a large flatboat and, after we had all embarked, we rowed down the Ohio and Mississippi rivers. In going down the rivers we often met large steamboats which would terribly frighten old mistress. All the way she was praying and crying. Among the boys there was one who was her favorite, named King, and when she saw one of the boats coming, she would cry to King to pull with all his might and see her out of danger, as she was sure they would kill them.

One day, while rowing down the Mississippi, there came blenching and blowing down the river a large steamer, with an Indian painted on the side, named Tecumseh. This so frightened old mistress that it threw her into hysterics. In fact, so completely did this voyage affect old mistress that by the time we reached Vicksburg she died. For this event the slaves did not feel sorry, for she had treated them very meanly.

Old master Crookesty did not commence operations here immediately, but hired all his slaves except one woman, who he kept to take care of his children. He hired me to a gentleman by the name of Mr. Bellfer, who had a large cotton farm. Here I entered on a new life, that of the plantation system. That is, every one had to be up with the blowing of the horn and be in the field by daylight. Every Sunday each one had their rations dealt out to them: three pounds of meat and one peck of corn for the week, which they had to grind and cook for themselves.

When cotton-picking time came, they talked of giving every one a stated task and told me I would have to pick a hundred pounds a day. I tried it for three days, but could not get over ninety pounds; but they put it down one hundred, and the Monday morning following they gave each one their task and told them that if they did not pick the amount they would have as many lashes as there were pounds short. I tried it and took my basket up to be weighed at noon. The overseer noticed that I was going to fall short of my number of pounds and exclaimed, to hurry me up, "Jatherous, jatherous, by the holy and just God, Israel, you will have to buy the rabbit agin night," meaning that I would get a whipping.

The overseer was an Irishman by birth, and was a singular old fellow. He kept a slate with each hand's name on it and would put each draft of cotton down as they brought it in. At night his voice could be heard at its loudest pitch, "All ye's, all ye's gather up your baskets and away to the cottonhouse." So we would gather up the baskets and go to the cottonhouse. As I was going I espied Mr. Bellfer coming to the cottonhouse with the lantern, bullwhip, and rope to tie the delinquents. I knew that my task was short, and that I would get as many lashes as my task was wanting pounds. I could not brave the settlement, so as the others went up I set my basket down and slipped behind the house and went into the woods. I remained there until I thought all the white people had retired; then I took my sack, which I used for picking cotton, and went into the sweet potato patch and digged some potatoes, which I took into the cook's house to roast. Hardly had I them covered, before Mr. Bellfer made his appearance at the door, and exclaimed, "Well Israel, is that you?"

"Yes, sir," I replied.

"Well, I will settle with you now," adding an oath for emphasis.

The overseer was not in the house, but was in the slave quarters, he having a fine black woman for a wife, he not having as much prejudice against color as many of our northern brethren. Mr. Bellfer aroused him, and soon after he made his appearance, "So you have him, have you, Doctor; by the holy and just God, he will buy the rabbit now."

They ordered me to cross my hands, and they fastened them and led me out into the yard. There was no whipping ground there, so while Mr. Bellfer held me, the overseer prepared the stakes to which to tie me while they were whipping me. Finding they were going to give me a hard whipping, I commenced begging and pleading that if they would only forgive me that time I would do better in future. But they were deaf to my cries. Mrs. Bellfer coming to the door at that time, I entreated her to plead for me, told her I would do better, and that I was sorry for what I had done.

Mistress Betsy had great influence with her husband, and, seeing that I was not as hardened as many of the other slaves, she stopped him and inquired into my case. The Doctor told her that I had not picked my task and had commenced running away.

Mistress Betsy then asked the Doctor not to whip me this time, for she was sure I would try and do better. But he told her to go away, that I had commenced running away, and if he did not break me all the niggers would do likewise.

But I kept on pleading and so awakened Mistress Betsy's feelings in my behalf that she begged the Doctor to let me off this time and offered to go my security that I would have my task hereafter and never run away any more. She asked me if I understood what she had promised.

"Yes ma'am," I replied.

Then Mr. Bellfer said, "Israel, if Mrs. Bellfer will go your security, I will let you off this time; but never expect it again." He then untied my hands, and I went into the kitchen and took my potatoes out of the fire and began to eat them.

While thus engaged I commenced revolving in my mind as to how I should make good my word and give myself a good character for promptness and energy. To pick a hundred pounds of cotton a day I knew I could not, and yet to break my word and lose my good name was equally as hard. I began thinking of some way by which I might succeed in always having my task made up. Thought I, we have a large watermelon patch near the field, and if I do not succeed in having a full quantity before the last load, I will slip one of them in the bottom of the basket. This settled, I went to sleep and dreamt my plan over.

The next morning we all started as usual to the cotton-field. All went on as usual. At eight o'clock we went to the cottonhouse and I had thirty-two pounds; after breakfast we picked until two o'clock and then I had twenty-eight pounds. The overseer, who could tell very near how much each one ought to average, said, "Jatherous, jatherous, Israel, by the holy and just God you will buy the rabbit agin night."

"The fast racehorse runs the fastest the last round," says I to myself and off I went to the field and picked hard until dark. Then the overseer's voice could be heard, "All ye's, all ye's, get up your baskets and away to the cottonhouse." During the time I was picking, I had selected a good sized melon and put it in the basket and went up to have it weighed.

I was among one of the first who put their baskets in the scales that night, and the result was announced as a hundred and five pounds for my day's work. "I knew you could reach a hundred pounds," said the Doctor.

"Hard work, sir, hard work," I replied. Thought I to myself, if you only knew how much less cotton there was, you would not look so pleased. I leapt into the cottonhouse and emptied my basket as far back as I possibly could. I succeeded this time without being caught, but I must confess I felt greatly afraid. Yet I knew that if I did not have the hundred pounds a whipping was sure, and if nothing ventured nothing would be gained, and this overbalanced my fear. I thought myself pretty smart to play such a trick upon as sharp persons as were master and the overseer.

I continued this whenever I thought my task was short and was never caught. When melons were gone I used pumpkins, and finally filled my sack with dirt and was equally successful.

It may be thought that this is exaggerated, as the melons would increase and then all would be brought to light. But when they all left the cottonhouse I would pretend to have forgotten something and go and get them out, take them into my house, and eat them.

There was another boy who was whipped nearly every day. I took pity on him and, he promising me faithfully not to expose my plan, I let him into my secret and thus saved him also. Before the season was over every one of the delinquents knew how to save their backs, and they found it much easier to pick melons and pumpkins than to have their backs cut to pieces.

But a day of reckoning was to come with master. Before the cotton was salable it had to be ginned—that is, cleaned of the seed and dirt and put up in bales of 450 pounds. It was then ready for market. As they always put down the amount picked, allowing so much for waste, they could calculate very nearly the amount it ought to make.

When the ginner had completed his work and had baled all the cotton, there were several bales short. Master accused him of stealing the cotton, but he proved to him that he had only got the ninth bale, which he was entitled to for ginning. The falling short was a mystery which was never solved.

About this time there occurred the following incident, which shows how little mercy the overseers have upon the slaves. There was a woman on the plantation named Mary, who was an extraordinary hand at picking cotton. Her task was put at a hundred and seventy-five pounds. She never had to be whipped for not getting her task, but was industrious and faithful. One day the overseer (generally they had rather see laziness and meanness), who had become uneasy under her good example, thought he would find some fault with her and whip her. Her husband seeing him, interfered. He then turned on him and, the husband resisting and trying to get out of his way, he took up his gun and deliberately fired at him. He did not kill him, but he was laid up a long time and cost master considerable to have him attended to and cured.

So ended my year on that farm.

HERMAN MELVILLE
(1819-1891)

Melville is well known by anyone who has studied American literature, though sometimes his work is more known than read. He suffered from something of the same mixture of fame and inattention during his lifetime. His first works, Typee: A Peep at Polynesian Life *(1846) and* Omoo *(1847), were widely read as examples of exotic South Sea Island tales and made Melville a popular writer. But his later works, including what would become his most famous novel,* Moby-Dick *(1851), never won him the same kind of wide audience, and it was almost impossible for him to make a living as a writer. In fact, after his strange and haunting novel,* The Confidence-Man: His Masquerade *(1857), Melville stopped publishing fiction, though he did compose poetry throughout the remainder of his life. He also wrote the novella* Billy Budd, *unpublished until the 1920s when Melville, who had been all but forgotten, was reestablished as one of America's preeminent novelists.*

Though initially known as a teller of sea tales, in fact Melville was one of the first writers in the United States to devote his creative talents to portraying the lives, including the work lives, of ordinary men and women. The novels Redburn *(1849) and* White-Jacket: or The World in a Man-of-War *(1850) offer pictures of beggar families in Liverpool, immigrants "packed like slaves" into ships from Europe, and navy sailors flogged and reduced to servile obedience. During the 1850s, Melville wrote a series of unsettling stories often focused on the conflicts between the comfortable and obtuse people who constituted his likely readership, whom he often represented by his narrators, and the men and women they ignorantly or indifferently oppressed. These included "Bartleby," "Benito Cereno," and the story reprinted here, "The Tartarus of Maids," which constitutes, with "The Paradise of Bachelors," a double story of comfort and misery.*

Melville was himself familiar with such conflicting conditions. Brought up with social position and material comfort, he was forced at age twelve by his father's bankruptcy and shortly thereafter by his death to drop out of school and to undertake a series of low-paying jobs as a clerk, a farm laborer, a rural teacher, and finally as a common sailor. From 1839 to 1844 he worked primarily at sea, first aboard a merchant ship, then aboard whalers, and finally on the warship United States. It was such experiences at sea—bleak working conditions, despotic authorities, brutal discipline, and yet the comradeship of men of every race, background, and condition—that provided both the material and the outlook for most of his fiction. As in many of his stories, the distance between the narrator of "The Tartarus of Maids" and the women workers he observes and comments upon marks the class divide that was rapidly becoming manifest in newly industrializing America. Just under the surface of the narrator's fascination with the mechanical details of papermaking lies a question necessary to ask and thorny to answer in ante-bellum America: what were the consequences and the possibilities for human life raised by the factories in which an increasing number of people in Europe and America would be toiling?

THE TARTARUS OF MAIDS

It lies not far from Woedolor Mountain in New England. Turning to the East, right out from among bright farms and sunny meadows, nodding in early June with odorous grasses, you enter ascendingly among bleak hills. These gradually close in upon a dusky pass, which, from the violent Gulf Stream of air unceasingly driving between its cloven walls of haggard rock, as well as from the tradition of a crazy spinster's hut having long ago stood somewhere hereabouts, is called the Mad Maid's Bellows-pipe.

Winding along at the bottom of the gorge is a dangerously narrow wheel-road, occupying the bed of a former torrent. Following this road to its highest point, you stand as within a Dantean gateway. From the steepness of the walls here, their strangely ebon hue, and the sudden contraction of the gorge, this particular point is called the Black Notch. The ravine now expandingly descends into a great, purple, hopper-shaped hollow, far sunk among many Plutonian, shaggy-wooded mountains. By the country people this hollow is called the Devil's Dungeon. Sounds of torrents fall on all sides upon the car. These rapid waters unite at last in one turbid brick-colored stream, boiling through a flume among enormous boulders. They call this strange-colored torrent Blood River. Gaining a dark precipice it wheels suddenly to the West, and makes one maniac spring of sixty feet into the arms of a stunted wood of gray-haired pines, between which it thence eddies on its further way down to the invisible low-lands.

Conspicuously crowning a rocky bluff high to one side, at the cataract's verge, is the ruin of an old saw-mill, built in those primitive times when vast pines and hemlocks superabounded throughout the neighboring region. The black-mossed bulk of those immense, rough-hewn, and spike-knotted logs, here and there tumbled all together, in long abandonment and decay, or left in solitary, perilous projection over the cataract's gloomy brink, impart to this rude wooden ruin not only much of the aspect of one of rough-quarried stone, but also a sort of feudal, Rhineland, and Thurmberg look, derived from the pinnacled wildness of the neighboring scenery.

Not far from the bottom of the Dungeon stands a large whitewashed building, relieved, like some great whited sepulchre, against the sullen background of mountain-side firs, and other hardy evergreens, inaccessibly rising in grim terraces for some two thousand feet.

The building is a paper-mill.

Having embarked on a large scale in the seedsman's business (so extensively and broadcast, indeed, that at length my seeds were distributed through all the Eastern and Northern States, and even fell into the far soil of Missouri and the Carolinas), the demand for paper at my place became so great, that the expenditure soon amounted to a most important item in the general account. It need hardly be hinted how paper comes into use with seedsmen, as envelopes. These are mostly made of yellowish paper, folded square; and when filled, are all but flat, and being stamped, and superscribed with the nature of the seeds contained, assume not a little the appearance of business-letters ready for the mail. Of these small envelopes I used an incredible quantity—several hundreds of thousands in a year. For a time I had purchased my paper from the wholesale dealers in a neighboring town. For economy's sake, and partly for the adventure of the trip, I now resolved to cross the mountains, some sixty miles, and order my future paper at the Devil's Dungeon paper-mill.

The sleighing being uncommonly fine toward the end of January, and promising to hold so for no small period, in spite of the bitter cold I started one gray Friday noon in my pung, well fitted with buffalo and wolf robes; and, spending one night on the road, next noon came in sight of Woedolor Mountain.

The far summit fairly smoked with frost; white vapors curled up from its whitewooded top, as from a chimney. The intense congelation made the whole country look like one petrifaction. The steel shoes of my pung craunched and gritted over the vitreous, chippy snow, as if it had been broken glass. The forests here and there skirting the route, feeling the same all-stiffening influence, their inmost fibres penetrated with the cold, strangely groaned—not in the swaying branches merely, but I likewise in the vertical trunk—as the fitful gusts remorselessly swept through them. Brittle with excessive frost, many colossal tough-grained maples, snapped in twain like pipestems, cumbered the unfeeling earth.

Flaked all over with frozen sweat, white as a milky ram, his nostrils at each breath sending forth two horn-shaped shoots of heated respiration, Black, my good horse, but six years old, started at a sudden turn, where, right across the track—not ten minutes fallen—an old distorted hemlock lay, darkly undulatory as an anaconda.

Gaining the Bellows-pipe, the violent blast, dead from behind, all but shoved my high-backed pung up-hill. The gust shrieked through the shivered pass, as if laden with lost spirits bound to the unhappy world. Ere gaining the summit, Black, my horse, as if exasperated by the cutting wind, slung out with his strong hind legs, tore the light pung straight up-hill, and sweeping grazingly through the narrow notch, sped downward madly past the ruined sawmill. Into the Devil's Dungeon horse and cataract rushed together.

With might and main, quitting my seat and robes, and standing backward, with one foot braced against the dashboard, I rasped and churned the bit, and stopped him just in time to avoid collision, at a turn, with the bleak nozzle of a rock, couchant like a lion in the way—a roadside rock.

At first I could not discover the paper-mill.

The whole hollow gleamed with the white, except, here and there, where a pinnacle of granite showed one wind-swept angle bare. The mountains stood pinned in shrouds—a pass of Alpine corpses. Where stands the mill? Suddenly a whirring, humming sound broke upon my ear. I looked, and there, like an arrested avalanche, lay the large white-washed factory. It was subordinately surrounded by a cluster of other and smaller buildings, some of which, from their cheap, blank air, great length, gregarious windows, and comfortless expression, no doubt were boarding-houses of the operatives. A snow-white hamlet amidst the snows. Various rude, irregular squares and courts resulted from the somewhat picturesque clusterings of these buildings, owing to the broken, rocky nature of the ground, which forbade all method in their relative arrangement. Several narrow lanes and alleys, too, partly blocked with snow fallen from the roof, cut up the hamlet in all directions.

When, turning from the traveled highway, jingling with bells of numerous farmers—who, availing themselves of the fine sleighing, were dragging their wood to market—and frequently diversified with swift cutters dashing from inn to inn of the scattered villages—when, I say, turning from that bustling main-road, I by degrees wound into the Mad Maid's Bellows-pipe, and saw the grim Black Notch beyond, then something latent, as well as something obvious in the time and scene, strangely brought back to my mind my first sight of dark and grimy Temple Bar. And when Black, my horse, went darting through the Notch, perilously grazing its rocky wall, I remembered being in a runaway London omnibus, which in much the same sort of style, though by no means at an equal rate, dashed through the ancient arch of Wren. Though the two objects did by no means completely correspond, yet this partial inadequacy but served to tinge the similitude not less with the vividness than the disorder of a dream. So that, when upon reining up at the protruding rock I at last caught sight of the quaint groupings of the factory-buildings, and with the traveled highway and the Notch behind, found myself all alone, silently and privily stealing through deep-cloven passages into this sequestered spot, and saw the long, high-gabled main factory edifice, with a rude tower—for hoisting heavy boxes—at one end, standing among its crowded outbuildings and boarding-houses, as the Temple Church amidst the surrounding offices and dormitories, and when the marvelous retirement of this mysterious mountain nook fastened its whole spell upon me, then, what memory lacked, all tributary imagination furnished, and I said to myself, "This is the very counterpart of the Paradise of Bachelors, but snowed upon, and frost-painted to a sepulchre."

Dismounting and warily picking my way down the dangerous declivity—horse and man both sliding now and then upon the icy ledges—at length I drove, or the blast drove me, into the largest square, before one side of the main edifice. Piercingly and shrilly the shotted blast blew by the corner; and redly and demoniacally boiled Blood River at one side. A long wood-pile, of many scores of cords, all glittering in mail of crusted ice, stood crosswise in the square. A row of horse-posts, their north sides plastered with adhesive snow, flanked the factory wall. The bleak frost packed and paved the square as with some ringing metal.

The inverted similitude recurred—"The sweet, tranquil Temple garden, with the Thames bordering its green beds," strangely meditated I.

But where are the gay bachelors?

Then, as I and my horse stood shivering in the wind-spray a girl ran from a neighboring dormitory door, and throwing her thin apron over her bare head, made for the opposite building.

"One moment, my girl; is there no shed hereabouts which I may drive into?"

Pausing, she turned upon me a face pale with work, and blue with cold; an eye supernatural with unrelated misery.

"Nay," faltered I, "I mistook you. Go on; I want nothing."

Leading my horse close to the door from which she had come, I knocked. Another pale, blue girl appeared, shivering in the doorway as, to prevent the blast, she jealously held the door ajar.

"Nay, I mistake again. In God's name shut the door. But hold, is there no man about?"

That moment a dark-complexioned, well-wrapped personage passed, making for the factory door, and spying him coming, the girl rapidly closed the other one.

"Is there no horse-shed here, sir?"

"Yonder, to the wood-shed," he replied, and disappeared inside the factory.

With much ado I managed to wedge in horse and pung between the scattered piles of wood all sawn and split. Then, blanketing my horse, and piling my buffalo on the blanket's top, and tucking in its edges well around the breast-band and breeching, so that the wind might not strip him bare, I tied him fast, and ran lamely for the factory door, stiff with frost, and cumbered with my driver's dread-naught.

Immediately I found myself standing in a spacious place intolerably lighted by long rows of windows, focusing inward the snowy scene without.

At rows of blank-looking counters sat rows of blank-looking girls, with blank, white folders in their blank hands, all blankly folding blank paper.

In one corner stood some huge frame of ponderous iron, with a vertical thing like a piston periodically rising and falling upon a heavy wooden block. Before it— its tame minister—stood a tall girl, feeding the iron animal with half-quires of rose-hued note-paper which, at every downward dab of the piston-like machine, received in the corner the impress of a wreath of roses. I looked from the rosy paper to the pallid cheek, but said nothing.

Seated before a long apparatus, strung with long, slender strings like any harp, another girl was feeding it with fools-cap sheets which, so soon as they curiously traveled from her on the cords, were withdrawn at the opposite end of the machine by a second girl. They came to the first girl blank; they went to the second girl ruled.

I looked upon the first girl's brow, and saw it was young and fair; I looked upon the second girl's brow, and saw it was ruled and wrinkled. Then, as I still looked, the two—for some small variety to the monotony—changed places; and where had stood the young, fair brow, now stood the ruled and wrinkled one.

Perched high upon a narrow platform, and still higher upon a high stool crowning it, sat another figure serving some other iron animal; while below the platform sat her mate in some sort of reciprocal attendance.

Not a syllable was breathed. Nothing was heard but the low, steady overruling hum of the iron animals. The human voice was banished from the spot. Machinery— that vaunted slave of humanity—here stood menially served by human beings, who served mutely and cringingly as the slave serves the Sultan. The girls did not so much seem accessory wheels to the general machinery as mere cogs to the wheels.

All this scene around me was instantaneously taken in at one sweeping glance— even before I had proceeded to unwind the heavy fur tippet from around my neck.

But as soon as this fell from me, the dark-complexioned man, standing close by, raised a sudden cry, and seizing my arm, dragged me out into the open air, and without pausing for a word instantly caught up some congealed snow and began rubbing both my cheeks.

"Two white spots like the whites of your eyes," he said; "man, your cheeks are frozen."

"That may well be," muttered I; "'tis some wonder the frost of the Devil's Dungeon strikes in no deeper. Rub away."

Soon a horrible, tearing pain caught at my reviving cheeks. Two gaunt bloodhounds, one on each side, seemed mumbling them. I seemed Actæon.

Presently, when all was over, I re-entered the factory, made known my business, concluded it satisfactorily, and then begged to be conducted throughout the place to view it.

"Cupid is the boy for that," said the dark-complexioned man. "Cupid!" and by this odd fancy-name calling a dimpled, red-cheeked, spirited-looking, forward little fellow, who was rather impudently, I thought, gliding about among the passive-looking girls—like a gold-fish through hueless waves—yet doing nothing in particular that I could see, the man bade him lead the stranger through the edifice.

"Come first and see the water-wheel," said this lively lad, with the air of boyishly-brisk importance.

Quitting the folding-room, we crossed some damp, cold boards, and stood beneath a great wet shed, incessantly showering with foam, like the green barnacled bow of some East Indiaman in a gale. Round and round here went the enormous revolutions of the dark colossal water-wheel, grim with its one immutable purpose.

"This sets our whole machinery a-going, sir; in every part of all these buildings; where the girls work and all."

I looked, and saw that the turbid waters of Blood River had not changed their hue by coming under the use of man.

"You make only blank paper; no printing of any sort, I suppose? All blank paper, don't you?"

"Certainly; what else should a paper-factory make?"

The lad here looked at me as if suspicious of my common-sense.

"Oh, to be sure!" said I, confused and stammering; "it only struck me as so strange that red waters should turn out pale chee—paper, I mean."

He took me up a wet and rickety stair to a great light room, furnished with no visible thing but rude, mangerlike receptacles running all round its sides; and up to these mangers, like so many mares haltered to the rack, stood rows of girls. Before each was vertically thrust up a long, glittering scythe, immovably fixed at bottom to the manger-edge. The curve of the scythe, and its having no snath to it, made it look exactly like a sword. To and fro, across the sharp edge, the girls forever dragged long strips of rags, washed white, picked from baskets at one side; thus ripping asunder every seam, and converting the tatters almost into lint. The air swam with the fine, poisonous particles, which from all sides darted, subtilely, as motes in sunbeams, into the lungs.

"This is the rag-room," coughed the boy.

"You find it rather stifling here," coughed I, in answer; "but the girls don't cough."

"Oh, they are used to it."

"Where do you get such hosts of rags?" picking up a handful from a basket.

"Some from the country round about; some from far over sea—Leghorn and London."

"'Tis not unlikely, then," murmured I, "that among these heaps of rags there may be some old shirts, gathered from the dormitories of the Paradise of Bachelors. But the buttons are all dropped off. Pray, my lad, do you ever find any bachelors' buttons hereabouts?"

"None grow in this part of the country. The Devil's Dungeon is no place for flowers."

"Oh! you mean the *flowers* so called—the Bachelor's Buttons?"

"And was not that what you asked about? Or did you mean the gold bosom-buttons of our boss, Old Bach, as our whispering girls all call him?"

"The man, then, I saw below is a bachelor, is he?"

"Oh, yes, he's a Bach."

"The edges of those swords, they are turned outward from the girls, if I see right; but their rags and fingers fly so, I can not distinctly see."

"Turned outward."

Yes, murmured I to myself; I see it now; turned outward; and each erected sword is so borne, edge-outward, before each girl. If my reading fails me not, just so, of old, condemned state-prisoners went from the hall of judgment to their doom: an officer before, bearing a sword, its edge turned outward, in significance of their fatal sentence. So, through consumptive pallors of this blank, raggy life, go these white girls to death.

"Those scythes look very sharp," again turning toward the boy.

"Yes; they have to keep them so. Look!"

That moment two of the girls, dropping their rags, plied each a whet-stone up and down the sword-blade. My unaccustomed blood curdled at the sharp shriek of the tormented steel.

Their own executioners; themselves whetting the very swords that slay them; meditated I.

"What makes those girls so sheet-white, my lad?"

"Why"—with a roguish twinkle, pure ignorant drollery, not knowing heartlessness—"I suppose the handling of such white bits of sheets all the time makes them so sheety."

"Let us leave the rag-room now, my lad."

More tragical and more inscrutably mysterious than any mystic sight, human or machine, throughout the factory, was the strange innocence of cruel-heartedness in this usage-hardened boy.

"And now," said he, cheerily, "I suppose you want to see our great machine, which cost us twelve thousand dollars only last autumn. That's the machine that makes the paper, too. This way, sir."

Following him, I crossed a large, bespattered place, with two great round vats in it, full of a white, wet, woolly-looking stuff, not unlike the albuminous part of an egg, soft-boiled.

"There," said Cupid, tapping the vats carelessly, "these are the first beginnings of the paper, this white pulp you see. Look how it swims bubbling round and round, moved by the paddle here. From hence it pours from both vats into that one common channel yonder, and so goes, mixed up and leisurely, to the great machine. And now for that."

He led me into a room, stifling with a strange, blood-like, abdominal heat, as if here, true enough, were being finally developed the germinous particles lately seen.

Before me, rolled out like some long Eastern manuscript, lay stretched one continuous length of iron frame-work—multitudinous and mystical, with all sorts of rollers, wheels, and cylinders, in slowly-measured and unceasing motion.

"Here first comes the pulp now," said Cupid, pointing to the highest end of the machine. "See; first it pours out and spreads itself upon this wide, sloping board; and then—look—slides, thin and quivering, beneath the first roller there. Follow on now, and see it as it slides from under that to the next cylinder. There; see how it has become just a very little less pulpy now. One step more, and it grows still more to some slight consistence. Still another cylinder, and it is so knitted—though as yet mere dragon-fly wing—that it forms an air-bridge here, like a suspended cobweb, between two more separated rollers; and flowing over the last one, and under again, and doubling about there out of sight for a minute among all those mixed cylinders you indistinctly see, it reappears here, looking now at last a little less like pulp and more like paper, but still quite delicate and defective yet awhile. But—a little further onward, sir, if you please—here now, at this further point, it puts on something of a real look, as if it might turn out to be something you might possibly handle in the end. But it's not yet done, sir. Good way to travel yet, and plenty more of cylinders must roll it."

"Bless my soul!" said I, amazed at the elongation, interminable convolutions, and deliberate slowness of the machine; "it must take a long time for the pulp to pass from end to end, and come out paper."

"Oh! not so long," smiled the precocious lad, with a superior and patronizing air; "only nine minutes. But look; you may try it for yourself. Have you a bit of paper? Ah! here's a bit on the floor. Now mark that with any word you please, and let me dab it on here, and we'll see how long before it comes out at the other end."

"Well, let me see," said I, taking out my pencil; "come, I'll mark it with your name."

Bidding me take out my watch, Cupid adroitly dropped the inscribed slip on an exposed part of the incipient mass.

Instantly my eye marked the second-hand on my dial-plate.

Slowly I followed the slip, inch by inch; sometimes pausing for full half a minute as it disappeared beneath inscrutable groups of the lower cylinders, but only gradually to emerge again; and so, on, and on, and on—inch by inch; now in open sight, sliding along like a freckle on the quivering sheet; and then again wholly vanished; and so, on, and on, and on—inch by inch; all the time the main sheet growing more and more to final firmness—when, suddenly, I saw a sort of paper-fall, not wholly unlike a water-fall; a scissory sound smote my ear, as of some cord being snapped; and down dropped an unfolded sheet of perfect foolscap, with my "Cupid" half faded out of it, and still moist and warm.

My travels were at an end, for here was the end of the machine.

"Well, how long was it?" said Cupid.

"Nine minutes to a second," replied I, watch in hand.

"I told you so."

For a moment a curious emotion filled me, not wholly unlike that which one might experience at the fulfillment of some mysterious prophecy. But how absurd, thought I again; the thing is a mere machine, the essence of which is unvarying punctuality and precision.

Previously absorbed by the wheels and cylinders, my attention was now directed to a sad-looking woman standing by.

"That is rather an elderly person so silently tending the machine-end here. She would not seem wholly used to it either."

"Oh," knowingly whispered Cupid, through the din, "she only came last week. She was a nurse formerly. But the business is poor in these parts, and she's left it. But look at the paper she is piling there."

"Aye, foolscap," handling the piles of moist, warm sheets, which continually were being delivered into the woman's waiting hands. "Don't you turn out anything but foolscap at this machine?"

"Oh, sometimes, but not often, we turn out finer work—cream-laid and royal sheets, we call them. But foolscap being in chief demand, we turn out foolscap most."

It was very curious. Looking at that blank paper continually dropping, dropping, dropping, my mind ran on in wonderings of those strange uses to which those thousand sheets eventually would be put. All sorts of writings would be writ on those now vacant things—sermons, lawyers' briefs, physicians' prescriptions, love-letters, marriage certificates, bills of divorce, registers of births, death-warrants, and so on, without end. Then, recurring back to them as they here lay all blank, I could not but bethink me of that celebrated comparison of John Locke, who, in demonstration of his theory that man had no innate ideas, compared the human mind at birth to a sheet of blank paper; something destined to be scribbled on, but what sort of characters no soul might tell.

Pacing slowly to and fro along the involved machine, still humming with its play, I was struck as well by the inevitability as the evolvement-power in all its motions.

"Does that thin cobweb there," said I, pointing to the sheet in its more imperfect stage, "does that never tear or break? It is marvelous fragile, and yet this machine it passes through is so mighty."

"It never is known to tear a hair's point."

"Does it never stop—get clogged?"

"No. It *must* go. The machinery makes it go just *so*, just that very way, and at that very pace you there plainly *see* it go. The pulp can't help going."

Something of awe now stole over me, as I gazed upon this inflexible iron animal. Always, more or less, machinery of this ponderous, elaborate sort strikes, in some moods, strange dread into the human heart, as some living, panting Behemoth might. But what made the thing I saw so specially terrible to me was the metallic necessity, the unbudging fatality which governed it. Though, here and there, I could not follow the thin, gauzy vail of pulp in the course of its more mysterious or entirely invisible advance, yet it was indubitable that, at those points where it eluded me, it still marched on in unvarying docility to the autocratic cunning of the machine. A fascination fastened on me. I stood spell-bound and wandering in my soul. Before my eyes—there, passing in slow procession along the wheeling cylinders, I seemed to see, glued to the pallid incipience of the pulp, the yet more pallid faces of all the pallid girls I had eyed that heavy day. Slowly, mournfully, beseechingly, yet unresistingly, they gleamed along, their agony dimly outlined on the imperfect paper, like the print of the tormented face on the handkerchief of Saint Veronica.

"Halloa! the heat of the room is too much for you," cried Cupid, staring at me.

"No—I am rather chill, if anything."

"Come out, sir—out—out," and, with the protecting air of a careful father, the precocious lad hurried me outside.

In a few moments, feeling revived a little, I went into the folding-room—the first room I had entered, and where the desk for transacting business stood, surrounded by the blank counters and blank girls engaged at them.

"Cupid here has led me a strange tour," said I to the dark-complexioned man before mentioned, whom I had ere this discovered not only to be an old bachelor, but also the principal proprietor. "Yours is a most wonderful factory. Your great machine is a miracle of inscrutable intricacy."

"Yes, all our visitors think it so. But we don't have many. We are in a very out-of-the-way corner here. Few inhabitants, too. Most of our girls come from far-off villages."

"The girls," echoed I, glancing round at their silent forms. "Why is it, sir, that in most factories, female operatives, of whatever age, are indiscriminately called girls, never women?"

"Oh! as to that—why, I suppose, the fact of their being generally unmarried—that's the reason, I should think. But it never struck me before. For our factory here, we will not have married women; they are apt to be off-and-on too much. We want none but steady workers: twelve hours to the day, day after day, through the three hundred and sixty-five days, excepting Sundays, Thanksgiving, and Fast-days. That's our rule. And so, having no married women, what females we have are rightly enough called girls."

"Then these are all maids," said I, while some pained homage to their pale virginity made me involuntarily bow.

"All maids."

Again the strange emotion filled me.

"Your cheeks look whitish yet, sir," said the man, gazing at me narrowly. "You must be careful going home. Do they pain you at all now? It's a bad sign, if they do."

"No doubt, sir," answered I, "when once I have got out of the Devil's Dungeon, I shall feel them mending."

"Ah, yes; the winter air in valleys, or gorges, or any sunken place, is far colder and more bitter than elsewhere. You would hardly believe it now, but it is colder here than at the top of Woedolor Mountain."

"I dare say it is, sir. But time presses me; I must depart."

With that, remuffling myself in dread-naught and tippet, thrusting my hands into my huge seal-skin mittens, I sallied out into the nipping air, and found poor Black, my horse, all cringing and doubled up with the cold.

Soon, wrapped in furs and meditations, I ascended from the Devil's Dungeon.

At the Black Notch I paused, and once more bethought me of Temple Bar. Then, shooting through the pass, all alone with inscrutable nature, I exclaimed—Oh! Paradise of Bachelors! and oh! Tartarus of Maids!

JOE HILL
(? - 1915)

Most songs associated with social movements were created anonymously, often by providing new words to well-known hymns and secular ditties. The familiar union song, "Solidarity Forever," written by Ralph Chaplin in 1915, uses the tune of "John Brown's Body," to which Union troops had marched during the Civil War; that tune had also served as the basis for Julia Ward Howe's stirring "Battle Hymn of the Republic": "Mine eyes have seen the glory of the coming of the Lord,/ He is trampling out the vintage where the grapes of wrath are stored." Joe Hill, perhaps the best-known poet and songwriter of the turn-of-the-nineteenth-century radicalism, used this tactic of adapting songs his listeners knew. "There Is Power in a Union" is set to the hymn "There Is Power in the Blood"; "It's a Long Way Down to the Soupline" parodies "Tipperary"; and one of his most famous take-offs, "The Preacher and the Slave," uses the tune for the sentimental song "In the Sweet By-and-By."

"Casey Jones—The Union Scab" is another case in point, for Hill took what had initially been a sad tale about a train engineer who had died in a wreck and turned it into a comical attack on those who devoted themselves to the company, in this case the Southern Pacific Railroad, rather than to their fellow workers. Hill's conversion of a familiar folktale into a political fable was characteristic of his life as poet, singer, and organizer for the Industrial Workers of the World (IWW). The Wobblies, as they were called, were the most militant organized force among American workers during the first two decades of the twentieth century. They dedicated themselves particularly to agitating among and organizing the men and women facing the most demanding, and often exploited, forms of labor: stevedores, lumberjacks, clothing workers, and miners.

Joe Hill came to the United States in 1901 from his native Sweden, where he had been named Joel Emmanuel Hagglund. He was working in the port of San Pedro, California, in 1910 when he joined up with the Wobblies. From that point on, he became an itinerant agitator, organizer, and singer for the movement, and many of his songs were printed in the Wobblies's Little Red Song Book, *which remains in print to this day. Early in 1914, Hill was arrested on a murder charge in Salt Lake City, Utah. He was convicted in a very controversial trial and, despite efforts by the labor movement, the Swedish government, and President Woodrow Wilson, Hill was executed by a firing squad November 19, 1915. His final words, contained in a telegram to Wobbly leader Big Bill Haywood, were "Don't waste time mourning. Organize." He was memorialized not only in a huge funeral in Chicago and by the scattering of his ashes across the United States (except in Utah) and overseas, but also in a well-known song by Earl Robinson and Alfred Hayes, "Joe Hill":*

> I dreamed I saw Joe Hill last night
> > Alive as you and me.
> Says I, "But Joe you're ten years dead."
> > "I never died," says he.
> > "I never died," says he.

CASEY JONES

1. The workers on the S. P. Line to strike sent out a call,
   But Casey Jones, the engineer, he wouldn't strike at all.
   His boiler it was leaking, and its drivers on the bum,
   And his engine and its bearings they were all out of plumb.

   CHORUS: Casey Jones kept his junk pile running;
             Casey Jones was working double time;
             Casey Jones got a wooden medal
             For being good and faithful on the S. P. Line.

2. The workers said to Casey, "Won't you help us win this strike?"
   But Casey said, "Let me alone; you'd better take a hike."
   Then someone put a bunch of railroad ties across the track,
   And Casey hit the river with an awful crack.

   CHORUS: Casey Jones hit the river bottom;
             Casey Jones broke his blooming spine;
             Casey Jones was an Angeleno:
             He took a trip to Heaven on the S. P. Line.

3. When Casey Jones got up to Heaven to the Pearly Gate,
   He said, "I'm Casey Jones, the guy that pulled the S. P. freight."
   "You're just the man," said Peter, "Our musicians went on strike;
   You can get a job a-scabbing any time you like."

   CHORUS: Casey Jones got a job in Heaven;
             Casey Jones was doing mighty fine;
             Casey Jones went scabbing on the angels
             Just like he did to workers on the S. P. Line.

4. The angels got together and they said it wasn't fair
   For Casey Jones to go around a-scabbing everywhere.
   The Angels' Union No. 23, they sure were there,
   And they promptly fired Casey down the Golden Stair.

   CHORUS: Casey Jones went to Hell aflying.
             "Casey Jones!" the Devil said. "Oh, fine!
             Casey Jones, get busy shoveling sulphur—
             That's what you get for scabbing on the S. P. Line!"

Boxcar Bertha Thompson
(b. 1903)

In the course of her life, "Boxcar Bertha" learned, as she put it at the end of her autobiography, "how it felt to be a hobo, a radical, a prostitute, a thief, a reformer, a social worker, and a revolutionist." She was born in 1903 to the daughter of a man, Moses Thompson, who had been an active abolitionist with John Brown, had fought in the Civil War, published a newspaper advocating voting rights for women and free love, and spent a couple of terms in jail for disseminating birth control information and publiclly encouraging his daughter to not marry her lover.

Bertha paints her mother as a hard-working, spunky, exuberant woman who migrated from man to man as the spirit moved her, and who claimed never to have taught her children values she did not practice. "Remember," Bertha reports her mother as saying as her daughter first sets out on her own, "I never made any sacrifice for you, nor did I give up any pleasure or good time for you." This philosophy of enjoying life to its fullest, even—or perhaps especially—when it is most seamy and apparently shameless, marks the life that Boxcar Bertha: An Autobiography *(later published as* Sister of the Road*) documents. The book was "told to" Dr. Ben Reitman, a well-known Chicago anarchist, tramp, reformer, physician, and sometimes lover of Emma Goldman. By then, 1933, Bertha was working in a New Deal project to record and support the lives of the thousands upon thousands of women and men "on the bum" during the Great Depression of the 1930s.*

As this selection indicates, she had the experience with which to carry out her job. It records part of her life as a prostitute, a form of employment often not thought about under the category of "work." In fact, selling sexual favors for money is among the most ancient of professions, especially for women; courtesans have played significant roles in many cultures, antique and modern. And for many poor and working-class women, prostitution has always been a potential anchor against hard times. Yet it is only in recent years that the term "sex workers" has come into vogue, as prostitutes have organized both to improve their own lot and to combat the outlook that has regarded them as moral lepers. Here, Bertha explores in convincing detail the class structure within the world of prostitution and its relationship to the world from which the "johns" (or "customers") come and to which they return.

FROM Boxcar Bertha,
An Autobiography

The cab stopped in front of the Globe, an old three-story brick building on Erie Street near Clark. It had once been run as a man's lodging house. I walked up the steps and was met by the clerk at the desk.

"Are you Bill's broad?"

I nodded affirmation and he pressed a button back of the desk and a door opened. The inside man, Rudy, a pock-marked individual with over-hanging brows and an unhealthy odor about his feet, appeared.

"Right this way. Take your clothes off in this room. Did you bring a teddy with you? Take your drugs out of your pocket-book, and your make-up. Put your clothes in a bundle. Don't keep any money on you."

I took the things out of my purse Bill had provided for me the night before—a small tube of vaseline, a bar of germicidal soap, a small bottle of antiseptic, and my lipstick, rouge, powder and comb. Rudy took my bundle and put it in a small room called the get-away room, a secret escape leading to the outside. One of the wainscoting panels was on hinges, and led to a small opening between the floors which gave a passage to the roof. The girls could walk along this roof to a ladder that led up to another roof, on top of which was a cupola where they could hide until the police had gone.

After Rudy had explained the get-away he took me back and introduced Margaret, the colored maid, a high-yellow in her early thirties. She asked me my name, and I told her "Bertha."

"Now, honey, we's already got a Bertha, so we'll call you Dottie," she told me. "We work in turns 'til every girl 'breaks luck,' and then it's choice. You'll take the next man that comes in, unless he's someone's friend. Sit down."

We were in a large room, the parlor, a room full of mirrors, with a linoleum floor. It was well lighted. There were no chairs, but it had benches on three sides. There were six girls waiting. The other three were busy, and I met them later.

"This is Edna, and she is going to show you how we does business here."

Edna, or French Edna, as the girls called her, broke in most of the new girls. She was a bleached blonde, weighing about two hundred and fifteen pounds. I was glad to see someone larger than myself.

Edna did more business than any of the others, but she did not make the most money, for she was strictly a two-dollar woman. The next girl was Lorraine, the broad of Pollack, the manager. She was tall, nicely formed, red-haired. She always "topped the house," that is, made the most money.

Next to her sat Jackie, a little girl with a hooked nose that made her look like a guinea pig. She was a "nigger lover." Her pimp was a colored man. She was a mediocre hustler, and was known as a "three-way broad." She had the best street clothes of any girl there.

Irene was a thin, dark little woman of about thirty. She didn't have so many tricks but was a hard worker and made pretty good money. Chickie, a bleached blonde, didn't look very young, and had a mousey face. She was the mother of two kids, and her man was a gambler. In the corner sat Dolly and June, who looked, both of them, like statues, with hair combed back and expressionless faces. "They're French, and lady lovers," Edna whispered. "They both live with Earl Walker, a 'jigaboo' pimp from the south side."

Katherine was a mature, thoughtful-looking girl of about thirty, always reading a book when she wasn't busy. Her pimp, Scotty, was a guard at the county jail.

"And so," she greeted me, "you want to be a two-dollar whore, huh? I congratulate you. If you stay here more than sixty days, you belong here. Anybody can get into one of these joints accidentally, but the girl who remains here was born for the job."

Peggy, a peppy, bleached blonde, was like a young panther. She had a great line of bull and would say to most any man who looked like he had money, "Daddy, you're wonderful! Oh, you're such a fine lover. Won't you please take me out of here? If you'll let me have twenty dollars, I'll pay my debts to this gang and I'll meet you on the outside." Sol Rubenstein was her pimp, and he came for her every evening in a big Lincoln.

The last girl I met the first day was Alabama, a thin brunette who looked as though she might be tubercular. She was a comedienne, singing and telling stories and playing jokes, half-drunk most of the time, although it was against the rules of the house for the girls to drink much. She was a good money-maker. All the customers liked her. She had two pimps, one a married man, a cab driver with two kids, that she was supporting, and the other a bartender named Kelly, in a Loop hotel. Katherine said, "She told Kelly that the cab driver was her husband. He knows she's a liar, but he's satisfied as long as she slips him most of the money."

The turn-over in girls was very large, Margaret told me. All of the girls had pimps. I found out that the Globe was a syndicate joint, bossed by a mysterious personage that I never saw. They called him "the old man." He never came to the joint, but the girls said they met him occasionally at his cabaret.

The manager of the house was Pollack, a big-nosed, syphilitic, squint-eyed, bald-headed man known affectionately as "the slaver-driver." Besides being paid for his job, he was kept by four women, one in our place, Lorraine, and one in each of the other three syndicate joints. Next in authority was Rudy, the inside man. And then came Pork Chops, an Italian with a lowering countenance and a greasy vest, who stood on the corner and watched for the cops. When they were coming he gave us the "Air-loft," or warning to get away. The "roper," who stood in front and solicited business was Bad Eye, a tall, goofy kid of about twenty who had lost his eye from a gonococci infection picked up on a towel carelessly tossed in his mother's bathroom. Bad eye was the only man working there who did not have a girl of his own, but was constantly, "on the make." The last man was Chew-Tobacco Rocky, a big Italian with a cud constantly in his mouth. He ran errands for the girls and carried messages from one joint to another. He was Irene's man, and the girls called him a "coffee and" pimp, because Irene just gave him a dollar a day.

The person we girls had the most to do with was Margaret, the maid. When a "John," or customer, came in he was ushered into the parlor where half a dozen girls sat around. He would take his choice and they would go to a room. The girl asked him for the money as soon as they were alone. Although this house was known as a two-dollar joint, when a stranger came in the girls would hustle him for more money and get all they could. We were taught to say to strangers, "We'll give you a good time for five dollars." If they hesitated, we were to say, "Give me three dollars, and I'll take off all my clothes."

When a cab load came the maid would always say, before the men came into the parlor, "Portier," which meant to get as much as you could, because the cab driver would have to be paid a commission, four dollars out of ten, two out of five, and one dollar out of three. We weren't supposed to take less than five dollars from each man in the cab load. There were exceptions. If a "good man," one who had plenty of money to spend, came in, the maid would say "Friday." If he was a five-dollar trick, she said, "Holiday," and if he was a ten-dollar trick, "Double Holiday." In this way strange girls would never cheapen the good trade. It was Margaret's duty to remember every customer, and what he spent.

Just as soon as we got the money from the customer we went out and bought aluminum checks from Margaret, similar to the old-time brass beer checks. A two-dollar check was marked "Five Cents in Trade," and a three-dollar check was a little larger and said, "Ten Cents in Trade." If there was a ten-dollar trick, she'd give us two threes and two deuces.

As soon as Margaret had a bank of a hundred dollars she passed it on to Pollack, who later gave it to the collector, Solly, who came twice a day with a little handbag and two heavily armed guards; Boyle, an ex-police sergeant and another called "The Indian." They took the money from there to the Newland Hotel belonging to The Old Man. He had charge of about thirty joints, houses of prostitution and gambling joints, and was then Chief of the North Side Syndicate. None of the joints was owned by him or his partners.

It was easy to start a joint, I learned. An old hotel was taken on commission and the former owner of the hotel might be kept right on to run the place. All the old man did was to conduct his business for him, furnish him the girls, a staff and police protection. The original owner or manager of the hotel got anywhere from twenty-five to fifty per cent of the old man's share of the day's receipts. The girls were told that police protection cost ten percent. But Pollack, who had been in the game for twenty years, said that the police got very little. The old man had an "in" at the City Hall. He contributed heavily to every campaign fund, Democratic or Republican. He donated to all the politicians, was good to the poor and divided about two hundred dollars a week for each joint to the police. The captain, harness bulls and squad men got the most of it.

The day and night crew of the Globe consisted of twenty girls. Each girl made on an average of thirty dollars a day for the house. When we were "going good," it wasn't unusual for the house to clear as their end four thousand or five thousand dollars a week.

I had thought a house of prostitution would be very exciting. I was surprised to learn how quiet it was. Edna showed me how to put the footpad on the bed. No man ever took off his shoes, and a piece of blanket was laid on to protect the spread. Then she showed me how to examine a man, and told me not to take him if he showed any signs of disease.

Before Edna was through breaking me in, I had a definite feeling of having to make good on my job, just as I have felt when I started a new typing job anywhere. I felt she and the other girls knew more than I did and that they expected me to keep up with them.

My first trick was a bit of a shock to me, however, a big Hunky, a man of about fifty with a handle-bar moustache. He was clumsy and rough. He put his hands under my teddy and pinched me. I didn't mind the roughness, but his fingernails were filthy and he had a vile garlic breath.

The next dozen men were fairly easy. Then an old smooth-faced man of about seventy came in. All his manhood had left him, but he wanted me to pet him and kiss him, and do things. I tried but failed completely. I found myself sorry for him and wishing that I could help him, but it was impossible.

Toward evening a big roughneck came in. The minute I looked at him I knew he would be trouble. I made my first mistake by asking him to spend five dollars, and my second by insisting that he spend an extra dollar to see me take off my teddy. He wasn't going to wait for anything. He wouldn't let me examine him. He handed me two dollars, and picked me up and threw me on the bed. I protested, but he fought with me and wouldn't let me up. I called for Margaret, and he began abusing her. Margaret pushed the buzzer for Rudy, the bouncer.

He came in with Pollack right behind him, and while Rudy pulled the fellow off, Pollack said, "Let him have it!" Rudy hit him over the head with a "sap," a soft black-jack with shot in the end of it. While he was unconscious they dragged him down the back steps and put him into a car, took him a few blocks away and dumped him into an alley under the "L" tracks.

Some of the men were embarrassed. They chose a girl quickly without hardly looking at her. Or they pretended to be tough and tried rough jokes. One well-dressed man with a long thoughtful face picked me out by coming over and putting a hand on my shoulder. Then, and when we were alone, he never said a single word. I let him rest a few minutes in my arms when he was through, and when he went out he gave me a look like you've seen on the face of a hungry dog after you've fed it. Another one, just a youngster really, a little drunk, cried after he was satisfied and said he'd never been in a place like that before. But most of them seemed old customers and used to the joint.

During the course of the day at least half of my customers asked me if I were French. I said "No." Some of them coaxed, some of them threatened to get someone else, but no one made any serious trouble, until a young stub-nosed Italian came in, and when I flatly refused, he went out to Margaret and said, "I want a French broad. I don't have to come here for the regular. I can get that at home."

Margaret said something to Rudy, and he came in and sat beside me, gave me a cigarette and lit one.

"Kid, a notch house is a place of business and the customer must be satisfied. Nowadays few men want it straight. They want it half and half. Don't blame me. I didn't invent human nature. We're in the business, and if you're going to hustle in any kind of a joint you've got to learn to be French, and maybe Greek. Now don't be a damned fool. You get on to the tricks, and it will be easier that way than any other."

I learned quickly. The rest of the girls thought nothing of it. Enda said, "The big money is in the 'queer' guys. And what freaks some of 'em are! But that's the way nature made them and what are you going to do about it?"

At the end of the day I had forty tricks, forty sex-hungry men that I had satisfied.

In common with all the girls, I kept track of all my tricks in a little notebook. Here is an account of my first day's work as a prostitute:

10 men at $2.00 each	$ 40.00
10 men at 3.00	30.00
5 men at 5.00	25.00
2 men at 4.00	8.00
3 men at 10.00	30.00
Total	$133.00

At half-past six Margaret sent me into the office to cash in. I had a hundred and thirty-three checks and naturally thought I was to get half that much, or $66.50. Instead Pollack and Rudy counted my checks and handed me $40.

"Why only $40?" I asked. "I gave you $133. Where I went to school in North Dakota half of $133 is $66.50."

"Don't you know how we do business here?" Pollack answered me. And he took a pencil and showed me.

Tricks	$133.00
50% for the house	66.50
	66.50
10% for protection	6.50
	$60.00

"You see, kid, if there's a pinch we take care of you. You don't have to worry about a thing. We get you bondsmen and everything."

"Well, that still leaves twenty dollars unaccounted for," I protested.

"What the hell difference does it make, as long as you don't have anything to worry about? And we took three dollars off for the maid. She's supposed to get fifty cents on every sixteen checks, but we only took three dollars from you to-night because you're new and you haven't many friends. We gave Bad Eye two bucks for bringing in the business. How would you make any money if it wasn't for the roper? You've got to give Chew-Tobacco a buck for getting your cigarettes, your java, and your eats. We took off two bucks for towels. You used about four dozen, and it costs two bits a dozen to get 'em laundered. If you'd like to bring your own towels from home, you can. Then we bought you a teddy, and four pairs of stockings . . . that cost twelve dollars. So there you are."

Protection	$ 6.50
Teddy and stockings	12.00
Maid	3.00
Roper	2.00
The Runner	1.00
Towels	2.00
	$26.50

"Now, do you understand? How long have you been hustling? You'll get along better if you don't ask so many questions."

My spirits somewhat dampened, I accepted the forty dollars without further question, and went wearily back to my hotel. I didn't feel that anything had changed in me because I had become a prostitute. I just felt completely worn-out, as though I'd finished an unusually hard day's work.

Bill came into my room that night just long enough to order up my supper and say, "Good girl," and "How's tricks?" and to take my money. He took all but two dollars. I was too tired to protest. All I wanted was to bathe and sleep. I remember thinking as I dozed off how easily I had fallen into Bill's system. Only one day, and I was a full-fledged prostitute. That's the way it happened to women. The routine of every day after that would carry them on, just like it does in an office or factory. When their day was over they would be too tired to think.

Bill didn't offer to sleep with me. I couldn't have let him touch me, then. He knew enough to know that. I tried to remember, lying there, how he had felt to me when he took me in his arms, but I couldn't. Instead, I kept seeing the faces of the men who had come in to me that day. And I knew I would go back again and again until I had learned what I wanted to know about them and about the girls who received them.

CARL SANDBURG

(1878-1967)

*No American poet is more closely identified with the fields and factories of the middle west than Carl Sandburg. Born and brought up in a working-class Swedish immigrant family, Sandburg quit school after eighth grade in 1891 and went to work delivering milk, harvesting ice, laying bricks, shining shoes, and threshing wheat. He also spent much of 1897 traveling across the United States as a hobo. During the Spanish-American War, he served in Puerto Rico for eight months. Returning to the United States, he entered Lombard (later Knox) College, where he was befriended by Phillip Green Wright, a professor of literary discernment and socialist convictions. Wright encouraged young Sandburg to develop his own free verse style and published his first three small books of poems—*Reckless Ecstasy *(1904),* Incidentals *(1907), and* The Plaint of a Rose *(1908)—on a basement press.*

Influenced by his own observations of life and work in America, as well as by his mentor, Wright, Sandburg became active in the Wisconsin Social Democratic party, organizing, writing pamphlets, and eventually becoming secretary to Milwaukee's first socialist mayor. In 1912, Sandburg and his family moved to Chicago, where he worked as a reporter and columnist for the Chicago Daily News *and continued to write verse. He became more widely known when his poems were published in 1914 in Harriet Monroe's new but influential Chicago magazine,* Poetry. *Sandburg's first major volume,* Chicago Poems, *came out in 1916, followed shortly by* Cornhuskers *(1918) and* Smoke and Steel *(1920). The last book was one of the first volumes of poetry to focus on the beauty and power of the mid-western industrial landscape.*

From that point, his literary reputation established, Sandburg branched out into a variety of forms. He continued to express his political commitments with a trenchant analysis of the 1919 race riot in Chicago. He wrote stories for children. And he began work on his multi-volume biography of Abraham Lincoln, The Prairie Years *(1926—two volumes) and* The War Years *(1940—four volumes); the second part would win the Pulitzer Prize in 1940, as did his* Complete Poems *in 1951. He had begun collecting and singing folksongs during his earlier travels across the United States; these he published in two anthologies,* The American Songbag *(1927) and* The New American Songbag *(1950). He often sang them, to his own guitar and banjo accompaniment, when he read his poetry. Aside from a number of other volumes of poetry and his verse celebration of ordinary Americans,* The People, Yes *(1936), Sandburg published a book on his wife's brother, the photographer Edward Steichen (1929); a novel,* Remembrance Rock *(1948); and an autobiography,* Always the Young Stranger.

WORK GANGS

Box cars run by a mile long.
And I wonder what they say to each other

When they stop a mile long on a sidetrack.
    Maybe their chatter goes:
I came from Fargo with a load of wheat up to the danger line.
I came from Omaha with a load of shorthorns and they splintered
    my boards.
I came from Detroit heavy with a load of flivvers.
I carried apples from the Hood river last year and this year
    bunches of bananas from Florida; they look for me with
    watermelons from Mississippi next year.

Hammers and shovels of work gangs sleep in shop comers
when the dark stars come on the sky and the night watchmen
    walk and look.

Then the hammer heads talk to the handles,
then the scoops of the shovels talk,
how the day's work nicked and trimmed them,
how they swung and lifted all day,
how the hands of the work gangs smelled of hope.
In the night of the dark stars
when the curve of the sky is a work gang handle,
in the night on the mile-long sidetracks,
in the night where the hammers and shovels sleep in corners,
the night watchmen stuff their pipes with dreams—
and sometimes they doze and don't care for nothin',
and sometimes they search their heads for meanings, stories, stars.
    The stuff of it runs like this:
A long way we come; a long way to go; long rests and long deep
    sniffs for our lungs on the way.
Sleep is a belonging of all; even if all songs are old songs and the
    singing heart is snuffed out like a switchman's lantern with the
    oil gone, even if we forget our names and houses in the
    finish, the secret of sleep is left us, sleep belongs to all, sleep
    is the first and last and best of all.

People singing; people with song mouths connecting with song
    hearts; people who must sing or die; people whose song hearts
    break if there is no song mouth; these are my people.

ELIZABETH BISHOP
(1911–1979)

Born in Worcester, Massachusetts, in 1911, Elizabeth Bishop spent much of
her childhood with grandparents in Nova Scotia and in Worcester, and with

an aunt in Boston. Her father, a successful contractor, had died when she was eight months old, and her mother was committed to a mental institution when she was four. Ill with asthma, she did not attend school until she was sixteen. Thereafter, she enrolled at Vassar, where she wrote for the school newspaper and helped found a literary magazine, Con Spirito, with future writers Mary McCarthy, Eleanor Clark, and Muriel Rukeyser. Toward the end of her Vassar years, she met Marianne Moore, who became a literary mentor and close friend. Before the outbreak of World War II, Bishop traveled extensively in Europe and North Africa, lived in New York and for four years in Key West, Florida, and then, with her friend Lota Costellat de Macedo Soares, for sixteen years in Brazil. She maintained touch with the literary scene in the United States through an extensive correspondence with Moore, Robert Lowell, Randall Jarrell, May Swenson, and others.

Bishop won virtually every poetry prize in the United States: her first book, North & South, *was given the Houghton Mifflin Poetry Award for 1946; her second book,* Poems: North & South—A Cold Spring, *won the 1955 Pulitzer Prize; and her third book,* Questions of Travel (1965), *won the National Book Award. In 1964, she was awarded the fellowship of the Academy of American Poets and served as chancellor of the Academy from 1966 to 1979. In addition to her poetry, her works include volumes of prose, a translation of the diary of a Brazilian woman, Helena Morley, and, after her death, a fascinating selection of her extensive correspondence. Never a prolific poet, she was increasingly seen as a precise and witty observer of the physical world, technically varied and brilliant in her formal experiments. "Filling Station" captures a sense of the place, its oily grime, the people and the dog that inhabit it, but it also wryly evokes the mystery of a kind of care and work that go into even so humble and "dirty" a world.*

FILLING STATION

Oh, but it is dirty!
—this little filling station,
oil-soaked, oil-permeated
to a disturbing, over-all
black translucency.
Be careful with that match!

Father wears a dirty,
oil-soaked monkey suit
that cuts him under the arms,
and several quick and saucy
and greasy sons assist him
(it's a family filling station),
all quite thoroughly dirty.

Do they live in the station?
It has a cement porch
behind the pumps, and on it

a set of crushed and grease-
impregnated wickerwork;
on the wicker sofa
a dirty dog, quite comfy.

Some comic books provide
the only note of color—
of certain color. They lie
upon a big dim doily
draping a taboret
(part of the set), beside
a big hirsute begonia.

Why the extraneous plant?
Why the taboret?
Why, oh why, the doily?
 (Embroidered in daisy stitch
with marguerites, I think,
and heavy with gray crochet.)

Somebody embroidered the doily.
Somebody waters the plant,
or oils it, maybe. Somebody
arranges the rows of cans
so that they softly say:
ESSO—SO—SO—SO
to high-strung automobiles.
Somebody loves us all.

                              —1965

PIETRO DI DONATO
(1911–1992)

Christ in Concrete *was initially a story based on the horrible death of the
author's father in a construction accident. In many ways, the story symbol-
izes the life of the Italian immigrant working man, striving to make a place
for himself and his family in the new world, sacrificed on the altars of
money and faith. It captures in remarkable English prose both the rhythms
of Italian speech and the deeply religious culture of Italian Catholics in
America.*

*In other ways, however, the story is only the beginning point of a longer
narrative, based on di Donato's own life, which became the novel* Christ in
Concrete. *It is a novel about a second generation immigrant boy growing
up in America between the old world outlooks and ideas of his parents' gen-*

eration, and the new world reality with which he must cope, and from which he must wrest a living. Di Donato himself achieved enormous initial success with the novel, first published in 1939: the Book-of-the-Month Club, for example, chose the novel over John Steinbeck's The Grapes of Wrath *for its monthly selection. It fit the mood of the time, especially in capturing the struggles of an immigrant generation of workers and the coming of age of a working-class boy. Di Donato, who had been on home relief (welfare) only a few years before, became something of a literary celebrity. That did not last: during World War II he became a conscientious objector, serving a term of alternative service in Cooperstown, New York. His subsequent novels met with little critical approval, though he was more successful writing journalism and religious biographies of Mother Cabrini and of Maria Goretti. Nevertheless,* Christ in Concrete *stands as a uniquely compelling parable of work and death.*

FROM CHRIST IN CONCRETE

GEREMIO

March whistled stinging snow against the brick walls and up the gaunt girders. Geremio, the foreman, swung his arms about, and gaffed the men on.

Old Nick, the "Lean," stood up from over a dust-flying brick pile, tapped the side of his nose and sent an oyster directly to the ground. "Master Geremio, the Devil himself could not break his tail any harder than we here."

Burly Julio of the walrus mustache and known as the "Snoutnose" let fall the chute door of the concrete hopper and sang over in the Lean's direction: "Mari-Annina's belly and the burning night will make of me once more a milk-mouthed stripling lad . . ."

The Lean loaded his wheelbarrow and spat furiously. "Sons of two-legged dogs . . . despised of even the Devil himself! Work! Sure! For America beautiful will eat you and spit your bones into the earth's hole! Work!" And with that his wiry frame pitched the barrow violently over the rough floor.

Snoutnose waved his head to and fro and with mock pathos wailed, "Sing on, O guitar of mine . . ."

Short, cheery-faced Tomas, the scaffoldman, paused with hatchet in hand and tenpenny spike sticking out from small dicelike teeth to tell the Lean as he went by, in a voice that all could hear, "Ah, father of countless chicks, the old age is a carrion!"

Geremio chuckled and called to him. "Hey, little Tomas, who are you to talk? You and big-titted Cola can't even hatch an egg, whereas the Lean has just to turn the doorknob of his bedroom and old Philomena becomes a balloon!"

Coarse throats tickled and mouths opened wide in laughter.

The Lean pushed his barrow on, his face cruelly furrowed with time and struggle. Sirupy sweat seeped from beneath his cap, down his bony nose and turned icy at its end. He muttered to himself. "Saints up, down, sideways and inside out! How many more stones must I carry before I'm overstuffed with the light of day! I don't understand . . . blood of the Virgin, I don't understand!"

Mike the "Barrel-mouth" pretended he was talking to himself and yelled out in his best English . . . he was always speaking English while the rest carried on in their native Italian. "I don't know myself, but somebodys whose gotta bigga buncha keeds and he alla times talka from somebodys elsa!"

Geremio knew it was meant for him and he laughed. "On the tomb of Saint Pimple-legs, this little boy my wife is giving me next week shall be the last! Eight hungry little Christians to feed is enough for any man."

Tomas nodded to the rest. "Sure, Master Geremio had a telephone call from the next bambino. Yes, it told him it had a little bell between instead of a rose bush. . . . It even told him its name!"

"Laugh, laugh all of you," returned Geremio, "but I tell you that all my kids must be boys so that they someday will be big American builders. And then I'll help them to put the gold away in the basements!"

A great din of riveting shattered the talk among the fast-moving men. Geremio added a handful of Honest tobacco to his corncob, puffed strongly, and cupped his hands around the bowl for a bit of warmth. The chill day caused him to shiver, and he thought to himself: Yes, the day is cold, cold . . . but who am I to complain when the good Christ Himself was crucified?

Pushing the job is all right (when has it been otherwise in my life?), but this job frightens me. I feel the building wants to tell me something; just as one Christian to another. Or perhaps the Easter week is making of me a spirit-seeing pregnant woman. I don't like this. Mr. Murdin tells me, Push it up! That's all he knows. I keep telling him that the underpinning should be doubled and the old material removed from the floors, but he keeps the inspector drunk and . . . "Hey, Ashes-ass! Get away from under that pilaster? Don't pull the old work. Push it away from you or you'll have a nice present for Easter if the wall falls on you!" . . . Well, with the help of God I'll see this job through. It's not my first, nor the . . . "Hey, Patsy number two! Put more cement in that concrete; we're putting up a building, not an Easter cake!"

Patsy hurled his shovel to the floor and gesticulated madly. "The padrone Murdin-sa tells me, 'Too much, too much! Lil' bit is plenty!' And you tell me I'm stingy! The rotten building can fall after I leave!"

Six floors below, the contractor called. "Hey, Geremio! Is your gang of dagos dead?"

Geremio cautioned the men. "On your toes, boys. If he writes out slips, someone won't have big eels on the Easter table."

The Lean cursed that the padrone could take the job and all the Saints for that matter and shove it . . . !

Curly-headed Lazarene, the roguish, pigeon-toed scaffold-man, spat a cloud of tobacco juice and hummed to his own music . . . "Yes, certainly yes to your face, master padrone . . . and behind, This to you and all your kind!"

The day, like all days, came to an end. Calloused and bruised bodies sighed, and numb legs shuffled toward shabby railroad flats . . .

"Ah, bella casa mio. Where my little freshets of blood and my good woman await me. Home where my broken back will not ache so. Home where midst the monkey chatter of my piccolinos I will float off to blessed slumber with my feet on the chair and the head on the wife's soft full breast."

These great child-hearted ones leave one another without words or ceremony, and as they ride and walk home, a great pride swells the breast . . .

"Blessings to Thee, O Jesus. I have fought winds and cold. Hand to hand I have locked dumb stones in place and the great building rises. I have earned a bit of bread for me and mine."

The mad day's brutal conflict is forgiven, and strained limbs prostrate themselves so that swollen veins can send the yearning blood coursing and pulsating deliciously as though the body mountained leaping streams.

The job alone remained behind . . . and yet, they also, having left the bigger part of their lives with it. The cold ghastly beast, the Job, stood stark, the eerie March wind wrapping it in sharp shadows of falling dusk.

That night was a crowning point in the life of Geremio. He bought a house! Twenty years he had helped to mold the New World. And now he was to have a house of his own! What mattered that it was no more than a wooden shack? It was his own!

He had proudly signed his name and helped Annunziata to make her X on the wonderful contract that proved them owners. And she was happy to think that her next child, soon to come, would be born under their own rooftree. She heard the church chimes, and cried to the children, "Children, to bed! It is near midnight. And remember, shut-mouth to the paesanos! Or they will send the evil eye to our new home even before we put foot."

The children scampered off to the icy yellow bedroom where three slept in one bed and three in the other. Coltishly and friskily they kicked about under the covers; their black iron-cotton stockings not removed . . . what! and freeze the peanut-little toes?

Said Annunziata, "The children are so happy, Geremio; let them be, for even I would dance a Tarantella." And with that she turned blushing. He wanted to take her on her word. She patted his hands, kissed them, and whispered. "Our children will dance for us . . . in the American style someday."

Geremio cleared his throat and wanted to sing. "Yes, with joy I could sing in a richer feeling than the great Caruso." He babbled little old-country couplets and circled the room until the tenant below tapped the ceiling.

Annunziata whispered, "Geremio, to bed and rest. Tomorrow is a day for great things . . . and the day on which our Lord died for us."

The children were now hard asleep. Heads under the cover, over . . . snotty noses whistling, and little damp legs entwined.

In bed Geremio and Annunziata clung closely to each other. They mumbled figures and dates until fatigue stilled their thoughts. And with chubby Johnny clutching fast his bottle and warmed between them . . . life breathed heavily, and dreams entertained in far, far worlds, the nation-builder's brood.

But Geremio and Annunziata remained for a long while staring into the darkness . . . silently.

At last Annunziata spoke. "Geremio?"

"Yes?"

"This job you are now working . . ."

"So?"

"You used always to tell me about what happened on the jobs . . . who was jealous, and who praised . . ."

"You should know by now that all work is the same . . ."

"Geremio. The month you have been on this job, you have not spoken a word about the work . . . And I have felt that I am walking into a dream. Is the work dangerous? Why don't you answer . . . ?"

2

Job loomed up damp, shivery gray. Its giant members waiting.

Builders donned their coarse robes, and waited.

Geremio's whistle rolled back into his pocket and the symphony of struggle began.

Trowel rang through brick and slashed mortar rivets were machine-gunned fast with angry grind Patsy number one check Patsy number two check the Lean three check Julio four steel bellowed back at hammer donkey engines coughed purple Ashes-ass Pietro fifteen chisel point intoned stone thin steel whirred and wailed through wood liquid stone flowed with dull rasp through iron veins and hoist screamed through space Rosario the Fat twenty-four and Giacomo Sangini check . . . The multitudinous voices of a civilization rose from the surroundings and melted with the efforts of the Job.

The Lean as he fought his burden on looked forward to only one goal, the end. The barrow he pushed, he did not love. The stones that brutalized his palms, he did not love. The great God Job, he did not love. He felt a searing bitterness and a fathomless consternation at the queer consciousness that inflicted the ever mounting weight of structures that he *had to! had to!* raise above his shoulders! When, when and where would the last stone be? Never . . . did he bear his toil with the rhythm of song! Never . . . did his gasping heart knead the heavy mortar with lilting melody! A voice within him spoke in wordless language.

The language of worn oppression and the despair of realizing that his life had been left on brick piles. And always, there had been hunger and her bastard, the fear of hunger.

Murdin bore down upon Geremio from behind and shouted:

"Goddammit, Geremio, if you're givin' the men two hours off today with pay, why the hell are they draggin' their tails? And why don't you turn that skinny old Nick loose, and put a young wop in his place?"

"Now listen-a to me, Mister Murdin—"

"Don't give me that! And bear in mind that there are plenty of good barefoot men in the streets who'll jump for a day's pay!"

"Padrone—padrone, the underpinning gotta be make safe and . . ."

"Lissenyawopbastard! if you don't like it, you know what you can do!" And with that he swung swaggering away.

The men had heard, and those who hadn't knew instinctively.

The new home, the coming baby, and his whole background, kept the fire from Geremio's mouth and bowed his head. "Annunziata speaks of scouring the ashcans for the children's bread in case I didn't want to work on a job where. . . . But am I not a man, to feed my own with these hands? Ah, but day will end and no boss in the world can then rob me the joy of my home!"

Murdin paused for a moment before descending the ladder.

Geremio caught his meaning and jumped to, nervously directing the rush of work. . . . No longer Geremio, but a machinelike entity.

The men were transformed into single, silent beasts. Snoutnose steamed through ragged mustache whip-lashing sand into mixer Ashes-ass dragged under four-by-twelve beam Lean clawed wall knots jumping in jaws masonry crumbled dust billowed thundered choked . . .

At noon, dripping noses were blown, old coats thrown over shoulders, and foot-long sandwiches were toasted at the end of wire over the flames. Shadows were once again personalities. Laughter added warmth.

Geremio drank his wine from an old-fashioned magnesia bottle and munched a great pepper sandwich . . . no meat on Good Friday.

Said one, "Are some of us to be laid off? Easter is upon us and communion dresses are needed and . . ."

That, while Geremio was dreaming of the new house and the joys he could almost taste. Said he, "Worry not. You should know Geremio." It then all came out. He regaled them with his wonderful joy of the new house. He praised his wife and children one by one. They listened respectfully and returned him well wishes and blessings. He went on and on. . . . "Paul made a radio—all by himself, mind you! One can bear *Barney Google* and many American songs!"

"A radio!"

"An electric machine like magic—yes."

"With music and Christian voices?"

"That is nothing to what he shall someday accomplish!"

"Who knows," suggested Giacomo amazed, "but that Dio has deigned to gift you with a Marconi . . ."

"I tell you, son of Geremio shall never never lay bricks! Paulie mine will study from books—he will be the great builder! This very moment I can see him . . . How proud he!"

Said they in turn: "Master Geremio, in my province it is told that for good luck in a new home, one is to sprinkle well with salt . . . especially the corners, and on moving day sweep with a new broom to the center and pick all up—but do not sweep it out over the threshold!"

"That may be, Pietro. But, Master Geremio, it would be better in my mind that holy water should bless. And also a holy picture of Saint Joseph guarding the door."

"The Americans use the shoe of a horse . . . there must be something in that. One may try. . ."

Snoutnose knew a better way. "You know, you know." He ogled his eyes and smacked his lips. Then, reaching out his hands over the hot embers . . . "To embrace a goosefat breast and bless the house with the fresh milk. And one that does not belong to the wife . . . that is the way!"

Acid-smelling di Nobilis were lit. Geremio preferred his corncob. And Lazarene "tobacco-eater" proudly chawed his quid . . . in the American style.

The ascent to labor was made, and as they trod the ladder, heads turned and eyes communed with the mute flames of the brazier whose warmth they were leaving, not with willing heart, and in that fleeting moment the breast wanted much to speak of hungers that never reached the tongue.

About an hour later, Geremio called over to Pietro, "Pietro, see if Mister Murdin is in the shanty and tell him I must see him! I will convince him that the work must not go on like this . . . just for the sake of a little more profit!"

Pietro came up soon. "The padrone is not coming up. He was drinking from a large bottle of whisky and cursed in American words that if you did not carry out his orders—"

Geremio turned away disconcerted, stared dumbly at the structure and mechanically listed in his mind's eye the various violations of construction safety. An uneasy sensation hollowed him. The Lean brought down an old piece of wall and the structure palsied. Geremio's heart broke loose and out-thumped the floor's vibrations, a rapid wave of heat swept him and left a chill touch in its wake. He looked about to the men, a bit frightened. They seemed usual, life-size, and moved about with the methodical deftness that made the moment then appear no different than the task of toil had ever been.

Snoutnose's voice boomed into him. "Master Geremio, the concrete is re-ady!"

"Oh yes, yes, Julio." And he walked gingerly toward the chute, but not without leaving behind some part of his strength, sending out his soul to wrestle with the limbs of Job, who threatened in stiff silence. He talked and joked with Snoutnose. Nothing said anything, nor seemed wrong. Yet a vague uneasiness was to him as certain as the foggy murk that floated about Job's stone and steel.

"Shall I let the concrete down now, Master Geremio?"

"Well, let me see—no, hold it a minute. Hey, Lazarene! Tighten the chute cables!"

Snoutnose straightened, looked about, and instinctively rubbed the sore small of his spine. "Ah," sighed he, "all the men feel as I—yes, I can tell. They are tired but happy that today is Good Friday and we quit at three o'clock—"And he swelled in human ecstasy at the anticipation of food, drink and the hairy flesh-tingling warmth of wife, and then, extravagant rest.

Geremio gazed about and was conscious of seeming to understand many things. He marveled at the strange feeling which permitted him to sense the familiarity of life. And yet—all appeared unreal, a dream pungent and nostalgic.

Life, dream, reality, unreality, spiraling ever about each other. "Ha," he chuckled, "how and from where do these thoughts come?"

Snoutnose had his hand on the hopper latch and was awaiting the word from Geremio. "Did you say something, Master Geremio?"

"Why yes, Julio, I was thinking—funny! A—yes, what is the time—yes, that is what I was thinking."

"My American can of tomatoes says ten minutes from two o'clock. It won't be long now, Master Geremio."

Geremio smiled. "No, about an hour . . . and then, home."

"Oh, but first we stop at Mulberry Street, to buy their biggest eels, and the other finger-licking stuffs."

Geremio was looking far off, and for a moment happiness came to his heart without words, a warm hand stealing over. Snoutnose's words sang to him pleasantly, and he nodded.

"And Master Geremio, we ought really to buy the sea-fruits with the shells—you know, for the much needed steam they put into the—"

He flushed despite himself and continued, "It is true, I know it—especially the juicy clams . . . uhmn, my mouth waters like a pump."

Geremio drew on his unlit pipe and smiled acquiescence. The men around him were moving to their tasks silently, feeling of their fatigue, but absorbed in contemplations the very same as Snoutnose's. The noise of labor seemed not to be noise, and as Geremio looked about, life settled over him a gray concert—gray forms, atmosphere and gray notes. . . . Yet his off-tone world felt so near, and familiar.

"Five minutes from two," swished through Snoutnose's mustache.

Geremio automatically took out his watch, rewound and set it. Lazarene had done with the cables. The tone and movement of the scene seemed to Geremio strange, differently strange, and yet, a dream familiar from a timeless date. His hand went up in motion to Julio. The molten stone gurgled low, and then with heightening rasp. His eyes followed the stone-cementy pudding, and to his ears there was no other sound than its flow. From over the roofs somewhere, the tinny voice of *Barney Google* whined its way, hooked into his consciousness and kept itself a revolving record beneath his skullplate.

"Ah, yes, *Barney Google,* my son's wonderful radio machine . . . wonderful Paul." His train of thought quickly took in his family, home and hopes. And with hope came fear. Something within asked, "Is it not possible to breathe God's air without fear dominating with the pall of unemployment? And the terror of production for Boss, Boss and Job? To rebel is to lose all of the very little. To be obedient is to choke. O dear Lord, guide my path."

Just then, the floor lurched and swayed under his feet. The slipping of the underpinning below rumbled up through the undetermined floors.

Was he faint or dizzy? Was it part of the dreamy afternoon? He put his hands in front of him and stepped back, and looked up wildly. "No! No!"

The men poised stricken. Their throats wanted to cry out and scream but didn't dare. For a moment they were a petrified and straining pageant. Then the bottom of their world gave way. The building shuddered violently, her supports burst with the crackling slap of wooden gunfire. The floor vomited upward. Geremio clutched at the air and shrieked agonizingly. "Brothers, what have we done? Ahhh-h, children of ours!" With the speed of light, balance went sickeningly awry and frozen men went flying explosively. Job tore down upon them madly. Walls, floors, beams became whirling, solid, splintering waves crashing with detonations that ground man and material in bonds of death.

The strongly shaped body that slept with Annunziata nights and was perfect in all the limitless physical quantities thudded as a worthless sack amongst the giant débris that crushed fragile flesh and bone with centrifugal intensity.

Darkness blotted out his terror and the resistless form twisted, catapulted insanely in its directionless flight, and shot down neatly and deliberately between the empty wooden forms of a foundation wall pilaster in upright position, his blue swollen face pressed against the form and his arms outstretched, caught securely through the meat by the thin round bars of reinforcing steel.

The huge concrete hopper that was sustained by an independent structure of thick timber wavered a breath or so, its heavy concrete rolling uneasily until a great sixteen-inch wall caught it squarely with all the terrific verdict of its dead weight and impelled it downward through joists, beams and masonry until it stopped short, arrested by two girders, an arm's length above Geremio's head; the gray concrete gushing from the hopper mouth, and sealing up the mute figure.

Giacomo had been thrown clear of the building and dropped six floors to the street gutter, where he lay writhing.

The Lean had evinced no emotion. When the walls descended, he did not move. He lowered his head. One minute later he was hanging in mid-air, his chin on his chest, his eyes tearing loose from their sockets, a green foam bubbling from his mouth and his body spasming, suspended by the shreds left of his mashed arms, pinned between a wall and a girder.

A two-by-four hooked little Tomas up under the back of his jumper and swung him around in a circle to meet a careening I-beam. In the flash that he lifted his frozen cherubic face, its shearing edge sliced through the top of his skull.

When Snoutnose cried beseechingly, "Saint Michael!" blackness enveloped him. He came to in a world of horror. A steady stream, warm, thick, and sickening as hot wine, bathed his face and clogged his nose, mouth, and eyes. The nauseous sirup that pumped over his face clotted his mustache red and drained into his mouth. He gulped for air, and swallowed blood. As he breathed, the pain shocked him to oppressive semiconsciousness. The air was wormingly alive with cries, screams, moans, and dust, and his crushed chest seared him with a thousand fires. He couldn't see, nor breathe enough to cry. His right hand moved to his face and wiped at the gelatinizing substance, but it kept coming on, and a heartbreaking moan wavered about him, not far. He wiped his eyes in subconscious despair. Where was he? What kind of a dream was he having? Perhaps he wouldn't wake up in time for work, and then what? But how queer; his stomach beating him, his chest on fire, he sees nothing but dull red, only one hand moving about, and a moaning in his face!

The sound and clamor of the rescue squads called to him from far off.

Ah, yes, he's dreaming in bed, and, far out in the streets, engines are going to a fire. Oh, poor devils! Suppose his house were on fire? With the children scattered about in the rooms he could not remember! He must do his utmost to break out of this dream! He's swimming under water, not able to raise his head and get to the air. He must get back to consciousness to save his children!

He swam frantically with his one right hand, and then felt a face beneath its touch. A face! It's Angelina alongside of him! Thank God, he's awake! He tapped her face. It moved. It felt cold, bristly, and wet. "It moves so. What is this?" His fingers slithered about grisly sharp bones and in a gluey, stringy, hollow mass, yielding as wet macaroni. Gray light brought sight, and hysteria punctured his heart. A girder lay across his chest, his right hand clutched a grotesque human mask, and suspended almost on top of him was the twitching, faceless body of Tomas. Julio fainted with an inarticulate sigh. His fingers loosed and the bodiless headless face dropped and fitted to the side of his face while the drippings above came slower and slower.

The rescue men cleaved grimly with pick and ax.

Geremio came to with a start . . . far from their efforts. His brain told him instantly what had happened and where he was. He shouted wildly. "Save me! Save me! I'm being buried alive!"

He paused exhausted. His genitals convulsed. The cold steel rod upon which they were impaled froze his spine. He shouted louder and louder. "Save me! I am hurt badly! I can be saved I can—save me before it's too late!" But the cries went no farther than his own ears. The icy wet concrete reached his chin. His heart appalled. "In a few seconds I will be entombed. If I can only breathe, they will reach me. Surely, they will!" His face was quickly covered, its flesh yielding to the solid sharp-cut stones. "Air! Air!" screamed his lungs as he was completely sealed. Savagely he bit into the wooden form pressed upon his mouth. An eighth of an inch of its surface splintered off. Oh, if he could only hold out long enough to bite even the smallest hole through to air! He must! There can be no other way! He must! There can be no other way! He is responsible for his family! He cannot leave them like this! He didn't want to die! This could not be the answer to life! He had bitten halfway through when his teeth snapped off to the gums in the uneven conflict. The pressure of the concrete was such, and its effectiveness so thorough, that the wooden splinters, stumps of teeth, and blood never left the choking mouth.

Why couldn't he go any farther?

Air! Quick! He dug his lower jaw into the little hollowed space and gnashed in choking agonized fury. Why doesn't it go through! Mother of Christ, why doesn't it give? Can there be a notch, or two-by-four stud behind it? Sweet Jesu! No! No! Make it give . . . Air! Air!

He pushed the bone-bare jaw maniacally; it splintered, cracked, and a jagged fleshless edge cut through the form, opening a small hole to air. With a desperate burst the lung-prisoned air blew an opening through the shredded mouth and whistled back greedily a gasp of fresh air. He tried to breathe, but it was impossible. The heavy concrete was settling immutably and its rich cement-laden grout ran into his pierced face. His lungs would not expand and were crushing in tighter and tighter under the settling concrete.

"Mother mine—mother of Jesu—Annunziata—children of mine—dear, dear, for mercy, Jesu-Giuseppe e' Mari," his blue foamed tongue called. It then distorted in a shuddering coil and mad blood vomited forth. Chills and fire played through him and his tortured tongue stuttered, "Mercy, blessed Father—salvation, most kind Father—Saviour—Saviour of His children, help me—adored Saviour—I kiss your feet eternally—you are my Lord—there is but one God—you are my God of infinite mercy—Hail Mary divine Virgin—our Father who art in heaven hallowed be thy— name—our Father—my Father," and the agony excrucited with never-ending mount, "our Father—Jesu, Jesu, soon Jesu, hurry dear Jesu Jesu! Je-sssu . . . !" His mangled voice trebled hideously, and hung in jerky whimperings. Blood vessels burst like mashed flower stems. He screamed. "Show yourself now, Jesu! Now is the time! Save me! Why don't you come! Are you there! I cannot stand it—ohhh, why do you let it happen—where are you? Hurry hurry hurry!"

His bones cracked mutely and his sanity went sailing distorted in the limbo of the subconscious. With the throbbing tones of an organ in the hollow background, the fighting brain disintegrated and the memories of a baffled lifetime sought outlet.

He moaned the simple songs of barefoot childhood, scenes flashed desperately on and off, and words and parts of words came pitifully high and low from his inaudible lips.

Paul's crystal-set earphones pressed the sides of his head tighter and tighter, the organ boomed the mad dance of the Tarentella, and the hysterical mind sang cringingly and breathlessly, "Jesu my Lord my God my all Jesu my Lord my God my all Jesu my Lord my God my all Jesu my Lord my God my all."

MERLE TRAVIS

(1 9 1 7 - 1 9 8 3)

Travis's father was originally a tobacco farmer, but unable to make a living at it, he moved the family to Ebenezer, Kentucky, in 1921, and took a job in the mines. One of his favorite expressions was "another day older and deeper in debt," a saying that became central to Travis's song "Sixteen Tons." During the 1930s, Travis hitch-hiked around the country, playing where he could, and eventually hooked up with a couple of country music groups, before establishing himself in Cincinnati with the Drifting Pioneers and on radio station WLW. During World War II, Travis served in the Marines, and afterwards settled in California. There he played with a variety of bands, working with artists like Tex Ritter and Tex Williams, who recorded "Smoke, Smoke, Smoke That Cigarette," a song Travis co-wrote and that sold a million copies.

The postwar period fostered a craze for folk music and Travis was asked by Capitol Records to record an album of Kentucky folksongs. He produced "Folk Songs of Our Hills," for which he wrote "Nine-Pound Hammer," "Dark as a Dungeon," and "Sixteen Tons." The last was recorded by Tennessee Ernie Ford in 1955 and sold over a million copies in a shorter time than any previous recording. Travis meanwhile had launched a movie career, playing a GI in the 1954 movie From Here to Eternity, *in which he sang "Re-Enlistment Blues." He also appeared in Clint Eastwood's* Honky-tonk Man, *worked as a scriptwriter for Johnny Cash's TV show, produced cartoons, and carried on his own stage act. But Travis was dogged by drug addiction and alcoholism, and though he was elected to the Country Music Hall of Fame, he was never able to sustain the career for which his great talent eminently suited him.*

SIXTEEN TONS

Now some people say a man's made out of mud,
But a poor man's made out of muscle and blood,
Muscle and blood, skin and bones,
A mind that's weak and a back that's strong.

[Chorus] You load sixteen tons and what do you get?
You get another day older and deeper in debt.
Saint Peter, don't you call me 'cause I can't go,
I owe my soul to the company store.

I was born one morning when the sun didn't shine,
I picked up my shovel and I walked to the mine.
I loaded sixteen tons of number nine coal,
And the straw boss hollered, "Well, bless my soul!"

I was born one morning in the drizzling rain;
Fighting and trouble is my middle name.
I was raised in the bottoms by a mama hound--
I'm as mean as a dog but I'm gentle as a lamb.

If you see me coming, you better step aside;
A lot of men didn't, and a lot of men died.
I got a fist of iron and a fist of steel,
If the right one don't get you then the left one will.

DEBORAH BOE

(B. 1951)

Deborah Boe's first book was Mojave: Poems *(1987). Her work has been published in* Poetry Magazine *and the* Ohio Review, *among other places. She has lived in Maine for much of her life.*

The poem that follows captures a sense of the changes, psychological and physical, that factory work imposes on people. The speaker does not directly voice protest at the dangers of her glue machine or the demands of management. Still, the poem works away from machine and factory to a very different world on the outside.

FACTORY WORK

All day I stand here, like this,
over the hot-glue machine,
not too close to the wheel
that brings up the glue,
and I take those metal shanks,
slide the backs of them in glue
and make them lie down
on the shoe-bottoms, before the sole
goes on. It's simple, but the lasts
weigh, give you big arms.
If I hit my boyfriend now,
in the supermarket parking lot,
he knows I hit him.

Phyllis, who stands next to me,
had long hair before the glue machine
got it. My machine ate up my shirt once.
I tried to get it out, the wheel
spinning on me, until someone with a brain
turned it off. It's not bad
here, people leave you alone,
don't ask you what you're thinking.

It's a good thing, too, because all this morning
I was remembering last night,
when I really thought my grandpa's soul
had moved into the apartment,
the way the eggs fell, and the lamp
broke, like someone was trying
to communicate to me, and he

just dead this week. I wouldn't
blame him. That man in the next aisle
reminds me of him, a little.

It's late October now, and Eastland
needs to lay some people off.
Last week they ran a contest
to see which shankers shanked fastest.
I'm not embarrassed to say
I beat them all. It's all
in economy of motion, all the moves
on automatic.
I almost
don't need to look at what
I'm doing. I'm thinking of the way
the leaves turn red when the cold
gets near them. They fall until
you're wading in red leaves up to your knees,
and the air snaps
in the tree-knuckles, and you begin
to see your breath rise
out of you like your own ghost
each morning you come here.

LLOYD ZIMPEL
(B.1929)

Lloyd Zimpel has approached work from the differing perspectives of a social scientist, an educator, and a creative writer. For a period of time, he worked in advertising in San Francisco, but in 1964 he became education director for the San Francisco office of California's Fair Employment Practices Commission, a position he retained until 1981. During this period, he wrote and edited a number of books about hardcore unemployment, disadvantaged workers, and the degradation of labor.

"Sand" is one of a two-part story titled Foundry Foreman, Foundrymen. *The story captures the explicit class structure of a traditional industrial workplace, a foundry, by focusing on the man in the middle between the boss and the workers. The boss is interested only in turning out as cheaply and quickly as possible the products he has contracted to sell; the workers' concern is to avoid injury in particular and, more generally, the brutality and dangerous conditions of their labor. The foreman is therefore torn between forces whose opposing demands place his job, his marriage, and his well-being in jeopardy. The story dramatizes the differing relationships to work and the different emotional reactions to that work established by the characters' class positions.*

SAND

While the night crew hustled, the new foreman, Prokop, watched through the haze of his own cigarette smoke from the catwalk halfway between the I-beams of the ceiling and the stained concrete of the foundry core room floor. Beside him the sand mixer throbbed gigantically, vibrating the rungs beneath his feet. Down the long alleyway below, the tank-like blowers clicked and hissed, pressuring sand into molds cut to the round contours of the differential housings the foundry day shift was pouring. These sounds had been in Prokop's ears for eight and nine hours each day, five and six days a week for six years—six sweaty years in the foundry core room at everything from dipping cores to handling the blowers. But the job on the catwalk was new: the growling mixer beside him and the nineteen men who hustled below had been his charges for less than a month.

This was as high as he hoped to go. "Mixing sand," he soberly confided to Price, a blower operator who had worked this same shift for three years, "is harder than you think. One bad batch and every core is ruined. . . . Whose fault is it? Who gets the blame?" he paused to make a mysterious pass at the button-studded control-panel, and answered himself: "The foreman's!"

When he got the promotion the superintendent told him that every core his shift turned out might as well be stamped *Made by Prokop*; he was that important. It was his shift, he had a free hand with it; the superintendent never rode him—if he came into the core room at all it was only to get a salt tablet and wave a friendly hand as he went out.

But this evening Prokop saw the super coming from the foundry—dark now because it ran no night shift—and he walked with a different purpose. His grease-stained hat was pushed back on his bald head; his broad flowered tie was loosened at the collar; his sleeves rolled up. With a heavy stride he passed the water fountain where the salt tablets were and came to stand with one boot on the lowest catwalk step. Prokop came down, bending toward the deep-pored face to hear what the super had to say.

"The day-men claim they're getting lots of hairline cracks." The super stared straight into Prokop's eyes. "Damn things are busting when they pour. It could be the sand and it could be the blowers." He gave his hat a further push with his thumb. "You might look into it," he said, and he walked away, pants stretched tight across his heavy thighs, back to his little office out of sight in the foundry's far north end.

"Well, it ain't the sand," Prokop mumbled to himself, but with no certainty. No one had ever criticized before.

Back on the catwalk he dipped a hand into the mixer and rubbed the moist sand between his fingers. Then he threw it back into the mixer and went down to warn his operators.

"Blow 'em tighter, they're falling apart."

On blower number one, Price told him: "I'm already blowing them as tight as they'll pack. If they get cracked, it's after they leave here. Talk to the ovenman, why don't you?"

Prokop gave him a long even look, enough to say he wouldn't be told his own business. But he checked the mix again, unsure if it was good or bad, and ran half a bucket of water which he poured into the sand as it rolled in great slow waves before the push of the mixer blades.

It looked fine, nothing wrong with it that he could see. Price might be right. His eyes roved to the far end of the alley where the new ovenman, Jay, in his colorless cap and asbestos gloves that reached to the elbow, moved a rack loaded with cores.

Prokop headed back into the hot shadows, watching as Jay rapidly emerged from one of the huge ovens with one asbestos-clad arm bent before his face to shield his eyes from the fierce heat, the other pulling the dolly that carried a rack loaded with smoking cores. As soon as the cores were clear, Jay grabbed the chain tackle and, hand moving swiftly over hand, brought the steel door down to cut off the heat that rolled furiously into the core room.

In the roasted air Prokop's eyes watered. He watched Jay who, dry-eyed as if all the juices had long since boiled out of him, moved the rack into position along the wall. Here the cores would cool until the dippers could handle them.

"Hey, Jay! Get this rack!" The shout came from one of the blower operators just as Jay lowered the dolly. Prokop heard him curse, watched him give the dolly a last angry pump so that the loaded rack dropped the last half-inch to the floor with a jar that trembled its tipper shelves.

"*Hey!*" yelled Prokop into the sting of smoke that drifted off the nick. "You can't do that! You're cracking the cores, dropping the racks like that."

Jay had already started toward the alleyway; but he stopped in mid-stride, the hand that pulled the now-empty dolly outstretched behind him.

"How's that?" he said roughly, his eyes sharp and hard in the heat-flushed face. "What's the matter with these cores?"

"They're *busting*, for God's sake," Prokop said. "They crumble at the smelter. You're cracking 'em with that dropping."

Jay's black bristled jaw came forward. "What the hell are you talking about?" he said coolly. Show me a busted core on that rack. Show me one." He dropped the dolly-handle and started toward the cores, confident enough to bet a week's wages there wasn't a hairline in any of them.

But as foreman Prokop need call no man's bluff. "Never mind that one rack. You run out fifty-sixty a night, and too damn many are coming through bad. I can't check every core in the place. You've got to watch—"

Jay waved one big asbestos glove, broad and flat as a shovel. "Listen," he said. "Those cores are done the best way these ovens can do them. You thought of checking the mix?"

"I'll worry about the mix," said Prokop, turning sharply away. Pant legs snapping, he walked off with the feel of Jay's eyes on his back.

He gave the sand five more minutes in the mixer, five minutes over the usual time and then stopped the blades. Beneath the mixing tank a chute opened and the sand, ready for the blowers, tumbled in huge damp chunks into the series of storage bins below.

With the mixer empty, Prokop came down to the floor, he plunged a hand wrist-deep into the sand in the first bin. If anything, it felt too damp. He checked each bin. The sand in each was damp. He snorted with disgust with himself. Too much water. The extra half-bucket did it.

When the loader came with his wheel-barrow, ready to load the power-shovel that fed the hoppers above the blowers, Prokop instructed him to use only sand from the previous mix. This last one was too wet, no doubt about it.

Back on the catwalk he punched the buttons that brought in a trolleyload of fresh sand. It emptied itself onto the naked steel mixer blades, burying them in one sudden splash of sand. He tossed water—less this time—and binder into the mixer and started it, watching closely as the sand began its sluggish motion.

When it was moving steadily, he crossed the core room through the archway to the foundry. Under the vast roof only one light burned and beneath it two of his men were jockeying a skidful of baked and dipped cores into position beside the idle smelter. Seeing him approach the men began to work faster. One of them, a dipper who sometimes came to work drunk, was sweating heavily, his khaki shirt soaked dark-brown.

"You guys taking care of these cores?" asked Prokop. "Lots of 'em cracking."

"Sure," the dipper said, and as if to prove it pulled the lowered jack from under the skid with the awkward care of a drunk trying to walk a line. With the jack between them the two went back to the core room.

Alone, Prokop edged between the skids, examining the bottle-shaped cores stacked on them. The third core he picked up broke in his hand; he was left holding the neck while the bottom smashed against the toe of his safety shoe.

He felt a cold touch of panic: was this the sort of work his shift was putting out? Every third core bad? He threw the neck down and carefully searched over each skid. By the time he had finished he was breathing easier. There was only one other bad core in the bunch. This was better than average, he told himself with relief.

But better than average or not, no one was going to compliment him on it, he knew that. He made his way back to the core room thinking that he had been mixing good sand every night for a month and not a good word reached him. One bad core and they were on his neck like a wood tick.

Slowly, he climbed the catwalk steps and poked a worried hand into the rolling sand. As he let it dribble away he saw Price coming down the alley.

"Hey, Prokop. Blower's plugged. Damn sand isn't dropping."

"Ain't empty, is it?"

"Just filled it," Price said, impatient that he should be credited with the stupidity of trying to work an empty blower.

"Probably nothing," Prokop muttered. But as he headed for the blower he passed the storage bins. At once he saw where the trouble lay. The door of the middle bin was up; that meant the loader was drawing from it, from the damp sand.

Under his breath Prokop cursed the stupid loader. He'd *told* him. It was far too wet for use. He slapped hopelessly at Price's blower chute. The sand had jammed in the hopper overhead.

Angrily swearing at blower, sand and loader alike, Prokop grabbed a broken broom from beside the water fountain: finding whatever handholds he could, he climbed to the top of the blower. With one hand he clung to the power shovel track that ran overhead, and with the other he jabbed the broomstick into the mound of firm damp sand, making hole after hole. For several minutes he worked with a scarcely controlled fury, until the mound collapsed like a balloon from which the air had been released.

"Try it now," he called, and jumped down as Price worked the lever that brought sand out in its normal hard stream. Without a word, Prokop threw the broom to the floor at Price's feet—a gesture of scorn for a man unable to solve his own petty problems—and turned back to the catwalk.

The guilty loader was nowhere in sight. Irritated, Prokop lighted a cigarette, watching the sand rise and fall in the mixer. Almost by itself his toe took up a nervous tapping against the pipe stanchion of the catwalk.

"Ho, Prokop!"

He knew what he would see even before he turned: another jammed blower. This time it was Crowley on number six who was gesturing angrily for him to come down.

"Use this for God's sake," Prokop said, grabbing the broomhandle from Price and throwing it to Crowley. "What's there to get so excited about?"

He waited until Crowley had slid and cursed his way to the top of the blower. Then he went back down the aisle, pausing to tell each operator that a bad batch of sand had got through and to watch for jam-ups. Price was waiting for him.

"Better get yourself some more brooms," he said drily. "This one's plugged again."

"Then dig it out with your hands."

Price frowned. I be damned, Prokop," he said. "I ain't a gopher." But he turned away, grumbling, and made a clumsy attempt at climbing the blower.

Angrier than ever, Prokop located the loader, slowly shoveling sand from his wheelbarrow into the power shovel. He jumped with alarm when the foreman grabbed his arm.

"What the hell you using this wet stuff for?" Prokop yelled. "Didn't I tell you?"

"I know it, Prokop, but it's all there is. Come on take a look."

Prokop waved him off. "Don't use any more." Tight-lipped he strode past the loader, toward Jay who stood in the alley watching Price bang uselessly on the blower chute. Just as he stepped over the ovenman's dolly, an operator down the alley yelled for a new rack. Prokop reached out and jabbed Jay's shoulder.

"Get a move on," he said, gesturing toward the yelling operator. "You're still getting paid by the hour."

The ovenman whirled. "Don't worry about me, Prokop," he snapped. "You got enough bad sand to worry about."

Already walking away, Prokop started to turn, ready with a sharp word; but instead he went on to climb the catwalk steps. What Jay said was true enough, and he wasn't proud of himself for riding a man with no good reason.

But he hadn't time to make excuses or apologies to himself or anyone; the clock over the water fountain told him that. While he had been fooling with the jammed blowers, the sand had been mixing and mixing, several minutes overtime already.

As quickly as he could reach the controls, he shot the mix into the bins, then ran down to see how it was.

Not as dry as he had expected: apparently he'd put in plenty of water to begin with. He motioned for the loader to come over. "Use this new batch," he told him.

"I already got them all loaded with the other batch, Prokop," he said.

Prokop looked away. "Good for you," he muttered under his breath. He'd hear from every damn blower now.

Price still didn't have number one working, he saw. While his helper lounged against the bench, arms folded, Price pounded at the chute and between blows turned black looks at the foreman. Prokop saw him speak out of the side of his mouth to his helper.

"Use the damn stick!" Prokop yelled, but Price only turned to spread his palms and point down the alley. Prokop saw that the operator on number three had the broom now and was making futile efforts to poke it into the sand while he awkwardly clung halfway up the side of the blower.

Prokop snorted at the sight. "Get *up* there!" he bellowed. "Quit that horsing around." With unutterable contempt he turned his back on them all, and fixed a cold stare at the new batch of sand in the mixer. Immediately he saw that something was wrong. The sand poured loosely as sugar against the sides of the mixer tank.

He had forgotten the binder. What kind of fool moves was he making anyhow? He might have sent this sand—useless without binder—into the storage bins, and he would never have lived it down, even if he mixed a million perfect batches afterward.

Furious and disgusted with himself, he dug a bucketful of binder from the barrel at the end of the catwalk and flung it smoothly over the sand. As the blades picked it up, blending it into the mix, he watched with squinted eyes. An oversight like that . . . there was no excuse. . . . He heard someone shouting—"You screwed up my production enough for one night, Prokop!" It was number three operator, his face flushed with anger at being ignored for what he must have thought to be the foreman's daydreams. "I might's well punch out and go home," he said. "Ain't making a dime with sand like that."

"Listen," Prokop said coldly, holding tight against the rage he felt. "So you lose a lousy nickel on piecework. You're getting your base rate. We got one bad batch. The next one is okay. It don't mean nothing."

"It means I got to diddle around half the night," the operator said, but he turned and went back to his machine.

On number one, Price had sent his helper up to the edge of the hopper with a spade. Perched at the lip of the blower, his head only inches from the ceiling, the man flung down spadeful after spadeful of wet sand. It hit the concrete floor with a liquid-like splash. Prokop watched as Price collared the loader to stand by with a wheelbarrowful of fresh sand, ready to fill the hopper as soon as the helper jumped down. On the floor the pile of sand mounted and spread into the alley.

That was the wisest thing—shoveling it out—Prokop admitted. He should have suggested it himself; it was the foreman's job. He caught himself from darting a look toward the foundry for signs of the super's presence, and turned to watch as the loader sent up the power shovel with its fresh mix into position over number one. Immediately Price opened the operating lever all the way, clearing the chamber with a belch of air. The last of the wet sand shot across the bench and the fresh mix came smoothly through. In a few minutes Price and his helper had finished filling the rack they were working on.

"Full rack on one!" Price's shout brought Jay and his dolly from the shadows of the oven. They came as far as the pile of sand now blocking the alley and stopped. Jay spoke to Price, then looked toward the catwalk. When he saw Prokop watching he stepped into the pile of sand on the floor, stubbornly pulling his empty dolly until it hung up on its low axles. Vigorously tugging, Jay got it free and rammed it under the filled rack. He rolled it out into the alley, up to the pile of sand once again.

Standing with both hands on the catwalk rail and staring down, Prokop saw the ovenman shrug, lean hard away from the dolly-handle and pull the load into the sand as far as his strength would take it. The wheels of the dolly ground halfway through, then stopped, jammed with sand. Jay dropped the handle and spread his hands toward the catwalk, an elaborate gesture to show his helplessness. Prokop took a deep breath and came down the steps.

"Okay, Prokop," Jay said. "What'dya want me to do, break my back on your wet sand?"

For a long moment the foreman eyed him levelly. "Suit yourself," he said. He wouldn't make an issue of Jay's childishness. "Just get that rack in the oven where it belongs."

Farther down the alley the operator of number five sat atop his machine and with short fast jabbing movements spaded another pile of wet sand onto the floor. Above the roar of the core room Prokop yelled up to him: "Get yourself a wheelbarrow to throw that in. You're blocking the alley."

He started toward the mixer, looking for an empty wheelbarrow the man could use. But halfway up the alley he drew up short. There on the catwalk was the white shirt and flowered tie again. The super, his face turned away from the turmoil in the core room, was examining the sand in the mixer. Dismayed, Prokop mounted the steps. Without turning, the super seemed aware that he had come onto the catwalk.

"How's it going?" he said, still without looking.

"Okay." Prokop winced to say it: anyone with eyes of his own could see the mess below. He tried to explain casually: "Well, we did have a little batch of bad sand. Just cleaning it out now."

"I noticed that," said the super with no particular weight to his words. He pushed back his hat. "That sand, what was the matter with it?"

"Little too wet, it seemed." Prokop matched the offhand quality of the super's voice as best he could. "We could probably have run it, but it was slow going."

The super pursed his lips and looked out over the room. Prokop followed his gaze to see the operator on number four climb up the side of his blower, spade in hand. Jay he noticed with furious annoyance, stood idle, waiting for the loader to finish shoveling the sand out of his way. Prokop strained forward, wanting to shout at the ovenman to give a hand, but he glanced sideways at the super and said nothing.

With Prokop following, the super started down the steps, wiping the sweat from beneath his soiled white collar. Back over his shoulder, in a voice Prokop had to strain to hear, he said: "Everything getting straightened out okay?"

"Sure," the foreman said. "No trouble."

"Fine." At the bottom of the steps the super stood for a moment looking down the alley, then he ambled back toward the foundry.

For the first time that night Prokop realized he was soaked with sweat. He hadn't been working that hard. It was the idea of the job that did it. Foreman. Suddenly Prokop saw himself a blower operator with no stake but piece-work in what the shift turned out.

"Prokop!" The loader was standing beneath the catwalk, shouting up at him. "What should I do with that old sand?"

"Dump it in the yard," said Prokop, and he went down to see which bins he could use for the batch that was now ready.

〜

When the shift moved into its last hour all the blowers were *whooshing* steadily and the molds clanked in tinny rhythm on the steel benches. Although he was reluctant to leave the mixer—as if something might again go wrong when he turned his back—Prokop made another trip to the dark foundry. He poked over the skids that held cores from the wet mix. They were a deep golden color from being baked extra long, but they seemed sturdy enough. All the same they showed more hairline cracks than usual.

Back in the core room he sought out Jay and warned him again: "Watch those racks. We're still getting hairlines—"

"You told me that once tonight," Jay said coldly. "I didn't forget."

"Okay," said Prokop. "Don't." But he went back to the mixer thinking he must sound like a nervous old woman, coming back again and again as he had with Jay, nagging away at something he couldn't settle neatly.

He had sand enough now for the time the shift had yet to run, and when he had emptied the mix into the storage bins he shut off the mixer. Its sound died, one part of the core room's roar gone, and the vibration of the catwalk ceased. Prokop felt strange without it. He leaned into the mixer tank and with a broom swept away the last damp chunks of sand: they would pit the velvet-smooth metal if they stood till morning.

With the inner surfaces of the mixer gleaming softly, Prokop came down to sweep the floor at the base of the mixer. He checked the bins, testing the sand that still remained. It was perfect, but no cores would ever be made from it: by morning it would be far too dry for the day shift to use. He turned his back on the useless sand and crossed the alley to watch Price at work.

"How's it going now?" he asked.

Price only nodded, as if reluctant to admit that everything was all right.

"That last batch was perfect, eh?" Prokop said.

But Price only shrugged, and the foreman turned away, unhappy with himself for begging praise: he didn't need it—that was why he had this job.

As he came back to the mixer the buzzer sounded. It was the end of the shift. Immediately all noise from the blowers died away. Into the disquieting silence rose the odd sound of the operators' gibing voices. Within a few minutes, all the men had disappeared for the washroom in the foundry, leaving only the loader who made hasty passes at the floor with a broom, and Jay, who always stayed until the last cores were baked and the oven turned down.

The foreman watched as the loader shoveled up the waste sand and carted it outside. Standing alone under the catwalk, cleaning the sand from his nails with a split matchstick, he heard the soft scrape of the ovenman's footsteps and the echoing *creak-creak-creak* of the dolly. Some word, some sign was due Jay, but Prokop could not find it. He walked quickly toward the foundry washroom, more relieved than he could ever remember to hear the last sounds of his shift fade behind him.

JACK LONDON
(1876-1916)

Few authors have in their careers and in their writing so fully dramatized class divisions and conflicts as Jack London. Born out of wedlock and raised in Oakland, California, by his mother and stepfather, young Jack dropped out of school, worked on a sealing ship, as an oyster pirate, and as an apprentice electrician before becoming a hobo for a period. During that time, he spent a month in a Buffalo jail, an experience that seems to have produced in him enormous sympathy for what he would later call "the people of the abyss" and an equally strong determination to lift himself from among them. After a short stint in the Yukon prospecting for gold, London settled on writ-

ing as the means for upward social movement, and he devoted himself with extraordinary pertinacity to learning and practicing his chosen craft. His second novel, The Call of the Wild (1903), made him famous and began to establish him as a celebrity. In all, he would write more than 50 volumes of stories, novels, and essays; would work with the fledgling movie industry; would become an agricultural innovator and an amateur anthropologist of Polynesian and Melanesian cultures; and would speak out for socialism and temperance—all in the brief 40 years he lived. London became one of the best-known and most popular writers of his time, though his fame and reputation have probably been greater outside his native land than in it.

Many of his best works struggle with the contradictions he faced in his own life. Nowhere is that more evident than in his semi-autobiographical novel, Martin Eden (1909), a book that powerfully captures the struggles of a working-class man both to retain contact with his social and cultural roots and yet to "move up" in the world. He advocated socialism and collective action as ways of combating the oppression of poor and working people. Indeed, some of his writings, like his exposé of poverty in London, The People of the Abyss (1903), his novel of the advent of a protofascist regime, The Iron Heel (1907), and his story "South of the Slot" (1909) have remained classics of left-wing literature. At the same time, he believed in the power of a strong, heroic individual to overcome adversity and to triumph in the world—he, after all, had done so. And he certainly practiced market capitalism in promoting his own career. But then again, excessive self-reliance served as the tragic flaw of his fictional heros, often leading them to disaster or death. In certain ways, the story we have included here, "The Apostate," seems a straightforward dramatization of the process by which a young working man comes to reject absolutely the assumptions and ties of capitalist society. But its cloudy final vision of a future "on the bum" is, as London knew by experience, no solution to the problem of oppressive and meaningless work. Still, London's title tells something of the almost religious power the idea of selling our labor for a wage has come to have in modern society.

THE APOSTATE

Now I wake me up to work;
I pray the Lord I may not shirk.
If I should die before the night,
I pray the Lord my work's all right.
                                        AMEN

"If you don't git up, Johnny, I won't give you a bite to eat!"

The threat had no effect on the boy. He clung stubbornly to sleep, fighting for its oblivion as the dreamer fights for his dream. The boy's hands loosely clenched themselves, and he made feeble, spasmodic blows at the air. These blows were intended for his mother, but she betrayed practised familiarity in avoiding them as she shook him roughly by the shoulder.

"Lemme 'lone!"

It was a cry that began, muffled, in the deeps of sleep, that swiftly rushed upward, like a wail, into passionate belligerence, and that died away and sank down into an inarticulate whine. It was a bestial cry, as of a soul in torment, filled with infinite protest and pain.

But she did not mind. She was a sad-eyed, tired-faced woman, and she had grown used to this task, which she repeated every day of her life. She got a grip on the bedclothes and tried to strip them down; but the boy, ceasing his punching, clung to them desperately. In a huddle, at the foot of the bed, he still remained covered. Then she tried dragging the bedding to the floor. The boy opposed her. She braced herself. Hers was the superior weight, and the boy and bedding gave, the former instinctively following the latter in order to shelter against the chill of the room that bit into his body.

As he toppled on the edge of the bed it seemed that he must fall head-first to the floor. But consciousness fluttered up in him. He righted himself and for a moment perilously balanced. Then he struck the floor on his feet. On the instant his mother seized him by the shoulders and shook him. Again his fists struck out, this time with more force and directness. At the same time his eyes opened. She released him. He was awake.

"All right," he mumbled.

She caught up the lamp and hurried out, leaving him in darkness.

"You'll be docked," she warned back at him.

He did not mind the darkness. When he had got into his clothes, he went out into the kitchen. His tread was very heavy for so thin and light a boy. His legs dragged with their own weight, which seemed unreasonable because they were such skinny legs. He drew a broken-bottomed chair to the table.

"Johnny!" his mother called sharply.

He arose as sharply from the chair, and, without a word went to the sink. It was a greasy, filthy sink. A smell came up from the outlet. He took no notice of it. That a sink should smell was to him part of the natural order, just as it was a part of the natural order that the soap should be grimy with dishwater and hard to lather. Nor did he try very hard to make it lather. Several splashes of the cold water from the running faucet completed the function. He did not wash his teeth. For that matter he had never seen a tooth-brush, nor did he know that there existed human beings in the world who were guilty of so great a foolishness as tooth washing.

"You might wash yourself wunst a day without bein' told," his mother complained.

She was holding a broken lid on the pot as she poured two cups of coffee. He made no remark, for this was a standing quarrel between them, and the one thing upon which his mother was hard as adamant. "Wunst" a day it was compulsory that he should wash his face. He dried himself on a greasy towel, damp and dirty and ragged, that left his face covered with shreds of lint.

"I wish we didn't live so far away," she said, as he sat down. "I try to do the best I can. You know that. But a dollar on the rent is such a savin', an we've more room here. You know that."

He scarcely followed her. He had heard it all before, many times, The range of her thought was limited, and she was ever harking back to the hardship worked upon them by living so far from the mills.

"A dollar means more grub," he remarked sententiously. "I'd sooner do the walkin' and git the grub."

He ate hurriedly, half chewing the bread and washing the unmasticated chunks down with coffee. The hot and muddy liquid went by the name of coffee. Johnny thought it was coffee—and excellent coffee. That was one of the few of life's illusions that remained to him. He had never drunk real coffee in his life.

In addition to the bread, there was a small piece of cold pork. His mother refilled his cup with coffee. As he was finishing the bread, he began to watch if more was forthcoming. She intercepted his questioning glance.

"Now, don't be hoggish, Johnny," was her comment. "You've had your share. Your brothers an' sisters are smaller 'n you."

He did not answer the rebuke. He was not much of a talker. Also, he ceased his hungry glancing for more. He was uncomplaining, with a patience that was as terrible as the school in which it had been learned. He finished his coffee, wiped his mouth on the back of his hand, and started to rise.

"Wait a second," she said hastily. "I guess the loaf can stand another slice—a thin un."

There was legerdemain in her actions. With all the seeming of cutting a slice from the loaf for him, she put loaf and slice back in the bread box and conveyed to him one of her own two slices. She believed she had deceived him, but he had noted her sleight-of-hand. Nevertheless, he took the bread shamelessly. He had a philosophy that his mother, what of her chronic sickliness, was not much of an eater anyway.

She saw that he was chewing the bread dry, and reached over and emptied her coffee cup into his.

"Don't set good somehow on my stomach this morning," she explained.

A distant whistle, prolonged and shrieking, brought both of them to their feet. She glanced at the tin alarm-clock on the shelf. The hands stood at half-past five. The rest of the factory world was just arousing from sleep. She drew a shawl about her shoulders, and on her head put a dingy hat, shapeless and ancient.

"We've got to run," she said, turning the wick of the lamp and blowing down the chimney.

They groped their way out and down the stairs. It was clear and cold, and Johnny shivered at the first contact with the outside air. The stars had not yet begun to pale in the sky, and the city lay in blackness. Both Johnny and his mother shuffled their feet as they walked. There was no ambition in the leg muscles to swing the feet clear of the ground.

After fifteen silent minutes, his mother turned off to the right.

"Don't be late," was her final warning from out of the dark that was swallowing her up.

He made no response, steadily keeping on his way. In the factory quarter, doors were opening everywhere, and he was soon one of a multitude that pressed onward through the dark. As he entered the factory gate the whistle blew again. He glanced at the east. Across a ragged sky-line of housetops a pale light was beginning to creep. This much he saw of the day as he turned his back upon it and joined his work-gang.

He took his place in one of many long rows of machines. Before him, above a bin filled with small bobbins, were large bobbins revolving rapidly. Upon these he wound the jute-twine of the small bobbins. The work was simple. All that was required was celerity. The small bobbins were emptied so rapidly, and there were so many large bobbins that did the emptying, that there were no idle moments.

He worked mechanically. When a small bobbin ran out, he used his left hand for a brake, stopping the large bobbin and at the same time, with thumb and forefinger, catching the flying end of twine. Also, at the same time, with his right hand, he caught up the loose twine-end of a small bobbin. These various acts with both hands were performed simultaneously and swiftly. Then there would come a flash of his hands as he looped the weaver's knot and released the bobbin. There was nothing difficult about the weaver's knots. He once boasted he could tie them in his sleep. And for that matter, he sometimes did, toiling centuries long in a single night at tying an endless succession of weaver's knots.

Some of the boys shirked, wasting time and machinery by not replacing the small bobbins when they ran out. And there was an overseer to prevent this. He caught Johnny's neighbor at the trick, and boxed his ears.

"Look at Johnny there—why ain't you like him?" the overseer wrathfully demanded.

Johnny's bobbins were running full blast, but he did not thrill at the indirect praise. There had been a time . . . but that was long ago, very long ago. His apathetic face was expressionless as he listened to himself being held up as a shining example. He was the perfect worker. He knew that. He had been told so, often. It was a commonplace, and besides it didn't seem to mean anything to him any more. From the perfect worker he had evolved into the perfect machine. When his work went wrong, it was with him as with the machine, due to faulty material. It would have been as possible for a perfect nail-die to cut imperfect nails as for him to make a mistake.

And small wonder. There had never been a time when he had not been in intimate relationship with machines. Machinery had almost been bred into him, and at any rate he had been brought up on it. Twelve years before, there had been a small flutter of excitement in the loom room of this very mill. Johnny's mother had fainted. They stretched her out on the floor in the midst of the shrieking machines. A couple of elderly women were called from their looms. The foreman assisted. And in a few minutes there was one more soul in the loom room than had entered by the doors. It was Johnny, born with the pounding, crashing roar of the looms in his ears, drawing with his first breath the warm, moist air that was thick with flying lint. He had coughed that first day in order to rid his lungs of the lint; and for the same reason he had coughed ever since.

The boy alongside of Johnny whimpered and sniffed. The boy's face was convulsed with hatred for the overseer who kept a threatening eye on him from a distance; but every bobbin was running full. The boy yelled terrible oaths into the whirling bobbins before him; but the sound did not carry half a dozen feet, the roaring of the room holding it in and containing it like a wall.

Of all this Johnny took no notice. He had a way of accepting things. Besides, things grow monotonous by repetition, and this particular happening he had witnessed many times. It seemed to him as useless to oppose the overseer as to defy the will of a machine. Machines were made to go in certain ways and to perform certain tasks. It was the same with the overseer.

But at eleven o'clock there was excitement in the room. In an apparently occult way the excitement instantly permeated everywhere The one-legged boy who worked on the other side of Johnny bobbed swiftly across the floor to a bin truck that stood empty. Into this he dived out of sight, crutch and all. The superintendent of the mill was coming along, accompanied by a young man. He was well dressed and wore a starched shirt—a gentleman, in Johnny's classification of men, and also, "the Inspector."

He looked sharp at the boys as he passed along. When he did so, he was compelled to shout at the top of his lungs, at which moments his face was ludicrously contorted with the strain of making himself heard. His quick eye noted the empty machine alongside of Johnny's, but he said nothing. Johnny also caught his eye, and he stopped abruptly. He caught Johnny by the arm to draw him back a step from the machine; but with an exclamation of surprise he released the arm.

"Pretty skinny," the superintendent laughed anxiously.

"Pipe stems," was the answer. "Look at those legs. The boy's got the rickets— incipient, but he's got them. If epilepsy doesn't get him in the end, it will be because tuberculosis gets him first."

Johnny listened, but did not understand. Furthermore he was not interested in future ills. There was an immediate and more serious ill that threatened him in the form of the inspector.

"Now, my boy, I want you to tell me the truth," the inspector said, or shouted, bending close to the boy's ear to make him hear. "How old are you?"

"Fourteen," Johnny lied, and he lied with the full force of his lungs. So loudly did he lie that it started him off in a dry, hacking cough that lifted the lint which had been settling in his lungs all morning.

"Looks sixteen at least," said the superintendent.

"Or sixty," snapped the inspector.

"He's always looked that way."

"How long ?" asked the inspector quickly.

"For years. Never gets a bit older."

"Or younger, I dare say. I suppose he's worked here all those years?"

"Off and on—but that was before the new law was passed," the superintendent hastened to add.

"Machine idle?" the inspector asked, pointing at the unoccupied machine beside Johnny's, in which the part filled bobbins were flying like mad.

"Looks that way." The superintendent motioned the overseer to him and shouted in his ear and pointed at the machine. "Machine's idle," he reported back to the inspector.

They passed on, and Johnny returned to his work, relieved in that the ill had been averted. But the one-legged boy was not so fortunate. The sharp-eyed inspector hauled him out at arm's length from the bin truck. His lips were quivering, and his face had all the expression of one upon whom was fallen profound and irremediable disaster. The overseer looked astounded, as though for the first time he had laid eyes on the boy, while the superintendent's face expressed shock and displeasure.

"I know him," the inspector said. "He's twelve years old. I've had him discharged from three factories inside the year. This makes the fourth."

He turned to the one-legged boy. "You promised me, word and honor, that you'd go to school."

The one-legged boy burst into tears. "Please, Mr. Inspector, two babies died on us, and we're awful poor."

"What makes you cough that way?" the inspector demanded, as though charging him with crime.

And as in denial of guilt, the one-legged boy replied: "It ain't nothin'. I jes' caught a cold last week, Mr. Inspector, that's all."

In the end the one-legged boy went out of the room with the inspector, the latter accompanied by the anxious and protesting superintendent. After that monotony settled down again. The long morning and the longer afternoon wore away and the whistle blew for quitting time. Darkness had already fallen when Johnny passed out through the factory gate. In the interval the sun had made a golden ladder of the sky, flooded the world with its gracious warmth, and dropped down and disappeared in the west behind a ragged sky-line of housetops.

Supper was the family meal of the day—the one meal at which Johnny encountered his younger brothers and sisters. It partook of the nature of an encounter, to him, for he was very old, while they were distressingly young. He had no patience with their excessive amazing juvenility. He did not understand it. His own childhood too far behind him. He was like an old and irritable man, annoyed by the turbulence of their young spirits that was to him arrant silliness. He glowered silently over his food, finding compensation in the thought that they would soon have to go to work. That would take the edge off of them and make them sedate and dignified—like him. Thus it was, after the fashion of the human, that Johnny made of himself a yardstick with which to measure the universe.

During the meal, his mother explained in various ways and with infinite repetition that she was trying to do the best she could; so that it was with relief, the scant meal ended, that Johnny shoved back his chair and arose. He debated for a moment between bed and the front door, and finally went out the latter. He did not go far. He sat down on the stoop, his knees drawn up and his narrow shoulders drooping forward, his elbows on his knees and the palms of his hand supporting his chin.

As he sat there, he did no thinking. He was just resting. So far as his mind was concerned, it was asleep. His brothers and sisters came out, and with other children played noisily about him. An electric globe on the corner lighted their frolics. He was peevish and irritable, that they knew; but the spirit of adventure lured them into teasing him. They joined hands before him, and, keeping time with their bodies, chanted in his face weird and uncomplimentary doggerel. At first he snarled curses at them—curses he had learned from the lips of various foremen. Finding this futile, and remembering his dignity, he relapsed into dogged silence.

His brother Will, next to him in age, having just passed his tenth birthday, was the ringleader. Johnny did not possess particularly kindly feelings toward him. His life had early been imbittered by continual giving over and giving way to Will. He had a definite feeling that Will was greatly in his debt and was ungrateful about it. In his own playtime, far back in the dim past, he had been robbed of a large part of that playtime by being compelled to take care of Will. Will was a baby then, and then, as now, their mother had spent her days in the mills. To Johnny had fallen the part of little father and little mother as well.

Will seemed to show the benefit of the giving over and the giving way. He was well-built, fairly rugged, as tall as his elder brother and even heavier. It was as though the lifeblood of the one had been diverted into the other's veins. And in spirits it was the same. Johnny was jaded, worn out, without resilience, while his younger brother seemed bursting and spilling over with exuberance.

The mocking chant rose louder and louder. Will leaned closer as he danced, thrusting out his tongue. Johnny's left arm shot out and caught the other around the neck. At the same time he rapped his bony fist to the other's nose. It was a pathetically bony fist, but that it was sharp to hurt was evidenced by the squeal of pain it produced. The other children were uttering frightened cries, while Johnny's sister, Jenny, had dashed into the house.

He thrust Will from him, kicked him savagely on the shins, then reached for him and slammed him face downward in the dirt. Nor did he release him till the face had been rubbed into the dirt several times. Then the mother arrived, an anaemic whirl-wind of solicitude and maternal wrath.

"Why can't he leave me alone?" was Johnny's reply to her upbraiding. "Can't he see I'm tired?"

"I'm as big as you," Will raged in her arms, his face a mess of tears, dirt, and blood. "I'm as big as you now, an' I'm goin' to git bigger. Then I'll lick you—see if I don't."

"You ought to be to work, seein' how big you are," Johnny snarled. "That's what's the matter with you. You ought to be to work. An' it's up to your ma to put you to work."

"But he's too young," she protested. "He's only a little boy."

"I was younger'n him when I started to work."

Johnny's mouth was open, further to express the sense of unfairness that he felt, but the mouth closed with a snap. He turned gloomily on his heel and stalked into the house and to bed. The door of his room was open to let in warmth from the kitchen. As he undressed in the semi-darkness he could hear his mother talking with a neighbor woman who had dropped in. His mother was crying, and her speech was punctuated with spiritless sniffles.

"I can't make out what's gittin' into Johnny," he could hear her say. "He didn't used to be this way. He was a patient little angel."

"An' he is a good boy," she hastened to defend. "He's worked faithful, an' he did go to work too young. But it wasn't my fault. I do the best I can, I'm sure."

Prolonged sniffling from the kitchen, and Johnny murmured to himself as his eyelids closed down, "You betcher life I've worked faithful."

The next morning he was torn bodily by his mother from the grip of sleep. Then came the meagre breakfast, the tramp through the dark, and the pale glimpse of day across the housetops as he turned his back on it and went in through the factory gate. It was another day, of all the days, and all the days were alike.

And yet there had been variety in his life—at the times he changed from one job to another, or was taken sick. When he was six, he was little mother and father to Will and the other children still younger. At seven he went into the mills—winding bobbins. When he was eight, he got work in another mill. His new job was marvel-lously easy. All he had to do was to sit down with a little stick in his hand and guide a stream of cloth that flowed past him. This stream of cloth came out of the maw of a machine, passed over a hot roller, and went on its way elsewhere. But he sat always in the one place, beyond the reach of daylight, a gas-jet flaring over him, him-self part of the mechanism.

He was very happy at that job, in spite of the moist heat, for he was still young and in possession of dreams and illusions. And wonderful dreams he dreamed as he watched the steaming cloth streaming endlessly by. But there was no exercise about the work, no call upon his mind, and he dreamed less and less, while his mind grew torpid and drowsy. Nevertheless, he earned two dollars a week, and two dol-lars represented the difference between acute starvation and chronic underfeeding.

But when he was nine, he lost his job. Measles was the cause of it. After he recovered, he got work in a glass factory. The pay was better, and the work demanded skill. It was piece-work, and the more skillful he was, the bigger wages he earned. Here was incentive. And under this incentive he developed into a remarkable worker.

It was simple work, the tying of glass stoppers into small bottles. At his waist he carried a bundle of twine. He held the bottles between his knees so that he might work with both hands. Thus, in a sitting position and bending over his own knees, his narrow shoulders grew humped and his chest was contracted for ten hours each day. This was not good for the lungs, but he tied three hundred dozen bottles a day.

The superintendent was very proud of him, and brought visitors to look at him. In ten hours three hundred dozen bottles passed through his hands. This meant that he had attained machine-like perfection. All waste movements were eliminated. Every motion of his thin arms, every movement of a muscle in the thin fingers, was swift and accurate. He worked at high tension, and the result was that he grew nervous. At night his muscles twitched in his sleep, and in the daytime he could not relax and rest. He remained keyed up and his muscles continued to twitch. Also he grew sallow and his lint-cough grew worse. Then pneumonia laid hold of the feeble lungs within the contracted chest, and he lost his job in the glassworks.

Now he had returned to the jute mills where he had first begun with winding bobbins. But promotion was waiting for him. He was a good worker. He would next go on the starcher, and later he would go into the loom room. There was nothing after that except increased efficiency.

The machinery ran faster than when he had first gone to work, and his mind ran slower. He no longer dreamed at all, though his earlier years had been full of dreaming. Once he had been in love. It was when he first began guiding the cloth over the hot roller, and it was with the daughter of the superintendent. She was much older than he, a young woman, and he had seen her at a distance only a paltry half-dozen times. But that made no difference. On the surface of the cloth stream that poured past him, he pictured radiant futures wherein he performed prodigies of toil, invented miraculous machines, won to the mastership of the mills, and in the end took her in his arms and kissed her soberly on the brow.

But that was all in the long ago, before he had grown too old and tired to love. Also, she had married and gone away, and his mind had gone to sleep. Yet it had been a wonderful experience, and he used often to look back upon it as other men and women look back upon the time they believed in fairies. He had never believed in fairies nor Santa Claus; but he had believed implicitly in the smiling future his imagination had wrought into the steaming cloth stream.

He had become a man very early in life. At seven, when he drew his first wages, began his adolescence. A certain feeling of independence crept up in him, and the relationship between him and his mother changed. Somehow, as an earner and breadwinner, doing his own work in the world, he was more like an equal with her. Manhood, full-blown manhood, had come when he was eleven, at which time he had gone to work on the night shift for six months. No child works on the night shift and remains a child.

There had been several great events in his life. One of these had been when his mother bought some California prunes. Two others had been the two times when she cooked custard. Those had been events. He remembered them kindly. And at that time his mother had told him of a blissful dish she would sometime make—"floating island," she had called it, "better than custard." For years he had looked forward to the day when he would sit down to the table with floating island before him, until at last he had relegated the idea of it to the limbo of unattainable ideals.

Once he found a silver quarter lying on the sidewalk. That, also, was a great event in his life, withal a tragic one. He knew his duty on the instant the silver flashed on his eyes, before even he had picked it up. At home, as usual, there was not enough to eat, and home he should have taken it as he did his wages every Saturday night. Right conduct in this case was obvious; but he never had any spending of his money, and he was suffering from candy hunger. He was ravenous for the sweets that only on red-letter days he had ever tasted in his life.

He did not attempt to deceive himself. He knew it was sin, and deliberately he sinned when he went on a fifteen-cent candy debauch. Ten cents he saved for a future orgy; but not being accustomed to the carrying of money, he lost the ten cents. This occurred at the time when he was suffering all the torments of conscience, and it was to him an act of divine retribution. He had a frightened sense of the closeness of an awful and wrathful God. God had seen, and God had been swift to punish, denying him even the full wages of sin.

In memory he always looked back upon that event as the one great criminal deed of his life, and at the recollection his conscience always awoke and gave him another twinge. It was the one skeleton in his closet. Also, being so made and circumstanced, he looked back upon the deed with regret. He was dissatisfied with the manner in which he had spent the quarter. He could have invested it better, and, out of his later knowledge of the quickness of God, he would have beaten God out by spending the whole quarter at one fell swoop. In retrospect he spent the quarter a thousand times, and each time to better advantage.

There was one other memory of the past, dim and faded, but stamped into his soul everlastingly by the savage feet of his father. It was more like a nightmare than a remembered vision of a concrete thing—more like the race-memory of man that makes him fall in his sleep and that goes back to his arboreal ancestry.

This particular memory never came to Johnny in broad daylight when he was wide awake. It came at night, in bed, at the moment that his consciousness was sinking down and losing itself in sleep. It always aroused him to frightened wakefulness, and for the moment, in the first sickening start, it seemed to him that he lay crosswise on the foot of the bed. In the bed were the vague forms of his father and mother. He never saw what his father looked like. He had but one impression of his father, and that was that he had savage and pitiless feet.

His earlier memories lingered with him, but he had no late memories. All days were alike. Yesterday or last year were the same as a thousand years—or a minute. Nothing ever happened. There were no events to mark the march of time. Time did not march. It stood always still. It was only the whirling machines that moved, and they moved nowhere—in spite of the fact that they moved faster.

When he was fourteen, he went to work on the starcher. It was a colossal event. Something had at last happened that could be remembered beyond a night's sleep or a week's pay-day. It marked an era. It was a machine Olympiad, a thing to date from. "When I went to work on the starcher," or, "after," or "before I went to work on the starcher," were sentences often on his lips.

He celebrated his sixteenth birthday by going into the loom room and taking a loom. Here was an incentive again, for it was piece-work. And he excelled, because the clay of him had been moulded by the mills into the perfect machine. At the end of three months he was running two looms, and, later, three and four.

At the end of his second year at the looms he was turning out more yards than any other weaver, and more than twice as much as some of the less skillful ones. And at home things began to prosper as he approached the full stature of his earning power. Not, however, that his increased earnings were in excess of need. The children were growing up. They ate more. And they were going to school, and schoolbooks cost money. And somehow, the faster he worked, the faster climbed the prices of things. Even the rent went up, though the house had fallen from bad to worse disrepair.

He had grown taller; but with his increased height he seemed leaner than ever. Also, he was more nervous. With the nervousness increased peevishness and irritability. The children had learned by many bitter lessons to fight shy of him. His mother respected him for his earning power, but somehow her respect was tinctured with fear.

There was no joyousness in life for him. The procession of the days he never saw. The nights he slept away in twitching unconsciousness. The rest of the time he worked, and his consciousness was machine consciousness. Outside this his mind was a blank. He had no ideals, and but one illusion; namely, that he drank excellent coffee. He was a work-beast. He had no mental life whatever; yet deep down in the crypts of his mind, unknown to him, were being weighed and sifted every hour in his toil, every movement of his hands, every twitch of his muscles, and preparations were making for a future course of action that would amaze him and all his little world.

It was in the late spring that he came home from work one night aware of unusual tiredness. There was a keen expectancy in the air as he sat down to the table, but he did not notice. He went through the meal in moody silence, mechanically eating what was before him. The children um'd and ah'd and made smacking noises with their mouths. But he was deaf to them.

"D'ye know what you're eatin'?" his mother demanded at last, desperately.

He looked vacantly at the dish before him, and vacantly at her.

"Floatin' island," she announced triumphantly.

"Oh," he said.

"Floating island!" the children chorused loudly.

"Oh," he said. And after two or three mouthfuls, he added, "I guess I ain't hungry to-night."

He dropped the spoon, shoved back his chair, and arose wearily from the table.

"An' I guess I'll go to bed."

His feet dragged more heavily than usual as he crossed the kitchen floor. Undressing was a Titan's task, a monstrous futility, and he wept weakly as he crawled into bed, one shoe still on. He was aware of a rising, swelling something inside his head that made his brain thick and fuzzy. His lean fingers felt as big as his wrist, while in the ends of them was a remoteness of sensation vague and fuzzy like his brain. The small of his back ached intolerably. All his bones ached. He ached everywhere. And in his head began the shrieking, pounding, crashing, roaring of a million looms. All space was filled with flying shuttles. They darted in and out, intricately, amongst the stars. He worked a thousand looms himself, and ever they speeded up, faster and faster, and his brain unwound, faster and faster, and became the thread that fed the thousand flying shuttles.

He did not go to work next morning. He was too busy weaving colossally on the thousand looms that ran inside his head. His mother went to work, but first she sent for the doctor. It was a severe attack of la grippe, he said. Jennie served as nurse and carried out his instructions.

It was a very severe attack, and it was a week before Johnny dressed and tottered feebly across the floor. Another week, the doctor said, and he would be fit to return to work. The foreman of the loom room visited him on Sunday afternoon, the first day of his convalescence. The best weaver in the room, the foreman told his mother. His job would be held for him. He could come back to work a week from Monday.

"Why don't you thank 'im, Johnny?" his mother asked anxiously.

"He's ben that sick he ain't himself yet," she explained apologetically to the visitor.

Johnny sat hunched up and gazing steadfastly at the floor. He sat in the same position long after the foreman had gone. It was warm outdoors, and he sat on the stoop in the afternoon. Sometimes his lips moved. He seemed lost in endless calculations.

Next morning, after the day grew warm, he took his seat on the stoop. He had pencil and paper this time with which to continue his calculations, and he calculated painfully and amazingly.

"What comes after millions?" he asked at noon, when Will came home from school. "An' how d'ye work 'em?"

That afternoon finished his task. Each day, but without paper and pencil, he returned to the stoop. He was greatly absorbed in the one tree that grew across the street. He studied it for hours at a time, and was unusually interested when the wind swayed its branches and fluttered its leaves. Throughout the week he seemed lost in a great communion with himself. On Sunday, sitting on the stoop, he laughed aloud, several times, to the perturbation of his mother, who had not heard him laugh in years.

Next morning, in the early darkness, she came to his bed to rouse him. He had had his fill of sleep all week, and awoke easily. He made no struggle, nor did he attempt to hold on to the bedding when she stripped it from him. He lay quietly, and spoke quietly.

"It ain't no use, ma."

"You'll be late," she said, under the impression that he was still stupid with sleep.

"I'm awake, ma, an' I tell you it ain't no use. You might as well lemme alone. I ain't goin' to git up."

"But you'll lose your job!" she cried.

"I ain't goin' to git up," he repeated in a strange, passionless voice.

She did not go to work herself that morning. This was sickness beyond any sickness she had ever known. Fever and delirium she could understand; but this was insanity. She pulled the bedding up over him and sent Jennie for the doctor.

When that person arrived Johnny was sleeping gently, and gently he awoke and allowed his pulse to be taken.

"Nothing the matter with him," the doctor reported. "Badly debilitated, that's all. Not much meat on his bones."

"He's always been that way," his mother volunteered.

"Now go 'way, ma, an' let me finish my snooze."

Johnny spoke sweetly and placidly, and sweetly and placidly he rolled over on his side and went to sleep.

At ten o'clock he awoke and dressed himself. He walked out into the kitchen, where he found his mother with a frightened expression on her face.

"I'm goin' away, ma," he announced, "an' I jes' want to say good-by."

She threw her apron over her head and sat down suddenly and wept. He waited patiently.

"I might a-known it," she was sobbing.

"Where?" she finally asked, removing the apron from her head and gazing up at him with a stricken face in which there was little curiosity.

"I don't know—anywhere."

As he spoke, the tree across the street appeared with dazzling brightness on his inner vision. It seemed to lurk just under his eyelids, and he could see it whenever he wished.

"An' your job?" she quavered.

"I ain't never goin' to work again."

"My God, Johnny!" she wailed, "don't say that!"

What he had said was blasphemy to her. As a mother who hears her child deny God, was Johnny's mother shocked by his words.

"What's got into you, anyway?" she demanded, with a lame attempt at imperativeness.

"Figures," he answered. "Jes' figures. I've ben doin' a lot of figurin' this week, an' it's most surprisin'."

"I don't see what that's got to do with it," she sniffled.

Johnny smiled patiently, and his mother was aware of a distinct shock at the persistent absence of his peevishness and irritability.

"I'll show you," he said. "I'm plum' tired out. What makes me tired? Moves. I've ben moving' ever since I was born. I'm tired of movin', an' I ain't goin' to move any more. Remember when I worked in the glass-house? I used to do three hundred dozen a day. Now I reckon I made about ten different moves to each bottle. That's thirty-six thousan' moves a day. Ten days, three hundred an' sixty thousan' moves a day. One month, one million an' eighty thousan' moves. Chuck out the eighty thousan'—" he spoke with the complacent beneficence of a philanthropist—"chuck out the eighty thousan', that leaves a million moves a month—twelve million moves a year.

"At the looms I'm movin' twic'st as much. That makes twenty-five million moves a year, an' it seems to me I've ben a-movin' that way 'most a million years.

"Now this week I ain't moved at all. I ain't made one move in hours an' hours. I tell you it was swell, jes' settin' there, hours an' hours, an' doin' nothin'. I ain't never ben happy before. I never had any time. I've ben movin' all the time. That ain't no way to be happy. An' I ain't goin' to do it any more. I'm jes' goin' to set, an' set, an' rest, an' rest, and then rest some more."

"But what's goin' to come of Will an' the children?" she asked despairingly.

"That's it, 'Will an' the children,'" he repeated.

But there was no bitterness in his voice. He had long known his mother's ambition for the younger boy, but the thought of it no longer rankled. Nothing mattered any more. Not even that.

"I know, ma, what you've ben plannin' for Will—keepin' him in school to make a bookkeeper out of him. But it ain't no use, I've quit. He's got to go to work."

"An' after I have brung you up the way I have," she wept, starting to cover her head with the apron and changing her mind.

"You never brung me up," he answered with sad kindliness. "I brung myself up, ma, an' I brung up Will. He's bigger'n me, an' heavier an' taller. When I was a kid, I reckon I didn't git enough to eat. When he come along an' was a kid, I was workin' an' earnin' grub for him too. But that's done with. Will can go to work, same as me, or he can go to hell, I don't care which. I'm tired. I'm goin' now. Ain't you goin' to say good-by?"

She made no reply. The apron had gone over her head again, and she was crying. He paused a moment in the doorway.

"I'm sure I done the best I knew how," she was sobbing.

He passed out of the house and down the street. A wan delight came into his face at the sight of the lone tree. "Jes' ain't goin' to do nothin'," he said to himself, half aloud, in a crooning tone. He glanced wistfully up at the sky, but the bright sun dazzled and blinded him.

It was a long walk he took, and he did not walk fast. It took him past the jute-mill. The muffled roar of the looms came to his ears, and he smiled. It was a gentle, placid smile. He hated no one, not even the pounding, shrieking machines. There was no bitterness in him, nothing but an inordinate hunger for rest.

The houses and factories thinned out and the open spaces increased as he approached the country. At last the city was behind him, and he was walking down a leafy lane beside the railroad track. He did not walk like a man. He did not look like a man. He was a travesty of the human. It was a twisted and stunted and nameless piece of life that shambled like a sickly ape, arms loose-hanging, stoop-shouldered, narrow-chested, grotesque and terrible.

He passed by a small railroad station and lay down in the grass under a tree. All afternoon he lay there. Sometimes he dozed, with muscles that twitched in his sleep. When awake, he lay without movement, watching the birds or looking up at the sky through the branches of the tree above him. Once or twice he laughed aloud, but without relevance to anything he had seen or felt.

After twilight had gone, in the first darkness of the night, a freight train rumbled into the station. When the engine was switching cars on to the sidetrack, Johnny crept along the side of the train. He pulled open the side-door of an empty box-car and awkwardly and laboriously climbed in. He closed the door. The engine whistled. Johnny was lying down, and in the darkness he smiled.

WOODY GUTHRIE

(1912-1967)

Woodrow Wilson Guthrie—"Woody" to anyone familiar with him—was among America's most prolific and best-known songwriters. He was unequaled among those who saw singing as a vital part of any movement for social change. Born and raised in Okemah, Oklahoma, Guthrie learned his music by listening to his father reciting poems, his mother singing songs she had gotten by heart, and from the itinerant musicians, with their homemade fiddles and banjos, who would stay in town long enough to earn a few bucks before moving on. Guthrie himself experienced all the hardships of a migrant worker and wandering minstrel, earning money sometimes by playing or dancing a jig, sometimes by picking strawberries, by fixing roofs, by painting signs, shining spittoons, selling papers. Like the "Okies" portrayed in John Steinbeck's

The Grapes of Wrath, he headed west to California, Oregon, and Washington when the dust storms of the Depression era of the 1930s made life all but unlivable, and family farming impossible, in Oklahoma and Texas. He was active in unions and in left-wing causes, was a sailor in the Merchant Marine in World War II (during which his ships were twice torpedoed), and walked and sang across North Africa and Europe, as well as the United States.

And always he made up songs. No one knows how many, perhaps one thousand or more. Many of them are about work or the lack of it, about the natural and manmade wonders of America, about the lives of ordinary people, and about organizing them for change. The titles are known to anyone even slightly familiar with the traditions of American balladeers: "Grand Coulee Dam," "This Land Is Your Land," "Reuben James," "Roll on, Columbia," "So Long, It's Been Good to Know You," "Union Maid," and "Hard Travelin'." The latter song is particularly emblematic of Guthrie's life, because despite facing personal hardships, disappointment, danger, and, eventually, mental problems, he sustained a sense of humor and hope in his singing. Of "Hard Travelin'," he wrote in his autobiography, Bound For Glory *(1943), that it is "the kind of song you would sing after you had been booted off your little place and had lost out, lost everything, hocked everything down at the pawnshop, and had bummed a lot of stems asking for work. . . . It is a song about the hard traveling of the working people, not the moonstruck traveling of the professional vacationers." Woody helped sustain in others, and particularly in those hit hardest by the Depression and war, a conviction that, despite dust and poverty and fascism and bombs, people singing with him could construct a future from their work, from a sense of their own and their neighbors' value, and from the pleasures of the singing.*

HARD TRAVELIN'

I've been having some hard traveling, I thought you knowed,
I've been having some hard traveling, way down the road,—
I've been having some hard traveling, hard rambling, hard gambling,
Been a-having some hard traveling, Lord.

I've been a-riding them fast rattlers, I thought you knowed,
I've been a-riding them flat wheelers way down the road,
I've been a-riding them blind passengers, dead enders, kicking up cinders,
I've been a-having some hard traveling, Lord.

I've been a-hitting some hard rock mining, I thought you knowed,
I've been a-leaning on a pressure drill way down the road,
Hammer flying, air hose sucking, six foot of mud and I sure been a-mucking,
And I've been a-hitting some hard traveling, Lord.

I've been a-hitting some hard harvesting, I thought you knowed,
North Dakota to Kansas City way down the road,
Cutting that wheat, stacking that hay, and I'm trying to make about a dollar a
    day,
And I've been a-having some hard traveling, Lord.

I've been a-working that Pittsburgh steel, I thought you knowed,
I've been a-dumping that red-hot slag way down the road,
I've been a-blasting, I've been a-firing, I've been a-pouring red-hot iron,
And I've been a-hitting some hard traveling, Lord.

I've been a-laying in a hard rock jail, I thought you knowed,
I've been a-laying out ninety days way down the road,
Damned old judge he said to me, "It's ninety days for vagrancy,"
And I've been a-hitting some hard traveling, Lord.

ALBERT MALTZ
(1908–1985)

During the Great Depression of the 1930s, as much as a third of the work-force was jobless, much more in some communities. Men—and women—wandered from place to place "on the bum," seeking a temporary job, a handout, anything to stave off hunger and the deep shame of unemploy-ment. President Roosevelt told the nation in his First Inaugural Address that the only thing Americans had to fear "was fear itself." Those were encouraging words, but in fact for many Americans the question came down to how to feed themselves and their families, to keep a roof over their heads, and to retain the skills and the sense of personal pride that only a job could provide. With the nation in economic and social crisis, and with new fascist movements on the march in countries like Italy and Germany, different questions and ideas about art began to develop. For some, art came to be seen as a weapon in political struggles, like those between cap-italism and socialism, or between fascism and communism. For others, art constituted a form of social protest, giving voice to those whose experiences had not previously been portrayed. Still others continued to see art as a way of providing meaning and a sense of order in what appeared an increasingly chaotic world.

Albert Maltz was among those who tried to express protest against the injustices of a system that left a third of the nation "ill-fed, ill-clad, and ill-housed," to use President Roosevelt's formulation. At the same time, he tried to sustain in his novels and stories a richness of charac-terization and a complexity of narrative not always achieved in social protest literature. Maltz's own life had something of the quality of a moral drama. In 1947, he was called before the House Un-American Activities Committee, which was then investigating alleged communist infiltration of the film industry. Maltz, along with nine other screen-writers and producers, refused to answer questions about his political affiliations and union activities; members of the group, which became known as the "Hollywood Ten," were indicted, fined, and imprisoned, and Maltz spent almost a year in a federal jail. Subsequently, he was blacklisted and was unable to find work in the movie industry or else-

where in the United States. He continued to write in Mexico, producing a number of books, including an account based on his prison experiences, A Long Day in a Short Life *(1957). The story that follows shows Maltz at his best. It combines a sense of outrage at the society that has so overwhelmed Jesse, with keen characterizations both of Jesse and his brother-in-law, Tom Brackett. Maltz's bitterly ironic narrative captures the despair of Depression life and the terrible meanings the idea of a job had taken on.*

THE HAPPIEST MAN ON EARTH

Jesse felt ready to weep. He had been sitting in the shanty waiting for Tom to appear, grateful for the chance to rest his injured foot, quietly, joyously anticipating the moment when Tom would say, "Why, of course, Jesse, you can start whenever you're ready!"

For two weeks he had been pushing himself, from Kansas City, Missouri, to Tulsa, Oklahoma, through nights of rain and a week of scorching sun, without sleep or a decent meal, sustained by the vision of that one moment. And then Tom had come into the office. He had come in quickly, holding a sheaf of papers in his hand; he had glanced at Jesse only casually, it was true—but long enough. He had not known him. He had turned away . . . And Tom Brackett was his brother-in-law.

Was it his clothes? Jesse knew he looked terrible. He had tried to spruce up at a drinking fountain in the park, but even that had gone badly; in his excitement he had cut himself shaving, an ugly gash down the side of his cheek. And nothing could get the red gumbo dust out of his suit even though he had slapped himself till both arms were worn out . . . Or was it just that he had changed so much?

True, they hadn't seen each other for five years; but Tom looked five years older, that was all. He was still Tom. God! Was he so different?

Brackett finished his telephone call. He leaned back in his swivel chair and glanced over at Jesse with small, clear, blue eyes that were suspicious and unfriendly. He was a heavy, paunchy man of forty-five, auburn-haired, rather dour-looking; his face was meaty, his features pronounced and forceful, his nose somewhat bulbous and reddish-hued at the tip. He looked like a solid, decent, capable businessman who was commander of his local branch of the American Legion—which he was. He surveyed Jesse with cold indifference, manifestly unwilling to spend time on him. Even the way he chewed his toothpick seemed contemptuous to Jesse.

"Yes?" Brackett said suddenly. "What do you want?"

His voice was decent enough, Jesse admitted. He had expected it to be worse. He moved up to the wooden counter that partitioned the shanty. He thrust a hand nervously through his tangled hair.

"I guess you don't recognize me, Tom," he said falteringly. "I'm Jesse Fulton."

"Huh?" Brackett said. That was all.

"Yes, I am, and Ella sends you her love."

Brackett rose and walked over to the counter until they were face to face. He surveyed Fulton incredulously, trying to measure the resemblance to his brother-in-law as he remembered him. This man was tall, about thirty. That fitted! He had straight good features and a lank erect body. That was right too. But the face was too gaunt, the body too spiny under the baggy clothes for him to be sure. His brother-in-law had been a solid, strong, young man with muscle and beef to him. It was like looking at a faded, badly taken photograph and trying to recognize the subject: The resemblance was there but the difference was tremendous. He searched the eyes. They at least seemed definitely familiar, gray, with a curiously shy but decent look in them. He had liked that about Fulton.

Jesse stood quiet. Inside he was seething. Brackett was like a man examining a piece of broken-down horseflesh; there was a look of pure pity in his eyes. It made Jesse furious. He knew he wasn't as far gone as all that.

"Yes, I believe you are," Brackett said finally, "but you sure have changed."

"By God, it's five years, ain't it?" Jesse said resentfully. "You only saw me a couple of times anyway." Then, to himself, with his lips locked together, in mingled vehemence and shame, "What if I have changed? Don't everybody? I ain't no corpse."

"You was solid looking," Brackett continued softly, in the same tone of incredulous wonder. "You lost weight, I guess?"

Jesse kept silent. He needed Brackett too much to risk antagonizing him. But it was only by deliberate effort that he could keep from boiling over. The pause lengthened, became painful. Brackett flushed. "Jiminy Christmas, excuse me," he burst out in apology. He jerked the counter up. "Come in. Take a seat. Good God, boy"—he grasped Jesse's hand and shook it—"I am glad to see you; don't think anything else! You just looked so peaked."

"It's all right," Jesse murmured. He sat down, thrusting his hand through his curly, tangled hair.

"Why are you limping?"

"I stepped on a stone; it jagged a hole through my shoe." Jesse pulled his feet back under the chair. He was ashamed of his shoes. They had come from the relief originally, and two weeks on the road had about finished them. All morning, with a kind of delicious, foolish solemnity, he had been vowing to himself that before anything else, before even a suit of clothes, he was going to buy himself a brand-new strong pair of shoes.

Brackett kept his eyes off Jesse's feet. He knew what was bothering the boy and it filled his heart with pity. The whole thing was appalling. He had never seen anyone who looked more down-and-out. His sister had been writing to him every week, but she hadn't told him they were as badly-off as this.

"Well now, listen," Brackett began, "tell me things. How's Ella?"

"Oh, she's pretty good," Jesse replied absently. He had a soft, pleasing shy voice that went with his soft gray eyes. He was worrying over how to get started.

"And the kids?"

"Oh, they're fine . . . Well, you know," Jesse added, becoming more attentive, "the young one has to wear a brace. He can't run around, you know. But he's smart. He draws pictures and he does things, you know."

"Yes," Brackett said. "That's good." He hesitated. There was a moment's silence. Jesse fidgeted in his chair. Now that the time had arrived, he felt awkward. Brackett leaned forward and put his hand on Jesse's knee. "Ella didn't tell me things were so bad for you, Jesse. I might have helped."

"Well, goodness," Jesse returned softly, "you been having your own troubles, ain't you?"

"Yes." Brackett leaned back. His ruddy face became mournful and darkly bitter. "You know I lost my hardware shop?"

"Well sure, of course," Jesse answered, surprised. "You wrote us. That's what I mean."

"I forgot," Brackett said. "I keep on being surprised over it myself. Not that it was worth much," he added bitterly. "It was running downhill for three years. I guess I just wanted it because it was mine." He laughed pointlessly, without mirth. "Well, tell me about yourself," he added. "What happened to the job you had?"

Jesse burst out abruptly, with agitation, "Let it wait, Tom, I got something on my mind."

"It ain't you and Ella?" Brackett interrupted anxiously.

"Why no!" Jesse sat back, "Why, however did you come to think that? Why Ella and me . . ." He stopped, laughing. "Why, Tom, I'm just crazy about Ella. Why she's just wonderful. She's just my whole life, Tom."

"Excuse me. Forget it." Brackett chuckled uncomfortably, turned away. The naked intensity of the youth's burst of love had upset him. It made him wish savagely that he could do something for them. They were too decent to have had it so hard. Ella was like this boy too, shy and a little soft.

"Tom, listen," Jesse said, "I come here on purpose." He thrust his hand through his hair, "I want you to help me."

"Damn it, boy," Brackett groaned. He had been expecting this. "I can't much. I only get thirty-five a week and I'm damn grateful for it."

"Sure, I know," Jesse emphasized excitedly. He was feeling once again the wild, delicious agitation that had possessed him in the early hours of the morning. "I know you can't help us with money! But we met a man who works for you! He was in our city! He said you could give me a job!"

"Who said?"

"Oh, why didn't you tell me?" Jesse burst out reproachfully. "Why, as soon as I heard of it I started out. For two weeks now I been pushing ahead like crazy."

Brackett groaned aloud. "You come walking from Kansas City in two weeks so I could give you a job?"

"Sure, Tom, of course. What else could I do?"

"God Almighty, there ain't no jobs, Jesse! It's a slack season. And you don't know this oil business. It's special. I got my Legion friends here, but they couldn't do nothing now. Don't you think I'd ask for you as soon as there was a chance?"

Jesse felt stunned. The hope of the last two weeks seemed rolling up into a ball of agony in his stomach. Then, frantically, he cried, "But listen, this man said you could hire! He told me! He drives trucks for you! He said you always need men!"

" Oh! . . . You mean my department?" Brackett said in a low voice.

"Yes, Tom. That's it!"

"Oh, no, you don't want to work in my department," Brackett told him in the same low voice. "You don't know what it is."

"Yes, I do," Jesse insisted. "He told me all about it, Tom. You're a dispatcher, ain't you? You send the dynamite trucks out?"

"Who was the man, Jesse?"

"Everett, Everett, I think."

"Egbert? Man about my size?" Brackett asked slowly.

"Yes, Egbert. He wasn't a phony, was he?"

Brackett laughed. For the second time his laughter was curiously without mirth. "No, he wasn't a phony." Then, in a changed voice: "Jiminy, boy, you should have asked me before you trekked all the way down here."

"Oh, I didn't want to," Jesse explained with naive cunning. "I knew you'd say no. He told me it was risky work, Tom. But I don't care."

Brackett locked his fingers together. His solid, meaty face became very hard. "I'm going to say no anyway, Jesse."

Jesse cried out. It had not occurred to him that Brackett would not agree. It had seemed as though reaching Tulsa were the only problem he had to face. "Oh no," he begged, "you can't. Ain't there any jobs, Tom?"

"Sure there's jobs. There's even Egbert's job if you want it."

"He's quit?"

"He's dead!"

"Oh!"

"On the job, Jesse. Last night if you want to know."

"Oh!" . . . Then, "I don't care!"

"Now you listen to me," Brackett said. "I'll tell you a few things that you should have asked before you started out. It ain't dynamite you drive. They don't use anything as safe as dynamite in drilling oil wells. They wish they could, but they can't. It's nitroglycerin! Soup!"

"But I know," Jesse told him reassuringly. "He advised me, Tom. You don't have to think I don't know."

"Shut up a minute," Brackett ordered angrily. "Listen! You just have to look at this soup, see? You just cough loud and it blows! You know how they transport it? In a can that's shaped like this, see, like a fan? That's to give room for compartments, because each compartment has to be lined with rubber. That's the only way you can even think of handling it."

"Listen, Tom . . ."

"Now wait a minute, Jesse. For God's sake just put your mind to this. I know you had your heart set on a job, but you've got to understand. This stuff goes only in special trucks! At night! They got to follow a special route! They can't go through any city! If they lay over, it's got to be in a special garage! Don't you see what that means? Don't that tell you how dangerous it is?"

"I'll drive careful," Jesse said. "I know how to handle a truck. I'll drive slow."

Brackett groaned. "Do you think Egbert didn't drive careful or know how to handle a truck?"

"Tom," Jesse said earnestly, "you can't scare me. I got my mind fixed on only one thing: Egbert said he was getting a dollar a mile. He was making five to six hundred dollars a month for half a month's work, he said. Can I get the same?"

"Sure you can get the same," Brackett told him savagely. "A dollar a mile. It's easy. But why do you think the company has to pay so much? It's easy—until you run over a stone that your headlights didn't pick out, like Egbert did. Or get a blowout! Or get something in your eye so the wheel twists and you jar the truck! Or any other God damn thing that nobody ever knows! We can't ask Egbert what happened to him. There's no truck to give any evidence. There's no corpse. There's nothing! Maybe tomorrow somebody'll find a piece of twisted steel way off in a cornfield. But we never find the driver. Not even a fingernail. All we know is that he don't come in on schedule. Then we wait for the police to call us. You know what happened last night? Something went wrong on a bridge. Maybe Egbert was nervous. Maybe he brushed the side with his fender. Only there's no bridge anymore. No truck. No Egbert. Do you understand now? That's what you get for your God damn dollar a mile!"

There was a moment of silence. Jesse sat twisting his long thin hands. His mouth was sagging open, his face was agonized. Then he shut his eyes and spoke softly. "I don't care about that, Tom. You told me. Now you got to be good to me and give me that job."

Brackett slapped the palm of his hand down on his desk. "No!"

"Listen, Tom," Jesse said softly, "you just don't understand." He opened his eyes. They were filled with tears. They made Brackett turn away. "Just look at me, Tom. Don't that tell you enough? What did you think of me when you first saw me? You thought: 'Why don't that bum go away and stop panhandling?' Didn't you, Tom? Tom, I just can't live like this any more. I got to be able to walk down the street with my head up."

"You're crazy," Brackett muttered. "Every year there's one out of five drivers gets killed. That's the average. What's worth that?"

"Is my life worth anything now? We're just starvin' at home, Tom. They ain't put us back on relief yet."

"Then you should have told me," Brackett exclaimed harshly. "It's your own damn fault. A man has no right to have false pride when his family ain't eating. I'll borrow some money and we'll telegraph it to Ella. Then you go home and get back on relief."

"And then what?"

"And then wait, God damn it! You're no old man. You got no right to throw your life away. Sometime you'll get a job."

"No!" Jesse jumped up. "No. I believed that too. But I don't now," he cried passionately. "I ain't getting a job no more than you're getting your hardware store back. I lost my skill, Tom. Linotyping is skilled work. I'm rusty now. I've been six years on relief. The only work I've had is pick and shovel. When I got that job this spring, I was supposed to be an A-1 man. But I wasn't. And they got new machines now. As soon as the slack started, they let me out."

"So what?" Brackett said harshly. "Ain't there other jobs?"

"How do I know?" Jesse replied. "There ain't been one for six years. I'd even be afraid to take one now. It's been too hard waiting so many weeks to get back on relief."

"Well, you got to have some courage," Brackett shouted. "You've got to keep up hope."

"I got all the courage you want," Jesse retorted vehemently, "but no, I ain't got no hope. The hope has dried up in me in six years waiting. You're the only hope I got."

"You're crazy," Brackett muttered. "I won't do it. For God's sake think of Ella for a minute."

"Don't you know I'm thinking about her?" Jesse asked softly. He plucked at Brackett's sleeve. "That's what decided me, Tom." His voice became muted into a hushed, pained, whisper. "The night Egbert was at our house I looked at Ella like I'd seen her for the first time. She ain't pretty anymore, Tom!" Brackett jerked his head and moved away. Jesse followed him, taking a deep, sobbing breath. "Don't that tell you, Tom? Ella was like a little doll or something, you remember. I couldn't walk down the street without somebody turning to look at her. She ain't twenty-nine yet, Tom, and she ain't pretty no more."

Brackett sat down with his shoulders hunched up wearily. He gripped his hands together and sat leaning forward, staring at the floor.

Jesse stood over him, his gaunt face flushed with emotion, almost unpleasant in its look of pleading and bitter humility. "I ain't done right for Ella, Tom. Ella deserved better. This is the only chance I see in my whole life to do something for her. I've just been a failure."

"Don't talk nonsense," Brackett commented without rancor. "You ain't a failure. No more than me. There's millions of men in the identical situation. It's just the depression, or the recession, or the God damn New Deal, or . . . !" He swore and lapsed into silence.

"Oh no," Jesse corrected him in a knowing, sorrowful tone, "those things maybe excuse other men. But not me. It was up to me to do better. This is my own fault!"

"Oh, beans!" Brackett said. "It's more sun spots than it's you!"

Jesse's face turned an unhealthy mottled red. It looked swollen. "Well I don't care," he cried wildly. "I don't care! You got to give me this! I got to lift my head up. I went through one stretch of hell, but I can't go through another. You want me to keep looking at my little boy's legs and tell myself if I had a job he wouldn't be like that? Every time he walks he says to me, 'I got soft bones from the rickets and you give it to me because you didn't feed me right.' Jesus Christ, Tom, you think I'm going to sit there and watch him like that another six years?"

Brackett leaped to his feet. "So what if you do?" he shouted. "You say you are thinking about Ella. How's she going to like it when you get killed?"

"Maybe I won't," Jesse pleaded. "I've got to have some luck sometime."

"That's what they all think," Brackett replied scornfully. "When you take this job, your luck is a question mark. The only thing certain is that sooner or later you get killed."

"Okay then," Jesse shouted back. "Then I do! But meanwhile I got something, don't I? I can buy a pair of shoes. Look at me! I can buy a suit that don't say 'Relief' by the way it fits. I can smoke cigarettes. I can buy some candy for the kids. I can eat some myself. Yes, by God, I want to eat some candy. I want a glass of beer once a day. I want Ella dressed up. I want her to eat meat three times a week, four times maybe. I want to take my family to the movies."

Brackett sat down. "Oh, shut up," he said wearily.

"No," Jesse told him softly, passionately, "you can't get rid of me. Listen, Tom," he pleaded, "I got it all figured out. On six hundred a month look how much I can save! If I last only three months, look how much it is . . . a thousand dollars . . . more! And maybe I'll last longer. Maybe a couple years. I can fix Ella up for life!"

"You said it," Brackett interposed. "I suppose you think she'll enjoy living when you're on a job like that?"

"I got it all figured out," Jesse answered excitedly. "She don't know, see? I tell her I make only forty. You put the rest in a bank account for her, Tom."

"Oh, shut up," Brackett said. "You think you'll be happy? Every minute, waking and sleeping, you'll be wondering if tomorrow you'll be dead. And the worst days will be your days off, when you're not driving. They have to give you every other day free to get your nerve back. And you lay around the house eating your heart out. That's how happy you'll be."

Jesse laughed. "I'll be happy! Don't you worry, I'll be so happy, I'll be singing. Lord God, Tom, I'm going to feel proud of myself for the first time in seven years!"

"Oh, shut up, shut up," Brackett said.

The little shanty became silent. After a moment Jesse whispered: "You got to, Tom. You got to. You got to."

Again there was silence. Brackett raised both hands to his head, pressing the palms against his temples.

"Tom, Tom . . ." Jesse said.

Brackett sighed. "Oh, God damn it," he said finally, "all right, I'll take you on, God help me." His voice was low, hoarse, infinitely weary. "If you're ready to drive tonight, you can drive tonight."

Jesse didn't answer. He couldn't. Brackett looked up. The tears were running down Jesse's face. He was swallowing and trying to speak, but only making an absurd, gasping noise.

"I'll send a wire to Ella," Brackett said in the same hoarse, weary voice. "I'll tell her you got a job, and you'll send her fare in a couple of days. You'll have some money then—that is, if you last the week out, you jackass!"

Jesse only nodded. His heart felt so close to bursting that he pressed both hands against it, as though to hold it locked within his breast.

"Come back here at six o'clock," Brackett said. "Here's some money. Eat a good meal."

"Thanks," Jesse whispered.

"Wait a minute," Brackett said. "Here's my address." He wrote it on a piece of paper, "Take any car going that way. Ask the conductor where to get off. Take a bath and get some sleep."

"Thanks," Jesse said. "Thanks, Tom."

"Oh, get out of here," Brackett said.

"Tom."

"What?"

"I just . . ." Jesse stopped. Brackett saw his face. The eyes were still glistening with tears, but the gaunt face was shining now with a kind of fierce radiance.

Brackett turned away. "I'm busy," he said.

Jesse went out. The wet film blinded him, but the whole world seemed to have turned golden. He limped slowly, with the blood pounding his temples and a wild, incommunicable joy in his heart. "I'm the happiest man in the world," he whispered to himself. "I'm the happiest man on the whole earth."

Brackett sat watching till finally Jesse turned the corner of the alley and disappeared. Then he hunched himself over with his head in his hands. His heart was beating painfully like something old and clogged. He listened to it as it beat. He sat in desperate tranquillity, gripping his head in his hands.

–1938

TILLIE OLSEN

(B. 1912?)

As writer, intellectual, teacher, and activist, Tillie Olsen has been a major force in the revival of interest in class as a category of thought in the United States. Much of her own writing, like this section of her short novel Yon-nondio: From the Thirties, *concerns the lives, especially the job lives, of* working-class women and men. Olsen brought to the attention of a whole generation of students of literature stories and poems of other writers, like many in this book, with similar concerns.

Olsen's involvement with working-class writing no doubt derives from her origins, the many jobs she has held, as well as her own activities on behalf of social justice. Her parents, Ida and Samuel Lerner, fled from Russia to escape the repression that followed the revolutionary uprising of 1905. Living mainly in Nebraska, they continued to be active in socialist causes, at a time in which the Socialist Party was a significant force on the American political landscape. Olsen was born in 1912 or 1913 in Nebraska. While she quit school in the eleventh grade, Olsen educated herself beyond what was normal for the time—and especially for women—by frequenting the public library and, on very rare occasions, buying a particularly cheap book or bound volume of a magazine. It was in such a magazine volume that she first found Rebecca Harding Davis's "Life in the Iron Mills." But her knowledge of work and the tensions and conflicts of jobs did not come primarily from books. For Olsen has worked as typist, teacher, laundress, solderer, waitress, hotel maid, and pork trimmer, among other things.

She also joined the Young Communist League (YCL) in the 1920s and participated in the YCL's efforts to organize packinghouse workers in Kansas City and, later, longshoremen in San Francisco. She was twice jailed in connection with these organizing efforts. She also began writing and, in 1934, publishing her poems and essays. From the beginning, works like "I Want You Women Up North to Know" and "The Strike" brought to the attention of her audience the struggles of working people for decent jobs and living conditions. But it was not Olsen's fortune to launch a writing career during the 1930s and 1940s; rather, the demands of bringing up four children, earning a living, and continuing when she could to participate in struggles for social justice often brought her to the "silences" about which she has eloquently written. It was not until 1953 that she was able to enroll in a writing course at San Francisco State University and shortly thereafter to win a writing fellowship at Stanford; those events helped her gain the time and contacts she needed to focus on literary production.

Olsen has not been a prolific writer. Still, stories like "Tell Me a Riddle" and "I Stand Here Ironing," essays like "Silences," and reading lists and bibliographies like those on "The Literature of Poverty, War, and the Struggle for Freedom" that she had initially prepared for a class she taught at Amherst College in 1968 have been unusually influential. They have all helped generations of people learn about, indeed experience, the real lives, the hopes and desires, of ordinary working women and men.

FROM YONNONDIO

"Just see," Tracy promised, "just see. I'll make a kick with that bastard today. Twelve foot he wants out of us, when ten's all anything on two legs can manage."

"All right," said Jim wearily, tugging off his soggy work pants. "All right."

"And calling this a dry house," Tracy muttered. "Give me a cloudburst anytime."

"Hell, the Mississipp's a road of concrete and the ocean's a dry bed."

"How you two can beef after the day's work you put in is beyond me," old man Albright butted in, "even my tongue's laid out."

"Well, this goddamn business of hangin up my work clothes in what they call a dry house and puttin em on the next morning twice as wet is just gettin under my skin."

"All right, son, wait'll you get the rheumatiz. Then you *will* have something under your skin to beef about."

"You wont see me doin any waitin," said Tracy. (I guess not, Jim thought, not till you got a woman and kids hangin around your neck.) "Look at those puckers—" pointing to his bare feet—"bigger'n on a washboard. Waterproof boots, hell. How you guys take it is beyond me."

"O.K.," said Jim, "put on the low needle and give our ears a vacation. Maybe we got something besides gettin canned up and steppin out a chippie to think about."

They dressed in silence. "Hey," Jim warned, "here comes the workingman's friend."

The contractor came in, puffed up like a balloon, with a smaller red balloon of a face wobbling on top. He spat his tobacco juice square into Jim's empty boot.

"So ten foot is all you women made today, huh? What I want to know is what the hell you do when you're on the job, suck titty?"

"Now boss," Albright said hurriedly, "we're doin' the best we can. We went like a redball all day."

"You mean a standstill, dont you? Well ten's the footage all right from now on, but for two of you to manage."

"Two?" came from all their startled throats.

"Two! A miner and a mucker to a job. Miller's tried it with his monkeys and they're doin it. My crews can do as good."

"Not and stay human," Jim said.

Tracy sputtered, "It cant be done."

"Shut up—I'm the one who says what can and cant get done. Tracy and Holbrook, Marello and Albright, that's the lineup."

"But say—"

"You heard me. There's plenty good concrete men and muckers with their tongues hangin out for a job. You'll make ten or you're out."

"Not me," exploded Tracy. "I'm throwin up this sh---y job."

"O.K. by me," the contractor said, "but dont come panhandlin when you're up against it . . . Anybody else feel like the breadline?"

Nobody said anything. Jim clenched his fists. "Dirty rat," he said in his teeth, "I hope his guts wither. I hope . . ." He flung his boots and mackinaw into the locker and walked out into the dwindling light. There was a darkness in him, a heavy darkness that wound into a hardness. When the slaughterhouse workers got on before the viaduct, he pushed his way viciously out of the packed streetcar and walked into a "soft drink" parlor. "A straight," he ordered. To himself, "Alright for Tracy to talk, he doesnt have a wife and brats. But no man has any business having 'em that wants to stay a man. Having to take all that goddamn crap . . . Not that they aren't worth it though," thinking of Jimmie. "What else you got?"

The sound of the two bits clamped down on the counter brought harshly the picture of Anna counting his pay money. "Goddamn woman—what's the matter with her anyhow? Dont even have a wife that's a wife anymore—just let her say one word to me and I'll bash her head in."

He thought he saw Mazie across the street, but he was not sure. No one greeted him at the gate—the dark walls of the kitchen enclosed him like a smothering grave. Anna did not raise her head.

In the other room Bess kept squalling and squalling, and Ben was piping an out-of-tune song to quiet her. There was a sour smell of wet diapers and burned pots in the air.

"Dinner ready?" he asked heavily.

"No, not yet."

Silence. Not a word from either.

"Say, cant you stop that damn brat's squallin? A guy wants a little rest once in a while."

No answer.

"Aw, this kitchen stinks. I'm going out on the porch. And shut that brat up, she's driving me nuts, you hear?" You hear, he reiterated to himself, stumbling down the steps, you hear, you hear. Driving me nuts.

> Alright for Tracy to talk, alright, he didn't have a wife and kids hangin round his neck like an anchor. Alright for him to talk, alright with nothing more important to worry about than getting canned up and stepping out a floosie.
>
> And Tracy was young, just twenty, still wet behind the ears, and the old blinders were on him so he couldn't really see what was around and he believed the bull about freedomofopportunity and a chancetorise and ifyoureallywanttoworkyoucanalwaysfindajob and ruggedindividualism and something about pursuitofhappiness.
>
> He didn't know, so the big sap threw it up, he threw up his job, thinking he was flinging his challenge into the teeth of life, proclaiming I'm a man, and I'm not taking crap offn anybody, I'm goin to live like a man. There's more to life than workin everything you got to live with outa you in order to keep a job, taking things no man should stand for to keep a job. So he threw it up, the big sap, not yet knowing a job was a straw and every man (having nothing to sell but his labor power) was the drowning man who had no choice but to hang onto it for notsodear life.
>
> So he threw it up, not yet knowing a job was God, and praying wasn't enough, you had to live for It, produce for It, prostrate yourself, take anything from It, for was it not God and what came was it not by Its Divine Providence, and nothing to do but bow to It and thank It for Its mercifulness to you, a poor sinner who has nothing to sell but your labor power. So he threw it up, the big sap (not knowing), he renounced God, he became an atheist and suffered the tortures of the damned, and God Job (being full up that generation) never took him back into the fold only a few days at a time, and he learned all right what it meant to be an infidel, he learned:
>
>> the little things gone: shoeshine and tailormades, tickets to a baseball game, and a girl, a girl to love up, whiskey down your gullet, and laughter, the happy belch of a full stomach, and walking with your shoulders back, tall and proud.
>>
>> He learned all right, the tortures of the damned: feet slapping the pavement, digging humbly into carpets, squatting wide apart in front of chairs and the nojobnojob nothingdointoday buzzing in his ears; eking the coffee–and out; shuffling along the frozen streets, buddy (they made a song out of it) can

you spare a dime, and the freights north east south west, getting vagged, keep movin, keep movin (the bulls dont need to tell you, your own belly yells it out, your own idle hands) *sing a song* of hunger the weather four below holes in your pockets and nowhere to go, the flophouses, the slophouses, a bowl of misery and a last month's cruller and the crabs have a good time spreading and spreading (you didn't know hell would be this bad, did you?).

Oh he learned alright. He never even got a chance to have a wife and kids hang round his neck like an anchor and make him grovel to God Job. (And I guess it's just as well, Jim Tracy, because even among the pious who heed and prostrate themselves It's wrath is visited, for Many Are Called but Few Are Chosen, and are not the Sins of the Fathers (having nothing to sell but their labor power) Visited on the Sons, and it's no fun to see the old lady nag and worry her life away, no fun to see the younguns pulpy with charity starches drowse and chant the lesson after the teacher: we-are-the-richest-country-in-the-worr-uld.)

So (not knowing) he threw it up, the big sap, thinking, the big sap, jobs grew on trees and (believing the old bull) a man didn't hafta take crap off'n anybody, he renounced God Job—and the tortures of the damned were visited upon him in full measure, he learned alright, alright, that last hour writhing in the "piano" in the chain gang down in Florida.

And there's nothing to say, Jim Tracy, I'm sorry, Jim Tracy, sorry as hell we weren't stronger and could get to you in time and show you that kind of individual revolt was no good, kid, no good at all, you had to bide your time and take it till there were enough of you to fight it all together on the job, and bide your time, and take it till the day millions of fists clamped in yours, and you could wipe out the whole thing, the whole goddamn thing, and a human could be a human for the first time on earth.

H A R V E Y   S W A D O S
(1 9 2 0 - 1 9 7 2)

Harvey Swados dedicated much of his career as an essayist, novelist, and writer of short stories to the idea of bringing about a better world, especially "for the people who made the things" others buy. The conditions of their labor, "the sweat, exhaustion, harrying, feverish haste, and stupid boredom," could, Swados firmly believed, be alleviated in a socialist order. And his work steadily reminds us of such possibilities . . . and as often, of their betrayal. Born into a physician's family in Buffalo, New York, Swados himself came from and remained in essentially middle-class circumstances. He graduated from the University of Michigan in 1940 and then served as a merchant seaman during World War II. For a time as he developed a writing career, he worked on an auto assembly line, an experience that provided the basis for his collection of linked stories, On the Line *(1957), from which the following title story is drawn. Afterwards, he taught at a number of colleges and universities, published a series of novels—the best known are probably* Standing Fast *(1970) and* Celebration *(1975)—story and essay collections, including* A Radical's America *(1962) and* A Radical at Large *(1968). Such essays and journalism constituted an effort to sustain a definition of "radical" that placed the humanization of work, in addition to racial equality and peace, at the center of a political agenda. Swados also published a biography of Senator Estes Kefauver,* Standing Up for the People *(1972), and worked in liberal Democratic campaigns.*

In On the Line, *a minor character from one story becomes the central figure of the next. It is a literary device, of course, but it is also one way of expressing Swados' view of how the lives of working people are interlinked one with another, on the line and off.*

ON THE LINE

When Orrin had been working on the line for about a year, his right hand began to stiffen. Instead of letting up, he tightened his grip on his tools and set to work even harder than before. Orrin was a stubborn man; he knew that he had been called a fanatic, and he took a certain pride in the knowledge.

Once, at the height of the auto production season, the men in the body shop were asked if they would come in not only on Saturday, but on Sunday also in order to meet the quota. Although they were entitled to double time for Sunday work, most of them were satisfied with the fifty hours' pay they had already earned, and one of the welders protested bitterly to Orrin.

"Now they want you to work on Sundays, for Christ's sakes. You don't even get to see your family. Are you going to come in, or are you going to tell them you have to go to church?"

Orrin held out his hands to the man, his fists loosely clenched.

He replied coldly, "I never go to church. Work is my religion."

When he saw the look on the welder's face, Orrin wished that he could have taken back the prideful, boasting words. But it was too late, and he knew that it would get around the shop, what he had said and the way he had acted, and it would be added to the already uncomplimentary picture most of the men had of him.

Orrin would have preferred to be liked, but he really didn't care. The men on the line came and went. What the transients thought of him made absolutely no difference. As for the others, the few who like himself made up the permanent backbone of the body shop, they had learned to take him as he was.

At first, when they observed the concentrated fury with which he worked, they muttered, "Company man," and one or two even approached the shop committeeman to find out if the union could get him to slow down. But they soon found out that Orrin did not work the way he did because he wanted to impress the bosses or because he was a brownnose by nature; although he had never belonged to a union before, he was perfectly willing to go along with everyone else on the line, even with their work standards—he was simply used to working hard and steady, and he took his pleasure from the plain fact that he could work better and harder and longer than anybody else around him.

Or so everyone came to understand. While he was not openly sneered at, Orrin knew as the months passed that he was not going to be liked here in the auto plant any more than he had been in the army or in any of the jobs he had held in the years between the end of the Second World War and his coming to work here. He made some casual friends, he earned respect for his severity and his skill and his fortitude, and finally he achieved a kind of neutral balance on the line. This was enough.

Orrin had always despised those who were physically his equals or better but who could not keep up with him; it had been so when he was nineteen and number-one man in his infantry outfit, and it was so now when he was losing his hair but was still number-one man on this line. When he listened to the big young fellows around him whining about how hard their work was, he could not keep the contempt he felt from showing in his face.

In a way it was paradoxical that he, as the one man who really enjoyed pressure, the one man who never complained when the cars moved so fast that they seemed to be rolling on their own fiendish motorless power or so close together that you could hardly squeeze between them to do your job, should have been the one who smiled the least. Those who bitched and those who griped often found occasion to laugh. They pulled practical jokes on each other like children, cutting off the gas to the solder flower's line, cutting off the air to the metal finishers' grinding discs, hiding each other's screwdrivers, rolling heavy buffing wheels like bowling balls down the aisles to bang one another in the shins; but not Orrin. He took his pleasure without showing it, he knew that they must envy him for being able to enjoy what he did without horsing around, and he smiled almost as seldom as he laughed.

As a result Orrin, whose face was long and rather pinched anyway, with two unhumorous vertical lines framing his thin hyphen of a mouth like parentheses, always looked sobersided. He wore a blue-striped railroad man's cap, in which his wife had taken a tuck, to protect his narrow balding head from dust, and baggy coveralls (still advertising LAKESIDE SERVICE STATION & REST., although no one but Orrin knew where it was) which hinted at an undertaker's figure, sad and lean but paunchy. When he changed in the locker room from the coveralls to the dark, conservative suit and tie he invariably wore to and from work, he looked even more like a mortician. Behind his back—he had heard it once—the youngsters called Orrin "The Gravedigger."

Nevertheless, inside he burned. He burned with the fire of youth, and he felt that those around him were no more men than the gutless boys who had come and gone, wounded, weary, or fleeing before the enemy in the French forest where he had fought for one hundred and seven days, senior man in his outfit at the age of nineteen. They groaned about coming in to work at all; they spat with disgust as the siren blew and they had to pick up their tools: it was all too much like the men in his company who had behaved as though Hitler was personally picking on them, when they would have preferred to stay home and let the enemy do as he pleased. For himself, Orrin faced each day with the conviction that he was setting an endurance record, not unlike the one he had set in France. After he had been invalided out of the line against his will, he was awarded an official commendation; at the bottom of his heart he felt that his unblemished attendance and punctuality record on this line would one day be recognized too.

He had always admired, ever since childhood, the flag-pole-sitters and marathon-dancers, the frozen explorers and solo fliers—all those who were able to clench their teeth and carry on indefinitely. His wife had even teased him about it early in their marriage when she learned how Orrin as a schoolboy had studied the box scores faithfully and tensely every day of Joe DiMaggio's marvelous consecutive-game hitting streak.

"I think you cared more about that hitting streak than you did about your own family," Edith had laughed, but then had quickly stopped when she saw his face.

"You don't understand," he had said, as calmly as possible. "Most women wouldn't. It's what makes a man unusual, doing something nobody else can do. It's why I was the last guy to stick it out on the line. They had to carry me back on a stretcher, did you know that?" But then it was his turn to stop, seeing by the expression on her face that she knew all right, knew so well that even though she would never understand, she was bored by the most important thing he'd ever done.

Orrin was driven to try to explain what it had been like, on the line, to men in the factory who cared no more about it than Edith. His fellow veterans cherished reminiscences of Calvados and cognac, of sudden dark encounters and complaisant girls, and they resented being reminded of the unpleasant things, which a lot of them hadn't even lived through anyway, but had only read about in the comfort of their heated barracks.

"Is that all you think about?" demanded Harold the pick-up man, one lunch hour as they were sitting in a semicircle on the floor, eating sandwiches. Aside from an annoying habit of handing out gratuitous advice, Harold was one of the more popular of the older men. He swallowed a small cookie, his large, pointed Adam's apple working up and down like a bobbin as he masticated, and then said: "In point of fact, I was considerably older than you and I was already married when I went off to the army. But that's past history, Orrin. People don't want to hear about it any more."

Stung bitterly, Orrin shot back, "Sure, you probably can't even remember getting hit. You were probably in a drunken fog."

There was an awful silence. Most of them knew that Harold was a drunkard—he had volunteered the information himself in a detached, almost scientific way—but for that very reason no one before had ever dared to mention it aloud.

Harold said coolly, "As a matter of fact, I was cold sober when I earned my Purple Heart. I got sprayed in the ass on Guadalcanal, bending over to pick up a booby-trapped bottle of Jap beer." When the laughter had subsided he added, "But I'm going to be forty years old come my next birthday, and I've got more to think about than that stuff that nicked me way the hell and gone back in 'forty-four."

Orrin was left with the boys recently out of high school, who didn't know what war was like and didn't know what work was like. At that only one of them, the kid named Walter who was saving up to go away to college, seemed willing to make the effort to understand. He was clumsy and slow to catch on, but he had a way of gritting his teeth that made Orrin suspect that he would stick no matter how miserable Buster made it for him. What's more, he would stick the way Orrin would have stuck if he'd found it hard: not because he had been starving, or his mother needed money for an operation, but simply as a point of honor.

So Orrin said to him, "Very few people take anything seriously but their own little pleasures. But it's the few that count. They're the ones that win the wars and keep production going."

"Yes, but in a democratic country you have to count on the majority, not just on those few," Walter replied, wiping his red, sweating freckled face against the already wet sleeve of his khaki shirt. "If we dropped dead tonight, the factory would open just the same tomorrow morning, and they'd turn out just as many cars."

Orrin shook his head. "There's always what they call key men. I don't care where it is, if those key men don't hold their end . . . things will fold. Take me. I'm no superman, far from it, but at least I know how to hold on. I'm not saying I won the war singlehanded or any of that boloney, but we would have been a lot worse off in my sector if I hadn't made up my mind I was going to stick it out on the line until they ordered me back or I got hit. And that's what happened. Guys came and went, they got hit, they went batty, they took off like rats, they faked everything from trench foot to clap. But I was there a hundred and seven days, and the longer I held out the more it bucked up the rest of the guys, and that's why I got my commendation after they took the shrapnel out of my legs."

"Those must have been the greatest days of your life," Walter said innocently.

"Well, they were," Orrin replied sharply. He pulled on his gloves and prepared to go back to work. "I don't mind looking back on them—why should I? I don't forget all the mud and slop and blood, or the stinking K rations and C rations, or shaving out of my helmet with cold water. That was part of the whole show. If there's no obstacles, there's no glory, right?"

Walter scuffed his feet through the debris before them, remains of sandwich wrappings, paper bags, cigarette packages, metal filings, stumps of lead. He seemed to be considering an answer. Finally he said, "I guess your life hasn't been very interesting since then if you think about the war so much."

Orrin felt his face getting red. Nervously he yanked off his cap, then jammed it back low on his forehead, so low that it almost covered his eyes. "It's different," he said. "When you're married and raise a family it's different."

"How many kids you got, Orrin?"

"Three. All girls." He took up his file and said aggressively, "Besides, that's what I like about this place. Never mind the money, aside from the fact that the rate is better here than you can get anyplace else. It's a challenge. It's not for sissies and it's not for old ladies. There's always obstacles, they keep the pressure on you all day from the time you punch in, the line keeps going like the tides or the earth turning, and it's up to you to keep up. Once you're on the line, it's up to you." And he went back to his job.

But the boy's question about the rest of his life was like a ladle stuck into a simmering stew—it set Orrin to thinking all over again. He was not happy at home. He couldn't put his finger on it; all he knew was that he looked forward to going to work more than he did to going home.

He had come home from overseas in '45 to the farm town where he had grown up. Everybody on Main Street had given him a big hello, and he had been invited to talk at a chicken dinner given for the GI's. Halting but not shy, he had spoken frankly of those climactic three months of the war when he had stuck it out on the line. His attitude had been so unusual that Mr. Haskins, who owned the feed and grain store, asked him about it.

"Tell me something, Orrin," he had said. "You're the only boy I know that's come back with a good word for the army. If you liked it so much, how's come you didn't reenlist?"

"No sense being in the army if there's no fighting going on, Mr. Haskins," Orrin had replied. "Besides, I've got a girl. I doubt if I could talk her into marrying a soldier."

Edith was the kid sister of his high-school buddy. Soon after her brother was discharged he had become a television repairman and started to put on weight. He turned out to be a fanny-pincher, the kind of man who was forever bragging about the hot reception he got from the lonely housewives whose antennas he mounted. But Edith was not at all like her brother. What attracted Orrin to her most of all was her intensity.

She was a slim, tallish girl, almost lean, bold-eyed, with ropelike veins in her forearms that protruded even more when she knotted her fingers together in moments of excitement. Although she was not conventionally attractive, Orrin was desperate to make love to her, perhaps because he could sense intuitively the depth and ferocity of her response. She was not the kind to hold him at bay: he had her two or three times in his dad's barn, and once even on her parents' bed, and the more he took her the more anxious he was to marry her quickly and keep her as his own.

Soon after the wedding they moved into a Quonset hut on the edge of the state college campus and Orrin enrolled in ag school under the GI Bill. Their days were dull and cramped; their nights were agonizingly wonderful. Clamped together on the studio couch under the arching metal roof, they grappled back and forth over tearing sheets, groaning and crying out in ecstasy, the floor around them a tangle of blankets, textbooks, and underclothing. Before the year was out Edith was pregnant.

She wanted above everything, even above success for Orrin, a healthy baby, and she decided that they would have to play it safe. What was more, Orrin's father had been failing on the farm; a fatal disease had wiped out most of his inadequately insured cattle, and he had finally gone to work as a machinist in a soft-drink bottling plant. Within two years he was forced to sell out the farm Orrin had been counting on, and Edith became pregnant again, unexpectedly.

"There's no sense our sticking around here," Orrin said to her one evening after she had put their daughter to sleep in her crib. "We've got no farm to go to. If we have to start from scratch, it might as well be in something with a future. I'm not going to be a farmer, Edie—it's a dying game. Let's pull out."

She sat on the edge of the mattress, winded from having pulled the studio couch apart and made up the bed. Her shoulders sagged; below her sunken chest her belly jutted out like a great globe; her thickly veined hands lay limply across her widespread knees. She grinned up at him, a cigarette dangling from one corner of her mouth. "Better to find out now than later on."

They moved back to her parents' house, into the attic bedroom. Their second daughter was born, and Orrin took a temporary job as a driver for the soft-drink firm where his father worked. The hours were long and the pay was ridiculous; Orrin was relieved when Edith herself suggested that he get the hell out of there and look for a decent job.

After a while—too long for his own comfort, with his father-in-law watching him out of the corner of his eye—Orrin caught on as a roofer's helper. This too paid next to nothing, but at least the government matched his earnings with on-the-job trainee checks. And there was a possibility that in time he might get set up on his own.

But the babies, noisier than little girls are supposed to be, were growing fast, and it was becoming impossible for them to stay on in his in-laws' attic. For the first time, Orrin sensed that Edith was starting tentatively to withdraw from the wholehearted commitment she had made to him during their very first nights together. He couldn't charge her with it, since it never came all the way up to the surface, and Edith went about the household routine as though nothing had changed. Nevertheless he knew absolutely that she was coming to he disappointed in him. He could feel it even in the different way she held him and closed her eyes in their most intimate moments together, and it was galling.

There were no houses to be had that year (or the year before or the year after). It was Edith's mother who finally found them the flat behind the church with which she was affiliated; just knowing how hard she'd had to work on her minister and his board to get them the rooms was enough to make Orrin clench his teeth. He cursed himself to his face while he shaved, observing with contempt how his hair was falling out, and thinking how eager his mother-in-law must have been to be rid of them.

The apartment behind the old white church was rent-free—there were even wages with it—but there was so much work to do in return that it was out of the question for him to hold on to his old job. The church itself had to be reroofed, for a start; the minister's drive had to be graded and graveled, the windows of his study had to be rehung and reputtied; the aisles of the church had to be mopped regularly, the sidewalks shoveled, the metal announcement board redleaded and repainted, the lawns mowed and trimmed. Orrin had become a handyman.

During the years that Orrin held the sexton's job he took on extra work here and there around town—hanging gutters and leaders, digging out septic tanks, installing automatic washing machines. Edith had become somewhat settled, now that she had her own place and her own two little girls; she was not quite so taut, although she remained ambitious for a better life for the four of them. She hinted strongly that she would be willing to get out and push Orrin's career, the way girls did that she knew—except that Orrin had no career.

He began to shop around. He wanted to make a move as badly as Edith, but he didn't want anything undemanding. "Being a sexton is strictly for an old man," he told his wife, "not for a young guy like me. There's nothing in it to drive you ahead."

Against his better judgment, he joined the local Legion post. As he had suspected, they talked politics and women—two subjects that bored the pants off him—and most of them were men who had no right to belong to the same organization as men who had been in combat. But it was in the Legion bowling alley that he got wind of the gas station partnership deal, so he had no reason to begrudge the dues he paid.

As soon as he was sure that the deal was open, and without telling Edith, he put his name down on the new housing development that was to go up not far from the service station itself. He could handle a GI mortgage, and on the ten-thousand-dollar model the down payment was negligible. Nevertheless he was uneasy, and he waited until the girls were soundly sleeping to talk to his wife. It was very quiet. Beyond their wall the choir was practicing hymns.

"The two-bedroom units are going up fast," he said. "We can move into one without waiting for the gas station deal to jell. If it falls through, so what? The worst that can happen is that I'll have to find another job."

Edith leaped up with that extraordinary agility she had when there was something she wanted to do in a hurry and flung herself onto his lap, her skirt flying up over her thighs. She yanked his tie down and ruffled his thinning hair.

"Tell me about the gas station, Orrin," she said excitedly. "I want to hear all about it—I know this is going to be it at last."

"It's called the Lakeside Service Station and Restaurant. It belongs to George Werlitz's uncle, who's getting too slow for a fourteen-hour grind between the gas pumps and the diner. What he wants is a younger fellow as a kind of junior partner that'll sooner or later buy him out."

"We don't know anything about running a diner. Is it a good spot?"

"It's on Route Ninety-three. All the people that want to go fishing at the north end of the lake have to go by there. And we can learn, can't we?"

Shortly after they had moved into their new house, Orrin took out a GI loan to establish himself as a partner in the Lakeside Service Station and Restaurant, and Edith took over main charge of the diner.

She liked the pressure almost as much as he did, and she was needed just as badly; nevertheless, deliberately this time, she became pregnant again. It was a gamble, and they both knew what she was gambling on. But, for the third time, Edith was delivered of a girl. Freshly shaved and scrubbed, Orrin arrived at her bedside and found her with her face turned to the wall; even after he had greeted her with an intimacy that was somewhat forced because of the eagerly listening mother at the other end of the semiprivate room, she refused to face him, but spoke in muffled tones, holding the bed sheet to her lips.

"What's the matter, Edie? I just saw the baby, it's cute as any I ever saw."

"It's a she. I suppose you're going to pretend you don't care."

Orrin would have been embarrassed even if he had been alone with his wife. He said placatingly, "I love the kids. You can't have a world without girls in it."

Edith twisted about convulsively. Ignoring her gaping roommate, she said loudly, "Don't hand me that crap. It's a man's world. I always wished I was a man. Now I can't even have a son." She began to sob. "What's the matter? Don't you know how to make boys?"

Orrin walked away. At the door he said, "Take care of yourself. I'll be back tonight after I close up."

Actually her bitter question was one he would have asked *her,* if he had dared. That was why she must have burst out at him, partly, to forestall him. She did not mention it again, nor did he, until after he had finally bought out old Werlitz and they were on their own at last, in their own home, with their own business. Edith had plunged back into the affairs of the diner as though she did not have three small children to care for; the life of business seemed to draw her now as Orrin's arms had drawn her in their first days together. She was happy, it seemed to him, even though by nightfall she was groggy with exhaustion; and when they turned off the floodlights and went to bed for their six hours' rest, she curled up dopily in his arms like a child kept up past its bedtime.

But then the blow fell. Without warning the state highway department announced that Route 93 was going to be straightened for a stretch of some twelve miles. When the job was done, the Lakeside Service Station would be standing on a semiabandoned country road, without a quarter of the traffic necessary to keep it solvent. And there was nothing that could be done.

In a blind rage Orrin raced over to old man Werlitz's and pounded on his front door; but his wife said that he was in bed with bursitis. She swore that he hadn't known of the road change when he had sold out. His nephew George, Orrin's Legion buddy, was equally positive that his uncle would never pull such a trick.

"It's the breaks of the game, Orrin."

"But I'm ruined," he cried, "Don't you see that? The oil company might finance me onto the new highway if they wanted to, but I'm tied up with the diner and all that land. How could I take on a new mortgage if I won't be able to liquidate this one?"

George's sympathy amounted to an arm around his shoulders, but that was all. As for Edith, she was unwilling even to give him that much. She only stared at him in cold despair.

"If you'd had your wits about you, you would have known the old man was getting ready to pull a swifty. I told you his price was too good to be true, didn't I?"

"You told me." He laughed shortly. "You've been in this just as deep."

"That's because I wanted to show you what I could do."

"You showed me already. You and your three girls."

"I knew you'd hold it against me for the rest of my life." She rubbed her hands together tautly; the veins began to coil at her wrists. "What good would it do you to have a son? You wouldn't have anything to pass on to him anyway. Except a bunch of debts."

It was after this that Orrin had realized that he and Edith were never going to have any more children, and that he was going to be years in crawling out from under the mountain of debts with which he had saddled himself. Without consulting Edith, he sold out the business and got himself two jobs: one on the assembly line at the new automobile plant, the other working evenings and Saturdays at a lumberyard, loading orders onto trucks for the following morning's deliveries.

He liked both jobs: the assembly line because he felt that once again, for the first time since the war, his endurance and his courage were being tested continually and found up to the mark; the lumberyard because it was startlingly quiet after the thunderous factory, his footfalls echoing emptily in the dimly lighted yard as he clumped about in his steel-toed shoes with the yellow order forms in his hand, balancing kegs of nails on one shoulder, swinging out ten-foot molding strips and swaying sheets of plywood.

Besides the extra pay check, he was able to buy lumber at wholesale for the dormer-windowed bedroom he was building in the expansion attic on Sundays for the two older girls. This too he was doing without consultation, for there were a jumble of things he wanted to show Edith, not simply to discuss with her: that they were not only not going to lose the house, but were going to make it a bigger and better one; that he was tough enough to handle three jobs at once; and that he cared enough about his daughters to want to make their life more comfortable.

Edith watched him in silence. She had never been much for small talk, any more than he; it was not easy to guess how she felt about his having gone from businessman to factory worker. Once she did say: "There's no point in your killing yourself, Orrin," but when he had replied sharply, "I'm healthy," she had simply commented, "I want you to stay that way. You don't prove anything by doing everything at once."

That was how things stood when his hand began to stiffen. He said nothing about it to anyone, figuring that it came from the use of muscles that had been inactive, just as a man's calves will ache when he attempts to walk after having done nothing but drive for years. He took it as a new test of his fortitude. Eventually, he was sure, it would work itself out.

The only trouble was that the hand did not get better. As the weeks on the line went by, it got so bad that when no one was looking he would whip off his thick cotton gloves and frantically massage the palm and fingers, pressing and pressing in an effort to relieve the agonizing throbs that were starting to travel all the way up his forearm when he clenched his file and set to work. It did not help.

After a while he began to think of the pain, as it burned its way through his hand, as a punishment and a trial, like the boils from which he had suffered without complaint during the last part of his hundred and seven days in the front lines. In his increasing loneliness, it became a companion to which he could talk silently. "Go away, you bastard," he would whisper to it; and if his attention were distracted, he would set to work and sometimes it really would go away. "Ah," he would say, "so I got rid of you that time."

But at night after he had fallen asleep all five fingers would stiffen like the legs of a crab, and they would remain that way until he had gotten into the car, driven to the factory, and begun to file, when they would gradually loosen up, only to be invaded by the returning pain. It became more and more difficult to conceal the stiffening from his wife, until one night, thrashing about in his sleep, he rolled over onto the tautened right hand and awoke with an irrepressible cry.

Wide-awake in an instant, as mothers are, Edith snapped on her lamp.

"Turn it off," he muttered. "It was me. I had a bad dream."

"Look at your hand," she said, sharp as a ferret. "What's wrong?"

"Nothing. It's just a little stiff. Turn off the light."

"A little stiff? It looks like a claw. Can I get you something? Does it hurt a lot?"

"Just sometimes," he replied, and could have kicked himself for his weakness. "Let's go to sleep, Edie. I'm tired."

"What do you mean, sometimes? How long has it been like that?"

"Off and on for a while." He turned over on his side, with his right arm hanging carefully over the edge of the bed, and closed his eyes.

"Go to see a doctor. Promise me you'll see a doctor."

"We'll see."

He had no intention of seeing a doctor even though, now that Edith knew about the fingers, which were beginning to snap back and forth uncontrollably, she began to nag him about it. For one thing, he saw no reason to go running for help just because she urged him to; for another, beyond all his pride in the record he was setting on the body-shop line was the fear that a doctor might do something to jeopardize it.

When he slashed his finger, though, catching his glove against the whirling edge of a grinding disc so that the cotton spun off and the disc bit into his flesh so viciously that blood spurted inside the torn glove all the way to the wrist, he had to go to the factory hospital. There the first-aid man wiped his hand clean and said, "Bend those fingers, will you, Mac, so I can make a neat bandage for you."

Wordlessly Orrin did as he was asked.

"Hey," the orderly said, "you got a trigger finger there, you know?"

"What's a trigger finger?"

"It clicks on you when you go to bend it, doesn't it, and then it won't come back by itself?"

"A couple of them are like that. It'll go away, won't it?"

"Can't prove it by me. You can soak it in the whirlpool, or better yet let the orthopedist see it—he comes in Wednesdays. Get a pass from your foreman next Wednesday for ten-thirty, okay?"

Orrin had no intention of seeing an orthopedist. But Edith saw the bandage and at once asked what they had said about his hand. When he told her, she was insistent that the practical thing to do was to cover himself against future disability and insure compensation by seeing the specialist.

Sheepishly, he asked Buster for a pass and walked on down to the hospital, past all those plant areas which seemed so soft and quiet, so clean and orderly, in comparison with the yelling, banging pressure of the body shop. It would be impossible for him, he thought, to stand around all day as these men did, clipping seat covers onto frames with small tools, spraying wheels with small guns as they swung silently by on overhead conveyers, or clamping cables onto batteries: this was woman's work, clean, dull, and deadly, and the men who did it looked incapable of getting down on their knees and working over a sheet of steel until the sweat streamed down and they remolded it to perfection. No wonder they earned less than he did—they were replaceable by anybody with two hands.

The orthopedist was a big bulky man in his forties, with a Masonic pin in the lapel of his tweed suit. He looked like a kindly former football player, and as Orrin extended his hand, palm up, for the examination, he knew that he would have to do what the doctor told him to—he felt, oddly, as though he were standing at attention before an officer about to give him orders. While the doctor poked and prodded gently, Orrin glanced at his own reflection in the gleaming chromium autoclave that stood against the tiled wall. He was astonished at how hangdog he looked, his bald forehead shining with the sweat of uneasiness, his body shrinking into the blue coveralls. My God, he thought, I look older than he does, and he turned his gaze hesitantly to the doctor's frank and friendly eyes.

"You've got a rare ailment," the doctor smiled, "known as tenosynovitis. Must be millions of people who have it."

"Is that what they call trigger finger?"

"The same. It's a callus growth around the sheath covering this tendon. The thicker it gets, the harder it is for the tendon to pull these fingers back and forth. In your case it'll probably become worse from the nature of your work, I regret to say."

"So there's nothing can be done?" Orrin asked, almost with relief.

"On the contrary, it's fairly easy to fix. Massage it with cocoa butter from the second palmar crease toward this finger tip for a week. If that won't help, we'll open the hand and scrape away the callus. Sounds bad, but there's nothing much to it, and it always does the trick."

Orrin simply did not have time to sit around smearing grease into his hand which he used more than twelve hours a day; but he did it while he ate and during his relief time, for it seemed to him now that this slippery expedient was his last hope of avoiding the operation that represented in some indefinable way a threat to the continuity of his life.

It did not work. The orthopedist, in a dark blue suit this time, as befitted one pronouncing sentence, took up Orrin's hand with the same smiling gentleness and shook his head.

"Let's get it over with. The company will have you driven over to the hospital, so you name the day. I'm there every morning, operating, except Wednesdays and Sundays."

"Will I lose any time?"

The doctor put his thumbs in his vest, disclosing a row of cigars. "No reason why you should. You'll be a little groggy from the local for a while, but if you rest up for an hour I don't see why you can't come back here and finish up the day."

"It isn't the money." Orrin swallowed; the hand was burning. "It's just that . . . I can't hang around and not work."

"I think they'll give you something to do. The way our Social Security system operates, a big company finds it cheaper to have you come in with one hand than for you to sit home until it heals, collecting compensation for lost time. That sends up their insurance premiums, you see?"

The intricacies of such large-scale bookkeeping were beyond Orrin, but he felt somewhat relieved. He reported to the hospital in good time and was led to the operating room, where he lay staring up at the great round light overhead, silently proffering his right arm up to anesthetist, surgeon, and nurse, half dreaming of the day he had lain like this in the base hospital cursing with shame and weariness as they picked the shell fragments out of his legs and behind.

In an hour they had finished injecting, cutting, scraping, and sewing, and he arose swaying from the table, remembering fleetingly Edith and her narrow pelvis and the three girl babies she had borne, moaning and gritting her teeth, in this same building. Then he found himself in the company station wagon, blinking in the unaccustomed noonday light, and before he knew it he was back in the ambitious noise and dirt of the body shop.

He was greeted by Buster the foreman, who removed the cigar from his mouth, glanced appraisingly at the bandaged hand, and asked, "How'd it go?"

Orrin shrugged. He felt uneasy in his street clothes, without the coveralls, almost like one of the tourists who came through the plant in batches. "All right, I guess. It'll be all right. Got a job for me?"

"You can't metal-finish with all them stitches. You know there's no work on this line for one hand. Go on into the office and ask Hawks."

Hawks was the superintendent of the entire body shop; Orrin had spoken to him only two or three times. His office was in a glass and metal island in the middle of the area; it had five desks and telephones in as many cubicles for the engineers, inspectors, and technicians who drifted in and out. Waiting for Hawks, Orrin stood inconspicuously in a corner behind the glass with his arms clasped behind him, the good one supporting the throbbing one, watching the welders on the line before him, their cracking, sputtering guns strangely muted behind this thin glass barrier.

Hawks walked in swiftly and with a side glance at Orrin picked up a telephone from an empty desk and muttered something into it, then hung up. He was a tall, sagging man with a broken nose and pendulous earlobes. Every day he wore a freshly starched immaculate white shirt with the cuffs turned back, and an incongruously flashy tie secured by a silver clasp in the shape of a dollar sign. He was by gossip a woman chaser.

He said somberly, "What's up?"

Orrin extended his bandaged hand. "Buster said you could find a job for me. I just had this opened up this morning."

"God *damn* it. What do they think this is, a convalescent home?" He looked sadly at Orrin, as though he were pleading for understanding. "*You* know there's nothing in the body shop for a man with one hand. Sit down and take it easy, you must be still groggy. I'll see what I can do."

Orrin sat tensely on the edge of a metal chair, waiting for his new assignment. He had no idea what they would ask him to do. What he really wondered was how Buster and the rest were making out without him.

Hawks came back from one of the little cubicles where he had been muttering into a telephone. He hitched up his expensive slacks. "They need a man over in the chassis department. Go over to where they drive the cars off the line, on the way over to the hospital, and ask for Big Tony. He's a big dago, always has his hat on, always chews gum. Don't forget to give him your clock number, or you won't get paid."

Orrin made for the chassis department and introduced himself to Big Tony, who put down his clipboard and looked at him dubiously.

"Can you drive with one hand?"

"I can use the arm to steer."

"This kid's partner is out today. Take every other job as it gets to the end of the line. Don't forget they've never been driven, they're stiff—the eights should start, the sixes you got to choke. Watch for the automatic shift and the regular shift.

There's only three places to take a job—over the pit for brake inspection, over onto that other line, or into the corner for repairs. I'll signal you which one to take. Go ahead, start this one up."

For Orrin it was exhilarating, bucking a line once again. The cars came off fast; sometimes he couldn't get them started, sometimes the automatic shift wouldn't work, sometimes there wasn't any seat inside and he had to steer from the floor, sometimes he drove into the wrong lane and had Big Tony howling curses at him. But it was good work for a one-armed man, and the time spun by so fast that he was astonished when the day was over.

"Boy, this was a tough one," sighed the youngster with whom he had been alternating jobs all day. "One of the toughest ever."

Orrin stared at him in disgust. The lad was no more than eighteen, myopic, with soft arms and a pimply forehead over his heavy eyeglasses. He said to him curiously, "How long have you been working here, anyway?"

"Two long months."

"Well, you ought to come on over to the body shop and find out what real work is like."

"No, thanks. I heard about it."

"This job was just right for me with one hand. If I had two hands, I'd fall asleep on it—and I'm practically twice your age."

Nevertheless, the following morning Orrin punched in quickly and hastened over to look up the boy. He saw him sitting by the huge air duct which sucked up the carbon monoxide as the cars came off the line.

"Okay, kid," he said. "I'm back to give you a hand again."

"Gee, I'm sorry," the boy replied, "but my partner's back today."

Orrin found himself waiting for an assignment once again on the edge of the metal chair in the body shop office. It was an hour and a half before Hawks came up and said absently, "See Buster. He'll give you something."

Until Hawks said these words Orrin had been shrinking down in the chair, avoiding the glances of the engineers and inspectors as they hurried in and out and mentally composing answers to some nonexistent executive who would come up to him and nudge him with his toe like someone tipping over a stone and say to him, *"What are you doing for your pay, sitting there and staring off into space when everyone else in this plant is working like a dog?"*

Now he arose, knowing that he had no answer, and walked slowly down the aisles to Buster, who stood at his desk painstakingly filling out requisition slips for tool repairs. Buster glanced up and said, "Oh, it's you," and at once led him away, as though afraid that Orrin would ask for permission to stay right there.

Orrin tagged after him silently, not walking alongside him so that Buster would feel that he had to make conversation. The foreman led him to a darkish corner at the rear end of the line at the beginning of the body shop, near the jigs where the bodies were first assembled, and indicated several barrels filled with small clips standing under a table.

"What you got to do is snap the green clips to the black ones, like this. Make sure the narrow end is on top. Then take this can and brush and give them a smear, it's an oxide for rust. Can you do it one-handed?"

Orrin nodded wordlessly.

"Main thing is to keep ahead of that colored guy. He works here alone, mounts these to every job as you get them ready." He indicated a ghostlike Negro, humped and talking to himself at the far end of the line. Orrin reached out and touched Buster's arm.

"Who usually does this job?"

"Generally the colored guy does the whole thing himself. But they gave him one extra operation and it got to be too much. So I told Hawks and the time-study man to let you do this until they re-evaluate the job."

So he was being given made work. Leaning his hip against the work bench, Orrin watched, his insides quivering, as Buster without troubling to take the cigar from his mouth casually assembled a few of the license-plate clips and painted them as a kind of demonstration.

Controlling his voice, Orrin asked, "What about my relief?"

Buster smiled. "You won't kill yourself on this job. I can't spare the relief man for it. Take a twelve-minute break whenever you feel like it and you're far enough ahead. Take it easy, Orrin."

In the days that followed, Orrin learned what it meant to be stupefied. Mindlessly he snapped the little clips together, hundreds of them, thousands of them, his fingertips doing the childish little endlessly repeated trick while his mind was utterly free to roam as it pleased. For a while he amused himself as, he thought, any intelligent man would—by devising new and simpler ways to do the work, by laying out the clips in overlapping rows before beginning to snap them together, by spreading out the finished groups so that they could all be painted at once—but then there was nothing left for him to improve upon, the whole operation was basically stupid, and he fell back on allowing himself to get behind, dawdling along until the Negro assembler looked nervously at the dwindling pile of clips, and then working frenziedly to catch up. That was a game that could not be repeated indefinitely, though, and finally he simply slouched over the table, slipping the pieces together and dreaming—dreaming of the exalted moments of his past life, dwindled away now to little trinkets that had to be fitted together and smeared anyhow with paint.

He was home early evenings, since he could not work at the lumberyard, but if he could have thought of another place to go, he would have. Edith wanted to mother him and claimed it was nice to have him around for a change, and it drove him wild, as if he were already an old man finishing out his life as a night watchman, with a wife who plumped up his pillows and cut his corns for him.

"Can't you see I'm sick of it all?" he burst out one night. "If you hadn't been after me to do something about the hand, this would never have happened. I was working hard, pulling us out of the hole. I was the key man on the line, and now they've got me sorting nuts and bolts."

"I don't see what's so terrible if you take it easy for a while. You're still on the payroll. And you'll get back the money you're losing at the lumberyard in your workmen's compensation. Besides"—she looked at him narrowly—"you didn't want to stay on that assembly line forever, did you? I bet those other men you worked with would give anything to trade jobs with you right now."

That was the truth. But it didn't say much for the rest of the men. The next day he took a walk over to the line during his relief period, for the first time since he had been put in the corner with the Negro. Buster was standing there with his cigar in one hand and a soft cloth in the other, feeling the jobs as they went by and cursing out the men who had missed low spots. The line was moving fast, and everyone was working hard and steady; occasionally Walter or Pop the inspector or one of the others would look up and wave to him, but no one had time to come over and talk until Harold the pick-up man, his long, drunkard's nose twitching and his big Adam's apple bobbing like an alligator's snout, brushed up to him for a moment. Harold pointed with his buffer to a tall, tawny Negro with oriental eyes who was grinding away at a high spot, his long legs bent in a catcher's stance.

"That's your replacement," Harold said. "Not as good as you, but he knows his stuff. Life goes on, eh, Orrin? In point of fact, no matter what you do or how well you do it, there's always somebody around waiting to take over."

In a sudden rage, Orrin wanted to turn his back and walk away without any answer at all. But before he could move, Harold himself went back to the job, waving negligently at him as he left. Orrin stood for an instant, then walked over to Buster, now chewing his cigar like a cud and staring vacantly into space beyond the moving line.

"Hi, Buster," Orrin said. "Thought I'd come over during my break."

"How you making out over there, Orrin?" Buster asked incuriously.

"To tell you the truth, I'm going crazy. It's not for me. I was wondering if—"

"Excuse me," Buster muttered, and sprang forward to the bonderizing booth, where Hawks had turned up, alternately waving for Buster to hurry and arguing heatedly with Halstein, the chief inspector. Orrin turned and walked slowly down the aisles to his little corner, where the silent Negro was helping himself to a handful of painted clips.

"Fixing to do some myself if you didn't get back soon."

"Yes, well, that's all right," said Orrin absently. He made up a little batch for the man and then pulled back the bandage from his palm, peering into the dark area to see how the stitches were healing. It would have to be soon, he thought; if it didn't heal soon . . . If I was a kid, he thought, I'd run away from home.

The next morning, as he mooned over the little metal snippets, remembering how Edith had once shown him the japanned box in which she kept all his V-mail from overseas, his commendation, and his ribbons, and wondering where that box was now, probably stuck away in a bottom drawer with a bunch of slips that needed mending, he was surprised to see Buster coming towards him with a young white-collar fellow in a brown gabardine suit, even balder than he was, whom he recognized as being from the payroll department.

"Fellow wants to talk to you for a minute, Orrin."

"I've got all day."

The payroll clerk laughed nervously. "If you remember last year, I came around to sign you up for your metal finisher's pay."

"I remember."

"I understand that since your injury and operation, you have been unable to perform metal finisher's work."

"Well, naturally . . . Say, wait a minute." Orrin flung aside the metal clips with which he had been toying. "Are you trying to tell me—"

"I'm only doing my job, fellow."

"Don't fellow me. You want to cut my pay, don't you? I ruin the damn hand metal-finishing and then you want to take away my metal finisher's pay. Well, you can take the stinking job and—"

"Take it easy, Orrin," Buster said uncomfortably. "It's nothing personal. This guy's got a job to do like anybody around here."

Orrin felt himself trembling from head to foot. "Is this the way they repay you for hard work? It's worse than the guards looking in your lunch box when you go out, to make sure you didn't steal five cents' worth of sandpaper. The hand's practically healed, I can go back to metal-finishing in a day or two, but that's not enough, is it? You got to take the lousy petty couple of dollars for these few days out of my hide. All right, take the money. And take the job too."

"It's got nothing to do with you or me. As soon as you go back on your old work, You go back on your old rate. You get paid for what you do—they can't make exceptions."

"I'm not talking about exceptions. I'm talking about whether a man is a human being or a piece of . . . My God," he cried out in anguish, "I might just as well have worked like all the others all year—nobody cares that I did my best."

Buster took him by the arm and led him away from the man in the brown suit. "Listen to me and don't be a jerk," he said intently. "You're not a kid to throw away a job just like that, you're a family man. Don't make a stink about the lousy five bucks, or whatever it is. They don't want to punish you for your operation, the place is too big, one hand doesn't know what the other one is doing. I wasn't supposed to tell you, but you're in line for a foreman's job on the night shift if you want. As soon as you get back on production again, Hawks is going to call you in." He nudged Orrin. "You know what I'm making, it's better than what you make. On salary, plus overtime, plus nightshift bonus, you'll do all right."

"Night shift," Orrin said slowly.

"They need bosses for nights. What do you care?" Buster added jocularly. "You're married a long time, you don't have to be home at night. You'll start fresh— new faces, you know? It's a break, Orrin. You don't want to be working all your life. I worked for sixteen years before they made me a boss."

Orrin thought of the living room where he hid from his wife behind the sports page of the paper at night; of the bedroom where she lay waiting for him when he worked alone in the lumberyard and came home late; of the half-finished children's room in the attic waiting for him to attack it once again, a final test of his fortitude. Then he looked at the bald-headed white-collar fellow as he stood waiting patiently with his ball-point pen and his little forms to be filled out, and he thought of the energy that he'd poured down the drain on job after job until now he was thirty-three and with nowhere to retreat beyond this ugly place where he had made his last-ditch resistance. Now he was being asked to sign his unconditional surrender.

He looked first at the payroll clerk, a little red in the face, then at Buster, holding a flaring lighter to his cigar stump, then at the solemn Negro, who had stopped work and was staring at the three of them, and he sighed.

"All right," he said at last. "Show me where to sign."

PATRICIA DOBLER

When Patricia Dobler writes about a rolling mill, she writes whereof she knows. She was born in Middletown, a small steel city on the main line between Dayton and Cincinnati, Ohio. In much of what is now the "rust belt" of the United States, it would have been a common practice of the post–World War II period to take school children through the local plant, where some fathers and uncles worked, and where the fortunate could manage not to. Dobler's earliest book of poetry, UXB *(1991), was published by Mill Hunk Books. Her* Talking to Strangers *(University of Wisconsin Press, 1986), won the Brittingham Prize in poetry. She has also issued* The Mill in Winter *(1986). A third full-length collection, entitled* The Body's Version, *has now been completed. Her poems have been published in journals like the* Mid-American Review, Ploughshares, Prairie Schooner, *and the* Southern Poetry Review. *She now teaches at Carlow College, a Catholic liberal arts institution for women founded by the Sisters of Mercy in Pittsburgh; she directs the Women's Creative Writing Center.*

Field Trip to the Rolling Mill, 1950

Sister Monica has her hands full
timing the climb to the catwalk
so the fourth-graders are lined up
before the next heat is tapped, "and no
giggling no jostling, you monkeys!
So close to the edge!" She passes out
sourballs for bribes, not liking
the smile on the foreman's face,
the way he pulls at his cap,
he's not Catholic. Protestant madness,
these field trips, this hanging from catwalks
suspended over an open hearth.

Sister Monica understands Hell
to be like this. If overhead cranes clawing
their way through layers of dark air
grew leathery wings and flew screeching
at them, it wouldn't surprise her.
And the three warning whistle blasts,
the blazing orange heat pouring out
liquid fire like Devil's soup
doesn't surprise her—she understands
Industry and Capital and Labor,
the Protestant trinity. That is why
she trembles here, the children clinging
to her as she watches them learn their future.

JEANNE BRYNER
(B. 1951)

Jeanne Bryner's volume of poetry Breathless *(1995) focuses on the world of nurses, patients, illness, and healing. Her poems explore the consciousness of nurses listening for the pulse of a dying child or caring for young men with AIDS. Other poems concern sexual abuse, rape, and other painful circumstances to which caregivers must attend. Bryner's poems have also appeared in the anthologies* Between the Heartbeats: Poetry and Prose by Nurses *and* Boomer Girls: Poems by Women from the Baby Boom Generation.

In the work that follows she celebrates a nurse midwife, who stands as a kind of model for a newer generation of those who work in and out of hospitals to sustain and comfort patients.

FOR MAUDE CALLEN: NURSE MIDWIFE, PINEVILLE, NC, 1951

I speak of a woman, blue black midwife
Of April fog, flood, swamp, and July nights
When Maude Callen's hands layered newsprint
In circles as a weaver works her loom,
Slow, to catch blood straw, placenta, save sheets.
I sing kitchen lamplight, clean cloths, Lysol,
Cord ties, gloves, gown and mask; she readies
For this crowning, first mother, purple cries.
I sing of sweat and gush and tear, open thighs
And triangle moons, ringlets, charcoal hair.
I sing sixteen-hour days, Maude's tires bare.
Mud country roads, no man doctor for miles.
I sing transition, collapse of mountains,
Crimson alluvium, the son untangled.

JAY PARINI
(B. 1948)

St. Andrews in Scotland; Hanover, New Hampshire; and Weybridge, Vermont; where Jay Parini has lived most of the last quarter century, are a very long cultural distance from his origins around the eastern Pennsylvania coalfields. That fact might be a source of some ironic fun to this novelist, poet, teacher, and literary critic. Parini has written feelingly about his youth among "coal miners and ditchdiggers," as he once put it in an interview, at a time and in a place where coal miners' unionism was gaining strength. His 1982 poetry collection, Anthracite Country, *and his 1986 novel,* The Patch Boys, *mine that vein of his life. He was the first in his extended family to attend college, much less to gain a Ph.D., which he accomplished at St. Andrews University by completing a dissertation, later an important critical study, on the poet Theodore Roethke. Roethke's straightforward irony and his interest in the lives of ordinary people are probably one influence on Parini's own practice of verse.*

Parini has also published two other books of poetry, as well as three novels, the most recent, The Last Station *(1990), a multinarrated story based on Tolstoy's final year. For a number of years before 1982, he taught at Dartmouth College, about which he wrote a wickedly funny* roman à clef, The Love Run *(1989), portraying the institution as a nest of preppy snobs. Since 1982, he has taught English at Middlebury College.*

PLAYING IN THE MINES

Never go down there, fathers told you,
over and over. The hexing cross
nailed onto the door read DANGER, DANGER.
But playing in the mines once every summer,
you ignored the warnings. The door
swung easier than you wished; the sunlight
followed you down the shaft a decent way.
No one behind you, not looking back,
you followed the sooty smell of coal dust,
Close damp walls with a thousand facets,
the vaulted ceiling with a crust of bats,
till the tunnel narrowed, and you came
to a point where the playing stopped.
You heard old voices pleading in the rocks;
they were all your fathers, longing to fix you
under their gaze and to go back with you.
But you said to them NEVER, NEVER,
as a chilly bile washed round your ankles.
You stood there wailing your own black fear.

GWENDOLYN BROOKS
(B. 1917)

Gwendolyn Brooks was born and raised in Topeka, Kansas, though as a mature artist she has been strongly identified with the African-American community of Chicago. Encouraged by her creative parents, she published her first poems at eleven and by age seventeen was regularly contributing poetry to the

Chicago Defender. *Early on, she was influenced by English and American romantic poets, by Emily Dickinson and Sara Teasdale, and after graduating from Chicago's Wilson Junior College, by American modernist experimenters. She had met Langston Hughes in 1933, and he provided her both with encouragement and with something of a model. Her first volume of poetry,* A Street in Bronzeville *(1945), was at once a lyrical evocation of the positive values of an African-American community and a protest against the segregated realities of American life in the 1930s and 1940s. Here she introduces people like "Satin-Legs Smith" and the Bronzeville women and their children, about whom she has continued to write throughout her career. Her poems bring together elements of African-American expressive traditions—the blues, the sermon, bop talk ("We real cool")—with elements she has derived from other formal traditions she has examined in her wide reading and travel.*

Brooks's second book, Annie Allen *(1949), won the Pulitzer Prize for poetry, the first volume by a black writer to be given that honor. Her novel* Maud Martha *(1953) remains one of her most influential texts, especially among black women writers, perhaps because it so forthrightly depicts the growing pains of a young black woman in urban America. Many of the poems in her 1960 volume* The Bean Eaters *deal with issues—like the Mississippi murder of Emmet Till in 1955, provoked by his supposedly whistling at a white woman—taken up by the civil rights movement. Brooks also became increasingly active as a teacher and speaker, offering workshops in local libraries, schools, and prisons, particularly for younger artists from the African-American community. Beginning around 1967, Brooks's outlook was considerably influenced by the Black Arts movement and particularly by the Black Nationalist views of Amiri Baraka and Haki R. Madhubuti. She began to publish exclusively with black-controlled presses, like Dudley Randall's Broadside Press and Madhubuti's Third World Press, thus providing a substantial degree of material support for these fledgling enterprises. She began to edit her own literary annual,* The Black Position, *and later started her own publishing house as part of an effort to retain profit from her work within the black community. Moving away from mainstream publishers, with their enormous promotional capabilities, may initially have cost Brooks a certain degree of recognition in the white community, but the level of excellence, the variety, and the sustained passion of her poetic output have insured that she be recognized as one of the major English-language poets of this century. She has always managed, through changing times and styles, to create a distinctive voice of her own, ironic, sometimes impatient, always caring—always committed to her community and to social change.*

BRONZEVILLE WOMAN IN A RED HAT

hires out to Mrs. Miles

I

They had never had one in the house before.
The strangeness of it all. Like unleashing

A lion, really. Poised
To pounce. A puma. A panther. A black
Bear.
There it stood in the door,
Under a red hat that was rash, but refreshing—
In a tasteless way, of course—across the dull dare,
The semi-assault of that extraordinary blackness.
The slackness
Of that light pink mouth told little. The eyes told of heavy
    care. . . .
But that was neither here nor there,
And nothing to a wage-paying mistress as should
Be getting her due whether life had been good
For her slave, or bad.
There it stood
In the door. They had never had
One in the house before.

But the Irishwoman had left!
A message had come.
Something about a murder at home.
A daughter's husband—"berserk," that was the phrase:
The dear man had "gone berserk"
And short work—
With a hammer—had been made
Of this daughter and her nights and days.
The Irishwoman (underpaid,
Mrs. Miles remembered with smiles),
Who was a perfect jewel, a red-faced trump,
A good old sort, a baker
Of rum cake, a maker
Of Mustard, would never return.
Mrs. Miles had begged the bewitched woman
To finish, at least, the biscuit blending,
To tarry till the curry was done,
To show some concern
For the burning soup, to attend to the tending
Of the tossed salad. "Inhuman,"
Patsy Houlihan had called Mrs. Miles.
"Inhuman." And "a fool."
And "a cool
One."

The Alert Agency had leafed through its files—
On short notice could offer
Only this dusky duffer
That now made its way to her kitchen and sat on her kitchen
    stool.

II

Her creamy child kissed by the black maid! square on the
    mouth!
World yelled, world writhed, world turned to light and
    rolled
Into her kitchen, nearly knocked her down.

Quotations, of course, from baby books were great
Ready armor; (but her animal distress
Wore, too and under, a subtler metal dress,
Inheritance of approximately hate.)
Say baby shrieked to see his finger bleed,
Wished human humoring—there was a kind
Of unintimate love, a love more of the mind
To order the nebulousness of that need.
—This was the way to put it, this the relief.
This sprayed a honey upon marvelous grime.
This told it possible to postpone the reef.
Fashioned a huggable darling out of crime.
Made monster personable in personal sight
By cracking mirrors down the personal night.

Disgust crawled through her as she chased the theme.
She, quite supposing purity despoiled,
Committed to sourness, disordered, soiled,
Went in to pry the ordure from the cream.
Cooing, "Come." (Come out of the cannibal wilderness,
Dirt, dark, into the sun and bloomful air.
Return to freshness of your right world, wear
Sweetness again. Be done with beast, duress.)

Child with continuing cling issued his No in final fire,
      Kissed back the colored maid,
      Not wise enough to freeze or be afraid.
      Conscious of kindness, easy creature bond.
      Love had been handy and rapid to respond.

Heat at the hairline, heat between the bowels,
Examining seeming coarse unnatural scene,
She saw all things except herself serene:
Child, big black woman, pretty kitchen towels.

DOLLY PARTON
(B. 1946)

Dolly Parton was one of twelve children, raised on a ratty farm in Locust Ridge, Tennessee, near the Smoky Mountains National Forest. Her mother, half Cherokee, played guitar, and her grandfather, the Rev. Jake Owens, wrote songs and fiddled. She was given a guitar at seven, and within a few years she was performing regularly on Knoxville's radio station WIVK. By age thirteen she had made her debut at the Grand Ole Opry and recorded her first single. Still in high school, she played snare drums in the marching band and continued to sing. When she graduated, she moved to Nashville and for about four years struggled to gain a foothold in the country music business. Her first hit, "Dumb Blonde," came in 1967, followed soon by "Something Fishy." Porter Waggoner signed her for his television show and for seven years she sang duets with his group on Grand Ole Opry, on tour, and on records. By the early seventies, she was sufficiently well known to strike out on her own, and by the late seventies, she had her own television show, was producing her own records, continuing to write songs, and had crossed over from country music to the top of the pop charts.

In 1980, she made her movie debut in 9 to 5, *with Lily Tomlin and Jane Fonda; she received an Oscar nomination for writing the title song for the film. She has also starred in movies including* The Best Little Whorehouse in Texas, Rhinestone *(with Sylvester Stallone), and* Steel Magnolias. *Her commercial successes through the seventies and eighties and her film notoriety allowed her to establish a multimillion dollar company, Dolly Parton Enterprises, which in 1986 opened Dollywood, a theme park focused on her upbringing in the Smoky Mountains.*

9 TO 5

Tumble out of bed and stumble to the kitchen;
pour myself a cup of ambition,
and stretch and try to come to life.
Jump in the shower and the blood starts pumping;
out on the street, the traffic starts jumping,
with folks like me on the job from nine to five.

[Chorus 1, 3, 5] Working nine to five, what a way to make a living;
barely getting by, it's all taking and no giving.
They just use your mind, and they never give you [you never get the] credit,
It's enough to drive you crazy if you let it.

They let you dream just to watch them shatter;
You're just a step on the boss man's ladder,
But you've got dreams he'll never take away,

In the same boat with a lot of your friends;
Waitin' for the day your ship'll come in,
And the tide's gonna turn, and it's all gonna roll your way.

[Chorus 2] Working nine to five, for service and devotion;
you would think that I would deserve a fair promotion;
want to move ahead but the boss won't seem to let me,
I swear sometimes, that man is out to get me.

[Chorus 4, 6] Nine to five, they've got you where they want you;
There's a better life, and you dream about it, don't you?
It's a rich man's game, no matter what they call it;
And you spend your life putting money in his pocket.

JUDY GRAHN

(B. 1940)

Judy Grahn's "Common Woman" poems (1969) express something of the frustration and anger about the position of women to which the feminist movement of the 1960s and 1970s addressed itself. But they also capture some of the pride and determination on which that movement for change was built. They describe, as Grahn put it, "everyday women without making us look either superhuman or pathetic." Growing up as a self-aware lesbian in a small town in New Mexico, Grahn learned much about pride and determination and developed the anger and humor her poems display.

Grahn has herself held many of the jobs at which her "common women" work: waitress, cook, maid, typist, secretary, lab technician, social service worker, poet. She has been active in the lesbian community in the United States, lecturing and reading her poems widely and recording a number of original videotapes. She has published a number of books concerned with issues of sexuality and gender; these include Another Mother Tongue: Gay Words, Gay Worlds *(1984),* The Highest Apple: Sappho and the Lesbian Poetic Tradition *(1985),* Blood, Bread, and Roses: How Menstruation Created the World *(1993), and* Butch/Femme *(1995), as well as works of poetry and myth, including* The Queen of Swords *(1987) and* The Queen of Wands *(1982). In many of these works, Grahn combines the study of ethnography, language, and religion to connect contemporary feminist ideas with ancient female rituals and myths. Her other volumes include* True to Life Adventure Stories *(1983); a novel,* Mundane's World *(1988); and books of poetry,* Edward the Dyke *(1970),* A Woman Is Talking to Death *(1974), and the collection* The Work of a Common Woman *(1978), from which the poem that follows is taken. Her own poems were gathered in* The Work of a Common Woman: The Collected Poetry of Judy Grahn, 1964-1977.*

ELLA, IN A SQUARE APRON, ALONG HIGHWAY 80

She's a copperheaded waitress,
tired and sharp-worded, she hides
her bad brown tooth behind a wicked
smile, and flicks her ass
out of habit, to fend off the pass
that passes for affection.
She keeps her mind the way men
keep a knife—keen to strip the game
down to her size. She has a thin spine,
swallows her eggs cold, and tells lies.
She slaps a wet rag at the truck drivers
if they should complain. She understands
the necessity for pain, turns away
the smaller tips, out of pride, and
keeps a flask under the counter. Once,
she shot a lover who misused her child.
Before she got out of jail, the courts had pounced
and given the child away. Like some isolated lake,
her flat blue eyes take care of their own stark
bottoms. Her hands are nervous, curled, ready
to scrape.
The common woman is as common
as a rattlesnake.

JOHN GILGUN
(B. 1935)

Gilgun was born and brought up in Malden, one of the Boston-area's Irish Catholic working-class redoubts. He makes powerful use of the scenes of his upbringing in his novel Music I Never Dreamed Of *(1989), a book about the coming of age of a gay working-class man during the height of Cold War anti-communism and homophobia. The novel was nominated for the Lambda Literary Award and the American Library Association Gay and Lesbian Task Force Award.*

For much of his post–graduate school life, Gilgun has taught literature at Missouri Western State College in Saint Joseph. He has published in a variety of forms. Everything That Has Been Shall Be Again *(1981), he describes as "reincarnation fables." From the Inside Out (1991) and* The Dooley Poems *(1991) are volumes of poetry, and* Your Buddy Misses You *(1994) is a collection of stories.*

COUNTING TIPS

for Janet Zandy

My mother came home from work,
sat down at the kitchen table
and counted her tips, nickel by nickel,
quarter by quarter, dime by dime.
I sat across from her reading Yeats.
No moonlight graced our window
and it wasn't Pre-Raphaelite pallor
that bleached my mother's cheeks.
I've never been able to forget
the moment she said—
interrupting *The Lake Isle of Innisfree*—
"I told him to go to hell."
A Back Bay businessman
had held back the tip, asking,
"How much do you think you're worth?"
And she'd said, "You can go to hell!"
All evening at the Winthrop Room she'd fed
stockbrokers, politicians, mafioso capos.
I was eighteen, a commuter student at BU,
riding the MTA to classes every day
and she was forty-one in her frilly cap,
pink uniform, and white waitress shoes.
"He just laughed but his wife was there
and she complained and the boss fired me."
Later, after a highball, she cried
and asked me not to tell my father
(at least not yet) and Ben Franklin
stared up from his quarter
looking as if he thought she deserved it,
and Roosevelt, from his dime, reminded her
she was twenty years shy of Social Security.
But the buffalo on the nickel, he—
he seemed to understand.

ELINOR LANGER

(B. 1939)

In the 1960s, Elinor Langer was among the young journalist-activists who helped redefine the character of journalism, and especially its relationships to movements for social change. She worked for the Washington Post *and then reported on politics for* Science *magazine. At the same time, she participated in civil rights and anti-war activities. She then became the New York editor for the activist and muckraking journal* Ramparts. *She has also written for the* Atlantic, The New York Review of Books, *and* The Nation, *on whose editorial board she continues to serve.*

She has written a major biographical study of an activist and writer of an earlier generation, Josephine Herbst, one of whose novels she has also edited. She has also taught at Goddard College in Vermont. In recent years, she has been working on a study of the rise of skinhead and neo-Nazi movements in the United States and the relationship of these movements to the rest of American society. Her essay "Inside the New York Telephone Company," in a book called Women at Work *(1972), was based on her employment there. While technologically outdated in some respects, it continues to capture much of the work ethos such companies demand—and produce.*

FROM INSIDE THE
NEW YORK TELEPHONE COMPANY

From October to December 1969 I worked for the New York Telephone Company as a Customer's Service Representative in the Commercial Department. My office was one of several in the Broadway–City Hall area of lower Manhattan, a flattened, blue-windowed commercial building in which the telephone company occupies three floors. The room was big and brightly lit—like the city room of a large newspaper—with perhaps one hundred desks arranged in groups of five or six around the desk of a Supervisor. The job consists of taking orders for new equipment and services and pacifying customers who complain, on the eleven exchanges (although not the more complex business accounts) in the area between the Lower East Side and 23rd Street on the North and bounded by Sixth Avenue on the West.

My Supervisor is the supervisor of five women. She reports to a Manager who manages four supervisors (about twenty women) and he reports to the District Supervisor along with two other managers. The offices of the managers are on the outer edge of the main room separated from the floor by glass partitions. The District Supervisor is down the hall in an executive suite. A job identical in rank to that of the district supervisor is held by four other men in Southern Manhattan alone. They report to the Chief of the Southern Division, himself a soldier in an army of division chiefs whose territories are the five boroughs, Long Island, Westchester, and the vast hinterlands vaguely referred to as "Upstate." The executives at——— Street were only dozens among the thousands in New York Tel alone.

Authority in their hierarchy is parceled out in bits. A Representative, for example, may issue credit to customers up to, say, $10.00; her supervisor, $25.00; her manager, $100.00; his supervisor, $300.00; and so forth. These employees are in the same relation to the centers of power in AT&T and the communications industry as the White House guard to Richard Nixon. They all believe that "The business of the telephone company is Service" and if they have ever heard of the ABM or AT&T's relation to it, I believe they think it is the Associated Business Machines, a particularly troublesome customer on the Gramercy-7 exchange.

I brought to the job certain radical interests. I knew I would see "bureaucratization," "alienation," and "exploitation." I knew that it was "false consciousness" of their true role in the imperialist economy that led the "workers" to embrace their oppressors. I believed those things and I believe them still. I know why, by my logic, the workers should rise up. But my understanding was making reality an increasing puzzle: Why didn't people move? What things, invisible to me, were holding them back? What I hoped to learn, in short, was something about the texture of the industrial system: what life within it meant to its participants.

I deliberately decided to take a job which was women's work, white collar, highly industrialized and bureaucratic. I knew that New York Tel was in a management crisis notorious both among businessmen and among the public and I wondered what effect the well-publicized breakdown of service was having on employees. Securing the position was not without hurdles. I was "overqualified," having confessed to college; I performed better on personnel tests than I intended to do; and I was inspected for symptoms of militance by a shrewd but friendly interviewer who noticed the several years' gap in my record of employment. "What have you been doing lately?" she asked me. "Protesting?" I said: "Oh, no, I've been married," as if that condition itself explained one's neglect of social problems. She seemed to agree that it did.

My problem was to talk myself out of a management traineeship at a higher salary while maintaining access to the job I wanted. This, by fabrications, I was able to do. I said: "Well, you see, I'm going through a divorce right now and I'm a little upset emotionally, and I don't know if I want a career with managerial responsibility." She said: "If anyone else said that to me, I'm afraid I wouldn't be able to hire them," but in the end she accepted me. I had the feeling it would have been harder for her to explain to her bosses why she had let me slip away, given my qualifications, than to justify to them her suspicions.

I nonetheless found as I began the job that I was viewed as "management material" and given special treatment. I was welcomed at length by both the District Supervisor and the man who was to be my Manager, and given a set of fluffy feminist speeches about "opportunities for women" at New York Tel. I was told in a variety of ways that I would be smarter than the other people in my class; "management" would be keeping an eye on me. Then the Manager led me personally to the back classroom where my training program was scheduled to begin.

The class consisted of five students and an instructor. Angela and Katherine were two heavy-set Italian women in their late forties. They had been promoted to Commercial after years of employment as clerks in the Repair Department where, as Angela said, "they were expected to be robots." They were unable to make the transition to the heavier demands of the Representative's job and returned to Repair in defeat after about a week.

Billy was a high-school boy of seventeen who had somehow been referred by company recruiters into this strange women's world. His lack of adult experience made even simple situations difficult for him to deal with: he could not tell a customer that she had to be in the apartment when an installer was coming without giggling uncontrollably about some imaginary tryst. He best liked "drinking with the boys," a pack of Brooklyn high schoolers whose alcoholism was at the Singapore Sling stage; he must have belonged to one of the last crowds in Brooklyn that had never smoked dope.

Betty was a pretty, overweight, intelligent woman in her mid-twenties who had been a Representative handling "Billing" and was now being "cross-trained" (as they say in the Green Berets) in Orders. She was poised, disciplined, patient, ladylike, competent in class and, to me, somewhat enigmatic outside it: liberal about Blacks, in spite of a segregated high-school education, but a virtual Minuteman about Reds, a matter wholly outside her experience. By the end of the class Betty and I had over-come our mutual skepticism enough to be almost friends and if there is anyone at the phone company to whom I feel slightly apologetic—for having listened always with a third ear and for masquerading as what I was not—it is Betty.

Sally, the instructor, was a pleasant, stocky woman in her early thirties with a frosted haircut and eyes made up like a raccoon. She had a number of wigs, includ-ing one with strange dangling curls. Sally's official role was to persuade us of the rationality of company policies and practices, which she did skillfully and faithfully. In her private life, however, she was a believer in magic, an aficionado rather than a practitioner only because she felt that while she understood how to conjure up the devil, she did not also know how to make him go away. To Sally a disagreeable female customer was not oppressed, wretched, impoverished in her own life, or merely bitchy: she was—literally—a witch. Sally explained to herself by demonology the existence of evils of which she was far too smart to be unaware.

The Representative's course is "programmed." It is apparent that the phone com-pany has spent millions of dollars for high-class management consultation on the best way to train new employees. The two principal criteria are easily deduced. First, the course should be made so routine that any employee can teach it. The teacher's material—the remarks she makes, the examples she uses—are all printed in a loose-leaf notebook that she follows. Anyone can start where anyone else leaves off. I felt that I could teach the course myself, simply by following the program. The second criterion is to assure the reproducibility of results, to guarantee that every part turned out by the system will be interchangeable with every other part. The system is to bureaucracy what Taylor was to the factory: it consists in breaking down every operation into discrete parts, then making verbal the discretions that are made.

At first we worked chiefly from programmed booklets organized around the principle of supplying the answer, then rephrasing the question. For instance:

It is annoying to have the other party to a conversation leave the line without an explanation.

Before leaving, you should excuse yourself and _____ what you are going to do.

Performing skillfully was a matter of reading, and not actual comprehension. Katherine and Angela were in constant difficulty. They "never read," they said. That's why it was hard for them.

Soon acting out the right way to deal with customers became more important than self-instruction. The days were organized into Lesson Plans, a typical early one being: How to Respond to a Customer If You Haven't Already Been Trained to Answer His Question, or a slightly more bureaucratic rendering of that notion. Sally explained the idea, which is that you are supposed to refer the call to a more experienced Repre-sentative or to the Supervisor. But somehow they manage to complicate this situation to the point where it becomes confusing even for an intelligent person to handle it. You mustn't say: "Gosh, that's tough. I don't know anything about that, let me give the phone to someone who does," though that in effect is what you do. Instead when the phone rings, you say: "Hello. This is Miss Langer. May I help you?" (The Rule is, get immediate "control of the contact" and hold it lest anything unexpected happen, like, for instance, a human transaction between you and the customer.)

He says: "This is Mr. Smith and I'd like to have an additional wall telephone installed in my kitchen."

You say: "I'll be very glad to help you, Mr. Smith (Rule the Second: Always express interest in the Case and indicate willingness to help), but I'll need more information. What is your telephone number?"

He tells you, then you confess: "Well, Mr. Smith, I'm afraid I haven't been trained in new installations yet because I'm a new representative, but let me give you some-one else who can help you." (Rule the Third: You must get his consent to this arrangement. That is, you must say: *May* I get someone else who can help you? *May* I put you on hold for a moment?)

The details are absurd but they are all prescribed. What you would do naturally becomes unnatural when it is codified, and the rigidity of the rules makes the Repre-sentatives in training feel they are stupid when they make mistakes. Another lesson, for example, was: What to Do If a Customer Calls and Asks for a Specific Person, such as Miss Smith, another Representative, or the Manager. Whatever the facts, you are to say "Oh, Miss Smith is busy but I have access to your records, may I help you?" A cus-tomer is never allowed to identify his interests with any particular employee. During one lesson, however, Sally said to Angela: "Hello, I'd like immediately to speak to Mrs. Brown," and Angela said, naturally, "Hold the line a minute, please. I'll put her on." A cardinal sin, for which she was immediately rebuked. Angela felt terrible.

Company rhetoric asserts that this rigidity does not exist, that Representatives are supposed to use "initiative" and "judgment," to develop their own language. What that means is that instead of using the precise words "Of course I'll be glad to help you but I'll need more information," you are allowed to "create" some individ-ual variant. But you must always (1) express willingness to help and (2) indicate the need for further investigation. In addition, while you are doing this, you must always write down the information taken from the customer, coded, on a yellow form called a CF-1, in such a way as to make it possible for a Representative in Florida to read and translate it. "That's the point," Sally told us. "You are doing it the same way a rep in Illinois or Alaska does it. We're one big monopoly."

The logic of training is to transform the trainees from humans into machines. The basic method is to handle any customer request by extracting "bits" of infor-mation: by translating the human problem he might have into bureaucratic language so that it can be processed by the right department. For instance, if a customer calls and says: "My wife is dying and she's coming home from the hospital today and I'd like to have a phone installed in her bedroom right away," you *say*, "Oh, I'm very sorry to hear that sir, I'm sure I can help you, would you be interested in our Princess model? It has a dial that lights up at night," meanwhile *writing* on your ever-present CF-1: "Csr wnts Prn inst bdrm immed," issuing the order, and placing it in the right-hand side of your work-file where it gets picked up every fifteen min-utes by a little clerk.

The knowledge that one is under constant observation (of which more later) I think helps to ensure that contacts are handled in this uniform and wooden man-ner. If you varied it, and said something spontaneous, you might well be overheard; moreover, it is probably not possible to be especially human when you are concen-trating so hard on extracting the bits, and when you have to deal with so many bits in one day. . . .

III

Daily life on the job at the New York Telephone Company consists largely of pressure. To a casual observer it might appear that much of the activity on the floor is random, but in fact it is not. The women moving from desk to desk are on missions of retrieving and refiling customers' records: the tête-à-têtes that look sociable are anxious conferences with a Supervisor in which a Representative is Thinking and Planning What to Do Next. Of course the more experienced women know how to use the empty moments that do occur for social purposes. But the basic working unit is one girl-one telephone, and the basic requirement of the job is to answer it, perhaps more than fifty times a day.

For every contact with a customer, the amount of paperwork is huge: a single contact can require the completion of three, four, or even five separate forms. No problems can be dispensed with handily. Even if, for example, you merely transfer a customer to Traffic or Repair you must still fill out and file as CF-1. At the end of the day you must tally up and categorize all the services you have performed on a little slip of paper and hand it in to the Supervisor, who completes a tally for the unit: it is part of the process of "taking credit" for services rendered by one unit vis-à-vis the others.

A Representative's time is divided into "open" and "closed" portions, according to a recent scientific innovation called FADS (for Force Administration Data System), of which the company is particularly proud; the innovation consists in establishing how many Representatives have to be available at any one moment to handle the volume of business anticipated for that month, that day, and that hour. Under this arrangement the contact with the customer and the processing of his request are carried out simultaneously: that is, the Representative does the paperwork needed to take care of a request while she is still on the line. For more complex cases, however, this is not possible and the processing is left for "closed" time: a time when no further calls are coming in.

This arrangement tends to create a constant low-level panic. There is a kind of act which it is natural to carry to its logical conclusion: brushing one's teeth, washing a dish, or filling out a form are things one does not leave half done. But the company's system stifles this natural urge to completion. Instead, during "open" time, the phone keeps ringing and the work piles up. You look at the schedule and know that you have only one hour of "closed" time to complete the work, and twenty minutes of that hour is a break.

The situation produces desperation: How am I to get it done? How can I call back all those customers, finish all that mail, write all those complicated orders, within forty minutes? Occasionally, during my brief time at the job, I would accidentally press the wrong button on my phone and it would become "open" again. Once, when I was feeling particularly desperate about time, I did that twice in a row and both times the callers were ordering new telephone service—a process which takes between eight and ten minutes to complete.

My feeling that time was slipping away, that I would never be able to "complete my commitment" on time was intense and hateful. Of course it was worse for me than for the experienced women—but not much worse. Another situation in which the pressure of time is universally felt is in the minutes before lunch and before five o'clock. At those times, if your phone is open, you sit hoping that a complex call will not arrive. A "new line" order at five minutes to five is a source of both resentment and frustration.

Given the pressure, it becomes natural to welcome the boring and routine—the simple suspensions or disconnections of service—and dread the unusual or complex. The women deal with the pressure by quietly getting rid of as many calls as they can, transferring them to another department although the proper jurisdiction may be a borderline matter. This transferring, the lightening of the load, is the bureaucratic equivalent of the "soldiering" that Taylor and the early scientific managers were striving to defeat. It is a subtle kind of slowdown, never discussed, but quickly transmitted to the new Representative as legitimate. Unfortunately, it does not slow things down very much.

As Daniel Bell points out in his extraordinary essay, "Work and Its Discontents," the rhythm of the job controls the time spent off the job as well: the breaks, the lunches, the holidays; even the weekends are scarcely long enough to reestablish a more congenial or natural path. The work rhythm controls human relationships and attitudes as well. For instance: there was a Puerto Rican worker in the Schrafft's downstairs whose job was to sell coffee-to-go to the customers: he spent his day doing nothing but filling paper cups with coffee, fitting on the lids, and writing out the checks. He was very surly and very slow and it looked to me as if the thoughts swirling in his head were those of an incipient murderer, not an incipient revolutionary. His slowness was very inconvenient to the thousands of workers in the building who had to get their coffee, take it upstairs, and drink it according to a precise timetable. We never had more than fifteen minutes to get there and back, and buying coffee generally took longer. The women resented him and called him "Speedy Gonzales," in tones of snobbery and hate. I know he hated us.

IV

The women of the phone company are middle class or lower middle class, come from a variety of ethnic backgrounds (Polish, Jewish, Italian, Irish, black, Puerto Rican), mainly high-school graduates or with a limited college education. They live just about everywhere except in Manhattan: the Bronx, Brooklyn, Staten Island, or Queens. Their leisure time is filled, first of all, with the discussion of objects. Talk of shopping is endless, as is the pursuit of it in lunch hours, after work, and on days off. The women have a fixation on brand names, and describe every object that way: it is always a London Fog, a Buxton, a White Stag. This fixation does not preclude bargain-hunting: but the purpose of hunting a bargain is to get the brand name at a lower price. Packaging is also important: the women will describe not only the thing but also the box or wrapper it comes in. They are especially fascinated by wigs. Most women have several wigs and are in some cases unrecognizable from day to day, creating the effect of a continually changing work force. The essence of wiggery is escapism: the kaleidoscopic transformation of oneself while everything else remains the same. Anyone who has ever worn a wig knows the embarrassing truth: it *is* transforming.

Consumerism is one of the major reasons why these women work. Their salaries are low in relation to the costs of necessities in American life, ranging from $95.00 to $132.50 *before* taxes: barely enough, if one is self-supporting, to pay for essentials. In fact, however, many of the women are not self-supporting, but live with their families or with husbands who also work, sometimes at more than one job.

Many of the women work overtime more than five hours a week (only for more than five extra hours do they get paid time and a half) and it seems from their visible spending that it is simply to pay for their clothes, which are expensive, their wigs, their color TV's, their dishes, silver, and so forth.

What the pressures of food, shelter, education, or medical costs contribute to their need to work I cannot tell, but it seems to me the women are largely trapped by their love of objects. What they think they need in order to survive and what they endure in order to attain it is astonishing. Why this is so is another matter. I think that the household appliances play a real role in the women's family lives: helping them to run their homes smoothly and in keeping with a (to them) necessary image of efficiency and elegance. As for the clothes and the wigs, I think they are a kind of tax, a tribute exacted by the social pressures of the work-place. For the preservation of their own egos against each other and against the system, they had to feel confident of their appearance on each and every day. Outside work they needed it too: to keep up, to keep their men, not to fall behind.

The atmosphere of passionate consuming was immeasurably heightened by Christmas, which also had the dismal effect of increasing the amount of stealing from the locker room. For a period of about three weeks nothing was safe: hats, boots, gloves. The women told me that the same thing happens every year: an overwhelming craving, a need for material goods that has to find an outlet, even in thievery from one another.

The women define themselves by their consumerism far more than by their work, as if they were compensating for their exploitation as workers by a desperate attempt to express their individuality as consumers. Much of the consuming pressure is generated by the women themselves: not only in shopping but in constant raffles, contests, and so forth in which the prize is always a commodity—usually liquor. The women are asked to participate in these raffles at least two or three times a week.

But the atmosphere is also deliberately fostered by the company itself. The company gave every woman a Christmas present: a little wooden doll, about four inches tall, with the sick-humor look that was popular a few years ago and still appears on greeting cards. On the outside the doll says "Joy is . . . " and when you press down the springs a little stick pops up that says "Extensions in Color" (referring to the telephone extensions we were trying to sell). Under that label is another sticker, the original one, which says "Knowing I wuv you." The doll is typical of the presents the company distributes periodically: a plastic shopping bag inscribed with the motto "Colorful Extensions Lighten the Load"; a keychain with a plastic Princess telephone saying "It's Little, It's Lovely, It Lights"; plastic rain bonnets with the telephone company emblem, and so forth.

There were also free chocolates at Thanksgiving and, when the vending machine companies were on strike, free coffee for a while in the cafeteria. The women are disgusted by the company's gift-giving policies. Last year, I was told, the Christmas present was a little gold-plated basket filled with velour fruit and adorned with a flag containing a company motto of the "Extensions in Color" type. They think it is a cheap trick—better not done at all—and cite instances of other companies which give money bonuses at Christmas.

It is obvious that the gifts are all programmed, down to the last cherry-filled chocolate, in some manual of Personnel Administration that is the source of all wisdom and policy; it is clear from their frequency that a whole agency of the company is devoted to devising these gimmicks and passing them out. In fact, apart from a standard assortment of insurance and pension plans, the only company policy I could discover which offers genuine advantage to the employees and which is not an attempt at manipulation is a tuition support program in which the company pays $1,000 out of $1,400 of the costs of continuing education.

Going still further, the company, for example, sponsors a recruiting game among employees, a campaign entitled "People Make the Difference." Employees who recruit other employees are rewarded with points: 200 for a recommendation, an additional thousand if the candidate is hired. Employees are stimulated to participate by the circulation of an S&H-type catalogue, a kind of encyclopedia of the post-scarcity society. There you can see pictured a GE Portable Color Television with a walnut-grained polystyrene cabinet (46,000 points), a Silver-Plated Hors d'Oeuvres Dish by Wallace (3,900 points), and a staggering assortment of mass-produced candelabra, linens, china, fountain pens, watches, clothing, luggage, and—for the hardy—pup tents, power tools, air mattresses.

Similarly, though perhaps less crudely, the company has institutionalized its practice of rewarding employees for longevity. After every two years with the company, the women receive a small gold charm, the men a "tie-tac." These grow larger with the years and after a certain period jewels begin to be added: rubies, emeralds, sapphires, and eventually diamonds and bigger diamonds. The tie-tac evolves over the years into a tie-clasp. After twenty-five years you may have either a ceremonial luncheon or an inscribed watch: the watches are pre-fixed, pre-selected, and pictured in a catalogue.

The company has "scientifically structured" its rewards just as it has scientifically "structured" its work. But the real point is that the system gets the women as consumers in two ways. If consumption were less central to them, they would be less likely to be there in the first place. Then, the company attempts to ensnare them still further in the mesh by offering as incentives goods and images of goods which are only further way stations of the same endless quest. . . .

VII

Perhaps the best way to think about the women of the telephone company is to ask the question: what reinforces company-minded behavior and what works against it? It is a difficult question. The reinforcement comes not from the work but from the externals of the job: the warmth of friendships, the mutual support, the opportunities for sharing and for gossip, the general atmosphere of company benevolence and paternalism; not to mention the need for money and the very human desire to do a good job.

I never heard any of the women mouth the company rhetoric about "service to the customer" but it was obvious to me that a well-handled contact could be satisfying in some way. You are the only person who has access to what the customer needs—namely, telephones—and if you can provide him with what he wants, on time and efficiently, you might reasonably feel satisfied about it. The mutual support—the sharing of closed time, helping one another out on commitments—is also very real. The continual raffles, sales contests, gimmicks, and parties are part of it, too. They simply make you feel part of a natural stream.

Working in that job one does not see oneself as a victim of "Capitalism." One is simply part of a busy little world which has its own pleasures and satisfactions as well as its own frustrations but, most important, it is a world, with a shape and an integrity all its own. The pattern of co-optation, in other words, rests on details: hundreds of trivial, but human, details.

What is on the other side? Everyone's consciousness of the iron fist, though what they usually see is the velvet glove; the deadening nature of the work; the low pay; what is going on in the outside world (to the extent that they are aware of it); the malfunctioning of the company; the pressure of supervision and observation. There was a sign that sat on the desk of one of the women while I was there, a Coney Island joke-machine sign: "Due to Lack of Interest, Tomorrow Will be Postponed." For a time I took it as an emblem and believed that was how the woman really felt. But now I am not sure.

I think that for these women to move they would have to have a sense of the possibility of change—not even to mention the desirability of change—which I am certain they do not feel. They are more satisfied with their lives than not, and to the extent that they are not, they cannot see even the dimmest possibility of remedial action through collective political effort. The reason they do not have "class-consciousness"—the magic ingredient—is that in fact they are middle class. If they feel oppressed by their situation, and I think many of them do, they certainly see it only as an individual problem, not as something which it is their human right to avoid or overcome.

How one would begin to change that, to free them to live more human lives, is very hard to know. Clearly it would require a total transformation of the way they think about the world and about themselves. What is impossible to know is whether the seeds of that transformation lie close beneath the surface and are accessible, or whether they are impossibly buried beyond rescue short of general social convulsion. It is hard to believe that the women are as untouched as they seem by the social pressures which seem so tangible to radicals. Yet I saw little evidence that would make any other conclusion possible.

I have a strong feeling of bad faith to have written this at all. I know the women will not recognize themselves in my account, but will nonetheless be hurt by it. They were, after all, warm and friendly: sympathetic about my troubles, my frustrations; helpful in the work; cheerful in a businesslike way. Betty, at least, was a friend. It is almost as if a breach of the paternalism of the company is involved. I fear a phone call asking "Was that a nice thing to do?" and I would say, perhaps not, perhaps the intellectual and political values of my life by which I was judging yours make equally little sense. Perhaps the skills which give me leverage to do it allow me only to express alienation and not to overcome it; perhaps I should merely be thankful that I was raised as an alpha and not a beta. Sometimes I am not sure. But I know that however it will seem to them, this piece is meant to be for the women of the telephone company, and that it is written for them with both love and hope.

PAULA GUNN ALLEN

(B. 1939)

*Born in Cubero, New Mexico, Paula Gunn Allen was brought up in unusu-
ally heterogeneous circumstances. Her mother, of Laguna Pueblo, Sioux,
and Scottish descent, told her five children stories drawn from Native American traditions. Her father, Lebanese American, added Arabic to the Spanish, Laguna, English, and German spoken in and around the household,
which was located next to the Laguna Pueblo itself. For eleven years, Allen
attended a convent school, yet in the long run she has returned, as she put
it, to her "mother's side, to the sacred hoop" of Indian female tradition. Yet,
as she told Joseph Bruchac in a 1987 interview, "My poetry has a haunted
sense to it and it has a sorrow and a grievingness that comes directly from
being split, not in two but in twenty, and never being able to reconcile all
the places that I am." It may well be the very complexity of her identity, and
the variety of her accomplishments, that have established her authority in
Native American, feminist, lesbian, and academic circles.*

*Allen earned her B.A. and M.F.A. degrees at the University of Oregon
and her Ph.D. from the University of New Mexico. She has taught at a number of institutions, including UNM, San Francisco State, and UC/Berkeley; she
is now professor of English at UCLA. She has edited a number of collections,
including* Studies in American Indian Literature *(1982),* Spider Woman's
Granddaughters: Traditional Tales and Contemporary Writing by Native
American Women *(1989), and* Studies in American Indian Literature: Critical Essays and Course Designs *(1983), a volume important to the development of teaching of Native American texts. Her own prose work includes* The
Sacred Hoop: Recovering the Feminine in American Indian Traditions
(1986); a novel, The Woman Who Owned the Shadows *(1983); and* Grand-
mothers of the Light: A Medicine Woman's Sourcebook *(1991) and* The
Voice of the Turtle *(1994). Allen has published eight books of poetry, including a collection,* Life Is a Fatal Disease: Collected Poems 1962–1995 *(1997).
Much of her writing has been devoted to reinvesting women's everyday lives
with the importance—and the mystery—she discovers in the rituals of the
Native American traditions that she has studied, taught, and transformed
for newer generations.*

WOMANWORK

some make potteries
some weave and spin
remember
the Woman/celebrate
webs and making
out of own flesh
earth
bowl and urn
to hold water

and ground corn
balanced on heads
and springs lifted
and rivers in our eyes
brown hands shaping
earth into earth
food for bodies
water for fields
they use
old pots
broken
fragments
castaway
bits
to make new
mixed with clay
it makes strong
bowls, jars
new
she
brought
light
we remember this
as we make
the water bowl
broken
marks the grandmother's grave
so she will shape water
for bowls
for food growing
for bodies
eating
at drink
thank her

SUSAN EISENBERG

(B. 1950)

Susan Eisenberg writes about rats electrocuted in switch boxes, elderly electrician partners on the job, blueprints, ceilings, and pliers. She is probably unique, not so much as a woman working in construction, nor even as a master electrician, but as a person who writes poetry about the world defined by the title of her second volume, Pioneering: Poems from the Construction Site *(1997). The title of her first volume provides some insight into her outlook and the tone of her verse,* It's a Good Thing I'm Not Macho *(1984). Her poems offer irony and self-awareness to go with the precision one needs to make firm connections that will withstand the changing weather.*

Eisenberg has also written a prose volume, We'll Call You If We Need You: Experiences of Women Working Construction *(1997), drawing on some twenty years of construction experience. She has also published essays and poetry in magazines like* Radical America, The Nation *and* The Utne Reader, *and created an interactive multimedia installation.*

HANGING IN, SOLO
(SO WHAT'S IT LIKE TO BE THE ONLY FEMALE ON THE JOB?)

On the sunshine rainbow days
womanhood
clothes me in a fuchsia velour jumpsuit
and crowns me with a diamond hardhat.
I flare my peacock feathers
and fly through the day's work.
    Trombones sizzle
as my drill glides through cement walls
    through steel beams.
Bundles of pipe rise through the air
at the tilt
    of my thumb.
Everything I do
    is perfect.

    The female of the species
    advances 10 spaces and
    takes an extra turn.

On the mudcold-gray-no-
sun-in-a-week days womanhood
weighs me down in colorless arctic fatigues;
hands me an empty survival kit;
and binds my head in an iron hardhat
    three sizes too small.
I burrow myself mole-like into my work, but
my tampax leaks;
my diamond-tip bit burns out after one hole;
my offsets are backwards;
all of my measurements are wrong.

At each mistake, a shrill siren
alerts all tradesmen on the job
    to come laugh at me.
Everything I do
    must be redone.

    The female of the species
    loses her next turn
    and picks a penalty card.

On most days, those
partly sunny days that bridge the
rainbow sunshine days and the mudcold-
gray days
    womanhood outfits me in a
flannel shirt and jeans
and hands me a hardhat just like
everyone else's. I go about my work like
a giraffe foraging the high branches:
stretching myself comfortably.
As I hang lighting fixtures and make splices,
I sing to myself
    and tell myself stories.
Everything I do
    is competent enough.

    The female of the species
    advances 1 space
    and awaits her next turn.

FRANCISCO JIMÉNEZ
(B. 1943)

Francisco Jiménez was born in San Pedro Tlaquepaque, Jalisco, México, the son of illiterate farm workers. The family immigrated to the United States shortly after World War II, working in the fields of California's Central Valley under conditions of brutal poverty. At six, young Francisco had to join other family members in the fields; school was a sometimes thing, at best, since the family would invariably have to move on from Bakersfield to Santa Maria to Fresno with the crops. Grasping the principle of words, as he relates in a story for children called "The Butterfly," became for him a

*key to opening a world beyond itinerant privation. His story "The Circuit"
captures this circle of poverty and hope, of desire and defeat; particularly
troubling is the moment in which the younger Francisco is able to go to
school while his older brother must return to work. While he was often
taunted and mocked and was frequently far behind his grade level, Jiménez
loved school: at the least it had floors, indoor plumbing, and electricity. At
fifteen, in his junior high school class, Jiménez was arrested by INS agents
as an illegal alien, and the family was sent to Mexico, from which they were
able to return with fresh visas. When his brother obtained a stable job in
Santa Maria, Jiménez could attend high school steadily; there he thrived,
becoming president of the student body and ultimately winning a scholarship to Santa Clara University. He later earned his doctorate at Columbia.*

*Since 1973, Jiménez has taught Spanish, Chicano/a and Latin Ameri-
can literatures at Santa Clara, directed the University's Institute of Poverty
and Conscience, and served as a senior administrator. With Gary Keller, he
edited a two-volume collection,* Hispanics in the United States: An Anthology of Creative Literature *(1980, 1982), a book on the* Identification and
Analysis of Chicano Literature *(1978), as well as a volume entitled* Poverty
and Social Justice: Critical Perspectives *(1987). He has also written and
edited a number of texts in Spanish, including* Mosaico de la vida: Prosa chicana, cubana y puertorriqueña *(1981).*

"The Circuit" won the annual award of the Arizona Quarterly, *in which
it was originally published. It is the title story of Jiménez's recent collection*
The Circuit: Stories from the Life of a Migrant Child *(1997).*

THE CIRCUIT

It was that time of year again. Ito, the strawberry sharecropper, did not smile. It was
natural. The peak of the strawberry season was over and the last few days the workers, most of them braceros, were not picking as many boxes as they had during the
months of June and July.

As the last days of August disappeared, so did the number of braceros. Sunday,
only one—the best picker—came to work. I liked him. Sometimes we talked during
our half-hour lunch break. That is how I found out he was from Jalisco, the same
state in Mexico my family was from. That Sunday was the last time I saw him.

When the sun had tired and sunk behind the mountains, Ito signaled us that it
was time to go home. "Ya esora," he yelled in his broken Spanish. Those were the
words I waited for twelve hours a day, every day, seven days a week, week after
week. And the thought of not hearing them again saddened me.

As we drove home Papá did not say a word. With both hands on the wheel, he
stared at the dirt road. My older brother, Roberto, was also silent. He leaned his
head back and closed his eyes. Once in a while he cleared from his throat the dust
that blew in from outside.

Yes, it was that time of year. When I opened the front door to the shack, I
stopped. Everything we owned was neatly packed in cardboard boxes. Suddenly I
felt even more the weight of hours, days, weeks, and months of work. I sat down on
a box. The thought of having to move to Fresno and knowing what was in store for
me there brought tears to my eyes.

That night I could not sleep. I lay in bed thinking about how much I hated this move.

A little before five o'clock in the morning, Papá woke everyone up. A few minutes later, the yelling and screaming of my little brothers and sisters, for whom the move was a great adventure, broke the silence of dawn. Shortly, the barking of the dogs accompanied them.

While we packed the breakfast dishes, Papá went outside to start the "Carcanchita." That was the name Papá gave his old '38 black Plymouth. He bought it in a used-car lot in Santa Rosa in the winter of 1949. Papá was very proud of his little jalopy. He had a right to be proud of it. He spent a lot of time looking at other cars before buying this one. When he finally chose the "Carcanchita," he checked it thoroughly before driving it out of the car lot. He examined every inch of the car. He listened to the motor, tilting his head from side to side like a parrot, trying to detect any noises that spelled car trouble. After being satisfied with the looks and sounds of the car, Papá then insisted on knowing who the original owner was. He never did find out from the car salesman, but he bought the car anyway. Papá figured the original owner must have been an important man because behind the rear seat of the car he found a blue necktie.

Papá parked the car out in front and left the motor running. "Listo," he yelled. Without saying a word, Roberto and I began to carry the boxes out to the car. Roberto carried the two big boxes and I carried the two smaller ones. Papá then threw the mattress on top of the car roof and tied it with ropes to the front and rear bumpers.

Everything was packed except Mamá's pot. It was an old large galvanized pot she had picked up at an army surplus store in Santa María the year I was born. The pot had many dents and nicks, and the more dents and nicks it acquired the more Mamá liked it. "Mi olla," she used to say proudly.

I held the front door open as Mamá carefully carried out her pot by both handles, making sure not to spill the cooked beans. When she got to the car, Papá reached out to help her with it. Roberto opened the rear car door and Papá gently placed it on the floor behind the front seat. All of us then climbed in. Papá sighed, wiped the sweat off his forehead with his sleeve, and said wearily: "Es todo."

As we drove away, I felt a lump in my throat. I turned around and looked at our little shack for the last time.

At sunset we drove into a labor camp near Fresno. Since Papá did not speak English, Mamá asked the camp foreman if he needed any more workers. "We don't need no more," said the foreman, scratching his head. "Check with Sullivan down the road. Can't miss him. He lives in a big white house with a fence around it."

When we got there, Mamá walked up to the house. She went through a white gate, past a row of rose bushes, up the stairs to the front door. She rang the doorbell. The porch light went on and a tall husky man came out. They exchanged a few words. After the man went in, Mamá clasped her hands and hurried back to the car. "We have work! Mr. Sullivan said we can stay there the whole season," she said, gasping and pointing to an old garage near the stables.

The garage was worn out by the years. It had no windows. The walls, eaten by termites, strained to support the roof full of holes. The dirt floor, populated by earthworms, looked like a gray road map.

That night, by the light of a kerosene lamp, we unpacked and cleaned our new home. Roberto swept away the loose dirt, leaving the hard ground. Papá plugged the holes in the walls with old newspapers and tin can tops. Mamá fed my little brothers and sisters. Papá and Roberto then brought in the mattress and placed it on the far corner of the garage. "Mamá, you and the little ones sleep on the mattress. Roberto, Panchito, and I will sleep outside under the trees," Papá said.

Early next morning Mr. Sullivan showed us where his crop was, and after breakfast, Papá, Roberto, and I headed for the vineyard to pick.

Around nine o'clock the temperature had risen to almost one hundred degrees. I was completely soaked in sweat and my mouth felt as if I had been chewing on a handkerchief. I walked over to the end of the row, picked up the jug of water we had brought, and began drinking. "Don't drink too much; you'll get sick," Roberto shouted. No sooner had he said that than I felt sick to my stomach. I dropped to my knees and let the jug roll off my hands. I remained motionless with my eyes glued on the hot sandy ground. All I could hear was the drone of insects. Slowly I began to recover. I poured water over my face and neck and watched the dirty water run down my arms to the ground.

I still felt a little dizzy when we took a break to eat lunch. It was past two o'clock and we sat underneath a large walnut tree that was on the side of the road. While we ate, Papá jotted down the number of boxes we had picked. Roberto drew designs on the ground with a stick. Suddenly I noticed Papá's face turn pale as he looked down the road. "Here comes the school bus," he whispered loudly in alarm. Instinctively, Roberto and I ran and hid in the vineyards. We did not want to get in trouble for not going to school. The neatly dressed boys about my age got off. They carried books under their arms. After they crossed the street, the bus drove away. Roberto and I came out from hiding and joined Papá. "Tienen que tener cuidado," he warned us.

After lunch we went back to work. The sun kept beating down. The buzzing insects, the wet sweat, and the hot dry dust made the afternoon seem to last forever. Finally the mountains around the valley reached out and swallowed the sun. Within an hour it was too dark to continue picking. The vines blanketed the grapes, making it difficult to see the bunches. "Vámonos," said Papá, signaling to us that it was time to quit work. Papá then took out a pencil and began to figure out how much we had earned our first day. He wrote down numbers, crossed some out, wrote down some more. "Quince," he murmured.

When we arrived home, we took a cold shower underneath a waterhose. We then sat down to eat dinner around some wooden crates that served as a table. Mamá had cooked a special meal for us. We had rice and tortillas with "carne con chile," my favorite dish.

The next morning I could hardly move. My body ached all over. I felt little control over my arms and legs. This feeling went on every morning for days until my muscles finally got used to the work.

It was Monday, the first week of November. The grape season was over and I could now go to school. I woke up early that morning and lay in bed, looking at the stars and savoring the thought of not going to work and of starting sixth grade for the first time that year. Since I could not sleep, I decided to get up and join Papá and Roberto for breakfast. I sat at the table across from Roberto, but I kept my head down, I did not want to look up and face him. I knew he was sad. He was not going to school today. He was not going tomorrow, or next week, or next month. He would not go until the cotton season was over, and that was sometime in February. I rubbed my hands together and watched the dry, acid stained skin fall to the floor in little rolls.

When Papá and Roberto left for work, I felt relief. I walked to the top of a small grade next to the shack and watched the "Carcanchita" disappear in the distance in a cloud of dust.

Two hours later, around eight o'clock, I stood by the side of the road waiting for school bus number twenty. When it arrived I climbed in. Everyone was busy either talking or yelling. I sat in an empty seat in the back.

When the bus stopped in front of the school, I felt very nervous. I looked out the bus window and saw boys and girls carrying books under their arms. I put my hands in my pant pockets and walked to the principal's office. When I entered I heard a woman's voice say: "May I help you?" I was startled. I had not heard English for months. For a few seconds I remained speechless. I looked at the lady who waited for an answer. My first instinct was to answer her in Spanish, but I held back. Finally, after struggling for English words, I managed to tell her that I wanted to enroll in the sixth grade. After answering many questions, I was led to the classroom.

Mr. Lema, the sixth-grade teacher, greeted me and assigned me a desk. He then introduced me to the class. I was so nervous and scared at that moment when everyone's eyes were on me that I wished I were with Papá and Roberto picking cotton. After taking roll, Mr. Lema gave the class the assignment for the first hour. "The first thing we have to do this morning is finish reading the story we begin yesterday," he said enthusiastically. He walked up to me, handed me an English book, and asked me to read. "We are on page 125," he said politely. When I heard this, I felt my blood pressure rush to my head; I felt dizzy. "Would you like to read?" he asked hesitantly. I opened the book to page 125. My mouth was dry. My eyes began to water. I could not begin. "You can read later," Mr. Lema said understandingly.

For the rest of the reading period I kept getting angrier and angrier with myself. I should have read, I thought to myself.

During recess I went into the restroom and opened my English book to page 125. I began to read in a low voice, pretending I was in class. There were many words I did not know. I closed the book and headed back to the classroom.

Mr. Lema was sitting at his desk correcting papers. When I entered he looked up at me and smiled. I felt better. I walked up to him and asked if he could help me with the new words. "Gladly," he said.

The rest of the month I spent my lunch hours working on English with Mr. Lema, my best friend at school.

One Friday during lunch hour Mr. Lema asked me to take a walk with him to the music room. "Do you like music?" he asked me as we entered the building.

"Yes, I like corridos," I answered. He then picked up a trumpet, blew on it and handed it to me. The sound gave me goose bumps. I knew that sound. I had heard it in many corridos. "How would you like to learn how to play it?" he asked. He must have read my face because before I could answer, he added: "I'll teach you how to play it during our lunch hours."

That day I could hardly wait to get home to tell Papá and Mamá the great news. As I got off the bus, my little brothers and sisters ran up to meet me. They were yelling and screaming. I thought they were happy to see me, but when I opened the door to our shack, I saw that everything we owned was neatly packed in cardboard boxes.

JIMMY SANTIAGO BACA

(B. 1952)

Jimmy Santiago Baca's resume includes a variety of prizes earned (Push-cart Prize, Vogelstein Award, American Book Award, among others), fel-lowships and endowed chairs held, books published, poetry competitions won, films written and produced. But his writing tells a different kind of story, a story of growing up in a divided and violent family in rural New Mexico, of years spent in an orphanage and on the streets of Albuquerque's barrio, of being sent up to the Florence, Arizona, penitentiary for six years on a dubious drug charge, of beginning to discover his voice and his self in the "pit of humiliation" into which he was shoved in jail. In prison he began to read poetry, first in English and then, as he taught himself the language, in Spanish. He began to write and eventually sent three of his poems to Denise Levertov, the poetry editor of the magazine Mother Jones. *She helped him find a publisher for his first collection of poems,* Immigrants in Our Own Land, *in 1979, the year of his release from prison.*

Baca's earlier poems focus on his prison experience, his struggle to sus-tain a sense of his own value in the face of his jailers' efforts to reduce him to a "nonentity." Subsequently, he has written more broadly about the expe-riences of brown and black people in late twentieth-century America, about his father and others whose oppressive conditions of life kept them separate from their children, about his own recent life at Black Mesa, New Mexico, parenting two sons and running a small farm. His own more recent vol-umes include Martín and Meditations on the South Valley *(1987), a verse autobiography, and* Black Mesa Poems *(1989). He has also written a play,* Los tres hijos de Julia, *produced in 1991, as well as scripts for films (*Bound by Honor*) and video productions, in which he has acted. Baca is very pop-ular on the poetry slam circuit, on which he was reigning World Heavy-weight Champion Poet for a number of years.*

SO MEXICANS ARE TAKING JOBS
FROM AMERICANS

0 Yes? Do they come on horses
with rifles, and say,
                      Ese gringo, gimmee your job?
And do you, gringo, take off your ring,
drop your wallet into a blanket
spread over the ground, and walk away?

I hear Mexicans are taking your jobs away.
Do they sneak into town at night,
and as you're walking home with a whore,
do they mug you, a knife at your throat,
saying, I want your job?

Even on TV, an asthmatic leader
crawls turtle heavy, leaning on an assistant,
and from a nest of wrinkles on his face,
a tongue paddles through flashing waves
of lightbulbs, of cameramen, rasping
"They're taking our jobs away."

Well, I've gone about trying to find them,
asking just where the hell are these fighters.
The rifles I hear sound in the night
are white farmers shooting blacks and browns
whose ribs I see jutting out
and starving children,
I see the poor marching for a little work,
I see small white farmers selling out
to clean-suited farmers living in New York,
who've never been on a farm,
don't know the look of a hoof or the smell
of a woman's body bending all day long in fields.

I see this, and I hear only a few people
got all the money in this world, the rest
count their pennies to buy bread and butter.

Below that cool green sea of money,
millions and millions of people fight to live,
search for pearls in the darkest depths
of their dreams, hold their breath for years
trying to cross poverty to just having something.

The children are dead already. We are killing them,
that is what America should be saying;
on TV, in the streets, in offices, should be saying,
    "We aren't giving the children a chance to live."

    Mexicans are taking our jobs, they say instead.
    What they really say is, let them die,
    and the children too.

GARY SOTO

(B. 1952)

Like many other Chicano working-class kids, Gary Soto initially intended to
work his way up the social ladder and help his people by becoming a con-

cerned professional, in his case an urban planner. Brought up in Fresno, California, in a largely working-class Mexican community, Soto attended schools there and then enrolled at Fresno State University. He became interested in literature while at college, particularly after studying with Philip Levine, and he published his first poem in 1973 while he was still an undergraduate. Subsequently Soto earned a master of fine arts degree from UC/Irvine in 1976. His first collection of poetry, The Elements of San Joaquin, appeared the following year and was met with wide praise. For a period of time, Soto lived in Mexico; he then took a teaching position at UC/Berkeley, which he retained for a number of years before deciding that "teaching is someone else's business." He cut loose to write, to read in school auditoriums, Chicano centers, and at parades in his honor, and "to make readers from nonreaders."

Since 1977, Soto has published eight books of poetry, including Black Hair (1985), Neighborhood Odes (1992), Canto Familiar/Familiar Song (1994), and New and Selected Poems, a 1995 finalist for both the Los Angeles Times Book Award and the National Book Award. As these titles suggest, much of his poetry has focused on his own life and that of his Mexican-American community. He writes about family relationships, the streets and houses of the barrio, dances and jobs, and the immigration and farm labor of people like his grandparents in direct, accessible, unsentimental language that appeals to a wide readership. He has also published three volumes of autobiographical sketches and essays, including Living up the Street (1985), a book-length memoir, an opera, Nerd-Landia, a 16mm film, The Bike, as well as a number of anthologies and books for children and young adults.

FIELD POEM

When the foreman whistled
My brother and I
Shouldered our hoes,
Leaving the field.
We returned to the bus
Speaking
In broken English, in broken Spanish
The restaurant food,
The tickets to a dance
We wouldn't buy with our pay.

From the smashed bus window,
I saw the leaves of cotton plants
Like small hands
Waving good-bye.

GISH JEN

(B. 1955)

Much of Gish Jen's writing focuses on the unstable, often hilarious incongruity of what we call "ethnicity" in late twentieth-century America. In her novel Mona in the Promised Land *(1996), for example, she writes about the misadventures of a daughter of highly educated Chinese immigrants who, like herself, grows up a rare Asian American in Scarsdale, a well-to-do, predominantly Jewish suburb of New York. In the novel, Mona's difference is the source both of comedy and a certain confused discomfort for herself and her schoolmates; she ultimately becomes Jewish, unlike her creator. Jen undertook her own form of "conversion," however, when she renamed herself from "Lillian" to "Gish," an event that marked her own perception that she was on track to become a writer.*

After her schooling in Scarsdale, Jen earned her B.A. at Harvard and then attended the Stanford Business School. She taught English to mining engineers in China for a year, then enrolled at the Iowa Writer's Workshop, from which she earned a master of fine arts degree in 1983. She began to publish stories in 1985; her first novel, Typical American, *came out in 1991, and her short story collection,* Who's Irish, *in 1999.*

She often attributes her ironic take on American life to her father. Trained as an engineer, he remained in the United States after the communist revolution in 1949, at a time when few white Americans thought of Chinese as professionals, much less active engineers. Her father's view of his own situation seems to have been marked by irony rather than anger, which is largely Jen's own response to ethnic difference and change. For instance, she notes the movement between her childhood and that of her own son by commenting about the celebration of Chinese New Year that it's no longer "this funny thing that his family does that nobody understands. It's something that's done inside his school auditorium." Difference, then, can be for her a source not only of tension but of amusement—or, perhaps, both together.

HIS OWN SOCIETY

When my father took over the pancake house, it was to send my little sister Mona and me to college. We were only in junior high at the time, but my father believed in getting a jump on things. "Those Americans always saying it," he told us. "Smart guys thinking in advance." My mother elaborated, explaining that businesses took bringing up, like children. They could take years to get going, she said, years.

In this case, though, we got rich right away. At two months we were breaking even, and at four, those same hotcakes that could barely withstand the weight of butter and syrup were supporting our family with ease. My mother bought a station wagon with air conditioning, my father an oversized, red vinyl recliner for the back room; and as time went on and the business continued to thrive, my father started to talk about his grandfather and the village he had reigned over in China—things my father had never talked about when he worked for other people. He told us about the bags of rice his family would give out to the poor at New Year's, and about the people who came to beg, on their hands and knees, for his grandfather to intercede for the more wayward of their relatives. "Like that Godfather in the movie," he would tell us as, his feet up, he distributed paychecks. Sometimes an employee would get two green envelopes instead of one, which meant that Jimmy needed a tooth pulled, say, or that Tiffany's husband was in the clinker again.

"It's nothing, nothing," he would insist, sinking back into his chair. "Who else is going to take care of you people?"

My mother would mostly just sigh about it. "Your father thinks this is China," she would say, and then she would go back to her mending. Once in a while, though, when my father had given away a particularly large sum, she would exclaim, outraged, "But this here is the U-S-of-A!"—this apparently having been what she used to tell immigrant stock boys when they came in late.

She didn't work at the supermarket anymore; but she had made it to the rank of manager before she left, and this had given her not only new words and phrases, but new ideas about herself, and about America, and about what was what in general. She had opinions, now, on how downtown should be zoned; she could pump her own gas and check her own oil; and for all she used to chide Mona and me for being "copycats," she herself was now interested in espadrilles, and wallpaper, and most recently, the town country club.

"So join already," said Mona, flicking a fly off her knee.

My mother enumerated the problems as she sliced up a quarter round of watermelon: There was the cost. There was the waiting list. There was the fact that no one in our family played either tennis or golf.

"So what?" said Mona.

"It would be waste," said my mother.

"Me and Callie can swim in the pool."

"Plus you need that recommendation letter from a member."

"Come on," said Mona. "Annie's mom'd write you a letter in *sec*."

My mother's knife glinted in the early summer sun. I spread some more newspaper on the picnic table,

"*Plus* you have to eat there twice a month. You know what that means." My mother cut another, enormous slice of fruit.

"No, I *don't* know what that means," said Mona.

"It means Dad would have to wear a jacket, dummy," I said.

"Oh! Oh! Oh!" said Mona, clasping her hand to her breast. "Oh! Oh! Oh! Oh! Oh!"

We all laughed: my father had no use for nice clothes, and would wear only ten-year-old shirts, with grease-spotted pants, to show how little he cared what anyone thought.

"Your father doesn't believe in joining the American society," said my mother. "He wants to have his own society."

"So go to dinner without him." Mona shot her seeds out in long arcs over the lawn. "Who cares what he thinks?"

But of course we all did care, and knew my mother could not simply up and do as she pleased. For in my father's mind, a family owed its head a degree of loyalty that left no room for dissent. To embrace what he embraced was to love; and to embrace something else was to betray him.

He demanded a similar sort of loyalty of his workers, whom he treated more like servants than employees. Not in the beginning, of course. In the beginning all he wanted was for them to keep on doing what they used to do, and to that end he concentrated mostly on leaving them alone. As the months passed, though, he expected more and more of them, with the result that for all his largesse, he began to have trouble keeping help. The cooks and busboys complained that he asked them to fix radiators and trim hedges, not only at the restaurant, but at our house; the waitresses that he sent them on errands and made them chauffeur him around. Our head waitress, Gertrude, claimed that he once even asked her to scratch his back.

"It's not just the blacks don't believe in slavery," she said when she quit.

My father never quite registered her complaint, though, nor those of the others who left. Even after Eleanor quit, then Tiffany, then Gerald, and Jimmy, and even his best cook, Eureka Andy, for whom he had bought new glasses, he remained mostly convinced that the fault lay with them.

"All they understand is that assembly line," he lamented. "Robots, they are. They want to be robots."

There *were* occasions when the clear running truth seemed to eddy, when he would pinch the vinyl of his chair up into little peaks and wonder if he was doing things right. But with time he would always smooth the peaks back down; and when business started to slide in the spring, he kept on like a horse in his ways.

By the summer our dishboy was overwhelmed with scraping. It was no longer just the hashbrowns that people were leaving for trash, and the service was as bad as the food. The waitresses served up French pancakes instead of German, apple juice instead of orange, spilt things on laps, on coats. On the Fourth of July some greenhorn sent an entire side of fries slaloming down a lady's *massif centrale.* Meanwhile in the back room, my father labored through articles on the economy.

"What is housing starts?" he puzzled. "What is GNP?"

Mona and I did what we could, filling in as busgirls and bookkeepers and, one afternoon, stuffing the comments box that hung by the cashier's desk. That was Mona's idea. We rustled up a variety of pens and pencils, checked boxes for an hour, smeared the cards up with coffee and grease, and waited. It took a few days for my father to notice that the box was full, and he didn't say anything about it for a few days more. Finally, though, he started to complain of fatigue; and then he began to complain that the staff was not what it could be. We encouraged him in this—pointing out, for instance, how many dishes got chipped—but in the end all that happened was that, for the first time since we took over the restaurant, my father got it into his head to fire someone. Skip, a skinny busboy who was saving up for a sportscar, said nothing as my father mumbled on about the price of dishes. My father's hands shook as he wrote out the severance check; and he spent the rest of the day napping in his chair once it was over.

As it was going on midsummer, Skip wasn't easy to replace. We hung a sign in the window and advertised in the paper, but no one called the first week, and the person who called the second didn't show up for his interview. The third week, my father phoned Skip to see if he would come back, but a friend of his had already sold him a Corvette for cheap.

Finally a Chinese guy named Booker turned up. He couldn't have been more than thirty, and was wearing a lighthearted seersucker suit, but he looked as though life had him pinned: his eyes were bloodshot and his chest sunken, and the muscles of his neck seemed to strain with the effort of holding his head up. In a single dry breath he told us that he had never bussed tables but was willing to learn, and that he was on the lam from the deportation authorities.

"I do not want to lie to you," he kept saying. He had come to the United States on a student visa, had run out of money, and was now in a bind. He was loath to go back to Taiwan, as it happened—he looked up at this point, to be sure my father wasn't pro-KMT—but all he had was a phony social security card and a willingness to absorb all blame, should anything untoward come to pass.

"I do not think, anyway, that it is against law to hire me, only to be me," he said, smiling faintly.

Anyone else would have examined him on this, but my father conceived of laws as speed bumps rather than curbs. He wiped the counter with his sleeve, and told Booker to report the next morning.

"I will be good worker," said Booker.

"Good," said my father.

"Anything you want me to do, I will do."

My father nodded.

Booker seemed to sink into himself for a moment. "Thank you," he said finally. "I am appreciate your help. I am very, very appreciate for everything." He reached out to shake my father's hand.

My father looked at him. "Did you eat today?" he asked in Mandarin.

Booker pulled at the hem of his jacket.

"Sit down," said my father. "Please, have a seat."

My father didn't tell my mother about Booker, and my mother didn't tell my father about the country club. She would never have applied, except that Mona, while over at Annie's, had let it drop that our mother wanted to join. Mrs. Lardner came by the very next day.

"Why, I'd be honored and delighted to write you people a letter," she said. Her skirt billowed around her.

"Thank you so much," said my mother. "But it's too much trouble for you, and also my husband is . . . "

"Oh, it's no trouble at all, no trouble at all. I tell you." She leaned forward so that her chest freckles showed. "I know just how it is. It's a secret of course, but you know, my natural father was Jewish. Can you see it? Just look at my skin."

"My husband," said my mother.

"I'd be honored and delighted," said Mrs. Lardner with a little wave of her hands. "Just honored and delighted."

Mona was triumphant. "See, Mom," she said, waltzing around the kitchen when Mrs. Lardner left. "What did I tell you? 'I'm just honored and delighted, just honored and delighted.'" She waved her hands in the air.

"You know, the Chinese have a saying," said my mother. "To do nothing is better than to overdo. You mean well, but you tell me now what will happen."

"I'll talk Dad into it," said Mona, still waltzing. "Or I bet Callie can. He'll do anything Callie says."

"I can try, anyway," I said.

"Did you hear what I said?" said my mother. Mona bumped into the broom closet door. "You're not going to talk anything; you've already made enough trouble." She started on the dishes with a clatter.

Mona poked diffidently at a mop.

I sponged off the counter. "Anyway," I ventured. "I bet our name'll never even come up."

"That's if we're lucky," said my mother.

"There's all these people waiting," I said.

"Good," she said. She started on a pot.

I looked over at Mona, who was still cowering in the broom closet. "In fact, there's some black family's been waiting so long, they're going to sue," I said.

My mother turned off the water. "Where'd you hear that?"

"Patty told me."

She turned the water back on, started to wash a dish, then put it back down and shut the faucet.

"I'm sorry," said Mona.

"Forget it," said my mother. "Just forget it."

Booker turned out to be a model worker, whose boundless gratitude translated into a willingness to do anything. As he also learned quickly, he soon knew not only how to bus, but how to cook, and how to wait table, and how to keep the books. He fixed the walk-in door so that it stayed shut, reupholstered the torn seats in the dining room, and devised a system for tracking inventory. The only stone in the rice was that he tended to be sickly; but, reliable even in illness, he would always send a friend to take his place. In this way we got to know Ronald, Lynn, Dirk, and Cedric, all of whom, like Booker, had problems with their legal status and were anxious to please. They weren't all as capable as Booker, though, with the exception of Cedric, whom my father often hired even when Booker was well. A round wag of a man who called Mona and me *shou hou*—skinny monkeys—he was a professed non-smoker who was nevertheless always begging drags off of other people's cigarettes. This last habit drove our head cook, Fernando, crazy, especially since, when refused a hit, Cedric would occasionally snitch one. Winking impishly at Mona and me, he would steal up to an ashtray, take a quick puff, and then break out laughing so that the smoke came rolling out of his mouth in a great incriminatory cloud. Fernando accused him of stealing fresh cigarettes too, even whole packs.

"Why else do you think he's weaseling around in the back of the store all the time," he said. His face was blotchy with anger. "The man is a frigging thief."

Other members of the staff supported him in this contention and joined in on an "Operation Identification," which involved numbering and initialing their cigarettes—even though what they seemed to fear for wasn't so much their cigarettes as their jobs. Then one of the cooks quit; and rather than promote someone, my fattier hired Cedric for the position. Rumors flew that he was taking only half the normal salary, that Alex had been pressured to resign, and that my father was looking for a position with which to placate Booker, who had been bypassed because of his health.

The result was that Fernando categorically refused to work with Cedric.

"The only way I'll cook with that piece of slime," he said, shaking his huge tattooed fist, "is if it's his ass frying on the grill."

My father cajoled and cajoled, to no avail, and in the end was simply forced to put them on different schedules.

The next week Fernando got caught stealing a carton of minute steaks. My father would not tell even Mona and me how he knew to be standing by the back door when Fernando was on his way out, but everyone suspected Booker. Everyone but Fernando, that is, who was sure Cedric had been the tip-off. My father held a staff meeting in which he tried to reassure everyone that Alex had left on his own, and that he had no intention of firing anyone. But though he was careful not to mention Fernando, everyone was so amazed that he was being allowed to stay that Fernando was incensed nonetheless.

"Don't you all be putting your bug eyes on me," he said. *"He's* the frigging crook." He grabbed Cedric by the collar.

Cedric raised an eyebrow. "Cook, you mean," he said.

At this Fernando punched Cedric in the mouth; and the words he had just uttered notwithstanding, my father fired him on the spot.

With everything that was happening, Mona and I were ready to be getting out of the restaurant. It was almost time: the days were still stuffy with summer, but our window shade had started flapping in the evening as if gearing up to go out. That year the breezes were full of salt, as they sometimes were when they came in from the East, and they blew anchors and docks through my mind like so many tumble-weeds, filling my dreams with wherries and lobsters and grainy-faced men who squinted, day in and day out, at the sky.

It was time for a change, you could feel it; and yet the pancake house was the same as ever. The day before school started my father came home with bad news.

"Fernando called police," he said, wiping his hand on his pant leg.

My mother naturally wanted to know what police; and so with much coughing and hawing, the long story began, the latest installment of which had the police call-ing immigration, and immigration sending an investigator. My mother sat stiff as whalebone as my father described how the man summarily refused lunch on the house and how my father had admitted, under pressure, that he knew there were "things" about his workers.

"So now what happens?

My father didn't know. "Booker and Cedric went with him to the jail," he said. "But me, here I am." He laughed uncomfortably.

The next day my father posted bail for "his boys" and waited apprehensively for something to happen. The day after that he waited again, and the day after that he called our neighbor's law student son, who suggested my father call the immigra-tion department under an alias. My father took his advice; and it was thus that he discovered that Booker was right: it was illegal for aliens to work, but it wasn't to hire them.

In the happy interval that ensued, my father apologized to my mother, who in turn confessed about the country club, for which my father had no choice but to for-give her. Then he turned his attention back to "his boys."

My mother didn't see that there was anything to do.

"I like to talking to the judge," said my father.

"This is not China," said my mother.

"I'm only talking to him. I'm not give him money unless he wants it."

"You're going to land up in jail."

"So what else I should do?" My father threw up his hands. "Those are my boys."

"Your boys!" exploded my mother. "What about your family? What about your wife?"

My father took a long sip of tea. "You know," he said finally. "In the war my father sent our cook to the soldiers to use. He always said it—the province comes before the town, the town comes before the family."

"A restaurant is not a town," said my mother.

My father sipped at his tea again. "You know, when I first come to the United States, I also had to hide-and-seek with those deportation guys. If people did not helping me, I'm not here today."

My mother scrutinized her hem.

After a minute I volunteered that before seeing a judge, he might try a lawyer.

He turned. "Since when did you become so afraid like your mother?"

I started to say that it wasn't a matter of fear, but he cut me off.

"What I need today," he said, "is a son."

My father and I spent the better part of the next day standing in lines at the immigration office. He did not get to speak to a judge, but with much persistence he managed to speak to a judge's clerk, who tried to persuade him that it was not her place to extend him advice. My father, though, shamelessly plied her with compliments and offers of free pancakes until she finally conceded that she personally doubted anything would happen to either Cedric or Booker.

"Especially if they're 'needed workers,'" she said, rubbing at the red marks her glasses left on her nose. She yawned. "Have you thought about sponsoring them to become permanent residents?"

Could he do that? My father was overjoyed, And what if he saw to it right away? Would she perhaps put in a good word with the judge?

She yawned again, her nostrils flaring. "Don't worry," she said. "They'll get a fair hearing."

My father returned jubilant. Booker and Cedric hailed him as their savior, their Buddha incarnate. He was like a father to them, they said; and laughing and clapping, they made him tell the story over and over, sorting over the details like jewels. And how old was the assistant judge? And what did she say?

That evening my father tipped the paperboy a dollar and bought a pot of mums for my mother, who suffered them to be placed on the dining room table. The next night he took us all out to dinner. Then on Saturday, Mona found a letter on my father's chair at the restaurant.

Dear Mr. Chang,

You are the grat boss. But, we do not like to trial, so will runing away now. Plese to excus us. People saying the law in America is fears like dragon. Here is only $140. We hope some day we can pay back the rest bale. You will getting intrest, as you diserving, so grat a boss you are. Thank you for every thing. In next life you will be burn in rich family, with no more pancaks.

Yours truley,
Booker + Cedric

In the weeks that followed my father went to the pancake house for crises, but otherwise hung around our house, fiddling idly with the sump pump and boiler in an effort, he said, to get ready for winter. It was as though he had gone into retirement, except that instead of moving south, he had moved to the basement. He even took to showering my mother with little attentions, and to calling her "old girl," and when we finally heard that the club had entertained all the applications it could for the year, he was so sympathetic that he seemed more disappointed than my mother.

TATO LAVIERA
(B. 1951)

Tato Laviera was born in Puerto Rico but has lived since 1960 in New York City. Like some other Latino writers, he really makes use of three languages: English, Spanish, and Spanglish. What distinguishes Laviera's work is his keen sense of how all these languages are actually spoken, used interactively to create identity, to establish value, and to construct daily life in "El Barrio." His poems are, like his plays, often performance pieces—indeed, he has performed them with salsa artists like Willie Colón. And eight of Laviera's plays have been produced and staged at the New York Federal Theater, the New York Shakespeare Festival, the Circle Repertory Theater, and the Teatro 4.

His books of poetry, La Carreta Made a U-Turn (1976), Enclave (1981), and AmeRícan (1985), suggest in their linguistically playful titles that while Laviera strongly attacks unemployment, discrimination, freezing buildings, chiseling landlords, and empty fridges, he does so with a certain humor, a playful grace, and a sense of optimism. His primary concern is, as he writes in AmeRícan, "integrating in new york and defining our/own destino, our own way of life." To that end, he blends elements from the Island and the City, from African as well as Caribbean culture, from the lives of Latinas as well as of Latinos. His most recent book of poems, Mainstram Ethics (1988), seems to suggest less that Latinos are adapting to life within the continental United States, but that America is itself being transformed by its rapidly growing Latino population. As "Latero's Story" illustrates, Laviera approaches his subject, America in the 1980s, with a bitter humor, a sense of the flagrant detail, and a dramatic style of delivery, for the poem is, no less than Browning's "My Last Duchess," a dramatic monologue—with rather a difference.

LATERO STORY

i am a twentieth-century welfare recipient
moonlighting in the sun as a latero
a job invented by national state laws
designed to re-cycle aluminum cans
returned to consumer's acid laden
gastric inflammation pituitary glands
coca diet rites low cal godsons
of artificially flavored malignant
indigestions somewhere down the line
of a cancerous cell

i collect garbage cans in outdoor facilities
congested with putrid residues
my hands shelving themselves
opening plastic bags never knowing
what they'll encounter

several times a day i touch evil rituals
cut throats of chickens
tongues of poisoned rats
salivating my index finger
smells of month old rotten foods
next to pamper's diarrhea
    dry blood infectious diseases
hypodermic needles tissued with
heroin water drops pilfered in
slimy greases hazardous waste materials
but i cannot use rubber gloves
they undermine my daily profits

i am a twentieth-century welfare recipient
moonlighting in the day as a latero
that is the only opportunity i have
to make it big in america
some day i might become experienced enough
to offer technical assistance
to other lateros
i am a thinking of publishing
my own guide to latero's collection
and founding a latero's union offering
medical dental benefits

i am a twentieth-century welfare recipient
moonlighting in the night as a latero
i am considered some kind of expert
at collecting cans during fifth avenue parades
i can now hire workers at twenty
five cents an hour guaranteed salary
and fifty per cent of two and one half cents
profit on each can collected

i am a twentieth-century welfare recipient
moonlighting in midnight as a latero
i am becoming an entrepreneur
an american success story
i have hired bag ladies to keep peddlers
from my territories
i have read in some guide to success
that in order to get rich
to make it big
i have to sacrifice myself
moonlighting until dawn by digging
deeper into the extra can
margin of profit
i am on my way up the opportunistic
ladder of success

in ten years i will quit welfare
to become a legitimate businessman
i'll soon become a latero executive
with corporate conglomerate intents
god bless america

-1988

PEGGY GIFFORD

(B. 1952)

Born in Rochester, Minnesota, to the rarefied and prestigious atmosphere of the Mayo Clinic, Gifford did not realize, until she moved to Cleveland at age 9, that everybody's father was not a doctor. This sense of privilege haunted her and her poetry as she began to write it in 1975. As early as 1965, as the poem included here expresses, she envisioned the bitter paradox that one person had to die on Christmas Eve so that another might gain a kidney and live—and a doctor thus achieve fame as a transplant pioneer.

Gifford earned her B.A. at Denison University and later a master of fine arts degree from the Iowa Writer's Workshop and an M.A. from the University of Southern Mississippi, where she taught. She edited the Mississippi Review *and the* Iowa Review *and worked for* Ms. *magazine. She also played Winnie-the-Pooh for a long time with a touring company in Ohio. She has published two poetry chapbooks,* The Rabbi's Daughter *(1982) and* Clean and Disappointed *(1987). She has worked as an acquisitions editor for the SUNY Press and worked on the Reconstructing American Literature project at The Feminist Press. Recently, she has learned to meet a payroll in Myrtle Beach, South Carolina.*

THE FIRST TRANSPLANT

Holidays were best
for the kind of death my father needed

and it was Christmas Eve.
The photographer waited with us

later he would put our picture
in LIFE magazine: *The surgeon*

and his family wait at home
for the phone to ring.

The photographer drank Amaretto
leaned against the mantel,

pretending he heard Santa
and telling me

about the New York blackout
the spring before—how frightened he had been

that Russians had really come and lights
were turned off purposely to make the city look

like some small seaboard town.
The MERRY CHRISTMAS embroidered

on my father's bowtie was interrupted
by his chin when he explained

that if the call should come
the helicopter would bring the kidney

frozen in a silver box
to the clinic roof. It would be difficult

to find a match; the donor must be young,
around sixteen and killed quite suddenly—

in a car perhaps with no damage
to his heart or spleen. Then my sister asked

if she could take a present to her boyfriend's house.
But the neighborhood was asleep

and mother said no one could leave,
and I went through the house in my socks

switching off every light
so it would seem

we were waiting, anxiously,
like everyone else on the street,

for Christmas morning. *The surgeon is seen*
rushing from his home
in the pre-dawn of December 25.

BARBARA GARSON

During 1966, when the Vietnam War was escalating and the subject, to those opposed to the war, seemed only desperate and painful, an off-off-Broadway play opened in New York City with the wonderfully irreverent title MacBird. *It took off from Shakespeare's tragedy to cartoon then-President Lyndon Johnson's bizarre claims to righteousness and justice in the war. The author, a young activist and writer, was Barbara Garson, and the play not only helped breathe some wit into the antiwar movement, but also helped begin the process of unraveling Johnson's credibility.*

Garson has continued throughout her writing career to take apart the self-serving claims of big shots and big money. Her 1989 book, The Electronic Sweatshop: How Computers Are Transforming the Office of the Future into the Factory of the Past, *from which the following selection is taken, early raised questions about how computers would change—and not for the better—the lives of those subject to increasing surveillance and control in sped-up offices. Her 1994* All the Livelong Day: The Meaning and Demeaning of Routine Work *explores the declining conditions of labor for fish packers, line workers, and others subject to downsizing, speed-up, and other manifestations of today's corporate production lines. Garson's approach to these subjects has been as a participant, taking the jobs she then has written about. Throughout the jobs, and in the writing, she has retained the ironic humor that made* MacBird *(and a subsequent take-off on Richard Nixon) both hilarious and sharply pointed.*

MCDONALD'S—WE DO IT ALL FOR YOU

Jason Pratt

"They called us the Green Machine," says Jason Pratt, recently retired McDonald's griddleman, "'cause the crew had green uniforms then. And that's what it is, a machine. You don't have to know how to cook, you don't have to know how to think. There's a procedure for everything and you just follow the procedures."

"Like?" I asked. I was interviewing Jason in the Pizza Hut across from his old McDonald's.

"Like, uh," the wiry teenager searched for a way to describe the all-encompassing procedures. "O.K., we'll start you off on something simple. You're on the ten-in-one grill, ten patties in a pound. Your basic burger. The guy on the bin calls, 'Six hamburgers.' So you lay your six pieces of meat on the grill and set the timer." Before my eyes Jason conjures up the gleaming, mechanized McDonald's kitchen. "Beep-beep, beep-beep, beep-beep. That's the beeper to sear 'em. It goes off in twenty seconds. Sup, sup, sup, sup, sup, sup." He presses each of the six patties down on the sizzling grill with an imaginary silver disk. "Now you turn off the sear beeper, put the buns in the oven, set the oven timer and then the next beeper is to turn the meat. This one goes beep-beep-beep, beep-beep-beep. So you turn your patties, and then you drop your re-cons on the meat, t-con, t-con, t-con." Here Jason takes two imaginary handfuls of reconstituted onions out of water and sets them out, two blops at a time, on top of the six patties he's arranged in two neat rows on our grill. "Now the bun oven buzzes [there are over a half dozen different timers with distinct beeps and buzzes in a McDonald's kitchen]. This one turns itself off when you open the oven door so you just take out your crowns, line 'em up and give 'em each a squirt of mustard and a squirt of ketchup." With mustard in his right hand and ketchup in his left, Jason wields the dispensers like a pair of six-shooters up and down the lines of buns. Each dispenser has two triggers. One fires the pre-measured squirt for ten-in-ones—the second is set for quarter-pounders.

"Now," says Jason, slowing down, "now you get to put on the pickles. Two if they're regular, three if they're small. That's the creative part. Then the lettuce, then you ask for a cheese count ('cheese on four please'). Finally the last beep goes off and you lay your burger on the crowns."

"On the *crown* of the buns?" I ask, unable to visualize. "On top?"

"Yeah, you dress 'em upside down. Put 'em in the box upside down too. They flip 'em over when they serve 'em."

"Oh, I think I see."

"Then scoop up the heels [the bun bottoms] which are on top of the bull warmer, take the heels with one hand and push the tray out from underneath and they land (plip) one on each burger, right on top of the re-cons, neat and perfect. [The official time allotted by Hamburger Central, the McDonald's headquarters in Oak Brook, Ill, is ninety seconds to prepare and serve a burger.] It's like I told you. The procedures makes the burgers. You don't have to know a thing."

◇　◇　◇

McDonald's employs 500,000 teenagers at any one time. Most don't stay long. About 8 million Americans—7 per cent of our labor force—have worked at McDonald's and moved on. Jason is not a typical ex-employee. In fact, Jason is a legend among the teenagers at the three McDonald's outlets in his suburban area. It seems he was so fast at the griddle (or maybe just fast talking) that he'd been taken back three times by two different managers after quitting.

But Jason became a real legend in his last stint at McDonald's. He'd been sent out the back door with the garbage, but instead of coming back in he got into a car with two friends and just drove away. That's the part the local teenagers love to tell. "No fight with the manager or anything . . . just drove away and never came back. . . . I don't think they'd give him a job again."

◇　◇　◇

"I would never go back to McDonald's," says Jason. "Not even as a manager." Jason is enrolled at the local junior college. "I'd like to run a real restaurant someday, but I'm taking data processing to fall back on." He's had many part-time jobs, the highest-paid at a hospital ($4.00 an hour), but that didn't last, and now dishwashing (at the $3.35 minimum). "Same as McDonald's. But I would never go back there. You're a complete robot."

"It seems like you can improvise a little with the onions," I suggested. "They're not premeasured." Indeed, the reconstituted onion shreds grabbed out of a container by the unscientific-looking wet handful struck me as oddly out of character in the McDonald's kitchen.

"There's supposed to be twelve onion bits per patty," Jason informed me. "They spot check."

"Oh come on."

"You think I'm kiddin'. They lift your heels and they say, 'You got too many onions.' It's portion control."

"Is there any freedom anywhere in the process?" I asked.

"Lettuce. They'll leave you alone as long as it's neat."

"So lettuce is freedom; pickles is judgment?"

"Yeah but you don't have time to play around with your pickles. They're never gonna say just six pickles except on the disk. [Each store has video disks to train the crew for each of about twenty work stations, like fries, register, lobby, quarter-pounder grill.] What you'll hear in real life is 'twelve and six on a turn-lay.' The first number is your hamburgers, the second is your Big Macs. On a turn-lay means you lay the first twelve, then you put down the second batch after you turn the first. So you got twenty-four burgers on the grill, in shifts. It's what they call a production mode. And remember you also got your fillets, your McNuggets. . . ."

"Wait, slow down." By then I was losing track of the patties on our imaginary grill. "I don't understand this turn-lay grill thing."

"Don't worry, you don't have to understand. You follow the beepers, you follow the buzzers and you turn your meat as fast as you can. It's like I told you, to work at McDonald's you don't need a face, you don't need a brain. You need to have two hands and two legs and move 'em as fast as you can. That's the whole system. I wouldn't go back there again for anything."

June Sanders

McDonald's french fries are deservedly the pride of their menu; uniformly golden brown all across America and in thirty-one other countries. However, it's difficult to standardize the number of fries per serving. The McDonald's fry scoop, perhaps their greatest technological innovation, helps to control this variable. The unique flat funnel holds the bag open while it aligns a limited number of fries so that they fall into the package with a paradoxically free, overflowing cornucopia look.

Despite the scoop, there's still a spread. The acceptable fry yield is 400 to 420 servings per 100-lb. bag of potatoes. It's one of the few areas of McDonald's cookery in which such a range is possible. The fry yield is therefore one important measure of a manager's efficiency. "Fluffy, not stuffy," they remind the young workers when the fry yield is running low.

No such variation is possible in the browning of the fries. Early in McDonald's history Louis Martino, the husband of the secretary of McDonald's founder Ray Kroc, designed a computer to be submerged in the fry vats. In his autobiography, *Grinding It Out*, Kroc explained the importance of this innovation. "We had a recipe . . . that called for pulling the potatoes out of the oil when they got a certain color and grease bubbles formed in a certain way. It was amazing that we got them as uniform as we did because each kid working the fry vats would have his own interpretation of the proper color and so forth. [The word "kid" was officially replaced by "person" or "crew person" in McDonald's management vocabulary in 1973 in response to union organizing attempts.] Louis's computer took all the guesswork out of it, modifying the frying to suit the balance of water to solids in a given batch of potatoes. He also engineered the dispenser that allowed us to squirt exactly the right amount of catsup and mustard onto our premeasured hamburger patties. . . ."

The fry vat probe is a complex miniature computer. The fry scoop, on the other hand, is as simple and almost as elegant as the wheel. Both eliminate the need for a human being to make "his own interpretation," as Ray Kroc puts it.

Together, these two innovations mean that a new worker can be trained in fifteen minutes and reach maximum efficiency in a half hour. This makes it economically feasible to use a kid for one day and replace him with another kid the next day.

June Sanders worked at McDonald's for one day.

"I needed money, so I went in and the manager told me my hours would be 4 to 10 P.M." This was fine with June, a well-organized black woman in her early twenties who goes to college full time.

"But when I came in the next day the manager said I could work till 10 for that one day. But from then on my hours would be 4 P.M. to 1 A.M. And I really wouldn't get off at 1 because I'd have to stay to clean up after they closed. . . . Yes it was the same manager, a Mr. O'Neil.

"I told him I'd have to check first with my family if I could come home that late. But he told me to put on the uniform and fill out the forms. He would start me out on french fries.

"Then he showed me an orientation film on a TV screen all about fries. . . . No, I still hadn't punched in. This was all in the basement. Then I went upstairs, and *then* I punched in and went to work. . . . No, I was not paid for the training downstairs. Yes, I'm sure."

I asked June if she had had any difficulty with the fries.

"No, it was just like the film. You put the french fries in the grease and you push a button which doesn't go off till the fries are done. Then you take them out and put them in a bin under a light. Then you scoop them into the bags with this thing, this flat, light metal—I can't really describe it—scoop thing that sits right in the package and makes the fries fill in place."

"Did they watch you for a while?" I asked. "Did you need more instruction?"

"Someone leaned over once and showed me how to make sure the fry scooper was set inside the opening of the bag so the fries would fall in right."

"And then?"

"And then, I stood on my feet from twenty after four till the manager took over my station at 10:35 P.M.

"When I left my legs were aching. I knew it wasn't a job for me. But I probably would have tried to last it out—at least more than a day—if it wasn't for the hours. When I got home I talked it over with my mother and my sister and then I phoned and said I couldn't work there. They weren't angry. They just said to bring back the uniform. . . . The people were nice, even the managers. It's just a rushed system."

"June," I said, "does it make any sense to train you and have you work for one day? Why didn't he tell you the real hours in the first place?"

"They take a chance and see if you're desperate. I have my family to stay with. That's why I didn't go back. But if I really needed the money, like if I had a kid and no family, I'd have to make arrangements to work any hours.

"Anyway, they got a full day's work out of me."

Damita

I waited on line at my neighborhood McDonald's. It was lunch hour and there were four or five customers at each of the five open cash registers. "May I take your order?" a very thin girl said in a flat tone to the man at the head of my line.

"McNuggets, large fries and a Coke," said the man. The cashier punched in the order. "That will be—".

"Big Mac, large fries and a shake," said the next woman on line. The cashier rang it up.

"Two cheeseburgers, large fries and a coffee," said the third customer. The cashier rang it up.

"How much is a large fries,"' asked the woman directly in front of me.

The thin cashier twisted her neck around trying to look up at the menu board.

"Sorry," apologized the customer, "I don't have my glasses."

"Large fries is seventy-nine," a round-faced cashier with glasses interjected from the next register.

"Seventy-nine cents," the thin cashier repeated.

"Well how much is a *small* fries?"

As they talked I leaned over the next register. "Say, can I interview you?" I asked the clerk with glasses, whose line was by then empty.

"Huh?"

"I'm writing a story about jobs at fast-food restaurants."

"O.K. I guess so."

"Can I have your phone number?"

"Well . . . I'll meet you when I get off. Should be sometime between 4 and 4:30."

By then it was my turn.

"Just a large fries," I said.

The thin cashier pressed "lge fries." In place of numbers, the keys on a McDonald's cash register say "lge fries," "reg fries," "med coke," "big mac," and so on. Some registers have pictures on the key caps. The next time the price of fries goes up (or down) the change will be entered in the store's central computer. But the thin cashier will continue to press the same button. I wondered how long she'd worked there and how many hundreds of "lge fries" she'd served without learning the price.

◇ ◇ ◇

Damita, the cashier with the glasses, came up from the crew room (a room in the basement with lockers, a table and a video player for studying the training disks) at 4:45. She looked older and more serious without her striped uniform.

"Sorry, but they got busy and, you know, here you get off when they let you."

The expandable schedule was her first complaint. "You give them your availability when you sign on. Mine I said 9 to 4. But they scheduled me for 7 o'clock two or three days a week. And I needed the money. So I got to get up 5 in the morning to get here from Queens by 7. And I don't get off till whoever's supposed to get here gets here to take my place. . . . It's hard to study with all the pressures."

Damita had come to the city from a small town outside of Detroit. She lives with her sister in Queens and takes extension courses in psychology at New York University. Depending on the schedule posted each Friday, her McDonald's paycheck for a five-day week has varied from $80 to $114.

"How long have you worked at McDonald's?" I asked.

"Well, see I only know six people in this city, so my manager from Michigan . . . yeah, I worked for McDonald's in high school . . . my manager from Michigan called this guy Brian who's the second assistant manager here. So I didn't have to fill out an application. Well, I mean the first thing I needed was a job," she seemed to apologize, "and I knew I could always work at McDonald's. I always say I'm gonna look for something else, but I don't get out till 4 and that could be 5 or whenever."

The flexible scheduling at McDonald's only seems to work one way. One day Damita had arrived a half hour late because the E train was running on the R track.

"The assistant manager told me not to clock in at all, just to go home. So I said O.K. and I left."

"What did you do the rest of the day?" I asked.

"I went home and studied, and I went to sleep."

"But how did it make you feel?"

"It's like a humiliating feeling 'cause I wasn't given any chance to justify myself. But when I spoke to the Puerto Rican manager he said it was nothing personal against me. Just it was raining that day, and they were really slow and someone who got here on time, it wouldn't be right to send them home."

"Weren't you annoyed to spend four hours traveling and then lose a day's pay?" I suggested.

"I was mad at first that they didn't let me explain. But afterwards I understood and I tried to explain to my sister: 'Time waits for no man.'"

"Since you signed on for 9 to 4," I asked Damita, "and you're going to school, why can't you say, 'Look, I have to study at night, I need regular hours'?"

"Don't work that way. They make up your schedule every week and if you can't work it, you're responsible to replace yourself. If you can't they can always get someone else."

"But Damita," I tried to argue with her low estimate of her own worth, "anyone can see right away that your line moves fast yet you're helpful to people. I mean, you're a valuable employee. And this manager seems to like you."

"Valuable! $3.35 an hour. And I can be replaced by any [pointing across the room] kid off the street." I hadn't noticed. At a small table under the staircase a manager in a beige shirt was taking an application from a lanky black teenager.

"But you know the register. You know the routine."

"How long you think it takes to learn the six steps? Step 1. Greet the customer, 'Good morning, can I help you?' Step 2. Take his order. Step 3. Repeat the order. They can have someone off the street working my register in five minutes."

"By the way," I asked, "on those cash registers without numbers, how do you change something after you ring it up? I mean if somebody orders a cheeseburger and then they change it to a hamburger, how do you subtract the slice of cheese?"

"I guess that's why you have step 3, repeat the order. One cheeseburger, two Cokes, three . . ."

"Yeah but if you punched a mistake or they don't want it after you get it together?"

"Like if I have a crazy customer, which I do be gettin' 'specially in this city, and they order hamburger, fries and shake, and it's $2.95 and then they just walk away?"

"I once did that here," I said. "About a week ago, when I first started my research. All I ordered was some french fries. And I was so busy watching how the computer works that only after she rang it up I discovered that I'd walked out of my house without my wallet. I didn't have a penny. I was so embarrassed."

"Are you that one the other day? Arnetta, this girl next to me, she said, 'Look at that crazy lady going out. She's lookin' and lookin' at everything and then she didn't have no money for a bag of fries.' I saw you leaving, but I guess I didn't recognize you. [I agreed it was probably me.] O.K., so say this crazy lady comes in and orders french fries and leaves. In Michigan I could just zero it out. I'd wait till I start the next order and press zero and large fries. But here you're supposed to call out 'cancel sale' and the manager comes over and does it with his key.

"But I hate to call the manager every time, 'specially if I got a whole line waiting. So I still zero out myself. They can tell I do it by the computer tape, and they tell me not to. Some of them let me, though, because they know I came from another store. But they don't show the girls here how to zero out. Everybody thinks you need the manager's key to do it."

"Maybe they let you because they can tell you're honest," I said. She smiled, pleased, but let it pass. "That's what I mean that you're valuable to them. You know how to use the register. You're good with customers."

"You know there was a man here," Damita said, a little embarrassed about bragging, "when I was transferred off night he asked my manager, 'What happened to that girl from Michigan?'"

"Did your manager tell you that?"

"No, another girl on the night shift told me. The manager said it to her. They don't tell you nothing nice themselves."

"But, see, you are good with people and he appreciates it."

"In my other McDonald's—not the one where they let me zero out but another one I worked in in Michigan—I was almost fired for my attitude. Which was helping customers who had arthritis to open the little packets. And another bad attitude of mine is that you're supposed to suggest to the customer, 'Would you like a drink with that?' or 'Do you want a pie?'—whatever they're pushing. I don't like to do it. And they can look on my tape after my shift and see I didn't push the suggested sell item."

McDonald's computerized cash registers allow managers to determine immediately not only the dollar volume for the store but the amount of each item that was sold at each register for any given period. Two experienced managers, interviewed separately, both insisted that the new electronic cash registers were in fact slower than the old mechanical registers. Clerks who knew the combinations—hamburger, fries, Coke: $2.45—could ring up the total immediately, take the cash and give change in one operation. On the new registers you have to enter each item and may be slowed down by computer response time. The value of the new registers, or at least their main selling point (McDonald's franchisers can choose from several approved registers), is the increasingly sophisticated tracking systems, which monitor all the activity and report with many different statistical breakdowns.

"Look, there," said Damita as the teenage job applicant left and the manager went behind the counter with the application, "If I was to say I can't come in at 7, they'd cut my hours down to one shift a week, and if I never came back they wouldn't call to find out where I was.

"I worked at a hospital once as an X-ray assistant. There if I didn't come in there were things that had to be done that wouldn't be done. I would call there and say, 'Remember to run the EKGs.' Here, if I called and said, 'I just can't come by 7 no more,' they'd have one of these high school kids off the street half an hour later. And they'd do my job just as good."

Damita was silent for a while and then she made a difficult plea. "This might sound stupid, I don't know," she said, "but I feel like, I came here to study and advance myself but I'm not excelling myself in any way. I'm twenty years old but— this sounds terrible to say—I'm twenty but I'd rather have a babysitting job. At least I could help a kid and take care. But I only know six people in this city. So I don't even know how I'd find a babysitting job."

"I'll keep my ears open," I said. "I don't know where I'd hear of one but . . ."

Damita seemed a little relieved. I suppose she realized there wasn't much chance of babysitting full-time, but at least she now knew seven people in the city.

Jon DeAngelo

Jon DeAngelo, twenty-two, has been a McDonald's manager for three years. He started in the restaurant business at sixteen as a busboy and planned even then to run a restaurant of his own someday. At nineteen, when he was the night manager of a resort kitchen, he was hired away by McOpCo, the McDonald's Operating Company.

Though McDonald's is primarily a franchise system, the company also owns and operates about 30 percent of the stores directly. These McOpCo stores, including some of the busiest units, are managed via a chain of command including regional supervisors, store managers and first and second assistants who can be moved from unit to unit. In addition, there's a network of inspectors from Hamburger Central who make announced and unannounced checks for QSC (quality, service, cleanliness) at both franchise and McOpCo installations.

Jon was hired at $14,000 a year. At the time I spoke with him his annual pay was $21,000—a very good salary at McDonald's. At first he'd been an assistant manager in one of the highest-volume stores in his region. Then he was deliberately transferred to a store with productivity problems.

"I got there and found it was really a great crew. They hated being hassled, but they loved to work. I started them having fun by putting the men on the women's jobs and vice versa. [At most McDonald's the women tend to work on the registers, the men on the grill. But everyone starts at the same pay.] Oh, sure, they hated it at first, the guys that is. But they liked learning all the stations. I also ran a lot of register races."

Since the computer tape in each register indicates sales per hour, per half hour or for any interval requested, the manager can revv the crew up for a real "on your mark, get set, go!" race with a printout ready as they cross the finish line, showing the dollars taken in at each register during the race.

The computer will also print out a breakdown of sales for any particular menu item. The central office can check, therefore, how many Egg McMuffins were sold on Friday from 9 to 9:30 two weeks or two years ago, either in the entire store or at any particular register.

This makes it possible to run a register race limited to Cokes for instance, or Big Macs. Cashiers are instructed to try suggestive selling ("Would you like a drink with that?") at all times. But there are periods when a particular item is being pushed. The manager may then offer a prize for the most danish sold.

A typical prize for either type of cash register race might be a Snoopy mug (if that's the current promotion) or even a $5 cash bonus.

"This crew loved to race as individuals," says Jon of his troubled store, "but even more as a team. They'd love to get on a production mode, like a chicken-pull-drop or a burger-turn-lay and kill themselves for a big rush.

"One Saturday after a rock concert we did a $1,900 hour with ten people on crew. We killed ourselves but when the rush was over everyone said it was the most fun they ever had in a McDonald's."

I asked Jon how managers made up their weekly schedule. How would he decide who and how many to assign?

"It comes out of the computer," Jon explained. "It's a bar graph with the business you're going to do that week already printed in."

"The business you're *going* to do, already printed in?"

"It's based on the last,week's sales, like maybe you did a $300 hour on Thursday at 3 P.M. Then it automatically adds a certain percent, say 15 percent, which is the projected annual increase for your particular store. . . . No, the person scheduling doesn't have to do any of this calculation. I just happen to know how it's arrived at. Really, it's simple, it's just a graph with the numbers already in it. $400 hour, $500 hour. According to Hamburger Central you schedule two crew members per $100 hour. So if you're projected for a $600 hour on Friday between 1 and 2, you know you need twelve crew for that lunch hour and the schedule sheet leaves space for their names."

"You mean you just fill in the blanks on the chart?"

"It's pretty automatic except in the case of a special event like the concert. Then you have to guess the dollar volume. Scheduling under could be a problem, but over would be a disaster to your crew labor productivity."

"Crew labor productivity?"

"Everything at McDonald's is based on the numbers. But crew labor productivity is pretty much the number a manager is judged by."

"Crew labor productivity? You have to be an economist."

"It's really simple to calculate. You take the total crew labor dollars paid out, divide that into the total food dollars taken in. That gives you your crew labor productivity. The more food you sell and the less people you use to do it, the better your percentage. It's pretty simple."

Apparently, I still looked confused.

"For example, if you take an $800 hour and you run it with ten crew you get a very high crew labor percent."

"That's good."

"Yes that's good. Then the manager in the next store hears Jon ran a 12 percent labor this week, I'll run a 10 percent labor. Of course you burn people out that way. But . . ."

"But Jon," I asked, "if the number of crew you need is set in advance and printed by the computer, why do so many managers keep changing hours and putting pressure on kids to work more?"

"They advertise McDonald's as a flexible work schedule for high school and college kids," he said, "but the truth is it's a high-pressure job, and we have so much trouble keeping help, especially in fast stores like my first one (it grossed $1.8 million last year), that 50 percent never make it past two weeks. And a lot walk out within two days.

"When I was a first assistant, scheduling and hiring was my responsibility and I had to fill the spots one way or another. There were so many times I covered the shifts myself. Times I worked 100 hours a week. A manager has to fill the spaces on his chart somehow. So if a crew person is manipulable they manipulate him."

"What do you mean?"

"When you first sign on, you give your availability. Let's say a person's schedule is weeknights, 4 to 10. But after a week the manager schedules him as a closer Friday night. He calls in upset, 'Hey, my availability isn't Friday night.' The manager says 'Well the schedule is already done. And you know the rule. If you can't work it's up to you to replace yourself.' At that point the person might quit, or he might not show up or he might have a fight with the manager."

"So he's fired?"

"No. You don't fire. You would only fire for cause like drugs or stealing. But what happens is he signed up for thirty hours a week and suddenly he's only scheduled for four. So either he starts being more available or he quits."

"Aren't you worried that the most qualified people will quit?"

"The only qualification to be able to do the job is to be able physically to do the job. I believe it says that in almost those words in my regional manual. And being there is the main part of being physically able to do the job."

"But what about your great crew at the second store? Don't you want to keep a team together?"

"Let me qualify that qualification. It takes a special kind of person to be able to move before he can think. We find people like that and use them till they quit."

"But as a manager don't you look bad if too many people are quitting?"

"As a manager I am judged by the statistical reports which come off the computer. Which basically means my crew labor productivity. What else can I really distinguish myself by? I could have a good fry yield, a low M&R [Maintenance and Repair budget]. But these are minor."

As it happens, Jon is distinguished among McDonald's managers in his area as an expert on the computerized equipment. Other managers call on him for cash register repairs. "They say, 'Jon, could you look at my register? I just can't afford the M&R this month.' So I come and fix it and they'll buy me a beer."

"So keeping M&R low is a real feather in a manager's cap," I deduced.

"O.K., it's true, you can over spend your M&R budget; you can have a low fry yield; you can run a dirty store; you can be fired for bothering the high school girls. But basically, every Coke spigot is monitored. [At most McDonald's, Coke doesn't flow from tips that turn on and off. Instead the clerk pushes the button "sm," "med" or "lge," which then dispenses the premeasured amount into the appropriate-size cup. This makes the syrup yield fairly consistent.] Every ketchup squirt is measured. My costs for every item are set. So my crew labor productivity is my main flexibility."

I was beginning to understand the pressures toward pettiness. I had by then heard many complaints about slight pilferage of time. For instance, as a safety measure no one was allowed to stay in a store alone. There was a common complaint that a closer would be clocked out when he finished cleaning the store for the night, even though he might be required to wait around unpaid till the manager finished his own nightly statistical reports. At other times kids clocked out and then waited hours (unpaid) for a crew chief training course (unpaid).

Overtime is an absolute taboo at McDonald's. Managers practice every kind of scheduling gymnastic to see that no one works over forty hours a week. If a crew member approaching forty hours is needed to close the store, he or she might be asked to check out for a long lunch. I had heard of a couple of occasions when, in desperation, a manager scheduled someone to stay an hour or two over forty hours. Instead of paying time-and-a-half, he compensated at straight time listing the extra hours as miscellaneous and paying through a fund reserved for things like register race bonuses. All of this of course to make his statistics look good.

"There must be some other way to raise your productivity," I suggested, "besides squeezing it out of the kids."

"I try to make it fun," Jon pleaded earnestly. "I know that people like to work on my shifts. I have the highest crew labor productivity in the area. But I get that from burning people out. Look, you can't squeeze a McDonald's hamburger any flatter. If you want to improve your productivity there is nothing for a manager to squeeze but the crew."

"But if it's crew dollars paid out divided by food dollars taken in, maybe you can bring in more dollars instead of using less crew."

"O.K., let me tell you about sausage sandwiches."

"Sausage sandwiches?" (Sounded awful.)

"My crew was crazy about sausage sandwiches. [Crew members are entitled to one meal a day at reduced prices. The meals are deducted from wages through a computerized link to the time clocks.] They made it from a buttered English muffin, a slice of sausage and a slice of cheese. I understand this had actually been a menu item in some parts of the country but never here. But the crew would make it for themselves and then all their friends came in and wanted them.

"So, I decided to go ahead and sell it. It costs about 9¢ to make and I sold it for $1.40. It went like hotcakes. My supervisor even liked the idea because it made so much money. You could see the little dollar signs in his eyes when he first came into the store. And he said nothing. So we kept selling it.

"Then someone came from Oak Brook and they made us stop it.

"Just look how ridiculous that is. A slice of sausage is 60¢ as a regular menu item, and an English muffin is 45¢. So if you come in and ask for a sausage and an English muffin I can still sell them to you today for $1.05. But there's no way I can add the slice of cheese and put it in the box and get that $1.40.

"Basically, I can't be any more creative than a crew person. I can't take any more initiative then the person on the register."

"Speaking of cash registers and initiative," I said . . . and told him about Damita. I explained that she was honest, bright and had learned how to zero out at another store. "Do you let cashiers zero out?" I asked.

"I might let her in this case," Jon said. "The store she learned it at was probably a franchise and they were looser. But basically we don't need people like her. Thinking generally slows this operation down.

"When I first came to McDonald's, I said, 'How mechanical! These kids don't even know how to cook.' But the pace is so fast that if they didn't have all the systems, you couldn't handle it. It takes ninety seconds to cook a hamburger. In those seconds you have to toast the buns, dress it, sear it, turn it, take it off the grill and serve it. Meanwhile you've got maybe twenty-four burgers, plus your chicken, your fish. You haven't got time to pick up a rack of fillet and see if it's done. You have to press the timer, drop the fish and know, without looking, that when it buzzes it's done.

"It's the same thing with management. You have to record the money each night before you close and get it to the bank the next day by 11 A.M. So you have to trust the computer to do a lot of the job. These computers also calculate the payrolls, because they're hooked into the time clocks. My payroll is paid out of a bank in Chicago. The computers also tell you how many people you're going to need each hour. It's so fast that the manager hasn't got time to think about it. He has to follow the procedures like the crew. And if he follows the procedures everything is going to come out more or less as it's supposed to. So basically the computer manages the store."

Listening to Jon made me remember what Ray Kroc had written about his own job (head of the corporation) and computers:

> We have a computer in Oak Brook that is designed to make real estate surveys. But those printouts are of no use to me. After we find a promising location, I drive around it in a car, go into the corner saloon and the neighborhood supermarket. I mingle with the people and observe their comings and goings. That tells me what I need to know about how a McDonald's store would do there.

By combining twentieth-century computer technology with nineteenth-century time-and-motion studies, the McDonald's corporation has broken the jobs of griddleman, waitress, cashier and even manager down into small, simple steps. Historically these have been service jobs involving a lot of flexibility and personal flare. But the corporation has systematically extracted the decision-making elements from filling french fry boxes or scheduling staff. They've siphoned the know-how from the employees into the programs. They relentlessly weed out all variables that might make it necessary to make a decision at the store level, whether on pickles or on cleaning procedures.

It's interesting and understandable that Ray Kroc refused to work that way. The real estate computer may be as reliable as the fry vat probe. But as head of the company Kroc didn't have to surrender to it. He'd let the computer juggle all the demographic variables, but in the end Ray Kroc would decide, intuitively, where to put the next store.

Jon DeAngelo, would like to work that way, too. So would Jason, June and Damita. If they had a chance to use some skill or intuition at their own levels, they'd not only feel more alive, they'd also be treated with more consideration. It's job organization, not malice, that allows (almost requires) McDonald's workers to be handled like paper plates. They feel disposable because they are.

I was beginning to wonder why Jon stayed on at McDonald's. He still yearned to open a restaurant. "The one thing I'd take from McDonald's to a French restaurant of my own is the fry vat computer. It really works." He seemed to have both the diligence and the style to run a personalized restaurant. Of course he may not have had the capital.

"So basically I would tell that girl [bringing me back to Damita] to find a different job. She's thinking too much and it slows things down. The way the system is set up, I don't need that in a register person, and they don't need it in me."

"Jon," I said, trying to be tactful, "I don't exactly know why you stay at McDonald's."

"As a matter of fact, I have already turned in my resignation.

"You mean you're not a McDonald's manager any more?" I was dismayed.

"I quit once before and they asked me to stay."

"I have had such a hard time getting a full-fledged manager to talk to me and now I don't know whether you count."

"They haven't actually accepted my resignation yet. You know I heard of this guy in another region who said he was going to leave and they didn't believe him. They just wouldn't accept his resignation. And you know what he did? One day, at noon, he just emptied the store, walked out, and locked the door behind him."

For a second Jon seemed to drift away on that beautiful image. It was like the kids telling me about Jason, the crewman who just walked out the back door.

"You know what that means to close a McDonald's at noon, to do a zero hour at lunch?"

"Jon," I said. "This has been fantastic. You are fantastic. I don't think anyone could explain the computers to me the way you do. But I want to talk to someone who's happy and moving up in the McDonald's system. Do you think you could introduce me to a manager who . . . "

"You won't be able to."

"How come?"

"First of all, there's the media hotline. If any press comes around or anyone is writing a book I'm supposed to call the regional office immediately and they will provide someone to talk to you. So you can't speak to a real corporation person except by arrangement with the corporation.

"Second, you can't talk to a happy McDonald's manager because 98 percent are miserable.

"Third of all, there is no such thing as a McDonald's manager. The computer manages the store."

KRISTIN KOVACIC

Kovacic was born and raised in Pittsburgh, where she has continued to work as a freelance editor and writer. Her story "A Place" appeared in the Cimarron Review, *and she has published other fiction and essays in* Kansas Quarterly, Carolina Quarterly, *and* River Styx. *She has studied contemporary working-class writing and worked on a television poetry project, "Woman to Woman on Lifetime."*

She writes about her family: "I come from a family of workers. We are all . . . excellent employees. We stay at jobs for lifetimes. Those of us who are not in unions get engraved pens and trivets from our employers. Dependable, our word" ("First Person: Being Pittsburgh," Pittsburgh Post-Gazette, *March 24, 1999). Her grandfather was a streetcar operator, her father, the focus of the selection that follows, an electrician.*

What her article relates about changes in the relationships between workers and management at Carnegie-Mellon University applies in many ways to other major private universities. These have become among the largest employers in cities like New Haven, Chicago, and Durham, and they have often imitated the most problematic features of corporate personnel policies, especially in relation to nonteaching staff.

"Proud to Work for the University"

In June 1958 Bogdan Kovacic, my father, emigrated from Zagreb, Yugoslavia, to Pittsburgh, Pennsylvania. As he likes to tell the story, he had a quarter in his pocket as the train rolled into Penn Station, and he used that to buy some crackers, hedging his bets against his next meal. He was twenty-six years old and spoke little English. He had left behind family, all of his good friends, his teammates from the professional handball team he played for. He was alone, he figured, and about to see the world.

This is part of the myth of my family, a story familiar to many Pittsburghers with immigrant roots. I'm afraid I am about to tell you a very old story.

Jobs, in 1958, were plentiful in Pittsburgh. Cousin Francie got him in at the plate factory. He hauled plates, dropping them now and then and making a big crash. He went to English classes at night, penciled neat meaningless sentences in a grammar book I have here—"Only a few friends are bidden to come," and, with emphasis, "You are never too old to learn." He signed his new American name, Andrew, over and over in the margins. He learned the questions he'd soon have to answer: "Are you a Bolshevik, anarchist, communist, or polygamist?" "What does Thanksgiving Day mean?" He met my mother, practiced his new words.

Trained as an electrician in Zagreb, he looked for work in his field. A friend told him he could get him in at the mill, and he went to have a look: the heat, the smoke, the filth over everything. He said no thanks; he'd have to work in hell soon enough. He found a job as an electrician at West Penn Hospital, good clean work. He was promoted to foreman. He bought a Chevy, sky blue.

Then we were born: my brother Andy, my sister Lara, and I. This, apparently, changed everything. He started night school again, and, with an electrical degree from Allegheny Technical Institute, he landed a job at Carnegie Mellon University (CMU) in 1969—two years before Richard Cyert assumed the presidency of the university. I remember the day Dad started, the new uniform my mother pressed off, and the first time the promise was made to us: you will get an education there. At that time, all Carnegie Mellon University employees were promised full undergraduate tuition for their children who were accepted there. That day, too, was the first time the challenge was set down: you will have to do well enough in school to be accepted. I was six, my brother seven, my sister was learning to crawl. It was a challenge we took very seriously; it was, we figured, our shot at seeing the world.

In those days we were required, on the first day of school, to say our names and what our fathers did for a living. One by one the kids would recite their names and then, simply, "J&L" or "Homestead," or "Duquesne Works." I would wait my turn, and then somewhat haughtily announce, "My dad is an electrician at Carnegie Mellon University. I'm going to college there, free." I told people even when they didn't ask me.

Carnegie Mellon became our identity, the greatest part of our family myth. While the men in the mills, our neighbors, were making much more money than Dad, locked into contracts in the glory days of steel, he, at least, had *invested*, had guaranteed our futures. We got Carnegie Mellon sweatshirts, tee-shirts, and notebooks for our birthdays. We cheered the buggys at carnival. When Dad worked weekends, we'd sometimes visit him on campus and ride in his little electric car, surveying what we knew would someday be ours—our library, our gymnasium, our student union. At night, passing by, we saw the beacon light in Hamerschlag Hall which Dad had installed. "That's my light," he'd say, and there it was, beckoning.

We also participated, through him, in Carnegie Mellon's road to academic glory. My dad didn't work at a factory, he worked for the university—among artists, engineers, and scientists. I didn't, for most of my early lifetime, see any fundamental difference between what my father and a professor of electrical engineering did for a living. They both worked for the university.

My father worked on experiments with monkeys and with robots. He helped harness energy from still water, bringing the physicist home for dinner after their hard day's work. Dad's work allowed Kathleen Mulcahy, the glass artist, to safely power her magnificent kiln. When he brought home the beautiful vase she made for him, my mother set it on the television set in the living room, eventually decorating the whole room around it—such colors we had never thought of bringing together. If my father was never going to see the world, Carnegie Mellon brought it closer to him and, by consequence, to us.

He was there when the computers arrived, the machines that would launch Carnegie Mellon's international star. I remember sitting at the dinner table while Dad told us about the computers, how, when we got to college, there would be a computer for every student; how we'd find a book in the library just by pushing a button; how there might not *be* any more books in the library, the computer taking over every aspect of our education. I remember being somewhat skeptical—this was long before *computer* was a household word, much less a household item. But, finally, I believed. Dad had the plans; he knew what was coming. He was the man who powered those glorious machines, who would later coordinate the installation of the "Andrew" computer network.

In 1981 I arrived and began my Carnegie Mellon education. On my first day of my first class—a core curriculum sociology course—we read about the concept of class in American society. We learned how to identify the working class from the middle class; there were just a few simple rules. The working class, my textbook said, works with its hands or, in the case of women, does clerical work like typing or filing. I did a little figuring. My mother is a secretary. My father is an electrician. His hands can get very dirty when he works, and he is scrupulous about washing them. He always carries Band-Aids in his wallet, ready for the daily cuts he gets at work, usually on his hands.

You can identify the working class, my textbook said, by the arrangement of their homes. The working class keeps its television set in the living room, for example, while the middle class keeps it in another place, like a den. I thought about our living room, Kathleen Mulcahy's vase crowning the television like a jewel. I thought for the very first time, that I was working-class. It was a genuine surprise.

I'm told that Andrew Carnegie founded Carnegie Institute of Technology for the education of the working classes of Pittsburgh. Long before I arrived, that mission had been abandoned as unprestigious and, more to the point, unprofitable. My classmates were from out of town, the daughters and sons of doctors, entrepreneurs, foreign financiers. Many of them rarely saw their parents, much less ran into them in Baker Hall, fixing a switch box. I learned the difference between an electrician and an electrical engineer. None of that bothered me; it surprised me, opening my picture of the world, and where I fit into it, much wider. Likewise, much about my life surprised my friends, whom I would bring home with me on holidays and weekends, introducing them to a genuine working-class home, television set and all. During my years in school my parents responded generously to CMU's requests for giving from parents, believing, in a way that other parents could not, that the money was going to the university's collective pot, whose assets were essentially our own. They also, I think, enjoyed the letters that came to the house afterwards: "Dear Mr. and Mrs. Kovacic, thank you for your generous gift."

In May 1985 I graduated, valedictorian of my college. I was selected to deliver the student commencement address, and on that day, under the big tent, a number of our family dreams came together. My father was sitting, suit and tie, in the audience. My sister, who had just been accepted for admission in the fall, sat next to him, checking out her campus. My brother, who, after receiving his associates' degree in forestry from Penn State University, was hired by CMU as a gardener—following my father's path—stood on the edge of the tent in his uniform. His boss had given him special permission to attend; normally the gardeners have to stay in their shop during the ceremonies. I dedicated the speech to my father, and I used my remarks to remind my classmates about the wonder, the absolute fortune, that we were going to do our work in life with questions, theories, problems, and poems—not with our backs, not with our bleeding hands. "Very well done," President Cyert said, shaking my hand on the dais. He told the audience that he was pleased to see the daughter of a staff member be so successful at the university.

When I think about that day now, the memory is very sweet, but I am also reminded that certain dread wheels were already in motion. The university, at the time of my graduation, was about to divide the workers' union (SEIU Local 29), selling off the janitors to a management firm (ABM) and cutting them off from Carnegie Mellon benefits, including tuition benefits. Those people, many of whom were Dad's friends, no longer worked for the university. Shortly after my graduation the administration dropped university from its official name, suggesting that it was more like a corporation than an institution of higher education, more like a factory than a school.

Contract battles for Dad's union became increasingly difficult to win. The administration, which for years claimed that its pay scale could never compete with the steel industry's, took advantage of the labor climate in the wake of steel's collapse to demand concessions. The administration hired outside firms to "consult" on the efficiency of the physical plant. There were layoffs. One of those firms became the manager of Carnegie Mellon's building and maintenance operations introducing suspicion among the physical plant workers—in spite of the administration's written assurances—that there would be further layoffs and that what had happened to the janitors might eventually happen to them.

In May 1990 my sister graduated with high honors, and we gathered again under the tent, to celebrate again the fulfillment of Dad's promise. President Cyert, saying his last farewells, recalled the achievements of his twenty-one years in office, the remarkable rise of Pittsburgh's Carnegie Tech to the global institution called Carnegie Mellon. My father, in the audience, could look back on those very same years, knowing that he had had a hand in all of it and that he had, in spite of all of the hard, physical work, made a very good investment in a growing institution. A steel mill might close, rust, and be razed to a clear toxic field, like the J&L South Side works he passed every day on his way to Oakland. But the university would always be there.

My sister and I were on our way. My brother was doing well in his job. Dad had three years until he could retire, and he was already planning. He would play more tennis (he is still, at sixty, a remarkable athlete). He and my mother would travel, back to Yugoslavia, where his family still lives, and to the other parts of the world they hadn't gotten around to seeing.

In June, after the tent had come down and the campus emptied out, the faculty and students returning to the cities that they come from, Dad reported to work, punched his clock. He was told not to work but to go directly through a door that closed behind him and seventeen other people, including two-thirds of all of the university's electricians, who were about to lose their jobs. They were told, for the first time, that there was a budget crisis that would require layoffs. They were told to turn in their keys and to be off the campus grounds by 10 A.M. They saw university police as they emerged, dazed by the blind-sided blow. "Like criminals," my mother told me, through tears, over the phone. She didn't think about the cost, the financial straits this would place them in. She thought about betrayal. "They treated him like a criminal, after all those years."

My father harbored no illusions about Carnegie Mellon's benevolence. He had seen, over the years, the university's antagonism toward its union. But in 1969 he had signed what he thought was a lifetime contract—he would give them a lifetime of hard labor; they would educate his children and allow him to retire, not comfortably, but in peace. It was not an extravagant plan.

Unfortunately for him, the Carnegie Mellon that let him go was not the university that had hired him, or perhaps, sadly, it was. How could he have known that the master plan of the global university, like that of a global corporation, included the abandonment of its responsibility to the blue-collar workers in its community, not to mention its utter disregard for their intelligence and pride? At the same moment that my father and sixteen other skilled construction and maintenance workers were shown, by an armed guard, the door, the administration announced the acceptance of a five million dollar gift from Paul Mellon toward new campus construction. Who, these men and women were forced to wonder, would be doing it? Who would design, construct, wire, and maintain the growth for which, as Dr. Cyert so elegantly phrased it for the reporters, "Carnegie Mellon's appetite continues to grow the larger [it] gets?" The arithmetic is tragically easy to do, even without a Carnegie Mellon education—why support loyal, lifetime employees when you can buy contracted work for less? At the same moment that my father faced the prospect of finding, at sixty, a new job, President Cyert eased into his retirement. The administration, as reported by the *Pittsburgh Post-Gazette*, was then finalizing plans to purchase a $1.9 million Sewickley estate for its new president, his wife, and their six horses.

"The emerging global company is divorced from where it produces its goods," Robert B. Reich, lecturer in public policy at the Harvard University Kennedy School of Government [now Secretary of Labor], told the *New York Times.* "It has no heart, and it has no soul. It is a financial enterprise designed to maximize profits. Many of the people who inhabit it may be fine, upstanding human beings, but the organization has its own merciless logic."

It was just this merciless logic, I have to believe, that caused my father to lose his job. Carnegie Mellon is a thriving, growing institution. It is not facing a budgetary crisis; it is facing a moral one—whether to cultivate the community of a university or the elite positioning of a corporation. My family felt, with great pride, a part of an educational community, until, without ceremony, Carnegie Mellon abandoned its role in it. Now, like too many other working-class families in Pittsburgh, we're left with the caution that it was foolish to have believed.

So now my father, writing in the workbook he received at his "transition" seminar, dutifully answers their questions. What do you feel is your greatest accomplishment? "My greatest accomplishment," he writes in the clipped, impossible language he has never learned to love, "is my family." What was most satisfying about your previous employment? "I was very proud," he says, carefully calling up the past tense, "to work for the university."

JUNOT DÍAZ

(B.1969)

Junot Díaz's first book, Drown *(1996), from which the following story is taken, moves between the different, yet equally grim, terrain of the barrios of the Dominican Republic and those of the Bronx and New Jersey. His narrators, mainly boys and young men, drug dealers, "illegal" workers, everhopeful laborers, trace a kind of cultural nausea generated by life in a community "separated from all other communities by a six-lane highway and the dump." Díaz is concerned with growing up between cultures, Spanish and English, the Caribbean and decaying suburbs, a fatherless home and one oppressed by fatherly officiousness and dishonesty. Díaz writes in prose some have characterized as "sociological," but in fact it sensitively registers the fears, desires, and anxieties of a variety of Dominican males, struggling to establish some foothold in the inescapable nation, the United States.*

Díaz graduated from Rutgers University and then completed the MFA program at Cornell. He has taught creative writing at Syracuse University and has worked in a copy store. His stories have appeared in the New Yorker, *among other magazines.*

EDISON, NEW JERSEY

The first time we try to deliver the Gold Crown the lights are on in the house but no one lets us in. I bang on the front door and Wayne hits the back and I can hear our double drum shaking the windows. Right then I have this feeling that someone is inside, laughing at us.

This guy better have a good excuse, Wayne says, lumbering around the newly planted rosebushes. This is bullshit.

You're telling me, I say but Wayne's the one who takes this job too seriously. He pounds some more on the door, his face jiggling. A couple of times he raps on the windows, tries squinting through the curtains. I take a more philosophical approach; I walk over to the ditch that has been cut next to the road, a drainage pipe half filled with water, and sit down. I smoke and watch a mama duck and her three ducklings scavenge the grassy bank and then float downstream like they're on the same string. Beautiful, I say but Wayne doesn't hear. He's banging on the door with the staple gun.

At nine Wayne picks me up at the showroom and by then I have our route planned out. The order forms tell me everything I need to know about the customers we'll be dealing with that day. If someone is just getting a fifty-two-inch card table delivered then you know they aren't going to give you too much of a hassle but they also aren't going to tip. Those are your Spotswood, Sayreville and Perth Amboy deliveries. The pool tables go north to the rich suburbs—Livingston, Ridgewood, Bedminster.

You should see our customers. Doctors, diplomats, surgeons, presidents of universities, ladies in slacks and silk tops who sport thin watches you could trade in for a car, who wear comfortable leather shoes. Most of them prepare for us by laying down a path of yesterday's *Washington Post* from the front door to the game room. I make them pick it all up. I say: Carajo, what if we slip? Do you know what two hundred pounds of slate could do to a floor? The threat of property damage puts the chop-chop in their step. The best customers leave us alone until the bill has to be signed. Every now and then we'll be given water in paper cups. Few have offered us more, though a dentist from Ghana once gave us a six-pack of Heineken while we worked.

Sometimes the customer has to jet to the store for cat food or a newspaper while we're in the middle of a job. I'm sure you'll be all right, they say. They never sound too sure. Of course, I say. Just show us where the silver's at. The customers ha-ha and we ha-ha and then they agonize over leaving, linger by the front door, trying to memorize everything they own, as if they don't know where to find us, who we work for.

Once they're gone, I don't have to worry about anyone bothering me. I put down the ratchet, crack my knuckles and explore, usually while Wayne is smoothing out the felt and doesn't need help. I take cookies from the kitchen, razors from the bathroom cabinets. Some of these houses have twenty, thirty rooms. On the ride back I figure out how much loot it would take to fill up all that space. I've been caught roaming around plenty of times but you'd be surprised how quickly someone believes you're looking for the bathroom if you don't jump when you're discovered, if you just say, Hi.

After the paperwork's been signed, I have a decision to make. If the customer has been good and tipped well, we call it even and leave. If the customer has been an ass—maybe they yelled, maybe they let their kids throw golf balls at us—I ask for the bathroom. Wayne will pretend that he hasn't seen this before; he'll count the drill bits while the customer (or their maid) guides the vacuum over the floor. Excuse me, I say. I let them show me the way to the bathroom (usually I already know) and once the door is shut I cram bubble bath drops into my pockets and throw fist-sized wads of toilet paper into the toilet. I take a dump if I can and leave that for them.

Most of the time Wayne and I work well together. He's the driver and the money man and I do the lifting and handle the assholes. Tonight we're on our way to Lawrenceville and he wants to talk to me about Charlene, one of the showroom girls, the one with the blowjob lips. I haven't wanted to talk about women in months, not since the girlfriend.

I really want to pile her, he tells me. Maybe on one of the Madisons.

Man, I say, cutting my eyes towards him. Don't you have a wife or something?

He gets quiet. I'd still like to pile her, he says defensively.

And what will that do?

Why does it have to *do* anything?

Twice this year Wayne's cheated on his wife and I've heard it all, the before and the after. The last time his wife nearly tossed his ass out to the dogs. Neither of the women seemed worth it to me. One of them was younger than Charlene. Wayne can be a moody guy and this is one of those nights; he slouches in the driver's seat and swerves through traffic, riding other people's bumpers like I've told him not to do. I don't need a collision or a four-hour silent treatment so I try to forget that I think his wife is good people and ask him if Charlene's given him any signals.

He slows the truck down. Signals like you wouldn't believe, he says.

On the days we have no deliveries the boss has us working at the showroom, selling cards and poker chips and mankala boards. Wayne spends his time skeezing the salesgirls and dusting shelves. He's a big goofy guy—I don't understand why the girls dig his shit. One of those mysteries of the universe. The boss keeps me in the front of the store, away from the pool tables. He knows I'll talk to the customers, tell them not to buy the cheap models. I'll say shit like, Stay away from those Bristols. Wait until you can get something real. Only when he needs my Spanish will he let me help on a sale. Since I'm no good at cleaning or selling slot machines I slouch behind the front register and steal. I don't ring anything up, and pocket what comes in. I don't tell Wayne. He's too busy running his fingers through his beard, keeping the waves on his nappy head in order. A hundred-buck haul's not unusual for me and back in the day, when the girlfriend used to pick me up, I'd buy her anything she wanted, dresses, silver rings, lingerie. Sometimes I blew it all on her. She didn't like the stealing but hell, we weren't made out of loot and I liked going into a place and saying, Jeva, pick out anything, it's yours. This is the closest I've come to feeling rich.

Nowadays I take the bus home and the cash stays with me. I sit next to this three-hundred-pound rock-and-roll chick who washes dishes at the Friendly's. She tells me about the roaches she kills with her water nozzle. Boils the wings right off them. On Thursday I buy myself lottery tickets—ten Quick Picks and a couple of Pick 4s. I don't bother with the little stuff.

The second time we bring the Gold Crown the heavy curtain next to the door swings up like a Spanish fan. A woman stares at me and Wayne's too busy knocking to see. Muñeca, I say. She's black and unsmiling and then the curtain drops between us, a whisper on the glass. She had on a t-shirt that said *No Problem* and didn't look like she owned the place. She looked more like the help and couldn't have been older than twenty and from the thinness of her face I pictured the rest of her skinny. We stared at each other for a second at the most, not enough for me to notice the shape of her ears or if her lips were chapped. I've fallen in love on less.

Later in the truck, on the way back to the showroom Wayne mutters, This guy is dead. I mean it.

The girlfriend calls sometimes but not often. She has found herself a new boyfriend, some zángano who works at a record store. *Dan* is his name and the way she says it, so painfully gringo, makes the corners of my eyes narrow. The clothes I'm sure this guy tears from her when they both get home from work—the chokers, the rayon skirts from the Warehouse, the lingerie—I bought with stolen money and I'm glad that none of it was earned straining my back against hundreds of pounds of raw rock. I'm glad for that.

The last time I saw her in person was in Hoboken. She was with *Dan* and hadn't yet told me about him and hurried across the street in her high clogs to avoid me and my boys, who even then could sense me turning, turning into the motherfucker who'll put a fist through anything. She flung one hand in the air but didn't stop. A month before the zángano, I went to her house, a friend visiting a friend, and her parents asked me how business was, as if I balanced the books or something. Business is outstanding, I said.

That's really wonderful to hear, the father said.

You betcha.

He asked me to help him mow his lawn and while we were dribbling gas into the tank he offered me a job. A real one that you can build on. Utilities, he said, is nothing to be ashamed of.

Later the parents went into the den to watch the Giants lose and she took me into her bathroom. She put on her makeup because we were going to a movie. If I had your eyelashes, I'd be famous, she told me. The Giants started losing real bad. I still love you, she said and I was embarrassed for the two of us, the way I'm embarrassed at those afternoon talk shows where broken couples and unhappy families let their hearts hang out.

We're friends, I said and Yes, she said, yes we are.

There wasn't much space so I had to put my heels on the edge of the bathtub. The cross I'd given her dangled down on its silver chain so I put it in my mouth to keep it from poking me in the eye. By the time we finished my legs were bloodless, broomsticks inside my rolled-down baggies and as her breathing got smaller and smaller against my neck, she said, I do, I still do.

Each payday I take out the old calculator and figure how long it'd take me to buy a pool table honestly. A top-of-the-line, three-piece slate affair doesn't come cheap. You have to buy sticks and balls and chalk and a score keeper and triangles and French tips if you're a fancy shooter. Two and a half years if I give up buying underwear and eat only pasta but even this figure's bogus. Money's never stuck to me, ever.

Most people don't realize how sophisticated pool tables are. Yes, tables have bolts and staples on the rails but these suckers hold together mostly by gravity and by the precision of their construction. If you treat a good table right it will outlast you. Believe me. Cathedrals are built like that. There are Incan roads in the Andes that even today you couldn't work a knife between two of the cobblestones. The sewers that the Romans built in Bath were so good that they weren't replaced until the 1950s. That's the sort of thing I can believe in.

These days I can build a table with my eyes closed. Depending on how rushed we are I might build the table alone, let Wayne watch until I need help putting on the slate. It's better when the customers stay out of our faces, how they react when we're done, how they run fingers on the lacquered rails and suck in their breath, the felt so tight you couldn't pluck it if you tried. Beautiful, is what they say and we always nod, talc on our fingers, nod again, beautiful.

The boss nearly kicked our asses over the Gold Crown. The customer, an asshole named Pruitt, called up crazy, said we were *delinquent.* That's how the boss put it. Delinquent. We knew that's what the customer called us because the boss doesn't use words like that. Look boss, I said, we knocked like crazy. I mean, we knocked like federal marshals. Like Paul Bunyan. The boss wasn't having it. You fuckos, he said. You butthogs. He tore us for a good two minutes and then *dismissed* us. For most of that night I didn't think I had a job so I hit the bars, fantasizing that I would bump into this cabrón out with that black woman while me and my boys were cranked but the next morning Wayne came by with that Gold Crown again. Both of us had hangovers. One more time, he said. An extra delivery, no overtime. We hammered on the door for ten minutes but no one answered. I jimmied with the windows and the back door and I could have sworn I heard her behind the patio door. I knocked hard and heard footsteps.

We called the boss and told him what was what and the boss called the house but no one answered. OK, the boss said. Get those card tables done. That night, as we lined up the next day's paperwork, we got a call from Pruitt and he didn't use the word delinquent. He wanted us to come late at night but we were booked. Two-month waiting list, the boss reminded him. I looked over at Wayne and wondered how much money this guy was pouring into the boss's ear. Pruitt said he was *contrite* and *determined* and asked us to come again. His maid was sure to let us in.

What the hell kind of name is Pruitt anyway? Wayne asks me when we swing onto the parkway.

Pato name, I say. Anglo or some other bog people.

Probably a fucking banker. What's the first name?

Just an initial, C. Clarence Pruitt sounds about right.

Yeah, Clarence, Wayne yuks.

Pruitt. Most of our customers have names like this, court case names: Wooley, Maynard, Gass, Binder, but the people from my town, our names, you see on convicts or coupled together on boxing cards.

We take our time. Go to the Rio Diner, blow an hour and all the dough we have in our pockets. Wayne is talking about Charlene and I'm leaning my head against a thick pane of glass.

Pruitt's neighborhood has recently gone up and only his court is complete. Gravel roams off this way and that, shaky. You can see inside the other houses, their newly formed guts, nailheads bright and sharp on the fresh timber. Wrinkled blue tarps protect wiring and fresh plaster. The driveways are mud and on each lawn stand huge stacks of sod. We park in front of Pruitt's house and bang on the door. I give Wayne a hard look when I see no car in the garage.

Yes? I hear a voice inside say.

We're the delivery guys, I yell.

A bolt slides, a lock turns, the door opens. She stands in our way, wearing black shorts and a gloss of red on her lips and I'm sweating.

Come in, yes? She stands back from the door, holding it open.

Sounds like Spanish, Wayne says.

No shit, I say, switching over. Do you remember me?

No, she says.

I look over at Wayne. Can you believe this?

I can believe anything, kid.

You heard us didn't you? The other day, that was you.

She shrugs and opens the door wider.

You better tell her to prop that with a chair. Wayne heads back to unlock the truck.

You hold that door, I say.

We've had our share of delivery trouble. Trucks break down. Customers move and leave us with an empty house. Handguns get pointed. Slate gets dropped, a rail goes missing. The felt is the wrong color, the Dufferins get left in the warehouse. Back in the day, the girlfriend and I made a game of this. A prediction game. In the mornings I rolled onto my pillow and said, What's today going to be like?

Let me check. She put her fingers up to her widow's peak and that motion would shift her breasts, her hair. We never slept under any covers, not in spring, fall or summer and our bodies were dark and thin the whole year.

I see an asshole customer, she murmured. Unbearable traffic. Wayne's going to work slow. And then you'll come home to me.

Will I get rich?

You'll come home to me. That's the best I can do. And then we'd kiss hungrily because this was how we loved each other.

The game was part of our mornings, the way our showers and our sex and our breakfasts were. We stopped playing only when it started to go wrong for us, when I'd wake up and listen to the traffic outside without waking her, when everything was a fight.

She stays in the kitchen while we work. I can hear her humming. Wayne's shaking his right hand like he's scalded his fingertips. Yes, she's fine. She has her back to me, her hands stirring around in a full sink, when I walk in.

I try to sound conciliatory. You're from the city?

A nod.

Where about?

Washington Heights.

Dominicana, I say. Quisqueyana. She nods. What street?

I don't know the address, she says. I have it written down. My mother and my brothers live there.

I'm Dominican, I say.

You don't look it.

I get a glass of water. We're both staring out at the muddy lawn.

She says, I didn't answer the door because I wanted to piss him off.

Piss who off?

I want to get out of here, she says.

Out of here?

I'll pay you for a ride.

I don't think so, I say.

Aren't you from Nueva York?

No.

Then why did you ask the address?

Why? I have family near there.

Would it be that big of a problem?

I say in English that she should have her boss bring her but she stares at me blankly. I switch over.

He's a pendejo, she says, suddenly angry. I put down the glass, move next to her to wash it. She's exactly my height and smells of liquid detergent and has tiny beautiful moles on her neck, all archipelago leading down into her clothes.

Here, she says, putting out her hand but I finish it and go back to the den.

Do you know what she wants us to do? I say to Wayne.

Her room is upstairs, a bed, a closet, a dresser, yellow wallpaper. Spanish *Cosmo* and *El Diario* thrown on the floor. Four hangers' worth of clothes in the closet and only the top dresser drawer is full. I put my hand on the bed and the cotton sheets are cool.

Pruitt has pictures of himself in his room. He's tan and probably has been to more countries than I know capitals for. Photos of him on vacations, on beaches, standing beside a wide-mouth Pacific salmon he's hooked. The size of his dome would have made Broca proud. The bed is made and his wardrobe spills out onto chairs and a line of dress shoes follows the far wall. A bachelor. I find an open box of Trojans in his dresser beneath a stack of boxer shorts. I put one of the condoms in my pocket and stick the rest under his bed.

I find her in her room. He likes clothes, she says.

A habit of money, I say but I can't translate it right; I end up agreeing with her. Are you going to pack?

She holds up her purse. I have everything I need. He can keep the rest of it.

You should take some of your things.

I don't care about that vaina. I just want to go.

Don't be stupid, I say. I open her dresser and pull out the shorts on top and a handful of soft bright panties fall out and roll down the front of my jeans. There are more in the drawer. I try to catch them but as soon as I touch their fabric I let everything go.

Leave it. Go on, she says and begins to put them back in the dresser, her square back to me, the movement of her hands smooth and easy.

Look, I say.

Don't worry. She doesn't look up.

I go downstairs. Wayne is sinking the bolts into the slate with the Makita. You can't do it, he says.

Why not?

Kid. We have to finish this.

I'll be back before you know it. A quick trip, in out.

Kid. He stands up slowly; he's nearly twice as old as me.

I go to the window and look out. New gingkoes stand in rows beside the driveway. A thousand years ago when I was still in college I learned something about them. Living fossils. Unchanged since their inception millions of years ago. You tagged Charlene, didn't you?

Sure did, he answers easily.

I take the truck keys out of the toolbox. I'll be right back, I promise.

My mother still has pictures of the girlfriend in her apartment. The girlfriend's the sort of person who never looks bad. There's a picture of us at the bar where I taught her to play pool. She's leaning on the Schmelke I stole for her, nearly a grand worth of cue, frowning at the shot I left her, a shot she'd go on to miss.

The picture of us in Florida is the biggest—shiny, framed, nearly a foot tall. We're in our bathing suits and the legs of some stranger frame the right. She has her butt in the sand, knees folded up in front of her because she knew I was sending the picture home to my moms; she didn't want my mother to see her bikini, didn't want my mother to think her a whore. I'm crouching next to her, smiling, one hand on her thin shoulder, one of her moles showing between my fingers.

My mother won't look at the pictures or talk about her when I'm around but my sister says she still cries over the breakup. Around me my mother's polite, sits quietly on the couch while I tell her about what I'm reading and how work has been.

Do you have anyone? she asks me sometimes.

Yes, I say.

She talks to my sister on the side, says, In my dreams they're still together.

We reach the Washington Bridge without saying a word. She's emptied his cupboards and refrigerator; the bags are at her feet. She's eating corn chips but I'm too nervous to join in.

Is this the best way? she asks. The bridge doesn't seem to impress her.

It's the shortest way.

She folds the bag shut. That's what he said when I arrived last year. I wanted to see the countryside. There was too much rain to see anything anyway.

I want to ask her if she loves her boss, but I ask instead, How do you like the States?

She swings her head across at the billboards. I'm not surprised by any of it, she says.

Traffic on the bridge is bad and she has to give me an oily fiver for the toll. Are you from the Capital? I ask.

No.

I was born there. In Villa Juana. Moved here when I was a little boy.

She nods, staring out at the traffic. As we cross over the bridge I drop my hand into her lap. I leave it there, palm up, fingers slightly curled. Sometimes you just have to try, even if you know it won't work. She turns her head away slowly, facing out beyond the bridge cables, out to Manhattan and the Hudson.

Everything in Washington Heights is Dominican. You can't go a block without passing a Quisqueya Bakery or a Quisqueya Supermercado or a Hotel Quisqueya. If I were to park the truck and get out nobody would take me for a deliveryman; I could be the guy who's on the street corner selling Dominican flags. I could be on my way home to my girl. Everybody's on the streets and the merengue's falling out of windows like TVs. When we reach her block I ask a kid with the sag for the building and he points out the stoop with his pinkie. She gets out of the truck and straightens the front of her sweatshirt before following the line that the kid's finger has cut across the street. Cuídate, I say.

Wayne works on the boss and a week later I'm back, on probation, painting the warehouse. Wayne brings me meatball sandwiches from out on the road, skinny things with a seam of cheese gumming the bread.

Was it worth it? he asks me.

He's watching me close. I tell him it wasn't.

Did you at least get some?

Hell yeah, I say.

Are you sure?

Why would I lie about something like that? Homegirl was an animal. I still have the teeth marks.

Damn, he says.

I punch him in the arm. And how's it going with you and Charlene?

I don't know, man. He shakes his head and in that motion I see him out on his lawn with all his things. I just don't know about this one.

We're back on the road a week later. Buckinghams, Imperials, Gold Crowns and dozens of card tables. I keep a copy of Pruitt's paperwork and when the curiosity finally gets to me I call. The first time I get the machine. We're delivering at a house in Long Island with a view of the Sound that would break you. Wayne and I smoke a joint on the beach and I pick up a dead horseshoe crab by the tail and heave it in the customer's garage. The next two times I'm in the Bedminster area Pruitt picks up and says, Yes? But on the fourth time she answers and the sink is running on her side of the phone and she shuts it off when I don't say anything.

Was she there? Wayne asks in the truck.

Of course she was.

He runs a thumb over the front of his teeth. Pretty predictable. She's probably in love with the guy. You know how it is.

I sure do.

Don't get angry.

I'm tired, that's all.

Tired's the best way to be, he says. It really is.

He hands me the map and my fingers trace our deliveries, stitching city to city. Looks like we've gotten everything, I say.

Finally. He yawns. What's first tomorrow?

We won't really know until the morning, when I've gotten the paperwork in order but I take guesses anyway. One of our games. It passes the time, gives us something to look forward to. I close my eyes and put my hand on the map. So many towns, so many cities to choose from. Some places are sure bets but more than once I've gone with the long shot and been right.

You can't imagine how many times I've been right.

Usually the name will come to me fast, the way the numbered balls pop out during the lottery drawings, but this time nothing comes: no magic, no nothing. It could be anywhere. I open my eyes and see that Wayne is still waiting. Edison, I say, pressing my thumb down. Edison, New Jersey.

CLOTHES MAKE THE WOMAN: THE SOCIAL DIMENSIONS OF CLASS

Section II concerns class and culture, in the broad, anthropological sense of that latter term. The works in this section concern the ways in which class inflects relationships, like those between parents and children (as in Olsen's "I Stand Here Ironing"), between siblings (as in Garland's "Up the Coulé"), between people and the institutions that often dominate their lives—schools, social agencies, stores (as in Yezierska's "Soap and Water" or Hunter's "Mom Luby and the Social Worker"). Here, too, writers ask and illustrate how factors such as clothing, where one lives and shops and takes vacations, what one buys and displays—what is often termed "lifestyle"—advertise, and also hide, class.

We are not only concerned in this section with divergences in consumption and exhibition—though those obviously play important roles in American society—but also with the ways in which the lessons of class are taught in everyday life (as in Forché's "As Children Together" or Allison's "Mama"), as well as how they are presented and studied in school and in the popular media. In other words, this section looks at the many forces apart from work that forge class, class consciousness, and class differences. While some of these texts are set in workplaces, many of them locate people at home (as in Jewett's "The Best China Saucer" or Gallagher's "3 A.M. Kitchen: My Father Talking"), in the neighborhood (as in Bambara's "The Lesson" or the excerpt from Galarza's *Barrio Boy*), and at schools (as in Smedley's *Daughter of Earth* and Glennon's essay about New Haven). Here we find people shopping, ironing, hanging out, growing up poor or rich, and coming to understand what such terms mean for them and for others.

CAROLYN STEEDMAN

(B. 1947)

Carolyn Steedman grew up in a working-class area of South London. That experience, and her mother's similar early life in Burnley, provide the basis for Landscapes for a Good Woman, *from which the following excerpt is taken. The book, partly autobiographical, deploys a variety of sociological, psychoanalytic, and historical methodologies in order better to understand the real dynamics of working-class women's lives. Steedman wishes to understand how it is, for example, that significant numbers of working people supported Conservative politicians, like Margaret Thatcher, despite the hostility of the Tories to the apparent self-interest of the working-class. Steedman is interested in exploring what to some has seemed the base materialism of many people of working-class origins, but which may better be seen as a legitimate desire for the good things in life that class inequality has denied them. She is also interested in exploring how gender produces profound differences in life-chances and outlook between working-class men and women.*

After graduating from the University of Sussex and Newnham College, Cambridge, Steedman taught in an elementary school, then worked at the Institute of Education in London, becoming a fellow in its Sociological Research Unit. Her first book, The Tidy House *(1983), won the Fawcett Society Book Award. It was followed by* Policing the Victorian Community *(1984), and by* Childhood, Culture, and Class in Britain *(1990). Steedman now teaches social history at the University of Warwick.*

FROM LANDSCAPE FOR A GOOD WOMAN

> . . . Stuff slippers and white cotton stockings,
> The lasses they mostly do wear,
> With a dimity corduroy petticoat,
> It is whiter than snow I declare;
> With a fringe or a flounce round the bottom
> These lasses they will have beside,
> And a sash for to go round their middle
> And to tie up in bunches behind.
>
> . . . The servant girls follow the fashions,
> As well as the best in the place:
> They'll dress up their heads like an owl, boys,
> And will think it no shame or disgrace.
> They will bind up their heads with fine ribbands,
> And a large bag of hair hangs behind;
> And when they do walk through the streets, boys,
> No peacock can touch them for pride.

('The Lasses' Resolution to Follow the Fashion',
c. 1870, in Roy Palmer,
*A Touch on the Times: Songs of Social Change,
1770–1914,* Penguin, 1974)

When I was three, before my sister was born, I had a dream. It remains quite clear across the years, the topography absolutely plain, so precise in details of dress that I can use them to place the dream in historical time. We were in a street, the street so wide and the houses so distant across the road that it might not have been a street at all; and the houses lay low with gaps between them, so that the sky filled a large part of the picture. Here, at the front, on this side of the wide road, a woman hurried along, having crossed from the houses behind. The perspective of the dream must have shifted several times, for I saw her once as if from above, moving through a kind of square, or crossing-place, and then again from the fixed point of the dream where I stood watching her, left forefront.

She wore the New Look, a coat of beige gaberdine which fell in two swaying, graceful pleats from her waist at the back (the swaying must have come from very high heels, but I didn't notice her shoes), a hat tipped forward from hair swept up at the back. She hurried, something jerky about her movements, a nervous, agitated walk, glancing round at me as she moved across the foreground. Several times she turned and came some way back towards me, admonishing, shaking her finger.

Encouraging me to follow in this way perhaps, but moving too fast for me to believe that this was what she wanted, she entered a revolving door of dark, polished wood, mahogany and glass, and started to go round and round, looking out at me as she turned. I wish I knew what she was doing, and what she wanted me to do.

In childhood, only the surroundings show, and nothing is explained. Children do not possess a social analysis of what is happening to them, or around them, so the landscape and the pictures it presents have to remain a background, taking on meaning later, from different circumstances. That dream is the past that lies at the heart of my present: it is my interpretative device, the means by which I can tell a story. My understanding of the dream built up in layers over a long period of time. Its strange lowered vista for instance, which now reminds the adult more than anything else of George Herriman's 'Krazy Kat' where buildings disappear and reappear from frame to frame, seems an obvious representation of London in the late forties and early fifties: all the houses had gaps in between because of the bombs, and the sky came closer to the ground than seemed right. I understood what I had seen in the dream when I learned the words 'gaberdine' and 'mahogany'; and I was born in the year of the New Look, and understood by 1951 and the birth of my sister, that dresses needing twenty yards for a skirt were items as expensive as children—more expensive really, because after 1948 babies came relatively cheap, on tides of free milk and orange juice, but good cloth in any quantity was hard to find for a very long time.

Detail like this provides retrospective labelling; but it is not evidence about a period of historical time. The only *evidence* that the dream offers is the feeling of childhood—all childhoods, probably—the puzzlement of the child watching from the pavement, wondering what's going on, what they, the adults, are up to, what they want from you, and what they expect you to do. It is evidence in this way, because as an area of feeling it is brought forward again and again to shape responses to quite different events. Memory alone cannot resurrect past time, because it is memory itself that shapes it, long after historical time has passed. The dream is not a fixed event of the summer of 1950; it has passed through many stages of use and exploration, and such reinterpretation gives an understanding that the child at the time can't possess: it's only recently that I've come to see who the woman in the New Look coat actually was.

Now, later, I see the time of my childhood as a point between two worlds: an older 'during the War', 'before the War', 'in the Depression', 'then'; and the place we inhabit now. The War was so palpable a presence in the first five years of my life that I still find it hard to believe that I didn't live through it. There were bomb-sites everywhere, prefabs on waste land, most things still on points, my mother tearing up the ration book when meat came off points, over my sister's pram, outside the library in the High Street in the summer of 1951, a gesture that still fills me with the desire to do something so defiant and final; and then looking across the street at a woman wearing a full-skirted dress, and then down at the forties straight-skirted navy blue suit she was still wearing, and longing, irritatedly, for the New Look; and then at us, the two living barriers to twenty yards of cloth. Back home, she said she'd be able to get it at the side door of the mill; but not here; not with you two . . .

My mother's story was told to me early on, in bits and pieces throughout the fifties, and it wasn't delivered to entertain, like my father's much later stories were, but rather to teach me lessons. There was a child, an eleven-year-old from a farm seven miles south of Coventry, sent off to be a maid-of-all-work in a parsonage in Burnley. She had her tin trunk, and she cried, waiting on the platform with her family seeing her off, for the through train to Manchester. They'd sent her fare, the people in Burnley; 'But think how she felt, such a little girl, she was only eleven, with nothing but her little tin box. Oh, she did cry.' I cry now over accounts of childhoods like this, weeping furtively over the reports of nineteenth-century commissions of inquiry into child labour, abandoning myself to the luxuriance of grief in libraries, tears staining the pages where Mayhew's little watercress girl tells her story. The lesson was, of course, that I must never, ever, cry for myself, for I was a lucky little girl: my tears should be for all the strong, brave women who gave me life. This story, which embodied fierce resentment against the unfairness of things, was carried through seventy years and three generations, and all of them, all the good women, dissolved into the figure of my mother, who was, as she told us, *a good mother*. She didn't go out dancing or drinking (gin, mother's ruin, was often specified. 'Your mother drank gin once,' my father told me years later, with nostalgic regret). She didn't go, as one mother she'd known, in a story of maternal neglect that I remember thinking was over the top at the time, and tie a piece of string round my big toe, dangle it through the window and down the front of the house, so that the drunken mother, returning from her carousing, she could tug at it, wake the child, get the front door open and send it down the shop for a basin of pie and peas. I still put myself to sleep by thinking about *not* lying on a cold pavement covered with newspapers.

The eleven-year-old who cried on Coventry station hated being a servant. She got out as soon as she could and found work in the weaving sheds—'she was a good weaver; six looms under her by the time she was sixteen'—married, produced nine children, eight of whom emigrated to the cotton mills of Massachusetts before the First World War, managed, 'never went before the Guardians'. It was much, much later that I learned from *One Hand Tied Behind Us* that four was the usual number of looms in Lancashire weaving towns. Burnley weavers were badly organized over the question of loom supervision, and my great-grandmother had six not because she was a good weaver, but because she was exploited. In 1916, when her daughter Carrie's husband was killed at the Somme, she managed that too, looking after the three-year-old, my mother, so that Carrie could go on working at the mill.

But long before the narrative fell into place, before I could dress the eleven-year-old of my imagination in the clothing of the 1870s, I knew perfectly well what that child had done, and how she had felt. She cried, because tears are cheap; and then she stopped, and got by, because no one gives you anything in this world. What was given to her, passed on to all of us, was a powerful and terrible endurance, the self-destructive defiance of those doing the best they can with what life hands out to them.

From a cotton town, my mother had a heightened awareness of fabric and weave, and I can date events by the clothes I wore as a child, and the material they were made of. Post-War children had few clothes, because of rationing, but not only scarcity, rather names like barathea, worsted, gaberdine, twill, jersey, lawn . . . fix them in my mind. The dream of the New Look must have taken place during or after the summer of 1950, because in it I wore one of my two summer dresses, one of green, one of blue gingham, which were made that year and which lasted me, with letting down, until I went to school.

Sometime during 1950, I think before the summer, before the dresses were made, I was taken north to Burnley and into the sheds, where one afternoon my mother visited someone she used to know as a child, now working there. The woman smiled and nodded at me, through the noise that made a surrounding silence. Afterwards, my mother told me that they had to lip-read: they couldn't hear each other speak for the noise of the looms. But I didn't notice the noise. The woman wore high platform-soled black shoes that I still believe I heard click on the bright polished floor as she walked between her looms. Whenever I hear the word 'tending' I always think of that confident attentiveness to the needs of the machines, the control over work that was unceasing, with half a mind and hands engaged, but the looms always demanding attention. When I worked as a primary-school teacher I sometimes retrieved that feeling with a particular clarity, walking between the tables on the hard floor, all the little looms working, but needing my constant adjustment.

The woman wore a dress that seemed very short when I recalled the picture through the next few years: broad shoulders, a straight skirt patterned with black and red flowers that hung the way it did—I know now—because it had some rayon in it. The post-War years were full of women longing for a full skirt and unable to make it. I wanted to walk like that, a short skirt, high heels, bright red lipstick, in charge of all that machinery.

This was the first encounter with the landscape of my mother's past. We came once again, on the last trip I made North before I was nineteen, during the autumn or winter of 1950 when, as I can now work out, my mother was pregnant with my sister. On this particular and first visit of the late spring, the world was still clear. On the edge of the town, it seemed like the top of the street, a little beck ran through some woods, with bluebells growing there, so that memory can tell that it was May. We paddled in the shallow water; this was the clean water that they used to use for the cotton; it came from another place, where the mills were before there was steam; you could see the gravel clear beneath. We didn't pick the flowers: we left them there for other people to enjoy. She wore her green tweed jacket; it was lucky she didn't have any stockings on otherwise she'd only have had to take them off; she laughed, she smiled: the last time.

At the back of the house, through the yard to the lane, the lavatory was perched over another stream; you could see the water running past if you looked down. In this back lane I played with another child, older than me, she was four: Maureen. She was a Catholic, my grandmother said, but I could play with her, she was a nice little girl, but they weren't like us: you could tell them by their eyes. It was the women who told you about the public world, of work and politics, the details of social distinction. My grandmother's lodger, the man who was to become her third husband when his wife died ten years later, stayed self-effacingly in the background as she explained these things. Anti-Catholicism propelled my mother's placing of herself in a public sphere. A few years later she often repeated the story of Molly, her best friend at school, the priest beckoning to the Catholic child from over the road, furtively passing a betting slip; the strain of the penny collections at church with a dozen mouths to feed at home.

As a teenage worker my mother had broken with a recently established tradition and on leaving school in 1927 didn't go into the sheds. She lied to me though when, at about the age of eight, I asked her what she'd done, and she said she'd worked in an office, done clerical work. Ten years later, on my third and last visit to Burnley and practising the accomplishments of the oral historian, I talked to my grandmother and she, puzzled, told me that Edna had never worked in any office, had in fact been apprenticed to a dry-cleaning firm that did tailoring and mending. On that same visit, the first since I was four, I found a reference written by the local doctor for my mother who, about 1930, applied for a job as a ward-maid at the local asylum, confirming that she was clean, strong, honest and intelligent. I wept over that, of course, for a world where some people might doubt her—my—cleanliness. I didn't care much about the honesty, and I knew I was strong; but there are people everywhere waiting for you to slip up, to show signs of dirtiness and stupidity, so that they can send you back where you belong.

She didn't finish her apprenticeship—I deduce that, rather than know it—sometime, it must have been 1934, came South, worked in Woolworth's on the Edgware Road, spent the War years in Roehampton, a ward-maid again, in the hospital where they mended fighter pilots' ruined faces. Now I can feel the deliberate vagueness in her accounts of those years: 'When did you meet daddy?'—'Oh, at a dance, at home.' There were no photographs. Who came to London first? I wish now that I'd asked that question. He worked on the buses when he arrived, showed me a canopy in front of a hotel once, that he'd pulled down on his first solo drive. He was too old to be called up (a lost generation of men who were too young for the first War, too old for the second). There's a photograph of him standing in front of the cabbages he'd grown for victory, wearing his Home Guard uniform. But what did he *do* after his time on the buses, and during the War years? Too late now to find out.

*

During the post-War housing shortage my father got an office job with a property company, and the flat to go with it. I was born in March 1947, at the peak of the Bulge, more babies born that month than ever before or after, and carried through the terrible winter of 1946–7. We moved to Streatham Hill in June 1951, to an estate owned by the same company (later to be taken over by Lambeth Council), and a few years after the move my father got what he wanted, which was to be in charge of the company's boiler maintenance. On his death certificate it says 'heating engineer'.

In the 1950s my mother took in lodgers. Streatham Hill Theatre (now a bingo hall) was on the pre-West End circuit, and we had chorus girls staying with us for weeks at a time. I was woken up in the night sometimes, the spare bed in my room being made up for someone they'd met down the Club, the other lodger's room already occupied.

I like the idea of being the daughter of a theatrical landlady, but that enterprise, in fact, provides me with my most startling and problematic memories. The girl from Aberdeen really did say 'Och, no, not on the table!' as my father flattened a bluebottle with his hand, but did he *really* put down a newspaper at the same table to eat his breakfast? I remember it happening, but it's so much like the books that I feel a fraud, a bit-part player in a soft and southern version of *The Road to Wigan Pier*.

I remember incidents like these, I think, because I was about seven, the age at which children start to notice social detail and social distinction, but also more particularly because the long lesson in hatred for my father had begun, and the early stages were in the traditional mode, to be found in the opening chapters of *Sons and Lovers* and Lawrence's description of the inculcated dislike of Mr Morrell, of female loathing for coarse male habits. The newspaper on the table is problematic for me because it was problematic for my mother, a symbol of all she'd hoped to escape and all she'd landed herself in. (It was at this time, I think, that she told me that her own mother, means-tested in the late 1920s, had won the sympathy of the Relieving Officer, who ignored the presence of the saleable piano because she kept a clean house, with a cloth on the table.)

Now, thirty years later, I feel a great regret for the father of my first four years, who took me out and who probably loved me, irresponsibly ('It's alright for him; he doesn't have to look after you'), and I wish I could tell him now, even though he really was a sod, that I'm sorry for the years of rejection and dislike. But we were forced to choose, early on, which side we belonged to, and children have to come down on the side that brings the food home and gets it on the table. By 1955 I was beginning to hate him—because *he* was to blame, for the lack of money, for my mother's terrible dissatisfaction at the way things were working out.

Changes in the market place, the growth of real income and the proliferation of consumer goods that marked the mid-1950s, were used by my mother to measure out her discontent: there existed a newly expanding and richly endowed material world in which she was denied a place. The new consumer goods came into the house slowly, and we were taught to understand that our material deprivations were due entirely to my father's meanness. We had the first fridge in our section of the street (which he'd got cheap, off the back of a lorry, contacts in the trade) but were very late to acquire a television. I liked the new vacuum cleaner at first, because it meant no longer having to do the stairs with a stiff brush. But in fact it added to my Saturday work because I was expected to clean more with the new machine. Now I enjoy shocking people by telling them how goods were introduced into households under the guise of gifts for children: the fridge in the house of the children we played with over the road was given to the youngest as a birthday present—the last thing an eight-year-old wants. My mother laughed at this, scornfully: the clothes and shoes she gave us as birthday presents were conventional gifts for all post-War children, but the record player also came into the house in this way, as my eleventh birthday present. I wasn't allowed to take it with me when I left, though: it really wasn't mine at all.

What happened at school was my own business, no questions ever asked, no encouragement nor discouragement ever given. It became just the thing I did, like my mother's going out to work. Later, the material conditions for educational success were provided: a table in my room, a pattern of domestic work that allowed homework to be done. From the earliest time I was expected to be competent: to iron a blouse, scrub a floor, learn to read, pass an exam; and I was. (There was, though, as my sister was to discover later, all hell to pay if you failed.) Indifference to what happened at school was useful: learning is the one untouched area of my life. So in reconstructing the pattern of this neglect, I am surprised to find myself walking up the hill with my mother from school one afternoon. She was smiling a pleased smile, and working things out, I think it must have been 1956, the day she was told that I'd be going into the eleven-plus class and so (because everyone in the class passed the exam) would be going to grammar school. I remember the afternoon because I asked her what class we were; or rather, I asked her if we were middle class, and she was evasive. I answered my own question, said I thought we must be middle class, and reflected very precisely in that moment on my mother's black, waisted coat with the astrakhan collar, and her high-heeled black suede shoes, her lipstick. She looked so much better than the fat, spreading, South London mothers around us, that I thought we had to be middle class.

The coat and the lipstick came from her own 'If you want something, you have to go out and work for it. Nobody gives you anything; nothing comes free in this world.' About 1956 or 1957 she got an evening job in one of the espresso bars opening along the High Road, making sandwiches and frying eggs. She saved up enough money to take a manicuring course and in 1958 got her diploma, thus achieving a certified skill for the first time in her forty-five years. When I registered her death I was surprised to find myself giving 'manicurist' as her trade, for the possibility of a trade was something she seemed to have left behind in the North. She always worked in good places, in the West End; the hands she did were in *Vogue* once. She came home with stories and imitations of her 'ladies'. She told me how she 'flung' a sixpenny piece back at a titled woman who'd given it her as a tip: 'If you can't afford any more than that Madam, I suggest you keep it.' Wonderful!—like tearing up the ration books.

She knew where we stood in relation to this world of privilege and possession, had shown me the place long before, in the bare front bedroom where the health visitor spoke haughtily to her. Many women have stood thus, at the window, looking out, their children watching their exclusion: 'I remember as it were but yesterday,' wrote Samuel Bamford in 1849, 'after one of her visits to the dwelling of that "fine lady"' (his mother's sister, who had gone up in the world):

> she divested herself of her wet bonnet, her soaked shoes, and changed her dripping outer garments and stood leaning with her elbow on the window sill, her hand up to her check, her eyes looking upon vacancy and the tears trickling over her fingers.

What we learned now, in the early 1960s, through the magazines and anecdotes she brought home, was how the goods of that world of privilege might be appropriated, with the cut and fall of a skirt, a good winter coat, with leather shoes, a certain voice; but above all with clothes, the best boundary between you and a cold world.

It was at this time that her voice changed, and her Lancashire accent began to disappear. Earlier, years before, she'd entertained us in the kitchen by talking really broad, not her natural dialect but a stagey variety that always preceded a rapid shift to music-hall cockney for a rendering of 'She Was Only a Bird in a Gilded Cage':

> It's the same the whole world over
> Ain't it a bleeding shame
> It's the rich what gets the pleasure,
> It's the poor what gets the blame.

*

We weren't, I now realize by doing the sums, badly off. My father paid the rent, all the bills, gave us our pocket money, and a fixed sum of seven pounds a week house-keeping money, quite a lot in the late 1950s went on being handed over every Fri-day until his death, even when estrangement was obvious, and he was living most of the time with somebody else. My mother must have made quite big money in tips, for the records of her savings, no longer a secret, show quite fabulous sums being stored away in the early 1960s. When she died there was over £40,000 in building-society accounts. Poverty hovered as a belief. It existed in stories of the thirties, in a family history. Even now when a bank statement comes in that shows I'm over-drawn or when the gas bill for the central heating seems enormous, my mind turns to quite inappropriate strategies, like boiling down the ends of soap, and lighting fires with candle ends and spills of screwed up newspaper to save buying wood. I think about these things because they were domestic economies that we practised in the 1950s. We believed we were badly off because we children were expensive items, and all these arrangements had been made for us. 'If it wasn't for you two,' my mother told us, 'I could be off somewhere else.' After going out manicuring she started spending Sunday afternoons in bed, and we couldn't stay in the house or play on the doorstep for fear of disturbing her. The house was full of her terrible tiredness and her terrible resentment; and I knew it was all my fault.

Later, in 1977, after my father's death, we found out that they were never married, that we were illegitimate. In 1934 my father left his wife and two-year-old daughter in the North, and came to London. He and my mother had been together for at least ten years when I was born, and we think now that I was her hostage to fortune, the fac-tor that might persuade him to get a divorce and marry her. But the ploy failed.

Just before my mother's death, playing about with the photographs on the front bedroom mantelpiece, my niece discovered an old photograph under one of me at three. A woman holds a tiny baby. It's the early 1930s, a picture of the half-sister left behind. But I think I knew about her and her mother long before I looked them both in the face, or heard about their existence, knew that the half-understood adult conversations around me, the two trips to Burnley in 1951, the quarrels about 'her', the litany of 'she', 'she', 'she' from behind closed doors, made up the figure in the New Look coat, hurrying away, wearing the clothes that my mother wanted to wear, angry with me yet nervously inviting me to follow, caught finally in the revolving door. We have proper birth certificates, because my mother must have told a sim-ple lie to the registrar, a discovery about the verisimilitude of documents that wor-ries me a lot as a historian.

*

What kind of secret was the illegitimacy? It was a real secret, that is, the product of an agreed silence on the part of two people about a real event (or absence of event), and it was an extremely well-kept secret. Yet it revealed itself at the time. Often, before I found out about it in 1977 and saw the documents, the sense of my child-hood that I carried through the years was that people knew something about me, something that was wrong with me, that I didn't know myself. The first dramatic enactment of the idea that I should not embarrass people with my presence came in 1954 when the children we played with in the street suggested that I go to Sun-day school with them. It is a measure of the extreme isolation of our childhood that this event took on the status of entering society itself. Tremulous for days, I then stood reluctantly on the doorstep after Sunday dinner when they called for me, clutching the hot, acrid penny that I'd been told I'd need for the collection, saying: they might not want me to come; they won't want me. From inside the house I was told to stop making a fuss and get up the road. It was a High Anglican church. We were given a little book with space for coloured stamps showing scenes from the Gospels that you received for each attendance.

> Every stamp cries duty done
> Every blank cries shame;
> Finish what you have begun
> In the Saviour's name

exhorted the book inside the front cover (a familiar message; the first social confirmation of the structures of endurance that the domestic day imparted). I stayed to win many Church of England hymnals.

It wasn't I think, the legal impropriety that I knew about, the illegitimacy; rather I felt the wider disjuncture of our existence, its lack of authorization.

*

In 1954 the *Pirates of Penzance* was playing at the Streatham Hill Theatre, and we had one of the baritones as a lodger instead of the usual girls. He was different from them, didn't eat in the kitchen with us, but had my mother bake him potatoes and grate carrots which he ate in the isolation of the dining-room. He converted my mother to Food Reform, and when she made a salad of grated vegetables for Christmas dinner in 1955, my father walked out and I wished he'd taken us with him.

I've talked to other people whose mothers came to naturopathy in the 1950s, and it's been explained as a way of eating posh for those who didn't know about continental food. I think it did have a lot to do with the status that being different conferred, for in spite of the austerity of our childhood, we believed that we were better than other people, the food we ate being a mark of this, because our mother told us so—so successfully that even now I have to work hard at actually seeing the deprivations. But much more than difference, our diet had to do with the need, wrenched from restricted circumstances, to be in charge of the body. Food Reform promised an end to sickness if certain procedures were followed, a promise that was not, of course, fulfilled. I spent a childhood afraid to fall ill, because being ill would mean that my mother would have to stay off work and lose money.

But more fundamental than this, I think, a precise costing of our childhood lay behind our eating habits. Brussel sprouts, baked potatoes, grated cheese, the variation of vegetables in the summer, a tin of vegetarian steak pudding on Sundays and a piece of fruit afterwards is a monotonous but healthy diet, and I can't think of many cheaper ways to feed two children and feel you're doing your best for them at the same time. We can't ever have cost very much. She looked at us sometimes, after we'd finished eating. 'Good, Kay, eh?' What I see on her face now is a kind of muted satisfaction; she'd done her best, though her best was limited: not her fault. Children she'd grown up with had died in the 1930s: 'They hadn't enough to eat.'

She brought the food home at night, buying each day's supply when she got off the bus from work. My sister's job was to meet her at the bus-stop with the wheel basket so she didn't have to carry the food up the road. We ate a day's supply at a time, so there was never much in the house overnight except bread for breakfast and the staples that were bought on Saturday. When I started to think about these things I was in a position to interpret this way of living and eating as a variation of the spending patterns of poverty described in Booth's and Rowntree's great surveys at the turn of the century; but now I am sure that it was the cheapness of it that propelled the practice. We were a finely balanced investment, threatening constantly to topple over into the realm of demand and expenditure. I don't think, though, that until we left home we ever cost more to feed and clothe than that seven pounds handed over each week.

Now I see the pattern of our nourishment laid down, like our usefulness, by an old set of rules. At six I was old enough to go on errands, at seven to go further to pay the rent and the rates, go on the long dreary walk to the Co-op for the divi. By eight I was old enough to clean the house and do the weekend shopping. At eleven it was understood that I washed the breakfast things, lit the fire in the winter and scrubbed the kitchen floor before I started my homework. At fifteen, when I could legally go out to work, I got a Saturday job which paid for my clothes (except my school uniform, which was part of the deal, somehow). I think that until I drop I will clean wherever I happen to be on Saturday morning. I take a furtive and secret pride in the fact that I can do all these things, that I am physically strong, can lift and carry things that defeat other women, wonder with some scorn what it must be like to learn to clean a house when adult, and not to have the ability laid down as part of the growing self. Like going to sleep by contrasting a bed with a pavement, I sometimes find myself thinking that if the worst comes to the worst, I can always earn a living by my hands; I can scrub, clean, cook and sew: all you have in the end is your labour.

I was a better deal than my sister, because I passed the eleven plus, went to grammar school, would get a good job, marry a man who would in her words 'buy me a house and you a house. There's no virtue in poverty.' In the mid-1960s the Sunday colour supplements were full of pictures of student life, and she came to see a university as offering the same arena of advantage as the good job had earlier done. The dreary curtailment of our childhood was, we discovered after my mother's death, the result of the most fantastic saving: for a house, the house that was never bought. When I was about seventeen I learned that V. S. Naipaul had written *A House for Mr Biswas* in Streatham Hill, a few streets away from where we lived. There are interpretations now that ask me to see the house, both the fictional one and the one my mother longed for through the years, as the place of undifferentiated and anonymous desire, to see it standing in her dream as the objects of the fairy-tales do—princesses, golden geese, palaces—made desirable in the story simply because someone wants them. But for my mother, as for Mr Biswas, the house was valuable in itself because of what it represented of the social world: a place of safety, wealth and position, a closed door, a final resting place. It was a real dream that dictated the pattern of our days.

It seems now to have been a joyless childhood. There were neighbours who fed us meat and sweets, sorry for us, tea parties we went to that we were never allowed to return. I recall the awful depression of Sunday afternoons, my mother with a migraine in the front bedroom, the house an absolute stillness. But I don't *remember* the oddness; it's a reconstruction. What I remember is what I read, and playing Annie Oakley by myself all summer long in the recreation ground, running up and down the hill in my brown gingham dress, wearing a cowboy hat and carrying a rifle. Saturday morning pictures confirmed it all: women worked hard, earned their own living; carried guns into the bargain.

The essence of being a good child is taking on the perspective of those who are more powerful than you, and I was good in this way as my sister never was. A house up the road, Sunday afternoon 1958, plates of roast lamb offered. My sister ate, but I refused; not out of sacrifice, nor because I was resisting temptation (I firmly believed that meat would make me ill, as my mother said) but because I understood (though this is the adult's formulation rather than the ten-year-old's) that the price of the meal was condemnation of my mother's oddness, and I wasn't having that. I was a very upright child.

At eight I had my first migraine (I could not please her; I might as well join her; they stopped soon after I left home) and I started to get rapidly and relentlessly short-sighted. I literally stopped seeing for a very long time. It is through the development of symptoms like these, some of them neurotic, that I can site the disasters of our childhood, and read it from an outsider's point of view. I think I passed those years believing that we were unnoticed, *unseen*; but of course we were seen, and the evidence of witnesses was retrievable by memory much later on. In 1956 when the first migraine opened a tunnel of pain one June morning, my little sister developed acute psoriasis. My teacher was worried at my failing sight, I couldn't see the board by the spring of 1957 and read a book under my desk during arithmetic lessons. Did he send a note to my mother? Surely he must have done; what else could have shaken her conviction that glasses would be bad for me? He said to me the morning after he'd seen her, 'Your mother says you're doing exercises for your eyes; make sure you do them properly.' I thought he was being kind, and he was; but I preserved the voice that I might later hear the disapproval in it. I think they must have used the eleven-plus and the amount of blackboard work it involved as a lever, because I got a pair of glasses before the exam.

That afternoon she walked up the road with me, what had they told her? The next year, standing by my new teacher's desk, now in the eleven-plus class, he showed my book to what must have been a student on teaching practice. 'This one,' he said, 'has an inferiority complex.' I didn't understand, had no dictionary in which to look up the words, but preserved them by my own invented syllabary, rehearsing them, to bring out for much later scrutiny. I must in fact have known that people were watching, being witnesses, for some years later I started to play a game of inviting their comment and disapproval and then withdrawing the spectacle I had placed before their eyes, making them feel ashamed of the pity they had felt. By the time I was fifteen we'd all three of us given up, huddled with tiredness and irritation in the house where my father was only now an intermittent presence. The house was a tip; none of us did any housework any more; broken china wasn't replaced; at meal times my mother, my sister and I shared the last knife between us. Responsible now for my own washing, I scarcely did any, spent the winter changing about the layers of five petticoats I wore to keep warm, top to bottom through the cold months. One morning, asked by the games mistress why I wasn't wearing my school blouse, I said I hadn't been able to find it in the place I'd put it down the night before (not true; I hadn't a clean one), presenting thus a scene of baroque household disorganization, daring her to disapprove, hoping she would.

Ten years before this, school had taught me to read, and I found out for myself how to do it fast. By the time I was six I read all the time, rapidly and voraciously. You couldn't join the library until you were seven, and before that I read my Hans Christian Andersen from back to front when I'd read it from start to finish. Kay was my name at home, and I knew that Kay, the boy in 'The Snow Queen', was me, who had a lump of ice in her heart. I knew that one day I might be asked to walk on the edge of knives, like the Little Mermaid, and was afraid that I might not be able to bear the pain. Foxe's *Book of Martyrs* was in the old library, a one-volume edition with coloured illustrations for Victorian children, the text pruned to a litany of death by flame. My imagination was furnished with the passionate martyrdom of the Protestant North '. . . Every blank cries shame; Finish what you have begun, In the Saviour's name.'

I see now the relentless laying down of guilt, and I feel a faint surprise that I must interpret it that way. My sister, younger than me, with children of her own and perhaps thereby with a clearer measure of what we lacked, tells me to recall a mother who never played with us, whose eruptions from irritation into violence were the most terrifying of experiences; and she is there, the figure of nightmares, though I do find it difficult to think about in this way. Such reworking of past time is new, infinitely surprising; and against it I must balance what it felt like then, and the implications of the history given me in small doses; that not being hungry and having a warm bed to lie in at night, I had a good childhood, was better than other people; was a *lucky* little girl.

*

My mother had wanted to marry a king. That was the best of my father's stories, told in the pub in the 1960s, of how difficult it had been to live with her in 1937, during the Abdication months. Mrs Simpson was no prettier than her, no more clever than her, no better than her. It wasn't fair that a king should give up his throne for her, and not for the weaver's daughter. From a traditional Labour background, my mother rejected the politics of solidarity and communality, always voted Conservative, for the left could not embody her desire for things to be *really* fair, for a full skirt that took twenty yards of cloth, for a half-timbered cottage in the country, for the prince who did not come. For my mother, the time of my childhood was the place where the fairy-tales failed.

AGNES SMEDLEY
(1892–1950)

Smedley grew up among poor farmers, first in Missouri, and then after the turn of the century in Colorado, to which her father had brought the family in hopes that mining might provide a better livelihood. It did not, and Smedley was forced to work as a child even while she attended school. School was a conflicted experience: while the young Agnes intensely desired its educational values, she found—as the following passage from her Daughter of Earth *suggests— that it also taught painful lessons about class inequalities. Though she could not complete formal schooling, she was able to obtain a teaching position in rural New Mexico, which stimulated her desire for further education. For a brief year she attended Tempe Normal School (now Arizona State University), where she worked on the student newspaper—the beginnings of her life-*

long occupation as journalist and writer. She also met and married Ernest Brundin, with whom she moved to California, where they became part of a young community interested in socialism. But marriage raised insuperable problems of sexuality and of power in a relationship, and after six years and a number of separations, Smedley divorced Brundin and moved to New York.

There she became part of the Greenwich Village bohemian scene, and also became active with Margaret Sanger's Birth Control Review *and in the movement for Indian independence from British rule. During World War I, she was harassed as an opponent of America's ally, Great Britain. After the war, she moved to Germany to live with one of the leaders of the Indian liberation movement, Viren Chattopadhyaya. But the personal, sexual, and political conflicts of that movement tore Smedley apart, and she suffered from a personal breakdown, which psychotherapy and the writing of her autobiographical novel,* Daughter of Earth, *seem to have alleviated.*

In 1929, Smedley headed to India, where she was not welcome by the British authorities. She never made it past Shanghai. There she became deeply involved in the ongoing revolution in China. She worked as a correspondent for newspapers and magazines in Germany, England, and the United States, reporting on the "Long March" of the Red Army to Yenan province; she also became engrossed with dissident Chinese intellectuals, like the writer Lu Hsun and his students. For a time she organized efforts to provide medical supplies to the Chinese revolutionaries. But her primary work was as a journalist: she wrote a series of books that were significant in introducing the Chinese communist movement and its leaders, like Mao-tse Tung, Chou En-lai, and Chu Teh (about whom she wrote a notable book) to western readers.

After World War II broke out, Smedley returned to the United States, where she continued to write about developments in China for journals like The New Republic *and* The Nation. *For a period of time she lived at the writers' colony, Yaddo, near Saratoga Springs. In the post-war anti-communist hysteria, Smedley was accused of espionage or at the very least communist sympathies. Though no evidence of spying was ever produced and though Smedley was herself too individualistic to submit to the discipline of any party, she painfully felt the antagonism of fellow writers at Yaddo and determined to return to China. Seriously ill, she traveled to England where, undergoing an operation, she died of complications. For a time, during the Cold War, her books were removed from many library shelves, but with the renewal of a feminist movement in the 1960s, Smedley's work was among the first from the 1920s and 1930s to be restored to significance.*

FROM DAUGHTER OF EARTH

The sea is gray and colorless today, and the sun is hidden behind these cold northern mists. So was my life in those long years that followed: gray, colorless, groping, unachieving. With many things begun and none finished; or if finished, failures. There was but one thing on which I could depend—poverty and uncertainty.

Our tent, as mud-colored as the packed earth on which it stood, was near the banks of the Purgatory River. My father had pitched it on the low land lying between the railway tracks and the back yards of a row of little two- and three-room houses on the outskirts of the town of Trinidad. The railway had been built on an embankment of stone, slate and slag from the coal fields. Each day Beatrice and I and our two little brothers dragged gunny sacks along the tracks and filled them with coal that had fallen from the passing engines. And when the trains came rumbling by, we rushed to the side and waved at the fine people framed in the flashing windows.

If you looked across the river, beyond the row of little houses, you saw the gray-purple hills that guarded the approaches to the mountain peak beyond. These were the foothills of the Rockies. The mountain peak—Fisher's Peak—was over a mile and a half high, my father told us proudly, and it was just as if he had said:

"Look at my mountain that I have found for you."

"In the fall," he continued, "I'll take you campin' there and I'll shoot deer and we'll eat venison."

Everything was new and wonderful about us. Inside our tent three beds were wedged nicely along one side. The other side was almost a parlor, for there stood the treasured sewing machine and the clock my mother had brought with her, and there was also a rocking-chair. A rocking-chair, a clock, a sewing machine, a mountain, and venison . . . I enumerated our luxuries proudly.

My father built a board shed in front of the door to serve as the kitchen. There my mother worked while he was away earning three dollars a day. He had his own team and wagon and he hauled sand from the river bed to some place or other. Sometimes he hauled bricks. I would stand on the bridge that stretched over the river and watch him drive by, and in the evening I would run to meet him. He would seat me astride one of his horses and I trotted proudly homeward, hoping all the neighbors would see.

My mother was in a state of quiet, suppressed excitement all the time and she was humble and modest before my father now. For he was really making tremendous money. He talked in much bigger terms than formerly . . . he was going to be real rich. My mother kept her silence again.

After a time, lured by enthusiastic letters from my mother, Aunt Helen came, flaming and vital, to join us. She had grown even more beautiful; no rose petal was silkier than her skin. No queen had more confidence than she. And her laugh! When she laughed everyone laughed too, even when they didn't know why. Awkward, ugly girls who might easily have hated her for her beauty, stood gossiping with her over the back fence, and when she came darting in at their back doors their eyes were wistful and hungry. She helped them make lotions to soften and bleach their skins, she shampooed their hair with eggs to make it grow and glisten, she cut dress patterns for them, and when they had company on Sunday evenings she did up their hair in puffs and sometimes even loaned them a skirt or a blouse. She could well afford to be generous to others, for she had more than her share of beauty!

She considered what work was worthy of her—for she knew her value. The neighboring girls argued for the laundry. She hesitated: what did it pay? They must remember she had been a hired girl making six dollars a month, with keep, the last years where she worked! And—with a shade of pink mounting to her checks—the eldest son of the family had been her beau and she was still engaged to him.

My mother and father urged her to go out again as a hired girl, for girls in the laundry "went bad." She flashed. She was not afraid of hard work, but she could take care of herself anywhere! They must remember that the laundry offered more money and only ten hours of work a day, instead of the sunrise-to-sunset or midnight work in a private home. After much arguing and consulting all the neighbors she decided on the laundry, starting on the mangle at seven dollars a week, with her goal as the stiff shirt machine that paid eleven a week.

From the first she placed her weekly wages before my mother, and only under protest would she keep two dollars for herself.

"I've got nice things, Elly; you an' the kids hain't. You can't live like tramps all the time. When you've got nice things I'll keep more."

She loved colors and beautiful things, and what it must have cost her to sacrifice them like this no one ever knew. Yet for years it was her money—earned in one way or another—that furnished us with most of the colorful and good clothing we had. When Helen began to draw weekly wages she took an equal place with my father in our home. She was as valuable and she was as respected as he. The two of them talked to each other as equals; they laughed or they quarreled as equals. My mother would listen wistfully, her hands folded across her stomach, and when one of us children interrupted, she would scold:

"Don't you see your father an' Aunt Helen are talkin'?"

When my father quarreled with my mother, Helen would invariably step in and meet him halfway. For she loved her sister. Her hair would shake loose when she tossed her head and her voice would rise high in excitement.

"You can't talk like that to *me*, John Rogers! An' you can't boss me around like you boss Elly, for I pay my room and board here!"

So it was! She paid for her room and board and no man had the right to "boss her around." My mother did not; she could never toss her head proudly and freely and say, "I'm payin' for my keep here!"

My father was never quite certain of his ground with Helen when she was angry. For beneath her beauty lay a wild, untamed spirit and she had never been "broke in to the bridle," as men spoke of broken wives. She often threatened to "scratch his eyes out," and she meant every word of it. She was capable of attacking him even if he were fully three times her size. Sometimes her anger was so deep that speech failed her; at such times she would resort to a primitive and vulgar insult that seemed almost instinctive, it was so far removed from the daintiness of her usual behavior. She would whirl with a rapid movement and, just before flinging out of the room would, with a flash of her hands, hoist her skirts to the waist in the back. My father was left speechless with rage. There seemed no answer to such an insult!

We were now city people. Trinidad had fully five thousand inhabitants, but claimed ten. It had a grade school building, and a high school building reared its head among trees on the hill across the river; over there rich people lived. The high school and riches seemed to go together. Anyway we, who lived beyond the tracks, knew that we could never dream of going to high school.

The grade school building stood on the other side of the town, on a hill directly facing the old historic Santa Fé Trail that had first been traveled by the Indians, then the early Spaniards, and later by the white pioneers to the great Southwest. It wound near the foot of a jutting peak on top of which slept one of the earliest pioneers of the West. The school was the first grade school I had ever seen. Each day I took my little brother George by the hand and guided him there and we knew that we were treading holy ground, for my mother constantly spoke of it as such. The teachers were clean and seemed smoothly ironed; they wore tailored suits and white waists and spoke a language that I could at first hardly understand. My mother had explained to one of them on the first day that I was near ten years old and had been in the "third reader" in my last school. The teacher had gazed at her for a long time, her eyes traveling down over the calico dress, over the hands so big-veined and worn that they were almost black, and then to the wistful, tired face lit up by the beautiful blue-black eyes. The eyes were young—but the hands might have belonged to a scrubwoman of fifty.

"Yes," the teacher had remarked at last, "I understand."

She was a kind, young teacher. When I read before her in a trembling voice she smiled encouragingly at my eagerness and at my attempt to forget the room filled with well-dressed little boys and girls. Then she sent me to the board and dictated figures. The fear of being sent to a lower grade drove me forward. Yet I was terror-stricken. Figures always were my enemies. I put down numbers at random . . . a certain native cunning coming to my aid—I knew she would think I had only made a mistake. And so it was.

"How can you make such a mistake!" she protested. I gazed at her blankly but did not reply. She took the chalk and worked out the simple problem. I watched her hand so intently that even now, nearly twenty years later, I see exactly the figures she wrote and her long white hand with a gold ring on the third finger.

For weeks she continued this method. I memorized what she said and wrote, but I never understood. A row of figures held before my eyes was, and remains, like a row of soldiers standing before me ready to shoot when the top one gives the command, "Fire!"

I felt very shy and humble in that school. In the front seat on the outside row sat a little girl. Her skin was white, her hair was thick and nearly white, and her dresses, shoes and stockings were always white. When the teacher had asked about her father, she had replied, "My father is a doctor!" and I had stared at her fascinated. She sat very straight in her seat and the teacher always took her copy book and held it up for the class to see. The handwriting was as prim and clean as she was; the margins were broad and even; there was not one mistake. One day after school my fascination led me to follow her home; she lived in a large, low brick bungalow surrounded by a lawn with many flowers. The grass was cut as smooth as a window pane, everything was peaceful, orderly and quiet. Even the fence and gate were painted white.

On Mother's Day the white girl's mother came and sat near the teacher and didn't associate with the other women. My mother had put on a new calico dress with a belt, and I had walked proudly by her side to the school. She stood in the back of the room, apart from the well-dressed women, and her frightened eyes watched as they talked so easily with each other. After that she never went again. Yet to her the school remained a sacred place to which it was an honor to send her children.

One day our teacher stepped aside while another one entered and read to us from a book on Manners. I learned about eating with a fork and keeping the mouth closed when you chew. Then she read something about washing the teeth, but I had never heard of that before except that my mother sometimes put yellow soap on her finger and washed her teeth with it. But I would have been ashamed to ask her to actually buy a brush for me to use only on my teeth! The teacher read about bathing daily. How that could be done I could not imagine. For my mother washed clothes only on Monday and we children had to bathe in the last, clean rinsing water; the oldest one bathed first and the youngest one last.

Then the teacher read a chapter about sleeplessness. If unable to sleep, one should get up and take a walk; or one should have two beds in a room and change from one to the other; the fresh sheets produced sleep! I had never seen sheets on a bed; we used only blankets. And to what bed I should change was a puzzle! For we only had four beds for eight people. Of course, I reflected, rich people like the little white girl did that. I pictured her arising in the middle of the night and crawling into another bed. Rich people perhaps could not sleep at night; it was aristocratic to be unable to sleep. I watched the little white girl, and she seemed to understand everything that was read.

But for all her perfection, victory was mine that year. The school year was not half finished before I sat in the back seat on the far outside row—and she only sat in the front seat. The back seat was the seat of honor! The child who sat there was the best in the room and needed little help or correction from the teacher. When all other children failed to answer a question the teacher would turn with confidence to the seat of honor with the word—

"Marie?"

With eyes that never left her face I arose and answered. The whole schoolroom watched and listened, waiting for a mistake. I, for all my faded dresses and stringy ugly hair, who had never seen a toothbrush or a bathtub, who had never slept between sheets or in a nightgown, stood with my hands glued to my sides and replied without one falter or one mistake! And the little white girl whose father was a doctor had to listen! Then it was that the little white girl invited me to her birthday party. My mother objected to buying bananas as a present, but after I had cried and said everyone else was taking things, she grudgingly bought three.

"They are rich people," she protested bitterly, looking at the precious bananas, "an' there's no use givin' 'em any more."

When I arrived at the little girl's home I saw that other children had brought presents of books, silver pieces, handkerchiefs and lovely things such as I had never seen in my life. Fairy tales mentioned them but I never thought they really existed. They were all laid out on a table covered with a cloth shot through with gold. I had to walk up before them all and place my three bananas there, covertly touching the cloth shot through with gold. Then I made my way to a chair against the wall and sat down, trying to hide my feet and wishing that I had never come.

The other little girls and boys were quite at ease,—they had been at parties before. They were not afraid to talk or laugh and their throats didn't become whispery and hoarse when anyone asked them a question. I became more and more miserable with each passing moment. In my own world I could reply and even lead, and down beyond the tracks no boy dared touch me or my brother George. If he did he faced me with a jimpson weed as a weapon. But this was a new kind of hurt. In school I had not felt like this before the little white girl: there I had learned an invaluable lesson—that she was clean and orderly, but that I could *do* and learn things that she couldn't. Because of that and because of my teacher's protecting attitude toward me, she had been ashamed not to invite me to her party.

"Of course, if you're too busy to come, you must not feel that you ought, just because I've invited you," she had said. She was not much over ten, yet she had been well trained. I felt vaguely that something was wrong, yet I looked gratefully at her and replied:

"I'll come. I ain't got nothin' to do!"

Now here I was in a gorgeous party where I wasn't wanted. I had brought three bananas at a great sacrifice only to find that no other child would have dreamed of such a cheap present. My dress, that seemed so elegant when I left home, was shamefully shabby here. I was disturbed in my isolation by a number of mothers who called us into another room and seated us at a long table covered with a white tablecloth, marvelous cakes and fruit such as made my heart sink when I compared them with my three bananas. Only my desire to tell my mother all about it, and my desire to know everything in the world even if it hurt, kept me from slipping out of the door when no one was looking, and rushing home. I was seated next to a little boy at the table.

"What street do you live on?" he asked, trying to start a polite conversation.

"Beyond th' tracks."

He looked at me in surprise. "Beyond the tracks! Only tough kids live there!"

I stared back trying to think of something to say, but failed. He sought other avenues of conversation.

"My papa's a lawyer—what's yours?"

"Hauls bricks."

He again stared at me. That made me long to get him over beyond the tracks—he with his eye-glasses and store-made clothes! We used our sling-shots on such sissies. He was stuck-up, that was what he was! But what about I couldn't see.

"*My* papa don't haul bricks!" he informed me, as if to rub it in. Wherein the insult lay I couldn't see, yet I knew one was meant. So I insulted back.

"My papa can lick your papa I bet!" I informed him, just as a pleasant elegant mother bent over us with huge plates of yellow ice cream in her hands.

"Well, Clarence, and what are you talking about?" she asked affectionately.

"Her father hauls bricks and she lives beyond the tracks and she says her father can lick my father!" Clarence piped.

"That doesn't matter, dear, that doesn't matter! Now, now, just eat your ice cream." But I saw her eyes rest disapprovingly on me and I knew it did matter.

Clarence plunged his spoon into his ice cream and henceforth ignored me. I picked up my spoon, but it clattered against the plate. A dainty little girl in blue, with flaring white silk ribbons on her braid of hair, glanced at me primly. I did not touch the spoon again, but sat with my hands under me watching the others eating in perfect self-possession and without noise. I knew I could never eat like that and if I tried to swallow, the whole table would hear. The mother returned and urged me to eat, but I said I didn't like ice cream or cake! She offered me fruit and I took it, thinking I could eat it at home. But when the children left the table I saw that they carried no fruit. So I left mine beside the precious ice cream and cake.

In the next room little boys and girls were choosing partners for a game, and the little white girl was actually sitting at the piano ready to play. My eyes were glued on her—to think of being able to play the piano! Everyone was chosen for the game but me. No little boy bowed to me and asked:

"Will you be my partner, please?" I saw them avoid me deliberately . . . some of them the same little boys who were so stupid in school!

The mother of my little hostess tried to be kind:

"Are you sick, Marie?" she asked. "Would you like to go home?"

"Yes, mam." My voice was hoarse and whispery.

She took me to the door and smiled kindly, saying she hoped I had had a nice time.

"Yes, mam," my hoarse voice replied.

The door closed behind me. The game had started inside and the voices of the children were shouting in laughter. In case anyone should be looking out of the window and think I cared, I turned my head and gazed sternly at a house across the street as I walked rapidly away.

And in case anyone I knew saw me with tears in my eyes I would say . . .

CAROLINE STANSBURY
KIRKLAND
(1801-1864)

Early in A New Home—Who'll Follow? *Caroline Kirkland writes "When my husband purchased two hundred acres of wild land on the banks of this to-be-celebrated stream [the Turnip River], and drew with a piece of chalk on the bar-room table at Danforth's the plan of a village, I little thought I was destined to make myself famous by handing down to posterity a faithful record of the advancing fortunes of that favored spot." The sentence captures the tone of her book, as well, perhaps, as the primary vein of her literary career: ironic, self-aware of her situation as a well-to-do yet vulnerable white woman of letters, somewhat bemused by the aspirations and antics of the male persuasion.*

Kirkland was born in New York City into a family both of female and male intellectuals, interested in education as well as literature. For a time she taught in a school that had been organized by an aunt and then, with her new husband, William Kirkland, opened a girls' school in Geneva, in the Finger Lakes district of New York. Soon, however, William wished to pursue his aspiration to found a city, or at least a town, on the frontier, and they moved to Michigan. There Kirkland experienced the people and events that form the basis for A New Home *and its sequel,* Forest Life *(1842). Her books offer an often ironic but not unsympathetic portrait of democracy in action on the frontier; the people she encounters are frequently self-interested, sometimes cruel, always determined to assert their equality with any and all. With some of the women, Mary Clavers—as Kirkland pseudonymously calls her narrator—establishes a relationship of community and support. At the same time, she observes that for most of the men, a newcomer was regarded "merely as an additional business-automaton—a somebody more with whom to try the race of enterprize, i.e., money-making."*

Returning to New York City after five years, Kirkland continued her literary career, made more urgent when, after her husband's death in 1846, she was forced to find means to support herself and her children. She taught, wrote, brought together gift books containing her essays, and became editor of the Union Magazine of Literature and Art. *Her reviews and the network of women writers that centered on her home established her as a significant figure in the mid-nineteenth-century literary world of New York and as an exponent of realism as a primary literary style for American writers.*

FROM A NEW HOME—WHO'LL FOLLOW?

My first care was to inquire where I might be able to procure a domestic, for I saw plainly I must not expect any aid from Miss Irene or her younger sister, who were just such "captive-princess" looking damsels as Miss Martineau mentions having seen at a country inn somewhere on her tour.

"Well, I don't know," said Mrs. Ketchum in reply to my questions; "there was a young lady here yesterday that was saying she didn't know but she'd live out a spell till she'd bought her a new dress."

"Oh! but I wish to get a girl who will remain with me; I should not like to change often."

Mrs. Ketchum smiled rather scornfully at this, and said there were not many girls about here that cared to live out long at a time.

My spirits fell at this view of the matter. Some of my dear theorizing friends in the civilized world had dissuaded me most earnestly from bringing a maid with me.

"She would always be discontented and anxious to return; and you'll find plenty of good farmer's daughters ready to live with you for the sake of earning a little money."

Good souls! how little did they know of Michigan! I have since that day seen the interior of many a wretched dwelling, with almost literally nothing in it but a bed, a chest, and a table; children ragged to the last degree, and potatoes the only fare; but never yet saw I one where the daughter was willing to own herself obliged to live out at service. She would "hire out" long enough to buy some article of dress perhaps, or "because our folks have been sick, and want a little money to pay the doctor," or for some such special reason; but never as a regular calling, or with an acknowledgement of inferior station.

This state of things appalled me at first; but I have learned a better philosophy since. I find no difficulty now in getting such aid as I require, and but little in retaining it as long as I wish, though there is always a desire of making an occasional display of independence. Since living with one for wages is considered by common consent a favour, I take it as a favour; and, this point once conceded, all goes well. Perhaps I have been peculiarly fortunate; but certainly with one or two exceptions, I have little or nothing to complain of on this essential point of domestic comfort.

To be sure, I had one damsel who crammed herself almost to suffocation with sweatmeats and other things which she esteemed very nice; and ate up her own pies and cake, to the exclusion of those for whom they were intended; who would put her head in at a door, with—"*Miss* Clavers, did you holler? I thought I *heered* a yell."

And another who was highly offended, because room was not made for her at table with guests from the city, and that her company was not requested for tea-visits. And this latter high-born damsel sent in from the kitchen a circumstantial account *in writing,* of the instances wherein she considered herself aggrieved; well written it was too, and expressed with much *naiveté,* and abundant respect. I answered it in the way which "turneth away wrath." Yet it was not long before this fiery spirit was aroused again, and I was forced to part with my country belle. But these instances are not very tremendous even to the city habits I brought with me; and I cannot say I regret having been obliged to relinquish what was, after all, rather a silly sort of pride. But bless me! how I get before my story! I viewed the matter very differently when I was at Ketchum's. My philosophy was of slow growth.

On reflection, it was thought best not to add another sleeper to the loft, and I concluded to wait on myself and the children while we remained at Ketchum's, which we hoped would be but for a day or two. I can only say, I contrived to *simplify* the matter very much, when I had no one to depend on but myself. The children had dirty faces, and aprons which would have effected their total exclusion from genteel society, more than half the time; and I was happy to encourage the closest intimacy between them and the calves and chickens, in order to gain some peace within doors. Mrs. Ketchum certainly had her own troubles during our sojourn under her leaky roof; for the two races commingled not without loud and long effervescence, threatening at times nothing short of a Kilkenny cat battle, ending in mutual extermination.

My office, on these occasions, was an humble imitation of the plan of the celestials in ancient times; to snatch away the combatant in whom I was most interested, and then to secrete him for a while, using as a desert island one of the beds in the loft, where the unfortunate had to dree a weary penance, and generally came down quite tame.

CHAPTER XIV

Down with the topmast; yare; lower, lower; bring her to try with main-course.—*The Tempest*

When Angeline left me, which she did after a few days, I was obliged to employ Mrs. Jennings to "chore round," to borrow her own expression; and as Mr. Clavers was absent much of the time, I had the full enjoyment of her delectable society with that of her husband and two children, who often came to meals very sociably, and made themselves at home with small urgency on my part. The good lady's habits required strong green tea at least three times a day; and between these three times she drank the remains of the tea from the spout of the tea-pot, saying "it tasted better so." "If she hadn't it," she said, "she had the 'sterics so that she wasn't able to do a chore." And her habits were equally imperious in the matter of dipping with her own spoon or knife into every dish on the table. She would have made out nobly on kibaubs, for even that unwieldly morsel a boiled ham, she grasped by the hock and cut off in mouthfuls with her knife, declining all aid from the carver, and saying cooly that she made out very well. It was in vain one offered her any thing, she replied invariably with a dignified nod; "I'll help myself, I thank ye. I never want no waitin' on." And this reply is the universal one on such occasions as I have since had vexatious occasion to observe.

Let no one read with all incredulous shake of the head, but rather let my sketch of these peculiar habits of my neighbours be considered as a mere beginning, a shadow of what might be told. I might

"Amaze indeed
The very faculty of eyes and ears,"

but I forbear.

If "grandeur hear with a disdainful smile"—thinking it would be far better to starve than to eat under such circumstances, I can only say such was not my hungry view of the case; and that I often found rather amusing exercise for my ingenuity in contriving excuses and plans to get the old lady to enjoy her meals alone. To have offered her outright a separate table, though the board should groan with all the delicacies of the city, would have been to secure myself the unenviable privilege of doing my own "chores," at least till I could procure a "help" from some distance beyond the reach of my friend Mrs. Jennings' tongue.

It did not require a very long residence in Michigan, to convince me that it is unwise to attempt to stem directly the current of society, even in the wilderness, but I have since learned many ways of *wearing round* which give me the opportunity of living very much after my own fashion, without offending, very seriously, any body's prejudices.

No settlers are so uncomfortable as those who, coming with abundant means as they suppose, to be comfortable, set out with a determination to live as they have been accustomed to live. They soon find that there are places where the "almighty dollar" is almost powerless; or rather, that powerful as it is, it meets with its conqueror in the jealous pride of those whose services must be had in order to live at all.

"Luff when it blows," is a wise and necessary caution. Those who forget it and attempt to carry all sail set and to keep an unvarying course, blow which way it will, always abuse Michigan, and are abused in their turn. Several whom we have known to set out with this capital mistake have absolutely turned about again in despair, revenging themselves by telling very hard stories about us nor'westers.

Touchstone's philosophy is your only wear for this meridian.

> "*Corin.* And how like you this shepherd's life, Master Touchstone?
> "*Touch.* Truly, shepherd, in respect of itself it is a good life; but in respect it is a shepherd's life, it is naught. In respect that it is solitary, I like it very well; but in respect that it is private, it is a very vile life. Now, in respect that it is in the fields, it pleaseth me well; but in respect it is not in the court, it is tedious. As it is a spare life, look you, it fits my humour well; but as there is no plenty in it, it goes much against my stomach. Hast any philosophy in thee, shepherd?

Nobody will quarrel with this view of things. You may say any thing you like of the country or its inhabitants: but beware how you raise a suspicion that you despise the homely habits of those around you. This is never forgiven.

It would be in vain to pretend that this state of society can ever be agreeable to those who have been accustomed to the more rational arrangements of the older world. The social character of the meals, in particular, is quite destroyed, by the constant presence of strangers, whose manners, habits of thinking, and social connexions are quite different from your own, and often exceedingly repugnant to your taste. Granting the correctness of the opinion which may be read in their countenances that they are "as good as you are," I must insist, that a greasy cook-maid, or a redolent stable-boy, can never be, to my thinking, an agreeable table companion—putting pride, that most terrific bug-bear of the woods, out of the question.

If the best man now living should honour my humble roof with his presence—if he should happen to have an unfortunate *penchant* for eating out of the dishes, picking his teeth with his fork, or using the fire-place for a pocket handkerchief, I would prefer he should take his dinner *solus* or with those who did as he did.

But, I repeat it; those who find these inconveniences most annoying while all is new and strange to them, will by the exertion of a little patience and ingenuity, discover ways and means of getting aside of what is most unpleasant, in the habits of their neighbours: and the silent influence of example is daily effecting much towards reformation in many particulars. Neatness, propriety, and that delicate forebearance of the least encroachment upon the rights or the enjoyments of others, which is the essence of true elegance of manner, have only to be seen and understood to be admired and imitated; and I would fain persuade those who are groaning under certain inflictions to which I have but alluded, that the true way of overcoming all the evils of which they complain is to set forth in their own manners and habits, all that is kind, forbearing, true, lovely, and of good report. They will find ere long that their neighbours have taste enough to love what is so charming, even though they see it exemplified by one who sits *all day* in a carpeted parlor, teaches her own children instead of sending them to the district school, hates "the breath of garlic eaters," and—oh fell climax!—knows nothing at all of soap-making.

CHAPTER XVIII

Lend me your *ears.*
—Shakespeare

Grant graciously what you cannot refuse safely.—*Lacon*

"Mother wants your sifter," said Miss Ianthe Howard, a young lady of six years' standing, attired in a tattered calico, thickened with dirt; her unkempt locks straggling from under that hideous substitute for a bonnet, so universal in the western country, a dirty cotton handkerchief, which is used, *ad nauseam,* for all sorts of purposes.

"Mother wants your sifter, and she says she guesses you can let her have some sugar and tea, 'cause you've got plenty."

This excellent reason, "'cause you've got plenty," is conclusive as to sharing with your neighbours. Whoever comes into Michigan with nothing, will be sure to better his condition; but wo to him that brings with him any thing like an appearance of abundance, whether of money or mere household conveniences. To have them, and not be willing to share them in some sort with the whole community, is an unpardonable crime. You must lend your best horse to *qui que ce soit,* to go ten miles over hill and marsh, in the darkest night, for a doctor; or your team to travel twenty after a "gal;" your wheel-barrows, your shovels, your utensils of all sorts, belong, not to yourself, but to the public, who do not think it necessary even to *ask* a loan, but take it for granted. The two saddles and bridles of Montacute spend most of their time travelling from house to house a-manback; and I have actually known a stray martingale to be traced to four dwellings two miles apart, having been lent from one to another, without a word to the original proprietor, who sat waiting, not very patiently, to commence a journey.

Then within doors, an inventory of your plenishing of all sorts, would scarcely more than include the articles which you are solicited to lend. Not only are all kitchen utensils as much your neighbours as your own, but bedsteads, beds, blankets, sheets, travel from house to house, a pleasant and effectual mode of securing the perpetuity of certain efflorescent peculiarities of the skin, for which Michigan is

becoming almost as famous as the land "'twixt Maidenkirk and John o'Groat's."
Sieves, smoothing irons, and churns run about as if they had legs; one brass kettle
is enough for a whole neighbourhood; and I could point to a cradle which has
rocked half the babies in Montacute. For my own part, I have lent my broom, my
thread, my tape, my spoons, my cat, my thimble, my scissors, my shawl, my shoes;
and have been asked for my combs and brushes: and my husband, for his shaving
apparatus and his pantaloons.

But the cream of the joke lies in the manner of the thing. It is so straight-forward
and honest, none of your hypocritical civility and servile gratitude! Your true republican, when he finds that you possess any thing which would contribute to his convenience, walks in with, "Are you going to use your horses *to-day?*" if horses happen to be the thing he needs.

"Yes, I shall probably want them."

"Oh, well; if you want them—I was thinking to get 'em to go up north a piece."

Or perhaps the desired article comes within the female department.

"Mother wants to get some butter: that 'ere butter you bought of Miss Barton this
mornin'."

And away goes your golden store, to be repaid perhaps with some cheesy, greasy
stuff, brought in a dirty pail with, "Here's your butter!"

A girl came in to borrow a "wash-dish," "because we've got company." Presently
she came back: "Mother says you've forgot to send a towel."

"The pen and ink and a sheet o' paper and a wafer," is no unusual request; and
when the pen is returned, you are generally informed that you sent "an awful bad pen."

I have been frequently reminded of one of Johnson's humorous sketches. A man
returning a broken wheel-barrow to a Quaker, with, "Here I've broke your rotten
wheel-barrow usin' on't. I wish you'd get it mended right off 'cause I want to borrow
it again this afternoon." The Quaker is made to reply, "Friend, it shall be done:" and
I wish I possessed more of his spirit.

CHAPTER XLVI

One must come quite away from the conveniences and refined indulgences of civilized life to know any thing about them. To be always inundated with comforts, is
but too apt to make us proud, selfish, and ungrateful. The mind's health, as well as
the body's, is promoted by occasional privation or abstinence. Many a sour-faced
grumbler I wot of, would be marvellously transformed by a year's residence in the
woods, or even in a Michigan village of as high pretensions as Montacute. If it were
not for casting a sort of dishonour on a country life, turning into a magnificent
"beterinhaus" these

> "Haunts of deer,
> And lanes in which the primrose ere her time
> Peeps through the moss"

I should be disposed to recommend a course of Michigan to the Sybarites, the puny
exquisites, the world-worn and sated Epicureans of our cities. If I mistake not, they
would make surprising advances in philosophy in the course of a few months' training. I should not be severe either. I should not require them to come in their strictly
natural condition as featherless bipeds. I would allow them to bring many a com-

fort—nay, even some real luxuries; books, for instance, and a reasonable supply of New-York Safety-Fund notes, the most tempting form which "world's gear" can possibly assume for our western, wild-cat wearied eyes. I would grant to each Neophyte a ready-made loggery, a garden fenced with tamarack poles, and every facility and convenience which is now enjoyed by the better class of our settlers, yet I think I might after all hope to send home a reasonable proportion of my subjects completely cured, sane for life.

I have in the course of these detached and desultory chapters, hinted at various deficiencies and peculiarities, which strike, with rather unpleasant force, the new resident in the back-woods; but it would require volumes to enumerate all the cases in which the fastidiousness, the taste, the pride, the self-esteem of the refined child of civilization, must be wounded by a familiar intercourse with the persons among whom he will find himself thrown, in the ordinary course of rural life. He is continually reminded in how great a variety of particular his necessities, his materials for comfort, and his sources of pain, are precisely those of the humblest of his neighbours. The humblest, did I say? He will find that he has no humble neighbours. He will very soon discover, that in his new sphere, no act of kindness, no offer of aid, will be considered as any thing short of insult, if the least suspicion of *condescension* peep out. Equality, perfect and practical, is the *sine qua non;* and any appearance of a desire to avoid this rather trying fraternization, is invariably met by a fierce and indignant resistance. The spirit in which was conceived the motto of the French revolution, "La fraternité ou la mort," exists in full force among us, though modified as to results. In cities we bestow charity—in the country we can only exchange offices, nominally at least. If you are perfectly well aware that your nearest neighbour has not tasted meat in a month, nor found in his pocket the semblance of a shilling to purchase it, you must not be surprised, when you have sent him a piece, to receive for reply,

"Oh! your pa wants to *change,* does he? Well, you may put it down." And this without the remotest idea that the time for repayment ever will arrive, but merely to avoid saying, "I thank you," a phrase especially eschewed, so far as I have had opportunity to observe.

This same republican spirit is evinced rather amusingly, in the reluctance to admire, or even to approve, any thing like luxury or convenience which is not in common use among the settlers. Your carpets are spoken of as "*one* way to hide dirt;" your mahogany table as "dreadful plaguy to scour;" your kitchen conveniences as "lumberin' up the house for nothin';" and so on to the end of the chapter. One lady informed me, that if she had such a pantry full of "dishes," under which general term is included every variety of china, glass, and earthenware, she should set up store, and "sell them off pretty quick," for she would not "be plagued with them." Another, giving a slighting glance at a French mirror of rather unusual dimensions, larger by two-thirds, I verily believe, than she had ever seen, remarked, "that would be quite a nice glass, if the frame was done over."

Others take up the matter reprovingly. They "don't think it right to spend money so;" they think too, that "pride never did nobody no good;" and some will go so far as to suggest modes of disposing of your superfluities.

"Any body that's got so many dresses, might afford to give away half on 'em;" or, "I should think you'd got so much land, you might give a poor man a lot, and never miss it." A store of any thing, however simple or necessary, is, as I have elsewhere observed, a subject of reproach, if you decline supplying whomsoever may be deficient.

This simplification of life, this bringing down the transactions of daily intercourse to the original principles of society, is neither very eagerly adopted, nor very keenly relished, by those who have been accustomed to the politer atmospheres. They rebel most determinedly, at first. They perceive that the operation of the golden rule, in circumstances where it is all *give* on one side, and all *take* on the other, must necessarily be rather severe; and they declare manfully against all impertinent intrusiveness. But, sooth to say, there are in the country so many ways of being made uncomfortable by one's most insignificant enemy, that it is soon discovered that warfare is even more costly than submission.

And all this forms part of the schooling which I propose for my spoiled child of refined civilization. And although many of these remarks and requisitions of our unpolished neighbours are unreasonable and absurd enough, yet some of them commend themselves to our better feelings in such a sort, that we find ourselves ashamed to refuse what it seemed at first impertinent to ask; and after the barriers of pride and prejudice are once broken, we discover a certain satisfaction in this homely fellowship with our kind, which goes far towards repaying whatever sacrifices or concessions we may have been induced to make. This has its limits of course; and one cannot help observing that "levelling upwards" is much more congenial to "human natur'," than levelling downwards. The man who thinks you ought to spare him a piece of ground for a garden, because you have more than he thinks you need, would be far from sharing with his poorer neighbour the superior advantages of his lot. He would tell him to work for them as *he* had done.

But then there are, in the one case, some absolute and evident superfluities, according to the primitive estimate of these regions; in the other, none. The doll of Fortune, who may cast a languid eye on this homely page, from the luxurious depths of a velvet-cushioned library-chair, can scarce be expected to conceive how natural it may be, for those who possess nothing beyond the absolute requisites of existence, to look with a certain degree of envy on the extra comforts which seem to cluster round the path of another; and to feel as if a little might well be spared, where so much would still be left. To the tenant of a log-cabin whose family, whatever be its numbers, must burrow in a single room, while a bed or two, a chest, a table, and a wretched handful of cooking utensils, form the chief materials of comfort, an ordinary house, small and plain it may be, yet amply supplied, looks like the very home of luxury. The woman who owns but a suit a-piece for herself and her children, considers the possession of an abundant though simple and inexpensive wardrobe, as needless extravagance; and we must scarcely blame her too severely, if she should be disposed to condemn as penurious, any reluctance to supply her pressing need, though she may have no shadow of claim on us beyond that which arises from her being a daughter of Eve. We look at the matter from opposite points of view. *Her* light shows her very plainly, as she thinks, what is *our* Christian duty; we must take care that ours does not exhibit too exclusively her envy and her impertinence.

The inequalities in the distribution of the gifts of fortune are not greater in the country than in town, but the contrary; yet circumstances render them more offensive to the less-favoured class. The denizens of the crowded alleys and swarming lofts of our great cities see, it is true, the lofty mansions, the splendid equipages of the wealthy—but they are seldom or never brought into contact or collision with the owners of these glittering advantages. And the extreme width of the great gulf between, is almost a barrier, even to all-reaching envy. But in the ruder stages of society, where no one has yet begun to expend any thing for show, the difference lies chiefly in the ordinary requisites of comfort; and this comes home at once "to men's business and bosoms." The keenness of their appreciation, and the strength of their envy, bear a direct proportion to the *real* value of the objects of their desire; and when they are in habits of entire equality and daily familiarity with those who own ten or twenty times as much of the *matériel* of earthly enjoyment as themselves, it is surely natural, however provoking, that they should not be studious to veil their belongings after a share of the good, which has been so bounteously showered upon their neighbours.

I am only making a sort of apology for the foibles of my rustic friends. I cannot say that I feel much respect for any thing which looks like a willingness to live at others' cost, save as a matter of the last necessity.

I was adverting to a certain unreservedness of communication on these points, as often bringing wholesome and much-needed instruction home to those whom prosperity and indulgence may have rendered unsympathizing, or neglectful of the kindly feelings which are among the best ornaments of our nature.

But I am aware that I have already been adventurous, far beyond the bounds of prudence. To hint that it may be better not to cultivate *too* far that haughty spirit of exclusiveness which is the glory of the fashionable world, is, I know, hazardous in the extreme. I have not so far forgotten the rules of the sublime *clique* as not to realize, that in acknowledging even a leaning toward the "vulgar" side, I place myself forever beyond its pale. But I am now a denizen of the wild woods—in my view, "no mean city" to own as one's home; and I feel no ambition to aid in the formation of a Montacute aristocracy, for which an ample field is now open, and all the proper materials are at hand. What lack we? Several of us have as many as three cows; some few, carpets and shanty-kitchens; and one or two, piano-fortes and silver tea-sets. I myself, as *dame de la seigneurie,* have had secret thoughts of an astral lamp! but even if I should go so far, I am resolved not to be either vain-glorious or over-bearing, although this kind of superiority forms the usual ground for exclusiveness. I shall visit my neighbours just as usual, and take care not to say a single word about dipped candles, if I can possibly help it.

LOUISA MAY ALCOTT
(1832–1888)

Alcott is usually thought about as a writer of children's books, and particularly that all-time best seller, Little Women *(1868). Indeed, she was an extremely successful and inventive writer in that genre, which is probably given too little appreciation by adult critics and readers. In addition to creating Jo, Meg, Beth, and Amy March, she wrote* Little Men *(1871), Jo's Boys (1886), and a variety of other works for children. Perhaps she thought that such books would help make the lives of young readers more stable and fun than her own had been. However that might be, her success brought to an end the struggle with poverty that she had maintained from adolescence.*

Alcott came to writing, like a number of other mid-nineteenth-century women, as an alternative to the limited kinds of work available to them. She herself had, as she dramatizes in her novel Work: A Story of Experience *(1873), served as a governess, companion, domestic servant, and, during the Civil War, nurse—an experience she powerfully described in* Hospital Sketches *(1863), a book that helped launch her on a literary career. Most of these efforts were directed to supporting her parents, her sisters, and their children.*

For Louisa was the daughter of Bronson Alcott, one of the most prominent of the Concord Transcendentalists, but a man all but constitutionally incapable of earning a living for himself and his family. Louisa described the poverty—and joys—of her childhood and adolescence with considerable satiric humor in Transcendental Wild Oats *(1873). By then, she could, as a successful author, afford to look back to those pre-Civil War days with a certain ironic distance. But during the previous decade she had devoted much of her energy to writing for a living, composing, generally under a pseudonym, gothic thrillers for popular publications like* Frank Leslie's Illustrated Magazine *and* The Flag of Our Union. *The narrative of* Work *reflects Alcott's own struggles for independence and a foothold in the world. It also celebrates in its heroine, Christie, and in her circle of women friends and co-workers an ideal of "a loving league of sisters."*

ACTRESS

Feeling that she had all the world before her where to choose, and that her next step ought to take her up at least one round higher on the ladder she was climbing, Christie decided not to try going out to service again. She knew very well that she would never live with Irish mates, and could not expect to find another Hepsey. So she tried to get a place as companion to an invalid, but failed to secure the only situation of the sort that was offered her, because she mildly objected to waiting on a nervous cripple all day, and reading aloud half the night. The old lady called her an "impertinent baggage," and Christie retired in great disgust, resolving not to be a slave to anybody.

Things seldom turn out as we plan them, and after much waiting and hoping for other work Christie at last accepted about the only employment which had not entered her mind.

Among the boarders at Mrs. Flint's were an old lady and her pretty daughter, both actresses at a respectable theatre. Not stars by any means, but good second-rate players, doing their work creditably and earning an honest living. The mother bad been kind to Christie in offering advice, and sympathizing with her disappointments. The daughter, a gay little lass, had taken Christie to the theatre several times, there to behold glories that surround the nymphs of spectacular romance.

To Christie this was a great delight, for, though she had pored over her father's Shakespeare till she knew many scenes by heart, she had never seen a play till Lucy led her into what seemed an enchanted world. Her interest and admiration pleased the little actress, and sundry lifts when she was hurried with her dresses made her grateful to Christie.

The girl's despondent face, as she came in day after day from her unsuccessful quest, told its own story, though she uttered no complaint, and these friendly souls laid their heads together, eager to help her in their own dramatic fashion.

"I've got it! I've got it! All hail to the queen!" was the cry that one day startled Christie as she sat thinking anxiously, while sewing mock-pearls on a crown for Mrs. Black.

Looking up she saw Lucy just home from rehearsal, going through a series of pantomimic evolutions suggestive of a warrior doing battle with incredible valor, and a very limited knowledge of the noble art of self-defence.

"What have you got? Who is the queen?" she asked, laughing, as the breathless hero lowered her umbrella, and laid her bonnet at Christie's feet.

"*You* are to be the Queen of the Amazons in our new spectacle, at half a dollar a night for six or eight weeks, if the piece goes well."

"No!" cried Christie, with a gasp.

"Yes!" cried Lucy, clapping her hands; and then she proceeded to tell her news with theatrical volubility. "Mr. Sharp, the manager, wants a lot of tallish girls, and I told him I knew of a perfect dear. He said 'Bring her on, then,' and I flew home to tell you. Now, don't look wild, and say no. You've only got to sing in one chorus, march in the grand procession, and lead your band in the terrific battle-scene. The dress is splendid! Red tunic, tiger-skin over shoulder, helmet, shield, lance, fleshings, sandals, hair down, and as much cork to your eyebrows as you like."

Christie certainly did look wild, for Lucy had burst into the room like a small hurricane, and her rapid words rattled about the listeners' ears as if a hail-storm had followed the gust. While Christie still sat with her mouth open, too bewildered to reply, Mrs. Black said in her cosey voice:

"Try it, me dear, it's just what you'll enjoy, and a capital beginning I assure ye; for if you do well old Sharp will want you again, and then, when some one slips out of the company, you can slip in, and there you are quite comfortable. Try it, me dear, and if you don't like it drop it when the piece is over, and there's no harm done."

"It's much easier and jollier than any of the things you are after. We'll stand by you like bricks, and in a week you'll say it's the best lark you ever had in your life. Don't be prim, now, but say yes, like a trump, as you are," added Lucy, waving a pink satin train temptingly before her friend.

"I will try it!" said Christie, with sudden decision, feeling that something entirely new and absorbing was what she needed to expend the vigor, romance, and enthusiasm of her youth upon.

With a shriek of delight Lucy swept her off her chair, and twirled her about the room as excitable young ladies are fond of doing when their joyful emotions need a vent. When both were giddy they subsided into a corner and a breathless discussion of the important step.

Though she had consented, Christie had endless doubts and fears, but Lucy removed many of the former, and her own desire for pleasant employment conquered many of the latter. In her most despairing moods she had never thought of trying this. Uncle Enos considered "play-actin'" as the sum of all iniquity. What would he say if she went calmly to destruction by that road? Sad to relate, this recollection rather strengthened her purpose, for a delicious sense of freedom pervaded her soul, and the old defiant spirit seemed to rise up within her at the memory of her Uncle's grim prophecies and narrow views.

"Lucy is happy, virtuous, and independent, why can't I be so too if I have any talent? It isn't exactly what I should choose, but any thing honest is better than idleness. I'll try it any way, and get a little fun, even if I don't make much money or glory out of it."

So Christie held to her resolution in spite of many secret misgivings, and followed Mrs. Black's advice on all points with a docility which caused that sanguine lady to predict that she would be a star before she knew where she was.

"Is this the stage? How dusty and dull it is by daylight!" said Christie next day, as she stood by Lucy on the very spot where she had seen Hamlet die in great anguish two nights before.

"Bless you, child, it's in curl-papers now, as I am of a morning. Mr. Sharp, here's an Amazon for you."

As she spoke, Lucy hurried across the stage, followed by Christie, wearing anything but an Amazonian expression just then.

"Ever on before?" abruptly asked a keen-faced, little man, glancing with an experienced eye at the young person who stood before him bathed in blushes.

"No, sir."

"Do you sing?"

"A little, sir."

"Dance, of course?"

"Yes, sir."

"Just take a turn across the stage, will you? Must walk well to lead a march."

As she went, Christie heard Mr. Sharp taking notes audibly:

"Good tread; capital figure; fine eye. She'll make up well, and behave herself, I fancy."

A strong desire to make off seized the girl; but, remembering that she had presented herself for inspection, she controlled the impulse, and returned to him with no demonstration of displeasure, but a little more fire in "the fine eye," and a more erect carriage of the "capital figure."

"All right, my dear. Give your name to Mr. Tripp, and your mind to the business, and consider yourself engaged,"—with which satisfactory remark the little man vanished like a ghost.

"Lucy, did you hear that impertinent 'my dear'?" asked Christie, whose sense of propriety had received its first shock.

"Lord, child, all managers do it. They don't mean any thing; so be resigned, and thank your stars he didn't say 'love' and, 'darling,' and kiss you, as old Vining used to," was all the sympathy she got.

Having obeyed orders, Lucy initiated her into the mysteries of the place, and then put her in a corner to look over the scenes in which she was to appear. Christie soon caught the idea of her part,—not a difficult matter, as there were but few ideas in the whole piece, after which she sat watching the arrival of the troop she was to lead. A most forlorn band of warriors they seemed, huddled together, and looking as if afraid to speak, lest they should infringe some rule; or to move, lest they be swallowed up by some unsuspected trap-door.

Presently the ballet-master appeared, the orchestra struck up, and Christie found herself marching and counter-marching at word of command. At first, a most uncomfortable sense of the absurdity of her position oppressed and confused her; then the ludicrous contrast between the solemn anxiety of the troop and the fantastic evolutions they were performing amused her till the novelty wore off; the martial music excited her; the desire to please sharpened her wits; and natural grace made it easy for her to catch and copy the steps and poses given her to imitate. Soon she forgot herself, entered into the spirit of the thing, and exerted every sense to please, so successfully that Mr. Tripp praised her quickness at comprehension. Lucy applauded heartily from a fairy car, and Mr. Sharp popped his head out of a palace window to watch the Amazon's descent from the Mountains of the Moon.

When the regular company arrived, the troop was dismissed till the progress of the play demanded their reappearance. Much interested in the piece, Christie stood aside under a palm-tree, the foliage of which was strongly suggestive of a dilapidated green umbrella, enjoying the novel sights and sounds about her.

Yellow-faced gentlemen and sleepy-eyed ladies roamed languidly about with much incoherent jabbering of parts, and frequent explosions of laughter. Princes, with varnished boots and suppressed cigars, fought, bled, and died, without a change of countenance. Damsels of unparalleled beauty, according to the text, gaped in the faces of adoring lovers, and crocheted serenely on the brink of annihilation. Fairies, in rubber-boots and woollen head-gear, disported themselves on flowery barks of canvas, or were suspended aloft with hooks in their backs like young Hindoo devotees. Demons, guiltless of hoof or horn, clutched their victims with the inevitable "Ha! ha!" and vanished darkly, eating pea-nuts. The ubiquitous Mr. Sharp seemed to pervade the whole theatre; for his voice came shrilly from above or spectrally from below, and his active little figure darted to and fro like a critical will-o-the-wisp.

The grand march and chorus in the closing scene were easily accomplished; for, as Lucy bade her, Christie "sung with all her might," and kept step as she led her band with the dignity of a Boadicea. No one spoke to her; few observed her; all were intent on their own affairs; and when the final shriek and bang died away without lifting the roof by its din, she could hardly believe that the dreaded first rehearsal was safely over.

A visit to the wardrobe-room to see her dress came next; and here Christie had a slight skirmish with the mistress of that department relative to the length of her classical garments. As studies from the nude had not yet become one of the amusements of the *élite* of Little Babel, Christie was not required to appear in the severe simplicity of a costume consisting of a necklace, sandals, and a bit of gold fringe about the waist, but was allowed an extra inch or two on her tunic, and departed, much comforted by the assurance that her dress would not be "a shock to modesty," as Lucy expressed it.

"Now, look at yourself, and, for my sake, prove an honor to your country and a terror to the foe," said Lucy, as she led her *protégée* before the green-room mirror on the first night of "The Demon's Daughter, or The Castle of the Sun!! The most Magnificent Spectacle ever produced upon the American Stage!!!"

Christie looked, and saw a warlike figure with glittering helmet, shield and lance, streaming hair and savage cloak. She liked the picture, for there was much of the heroic spirit in the girl, and even this poor counterfeit pleased her eye and filled her fancy with martial memories of Joan of Arc, Zenobia, and Britomarte.

"Go to!" cried Lucy, who affected theatrical modes of speech. "Don't admire yourself any longer, but tie up your sandals and come on. Be sure you rush down the instant I cry, 'Demon, I defy thee!' Don't break your neck, or pick your way like a cat in wet weather, but come *with effect*, for I want that scene to make a hit."

Princess Caremfil swept away, and the Amazonian queen climbed to her perch among the painted mountains, where her troop already sat like a flock of pigeons shining in the sun. The gilded breast-plate rose and fell with the quick beating of her heart, the spear shook with the trembling of her hand, her lips were dry, her head dizzy, and more than once, as she waited for her cue, she was sorely tempted to run away and take the consequences.

But the thought of Lucy's good-will and confidence kept her, and when the cry came she answered with a ringing shout, rushed down the ten-foot precipice, and charged upon the foe with an energy that inspired her followers, and quite satisfied the princess struggling in the demon's grasp.

With clashing of arms and shrill war-cries the rescuers of innocence assailed the sooty fiends who fell before their unscientific blows with a rapidity which inspired in the minds of beholders a suspicion that the goblins' own voluminous tails tripped them up and gallantry kept them prostrate. As the last groan expired, the last agonized squirm subsided, the conquerors performed the intricate dance with which it appears the Amazons were wont to celebrate their victories. Then the scene closed with a glare of red light and a "grand tableau" of the martial queen standing in a bower of lances, the rescued princess gracefully fainting in her arms, and the vanquished demon scowling fiercely under her foot, while four-and-twenty dishevelled damsels sang a song of exultation, to the barbaric music of a tattoo on their shields.

All went well that night, and when at last the girls doffed crown and helmet, they confided to one another the firm opinion that the success of the piece was in a great measure owing to their talent, their exertions, and went home predicting for themselves careers as brilliant as those of Siddons and Rachel.

It would be a pleasant task to paint the vicissitudes and victories of a successful actress; but Christie was no dramatic genius born to shine before the world and leave a name behind her. She had no talent except that which may be developed in any girl possessing the lively fancy, sympathetic nature, and ambitious spirit which make such girls naturally dramatic. This was to be only one of many experiences which were to show her her own weakness and strength, and through effort, pain, and disappointment fit her to play a nobler part on a wider stage.

For a few weeks Christie's illusions lasted; then she discovered that the new life was nearly as humdrum as the old, that her companions were ordinary men and women, and her bright hopes were growing as dim as her tarnished shield. She grew unutterably weary of "The Castle of the Sun," and found the "Demon's Daughter" an unmitigated bore. She was not tired of the profession, only dissatisfied with the place she held in it, and eager to attempt a part that gave some scope for power and passion.

Mrs. Black wisely reminded her that she must learn to use her wings before she tried to fly, and comforted her with stories of celebrities who had begun as she was beginning, yet who had suddenly burst from their grub-like obscurity to adorn the world as splendid butterflies.

"We'll stand by you, Kit; so keep up your courage, and do your best. Be clever to every one in general, old Sharp in particular, and when a chance comes, have your wits about you and grab it. That's the way to get on," said Lucy, as sagely as if she had been a star for years.

"If I had beauty I should stand a better chance," sighed Christie, surveying herself with great disfavor, quite unconscious that to a cultivated eye the soul of beauty was often visible in that face of hers, with its intelligent eyes, sensitive mouth, and fine lines about the forehead, making it a far more significant and attractive countenance than that of her friend, possessing only piquant prettiness.

"Never mind, child; you've got a lovely figure, and an actress's best feature,—fine eyes and eyebrows. I heard old Kent say so, and he's a judge. So make the best of what you've got, as I do," answered Lucy, glancing at her own comely little person with an air of perfect resignation.

Christie laughed at the adviser, but wisely took the advice, and, though she fretted in private, was cheerful and alert in public. Always modest, attentive, and obliging, she soon became a favorite with her mates, and, thanks to Lucy's good offices with Mr. Sharp, whose favorite she was, Christie got promoted sooner than she otherwise would have been.

A great Christmas spectacle was brought out the next season, and Christie had a good part in it. When that was over she thought there was no hope for her, as the regular company was full and a different sort of performance was to begin. But just then her chance came, and she "grabbed it." The first soubrette died suddenly, and in the emergency Mr. Sharp offered the place to Christie till he could fill it to his mind. Lucy was second soubrette, and had hoped for this promotion; but Lucy did not sing well. Christie had a good voice, had taken lessons and much improved of late, so she had the preference and resolved to stand the test so well that this temporary elevation should become permanent.

She did her best, and though many of the parts were distasteful to her she got through them successfully, while now and then she had one which she thoroughly enjoyed. Her Tilly Slowboy was a hit, and a proud girl was Christie when Kent, the comedian, congratulated her on it, and told her he had seldom seen it better done.

To find favor in Kent's eyes was an honor indeed, for he belonged to the old school, and rarely condescended to praise modern actors. His own style was so admirable that he was justly considered the first comedian in the country, and was the pride and mainstay of the old theatre where he had played for years. Of course he possessed much influence in that little world, and being a kindly man used it generously to help up any young aspirant who seemed to him deserving.

He had observed Christie, attracted by her intelligent face and modest manners, for in spite of her youth there was a native refinement about her that made it impossible for her to romp and flirt as some of her mates did. But till she played Tilly he had not thought she possessed any talent. That pleased him, and seeing how much she valued his praise, and was flattered by his notice, he gave her the wise but unpalatable advice always offered young actors. Finding that she accepted it, was willing to study hard, work faithfully, and wait patiently, he predicted that in time she would make a clever actress, never a great one.

Of course Christie thought he was mistaken, and secretly resolved to prove him a false prophet by the triumphs of her career. But she meekly bowed to his opinion; this docility pleased him, and he took a paternal sort of interest in her, which, coming from the powerful favorite, did her good service with the higher powers, and helped her on more rapidly than years of meritorious effort.

Toward the end of that second season several of Dickens's dramatized novels were played, and Christie earned fresh laurels. She loved those books, and seemed by instinct to understand and personate the humor and pathos of many of those grotesque creations. Believing she had little beauty to sacrifice, she dressed such parts to the life, and played them with a spirit and ease that surprised those who had considered her a dignified and rather dull young person.

"I'll tell you what it is, Sharp, that girl is going to make a capital character actress. When her parts suit, she forgets herself entirely and does admirably well.

Her Miggs was nearly the death of me to-night. She's got that one gift, and it's a good one. You'd better give her a chance, for I think she'll be a credit to the old concern."

Kent said that,—Christie heard it, and flew to Lucy, waving Miggs's cap for joy as she told the news.

"What did Mr. Sharp say?" asked Lucy, turning round with her face half "made up."

"He merely said 'Hum,' and smiled. Wasn't that a good sign?" said Christie, anxiously.

"Can't say," and Lucy touched up her eyebrows as if she took no interest in the affair.

Christie's face fell, and her heart sunk at the thought of failure; but she kept up her spirits by working harder than ever, and soon had her reward. Mr. Sharp's "Hum" did mean yes, and the next season she was regularly engaged, with a salary of thirty dollars a week.

It was a grand step, and knowing that she owed it to Kent, Christie did her utmost to show that she deserved his good opinion. New trials and temptations beset her now, but hard work and an innocent nature kept her safe and busy. Obstacles only spurred her on to redoubled exertion, and whether she did well or ill, was praised or blamed, she found a never-failing excitement in her attempts to reach the standard of perfection she had set up for herself. Kent did not regret his patronage. Mr. Sharp was satisfied with the success of the experiment, and Christie soon became a favorite in a small way, because behind the actress the public always saw a woman who never "forgot the modesty of nature."

But as she grew prosperous in outward things, Christie found herself burdened with a private cross that tried her very much. Lucy was no longer her friend; something had come between them, and a steadily increasing coldness took the place of the confidence and affection which had once existed. Lucy was jealous for Christie had passed her in the race. She knew she could not fill the place Christie had gained by favor, and now held by her own exertions, still she was bitterly envious, though ashamed to own it.

Christie tried to be just and gentle, to prove her gratitude to her first friend, and to show that her heart was unchanged. But she failed to win Lucy back and felt herself injured by such unjust resentment. Mrs. Black took her daughter's part, and though they preserved the peace outwardly the old friendliness was quite gone.

Hoping to forget this trouble in excitement Christie gave herself entirely to her profession, finding in it a satisfaction which for a time consoled her.

But gradually she underwent the sorrowful change which comes to strong natures when they wrong themselves through ignorance or wilfulness.

Pride and native integrity kept her from the worst temptations of such a life, but to the lesser ones she yielded, growing selfish, frivolous, and vain,—intent on her own advancement, and careless by what means she reached it. She had no thought now beyond her art, no desire beyond the commendation of those whose opinion was serviceable, no care for any one but herself.

Her love of admiration grew by what it fed on, till the sound of applause became the sweetest music to her ear. She rose with this hope, lay down with this satisfaction, and month after month passed in this feverish life, with no wish to change it, but a growing appetite for its unsatisfactory delights, an ever-increasing forgetfulness of any higher aspiration than dramatic fame.

"Give me joy, Lucy, I'm to have a benefit next week! Everybody else has had one, and I've played for them all, so no one seemed to begrudge me my turn when dear old Kent proposed it," said Christie, coming in one night still flushed and excited with the good news.

"What shall you have?" asked Lucy, trying to look pleased, and failing decidedly.

"'Masks and Faces.' I've always wanted to play Peg and it has good parts for you and Kent, and St. George. I chose it for that reason, for I shall need all the help I can get to pull me through, I dare say."

The smile vanished entirely at this speech, and Christie was suddenly seized with a suspicion that Lucy was not only jealous of her as an actress, but as a woman. St. George was a comely young actor who usually played lovers' parts with Christie, and played them very well, too, being possessed of much talent, and a gentleman. They had never thought of falling in love with each other, though St. George wooed and won Christie night after night in vaudeville and farce. But it was very easy to imagine that so much mock passion had a basis of truth, and Lucy evidently tormented herself with this belief.

"Why didn't you choose Juliet: St. George would do Romeo so well?" said Lucy, with a sneer.

"No, that is beyond me. Kent says Shakespeare will never be my line, and I believe him. I should think you'd be satisfied with 'Masks and Faces,' for you know Mabel gets her husband safely back in the end," answered Christie, watching the effect of her words.

"As if I wanted the man! No, thank you, other people's leavings won't suit me," cried Lucy, tossing her head, though her face belied her words.

"Not even though he has 'heavenly eyes,' 'distracting legs,' and 'a melting voice?'" asked Christie maliciously, quoting Lucy's own rapturous speeches when the new actor came.

"Come, come, girls, don't quarrel. I won't 'ave it in me room. Lucy's tired to death, and it's not nice of you, Kitty, to come and crow over her this way," said Mamma Black, coming to the rescue, for Lucy was in tears, and Christie looking dangerous.

"It's impossible to please you, so I'll say good-night," and Christie went to her room with resentment burning hotly in her heart.

As she crossed the chamber her eye fell on her own figure reflected in the long glass, and with a sudden impulse she turned up the gas, wiped the rouge from her cheeks, pushed back her hair, and studied her own face intently for several moments. It was pale and jaded now, and all its freshness seemed gone; hard lines had come about the mouth, a feverish disquiet filled the eyes, and on the forehead seemed to lie the shadow of a discontent that saddened the whole face. If one could believe the testimony of that countenance things were not going well with Christie, and she owned it with a regretful sigh, as she asked herself, "Am I what I hoped I should be? No, and it is my fault. If three years of this life have made me this, what shall I be in ten? A fine actress perhaps, but how good a woman?"

With gloomy eyes fixed on her altered face she stood a moment struggling with herself. Then the hard look returned, and she spoke out defiantly, as if in answer to some warning voice within herself. "No one cares what I am, so why care myself? Why not go on and get as much fame as I can? Success gives me power if it cannot give me happiness, and I must have some reward for my hard work. Yes! a gay life and a short one, then out with the lights and down with the curtain!"

But in spite of her reckless words Christie sobbed herself to sleep that night like a child who knows it is astray, yet cannot see the right path or hear its mother's voice calling it home.

On the night of the benefit, Lucy was in a most exasperating mood, Christie in a very indignant one, and as they entered their dressing-room they looked as if they might have played the Rival Queens with great effect. Lucy offered no help and Christie asked none, but putting her vexation resolutely out of sight fixed her mind on the task before her.

As the pleasant stir began all about her, actress-like, she felt her spirits rise, her courage increase with every curl she fastened up, every gay garment she put on, and soon smiled approvingly at herself, for excitement lent her cheeks a better color than rouge, her eyes shone with satisfaction, and her heart beat high with the resolve to make a hit or die.

Christie needed encouragement that night, and found it in the hearty welcome that greeted her, and the full house, which proved how kind a regard was entertained for her by many who knew her only by a fictitious name. She felt this deeply, and it helped her much, for she was vexed with many trials those before the footlights knew nothing of.

The other players were full of kindly interest in her success, but Lucy took a naughty satisfaction in harassing her by all the small slights and unanswerable provocations which one actress has it in her power to inflict upon another.

Christie was fretted almost beyond endurance, and retaliated by an ominous frown when her position allowed, threatening asides when a moment's by-play favored their delivery, and angry protests whenever she met Lucy off the stage.

But in spite of all annoyances she had never played better in her life. She liked the part, and acted the warm-hearted, quick-witted, sharp-tongued Peg with a spirit and grace that surprised even those who knew her best. Especially good was she in the scenes with Triplet, for Kent played the part admirably, and cheered her on with many an encouraging look and word. Anxious to do honor to her patron and friend she threw her whole heart into the work; in the scene where she comes like a good angel to the home of the poor play-wright, she brought tears to the eyes of her audience; and when at her command Triplet strikes up a jig to amuse the children she "covered the buckle" in gallant style, dancing with all the frolicsome *abandon* of the Irish orange-girl who for a moment forgot her grandeur and her grief.

That scene was her best, for it is full of those touches of nature that need very little art to make them effective; and when a great bouquet fell with a thump at Christie's feet, as she paused to bow her thanks for an encore, she felt that she had reached the height of earthly bliss.

In the studio scene Lucy seemed suddenly gifted with unsuspected skill; for when Mabel kneels to the picture, praying her rival to give her back her husband's heart, Christie was amazed to see real tears roll down Lucy's cheeks, and to hear real love and longing thrill her trembling words with sudden power and passion.

"That is not acting. She does love St. George, and thinks I mean to keep him from her. Poor dear! I'll tell her all about it to-night, and set her heart at rest," thought Christie; and when Peg left the frame, her face expressed the genuine pity that she felt, and her voice was beautifully tender as she promised to restore the stolen treasure.

Lucy felt comforted without knowing why, and the piece went smoothly on to its last scene. Peg was just relinquishing the repentant husband to his forgiving wife with those brave words of hers, when a rending sound above their heads made all look up and start back; all but Lucy, who stood bewildered. Christie's quick eye saw the impending danger, and with a sudden spring she caught her friend from it. It was only a second's work, but it cost her much; for in the act, down crashed one of the mechanical contrivances used in a late spectacle, and in its fall stretched Christie stunned and senseless on the stage.

A swift uprising filled the house with tumult; a crowd of actors hurried forward, and the panic-stricken audience caught glimpses of poor Peg lying mute and pallid in Mabel's arms, while Vane wrung his hands, and Triplet audibly demanded, "Why the devil somebody didn't go for a doctor?"

Then a brilliant view of Mount Parnassus, with Apollo and the Nine Muses in full blast, shut the scene from sight, and soon Mr. Sharp appeared to ask their patience till the after-piece was ready, for Miss Douglas was too much injured to appear again. And with an unwonted expression of feeling, the little man alluded to "the generous act which perhaps had changed the comedy to a tragedy and robbed the beneficiary of her well-earned reward at their hands."

All had seen the impulsive spring toward, not from, the danger, and this unpremeditated action won heartier applause than Christie ever had received for her best rendering of more heroic deeds.

But she did not hear the cordial round they gave her. She had said she would "make a hit or die;" and just then it seemed as if she had done both, for she was deaf and blind to the admiration and the sympathy bestowed upon her as the curtain fell on the first, last benefit she ever was to have.

HAMLIN GARLAND

(1860-1940)

Garland's writing directly reflected the struggle of his family and himself to wrest a living from farms in Wisconsin, Minnesota, Iowa, and the Dakota Territory. There he experienced the frustrations of limited horizons, the bitterness of economic inequity before the power of banks and railroads, and the banal hardships of women's daily lives that are dramatized in "Up the Coulé." In Osage, Iowa, he had attended Cedar Valley Seminary before staking a claim to a prairie farm in the Dakotas. But he came to feel that there was little future for him there and in 1884 he determined to move east to Boston to educate himself and pursue a career. He read Whitman, Darwin, Herbert Spencer, and Henry George, whose economic theories about tax reform influenced his future writing.

Garland began to teach, first at the Boston School of Oratory, and then to write, producing a series of stories based upon midwestern farm life. A first collection, Main-Travelled Roads (1891), which included "Up the Coulé," was very positively received for its realistic, often harsh portrait of ordinary farming people caught in an uneven struggle for survival. A second set of stories, Prairie Folks (1893), and a series of novels established Garland as a writer committed to the social and political reforms advocated

by George and by farmers' organizations of the late nineteenth century. His
1895 novel, Rose of Dutcher's Coolly, *presents a woman in situations much*
like his own, desiring a wider life, guilty at abandoning the family back
home, setting out to become a successful author; the novel also reflects Gar-
land's own sensitivity to the distinctive constraints faced by women.

Garland also wrote a number of significant essays on literary and social
theory, collected in Crumbling Idols *(1894), as well as a series of autobi-*
ographies, beginning with A Son of the Middle Border *(1917). His personal*
narratives are among the most enduring of such American works and
deserve to be more widely read. He also published an important collection
of Native American stories in the Book of the American Indian *(1923).*
Unfortunately, however, Garland's ideas about social and fiscal reform
seemed to those who set the tone of modernism in the 1920s to be cranky;
he was made out to be an intellectual relic from another era, an unfair and
inaccurate judgment, but one that nevertheless undermined his reputation
and made his work less influential than it might otherwise have been.

UP THE COULÉ

"Keep the main-travelled road up the Coolly—it's the second house after crossin'
the crick."

The ride from Milwaukee to the Mississippi is a fine ride at any time, superb in
summer. To lean back in a reclining-chair and whirl away in a breezy July day, past
lakes, groves of oak, past fields of barley being reaped, past hay-fields, where the
heavy grass is toppling before the swift sickle, is a panorama of delight, a road full
of delicious surprises, where down a sudden vista lakes open, or a distant wooded
hill looms darkly blue, or swift streams, foaming deep down the solid rock, send
whiffs of cool breezes in at the window.

It has majesty, breadth. The farming has nothing apparently petty about it. All
seems vigorous, youthful, and prosperous. Mr. Howard McLane in his chair let his
newspaper fall on his lap, and gazed out upon it with dreaming eyes. It had a certain mysterious glamour to him; the lakes were cooler and brighter to his eye, the
greens fresher, and the grain more golden than to any one else, for he was coming
back to it all after an absence of ten years. It was, besides, *his* West. He still took
pride in being a Western man.

His mind all day flew ahead of the train to the little town far on toward the Mississippi, where he had spent his boyhood and youth. As the train passed the Wisconsin River, with its curiously carved cliffs, its cold, dark, swift-swirling water eating slowly under cedar-clothed banks, Howard began to feel curious little
movements of the heart, like a lover as he nears his sweetheart.

The hills changed in character, growing more intimately recognizable. They rose
higher as the train left the ridge and passed down into the Black River valley, and
specifically into the La Crosse valley. They ceased to have any hint of upheavals of
rock, and became simply parts of the ancient level left standing after the water had
practically given up its post-glacial, scooping action.

It was about six o'clock as he caught sight of the dear broken line of hills on
which his baby eyes had looked thirty-five years ago. A few minutes later and the

train drew up at the grimy little station set in at the hillside, and, giving him just time to leap off, plunged on again toward the West. Howard felt a ridiculous weakness in his legs as he stepped out upon the broiling hot splintery planks of the station, and faced the few idlers lounging about. He simply stood and gazed with the same intensity and absorption one of the idlers might show standing before the Brooklyn Bridge.

The town caught and held his eyes first. How poor and dull and sleepy and squalid it seemed! The one main street ended at the hillside at his left, and stretched away to the north, between two rows of the usual village stores, unrelieved by a tree or a touch of beauty. An unpaved street, drab-colored, miserable, rotting wooden buildings, with the inevitable battlements—the same, only worse, was the town.

The same, only more beautiful still, was the majestic amphitheatre of green wooded hills that circled the horizon, and toward which he lifted his eyes. He thrilled at the sight.

"Glorious!" he cried involuntarily.

Accustomed to the White Mountains, to the Alleghanies, he had wondered if these hills would retain their old-time charm. They did. He took off his hat to them as he stood there. Richly wooded, with gently-sloping green sides, rising to massive square or rounded tops with dim vistas, they glowed down upon the squalid town, gracious, lofty in their greeting, immortal in their vivid and delicate beauty.

He was a goodly figure of a man as he stood there beside his valise. Portly, erect, handsomely dressed, and with something unusually winning in his brown mustache and blue eyes, something scholarly suggested by the pinch-nose glasses, something strong in the repose of the head. He smiled as he saw how unchanged was the grouping of the old loafers on the salt-barrels and nail-kegs. He recognized most of them—a little dirtier, a little more bent, and a little graver.

They sat in the same attitudes, spat tobacco with the same calm delight, and joked each other, breaking into short and sudden fits of laughter, and pounded each other on the back, just as when he was a student at the La Crosse Seminary, and going to and fro daily on the train.

They ruminated on him as he passed, speculating in a perfectly audible way upon his business.

"Looks like a drummer."

"No, he ain't no drummer. See them Boston glasses?"

"That's so. Guess he's a teacher."

"Looks like a moneyed cuss."

"Bos'n, I *guess*."

He knew the one who spoke last—Freeme Cole, a man who was the fighting wonder of Howard's boyhood, now degenerated into a stoop-shouldered, faded, garrulous, and quarrelsome old man. Yet there was something epic in the old man's stories, something enthralling in the dramatic power of recital.

Over by the blacksmith shop the usual game of "quaits" was in progress, and the drug-clerk on the corner was chasing a crony with the squirt-pump, with which he was about to wash the windows. A few teams stood ankle-deep in the mud, tied to the fantastically-gnawed pine pillars of the wooden awnings. A man on a load of hay was "jawing" with the attendant of the platform scales, who stood below, pad and pencil in hand.

"Hit 'im! hit 'im! jump off and knock 'im!" suggested a bystander, jovially.

Howard knew the voice.

"Talk's cheap. Takes money t' buy whiskey," he said, when the man on the load repeated his threat of getting off and whipping the scales-man.

"You're William McTurg," Howard said, coming up to him.

"I am, sir," replied the soft-voiced giant, turning and looking down on the stranger, with an amused twinkle in his deep brown eyes. He stood as erect as an Indian, though his hair and beard were white.

"I'm Howard McLane."

"Ye begin t' look it," said McTurg, removing his right hand from his pocket. "How are yeh?"

"I'm first-rate. How's mother and Grant?"

"Saw 'im ploughing corn as I came down. Guess he's all right. Want a boost?"

"Well, yes. Are you down with a team?"

"Yep. 'Bout goin' home. Climb right in. That's my rig, right there," nodding at a sleek bay colt hitched in a covered buggy. "Heave y'r grip under the seat."

They climbed into the seat after William had lowered the buggy-top and un-hitched the horse from the post. The loafers were mildly curious. Guessed Bill had got hooked onto by a lightnin'-rod peddler, or somethin' o' that kind.

"Want to go by river, or 'round by the hills?"

"Hills, I guess."

The whole matter began to seem trivial, as if he had only been away for a month or two.

William McTurg was a man little given to talk. Even the coming back of a nephew did not cause any flow of questions or reminiscences. They rode in silence, he sat a little bent forward. the lines held carelessly in his hands, his great leonine head swaying to and fro with the movement of the buggy.

As they passed familiar spots, the younger man broke the silence with a question.

"That's old man McElvaine's place, ain't it?"

"Yep."

"Old man living?"

"I *guess* he is. Husk more corn 'n any man he c'n hire."

In the edge of the village they passed an open lot on the left, marked with cir-cus-rings of different eras.

"There's the old ball-ground. Do they have circuses on it just the same as ever?"

"Just the same."

"What fun that field calls up! The games of ball we used to have! Do you play yet?"

"Sometimes. Can't stoop so well as I used to." He smiled a little. "Too much fat."

It all swept back upon Howard in a flood of names and faces and sights and sounds; something sweet and stirring somehow, though it had little of aesthetic charm at the time. They were passing along lanes now, between superb fields of corn, wherein ploughmen were at work. Kingbirds flew from post to post ahead of them; the insects called from the grass. The valley slowly outspread below them. The workmen in the fields were "turning out" for the night. They all had a word of chaff with McTurg.

Over the western wall of the circling amphitheatre the sun was setting. A few scattering clouds were drifting on the west wing, their shadows sliding down the green and purpled slopes. The dazzling sunlight flamed along the luscious velvety grass, and shot amid the rounded, distant purple peaks, and streamed in bars of gold and crimson across the blue mist of the narrower upper Coulés.

The heart of the young man swelled with pleasure almost like pain, and the eyes of the silent older man took on a far-off, dreaming look, as he gazed at the scene which had repeated itself a thousand times in his life, but of whose beauty he never spoke.

Far down to the left was the break in the wall, through which the river ran, on its way to join the Mississippi. As they climbed slowly among the hills, the valley they had left grew still more beautiful, as the squalor of the little town was hid by the dusk of distance. Both men were silent for a long time. Howard knew the peculiarities of his companion too well to make any remarks or ask any questions, and besides it was a genuine pleasure to ride with one who could feel that silence was the only speech amid such splendors.

Once they passed a little brook singing in a mournfully sweet way its eternal song over its pebbles. It called back to Howard the days when he and Grant, his younger brother, had fished in this little brook for trout, with trousers rolled above the knee and wrecks of hats upon their heads.

"Any trout left?" he asked.

"Not many. Little fellers." Finding the silence broken, William asked the first question since he met Howard. "Less see: you're a show feller now? B'long to a troupe?"

"Yes, yes; I'm an actor."

"Pay much?"

"Pretty well."

That seemed to end William's curiosity about the matter.

"Ah, there's our old house, ain't it?" Howard broke out, pointing to one of the houses farther up the Coulé. It'll be a surprise to them, won't it?"

"Yep; only they don't live there."

"What! They don't!"

"No."

"Who does?"

"Dutchman."

Howard was silent for some moments. "Who lives on the Dunlap place?"

"'Nother Dutchman."

"Where's Grant living, anyhow?"

"Farther up the Coolly."

"Well, then I'd better get out here, hadn't I?"

"Oh, I'll drive yeh up."

"No, I'd rather walk."

The sun had set, and the Coulé was getting dusk when Howard got out of McTurg's carriage, and set off up the winding lane toward his brother's house. He walked slowly to absorb the coolness and fragrance and color of the hour. The katydids sang a rhythmic song of welcome to him. Fireflies were in the grass. A whippoorwill in the deep of the wood was calling weirdly, and an occasional nighthawk, flying high gave his grating shriek, or hollow boom, suggestive and resounding.

He had been wonderfully successful, and yet had carried into his success as a dramatic author as well as actor a certain puritanism that made him a paradox to his fellows. He was one of those actors who are always in luck, and the best of it was he kept and made use of his luck. Jovial as he appeared, he was inflexible as granite against drink and tobacco. He retained through it all a certain freshness of enjoyment that made him one of the best companions in the profession; and now as he walked on, the hour and the place appealed to him with great power. It seemed to sweep away the life that came between.

How close it all was to him, after all! In his restless life, surrounded by the glare of electric lights, painted canvas, hot colors, creak of machinery, mock trees, stones, and brooks, he had not lost but gained appreciation for the coolness, quiet and low tones, the shyness of the wood and field.

In the farm-house ahead of him a light was shining as he peered ahead, and his heart gave another painful movement. His brother was awaiting him there, and his mother, whom he had not seen for ten years and who had grown unable to write. And when Grant wrote, which had been more and more seldom of late, his letters had been cold and curt.

He began to feel that in the pleasure and excitement of his life he had grown away from his mother and brother. Each summer he had said, "Well, now I'll go home *this* year sure." But a new play to be produced, or a yachting trip, or a tour of Europe, had put the home-coming off; and now it was with a distinct consciousness of neglect of duty that he walked up to the fence and looked into the yard, where William had told him his brother lived.

It was humble enough—a small white house, story-and-a-half structure, with a wing, set in the midst of a few locust-trees; a small drab-colored barn, with a sagging ridge-pole; a barnyard full of mud, in which a few cows were standing, fighting the flies and waiting to be milked. An old man was pumping water at the well; the pigs were squealing from a pen near by; a child was crying.

Instantly the beautiful, peaceful valley was forgotten. A sickening chill struck into Howard's soul as he looked at it all. In the dim light he could see a figure milking a cow. Leaving his valise at the gate, he entered, and walked up to the old man, who had finished pumping and was about to go to feed the hogs.

"Good-evening," Howard began. "Does Mr. Grant McLane live here?"

"Yes, sir, he does. He's right over there milkin'."

"I'll go over there an—"

"Don't b'lieve I would. It's darn muddy over there. It's been turrible rainy. He'll be done in a minute, anyway."

"Very well; I'll wait."

As he waited, he could hear a woman's fretful voice, and the impatient jerk and jar of kitchen things, indicative of ill-temper or worry. The longer he stood absorbing this farm-scene, with all its sordidness, dulness, triviality, and its endless drudgeries, the lower his heart sank. All the joy of the home-coming was gone, when the figure arose from the cow and approached the gate, and put the pail of milk down on the platform by the pump.

"Good-evening," said Howard, out of the dusk.

Grant stared a moment. "Good-evening."

Howard knew the voice, though it was older and deeper and more sullen. "Don't you know me, Grant? I am Howard."

The man approached him, gazing intently at his face. "You are?" after a pause. "Well, I'm glad to see yeh, but I can't shake hands. That damned cow had laid down in the mud."

They stood and looked at each other. Howard's cuffs, collar, and shirt, alien in their elegance, showed through the dusk, and a glint of light shot out from the jewel of his necktie, as the light from the house caught it at the right angle. As they gazed in silence at each other, Howard divined something of the hard, bitter feeling which came into Grant's heart, as he stood there, ragged, ankle-deep in muck, his sleeves rolled up, a shapeless old straw hat on his head.

The gleam of Howard's white hands angered him. When he spoke, it was in a hard, gruff tone, full of rebellion.

"Well, go in the house and set down. I'll be in soon's I strain the milk and wash the dirt off my hands."

"But Mother—"

"She's 'round somewhere. Just knock on the door under the porch round there."

Howard went slowly around the corner of the house, past a vilely smelling rain-barrel, toward the west. A gray-haired woman was sitting in a rocking-chair on the porch, her hands in her lap, her eyes fixed on the faintly yellow sky, against which the hills stood dim purple silhouettes, and the locust-trees were etched as fine as lace. There was sorrow, resignation, and a sort of dumb despair in her attitude.

Howard stood, his throat swelling till it seemed as if he would suffocate. This was his mother—the woman who bore him, the being who had taken her life in her hand for him; and he, in his excited and pleasurable life, had neglected her!

He stepped into the faint light before her. She turned and looked at him without fear. "Mother!" he said. She uttered one little, breathing, gasping cry, called his name, rose, and stood still. He bounded up the steps and took her in his arms.

"Mother! Dear old mother!"

In the silence, almost painful, which followed, an angry woman's voice could be heard inside: "I don't care. I ain't goin' to wear myself out fer him. He c'n eat out here with us, or else—"

Mrs. McLane began speaking. "Oh, I've longed to see yeh, Howard. I was afraid you wouldn't come till—too late."

"What do you mean, mother? Ain't you well?"

"I don't seem to be able to do much now 'cept sit around and knit a little. I tried to pick some berries the other day, and I got so dizzy I had to give it up."

"You mustn't work. You *needn't* work. Why didn't you write to me how you were?" Howard asked in an agony of remorse.

"Well, we felt as if you probably had all you could do to take care of yourself."

"Are you married, Howard?"

"No, mother; and there ain't any excuse for me—not a bit," he said, dropping back into her colloquialisms. "I'm ashamed when I think of how long it's been since I saw you. I could have come."

"It don't matter now," she interrupted gently. "Its the way things go. Our boys grow up and leave us."

"Well, come in to supper," said Grant's ungracious voice from the doorway. "Come, mother."

Mrs. McLane moved with difficulty. Howard sprang to her aid, and leaning on his arm she went through the little sitting-room, which was unlighted, out into the kitchen, where the supper-table stood near the cook-stove.

"How, this is my wife," said Grant, in a cold, peculiar tone.

Howard bowed toward a remarkably handsome young woman, on whose forehead was a scowl, which did not change as she looked at him and the old lady.

"Set down, anywhere," was the young woman's cordial invitation.

Howard sat down next to his mother, and facing the wife, who had a small, fretful child in her arms. At Howard's left was the old man, Lewis. The supper was spread upon a gay-colored oilcloth, and consisted of a pan of milk, set in the midst, with bowls at each plate. Beside the pan was a dipper and a large plate of bread, and at one end of the table was a dish of fine honey.

A boy of about fourteen leaned upon the table, his bent shoulders making him look like an old man. His hickory shirt, like that of Grant, was still wet with sweat, and discolored here and there with grease, or green from grass. His hair, freshly wet and combed, was smoothed away from his face, and shone in the light of the kerosene lamp. As he ate, he stared at Howard, as if he would make an inventory of each thread of the visitor's clothing.

"Did I look like that at his age?" thought Howard.

"You see we live jest about the same's ever," said Grant, as they began eating, speaking with a grim, almost challenging inflection.

The two brothers studied each other curiously, as they talked of neighborhood scenes. Howard seemed incredibly elegant and handsome to them all, with his rich, soft clothing, his spotless linen, and his exquisite enunciation and ease of speech. He had always been "smooth-spoken," and he had become "elegantly persuasive," as his friends said of him, and it was a large factor in his success.

Every detail of the kitchen, the heat, the flies buzzing aloft, the poor furniture, the dress of the people—all smote him like the lash of a wire whip. His brother was a man of great character. He could see that now. His deep-set, gray eyes and rugged face showed at thirty a man of great natural ability. He had more of the Scotch in his face than Howard, and he looked much older.

He was dressed, like the old man and the boy, in a checked shirt without vest. His suspenders, once gay-colored, had given most of their color to his shirt, and had marked irregular broad bands of pink and brown and green over his shoulders. His hair was uncombed, merely pushed away from his face. He wore a mustache only, though his face was covered with a week's growth of beard. His face was rather gaunt, and was brown as leather.

Howard could not eat much. He was disturbed by his mother's strange silence and oppression, and sickened by the long-drawn gasps with which the old man ate his bread and milk, and by the way the boy ate. He had his knife gripped tightly in his fist, knuckles up, and was scooping honey upon his bread.

The baby, having ceased to be afraid, was curious, gazing silently at the stranger.

"Hello, little one! Come and see your uncle. Eh? Course 'e will," cooed Howard in the attempt to escape the depressing atmosphere. The little one listened to his inflections as a kitten does, and at last lifted its arms in sign of surrender.

The mother's face cleared up a little. "I declare, she wants to go to you."

"Course she does. Dogs and kittens always come to me when I call 'em. Why shouldn't my own niece come?"

He took the little one and began walking up and down the kitchen with her, while she pulled at his beard and nose. "I ought to have you, my lady, in my new comedy. You'd bring down the house."

"You don't mean to say you put babies on the stage, Howard," said his mother in surprise.

"Oh, yes. Domestic comedy must have a baby these days."

"Well, that's another way of makin' a livin', sure," said Grant. The baby had cleared the atmosphere a little. "I s'pose you fellers make a pile of money."

"Sometimes we make a thousand a week; oftener we don't."

"A thousand dollars!" They all stared.

"A thousand dollars sometimes, and then lose it all the next week in another town. The dramatic business is a good deal like gambling—you take your chances."

"I wish you weren't in it, Howard. I don't like to have my son—"

"I wish I was in somethin' that paid better'n farmin'. Anything under God's heavens is better'n farmin'," said Grant.

"No, I ain't laid up much," Howard went on, as if explaining why he hadn't helped them. "Costs me a good deal to live, and I need about ten thousand dollars leeway to work on. I've made a good living, but I—I ain't made any money."

Grant looked at him, darkly meditative.

Howard went on:

"How'd ye come to sell the old farm? I was in hopes—"

"How'd we come to sell it?" said Grant with terrible bitterness. "We had something on it that didn't leave anything to sell. You probably don't remember anything about it, but there was a mortgage on it that eat us up in just four years by the almanac. 'Most killed mother to leave it. We wrote to you for money, but I don't s'pose you remember *that*."

"No, you didn't."

"Yes, I did."

"When was it? I don't—why, it's—I never received it. It must have been that summer I went with Rob Manning to Europe." Howard put the baby down and faced his brother. "Why, Grant, you didn't think I refused to help?"

"Well, it looked that way. We never heard a word from yeh all summer, and when y' did write, it was all about yerself'n plays 'n things we didn't know anything about. I swore to God I'd never write to you again, and I won't."

"But, good heavens! I never got it."

"Suppose you didn't. You might of known we were poor as Job's off-ox. Everybody is that earns a living. We fellers on the farm have to earn a livin' for ourselves and you fellers that don't work. I don't blame yeh. I'd do it if I could."

"Grant, don't talk so! Howard didn't realize—"

"I tell yeh I don't blame 'im. Only I don't want him to come the brotherly business over me, after livin' as he has—that's all." There was a bitter accusation in the man's voice.

Howard leaped to his feet, his face twitching. "By God, I'll go back to-morrow morning!" he threatened.

"Go, an' be damned! I don't care what yeh do," Grant growled, rising and going out.

"Boys," called the mother, piteously, "it's terrible to see you quarrel."

"But I'm not to blame, mother," cried Howard in a sickness that made him white as chalk. "The man is a savage. I came home to help you all, not to quarrel."

"Grant's got one o' his fits on," said the young wife, speaking for the first time. "Don't pay any attention to him. He'll be all right in the morning."

"If it wasn't for you, mother, I'd leave now, and never see that savage again."

He lashed himself up and down in the room, in horrible disgust and hate of his brother and of this home in his heart. He remembered his tender anticipations of the home-coming with a kind of self-pity and disgust. This was his greeting!

He went to bed, to toss about on the hard, straw-filled mattress in the stuffy little best room. Tossing, writhing under the bludgeoning of his brother's accusing inflections, a dozen times he said, with a half-articulate snarl:

"He can go to hell! I'll not try to do anything more for him. I don't care if he *is* my brother; he has no right to jump on me like that. On the night of my return, too. My God! he is a brute, a savage!"

He thought of the presents in his trunk and valise which he couldn't show to him that night, after what had been said. He had intended to have such a happy evening of it, such a tender reunion! It was to be so bright and cheery!

In the midst of his cursings, his hot indignation, would come visions of himself in his own modest rooms. He seemed to be yawning and stretching in his beautiful bed, the sun shining in, his books, foils, pictures around him, to say good-morning and tempt him to rise, while the squat little clock on the mantel struck eleven warningly.

He could see the olive walls, the unique copper-and-crimson arabesque frieze (his own selection), and the delicate draperies; an open grate full of glowing coals, to temper the sea-winds; and in the midst of it, between a landscape by Enneking and an Indian in a canoe in a cañon, by Brush, he saw a sombre landscape by a master greater than Millet, a melancholy subject, treated with pitiless fidelity.

A farm in the valley! Over the mountains swept jagged, gray, angry, sprawling clouds, sending a freezing, thin drizzle of rain, as they passed, upon a man following a plough. The horses had a sullen and weary look, and their manes and tails streamed sidewise in the blast. The ploughman clad in a ragged gray coat, with uncouth, muddy boots upon his feet, walked with his head inclined towards the sleet, to shield his face from the cold and sting of it. The soil rolled away, black and sticky and with a dull sheen upon it. Near by, a boy with tears on his cheeks was watching cattle, a dog seated near, his back to the gale.

As he looked at this picture, his heart softened. He looked down at the sleeve of his soft and fleecy night-shirt, at his white, rounded arm, muscular yet fine as a woman's, and when he looked for the picture it was gone. Then came again the assertive odor of stagnant air, laden with camphor; he felt the springless bed under him, and caught dimly a few soap-advertising lithographs on the walls. He thought of his brother, in his still more inhospitable bedroom, disturbed by the child, condemned to rise at five o'clock and begin another day's pitiless labor. His heart shrank and quivered, and the tears started to his eyes.

"I forgive him, poor fellow! He's not to blame."

II

He woke, however, with a chill, languid pulse, and an oppressive melancholy on his heart. He looked around the little room, clean enough, but oh, how poor! how barren! Cold plaster walls, a cheap wash-stand, a wash-set of three pieces, with a blue band around each; the windows, rectangular, and fitted with fantastic green shades.

Outside he could hear the bees humming. Chickens were merrily moving about. Cow-bells far up the road were sounding irregularly. A jay came by and yelled an insolent reveille, and Howard sat up. He could hear nothing in the house but the rattle of pans on the back side of the kitchen. He looked at his watch and saw it was half-past seven. His brother was in the field by this time, after milking, currying the horses, and eating breakfast—had been at work two hours and a half.

He dressed himself hurriedly in a négligé shirt with a windsor scarf, light-colored, serviceable trousers with a belt, russet shoes and a tennis hat—a knock-about costume, he considered. His mother, good soul, thought it a special suit put on for her benefit, and admired it through her glasses.

He kissed her with a bright smile, nodded at Laura the young wife, and tossed the baby, all in a breath, and with the manner as he himself saw, of the returned captain in the war-dramas of the day.

"Been to breakfast?" He frowned reproachfully. "Why didn't you call me? I wanted to get up, just as I used to, at sunrise."

"We thought you was tired, and so we didn't—"

"Tired! Just wait till you see me help Grant pitch hay or something. Hasn't finished his haying, has he?"

"No, I guess not. He will to-day if it don't rain again."

"Well, breakfast is all ready—Howard," said Laura, hesitating a little on his name.

"Good! I am ready for it. Bacon and eggs, as I'm a jay! Just what I was wanting. I was saying to myself: 'Now if they'll only get bacon and eggs and hot biscuits and honey—' Oh, say, mother, I heard the bees humming this morning; same noise they used to make when I was a boy, exactly. Must be the same bees.— Hey, you young rascal! come here and have some breakfast with your uncle."

"I never saw her take to any one so quick," Laura smiled. Howard noticed her in particular for the first time. She had on a clean calico dress and a gingham apron, and she looked strong and fresh and handsome. Her head was intellectual, her eyes full of power. She seemed anxious to remove the impression of her unpleasant looks and words the night before. Indeed it would have been hard to resist Howard's sunny good-nature.

The baby laughed and crowed. The old mother could not take her dim eyes off the face of her son, but sat smiling at him as he ate and rattled on. When he rose from the table at last, after eating heartily and praising it all, he said, with a smile:

"Well, now I'll just telephone down to the express and have my trunk brought up. I've got a few little things in there you'll enjoy seeing. But this fellow," indicating the baby, "I didn't take into account. But never mind; Uncle How'll make that all right."

"You ain't goin' to lay it up agin Grant, be you, my son?" Mrs. McLane faltered, as they went out into the best room.

"Of course not! He didn't mean it. Now can't you send word down and have my trunk brought up? Or shall I have to walk down?"

"I guess I'll see somebody goin' down," said Laura,

"All right. Now for the hay-field," he smiled, and went out into the glorious morning.

The circling hills the same, yet not the same as at night. A cooler, tenderer, more subdued cloak of color upon them. Far down the valley a cool, deep, impalpable, blue mist lay, under which one divined the river ran, under its elms and basswoods and wild grapevines. On the shaven slopes of the hills cattle and sheep were feeding, their cries and bells coming to the ear with a sweet suggestiveness. There was something immemorial in the sunny slopes dotted with red and brown and gray cattle.

Walking toward the haymakers, Howard felt a twinge of pain and distrust. Would he ignore it all and smile—

He stopped short. He had not seen Grant smile in so long—he couldn't quite see him smiling. He had been cold and bitter for years. When he came up to them, Grant was pitching on; the old man was loading, and the boy was raking after.

"Good-morning," Howard cried cheerily. The old man nodded, the boy stared. Grant growled something, without looking up. These "finical" things of saying good-morning and good-night are not much practised in such homes as Grant McLane's.

"Need some help? I'm ready to take a hand. Got on my regimentals this morning."

Grant looked at him a moment.

"You look like it."

"Gimme a hold on that fork, and I'll show you. I'm not so soft as I look, now you bet."

He laid hold upon the fork in Grant's hands, who released it sullenly and stood back sneering. Howard stuck the fork into the pile in the old way, threw his left hand to the end of the polished handle, brought it down into the hollow of his thigh, and laid out his strength till the handle bent like a bow. "Oop she rises!" he called laughingly, as the whole pile began slowly to rise, and finally rolled upon the high load.

"Oh, I ain't forgot how to do it," he laughed, as he looked around at the boy, who was studying the jacket and hat with a devouring gaze.

Grant was studying him too, but not in admiration.

"I shouldn't say you had," said the old man, tugging at the forkful.

"Mighty funny to come out here and do a little of this. But if you had to come here and do it all the while, you wouldn't look so white and soft in the hands," Grant said, as they moved on to another pile. "Give me that fork. You'll be spoiling your fine clothes."

"Oh, these don't matter. They're made for this kind of thing."

"Oh, are they? I guess I'll dress in that kind of a rig. What did that shirt cost? I need one."

"Six dollars a pair; but then it's old."

"And them pants," he pursued; "they cost six dollars too, didn't they?"

Howard's face darkened. He saw his brother's purpose. He resented it. "They cost fifteen dollars, if you want to know, and the shoes cost six-fifty. This ring on my cravat cost sixty dollars and the suit I had on last night cost eighty-five. My suits are made by Breckstein, on Fifth Avenue and Twentieth Street, if you want to patronize him," he ended brutally, spurred on by the sneer in his brother's eyes. "I'll introduce you."

"Good idea," said Grant, with a forced, mocking smile. "I need just such a get-up for haying and corn-ploughing. Singular I never thought of it. Now my pants cost eighty-five cents, s'penders fifteen, hat twenty, shoes one-fifty; stockin's I don't bother about."

He had his brother at a disadvantage, and he grew fluent and caustic as he went on, almost changing places with Howard, who took the rake out of the boy's hands and followed, raking up the scatterings.

"Singular we fellers here are discontented and mulish, ain't it? Singular we don't believe your letters when you write, sayin', 'I just about make a live of it'? Singular we think the country's goin' to hell, we fellers, in a two-dollar suit, wadin' around in the mud or sweatin' around in the hay-field, while you fellers lay around New York and smoke and wear good clothes and toady to millionaires?"

Howard threw down the rake and folded his arms. "My God! you're enough to make a man forget the same mother bore us!"

"I guess it wouldn't take much to make you forget that. You ain't put much thought on me nor her for ten years."

The old man cackled, the boy grinned, and Howard, sick and weak with anger and sorrow, turned away and walked down toward the brook. He had tried once more to get near his brother, and had failed. Oh, God! how miserably, pitiably! The hot blood gushed all over him as he thought of the shame and disgrace of it.

He, a man associating with poets, artists, sought after by brilliant women, accustomed to deference even from such people, to be sneered at, outfaced, shamed, shoved aside, by a man in a stained hickory shirt and patched overalls, and that man his brother! He lay down on the bright grass, with the sheep all around him, and writhed and groaned with the agony and despair of it.

And worst of all, underneath it was a consciousness that Grant was right in distrusting him. He *had* neglected him; he *had* said, "I guess they're getting along all right." He had put them behind him when the invitation to spend summer on the Mediterranean or in the Adirondacks, came.

"What can I do? What can I do?" he groaned.

The sheep nibbled the grass near him, the jays called pertly, "Shame, shame," a quail piped somewhere on the hillside, and the brook sung a soft, soothing melody that took away at last the sharp edge of his pain, and he sat up and gazed down the valley, bright with the sun and apparently filled with happy and prosperous people.

Suddenly a thought seized him. He stood up so suddenly the sheep fled in affright. He leaped the brook, crossed the flat, and began searching in the bushes on the hillside. "Hurrah!" he said, with a smile.

He had found an old road which he used to travel when a boy—a road that skirted the edge of the valley, now grown up to brush, but still passable for footmen. As he ran lightly along down the beautiful path, under oaks and hickories, past masses of poison-ivy, under hanging grapevines, through clumps of splendid hazelnut bushes loaded with great sticky, rough, green burs, his heart threw off part of its load.

How it all came back to him! How many days, when the autumn sun burned the frost off the bushes, had he gathered hazel-nuts here with his boy and girl friends— Hugh and Shelley McTurg, Rome Sawyer, Orrin McIlvaine, and the rest! What had become of them all? How he had forgotten them!

This thought stopped him again, and he fell into a deep muse, leaning against an oak-tree and gazing into the vast fleckless space above. The thrilling, inscrutable mystery of life fell upon him like a blinding light. Why was he living in the crush and thunder and mental unrest of a great city, while his companions, seemingly his equals, in powers, were milking cows, making butter, and growing corn and wheat in the silence and drear monotony of the farm?

His boyish sweethearts! their names came back to his ear now, with a dull, sweet sound as of faint bells. He saw their faces, their pink sunbonnets tipped back upon their necks, their brown ankles flying with the swift action of the scurrying partridge. His eyes softened: he took off his hat. The sound of the wind and the leaves moved him almost to tears.

A woodpecker gave a shrill, high-keyed, sustained cry. "Ki, ki, ki!" and he started from his revery, the dapples of sun and shade falling upon his lithe figure as he hurried on down the path.

He came at last to a field of corn that ran to the very wall of a large weather-beaten house, the sight of which made his breathing quicker. It was the place where he was born. The mystery of his life began there. In the branches of those poplar and hickory trees he had swung and sung in the rushing breeze, fearless as a squirrel. Here was the brook where, like a larger Kildee, he with Grant had waded after crawfish, or had stolen upon some wary trout, rough-cut pole in hand.

Seeing someone in the garden, he went down along the corn-row through the rustling ranks of green leaves. An old woman was picking berries, a squat and shapeless figure.

"Good-morning," he called cheerily.

"Morgen," she said, looking up at him with a startled and very red face. She was German in every line of her body.

"Ich bin Herr McLane," he said, after a pause.

"So?" she replied, with a questioning inflection.

"Yah; ich bin Herr Grant's Bruder."

"Ach, so!" she said, with a downward inflection. "Ich no spick Inglish. No spick Inglis."

"Ich bin durstig," he said. Leaving her pans, she went with him to the house, which was what he wanted to see.

"Ich bin hier geboren."

"Ach, so!" She recognized the little bit of sentiment, and said some sentences in German whose general meaning was sympathy. She took him to the cool cellar where the spring had been trained to run into a tank containing pans of cream and milk, she gave him a cool draught from a large tin cup, and then at his request they went upstairs. The house was the same, but somehow seemed cold and empty. It was clean and sweet, but it had so little evidence of being lived in. The old part, which was built of logs, was used as best room, and modelled after the best rooms of the neighboring Yankee homes, only it was emptier, without the cabinet organ and the rag-carpet and the chromos.

The old fireplace was bricked up and plastered—the fireplace beside which in the far-off days he had lain on winter nights, to hear his uncles tell tales of hunting, or to hear them play the violin, great dreaming giants that they were.

The old woman went out and left him sitting there, the centre of a swarm of memories coming and going like so many ghostly birds and butterflies.

A curious heartache and listlessness, a nerveless mood came on him. What was it worth, anyhow—success? Struggle, strife, trampling on some one else. His play crowding out some other poor fellow's hope. The hawk eats the partridge, the partridge eats the flies and bugs, the bugs eat each other and the hawk, when he in his turn is shot by man. So, in the world of business, the life of one man seemed to him to be drawn from the life of another man, each success to spring from other failures.

He was like a man from whom all motives had been withdrawn. He was sick, sick to the heart. Oh, to be a boy again! An ignorant baby, pleased with a block and string, with no knowledge and no care of the great unknown! To lay his head again on his mother's bosom and rest! To watch the flames on the hearth!—

"Why not? Was not that the very thing to do? To buy back the old farm? It would cripple him a little for the next season, but he could do it. Think of it! To see his mother back in the old home, with the fireplace restored, the old furniture in the sitting-room around her, and fine new things in the parlor!

His spirits rose again. Grant couldn't stand out when he brought to him a deed of the farm. Surely his debt would be cancelled when he had seen them all back in the wide old kitchen. He began to plan and to dream. He went to the windows, and looked out on the yard to see how much it had changed.

He'd build a new barn, and buy them a new carriage. His heart glowed again, and his lips softened into their usual feminine grace—lips a little full and falling easily into curves.

The old German woman came in at length, bringing some cakes and a bowl of milk, smiling broadly and hospitably as she waddled forward.

"Ach! Goot!" he said, smacking his lips over the pleasant draught.

"Wo ist ihre goot mann?" he inquired, ready for business.

III

When Grant came in at noon Mrs. McLane met him at the door, with a tender smile on her face.

"Where's Howard, Grant?"

"I don't know," he replied in a tone that implied "I don't care."

The dim eyes clouded with quick tears.

"Ain't you seen him?"

"Not since nine o'clock."

"Where d'you think he is?"

"I tell yeh I don't know. He'll take care of himself; don't worry."

He flung off his hat and plunged into the washbasin. His shirt was wet with sweat and covered with dust of the hay and fragments of leaves. He splashed his burning face with the water, paying no further attention to his mother. She spoke again, very gently, in reproof:

"Grant, why do you stand out against Howard so?"

"I don't stand out against him," he replied harshly, pausing with the towel in his hands. His eyes were hard and piercing. "But if he expects me to gush over his coming back, he's fooled, that's all. He's left us to paddle our own canoe all this while, and, so far as *I'm* concerned, he can leave us alone hereafter. He looked out for his precious hide mighty well, and now he comes back here to play big-gun and pat us on the head. I don't propose to let him come that over me."

Mrs. McLane knew too well the temper of her son to say any more, but she inquired about Howard of the old hired man.

"He went off down the valley. He 'n' Grant had s'm *words*, and he pulled out down toward the old farm. That's the last I see of 'im."

Laura took Howard's part at the table. "Pity you can't be decent," she said, brutally direct as usual. "You treat Howard as if he was a—a—I do' know what."

"Will you let me alone?"

"No, I won't. If you think I'm going to set by an' agree to your bullyraggin him, you're mistaken. It's a shame! You're mad 'cause he's succeeded and you ain't. He ain't to blame for his brains. If you and I'd had any, we'd 'a 'succeeded too. It ain't our fault and it ain't his; so what's the use?"

There was a look came into Grant's face that the wife knew. It meant bitter and terrible silence. He ate his dinner without another word.

It was beginning to cloud up. A thin, whitish, all-pervasive vapor which meant rain was dimming the sky, and he forced his hands to their utmost during the afternoon in order to get most of the down hay in before the rain came. He was pitching hay up into the barn when Howard came by just before one o'clock.

It was windless there. The sun fell through the white mist with undiminished fury, and the fragrant hay sent up a breath that was hot as an oven-draught. Grant was a powerful man, and there was something majestic in his action as he rolled the huge flakes of hay through the door. The sweat poured from his face like rain, and he was forced to draw his dripping sleeve across his face to clear away the blinding sweat that poured into his eyes.

Howard stood and looked at him in silence, remembering how often he had worked there in that furnace-heat, his muscles quivering, cold chills running over his flesh, red shadows dancing before his eyes.

His mother met him at the door, anxiously, but smiled as she saw his pleasant face and cheerful eyes.

"You're a little late, m' son."

Howard spent most of the afternoon sitting with his mother on the porch, or under the trees, lying sprawled out like a boy, resting at times with sweet forgetfulness of the whole world, but feeling a dull pain whenever he remembered the stern, silent man pitching hay in the hot sun on the torrid side of the barn.

His mother did not say anything about the quarrel; she feared to reopen it. She talked mainly of old times in a gentle monotone of reminiscence, while he listened, looking up into her patient face.

The heat slowly lessened as the sun sank down toward the dun clouds rising like a more distant and majestic line of mountains beyond the western hills. The sound of cow-bells came irregularly to the ear, and the voices and sounds of the haying-fields had a jocund, thrilling effect on the ear of the city-dweller.

He was very tender. Everything conspired to make him simple, direct, and honest.

"Mother, if you'll only forgive me for staying away so long, I'll surely come to see you every summer."

She had nothing to forgive. She was so glad to have him there at her feet—her great, handsome, successful boy! She could only love him and enjoy him every moment of the precious days. If Grant would only reconcile himself to Howard! That was the great thorn in her flesh.

Howard told her how he had succeeded.

"It was luck, mother. First I met Cooke, and he introduced me to Jake Saulsman of Chicago. Jake asked me to go to New York with him, and—I don't know why—took a fancy to me some way. He introduced me to a lot of the fellows in New York, and they all helped me along. I did nothing to merit it. Everybody helps me. Anybody can succeed in that way."

The doting mother thought it not at all strange that they all helped him.

At the supper-table Grant was gloomily silent, ignoring Howard completely. Mrs. McLane sat and grieved silently, not daring to say a word in protest. Laura and the baby tried to amuse Howard, and under cover of their talk the meal was eaten.

The boy fascinated Howard. He "sawed wood" with a rapidity and uninterruptedness which gave alarm. He had the air of coaling up for a long voyage.

"At that age," Howard thought, "I must have gripped my knife in my right hand so, and poured my tea into my saucer so. I must have buttered and bit into a huge slice of bread just so, and chewed at it with a smacking sound in just that way. I must have gone to the length of scooping up honey with my knife-blade."

It was magically, mystically beautiful over all this squalor and toil and bitterness, from five till seven—a moving hour. Again the falling sun streamed in broad banners across the valleys; again the blue mist lay far down the Coulé over the river; the cattle called from the hills in the moistening, sonorous air; the bells came in a pleasant tangle of sound; the air pulsed with the deepening chorus of katydids and other nocturnal singers.

Sweet and deep as the very springs of his life was all this to the soul of the elder brother; but in the midst of it, the younger man, in ill-smelling clothes and great boots that chafed his feet, went out to milk the cows—on whose legs the flies and mosquitoes swarmed, bloated with blood,—to sit by the hot side of the cow and be lashed with her tail as she tried frantically to keep the savage insects from eating her raw.

"The poet who writes of milking the cows does it from the hammock, looking on," Howard soliloquized, as he watched the old man Lewis racing around the filthy yard after one of the young heifers that had kicked over the pail in her agony with the flies and was unwilling to stand still and be eaten alive.

"So, so! you beast!" roared the old man, as he finally cornered the shrinking, nearly frantic creature.

"Don't you want to look at the garden?" asked Mrs. McLane of Howard; and they went out among the vegetables and berries.

The bees were coming home heavily laden and crawling slowly into the hives. The level, red light streamed through the trees, blazed along the grass, and lighted a few old-fashioned flowers into red and gold flame. It was beautiful, and Howard looked at it through his half-shut eyes as the painters do, and turned away with a sigh at the sound of blows where the wet and grimy men were assailing the frantic cows.

"There's Wesley with your trunk," Mrs. McLane said, recalling him to himself.

Wesley helped him carry the trunk in, and waved off thanks.

"Oh, that's all right," he said; and Howard knew the Western man too well to press the matter of pay.

As he went in an hour later and stood by the trunk, the dull ache came back into his heart. How he had failed! It seemed like a bitter mockery now to show his gifts.

Grant had come in from his work, and with his feet released from his chafing boots, in his wet shirt and milk-splashed overalls, sat at the kitchen table reading a newspaper which he held close to a small kerosene lamp. He paid no attention to anyone. His attitude, curiously like his father's, was perfectly definite to Howard. It meant that from that time forward there were to be no words of any sort between them. It meant that they were no longer brothers, not even acquaintances. "How inexorable that face!" thought Howard.

He turned sick with disgust and despair, and would have closed his trunk without showing any of the presents, only for the childish expectancy of his mother and Laura.

"Here's something for you, mother," he said, assuming a cheerful voice, as he took a fold of fine silk from the trunk and held it up. "All the way from Paris."

He laid it on his mother's lap and stooped and kissed her, and then turned hastily away to hide the tears that came to his own eyes as he saw her keen pleasure.

"And here's a parasol for Laura. I don't know how I came to have that in here. And here's General Grant's autobiography for his namesake," he said, with an effort at carelessness, and waited to hear Grant rise.

"Grant, won't you come in?" asked his mother, quaveringly.

Grant did not reply nor move. Laura took the handsome volumes out and laid them beside him on the table. He simply pushed them one side and went on with his reading.

Again that horrible anger swept hot as flame over Howard. He could have cursed him. His hands shook as he handed out other presents to his mother and Laura and the baby. He tried to joke.

"I didn't know how old the baby was, so she'll have to grow to some of these things."

But the pleasure was all gone for him and for the rest. His heart swelled almost to a feeling of pain as he looked at his mother. There she sat with the presents in her lap. The shining silk came too late for her. It threw into appalling relief her age, her poverty, her work-weary frame. "My God!" he almost cried aloud, "how little it would have taken to lighten her life!"

Upon this moment, when it seemed as if he could endure no more, came the smooth voice of William McTurg:

"Hello, folkses!"

"Hello, Uncle Bill! Come in."

"That's what we came for," laughed a woman's voice.

"Is that you, Rose?" asked Laura.

"Its me—Rose," replied the laughing girl, as she bounced into the room and greeted everybody in a breathless sort of way.

"You don't mean little Rosy?"

"Big Rosy now," said William.

Howard looked at the handsome girl and smiled, saying in a nasal sort of tone, "Wal, wal! Rosy, how you've growed since I saw yeh!"

"Oh, look at all this purple and fine linen! Am I left out?"

Rose was a large girl of twenty-five or there-abouts, and was called an old maid. She radiated good-nature from every line of her buxom self. Her black eyes were full of drollery, and she was on the best of terms with Howard at once. She had been a teacher, but that did not prevent her from assuming a peculiar directness of speech. Of course they talked about old friends.

"Where's Rachel?" Howard inquired. Her smile faded away.

"Shellie married Orrin McIlvaine. They're way out in Dakota. Shellie's havin' a hard row of stumps."

There was a little silence,

"And Tommy?"

"Gone West. Most all the boys have gone West. That's the reason there's so many old maids."

"You don't mean to say—"

"I don't *need* to say—I'm an old maid. Lots of the girls are."

"It don't pay to marry these days."

"Are you married?"

"Not *yet*." His eyes lighted up again in a humorous way.

"Not yet! That's good! That's the way old maids all talk."

"You don't mean to tell me that no young fellow comes prowling around—"

"Oh, a young Dutchman or Norwegian once in a while. Nobody that counts. Fact is, we're getting like Boston—four women to one man; and when you consider that we're getting more particular each year, the outlook is—well, it's dreadful!"

"It certainly is."

"Marriage is a failure these days for most of us. We can't live on the farm, and can't get a living in the city, and there we are." She laid her hand on his arm. "I declare, Howard, you're the same boy you used to be. I ain't a bit afraid of you, for all your success."

"And you're the same girl? No, I can't say that. It seems to me you've grown more than I have—I don't mean physically, I mean mentally," he explained, as he saw her smile in the defensive way a fleshy girl has, alert to ward off a joke.

They were in the midst of talk. Howard telling one of his funny stories, when a wagon clattered up to the door, and merry voices called loudly:

"Whoa, there, Sampson!"

"Hullo, the house!"

Rose looked at her father with a smile in her black eyes exactly like his. They went to the door.

"Hullo! What's wanted?"

"Grant McLane live here?"

"Yup. Right here."

A moment later there came a laughing, chatting squad of women to the door. Mrs. McLane and Laura stared at each other in amazement. Grant went out-doors.

Rose stood at the door as if she were hostess.

"Come in, Nettie. Glad to see yeh—glad to see yeh! Mrs. McIlvaine, come right in! Take a seat. Make yerself to home, *do!* And Mrs. Peavey! Wal, I never! This must be a surprise-party. Well, I swan! How many more o' ye air they?"

All was confusion, merriment, hand-shakings as Rose introduced them in her roguish way.

"Folks, this is Mr. Howard McLane of New York. He's an actor, but it hain't spoiled him a bit as I can see. How, this is Nettie McIlvaine—Wilson that was."

Howard shook hands with Nettie, a tall, plain girl with prominent teeth.

"This is Ma McIlvaine."

"She looks just the same," said Howard, shaking her hand and feeling, how hard and work-worn it was.

And so amid bustle, chatter, and invitations "to lay off y'r things an' stay awhile," the women got disposed about the room at last. Those that had rocking-chairs rocked vigorously to and fro to hide their embarrassment. They all talked in loud voices.

Howard felt nervous under this furtive scrutiny. He wished his clothes didn't look so confoundedly dressy. Why didn't he have sense enough to go and buy a fif-teen-dollar suit of diagonals for every-day wear.

Rose was the life of the party. Her tongue rattled on in the most delightful way.

"It's all Rose an' Bill's doin's," Mrs. McIlvaine explained. "They told us to come over an' pick up anybody we see on the road. So we did."

Howard winced a little at her familiarity of tone. He couldn't help it for the life of him.

"Well, I wanted to come to-night because I'm going away next week, and I wanted to see how he'd act at a surprise-party again," Rose explained.

"Married, I s'pose," said Mrs. McIlvaine, abruptly.

"No, not yet."

"Good land! Why, y' mus' be thirty-five, How. Must 'a' dis'p'inted y'r mam not to have a young 'un to call 'er granny."

The men came clumping in, talking about haying and horses. Some of the older ones Howard knew and greeted, but the younger ones were mainly too much changed.

They were all very ill at ease. Most of them were in compromise dress—something lying between working "rig" and Sunday dress. Most of them had on clean shirts and paper collars, and wore their Sunday coats (thick woollen garments) over rough trousers. All of them crossed their legs at once, and most of them sought the wall and leaned back perilously upon the hind legs of their chairs, eyeing Howard slowly.

For the first few minutes the presents were the subjects of conversation. The women especially spent a good deal of talk upon them.

Howard found himself forced to taking the initiative, so he inquired about the crops and about the farms.

"I see you don't plough the hills as we used to. And reap! *What* a job it ust to be. It makes the hills more beautiful to have them covered with smooth grass and cattle."

There was only dead silence to this touching upon the idea of beauty.

"I s'pose it pays reasonably."

"Not enough to kill," said one of the younger men. "You c'n see that by the houses we live in—that is, most of us. A few that came in early an' got land cheap, like McIlvaine, here—he got a lift that the rest of us can't get."

"I'm a free-trader, myself," said one young fellow, blushing and looking away as Howard turned and said cheerily:

"So 'm I."

The rest seemed to feel that this was a tabooed subject—a subject to be talked out of doors, where one could prance about and yell and do justice to it.

Grant sat silently in the kitchen doorway, not saying a word, not looking at his brother.

"Well, I don't never use hot vinegar for mine," Mrs. McIlvaine was heard to say. "I jest use hot water, an' I rinse 'em out good, and set 'em bottom-side up in the sun. I do' know but what hot vinegar *would* be more cleansin'."

Rose had the younger folks in a giggle with a droll telling of a joke on herself.

"How'd y' stop 'em from laffin'?"

"I let 'em laugh. Oh, my school is a disgrace—so one director says. But I like to see children laugh. It broadens their cheeks."

"Yes, that's all hand-work." Laura was showing the baby's Sunday clothes.

"Goodness Peter! How do you find time to do so much?"

"I take time."

Howard, being the lion of the evening, tried his best to be agreeable. He kept near his mother, because it afforded her so much pride and satisfaction, and because he was obliged to keep away from Grant, who had begun to talk to the men. Howard talked mainly about their affairs, but still was forced more and more into talking of life in the city. As he told of the theatre and the concerts, a sudden change fell upon them; they grew sober, and he felt deep down in the hearts of these people a melancholy which was expressed only elusively with little tones or sighs. Their gayety was fitful.

They were hungry for the world, for art—these young people. Discontented and yet hardly daring to acknowledge it; indeed, few of them could have made definite statement of their dissatisfaction. The older people felt it less. They practically said, with a sigh of pathetic resignation:

"Well, I don't expect ever to see these things *now*."

A casual observer would have said, "What a pleasant bucolic—this little surprise-party of welcome!" But Howard with his native ear and eye had no such pleasing illusion. He knew too well these suggestions of despair and bitterness. He knew that, like the smile of the slave, this cheerfulness was self-defence; deep down was another self.

Seeing Grant talking with a group of men over by the kitchen door, he crossed over slowly and stood listening. Wesley Cosgrove—a tall, raw-boned young fellow with a grave, almost tragic face—was saying:

"Of course I ain't. Who is? A man that's satisfied to live as we do is a fool."

"The worst of it is," said Grant, without seeing Howard, "a man can't get out of it during his lifetime, and *I* don't know that he'll have any chance in the next—the speculator'll be there ahead of us."

The rest laughed, but Grant went on grimly:

"Ten years ago Wess, here, could have got land in Dakota pretty easy, but now it's about all a feller's life's worth to try it. I tell you things seem shuttin' down on us fellers."

"Plenty o' land to rent?" suggested some one.

"Yes, in terms that skin a man alive. More than that, farmin' ain't so free a life as it used to be. This cattle-raisin' and butter-makin' makes a nigger of a man. Binds him right down to the grindstone, and he gets nothin' out of it—that's what rubs it in. He simply wallers-around in the manure for somebody else. I'd like to know what a man's life is worth who lives as we do? How much higher is it than the lives the niggers used to live?"

These brutally bold words made Howard thrill with emotion like some great tragic poem. A silence fell on the group.

"That's the God's truth, Grant," said young Cosgrove, after a pause.

"A man like me is helpless," Grant was saying. "Just like a fly in a pan of molasses. There ain't any escape for him. The more he tears around the more liable he is to rip his legs off."

"What can he do?"

"Nothin'."

The men listened in silence.

"Oh come, don't talk politics all night!" cried Rose, breaking in. "Come, let's have a dance. Where's that fiddle?"

"Fiddle!" cried Howard, glad of a chance to laugh. "Well, now! Bring out that fiddle. Is it William's?"

"Yes, pap's old fiddle."

"O Gosh! he don't want to hear me play," protested William. "He's heard s' many fiddlers."

"Fiddlers! I've heard a thousand violinists, but not fiddlers. Come, give us 'Honest John.'"

William took the fiddle in his work-calloused and crooked hands and began tuning it. The group at the kitchen door turned to listen, their faces lighting up a little. Rose tried to get a set on the floor.

"Oh, good land!" said some. "We're all tuckered out. What makes you so anxious?"

"She wants a chance to dance with the New Yorker."

"That's it exactly," Rose admitted.

"Wal, if you'd churned and mopped and cooked for hayin' hands as I have today, you wouldn't be so full o' nonsense."

"Oh, bother! Life's short. Come quick, get Bettie out. Come, Wess, never mind your hobby-horse."

By incredible exertion she got a set on the floor, and William got the fiddle in tune. Howard looked across at Wesley, and thought the change in him splendidly dramatic. His face had lighted up into a kind of deprecating, boyish smile. Rose could do anything with him.

William played some of the old tunes that had a thousand associated memories in Howard's brain, memories of harvest-moons, of melon-feasts, and of clear, cold winter nights. As he danced, his eyes filled with a tender, luminous light. He came closer to them all than he had been able to do before. Grant had gone out into the kitchen.

After two or three sets had been danced, the company took seats and could not be stirred again. So Laura and Rose disappeared for a few moments, and returning, served strawberries and cream, which Laura said she "just happened to have in the house."

And then William played again. His fingers, now grown more supple, brought out clearer, firmer tones. As he played, silence fell on these people. The magic of music sobered every face; the women looked older and more care-worn, the men slouched sullenly in their chairs, or leaned back against the wall.

It seemed to Howard as if the spirit of tragedy had entered this house. Music had always been William's unconscious expression of his unsatisfied desires. He was never melancholy except when he played. Then his eyes grew sombre, his drooping face full of shadows.

He played on slowly, softly, wailing Scotch tunes and mournful Irish songs. He seemed to find in the songs of these people, and especially in a wild, sweet, low-keyed negro song, some expression for his indefinable inner melancholy.

He played on, forgetful of everybody, his long beard sweeping the violin, his toil-worn hands marvellously obedient to his will.

At last he stopped, looked up with a faint, deprecating smile, and said with a sigh: "Well, folkses, time to go home."

The going was quiet. Not much laughing. Howard stood at the door and said good-night to them all, his heart very tender.

"Come and see us," they said.

"I will," he replied cordially. "I'll try and get around to see everybody, and talk over old times, before I go back."

After the wagons had driven out of the yard, Howard turned and put his arm about his mother's neck.

"Tired?"

"A little."

"Well, now good-night. I'm going for a little stroll."

His brain was too active to sleep. He kissed his mother good-night, and went out into the road, his hat in his hand, the cool, moist wind on his hair.

It was very dark, the stars being partly hidden by a thin vapor. On each side the hills rose, every line familiar as the face of an old friend. A whippoorwill called occasionally from the hillside, and the spasmodic jangle of a bell now and then told of some cow's battle with the mosquitoes.

As he walked, he pondered upon the tragedy he had re-discovered in these people's lives. Out here under the inexorable spaces of the sky, a deep distaste of his own life took possession of him. He felt like giving it all up. He thought of the infinite tragedy of these lives which the world loves to call "peaceful and pastoral." His mind went out in the aim to help them. What could he do to make life better worth living? Nothing. They must live and die practically as he saw them to-night.

And yet he knew this was a mood, and that in a few hours the love and the habit of life would come back upon him and upon them; that he would go back to the city in a few days; that these people would live on and make the best of it.

"I'll make the best of it," he said at last, and his thought came back to his mother and Grant.

IV

The next day was a rainy day; not a shower, but a steady rain—an unusual thing in mid-summer in the West. A cold, dismal day in the fireless, colorless farm-houses. It came to Howard in that peculiar reaction which surely comes during a visit of this character, when thought is a weariness, when the visitor longs for his own familiar walls and pictures and books, and longs to meet his friends, feeling at the same time the tragedy of life which makes friends nearer and more congenial than blood-relations.

Howard ate his breakfast alone, save Baby and Laura, its mother, going about the room. Baby and mother alike insisted on feeding him to death. Already dyspeptic pangs were setting in.

"Now ain't there something more I can—"

"Good heavens! No!" he cried in dismay. "I'm likely to die of dyspepsia now. This honey and milk, and these delicious hot biscuits—"

"I'm afraid it ain't much like the breakfasts you have in the city."

"Well, no, it ain't," he confessed. "But this is the kind a man needs when he lives in the open air."

She sat down opposite him, with her elbows on the table, her chin in her palm, her eyes full of shadows.

"I'd like to go to a city once. I never saw a town bigger'n Lumberville. I've never seen a play, but I've read of 'em in the magazines. It must be wonderful; they say they have wharves and real ships coming up to the wharf, and people getting off and on. How do they do it?"

"Oh, that's too long a story to tell. It's a lot of machinery and paint and canvas. If I told you how it was done, you wouldn't enjoy it so well when you come on and see it."

"Do you ever expect to see *me* in New York?"

"Why, yes. Why not? I expect Grant to come on and bring you all some day, especially Tonikins here. Tonikins, you hear, sir? I expect you to come on you' forf birf-day, sure." He tried thus to stop the woman's gloomy confidence.

"I hate farm-life," she went on with a bitter inflection. "It's nothing but fret, fret and work the whole time, never going any place, never seeing anybody but a lot of neighbors just as big fools as you are. I spend my time fighting flies and washing dishes and churning. I'm sick of it all."

Howard was silent. What could he say to such an indictment? The ceiling swarmed with flies which the cold rain had driven to seek the warmth of the kitchen. The gray rain was falling with a dreary sound outside, and down the kitchen stovepipe an occasional drop fell on the stove with a hissing, angry sound.

The young wife went on with a deeper note:

"I lived in Lumberville two years, going to school, and I know a little something of what city life is. If I was a man, I bet I wouldn't wear my life out on a farm, as

Grant does. I'd get away and I'd do something. I wouldn't care what, but I'd get away."

There was a certain volcanic energy back of all the woman said, that made Howard feel she'd make the attempt. She didn't know that the struggle for a place to stand on this planet was eating the heart and soul out of men and women in the city, just as in the country. But he could say nothing. If he had said in conventional phrase, sitting there in his soft clothing, "We must make the best of it all," the woman could justly have thrown the dish-cloth in his face. He could say nothing.

"I was a fool for ever marrying," she went on, while the baby pushed a chair across the room. "I made a decent living teaching, I was free to come and go, my money was my own. Now I'm tied right down to a churn or a dish-pan, I never have a cent of my own. *He's* growlin' round half the time, and there's no chance of his ever being different."

She stopped with a bitter sob in her throat. She forgot she was talking to her husband's brother. She was conscious only of his sympathy.

As if a great black cloud had settled down upon him, Howard felt it all—the horror, hopelessness, immanent tragedy of it all. The glory of nature, the bounty and splendor of the sky, only made it the more benumbing. He thought of a sentence Millet once wrote:

"I see very well the aureole of the dandelions, and the sun also, far down there behind the hills, flinging his glory upon the clouds. But not alone that—I see in the plains the smoke of the tired horses at the plough, or, on a stony-hearted spot of ground, a back-broken man trying to raise himself upright for a moment to breathe. The tragedy is surrounded by glories—that is no invention of mine."

Howard arose abruptly and went back to his little bedroom, where he walked up and down the floor till he was calm enough to write, and then he sat down and poured it all out to "Dearest Margaret," and his first sentence was this:

"If it were not for you (just to let you know the mood I'm in)—if it were not *for* you, and I had the world in my hands, I'd crush it like a puffball; evil so predominates, suffering is so universal and persistent, happiness so fleeting and so infrequent."

He wrote on for two hours, and by the time he had sealed and directed several letters he felt calmer, but still terribly depressed. The rain was still falling, sweeping down from the half-seen hills, wreathing the wooded peaks with a gray garment of mist, and filling the valley with a whitish cloud.

It fell around the house drearily. It ran down into the tubs placed to catch it, dripped from the mossy pump, and drummed on the upturned milk-pails, and upon the brown and yellow beehives under the maple-trees. The chickens seemed depressed, but the irrepressible bluejay screamed amid it all, with the same insolent spirit, his plumage untarnished by the wet. The barnyard showed a horrible mixture of mud and mire, through which Howard caught glimpses of the men, slumping to and fro without more additional protection than a ragged coat and a shapeless felt hat.

In the sitting-room where his mother sat sewing there was not an ornament, save the etching he had brought. The clock stood on a small shelf, its dial so much defaced that one could not tell the time of day; and when it struck, it was with noticeably disproportionate deliberation, as if it wished to correct any mistake into which the family might have fallen by reason of its illegible dial.

The paper on the walls showed the first concession of the Puritans to the Spirit of Beauty, and was made up of a heterogeneous mixture of flowers of unheard-of shapes and colors, arranged in four different ways along the wall. There were no books, no music, and only a few newspapers in sight—a bare, blank, cold, drab-colored shelter from the rain, not a home. Nothing cosey, nothing heart-warming; a grim and horrible shed.

"What are they doing? It can't be they're at work such a day as this," Howard said, standing at the window.

"They find plenty to do, even on rainy days," answered his mother. "Grant always has some job to set the men at. It's the only way to live."

"I'll go out and see them," he turned suddenly. "Mother, why should Grant treat me so? Have I deserved it?"

Mrs. McLane sighed in pathetic hopelessness. "I don't know, Howard. I'm worried about Grant. He gets more an' more down-hearted an' gloomy every day. Seems if he'd go crazy. He don't care how he looks any more, won't dress up on Sunday. Days an' days he'll go aroun' not sayin' a word. I was in hopes you could help him, Howard."

"My coming seems to have had an opposite effect. He hasn't spoken a word to me, except when he had to, since I came. Mother, what do you say to going home with me to New York?"

"Oh, I couldn't do that!" she cried in terror. "I couldn't live in a big city—never!"

"There speaks the truly rural mind," smiled Howard at his mother, who was looking up at him through her glasses with a pathetic forlornness which sobered him again. "Why, mother, you could live in Orange, New Jersey, or out in Connecticut, and be just as lonesome as you are here. You wouldn't need to live in the city. I could see you then every day or two."

"Well, I couldn't leave Grant an' the baby, anyway," she replied, not realizing how one could live in New Jersey and do business daily in New York.

"Well, then, how would you like to go back into the old house?" he said, facing her.

The patient hands fell to the lap, the dim eyes fixed in searching glance on his face. There was a wistful cry in the voice.

"Oh, Howard! Do you mean—"

He came and sat down by her, and put his arm about her and hugged her hard. "I mean, you dear, good, patient, work-weary old mother, I'm going to buy back the old farm and put you in it."

There was no refuge for her now except in tears, and she put up her thin, trembling old hands about his neck, and cried in that easy, placid, restful way age has.

Howard could not speak. His throat ached with remorse and pity. He saw his forgetfulness of them all once more without relief,—the black thing it was!

"There, there mother, don't cry!" he said, torn with anguish by her tears. Measured by man's tearlessness, her weeping seemed terrible to him. "I didn't realize how things were going here. It was all my fault—or at least, most of it. Grant's letter didn't reach me. I thought you were still on the old farm. But no matter; it's all over now. Come, don't cry any more, mother dear. I'm going to take care of you now."

It had been years since the poor, lonely woman had felt such warmth of love. Her sons had been like her husband, chary of expressing their affection; and like most

Puritan families, there was little of caressing among them. Sitting there with the rain on the roof and driving through the trees, they planned getting back into the old house. Howard's plan seemed to her full of splendor and audacity. She began to understand his power and wealth now, as he put it into concrete form before her.

"I wish I could eat Thanksgiving dinner there with you," he said at last, "but it can't be thought of. However, I'll have you all in there before I go home. I'm going out now and tell Grant. Now don't worry any more; I'm going to fix it all up with him, sure." He gave her a parting hug.

Laura advised him not to attempt to get to the barn; but as he persisted in going, she hunted up an old rubber coat for him. "You'll mire down and spoil your shoes," she said, glancing at his neat calf gaiters.

"Darn the difference!" he laughed in his old way. "Besides, I've got rubbers."

"Better go round by the fence," she advised, as he stepped out into the pouring rain.

How wretchedly familiar it all was! The miry cow-yard, with the hollow trampled out around the horse-trough, the disconsolate hens standing under the wagons and sheds, a pig wallowing across its sty, and for atmosphere the desolate, falling rain. It was so familiar he felt a pang of the old rebellious despair which seized him on such days in his boyhood.

Catching up courage, he stepped out on the grass, opened the gate and entered the barnyard. A narrow ribbon of turf ran around the fence, on which he could walk by clinging with one hand to the rough boards. In this way he slowly made his way around the periphery, and came at last to the open barn-door without much harm.

It was a desolate interior. In the open floorway Grant, seated upon a half-bushel, was mending a harness. The old man was holding the trace in his hard brown hands; the boy was lying on a wisp of hay. It was a small barn, and poor at that. There was a bad smell, as of dead rats, about it, and the rain fell through the shingles here and there. To the right, and below, the horses stood, looking up with their calm and beautiful eyes, in which the whole scene was idealized.

Grant looked up an instant and then went on with his work.

"Did yeh wade through?" grinned Lewis, exposing his broken teeth.

"No, I kinder circumambiated the pond." He sat down on the little tool-box near Grant. "Your barn is a good deal like that in 'The Arkansas Traveller.' Needs a new roof, Grant." His voice had a pleasant sound, full of the tenderness of the scene through which he had just been. "In fact, you need a new barn."

"I need a good many things more'n I'll ever get," Grant replied shortly.

"How long did you say you'd been on this farm?"

"Three years this fall."

"I don't s'pose you've been able to think of buying—Now hold on, Grant," he cried, as Grant threw his head back. "For God's sake, don't get mad again! Wait till you see what I'm driving at."

"I don't see what you're drivin' at, and I don't care. All I want you to do is to let us alone. That ought to be easy enough for you."

"I tell you, I didn't get your letter. I didn't know you'd lost the old farm." Howard was determined not to quarrel. "I didn't suppose—"

"You might 'a' come to see."

"Well, I'll admit that. All I can say in excuse is that since I got to managing plays I've kept looking ahead to making a big hit and getting a barrel of money—just as the old miners used to hope and watch. Besides, you don't understand how much pressure there is on me. A hundred different people pulling and hauling to have me go here or go there, or do this or do that. When it isn't yachting, it's canoeing, or—"

He stopped. His heart gave a painful throb, and a shiver ran through him. Again he saw his life, so rich, so bright, so free, set over against the routine life in the little low kitchen, the barren sitting-room, and this still more horrible barn. Why should his brother sit there in wet and grimy clothing mending a broken trace, while he enjoyed all the light and civilization of the age?

He looked at Grant's fine figure, his great strong face; recalled his deep, stern, masterful voice. "Am I so much superior to him? Have not circumstances made me and destroyed him?"

"Grant, for God's sake, don't sit there like that! I'll admit I've been negligent and careless. I can't understand it all myself. But let me do something for you now. I've sent to New York for five thousand dollars. I've got terms on the old farm. Let me see you all back there once more before I return."

"I don't want any of your charity."

"It ain't charity. It's only justice to you." He rose. "Come now, let's get at an understanding, Grant. I can't go on this way. I can't go back to New York and leave you here like this."

Grant rose too. "I tell you, I don't ask your help. You can't fix this thing up with money. If you've got more brains 'n I have, why it's all right. I ain't got any right to take anything that I don't earn."

"But you don't get what you do earn. It ain't your fault. I begin to see it now. Being the oldest, I had the best chance. I was going to town to school,while you were ploughing and husking corn. Of course I thought you'd be going soon, yourself. I had three years the start of you. If you'd been in my place, *you* might have met a man like Cooke, *you* might have gone to New York and have been where I am."

"Well, it can't be helped now. So drop it."

"But it must be!" Howard said, pacing about, his hands in his coat-pockets. Grant had stopped work, and was gloomily looking out of the door at a pig nosing in the mud for stray grains of wheat at the granary door:

"Good God! I see it all now," Howard burst out in an impassioned tone. "I went ahead with *my* education, got *my* start in life, then father died, and you took up his burdens. Circumstances made me and crushed you. That's all there is about that. Luck made me and cheated you. It ain't right."

His voice faltered. Both men were now oblivious of their companions and of the scene. Both were thinking of the days when they both planned great things in the way of an education, two ambitious, dreamful boys.

"I used to think of you, Grant, when I pulled out Monday morning in my best suit—cost fifteen dollars in those days." He smiled a little at the recollection. "While you in overalls and an old 'wammus' was going out into the field to plough, or husk corn in the mud. It made me feel uneasy, but, as I said, I kept saying to myself, 'His turn'll come in a year or two.' But it didn't."

His voice choked. He walked to the door, stood a moment, came back. His eyes were full of tears.

"I tell you, old man, many a time in my boarding-house down to the city, when I thought of the jolly times I was having, my heart hurt me. But I said: 'It's no use to cry. Better go on and do the best you can, and then help them afterwards. There'll only be one more miserable member of the family if you stay at home.' Besides, it seemed right to me to have first chance. But I never thought you'd be shut off,

Grant. If I had, I never would have gone on. Come, old man, I want you to believe that." His voice was very tender now and almost humble.

"I don't know as I blame yeh for that, How," said Grant, slowly. It was the first time he had called Howard by his boyish nickname. His voice was softer, too, and higher in key. But he looked steadily away.

"I went to New York. People liked my work. I was very successful, Grant; more successful than you realize. I could have helped you at any time. There's no use lying about it. And I ought to have done it; but some way—it's no excuse, I don't mean it for an excuse, only an explanation—some way I got in with the boys. I don't mean I was a drinker and all that. But I bought pictures and kept a horse and a yacht, and of course I had to pay my share of all expeditions, and—oh, what's the use!"

He broke off, turned, and threw his open palms out toward his brother, as if throwing aside the last attempt at an excuse.

"I *did* neglect you, and it's a damned shame! and I ask your forgiveness. Come, old man!"

He held out his hand, and Grant slowly approached and took it. There was a little silence. Then Howard went on, his voice trembling, the tears on his face.

"I want you to let me help you, old man. That's the way to forgive me. Will you?"

"Yes, if you can help me."

Howard squeezed his hand. "That's right, old man. Now you make me a boy again. Course I can help you. I've got ten—"

"I don't mean that, How." Grant's voice was very grave. "Money can't give me a chance now."

"What do you mean?"

"I mean life ain't worth very much to me. I'm too old to take a new start. I'm a dead failure. I've come to the conclusion that life's a failure for ninety-nine per cent of us. You can't help me now. It's too late."

The two men stood there, face to face, hands clasped, the one fair-skinned, full-lipped, handsome in his neat suit; the other tragic, sombre in his softened mood, his large, long, rugged Scotch face bronzed with sun and scarred with wrinkles that had histories, like sabre-cuts on a veteran, the record of his battles.

–1891

ANONYMOUS

According to Edith Fowkes and Joe Glazer, this ditty was printed in a number of nineteenth-century songbooks. It was also found in the diary of Mrs. Sara A. Price, some of whose sons had been killed in the Civil War. It therefore appears to have been a product of the mid-century. In any case, it captures something of the saying that "women's work is never done."

THE HOUSEKEEPER'S LAMENT

1. One day as I wandered, I heard a complaining,
   and saw an old woman, the picture of gloom.
   She gazed at the mud on her doorstep ('twas raining)
   and this was her song as she wielded her broom:
   "Oh life is a toil and love is a trouble,
   And beauty will fade and riches will flee,
   Oh, pleasures they dwindle and prices they double,
   And nothing is as I wish it to be.

2. "It's sweeping at six and it's dusting at seven;
   It's victuals at eight and it's dishes at nine.
   It's potting and panning from ten to eleven;
   We scarce break our fast till we plan how to dine.

3. "There's too much of worriment goes in a bonnet;
   There's too much of ironing goes in a shirt.
   There's nothing that pays for the time you waste on it;
   There's nothing that lasts us but trouble and dirt.

4. "In March it is mud, it is snow in December;
   The mid-summer breezes are loaded with dust.
   In fall the leaves litter; in rainy September
   The wallpaper rots and the candlesticks rust.

5. "Last night in my dreams I was stationed forever
   On a far little isle in the midst of the sea.
   My one chance for life was a ceaseless endeavor
   To sweep off the waves ere they swept over me.

6. "Alas, 'twas no dream, for ahead I behold it;
   I know I am helpless my fate to avert."
   She put down her broom and her apron she folded,
   Then lay down and died, and was buried in dirt.

MARY WILKINS FREEMAN

(1852–1930)

For about forty years after her death in 1930, Mary Wilkins Freeman functionally disappeared from the pages of American literature. To be sure, some older critics, like Fred Lewis Pattee, continued to teach and write about her. But for the modernist generation of the 1920s and their immediate successors, she represented all that they rejected about the "genteel tradition": she wrote about poor and working rural women, she celebrated small triumphs of small people, she placed her characters in a region, New England, increasingly seen by urban readers as quaint. And she wrote in what seemed, at least, unaffected, straightforward prose. It took the renewal of a feminist movement in the 1960s to bring Freeman back into fashion. For then it was discovered that many of her stories were about the resourcefulness and strength of poor and working women: the title character of "Mother," who "revolts" by moving her household into a new barn; the protagonist of "A New England Nun," who rejects the prescribed marriage for the comforts of spinsterhood; and the sisters of "A Mistaken Charity," who turn down the unwanted comforts of a old people's home for the pleasure of their own, their very own, hovel.

For Freeman, writing about such people basically constituted a way of making a living. She wrote to Pattee, "I had to earn a living. . . . No 'realistic rush,' no 'Kipling freshness' swept me along in spite of myself. Pen and ink and paper involved slight capital and were most obviously at hand. I sat down and wrote my little stories about the types I knew. They sold. That is really all. Very simple." But it was finally not so simple. To be sure, in some degree Freeman saw herself in the constrained and limited characters she created. And certainly she took advantage of the growing market before and after the turn of the century for regionally inflected fiction. But Freeman's stories are more than innocent tales of rural poverty. Rather, she explores the inner lives of women, the often bitter politics of small communities and families, the contradictory imperatives that trap working people between desire and obligation.

She herself knew about labor and responsibility. Her first twenty-five years were marked by family disasters and obstacles to her development as a writer. She did not publish her first piece of writing until she was almost thirty. A few years after her mother's death in 1880, she moved into the home of a childhood friend in Randolph, Massachusetts, where she was to remain for twenty years. There she wrote many of her best stories, the first collection of which, A Humble Romance and Other Stories, was published in 1887. A huge amount of work was soon to issue from her pen: fifteen volumes of stories, fourteen novels, three collections of poetry, eight children's books, and numerous uncollected tales. Only late in life did she put aside her doubts and marry Charles Freeman. The marriage in many ways proved a disaster: he was alcoholic, she was forced to separate herself from the place and people about which she wrote, and the taste for regionally based fiction began to decline. Nevertheless, Freeman sustained her success into the 1920s, winning a number of prizes and becoming, with Edith Wharton, the first women accepted into the National Institute of Arts and Letters. Today, ironically, many of her most avid readers are those who have never seen a working farm, faced the question of where to find a home, or imagined life in a poorhouse. That fact is one measure of her success.

A Mistaken Charity

There were in a green field a little, low, weather-stained cottage, with a foot-path leading to it from the highway several rods distant, and two old women—one with a tin pan and old knife searching for dandelion greens among the short young grass, and the other sitting on the door-step watching her, or, rather, having the appearance of watching her.

"Air there enough for a mess, Harriét?" asked the old woman on the door-step. She accented oddly the last syllable of the Harriet, and there was a curious quality in her feeble, cracked old voice. Besides the question denoted by the arrangement of her words and the rising inflection, there was another, broader and subtler, the very essence of all questioning, in the tone of her voice itself; the cracked, quavering notes that she used reached out of themselves, and asked, and groped like fingers in the dark. One would have known by the voice that the old woman was blind.

The old woman on her knees in the grass searching for dandelions did not reply; she evidently had not heard the question. So the old woman on the door-step, after waiting a few minutes with her head turned expectantly, asked again, varying her question slightly, and speaking louder:

"Air there enough for a mess, do ye s'pose, Harriét?"

The old woman in the grass heard this time. She rose slowly and laboriously; the effort of straightening out the rheumatic old muscles was evidently a painful one; then she eyed the greens heaped up in the tin pan, and pressed them down with her hand.

"Wa'al, I don't know, Charlotte," she replied, hoarsely. "There's plenty on 'em here, but I 'ain't got near enough for a mess; they do bile down so when you get 'em in the pot an' it's all I can do to bend my j'ints enough to dig 'em."

"I'd give consider'ble to help ye, Harriét," said the old woman on the door-step.

But the other did not hear her; she was down on her knees in the grass again, anxiously spying out the dandelions.

So the old woman on the door-step crossed her little shrivelled hands over her calico knees, and sat quite still, with the soft spring wind blowing over her.

The old wooden door-step was sunk low down among the grasses, and the whole house to which it belonged had an air of settling down and mouldering into the grass as into its own grave.

When Harriet Shattuck grew deaf and rheumatic, and had to give up her work as tailoress, and Charlotte Shattuck lost her eyesight, and was unable to do any more sewing for her livelihood, it was a small and trifling charity for the rich man who held a mortgage on the little house in which they had been born and lived all their lives to give them the use of it, rent and interest free. He might as well have taken credit to himself for not charging a squirrel for his tenement in some old decaying tree in his woods.

So ancient was the little habitation, so wavering and mouldering, the hands that had fashioned it had lain still so long in their graves, that it almost seemed to have fallen below its distinctive rank as a house. Rain and snow had filtered through its roof, mosses had grown over it, worms had eaten it, and birds built their nests under its eaves; nature had almost completely overrun and obliterated the work of man, and taken her own to herself again, till the house seemed as much a natural ruin as an old tree-stump.

The Shattucks had always been poor people and common people; no especial grace and refinement or fine ambition had ever characterized any of them; they had always been poor and coarse and common. The father and his father before him had simply lived in the poor little house, grubbed for their living, and then unquestion-ingly died. The mother had been of no rarer stamp, and the two daughters were cast in the same mould.

After their parents' death Harriet and Charlotte had lived along in the old place from youth to old age, with the one hope of ability to keep a roof over their heads, covering on their backs, and victuals in their mouths—an all-sufficient one with them.

Neither of them had ever had a lover; they had always seemed to repel rather than attract the opposite sex. It was not merely because they were poor, ordinary, and homely; there were plenty of men in the place who would have matched them well in that respect; the fault lay deeper—in their characters. Harriet, even in her girlhood, had a blunt, defiant manner that almost amounted to surliness, and was well calculated to alarm timid adorers, and Charlotte had always had the reputation of not being any too strong in her mind.

Harriet had gone about from house to house doing tailor-work after the primitive country fashion, and Charlotte had done plain sewing and mending for the neigh-bors. They had been, in the main, except when pressed by some temporary anxiety about their work or the payment thereof, happy and contented, with that negative kind of happiness and contentment which comes not from gratified ambition, but a lack of ambition itself. All that they cared for they had had in tolerable abundance, for Harriet at least had been swift and capable about her work. The patched, mossy old roof had been kept over their heads, the coarse, hearty food that they loved had been set on their table, and their cheap clothes had been warm and strong.

After Charlotte's eyes failed her, and Harriet had the rheumatic fever, and the little hoard of earnings went to the doctors, times were harder with them, though still it could not be said that they actually suffered.

When they could not pay the interest on the mortgage they were allowed to keep the place interest free; there was as much fitness in a mortgage on the little house, anyway, as there would have been on a rotten old apple-tree; and the people about, who were mostly farmers, and good friendly folk, helped them out with their living. One would donate a barrel of apples from his abundant harvest to the two poor old women, one a barrel of potatoes, another a load of wood for the winter fuel, and many a farmer's wife had bustled up the narrow foot-path with a pound of butter, or a dozen fresh eggs, or a nice bit of pork. Besides all this, there was a tiny garden patch behind the house, with a straggling row of currant bushes in it, and one of goose-berries, where Harriet contrived every year to raise a few pumpkins, which were the pride of her life. On the right of the garden were two old apple-trees, a Baldwin and a Porter, both yet in a tolerably good fruit-bearing state.

The delight which the two poor old souls took in their own pumpkins, their apples and currants, was indescribable. It was not merely that they contributed largely towards their living; they were their own, their private share of the great wealth of nature, the little taste set apart for them alone out of her bounty, and worth more to them on that account, though they were not conscious of it, than all the richer fruits which they received from their neighbors' gardens.

This morning the two apple-trees were brave with flowers, the currant bushes looked alive, and the pumpkin seeds were in the ground. Harriet cast complacent glances in their direction from time to time, as she painfully dug her dandelion greens. She was a short, stoutly built old woman, with a large face coarsely wrinkled, with a suspicion of a stubble of beard on the square chin.

When her tin pan was filled to her satisfaction with the sprawling, spidery greens, and she was hobbling stiffly towards her sister on the door-step, she saw another woman standing before her with a basket in her hand.

"Good-morning, Harriet," she said, in a loud, strident voice, as she drew near. "I've been frying some doughnuts, and I brought you over some warm."

"I've been tellin' her it was real good in her," piped Charlotte from the door-step, with an anxious turn of her sightless face towards the sound of her sister's footstep.

Harriet said nothing but a hoarse "Good-mornin', Mis' Simonds." Then she took the basket in her hand, lifted the towel off the top, selected a doughnut, and deliberately tasted it.

"Tough," said she. "I s'posed so. If there is anything I 'spise on this airth it's a tough doughut."

" Oh, Harriét!" said Charlotte with a frightened look.

"They air tough," said Harriet, with hoarse defiance, "and if there is anything I 'spise on this airth it's a tough doughnut."

The woman whose benevolence and cookery were being thus ungratefully received only laughed. She was quite fleshy, and had a round, rosy, determined face.

"Well, Harriet," said she, "I am sorry they are tough, but perhaps you had better take them out on a plate, and give me my basket. You may be able to eat two or three of them if they are tough."

"They air tough—turrible tough," said Harriet, stubbornly; but she took the basket into the house and emptied it of its contents nevertheless.

"I suppose your roof leaked as bad as ever in that heavy rain day before yesterday?" said the visitor to Harriet, with an inquiring squint towards the mossy shingles, as she was about to leave with her empty basket.

"It was turrible," replied Harriet, with crusty acquiescence—"turrible. We had to set pails an' pans everywheres, an' move the bed out."

"Mr. Upton ought to fix it."

"There ain't any fix to it; the old ruff ain't fit to nail new shingles on to; the hammerin' would bring the whole thing down on our heads," said Harriet, grimly.

"Well, I don't know as it can be fixed, it's so old. I suppose the wind comes in bad around the windows and doors too?"

"It's like livin' with a piece of paper, or mebbe a sieve, 'twixt you an' the wind an' the rain," quoth Harriet, with a jerk of her head.

"You ought to have a more comfortable home in your old age," said the visitor, thoughtfully.

"Oh, it's well enough," cried Harriet, in quick alarm, and with a complete change of tone; the woman's remark had brought an old dread over her. "The old house 'll last as long as Charlotte an' me do. The rain ain't so bad, nuther is the wind; there's room enough for us in the dry places, an' out of the way of the doors an' windows. It's enough sight better than goin' on the town." Her square, defiant old face actually looked pale as she uttered the last words and stared apprehensively at the woman.

"Oh, I did not think of your doing that," she said, hastily and kindly. "We all know how you feel about that, Harriet, and not one of us neighbors will see you and Charlotte go to the poorhouse while we've got a crust of bread to share with you."

Harriet's face brightened. "Thank ye, Mis' Simonds," she said, with reluctant courtesy. "I'm much obleeged to you an' the neighbors. I think mebbe we'll be able to eat some of them doughnuts if they air tough," she added, mollifyingly, as her caller turned down the foot-path.

"My, Harriét," said Charlotte, lifting up a weakly, wondering, peaked old face, "what did you tell her them doughnuts was tough fur?"

"Charlotte, do you want everybody to look down on us, an' think we ain't no account at all, just like any beggars, 'cause they bring us in vittles?" said Harriet, with a grim glance at her sister's meek, unconscious face.

"No, Harriét," she whispered.

"Do you want *to go to the poor-house?*"

"No, Harriét." The poor little old woman on the doorstep fairly cowered before her aggressive old sister.

"Then don't hender me agin when I tell folks their doughnuts is tough an' their pertaters is poor. If I don't kinder keep up an' show some sperrit, I sha'n't think nothing of myself, an' other folks won't nuther, and fust thing we know they'll kerry us to the poorhouse. You'd 'a been there before now if it hadn't been for me, Charlotte."

Charlotte looked meekly convinced, and her sister sat down on a chair in the doorway to scrape her dandelions.

"Did you git a good mess, Harriét?" asked Charlotte, in a humble tone.

"Toler'ble."

"They'll be proper relishin' with that piece of pork Mis' Mann brought in yesterday. O Lord, Harriet, it's a chink!"

Harriet sniffed.

Her sister caught with her sensitive ear the little contemptuous sound. "I guess," she said, querulously, and with more pertinacity than she had shown in the matter of the doughnuts, "that if you was in the dark, as I am, Harriet, you wouldn't make fun an' turn up your nose at chinks. If you had seen the light streamin' in all of a sudden through some little hole that you hadn't known of before when you set down on the door-step this mornin', and the wind with the smell of the apple blows in it came in your face, an' when Mis' Simonds brought them hot doughnuts, an' when I thought of the pork an' greens jest now—O Lord, how it did shine in! An' it does now. If you was me, Harriét, you would know there was chinks."

Tears began starting from the sightless eyes, and streaming pitifully down the pale old checks.

Harriet looked at her sister, and her grim face softened.

"Why, Charlotte, hev it that thar *is* chinks if you want to. Who cares?"

"Thar *is* chinks, Harriét."

"Wa'al, thar *is* chinks, then. If I don't hurry, I sha'n't get these greens in in time for dinner,"

When the two old women sat down complacently to their meal of pork and dandelion greens in their little kitchen they did not dream how destiny slowly and surely was introducing some new colors into their web of life, even when it was almost completed, and that this was one of the last meals they would eat in their old home for many a day. In about a week from that day they were established in the "Old Ladies' Home" in a neighboring city. It came about in this wise: Mrs. Simonds, the woman who had brought the gift of hot doughnuts, was a smart, energetic person, bent on doing good, and she did a great deal. To be sure, she always did it in her own way. If she chose to give hot doughnuts, she gave hot doughnuts; it made not the slightest difference to her if the recipients of her charity would infinitely have preferred ginger cookies. Still, a great many would like hot doughnuts, and she did unquestionably a great deal of good.

She had a worthy coadjutor in the person of a rich and childless elderly widow in the place. They had fairly entered into a partnership in good works, with about an equal capital on both sides, the widow furnishing the money, and Mrs. Simonds, who had much the better head of the two, furnishing the active schemes of benevolence.

The afternoon after the doughnut episode she had gone to the widow with a new project, and the result was that entrance fees had been paid, and old Harriet and Charlotte made sure of a comfortable home for the rest of their lives. The widow was hand in glove with officers of missionary boards and trustees of charitable institutions. There had been an unusual mortality among the inmates of the "Home" this spring, there were several vacancies, and the matter of the admission of Harriet and Charlotte was very quickly and easily arranged. But the matter which would have seemed the least difficult—inducing the two old women to accept the bounty which Providence, the widow, and Mrs. Simonds were ready to bestow on them— proved the most so. The struggle to persuade them to abandon their tottering old home for a better was a terrible one. The widow had pleaded with mild surprise, and Mrs. Simonds with benevolent determination; the counsel and reverend eloquence of the minister had been called in; and when they yielded at last it was with a sad grace for the recipients of a worthy charity.

It had been hard to convince them that the "Home" was not an almshouse under another name, and their yielding at length to anything short of actual force was only due probably to the plea, which was advanced most eloquently to Harriet, that Charlotte would be so much more comfortable.

The morning they came away, Charlotte cried pitifully, and trembled all over her little shrivelled body. Harriet did not cry. But when her sister had passed out the low, sagging door she turned the key in the lock, then took it out and thrust it slyly into her pocket, shaking her head to herself with an air of fierce determination.

Mrs. Simonds's husband, who was to take them to the depot, said to himself, with disloyal defiance of his wife's active charity, that it was a shame, as he helped the two distressed old souls into his light wagon, and put the poor little box, with their homely clothes in it, in behind.

Mrs. Simonds, the widow, the minister, and the gentleman from the "Home" who was to take charge of them, were all at the depot, their faces beaming with the delight of successful benevolence. But the two poor old women looked like two forlorn prisoners in their midst. It was an impressive illustration of the truth of the saying "that it is more blessed to give than to receive."

Well, Harriet and Charlotte Shattuck went to the "Old Ladies' Home" with reluctance and distress. They stayed two months, and then—they ran away.

The "Home" was comfortable, and in some respects even luxurious; but nothing suited those two unhappy, unreasonable old women.

The fare was of a finer, more delicately served variety than they had been accustomed to; those finely flavored nourishing soups for which the "Home" took great credit to itself failed to please palates used to common, coarser food.

"O Lord, Harriét, when I set down to the table here there ain't no chinks," Charlotte used to say. "If we could hev some cabbage or some pork an' greens, how the light would stream in!"

Then they had to be more particular about their dress. They had always been tidy enough, but now it had to be something more; the widow, in the kindness of her heart, had made it possible, and the good folks in charge of the "Home," in the kindness of their hearts, tried to carry out the widow's designs.

But nothing could transform these two unpolished old women into two nice old ladies. They did not take kindly to white lace caps and delicate neckerchiefs. They liked their new black cashmere dresses well enough, but they felt as if they broke a commandment when they put them on every afternoon. They had always worn calico with long aprons at home, and they wanted to now; and they wanted to twist up their scanty gray locks into little knots at the back of their heads, and go without caps, just as they always had done.

Charlotte in a dainty white cap was pitiful, but Harriet was both pitiful and comical. They were totally at variance with their surroundings, and they felt it keenly, as people of their stamp always do. No amount of kindness and attention—and they had enough of both—sufficed to reconcile them to their new abode. Charlotte pleaded continually with her sister to go back to their old home.

"O Lord, Harriét, she would exclaim (by the way, Charlotte's "O Lord," which, as she used it, was innocent enough, had been heard with much disfavor in the "Home," and she, not knowing at all why, had been remonstrated with concerning it), "let us go home. I can't stay here no ways in this world. I don't like their vittles, an' I don't like to wear a cap; I want to go home and do different. The currants will be ripe, Harriét. O Lord, thar was almost a chink, thinking about 'em. I want some of 'em; an' the Porter apples will be gittin' ripe, an' we could have some apple-pie. This here ain't good; I want merlasses fur sweeting. Can't we get back no ways, Harriét? It ain't far, an' we could walk, an' they don't lock us in, nor nothin'. I don't want to die here; it ain't so straight up to heaven from here. O Lord, I've felt as if I was slantendicular from heaven ever since I've been here, an' it's been so awful dark. I ain't had any chinks. I want to go home, Harriét."

"We'll go to-morrow mornin'," said Harriet, finally; "we'll pack up our things an' go; we'll put on our old dresses, an' we'll do up the new ones in bundles, an' we'll jest shy out the back way to-morrow mornin'; an' we'll go. I kin find the way, an' I reckon we kin git thar, if it is fourteen mile. Mebbe somebody will give us a lift."

And they went. With a grim humor Harriet hung the new white lace caps with which she and Charlotte had been so pestered, one on each post at the head of the bedstead, so they would meet the eyes of the first person who opened the door. Then they took their bundles, stole slyly out, and were soon on the high-road, hobbling along, holding each other's hands, as jubilant as two children, and chuckling to themselves over their escape, and the probable astonishment there would be in the "Home" over it.

"O Lord, Harriét, what do you s'pose they will say to them caps?" cried Charlotte, with a gleeful cackle.

"I guess they'll see as folks ain't goin' to be made to wear caps agin their will in a free kentry," returned Harriet, with an echoing cackle, as they sped feebly and bravely along.

The "Home" stood on the very outskirts of the city, luckily for them. They would have found it a difficult undertaking to traverse the crowded streets. As it was, a short walk brought them into the free country road—free comparatively, for even here at ten o'clock in the morning there was considerable travelling to and from the city on business or pleasure.

People whom they met on the road did not stare at them as curiously as might have been expected. Harriet held her bristling chin high in air, and hobbled along with an appearance of being well aware of what she was about, that led folks to doubt their own first opinion that there was something unusual about the two old women.

Still their evident feebleness now and then occasioned from one and another more particular scrutiny. When they had been on the road a half-hour or so, a man in a covered wagon drove up behind them. After he had passed them, he poked his head around the front of the vehicle and looked back. Finally he stopped, and waited for them to come up to him.

"Like a ride, ma'am?" said he, looking at once bewildered and compassionate.

"Thankee," said Harriet, "we'd be much obleeged."

After the man had lifted the old women into the wagon, and established them on the back seat, he turned around, as he drove slowly along, and gazed at them curiously.

"Seems to me you look pretty feeble to be walking far," said he. "Where were you going?"

Harriet told him with an air of defiance.

"Why," he exclaimed, "it is fourteen miles out. You could never walk it in the world. Well, I am going within three miles of there, and I can go on a little farther as well as not. But I don't see— Have you been in the city?"

"I have been visitin' my married darter in the city," said Harriet, calmly.

Charlotte started, and swallowed convulsively.

Harriet had never told a deliberate falsehood before in her life, but this seemed to her one of the tremendous exigencies of life which justify a lie. She felt desperate. If she could not contrive to deceive him in some way, the man might turn directly around and carry Charlotte and her back to the "Home" and the white caps.

"I should not have thought your daughter would have let you start for such a walk as that," said the man. "Is this lady your sister? She is blind, isn't she? She does not look fit to walk a mile."

"Yes, she's my sister," replied Harriet, stubbornly: "an' she's blind; an' my darter didn't want us to walk. She felt reel bad about it. But she couldn't help it. She's poor, and her husband's dead, an' she's got four leetle children."

Harriet recounted the hardships of her imaginary daughter with a glibness that was astonishing. Charlotte swallowed again.

"Well," said the man, " I am glad I overtook you, for I don't think you would ever have reached home alive."

About six miles from the city an open buggy passed them swiftly. In it were seated the matron and one of the gentlemen in charge of the "Home." They never thought of looking into the covered wagon—and indeed one can travel in one of those vehicles, so popular in some parts of New England, with as much privacy as he could in his tomb. The two in the buggy were seriously alarmed, and anxious for the safety of the old women, who were chuckling maliciously in the wagon they soon left far behind. Harriet had watched them breathlessly until they disappeared on a curve of the road; then she whispered to Charlotte.

A little after noon the two old women crept slowly up the foot-path across the field to their old home.

"The clover is up to our knees," said Harriet; "an' the sorrel and the white-weed; an' there's lots of yaller butterflies."

"O Lord, Harriét, thar's a chink, an' I do believe I saw one of them yaller butterflies go past it," cried Charlotte, trembling all over, and nodding her gray head violently.

Harriet stood on the old sunken door-step and fitted the key, which she drew triumphantly from her pocket, in the lock, while Charlotte stood waiting and shaking behind her.

Then they went in. Everything was there just as they had left it. Charlotte sank down on a chair and began to cry. Harriet hurried across to the window that looked out on the garden.

"The currants air ripe," said she; "*an*' them pumpkins hev run all over everything."

"O Lord, Harriét," sobbed Charlotte, "thar is so many chinks that they air all runnin' together!"

SARAH ORNE JEWETT
(1849-1909)

Much of Jewett's life and writing centered on the small Maine community of South Berwick, where she was raised. Her family on both sides dated back to prerevolutionary times, people who had established comfortable livings by building and using ships. She wished at first to follow in her father's footsteps and become a physician, but poor health blocked that path. Instead she took up writing shortly after she had graduated from Berwick Academy in 1865. She was able to combine her interest in medicine and her skill in writing in one of her two novels, A Country Doctor *(1884), a story about a woman who decides for a career in medicine rather than marriage.*

But she is primarily known for her short stories, many of which were collected in Deephaven *(1877) and* A White Heron and Other Stories *(1886), and for* The Country of the Pointed Firs *(1896), a set of interlinked narratives that anticipated in its innovative form related later works such as Sherwood Anderson's* Winesburg, Ohio *and Ernest Hemingway's* In Our Time. The Country of the Pointed Firs *and many of Jewett's other works are narrated by a sophisticated Boston visitor to Maine who relates the stories she herself hears, primarily from Mrs. Almira Todd, a downeast native, purveyor of herbs and advice, and central figure in the community. In many of her stories, Jewett explores the social class structure of the small Maine communities about which she writes, as well as the relationships among women that lie at the emotional center of those structures.*

Jewett herself divided her life between Boston's active literary and publishing world and Maine. She lived in a long-term relationship with Annie Fields, widow of James T. Fields, one of the most influential publishers of the nineteenth century. And she counted among her friends many of the best-known women and men of the New England literary scene.

She also wrote stories for children. The one that follows captures for adult readers as well as for children the process by which the central figure, Nelly, learns about class differences and their consequences for play, friendships, and self-image.

THE BEST CHINA SAUCER

This is a story with a moral, but I will not keep you waiting to hear it until you come to the end. I will put my moral at the beginning. It is—

Mind your mother,—unless, of course, you are perfectly sure she is a foolish and unwise woman, and that you are always the more sensible of the two.

My friend, Miss Nelly Willis, was a little late at breakfast one morning, and as she took her chair she found the rest of the family talking over their plans for the day. Papa was going to his business, and Tom to his school in the city, as usual. Mamma was going to do some shopping and lunch with a friend, and said that she should not be home until late in the afternoon. And Maggie, Nelly's elder sister, was to spend the day with her aunt, who lived a few miles away, farther out in the country.

"So we shall leave the little girl all alone," said Mrs. Willis to Nelly, "and what does she mean to do? I wish there was some one near who could come to play with you."

"Mamma, dear," said Nelly, "just this once call I have Jane Simmons for a little while? I won't bring her into the house, and we won't go out of sight, or carry out the best playthings, or do a bit of mischief. I don't see why Mrs. Duncan stays away so long. I do miss Grace and Georgie so."

"Nelly, dear," said Mrs. Willis, "I am very sorry to hinder any pleasure of yours, but I don't wish you to play with Jane. I wonder why you ask me, when I have told you so many times. She is a very naughty girl, and always teaches you bad words and bad manners, and tries to make you disobey me. I will tell you what I am going to do, though I meant it should be a surprise. I have asked Alice Russell to come out with me from town and make you a little visit." (Alice was a very dear friend of Nelly's.) "Now I think you had better put the play-room in order, because you will be there to-morrow, and you know Alice keeps her playthings looking very nice. I shall not be worried about you, for I am sure you will be good while I am gone."

Just then the carriage was driven around to the door, and there was a great hurrying and running up and down stairs, and in a few minutes everybody had gone, and Nelly was left to her own devices. She went back to the breakfast room and had another saucerful of strawberries, with a great deal of sugar on them; then she watched Ann while she cleared away the table and washed the china and silver, shut the blinds, and pulled down the curtains, and hung the linnet's cage and the parrot's out on the west piazza, in the shade. Then our friend went up to the playroom, but unfortunately it was in better order than usual, so she did not find much to do. She had been dress-making the day before, and had left her work scattered on the floor, by one of the windows, but it does not take long to roll up pieces of cloth and put them into one of the doll's trunks. Some she carried out to the rag-bag, and then went out to bring them back, thinking that she might wish some time to alter the over-skirt she had been making for Dora Mary. She dressed all the dolls in their best clothes, because some of Alice's family would be sure to come, and they were dolls who thought a great deal of dress.

All this did not take long, and Nelly sat down in her rocking-chair in front of the doll-house, and wondered what she should do next. She thought of dressing herself in her mother's or Maggie's clothes, and parading about the house in great majesty with her long trains. She was very fond of this; but where would be the fun to-day, with nobody to see her? She had some worsted-work, in which she had been interested, but she had used up all the worsted, and her mother was to buy more in town that day. She called to Susan, who was putting Maggie's room in order, to ask if she wouldn't tell a story. Susan's stories were always so interesting. But Susan said, "Bless you, dear! I can't stop to talk in the middle of the forenoon. I promised to hurry with my work so as to help Nancy,—she's dreadful busy; but I'm coming up by and by to sew, and perhaps I'll think of a story then."

Nelly was disappointed, and looked out of the window, and drummed with her feet against the chair. Anything was better than sitting there, so she went to the doll's house and took dear Amelia, who had a very fair complexion and light hair, and looked so faded that Nelly always said she was ill. Poor thing! she had to take such quantities of medicine, and go without her dinner and stay in bed half her time. When she sat up it was only in an easy-chair, with pillows behind her and one of the largest doll's blankets wrapped around her; and when she went out, she was made into such a bundle with shawls that I am afraid the fresh air did her no good.

"I think I will carry you out for a while, dear," said Nelly, and poor Amelia was dressed warmer than usual, just to take up the time. She even had to wear a thick blue and white worsted scarf around her face and throat. They walked up and down the garden some time, but it was stupid, and when they went down by the carriage-gate to hunt for a bird's nest which Tom had said was near there in the hedge, whom should they see coming up the street but the Simmons girl. Nelly was delighted, and thought, "I'll call her in for just a few minutes, and then I can go into the house and leave her; she doesn't dare to come near the house." Then she remembered what her mother had said that morning, and with a great effort turned and walked away up the avenue. She had not gone far when she heard the little side-gate open, and looked back to see Jane coming in and bringing her brother with her. Jane looked unusually dirty that morning and very naughty. She was carrying her mother's parasol, and the brother, who was never called anything but "The Baby," was unbecomingly dressed in an old shawl, folded as small as possible; because he was so very short it trailed several inches upon the ground, and there were some little sticks and several bur-dock burrs tangled into the fringe. Jane had put a cast-off Shaker bonnet of her own on his head; there was a great crack in the top of it, through which a tuft of hair showed itself, and fluttered in the wind. He had the dirtiest face you ever saw, and it always seemed to be the same dirt. Nelly hated The Baby. "What made her play with Jane?" Oh, I'm sure I don't know. If Jane had not known any better, it would have been different; one would have pitied her; but she did know better than to be so naughty and so careless. There was certainly nothing to hinder her being good and kind and honest and clean, except that she would not take the trouble. In her heart, that day, Nelly was glad to see Jane, but she did not say much at first. "You're p'lite, ain't you?" said Jane. "See me coming and made believe you didn't. I saw all the folks riding off to town a while ago, and Mother said I might come over and play."

Nelly always tried to be polite, and this was not without effect. "What will she say if I tell her to go home?" she thought. "Mamma never tells her visitors to go home, even if she doesn't like them," and here there came a thought of how sorry she had been after the last time Jane came, and what sad mischances there had been. "But perhaps I had better keep her a little while and be pleasant to her, and then tell her I must go into the house, and that I am never going to play with her any more." "I don't see what made you bring The Baby, though," said she, aloud.

"Oh, dear!" said Jane, "I have to lug him everywhere. Long as he couldn't talk I wasn't bothered with him, for if worst came to worst, I used to tie him to the lilac-bush and clear out, and only be sure to get back in time to unhitch him before mother came; now he goes and tells everything, but he is real good to-day, and you needn't mind him. Going to play dolls, aren't you?"

"No, I'd rather do something else," said Nelly. "I have just finished clearing up the play-room, and I'm going to have company to-night."

"Well, ain't you got company now? You didn't use to be so 'fraid of your old dolls. I thought we would have a real nice party, and I've brought something splendid in my pocket that my aunt gave me last night. I've been saving it."

"Poor thing!" thought Nelly. "It would be so cross in me not to let her have a good time. Mamma said I must always be kind to her. She's very pleasant, and perhaps she is trying to be good, after all. Here; you take care of Amelia and I'll go in and get the tea-set and one or two dolls. Amelia is my sick doll, you know, and you must be very careful of her."

"Yes 'm," said Jane, meekly, and as soon as Nelly was out of sight, she looked at poor Amelia's clothes and robbed her of her flannel petticoat, which was prettily embroidered and new only the week before. When Nelly found out a few days later that it was gone, the doll was at once taken very ill, and did not sit up much for half the summer. One of the rooms in the baby-house was kept dark, and the dolls took turns in sitting up with her at night.

Nelly soon came back, carrying the tea-set box and the little tea-table, and a doll beside under each arm. "Here's the table-cloth in my pocket," said she, "and I brought a piece of pine-apple; there's sugar in the sugar-bowl that we can put on after we have sliced it. It shall be your party, and you are Mrs. Simmons and must sit at the head of the table, and I am Mrs. Willis come to spend the day with you."

This pleased Jane, and she was as good-natured as possible, and they set the table, while The Baby sat quietly on the ground and poked up ant-hills with a little stick.

"Now," said Mrs. Simmons, when the table was ready, "let's see what you have in your pocket."

"I!" said Nelly, with surprise. "Why, I brought out nothing but the pine-apple. It's your party, you know, and I thought you had your pocket full of something that your aunt gave you."

"So I have," said Jane, "but I guess I'm not going to let you eat it all up."

"I'm not a bit hungry," answered Mrs. Willis. "I had a splendid breakfast. I don't want any of your candy, or whatever it is. Mamma will bring me some from town."

Mrs. Simmons was very angry. Her breakfast had not been "splendid," though she had had enough of it, and she had counted on Nelly's bringing out a quantity of good things, as she sometimes had before.

"Oh," thought Nelly, "now she's going to act, and be cross. I wish I had thought to hide when I saw her coming. I must bring out something to eat, or nobody knows what she will do." And off she went to the house again, while Mrs. Simmons asked her to look for some cake with sugar on it.

She hunted in the china-closet and on the sideboard and could find no cake at all. Nancy told her there was not a bit in the house; Mrs. Willis was to bring some out from the city. "You're not hungry again so quick as this?" said Ann, who came into the dining-room just then. Nelly did not dare to tell them that a tea-party was going on, or who the guests were, but after some search she carried out some macaroons and some plum-pudding, which she had not eaten at dinner the evening before, and was saving for her lunch that day. "It's too bad to let her eat this all up," thought Nelly. "Perhaps Nancy has some more put away. I've a great mind to tell Nancy to go out and send them home," and all the time she was hurrying so Nancy would not call her back or follow her. Foolish child!

Mrs. Simmons was satisfied when Nelly showed the pudding and while they finished arranging the table she told of a shop she was going to open in her wood-shed the next week, with wind-mills and darts and fly-boxes, and all sorts of delightful and useless things made of paper, besides molasses and water, at five pins for a drink in a toy tin dipper, or one cent for a large mugful. Jane liked to get cents, and Nelly almost always had some in her pocket. "I'll take down a whole paper of pins," thought Nelly, "and buy ever so much." Jane was so friendly and quiet that her heart warmed toward her. "Poor thing!" she thought, "she doesn't know any people but bad ones, and no wonder she swears, and throws stones, and does all sorts of things." Just now Mrs. Simmons happened to come closer to her, and Nelly saw for the first time a most shocking and heathenish decoration. "Oh, Jane!" she cried, "what have you been doing to those poor flies, you horrid girl?"

"Want me to string you some?" said Mrs. Simmons, with a grin. "I did every bit of this this morning, before I came over. I'll bring you one that will go round your neck twice, to-morrow, if you will give me two cents."

It was a necklace of flies, on a long piece of white thread, to which the needle was still hanging. Oh! those dozens of poor flies. Some were dead, but others faintly buzzed.

"Jane Simmons," said Nelly, "you can eat that pudding, and then you go right straight home, and I never will play with you any more. How could you be so awful. Hurry up, or I will call Nancy."

"I was going pretty soon, anyway," said Jane. "I guess there are flies enough left; you needn't make such a fuss. They let them stick on papers and die, in your house. You're an awful little 'fraid cat. Who wants to play with you, anyway?"

Nelly sat down on the grass, and would not say another word, and Jane ate the pudding as fast as she could. The Baby had not been satisfied with his share of the feast, and as she laid the best china saucer down he snatched it, and also the little cream-pitcher that belonged to the doll's tea-set, and ran away with them.

"Oh, please stop him!" begged Nelly, and Jane tried to catch him, and (how can I tell it?) stepped on his trailing shawl. The Baby fell down and rolled over and over in the gravel, and the best china saucer and the cream-pitcher were both broken.

"What *will* mamma say?" said Nelly. "O Jane! it is one of the very best saucers that she likes so much, and I heard her tell Mrs. Duncan, the other day, that she couldn't get any more, for she had tried a great many times."

If Jane had been at all sorry, Nelly would have considered her only her companion in misfortune, but instead of that she seemed to think it was a great joke, and said something very provoking. Nelly shouted at the top of her voice for Thomas, forgetting that he had gone to get Maggie's saddle horse a pair of new shoes at the blacksmith's. But Jane, for a wonder, was a little frightened, and seizing The Baby's hand, she hurried him home. She expected a messenger from Mrs. Willis for several days, and kept watch, whenever she was at home, so that if she saw anybody coming she could climb the fence behind the house and run.

Poor Nelly was very miserable. She gathered up the bits of china carefully, and put them in her pocket, and then sat down and cried a little, for it was such a dear cream-pitcher, with a blue and gold flower on each side, and a slender black handle.

There was nobody in the garden, and nobody saw her. It was very lonely. The dolls, in their best dresses, sat around the tea-table, and Nelly was almost provoked with them for looking just as they always did, and sitting up so straight and consequential when such a terrible thing had happened. Amelia, at least, ought to have been sympathizing, for was she not regretting the loss of her new petticoat? The corners of the table-cloth waved cheerfully in the wind, and some bright leaves from a red rose-bush near by came fluttering through the air, and a few lodged on the table among the tiny china dishes.

Just then Nelly happened to see The Baby's Shaker bonnet lying on the grass at a little distance, and she jumped up, and taking it by the end of one string she ran to the gate and threw it as far as she could out into the street. When she came back she took the dolls and the tea-set box and the table in her arms, and went into the house. She hid the pieces of china down under some stockings at the back of one of her bureau drawers, and felt very guilty and sad. After a little while she had lunch alone and then she tried to play with the dolls; but it was no fun at all, even though two had scarlet-fever, and the black tea-poy was doctor, and usually had a good deal to say. But Susan told a story after a while as she sat at her sewing, and Mrs. Willis came home earlier than was expected, bringing Alice with her. It was very naughty of Nelly, but she did not tell her mother what had happened, and all through the evening she was miserable whenever any one went up-stairs, for fear they might go to her lower drawer and find the broken china. Still, she had a good time, for her sister Maggie had brought home a young lady to spend the night, who was very bright and funny, and she sang and played for the children to dance in the evening.

"Has Nelly been a good girl to-day?" Mrs. Willis asked Susan.

"Indeed, yes, ma'am," said Susan. "As good as a kitten, playing with her little dolls in the garden, and I told her a story this afternoon while I was mending the ruffles on her blue dress."

And Mrs. Willis smiled at Nelly in a way that made her feel like crying.

She and Alice had not seen each other for several weeks, and had a great deal to talk about and laugh about, so it was late before they were quiet. Alice went to sleep first, but Nelly was awake awhile, for she was so worried about what had happened. What would her mother say? and how sorry and grieved she would be to find that her little girl had done exactly what she asked her not to do, just before she went away. And Nelly wondered why she had played with Jane, and she remembered the fly-necklace with a shiver, and after a long time she went to sleep. Then she had a sad dream, and it was such an odd dream that I must tell you about it.

She thought that she heard a great rattling and clinking out in the hall, and she got up to look out and see what the matter was, and noticed, on the way, that the lowest bureau drawer was open. The moon was shining in brightly through the large hall windows, and Nelly dreamed that she saw the funeral procession of the best china saucer.

It was plain that he had been a favorite in the china-closet, for there was such a large attendance. Even the great punch-bowl had come from off the side-board, and that was a great honor. The silver was always locked up at night, but one tea-spoon was there, which had been overlooked. The dead saucer was in a little black Japanese tray, carried by the cruets from the castor, and next came the cup, the poor lonely widow. It is not the fashion for china to wear mourning, and she was dressed as usual in white with brilliant pictures of small Chinese houses and tall men and women. After her came the rest of the near relations, walking two and two, and after them the punch-bowl, looking large and grand, and as if he felt very sorry. It was a large and elegant company, and reached from Nelly's door far along the hall, to the head of the staircase, and how much farther than that she could not see.

"How will that clumsy punch-bowl go so far and get down the stairs again without cracking himself?" thought our friend, and wondered what they were waiting for.

But in a few moments the play-room door opened, and out came the poor, sad little dolls' tea-set. The tea-pots first, and then the sugar-bowl, and the cups and saucers, and the plates, all walking two by two, and then the little glass tumblers. It was remarkable that the cream-pitcher was the first of the family who had been broken, but Nelly had been very careful. There was one little plate badly cracked, and how dreadful if it should fall down the stairs and die on the way!

It worried her terribly, the thought of this, as foolish things do worry us in dreams. And next she thought, what if some of the other china should trip and fall, or if one of the heavy soup-tureens should go crashing down among the rest. She did not dare to watch any longer, and when the doll's tea-set came up, and the great procession began to move, she rushed back to bed and opened her eyes to find that instead of moonlight it was morning, and Susan had come in to wake Alice and herself, and help them dress. Nelly did not wait until Alice had gone, to tell her mother, as she had meant to do the evening before. Mrs. Willis was very sorry indeed, you may be sure of that, when she heard Nelly's story. "Poor Jane!" said she. "I am sorry for the naughty little girl. I wish I could have done something for her; I tried, but she always made you naughty, and I am afraid you cannot do her any good."

This was the end of Nelly's playing with Jane, at any rate, for the Simmonses moved away the very next week. The Duncans came back soon after, and they were Nelly's best friends, so she was no longer solitary, but she always has wondered what it was that Jane had in her pocket for the party.

JACK LONDON
(1876–1916)

In this story, London dramatizes class divisions and ways of life in terms of a split in the personality and loyalties of his central character, Freddie Drummond/Bill Totts. That divide is as sharp as the famous one between Dr. Jekyll and Mr. Hyde. But in this case, the "monster," from conventional, middle-class points of view, turns out to be London's hero. (See entry for London in section I for biographical information.)

SOUTH OF THE SLOT

Old San Francisco, which is the San Francisco of only the other day, the day before the Earthquake, was divided midway by the Slot. The Slot was an iron crack that ran along the center of Market Street, and from the Slot arose the burr of the ceaseless, endless cable that was hitched at will to the cars it dragged up and down. In truth, there were two Slots, but, in the quick grammar of the West, time was saved by calling them, and much more that they stood for, The Slot. North of the Slot were the theaters, hotels and shopping district, the banks and the staid, respectable business houses. South of the Slot were the factories, slums, laundries, machine-shops, boiler-works and the abodes of the working class.

The Slot was the metaphor that expressed the class cleavage of Society, and no man crossed this metaphor, back and forth, more successfully than Freddie Drummond. He made a practice of living in both worlds and in both worlds he lived signally well. Freddie Drummond was a professor in the Sociology Department of the University of California, and it was as a professor of sociology that he first crossed over the Slot, lived for six months in the great labor ghetto and wrote The Unskilled Laborer—a book that was hailed everywhere as an able contribution to the Literature of Progress and as a splendid reply to the Literature of Discontent. Politically and economically, it was nothing if not orthodox. Presidents of great railway systems bought whole editions of it to give to their employees. A manufacturers' association alone distributed fifty thousand copies of it. In its preachment of thrift and content it ran Mrs. Wiggs of the Cabbage Patch a close second.

At first, Freddie Drummond found it monstrously difficult to get along among the working people. He was not used to their ways, and they certainly were not used to his. They were suspicious. He had no antecedents. He could talk of no previous jobs. His hands were soft. His extraordinary politeness was ominous. His first idea of the rôle he would play was that of a free and independent American who chose to work with his hands and no explanations given. But it wouldn't do, as he quickly discovered. At the beginning they accepted him, very provisionally, as a freak. A little later, as he began to know his way about better, he insensibly drifted into the only rôle that he could play with some degree of plausibility—namely, that of a man who had seen better days, very much better days, but who was down in his luck, though, to be sure, only temporarily.

He learned many things and generalized much and often erroneously, all of which can be found in the pages of The Unskilled Laborer. He saved himself, however, after the sane and conservative manner of his kind, by labeling his generalizations as "tentative." One of his first experiences was in the great Wilmax Cannery, where he was put on piecework making small packing-cases. A box-factory supplied the parts, and all Freddie Drummond had to do was to fit the parts into a form and drive in the wire nails with a light hammer.

It was not skilled labor, but it was piecework. The ordinary laborers in the cannery got a dollar and a half a day. Freddie Drummond found the other men on the same job with him jogging along and earning a dollar and seventy-five cents a day. By the third day he was able to earn the same. But he was ambitious. He did not care to jog along, and, being unusually able and fit, on the fourth day earned two dollars. The next day, having keyed himself up to an exhausting high tension, he earned two dollars and a half. His fellow-workers favored him with scowls and black looks and made remarks, slangily witty and which he did not understand, about sucking up to the boss, and pace-making, and holding her down when the rains set in. He was astonished at their malingering on piecework, generalized about the laziness of the unskilled laborer, and proceeded next day to hammer out three dollars' worth of boxes.

And that night, coming out of the cannery, he was interviewed by his fellow-workmen, who were very angry and incoherently slangy. He failed to comprehend the motive behind their action. The action itself was strenuous. When he refused to ease down his pace and bleated about freedom of contract, independent American-ism and the dignity of toil they proceeded to spoil his pace-making ability. It was a fierce battle, for Drummond was a large man and an athlete; but the crowd finally jumped on his ribs, walked on his face and stamped on his fingers, so that it was only after lying in bed for a week that he was able to get up and look for another job. All of this is duly narrated in that first book of his, in the chapter entitled The Tyranny of Labor.

A little later, in another department of the Wilmax Cannery, lumping as a fruit-dis-tributor among the women, he essayed to carry two boxes of fruit at a time and was promptly reproached by the other fruit-lumpers. It was palpable malingering; but he was there, he decided, not to change conditions, but to observe. So he lumped one box thereafter, and so well did he study the art of shirking that he wrote a special chap-ter on it, with the last several paragraphs devoted to tentative generalizations.

In those six months he worked at many jobs and developed into a very good imi-tation of a genuine worker. He was a natural linguist and he kept notebooks, mak-ing a scientific study of the workers' slang or argot until he could talk quite intelli-gibly. This language also enabled him more intimately to follow their mental processes and thereby to gather much data for a projected chapter in some future book which he planned to entitle Synthesis of Working-Class Psychology.

Before he arose to the surface from that first plunge into the underworld, he dis-covered that he was a good actor and demonstrated the plasticity of his nature. He was himself astonished at his own fluidity. Once having mastered the language and conquered numerous fastidious qualms he found that he could flow into any nook of working-class life and fit it so snugly as to feel comfortably at home. As he said in the preface to his second book, The Toiler, he endeavored really to know the working people; and the only possible way to achieve this was to work beside them, eat their food, sleep in their beds, be amused with their amusements, think their thoughts and feel their feelings.

He was not a deep thinker. He had no faith in new theories. All his norms and criteria were conventional. His Thesis on the French Revolution was noteworthy in college annals, not merely for its painstaking and voluminous accuracy, but for the fact that it was the dryest, deadest, most formal and most orthodox screed ever written on the subject. He was a very reserved man, and his natural inhibition was large in quantity and steel-like in quality. He had but few friends. He was too undemonstrative, too frigid. He had no vices, nor had any one ever discovered any temptations. Tobacco he detested, beer he abhorred, and he was never known to drink anything stronger than an occasional light wine at dinner.

When a freshman he had been baptized Ice-Box by his warmer-blooded fellows. As a member of the Faculty he was known as Cold-Storage. He had but one grief, and that was Freddie. He had earned it when he played fullback on the Varsity eleven, and his formal soul had never succeeded in living it down. Freddie he would ever be, except officially, and through nightmare vistas he looked into a future when his world would speak of him as Old Freddie.

For he was very young to be a doctor of sociology—only twenty-seven, and he looked younger. In appearance and atmosphere he was a strapping big college man, smooth-faced and easy-mannered, clean and simple and wholesome, with a known record of being a splendid athlete and an implied vast possession of cold culture of the inhibited sort. He never talked shop out of class and committee-rooms, except later when his books showered him with distasteful public notice and he yielded to the extent of reading occasional papers before certain literary and economic societies.

He did everything right—too right; and in dress and comportment was inevitably correct. Not that he was a dandy. Far from it. He was a college man, in dress and carriage as like as a pea to the type that of late years is being so generously turned out of our institutions of higher learning. His handshake was satisfyingly strong and stiff. His blue eyes were coldly blue and convincingly sincere. His voice, firm and masculine, clean and crisp of enunciation, was pleasant to the ear. The one drawback to Freddie Drummond was his inhibition. He never unbent. In his football days the higher the tension of the game the cooler he grew. He was noted as a boxer, but he was regarded as an automaton, with the inhuman action of a machine judging distance and timing blows, guarding, blocking and stalling. He was rarely punished himself, while he rarely punished an opponent. He was too clever and too controlled to permit himself to put a pound more weight into a punch than he intended. With him it was a matter of exercise. It kept him fit.

As time went by Freddie Drummond found himself more frequently crossing the Slot and losing himself in South of Market. His summer and winter holidays were spent there, and, whether it was a week or a week-end, he found the time spent there to be valuable and enjoyable. And there was so much material to be gathered. His third book, Mass and Master, became a textbook in the American universities, and almost before he knew it he was at work on a fourth one, The Fallacy of the Inefficient.

Somewhere in his make-up there was a strange twist or quirk. Perhaps it was a recoil from his environment and training, or from the tempered seed of his ancestors, who had been bookmen generation preceding generation; but, at any rate, he found enjoyment in being down in the working-class world. In his own world he was Cold-Storage, but down below he was Big Bill Totts, who could drink and smoke and slang and fight and be an all-around favorite. Everybody liked Bill, and more than one working-girl made love to him. At first he had been merely a good actor, but as time went on simulation became second nature. He no longer played a part, and he loved sausages—sausages and bacon, than which, in his own proper sphere, there was nothing more loathsome in the way of food.

From doing the thing for the need's sake he came to doing the thing for the thing's sake. He found himself regretting it as the time drew near for him to go back to his lecture-room and his inhibition. And he often found himself waiting with anticipation for the dreary time to pass when he could cross the Slot and cut loose and play the devil. He was not wicked, but as Big Bill Totts he did a myriad of things that Freddie Drummond would never have been permitted to do. Moreover, Freddie Drummond never would have wanted to do them. That was the strangest part of his discovery. Freddie Drummond and Bill Totts were two totally different creatures. The desires and tastes and impulses of each ran counter to the other's. Bill Totts could shirk at a job with a clear conscience, while Freddie Drummond condemned shirking as vicious, criminal and un-American, and devoted whole chapters to condemnation of the vice. Freddie Drummond did not care for dancing, but Bill Totts never missed the nights at the various dancing clubs, such as The Magnolia, The Western Star, and The Élite; while he won a massive silver cup standing thirty inches high for being the best-sustained character at the butchers' and meat-workers' annual grand masked ball. And Bill Totts liked the girls, and the girls liked him while Freddie Drummond enjoyed playing the ascetic in this particular, was open in his opposition to equal suffrage and cynically bitter in his secret condemnation of co-education.

Freddie Drummond changed his manners with his dress and without effort. When he entered the obscure little room used for his transformation scenes he carried himself just a bit too stiffly. He was too erect, his shoulders were an inch too far back, while his face was grave, almost harsh, and practically expressionless. But when he emerged in Bill Totts' clothes he was another creature. Bill Totts did not slouch, but somehow his whole form limbered up and became graceful. The very sound of the voice was changed and the laugh was loud and hearty, while loose speech and an occasional oath were as a matter of course on his lips. Also Bill Totts was a trifle inclined to late hours, and at times, in saloons, to be good-naturedly bellicose with other workmen. Then, too, at Sunday picnics or when coming home from the show either arm betrayed a practiced familiarity in stealing around girls' waists, while he displayed a wit keen and delightful in the flirtatious badinage that was expected of a good fellow in his class.

So thoroughly was Bill Totts himself, so thoroughly a workman, a genuine denizen of South of the Slot, that he was as class-conscious as the average of his kind, and his hatred for a scab even exceeded that of the average loyal union man. During the water-front strike Freddie Drummond was somehow able to stand apart from the unique combination, and, coldly critical, watch Bill Totts hilariously slug scab longshoremen. For Bill Totts was a dues-paying member of the Longshoremen's Union and had a right to be indignant with the usurpers of his job. Big Bill Totts was so very big and so very able that it was Big Bill to the front when trouble was brewing. From acting outraged feelings Freddie Drummond, in the rôle of his other self, came to experience genuine outrage, and it was only when he returned to the classic atmosphere of the university that he was able, sanely and conservatively, to generalize upon his underworld experiences and put them down on paper as a trained sociologist should. That Bill Totts lacked the perspective to raise him above class-consciousness Freddie Drummond clearly saw. But Bill Totts could not see it. When he saw a scab taking his job away he saw red at the same time and little else did he see. It was Freddie Drummond, irreproachably clothed and comported, seated at his study desk or facing his class in Sociology 17, who saw Bill Totts and all around Bill Totts, and all around the whole scab and union-labor problem and its relation to the economic welfare of the United States in the struggle for the world-market. Bill Totts really wasn't able to see beyond the next meal and the prize-fight the following night at the Gayety Athletic Club.

It was while gathering material for Women and Work that Freddie received his first warning of the danger he was in. He was too successful at living in both worlds. This strange dualism he had developed was, after all, very unstable, and as he sat in his study and meditated he saw that it could not endure. It was really a transition stage; and if he persisted he saw that he would inevitably have to drop one world or the other. He could not continue in both. And as he looked at the row of volumes that graced the upper shelf of his revolving bookcase, his volumes, beginning with his Thesis and ending with Women and Work, he decided that that was the world he would hold on to and stick by. Bill Totts had served his purpose, but he had become a too-dangerous accomplice. Bill Totts would have to cease.

Freddie Drummond's fright was due to Mary Condon, president of the International Glove-Workers' Union No. 974. He had seen her first from the spectators' gallery at the annual convention of the Northwest Federation of Labor, and he had seen her through Bill Totts' eyes, and that individual had been most favorably impressed by her. She was not Freddie Drummond's sort at all. What if she were a royal-bodied woman, graceful and sinewy as a panther, with amazing black eyes that could fill with fire or laughter-love, as the mood might dictate? He detested woman with a too-exuberant vitality and a lack of—well, of inhibition. Freddie Drummond accepted the doctrine of evolution because it was quite universally accepted by college men, and he flatly believed that man had climbed up the ladder of life out of the weltering muck and mess of lower and monstrous organic things. But he was a trifle ashamed of their genealogy. Wherefore, probably, he practiced his iron inhibition and preached it to others, and preferred women of his own type who could shake free of this bestial and regrettable ancestral line and by discipline and control emphasize the wideness of the gulf that separated them from what their dim forebears had been.

Bill Totts had none of these considerations. He had liked Mary Condon from the moment his eyes first rested on her in the convention hall, and he had made it a point, then and there, to find out who she was. The next time he met her, and quite by accident, was when he was driving an express wagon for Pat Morrissey. It was in a lodging-house in Mission Street, where he had been called to take a trunk into storage. The landlady's daughter had called him and led him to the little bedroom, the occupant of which, a glove-maker, had just been removed to a hospital. But Bill did not know this. He stooped, upended the trunk, which was a large one, got it on his shoulder and struggled to his feet with his back toward the open door. At that moment he heard a woman's voice.

"Belong to the union?" was the question asked.

"Aw, what's it to you?" he retorted. "Run along now, an' git outa my way. I wanta turn 'round."

The next he knew, big as he was, he was whirled half around and sent reeling backward, the trunk overbalancing him, till he fetched up with a crash against the wall. He started to swear, but at the same instant found himself looking into Mary Condon's flashing, angry eyes.

"Of course I b'long to the union," he said. "I was only kiddin' you."

"Where's your card?" she demanded in businesslike tones.

"In my pocket. But I can't git it out now. This trunk's too damn heavy. Come on down to the wagon an' I'll show it to you."

"Put that trunk down," was the command.

"What for? I got a card, I'm tellin' you."

"Put it down, that's all. No scab's going to handle that trunk. You ought to be ashamed of yourself, you big coward, scabbing on honest men. Why don't you join the union and be a man?"

Mary Condon's color had left her face and it was apparent that she was in a white rage.

"To think of a big man like you turning traitor to his class. I suppose you're aching to join the militia for a chance to shoot down union drivers the next strike. You may belong to the militia already, for that matter. You're the sort—"

"Hold on now; that's too much!" Bill dropped the trunk to the floor with a bang, straightened up and thrust his hand into his inside coat pocket. "I told you I was only kiddin'. There, look at that."

It was a union card properly enough.

"All right, take it along," Mary Condon said. "And the next time don't kid."

Her face relaxed as she noticed the ease with which he got the big trunk to his shoulder and her eyes glowed as they glanced over the graceful massiveness of the man. But Bill did not see that. He was too busy with the trunk.

The next time he saw Mary Condon was during the laundry strike. The laundry workers, but recently organized, were green at the business, and had petitioned Mary Condon to engineer the strike. Freddie Drummond had had an inkling of what was coming and had sent Bill Totts to join the union and investigate. Bill's job was in the washroom, and the men had been called out first that morning in order to stiffen the courage of the girls; and Bill chanced to be near the door to the mangle-room when Mary Condon started to enter. The superintendent, who was both large and stout, barred her way. He wasn't going to have his girls called out and he'd teach her a lesson to mind her own business. And as Mary tried to squeeze past him he thrust her back with a fat hand on her shoulder. She glanced around and saw Bill.

"Here you, Mr. Totts," she called. "Lend a hand. I want to get in."

Bill experienced a startle of warm surprise. She had remembered his name from his union card. The next moment the superintendent had been plucked from the doorway, raving about rights under the law, and the girls were deserting their machines. During the rest of that short and successful strike, Bill constituted himself Mary Condon's henchman and messenger, and when it was over returned to the university to be Freddie Drummond and to wonder what Bill Totts could see in such a woman.

Freddie Drummond was entirely safe, but Bill had fallen in love. There was no getting away from the fact of it, and it was this fact that had given Freddie Drummond his warning. Well, he had done his work and his adventures could cease. There was no need for him to cross the Slot again. All but the last three chapters of his latest, Labor Tactics and Strategy, was finished, and he had sufficient material on hand adequately to supply those chapters.

Another conclusion he arrived at was that, in order to sheet-anchor himself as Freddie Drummond, closer ties and relations in his own social nook were necessary. It was time that he was married, anyway, and he was fully aware that if Freddie Drummond didn't get married Bill Totts assuredly would, and the complications were too awful to contemplate. And so enters Catherine Van Vorst. She was a college woman herself, and her father, the one wealthy member of the Faculty, was the head of the philosophy department. It would be a wise marriage from every standpoint, Freddie Drummond concluded when the engagement was entered into and announced. In appearance, cold and reserved, aristocratic and wholesomely conservative, Catherine Van Vorst, though warm in her way, possessed an inhibition equal to Drummond's.

All seemed well with him, but Freddie Drummond could not quite shake off the call of the underworld, the lure of the free and open, of the unhampered, irresponsible life South of the Slot. As the time of his marriage approached he felt that he had indeed sowed wild oats, and he felt, moreover, what a good thing it would be if he could have but one wild fling more, play the good fellow and the wastrel one last time ere he settled down to gray lecture-rooms and sober matrimony. And, further to tempt him, the very last chapter of Labor Tactics and Strategy remained unwritten for lack of a trifle more of essential data which he had neglected to gather.

So, Freddie Drummond went down for the last time as Bill Totts, got his data, and, unfortunately, encountered Mary Condon. Once more installed in his study it was not a pleasant thing to look back upon. It made his warning doubly imperative. Bill Totts had behaved abominably. Not only had he met Mary Condon at the Central Labor Council, but he had stopped in at a creamery with her, on the way home, and treated her to oysters. And before they parted at her door his arms had been about her and he had kissed her on the lips and kissed her repeatedly. And her last words in his ear, words uttered softly with a catchy sob in the throat that was nothing more nor less than a love-cry, were, "Bill—dear, dear Bill."

Freddie Drummond shuddered at the recollection. He saw the pit yawning for him. He was not by nature a polygamist, and he was appalled at the possibilities of the situation. It would have to be put an end to, and it would end in one only of two ways: either he must become wholly Bill Totts and be married to Mary Condon, or he must remain wholly Freddie Drummond and be married to Catherine Van Vorst. Otherwise, his conduct would be horrible and beneath contempt.

In the several months that followed, San Francisco was torn with labor strife. The unions and the employers' associations had locked horns with a determination that looked as if they intended to settle the matter one way or the other for all time. But Freddie Drummond corrected proofs, lectured classes and did not budge. He devoted himself to Catherine Van Vorst and day by day found more to respect and admire in her—nay, even to love in her. The street-car strike tempted him, but not so severely as he would have expected; and the great meat strike came on and left him cold. The ghost of Bill Totts had been successfully laid, and Freddie Drummond with rejuvenescent zeal tackled a brochure, long planned, on the topic of Diminishing Returns.

The wedding was two weeks off when, on one afternoon, in San Francisco, Catherine Van Vorst picked him up and whisked him away to see a Boys' Club recently instituted by the settlement workers with whom she was interested. They were in her brother's machine, but they were alone except for the chauffeur. At the junction with Kearny Street, Market and Geary Streets intersect like the sides of a sharp-angled letter V. They, in the auto, were coming down Market with the intention of negotiating the sharp apex and going up Geary. But they did not know what was coming down Geary, timed by Fate to meet them at the apex. While aware from the papers that the meat strike was on and that it was an exceedingly bitter one, all thought of it at that moment was farthest from Freddie Drummond's mind. Was he not seated beside Catherine? And besides, he was carefully expounding to her his views on settlement work—views that Bill Totts' adventures had played a part in formulating.

Coming down Geary Street were six meat wagons. Beside each scab driver sat a policeman. Front and rear, and along each side of this procession, marched a protecting escort of one hundred police. Behind the police rear-guard, at a respectful distance, was an orderly but vociferous mob several blocks in length, that congested the street from sidewalk to sidewalk. The Beef Trust was making an effort to supply the hotels and, incidentally, to begin the breaking of the strike. The St. Francis had already been supplied at a cost of many broken windows and broken heads, and the expedition was marching to the relief of the Palace Hotel.

All unwitting, Drummond sat beside Catherine talking settlement work as the auto, honking methodically and dodging traffic, swung in a wide curve to get around the apex. A big coal wagon, loaded with lump coal and drawn by four huge horses, just debouching from Kearny Street as though to turn down Market, blocked their way. The driver of the wagon seemed undecided, and the chauffeur, running slow but disregarding some shouted warning from the policemen, swerved the auto to the left, violating the traffic rules in order to pass in front of the wagon.

At that moment Freddie Drummond discontinued his conversation. Nor did he resume it again, for the situation was developing with the rapidity of a transformation scene. He heard the roar of the mob at the rear and caught a glimpse of the helmeted police and the lurching meat wagons. At the same moment, laying on his whip and standing up to his task, the coal-driver rushed horses and wagon squarely in front of the advancing procession, pulled the horses up sharply and put on the brake. Then he made his lines fast to the brake-handle and sat down with the air of one who had stopped to stay. The auto had been brought to a stop, too, by his big, panting leaders.

Before the chauffeur could back clear, an old Irishman, driving a rickety express wagon and lashing his one horse to a gallop, had locked wheels with the auto. Drummond recognized both horse and wagon, for he had driven them often himself. The Irishman was Pat Morrissey. On the other side a brewery wagon was locking with the coal wagon, and an east-bound Kearny Street car, wildly clanging its gong, the motorman shouting defiance at the crossing policemen, was dashing forward to complete the blockade. And wagon after wagon was locking and blocking and adding to the confusion. The meat wagons halted. The police were trapped. The roar at the rear increased as the mob came on to the attack, while the vanguard of the police charged the obstructing wagons.

"We're in for it," Drummond remarked coolly to Catherine.

"Yes," she nodded with equal coolness. "What savages they are!"

His admiration for her doubled on itself. She was indeed his sort. He would have been satisfied with her even if she had screamed and clung to him, but this—this was magnificent. She sat in that storm-center as calmly as if it had been no more than a block of carriages at the opera.

The police were struggling to clear a passage. The driver of the coal wagon, a big man in shirt sleeves, lighted a pipe and sat smoking. He glanced down complacently at a captain of police who was raving and cursing at him, and his only acknowledgment was a shrug of the shoulders. From the rear arose the rat-tat-tat of clubs on heads and a pandemonium of cursing, yelling and shouting. A violent accession of noise proclaimed that the mob had broken through and was dragging a scab from a wagon. The police captain was reënforced from his vanguard and the mob at the rear was repelled. Meanwhile, window after window in the high office-building on the right had been opened and the class-conscious clerks were raining a shower of office furniture down on the heads of police and scabs. Waste-baskets, ink-bottles, paper-weights, typewriters—anything and everything that came to hand was filling the air.

A policeman, under orders from his captain, clambered to the lofty seat of the coal wagon to arrest the driver. And the driver, rising leisurely and peacefully to meet him, suddenly crumpled him in his arms and threw him down on top of the captain. The driver was a young giant, and when he climbed on top his load and poised a lump of coal in both hands a policeman, who was just scaling the wagon from the side, let go and dropped back to earth. The captain ordered half a dozen of his men to take the wagon. The teamster, scrambling over the load from side to side, beat them down with huge lumps of coal.

The crowd on the sidewalks and the teamsters on the locked wagons roared encouragement and their own delight. The motorman, smashing helmets with his controller-bar, was beaten into insensibility and dragged from his platform. The captain of police, beside himself at the repulse of his men, led the next assault on the coal wagon. A score of police were swarming up the tall-sided fortress. But the teamster multiplied himself. At times there were six or eight policemen rolling on the pavement and under the wagon. Engaged in repulsing an attack on the rear end of his fortress the teamster turned about to see the captain just in the act of stepping on to the seat from the front end. He was still in the air and in most unstable equilibrium when the teamster hurled a thirty-pound lump of coal. It caught the captain fairly on the chest and he went over backward, striking on a wheeler's back, tumbling to the ground and jamming against the rear wheel of the auto.

Catherine thought he was dead, but he picked himself up and charged back. She reached out her gloved hand and patted the flank of the snorting, quivering horse. But Drummond did not notice the action. He had eyes for nothing save the battle of the coal wagon, while somewhere in his complicated psychology one Bill Totts was heaving and straining in an effort to come to life. Drummond believed in law and order and the maintenance of the established; but this riotous savage within him would have none of it. Then, if ever, did Freddie Drummond call upon his iron inhibition to save him. But it is written that the house divided against itself must fall. And Freddie Drummond found that he had divided all the will and force of him with Bill Totts, and between them the entity that constituted pair of them was being wrenched in twain.

Freddie Drummond sat in the auto quite composed, alongside Catherine Van Vorst; but looking out of Freddie Drummond's eyes was Bill Totts, and somewhere behind those eyes, battling for the control of their mutual body, was Freddie Drummond, the sane and conservative sociologist, and Bill Totts, the class-conscious and bellicose union working-man. It was Bill Totts looking out of those eyes who saw the inevitable end of the battle on the coal wagon. He saw a policeman gain the top of the load, a second and a third. They lurched clumsily on the loose footing, but their long riot-clubs were out and swinging. One blow caught the teamster on the head. A second he dodged, receiving it on the shoulder. For him the game was plainly up. He dashed in suddenly, clutched two policemen in his arms, and hurled himself a prisoner to the pavement.

Catherine Van Vorst was sick and faint at sight of the blood and brutal fighting. But her qualms were vanquished by the sensational and most unexpected happening that followed. The man beside her emitted an unearthly yell and rose to his feet. She saw him spring over the front seat, leap to the broad rump of the wheeler and from there gain the wagon. His onslaught was like a whirlwind. Before the bewildered officer on top the load could guess the errand of this conventionally-clad but excited-seeming gentleman he was the recipient of a punch that arched him back through the air to the pavement. A kick in the face led an ascending policeman to follow his example. A rush of three more gained the top and locked with Bill Totts in a gigantic clinch, during which his scalp was opened up by a club, and coat, vest and half his starched shirt were torn from him. But the three policemen were flung wide and far, and Bill Totts, raining down lumps of coal, held the fort.

The captain led gallantly to the attack, but was bowled over by a chunk of coal that burst on his head in black baptism. The need of the police was to break the blockade in front before the mob could break in at the rear, and Bill Totts' need was to hold the wagon till the mob did break through. So the battle of the coal went on.

The crowd had recognized its champion. Big Bill, as usual, had come to the front, and Catherine Van Vorst was bewildered by the cries of "Bill! Oh, you Bill!" that arose on every hand. Pat Morrissey, on his wagon-seat, was jumping and screaming in an ecstasy: "Eat 'em, Bill! Eat 'em! Eat 'em alive!" From the sidewalk she heard a woman's voice cry out, "Look out, Bill—front end!" Bill took the warning, and with well-directed coal cleaned the front end of the wagon of assailants. Catherine Van Vorst turned her head and saw on the curb of the sidewalk a woman with vivid coloring and flashing black eyes who was staring with all her soul at the man who had been Freddie Drummond a few minutes before.

The windows of the office-building became vociferous with applause. The mob had broken through on one side the line of wagons and was advancing, each segregated policeman the center of a fighting group. The scabs were torn from their seats, the traces of the horses cut and the frightened animals put in flight. Many policemen crawled under the coal wagon for safety, while the loose horses, with here and there a policeman on their backs or struggling at their heads to hold them, surged across the sidewalk opposite the jam and broke into Market Street.

Catherine Van Vorst heard the woman's voice calling in warning. She was back on the curb again and crying out:

"Beat it, Bill! Now's your time! Beat it!"

The police for the moment had been swept away. Bill Totts leaped to the pavement and made his way to the woman on the sidewalk. Catherine Van Vorst saw her throw her arms around him and kiss him on the lips; and Catherine Van Vorst watched him curiously as he went on down the sidewalk, one arm around the woman, both talking and laughing, and he with a volubility and abandon she could never have dreamed possible.

The police were back again and clearing the jam while waiting for reënforcements and new drivers and horses. The mob had done its work and was scattering, and Catherine Van Vorst, still watching, could see the man she had known as Freddie Drummond. He towered a head above the crowd. His arm was still about the woman. And she in the motor car, watching, saw the pair cross Market Street, cross the Slot and disappear down Third Street into the labor ghetto.

In the years that followed no more lectures were given in the University of California by one Freddie Drummond and no more books on economics and the labor question appeared over the name of Frederick A. Drummond. On the other hand, there arose a new labor leader, William Totts by name. He it was who married Mary Condon, president of the International Glove-Workers' Union No. 974, and he it was who called the notorious cooks' and waiters' strike, which, before its successful termination, brought out with it scores of other unions, among which, of the more remotely allied, were the chicken-pickers and the undertakers.

JAMES OPPENHEIM

(1882–1932)

Oppenheim is known today, if at all, as the composer of the poem that follows, "Bread and Roses." During the first two decades of the twentieth century, however, he published widely, stories, poems, and, in the 1920s, volumes about psychiatry and self-help. Many of his books, like the collection

of stories, Pay Envelopes: Tales of the Mill, the Mine, and the City Street
*(1911), concerned the everyday lives of working people in New York and
Pittsburgh. He also wrote about poor Jewish immigrants struggling to find
a place in America in books like* Dr. Rast *(1909). Oppenheim also served as
the editor of a short-lived but influential magazine of the World War I
period,* Seven Arts; *many of the significant writers of the pre-war period—
Lowell, Anderson, Dreiser, O'Neill, among them—contributed to the magazine, though its adventurous literary character as well as its pacifist politics
were primarily shaped by the editor.*

*Oppenheim was, in fact, active in a number of political causes of the
time. He served as head of the Hudson Settlement on New York's Lower East
Side from 1903 to 1905, was involved in various socialist groupings of the
period, wrote what he thought of as revolutionary poems, as in* Songs for
the New Age *(1914), and also prepared a number of volumes in the Little
Blue Book series issued by the Kansas socialist publisher Haldeman-Julius.
"Bread and Roses" was written as his response to the 1912 strike of 20,000
workers in the Lawrence, Massachusetts, mills. One of the great triumphs of
the Industrial Workers of the World and of the 27 nationalities represented
on the strike committee, the ten-week action proved a watershed for reduc-
ing hours and raising wages among a quarter million textile workers in
New England. During one of the numerous strike parades a contingent of
young girls carried a banner saying "We want bread and roses too." The
slogan inspired Oppenheim's poem, which was set to music by Caroline
Kohlsaat, and has remained as a kind of feminist anthem.*

BREAD AND ROSES

As we come marching, marching in the beauty of the day,
A million darkened kitchens, a thousand mill lofts gray,
Are touched with all the radiance that a sudden sun discloses,
For the people hear us singing: "Bread and roses! Bread and roses!"

As we come marching, marching, we battle too for men,
For they are women's children, and we mother them again.
Our lives shall not be sweated from birth until life closes;
Hearts starve as well as bodies; give us bread, but give us roses!

As we come marching, marching, unnumbered women dead
Go crying through our singing their ancient cry for bread.
Small art and love and beauty their drudging spirits knew.
Yes, it is bread we fight for—but we fight for roses, too!

As we come marching, marching, we bring the greater days.
The rising of the women means the rising of the race.
No more the drudge and idler—ten that toil where one reposes,
But a sharing of life's glories: Bread and roses! Bread and roses!

ANZIA YEZIERSKA

(1881?–1970)

When in about 1908 Yezierska started to take her writing seriously, she began to use the name by which she has become known rather than the name, Hattie Mayer, she had been given at Ellis Island when she and her family had arrived from Poland. The return to her European identity represented a conscious choice of voice by the writer. For while she was well-read, held a degree from Columbia College's domestic science program, and had taught that subject in New York City schools, she wished to capture in her fiction the experiences of poor urban Jewish working people, especially of women. Therefore she often adopted a nonstandard dialect in which to narrate her stories. From her first published story, "The Free Vacation House" (1915), her subject was existence in the ghetto and the struggles of its inhabitants for fuller lives.

It was a struggle with which Yezierska was familiar by experience. She had worked in garment industry sweatshops, as a housemaid, and in a laundry, studying English at night and helping support her family. After the failure of two early marriages, and frustrated by sporadic teaching of a subject she hated, Yezierska sought out the philosopher John Dewey at his Columbia University office to get his aid in obtaining a regular teaching job. She audited his seminars in 1917 and 1918, and while their relationship did not last, he did help her find publishers for her writing. One of her best-known stories, "The Fat of the Land," was chosen for the Best Short Stories *of 1919, and the following year her first collection,* Hungry Hearts, *was published. She was hired by Goldwyn movie studios to write scripts, and her stories and her first novel,* Salome of the Tenements *(1922), were made into films (now sadly lost).*

But she felt stifled in Hollywood and returned to New York, where she spent much of the rest of her creative life. A series of novels followed, the best known of which, Bread Givers *(1925), concerns the conflicts within a family in which the father devotes himself to study, expecting, therefore, that the women will provide. After the publication of the novel* All I Could Never Be *(1932), which is based on her relationship with Dewey, Yezierska seems to have stopped writing fiction for a time, though she worked for the WPA Writer's Project during the Depression. In 1950, she published a fictionalized autobiography,* Red Ribbon on a White Horse; *that book helped spark a renewal of interest in her work, which was given further impetus by the feminist movement of the 1960s. In her older years she adopted as her narrative voice an elderly woman who spoke for the poor, the aged, and the marginalized.*

SOAP AND WATER

What I so greatly feared, happened! Miss Whiteside, the dean of our college, withheld my diploma. When I came to her office, and asked her why she did not pass me, she said that she could not recommend me as a teacher because of my personal appearance.

She told me that my skin looked oily, my hair unkempt, and my finger-nails sadly neglected. She told me that I was utterly unmindful of the little niceties of the well-groomed lady. She pointed out that my collar did not set evenly, my belt was awry, and there was a lack of freshness in my dress. And she ended with: "Soap and water are cheap. Any one can be clean."

In those four years while I was under her supervision, I was always timid and diffident. I shrank and trembled when I had to come near her. When I had to say something to her, I mumbled and stuttered, and grew red and white in the face with fear.

Every time I had to come to the dean's office for a private conference, I prepared for the ordeal of her cold scrutiny, as a patient prepares for a surgical operation. I watched her gimlet eyes searching for a stray pin, for a spot on my dress, for my unpolished shoes, for my uncared-for finger-nails, as one strapped on the operating table watches the surgeon approaching with his tray of sterilized knives.

She never looked into my eyes. She never perceived that I had a soul. She did not see how I longed for beauty and cleanliness. How I strained and struggled to lift myself from the dead toil and exhaustion that weighed me down. She could see nothing in people like me, except the dirt and the stains on the outside.

But this last time when she threatened to withhold my diploma, because of my appearance, this last time when she reminded me that "Soap and water are cheap. Any one can be clean," this last time, something burst within me.

I felt the suppressed wrath of all the unwashed of the earth break loose within me. My eyes blazed fire. I didn't care for myself, nor the dean, nor the whole laundered world. I had suffered the cruelty of their cleanliness and the tyranny of their culture to the breaking point. I was too frenzied to know what I said or did. But I saw clean, immaculate, spotless Miss Whiteside shrivel and tremble and cower before me, as I had shriveled and trembled and cowered before her for so many years.

Why did she give me my diploma? Was it pity? Or can it be that in my outburst of fury, at the climax of indignities that I had suffered, the barriers broke, and she saw into the world below from where I came?

Miss Whiteside had no particular reason for hounding and persecuting me. Personally, she didn't give a hang if I was clean or dirty. She was merely one of the agents of clean society, delegated to judge who is fit and who is unfit to teach.

While they condemned me as unfit to be a teacher, because of my appearance, I was slaving to keep them clean. I was slaving in a laundry from five to eight in the morning, before going to college, and from six to eleven at night, after coming from college. Eight hours of work a day, outside my studies. Where was the time and the strength for the "little niceties of the well-groomed lady"?

At the time when they rose and took their morning bath, and put on their fresh-laundered linen that somebody had made ready for them, when they were being served with their breakfast, I had already toiled for three hours in a laundry.

When college hours were over, they went for a walk in the fresh air. They had time to rest, and bathe again, and put on fresh clothes for dinner. But I, after college hours, had only time to bolt a soggy meal, and rush back to the grind of the laundry till eleven at night.

At the hour when they came from the theater or musicale, I came from the laundry. But I was so bathed in the sweat of exhaustion that I could not think of a bath of soap and water. I had only strength to drag myself home, and fall down on the bed and sleep. Even if I had had the desire and the energy to take a bath, there were no such things as bathtubs in the house where I lived.

Often as I stood at my board at the laundry, I thought of Miss Whiteside, and her clean world, clothed in the snowy shirt-waists I had ironed. I was thinking—I, soaking in the foul vapors of the steaming laundry, I, with my dirty, tired hands, I am ironing the clean, immaculate shirt-waists of clean, immaculate society. I, the unclean one, am actually fashioning the pedestal of their cleanliness, from which they reach down, hoping to lift me to the height that I have created for them.

I look back at my sweatshop childhood. One day, when I was about sixteen, some one gave me Rosenfeld's poem, "The Machine," to read. Like a spark thrown among oily rags, it set my whole being aflame with longing for self-expression. But I was dumb. I had nothing but blind, aching feeling. For days I went about with agonies of feeling, yet utterly at sea how to fathom and voice those feelings—birth-throes of infinite worlds, and yet dumb.

Suddenly, there came upon me this inspiration. I can go to college! There I shall learn to express myself, to voice my thoughts. But I was not prepared to go to college. The girl in the cigar factory, in the next block, had gone first to a preparatory school. Why shouldn't I find a way, too?

Going to college seemed as impossible for me, at that time, as for an ignorant Russian shopgirl to attempt to write poetry in English. But I was sixteen then, and the impossible was a magnet to draw the dreams that had no outlet. Besides, the actual was so barren, so narrow, so strangling, that the dream of the unattainable was the only air in which the soul could survive.

The ideal of going to college was like the birth of a new religion in my soul. It put new fire in my eyes, and new strength in my tired arms and fingers.

For six years I worked daytimes and went at night to a preparatory school. For six years I went about nursing the illusion that college was a place where I should find self-expression, and vague, pent-up feelings could live as thoughts and grow as ideas.

At last I came to college. I rushed for it with the outstretched arms of youth's aching hunger to give and take of life's deepest and highest, and I came against the solid wall of the well-fed, well-dressed world—the frigid whitewashed wall of cleanliness.

Until I came to college I had been unconscious of my clothes. Suddenly I felt people looking at me at arm's length, as if I were crooked or crippled, as if I had come to a place where I didn't belong, and would never be taken in.

How I pinched, and scraped, and starved myself, to save enough to come to college! Every cent of the tuition fee I paid was drops of sweat and blood from underpaid laundry work. And what did I get for it? A crushed spirit, a broken heart, a stinging sense of poverty that I never felt before.

The courses of study I had to swallow to get my diploma were utterly barren of interest to me. I didn't come to college to get dull learning from dead books. I didn't come for that dry, inanimate stuff that can be hammered out in lectures. I came because I longed for the larger life, for the stimulus of intellectual associations. I came because my whole being clamored for more vision, more fight. But everywhere I went I saw big fences put up against me, with the brutal signs: "No trespassing. Get off the grass."

I experienced at college the same feeling of years ago when I came to this country, when after months of shut-in-ness, in dark tenements and stifling sweatshops, I had come to Central Park for the first time. Like a bird just out from a cage, I stretched out my arms, and then flung myself in ecstatic abandon on the grass. Just as I began to breathe in the fresh-smelling earth, and lift up my eyes to the sky, a big, fat policeman with a club in his hand, seized me, with: "Can't you read the sign? Get off the grass!" Miss Whiteside, the dean of the college, the representative of the clean, the educated world, for all her external refinement, was to me like that brutal policeman, with the club in his hand, that drove me off the grass.

The death-blows to all aspiration began when I graduated from college and tried to get a start at the work for which I had struggled so hard to fit myself. I soon found other agents of clean society, who had the power of giving or withholding the positions I sought, judging me as Miss Whiteside judged me. One glance at my shabby clothes, the desperate anguish that glazed and dulled my eyes and I felt myself condemned by them before I opened my lips to speak.

Starvation forced me to accept the lowest-paid substitute position. And because my wages were so low and so unsteady, I could never get the money for the clothes to make an appearance to secure a position with better pay. I was tricked and foiled. I was considered unfit to get decent pay for my work because of my appearance, and it was to the advantage of those who used me that my appearance should damn me, so as to get me to work for the low wages I was forced to accept. It seemed to me the whole vicious circle of society's injustices was thrust like a noose around my neck to strangle me.

The insults and injuries I had suffered at college had so eaten into my flesh that I could not bear to get near it. I shuddered with horror whenever I had to pass the place blocks away. The hate which I felt for Miss Whiteside spread like poison inside my soul, into hate for all clean society. The whole clean world was massed against me. Whenever I met a well-dressed person, I felt the secret stab of a hidden enemy.

I was so obsessed and consumed with my grievances that I could not get away from myself and think things out in the light. I was in the grip of that blinding, destructive, terrible thing—righteous indignation. I could not rest. I wanted the whole world to know that the college was against democracy in education, that clothes form the basis of class distinctions, that after graduation the opportunities for the best positions are passed out to those who are best-dressed, and the students too poor to put up a front are pigeon-holed and marked unfit and abandoned to the mercy of the wind.

A wild desire raged in the corner of my brain. I knew that the dean gave dinners to the faculty at regular intervals. I longed to burst in at one of those feasts, in the midst of their grand speech-making, and tear down the fine clothes from these well-groomed ladies and gentlemen, and trample them under my feet, and scream like a lunatic: "Soap and water are cheap! Soap and water are cheap! Look at me! See how cheap it is!"

There seemed but three avenues of escape to the torments of my wasted life, madness, suicide, or a heart-to-heart confession to someone who understood. I had not energy enough for suicide. Besides, in my darkest moments of despair, hope clamored loudest. Oh, I longed so to live, to dream my way up on the heights, above the unreal realities that ground me and dragged me down to earth.

Inside the ruin of my thwarted life, the *unlived* visionary immigrant hungered and thirsted for America. I had come a refugee from the Russian pogroms, aflame with dreams of America. I did not find America in the sweatshops, much less in the schools and colleges. But for hundreds of years the persecuted races all over the world were nurtured on hopes of America. When a little baby in my mother's arms, before I was old enough to speak, I saw all around me weary faces light up with thrilling tales of the far-off "golden country." And so, though my faith in this so-called America was shattered, yet underneath, in the sap and roots of my soul, burned the deathless faith that America is, must be, somehow, somewhere. In the midst of my bitterest hates and rebellions, visions of America rose over me, like songs of freedom of an oppressed people.

My body was worn to the bone from overwork, my footsteps dragged with exhaustion, but my eyes still sought the sky, praying, ceaselessly praying, the dumb, inarticulate prayer of the lost immigrant: "America! Ach, America! Where is America?"

It seemed to me if I could only find some human being to whom I could unburden my heart, I would have new strength to begin again my insatiable search for America.

But to whom could I speak? The people in the laundry? They never understood me. They had a grudge against me because I left them when I tried to work myself up. Could I speak to the college people? What did these icebergs of convention know about the vital things of the heart?

And yet, I remembered, in the freshman year, in one of the courses in chemistry, there was an instructor, a woman, who drew me strangely. I felt she was the only real teacher among all the teachers and professors I met. I didn't care for the chemistry, but I liked to look at her. She gave me life, air, the unconscious emanation of her beautiful spirit. I had not spoken a word to her, outside the experiments in chemistry, but I knew her more than the people around her who were of her own class. I felt in the throb of her voice, in the subtle shading around the corner of her eyes, the color and texture of her dreams.

Often in the midst of our work in chemistry I felt like crying out to her: "Oh, please be my friend. I'm so lonely." But something choked me. I couldn't speak. The very intensity of my longing for her friendship made me run away from her in confusion the minute she approached me. I was so conscious of my shabbiness that I was afraid maybe she was only trying to be kind. I couldn't bear kindness. I wanted from her love, understanding, or nothing.

About ten years after I left college, as I walked the streets bowed and beaten with the shame of having to go around begging for work, I met Miss Van Ness. She not only recognized me, but stopped to ask how I was, and what I was doing.

I had begun to think that my only comrades in this world were the homeless and abandoned cats and dogs of the street, whom everybody gives another kick, as they slam the door on them. And here was one from the clean world human enough to be friendly. Here was one of the well-dressed, with a look in her eyes and a sound in her voice that was like healing oil over the bruises of my soul. The mere touch of that woman's hand in mine so overwhelmed me, that I burst out crying in the street.

The next morning I came to Miss Van Ness at her office. In those ten years she had risen to a professorship. But I was not in the least intimidated by her high office. I felt as natural in her presence as if she were my own sister. I heard myself telling her the whole story of my life, but I felt that even if I had not said a word she would have understood all I had to say as if I had spoken. It was all so unutterable, to find one from the other side of the world who was so simply and naturally that miraculous thing—a friend. Just as contact with Miss Whiteside had tied and bound all my thinking processes, so Miss Van Ness unbound and freed me and suffused me with light.

I felt the joy of one breathing on the mountain-tops for the first time. I looked down at the world below. I was changed and the world was changed. My past was the forgotten night. Sunrise was all around me.

I went out from Miss Van Ness's office, singing a song of new life: "America! I found America."

ROBERT FROST
(1874-1963)

Frost may well have been the best-known of American poets, certainly of the twentieth century, and one who distinctively focused on a particular area of the American landscape, rural New England. It is therefore ironic that his first two books, A Boy's Will *(1913) and* North of Boston *(1914), were published first in England, where he was then living. But many things about him were paradoxical: he spoke as a farmer, but seldom had actually farmed; he spoke about rural New Englanders, but had been born in San Francisco, grew up in the industrial city of Lawrence, and spent much of his life on or around college campuses. He was enormously popular as a reader and poet in residence, went on many lecture tours at home and overseas, read one of his poems at the inaugural of President John F. Kennedy, and generally won more accolades—including four Pulitzer prizes—than any of his contemporaries.*

For all that, a deep streak of pessimism and pain runs through his poetry, some of it perhaps related to a long series of family tragedies and some to a view of life as inevitably "a diminished thing." Still, Frost had an acute ear for the speech of the men and women about whom he chose to write and also a gift for telling a good story in traditional poetic forms, like blank verse and tightly rhymed stanzas. He was able to capture in colloquial, direct language the power and limits of his Yankee men and women and to bring their obsessions, pleasures, and work to an audience increasingly unfamiliar with anything like an "Axe-Helve," much less a plough.

THE AX-HELVE

I've known ere now an interfering branch
Of alder catch my lifted ax behind me.
But that was in the woods, to hold my hand
From striking at another alder's roots,
And that was, as I say, an alder branch.
This was a man, Baptiste, who stole one day
Behind me on the snow in my own yard
Where I was working at the chopping block,
And cutting nothing not cut down already.
He caught my ax expertly on the rise,
When all my strength put forth was in his favor,
Held it a moment where it was, to calm me,
Then took it from me—and I let him take it.
I didn't know him well enough to know
What it was all about. There might be something
He had in mind to say to a bad neighbor
He might prefer to say to him disarmed.
But all he had to tell me in French-English
Was what he thought of—not me, but my ax,
Me only as I took my ax to heart.
It was the bad ax-helve someone had sold me—

"Made on machine," he said, plowing the grain
With a thick thumbnail to show how it ran
Across the handle's long-drawn serpentine,
Like the two strokes across a dollar sign.
"You give her one good crack, she's snap raght off.
Den where's your hax-ead flying t'rough de hair?"
Admitted; and yet, what was that to him?

"Come on my house and I put you one in
What's las' awhile—good hick'ry what's grow crooked,
De second growt' I cut myself—tough, tough!"

Something to sell? That wasn't how it sounded.

"Den when you say you come? It's cost you nothing.
Tonaght?"

      As well tonight as any night.

Beyond an over-warmth of kitchen stove
My welcome differed from no other welcome.
Baptiste knew best why I was where I was.
So long as he would leave enough unsaid,
I shouldn't mind his being overjoyed
(If overjoyed he was) at having got me
Where I must judge if what he knew about an ax
That not everybody else knew was to count
For nothing in the measure of a neighbor.
Hard if, though cast away for life with Yankees,
A Frenchman couldn't get his human rating!

Mrs. Baptiste came in and rocked a chair
That had as many motions as the world:
One back and forward, in and out of shadow,
That got her nowhere; one more gradual,
Sideways, that would have run her on the stove
In time, had she not realized her danger
And caught herself up bodily, chair and all,
And set herself back where she started from.
"She ain't spick too much Henglish—dat's too bad."
I was afraid, in brightening first on me,
Then on Baptiste, as if she understood
What passed between us, she was only feigning.
Baptiste was anxious for her; but no more
Than for himself, so placed he couldn't hope
To keep his bargain of the morning with me
In time to keep me from suspecting him
Of really never having meant to keep it.

Needlessly soon he had his ax-helves out,
A quiverful to choose from, since he wished me
To have the best he had, or had to spare—
Not for me to ask which, when what he took
Had beauties he had to point me out at length
To insure their not being wasted on me.
He liked to have it slender as a whipstock,
Free from the least knot, equal to the strain
Of bending like a sword across the knee.
He showed me that the lines of a good helve
Were native to the grain before the knife
Expressed them, and its curves were no false curves
Put on it from without. And there its strength lay
For the hard work. He chafed its long white body
From end to end with his rough hand shut round it.
He tried it at the eyehole in the ax-head.
"Hahn, hahn," he mused, "don't need much taking down."
Baptiste knew how to make a short job long
For love of it, and yet not waste time either.

Do you know, what we talked about was knowledge?
Baptiste on his defense about the children
He kept from school, or did his best to keep—
Whatever school and children and our doubts
Of laid-on education had to do
With the curves of his ax-helves and his having
Used these unscrupulously to bring me
To see for once the inside of his house.
Was I desired in friendship, partly as someone
To leave it to, whether the right to hold
Such doubts of education should depend
Upon the education of those who held them?

But now he brushed the shavings from his knee
And stood the ax there on its horse's hoof,
Erect, but not without its waves, as when
The snake stood up for evil in the Garden—
Top-heavy with a heaviness his short,
Thick hand made light of, steel-blue chin drawn down
And in a little—a French touch in that.
Baptiste drew back and squinted at it, pleased:
"See how she's cock her head!"

                         1923

EDITH SUMMERS KELLEY

(1884-1956)

Edith Summers Kelley wrote about what she had experienced. Born in Canada and educated at the University of Toronto, she moved to New York early in the century. After a series of menial jobs, she became secretary for Upton Sinclair, who had just written The Jungle. *Involved in the Greenwich Village bohemian world of the prewar period, she was for a time engaged to the youthful Sinclair Lewis, though she actually married his roommate. That marriage did not last, and she ultimately established a fifty-year-long relationship with a young sculptor, C. Fred Kelley. The couple found, however, that sculpture and writing did not, at least for them, pay the grocery bills, and so they decided to try farming as a way of making a living. In Kentucky they tried to raise tobacco and later in California, chickens. None of these attempts was particularly successful, and the growing family lived in poverty, unrelieved by efforts to restart their artistic careers. During the 1930s, Kelley worked as a housemaid in the San Diego area.*

Weeds (1923), from which the following excerpt is taken, is based on some of these draining farm experiences. When it was published, the novel received many favorable reviews, but it never caught on, perhaps because the nation's readers were not in 1923 interested in poverty, deprivation, and struggle. Kelley's subsequent novel, The Devil's Hand, *was not published during her lifetime. In the early 1970s, a different reading public, generated by the second wave of feminism, found the struggles of the central figure of* Weeds, *Judith Pippinger, painfully compelling, and Kelley's realistic work began to find its way into college syllabi and reading lists as well as onto bookstore shelves.*

FROM WEEDS

Jerry had a fine bed of tobacco plants that year and together he and Judith set out four acres. Now that the baby was weaned, Judith could leave him with Luella or Aunt Mary while she worked in the field. Her help was badly needed this year, for Jerry had no money left to pay a hired hand. She was glad to do this, for even setting tobacco was a change from the dreary sameness of the household. At a cost of oozing rivers of sweat, of untellable weariness, stiffness, lame backs, and aching necks and hands worn almost to bleeding, the four acres were set at last and they sighed with relief.

"Naow if there on'y comes a good rain," said Jerry, "they'll git a start."

But the good rain did not come. Day after day the sky was cloudless, the flame of the sun clear and hot. Day after day the hard clay hillsides baked harder and the tobacco plants shrank into themselves, turned from green to gray, from gray to brown, shriveled and dried up and blew away in dust.

"Gawd, hain't it discouragin'!" Jerry would say, looking darkly at the clear, blue expanse of sky.

At last it rained. It rained all day and all night; and the next day the "season" was on.

With the infinite patience of those who have to humor the caprices of nature in order to wrest a living from the earth, they went over the whole four acres once more. Jerry had kept his tobacco bed well watered and there were plenty of plants.

"Bejasus, if Luke had stole 'em this time," he said to Judith, "I'd a gone daown there an' bust his jaw fer him. On'y reason he didn't steal 'em, he made his bed clost by a spring this year an' he's got lots of his own."

More than two thirds of the plants were dead and had to be replaced.

"They're a bit late," commented Jerry, "but if the season's any good, they'll grow into good terbaccer yet. It don't take terbaccer long to make itsse'f."

It rained several times through June and the plants began to spread out green and lusty. Then with July the weather turned dry again and intensely hot. The clay hillsides baked harder than ever, so hard that the clods were more like stones than lumps of dried earth. Jerry, in an attempt to save his crop by making cultivation take the place of rain, went through his corn and tobacco again and again with the cultivator, then followed the rows of tobacco with his great sharp hoe, loosening up the ground around each plant. Judith tried to help him at this task but had to give it up. The ground was too flinty, the hoe too heavy; and the sickness of pregnancy which was coming upon her for the second time made her arms weak and nerveless.

No rain fell during July; and in blinding light and blazing heat August set in. It seemed to Jerry, who anxiously watched he sky, as though nature, not content with defrauding him out of the fruit of his labors, was amusing herself by making a fool of him and playing with him as a cat plays with a mouse. Sometimes the sky would grow overcast and all the signs of approaching rain appear, only to be swept away with the next wind. Occasionally even a light shower would fall, enough to partly lay the dust and irritate the anxious tobacco rowers. Then the sky would clear again. Often they would see it raining on the horizon, over near Cynthiana or Georgetown or up toward Cincinnati. But no rain fell to refresh their own thirsty fields. Sometimes on hot afternoons great black storm clouds gathered in the west and rolled up into the sky, then passed away obliquely and disappeared toward the south. Through the heavy, sultry night, when it was hard to get to sleep, heat lightning played incessantly around the horizon. This long continued strain of watching for rain and seeing it approach only to go away again began to wear on the nerves of both Jerry and Judith. They became touchy and irritable and snapped at each other over trifling matters.

Judith tried to keep her garden alive by frequent hoeings. But with the increasing heat and drought it wilted and withered up till there was nothing left but a few dried stalks. They had the milk from their cow, some salt meat left over from the winter before and some dried beans. These with corn meal cakes and coffee made up their daily fare.

By the middle of August wells and cisterns were getting low and springs and streams were drying up. Some of these latter were already bone dry, with the hoofprints of the cattle that used to drink in them baked hard into the flinty clay. Water for stock was growing scarce. The Blackfords' well was dropping lower every day, and Jerry, afraid that it might go dry altogether, would not let Judith use any of the precious water for washing clothes. When wash day came, he would hook up Nip or Tuck to the cart and drive her and the baby and the tubs and the bundle of clothes to a spring further down the hollow where water was still to be had. The spring was low and the scant water fouled by the feet of cattle; but it had to serve. Here he had put up a rude bench on which to set the tubs, and here, as there was now nothing for him to do in the field, he would help Judith to rub and rinse the clothes through the muddy water and spread them on the grass to dry, while the baby crawled about through the wild weed jungle and grasped with his helpless, chubby hands at butterflies and flecks of sunlight.

These little excursions were not picnics, as they might have been under more favorable conditions. The failure of their crops had cast a gloom upon the young couple which was deepened by the change that had come over Judith. The debilitating effect of the long continued heat added to the nausea and nervous irritability of an unwelcome pregnancy had induced in her a state of body and mind in which, in order to endure life at all, she instinctively closed herself up from it as much as she could. With something of the feeling of a creature of the woods, she sought to shut herself up with her weakness and misery. She plodded through the round of her daily tasks like an automaton. Even to the lifting of an eyelid, she made no motion that was not necessary. Her feet dragged, her eyes seemed as if covered by a film and her face wore a heavy, sullen expression. She avoided meeting people, answered them in monosyllables when they spoke to her, and took no interest whatever in the doings of the neighborhood. When Jerry tried to talk to her, she scarcely looked at him or answered him, until, chilled by her lack of response, he too would fall into gloomy silence. Sometimes when Jerry, in his inexperience with the washing of clothes, did something particularly clumsy and awkward, she would scold him sharply then relapse into her habitual impassivity. When the clothes were dried and gathered up, they rode home in silence, Jerry driving, Judith holding the baby on her lap.

Beat upon by the fierce heat and the hard, white light, the face of the country took on every day more of the appearance of drought. Each day vegetation shrank and the exposed surface of bare, caked earth increased. Corn dwindled and yellowed and bluegrass turned dry and brown. The alfalfa stretched its deep roots far down into the soil and managed to keep its rich dark green color, but grew never an inch. The roads lay under a thick coating of this fine powdery dust, soft as velvet to bare feet. When a wagon or buggy passed along it traveled hidden from sight by its own dust and left a diminishing trail behind like a comet. Hens held their wings out from their bodies and panted in the deepest shade of the barnyard. In the pastures cattle and sheep stood all day under trees; and even horses rarely ventured forth into the full glare of the sun. In the evening when the sun slanted low and a grateful coolness stole across the fields, all these creatures, like their human brothers, shook off the torpor of the heat and began to feel more like themselves. The hens scratched for a living among the chaff and dung. The sheep and cattle, banded together after their kind and with their heads all turned in one direction, cropped the scant bluegrass. The horses, aristocrats of the pasture, went apart by themselves, scorning the company of these humbler creatures.

The tobacco plants, owing to their sturdy weed nature, lived through the heat and drought; but they might as well have died, for their leaves were as thin as paper. By the middle of August the tobacco growers, including even Jerry, had given up all hope of getting a crop that year.

With the failure of their crops, every day became Sunday for the men; and they began to visit in each other's barnyards. Different degrees of success, with the inevitable accompaniment of work, self-seeking, greed, jealousy, and disappointment, would have divided them. But the universal bad luck brought them into community of spirit and ushered in an era of neighborliness and good feeling. Lounging on the shady side of each other's barns, whittling aimlessly at bits of stick, chewing straws and tobacco, the men talked about the springs that had gone dry and those that were going dry, inquired about the state of each other's wells and cisterns, and complained about how far they had to drive their cattle to water. They compared notes on the subject of prickly heat and other skin rashes, and talked of the hotness of beds at night. Uncle Jabez Moorhouse quoted copiously from his one book on the subject of drought, a favorite topic with the prophets, and all the old men called to mind former dry years, citing chapter and verse as to the exact date of the arid year, the time the drought began and the number of weeks it had lasted. The calendar for the past fifty years was thoroughly gone over from this point of view and each dry year carefully compared in all respects with the current one. There was matter here for much discussion and argument among the older men, their memories often telling stories that were widely at variance with each other.

The first days of August brought news that sent a buzz of excitement through the groups of barnyard loungers. Although there was no newspaper to carry it, this news flashed rapidly into even the innermost recesses of Scott County. The most unschooled tobacco grower living in the loneliest hollow did not have to wait long for its arrival. The more advanced and intellectual, who subscribed to a religious or agricultural monthly, got the tidings long before the next issue of their magazine was dropped in the rural mail box. The magic word *war* is powerfully and swiftly winged and scorns modern methods of broadcasting. Standing about the coldly monumental August stove, the loiterers in Peter Akers' store spat into last winter's sawdust and talked over the news that the Cincinnati-Lexington train had brought. Driving homeward in their several directions, they pulled up alongside of every passing wagon.

"Hey, d'yuh know there's a big war on?"

At home they told their wives, their neighbors, everybody who passed by the house.

Having done this, they had, however, told all they knew. The words Germans, French, Russians, floated about in the air, but to most of the tobacco growers meant nothing whatever except that the war was a long way off. There was, however, a general realization that it was a big one, that somewhere far away the world was in great turmoil and excitement. The outermost ripples of this excitement shivered through Scott County.

The women inquired anxiously as to the likelihood of their sons and husbands having to go to war. Their fears relieved on this vital point, they poohhooed the whole matter and went on about their housework, instantly transferring their attention to matters of real importance, such as the rendering out of hog fat and the patching of overalls.

"It's ridiclus," said Aunt Abigail, on one of her visits to Judith, "the idee o' them folks a-goin' to fightin' each other. It's a shame an' a disgrace an' it'd otta be put a stop to. Even if they air on'y ignernt furrin folks, they'd otta know better."

To the men it was meat and drink. When they gathered in each other's barnyards, the talk was all of war. To sit in the peaceful warmth of a summer afternoon, placidly chewing the mild Burley of their own fields and express their views about the fighting of the foreigners was a rare treat, combining luxuriously the thrills and excitements of war with the comfort and security of peace. They had virtually no basis upon which to form opinions; but opinions they had, none the less. They were as excitable, argumentative, and dogmatic as any group of men in any other walk of life. Each man held his own convictions in as high esteem and those of his neighbor in as thorough despisal as if he were a successful manufacturer of toothpaste or a United States senator. The discussions on the war were as animated, as heated, as intelligent, and as generally representative of the different types of male humanity as if they had occurred in a metropolitan club. The fact that on the shady side of Jerry Blackford's cowshed the basis of fact was somewhat more vague and flimsy than that in a Union League clubroom made no essential difference. Each man aired his own ideas as loudly and impressively as he could, and paid no attention whatever to those of any of the others; and there was much honest joy and satisfaction.

"They'd otta have us fellers go on over there an' beat 'em all up. We cud do it easy," opined Ziemer Whitmarsh, who had a prominent chin and the long arms and heavy shoulders of a prize fighter. "'Twouldn't be no chore fer us, would it, Bob?"

"No, siree," chimed in young Bob Crupper. "They'd otta let us at 'em." Bob's chin did not protrude unduly; but he had eyes fearless and dreamy, like those of his father. He was ripe for adventure of any kind: war, women, anything. His eyes wistfully sought the horizon.

"I wish 'twa'n't so durn fur away," he fretted.

Bob's father, old Amos, who was a veteran of the Civil War, had subscribed to a Georgetown paper, and was thus placed in a position of authority as regards facts. But it was the romantic and chivalrous aspects of the war that most appealed to the old soldier, as in the days of his youth; and out of his rich nature he was quick to set up heroes to worship and weave a mythical fabric of glory and chivalry.

"Some o' them generals must be powerful men," he would thunder out in a deep rumble of bass ecstasy. "This here von Kluck, he must be a mighty powerful man. An' the Roosians is a fine people, a strong, powerful people. Them Roosians hain't afraid to die fer their country."

"It'll fetch up the price of tebaccer," mused Uncle Sam Whitmarsh, sagely stroking his lean jaw, "—an' hosses. Terbaccer and hosses is things they used up fast in war. An' terbaccer an' hosses is what we got here in Kentucky. An' everything else'll go up too: hog meat and butter and eggs."

"Yaas, an' flour an' sorghum an' coffee alongside of 'em," grunted old Jonah Cobb pessimistically. "I mind me in Civil War times—"

"Aw, don't croak, Jonah. War times is good times fer the farmer. If we kin git a good price for our terbaccer, we hain't a-goin' to kick about payin' a little extry fer a sack o' biscuit flour."

"A sound of battle is in the land and of great destruction," quoted Uncle Jabez Moorhouse. "Woe onto them, for their time is come, the time of their visitation. The earth shall be utterly emptied and utterly laid waste. Behold, Jehovah maketh the earth empty and maketh it waste and turneth it upside down and scattereth abroad the inhabitants thereof. The earth shall stagger like a drunken man."

He loved the sound of the sonorous rhythms and rolled them on his tongue ecstatically.

"I done heard it was a-coming' this way," hazarded Gus Dibble timorously. "Did any o' you folks hear it was a-comin' this way? If it comes this way, they say we'll all hev to go into it."

Gus Dibble was a skinny, pallid fellow with very bad teeth. He had a wife and two small children and tried to raise tobacco to support them. He also had consumption, asthma, and a hernia.

"Aw, what kind of a notion hev you got, Gus?" scoffed Bob Crupper, who from association with his father had become enlightened. "Don't you know you gotta go acrost the ocean to git to where they're a-fightin'?"

"I dunno," answered Gus, humbly and vaguely. "All I know is they said it was a-comin' this way."

For Judith Blackford and the rest of the women in the solitude of their isolated shanties life moved on as stagnantly as usual, except that the heat and the scarcity of water made it somewhat more disagreeable and difficult. For them there was no such thing as change nor anything even vaguely resembling a holiday season. Families must be fed after some fashion or other and dishes washed three times a day, three hundred and sixty-five days in the year. Babies must be fed and washed and dressed and "changed" and rocked when they cried and watched and kept out of mischief and danger. The endless wrangles among older children must be arbitrated in some way or other, if only by cuffing the ears of both contestants; and the equally endless complaints stilled by threats, promises, whatever lies a harassed mother could invent to quiet the fretful clamor of discontented childhood. Fires must be lighted and kept going as long as needed for cooking, no matter how great the heat. Cows must be milked and cream skimmed and butter churned. Hens must be fed and eggs gathered and the filth shoveled out of henhouses. Diapers must be washed, and grimy little drawers and rompers and stiff overalls and sweaty work shirts and grease-bespattered dresses and kitchen aprons and filthy, sour-smelling towels and socks stinking with the putridity of unwashed feet and all the other articles that go to make up a farm woman's family wash. Floors must be swept and scrubbed and stoves cleaned and a never ending war waged against the constant encroaches of dust, grease, stable manure, flies, spiders, rats, mice, ants, and all the other breeders of filth that are continually at work in country households. These activities, with the occasional variation of Sunday visiting, made up the life of the women, a life that was virtually the same every day of the year, except when their help was needed in the field to set tobacco or shuck corn, or when fruit canning, hog killing, or house cleaning crowded the routine.

Late in August, when the tobacco and corn were past saving, the rains came in floods and filled up the wells and cisterns, set the creeks to running again, washed great gullies in the plowed hillsides and refreshed the thirsty pastures.

There followed a lean fall and winter. There was no corn to fatten hogs; so the tenant farmers had to get rid of what hogs they had. The hogs, being lean and forced upon the market, brought only a poor price. The stunted, half filled out nubbins that the corn fields had produced that year were all carefully saved to make into meal for household use. The hens, too, had to go; for hens are too greedy-natured to keep through a time of scarcity. Jerry bundled them into a coop and took them to Clayton and sold them for thirty-five cents apiece, all but a dozen or so which Judith insisted upon keeping "for company," as she expressed it. These scratched and ranged for a living, and kept alive, though they laid never an egg.

Jerry dug his potatoes, most of them not much bigger than marbles, a slow and disheartening task; and Judith cooked them, while they lasted, with the skins on, so that no part of them might be wasted. They were greenish and bitter; but when they were all gone they were sorely missed. The few dried beans and peas that had managed to come to fruit before the dry spell caught them were carefully pulled and shelled and stored away. Hickory nuts and black walnuts were gathered and spread out on the floor of the loft to dry. There were no blackberries that year and only a few stunted apples. Jerry searched through the woods looking for stray apple trees that had sprung up from seed, and brought home an occasional bushel or so of wormy runts. These Judith made up into apple butter which she stored away in crocks and jars.

By January all these things were gone and there was nothing left but some corn.

Work by the day was hard to get; for there were many more men than jobs, and would continue so until the spring rush came on. jerry fretted at his forced idleness and was always on the watch for a chance to earn a day's wages. When he managed to pick up an occasional job, he bought flour for biscuits, canned salmon or a piece of bacon. Then there was a feast royal. These feasts, however, were widely scattered oases on a great desert of corn meal. This had to be eaten without milk; for there was not much food for the cow, and the small amount of milk she gave was all taken by the baby.

Judith was big with her second child. She had recovered from the sickness of early pregnancy and regained some of her old health and spirits. Grown accustomed perforce to the life made necessary by the baby, she chafed less at the monotony and restrictions of the household. But she was no longer the Judith that Jerry had married. The year and a half since the birth of the baby, which had made no noticeable change in Jerry, had left their print upon on her. The youthful curves of her face and body were still there; the youthful color was in her cheeks in spite of the spare diet. But her body had lost its elasticity, her eyes their light and sparkle. The buoyancy and effervescence of youth were gone. It was as if the life spirit in the still young body had grown tired. She rarely sang any more, and was not often heard to laugh. Sometimes, in a feverish burst of gaiety, she would romp uproariously with the baby and seem for a little while like a child again. Then all at once she would let her arms fall at her sides as though suddenly tired and go about her work a little more soberly than before. Sometimes she would sit for a long time abstractedly looking out of the window at the sweep of hillside lined against the sky and take no notice that the baby was crying or tugging at her dress with his strong little fists or eating out of the dog's plate on the floor. Then she would rouse herself with a start, as though shaking something from her, and go on about her sweeping or washing or whatever she had to do.

One Saturday night in late February, the Blackford's door was flung open and Jabez Moorhouse stalked across the floor and stood warming himself by the stove. Snow was falling outside and his cloth cap and broad, stooping shoulders were powdered with white. He loosened the ragged gray woolen muffler that was knotted about his neck and beat the snow from his mittens on the side of the woodbox.

"The wind's sholy keen to-night," he said, spreading out his big hands over the grateful warmth of the stove. "It goes through clothes that hain't none too new like that much tissue paper. 'Tain't no night to be a-travelin' the roads. But I come on a special errand. I want you two and the young un to come over to my place to-morrer long about 'leven o'clock. There's a-goin' to be a s'prise party. Now I gotta be a-gittin' on, 'cause there's others I wanta bid. To-morrer 'bout 'leven, or any time in the forenoon fer that matter. The earlier the welcomer. Don't say nothin' to nobody."

He was gone, with a significant parting smile and wink; and Jerry and Judith looked at each other in astonishment. Behind him he had left an air of mystery, of wonder, and surmise.

"A s'prise party," mused Jerry. "What the devil has Uncle Jabez got to make a s'prise party with? He hain't had no work this winter."

"We'll go an' see anyway," said Judith, a glow in her cheeks. Breaking thus unexpectedly into the dull monotony of their lives, the suddenness and mystery of the invitation thrilled her with excitement.

Next morning, when they arrived at the little shanty behind the big hemlock trees, Judith was surprised to find her father and Uncle Sam Whitmarsh standing talking together just outside the kitchen door where two walls meeting at right angles formed a sheltered nook, pleasantly warmed by the midday winter sun.

"What *you* a-doin' here, Dad?"

"I dunno yet, Judy," answered Bill. "I seem to be a-waitin.'"

Judith pushed open the door and stepped inside, the baby on her arm. She was greeted by a smell, an all-pervading, ineffable, intoxicating smell, the most delicious aroma that ever set a hungry mouth to watering. As she eagerly sniffed the savory odor, she felt a soft, pleasurable, almost erotic sensation tingle through her body, and her lips curved into a smile, such a smile as might have answered a lover's kiss.

"Looky here, Judy, my gal."

Jabez opened the oven door, which had lost its handle and had to be operated by means of a pair of pliers, and drew toward the front of the oven two large sizzling pans, one on the oven floor, the other above it on the grating. As she looked at these pans and sniffed the appetizing smell that steamed up from them, Judith felt once more creeping over her body the same soft, pleasurable, almost erotic sensation and her lips fell again into that smile which might have answered a lover's kiss. In each pan was a large, upcurving mass, delicately brown, casting up a savory steam and oozing succulent juices into the rich, bubbling gravy beneath. With a big tin spoon Jabez lifted this steaming essence from the bottom of the pan and poured it over the big brown mounds. Some of it penetrated into the meat; some trickled appetizingly down the sides and back into the gravy pool.

"Is it near done, Uncle Jabez?"

There was a strained tenseness in the question.

"You damn betcha. We'll be a-lightin' into it afore ten minutes is past. The Bible says the full belly loathes the honeycomb; but to the hungry every bitter thing is sweet. So I reckon them two hind quarters'll slide daown kinder easy."

Uncle Jonah Cobb, who had been pacing up and down the floor, stopped at the arresting word *honey* and looked disappointed when nothing further was said about it.

"They don't do good 'ithout salt," he mumbled to himself, continuing his walk.

Corn cakes were frying on the top of the stove. The big table, roughly made of unplaned pine boards, was drawn into the middle of the room; and Jabez had unearthed from somewhere a tablecloth that had once been white. It was yellowed from long lying away and much creased and crumpled. But it was a tablecloth, and as such suggestive of feasts and holidays. With a strange assortment of broken handled knives and forks and cracked and crazed plates, the table was set for eight.

The overpowering aroma, acting upon the intensity of her craving appetite, affected Judith like a drug which makes the near and real seem vague and far away. She had afterwards a dim recollection of people moving restlessly about, striding up and down the floor and asking if it was time to sit down. But she hardly realized what was going on about her until she found herself seated at the table. Silently as if they had sprung out of the earth, Uncle Jonah and Aunt Selina were found sitting opposite her. Uncle Sam Whitmarsh was at her right hand and Jerry at her left. Her father and Uncle Amos Crupper were at the other end of the table.

Jabez brought one of the big roasting pans and setting it down at his end of the table on top of a piece of pine board began to carve. It must have been that all the others seated there felt like herself; for they seemed rapt and taken out of themselves as though they were religious devotees assisting at some sacred rite. There was a tense look in every face and every eye gleamed and glittered. Judith thought she had never seen such a light in any eyes before. She had seen the light of love, of anger, of jealousy shining from people's eyes. But such expressions were weak and volatile compared with this. It was a look that expressed something more basic than anger, more enduring than love, more all-compelling than jealousy. The eyes were all fixed steadily upon one object, the roasting pan at Jabez' end of the table. The silence was tense with ravenous expectancy.

As each guest was served, he fell to eating, without waiting for the others. Those who were still waiting began to shift uneasily in their chairs, while their eyes ranged restlessly from the diminished hind quarter to the plates of their more fortunate neighbors.

At last everybody was eating and Jabez filled his own plate and fell upon the contents. A silence followed, broken only by the crackle of the fire and the click of the knives and forks. In a patch of sunlight on the floor the baby sat and played with a skunk skin that Jabez was saving to make into a cap.

"Ki-ki, ki-ki, nice ki-ki," he kept saying, as he stroked the soft fur. When a large cat walked out from behind the stove, purring and arching her back, he forsook the skin for the living animal.

A heaping plate of corn cakes was set at each end of the table, from which the guests helped themselves at their will. These, with the meat, formed the whole meal.

For a long time no voice spoke, no eye was lifted. There was nothing but the play of knives and forks, the sound of munching, and the constant reaching out of hands toward the corn cakes.

It was only when the second hind quarter had been carved, served, and partly eaten that the diners began to lift their eyes from their plates, lean back in their chairs, and exchange occasional remarks.

Coffee, which had been boiling on the stove in a big granite stewpan, was now served by Jabez in whatever utensils he could find. Judith got hers in a jelly glass. Aunt Selina had a granite mug, Jerry a tin cup. Uncle Jonah was honored with a large, imposing, and very substantial mustache cup ornamented with pink roses tastefully combined with pale blue true lovers' knots and bearing the legend "Father" in large gilt letters.

Down at the far end of the table, Judith glimpsed her father's familiar habit of turning a spoon over in his mouth. He liked to soak his corn cakes in coffee and eat them with a teaspoon. He put the spoon in his mouth in the usual way and invariably brought it out bottom side up.

When Jabez had served everybody else, he used the dipper to hold his own portion of coffee; and holding it aloft by the long handle, he stood up at the end of the table and rapped for attention.

"Neighbors," he began, "I wish I might give you all sumpin' better'n coffee to drink a toast in. But this here's a dry year. I never reckoned the winter'd come that I'd spend 'ithout a drop o' whiskey on the shelf. But this is that winter. The Bible says that he that tilleth the soil shall have plenty o' bread; an' anybody'd think he'd otta. But you an' me knows, none better, that he don't allus have plenty o' bread, an' still less o' meat. Another thing the Bible says is that the poor man is hated even of his own neighbor; an' I reckon there's heap more truth in that sayin' than in the other one. The earth's a mean an' stingy stepmother, an' she makes the most of her stepchillun pretty mean an' stingy too. A hard life makes 'em hard an' close an' suspicious of each other. They cheat an' they git cheated, an' oftener'n not they hate their neighbors. But if a hard life breeds hates, it breeds likin's too; an' it's because you all is folks that I'm praoud to call my friends, that I ast you to come here to-day. Friends, let's drink a toast to the health of our landlord an' neighbor, Uncle Ezry Pettit. This here is his treat."

A perceptible tremor went around the table. Everybody started slightly and looked half apprehensively at everybody else to see how they took it; then at the door as if Uncle Ezra might be expected to appear there at any moment and claim his property. Uncle Sam Whitmarsh chuckled into his tin mug. Uncle Amos Crupper held his cup poised half way between the table and his lips, deliberate, thoughtful, turning it over in his mind. Judith, glancing sidewise at Jerry, saw a look of shock pass across his face and felt a disturbing aura of disapproval suddenly surround him. But he went on eating.

"Haow did yuh come to git away with her, Jabez?"

It was her father asking the question. He tried to make his voice sound off-handed, but it had a strained, unnatural sound.

"Waal, Bill, it was this way. Friday evenin' on towards night I was a-comin' home raound by the back of Uncle Ezry's old terbaccer barn; an' there she stud caught in the wire fence. I was jes' fixin' to pull her aout, when it come over me all of a sudden haow good she'd eat. After that idear'd took a holt of me, I jes' didn't hev the heart to turn her loose. I tuk a good look all raound, an' there wa'n't a soul to be seen on hill ner holler. It come into my mind haow Abraham when he wanted sumpin to offer up to the Lord fer a burnt offerin', faound a ram caught in the thicket. An' I ses to myse'f a wire fence was jes as good as a thicket any day fer ketchin' sech critters, an' mos' likely I needed the ewe more'n Abraham did the ram. So I jes hit her a whack atween the eyes with the hammer I was a-carryin'. She dropped like a sack o' meal, an' I drug her into the brush. Come dark night I went an' fetched her; an' here she is. She was a fat ewe."

"She was that," assented Uncle Sam Whitmarsh, wiping the grease from his mouth with his pocket handkerchief.

"Waal, I reckon Uncle Ezry won't die in the county house fer lack of her," opined Bill in the tone of one who has justified himself to his conscience. "Gawd, there hain't nothin' like a good meal o' meat to make a feller feel like a man agin. I didn't have no idear I was that meat hungry till I smelt her a-roastin'. Then wild hosses wouldn't 'a' helt me back. It sholy feels good to have yer belly well lined."

Bill sighed, stretched out his long legs luxuriously, and reached into his pocket for a chew of tobacco. The other men pushed back their chairs and also sought their pockets. Aunt Selina brought out her corn cob pipe from the pocket of her patched skirt and filled it with swift, practised movements of her small fingers. Having done so she approached Judith and sitting down beside her plied her with questions about herself and the baby.

All the time the old woman's bright, youthful brown eyes sought Judith's face, as though trying to bridge the gulf of years.

From a child, Judith had been fond of Aunt Selina. There was something about her alert, birdlike, patched little person, so frail and skinny, yet so full of a certain humming, quick pulsating life that drew all children to her, as like is drawn to like. For Aunt Selina, in spite of her years, her corn cob pipe and her ability to spit like a man, was still more than half a child. Judith's early liking for her had persisted through the years; but to-day the old woman seemed a more than usually attractive person. Judith answered all her questions with great animation. She told all about the trouble the baby had had cutting his teeth. She was enthusiastic over plans for raising a big flock of chickens in the spring; and she discussed exhaustively the relative merits of stripes, checks, sprays, spots, and all over patterns in dress goods.

She scarcely knew what she was saying and could remember almost nothing of it afterward. She only knew that she felt warm, strong, happy, full of life and vigor, alive with interest in everything. She seemed to be surrounded by a rosy mist through which things appeared vague and somewhat removed but replete with infinite possibilities for joy and achievement. A small amount of alcohol would have had a similar effect. She was meat drunk. It was the second time in her life that she had tasted mutton.

The others seemed to be affected in much the same way. From about the stove where the men had collected came the sound of animated talk and of bold, assured, unrestrained laughter, such talk and laughter as were rarely heard in a tenant farmer's house except when whiskey was one of the guests. The language, however, out of deference to the two women present, was somewhat restrained and guarded.

"Mebbe you'll call to mind, Amos," Uncle Sam Whitmarsh was saying, "the day we helped tote Uncle Ezry's bar'l o' whiskey daown into his cellar. I reckon it's a good thirty-five year past; but it seems on'y like yestiddy to me. My haow time goes. There was you an' me, an' there was Ned Tyler that left here an' went over into Indianny an' there was Abner Sykes that's dead an' buried this thirty year. You mind that day, Amos?"

"Yaas, I mind that day, Sam; an' I mind well the heft o' that bar'l o' whiskey." Uncle Amos smiled reminiscently. "We was young men them days, Sam."

"Yaas, we was young, an' Ezry was young, an' he drunk a heap o' whiskey in them days afore he got so old he couldn't hold it no more. It was terbaccer harvest an' we was all there a-helpin' to cut. The bar'l come that mornin'. After dinner Ezry ses: 'Boys,' ses he, 'I wish you'd gimme a hand with this here bar'l afore you go back to field.'"

"There stud the bar'l as big as a maounting; an' there stud the cellar steps, steep an' narrer. Ezry never so much as laid hand to it; he jes stud there an' told us what he wanted did. Waal, we four took a holt o' that there bar'l an' we tugged an' pulled an' wrestled an' strained an' sweat till we got her daown them steep narrer stairs. Then Ezry wa'n't satisfied with that; but he had to hev it put way back into the fur corner where it was dark an' cool. After we'd got her there an' blocks set under her to hold her level an' everything all ship-shape, Ezry ses: 'Thanks, boys, you kin go naow.' An' we all troops back up the cellar stairs as dry as we come. I kin see the look on Abner Sykes' face to this day. He's dead an' gone, but that look is a-livin' yet. Yaas, he's got a close fist, has Ezry."

Judith, who had heard this story more than once before, felt herself dropping to sleep again and again. She would catch herself napping, straighten up with a sudden start and open her eyes very wide, only to fall into another doze. The sound of a snore roused her from one of these naps, and looking in the direction from which it had come, she saw that Uncle Jonah, sunk into the depths of an old rocking chair, had fallen fast asleep with his chin resting on his breast. The air in the room was close and heavy with Sunday afternoon dullness. Her eyelids kept falling over her eyes of their own weight. She longed with an intense physical craving to throw herself down somewhere—anywhere—and sleep, sleep, sleep.

Gradually the men stopped talking and lost interest in what their companions were saying. More and more they sagged in their chairs, their legs stretched out lazily toward the stove. Chins dropped, and the sound of muffled, fragmentary voices grew faint and far away. At length even these ceased, and only an occasional faint snore stirred the silence.

Judith was aroused by Jerry gently shaking her shoulder.

"Judy, Judy, it's near night an' time we was home. The baby's awake an' cryin'."

She roused herself with an effort and fetched the baby from the inner room where she had laid him on Jabez's bed. The others were all preparing to go, except Uncle Jonah and Aunt Selina, who still slept on peacefully.

"Leave 'em take their rest," said Jabez. "They hain't got nothin' to go home for."

As they were driving home, Jerry suddenly broke the silence.

"Uncle Jabez hadn't oughter of stole that ewe. I'm sorry I et any."

"But you kep' on a-eatin' after you knowed she was stole."

"Well, God damn it all, Judy, I was hungry."

"So was we all. So was Jabez when he knocked her in the head."

Her voice had a dry and final sound.

Jerry could find no words with which to express the complexity of his feelings. So he kept silence. From time to time he glanced sidewise at his wife with a look of uneasiness and mistrust. She gave him never a look, but sat staring straight in front of her over the baby's head. His mind stirred uneasily with a baffled, futile feeling, very disquieting to his male vanity, that she did not think it worth her while to discuss the matter with him. An intangible film which, ever since the Georgetown Court Day had been spreading itself between them, seemed to grow momently denser and more permanent in quality.

DAVID BUDBILL
(B. 1940)

Born in Cleveland to a street car driver and a minister's daughter, Budbill has mainly lived in the rural area of Vermont about which he has extensively written. He says of himself that "he has worked as a carpenter's apprentice, short order cook, manager of a coffee house, day laborer on a Christmas tree farm, street gang worker, attendant in a mental hospital, forester, gardener, pastor of a church, high school and college teacher."

His six books of poetry include The Chain Saw Dance *(1977),* Why I Came to Judevine *(1987),* Judevine: The Complete Poems, 1970–1990 *(1991, revised and expanded, 1999), and* Moment to Moment: Poems of a Mountain Recluse *(1999). He has also written fiction, including stories in* Snowshoe Trek to Otter River *(1976) and a novel,* Bones on Black Spruce Mountain *(1978). He is perhaps most widely known for his eight plays, a number of which have been presented in venues across the United States. His drama includes* Judevine *(1984) and* Pulp Cutters' Nativity *(1981), a contemporary adaptation of the medieval English miracle play,* The Second Shepherds' Play. *He has regularly performed his work* Zen Mountains-Zen Streets: A Duet for Poet and Improvised Bass *(1984). He founded and now edits* The Judevine Mountain Emailite: A Cyberzine: An Online and Ongoing Journal of Politics and Opinion.

BOBBIE

For years Bobbie drove the pickup truck to Morrisville
every day to sew the flys in men's pajamas at a factory
down there. When you spoke to her about the job,
she'd blush and turn on her heel like a little girl.
She was good. The best one down there.
It was piecework and she was fast.
She quit the sewing when she and Doug went to farming.

Bobble is beautiful, or could be.
Under thirty years of work and plainness you can see
her body, see her face,
those definite, delicate features
glowing.
She strides like a doe.
In spite of two brown teeth
her smile is warm and liquid.

Last summer she cut off a finger in the baler,
paid her farmer's dues.

Now she holds her missing finger behind her when she talks.
She's got something new to blush for.

EDITH WHARTON
(1862–1937)

It is perhaps paradoxical that a person from a background of long-estab-
lished wealth and privilege could write so aptly about decline and impover-
ishment. Edith Wharton achieved this in her novel The House of Mirth *not*
only because she was a consummate artist but because she herself had had
to think long and deep about the alternatives—or rather the lack of them—
to marriage for a woman of her class. She knew privilege well, having been
born and bred to it in the "Old New York" society family of George Freder-
ick and Lucretia Stevens Rhinelander Jones. But after her conventional mar-
riage to Edward Wharton began to fail, and Edith had come to feel utterly
trapped by privilege and boredom, she had to consider where alternatives
might lead her. They led her particularly to writing, which she initially saw
as an outlet for her stifled intellect.

She began by writing about the decoration of houses, started composing short stories in the 1890s, then added longer fiction to her repertoire. The publication of The House of Mirth *in 1905 brought her recognition as one of America's major novelists, and a series of important books emerged in the following two decades:* Ethan Frome, The Reef, The Custom of the Country, Summer, *and* The Age of Innocence, *all by 1921. The last novel won her the Pulitzer Prize. In all, she wrote eighty-six stories, nineteen novels and novellas, a number of books on decoration, architecture, and the like, as well as reviews and essays. In 1910 she moved to France, where she lived the remainder of her life; and then, to the shock of her family, she divorced her husband in 1913. During World War I she was active with medical relief efforts in her adopted country and was considered something of a heroine for her efforts.*

Many of her most important stories and novels focus on the issues of women's entrapment by social conventions, the sexual double standard, and poverty. In The House of Mirth *particularly, her central figure, Lily Bart, cannot take the steps that would effectively mean selling herself into marriage. Having no financial resources of her own, and only the skills and charm necessary to make her marriageable, she is forced by circumstances to attempt to earn her living by producing what she had previously consumed: millinary. The disastrous results are brought alive by Wharton in the excerpt that follows.*

FROM THE HOUSE OF MIRTH

"Look at those spangles, Miss Bart—every one of 'em sewed on crooked."

The tall forewoman, a pinched perpendicular figure, dropped the condemned structure of wire and net on the table at Lily's side, and passed on to the next figure in the line.

There were twenty of them in the work-room, their fagged profiles, under exaggerated hair, bowed in the harsh north light above the utensils of their art; for it was something more than an industry, surely, this creation of ever-varied settings for the face of fortunate womanhood. Their own faces were sallow with the unwholesomeness of hot air and sedentary toil, rather than with any actual signs of want: they were employed in a fashionable millinery establishment, and were fairly well clothed and well paid; but the youngest among them was as dull and colourless as the middle-aged. In the whole work-room there was only one skin beneath which the blood still visibly played; and that now burned with vexation as Miss Bart, under the lash of the forewoman's comment, began to strip the hat-frame of its over-lapping spangles.

To Gerty Farish's hopeful spirit a solution appeared to have been reached when she remembered how beautifully Lily could trim hats. Instances of young lady-milliners establishing themselves under fashionable patronage, and imparting to their "creations" that indefinable touch which the professional hand can never give, had flattered Gerty's visions of the future, and convinced even Lily that her separation from Mrs. Norma Hatch need not reduce her to dependence on her friends.

The parting had occurred a few weeks after Selden's visit, and would have taken place sooner had it not been for the resistance set up in Lily by his ill-starred offer of advice. The sense of being involved in a transaction she would not have cared to examine too closely had soon afterward defined itself in the light of a hint from Mr. Stancy that, if she "saw them through," she would have no reason to be sorry. The implication that such loyalty would meet with a direct reward had hastened her flight, and flung her back, ashamed and penitent, on the broad bosom of Gerty's sympathy. She did not, however, propose to be there prone, and Gerty's inspiration about the hats at once revived her hopes of profitable activity. Here was, after all, something that her charming listless hands could really do; she had no doubt of their capacity for knotting a ribbon or placing a flower to advantage. And of course only these finishing touches would be expected of her: subordinate fingers, blunt, grey, needle-pricked fingers, would prepare the shapes and stitch the linings, while she presided over the charming little front shop—a shop all white panels, mirrors, and moss-green hangings—where her finished creations, hats, wreaths, aigrettes and the rest, perched on their stands like birds just poising for flight.

But at the very outset of Gerty's campaign this vision of the green-and-white shop had been dispelled. Other young ladies of fashion had been thus "set-up," selling their hats by the mere attraction of a name and the reputed knack of tying a bow; but these privileged beings could command a faith in their powers materially expressed by the readiness to pay their shop-rent and advance a handsome sum for current expenses. Where was Lily to find such support? And even could it have been found, how were the ladies on whose approval she depended to be induced to give her their patronage? Gerty learned that whatever sympathy her friend's case might have excited a few months since had been imperilled, if not lost, by her associations with Mrs. Hatch. Once again, Lily had withdrawn from an ambiguous situation in time to save her self-respect, but too late for public vindication. Freddy Van Osburgh was not to marry Mrs. Hatch; he had been rescued at the eleventh hour—some said by the efforts of Gus Trenor and Rosedale—and despatched to Europe with old Ned Van Alstyne; but the risk he had run would always be ascribed to Miss Bart's connivance, and would somehow serve as a summing-up and corroboration of the vague general distrust of her. It was a relief to those who had hung back from her to find themselves thus justified, and they were inclined to insist a little on her connection with the Hatch case in order to show that they had been right.

Gerty's guest, at any rate, brought up against a solid wall of resistance; and even when Carry Fisher, momentarily penitent for her share in the Hatch affair, joined her efforts to Miss Farish's, they met with no better success. Gerty had tried to veil her failure in tender ambiguities; but Carry, always the soul of candour, put the case squarely to her friend.

"I went straight to Judy Trenor; she has fewer prejudices than the others, and besides she's always hated Bertha Dorset. But what *have* you done to her, Lily? At the very first word about giving you a start she flamed out about some money you'd got from Gus; I never knew her so hot before. You know she'll let him do anything but spend money on his friends: the only reason she's decent to me now is that she knows I'm not hard up.—He speculated for you, you say? Well, what's the harm? He had no business to lose. He *didn't* lose? Then what on earth—but I never *could* understand you, Lily!"

The end of it was that, after anxious enquiry and much deliberation, Mrs. Fisher and Gerty, for once oddly united in their effort to help their friend, decided on placing her in the work-room of Mme. Regina's renowned millinery establishment. Even this arrangement was not effected without considerable negotiation, for Mme.

Regina had a strong prejudice against untrained assistance, and was induced to yield only by the fact that she owed the patronage of Mrs. Bry and Mrs. Gormer to Carry Fisher's influence. She had been willing from the first to employ Lily in the show-room: as a displayer of hats, a fashionable beauty might be a valuable asset. But to this suggestion Miss Bart opposed a negative which Gerty emphatically supported, while Mrs. Fisher, inwardly unconvinced, but resigned to this latest proof of Lily's unreason, agreed that perhaps in the end it would be more useful that she should learn the trade. To Regina's work-room Lily was therefore committed by her friends, and there Mrs. Fisher left her with a sigh of relief, while Gerty's watchfulness continued to hover over her at a distance.

Lily had taken up her work early in January: it was now two months later, and she was still being rebuked for her inability to sew spangles on a hat-frame. As she returned to her work she heard a titter pass down the tables. She knew she was an object of criticism and amusement to the other work-women. They were, of course, aware of her history—the exact situation of every girl in the room was known and freely discussed by all the others—but the knowledge did not produce in them any awkward sense of class distinction: it merely explained why her untutored fingers were still blundering over the rudiments of the trade. Lily had no desire that they should recognize any social difference in her; but she had hoped to be received as their equal, and perhaps before long to show herself their superior by a special deftness of touch, and it was humiliating to find that, after two months of drudgery, she still betrayed her lack of early training. Remote was the day when she might aspire to exercise the talents she felt confident of possessing; only experienced workers were entrusted with the delicate art of shaping and trimming the hat, and the forewoman still held her inexorably to the routine of preparatory work.

She began to rip the spangles from the frame, listening absently to the buzz of talk which rose and fell with the coming and going of Miss Haines's active figure. The air was closer than usual, because Miss Haines, who had a cold, had not allowed a window to be opened even during the noon recess; and Lily's head was so heavy with the weight of a sleepless night that the chatter of her companions had the incoherence of a dream.

"I *told* her he'd never look at her again; and he didn't. I wouldn't have, either—I think she acted real mean to him. He took her to the Arion Ball, and had a hack for her both ways. . . . She's taken ten bottles, and her headaches don't seem no better— but she's written a testimonial to say the first bottle cured her, and she got five dollars and her picture in the paper. . . . Mrs. Trenor's hat? The one with the green Paradise? Here, Miss Haines—it'll be ready right off. . . . That was one of the Trenor girls here yesterday with Mrs. George Dorset. How'd I know? Why, Madam sent for me to alter the flower in that Virot hat—the blue tulle: she's tall and slight, with her hair fuzzed out—a good deal like Mamie Leach, on'y thinner. . . ."

On and on it flowed, a current of meaningless sound, on which, startlingly enough, a familiar name now and then floated to the surface. It was the strangest part of Lily's strange experience, the hearing of these names, the seeing the fragmentary and distorted image of the world she had lived in reflected in the mirror of the working-girls' minds. She had never before suspected the mixture of insatiable curiosity and contemptuous freedom with which she and her kind were discussed in this underworld of toilers who lived on their vanity and self-indulgence. Every girl in Mme. Regina's work-room knew to whom the headgear in her hands was destined, and had her opinion of its future wearer, and a definite knowledge of the latter's place in the social system. That Lily was a star fallen from that sky did not, after the first stir of curiosity had subsided, materially add to their interest in her. She had fallen, she had "gone under," and true to the ideal of their race, they were awed only by success—by the gross tangible image of material achievement. The consciousness of her different point of view merely kept them at a little distance from her, as though she were a foreigner with whom it was an effort to talk.

"Miss Bart, if you can't sew those spangles on more regular I guess you'd better give the hat to Miss Kilroy."

Lily looked down ruefully at her handiwork. The forewoman was right: the sewing on of the spangles was inexcusably bad. What made her so much more clumsy than usual? Was it a growing distaste for her task, or actual physical disability? She felt tired and confused: it was an effort to put her thoughts together. She rose and handed the hat to Miss Kilroy, who took it with a suppressed smile.

"I'm sorry; I'm afraid I am not well," she said to the forewoman.

Miss Haines offered no comment. From the first she augured ill of Mme. Regina's consenting to include a fashionable apprentice among her workers. In that temple of art no raw beginners were wanted, and Miss Haines would have been more than human had she not taken a certain pleasure in seeing her forebodings confirmed.

"You'd better go back to binding edges," she said drily.

Lily slipped out last among the band of liberated work-women. She did not care to be mingled in their noisy dispersal: once in the street, she always felt an irresistible return to her old standpoint, an instinctive shrinking from all that was unpolished and promiscuous. In the days—how distant they now seemed!—when she had visited the Girls' Club with Gerty Farish, she had felt an enlightened interest in the working-classes; but that was because she looked down on them from above, from the happy altitude of her grace and her beneficence. Now that she was on a level with them, the point of view was less interesting.

She felt a touch on her arm, and met the penitent eye of Miss Kilroy.

"Miss Bart, I guess you can sew those spangles on as well as I can when you're feeling right. Miss Haines didn't act fair to you."

Lily's colour rose at the unexpected advance: it was a long time since real kindness had looked at her from any eyes but Gerty's.

"Oh, thank you: I'm not particularly well, but Miss Haines was right. I *am* clumsy."

"Well, it's mean work for anybody with a headache." Miss Kilroy paused irresolutely. "You ought to go right home and lay down. Ever try orangeine?"

"Thank you." Lily held out her hand. "It's very kind of you—I mean to go home."

She looked gratefully at Miss Kilroy, but neither knew what more to say. Lily was aware that the other was on the point of offering to go home with her, but she wanted to be alone and silent—even kindness, the sort of kindness that Miss Kilroy could give, would have jarred on her just then.

"Thank you," she repeated as she turned away.

She struck westward through the dreary March twilight, toward the street where her boarding-house stood. She had resolutely refused Gerty's offer of hospitality. Something of her mother's fierce shrinking from observation and sympathy was beginning to develop in her, and the promiscuity of small quarters and close intimacy seemed, on the whole, less endurable than the solitude of a hall bedroom in a house where she could come and go unremarked among other workers. For a while she had been sustained by this desire for privacy and independence; but now, perhaps from increasing physical weariness, the lassitude brought about by hours of unwonted confinement, she was beginning to feel acutely the ugliness and discomfort of her surroundings. The day's task done, she dreaded to return to her narrow room, with its blotched wall-paper and shabby paint; and she hated every step of the walk thither, through the degradation of a New York street in the last stages of decline from fashion to commerce.

But what she dreaded most of all was having to pass the chemist's at the corner of Sixth Avenue. She had meant to take another street: she had usually done so of late. But today her steps were irresistibly drawn toward the flaring plate-glass corner; she tried to take the lower crossing, but a laden dray crowded her back, and she struck across the street obliquely, reaching the sidewalk just opposite the chemist's door.

Over the counter she caught the eye of the clerk who had waited on her before, and slipped the prescription into his hand. There could be no question about the prescription: it was a copy of one of Mrs. Hatch's, obligingly furnished by that lady's chemist. Lily was confident that the clerk would fill it without hesitation; yet the nervous dread of a refusal, or even of an expression of doubt, communicated itself to her restless hands as she affected to examine the bottles of perfume stacked on the glass case before her.

The clerk had read the prescription without comment; but in the act of handing out the bottle he paused.

"You don't want to increase the dose, you know," he remarked.

Lily's heart contracted. What did he mean by looking at her in that way?

"Of course not," she murmured, holding out her hand.

"That's all right: it's a queer-acting drug. A drop or two more, and off you go— the doctors don't know why."

The dread lest he should question her, or keep the bottle back, choked the murmur of acquiescence in her throat; and when at length she emerged safely from the shop she was almost dizzy with the intensity of her relief. The mere touch of the packet thrilled her tired nerves with the delicious promise of a night of sleep, and in the reaction from her momentary fear she felt as if the first fumes of drowsiness were already stealing over her.

In her confusion she stumbled against a man who was hurrying down the last steps of the elevated station. He drew back, and she heard her name uttered with surprise. It was Rosedale, fur-coated, glossy and prosperous—but why did she seem to see him so far off, and as if through a mist of splintered crystals? Before she could account for the phenomenon she found herself shaking hands with him. They had parted with scorn on her side and anger upon his; but all trace of these emotions seemed to vanish as their hands met, and she was only aware of a confused wish that she might continue to hold fast to him.

"Why, what's the matter, Miss Lily? You're not well!" he exclaimed; and she forced her lips into a pallid smile of reassurance.

"I'm a little tired—it's nothing. Stay with me a moment, please," she faltered. That she should be asking this service of Rosedale!

He glanced at the dirty and unpropitious corner on which they stood, with the shriek of the "elevated" and the tumult of trams and waggons contending hideously in their ears.

"We can't stay here; but let me take you somewhere for a cup of tea. The *Longworth* is only a few yards off, and there 'll be no one there at this hour."

A cup of tea in quiet, somewhere out of the noise and ugliness, seemed for the moment the one solace she could bear. A few steps brought them to the ladies' door of the hotel he had named, and a moment later he was seated opposite to her, and the waiter had placed the tea-tray between them.

"Not a drop of brandy or whiskey first? You look regularly done up, Miss Lily. Well, take your tea strong, then; and, waiter, get a cushion for the lady's back."

Lily smiled faintly at the injunction to take her tea strong. It was the temptation she was always struggling to resist. Her craving for the keen stimulant was forever conflicting with that other craving for sleep—the midnight craving which only the little phial in her hand could still. But today, at any rate, the tea could hardly be too strong: she counted on it to pour warmth and resolution into her empty veins.

As she leaned back before him, her lids drooping in utter lassitude, though the first warm draught already tinged her face with returning life, Rosedale was seized afresh by the poignant surprise of her beauty. The dark pencilling of fatigue under her eyes, the morbid blue-veined pallour of the temples, brought out the brightness of her hair and lips, as though all her ebbing vitality were centred there. Against the dull chocolate-coloured background of the restaurant, the purity of her head stood out as it had never done in the most brightly-lit ball-room. He looked at her with a startled uncomfortable feeling, as though her beauty were a forgotten enemy that had lain in ambush and now sprang out on him unawares.

To clear the air he tried to take an easy tone with her. "Why, Miss Lily, I haven't seen you for an age. I didn't know what had become of you."

As he spoke he was checked by an embarrassing sense of the complications to which this might lead. Though he had not seen her he had heard of her; he knew of her connection with Mrs. Hatch, and of the talk resulting from it. Mrs. Hatch's milieu was one which he had once assiduously frequented, and now as devoutly shunned.

Lily, to whom the tea had restored her usual clearness of mind, saw what was in his thoughts and said with a slight smile: "You would not be likely to know about me. I have joined the working classes."

He stared in genuine wonder. "You don't mean——? Why, what on earth are you doing?"

"Learning to be a milliner—at least trying to learn," she hastily qualified the statement.

Rosedale suppressed a low whistle of surprise. "Come off—you ain't serious, are you?"

"Perfectly serious. I'm obliged to work for my living."

"But I understood—I thought you were with Norma Hatch."

"You heard I had gone to her as her secretary?"

"Something of the kind, I believe." He leaned forward to refill her cup.

Lily guessed the possibilities of embarrassment which the topic held for him, and raising her eyes to his, she said suddenly: "I left her two months ago."

Rosedale continued to fumble awkwardly with the tea-pot, and she felt sure that he had heard what had been said of her. But what was there that Rosedale did not hear?

"Wasn't it a soft berth?" he enquired, with an attempt at lightness.

"Too soft—one might have sunk in too deep." Lily rested one arm on the edge of the table, and sat looking at him more intently than she had ever looked before. An uncontrollable impulse was urging her to put her case to this man, from whose curiosity she had always so fiercely defended herself.

"You know Mrs. Hatch, I think? Well, perhaps you can understand that she might make things too easy for one."

Rosedale looked faintly puzzled, and she remembered that allusiveness was lost on him.

"It was no place for you, anyhow," he agreed, so suffused and immersed in the light of her full gaze that he found himself being drawn into strange depths of intimacy. He who had had to subsist on mere fugitive glances, looks winged in flight and swiftly lost under covert, now found her eyes settling on him with a brooding intensity that fairly dazzled him.

"I left," Lily continued, "lest people should say I was helping Mrs. Hatch to marry Freddy Van Osburgh—who is not in the least too good for her—and as they will continue to say it, I see that I might as well have stayed where I was."

"Oh, Freddy———" Rosedale brushed aside the topic with an air of its unimportance which gave a sense of the immense perspective he had acquired. "Freddy don't count but I knew *you* weren't mixed up in that. It ain't your style."

Lily coloured slightly: she could not conceal from herself that the words gave her pleasure. She would have liked to sit there, drinking more tea, and continuing to talk of herself to Rosedale. But the old habit of observing the conventions reminded her that it was time to bring their colloquy to an end, and she made a faint motion to push back her chair.

Rosedale stopped her with a protesting gesture. "Wait a minute—don't go yet; sit quiet and rest a little longer. You look thoroughly played out. And you haven't told me———" He broke off, conscious of going farther than he had meant. She saw the struggle and understood it; understood also the nature of the spell to which he yielded as, with his eyes on her face, he began again abruptly: "What on earth did you mean by saying just now that you were learning to be a milliner?"

"Just what I said. I am an apprentice at Regina's."

"Good Lord—*you*? But what for? I knew your aunt had turned you down: Mrs. Fisher told me about it. But I understood you got a legacy from her———"

"I got ten thousand dollars; but the legacy is not to be paid till next summer."

"Well, but—look here: you could *borrow* on it any time you wanted."

She took her head gravely. "No; for I owe it already."

"Owe it? The whole ten thousand?"

"Every penny." She paused, and then continued abruptly, with her eyes on his face: "I think Gus Trenor spoke to you once about having made some money for me in stocks."

She waited, and Rosedale, congested with embarrassment, muttered, that he remembered something of the kind.

"He made about nine thousand dollars," Lily pursued, in the same tone of eager communicativeness. "At the time, I understood that he was speculating with my own money: it was incredibly stupid of me, but I knew nothing of business. Afterward I found out that he had *not* used my money—that what he said he had made for me he had really given me. It was meant in kindness, of course; but it was not the sort of obligation one could remain under. Unfortunately I had spent the money before I discovered my mistake; and so my legacy will have to go to pay it back. That is the reason why I am trying to learn a trade."

She made the statement clearly, deliberately, with pauses between the sentences, so that each should have time to sink deeply into her hearer's mind. She had a passionate desire that someone should know the truth about this transaction, and also that the rumour of her intention to repay the money should reach Judy Trenor's ears.

And it had suddenly occurred to her that Rosedale, who had surprised Trenor's confidence, was the fitting person to receive and transmit her version of the facts. She had even felt a momentary exhilaration at the thought of thus relieving herself of her detested secret; but the sensation gradually faded in the telling, and as she ended her pallour was suffused with a deep blush of misery.

Rosedale continued to stare at her in wonder; but the wonder took the turn she had least expected.

"But see here—if that's the case, it cleans you out altogether?"

He put it to her as if she had not grasped the consequences of her act; as if her incorrigible ignorance of business were about to precipitate her into a fresh act of folly.

"Altogether—yes," she calmly agreed.

He sat silent, his thick hands clasped on the table, his little puzzled eyes exploring the recesses of the deserted restaurant.

"See here—that's fine," he exclaimed abruptly.

Lily rose from her seat with a deprecating laugh. "Oh, no—it's merely a bore," she asserted, gathering together the ends of her feather scarf.

Rosedale remained seated, too intent on his thoughts to notice her movement. "Miss Lily, if you want any backing—I like pluck——" broke from him disconnectedly.

"Thank you." She held out her hand. "Your tea has given me a tremendous backing. I feel equal to anything now."

Her gesture seemed to show a definite intention of dismissal, but her companion had tossed a bill to the waiter, and was slipping his short arms into his expensive overcoat.

"Wait a minute—you've got to let me walk home with you," he said.

Lily uttered no protest, and when he had paused to make sure of his change they emerged from the hotel and crossed Sixth Avenue again. As she led the way westward past a long line of areas which, through the distortion of their paintless rails, revealed with increasing candour the *disjecta membra* of bygone dinners, Lily felt that Rosedale was taking contemptuous note of the neighbourhood; and before the doorstep at which she finally paused he looked up with an air of incredulous disgust.

"This isn't the place? Some one told me you were living with Miss Farish."

"No: I am boarding here. I have lived too long on my friends."

He continued to scan the blistered brown stone front, the windows draped with discoloured lace, and the Pompeian decoration of the muddy vestibule; then he looked back at her face and said with a visible effort: "You'll let me come and see you some day?"

She smiled, recognizing the heroism of the offer to the point of being frankly touched by it. "Thank you—I shall be very glad," she made answer, in the first sincere words she had ever spoken to him.

That evening in her own room Miss Bart—who had fled early from the heavy fumes of the basement dinner-table—sat musing upon the impulse which had led her to unbosom herself to Rosedale. Beneath it she discovered an increasing sense of loneliness—a dread of returning to the solitude of her room, while she could be anywhere else, or in any company but her own. Circumstances, of late, had combined to cut her off more and more from her few remaining friends. On Carry Fisher's part the withdrawal was perhaps not quite involuntary. Having made her final effort on Lily's behalf, and landed her safely in Mme. Regina's work-room, Mrs. Fisher seemed disposed to rest from her labours; and Lily, understanding the reason, could not condemn her. Carry had in fact come dangerously near to being involved in the episode of Mrs. Norma Hatch, and it had taken some verbal ingenuity to extricate herself. She frankly owned to having brought Lily and Mrs. Hatch together, but then she did not know Mrs. Hatch—she had expressly warned Lily that she did not know Mrs. Hatch—and besides, she was not Lily's keeper, and really the girl was old enough to take care of herself. Carry did not put her own case so brutally, but she allowed it to be thus put for her by her latest bosom friend, Mrs. Jack Stepney: Mrs. Stepney, trembling over the narrowness of her only brother's escape, but eager to vindicate Mrs. Fisher, at whose house she could count on the "jolly parties" which had become a necessity to her since marriage had emancipated her from the Van Osburgh point of view.

Lily understood the situation and could make allowances for it. Carry had been a good friend to her in difficult days, and perhaps only a friendship like Gerty's could be proof against such an increasing strain. Gerty's friendship did indeed hold fast; yet Lily was beginning to avoid her also. For she could not go to Gerty's without risk of meeting Selden; and to meet him now would be pure pain. It was pain enough even to think of him, whether she considered him in the distinctness of her waking thoughts, or felt the obsession of his presence through the blur of her tormented nights. That was one of the reasons why she had turned again to Mrs. Hatch's prescription. In the uneasy snatches of her natural dreams he came to her sometimes in the old guise of fellowship and tenderness; and she would rise from the sweet delusion mocked and emptied of her courage. But in the sleep which the phial procured she sank far below such half-waking visitations, sank into depths of dreamless annihilation from which she woke each morning with an obliterated past.

Gradually, to be sure, the stress of the old thoughts would return; but at least they did not importune her waking hour. The drug gave her a momentary illusion of complete renewal, from which she drew strength to take up her daily work. The strength was more and more needed as the perplexities of her future increased. She knew that to Gerty and Mrs. Fisher she was only passing through a temporary period of probation, since they believed that the apprenticeship she was serving at Mme. Regina's would enable her, when Mrs. Peniston's legacy was paid, to realize the vision of the green-and-white shop with the fuller competence acquired by her preliminary training. But to Lily herself, aware that the legacy could not be put to such a use, the preliminary training seemed a wasted effort. She understood clearly enough that, even if she could ever learn to compete with hands formed from childhood for their special work, the small pay she received would not be a sufficient addition to her income to compensate her for such drudgery. And the realization of this fact brought her recurringly face to face with the temptation to use the legacy in establishing her business. Once installed, and in command of her own workwomen, she believed she had sufficient tact and ability to attract a fashionable *clientèle*; and if the business succeeded she could gradually lay aside money enough to discharge her debt to Trenor. But the task might take years to accomplish, even if she continued to stint herself to the utmost; and meanwhile her pride would be crushed under the weight of an intolerable obligation.

These were her superficial considerations; but under them lurked the secret dread that the obligation might not always remain intolerable. She knew she could not count on her continuity of purpose, and what really frightened her was the thought that she might gradually accommodate herself to remaining indefinitely in Trenor's debt, as she had accommodated herself to the part allotted her on the Sabrina, and as she had so nearly drifted into acquiescing with Stancy's scheme for the advancement of Mrs. Hatch. Her danger lay, as she knew, in her old incurable dread of discomfort and poverty; in the fear of that mounting tide of dinginess against which her mother had so passionately warned her. And now a new vista of peril opened before her. She understood that Rosedale was ready to lend her money; and the longing to take advantage of his offer began to haunt her insidiously. It was of course impossible to accept a loan from Rosedale; but proximate possibilities hovered temptingly before her. She was quite sure that he would come and see her again, and almost sure that, if he did, she could bring him to the point of offering to marry her on the terms she had previously rejected. Would she still reject them if they were offered? More and more, with every fresh mischance befalling her, did the pursuing furies seem to take the shape of Bertha Dorset; and close at hand, safely locked among her papers, lay the means of ending their pursuit. The temptation, which her scorn of Rosedale had once enabled her to reject, now insistently returned upon her; and how much strength was left her to oppose it?

What little there was must at any rate be husbanded to the utmost; she could not trust herself again to the perils of a sleepless night. Through the long hours of silence the dark spirit of fatigue and loneliness crouched upon her breast, leaving her so drained of bodily strength that her morning thoughts swam in a haze of weakness. The only hope of renewal lay in the little bottle at her bed-side; and how much longer that hope would last she dared not conjecture.

WILLIAM CARLOS WILLIAMS
(1883–1963)

The term "modernism" generally evokes images of experimental art and literature. It also has often implied elitist, if not fascist, politics. William Carlos Williams was among the most innovative of the writers of the first half of the twentieth century. But while Williams shared the injunction of his friend Ezra Pound to "make it new," he did not at all share Pound's fascist political ideas. On the contrary, Williams wrote sympathetically and with insight about the lives of poor and working people, about immigrants and minorities in his native northern New Jersey. Though his family spoke Spanish at home when Williams was young, he became extraordinarily adept at capturing the cadences of American English. Like his contemporary, Robert Frost, Williams used a poetic diction marked by everyday speech, but Frost's is that of rural people whereas Williams's has the brassy, sometimes quirky quality of fast urban life. A certain strain in Frost attaches him to earlier poets of the English romantic tradition, like William Wordsworth; Williams's mode is decidedly antiromantic. Where there is an underlying gloom, even cynicism, in some of Frost's work, Williams retains a certain forward-looking power, even in the face of the ugliness and corruption of small city life.

Through much of his adult life, Williams was a practicing physician in northern New Jersey. But he lived in Europe for periods of time, and was influenced not only by modernist writers like Pound and Marianne Moore, but also by visual artists like Alfred Stieglitz and Cubist painters. His wide knowledge of modern art and the theories of its creation is reflected in the variety of forms in which he wrote, including, besides poetry short and long, four novels, drama, other kinds of fiction, autobiography and innovative nonfictional books like Kora in Hell: Improvisations *(1920) and* In the American Grain *(1925). He developed quite distinctive styles, designed to capture the fragmented, disconnected qualities of modern urban life.*

Like the Imagists, Williams insisted upon specificity in language or, as he put it, "no ideas but in things." Some of his most familiar poems, like the eight-line work about "a red wheel/barrow/glazed with rain/water" (half the poem) are as short and intense as any in the language. Later in his life, however, he composed an epic-length poem, titled after the major city of northern New Jersey, Paterson *(1946–1963). Here Williams works into a kind of collage a variety of materials, some composed, some found in newspapers, letters, and other documents, to create a poetic portrait of the history and culture of what becomes a symbolic American city, and of a poet's search for ways of fathoming and expressing the lives, many quite ordinary, comprehended in it.*

To Elsie

The pure products of America
go crazy—
mountain folk from Kentucky

or the ribbed north end of
Jersey
with its isolate lakes and

valleys, its deaf-mutes, thieves
old names
and promiscuity between

devil-may-care men who have taken
to railroading
out of sheer lust of adventure—

and young slatterns, bathed
in filth
from Monday to Saturday

to be tricked out that night
with gauds
from imaginations which have no

peasant traditions to give them
character
but flutter and flaunt

sheer rags—succumbing without
emotion
save numbed terror

under some hedge of choke-cherry
or viburnum—
which they cannot express—

Unless it be that marriage
perhaps
with a dash of Indian blood

will throw up a girl so desolate
so hemmed round
with disease or murder

that she'll be rescued by an
agent—
reared by the state and

sent out at fifteen to work in
some hard-pressed
house in the suburbs—

some doctor's family, some Elsie—
voluptuous water
expressing with broken

brain the truth about us—
her great
ungainly hips and flopping breasts

addressed to cheap
jewelry
and rich young men with fine eyes

as if the earth under our feet
were
an excrement of some sky

and we degraded prisoners
destined
to hunger until we eat filth

while the imagination strains
after deer
going by fields of goldenrod in

the stifling heat of September
Somehow
it seems to destroy us

It is only in isolate flecks that
something
is given off

No one
to witness
and adjust, no one to drive the car.

1923

KENNETH FEARING

(1902-1961)

If one were miscellaneously to take some of Kenneth Fearing's books off a library shelf, one might think that there were two twentieth-century American writers by that name. One was the writer of thrillers and hard-boiled detective novels, somewhat in the style of Dashiell Hammett and Raymond Chandler; the other a political poet who used the idiom of the city—the slick ad, the shouted slogan, the overheard newsroom conversation—to capture a sense of the disaster America had become in the 1930s Depression. Actually, Fearing had other careers as well: film critic for The New Masses, *publicist, founding editor of* Partisan Review, *writer for* The New Yorker, *and, under various pseudonyms, for many less exalted magazines. He was brought up in comfortable circumstances in Oak Park, Illinois, and graduated from the University of Wisconsin in 1924. After working briefly for a Chicago newspaper, he moved to New York, where he was active in circles that were radical both in politics and in artistic modes.*

His novels are marked by their use of multiple narrative points of view and a staccato style that provides an edgy sense of the instability and potential for violence of the modern urban world. His best-known work of fiction, The Big Clock *(1946), was made into a movie and reissued as a popular paperback twenty years after Fearing's death. Other novels also reflect his efforts to combine modernist narrative tactics with the scary psychological details characteristic of pulp thrillers.*

His poetry, Fearing himself claimed, was influenced by Walt Whitman and Carl Sandburg. He preferred to use short lines, the lingo of mass culture, and abrupt shifts to portray middle and working-class people caught in economic and political traps not of their own devising. Perhaps no poet of the Depression period so successfully used the vernacular to mourn and to protest what was becoming of ordinary American women and men in a nation ill-fed, ill-housed, and ill-used.

DIRGE

1-2-3 was the number he played but today the number came 3-2-1;
Bought his Carbide at 30 and it went to 29; had the favorite at
    Bowie but the track was slow—

O executive type, would you like to drive a floating-power, knee-
    action, silk-upholstered six? Wed a Hollywood star? Shoot
    the course in 58? Draw to the ace, king, jack?
O fellow with a will who won't take no, watch out for three
    cigarettes on the same, single match; O democratic voter
    born in August under Mars, beware of liquidated rails—

Denouement to denouement, he took a personal pride in the certain, cer-
    tain way he lived his own, private life,
But nevertheless, they shut off his gas; nevertheless, the bank fore-
    closed; nevertheless, the landlord called; nevertheless, the
    radio broke,

And twelve o'clock arrived just once too often,
Just the same he wore one gray tweed suit, bought one straw hat,
    drank one straight Scotch, walked one short step, took one
    long look, drew one deep breath,
Just one too many,

    And wow he died as wow he lived,
    Going whop to the office and blooie home to sleep and biff got
        married and bam had children and oof got fired,
    Zowie did he live and zowie did he die,

    With who the hell are you at the corner of his casket, and where
        the hell're we going on the right-hand silver knob, and who
        the hell cares walking second from the end with an Amer-
        ican Beauty wreath from why the hell not,

    Very much missed by the circulation staff of the New York Eve-
        ning Post; deeply, deeply mourned by the B.M.T.
    Wham, Mr. Roosevelt; pow, Sears Roebuck; awk, big dipper;
        bop, summer rain;
    Bong, Mr., bong, Mr., bong, Mr., bong.

                      1935

TILLIE OLSEN

(B. 1912?)

In this story, Olsen dramatizes the impact of class position in terms of the attention a mother can provide for her child. Thus she is able to render in a situation rich with echoes for our own time the ways in which class shapes life chances, or, in Olsen's now well-known phrase, "So all that is in her will not bloom—but in how many does it? There is still enough left to live by."
(For biographical information about Olsen, see the headnote in section I.)

I STAND HERE IRONING

I stand here ironing, and what you asked me moves tormented back and forthwith the iron.

"I wish you would manage the time to come in and talk with me about your daughter. I'm sure you can help me understand her. She's a youngster who needs help and whom I'm deeply interested in helping."

"Who needs help." . . . Even if I came, what good would it do? You think because I am her mother I have a key, or that in some way you could use me as a key? She has lived for nineteen years. There is all that life that has happened outside of me, beyond me.

And when is there time to remember, to sift, to weigh, to estimate, to total? I will start and there will be an interruption and I will have to gather it all together again. Or I will become engulfed with all I did or did not do, with what should have been and what cannot be helped.

She was a beautiful baby. The first and only one of our five that was beautiful at birth. You do not guess how new and uneasy her tenancy in her now-loveliness. You did not know her all those years she was thought homely, or see her poring over her baby pictures, making me tell her over and over how beautiful she had been—and would be, I would tell her—and was now, to the seeing eye. But the seeing eyes were few or nonexistent. Including mine.

I nursed her. They feel that's important nowadays. I nursed all the children, but with her, with all the fierce rigidity of first motherhood, I did like the books then said. Though her cries battered me to trembling and my breasts ached with swollenness, I waited till the clock decreed.

Why do I put that first? I do not even know if it matters, or if it explains anything.

She was a beautiful baby. She blew shining bubbles of sound. She loved motion, loved light, loved color and music and textures. She would lie on the floor in her blue overalls patting the surface so hard in ecstasy her hands and feet would blur. She was a miracle to me, but when she was eight months old I had to leave her daytimes with the woman downstairs to whom she was no miracle at all, for I worked or looked for work and for Emily's father, who "could no longer endure" (he wrote in his good-bye note) "sharing want with us."

I was nineteen. It was the pre-relief, pre-WPA world of the depression. I would start running as soon as I got off the streetcar, running up the stairs, the place smelling sour, and awake or asleep to startle awake, when she saw me she would break into a clogged weeping that could not be comforted, a weeping I can hear yet.

After a while I found a job hashing at night so I could be with her days, and it was better. But it came to where I had to bring her to his family and leave her.

It took a long time to raise the money for her fare back. Then she got chicken pox and I had to wait longer. When she finally came, I hardly knew her, walking quick and nervous like her father, looking like her father, thin, and dressed in a shoddy red that yellowed her skin and glared at the pockmarks. All the baby loveliness gone.

She was two. Old enough for nursery school they said, and I did not know then what I know now—the fatigue of the long day, and the lacerations of group life in the kinds of nurseries that are only parking places for children.

Except that it would have made no difference if I had known. It was the only place there was. It was the only way we could be together, the only way I could hold a job.

And even without knowing, I knew. I knew the teacher that was evil because all these years it has curdled into my memory, the little boy hunched in the corner, her rasp, "why aren't you outside, because Alvin hits you? that's no reason, go out, scaredy." I knew Emily hated it even if she did not clutch and implore "don't go Mommy" like the other children, mornings.

She always had a reason why we should stay home. Momma, you look sick. Momma, I feel sick. Momma, the teachers aren't there today, they're sick. Momma, we can't go, there was a fire there last night. Momma, it's a holiday today, no school, they told me.

But never a direct protest, never rebellion. I think of our others in their three-, four-year-oldness—the explosions, the tempers, the denunciations, the demands—and I feel suddenly ill. I put the iron down. What in me demanded that goodness in her? And what was the cost, the cost to her of such goodness?

The old man living in the back once said in his gentle way: "You should smile at Emily more when you look at her." What *was* in my face when I looked at her? I loved her. There were all the acts of love.

It was only with the others I remembered what he said, and it was the face of joy, and not of care or tightness or worry I turned to them—too late for Emily. She does not smile easily, let alone almost always as her brothers and sisters do. Her face is closed and sombre, but when she wants, how fluid. You must have seen it in her pantomimes, you spoke of her rare gift for comedy on the stage that rouses a laughter out of the audience so dear they applaud and applaud and do not want to let her go.

Where does it come from, that comedy? There was none of it in her when she came back to me that second time, after I had had to send her away again. She had a new daddy now to learn to love, and I think perhaps it was a better time.

Except when we left her alone nights, telling ourselves she was old enough.,

"Can't you go some other time, Mommy, like tomorrow?" she would ask. "Will it be just a little while you'll be gone? Do you promise?"

The time we came back, the front door open, the clock on the floor in the hall. She rigid awake. "It wasn't just a little while. I didn't cry. Three times I called you, just three times, and then I ran downstairs to open the door so you could come faster. The clock talked loud. I threw it away, it scared me what it talked."

She said the clock talked loud again that night I went to the hospital to have Susan. She was delirious with the fever that comes before red measles, but she was fully conscious all the week I was gone and the week after we were home when she could not come near the new baby or me.

She did not get well. She stayed skeleton thin, not wanting to eat, and night after night she had nightmares. She would call for me, and I would rouse from exhaustion to sleepily call back: "You're all right, darling, go to sleep, it's just a dream," and if she still called, in a sterner voice, "now go to sleep, Emily, there's nothing to hurt you." Twice, only twice, when I had to get up for Susan anyhow, I went in to sit with her.

Now when it is too late (as if she would let me hold and comfort her like I do the others) I get up and go to her at once at her moan or restless stirring. "Are you awake, Emily? Can I get you something?" And the answer is always the same: "No, I'm all right, go back to sleep, Mother."

They persuaded me at the clinic to send her away to a convalescent home in the country where "she can have the kind of food and care you can't manage for her, and you'll be free to concentrate on the new baby." They still send children to that place. I see pictures on the society page of sleek young women planning affairs to raise money for it, or dancing at the affairs, or decorating Easter eggs or filling Christmas stockings for the children.

They never have a picture of the children so I do not know if the girls still wear those gigantic red bows and the ravaged looks on the every other Sunday when parents can come to visit "unless otherwise notified"—we were notified the first six weeks.

Oh it is a handsome place, green lawns and tall trees and fluted flower beds. High up on the balconies of each cottage the children stand, the girls in their red bows and white dresses, the boys in white suits and giant red ties. The parents stand below shrieking up to be heard and the children shriek down to be heard, and between them the invisible wall "Not To Be Contaminated by Parental Germs or Physical Affection."

There was a tiny girl who always stood hand in hand with Emily. Her parents never came. One visit she was gone. "They moved her to Rose Cottage" Emily shouted in explanation. "They don't like you to love anybody here."

She wrote once a week, the labored writing of a seven-year-old. "I am fine. How is the baby. If I write my leter nicly I will have a star. Love." There never was a star. We wrote every other day, letters she could never hold or keep but only hear read— once. "We simply do not have room for children to keep any personal possessions," they patiently explained when we pieced one Sunday's shrieking together to plead how much it would mean to Emily, who loved so to keep things, to be allowed to keep her letters and cards.

Each visit she looked frailer. "She isn't eating," they told us.

(They had runny eggs for breakfast or mush with lumps, Emily said later, I'd hold it in my mouth and not swallow. Nothing ever tasted good, just when they had chicken.)

It took us eight months to get her released home, and only the fact that she gained back so little of her seven lost pounds convinced the social worker.

I used to try to hold and love her after she came back, but her body would stay stiff, and after a while she'd push away. She ate little. Food sickened her, and I think much of life too. Oh she had physical lightness and brightness, twinkling by on skates, bouncing like a ball up and down up and down over the jump rope, skimming over the hill; but these were momentary.

She fretted about her appearance, thin and dark and foreign-looking at a time when every little girl was supposed to look or thought she should look a chubby blonde replica of Shirley Temple. The doorbell sometimes rang for her, but no one seemed to come and play in the house or be a best friend. Maybe because we moved so much.

There was a boy she loved painfully through two school semesters. Months later she told me how she had taken pennies from my purse to buy him candy. "Licorice was his favorite and I brought him some every day, but he still liked Jennifer better'n me. Why, Mommy?" The kind of question for which there is no answer.

School was a worry to her. She was not glib or quick in a world where glibness and quickness were easily confused with ability to learn. To her overworked and exasperated teachers she was an overconscientious "slow learner" who kept trying to catch up and was absent entirely too often.

I let her be absent, though sometimes the illness was imaginary. How different from my now-strictness about attendance with the others. I wasn't working. We had a new baby, I was home anyhow. Sometimes, after Susan grew old enough, I would keep her home from school, too, to have them all together.

Mostly Emily had asthma, and her breathing, harsh and labored, would fill the house with a curiously tranquil sound. I would bring the two old dresser mirrors and her boxes of collections to her bed. She would select beads and single earrings, bottle tops and shells, dried flowers and pebbles, old postcards and scraps, all sorts of oddments; then she and Susan would play Kingdom, setting up landscapes and furniture, peopling them with action.

Those were the only times of peaceful companionship between her and Susan. I have edged away from it, that poisonous feeling between them, that terrible balancing of hurts and needs I had to do between the two, and did so badly, those earlier years.

Oh there are conflicts between the others too, each one human, needing, demanding, hurting, taking—but only between Emily and Susan, no, Emily toward Susan that corroding resentment. It seems so obvious on the surface, yet it is not obvious. Susan, the second child, Susan, golden- and curly-haired and chubby, quick and articulate and assured, everything in appearance and manner Emily was not; Susan, not able to resist Emily's precious things, losing or sometimes clumsily breaking them; Susan telling jokes and riddles to company for applause while Emily sat silent (to say to me later: that was *my* riddle, Mother, I told it to Susan); Susan, who for all the five years' difference in age was just a year behind Emily in developing physically.

I am glad for that slow physical development that widened the difference between her and her contemporaries, though she suffered over it. She was too vulnerable for that terrible world of youthful competition, of preening and parading, of constant measuring of yourself against every other, of envy, "If I had that copper hair," "If I had that skin. . . ." She tormented herself enough about not looking like the others, there was enough of the unsureness, the having to be conscious of words before you speak, the constant caring—what are they thinking of me? without having it all magnified by the merciless physical drives.

Ronnie is calling. He is wet and I change him. It is rare there is such a cry now. That time of motherhood is almost behind me when the ear is not one's own but must always be racked and listening for the child cry, the child call. We sit for a while and I hold him, looking out over the city spread in charcoal with its soft aisles of light. "*Shoogily*," he breathes and curls closer. I carry him back to bed, asleep. *Shoogily.* A funny word, a family word, inherited from Emily, invented by her to say: *comfort.*

In this and other ways she leaves her seal, I say aloud. And startle at my saying it. What do I mean? What did I start to gather together, to try and make coherent? I was at the terrible, growing years. War years. I do not remember them well. I was working, there were four smaller ones now, there was not time for her. She had to help be a mother, and housekeeper, and shopper. She had to set her seal. Mornings of crisis and near hysteria trying to get lunches packed, hair combed, coats and shoes found, everyone to school or Child Care on time, the baby ready for transportation. And always the paper scribbled on by a smaller one, the book looked at by Susan then mislaid, the homework not done. Running out to that huge school where she was one, she was lost, she was a drop; suffering over her unpreparedness, stammering and unsure in her classes.

There was so little time left at night after the kids were bedded down. She would struggle over books, always eating (it was in those years she developed her enormous appetite that is legendary in our family) and I would be ironing, or preparing food for the next day, or writing V-mail to Bill, or tending the baby. Sometimes, to make me laugh, or out of her despair, she would imitate happenings or types at school.

I think I said once: "Why don't you do something like this in the school amateur show?" One morning she phoned me at work, hardly understandable through the weeping: "Mother, I did it. I won, I won; they gave me first prize; they clapped and clapped and wouldn't let me go."

Now suddenly she was Somebody, and as imprisoned in her difference as she had been in her anonymity.

She began to be asked to perform at other high schools, even in colleges, then at city and statewide affairs. The first one we went to, I only recognized her that first moment when thin, shy, she almost drowned herself into the curtains. Then: Was this Emily? The control, the command, the convulsing and deadly clowning, the spell, then the roaring, stamping audience, unwilling to let this rare and precious laughter out of their lives.

Afterwards: You ought to do something about her with a gift like that—but without money or knowing how, what does one do? We have left it all to her, and the gift has as often eddied inside, clogged and clotted, as been used and growing.

She is coming. She runs up the stairs two at a time with her light graceful step, and I know she is happy tonight. Whatever it was that occasioned your call did not happen today.

"Aren't you ever going to finish the ironing, Mother? Whistler painted his mother in a rocker. I'd have to paint mine standing over an ironing board." This is one of her communicative nights and she tells me everything and nothing as she fixes herself a plate of food out of the icebox.

She is so lovely. Why did you want me to come in at all? Why were you concerned? She will find her way.

She starts up the stairs to bed. "Don't get *me* up with the rest in the morning." "But I thought you were having midterms." "Oh, those," she comes back in, kisses me, and says quite lightly, "in a couple of years when we'll all be atom-dead they won't matter a bit."

She has said it before. She *believes* it. But because I have been dredging the past, and all that compounds a human being is so heavy and meaningful in me, I cannot endure it tonight.

I will never total it all. I will never come in to say: She was a child seldom smiled at. Her father left me before she was a year old. I had to work her first six years when there was work, or I sent her home and to his relatives. There were years she had care she hated. She was dark and thin and foreign-looking in a world where the prestige went to blondeness and curly hair and dimples, she was slow where glibness was prized. She was a child of anxious, not proud, love. We were poor and could not afford for her the soil of easy growth. I was a young mother, I was a distracted mother. There were the other children pushing up, demanding. Her younger sister seemed all that she was not. There were years she did not let me touch her. She kept too much in herself, her life was such she had to keep too much in herself. My wisdom came too late. She has much to her and probably little will come of it. She is a child of her age, of depression, of war, of fear.

Let her be. So all that is in her will not bloom—but in how many does it? There is still enough left to live by. Only help her to know—help make it so there is cause for her to know—that she is more than this dress on the ironing board, helpless before the iron.

ERNESTO GALARZA
(1905-1984)

During an amazingly productive life, Galarza published some twenty-six books. Some of their titles offer a sense of the variety of his writing as a poet, social scientist, agitator, educator, and labor organizer. They include, most famously, his autobiography, Barrio Boy *(1971), but also his first,* The Roman Catholic Church as a Factor in the Political and Social History of Mexico *(1928), which began as his senior thesis at Occidental College; his Ph.D. dissertation,* La industria eléctrica en México *(1941); an account of U.S. intervention in Bolivia,* The Case of Bolivia *(1949);* Strangers in Our Fields *(1956), a powerful attack on the* bracero *system; poems in Spanish (e.g.,* Poemas párvulos*—1971) and English (e.g.,* Kodachromes in Rhyme: Poems*—1982); and other bilingual books for children as well as accounts of organizing campaigns.*

Galarza was born and grew up in the village of Jalcocotán, Nayarit, Mexico. The village was a pueblo libre—that is to say, its people worked for themselves, as they had done since before the Spanish conquest, rather than for a rich landowner. Perhaps their spirit of independence set the tone for Galarza's life, which was in many ways a never-ending struggle to achieve and to secure independence for Mexican-Americans. Galarza gradually moved north with his family during the Mexican Revolution, ending the journey in Sacramento. There he worked a great variety of jobs part-time and summers in order to accomplish what was then, for Mexican-American boys, the unusual feat of completing high school. He continued that pattern of hard work and successful study at Occidental, where he graduated Phi Beta Kappa. Afterward, he became the first Mexican-American to enroll in graduate study at Stanford, at which he received his M.A. in history and political science. He and his new wife then moved on to

Columbia, where Galarza received his Ph.D. in 1944. But academic work did not take up all of his time: he published a book of poems, Thirty Poems *(1935), and he and his wife served as co-principals of an experimental school on Long Island from 1932 to 1936.*

For the following eleven years, Galarza worked for the Pan American Union—what would become the Organization of American States—as a research associate and then as director of the Division of Labor and Social Information. He was involved in two highly controversial episodes concerning Bolivian tin workers and the bracero *labor program, which brought "temporary"—and cheap—Mexican laborers to the U.S. His principled positions on these issues ultimately led him to resign from the organization. He then became director of research and education, and later one of the main organizers of the National Farm Labor Union (NFLU), an ill-supported effort of the AFL-CIO to organize farm workers in the face of so-called "Right-to-work" laws and the* bracero *program itself, which functionally sanctioned the exploitation of Mexican workers.*

From 1960 on, Galarza was based in San Jose. Though no longer formally involved in the labor movement, he continued to investigate and write about farmworkers, as, for example, in Merchants of Labor *(1964). But increasingly his attention was directed to the issues faced by a newly urbanized Chicano/a population. Some of his most important work concerned his development of a strategy for fulfilling the educational needs of urbanized Mexican children in the United States. To that end, he wrote bilingual and bicultural books for children, which he published from a press he had begun in San Jose. And he continued to serve on the boards of virtually every major Mexican-American organization devoted—as he had long been—to the social and political advancement of* la raza.

FROM B A R R I O B O Y

To make room for a growing family it was decided that we should move, and a house was found in Oak Park, on the far side of town where the open country began. The men raised the first installment for the bungalow on Seventh Avenue even after Mrs. Dodson explained that if we did not keep up the monthly payments we would lose the deposit as well as the house.

The real estate broker brought the sale contract to the apartment one evening. Myself included, we sat around the table in the living room, the gringo explaining at great length the small print of the document in a torrent of words none of us could make out. Now and then he would pause and throw in the only word he knew in Spanish: "Sabee?" The men nodded slightly as if they had understood. Doña Henriqueta was holding firmly to the purse which contained the down payment, watching the broker's face, not listening to his words. She had only one question. Turning to me she said: "Ask him how long it will take to pay all of it." I translated, shocked by the answer: "Twenty years." There was a long pause around the table, broken by my stepfather: "What do you say?" Around the table the heads nodded agreement. The broker passed his fountain pen to him. He signed the contract and after him Gustavo and José. Doña Henriqueta opened the purse and counted out the greenbacks. The broker pocketed the money, gave us a copy of the document, and left.

The last thing I did when we moved out of 418 L was to dig a hole in the corner of the backyard for a tall carton of Quaker Oats cereal, full to the brim with the marbles I had won playing for keeps around the *barrio*. I tamped the earth over my buried treasure and laid a curse on whoever removed it without my permission.

Our new bungalow had five rooms, and porches front and back. In the way of furniture, what friends did not lend or Mrs. Dodson gave us we bought in the secondhand shops. The only new item was an elegant gas range, with a high oven and long, slender legs finished in enamel. Like the house, we would be paying for it in installments.

It was a sunny, airy spot, with a family orchard to one side and a vacant lot on the other. Back of us there was a pasture. With chicken wire we fenced the back yard, turned over the soil, and planted our first vegetable garden and fruit trees. José and I built a palatial rabbit hutch of laths and two-by-fours he gathered day by day on the waterfront. A single row of geraniums and carnations separated the vegetable garden from the house. From the vacant lots and pastures around us my mother gathered herbs and weeds which she dried and boiled the way she had in the pueblo. A thick green fluid she distilled from the mallow that grew wild around us was bottled and used as a hair lotion. On every side our windows looked out on family orchards, platinum stretches of wild oats and quiet lanes, shady and unpaved.

We could not have moved to a neighborhood less like the *barrio*. All the families around us were Americans. The grumpy retired farmer next door viewed us with alarm and never gave time of day, but the Harrisons across the street were cordial. Mr. Harrison loaned us his tools, and Roy, just my age but twice my weight, teamed up with me at once for an exchange of visits to his mother's kitchen and ours. I astounded him with my Mexican rice, and Mrs. Harrison baked my first waffle. Roy and I also found a common bond in the matter of sisters. He had an older one and by now I had two younger ones. It was a question between us whether they were worse as little nuisances or as big bosses. The answer didn't make much difference but it was a relief to have another man to talk with.

Some Sundays we walked to Joyland, an amusement park where my mother sat on a bench to watch the children play on the lawn and I begged as many rides as I could on the roller coaster, which we called in elegant Spanish "the Russian Mountain." José liked best the free vaudeville because of the chorus girls who danced out from the stage on a platform and kicked their heels over his head.

Since Roy had a bicycle and could get away from his sister by pedaling off on long journeys I persuaded my family to match my savings for a used one. Together we pushed beyond the boundaries of Oak Park miles out, nearly to Perkins and the Slough House. It was open country, where we could lean our wheels against a fence post and walk endlessly through carpets of golden poppies and blue lupin. With a bike I was able to sign on as a carrier of the *Sacramento Bee*, learning in due course the art of slapping folded newspapers against people's porches instead of into the bushes or on their roofs. Roy and I also became assistants to a neighbor who operated a bakery in his basement, taking our pay partly in dimes and partly in broken cookies for our families.

For the three men of the household as well as for me the bicycle became the most important means for earning a living. Oak Park was miles away from the usual places where they worked and they pedaled off, in good weather and bad, in the early morning. It was a case of saving carfare.

I transferred to the Bret Harte School, a gingerbread two-story building in which there was a notable absence of Japanese, Filipinos, Koreans, Italians, and the other nationalities of the Lincoln School. It was at Bret Harte that I learned how an English sentence could be cut up on the blackboard and the pieces placed on different lines connected by what the teacher called a diagram. The idea of operating on a sentence and rearranging its members as a skeleton of verbs, modifiers, subject, and prepositions set me off diagraming whatever I read, in Spanish and English. Spiderwebs, my mother called them, when I tried to teach her the art.

My bilingual library had grown with some copies of old magazines from Mexico, a used speller Gustavo had bought for me in Stockton, and the novels my mother discarded when she had read them. Blackstone was still the anchor of my collection and I now had a paperback dictionary called *El Inglés sin Maestro*. By this time there was no problem of translating or interpreting for the family I could not tackle with confidence.

It was Gustavo, in fact, who began to give my books a vague significance. He pointed out to me that with diagrams and dictionaries I could have a choice of becoming a lawyer or a doctor or an engineer or a professor. These, he said, were far better careers than growing up to be a *camello,* as he and José always would be. *Camellos,* I knew well enough, was what the *chicanos* called themselves as the worker on every job who did the dirtiest work. And to give our home the professional touch he felt I should be acquiring, he had a telephone installed.

It came to the rest of us as a surprise. The company man arrived one day with our name and address on a card, a metal tool box and a stand-up telephone wound with a cord. It was connected and set on the counter between the dining room and the parlor. There the black marvel sat until we were gathered for dinner that evening. It was clearly explained by Gustavo that the instrument was to provide me with a quick means of reaching the important people I knew at the Y.M.C.A., the boy's band, or the various public offices where I interpreted for *chicanos* in distress. Sooner or later some of our friends in the *barrio* would also have telephones and we could talk with them.

"Call somebody," my mother urged me.

With the whole family watching I tried to think of some important person I could ring for a professional conversation. A name wouldn't come. I felt miserable and hardly like a budding engineer or lawyer or doctor or professor.

Gustavo understood my predicament and let me stew in it a moment. Then he said: "Mrs. Dodson." My pride saved by this ingenious suggestion, I thumbed through the directory, lifted the earpiece from the hook, and calmly asked central for the number. My sisters, one sitting on the floor and the other in my mother's arms, never looked less significant; but they, too, had their turn saying hello to the patient Señora Dodson on the other end of the line.

Every member of the family, in his own way, missed the *barrio*. José and Gustavo could no longer join the talk of the poolrooms and the street corners by walking two blocks down the street. The sign language and simple words my mother had devised to communicate with the Americans at 418 L didn't work with the housewives on 7th Avenue. The families we had known were now too far away to exchange visits. We knew no one in Oak Park who spoke Spanish. Our street was always quiet and often lonely with little to watch from our front porch other than boys riding bicycles or Mrs. Harrison hanging out her wash. Pork Chops and the Salvation Army never played there.

I, too, knew that things were different. There was no corner where I could sell the *Union* and my income from running errands and doing chores around the rooming house stopped. There were no alleys I could comb for beer bottles or docks where I could gather saleable or edible things. The closest to Big Singh I could find was a runty soothsayer in Joyland who sat on a rug with a feather in his turban and told your fortune.

We now had an infant boy in the family who with my two sisters made four of us. The baby was himself no inconvenience to me, but it meant that I had to mind the girls more, mostly chasing them home from the neighbors. If I had been the eldest girl in the family I would have stepped into my mother's place and taken over the management of all but the youngest. But being a boy, the female chores seemed outrageous and un-Mexican. Doña Henriqueta tried telling me that I was now the *jefe de familia* of all the juniors. But she was a gentle mother and the freedom of the house, the yard, and my personal property that she gave the two girls did nothing to make them understand that I was their *jefe.* When Nora, the oldest of the two, demolished my concertina with a hammer (no doubt to see where the notes came from) I asked for permission to strangle her. Permission was denied.

During the first year we lived at Oak Park we began to floor and partition the basement. Some day, we knew, the López's would come through and we would have a temporary home ready for them. With three-and-a-half men in the house earning wages, if work was steady, we were keeping up with the installments and saving for the reunion.

An epidemic erased the quiet life on 7th Avenue and the hopes we had brought with us.

I had been reading to the family stories in the *Bee* of the Spanish influenza. At first it was far off, like the war, in places such as New York and Texas. Then the stories told of people dying in California towns we knew, and finally the *Bee* began reporting the spread of the "flu" in our city.

One Sunday morning we saw Gustavo coming down the street with a suitcase in his hand, walking slowly. I ran out to meet him. By the front gate, he dropped the suitcase, leaned on the fence, and fainted. He had been working as a sandhog on the American River, and had come home weak from fever.

Gustavo was put to bed in one of the front rooms. José set out to look for a doctor, who came the next day, weary and nearly sick himself. He ordered Gustavo to the hospital. Three days later I answered the telephone call from the hospital telling us he was dead. Only José went to Gustavo's funeral. The rest of us, except my stepfather, were sick in bed with the fever.

In the dining room, near the windows where the sunlight would warm her, my mother lay on a cot, a kerosene stove at her feet. The day Gustavo died she was delirious. José bicycled all over the city, looking for oranges, which the doctor said were the best medicine we could give her. I sweated out the fever, nursed by José, who brought me glasses of steaming lemonade and told me my mother was getting better. The children were quarantined in another room, lightly touched by the fever, more restless than sick.

Late one afternoon José came into my room, wrapped me in blankets, pulled a cap over my ears, and carried me to my mother's bedside. My stepfather was holding a hand mirror to her lips. It didn't fog. She had stopped breathing. In the next room my sister was singing to the other children, "A birdie with a yellow bill/hopped upon my windowsill/cocked a shiny eye and said/Shame on you you sleepy head."

The day we buried Doña Henriqueta, Mrs. Dodson took the oldest sister home with her. The younger children were sent to a neighbor. That night José went to the *barrio,* got drunk, borrowed a pistol, and was arrested for shooting up Second Street.

We did not find out what had happened until I bicycled the next morning to Mrs. Dodson to report that José had not come home. By this time our friends in the *barrio* knew of José's arrest and a telephone call to a bartender who knew us supplied the details. Nothing serious, Mrs. Dodson repeated to me. Nobody had been hurt. She left me in charge of my sister and went to bail out my uncle.

They returned together. Gently, Mrs. Dodson scolded José, who sat dejectedly, his eyes closed so he would not have to look her in the eye, cracking the joint of his fingers, chewing on his tight lips, a young man compressing years of hard times and the grief of the past days in a show of manhood.

When the lecture was nearly over, Mrs. Dodson was not talking of drunkenness and gunplay, but of the future, mostly of mine, and of José's responsibility for it. She walked with us down the front stairway. Pushing my bicycle I followed him on foot the miles back to Oak Park, keeping my distance, for I knew he did not want me to see his face. As he had often told me, "Men never cry, no matter what."

A month later I made a bundle of the family keepsakes my stepfather allowed me to have, including the butterfly sarape, my books, and some family pictures. With the bundle tied to the bars of my bicycle, I pedaled to the basement room José had rented for the two of us on O Street. near the corner of Fifth, on the edge of the *barrio.*

José was now working the riverboats and, in the slack season, following the round of odd jobs about the city. In our basement room, with a kitchen closet, bathroom, and laundry tub on the back porch and a woodshed for storage, I kept house. We bought two cots, one for me and the other for José when he was home.

Our landlords lived upstairs, a middle-aged brother and sister who worked and rented rooms. As part payment on our rent I kept the yard trim. They were friends of Doña Tránsito, the grandmother of a Mexican family that lived in a weather-beaten cottage on the corner. Doña Tránsito was in her sixties, round as a barrel, and she wore her gray hair in braids and smoked hand-rolled cigarettes on her rickety front porch. To her tiny parlor *chicanos* in trouble came for advice, and the firm old lady with the rasping voice and commanding ways often asked me to interpret or translate for them in their encounters with the *Autoridades.* Since her services were free, so were mine. I soon became a regular visitor and made friends with her son, Kid Felix, a prizefighter who gave free boxing lessons to the boys in the neighborhood.

Living only three houses from Doña Tránsito, saying my *saludos* to her every time I passed the corner, noticing how even the Kid was afraid to break her personal code of *barrio* manners, I lived inside a circle of security when José was away. On her front porch, summer evenings, the old Mexican dame talked about people such as I had known in the pueblo and asked how I was doing in school and where I was working.

It was Doña Tránsito who called in the *curandera* once when the child of a neighbor was dying. I had brought a doctor to the house and was in the sick room when he told the family there was nothing more he could do. Doña Tránsito ordered me at once to fetch the old crone who lived on the other side of the railroad tracks towards the river and who practiced as a healer.

With Doña Tránsito I watched the ritual from a corner of the sick room. The healer laid on a side table an assortment of bundled weeds, small glass jars, candles, and paper bags tied with strings. On the floor next to her she placed a canvas satchel. A bowl and some cups were brought to her from the kitchen. She crumpled stems of herbs into one of the cups and mixed them with oil from one of her jars. She hooked her finger into another jar and pulled out a dab of lard which she worked into a powder in another cup to make a dark paste. Two candles were lighted and placed at the head of the bed. The electric light was turned off. She opened the satchel and took out a framed picture of the Virgin of Guadalupe, which was hung on the wall over the sick child's head. The window blind pulled down.

The little girl was uncovered. She lay naked, pale and thin on the sheet, her arms straight down her sides. Around her the healer arranged a border of cactus leaves, which she took out of her satchel one by one, cutting them open around the edge. She warmed the cup with the powdered herbs and rubbed the concoction on the soles of the child's bare feet. With the paste, which she also warmed over the candle, the healer made a cross on the forehead of the patient and another on her chest. A blanket was then laid over her, leaving only the head uncovered.

The healer knelt before the picture of the Virgin and began to pray. The parents of the child, some relatives who were there, Doña Tránsito and I formed a circle around the room, on our knees.

We had been praying a long while when the healer arose and bent over the bed, looking intently at the wasted face. To nobody in particular she said the child was not sweating. She wrapped her black shawl around her head and shoulders, left the room, and closed the street door quietly behind her. In the morning the child died.

Through Doña Tránsito I met other characters of the *barrio*. One of them was Don Crescencio, stooped and bony, who often stopped to chat with my neighbor. He told us stories of how he had found buried treasure with two twigs cut from a weeping willow, and how he could locate an underground spring in the same way, holding the twigs just so, feeling his way on bare feet over the ground, watching until the twigs, by themselves, crossed and dipped. There were the Ortegas, who raised vegetables on a sandlot they had bought by the levee, and explained to Doña Tránsito, who knew a great deal about such matters herself, what vegetables did better when planted according to different shapes of the moon. The Kid gave us lectures and exhibitions explaining jabs and left hooks and how he planned to become the world's Mexican champion. In our basement José gathered his friends to listen to songs of love, revenge, and valor, warmed with beer and tequila.

When troubles made it necessary for the *barrio* people to deal with the Americans uptown, the *Autoridades,* I went with them to the police court, the industrial accident office, the county hospital, the draft board, the county clerk. We got lost together in the rigamarole of functionaries who sat, like *patrones,* behind desks and who demanded licenses, certificates, documents, affidavits, signatures, and witnesses. And we celebrated our successes, as when the worker for whom I interpreted in interviews that lasted many months, was awarded a thousand dollars for a disabled arm. Don Crescendo congratulated me, saying that in Mexico for a thousand American dollars you could buy the lives of many peons.

José had chosen our new home in the basement on O Street because it was close to the Hearkness Junior High School, to which I transferred from Bret Harte.

As the *jefe de familia* he explained that I could help earn our living but that I was to study for a high school diploma. That being settled, my routine was clearly divided into schooltime and worktime, the second depending on when I was free from the first.

Few Mexicans of my age from the *barrio* were enrolled at the junior high school when I went there. At least, there were no other Mexican boys or girls in Mr. Everett's class in civics, or Miss Crowley's English composition, or Mrs. Stevenson's course. Mrs. Stevenson assigned me to read to the class and to recite poems by Amado Nervo, because the poet was from Tepic and I was, too. Miss Crowley accepted my compositions about Jalcocotán and the buried treasure of Acaponeta while the others in the class were writing about Sir Patrick Spence and the Beautiful Lady without Mercy, whom they had never met. For Mr. Everett's class, the last of the day, I clipped pieces from the *Sacramento Bee* about important events in Sacramento. From him I learned to use the ring binder in which I kept clippings to prepare oral reports. Occasionally he kept me after school to talk. He sat on his desk, one leg dangling over a corner, behind him the frame of a large window and the arching elms of the school yard, telling me he thought I could easily make the debating team at the high school next year, that Stanford University might be the place to go after graduation, and making other by-the-way comments that began to shape themselves into my future.

Afternoons, Saturdays, and summers allowed me many hours of worktime I did not need for study. José explained how things now stood. There were two funerals to pay for. More urgently than ever, Doña Esther and her family must be brought to live with us. He would pay the rent and buy the food. My clothes, books and school expenses would be up to me.

On my vacations, and when he was not on the riverboats, he found me a job as water boy on a track gang. We chopped wood together near Woodland and stacked empty lug boxes in a cannery yard. Cleaning vacant houses and chopping weeds were jobs we could do as a team when better ones were not to be had. As the apprentice, I learned from him how to brace myself for a heavy lift, to lock my knee under a loaded hand-truck, to dance rather than lift a ladder and to find the weakest grain in a log. Like him I spit into my palms to get the feel of the axe handle and grunted as the blade bit into the wood. Imitating him I circled a tree several times, sizing it up, *tante-ando,* as he said, before pruning or felling it.

Part of one summer my uncle worked on the river while I hired out a farmhand on a small ranch south of Sacramento. My senior on the place was Roy, a husky Oklahoman who was part-time taxi driver and full-time drinker of hard whiskey. He was heavy-chested, heavy-lipped and jowly, a grumbler rather than a talker and a man of great ingenuity with tools and automobile engines. Under him I learned to drive the Fordson tractor on the place, man the gasoline pump, feed the calves, check an irrigation ditch, make lug boxes for grapes and many other tasks on a small farm. Roy used Bull Durham tobacco which he rolled into the same droopy cigarettes that Doña Eduvijes smoked in Jalco and Doña Tránsito on her front porch.

Roy and I sat under the willow tree in front of the ranch house after work, I on the grass, he on a creaky wicker chair, a hulking, sour man glad for the company of a boy. He counseled me on how to avoid the indulgences he was so fond of, beginning his sentences with a phrase he repeated over and over, "as the feller says." "Don't aim to tell you your business," he explained, "but, as the feller says, get yourself a good woman, don't be no farmhand for a livin', be a lawyer or a doctor, and don't get to drinkin' nohow. And there's another thing, Ernie. If nobody won't listen to you, go on and talk to yourself and hear what a smart man has to say."

And Roy knew how to handle boys, which he showed in an episode that could have cost me my life or my self-confidence. He had taught me to drive the tractor, walking along side during the lessons as I maneuvered it, shifting gears, stopping and starting, turning and backing, raising a cloud of dust wherever we went. Between drives Roy told me about the different working parts of the machine, giving me instructions on oiling and greasing and filling the radiator. "She needs to be took care of, Ernie," he admonished me, "like a horse. And another thing, she's like to buck. She can turn clear over on you if you let 'er. If she starts to lift from the front even a mite, you turn her off. You hear?"

"Yes, sir," I said, meaning to keep his confidence in me as a good tractor man.

It was a few days after my first solo drive that it happened. I was rounding a telephone pole on the slightly sloping bank of the irrigation ditch. I swung around too fast for one of the rear tracks to keep its footing. It spun and the front began to lift. Forgetting Roy's emphatic instructions I gunned the engine, trying to right us to the level ground above the ditch. The tractor's nose kept climbing in front of me. We slipped against the pole, the tractor, bucking, as Roy said it would.

Roy's warning broke through to me in my panic, and I reached up to turn off the ignition. My bronco's engine sputtered out and it settled on the ground with a thump.

I sat for a moment in my sweat. Roy was coming down the ditch in a hurry. He walked up to me and with a quick look saw that neither I nor the tractor was damaged.

"Git off" he said.

I did, feeling that I was about to be demoted, stripped of my rank, bawled out, and fired.

Roy mounted the machine, started it, and worked it off the slope to flat ground. Leaving the engine running, he said: "Git on."

I did.

"Now finish the discing," he said. Above the clatter of the machine, he said: "Like I said, she can buck. If she does, cut 'er. You hear?" And he waved me off to my work.

Except for food and a place to live, with which José provided me, I was on my own. Between farm jobs I worked in town, adding to my experience as well as to my income. As a clerk in a drug store on Second and J, in the heart of the lower part of town, I waited on *chicanos* who spoke no English and who came in search of remedies with no prescription other than a recital of their pains. I dispensed capsules, pills, liniments, and emulsions as instructed by the pharmacist, who glanced at our customers from the back of the shop and diagnosed their ills as I translated them. When I went on my shift, I placed a card in the window that said "Se habla Español." So far as my *chicano* patients were concerned it might as well have said "Dr. Ernesto Galarza."

From drugs I moved to office supplies and stationery sundries, working as delivery boy for Wahl's, several blocks uptown from skid row. Between deliveries I had no time to idle. I helped the stock clerk, took inventory, polished desks, and hopped when a clerk bawled an order down the basement steps. Mr. Wahl, our boss, a stocky man with a slight paunch, strutted a little as he constantly checked on the smallest details of his establishment, including myself. He was always pleasant and courteous, a man in whose footsteps I might possibly walk into the business world of Sacramento.

But like my uncles, I was looking for a better *chanza*, which I thought I found with Western Union, as a messenger, where I could earn tips as well as wages. Since I knew the lower part of town thoroughly, whenever the telegrams were addressed to that quarter the dispatcher gave them to me. Deliveries to the suites on the second floor of saloons paid especially well, with tips of a quarter from the ladies who worked there. My most generous customer was tall and beautiful Miss Irene, who always asked how I was doing in school. It was she who gave me an English dictionary, the first I ever possessed, a black bound volume with remarkable little scallops on the pages that made it easy to find words. Half smiling, half commanding, Miss Irene said to me more than once: "Don't you stop school without letting me know." I meant to take her advice as earnestly as I took her twenty-five cent tip.

It was in the lower town also that I nearly became a performing artist. My instructor on the violin had stopped giving me lessons after we moved to Oak Park. When we were back on O Street he sent word through José that I could work as second fiddler on Saturday nights in the dancehall where he played with a mariachi. Besides, I could resume my lessons with him. A dollar a night for two hours as a substitute was the best wages I had ever made. Coached by my teacher, I second-fiddled for sporting *chicanos* who swung their ladies on the dance floor and sang to our music. Unfortunately I mentioned my new calling to Miss Crowley when I proposed it to her as a subject for a composition. She kept me after school and persuaded me to give it up, on the ground that I could earn more decorating Christmas cards during the vacation than at the dancehall. She gave me the first order for fifty cards and got subscriptions for me from the other teachers. I spent my Christmas vacation as an illustrator, with enough money saved to quit playing in the saloon.

MARY McCARTHY
(1912-1989)

McCarthy began her writing career as an acerbic critic of drama and human mores. And she continued in that mode, whether she was writing stories, novels, autobiography, or cultural criticism. Initially, after her graduation from Vassar College in 1933, she wrote for what were then left or liberal journals, The New Republic, The Nation, *and* Partisan Review, *for which she became drama critic. Encouraged by her then husband, the critic Edmund Wilson, she composed a series of what came to be interrelated stories, which she published as her first book of fiction,* The Company She Keeps *(1942). The experiences of the central figure of the book, Margaret Sargent, are probably based on some of McCarthy's own. Her women characters are often intellectuals searching for a sense of identity and vocation, and often unable to reconcile the ideals of social movements and personal relationships with lived reality. Such divisions constitute central elements in her narratives.*

McCarthy herself grew up in Seattle and Minneapolis in a family divided by religion and outlook. Her parents died in the flu epidemic of 1918; thereafter McCarthy was raised by culturally conservative relatives, attending boarding school whenever she could. After World War II, she taught briefly at Bard and Sarah Lawrence Colleges, but found them unsatisfying. Increasingly, she devoted herself to writing, particularly novels and polemical essays in Partisan Review *and elsewhere. A series of clever and cutting novels followed:* The Groves of Academe *(1952), which satirized the pretentiousness of the academic world and the dishonesty of an academic leftist;* A Charmed Life *(1955), which mocked the conventions of Cape Cod Bohemians (of whom McCarthy had been one); and finally* The Group *(1963), probably McCarthy's best and certainly most popular novel.* The Group *traces in often painfully explicit detail the post-college lives of a group of mostly privileged Vassar graduates. Between the novels, she had also published an explicitly autobiographical volume,* Memories of a Catholic Girlhood *(1957) and two striking volumes of art history and travel,* Venice Observed *(1956) and* The Stones of Florence *(1959).*

Later in life she wrote about Vietnam and also the Watergate scandal, in addition to fiction. But she was never comfortable with those committed to actions against the war, nor, indeed, with any left-leaning social movement. Indeed, she devoted many of her considerable invective skills to attacking those, like Lillian Hellman, she considered to be Stalinists or blind adherents to left-wing causes. If many of her essays are now part of history, her portraits of well-intentioned and often well-heeled people continue to ring true.

FROM THE GROUP

It was June, 1933, one week after Commencement, when Kay Leiland Strong, Vassar '33, the first of her class to run around the table at the Class Day dinner, was married to Harald Petersen, Reed '27, in the chapel of St. George's Church, P.E., Karl F. Reiland, Rector. Outside, on Stuyvesant Square, the trees were in full leaf, and the wedding guests arriving by twos and threes in taxis heard the voices of children playing round the statue of Peter Stuyvesant in the park. Paying the driver, smoothing out their gloves, the pairs and trios of young women, Kay's classmates, stared about them curiously, as though they were in a foreign city. They were in the throes of discovering New York, imagine it, when some of them had actually lived here all their lives, in tiresome Georgian houses full of waste space in the Eighties or Park Avenue apartment buildings, and they delighted in such out-of-the-way corners as this, with its greenery and Quaker meeting-house in red brick, polished brass, and white trim next to the wine-purple Episcopal church—on Sundays, they walked with their beaux across Brooklyn Bridge and poked into the sleepy Heights section of Brooklyn; they explored residential Murray Hill and is quaint MacDougal Alley and Patchin Place and Washington Mews with all the artists' studios; they loved the Plaza Hotel and the fountain there and the green mansarding of the Savoy Plaza and the row of horse-drawn hacks and elderly coachmen, waiting, as in a French *place*, to tempt them to a twilight ride through Central Park.

The sense of an adventure was strong on them this morning, as they seated themselves softly in the still, near-empty chapel; they had never been to a wedding quite like this one before, to which invitations had been issued orally by the bride herself, without the intervention of a relation or any older person, friend of the family. There was to be no honeymoon, they had heard, because Harald (that was the way he spelled it—the old Scandinavian way) was working as an assistant stage manager for a theatrical production and had to be at the theatre as usual this evening to call "half hour" for the actors. This seemed to them very exciting and of course it justified the oddities of the wedding: Kay and Harald were too busy and dynamic to let convention cramp their style. In September, Kay was going to start at Macy's, to be trained, along with other picked college graduates, in merchandising techniques, but instead of sitting around all summer, waiting for the job to begin, she had already registered for a typing course in business school, which Harald said would give her a tool that the other trainees wouldn't have. And, according to Helena Davison, Kay's roommate junior year, the two of them had moved right into a summer sublet, in a nice block in the East Fifties, without a single piece of linen or silver of their own, and had spent the last week, ever since graduation (Helena had just been there and seen it), on the regular tenant's sublet sheets!

How like Kay, they concluded fondly, as the tale passed along the pews. She had been amazingly altered, they felt, by a course in Animal Behavior she had taken with old Miss Washburn (who had left her brain in her will to Science) during their junior year. This and her work with Hallie Flanagan in Dramatic Production had changed her from a shy, pretty, somewhat heavy Western girl with black lustrous curly hair and a wild-rose complexion, active in hockey, in the choir, given to large tight brassiéres and copious menstruations, into a thin, hard-driving, authoritative young woman, dressed in dungarees, sweat shirt, and sneakers, with smears of paint in her unwashed hair, tobacco stains on her fingers, airily talking of "Hallie" and "Lester," Hallie's assistant, of flats and stippling, of oestrum and nymphomania, calling her friends by their last names loudly—"Eastlake," "Renfrew," "MacAusland"—counseling pre-marital experiment and the scientific choice of a mate. Love, she said, was an illusion.

To her fellow group members, all seven of whom were now present, in the chapel, this development in Kay, which they gently labeled a "phase," had been, nevertheless, disquieting. Her bark was worse than her bite, they used to reiterate to each other, late at night in their common sitting room in the South Tower of Main Hall, when Kay was still out, painting flats or working on the electricity with Lester in the theatre. But they were afraid that some man, who did not know the old dear as they did, would take her at her word. They had pondered about Harald; Kay had met him last summer when she was working as an apprentice at a summer theatre in Stamford and both sexes had lived in a dormitory together. She said he wanted to marry her, but that was not the way his letters sounded to the group. They were not love letters at all, so far as the group could see, but accounts of personal successes among theatrical celebrities, what Edna Ferber had said to George Kaufman in his hearing, how Gilbert Miller had sent for him and a woman star had begged him to read his play to her in bed. "Consider yourself kissed," they ended, curtly, or just "C.Y.K."—not another word. In a young man of their own background, as the girls vaguely phrased it, such letters would have been offensive, but their education had impressed on them the unwisdom of making large judgments from one's own narrow little segment of experience. Still, they could tell that Kay was not as sure of him as she pretended she was; sometimes he did not write for weeks, while poor Kay went on whistling in the dark. Polly Andrews, who shared a mailbox with her, knew this for a fact. Up to the Class Day dinner, ten days ago, the girls had had the feeling that Kay's touted "engagement" was pretty much of a myth. They had almost thought of turning to some wiser person for guidance, a member of the faculty or the college psychiatrist—somebody Kay could talk it out to, frankly. Then, that night, when Kay had run around the long table, which meant you were announcing your engagement to the whole class, and produced from her winded bosom a funny Mexican silver ring to prove it, their alarm had dissolved into a docile amusement; they clapped, dimpling and twinkling, with an air of prior knowledge. More gravely, in low posh tones, they assured their parents, up for the Commencement ceremonies, that the engagement was of long standing, that Harald was "terribly nice" and "terribly in love" with Kay. Now, in the chapel, they rearranged their fur pieces and smiled at each other, noddingly, like mature little martens and sables: they had been right, the hardness was only a phase; it was certainly a point for *their* side that the iconoclast and scoffer was the first of the little band to get married.

"Who would have thunk it?" irrepressibly remarked "Pokey" (Mary) Prothero, a fat cheerful New York society girl with big red checks and yellow hair, who talked like a jolly beau of the McKinley period, in imitation of her yachtsman father. She was the problem child of the group, very rich and lazy, having to be coached in her subjects, cribbing in examinations, sneaking weekends, stealing library books, without morals or subtleties, interested only in animals and hunt dances; her ambition, recorded in the yearbook, was to become a vet; she had come to Kay's wedding good-naturedly because her friends had dragged her there, as they had dragged her to college assemblies, throwing stones up at her window to rouse her and then thrusting her into her cap and rumpled gown. Having now got her safely to the church, later in the day they would propel her into Tiffany's, to make sure that Kay got one good, thumping wedding present, a thing Pokey, by herself, would not understand the necessity of, since to her mind wedding presents were a part of the burden of privilege, associated with detectives, bridesmaids, fleets of limousines, reception at Sherry's or the Colony Club. If one was not in society, what was the point of the folderol? She herself, she proclaimed, hated being fitted for dresses, hated her coming-out party, would hate her wedding, when she had it, which, as she said, was bound to happen since, thanks to Daddy's money, she had her pick of beaux. All these objections she had raised in the taxicab on the way down, in her grating society caw, till the taxi driver turned round at a stop light to look at her, fat and fair, in a blue faille suit with sables and a *lorgnon* of diamonds, which she raised to her weak sapphire eyes to peer at him and at his picture, concluding, in a loud firm whisper, to her roommates, "It's *not* the same man."

"What perfect pets they look!" murmured Dottie Renfrew, of Boston, to quiet her, as Harald and Kay came in from the vestry and took their places before the surpliced curate, accompanied by little Helena Davison, Kay's ex-roommate from Cleveland, and by a sallow blond young man with a mustache. Pokey made use of her *lorgnon,* squinting up her pale-lashed eyes like an old woman; this was her first appraisal of Harald, for she had been away hunting for the weekend the one time he had come to college. "Not too bad," she pronounced. "Except for the shoes." The groom was a thin, tense young man with black straight hair and a very good, supple figure, like a fencer's; he was wearing a blue suit, white shirt, brown suède shoes, and dark-red tie. Her scrutiny veered to Kay, who was wearing a pale-brown thin silk dress with a big white *mous-seline de soie* collar and a wide black taffeta hat wreathed with white daisies; around one tan wrist was a gold bracelet that had belonged to her grandmother; she carried a bouquet of field daisies mixed with lilies of the valley. With her glowing cheeks, vivid black curly hair, and tawny hazel eyes, she looked like a country lass on some old tinted post card; the seams of her stockings were crooked, and the backs of her black suède shoes had worn spots, where she had rubbed them against each other. Pokey scowled. "Doesn't she know," she lamented, "that black's bad luck for weddings?" "*Shut up*," came a furious growl from her other side. Pokey, hurt, peered around, to find Elinor Eastlake, of Lake Forest, the taciturn brunette beauty of the group, staring at her with murder in her long, green eyes. "But Lakey!" Pokey cried, protesting. The Chicago girl, intellectual, impeccable, disdainful, and nearly as rich as herself, was the only one of the group she stood in awe of. Behind her blinking good nature, Pokey was a logical snob. She assumed that it was taken for granted that of the other seven roommates, only Lakey could expect to be in *her* wedding, and vice versa, of course; the others would come to the reception. "*Fool*," spat out the Madonna from Lake Forest, between gritted pearly teeth. Pokey rolled her eyes. "Temperamental," she observed to Dottie Renfrew. Both girls stole amused glances at Elinor's haughty profile; the fine white Renaissance nostril was dinted with a mark of pain.

To Elinor, this wedding was torture. Everything was so jaggedly ill-at-ease: Kay's costume, Harald's shoes and necktie, the bare altar, the sparsity of guests on the groom's side (a couple and a solitary man), the absence of any family connection. Intelligent and morbidly sensitive, she was inwardly screaming with pity for the principals and vicarious mortification. Hypocrisy was the sole explanation she could find for the antiphonal bird twitter of "Terribly nice," and "Isn't this exciting?" that had risen to greet the couple in lieu of a wedding March. Elinor was always firmly convinced of other people's hypocrisy since she could not believe that they noticed less than she did. She supposed now that the girls all around her *must* see what she saw, *must* suffer for Kay and Harald a supreme humiliation.

Facing the congregation, the curate coughed. "Step forward!" he sharply admonished the young couple, sounding, as Lakey observed afterward, more like a bus conductor than a minister. The back of the groom's neck reddened; he had just had a haircut. All at once, the fact that Kay was a self-announced scientific atheist came home to her friends in the chapel; the same thought crossed every mind: what had happened in the interview in the rectory? Was Harald a communicant? It seemed very unlikely. How had they worked it, then, to get married in a rock-ribbed Episcopal church? Dottie Renfrew, a devout Episcopal communicant, drew her clasped furs closer around her susceptible throat; she shivered. It occurred to her that she might be compounding a sacrilege: to her certain knowledge, Kay, the proud daughter of an agnostic doctor and a Mormon mother, had not even been baptized. Kay, as the group knew too, was not a very truthful person; could she have lied to the minister? In that case, was the marriage invalid? A flush stole up from Dottie's collarbone, reddening the patch of skin at the V opening of her handmade crepe de Chine blouse; her perturbed brown eyes canvassed her friends; her eczematous complexion spotted. She knew by heart what was coming. "If any man can show just cause, why they may not be lawfully joined together, let him now speak, or else hereafter for ever hold his peace." The curate's voice halted, on a questioning note; he glanced up and down the pews. Dottie shut her eyes and prayed, conscious of a dead hush in the chapel. Would God or Dr. Leverett, her clergyman, really want her to speak up? She prayed that they would not. The opportunity passed, as she heard the curate's voice resume, loud and solemn, as if almost in reprobation of the couple, to which he now turned. "I require and charge you both, as ye will answer at the dreadful day of judgment, when the secrets of all hearts shall be disclosed, that if either of you know any impediment, why ye may not be lawfully joined together in Matrimony, ye do now confess it. For be ye well assured, that if any persons are joined together otherwise than as God's Word doth allow, their Marriage is not lawful."

You could have heard a pin drop, as the girls agreed later. Every girl was holding her breath. Dottie's religious scruples had given way to a new anxiety, which was common to the whole group. The knowledge, shared by them of Kay's having "lived with" Harald filled them with a sudden sense of the unsanctioned. They glanced stealthily around the chapel and noted for the nth time the absence of parents or *any older person*; and this departure from convention, which had been "such fun" before the service began, struck them now as queer and ominous. Even Elinor Eastlake, who knew scornfully well that fornication was not the type of impediment alluded to in the service, half expected an unknown presence to rise and stop the ceremony. To her mind, there was a spiritual obstacle to the marriage; she considered Kay a *cruel, ruthless, stupid* person who was marrying Harald for ambition.

Everyone in the chapel had now noticed something a little odd, or so it seemed, in the curate's pauses and stresses; they had never heard "their marriage is not lawful" delivered with such emphasis. On the groom's side, a handsome, auburn-haired, dissipated-looking young man clenched his fist suddenly and muttered something under his breath. He smelled terribly of alcohol and appeared extremely nervous; all through the ceremony, he had been clasping and unclasping his well-shaped, strong-looking hands and biting his chiseled lips. "He's a painter; he's just been divorced," whispered fair-haired Polly Andrews, who was the quiet type but who knew everything, on Elinor Eastlake's right. Elinor, like a young queen, leaned forward and deliberately caught his eye; here was someone, she felt, who was as disgusted and uncomfortable as she was. He responded with a stare of bitter, encompassing irony, followed by a wink directed, unmistakably, at the altar. Having moved into the main part of the service, the curate had now picked up speed, as though he had suddenly discovered another appointment and were running off this couple as rapidly as possible: this was only a $10 wedding, his manner seemed to imply. Behind her large hat, Kay appeared to be oblivious of all slights, but Harald's ears and neck had turned a darker red, and, in his responses, he began, with a certain theatrical flourish, to slow down and correct the minister's intonations.

This made the couple on the groom's side smile, as if at a familiar weakness or fault, but the girls, in *their* pews, were scandalized by the curate's rudeness and applauded what they called Harald's victory over which they firmly intended to make the center of congratulations after the ceremony. There were some who, then and there, resolved to speak to Mother and get her to speak to Dr. Reiland, the rector, about it, a capacity for outrage, their social birthright, had been redirected, as it were, by education. The fact that Kay and Harald were going to be poor as church mice was no excuse, they thought staunchly, for such conduct on the part of a priest, in these times especially, when everybody was having to retrench. Even among their own number, one girl had had to accept a scholarship to finish college, and nobody thought the worse of her for it: Polly Andrews remained one of their *very* dearest friends. They were a different breed, they could assure the curate, from the languid buds of the previous decade: there was not one of them who did not propose to work this coming fall, at a volunteer job if need be. Libby MacAusland had a promise from a publisher; Helena Davison, whose parents, out in Cincinnati, no, Cleveland, lived on the income of their income, was going into teaching—she already had a job sewed up at a private nursery school; Polly Andrews, more power to her, was to work as a technician in the new Medical Center; Dottie Renfrew was slated for social work in a Boston settlement house; Lakey was off to Paris to study art history, working toward an advanced degree; Pokey Prothero, who had been given a plane for graduation, was getting her pilot's license so as to be able to commute three days a week to Cornell Agricultural School, and, last but not least, yesterday little Priss Hartshorn, the group grind, had simultaneously announced her engagement to a young doctor and landed a job with the N.R.A. Not bad, they conceded, for a group that had gone through college with the stigma of being high-hat. And elsewhere in the class, in the wider circle of Kay's friends, they could point out girls of perfectly good background who were going into business, anthropology, medicine, not because they had to, but because they knew they had something to contribute to our emergent America. The group was not afraid of being radical either; they could see the good Roosevelt was doing, despite what Mother and Dad said; they were not taken in by party labels and thought the Democrats should be given a chance to show what they had up their sleeve. Experience was just a question of learning through trial and error; the most conservative of them, pushed to the wall, admitted that an honest socialist was entitled to a hearing.

The worst fate, they utterly agreed, would be to become like Mother and Dad, stuffy and frightened. Not one of them, if she could help it, was going to marry a broker or a banker or a cold-fish corporation lawyer, like so many of Mother's generation. They would rather be wildly poor and live on salmon wiggle than be forced to marry one of those dull purplish young men of their own set, with a seat on the Exchange and bloodshot eyes, interested only in squash and cockfighting and drinking at the Racquet Club with his cronies, Yale or Princeton '29. It would be better, yes, they were not afraid to say it, though Mother gently laughed, to marry a Jew if you loved him—some of them were awfully interesting and cultivated, though terribly ambitious and inclined to stick together, as you saw very well at Vassar: if you knew them you had to know their friends. There was one thing, though, truthfully, that made the group feel a little anxious for Kay. It was a pity in a way that a person as gifted as Harald and with a good education had had to pick the stage, rather than medicine or architecture or museum work, where the going was not so rough. To hear Kay talk, the theatre was pretty red in tooth and claw, though of course there were some nice people in it, like Katharine Cornell and Walter Hampden (he had a niece in the Class of '32) and John Mason Brown, the thingummy, who talked to Mother's club every year. Harald had done graduate work at the Yale Drama School, under Professor Baker, but then the depression had started, and he had had to come to New York to be a stage manager instead of just writing plays. That was like starting from the bottom in a factory, of course, which lots of nice boys were doing, and there was probably no difference between backstage in a theatre, where a lot of men in their undershirts sat in front of a mirror putting on make-up, and a blast furnace or a coal mine, where the men were in their undershirts too. Helena Davison said that when Harald's show came to Cleveland that spring, he spent all his time playing poker with the stage hands and the electricians, who were the nicest people in the show, and Helena's father said he agreed with him, especially after seeing the play—Mr. Davison was a bit of a card and more democratic than most fathers, being from the West and more or less self-made. Still nobody could afford to be standoffish nowadays. Connie Storey's fiancé, who was going into journalism, was working as an office boy at *Fortune*, and her family, instead of having conniptions, was taking it very calmly and sending her to cooking school. And lots of graduate architects, instead of joining a firm and building rich men's houses, had gone right into the factories to study industrial design. Look at Russel Wright, whom everybody thought quite the thing now; he was using industrial materials, like the wonderful new spun aluminum, to make all sorts of useful objects like cheese trays and water carafes. Kay's first wedding present, which she had picked out herself, was a Russel Wright cocktail shaker in the shape of a skyscraper and made out of oak ply and aluminum with a tray and twelve little round cups to match—light as a feather and nontarnishable, of course. The main point was, Harald was a natural gentleman—though inclined to show off in his letters, which was probably to impress Kay, who was inclined to drop names herself and talk about people's butlers and Fly and A.D. and Porcellian and introduce poor Harald as a Yale man when he had only gone to graduate school at New Haven. . . . That was a side of Kay that the group did its best to deprecate and that drove Lakey wild. A lack of fastidiousness and consideration for the other person; she did not seem to realize the little social nuances. She was always coming into people's rooms, for instance, and making herself at home and fiddling with things on their bureaus and telling them about their inhibitions if they objected; it was she who insisted on playing Truth and on getting everybody in the group to make lists of their friends in the order of preference and then compare the lists. What she did not stop to think about was that somebody had to be on the bottom of every list, and when that somebody cried and refused to be consoled, Kay was always honestly surprised; *she* would not mind, she said hearing the truth about herself. Actually, she never did hear it because the others were too tactful ever to put her at the bottom, even if they wanted to, because Kay was a little bit of an outsider and nobody wanted her to feel that. So instead they would put Libby MacAusland or Polly Andrews—someone they had known all their lives or gone to school with or something. Kay did get a bit of a shock, though, to find that she was not at the top of Lakey's list. She was crazy about Lakey, whom she always described as her best friend. Kay did not know it, but the group had had a pitched battle with Lakey over Easter vacation, when they had drawn straws to see who was to invite Kay home for the holidays and Lakey had got the shortest straw and then refused to play. The group had simply borne down on Lakey in a body and accused her of being a poor sport, which was true. After all, as they had swiftly pointed out to her, it was she who had invited Kay to group with them in the first place; when they saw that they could get the South Tower for themselves if they had eight in the group instead of six, it was Lakey's idea that they should invite Kay and Helena Davison to join forces with them and take the two small single rooms.

If you were going to use a person, then you had to make the best of them. And it was not "using," anyway; they all liked Kay and Helena, including Lakey herself, who had discovered Kay as a sophomore, when they were both on the Daisy

Chain. She had taken Kay up for all she was worth, because Kay, as she said, was "malleable" and "capable of learning." Now she claimed to have detected that Kay had feet of clay, which was rather a contradiction, since wasn't clay malleable? But Lakey was very contradictory; that was her charm. Sometimes she was a frightful snob and sometimes just the opposite. She was looking so furious this morning, for instance, because Kay, according to her, should have got married quietly in City Hall instead of making Harald, who was not to the manor born, try to carry off a wedding in J. P. Morgan's church. Now was this snobbish of Lakey or wasn't it? Naturally, she had not said any of this to Kay; she had expected Kay to feel it for herself, which was just what Kay couldn't do and remain the blunt, natural, unconscious Kay they all loved, in spite of her faults. Lakey had the weirdest ideas about people. She had got the bee in her bonnet, last fall, that Kay had worked her way into the group out of a desire for social prestige; this was not at all the way it had happened, and it was a peculiar thing, really, to think about a girl who was so unconventional that she had not even bothered to have her own parents to her wedding, though her father was very prominent in Salt Lake City affairs.

It was true, Kay had rather angled to get Pokey Prothero's town house for the reception, but she had taken it with good grace when Pokey had loudly lamented that the house was in dust covers for the summer, with only a caretaking couple to look after Father on the nights he spent in town. Poor Kay—some of the girls thought that Pokey might have been a little more generous and offered her a card to the Colony. In fact, on this score, nearly all the group felt a little bit conscience-stricken. Each one of them, as the others knew, had a house or a big apartment or a club member-ship, if it was only the Cosmopolitan, or a cousin's digs or a brother's that might pos-sibly have been put at Kay's disposal. But that would have meant punch, champagne, a cake from Sherry's or Henri's, extra help—before one knew it one would have found oneself giving the wedding and supplying a father or a brother to take Kay down the aisle. In these times, in sheer self-protection, one had to think twice, as Mother said, fatigued; there were so many demands. Fortunately, Kay had decided that she and Harald should give the wedding breakfast themselves, at the old Hotel Brevoort down on Eighth Street: so much nicer, so much more appropriate.

JOHN CHEEVER
(1912-1982)

Cheever is in many ways identified with The New Yorker *magazine. It is not only that the magazine published more of his stories than any other writer's, nor that his style—comic, precise, angular, hopeful—characterized some fifty years of the magazine's. It was, as well, that the people Cheever wrote about, the upper-middle-class of the Upper East Side and its Westch-ester suburban extensions, were for many years* The New Yorker's *audience as well as its subject. Cheever's very first story, "Expelled," was published in 1930 in* The New Republic *less than a year after the incident on which the story is based: Cheever's expulsion from Thayer Academy. In a way, most of Cheever's fictions replicate the core of that very first story: his people have been expelled from the comfortable, sensible world they had reason to expect, and here they are, trying to reassemble their lives, or at least their careers or marriages or identities, in a world grown increasingly, dangerously, and often hilariously, out of control.*

Cheever himself never quite got it under control, either. He did not go back to school after Thayer but lived in a roach den in New York while producing a string of stories in the 1930s, many of them initially printed in The New Yorker. *His first collection,* The Way Some People Live *(1943), came out while Cheever was serving out a four-year hitch in the Army during World War II. After the war, he continued to produce stories and write scripts for the television series* Life with Father *until he launched into his first novel,* The Wapshot Chronicle *(1957). While he wrote other novels, including a sequel,* The Wapshot Scandal *(1964), the short story remained his forte; in many ways his most successful book was the collection* The Stories of John Cheever *(1978), which was a best seller.*

But Cheever never seemed satisfied with the work he produced and he was for a time plagued with depression and alcoholism sufficient to be hospitalized. That experience, and a period of teaching at New York's maximum security prison, Sing Sing, led to the novel Falconer *(1977), set in a prison of that name and concerned, as Cheever himself put it, with "incarceration, homosexuality, and addiction." The novel is unusual in a number of ways, not least because it is more sympathetic to its central character, a forty-eight-year-old college professor and fratricide; but it also contains one of Cheever's most ugly in a long line of demeaning portraits of women. While the novel took him into new terrain, Cheever has continued to be seen, rightly or wrongly, as a chronicler of a sophisticated if baffled upper-middle-class in and around a rapidly changing New York.*

THE CHILDREN

Mr. Hatherly had many old-fashioned tastes. He wore high yellow boots, dined at Lüchow's in order to hear the music, and slept in a woolen nightshirt. His urge to establish in business a patriarchal liaison with some young man who would serve as his descendant, in the fullest sense of the word, was another of these old-fashioned tastes. Mr. Hatherly picked for his heir a young immigrant named Victor Mackenzie, who had made the crossing from England or Scotland—a winter crossing, I think—when he was sixteen or seventeen. The winter crossing is a guess. He may have worked his way or borrowed passage money or had some relation in this country to help him, but all this was kept in the dark, and his known life began when he went to work for Mr. Hatherly. As an immigrant, Victor may have cherished an obsolete vision of the American businessman. Here and there one saw in Mr. Hatherly a touch of obsolescence. His beginnings were obscure, and, as everyone knows, he got rich enough to be an ambassador. In business, he was known as a harsh and unprincipled trader. He broke wind when he felt like it and relished the ruin of a competitor. He was very short—nearly a dwarf. His legs were spindly and his large belly had pulled his spine out of shape. He decorated his bald skull by combing across it a few threads of gray hair, and he wore an emerald fob on his watch chain. Victor was a tall man, with the kind of handsomeness that is sooner or later disappointing. His square jaw and all his other nicely proportioned features might at first have led you to expect a man of exceptional gifts of character, but you felt in the end that he was merely pleasant, ambitious, and a little ingenuous. For years, this curmudgeon and the young immigrant walked side by side confidently, as if they might have been accepted in the ark.

Of course, it all took a long time; it took years and years. Victor began as an office boy with a hole in his sock. Like the immigrants of an earlier generation, he had released great stores of energy and naïveness through the act of expatriation. He worked cheerfully all day. He stayed cheerfully at night to decorate the showcases in the waiting room. He seemed to have no home to go to. His eagerness reminded Mr. Hatherly, happily, of the apprentices of his own youth. There was little enough in business that did remind him of the past. He kept Victor in his place for a year or two, speaking to him harshly if he spoke to him at all. Then in his crabbed and arbitrary way he began to instruct Victor in the role of an heir. Victor was sent on the road for six months. After this he worked in the Rhode Island mills. He spent a season in the advertising department and another in the sales division. His position in the business was difficult to assess, but his promotions in Mr. Hatherly's esteem were striking. Mr. Hatherly was sensitive about the odd figure he cut, and disliked going anywhere alone. When Victor had worked with him for a few years, he was ordered to get to the old man's apartment, on upper Fifth Avenue, at eight each morning and walk him to work. They never talked much along the way, but then Hatherly was not loquacious. At the close of the business day, Victor either put him into a taxi or walked him home. When the old man went off to Bar Harbor without his eyeglasses, it was Victor who got up in the middle of the night and put the glasses on the early-morning plane. When the old man wanted to send a wedding present, it was Victor who bought it. When the old man was ailing, it was Victor who got him to take his medicine. In the gossip of the trade Victor's position was naturally the target for a lot of jocularity, criticism, and downright jealousy. Much of the criticism was unfair, for he was merely an ambitious young man who expressed his sense of business enterprise by feeding pills to Mr. Hatherly. Running through all his amenability was an altogether charming sense of his own identity. When he felt that he had grounds for complaint, he said so. After working for eight years under Mr. Hatherly's thumb, he went to the old man and said that he thought his salary was inadequate. The old man rallied with a masterful blend of injury, astonishment, and tenderness. He took Victor to his tailor and let him order four suits. A few months later, Victor again complained—this time about the vagueness of his position in the firm. He was hasty, the old man said, in objecting to his lack of responsibility. He was scheduled to make a presentation, in a week or two, before the board of directors. This was more than Victor had expected, and he was content. Indeed, he was grateful. This was America! He worked hard over his presentation. He read it aloud to the old man, and Mr. Hatherly instructed him when to raise and when to lower his voice, whose eye to catch and whose to evade, when to strike the table and when to pour himself a glass of water. They discussed the clothing that he would wear. Five minutes before the directors' meeting began, Mr. Hatherly seized the papers, slammed the door in Victor's face, and made the presentation himself.

He called Victor into his office at the end of that trying day. It was past six, and the secretaries had locked up their teacups and gone home. "I'm sorry about the presentation," the old man mumbled. His voice was heavy. Then Victor saw that he had been crying. The old man slipped off the high desk chair that he used to increase his height and walked around the large office. This was, in itself, a demonstration of intimacy and trust. "But that isn't what I want to talk about," he said. "I want to talk about my family. Oh, there's no misery worse than bad blood in a family! My wife"—he spoke with disgust—"is a stupid woman. The hours of pleasure I've had from my children I can count on the fingers of one hand. It may be my fault," be said, with manifest insincerity. "What I want you to do now is to help me with my boy, Junior. I've brought Junior up to respect money. I made him earn every nickel he got until he was sixteen, so it isn't my fault that he's a damn fool with money, but he is. I just don't have the time to bother with his bad checks any more. I'm a busy man. You know that. What I want you to do is act as Junior's business adviser. I want you to pay his rent, pay his alimony, pay his maid, pay his household expenses, and give him a cash allowance once a week."

For a moment, anyhow, Victor seemed to breathe the freshness of a considerable skepticism. He had been cheated, that afternoon, out of a vital responsibility and was being burdened now with a foolish one. The tears could be hypocritical. The fact that this request was made to him in a building that had been emptied and was unnaturally quiet and at a time of day when the fading light outside the windows might help to bend his decision were all tricks in the old man's hand. But, even seen skeptically, the hold that Hatherly had on him was complete. "Mr. Hatherly told me to tell you," Victor could always say. "I come from Mr. Hatherly." "Mr. Hatherly . . ." Without this coupling of names his own voice would sound powerless. The comfortable and becoming shirt whose cuffs he shot in indecision had been given to him by Mr. Hatherly. Mr. Hatherly had introduced him into the 7th Regiment. Mr. Hatherly was his only business identity, and to separate himself from this source of power might be mortal. He didn't reply.

"I'm sorry about the presentation," the old man repeated. "I'll see that you make one next year. Promise." He gave his shoulders a hitch to show that he was moving on from this subject to another. "Meet me at the Metropolitan Club tomorrow at two," he said briskly. "I have to buy out Worden at lunch. That won't take long. I hope he brings his lawyer with him. Call his lawyer in the morning and make sure that his papers are in order. Give him hell for me. You know how to do it. You'll help me a great deal by taking care of Junior," he said with great feeling. "And take care of yourself, Victor. You're all I have."

After lunch the next day, the old man's lawyer met them at the Metropolitan Club and went with them to an apartment, where Junior was waiting. He was a thick-set man a good ten years older than Victor, and be seemed resigned to having his income taken out of his hands. He called Mr. Hatherly Poppa and sadly handed over to his father a bundle of unpaid bills. With Victor and the lawyer, Mr. Hatherly computed Junior's income and his indebtedness, took into consideration his alimony payments, and arrived at a reasonable estimate for his household expenses and the size of his allowance, which he was to get at Victor's office each Monday morning. Junior's goose was cooked in half an hour.

He came around for his allowance every Monday morning and submitted his household bills to Victor. He sometimes hung around the office and talked about his father—uneasily, as if he might be overheard. All the minutiae of Mr. Hatherly's life—that he was sometimes shaved three times a day and that he owned fifty pairs of shoes—interested Victor. It was the old man who cut these interviews short. "Tell him to come in and get his money and go," the old man said. "This is a business office. That's something he's never understood."

Meanwhile, Victor had met Theresa and was thinking of getting married. Her full name was Theresa Mercereau; her parents were French but she had been born in the United States. Her parents had died when she was young, and her guardian had put her into fourth-string boarding schools. One knows what these places are like. The headmaster resigns over the Christmas holidays. He is replaced by the gymnastics instructor. The heating plant breaks down in February and the water pipes freeze. By this time, most of the parents who are concerned about their children have transferred them to other schools, and by spring there are only twelve or thirteen boarders left. They wander singly or in pairs around the campus, killing time before supper. It has been apparent to them for months that Old Palfrey Academy is dying, but in the first long, bleakly lighted days of spring this fact assumes new poignancy and force. The noise of a quarrel comes from the headmaster's quarters, where the Latin instructor is threatening to sue for back wages. The smell from the kitchen windows indicates that there will be cabbage again. A few jonquils are in bloom, and the lingering light and the new ferns enjoin the stranded children to look ahead, ahead, but at the back of their minds there is a suspicion that the jonquils and the robins and the evening star imperfectly conceal the fact that this hour is horror, naked horror. Then a car roars up the driveway. "I am Mrs. Hubert Jones," a woman exclaims, "and I have come to get my daughter . . ." Theresa was always one of the last to be rescued, and these hours seemed to have left some impression on her. It was the quality of an especial sadness, a delicacy that was never forlorn, a charming air of having been wronged, that one remembered about her.

That winter, Victor went to Florida with Mr. Hatherly to hoist his beach umbrella and play rummy with him, and while they were there he said that he wanted to get married. The old man yelled his objections. Victor stood his ground. When they returned to New York, the old man invited Victor to bring Theresa to his apartment one evening. He greeted the young woman with great cordiality and then introduced her to Mrs. Hatherly—a wasted and nervous woman who kept her hands at her mouth. The old man began to prowl around the edges of the room. Then he disappeared. "It's all right," Mrs. Hatherly whispered. "He's going to give you a present." He returned in a few minutes and hung a string of amethysts around Theresa's beautiful neck. Once the old man had accepted her, he seemed happy about the marriage. He made all the arrangements for the wedding, of course, told them where to go for a honeymoon, and rented and furnished an apartment for them one day between a business lunch and a plane to California. Theresa seemed, like her husband, to be able to accommodate his interference. When her first child was born, she named it Violet—this was her own idea—after Mr. Hatherly's sainted mother.

When the Mackenzies gave a party, in those years, it was usually because Mr. Hatherly had told them to give a party. He would call Victor into his office at the end of the day, tell him to entertain, and set a date. He would order the liquor and the food, and overhaul the guest list with the Mackenzies' business and social welfare in mind. He would rudely refuse an invitation to come to the party himself, but he would appear before any of the guests, carrying a bunch of flowers that was nearly as tall as he was. He would make sure that Theresa put the flowers in the right vase. Then he would go into the nursery and let Violet listen to his watch. He would go through the apartment, moving a lamp here or an ashtray there and giving the curtains a poke. By this time the Mackenzies' guests would have begun to arrive, but Mr. Hatherly would show no signs of going. He was a distinguished old man and everyone liked to talk with him. He would circle the room, making sure that all the glasses were filled, and if Victor told an anecdote the chances were that Mr. Hatherly had drilled him in how to tell it. When the supper was served, the old man would be anxious about the food and the way the maid looked.

He was always the last to go. When the other guests had said good night, he would settle down and all three would have a glass of milk and talk about the evening. Then the old man would seem happy—with a kind of merriment that his enemies would never have believed him capable of. He would laugh until the tears rolled down his cheeks. He sometimes took off his boots. The small room seemed to be the only room in which he was content, but it must always have been at the back of Mr. Hatherly's mind that these young people were in substance nothing to him, and that it was because his own flesh and blood had been such a bitter disappointment that he found himself in so artificial a position. At last he would get up to go. Theresa would straighten the knot in his tie, brush the crumbs off his vest, and bend down to be kissed. Victor would help him into his fur coat. All three of them would be deep in the tenderness of a family parting. "Take good care of yourselves," the old man would mumble. "You're all I have."

One night, after a party at the Mackenzies, Mr. Hatherly died in his sleep. The funeral was in Worcester, where he was born. The family seemed inclined to keep the arrangements from Victor, but he found out what they were easily enough, and went, with Theresa, to the church and the cemetery. Old Mrs. Hatherly and her unhappy children gathered at the edge of the grave. They must have watched the old man's burial with such conflicting feelings that it would be impossible to extricate from the emotional confusion anything that could be named. "Goodbye, goodbye," Mrs. Hatherly called, halfheartedly, across the earth, and her hands flew to her lips—a habit that she had never been able to break, although the dead man had often threatened to strike her for it. If the full taste of grief is a privilege, this was now the privilege of the Mackenzies. They were crushed. Theresa had been too young when her parents died for her to have, as a grown person, any clear memories of grieving for them, and Victor's parents—whoever they were—had died a few years back, in England or Scotland, and it seemed at Hatherly's grave that she and Victor were in the throes of an accrual of grief and that they were burying more than the bones of one old man. The real children cut the Mackenzies.

The Mackenzies were indifferent to the fact that they were not mentioned in Mr. Hatherly's will. A week or so after the funeral, the directors elected Junior to the presidency of the firm, and one of the first things he did was to fire Victor. He had been compared with this industrious immigrant for years, and his resentment was understandable and deep. Victor found another job, but his intimate association with Mr. Hatherly was held against him in the trade. The old man had a host of enemies, and Victor inherited them all. He lost his new job after six or eight months, and found another that he regarded as temporary—an arrangement that would enable him to meet his monthly bills while he looked around for something better. Nothing better turned up. He and Theresa gave up the apartment that Mr. Hatherly had taken for them, sold all their furniture, and moved around from place to place, but all this—the ugly rooms they lived in, the succession of jobs that Victor took— is not worth going into. To put it simply, the Mackenzies had some hard times; the Mackenzies dropped out of sight.

The scene changes to a fund-raising party for the Girl Scouts of America, in a suburb of Pittsburgh. It is a black-tie dance in a large house—Salisbury Hall—that has been picked by the dance committee with the hope that idle curiosity about this edifice will induce a lot of people to buy the twenty-five dollar tickets. Mrs. Brownlee, the nominal hostess, is the widow of a pioneer steel magnate. Her house is strung for half a mile along the spine of one of the Allegheny hills. Salisbury Hall is a castle, or, rather, a collection of parts of castles and houses. There is a tower, a battlement, and a dungeon, and the postern gate is a reproduction of the gate at Château Gaillard. The stones and timber for the Great Hall and the armory were brought from abroad. Like most houses of its kind, Salisbury Hall presents insuperable problems of maintenance. Touch a suit of chain mail in the armory and your hand comes away black with rust. The copy of a Mantegna fresco in the ballroom is horribly stained with water. But the party is a success. A hundred couples are dancing. The band is playing a rhumba. The Mackenzies are here.

Theresa is dancing. Her hair is still fair—it may be dyed by now—and her arms and her shoulders are still beautiful. The air of sadness, of delicacy, still clings to her. Victor is not on the dance floor. He is in the orangery, where watery drinks are being sold. He pays for four drinks, walks around the edge of the crowded dance floor, and goes through the armory, where a stranger stops to ask him a question. "Why, yes," Victor says courteously, "I do happen to know about it. It's a suit of mail that was made for the coronation of Philip II. Mr. Brownlee had it copied . . ." He continues along another quarter of a mile of halls and copied parlors, through the Great Hall, to a small parlor, where Mrs. Brownlee is sitting with some friends. "Here's Vic with our drinks!" she cries. Mrs. Brownlee is an old lady, plucked and painted and with her hair dyed an astonishing shade of pink. Her fingers and her forearms are loaded with rings and bracelets. Her diamond necklace is famous. So, indeed, are most of her jewels—most of them have names. There are the Taphir emeralds, the Bertolotti rubies, and the Demidoff pearls, and, feeling that a look at this miscellany should be included in the price of admission, she has loaded herself unsparingly for the benefit of the Girl Scouts. "Everybody's having a good time, aren't they, Vic?" she asks. "Well, they should be having a good time. My house has always been known for its atmosphere of hospitality as well as for its wealth of artistic treasures. Sit down, Vic," she says. "Sit down. Give yourself a little rest. I don't know what I'd do without you and Theresa." But Victor doesn't have time to sit down. He has to run the raffle. He goes back through the Great Hall, the Venetian Salon, and the armory, to the ballroom. He climbs onto a chair. There is a flourish of music. "Ladies and gentlemen!" he calls through a megaphone. "Ladies and gentlemen, can I have your attention for a few minutes . . ." He raffles off a case of Scotch, a case of bourbon, a Waring mixer, and a power lawn mower. When the raffle is over and the dancing begins again, he goes out onto the terrace for a breath of air, and we follow him and speak to him there.

"Victor?"

"Oh, how nice to see you again," he exclaims. "What in the world are you doing in Pittsburgh?" His hair has grayed along conventionally handsome lines. He must have had some work done on his teeth, because his smile is whiter and more dazzling than ever. The talk is the conversation of acquaintances who have not met for ten or fifteen years—it has been that long—about this and that, then about Theresa, then about Violet. At the mention of Violet, he seems very sad. He sets the megaphone on the stone terrace and leans on its metal rim. He bows his head. "Well, Violet is sixteen now, you know," he says. "She's given me a lot to worry about. She was suspended from school about six weeks ago. Now I've got her into a new school in Connecticut. It took a lot of doing." He sniffs.

"How long have you been in Pittsburgh, Victor?"

"Eight years," he says. He swings the megaphone into the air and peers through it at a star. "Nine, actually," he says.

"What are you doing, Victor?"

"I'm between jobs now." He lets the megaphone fall.

"Where are you living, Victor?"

"Here," he says.

"I know. But where in Pittsburgh?"

"Here," he says. He laughs. "We live here. At Salisbury Hall. Here's the head of the dance committee, and if you'll excuse me, I'll make my report on the raffle. It's been very nice to see you again."

Anyone—anyone, that is, who did not eat peas off a knife—might have been invited to Salisbury Hall when the Mackenzies first went there. They had only just arrived in Pittsburgh, and were living in a hotel. They drove out with some friends for a weekend. There were fourteen or fifteen guests in the party, and Prescott Brownlee, the old lady's eldest son. There was some trouble before dinner. Prescott got drunk at a roadhouse near the estate, and the bartender called Mrs. Brownlee and told her to have him removed before he called the police. The old lady was used to this kind of trouble. Her children were in it most of the time, but that afternoon she did not know where to turn for help. Nils, the houseman, hated Prescott. The gardener had gone home. Ernest, the butler, was too old. Then she remembered Victor's face, although she had only glimpsed it in the hall when they were introduced. She found him in the Great Hall and called him aside. He thought he was going to be asked to mix the cocktails. When she made her request, he said that he would be glad to help. He drove to the roadhouse, where he found Prescott sitting at a table. Someone had given him a bloody nose, and his clothing was splattered with blood, but he was still pugnacious, and when Victor told him to come home, he got up swinging. Victor knocked him down. This subdued Prescott, who began to cry and stumbled obediently out to the car. Victor returned to Salisbury Hall by a service driveway. Then, supporting Prescott, who could not walk, he got him into a side door that opened into the armory. No one saw them. The air in the unheated room was harsh and bitter. Victor pushed the sobbing drunk under the rags of royal battle flags and pennants that hung from the rafters and past a statue of a man on horseback that displayed a suit of equestrian armor. He got Prescott up a marble staircase and put him to bed. Then he brushed the sawdust off his own evening clothes and went down to the Great Hall and made the cocktails.

He didn't mention this incident to anyone—not even to Theresa—and on Sunday afternoon Mrs. Brownlee took him aside again, to thank him. "Oh, bless your heart, Mr. Mackenzie!" she said. "You're a good Samaritan. When that man called me up yesterday, I didn't know where to turn." They heard someone approaching across the Great Hall. It was Prescott. He had shaved, dressed his wounds, and soaked his hair down with water, but he was drunk again. "Going to New York," he mumbled to his mother. "Ernest's going to drive me to the plane. *See* you." He turned and wandered back across the library into the Venetian Salon and out of sight, and his mother set her teeth as she watched him go. Then she seized Victor's hand and said, "I want you and your lovely wife to come and live at Salisbury Hall. I know that you're living in a hotel. My house has always been known for its atmosphere of hospitality as well as for its wealth of artistic treasures. You'll be doing me a favor. That's what it amounts to."

The Mackenzies gracefully declined her offer and returned to Pittsburgh on Sunday night. A few days later, the old lady, hearing that Theresa was sick in bed, sent flowers, and a note repeating her invitation. The Mackenzies discussed it that night. "We must think of it as a business arrangement, if we think of it at all," Victor said. "We must think of it as the practical answer to a practical problem." Theresa had always been frail, and living in the country would be good for her. This was the first thing they thought of. Victor had a job in town, but he could commute from the railroad station nearest Salisbury Hall. They talked with Mrs. Brownlee again and got her to agree to accept from them what they would have paid for rent and food, so that the arrangement would be kept impersonal. Then they moved into a suite of rooms above the Great Hall.

It worked out very well. Their rooms were large and quiet, and the relationship with Mrs. Brownlee was easygoing. Any sense of obligation they may have felt was dispelled by their knowing that they were useful to their hostess in a hundred ways. She needed a man around the place, and who else would want to live in Salisbury Hall? Except for gala occasions, more than half the rooms were shut, and there were not enough servants to intimidate the rats that lived in the basement. Theresa undertook the herculean task of repairing Mrs. Brownlee's needlepoint; there were eighty-six pieces. The tennis court at Salisbury Hall had been neglected since the war, and Victor, on his weekends, weeded and rolled it and got it in shape again. He absorbed a lot of information about Mrs. Brownlee's house and her scattered family, and when she was too tired to take interested guests around the place, he was always happy to. "This hall," he would say, "was removed panel by panel and stone by stone from a Tudor house near the cathedral in Salisbury. The marble floor is part of the lobby floor of the old First National Bank. . . . Mr. Brownlee gave Mrs. Brownlee the Venetian Salon as a birthday present, and these four columns of solid onyx came from the ruins of Herculaneum. They were floated down Lake Erie from Buffalo to Ashtabula. . . ." Victor could also point out the scar on a tree where Spencer Brownlee had wrecked his car, and the rose garden that had been planted for Hester Brownlee when she was so sick. We have seen how helpful he was on occasions like the dance for the Girl Scout fund.

Violet was away in camps and schools. "Why do you live here?" she asked the first time she came to visit her parents in Salisbury Hall. "What a moldy old wreck! What a regular junk heap!" Mrs. Brownlee may have heard Violet laughing at her house. In any event, she took a violent dislike to the Mackenzies' only child, and Violet's visits were infrequent and brief. The only one of Mrs. Brownlee's children who returned from time to time was Prescott. Then, one evening not long after the Girl Scout dance, Mrs. Brownlee got a wire from her daughter Hester, who had been living in Europe for fifteen years. She had arrived in New York and was coming on to Pittsburgh the following day.

Mrs. Brownlee told the Mackenzies the good news at dinner. She was transported. "Oh, you'll love Hester," she said. "You'll both love her! She was always just like Dresden china. She was sickly when she was a child and I guess that's why she's always been my favorite. Oh, I hope she'll stay! I wish there was time to have her rooms painted! You must urge her to stay, Victor. It would make me so happy. You urge her to stay. I think she'll like you."

Mrs. Brownlee's words echoed through a dining room that had the proportions of a gymnasium; their small table was pushed against a window and separated from the rest of the room by a screen, and the Mackenzies liked to have dinner there. The window looked down the lawns and stairways to the ruin of a formal garden. The iron lace on the roof of the broken greenhouses, the noise of the fountains whose basins were disfigured and cracked, the rattle of the dumbwaiter that brought their tasteless dinner up from the basement kitchens, where the rats lived—the Mackenzies regarded all this foolishness with the deepest respect, as if it had some genuine significance. They may have suffered from an indiscriminate sense of the past or from an inability to understand that the past plays no part in our happiness. A few days earlier, Theresa had stumbled into a third-floor bedroom that was full of old bon-voyage baskets—gilded, and looped with dog-eared ribbons—that had been saved from Mrs. Brownlee's many voyages.

While Mrs. Brownlee talked about Hester that evening, she kept her eye on the garden and saw, in the distance, a man climbing over one of the marble walls. Then a girl handed him down a blanket, a picnic hamper, and a bottle, and jumped into his arms. They were followed by two more couples. They settled themselves in the Temple of Love and, gathering a pile of broken latticework, built a little fire.

"Drive them away, Victor," Mrs. Brownlee said.

Victor left the table and crossed the terrace and went down to the garden and told the party to go.

"I happen to be a very good friend of Mrs. Brownlee's," one of the men said.

"That doesn't matter," Victor said. "You'll have to get out."

"Who says so?"

"I say so."

"Who are you?"

Victor didn't answer. He broke up their fire and stamped out the embers. He was outnumbered and outweighed, and he knew that if it came to a fight, he would probably get hurt, but the smoke from the extinguished fire drove the party out of the temple and gave Victor an advantage. He stood on a flight of steps above them and looked at his watch. "I'll give you five minutes to get over the wall and out," he said.

"But I'm a friend of Mrs. Brownlee's!"

"If you're a friend of Mrs. Brownlee's," Victor said, "come in the front way. I give you five minutes." They started down the path toward the wall, and Victor waited until one of the girls—they were all pretty—had been hoisted over it. Then he went back to the table and finished his dinner while Mrs. Brownlee talked on and on about Little Hester.

The next day was Saturday, but Victor spent most of it in Pittsburgh, looking for work. He didn't get out to Salisbury Hall until about four, and he was hot and dirty. When he stepped into the Great Hall, he saw that the doors onto the terrace were open and the florist's men were unloading a truck full of tubbed orange trees. A maid came up to him excitedly. "Nils is sick and can't drive!" she exclaimed. "Mrs. Brownlee wants you to go down to the station and meet Miss Hester. You'd better hurry. She's coming on the four-fifteen. She doesn't want you to take your car. She wants you to take the Rolls-Royce. She says you have permission to take the Rolls-Royce."

The four-fifteen had come and gone by the time Victor arrived at the station. Hester Brownlee was standing in the waiting room, surrounded by her luggage. She was a middle-aged woman who had persevered with her looks, and might at a distance have seemed pretty. "How do you do, Miss Brownlee?" Victor said. "I'm Victor Mackenzie. I'm—"

"Yes, I know," she said. "I've heard all about you from Prescott." She looked past his shoulder. "You're late."

"I'm sorry," Victor said, "but your mother—"

"These are my bags," she said. She walked out to the Rolls-Royce and got into the back seat.

Victor lighted a cigarette and smoked it halfway down. Then he carried her bags out to the car and started home to Salisbury Hall along a back road.

"You're going the wrong way," Miss Brownlee called. "Don't you *even* know the way?"

"I'm not going the usual way," Victor said patiently, "but a few years ago they built a factory down the road, and the traffic is heavy around closing time. It's quicker this way. But I expect that you'll find a good many changes in the neighborhood. How long has it been, Miss Brownlee, since you've seen Salisbury Hall?" There was no answer to his question, and, thinking that she might not have heard him, he asked again, "How long has it been, Miss Brownlee, since you've seen Salisbury Hall?"

They made the rest of the trip in silence. When they got to the house, Victor unloaded her bags and stood them by the door. Miss Brownlee counted them aloud. Then she opened her purse and handed Victor a quarter. "Why, thank you!" Victor said. "Thank you very much!" He went down into the garden to walk off his anger. He decided not to tell Theresa about this meeting. Finally, he went upstairs. Theresa was at work on one of the needlepoint stools. The room they used for a parlor was cluttered with half-repaired needlepoint. She embraced Victor tenderly, as she always did when they had been separated for a day. Victor had dressed when a maid knocked on the door. "Mrs. Brownlee wants to see you, both of you," she said. "She's in the office. At once."

Theresa clung to Victor's arm as they went downstairs. The office, a cluttered and dirty room beside the elevator, was brightly lighted. Mrs. Brownlee, in *grande tenue,* sat at her husband's desk. "You're the straw that broke the camel's back—both of you," she said harshly when they came in. "Shut the door. I don't want everybody to hear me. Little Hester has come home for the first time in fifteen years, and the first thing she gets off the train, you have to insult her. For nine years, you've had the privilege of living in this beautiful house—a wonder of the world—and how do you repay me? Oh, it's the straw that breaks the camel's back! Prescott's told me often enough that you weren't any good, either of you, and Hester feels the same way, and gradually I'm beginning to see it myself."

The harried and garishly painted old lady wielded over the Mackenzies the power of angels. Her silver dress glittered like St. Michael's raiment, and thunder and lightning, death and destruction, were in her right hand. "Everybody's been warning me about you for years," she said. "And you may not mean to do wrong—you may just be unlucky—but one of the first things Hester noticed is that half the needlepoint is missing. You're always repairing the chair that I want to sit down in. And you, Victor—you told me that you fixed the tennis court, and, of course, I don't know about that because I can't play tennis, but when I asked the Beardons over to play tennis last week, they told me that the court wasn't fit to play on, and you can imagine how embarrassed I was, and those people you drove out of the garden last night turned out to be the children of a very dear friend of the late Mr. Brownlee's. And you're two weeks behind with your rent."

"I'll send you the rent," Victor said. "We will go."

Theresa had not taken her arm out of his during the interview, and they left the office together. It was raining, and Ernest was putting out pails in the Venetian Salon, where the domed ceiling had sprung a leak. "Could you help me with some suitcases?" Victor asked. The old butler must have overheard the interview, because he didn't answer.

There was in the Mackenzies' rooms an accumulation of sentimental possessions—photographs, pieces of silver, and so forth. Theresa hastily began to gather these up. Victor went down to the basement and got their bags. They packed hurriedly—they did not even stop to smoke a cigarette—but it took them most of the evening. When they had finished, Theresa stripped the bed and put the soiled towels into a hamper, and Victor carried the bags down. He wrote a postcard to Violet's school, saying that his address was no longer Salisbury Hall. He waited for Theresa by the front door. "Oh, my darling, where will we go?" she murmured when she met him there. She waited in the rain for him to bring their car around, and they drove away, and God knows where they did go after that.

God knows where they went after that, but for our purposes they next appeared, years later, at a resort on the coast of Maine called Horsetail Beach. Victor had some kind of job in New York, and they had driven to Maine for his vacation. Violet was not with them. She had married and was living in San Francisco. She had a baby. She did not write to her parents, and Victor knew that she thought of him with bitter resentment, although he did not know why. The waywardness of their only child troubled Victor and Theresa, but they could seldom bring themselves to discuss it. Helen Jackson, their hostess at Horsetail Beach, was a spirited young woman with four children. She was divorced. Her house was tracked with sand, and most of the furniture was broken. The Mackenzies arrived there on a stormy evening when the north wind blew straight through the walls of the house. Their hostess was out to dinner, and as soon as they arrived, the cook put on her hat and coat and went off to the movies, leaving them in charge of the children. They carried their bags upstairs, stepping over several wet bathing suits, put the four children to bed, and settled themselves in a cold guest room.

In the morning, their hostess asked them if they minded if she drove into Camden to get her hair washed. She was giving a cocktail party for the Mackenzies that afternoon, although it was the cook's day off. She promised to be back by noon, and when she had not returned by one, Theresa cooked lunch. At three, their hostess telephoned from Camden to say that she had just left the hairdresser's and would Theresa mind getting a head start with the canapés? Theresa made the canapés. Then she swept the sand out of the living room and picked up the wet bathing suits. Helen Jackson finally returned from Camden, and the guests began to arrive at five. It was cold and stormy. Victor shivered in his white silk suit. Most of the guests were young, and they refused cocktails and drank ginger ale, gathered around the piano, and sang. It was not the Mackenzies' idea of a good party. Helen Jackson tried unsuccessfully to draw them into the circle of hearty, if meaningless, smiles, salutations, and handshakes upon which that party, like every other, was rigged. The guests all left at half past six, and the Mackenzies and their hostess made a supper of leftover canapés. "Would you mind dreadfully taking the children to the movies?" Helen Jackson asked Victor. "I promised them they could go to the movies if they were good about the party, and they've been perfect angels, and I hate to disappoint them, and I'm dead myself."

The next morning, it was still raining. Victor could see by his wife's face that the house and the weather were a drain on her strength. Most of us are inured to the inconveniences of a summer house in a cold rain, but Theresa was not. The power that the iron bedsteads and the paper window curtains had on her spirit was out of proportion, as if these were not ugly objects in themselves but threatened to over-whelm her common sense. At breakfast, their hostess suggested that they take a drive in the rain. "I know that it's vile out," she said, "but you could drive to Cam-den, and it's a way of killing time, isn't it, and you go through a lot of enchanting little villages, and if you did go down to Camden, you could go to the rental library and get *The Silver Chalice*. They've been reserving it for days and days, and I never find the time to get it. The rental library is on Estrella Lane." The Mackenzies drove to Camden and got *The Silver Chalice*. When they returned, there was another chore for Victor. The battery in Helen Jackson's car was dead. He took it to the garage and got a rental battery and installed it. Then, in spite of the weather, he tried to go swimming, but the waves were high and full of gravel, and after diving once he gave up and went back to the house. When he walked into the guest room in his wet bathing trunks, Theresa raised her face and he saw that it was stained with tears. "Oh, my darling," she said, "I'm homesick."

It was, even for Victor, a difficult remark to interpret. Their only home then was a one-room apartment in the city, which, with its kitchenette and studio couch, seemed oddly youthful and transitory for these grandparents. If Theresa was home-sick, it could only be for a collection of parts of houses. She must have meant some-thing else.

"Then we'll go," he said. "We'll leave the first thing in the morning." And then, seeing how happy his words had made her, he went on. "We'll get into the car and we'll drive and we'll drive and we'll drive. We'll go to Canada."

When they told Helen Jackson, at dinner, that they were leaving in the morning, she seemed relieved. She got out a road map and marked with a pencil the best route up through the mountains to Ste. Marie and the border. The Mackenzies packed after dinner and left early in the morning. Helen came out to the driveway to say goodbye. She was wearing her wrapper and carrying a silver coffeepot. "It's been perfectly lovely to have you," she said, "even if the weather has been so vile and disagreeable and horrid, and since you've decided to go through Ste. Marie, would you mind terribly stopping for a minute and returning Aunt Marly's silver coffeepot? I borrowed it years ago, and she's been writing me threatening letters and telephoning, and you can just leave it on the doorstep and run. Her name is Mrs. Sauer. The house is near the main road." She gave the Mackenzies some sketchy directions, kissed Theresa, and handed her the coffeepot. "It's been simply won-derful having you," she called as they drove away.

The waves at Horsetail Beach were still high and the wind was cold when the Mackenzies turned their back on the Atlantic Ocean. The noise and the smell of the sea faded. Inland, the sky seemed to be clearing. The wind was westerly and the overcast began to be displaced with light and motion. The Mackenzies came into hilly farmland. It was country they had never seen before, and as the massive clouds broke and the dilated light poured onto it, Theresa felt her spirits rising. She felt as if she were in a house on the Mediterranean, opening doors and windows. It was a house that she had never been in. She had only seen a picture of it, years ago, on a postcard. The saffron walls of the house continued straight down into the blue water, and all the doors and windows were shut. Now she was opening them. It was at the beginning of summer. She was opening doors and windows, and leaning into the light from one of the highest, she saw a single sail, disappearing in the direction of Africa, carrying the wicked King away. How else could she account for the feeling of perfect contentment that she felt? She sat in the car with her arm and her shoulder against her husband's, as she always did. As they came into the mountains, she noticed that the air seemed cooler and lighter, but the image of opening doors and windows—doors that stuck at the sill, shuttered windows, casement windows, windows with sash weights, and all of them opening onto the water—stayed in her mind until they came down, at dusk, into the little river resort of Ste. Marie.

"God damn that woman," Victor said; Mrs. Sauer's house was not where Helen Jackson had said it would be. If the coffeepot had not looked valuable, he would have thrown it into a ditch and driven on. They turned up a dirt road that ran parallel to the river, and stopped at a gas station and got out of the car to ask directions. "Sure, sure," the man said. "I know where the Sauers' place is. Their landing's right across the road, and the boatman was in here a minute ago." He threw open the screen door and shouted through his hands. "Perley! There's some people here want to get over to the island."

"I want to leave something," Victor said.

"He'll take you over. It makes a pretty ride this time of day. He don't have nothing to do. He's in here talking my ear off most of the time. Perley! Perley!"

The Mackenzies crossed the road with him to where a crooked landing reached into the water. An old man was polishing the brass on a launch. "I'll take you over and bring you right back," he said.

"I'll wait here," Theresa said.

Trees grew down to the banks on both shores; they touched the water in places. The river at this point was wide, and as it curved between the mountains she could see upstream for miles. The breadth of the view pleased her, and she hardly heard Victor and the boatman talking. "Tell the lady to come," the old man said.

"Theresa?"

She turned, and Victor gave her a hand into the boat. The old man put a dirty yachting cap on his head, and they started upstream. The current was strong, and the boat moved against it slowly, and at first they could not make out any islands, but then they saw water and light separate from the mainland what they had thought was a peninsula. They passed through some narrows and, swinging around abruptly—it was all strange and new to them—came up to a landing in a cove. Victor followed a path that led from the landing up to an old-fashioned frame camp stained the color of molasses. The arbor that joined the house to the garden was made of cedar posts, from which the bark hung in strips among the roses. Victor rang the bell. An old servant opened the door and led him through the house and out to the porch, where Mrs. Sauer was sitting with some sewing in her lap. She thanked him for bringing the coffeepot and, as he was about to leave, asked him if he were alone.

"Mrs. Mackenzie is with me," Victor said. "We're driving to Quebec."

"Well, as Talbot used to say, the time has come for the drinking to begin," the old lady said. "If you and your wife would stop long enough to have a cocktail with me, you would be doing me a great favor. That's what it amounts to."

Victor got Theresa, who was waiting in the arbor, and brought her to the porch.

"I know how rushed you children always are," the old lady said. "I know what a kindness it is for you to stop, but Mr. Sauer and I've been quite lonely up here this season. Here I sit, hemming curtains for the cook's room. What a bore!" She held up her sewing, and let it fall. "And since you've been kind enough to stay for a cocktail, I'm going to ask another favor. I'm going to ask you to mix the cocktails. Agnes, who let you in, usually makes them, and she waters the gin. You'll find everything in the pantry. Go straight through the dining room."

Navajo rugs covered the floor of the big living room. The fireplace chimney was made of fieldstone, and fixed to it was, of course, a pair of antlers. At the end of a large and cheerless dining room, Victor found the pantry. The old servant brought him the shaker and the bottles.

"Well, I'm glad you're staying," she said. "I knew she was going to ask you. She's been so lonely this season that I'm worried for her. She's a lovely person—oh, she's a lovely person—but she hasn't been like herself. She begins to drink at about eleven in the morning. Sometimes earlier." The shaker was a sailing trophy. The heavy silver tray had been presented to Mr. Sauer by his business associates.

When Victor returned to the porch, Theresa was hemming the curtains. "How good it is to taste gin again," old Mrs. Sauer exclaimed. "I don't know what Agnes thinks she's accomplishing by watering the cocktails. She's a most devoted and useful servant, and I would be helpless without her, but she's growing old, she's growing old. I sometimes think she's lost her mind. She hides the soap chips in the icebox and sleeps at night with a hatchet under her pillow."

"To what good fortune do we owe this charming visitation?" the old gentleman asked when he joined them. He drew off his gardening gloves and slipped his rose shears into the pocket of his checked coat.

"Isn't it generous of these children to stop and have a drink with us?" Mrs. Sauer said, when they had been introduced. The old man did not seem surprised at hearing the Mackenzies described as children. "They've come from Horsetail Beach and they're on their way to Quebec."

"Mrs. Sauer and I have always detested Horsetail Beach," the old gentleman said. "When do you plan to reach Quebec?"

"Tonight," Victor said.

"Tonight?" Mrs. Sauer asked.

"I doubt that you can reach Quebec tonight," the old gentleman said.

"I suppose you can do it," the old lady said, "the way you children drive, but you'll be more dead than alive. Stay for dinner. Stay the night."

"Do stay for dinner," the old man said.

"You will, won't you?" Mrs. Sauer said. "I will not take no for an answer! I am old and privileged, and if you say no, I'll claim to be deaf and pretend not to hear you. And now that you've decided to stay, make another round of these delicious cocktails and tell Agnes that you are to have Talbot's room. Tell her tactfully. She hates guests. Remember that she's very old."

Victor carried the sailing trophy back into the house, which, in spite of its many large windows, seemed in the early dark like a cave. "Mrs. Mackenzie and I are staying for dinner and the night," he told Agnes. "She said that we were to have Talbot's room."

"Well, that's nice. Maybe it will make her happy. She's had a lot of sorrow in her life. I think it's affected her mind. I knew she was going to ask you, and I'm glad you can stay. It makes me happy. It's more dishes to wash and more beds to make, but it's more—it's more—"

"It's more merrier?"

"Oh, that's it, that's it." The old servant shook with laughter. "You remind me a little of Mr. Talbot. He was always making jokes with me when he came out here to mix the cocktails. God have mercy on his soul. It's hard to realize," she said sadly.

Walking back through the cavelike living room, Victor could hear Theresa and Mrs. Sauer discussing the night air, and he noticed that the cold air had begun to come down from the mountains. He felt it in the room. There were flowers somewhere in the dark, and the night air had heightened their smell and the smell of the boulders in the chimney, so the room smelled like a cave with flowers in it. "Everyone says that the view looks like Salzburg," Mrs. Sauer said, "but I'm patriotic and I can't see that views are improved by such comparisons. They do seem to be improved by good company, however. We used to entertain, but now—"

"Yes, yes," the old gentleman said, and sighed. He uncorked a bottle of citronella and rubbed his wrists and the back of his neck.

"There!" Theresa said. "The cook's curtains are done!"

"Oh, how can I thank you!" Mrs. Sauer said. "Now if someone would be kind enough to get my glasses, I could admire your needlework. They're on the mantelpiece."

Victor found her glasses—not on the mantelpiece but on a nearby table. He gave them to her and then walked up and down the porch a few times. He managed to suggest that he was no longer a chance guest but had become a member of the family. He sat down on the steps, and Theresa joined him him there. "Look at them," the old lady said to her husband. "Doesn't it do you good to see, for a change, young people who love one another? . . . There goes the sunset gun. My brother George bought that gun for the yacht club. It was his pride and his joy. Isn't it quiet this evening?"

But the tender looks and attitudes that Mrs. Sauer took for pure love were only the attitudes of homeless summer children who had found a respite. Oh, how sweet, how precious the hour seemed to them! Lights burned on another island. Stamped on the twilight was the iron lace of a broken greenhouse roof. What poor magpies. Their ways and airs were innocent; their bones were infirm. Indeed, they impersonated the dead. Come away, come away, sang the wind in the trees and the grass, but it did not sing to the Mackenzies. They turned their heads instead to hear old Mrs. Sauer. "I'm going up to put on my green velvet," she said, "but if you children don't feel like dressing . . ."

Waiting on table that night Agnes thought that she had not seen such a gay dinner in a long time. She heard them go off after dinner to play billiards on the table that had been bought for poor, dead Talbot. A little rain fell, but, unlike the rain at Horsetail Beach, this was a gentle and excursive mountain shower. Mrs. Sauer yawned at eleven, and the game broke up. They said good night in the upstairs hall, by the pictures of Talbot's crew, Talbot's pony, and Talbot's class. "Good night, good night," Mrs. Sauer exclaimed, and then set her face, determined to overstep her manners, and declared, "I am delighted that you agreed to stay. I can't tell you how much it means. I'm—" Tears started from her eyes.

"It's lovely to be here," Theresa said.

"Good night, children," Mrs. Sauer said.

"Good night, good night," Mr. Sauer said.

"Good night," Victor said.

"Good night, good night," Theresa said.

"Sleep well," Mrs. Sauer said. "And pleasant dreams."

Ten days later, the Sauers were expecting some other guests—some young cousins named Wycherly. They had never been to the house before, and they came up the path late in the afternoon. Victor opened the door to them. "I'm Victor Mackenzie," he said cheerfully. He wore tennis shorts and a pullover, but when he bent down to pick up a suitcase, his knees creaked loudly: "The Sauers are out driving with my wife," he explained. "They'll be back by six, when the drinking begins." The cousins followed him across the big living room and the stairs. "Mrs. Sauer is giving you Uncle George's room," he said, "because it has the best view and the most hot water. It's the only room that's been added to the house since Mr. Sauer's father built the place in 1903. . . ."

The young cousins did not quite know what to make of him. Was he a cousin himself? an uncle, perhaps? a poor relation? But it was a comfortable house and a brilliant day, and in the end they would take Victor for what he appeared to be, and he appeared to be very happy.

CAROLYN FORCHÉ
(B. 1950)

Forché derives from a working-class family of Slovak immigrants. Her father worked long hours as a tool and die maker in Detroit, and her mother had seven children before she was able to attend college. Forché went to Catholic schools for her own education, then attended Michigan State University, from which she earned the B.A. in 1972. She then took an M.F.A. degree from Bowling Green State University in 1975. By then, she had produced her first book of poems, Gathering the Tribes *(1976), which won the Yale Series of Younger Poets Award.*

For a time in 1977, Forché lived in Spain in order to translate the work of the exiled Salvadoran poet Claribel Alegría, a volume of whose poems in English, Flowers from the Volcano, *she published in 1982. A Guggenheim fellowship allowed her to live for most of two years in El Salvador, where she served as a human rights activist for Amnesty International, working closely with Msgr. Oscar Romero, the Archbishop of San Salvador, who would be assassinated by a right-wing death squad. Her own life was threatened on a number of occasions, and at Romero's insistence that she "tell the American people what is happening," she left the country. Seven of the poems in her second book,* The Country Between Us *(1982), were written in El Salvador, a number of them dealing in terrifying detail with figures in the military and in the ongoing struggle for justice and peace. She also wrote "El Salvador: An Aide Memoire" (1981) and the text for a volume of the work of thirty Salvadoran photographers (1983).*

Subsequently, Forché worked as a correspondent in Beirut, Lebanon, for National Public Radio, as a human rights liaison in South Africa, as a translator, and as an editor of an unusual international collection of poetry, Against Forgetting: Twentieth-Century Poetry of Witness *(1991). Her most recent book of poetry is* The Angel of History *(1994), a series of narratives*

*and fragments concerned with the atrocities of twentieth-century wars,
from the Holocaust to Hiroshima, seen particularly from the perspective of
women struggling to reassemble lives torn apart by these events.*

AS CHILDREN TOGETHER

Under the sloped snow
pinned all winter with Christmas
lights, we waited for your father
to whittle his soap cakes
away, finish the whisky,
your mother to carry her coffee
from room to room closing lights
cubed in the snow at our feet.
Holding each other's
coat sleeves we slid down
the roads in our tight
black dresses, past
crystal swamps and the death
face of each dark house,
over the golden ice
of tobacco spit, the blue
quiet of ponds, with town
glowing behind the blind
white hills and a scant
snow ticking in the stars.
You hummed *blanche comme
la neige* and spoke of Montreal
where a *quebeçoise* could sing,
take any man's face
to her unfastened blouse
and wake to wine
on the bedside table.
I always believed this,
Victoria, that there might
be a way to get out.

You were ashamed of that house,
its round tins of surplus flour,
chipped beef and white beans,
relief checks and winter trips
that always ended in deer
tied stiff to the car rack,
the accordion breath of your uncles
down from the north, and what
you called the stupidity
of the Michigan French.

Your mirror grew ringed
with photos of servicemen
who had taken your breasts
in their hands, the buttons
of your blouses in their teeth,
who had given you the silk
tassles of their graduation,
jackets embroidered with dragons
from the Far East. You kept
the corks that had fired
from bottles over their beds,
their letters with each city
blackened, envelopes of hair
from their shaved heads.
I am going to have it, you said.
Flowers wrapped in paper from carts
in Montreal, a plane lifting out
of Detroit, a satin bed, a table
cluttered with bottles of scent.

So standing in a platter of ice
outside a Catholic dance hall
you took their collars
in your fine chilled hands
and lied your age to adulthood.

I did not then have breasts of my own,
nor any letters from bootcamp
and when one of the men who had
gathered around you took my mouth
to his own there was nothing
other than the dance hall music
rising to the arms of iced trees.

I don't know where you are now, Victoria.
They say you have children, a trailer
in the snow near our town,
and the husband you found as a girl
returned from the Far East broken
cursing holy blood at the table
where nightly a pile of white shavings
is paid from the edge of his knife.

If you read this poem, write to me.
I have been to Paris since we parted.

                              –1982

TESS GALLAGHER

(B. 1943)

Tess Gallagher's roots as well as her home are located in Port Angeles, Washington, an area of lumbering, shipping, and fishing. In her childhood, she helped her father, who worked as a logger, longshoreman, and farmer. She also went salmon fishing with him in the Straits of Juan de Fuca. These experiences constitute significant elements in her writing, particularly in the poem that follows, "3 A.M. Kitchen: My Father Speaking," which evokes his voice telling his own story almost without comment.

Gallagher began writing as a sixteen-year-old journalist for the Port Angeles Daily News. *She attended the University of Washington, obtaining both B.A. and M.A. from that institution. Subsequently, she received the M.F.A. from the well-known Iowa Writers' Workshop. She taught at about ten colleges and universities, including a longer-term position at Syracuse, before resettling in Port Angeles. She has published in a variety of forms, including poetry, short stories, and essays. She also wrote two screenplays with her late husband, poet and short story writer Raymond Carver.*

One of Gallagher's earliest books of poems, Instructions to the Double *(1976), concerns her conflicts between her working-class origins, with all its limitations and power, and the life of a poet, to which her training and graduation from Iowa (1974) seemed to have committed her. In her writing, this conflict is often represented by a certain tension between straightforward language and diction and surrealistic poetic forms and images. Her evocation of her past and of her efforts to establish her own identity as a woman and a poet have often been expressed in forms that shift rapidly between worry, nostalgia, humor, and compassion.*

3 A.M. KITCHEN: MY FATHER TALKING

For years it was land working me, oil fields,
cotton fields, then I got some land. I
worked it. Them days you could just about
make a living. I was logging.

Then I sent to Missouri. Momma
come out. We got married.
We got some kids. Five kids.
That kept us going.

We bought some land near the water.
It was cheap then. The water
was right there. You just looked out
the window. It never left the window.

I bought a boat. Fourteen footer.
There was fish out there then.
You remember, we used to catch
six, eight fish, clean them right
out in the yard. I could of fished to China.

I quit the woods. One day just
walked out, took off my corks, said that's
it. I went to the docks.
I was driving winch. You had to watch
to see nothing fell out of the sling. If
you killed somebody you'd
never forget it. All
those years I was just working
I was on edge, every day. Just working.

You kids, I could tell you
a lot. But I won't.
It's winter. I play a lot of cards
down at the tavern. Your mother.
I have to think of excuses
to get out of the house. You're
wasting your time, she says. You're wasting
your money.

You don't have no idea, Threasie.
I run out of things
to work for. Hell, why shouldn't I
play cards? Threasie,
some days now I just don't know.

DAVID CITINO
(B. 1947)

David Citino has published eight books of poetry. Among them are three in which the speaker is Sister Mary Appassionata, The Appassionata Poems *(1983),* The Appassionata Doctrines *(1986), and most recently,* The Book of Appassionata: Collected Poems *(1998). Other books evoke the landscapes of rural and urban Ohio, with both of which Citino is personally familiar. Citino's poems have been published in many magazines, including* The Antioch Review, Chicago Review, The Kenyon Review, Michigan Quarterly Review, Poetry, Prairie Schooner, The Southern Review, Threepenny

Review, *and* Yale Review. *He has taught English and creative writing at the Ohio State University for over twenty years. He has won fellowships from the National Endowment for the Arts as well as from the Ohio Arts Council. He is poetry editor and member of the board of the Ohio State University Press, and a member of the board of trustees of the Greater Columbus Arts Council and of the board of trustees of Thurber House, the writers' center located in downtown Columbus.*

His poems are in general accessible and immediate in their impact. He has a particular facility for capturing varied speaking voices and conversations.

VISITING MY FATHER IN FLORIDA

Forty years, every working day he drove
through the rolling haze of Cleveland streets
to the Harshaw Chemical Co., past Union Carbide,
Rockwell International, Bethlehem Steel, all the
barbed-wire, bricked-windowed plants, sulfur
rising from their stacks to rain on playgrounds
and reservoirs, the states downwind. He knew

the neighborhoods of Italians and Poles, Greeks
and Slovenes, Slovaks and Croats before they moved
their kitchen tables, photo albums and ceramic jockeys
to the suburbs. He couldn't understand the girls
in platform heels and slit skirts who'd whisper
"Hey Mister" from bleak doorways. "Go home to
your mother," he told one once. "Your white ass,"

she answered. He persisted so long even he changed.
Now we drive through his new "planned community,"
banks and K Marts garish as modern churches,
acres of offices of oncologists, proctologists,
urologists, ancient women pedaling tricycles,
Lincoln and Cadillac dealers, the old in bunches
raising blouses and shirts to show their latest scars.

Later we fish his new canal. Caloosahatchee mullet
leap stiffly toward the sky. He lifts his rod
and a whiskered, flat-headed catfish the color
of sludge lands between us, writhing. I've never
seen a thing so old, so ugly. It leaves a trail
of slime on the new dock, lost in so much sudden light,
blind. Its mouth gulps the precious, useless air.

JIM DANIELS

(B. 1946)

No contemporary poet has so steadily and forcefully portrayed the world of industrial labor as Jim Daniels. Like his grandfather and brothers, Daniels worked in the automobile industry before enrolling in Alma College in Michigan, from which he graduated in 1978, later earning his M.F.A. at Bowling Green State University. He became writer in residence at Carnegie-Mellon University in Pittsburgh in 1981, and has remained there.

The titles of his earliest chapbooks evoke his industrial background, Factory Poems *(1979) and* On the Line *(1981). The poems deal with life in and around the factories of Detroit, with the jobs and tools, the bars and bosses, the pressure of the line and the rage at those who control and enforce its pace. Daniels also creates a character, Digger, who reappears in a number of his books, most notably* Digger's Territory *(1989) and* Punching Out *(1990). Digger, who is the central figure in the poem that follows, often seems to be a stand-in for Daniels himself, though his creator no doubt has a certain distance on the exasperating and demanding factory life Digger tries, often without much success, to resist.*

Daniels's first full-length book of poetry, Places/Everyone *(1985), attracted a good deal of critical attention for its straightforward, unsentimental style, its evocation of working-class life from the point of view of working-class people, its ways of blending factory language and imagery into every aspect of life. Daniels is never nostalgic, but neither does he present a landscape only of fear and defeat; his people never can escape conflict but neither can they be reduced, however pervasive the time-and-motion study men, to automatons or abstractions. His descriptions match their own determination to live, in spite of all.*

DIGGER GOES ON VACATION

The maps from AAA, the tourbooks,
you are well-prepared:
Florida here we come.
For the first time
your son will not go with you.
He has a legitimate excuse:
a job at the corner store.
It is only you and the girls.
You think of your wife
as a girl.
You think
that you have given her nothing.
At the first Stuckey's on the road
you buy her a box of peanut brittle
and smile weakly
as she kisses your cheek.

Then you think of the plant
she is kissing you good-bye
in the morning.
You feel a chill
maybe wind on your neck.
You have two weeks.
Your body shakes
as you pull back on the road:
you have fifteen more years.

First night
you stop at a motel
off of 1-75 in Kentucky.
At a diner
you eat a late dinner
the girls nodding off to sleep
in their hamburgers.
You look at your wife.
If somehow she could lose some weight.
Then you look at your belly
hanging over your belt:
but mine's hard, you tell yourself,
muscle.

You punch your gut:
if we could just lose
all this weight.

"Digger?"
"Oh . . . yeah."
You pay the bill
and walk across the street
to the motel
squeezing your wife's hand
like a snowball
you want to melt.

You lie in the sand
the sun crisp on your back.
You will get burned.
You always do.
You try to read a book
in the bright glare—
the same book you brought
on vacation last year:
The Godfather.

At a cabin in Northern Michigan
you read 150 pages
and killed mosquitoes.
She packed it to keep me busy,
keep my eyes off the women.

You look over at your wife
wearing a floppy sun hat and bulging out
from her bathing suit.
You throw sand on her belly:
"hey Loretta, gimme a beer."
She hands you one
from the cooler by her side.

She really does
care about me,
you think, and suddenly
you are happy and smile.
You put the cold beer
against her neck
and she jumps up screaming.
"Hey baby, I love you."
"What?"
She takes off her sunglasses
and smiles, hugging you.
"You haven't said that since . . .
last year's vacation!"

You stare out at the sea of skin
and wonder when
you'll say it again.

At the beach
your foot in the sand
outlines the part
you weld onto axles.
"What's that, Daddy?"
You kick sand
over the drawing,
"Nothin'."
But no matter how many times
you kick the sand
it still looks like
something.

In a motel in Tennessee
you peel off your skin
to gross your daughters out.
"Oh Daddy, that's sick!"
You laugh
and rub your vacation beard:
"when all this skin is gone
I'll be a new person."
"Who will you be then, Daddy?"
"I'll be an astronaut.
So I could get lost in space."
"You're already lost in space,"
your wife shouts from the bathroom.

That night after dinner
you drink alone
at a local bar.
Your hands hold up your head
like obedient stilts.
This is how you always
become a new person.
You talk to the bartender:
"I used to be an astronaut."
And he believes you.

TONI CADE BAMBARA
(1939-1995)

Born Toni Cade, the writer adopted Bambara from the signature on a sketchbook she found in her grandmother's trunk. In a sense, adopting the name represented an act characteristic of Bambara: finding meaning and sustenance in the African-American past. Like many of the writers of the Black Arts movement of the 1960s, she looked, in part, to that past as a source of inspiration, subject matter, and intellectual models.

But she also looked, and perhaps more substantively, to the urban life in which she grew up and also to the movement for black rights that had developed in the 1950s and flourished through the 1960s. She was a New Yorker, living in Harlem, Bed-Stuy, and Queens, attending public schools, and receiving both a B.A. from Queens College of the City University and an M.A. from City College in 1963. After, she also studied theater at the Commedia del'Arte in Milan, filmmaking in England, and modern dance and painting in the United States and abroad.

Bambara's active participation in the Black Arts and civil rights movements helped shape her fiction. Her protagonists often learn the lessons of

*inequality in American society, as in the story that follows. As often, how-
ever, they learn to cope and also to triumph, breaking through the limitations imposed by conventional attitudes about class, race, and other
imposed categories of identity, like disability, as in her familiar story "Raymond's Run." But her stories are hardly didactic; rather they are written
with a keen sense of urban black vernacular, of the way real people speak
and interact in real situations. She was particularly successful in bringing
alive young black girls, of the irreverent, determined sort portrayed in "The
Lesson."*

*Much of Bambara's own work was directed toward the movement's
goals: she read her work at rallies and at meetings, she developed film projects focused on the demands and hopes of African-American life, she
taught not only in colleges but in community schools—and she worked as
an activist and organizer. Her literary production included two volumes of
stories,* Gorilla My Love *(1972) and* The Sea Birds Are Still Alive *(1977), as
well as a novel,* The Salt Eaters *(1980), which won the American Book
Award, and numerous essays on cultural and political topics.*

THE LESSON

Back in the days when everyone was old and stupid or young and foolish and me
and Sugar were the only ones just right, this lady moved on our block with nappy
hair and proper speech and no makeup. And quite naturally we laughed at her,
laughed the way we did at the junk man who went about his business like he was
some big-time president and his sorry-ass horse his secretary. And we kinda hated
her too, hated the way we did the winos who cluttered up our parks and pissed on
our handball walls and stank up our hallways and stairs so you couldn't halfway
play hide-and-seek without a goddamn gas mask. Miss Moore was her name. The
only woman on the block with no first name. And she was black as hell, cept for her
feet, which were fish-white and spooky. And she was always planning these boring-
ass things for us to do, us being my cousin, mostly, who lived on the block cause
we all moved North the same time and to the same apartment then spread out gradual to breathe. And our parents would yank our heads into some kinda shape and
crisp up our clothes so we'd be presentable for travel with Miss Moore, who always
looked like she was going to church, though she never did. Which is just one of the
things the grownups talked about when they talked behind her back like a dog. But
when she came calling with some sachet she'd sewed up or some gingerbread she'd
made or some book, why then they'd all be too embarrassed to turn her down and
we'd get handed over all spruced up. She'd been to college and said it was only right
that she should take responsibility for the young ones' education, and she not even
related by marriage or blood. So they'd go for it. Specially Aunt Gretchen. She was
the main gofer in the family. You got some ole dumb shit foolishness you want
somebody to go for, you send for Aunt Gretchen. She been screwed into the go-
along for so long, it's a blood-deep natural thing with her. Which is how she got saddled with me and Sugar and Junior in the first place while our mothers were in a la-
de-da apartment up the block having a good ole time.

So this one day Miss Moore rounds us all up at the mailbox and it's purdee hot and she's knockin herself out about arithmetic. And school suppose to let up in summer I heard, but she don't never let up. And the starch in my pinafore scratching the shit outta me and I'm really hating this nappy-head bitch and her goddamn college degree. I'd much rather go to the pool or to the show where it's cool. So me and Sugar leaning on the mailbox being surly, which is a Miss Moore word. And Flyboy checking out what everybody brought for lunch. And Fat Butt already wasting his peanut-butter-and-jelly sandwich like the pig he is. And Junebug punchin on Q.T.'s arm for potato chips. And Rosie Giraffe shifting from one hip to the other waiting for somebody to step on her foot or ask her if she from Georgia so she can kick ass, preferably Mercedes'. And Miss Moore asking us do we know what money is, like we a bunch of retards. I mean real money, she say, like it's only poker chips or monopoly papers we lay on the grocer. So right away I'm tired of this and say so. And would much rather snatch Sugar and go to the Sunset and terrorize the West Indian kids and take their hair ribbons and their money too. And Miss Moore files that remark away for next week's lesson on brotherhood, I can tell. And finally I say we oughta get to the subway cause it's cooler and besides we might meet some cute boys. Sugar done swiped her mama's lipstick, so we ready.

So we heading down the street and she's boring us silly about what things cost and what our parents make and how much goes for rent and how money ain't divided up right in this country. And then she gets to the part about we all poor and live in the slums, which I don't feature. And I'm ready to speak on that, but she steps out in the street and hails two cabs just like that. Then she hustles half the crew in with her and hands me a five-dollar bill and tells me to calculate 10 percent tip for the driver. And we're off. Me and Sugar and Junebug and Flyboy hangin out the window and hollering to everybody, putting lipstick on each other cause Flyboy a faggot anyway, and making farts with our sweaty armpits. But I'm mostly trying to figure how to spend this money. But they all fascinated with the meter ticking and Junebug starts laying bets as to how much it'll read when Flyboy can't hold his breath no more. Then Sugar lays bets as to how much it'll be when we get there. So I'm stuck. Don't nobody want to go for my plan, which is to jump out at the next light and run off to the first bar-b-que we can find. Then the driver tells us to get the hell out cause we there already. And the meter reads eighty-five cents. And I'm stalling to figure out the tip and Sugar say give him a dime. And I decide he don't need it bad as I do, so later for him. But then he tries to take off with Junebug foot still in the door so we talk about his mama something ferocious. Then we check out that we on Fifth Avenue and everybody dressed up in stockings. One lady in a fur coat, hot as it is. White folks crazy.

"This is the place," Miss Moore say, presenting it to us in the voice she uses at the museum. "Let's look in the windows before we go in."

"Can we steal?" Sugar asks very serious like she's getting the ground rules squared away before she plays. "I beg your pardon," say Miss Moore, and we fall out. So she leads us around the windows of the toy store and me and Sugar screamin, "This is mine, that's mine, I gotta have that, that was made for me, I was born for that," till Big Butt drowns us out.

"Hey, I'm goin to buy that there."

"That there? You don't even know what it is, stupid."

"I do so," he say punchin on Rosie Giraffe. "It's a microscope."

"Whatcha gonna do with a microscope, fool?"

"Look at things."

"Like what, Ronald?" ask Miss Moore. And Big Butt ain't got the first notion. So here go Miss Moore gabbing about the thousands of bacteria in a drop of water and the somethinorother in a speck of blood and the million and one living things in the air around us is invisible to the naked eye. And what she say that for? Junebug go to town on that "naked" and we rolling. Then Miss Moore ask what it cost. So we all jam into the window smudgin it up and the price tag say $300. So then she ask how long'd take for Big Butt and Junebug to save up their allowances. "Too long," I said. "Yeh," adds Sugar, "outgrown it by that time." And Miss Moore say no, you never outgrow learning instruments. "Why, even medical students and interns and," blah, blah, blah. And we ready to choke Big Butt for bringing it up in the first damn place.

"This here costs four hundred eighty dollars," say Rosie Giraffe. So we pile up all over her to see what she pointin out. My eyes tell me it's a chunk of glass cracked with something heavy and different-color inks dripped into the splits, then the whole thing put into a oven or something. But for $480 it don't make sense.

"That's a paperweight made of semi-precious stones fused together under tremendous pressure," she explains slowly, with her hands doing the mining and all the factory work.

"So what's a paperweight?" asks Rosie Giraffe.

"To weigh paper with, dumbbell," say Flyboy, the wise man from the East.

"Not exactly," say Miss Moore, which is what she say when you warm or way off too. "It's to weigh paper down so it won't scatter and make your desk untidy." So right away me and Sugar curtsy to each other and then to Mercedes who is more the tidy type.

"We don't keep paper on top of the desk in my class," say Junebug, figuring Miss Moore crazy or lyin one.

"At home, then," she say. "Don't you have a calendar and a pencil case and a blotter and a letter-opener on your desk at home where you do your homework?" And she know damn well what our homes look like cause she nosys around in them every chance she gets.

"I don't even have a desk," say Junebug. "Do we?"

"No. And I don't get no homework neither," say Big Butt.

"And I don't even have a home," say Flyboy like he do at school to keep the white folks off his back and sorry for him. Send this poor kid to camp posters, is his specialty.

"I do," say Mercedes. "I have a box of stationery on my desk and a picture of my cat. My godmother bought the stationery and the desk. There's a big rose on each sheet and the envelopes smell like roses."

"Who wants to know about your smelly-ass stationery," say Rosie Giraffe fore I can get my two cents in.

"It's important to have a work area all your own so that . . ."

"Will you look at this sailboat, please," say Flyboy, cuttin her off and pointin to the thing like it was his. So once again we tumble all over each other to gaze at this magnificent thing in the toy store which is just big enough to maybe sail two kittens across the pond if you strap them to the posts tight. We all start reciting the price tag like we in assembly. "Handcrafted sailboat of fiberglass at one thousand one hundred ninety-five dollars."

"Unbelievable," I hear myself say and am really stunned. I read it again for myself just in case the group recitation put me in a trance. Same thing. For some reason this pisses me off. We look at Miss Moore and she lookin at us, waiting for I dunno what.

"Who'd pay all that when you can buy a sailboat set for a quarter at Pop's, a tube of glue for a dime, and a ball of string for eight cents? "It must have a motor and a whole lot else besides," I say. "My sailboat cost me about fifty cents."

"But will it take water?" say Mercedes with her smart ass.

"Took mine to Alley Pond Park once," say Flyboy. "String broke, lost it. Pity."

"Sailed mine in Central Park and it keeled over and sank. Had to ask my father for another dollar."

"And you got the strap," laugh Big Butt. "The jerk didn't even have a string on it. My old man wailed on his behind."

Little Q.T. was staring hard at the sailboat and you could see he wanted it bad. But he too little and somebody'd just take it from him. So what the hell. "This boat for kids, Miss Moore?"

"Parents silly to buy something like that just to get all broke up," say Rosie Giraffe.

"That much money it should last forever," I figure.

"My father'd buy it for me if I wanted it."

"Your father, my ass," say Rosie Giraffe getting a chance to finally push Mercedes.

"Must be rich people shop here," say Q.T.

"You are a very bright boy," say Flyboy. "What was your first clue?" And he rap him on the head with the back of his knuckles, since Q.T. the only one he could get away with. Though Q.T. liable to come up behind you years later and got his licks in when you half expect it.

"What I want to know is," I say to Miss Moore though I never talk to her, I wouldn't give the bitch that satisfaction, "is how much a real boat costs? I figure a thousand'd get you a yacht any day."

"Why don't you check that out," she say, "and report back to the group?" Which really pains my ass. If you gonna mess up a perfectly good swim day least you could do is have some answers. "Lets go in," she say like she got something up her sleeve. Only she don't lead the way. So me and Sugar turn the corner to where the entrance is, but when we get there I kinda hang back. Not that I'm scared, what's there to be afraid of, just a toy store. But I feel funny, shame. But what I got to be shamed about? Got as much right to go in as anybody. But somehow I can't seem to got hold of the door, so I step away for Sugar to lead. But she hangs back too. And I look at her and she looks at me and this is ridiculous. I mean, damn, I have never ever been shy about doing nothing or going nowhere. But then Mercedes steps up and then Rosie Giraffe and Big Butt crowd in behind and shove, and next thing we all stuffed into the doorway with only Mercedes squeezing past us, smoothing out her jumper and walking right down the aisle. Then the rest of us tumble in like a glued-together jigsaw done all wrong. And people lookin at us. And it's like the time me and Sugar crashed into the Catholic church on a dare. But once we got in there and everything so hushed and holy and the candles and the bowin and the handkerchiefs on all the drooping heads, I just couldn't go through with the plan. Which was for me to run up to the altar and do a tap dance while Sugar played the nose flute and messed around in the holy water. And Sugar kept givin me the elbow. The later teased me so bad I tied her up in the shower and turned it on and locked her in. And she'd be there till this day if Aunt Gretchen hadn't finally figured I was lyin about the boarder takin a shower.

Same thing in the store. We all walkin on tiptoe and hardly touchin the games and puzzles and things. And I watched Miss Moore who is steady watchin us like she waitin for a sign. Like Mama Drewery watches the sky and sniffs the air and takes note of just how much slant is in the bird formation. Then me and Sugar bump smack into each other, so busy gazing at the toys, 'specially the sailboat. But we don't laugh and go into our fat-lady bump-stomach routine. We just stare at that price tag. Then Sugar run a finger over the whole boat. And I'm jealous and want to hit her. Maybe not her, but I sure want to punch somebody in the mouth.

"Watcha bring us here for, Miss Moore?"

"You sound angry, Sylvia. Are you mad about something?" Givin me one of them grins like she tellin a grown-up joke that never turns out to be funny. And she's lookin very closely at me like maybe she plannin to do my portrait from memory. I'm mad, but I won't give her that satisfaction. So I slouch around the store being very bored and say, "Let's go."

Me and Sugar at the back of the train watchin the tracks whizzin by large then small then gettin gobbled up in the dark. I'm thinkin about this tricky toy I saw in the store. A clown that somersaults on a bar then does chin-ups just cause you yank lightly at his leg. Cost $35. I could see me askin my mother for a $35 birthday clown. "You wanna who that costs what?" she'd say, cocking her head to the side to get a better view of the hole in my head. Thirty-five dollars could buy new bunk beds for Junior and Gretchen's boy. Thirty-five dollars and the whole household could go visit Granddaddy Nelson in the country. Thirty-five dollars would pay for the rent and the piano bill too. Who are these people that spend that much for performing clowns and $1,000 for toy sailboats? What kinda work they do and how they live and how come we ain't in on it? Where we are is who we are, Miss Moore always pointin out. But it don't necessarily have to be that way, she always adds then waits for somebody to say that poor people have to wake up and demand their share of the pie and don't none of us know what kind of pie she talkin about in the first damn place. But she ain't so smart cause I still got her four dollars from the taxi and she sure ain't gettin it. Messin up my day with this shit. Sugar nudges me in my pocket and winks.

Miss Moore lines us up in front of the mailbox where we started from, seem like years ago, and I got a headache for thinkin so hard. And we lean all over each other so we can hold up under the draggy-ass lecture she always finishes us off with at the end before we thank her for borin us to tears. But she just looks at us like she readin tea leaves. Finally she say, "Well, what did you think of F.A.O. Schwarz?"

Rosie Giraffe mumbles, "White folks crazy."

"I'd like to go there again when I get my birthday money," says Mercedes, and we shove her out the pack so she has to lean on the mailbox by herself.

"I'd like a shower. Tiring day," said Flyboy.

Then Sugar surprises me by sayin, "You know, Miss Moore, I don't think all of us here put together eat in a year what that sailboat costs." And Miss Moore lights up like somebody goosed her. "And?" she say, urging Sugar on. Only I'm standin on her foot so she don't continue.

"Imagine for a minute what kind of society it is in which some people can spend on a toy what it would cost to feed a family of six or seven. What do you think?"

"I think," say Sugar pushing me off her feet like she never done before, cause I whip her ass in a minute, "that this is not much of a democracy if you ask me. Equal chance to pursue happiness means an equal crack at the dough, don't it?" Miss Moore is besides herself and I am disgusted with Sugar's treachery. So I stand on her foot one more time to see if she'll shove me. She shuts up, and Miss Moore looks at me, sorrowfully I'm thinkin. And somethin weird is goin on, I can feel it in my chest.

"Anybody else learn anything today?" lookin dead at me. I walk away and Sugar has to run to catch up and don't even seem to notice when I shrug her arm off my shoulder.

"Well, we got four dollars anyway," she said.

"Uh hunh."

"We could go to Hascombs and get half a chocolate layer and then go to the Sunset and still have plenty money for potato chips and ice-cream sodas."

"Uh hunh."

"Race you to Hascombs," she say.

We start down the block and she gets ahead which is O.K. by me cause I'm goin to the West End and then over to the Drive to think this day through. She can run if she want to and even run faster. But ain't nobody gonna beat me at nuthin.

LYNDA GLENNON
(B. 1940)

Glennon was raised in a blue-collar Irish neighborhood in New Haven, Connecticut. In junior high school she became the leader of the Black Rebellion Girls' Club, modeled after Marlon Brando's gang in The Wild Ones, *but in senior year in high school she was both captain of the cheerleaders and class salutatorian. She became fascinated with studying, as well as acting out, such contradictions, as well as with the social differences manifest in town-gown tensions.*

After college, Glennon took a master's degree in sociology, though she found the dominant quantitative paradigms uninteresting. At the New School for Social Research, she found renewed interest in phenomenology and critical studies, and she has worked since to synthesize instrumental and expressive orientations in social thought and in significant social arrangements of family, sex roles, media, and the like. She is professor of sociology at Rollins College in Florida, where she has been a member of the faculty since 1980. Glennon is the author of Women and Dualism: A Sociology of Knowledge Analysis *(1979).*

YALE: REFLECTIONS ON
CLASS IN NEW HAVEN

For a long time I've avoided writing about my social-class experiences with Yale. What of my parents and friends back in New Haven? They will be scandalized by my unearthing this whole business of class conflict. But one of my personal and professional interests has become the study of social-class life styles, and, oh, how Yale plays a part in my personal struggles and in my very education!

YALE. Townspeople sound ambivalent when they say the word. "Yay'-illll," they intone, partly in resentment, partly in pride that the fancy university is in their home town. "Yay'-illll?" the stranger searches. "Oh yeah, that's that Ivy-Leaguer place, the one with the boola boola, bulldog bow wow wow, Eli Yale and all that, from 'the tables down at Mory's to the place where Louie dwells.'" What these names meant few of us knew, even though they were familiar in our world of working-class New Haveners. As a child hearing "We are poor little lambs who have lost our way," I would think of Little Bo Peep, and of "Black sheep black sheep have you any wool, Yes sir (or mam), yes sir, three bags full." Whenever I would ask my mother, "Who's Louie, Ma?" or "Who's Mory?" she would say she didn't know. I didn't know until my college years that Mory's "restaurant" was an exclusive association located on York Street next to the Yorkside restaurant where we would go for coffee after the movies and football games and next to where the old Yale Co-op used to be. In those days the Co-op's clothing and sporting goods sections were located at the far end of the building on York Street. I found magic in the window displays of blue-and-white striped scarves that Yale steadies wore and that for a time became the uniform of upper-middle-class females in New Haven, along with the required camel's hair polo coats. I could never afford to buy one, though I remember beginning to knit one and giving up after fifteen rows of the six feet required.

When I was a child I had only vague notions of what Yale was. I knew, of course, that it had a major presence in New Haven. "What's that building?" I'd ask my mother, spotting something that looked interesting. "Oh, that's part of Yale," she'd answer. "But what do they do in there?" I'd persist. "What's it for?" "I don't know; it's just part of Yale," she'd repeat. The tone of her voice would signal me to stop; I was treading on shaky grounds. I was not to ask her anything more about things she didn't know about and felt intimidated by. She did know Woolsey Hall, the Yale Bowl, and Peabody Museum. But these even I knew then. These were the buildings that entered into the daily lives of townspeople, even us working-class ones. Practically everybody knew Yale Bowl—the local radio station covered the games there, and besides we couldn't visit Aunt Josephine on those Saturdays when home football games were scheduled, the traffic was so bad. "Oh, it's Bowl traffic," was a common phrase. A lot of us knew that famous singers or musicians performed in Woolsey Hall from reading the placards in front of the building or their advertisements on the movie pages of *The New Haven Register.* And Peabody Museum was open to the public. We went there on Sunday afternoons once in a while, when my mother had exhausted the supply of stores that we could "window shop" in the downtown area of New Haven. Peabody Museum didn't have a "keep out" aura about it and we didn't feel unwelcome—there were too many other townspeople there for us to feel conspicuous, and lots of kids racing around hooting and hollering made the place very hang-loose. I never knew Yale had an art gallery until many years later when I was in college.

Somehow, even now, I can't imagine the presence of noisy, messy children at most of the rest of Yale. The images are just too contradictory. The only children I ever saw rode papoose style on their parents' backs even then, or they were the velvet-clad hothouse variety who looked like the twentieth-century version of Little Boy Blue. These children were different from the children I grew up with, and, more than their clothing, their language style set them apart from the rest of us kids, a style that one now hears from articulate child actors on some television commercials. These children at Yale speak the Queen's English at ages five and six, by God: "Pardon me, Auntie Emily, but may I have another dollop of sour cream on my baked potato?" Most of the kids I grew up with could hardly manage to keep the food in their mouths at that age, and were constantly getting walloped verbally or manually and told to be quiet, sit still, mind your manners, and eat what's on your plate. The poor starving children in China (then) would suffer worse hunger pains if I didn't finish my yellow waxed beans and unseasoned potato. (So I tried to sit still, be quiet, and save the world with every mouthful.) This was not the scene at the Yale family table, though. That conversation was erudite, worldly wise, and had shape. Most working-class children learn to speak that way, if at all, as a second language.

Any unusual, old, or expensive-looking architecture in New Haven almost invariably turned out to be Yale-connected. My family, like most other working-class families in New Haven, came to know the Yale campus in fragmented but personally relevant ways. When I went to college I began to match such names as Vanderbilt and Wright with the freshman buildings in the quadrangle of the Old Campus. Until then I had thought that these somber structures, up by where we used to park the family car for movie matinees as young high school girls, were either classroom buildings where mysterious mathematical formulae covered the blackboards, or that these were the offices where all the administrators could be found. The Forestry School up on Prospect Street became real to me after I had gotten an after-school job of picking up and delivering dictaphone tapes to a woman in my neighborhood who transcribed them. I had half-expected to run into Paul Bunyan in the halls, and I was disappointed to find dull, ordinary-looking, bureaucratic types in there, although once I did catch a glimpse of a man in a red-and-black plaid flannel shirt and field boots that fed my fantasy for weeks about what went on in that building. Ingalls Hockey Rink was built during my adolescence, and it was so unusual in shape that everybody in town commented on it. To some it was the whale, to some the turtle, to others Noah's Ark. "Ugh," my parents used to say, "that building is hideous, why would they ever build anything so crazy?" I thought it was kind of nice, partly in rebellion against my parents, partly because I was beginning to experience the social-class ambivalence that plagues working-class kids who find themselves in two social worlds.

My family came to know those Yale buildings in the passageways of our everyday life; buildings we passed on the way from our relatives' homes in one working-class district to our own in Fair Haven. Unlike the legally recognized East, West, and North Havens, Fair Haven was known only to old-time New Haveners, and sometimes only those who had some working-class ties, for it was the Irish-Italian enclave whose roots went back generations. It was thoroughly working-class in flavor; a few scattered lower-middle-class homes could be found there (lace-curtain Irish, especially), but the blood and guts were blue-collar. So when a Yale student asked me what part of New Haven I lived in, "Fair Haven" was never enough of a reply. At that time I thought merely that Yalies were out-of-towners and couldn't be expected to know the districts in a strange city. I realized much later that besides being out-of-towners they were also "out-of-classers." Certain knowing elites would reply "Oh, how very interesting," with that tone all working-class people know, and then politely excuse themselves. I was the exception in their lives, just as they were in mine. But for them New Haven was synonymous with Yale, and the city's inhabitants were simply nuisances that got in their way from time to time. I was the one made to feel odd and out of place.

The Yalies were a lot of trouble to townspeople. They would practically take over at meal times the streets bounding their dining halls; at class-changing times the streets throughout the campus would be congested with moving bodies. Elm Street was always very bad, up by Liggetts at York and Elm down to College Street. The

Yalies always seemed quietly ruthless and unself-consciously confident in their khaki slacks, blue oxford-cloth shirts, sleeves rolled twice, ties flapping in the breeze, running off to classes or dinner, crossing Elm Street, not bothering about traffic, oblivious. The townspeople resented this terribly. My father called them "rich boys" or "smart alecks." My young working-class dates would get furious if a Yalie crossed in front of a car they were driving without seeming to notice. "Get a Yalie," they'd yell, revving up the engine, while I would cry, "Don't do that," or "Stop it," giving them the perfect excuse to spare the life of the enemy. It was a ritual we took for granted. As these working-class males grew older and calmer they stopped noticing the insult of going unnoticed, stopped hoping a Yalie would run in front of their cars. Then it would take a real affront for one of them to rile one of us; we learned to call them names rather than to wish their demise. So "wise guy" and "smart aleck" (and their obscene renditions) peppered the air down Elm Street every day at these regular intervals. It was especially marked at the dinner hour because then the working-class folks would be coming home from work—hard, uninspiring work in jobs that did not allow them to control the rhythm of work, the breaks, or the pacing. This is the most difficult thing to take, the thing that most social critics miss who have never themselves had to survive working-class jobs. It's seldom the repetitiveness or the monotony of the job that causes alienation and demoraliza-tion, that erodes one's sense of pride and independence. It's being told when to start work, when to have a cigarette break; it's having to make an issue out of going to the toilet, and having gongs, bells, or even music dictate what has to be done next. And then driving home in cars that are falling apart but not yet paid for, the last straw for these working-class people is for some smart-ass-rich-Yalie to cross in front of a car in defiance of traffic rules, courtesy, or decent responsibility. It is too much. These privileged creatures seemed to make the whole world stop for them, wait for them, fear them.

Yalies seemed to be oblivious of the feelings of the townspeople, particularly the working-class ones. They took it for granted that these were their streets, that cars were intruders that didn't belong there. Townspeople feel that Yalies are guests of the town, that they come and go, but the people stay on. Yalies seem to think that they are New Haven.

The "townie" syndrome is vicious, but it was a long time before I got the full impact of its class dynamics. Coming into puberty, I began to look at Yalies as some-thing other than the "smart alecks" my father called them. I began to find them attractive. I first "discovered" Yale men one day in my first or second year of high school. Three of my girlfriends and I had gotten all the way to the College movie the-atre ticket booth one Sunday afternoon when we discovered we were short of money. It was a freezing cold day in late September, and we began to look for shelter from the wind. We started to saunter into an entranceway, just past what I later came to identify as Bingham Hall on Chapel Street. We felt very brave, as ex-members of The Black Rebellion Girls' Club (after Brando's Black Rebellion Motorcycle Club in *The Wild Ones)*, and we were still wearing B.R.G.C. uniforms—skintight jeans, navy shirts over yellow turtlenecks, dungaree jackets, and brown Western-style ankle boots. We found ourselves surrounded by two- and three-story long buildings, old and ivy-cov-ered. Like a spark hitting tinder the place was suddenly alive with hooting, hollering, catcalls, and whistling. Since this was the 'fifties, we were flattered. I thought, "Oh gee, I might get to meet a Yalie." They all seemed to be falling in love with us. "If you can't get a date get a Yalie"—a maxim that seemed to spring from a rage at being ignored was forgotten in that instant. And I did not know then that while sex and love are polarities for many men, they are so especially for Yalies and townies.

We somehow sensed that parading through the campus getting whistled at was not a good idea, so we never repeated that first experience. We had a gut-level intuition that such conduct would get us into trouble, although no one of us ever articulated what was wrong. Other working-class girls may not have been so lucky as to have such a strong peer group. For example, around the time of my freshman year in college the story of a girl who regularly held "court" in Yale dormitories, and offered her services to a line of eager young Yalies, was published locally. Those men who were caught were dismissed from Yale. The girl was charged with "lascivious carriage," and because she was only fifteen or sixteen was remanded to juvenile authorities.

Just as in the Elizabeth Ray scandal, one must understand that there is a strong pull by very virtue of class differences toward the men from the higher classes. It is not a matter of a woman's scanning several options and selecting the one that best advances self-interest. The life style of the working class does not include this middle-class emphasis on actively mastering one's environment, on rational calculation and primacy of self-interested action. In a society that makes those from the poorer classes feel shabby and as if they did not count for anything, it is easy for a girl to feel flattered by sexual attention from one of the privileged classes. Such attention can seem more desirable than being ignored, as though social class differences were temporarily equalized. The rude awakening comes much later when it becomes apparent that sex was mistaken for love. I struggled through these confusions along with my friends throughout adolescence. Any one of us might have come to the same fate had we not had the support of one another.

I used to find myself describing my home town to strangers as "New Haven—you know, the place where Yale is," with a sense of pride at having grown up next to so famous and fancy a place as Yale. I also used to say we had great cultural advantages—music, films, lectures, and theatre—"because of Yale." This went along with describing my alma mater, a small Catholic women's college (we called it a "girls'" college in those days), Albertus Magnus, as intellectually superior because it had some Yale professors on the staff who were induced by economic pressure or by the personal pleading of the "good nuns" to teach a course or two there. I now wonder what those teachers thought of the Aggie Maggies, as polarized a bunch were we: the suave but not so bright upper-middle-class girls and the socially inept but bright working-class girls. The temper of the place has changed since my four years that bridged the 'fifties and 'sixties, but then the school was geared to the needs and interests of the upper middle class, socially at least, and we commuters were always made to feel as though we were the poor relatives. It was here that I learned that verbal proficiency could masquerade as intelligence. It took years for me to speak without self-consciousness, trying to make some sense of the confusion of speech between working class and upper middle class.

Most of the commuters were from working-class backgrounds. We had to be unusually bright in order for someone besides our parents, already economically strapped and not enthusiastic about our spending four years in college, to notice us and spur us on to get a college education. I remember my mother's saying offhandedly that girls didn't really need to go to college; they could get good jobs without it. I just "happened" into college, having graduated second in my class in high school, and having taken to heart the assumption of everybody there that I should go to college. I was not a supermotivated achiever, although I liked theoretical discussions and social criticism, and had even then a satiric view of the world, having been the leader of the B.R.G.C. and then in my senior year captain of cheerleaders.

By the time of my graduation from high school the teachers had convinced my parents that I needed a good academic college, and one that was Catholic, too. The nuns at high school and my parents communicated to me that if I went to a secular school I'd lose the faith (like a wallet or a pair of mittens, I thought). So I chose Albertus Magnus, where for the first time I was exposed to an upper-middle-class life style.

I was convinced during my first two years there that I was hopelessly stupid, that all the work I had done up until now had been completely misjudged, and that a terrible mistake had been made, that I was actually quite stupid, if not retarded. It wasn't until later in my junior year that I was discovered and defined as a nascent intellectual by three of my teachers, a philosopher, a sociologist, and an English professor. I had also by my junior year become the reigning bohemian at the college, the president of the debate club, and the distress of the administrators, who were constantly reminding me that I represented the college and that I would simply have to do something about my appearance and manner. That meant that I was to become more like the upper-middle-class students, the ones who talked "nice," dressed sedately, and who smiled when they got in sticky situations. The administration didn't know what to make of my black leotards and turtlenecks, waist-length hair, and direct, unsmiling eye contact. One of the deans, a lace-curtain-Irish nun, asked me in each of the many confrontations in her office, "What are you staring at?" Staring was an un-middle-class thing to do; it made her ill at ease. I had no idea why she was so upset. I have since come to understand better the profound differences between social classes on this whole matter of self-presentation.

The college threw me into direct contact with Yale, especially through the mixers it arranged or got us invited to in our freshman year. I remember one such mixer in particular, held at some official-looking hall at Yale during our freshman orientation week. It was just terrible. I was asked to dance by a guy who looked like Mack the Knife, very slick—very clean lines—but a bit leering and sinister. Those days the typical Yalie was light-haired and crew-cutted, wearing the basic Ivy League uniform: khaki slacks, muted blue oxford-cloth button-down shirt, dark or striped knit tie, brown loafers or maybe desert boots—decidedly low-key or what they now call "laid back." This guy I met at the mixer was another basic Yalie type: headed for a career in finance management or corporate law. I didn't like him at all. He was wearing a navy blue flannel blazer with a crest on the pocket, and a navy and maroon rep tie. He said he lived in New York. No, actually he said he lived in Manhattan. I remember thinking "How unusual, calling New York 'Manhattan'," and I picked up that habit myself right then and there, and kept it for years afterward. Being marginal, I was always alert to the nuances of language. At that time I was uncritical of the very idea of social hierarchy so I tried my best to erase any traces of my "lower station." And calling Manhattan "New York" seemed by his very tone to be a gaffe, a sign that one was not knowing, was not "shoe," or, in short, had no class. I, the working-class child, felt ill at ease.

The sensitivity to being "in," to not being gauche, is not restricted to, but is particularly acute for, the working-class youngster. As a matter of fact, some working-class kids have little or no contact with the world of the upper or middle class, except on television, and escape that conflict, because class oppression requires a person-to-person encounter to be experienced as personal pain. The marginal youngster is torn between the desire to be welcomed in the group judged superior, and the desire to repudiate the group completely for its strangeness and for its presumption in judging. So I began to call New York "Manhattan" because I was afraid I'd be found out as a clod. At the same time I was beginning to question the whole system of class differences that could do such injury to the spirits of those caught in the ambiguities of the hierarchy.

It took much more exposure to Yale to begin to detect the finer points of class membership, which were glaringly obvious to class insiders. But this working-class child, who was just beginning to recognize that the working-class was considered less good than people who lived in the fancy houses and bought their clothes from the little shops near the campus, was in very strange territory.

My dancing partner's preparatory school was Andover. I had a vague notion that finishing or preparatory schools were for those who were deficient scholastically, as summer school provided a second chance to pass courses flunked during the regular year. I also remembered that a boy I had gone to school with was admitted to Yale on a scholarship on condition that he spend a year in a preparatory school to make up subjects lacking in his background. He was bright enough, but I had prided myself on being brighter. I thought indeed that he was being penalized for not being bright enough; that he was being sent to some detention station for scholastic deficiency. So this was my image of preparatory schools. It took about two years into college, some further abrasive encounters with the elites, and a sociology course for me to begin to make sense out of this alien system.

So this guy that I met at the mixer had gone to Andover, and was smooth as oil. I was wearing a dress I had made from some paisley cotton fabric cut from a Vogue pattern. The picture on the package looked very elegant indeed, but the actual dress looked ordinary, if not downright dowdy. I was also wearing a pin made out of some brass-alloy type metal molded into a cuckoo clock, with pendulums hanging on little chains and a bird perched atop the roof, the whole thing one-and-a-half by two-and-a-half inches (four inches if you count the pendulums). The stiffly painful conversation between this guy and me went from bad to worse. He asked if my pin (he called it a "brooch") was an heirloom. Lord, I got it from a box of junk jewelry my Aunt gave us kids to play with years before. So I was wearing this piece of discarded junk to hide the uneven stitching around the collar of my homemade dress and Mack the Elite asks me if it's an heirloom. I'll never forget how I felt. In my nervousness, I blurted out that it was my grandmother's. So then he talked about his grandmama and how she was very wealthy but in poor health, and that she was very slow to give out any of her precious jewelry for fear that the relatives would take advantage of her situation. Another blow. I tried to get the conversation back to my reality but to no avail. Saying that the pin was just "an old thing" didn't help much. Long silence. He then said he liked my dress. I said I had made it. Another long silence. He tried again with how nice it was to be able to sew; what a nice change it was from having to go and be fitted at tailor shops. Lord, I sewed because my parents couldn't afford any really decent dresses, what with taking out a loan for my tuition. I said his blazer was nice, but he just looked startled. I tried to change the conversation to sports. Did he play any, I asked. Oh yes, he leaped at this, he hoped to get on the lacrosse team. "What the hell is lacrosse?" I asked myself. And he was rather good at cricket, he added. I felt hopelessly unable to say I didn't have a clue as to what he was talking about. But it wasn't so much a lack of courage on my part;

we just had no common ground whatsoever. Nowadays I have the presence of self to treat such differences as interesting, and the upper-class person as somewhat provincial and sheltered not to realize that such cultural oddities are just that to the majority of the population. But not then. I was thoroughly intimidated and all I wanted to do was to get out of there, to get to a place where I could feel comfortable and sure of my signals, where everything I said wouldn't be misread, where the assumptions about me and my background would be the correct ones. At some point in the encounter I noticed the slow turning of Mack the Elite. He began to look at me as though I was slightly untouchable. I began to feel vermin-ridden. It was not a good feeling.

Mack the Elite was one of the few genuine stereotypes I met at Yale. I did meet many Yalies during my college years, but out of that number only a few fit the pure type. The others were those on scholarship, or those who had become steadies of upper-middle-class students at Albertus Magnus, or those who had some tie with organizations I belonged to: political clubs and the debating team. The pure types— the upper-class WASP's who had impeccable credentials prepped at the best schools, had had money in the family for generations, were listed in the Social Register, and had dinner rights to all the other families in the elite circle—these I would meet by some fluke. One such fluke might be that their hometown sweethearts were taken ill and couldn't visit that weekend, so the guy ended up at a fraternity party or room party, or occasionally at one of the two or three mixers the college sponsored for us our first few years there. (Dick Cavett labeled Albertus Magnus, along with the Nursing School and Hillhouse High, as "frontiers of desperation" for dateless Yalies, in his memoirs, a piece of snobbery most take for granted at Yale.) I watched with dismay as several of my friends got their hearts broken as it finally dawned on them that their great loves at Yale only saw them during the week and that big weekends were reserved for their serious attachments back home. "We're a geographical convenience, that's all we are," one of my friends used to chant.

Two of my commuter friends and I were almost tossed out of school one time for sending personal invitations to a mixer in the old stable at the college. We decided that the general invitation to the Thomas More Club was just not good enough. We went through the Yale Directory of the Class of '62 and picked out the most attractive looking Yalies we found and sent out forty or so invitations. Our Dean of Students was appalled. One of us got the penalty of stuffing envelopes for fifteen hours in the Alumnae Office for this misdeed and we were spared suspension. Through this mixer, though, I met another one of the genuine articles. He even belonged to a secret society, housed in one of those coffins of a building, vaguely Egyptian, with no windows; it looked like a huge mausoleum, a tomb covered with ivy. One rumor among us kids as we were growing up was that the building was entirely filled with water—a cubic swimming pool, we imagined, that rose three stories. We half expected to see a Pharaoh emerge dressed in Harris tweed with a pipe clenched in his teeth, wearing royal headdress, and leading a sphinx on a chain. When I was a child my fantasy hodgepodge had little relationship to reality once I moved outside my neighborhood. My comic-book diet ran to *Archie, Casper the Friendly Ghost, Little Lulu, Superman,* and *Wonder Woman,* with an occasional horror diversion or true romance saga. I did not grow up reading those educational books middle-class uncles and aunts give for birthday and Christmas presents, books about pyramids, butterflies, how airplanes work, and where Japan, Egypt, and the Persian Gulf are. Remember, also, that I didn't grow up with television. I was almost adolescent before my parents were convinced TV wasn't a crazy thing to buy, and had saved up enough for a down payment. Up until then I watched television only occasionally at a friend's whose father worked as a delivery man for an appliance store and got a discount on a set. On Sunday nights we would sometimes visit acquaintances of my parents who had a rumpus room (that is, a cellar with linoleum) and would tune into Ted Mack's Amateur Hour.

It was very difficult growing up in the shadow of Yale, attending a school that was on the receiving end of its class bias but yet was so totally uncritical of Yale and all it represented. Yale had, of course, professional giants, and perhaps even a few geniuses. No doubt many of its people were free from class bias, but the image it projected was one of cultural imperialism, impressing the young Yalies with its sophistication and erudition. They tried frantically to fit the style, but those I met came off like a bad imitation: silly, bitchy, or just plain unfunny.

A friend recently called my attention to an article in *The New York Times Magazine* (February 1, 1976) on Yale's elitism. In fact, the subject of the article was not Yale, but Brown. Such is my ambivalence still that I thought, first, "How could anyone confuse Yale with Brown! Yale stands alone," and then, as I skimmed the actual article and read about the fashionably initialed luggage, the mutual checking out of one another that takes place as students return to classes in September, I remembered the old feelings of being poor, of being judged unworthy of respect because I didn't have all those things the others had: the tailored tweeds, the little leather clutch bags, the Pendleton plaids, or any of those things that were advertised in *The New Yorker*. (Ah, *The New Yorker!* They put in all those cartoons to keep working-class people from getting completely depressed over the insurmountable gap between their life style and that represented by the commodities pictured in its ads.)

The Brown article triggered those old feelings of envy, inadequacy, and outrage I had growing up next to Yale. Yale's style was so alien to us that it was almost like having another country in the middle of town. New Haven felt like an occupied zone. From this vantage point it is easy to understand the hatred colonized people have toward the colonizer. It is also easy to understand how colonized people have to struggle with the problem of identifying with the colonizers. I and most of my friends went through stages where we felt that the Yale way was superior; that that way of dressing, talking, holding conversations, being witty, entertaining, relaxing—the whole works—was better than ours. We all, at one time or another, felt that we were inferior, of no use at all; that their oak-paneled life was the best this world had to offer.

What nonsense all this has become. But as a child riding past its old, expensive, and mysterious-looking buildings I would almost feel the sacredness emanating. And the ivy-covered walls! God, those were really there, just as in all those old songs and stories. The buildings seemed too fine for me, and I would get the same feeling for the entire building that I would get if I dreamed of being in the wrong upper-middle-class home facing its little tea tables, the linen napkins, the crystal and silver nut dishes and porcelain ashtrays, the muted pastels, oriental rugs, bud vases, silk and velvet upholstery, and petits fours on silver dessert trays. An after-dinner-mint wonderland. I felt out of place, the bull in the china shop, the screaming red in a world of pastel gentility. Yale was much more solid oak, vibrant earth tones, marble and gold, parchment and antiquity. Nonetheless, I felt the same way in both social circles.

When I was a child these Yale buildings looked like magic castles, but after living with a sacred object so long, it becomes taken for granted. But some took longer to fade into acceptance than others. Woolsey Hall for a long time looked like a magnificent Byzantine mosque to me. It had huge pillars lining the entranceway, ten or fifteen of them, tile mosaic floors, and a massive dome all gold and gleaming. Once or twice our College Glee Club performed there, and I remember going to an Erich Fromm lecture there once. The fortress-like entrances to the residential colleges had archways, each with a coat of arms emblazoned on the top, through which one peeped into another magic world of ivy and brick and neat rectangles of grass. Most entrances had formidable looking iron gates. I always had the feeling I would be arrested the minute I set foot past the gate, even those times that I was escorted by a Yalie date, by the gatekeepers who lived in little stone cubicles just past the iron gates.

The out-of-town women, or those who looked affluent and self-confident, like a rich Nancy Drew, always seemed to float past such barriers. After the scandal of the young girl in the college, I and my working-class friends were questioned thoroughly if we went to meet our dates unescorted. Not Nancy Drew, though. She got a smile and was waved on. Her tweed skirt, Gucci shoes, camel's hair coat and Yale-striped scarf, like the one we used to ooh and aah over at the Yale Co-op, assured her immediate entry anywhere on campus. Her spring uniform in the early 'sixties consisted of the Cos Cob look, straight from the pages of *The New Yorker:* tiny rosebud prints in pastel on cream-colored duck fabric, pastel cashmere cardigans, A-lines and Peter Pan collars, accented with circle pins and matching barrettes. The style has changed now (working-class Mary Hartman is dressed this way in the 'seventies, appropriately), but the manner is consistently self-confident and unself-conscious. These women looked Yale, we didn't, even though the guards had never been given instructions that Pendleton, Gucci, J. Press, Abercrombie and Fitch, and Cos Cob were to be given first-class treatment. They just knew, just as the rest of the society learns that there are different social classes and that people are to be treated as befits their station. Never in these words, though. The lesson is always couched in such terms as someone's belonging to a "better class of people," as someone else's being "rough-cut" or "unpolished," or as being "riff-raff." No matter. When these terms are correlated with specific status possessions and life styles it is social classes that are being referred to. All this in a country that declares that we have no social classes. This blindness to the realities of class is not an affliction of the average citizen alone. The head of all research activities at one of the major television networks recently told me that America had no social-class system at all. Having come from a European country where class distinctions are blatant he found America classless by contrast. But this is rather like declaring that the Northern United States is free of racism because its manifestations are not so obvious as they are in the South. So too it is with social class, except that few are willing to define the problem as one of class. It seems to be a difficult step to take to substitute the terms lower, middle and upper classes for the folksy terms in use now. For if the objective conditions of class are understood as tied to social fate, we could stop assuming that ineptness, self-consciousness, and lack of polish are random, and that polish is a sign of moral superiority. The polish or lack of polish results simply from being born into a particular family at a particular time in history. Simply that.

GLORIA NAYLOR

(B. 1950)

In an interview with Toni Morrison, Naylor said that reading Morrison's novel The Bluest Eye *in 1977 was key to enabling her to begin writing about her own experiences. Up to that point, Naylor said, all the great writers she had read were male or white, or both, so she had to wonder whether her own story was worth telling. The inspiration supplied by Morrison rapidly brought fruit; Naylor submitted her first story to* Essence *magazine in 1979, and finished her first book,* The Women of Brewster Place, *in 1981, the same year that she completed a B.A. at Brooklyn College.*

She had come to Brooklyn College, and before that to Medgar Evers College, after leaving the Jehovah's Witnesses, with which she had been affiliated for seven years, and in which she had served as a full-time worker in New York, North Carolina, and Florida. But while the Witnesses helped her overcome her initial shyness, they did not finally solve the problems of her life, and after a period of personal difficulties, Naylor left the religion and began college, although she continued to work throughout as a switchboard operator. After graduating from Brooklyn and completing her first book, Naylor took a master's degree in African-American studies at Yale; her second book, Linden Hills *(1985), also served as her master's thesis. With its publication, she was firmly launched on a literary career, receiving National Endowment for the Arts and later Guggenheim fellowships and serving in a variety of positions as lecturer, visiting writer, and fellow. Her fourth book,* Bailey's Cafe *(1992), was produced by the Hartford Stage Company in 1994. Her other works include* Mama Day *(1988) and* The Men of Brewster Place *(1998).*

Naylor has drawn on her family and her experiences as a Jehovah's Witness in her books, but they are not really autobiographical. She links the stories of The Women of Brewster Place *by turning characters and events mentioned in one story into the centers of another. As in most of Naylor's work, the stories reflect the struggles of their black female protagonists to live in a corrupt and dangerous world where safety, much less stability, is often an illusion, and hope and mutual support the only avenues to survival.*

KISWANA BROWNE

From the window of her sixth-floor studio apartment, Kiswana could see over the wall at the end of the street to the busy avenue that lay just north of Brewster Place. The late-afternoon shoppers looked like brightly clad marionettes as they moved between the congested traffic, clutching their packages against their bodies to guard them from sudden bursts of the cold autumn wind. A portly mailman had abandoned his cart and was bumping into indignant windowshoppers as he puffed behind the cap that the wind had snatched from his head. Kiswana leaned over to see if he was going to be successful, but the edge of the building cut him off from her view.

A pigeon swept across her window, and she marveled at its liquid movements in the air waves. She placed her dreams on the back of the bird and fantasized that it would glide forever in transparent silver circles until it ascended to the center of the universe and was swallowed up. But the wind died down, and she watched with a sigh as the bird beat its wings in awkward, frantic movements to land on the corroded top of a fire escape on the opposite building. This brought her back to earth.

Humph, it's probably sitting over there crapping on those folks' fire escape, she thought. Now, that's a safety hazard. . . . And her mind was busy again, creating flames and smoke and frustrated tenants whose escape was being hindered because they were slipping and sliding in pigeon shit. She watched their cussing, haphazard descent on the fire escapes until they had reached the bottom. They were milling around, oblivious to their burning apartments, angrily planning to march on the mayor's office about the pigeons. She materialized placards and banners for them, and they had just reached the corner, boldly sidestepping fire hoses and broken glass, when they all vanished.

A tall copper-skinned woman had met this phantom parade at the corner, and they had dissolved in front of her long, confident strides. She plowed through the remains of their faded mists, unconscious of the lingering wisps of their presence on her leather bag and black fur-trimmed coat. It took a few seconds for this transfer from one realm to another to reach Kiswana, but then suddenly she recognized the woman.

"Oh, God, it's Mama!" She looked down guiltily at the forgotten newspaper in her lap and hurriedly circled random job advertisements.

By this time Mrs. Browne had reached the front of Kiswana's building and was checking the house number against a piece of paper in her hand. Before she went into the building she stood at the bottom of the stoop and carefully inspected the condition of the street and the adjoining property. Kiswana watched this meticulous inventory with growing annoyance but she involuntarily followed her mother's slowly rotating head, forcing herself to see her new neighborhood through the older woman's eyes. The brightness of the unclouded sky seemed to join forces with her mother as it highlighted every broken stoop railing and missing brick. The afternoon sun glittered and cascaded across even the tiniest fragments of broken bottle, and at that very moment the wind chose to rise up again, sending unswept grime flying into the air, as a stray tin can left by careless garbage collectors went rolling noisily down the center of the street.

Kiswana noticed with relief that at least Ben wasn't sitting in his usual place on the old garbage can pushed against the far wall. He was just a harmless old wino, but Kiswana knew her mother only needed one wino or one teenager with a reefer within a twenty-block radius to decide that her daughter was living in a building seething with dope factories and hang-outs for derelicts. If she had seen Ben, nothing would have made her believe that practically every apartment contained a family, a Bible, and a dream that one day enough could be scraped from those meager Friday night paychecks to make Brewster Place a distant memory.

As she watched her mother's head disappear into the building, Kiswana gave silent thanks that the elevator was broken. That would give her at least five minutes' grace to straighten up the apartment. She rushed to the sofa bed and hastily closed it without smoothing the rumpled sheets and blanket or removing her nightgown. She felt that somehow the tangled bedcovers would give away the fact that she had not slept alone last night. She silently apologized to Abshu's memory as she heartlessly crushed his spirit between the steel springs of the couch. Lord, that man was sweet. Her toes curled involuntarily at the passing thought of his full lips moving slowly over her instep. Abshu was a foot man, and he always started his lovemaking from the bottom up. For that reason Kiswana changed the color of the polish on her toenails every week. During the course of their relationship she had gone from shades of red to brown and was now into the purples. I'm gonna have to start mixing them soon, she thought aloud as she turned from the couch and raced into the bathroom to remove any traces of Abshu from there. She took up his shaving cream and razor and threw them into the bottom drawer of her dresser beside her diaphragm. Mama wouldn't dare pry into my drawers right in front of me, she thought as she slammed the drawer shut. Well, at least not the *bottom* drawer. She may come up with some sham excuse for opening the top drawer, but never the bottom one.

When she heard the first two short raps on the door, her eyes took a final flight over the small apartment, desperately seeking out any slight misdemeanor that might have to be defended. Well, there was nothing she could do about the crack in the wall over that table. She had been after the landlord to fix it for two months now. And there had been no time to sweep the rug, and everyone knew that off-gray always looked dirtier than it really was. And it was just too damn bad about the kitchen. How was she expected to be out job-hunting every day and still have time to keep a kitchen that looked like her mother's, who didn't even work and still had someone come in twice a month for general cleaning. And besides . . .

Her imaginary argument was abruptly interrupted by a second series of knocks, accompanied by a penetrating, "Melanie, Melanie, are you there?"

Kiswana strode toward the door. She's starting before she even gets in here. She knows that's not my name anymore.

She swung the door open to face her slightly flushed mother. "Oh, hi, Mama. You know, I thought I heard a knock, but I figured it was for the people next door, since no one hardly ever calls me Melanie." Score one for me, she thought.

"Well it's awfully strange you can forget a name you answered to for twenty-three years," Mrs. Browne said, as she moved past Kiswana into the apartment. "My, that was a long climb. How long has your elevator been out? Honey, how do you manage with your laundry and groceries up all those steps? But I guess you're young, and it wouldn't bother you as much as it does me." This long string of questions told Kiswana that her mother had no intentions of beginning her visit with another argument about her new African name.

"You know I would have called before I came, but you don't have a phone yet. I didn't want you to feel that I was snooping. As a matter of fact, I didn't expect to find you home at all. I thought you'd be out looking for a job." Mrs. Browne had mentally covered the entire apartment while she was taking off her coat.

"Well, I got up late this morning. I thought I'd buy the afternoon paper and start early tomorrow."

"That sounds like a good idea." Her mother moved toward the window and picked up the discarded paper and glanced over the hurriedly circled ads. "Since when do you have experience as a fork-lift operator?"

Kiswana caught her breath and silently cursed herself for her stupidity. "Oh, my hand slipped—I meant to circle file clerk." She quickly took the paper before her mother could see that she had also marked cutlery salesman and chauffeur.

"You're sure you weren't sitting here moping and day-dreaming again?" Amber specks of laughter flashed in the corner of Mrs. Browne's eyes.

Kiswana threw her shoulders back and unsuccessfully tried to disguise her embarrassment with indignation.

"Oh, God, Mama! I haven't done that in years—it's for kids. When are you going to realize that I'm a woman now?" She sought desperately for some womanly thing to do and settled for throwing herself on the couch and crossing her legs in what she hoped looked like a nonchalant arc.

"Please, have a seat," she said, attempting the same tones and gestures she'd seen Bette Davis use on the late movies.

Mrs. Browne, lowering her eyes to hide her amusement, accepted the invitation and sat at the window, also crossing her legs. Kiswana saw immediately how it should have been done. Her celluloid poise clashed loudly against her mother's quiet dignity, and she quickly uncrossed her legs. Mrs. Browne turned her head toward the window and pretended not to notice.

"At least you have a halfway decent view from here. I was wondering what lay beyond that dreadful wall—it's the boulevard. Honey, did you know that you can see the trees in Linden Hills from here?"

Kiswana knew that very well, because there were many lonely days that she would sit in her gray apartment and stare at those trees and think of home, but she would rather have choked than admit that to her mother.

"Oh, really, I never noticed. So how is Daddy and things at home?"

"Just fine. We're thinking of redoing one of the extra bedrooms since you children have moved out, but Wilson insists that he can manage all that work alone. I told him that he doesn't really have the proper time or energy for all that. As it is, when he gets home from the office, he's so tired he can hardly move. But you know you can't tell your father anything. Whenever he starts complaining about how stubborn you are, I tell him the child came by it honestly. Oh, and your brother was by yesterday," she added, as if it had just occurred to her.

So that's it, thought Kiswana. That's why she's here.

Kiswana's brother, Wilson, had been to visit her two days ago, and she had borrowed twenty dollars from him to get her winter coat out of layaway. That son-of-a-bitch probably ran straight to Mama—and after he swore he wouldn't say anything. I should have known, he was always a snotty-nosed sneak, she thought.

"Was he?" she said aloud. "He came by to see me, too, earlier this week. And I borrowed some money from him because my unemployment checks hadn't cleared in the bank, but now they have and everything's just fine." There, I'll beat you to that one.

"Oh, I didn't know that," Mrs. Browne lied. "He never mentioned you. He had just heard that Beverly was expecting again, and he rushed over to tell us."

Damn. Kiswana could have strangled herself.

"So she's knocked up again, huh?" she said irritably.

Her mother started. "Why do you always have to be so crude?"

"Personally, I don't see how she can sleep with Willie. He's such a dishrag."

Kiswana still resented the stance her brother had taken in college. When everyone at school was discovering their blackness and protesting on campus, Wilson never took part; he had even refused to wear an Afro. This had outraged Kiswana because, unlike her, he was dark-skinned and had the type of hair that was thick and kinky enough for a good "Fro." Kiswana had still insisted on cutting her own hair, but it was so thin and fine-textured, it refused to thicken even after she washed it. So she had to brush it up and spray it with lacquer to keep it from lying flat. She never forgave Wilson for telling her that she didn't look African, she looked like an electrocuted chicken.

"Now that's some way to talk. I don't know why you have an attitude against your brother. He never gave me a restless night's sleep, and now he's settled with a family and a good job."

"He's an assistant to an assistant junior partner in a law firm. What's the big deal about that?"

"The job has a future, Melanie. And at least he finished school and went on for his law degree."

"In other words, not like me, huh?"

"Don't put words into my mouth, young lady. I'm perfectly capable of saying what I mean."

Amen, thought Kiswana.

"And I don't know why you've been trying to start up with me from the moment I walked in. I didn't come here to fight with you. This is your first place away from home, and I just wanted to see how you were living and if you're doing all right. And I must say, you've fixed this apartment up very nicely."

"Really, Mama?" She found herself softening in the light of her mother's approval.

"Well, considering what you had to work with." This time she scanned the apartment openly.

"Look, I know it's not Linden Hills, but a lot can be done with it. As soon as they come and paint, I'm going to hang my Ashanti print over the couch. And I thought a big Boston Fern would go well in that corner, what do you think?"

"That would be fine, baby. You always had a good eye for balance."

Kiswana was beginning to relax. There was little she did that attracted her mother's approval. It was like a rare bird, and she had to tread carefully around it lest it fly away.

"Are you going to leave that statue out like that?"

"Why, what's wrong with it? Would it look better somewhere else?"

There was a small wooden reproduction of a Yoruba goddess with large protruding breasts on the coffee table.

"Well," Mrs. Browne was beginning to blush, "it's just that it's a bit suggestive, don't you think? Since you live alone now, and I know you'll be having male friends stop by, you wouldn't want to be giving them any ideas. I mean, uh, you know, there's no point in putting yourself in any unpleasant situations because they may get the wrong impressions and uh, you know, I mean, well . . ." Mrs. Browne stammered on miserably.

Kiswana loved it when her mother tried to talk about sex. It was the only time she was at a loss for words.

"Don't worry, Mama." Kiswana smiled. "That wouldn't bother the type of men I date. Now maybe if it had big feet . . ." And she got hysterical, thinking of Abshu.

Her mother looked at her sharply. "What sort of gibberish is that about feet? I'm being serious, Melanie."

"I'm sorry, Mama." She sobered up. "I'll put it away in the closet," she said, knowing that she wouldn't.

"Good," Mrs. Browne said, knowing that she wouldn't either. "I guess you think I'm too picky, but we worry about you over here. And you refuse to put in a phone so we can call and see about you."

"I haven't refused, Mama. They want seventy-five dollars for a deposit, and I can't swing that right now."

"Melanie I can give you the money."

"I don't want you to be giving me money—I've told you that before. Please, let me make it by myself."

"Well, let me lend it to you, then."

"No!"

"Oh, so you can borrow money from your brother, but not from me."

Kiswana turned her head from the hurt in her mother's eyes. "Mama, when I borrow from Willie, he makes me pay him back. You never let me pay you back," she said into her hands.

"I don't care. I still think it's downright selfish of you to be sitting over here with no phone, and sometimes we don't hear from you in two weeks—anything could happen—especially living among these people."

Kiswana snapped her head up. "What do you mean, *these people*. They're my people and yours, too, Mama—we're all black. But maybe you've forgotten that over in Linden Hills."

"That's not what I'm talking about, and you kow it. These streets—this building—it's so shabby and rundown. Honey, you don't have to live like this."

"Well, this is how poor people live."

"Melanie, you're not poor."

"No, Mama, *you're* not poor. And what you have and I have are two totally different things. I don't have a husband in real estate with a five-figure income and a home in Linden Hills—*you* do. What I have is a weekly unemployment check and an overdrawn checking account at United Federal. So this studio on Brewster is all I can afford."

"Well, you could afford a lot better," Mrs. Browne snapped, "if you hadn't dropped out of college and had to resort to these dead-end clerical jobs."

"Uh-huh, I knew you'd get around to that before long." Kiswana could feel the rings of anger begin to tighten around her lower backbone, and they sent her forward onto the couch. "You'll never understand, will you? Those bourgie schools were counterrevolutionary. My place was in the streets with my people, fighting for equality and a better community."

"Counterrevolutionary!" Mrs. Browne was raising her voice. "Where's your revolution now, Melanie? Where are all those black revolutionaries who were shouting and demonstrating and kicking up a lot of dust with you on that campus? Huh? They're sitting in wood-paneled offices with their degrees in mahogany frames, and they won't even drive their cars past this street because the city doesn't fix potholes in this part of town."

"Mama," she said, shaking her head slowly in disbelief, "how can you—a black woman—sit there and tell me that what we fought for during the Movement wasn't important just because some people sold out?"

"Melanie, I'm not saying it wasn't important. It was damned important to stand up and say that you were proud of what you were and to get the vote and other social opportunities for every person in this country who had it due. But you kids thought you were going to turn the world upside down, and it just wasn't so. When the smoke had cleared, you found yourself with a fistful of new federal laws and a country still full of obstacles for black people to fight their way over just because they're black. There was no revolution, Melanie, and there will be no revolution."

"So what am I supposed to do, huh? Just throw up my hands and not care about what happens to my people? I'm not supposed to keep fighting to make things better?"

"Of course, you can. But you're going to have to fight within the system, because it and these so-called 'bourgie' schools are are going to be here for a long time. And that means that you get smart like a lot of your old friends and get an important job where you you can have some influence. You don't have to sell out, as you say, and work for some corporation, but you could become an assemblywoman or a civil liberties lawyer or open a freedom school in this very neighborhood. That way you could really help the community. But what help are you going to be to these people on Brewster while you're living hand-to-mouth on file-clerk jobs waiting for a revolution? You're wasting your talents, child."

"Well, I don't think they're being wasted. At least I'm here in day-to-day contact with the problems of my people. What good would I be after four or five years of a lot of white brainwashing in some phony, prestige institution, huh? I'd be like you and Daddy and those other educated blacks sitting over there in Linden Hills with a terminal case of middle-class amnesia."

"You don't have to live in a slum to be concerned about social conditions, Melanie. Your father and I have been charter members of the NAACP for the last twenty-five years."

"Oh, God!" Kiswana threw her head back in exaggerated disgust. "That's being concerned? That middle-of-the-road, Uncle Tom dumping ground for black Republicans!"

"You can sneer all you want, young lady, but that organization has been working for black people since the turn of the century, and it's still working for them. Where are all those radical groups of yours that were going to put a Cadillac in every garage and Dick Gregory in the White House? I'll tell you where."

I knew you would, Kiswana thought angrily.

"They burned themselves out because they wanted too much too fast. Their goals weren't grounded in reality. And that's always been your problem."

"What do you mean, my problem? I know exactly what I'm about."

"No, you don't. You constantly live in a fantasy world—always going to extremes—turning butterflies into eagles, and life isn't about that. It's accepting what is and working from that. Lord, I remember how worried you had me, putting all that lacquered hair spray on your head. I thought you were going to get lung cancer—trying to be what you're not."

Kiswana jumped up from the couch. "Oh, God, I can't take this anymore. Trying to be something I'm not—trying to be something I'm not, Mama! Trying to be proud of my heritage and the fact that I was of African descent. If that's being what I'm not, then I say fine. But I'd rather be dead than be like you—a white man's nigger who's ashamed of being black!"

Kiswana saw streaks of gold and ebony light follow her mother's flying body out of the chair. She was swung around by the shoulders and made to face the deadly stillness in the angry woman's eyes. She was too stunned to cry out from the pain of the long fingernails that dug into her shoulders, and she was brought so close to her mother's face that she saw her reflection, distorted and wavering, in the tears that stood in the older woman's eyes. And she listened in that stillness to a story she had heard from a child.

"My grandmother," Mrs. Browne began slowly in a whisper, "was a full-bloodied Iroquois, and my grandfather a free black from a long line of journeymen who had lived in Connecticut since the establishment of the colonies. And my father was a Bajan who came to this country as a cabin boy on a merchant mariner."

"I know all that," Kiswana said, trying to keep her lips from trembling.

"Then, know this." And the nails dug deeper into her flesh. "I am alive because of the blood of proud people who never scraped or begged or apologized for what they were. They lived asking only one thing of this world—to be allowed to be. And I learned through the blood of these people that black isn't beautiful and it isn't ugly—black is! It's not kinky hair and it's not straight hair—it just is.

"It broke my heart when you changed your name. I gave you my grandmother's name, a woman who bore nine children and educated them all, who held off six white men with a shotgun when they tried to drag one of her sons to jail for 'not knowing his place.' Yet you needed to reach into an African dictionary to find a name to make you proud.

"When I brought my babies home from the hospital, my ebony son and my golden daughter, I swore before whatever gods would listen—those of my mother's people or those of my father's people—that I would use everything I had and could ever get to see that my children were prepared to meet this world on its own terms, so that no one could sell them short and make them ashamed of what they were or how they looked—whatever they were or however they looked. And Melanie, that's not being white or red or black—that's being a mother."

Kiswana followed her reflection in the two single tears that moved down her mother's cheeks until it blended with them into the woman's copper skin. There was nothing and then so much that she wanted to say, but her throat kept closing up every time she tried to speak. She kept her head down and her eyes closed, and thought, Oh, God, just let me die. How can I face her now?

Mrs. Browne lifted Kiswana's chin gently. "And the one lesson I wanted you to learn is not to be afraid to face anyone, not even a crafty old lady like me who can outtalk you." And she smiled and winked.

"Oh, Mama, I . . ." and she hugged the woman tightly.

"Yeah, baby." Mrs. Browne patted her back. "I know."

She kissed Kiswana on the forehead and cleared her throat. "Well, now, I better be moving on. It's getting late, there's dinner to be made, and I have to get off my feet—these new shoes are killing me."

Kiswana looked down at the beige leather pumps. "Those are really classy. They're English, aren't they?"

"Yes, but, Lord, do they cut me right across the instep." She removed the shoe and sat on the couch to massage her foot.

Bright red nail polish glared at Kiswana through the stockings. "Since when do you polish your toenails?" she gasped. "You never did that before."

"Well . . ." Mrs. Browne shrugged her shoulders, "your father sort of talked me into it, and, uh, you know, he likes it and all, so I thought, uh, you know, why not, so . . ." And she gave Kiswana an embarrassed smile.

I'll be damned, the young woman thought, feeling her whole face tingle. Daddy's into feet! And she looked at the blushing woman on her couch and suddenly realized that her mother had trod through the same universe that she herself was now traveling. Kiswana was breaking no new trails and would eventually end up just two feet away on that couch. She stared at the woman she had been and was to become.

"But I'll never be a Republican," she caught herself saying aloud.

"What are you mumbling about, Melanie?" Mrs. Browne slipped on her shoe and got up from the couch.

She went to get her mother's coat. "Nothing, Mama. It's really nice of you to come by. You should do it more often."

"Well, since it's not Sunday, I guess you're allowed at least one lie."

They both laughed.

After Kiswana had closed the door and turned around, she spotted an envelope sticking between the cushions of her couch. She went over and opened it up; there was seventy-five dollars in it.

"Oh, Mama, darn it!" She rushed to the window and started to call to the woman, who had just emerged from the building, but she suddenly changed her mind and sat down in the chair with a long sigh that caught in the upward draft of the autumn wind and disappeared over the top of the building.

ROBERT COLES

(B. 1929)

As an undergraduate at Harvard, Robert Coles wrote his senior thesis on the work of William Carlos Williams, both a doctor and a poet. Like Williams, Coles has combined writing with medicine, specifically psychiatry, and more specifically yet, the lives of children and young people facing the anxieties, threats, and opportunities presented by social change.

Coles received his medical degree from Columbia's College of Physicians and Surgeons, interned at the University of Chicago hospital, and did his residency in psychiatry at Massachusetts General Hospital and at McLean Hospital. He held a number of positions at Boston-area psychiatric clinics, then served as a physician in the Air Force from 1958 to 1960. In 1963, he became a researcher at Harvard University Health Services as well as a lecturer in general education at Harvard University.

His first major project was to study the psychiatric impact of school desegregation on southern students, white and black. His report on his findings, The Desegregation of Southern Schools: A Psychiatric Study *(1963), was important in setting to rest notions that the process or the results of desegregation would be harmful to youths undergoing it. Subsequently, he studied the young people involved in the civil rights movement, concluding that, despite the threats of violence and jail many faced, the activists were healthy, ethical people who displayed strength of character and purpose. Coles did hundreds of interviews with young people involved in the processes of integrating schools, north as well as south, and beginning in 1967 published his findings in a series of important and highly readable studies,* Children of Crisis: A Study of Courage and Fear, *from which the following selection is drawn. Volumes II and III of that study won the Pulitzer Prize for 1973.*

Coles has continued to write books on a variety of controversial issues affecting youth: marijuana, schooling, and hunger, for example. His work represents an unusual combination of carefully researched documentation and fresh style, as well as his lifelong commitment to the amelioration of America's social problems.

MONEY AND LUCK

The boy Raymond was five when he was told that he was a Negro, and that most people in the United States of America are white. Raymond hadn't seen all that many white people as a baby; just before he was born, in 1958, his parents had built a large brick home on eight acres of land at the edge of a section of Atlanta where the most prosperous of black families live. The boy's father is quite well-to-do. He was the only child of a Pullman porter. He was sent to a school run by a black college for children of upper-middle-class black parents. He went to college. He opened up an insurance agency after he graduated. He married the daughter of a professor. He invested his profits in real estate. He opened up a "finance company." He was the chief backer of a large shopping center, for working-class black families. He opened up a store that featured hi-fi equipment, radios, televisions, records. He expanded, soon owned a chain of such stores throughout black Atlanta—and the black sections of other, smaller Georgia cities. He moved on into Alabama, opened up music stores in Birmingham and Montgomery, bought land near those cities, sold it, bought more land, sold it. He opened up branches of his finance company in various cities of Alabama, and eventually decided to do the same in Mississippi and South Carolina.

No one in his family, however, is allowed to talk about money at the table, just as no one is allowed to call himself or herself "black." When the boy Raymond was three his older brother was about to be one of Atlanta's "pioneers"; leaders of the Negro community had urged that the youth help initiate school desegregation in 1961. But the father, finally, would not allow his son to take part in such an effort. He did not want his son to "suffer." He also did not especially welcome the publicity. He was a private man. But he was willing to spend a lot of money on behalf of other Negro children; he contributed heavily to the NAACP, and to its legal struggles against segregation. And he gave his blessing, as a leader of his people, to those young men and women who did enter Atlanta's all-white high schools in the late summer of 1961. Two years later the city was no longer the same, as the boy Raymond was told when he heard from his father "the facts of life." That was the expression the father had used; and that was the expression the boy remembered a few weeks afterward: "My Daddy told me it was my turn to be told; so we went outside to the pool, and he told me. He said I had to know the facts of life. He told me I was Negro, and I'd never turn out to be white. I guess it was my fault that he had to tell me. I'd seen a television program, and there was a kid on it, and he was nice. So I told my brother I'd like to go play with him. My brother said I couldn't, because it's just a program; and besides, he said, the boy's white, and we're Negroes. I told my brother that maybe we'd turn white, and then there wouldn't be any difference. Then I could play with the boy. It was the next day that Daddy talked with me. He said I shouldn't be expecting to be white, because it won't happen."

When Raymond was seven he was still noticing white children on television and asking his parents why he didn't see them in real life. One day the father took the boy aside and said they were going on a trip together, into parts of Atlanta Raymond had never seen. They left an hour later, and toured the "poor white" section of the city, as the father described the neighborhoods he pointed out to his son. The boy was fascinated: everyone was white, just as everyone was black where he lived. On the way home the father gave his son a "talk," and it was one the boy would never

forget. A year later, at eight, he could still vividly remember what the weather outside was like, as his father spoke and he listened without once interrupting: "We
kept driving down a road where the white people go to get the bus for work; it was
raining, I remember, because Daddy told me some of them don't have cars, and they
need a bus to get to work. He told me that a lot of Negro people don't have cars
either, but I should never be ashamed of my own people, because the white people,
a lot of them, aren't any better than we are. He told me that the most important
thing is how you live. If you're poor, it doesn't make any difference whether you're
Negro or you're white. If you've got enough money, it doesn't make any difference
either—because you've got what you need: money. That's why Daddy works so hard;
he told me that. He said that my mother will tell him, a lot of the time, that he
should slow down, because he's got all the money he'll ever need. But he answers
her right back; he says a Negro without money is in a bad way. My mother doesn't
argue with my Daddy; she agrees with him."

At the age of eight he drew a picture of himself. He made his legs quite long, his
arms quite short. He gave himself eyes and a mouth, but no nose and no ears—and
no hair. He used a brown crayon while drawing his self-portrait. He placed himself
on a hill, pleading the desire to see "far off." (His home is located on a hill.) He furnished the hill with a few pine trees, none of which is as tall as he is. There is no sky,
no sun. He has a telescope in one hand, but is not using it. No distant (or, for that
matter nearby) view is provided. A week later he drew another picture, this one of a
white boy, the son of a banker his father knows. Once Raymond had gone with his
father to meet the banker at his office, and had met the banker's son. The two boys
had talked, but not played. The white boy had actually left rather abruptly, saying he
had to shop with his mother. Raymond drew the boy as short, with a small round
head, possessed of a mouth, no nose, and eyes located strangely high up on the
face—at the roots, virtually, of the boy's yellow hair, which was made rather obvious.
The eyes are blue. The boy lacks ears. He also lacks hands. He has short stumps for
arms. He is placed on some earth; no grass is visible, no trees are provided. There is,
however, a sky above, and a rather fat sun, which also has eyes and a mouth. The boy
starts to draw some buildings, but stops and decides that he is done. The result: a
bleak landscape of seemingly half built or half destroyed buildings.

The boy talked about white people and himself after he finished his drawings: "I
wouldn't want to be a redneck. They're the worst people alive. A lot of white people
are poor, and they are no good. They live in slums. When they drink beer they call the
Negroes bad names. The Negroes have a lot of patience. They're always putting up
with the bad manners of the white people. My grandfather worked on the railroads,
and he served the white people—the rich ones. Even they didn't have the manners
they should have had. He'd have to clean up after them. He used to tell my father: The
white man is an animal, and it's best to watch him all the time, and stay clear of him,
if you can. My father says once his father came home and said he'd never go back to
work, because he'd been waiting on some rich folks from New Orleans, and they kept
asking him to do things, and they never said please or thank you, and they were sweet
to their friends and real sour to him. But he did go back to work, I know; he died on
a train that was going to Washington, I believe, from Atlanta.

"My Daddy was never allowed to go on a train. My grandfather told him he had
to be his own boss, and never work for the white man. My Daddy works for himself.
He says he'd like to have some white people working for him, but it would only
mean a lot of trouble. The police always believe the white man. My Daddy says there

are Negro police, but sometimes they will favor the white man too. He's always getting the Negro into a jam, and he's always hurting us, one way or the other. As soon as we try to build ourselves up, he's trying to tear us down. But Daddy says it's getting better and better, and by the time I grow up we'll be living better. Daddy says I was lucky to be born when I was born, and not a long time ago."

Though he has learned to criticize white people and to fear, even loathe, them, he has also learned to keep a sharp eye on them—through television and the movies, through the things said about them by his parents, relatives, friends. A cousin of his, also from a well-off family, attended a private integrated school—integrated in the sense that the boy is one of ten blacks in a school of two hundred white children. Raymond has asked his cousin rather often about "the white kids": What are they like? What do they do in their spare time? Can one make friends with them? Are they loyal friends? Do they all of a sudden turn on you? How do they dress, or talk? What do they read? And are they any good at sports? And do they go to the Cub Scouts, the Boy Scouts?

Raymond received answers; and by the age of nine he had come to the conclusion that there was no point, really, in even asking any more questions. White people are of many kinds, he began to realize; it is risky to generalize. Anyway (so he had also decided) race is important, but class is also important: "I got a railroad set, and Daddy says it cost as much as his Daddy used to get for a salary in a whole year! Well, maybe a half a year! We have a big playroom. It's the best railroad set there is. Daddy has bought stocks in railroad companies. He says he doesn't make much money on the stocks, but he enjoys sitting in his office and getting letters from the president or the treasurer of a railroad company addressed to him, asking for his vote, I guess, or telling him what the company is doing. Daddy wishes his Daddy had lived to be able to see those letters. Daddy says he wishes he could buy a whole railroad company, but he doesn't have the money. He buys a lot of stocks in the airplane companies. We travel first-class on the planes. We get treated like the best. You have these ladies, and they are white, and they wait on you. They keep on offering you something to eat and something to drink. My mother says she has to go on a diet after every plane trip we take. My father tells her not to eat anything, and ask for a diet cola. But she says she gets a big kick out of sitting there and having the white girls come in to her and ask her what she wants and ask if she's happy. We all laugh, but Mom and Daddy get angry at us. They tell us to behave ourselves and act serious, or we'll be in real trouble later, when we get off the plane, and we're away from the white people waiting on us."

When Raymond was nine his father opened up a savings account for him. The boy was taken to the bank, introduced to a bank officer, told about what would happen (in the way of interest accrued) to the fifty dollars his father had deposited and to the future sums that would be added later on. The father was quite solemn with the boy; in fact, gave him a lecture on the importance of money in our society. The boy asked why some people had a lot of money and some people none; he asked why those who have no money don't try to print some up; he asked what happens to those who lack enough money to buy food or pay for clothes; he wondered whether whites have more money than blacks, and if so, why. His father tried to explain the country's economic system; he told the boy about "the free enterprise system," how it permitted "anyone" to work his way up. The boy wondered out loud why so few had actually done so. After all, his father had told him that there are relatively few rich, and many, many poor in the country.

The father explained further: it takes considerable energy, dedication, and intelligence for someone to "rise high" in this country. Those who do so deserve what they get. The boy asked about the Negroes, millions of them, who have given their energy and dedication to the white man—and no small amount of intelligence too. What about his grandfather, who has been described so often as "shrewd" and who gave all he had, for decades, to his job, to the white people? The father was silent for a long time. He acknowledged his own father's many virtues, but insisted that he "might have become a millionaire" if he had been even shrewder, smarter—or luckier. The boy stopped asking questions at that point. He told his father that he was grateful, that he realized how lucky he was, how very lucky. He wished there were more Negro boys and girls of his age who had savings accounts, and lived in houses like the one he had. The father said an amen to the boy's declaration, adding only the conviction that such a life can be anyone's who tries hard enough to obtain it. The boy was in no mood then to disagree.

A month or so later, in an English class of the private Episcopal school he attended, Raymond wrote a composition that surprised and unnerved his teacher. She gave him an A, but worried that he was "too hard" on his family and on his friends and neighbors, not to mention classmates. The composition went like this: "In our country anyone can become rich. All he has to do is be smart and be lucky, and be determined. He has to be smart enough to beat the next guy. If he isn't he'll be left behind. He has to be lucky, too. If he has an idea, and it's the right time, he'll hit a home run. If it's not the right time, he'll strike out.

"What about all the people who work all the time, but don't get rich? They may be smart, but they're not very lucky. They're not determined enough. They may be good to have working for you, but they aren't the leaders. It's the leaders who make the money. My mother said that a lot of people who have made a lot of money have cheated, and they've been crooked. But it's not fair to say that everyone who has a lot of money has done wrong. I do know some rich people who have done wrong. I have some friends, and they talk about their fathers. They aren't as honest as the police. But the police aren't so honest either. My father has given them very big Christmas presents. Like he says, he even gives them Christmas presents in July, as well as in December. I don't want to make a lot of money. People might think I wasn't nice to a lot of other people."

The teacher asked the boy to be more "specific." She told him he had indulged in "generalities." She also said he offered a lot of "hearsay evidence," rather than "concrete facts." She told him that he had unquestionably "misinterpreted" what his parents had said, and that it was "too bad" he had done so, because the "subject matter" of his composition was "excellent." She suggested that he go home, show the paper to his parents, discuss its contents with them, come back and discuss them with her; then he would be in a position to write the essay once again. Even so, he received a B–, a good grade from that particular teacher. She waited in vain, however, for the boy to come to her for a discussion of the composition. He did show it to his parents, but they became upset enough to frighten their son. He was told that he had somehow come up with "crazy" ideas, with "communist" thoughts, with "confused" thinking. He was told that he had managed to "discredit" his race— in the eyes of white people, meaning his teacher and the other teachers who (so the parents believed) had read what the boy had written.

The father gave Raymond a long "lecture." He told the boy that he had to be doubly careful; he was black and he was the son of rather well-off parents. For being the former, he was always "on display," so far as white people go; for being the latter, he was likely to be envied and even hated by both whites and blacks who are less prosperous—including schoolteachers. The father and mother also went to Raymond's teacher and talked with her. They wanted to know how their son had managed to get such ideas into his head. They wanted to express their concern, their worry, their disapproval. The teacher was of no help; she sympathized with the boy's parents, told them what she had come to realize, in years of teaching—that children come up with surprising, even shocking lines of reasoning, and that it is not wise to argue strenuously with a boy like Raymond. Best to let him "outgrow" the vexing "ideas" expressed in the composition.

Yet the boy wanted to talk about what he had written. When the father, keeping in mind the teacher's advice, indicated a lack of interest in a "discussion," Raymond sought out his mother, and, in time, his best friend: "I talked to my mother. She said she knew what was bothering me. She told me her Daddy had once swept floors, and she remembers him being glad that he had that job! She said I was right to worry about the poor people. But she said it's not right to denounce people, just because they've made money. It's better to have money than not to have money. I reminded her that she was the one who told me that a lot of rich people are cheaters, and they know how to be crooked and not get caught. She said I was exaggerating what she told me, and that I'd better not go around quoting her, or she'll get in trouble, and then I'd be in even worse trouble! My best friend said my mother is right. His father is my father's best friend and he is my best friend. He's ten; my mother says he could almost pass for white, but he can't. If he married a white woman when he grows up, then his children would probably be white. They'd look white, at least. He says he doesn't want to look white; he says he's glad he's a Negro. I am, too. I guess I am.

"My Dad always tells us that we should be glad that we can live the way we do—real comfortable. He says a lot of Negro people spend half their lives wishing they were white, or trying to look just a little whiter. They straighten their hair, or they even try to make their skin look lighter. Some dye their hair! According to my father, it's foolish to try to look white if you're Negro. You can't do it. But you can make some money, and then you can live as good as the white man—and better than a lot of whites, if you make enough dollars. My friend says he'd like to be a millionaire. I asked my father if he is one. He said it's none of my business. He's set some money aside for me, I know that. He's told me; and I heard him talking to his lawyer. He said that if I ever went to a good college—like Harvard or Yale, someplace like that—then he wanted me to be able to keep up with anyone who goes there. I don't think I get the money until I'm twenty-five, some age like that. I'll be halfway through my life by then!

"They got all upset at school because they thought I was being fresh; they thought I wasn't being fair to all the rich folks! But it was my father who told me not to trust anyone who made a lot of money, because you don't make a lot of money by being honest all day and all night. He joked with me; he said he'd 'turned a few tricks' to get where he was. But he's a real good man. He tells the truth. He doesn't pretend. At the church they gave him a cup, and said he was the best, the most outstanding man in the whole Negro community. We were all there. We were proud of him. They took his picture, and they showed him on television later, accepting the cup. But they didn't show him giving his speech.

"My Daddy got up and said thank you, and then he made everyone nervous, because he said he remembered his own Daddy, and how he'd told him that if he wants people to pay attention to him and recognize him, then the thing to do was make a lot of money. He said that he'd fought his way up, and he wanted to give money to the church, and he hoped the church would give the money to good kids, who are smart and ambitious, and want to work their way up, the way my Daddy did. And he said he hoped those kids didn't make any mistakes, or hurt anyone on the way; but they most likely would, he said, because that's what you have to do to win. He said he was sorry if he'd been bad to anyone; and he hoped God would forgive him, and he asked for everyone to pray for his family and him, and he promised to give more money away. Later he asked me if I'd be worried if he gave *all* his money away. I said he wouldn't give too much of his money away, but even if he did, I wouldn't worry because he'd just go and make some more, because that's how he is!"

About a year after the boy's composition had stirred up confusion and apprehension at school and home, the father agreed with his son's earlier judgment. The boy was twelve, was becoming a young man. His father took him for a walk, talked with him about matters of money, race, class, and sex; told him that he had been right a while back to be suspicious of those with money, but emphasized how vulnerable and sad it was for anyone to be without a substantial amount of money—"especially Negroes." The boy was touched by his father's candor, by his willingness to subject himself to his own keen, critical eye. It would be no joy being a Negro in America, but with "money and luck," a twosome repeatedly mentioned by his father, it could be "pretty good, most of the time." The boy liked that cautious, guarded, tentative kind of optimism. He made it his own. He kept on telling his close friend that "money and luck" are what matter; that they make all the difference; that a Negro, and especially a poor Negro, needs both badly; that with both one can "forget" a lot of things, and enjoy a lot of other things, and somehow, get the "kick" out of life a Pullman porter once saw white people get, and an Atlanta businessman and his son are sure they are both getting.

DOROTHY ALLISON
(B. 1949)

Because Dorothy Allison's fiction has a highly autobiographical quality, one might not imagine that the author holds both a B.A. and a master's degree in anthropology, the latter from the New School of Social Research. The fictional voice is generally that of a "white trash" woman, part of a culture of poverty, violence, and displacement. The reality is that the voice is the creation of a powerful artist who learned her craft at the Sagaris Institute in Vermont and at George Washington University, and who has practiced it by writing for many of the most significant feminist, lesbian, and mainstream magazines of the 1980s and 1990s.

Allison's first book was a collection of poetry, The Women Who Hate Me *(1983; an expanded version was published in 1991). The poetry shares many of the qualities of Allison's prose: a sharp and often ironic focus on the real events of everyday life, however violent, ugly, and bitter.* Trash: Short Stories *came out in 1988 and her well-known novel,* Bastard Out of Carolina, *in 1992. Both the stories and the novel, including "Mama," printed here, are concerned with the painful lessons of class oppression: rage, fam-*

ily violence, ignorance, and the creation of survival skills. Allison's descrip-
tion of the narrative voice of Trash *captures something of her outlook as*
well as the quality of her prose; she is "a cross-eyed working-class lesbian,
addicted to violence, language, and hope, who has made the decision to live,
is determined to live, on the page and on the street, for me and mine." Alli-
son speaks in her own voice in Skin: Talking about Sex, Class and Literature *(1993). Here she argues not only for a society less obsessed with sexual*
repression, but for the importance of class as a determining factor in the
life chances and real conditions of women in the United States.

MAMA

Above her left ankle my mother has an odd star-shaped scar. It blossoms like a violet above the arch, a purple pucker riding the muscle. When she was a little girl in
South Carolina they still bled people in sickness, and they bled her there. I thought
she was just telling a story, when she first told me, teasing me or covering up some
embarrassing accident she didn't want me to know about. But my aunt supported her.

"It's a miracle she's alive, girl. She was such a sickly child, still a child when she
had you, and then there was the way you were born."

"How's that?"

"Assbackward," Aunt Alma was proud to be the first to tell me, and it showed in
the excitement in her voice. "Your mama was unconscious for three days after you
were born. She'd been fast asleep in the back of your Uncle Lucius's car when they
hit that Pontiac right outside the airbase. Your mama went right through the windshield and bounced off the other car. When she woke up three days later, you were
already out and named, and all she had was a little scar on her forehead to show
what had happened. It was a miracle like they talk about in Bible school, and I know
there's something your mama's meant to do because of it."

"Oh, yeah," Mama shrugged when I asked her about it. "An't no doubt I'm meant
for greater things—bigger biscuits, thicker gravy. What else could God want for
someone like me, huh?" She pulled her mouth so tight I could see her teeth pushing her upper lip, but then she looked into my face and let her air out slowly.

"Your aunt is always laying things to God's hand that he wouldn't have interest in
doing anyway. What's true is that there was a car accident and you got named before
I could say much about it. Ask your aunt why you're named after her, why don't you?"

On my stepfather's birthday I always think of my mother. She sits with her coffee and cigarettes, watches the sun come up before she must leave for work. My
mama lives with my stepfather still, though she spent most of my childhood swearing that as soon as she had us up and grown, she'd leave him flat. Instead, we left,
my sister and I, and on my stepfather's birthday we neither send presents nor visit.
The thing we do—as my sister has told me and as I have told her—is think about
Mama. At any moment of the day we know what she will be doing, where she will
be, and what she will probably be talking about. We know, not only because her days
are as set and predictable as the schedule by which she does the laundry, we know
in our bodies. Our mother's body is with us in its details. She is recreated in each of
us, strength of bone and the skin curling over the thick flesh the women of our family have always worn.

When I visit Mama, I always look first to her hands and feet to reassure myself. The skin of her hands is transparent—large-veined, wrinkled and bruised—while her feet are soft with the lotions I rubbed into them every other night of my childhood. That was a special thing between my mother and me, the way she'd give herself the care of my hands, lying across the daybed, telling me stories of what she'd served down at the truckstop, who had complained and who tipped specially well, and most important, who had said what and what she'd said back. I would sit at her feet, laughing and nodding and stroking away the tightness in her muscles, watching the way her mouth would pull taut while under her pale eyelids the pulse of her eyes moved like kittens behind a blanket. Sometimes my love for her would choke me, and I would ache to have her open her eyes and see me there, to see how much I loved her. But mostly I kept my eyes on her skin, the fine traceries of the veins and the knotted cords of ligaments, seeing where she was not beautiful and hiding how scared it made me to see her close up, looking so fragile, and too often, so old.

When my mama was twenty-five she already had an old woman's hands, and I feared them. I did not know then what it was that scared me so. I've come to understand since that it was the thought of her growing old, of her dying and leaving me alone. I feared those brown spots, those wrinkles and cracks that lined her wrists, ankles, and the soft shadowed sides of her eyes. I was too young to imagine my own death with anything but an adolescent's high romantic enjoyment; I pretended often enough that I was dying of a wasting disease that would give lots of time for my aunts, uncles, and stepfather to mourn me. But the idea that anything could touch my mother, that anything would dare to hurt her was impossible to bear, and I woke up screaming the one night I dreamed of her death—a dream in which I tried bodily to climb to the throne of a Baptist god and demand her return to me. I thought of my mama like a mountain or a cave, a force of nature, a woman who had saved her own life and mine, and would surely save us both over and over again. The wrinkles in her hands made me think of earthquakes and the lines under her eyes hummed of tidal waves in the night. If she was fragile, if she was human, then so was I, and anything might happen. if she was not the backbone of creation itself, then fear would overtake me. I could not allow that, would not. My child's solution was to try to cure my mother of wrinkles in the hope of saving her from death itself.

Once, when I was about eight and there was no Jergens lotion to be had, I spooned some mayonnaise out to use instead. Mama leaned forward, sniffed, lay back and laughed into her hand.

"If that worked," she told me, still grinning, "I wouldn't have dried up to begin with—all the mayonnaise I've eaten in my life."

"All the mayonnaise you've spread—like the butter of your smile, out there for everybody," my stepfather grumbled. He wanted his evening glass of tea, wanted his feet put up, and maybe his neck rubbed. At a look from Mama, I'd run one errand after another until he was settled with nothing left to complain about. Then I'd go back to Mama. But by that time we'd have to start on dinner, and I wouldn't have any more quiet time with her till a day or two later when I'd rub her feet again.

I never hated my stepfather half as much for the beatings he gave me as for those stolen moments when I could have been holding Mama's feet in my hands. Pulled away from Mama's side to run get him a pillow or change the television channel and forced to stand and wait until he was sure there was nothing else he wanted me to do, I entertained myself with visions of his sudden death. Motorcycle outlaws would come to the door, mistaking him for a Drug Enforcement Officer, and blow his head off with a sawed-off shotgun just like the one my Uncle Bo kept under the front seat in his truck. The lawn mower would explode, cutting him into scattered separate pieces the emergency squad would have to collect in plastic bags. Standing and waiting for his orders while staring at the thin black hairs on his balding head, I would imagine his scalp seen through blood-stained plastic, and smile wide and happy while I thought out how I would tell that one to my sister in our dark room at night, when she would whisper back to me her own version of our private morality play.

When my stepfather beat me I did not think, did not imagine stories of either escape or revenge. When my stepfather beat me I pulled so deeply into myself I lived only in my eyes, my eyes that watched the shower sweat on the bathroom walls, the pipes under the sink, my blood on the porcelain toilet seat, and the buckle of his belt as it moved through the air. My ears were disconnected so I could understand nothing—neither his shouts, my own hoarse shameful strangled pleas, nor my mother's screams from the other side of the door he locked. I would not come back to myself until the beating was ended and the door was opened and I saw my mother's face, her hands shaking as she reached for me. Even then, I would not be able to understand what she was yelling at him, or he was yelling at both of us. Mama would take me into the bedroom and wash my face with a cold rag, wipe my legs and, using the same lotion I had rubbed into her feet, try to soothe my pain. Only when she had stopped crying would my hearing come back, and I would lie still and listen to her voice saying my name—soft and tender, like her hand on my back. There were no stories in my head then, no hatred, only an enormous gratitude to be lying still with her hand on me and, for once, the door locked against him.

Push it down. Don't show it. Don't tell anyone what is really going on. We are not safe, I learned from my mama. There are people in the world who are, but they are not us. Don't show your stuff to anyone. Tell no one that your stepfather beats you. The things that would happen are too terrible to name.

Mama quit working honkytonks to try the mill as soon as she could after her marriage. But a year in the mill was all she could take; the dust in the air got to her too fast. After that there was no choice but to find work in a diner. The tips made all the difference, though she could have made more money if she'd stayed with the honkytonks or managed a slot as a cocktail waitress. There was always more money serving people beer and wine, more still in hard liquor, but she'd have had to go outside Greenville County to do that. Neither she nor her new husband could imagine going that far.

The diner was a good choice anyway, one of the few respectable ones downtown, a place where men took their families on Sunday afternoon. The work left her tired, but not sick to death like the mill, and she liked the people she met there, the tips and the conversation.

"You got a way about you," the manager told her.

"Oh yeah, I'm known for my ways," she laughed, and no one would have known she didn't mean it. Truckers or judges, they all liked my mama. And when they weren't slipping quarters in her pocket, they were bringing her things, souvenirs or friendship cards, once or twice a ring. Mama smiled, joked, slapped ass, and firmly passed back anything that looked like a down payment on something she didn't want to sell. She started taking me to work with her when I was still too short to see over the counter, letting me sit up there to watch her some, and tucking me away in the car when I got cold or sleepy.

"That's my girl," she'd brag. "Four years old and reads the funny papers to me every Sunday morning. She's something, an't she?"

"Something," the men would nod, mostly not even looking at me, but agreeing with anything just to win Mama's smile. I'd watch them closely, the wallets they pulled out of their back pockets, the rough patches on their forearms and scratches on their chins. Poor men, they didn't have much more than we did, but they could buy my mama's time with a cup of coffee and a nickel slipped under the saucer. I hated them, each and every one.

My stepfather was a truck driver—a little man with a big rig and a bigger rage. He kept losing jobs when he lost his temper. Somebody would say something, some joke, some little thing, and my little stepfather would pick up something half again his weight and try to murder whoever had dared to say that thing. "Don't make him angry," people always said about him. "Don't make him angry," my mama was always saying to us.

I tried not to make him angry. I ran his errands. I listened to him talk, standing still on one leg and then the other, keeping my face empty, impartial. He always wanted me to wait on him. When we heard him yell, my sister's face would break like a pool of water struck with a handful of stones. Her glance would fly to mine. I would stare at her, hate her, hate myself. She would stare at me, hate me, hate herself. After a moment, I would sigh—five, six, seven, eight years old, sighing like an old lady—tell her to stay there, get up and go to him. Go to stand still for him, his hands, his big hands on his little body. I would imagine those hands cut off by marauders sweeping down on great black horses, swords like lightning bolts in the hands of armored women who wouldn't even know my name but would kill him anyway. Imagine boils and blisters and wasting diseases; sudden overturned cars and spreading gasoline. Imagine vengeance. Imagine justice. What is the difference anyway when both are only stories in your head? In the everyday reality you stand still. I stood still. Bent over. Laid down.

"Yes, Daddy."
"No, Daddy."
"I'm sorry, Daddy"
"Don't do that, Daddy."
"Please, Daddy."

Push it down. Don't show it. Don't tell anyone what is really going on. We are not safe. There are people in the world who are, but they are not us. Don't show your fear to anyone. The things that would happen are too terrible to name.

Sometimes I wake in the middle of the night to the call of my name shouted in my mama's voice, rising from silence like an echo caught in the folds of my brain. It is her hard voice I hear, not the soft one she used when she held me tight, the hard voice she used on bill collectors and process servers. Sometimes her laugh comes too, that sad laugh, thin and foreshadowing a cough, with her angry laugh following. I hate that laugh, hate the sound of it in the night following on my name like shame. When I hear myself laugh like that, I always start to curse, to echo what I know was the stronger force in my mama's life.

As I grew up my teachers warned me to clean up my language, and my lovers became impatient with the things I said. Sugar and honey, my teachers reminded me when I sprinkled my sentences with the vinegar of my mama's rage—as if I was sup-posed to want to draw flies. And, "Oh honey," my girlfriends would whisper, "do you have to talk that way?" I did, I did indeed. I smiled them my mama's smile and played for them my mama's words while they tightened up and pulled back, seeing me for someone they had not imagined before. They didn't shout, they hissed; and even when they got angry, their language never quite rose up out of them the way my mama's rage would fly.

"Must you? Must you?" they begged me. And then, "For God's sake!"

"Sweet Jesus!" I'd shout back but they didn't know enough to laugh.

"Must you? Must you?"

Hiss, hiss.

"For God's sake, do you have to end everything with *ass?* An anal obsession, that's what you've got, a goddamn anal obsession!"

"I do, I do," I told them, "and you don't even know how to say *goddamn.* A woman who says *goddamn* as soft as you do isn't worth the price of a meal of shit!"

Coarse, crude, rude words, and ruder gestures—Mama knew them all. *You ass-fucker, get out of my yard,* to the cop who came to take the furniture. *Shitsucking bastard!* to the man who put his hand under her skirt. *Jesus shit a brick,* every day of her life. Though she slapped me when I used them, my mama taught me the power of nasty words. Say *goddamn.* Say anything but begin it with *Jesus* and end it with *shit.* Add that laugh, the one that disguises your broken heart. Oh, never show your broken heart! Make them think you don't have one instead.

"If people are going to kick you, don't just lie there. Shout back at them."

"Yes, Mama."

Language then, and tone, and cadence. Make me mad, and I'll curse you to the seventh generation in my mama's voice. But you have to work to get me mad. I mea-sure my anger against my mama's rages and her insistence that most people aren't even worth your time. "We are another people. Our like isn't seen on the earth that often," my mama told me, and I knew what she meant. I know the value of the hard asses of this world. And I am my mama's daughter—tougher than kudzu, meaner than all the ass-kicking, bad-assed, cold-assed, saggy-assed fuckers I have ever kown. But it's true that sometimes I talk that way just to remember my mother, the survivor, the endurer, but the one who could not always keep quiet about it.

We are just like her, my sister and I. That March when my sister called, I thought for a moment it was my mama's voice. The accent was right, and the language—the slow drag of matter-of-fact words and thoughts, but the beaten-down quality wasn't Mama, couldn't have been. For a moment I felt as if my hands were gripping old and tender flesh, the skin gone thin from age and wear, my granny's hands, perhaps, on the day she had stared out at her grandsons and laughed lightly, insisting I take a good look at them. "See, see how the blood thins out." She spit to the side and clamped a hand down on my shoulder. I turned and looked at her hand, that hand as strong as heavy cord rolled back on itself, my bare shoulder under her hand and the muscles there rising like bubbles in cold milk. I had felt thick and strong beside her, thick and strong and sure of myself in a way I have not felt since. That March when my sister called I felt old; my hands felt wiry and worn, and my blood seemed hot and thin as it rushed through my veins.

My sister's voice sounded hollow; her words vibrated over the phone as if they had iron edges. My tongue locked to my teeth, and I tasted the fear I thought I had put far behind me.

"They're doing everything they can—surgery again this morning and chemotherapy and radiation. He's a doctor, so he knows, but Jesus . . ."

"Jesus shit."

"Yeah."

Mama woke up alone with her rage, her grief. "Just what I'd always expected," she told me later. "You think you know what's going on, what to expect. You relax a minute and that's when it happens. Life turns around and kicks you in the butt."

Lying there, she knew they had finally gotten her, the *they* that had been dogging her all her life, waiting for the chance to rob her of all her tomorrows. Now they had her, her body pinned down under bandages and tubes and sheets that felt like molten lead. She had not really believed it possible. She tried to pull her hands up to her neck, but she couldn't move her arms. "I was so mad I wanted to kick holes in the sheets, but there wasn't no use in that." When my stepfather came in to sit and whistle his sobs beside the bed, she took long breaths and held her face tight and still. She became all eyes, watching everything from a place far off inside herself.

"Never want what you cannot have," she'd always told me. It was her rule for survival, and she grabbed hold of it again. She turned her head away from what she could not change and started adjusting herself to her new status. She was going to have to figure out how to sew herself up one of those breast forms so she could wear a bra. "Damn things probably cost a fortune," she told me when I came to sit beside her. I nodded slowly. I didn't let her see how afraid I was, or how uncertain, or even how angry. I showed her my pride in her courage and my faith in her strength. But underneath I wanted her to be angry, too. "I'll make do," she whispered, showing me nothing, and I just nodded.

"Everything's going to be all right," I told her.

"Everything's going to be all right," she told me. The pretense was sometimes the only thing we had to give each other.

When it's your mama and it's an accomplished fact, you can't talk politics into her bleeding. You can't quote from last month's article about how a partial mastectomy is just as effective. You can't talk about patriarchy or class or confrontation strategies. I made jokes on the telephone, wrote letters full of healthy recipes and vitamin therapies, I pretended for her sake and my own that nothing was going to happen, that cancer is an everyday occurrence (and it is) and death is not part of the scenario.

Push it down. Don't show it. Don't tell anybody what is really going on. My mama makes do when the whole world cries out for things to stop, to fall apart, just once for all of us to let our anger show. My mama clamps her teeth, laughs her bitter laugh, and does whatever she thinks she has to do with no help, thank you, from people who only want to see her wanting something she can't have anyway.

Five, ten, twenty years—my mama has had cancer for twenty years. "That doctor, the one in Tampa in '71, the one told me I was gonna die, that sucker choked himself on a turkey bone. People that said what a sad thing it was—me having cancer, and surely meant to die—hell, those people been run over by pickups and dropped down dead with one thing and another, while me, I just go on. It's something, an't it?"

It's something. Piece by piece, my mother is being stolen from me. After the hysterectomy, the first mastectomy, another five years later, her teeth that were easier to give up than to keep, the little toes that calcified from too many years working waitress in bad shoes, hair and fingernails that drop off after every bout of chemotherapy, my mama is less and less the mountain, more and more the cave—the empty place from which things have been removed.

"With what they've taken off me, off Granny, and your Aunt Grace—shit, you could almost make another person."

A woman, a garbage creation, an assembly of parts. When I drink I see her rising like bats out of deep caverns, a gossamer woman—all black edges, with a chrome uterus and molded glass fingers, plastic wire rib cage and red unblinking eyes. My mama, my grandmother, my aunts, my sister and me—every part of us that can be taken has been.

"Flesh and blood needs flesh and blood," my mama sang for me once, and laughing added, "but we don't need as much of it as we used to, huh?"

When Mama talked, I listened. I believed it was the truth she was telling me. I watched her face as much as I listened to her words. She had a way of dropping her head and covering her bad teeth with her palm. I'd say, "Don't do that." And she'd laugh at how serious I was. When she laughed with me, that shadow, so grey under her eyes, lightened, and I felt for a moment—powerful, important, never so important as when I could make her laugh.

I wanted to grow up to do the poor-kid-done-good thing, the Elvis Presley/Ritchie Valens movie, to buy my mama her own house, put a key in her hand and say, "It's yours—from here to there and everything in between, these walls, that door, that gate, these locks. You don't ever have to let anyone in that you don't want. You can lay in the sun if you want or walk out naked in the moonlight if you take the mood. And if you want to go into town to mess around, we can go do it together."

I did not want to be my mother's lover; I wanted more than that. I wanted to rescue her the way we had both wanted her to rescue me. *Do not want what you cannot have,* she told me. But I was not as good as she was. I wanted that dream. I've never stopped wanting it.

The day I left home my stepfather disappeared. I scoured him out of my life, exorcising every movement or phrase in which I recognized his touch. All he left behind was a voice on a telephone line, a voice that sometimes answered when I called home. But Mama grew into my body like an extra layer of warm protective fat, closing me around. My muscles hug my bones in just the way hers do, and when I turn my face, I have that same bulldog angry glare I was always ashamed to see on her. But my legs are strong, and I do not stoop the way she does; I did not work waitress for thirty years, and my first lover taught me the importance of buying good shoes. I've got

Mama's habit of dropping my head, her quick angers, and that same belly-gutted scar she was so careful to hide. But nothing marks me so much her daughter as my hands—the way they are aging, the veins coming up through skin already thin. I tell myself they are beautiful as they recreate my mama's flesh in mine.

My lovers laugh at me and say, "Every tenth word with you is mama. Mama said. Mama used to say. My mama didn't raise no fool."

I widen my mouth around my drawl and show my mama's lost teeth in my smile.

Watching my mama I learned some lessons too well. Never show that you care, Mama taught me, and never want something you cannot have. Never give anyone the satisfaction of denying you something you need, and for that, what you have to do is learn to need nothing. Starve the wanting part of you. In time I understood my mama to be a kind of Zen Baptist—rooting desire out of her own heart as ruthlessly as any mountaintop ascetic. The lessons Mama taught me, like the lessons of Buddha, were not a matter of degree but of despair. My mama's philosophy was bitter and thin. She didn't give a damn if she was ever born again, she just didn't want to be born again poor and wanting.

I am my mama's daughter, her shadow on the earth, the blood thinned down a little so that I am not as powerful as she, as immune to want and desire. I am not a mountain or a cave, a force of nature or a power on the earth, but I have her talent for not seeing what I cannot stand to face. I make sure that I do not want what I do not think I can have, and I keep clearly in mind what it is I cannot have. I roll in the night all the stories I never told her, cannot tell her still—her voice in my brain echoing love and despair and grief and rage. When, in the night, she hears me call her name, it is not really me she hears, it is the me I constructed for her—the one who does not need her too much, the one whose heart is not too tender, whose insides are iron and silver, whose dreams are cold ice and slate—who needs nothing, nothing. I keep in mind the image of a closed door, Mama weeping on the other side. She could not rescue me. I cannot rescue her. Sometimes I cannot even reach across the wall that separates us.

On my stepfather's birthday I make coffee and bake bread pudding with bourbon sauce. I invite friends over, tell outrageous stories, and use horrible words. I scratch my scars and hug my lover, thinking about Mama twelve states away. My accent comes back and my weight settles down lower, until the ache in my spine is steady and hot. I remember Mama sitting at the kitchen table in the early morning, tears in her eyes, lying to me and my sister, promising us that the time would come when she would leave him—that as soon as we were older, as soon as there was a little more money put by and things were a little easier—she would go.

I think about her sitting there now, waiting for him to wake up and want his coffee, for the day to start moving around her, things to get so busy she won't have to think. Sometimes, I hate my mama. Sometimes, I hate myself. I see myself in her, and her in me. I see us too clearly sometimes, all the little betrayals that cannot be forgotten or changed.

When Mama calls, I wait a little before speaking.

"Mama," I say, "I knew you would call."

KRISTIN HUNTER

(B. 1931)

For many years, Hunter lived and worked in Philadelphia, where she had been born and had graduated from the University of Pennsylvania. Indeed, South Street, at the center of one of the city's main African-American districts, functions as a kind of character in her work. She had been raised in Camden and in Magnolia, New Jersey, a middle-class black suburb, where as a lonely teenager she had written a youth column for the Pittsburgh Courier, an African-American newspaper. After graduation from Penn she taught for a time and worked in advertising and as a freelance writer. One of her pieces, her 1955 script for A Minority of One, *was presented on nationwide television.*

Her first novel, God Bless the Child *(1964), constituted a kind of bridge between an older generation of black writers and the soon to emerge flourishing of black women's fiction. A second novel,* The Landlord, *followed in 1966; that book was made into a successful film by the same title. Later books for adult readers included the story collection* Guests in the Promised Land *(1973), which was a National Book Award finalist, and a number of novels. "Mom Luby and the Social Worker" is taken from the 1973 volume. Hunter also has written books for younger readers, including her first, the prize-winning* The Soul Brothers and Sister Lou *(1968), about a young singing group.*

Her stories focus on people negotiating the urban landscape of places like Philadelphia, and while she presents that world without excess or sentimentality, she also does so with humor and a keen ear for the satirical comment.

MOM LUBY AND THE SOCIAL WORKER

Puddin' and I been livin' with Mom Luby three years, ever since our mother died. We like it fine. But when Mom Luby took us down to the Welfare, we thought our happy days were over and our troubles about to begin.

"Chirren," she said that day, "I got to get some of this State Aid so I can give you everything you need. Shoes for you, Elijah, and dresses for Puddin' now she's startin' school. And lunch money and carfare and stuff like that. But the only way I can get it is to say I'm your mother. So don't mess up my lie."

Mom Luby is old as Santa Claus, maybe older, with hair like white cotton and false teeth that hurt so much she takes them out and gums her food. But she's strong as a young woman and twice as proud. Much too proud to say she's our grandmother, which is something the Welfare people might believe.

So we went down there scared that morning, Puddin' holding tight onto both our hands. But we was lucky. The lady behind the desk didn't even look at us, and we got out of that gloomy old State Building safe and free. Man! Was I glad to get back to Division Street where people don't ask questions about your business.

When we got home, a whole bunch of people was waiting for Mom to let them in the speakeasy she runs in the back room. Jake was there, and Sissiemae, and Bobo and Walter and Lucas and Mose and Zerline. They are regular customers who come every evening to drink the corn liquor Mom gets from down South and eat the food she fixes, gumbo and chicken wings and ribs and potato salad and greens.

Bobo picked Puddin' up to see how much she weighed (a lot), until she hollered to be let down. Jake gave me a quarter to take his shoes down to Gumby's Fantastic Shoe Shine Parlor and get them shined and keep the change. We let the people in the front door and through the red curtain that divides the front room from the back. Soon they were settled around the big old round table with a half-gallon jar of corn. Then Sissiemae and Lucas wanted chicken wings, and I had to collect the money while Mom heated them up on the stove. There was so much to do, I didn't pay no attention to the tapping on the front door.

But then it came again, louder, like a woodpecker working on a tree.

"Elijah," Mom says, "run see who it is trying to chip a hole in that door. If it be the police, tell them I'll see them Saturday."

But it wasn't the cops, who come around every Saturday night to get their money and drink some of Mom's corn and put their big black shoes up on the table. It was a little brownskin lady with straightened hair and glasses and black high-top shoes. She carried a big leather envelope and was dressed all in dark blue.

"Good afternoon," she says. "I am Miss Rushmore of the Department of Child Welfare, Bureau of Family Assistance. Is Mrs. Luby at home?"

"I am she," says Mom. "Never been nobody else. Come in, honey, and set yourself down. Take off them shoes, they do look like real corn-crushers to me."

"No thank you," says Miss Rushmore. She sits on the edge of one of Mom's chairs and starts pulling papers out of the envelope. "This must be Elijah."

"Yes ma'am," I say.

"And where is Arlethia?"

"Taking her nap," says Mom, with a swat of the broom at the middle of the curtain, which Puddin' was peeking through. She's five and fat, and she loves to hang around grownups. Especially when they eating.

Mom hit the curtain with the broom again, and Puddin' ran off. The lady didn't even notice. She was too busy peeking under the lids of the pots on the stove.

"Salt pork and lima beans," she says. "Hardly a proper diet for growing children."

"Well," says Mom, "when I get me some of this State Aid, maybe I can afford to get them canned vegetables and box cereal. Meanwhile you welcome to what we have."

The lady acted like she didn't hear that. She just wrinkled up her nose like she smelled something bad.

"First," she says, "we must have a little talk about your budget. Do you understand the importance of financial planning?"

"Man arranges and God changes," says Mom. "When I got it, I spends it, when I don't, I do without."

"That," says the lady, "is precisely the attitude I am here to correct." She pulls out a big yellow sheet of paper. "Now this is our Family Budget Work Sheet. What is your rent?"

"I ain't paid it in so long I forgot," Mom says. Which set me in a fit because everybody but this dumb lady knows Mom owns the house. Behind her back Mom gave me a whack that stopped my giggles.

The lady sighed. "We'll get to the budget later," she says. "First, there are some questions you left blank today. How old were you when Elijah was born?"

"Thirty-two," says Mom.

"And he is now thirteen, which would make you forty-five," says the lady.

"Thirty-eight," says Mom without batting an eye.

"I'll put down forty-five," says the lady, giving Mom a funny look. "No doubt your hard life has aged you beyond your years. Now, who is the father, and where is he?"

"Lemme see," says Mom, twisting a piece of her hair. "I ain't seen Mr. Luby since 1942. He was a railroad man, you see, and one time he just took a train out of here and never rode back."

"1942," Miss Rushmore wrote on the paper. And then said, "But that's impossible!"

"The dear Lord do teach us," says Mom, "that nothing in life is impossible if we just believe enough."

"Hey, Mom, we're out of corn!" cries Lucas from the back room.

Miss Rushmore looked very upset. "Why," she says, "you've got a man in there."

"Sure do sound like it, don't it?" Mom says. "Sure do. You got one too, honey?"

"That's my business," says the lady.

"I was just trying to be sociable," says Mom pleasantly. "You sure do seem interested in mine."

I ran back there and fetched another mason jar of corn from the shed kitchen. I told Lucas and Bobo and them to be quiet. Which wasn't going to be easy, cause them folks get good and loud when they get in a card game. I also dragged Puddin' away from the potato salad bowl, where she had stuck both her hands, and brought her in the front room with me. She was bawling. The lady gave her a weak smile.

"Now," Mom says. "About these shoes and school clothes."

"I am not sure," Miss Rushmore says, "that you can get them. There is something wrong in this house that I have not yet put my finger on. But this is what you do. First you fill out Form 905, which you get at the Bureau of Family Assistance, room 1203. Then you call the Division of Child Welfare and make an appointment with Mr. Jenkins. He will give you Form 202 to fill out. Then you go to the fifth floor, third corridor on the left, turn right, go in the second door. You stand at the first desk and fill out Form 23-B, Requisition for Clothing Allowance. You take *that* to Building Three, room 508, third floor, second door, fourth desk and then—"

"Lord," Mom says, "By the time we get clothes for these chirren, they will have done outgrowed them."

"I don't make the rules," the lady says.

"Well, honey," says Mom, "I ain't got time to do all that, not right now, Tonight I got to go deliver a baby. Then I got to visit a sick old lady and work on her with some herbs. Then I got to go down to the courthouse and get a young man out of jail. He's not a bad boy, he's just been keepin' bad company. *Then* I got to preach a funeral."

The lady looked at Mom like she was seeing a spirit risen from the dead. "But you can't do those things!" she says.

But I happen to know Mom Luby *can*. She's a midwife and a herb doctor and an ordained minister of the Gospel, besides running a place to eat and drink after hours. And she wouldn't need Welfare for us if people would only pay her sometimes.

Mom says, "Honey, just come along and watch me."

She picked up her old shopping bag full of herbs and stuff. Miss Rushmore picked up her case and followed like somebody in a trance. Mom has that effect on people sometimes.

They were gone about two hours, and me and Puddin' had a good time eating and joking and looking into everybody's card hands.

I was surprised to see Mom bring Miss Rushmore straight into the back room when they got back. She sat her down at the table and poured her a drink of corn. To tell the truth, that lady looked like she needed it. Her glasses was crooked, and her shoes were untied, and her hair had come loose from its pins. She looked kind of pretty, but lost.

"Mrs. Luby," she said after a swallow of corn, "you don't need my help."

"Ain't it the truth," says Mom.

"I came here to help you solve your problems. But now I don't know where to begin."

"What problems?" Mom asks.

"You are raising these children in an unhealthy atmosphere. I am not even sure they are yours. And you are practicing law, medicine, and the ministry without a license. I simply can't understand it."

"Can't understand what, honey?"

The lady sighed. "How you got more done in two hours than I ever get done in two years."

"You folks oughta put me on the payroll," says Mom with a chuckle.

"We can't," says Miss Rushmore. "You're not qualified."

Lucas started laughing, and Bobo joined in, and then we all laughed, Mose and Zerline and Jake and Sissiemae and Puddin' and me. We laughed so hard we rocked the room and shook the house and laughed that social worker right out the door.

"She got a point though," Mom says after we finished laughing. "You need an education to fill out forty pieces of paper for one pair of shoes. Never you mind, chirren. We'll make out fine, like we always done. Cut the cards, Bobo. Walter, deal."

NTOZAKE SHANGE

(B. 1948)

Shange is best known as a playwright and performance artist, especially for her first piece, which achieved great success on Broadway, for colored girls who have considered suicide/when the rainbow is enuf *(1976). That work, built around an interlinked series of powerful poetic monologues about the life crises of seven black women characters, embodies elements of song, dance, improvisation, and story-telling. Within the decade following, Shange had produced four other unconventional choreographed dramas, and in 1989, a conventional one-act play. She has also written two novellas, Sas-safras (1976) and* Melissa and Smith *(1985), and two novels, Sassafras, Cypress & Indigo (1982) and* Betsey Brown *(1985), from which the follow-ing selection is taken. She has also published a number of volumes of poetry and a collection of essays about her writing, performances, installations, and dramatic ideas,* See No Evil: Prefaces, Essays & Accounts *(1984).*

Shange was born in Trenton, New Jersey, and originally named Paulette Williams by her father, a successful surgeon, and her mother, a psychiatric social worker. She graduated from Barnard College with a B.A. in Ameri-

can studies in 1970. At about the same time, at the height of an African revival among black American intellectuals, she decided to adopt the Zulu names Ntozake (she who comes with her own things) and Shange (one who walks like a lion). Though she completed a master's degree in American studies at the University of Southern California in 1973, she was already deeply involved in theatrical experiments as well as in the struggles of people of the African diaspora for identity and living space. Her work has adapted forms of African-American oral culture and has, she says, particularly been addressed to women. She has been a successful participant in early forms of poetry slams and has otherwise been active as a black feminist as well as a performer and playwright.

FROM B E T S E Y B R O W N

Not too much was happening round Mrs. Maureen's at that early hour of the morning. Mr. Tavaneer was winding the gates up in fronta his liquor store. The grease wasn't even hot yet in Mrs. Jackson's "We Know You Like Jackson's Chicken House." Mrs. Maureen didn't have her blinking lights on either. Mrs. Maureen's blinking lights were a silhouette of a bouffant hairdo with the words "Maureen Can Do This For You" underneath in blue and red. The hairdo was purple and didn't blink. Some of the lights were out, but everybody knew where Mrs. Maureen's was. Betsey had to shout "Hello" to Mr. Tavaneer cause one time some robbers shot a pistol right upside his head for not moving fast enough. Mr. Tavaneer said he never had no intentions of moving, but no one knew the rest of the story cause the robbers hightailed it on away. Just Mr. Tavaneer couldn't hear.

"Hello, Mr. Tavaneer!" Betsey walked closer to him. "Good Morning, Mr. Tavaneer!" Betsey was almost shouting by now. Mr. Tavaneer turned round gruffly. "Must you be blasting the daylights out of the ground, Betsey? It's the other side I can't hear out of, not this one. What you doing round here so early in the morning? Mrs. Maureen aint open to customers at this hour."

"Oh, I'm not coming as a customer, Mr. Tavaneer. I'm looking for work."

Betsey set her things down as Mr. Tavaneer opened the Spirit Shop.

"Aint your father still a doctor?"

"Yes, Sir."

"Don't your mama work round to the hospital with them crazy folks?"

"Yes, Sir."

"Then why do you need work?"

"That's how come I came to see Mrs. Maureen."

"At this hour?" Mr. Tavaneer swept the debris from in front of his store and stepped back, surveying the neighborhood. The crap games would start soon. The laundrymats'd be open. The numbers man would be coming by a few times. The winos would find their way to his shop and the smell would lift him high unto heaven's gate.

"Well, you keep a good ten feet from either side of my store, Betsey. That's all I need is for the police to say I been catering to minors. Sides, I gotta mind to call your papa. I know he don't think you out this way looking for no job. I just might do that. Silly gal. You'll find out soon enough St. Louis is a dangerous place."

Betsey wasn't thrilled with Mr. Tavaneer's words for the day, but she went on up the stairs to Mrs. Maureen's anyway. At first there was no answer. Betsey rang the bell again and still nobody came.

"I told you it was a peculiar hour to come round Mrs. Maureen's to 'work.'" Mr. Tavaneer shouted from his bad side, thinking Betsey couldn't hear him.

By the third ring, Betsey was beginning to feel a little scared. It was awfully quiet and dingy. There were ill-meaning folks cluttering up the street. Mrs. Maureen's looked worn-out, or needing something like the Saturday customers to spruce it up. Finally Mrs. Maureen came down the many steps to the door. Her face wasn't as pleasant as usual. That's cause all the make-up from the night before hadn't been properly oiled away yet. Then, too, Mrs. Maureen didn't have on her beauty salon uniform. She had on a robe of some sort that twisted round her body like the ripples in some kinds of soda bottles, round and round, till they reached her bosom where they stopped all of a sudden and all this flesh hung out in two great mounds, dusted with little red feathers.

"Betsey Brown, is that you?" Mrs. Maureen managed to whisper through a wig that was sitting on her head the wrong way, or at least lopsided. "Well, Betsey, I aint open now. I mean, aint it a bit early to come callin?"

"Yes, Mrs. Maureen. I'm very sorry to disturb you, but I didn't know where else to go. I ran away and you're the only person I know who might help me."

Mrs. Maureen put her hand on her hip to help herself stand up.

"You say you ran away. You ran away from where?"

"From home, Mrs. Maureen. I ran away from home. Nobody understands me there. They all want me to be somebody else. And I'm just Betsey Brown, Mrs. Maureen. You understand, don't you?"

Mrs. Maureen's eyes were finally beginning, to come open. She coughed to wake up and shifted the tottering wig to the other side of her head.

"Un, hum. You say you ran away and came here." It took a long time for Mrs. Maureen to grasp the reality of Betsey's announcement. Now Mrs. Maureen had all kinds of girls coming in and out, but they weren't thirteen, or plain old "Betsey Browns." "Yes, you come on in heah while I think on this some. Run away, hum? And you ran away over heah?"

"Yes, M'am."

Mrs. Maureen's eyes kept opening and shutting as she led Betsey up the stairs to the beauty parlor, or what Betsey knew of the beauty parlor. Behind the French doors where Betsey assumed Mrs. Maureen lived, there was indeed a kitchen, but there were also some roomers or callers or men and women in the midst of all sorts of transactions. Betsey most forgot where she was and was fixing to run home till she remembered she was running away from home.

Mrs. Maureen shooed everyone out her way. Made herself a pot of coffee.

"You eat?"

"Yes, M'am." Betsey was having second thoughts about coming to Mrs. Maureen's. Seemed like there was more going on than usual: There were never any men at Mrs. Maureen's, and the girls who helped out wore uniforms from the uniform store like Mrs. Maureen's. It didn't smell old and tired. Mrs. Maureen never looked so old, either.

Once she had her coffee and her body stopped this persistent heaving and swaying with every sigh, Mrs. Maureen took Betsey's hands up in hers and said, "Chile, I know folks that love you can't always see exactly what you mean, or feel exactly how you feel, but I can't let you stay here in a place like this. Why I wouldn't even let one of my own daughters stay here, Betsey."

"But, Mrs. Maureen, you said I was almost like kinfolk. You said there was folks in Mississippi who looked like me. You said you'd love to have a child like me around to chat with and grow up."

"Oh, Betsey, chile, I know your mama's missing you."

Mrs. Maureen kept rubbing her hands together with Betsey's, as if rubbing hands together would rub the knowledge of the world into Betsey's head.

"But Mrs. Maureen, please, please don't call Mama. She doesn't even know I'm gone yet. They think I'm at school."

"And that's where you should be."

"I'm tired of those white folks."

"Who you think aint tired of white folks?"

Mrs. Maureen was beginning to get mad at Betsey now. Of all the very last nerve, to be running away from a family as nice as the Browns. Betsey needed a good talking to.

"Well, now that you've run off and all, what are you gointa do?" Mrs. Maureen shoved a plate of grits and eggs and sausage under Betsey's chin, while she waited for a response.

"I was gonna help you out in the shop until I eloped."

Mrs. Maureen liked to fell off her chair which would have been quite something, seeing how Mrs. Maureen was quite something.

"Elope?"

"Yes, M'am." Betsey's eyes gleamed as she said the word and tasted the peppers in the sausage.

Mrs. Maureen, who knew she was getting on in years and had heard just about everything there was to hear and seen more than there was to see, let herself light up the kitchen with laughter. "Elope." Mrs. Maureen jumped up like she was twirling crepe paper for a wedding screaming: "Elope," and trailing it with, "Where you goin'? To Arkansas? Chirren can't get married in Missouri and believe me, I know about the law. And that's the law."

When she'd tired herself out, Mrs. Maureen asked Betsey: "Isn't elopin a bit ol' fashioned? How old is this boy and does he know too, or is this thing just a secret tween me and you?"

Betsey didn't see anything funny about her situation. She especially didn't think her friend, Mrs. Maureen, should be laughing at her this way. Eugene Boyd was a fine boy and thirteen was just a little way from being full grown. But it was Mrs. Maureen's or she didn't know what, so Betsey kept her mouth shut.

"Hum, elope? Hum. I've heard that one before. Sorry to say."

Mrs. Maureen started to clear the dishes away. The morning throng began to mill about once again in tee-shirts and robes, nighties and nothing.

"If you're gonna stay with us, you might as well see it in the raw, honey." Mrs. Maureen rubbed Betsey's back, which was stiff as a rail. "Don't worry, nobody's gonna hurt you."

Betsey wisht she was home. Right now. Away from these men with stocking caps on and curlers in their heads. These women with too much rouge and not enough clothes.

"Betsey, I think a friend of yours ran away to me some time ago—I think she's still here. Let me go see. She was gointa elope, too, I recollect. Folks round your way sho' don't be keepin up with the times. Elope. Two colored chirren elopin. I swear I hear all the bad news first. Even 'fore the President, they let me in on it. REGINA! Regina, bring your hot lil tail out here and talk some sense to this gal bout love and romance. Regina!"

Betsey watched as women passed by the kitchen table leaving wads of money in the center. The men with rollers strolled by too, pulling folds of dollar bills from their money clips. There was a lot of money on that table. More money than when she and Margot and Sharon emptied Greer's pockets and Jane's purses in order to go to the movies that time Jane and Greer went to Paris and left them with some skinny woman whose baby stank. There was really a lot of money on that table by the time Mrs. Maureen appeared with Regina. It hadn't occurred to Betsey that Regina could be Roscoe's Regina from love and kisses, but there she was in a awful flimsy red negligee, deep holes under her eyes, and a shame on her that made Betsey's skin cringe. Regina was pregnant. She laid her money on Mrs. Maureen's table too.

"Now do like I tol' you and tell this girl bout runnin off and elopin and carryin on like a fool over some no count niggah with his head fulla dreams. Go on, do like I say."

Regina and Betsey hugged and hugged. Regina's tummy bumping Betsey's head. Betsey thought she could hear the baby singing. She knew she could hear it moving. Regina's stomach was so hard, like a drum. Betsey knew from the tears in Regina's eyes that the baby was Roscoe's.

"Gina, where's Roscoe? I thought you all were going to Chicago to have your family?"

"Guess who's in Chi-town, Betsey?" Mrs. Maureen asked, counting her money.

"Roscoe's getting things ready for us, Betsey. Honest he is. He told me to stay here till he could send for me. Said it wouldn't take long."

"And how many weeks you been here now? You'll still be here when that baby comes flying outta ya."

"He told me I was coming here to work for you."

"He didn't tell me you couldn't press heads, so I put you to work doing what you obviously knew how to do awready."

Betsey helped Regina sit down. Gina couldn't stop crying or holding her tummy, her baby. She kept whispering Roscoe's name, praying for him to come get her. She was bout to lose her mind. Betsey held onto her real tight. She remembered Roscoe standing up to Grandma. She was sure Roscoe loved Regina. She was sure Roscoe didn't know the kinda trouble Regina was in.

"Regina, I know Roscoe loves you. I was there. I saw you kiss. He's gonna send for you. Believe me." Betsey pulled closer to Regina's naked legs, swollen and over-perfumed.

"You think so, Betsey? You think he's gonna get me outta heah?"

"You can get outta heah anytime you pay me the money you owe me for your room and board."

"Mrs. Maureen, I could stay and help you press heads. Mommy lets me press Margot and Sharon's sometimes when they need a touch-up. I'll help Regina and that way I could stay with you, too. Would that be awright with you, Gina?"

"Oh, Betsey, you can't stay here. There's too much going on that I don't want you to see, ever. Things I never want you or my baby to see."

"Looks to me like you saw a bit too much 'fore you came prancin through my front door, missie. Don't you be holdin me responsible for your behavior."

Mrs. Maureen divided the money in small stacks, which were picked up by the strangely clad women who'd put it there. The largest portion went right in the cleft of Mrs. Maureen's bosom. She patted it over and over, smiling at Betsey. She did like Betsey.

"Girl, why don't we go in the other room and I'll do your head up real pretty, with some bumper curls we'll comb out together. You got to go home, chile. I know your mama's missing you. A sweet chile like you got no business here 'cept on Saturday mornings when your head needs doing. C'mon, let's get the combs heated up."

"No, Mrs. Maureen. Let me stay at least long enough to help with Regina's baby. I could baby-sit, you know that, and help you keep the place straight." Betsey was frightened. How could Roscoe leave Regina like this? What was Gina doing with all that money and the baby? How could being in love leave you so sad and alone? "Mrs. Maureen, please let me stay, just a few days? Mama won't be mad when she knows I've been with you."

"Your mama aint never gointa know you been with me. Her heart's probably breaking right this minute, wondering where is that bright sweet girl she loves so much. And here you are making a fuss over a fool gal got herself knocked-up and left behind."

Mrs. Maureen was fiddling with Betsey's braids now. Taking them down one by one and running her fingers through the hair looking for split ends she'd have to cut.

"You think that school won't call your mama and tell her you aint there? What you think she's gonna imagine? Well, let me tell you. She's gointa think some crack-ers got hold to you and beat you good! That's what! This city is going to the dogs these days. I'm tellin you. Gina, go on and tell her what I tol' you. Do like I say, now."

Regina's eyes were sunken and swollen now. She knew Betsey couldn't stay at Mrs. Maureen's. That was out of the question, but she didn't want Betsey to think that love left you pitiful like that song went, "They Call Me, Mr. Pitiful." Gina wanted Betsey to remember the joy and the hope of two hands joined, swinging down the street. She also wanted Betsey to have hope for her.

"Listen, I've got an idea. Mrs. Maureen, why don't you do Betsey's hair, while I give her a manicure."

"Least you learned to do that."

"No, now let me finish. I'll give Betsey a manicure and a pedicure. Then we could do her face up like in the Ebony Fashion Fair. That way, when she does get home, she'll be looking so pretty her mama will forget how mad she is. You know she's going to be mad, don't you, Betsey?"

"Yeah, but it's her fault. She won't let me play the music I want to hear or dance the way I want to dance. You know, Regina, how we usedta fool around at Soldan when Smokey Robinson came, or the time you took us to see the Olympics. We danced in the aisles with everybody else. It was so wonderful when you were there, Regina. Remember, we did routines from the Shirelles and you rolled our hair up like the Ronettes with those false hairpieces from Mr. Robinson's. She doesn't want me to be like everybody else, Regina. She wants me to be special, like I lived inside a glass cage or something. She actually thinks those white kids where I go to school think I'm alive. Gina, they hardly speak to me. And the one time I had a spend-the-night party only one of them showed up, and she was Jewish. They don't like her, either. But I can't tell anybody these things cause how would that look, to say we weren't up to white folks. I know we got to fight the white people and be better than them, Gina. It's just I'm so tired of them and I feel so much better when I'm with the colored. I feel so much better when I'm like everybody else."

Betsey wept on Gina's thighs just where the baby was jutting out. Mrs. Maureen was mixing egg yolks and beer to give Betsey a conditioner, shaking her head, mumbling bout the things children had on their minds these days. A child had a right to be a child. Even in Mississippi a girl was a girl till her time came. White folks or no white folks. Nobody sent a little ol' thing out to take up for the whole damn race. That's what was wrong with the colored, always putting it off to the next generation to do battle with the white man.

"Betsey, honey, that's called loneliness. You're gonna be lonely sometimes, sweetie. Cause you are special. Your mama's not making that up. You are different and it's not the color of your skin, either. You have a good time the way nobody else can, and you feel things the way nobody else can. There is no such thing as ordinary, Betsey. Nobody's ordinary. Each one of us is special and it's the coming together of alla that that makes the world so fine."

Mrs. Maureen almost dropped her egg yolks and beer concoction, listening to Gina. Then she motioned for Gina to move Betsey's head round so they could condition it real good.

"Betsey, I'm not saying that there's not different kinds of folks. You and me, we're different."

"You better believe that," Mrs. Maureen added, her fingers gooey with the yolk and malt coating Betsey's head.

"That's not what I meant, but in a way it is. Betsey, you and I can do certain kinds of things together and then there are other things we can never do together. It's hard to explain, but there's all different kinds of colored folks. You're one kind and I'm another, that's all."

"But don't you like me, Regina?"

"Oh Betsey, I love you. You're like my own sister. Why if the baby is a girl, I'ma gonna name her Elizabeth and call her Betsey with a 'e.' Cross my heart."

"She's ready for a rinse now," Mrs. Maureen wrapped Betsey's head in a towel, while Regina threw an old shirt around Betsey's very Lord and Taylor school outfit.

Regina laughed silently. Betsey even ran off like a doctor's daughter. How was she going to be ordinary when there weren't but five thousand Negro doctors in the whole country. Gina'd heard Dr. Brown say that to Charlie one time, when Charlie said he wanted to be like Jackie Robinson. What a whipping that was. Thinking bout the Browns took Regina's mind off Betsey and to her baby.

How was she gonna feed her child? How could she ever have a child like Betsey, who heard the word colored and thought of something good? How was she gonna explain who or where Daddy was, when she'd planned for Daddy to be right there?

The rinse was set and Betsey was under the dryer in the front of Mrs. Maureen's, where the hincty Negro ladies lined up with their furs and polished faces. Mrs. Maureen's demeanor had changed entirely, as had her clothes. She was in her little pink uniform with the appliquéd flower on the collar and the white nurse's shoes she wore every day as she stood over the doctor's wife, the lawyer's wife, the minister's wife, and the undertaker's wife. The helpers were clad in smart white jackets moving quickly from hand to hand, foot to foot. It was the only place in town a Negro woman could get a manicure, or a pedicure, if she was brave enough. They lived in a world of their own and never ventured past the French doors where Mrs. Maureen's other world thrived.

Betsey was as pampered as a princess. Mrs. Maureen explained her presence on a school day as a mixture of a birthday present and as a prelude to Betsey's solo clarinet performance in front of the white people at one of those "schools."

The women nodded their heads. Yes, it was important to look good if you're dealing with white folks. Yes, it was lovely of Mrs. Brown to think of letting Betsey have a manicure when her hands were going to be so prominently displayed.

Betsey couldn't hear, but she could see some of what Regina meant. There were different kinds of Negroes. She bet money some of these Negroes wouldn't give a stone's throw if something happened to Roscoe, they didn't care what was gonna happen to Regina's baby. "Niggahs" they'd say and leave it to the will of God that people, especially colored people, suffered. Yet, they couldn't go anywhere else to have their hands done but a bordello. Betsey burst out laughing. She could tell by the looks on the women's faces that it was an "inappropriate" laugh. As if being a Negro was appropriate. Betsey knew they'd never get that joke. So she went back to reading bout a murder in *Tan.*

Mrs. Maureen sent Regina for Little John to come do Betsey's make-up. It was Mrs. Maureen's way of saying to Mrs. Brown that there's a growing girl here, lady, pay attention. The minister's wife left just in time. The other ladies were puzzled, but calmed when Mrs. Maureen went on bout stagelights and bone structure. Little John just hovered with brushes of mink and fox hair. He was in his world. A face with no wrinkles. No blemishes. Purity. He was beside himself. Mrs. Maureen had to remind him, "Little John, she a child playing a clarinet, this is not the Jewel Box Revue."

The pedicure Regina executed herself. She wanted Betsey to feel relaxed and cared about. The way all little Negro girls should feel. Not cramped or out of place, or funny-looking or easy. Just lovely and well-loved. Gina gave Betsey a very special pedicure cause she knew she'd never have one, and probably her little girl wouldn't either. Not the way this world was bout folks born on the other side of the tracks, colored or white. You could forget it, the sweetness, that is.

Betsey could hardly believe it was her when she looked in the mirror. What a woman she was going to be! Regina gave her five dollars to take a cab home, cause dusk was falling and it was getting late. Regina made her promise not to come back or mention to her mama about the baby or Roscoe. Mrs. Maureen was more explicit.

"If your mother so much as dreams you were here before the shop opened, you gonna get a licking the likes of which you've never felt."

Regina held Betsey real close to her. "Betsey, your life isn't gonna be like mine. Don't you grow up too soon. Take your time. There's something so special when you're really in love, let it come to you. Don't chase it. Okay? You be good, now. I love you."

With that Betsey was sent down the stairs and out the door, escorted by Little John, who was still dabbing and brushing her face. "You are just too beautiful, my dear."

Betsey felt beautiful. She felt brave. She knew it now. There was a difference between being a little girl and being a woman. She knew now. She'd never see Regina again, but they'd never be separate, either. Women who can see over the other side are never far from each other.

Betsey took her five dollars to a very special place. A Yellow cab carried her to the boulevard where the white folks had their parade each fall and crowned a queen of the Veiled Prophet, who was a white man no one ever saw. Then they had a big ball with pictures in the newspapers for days of this white girl and that white girl. The regular people could come and watch, even the colored. Betsey did it every year, looked at the floats of the ladies in waiting in their satin gowns and laced gloves, the clowns and musicians longside the floats entertaining one and all. The whole city in a Mardi Gras out of season and out of time, with young girls of every color wishing the man behind the jeweled mask had chosen them to ride about the city that night, a night the stars were sapphires, opals, and diamonds, a tiara for a queen.

Betsey paid the cab driver $4.25 and gave him the rest as a tip. She was feeling regal. Then she marched as grandly as possible to the middle of the street where she proceeded to stop traffic and create a great stir while she declared herself Queen of the Negro Veiled Prophet and his entourage.

The police only asked her her name and address, and went on about how St. Louis was a dangerous place to be roaming about alone at dusk. They didn't understand she reigned on her own streets for the first time in her life. She wasn't afraid anymore. The city was hers.

GARRETT HONGO
(B. 1951)

Hongo was born into a family of Japanese origins in the small, lush community of Volcano, on the Big Island of Hawaii. Early in his life, his family moved elsewhere in Hawaii, then to California, settling finally in Gardena, a Japanese-American community adjacent to Watts. Hongo graduated from Pomona College, traveled to Japan on a Watson fellowship, studied at the University of Michigan, then earned an M.F.A. degree at the University of California/ Irvine. He has taught at a number of colleges, mainly at the University of Missouri, where he also served as editor of the Missouri Review, *and more recently at the University of Oregon.*

Hongo was initially inspired by a group of writers—Frank Chin, Lawson Fusao Inada, and Wakako Yamauchi—who conceived the category "Asian-American," as distinct from the particularity of a single national origin. He directed a theater group in Seattle from 1976–1978 with the wonderful title of the Asian Exclusion Act, staging a number of important Asian-American dramas. He also published an initial volume of poetry with Inada and Alan Chong Lau titled Buddha Bandits Down Highway 99 *(1978). His own first book of poems was* Yellow Light *(1982), which won the Wesleyan Poetry Prize. It was followed by* The River of Heaven *(1988), which was widely praised. His memoir,* Volcano, *came out in 1995. At the same time, he was active as an editor and promoter of Asian-American literature:* The Open Boat *(1993) includes thirty-one Asian-American poets;* Under Western Eyes *(1995) is a volume of personal stories by Asian-American writers. And Hongo expressed his indebtedness to Wakako Yamauchi by editing and writing an introduction to her collection* Songs My Mother Taught Me *(1994).*

Hongo's own poetry uses details of Japanese-American life, from food to family relations to work, to express his quest for a sense of his origins and his identity as at once American, Japanese, Hawaiian, and the various hyphenates that can be constructed from those terms. He has been a tireless experimenter with aspects of Asian-American cultures, from music to poetic forms, in his effort to capture the lives and forms of work of those from whom he is descended.

OFF FROM SWING SHIFT

Late, just past midnight,
freeway noise from the Harbor
and San Diego leaking in
from the vent over the stove,
and he's off from swing shift at Lear's.
Eight hours of twisting circuitry,
charting ohms and maximum gains
while transformers hum
and helicopters swirl
on the roofs above the small factory.
He hails me with a head-fake,
then the bob and weave
of a weekend middleweight
learned at the Y on Kapiolani
ten years before I was born.

The shoes and gold London Fogger
come off first, then the easy grin
saying he's lucky as they come.
He gets into the slippers
my brother gives him every Christmas,
carries his Thermos over to the sink,
and slides into the one chair at the table
that's made of wood and not yellow plastic.
He pushes aside stacks
of *Sporting News* and *Outdoor Life,*
big round tins of Holland butter cookies,
and clears a space for his elbows, his pens,
and the *Racing Form's* Late Evening Final.

His left hand reaches out,
flicks on the Sony transistor
we bought for his birthday
when I was fifteen.
The right ferries in the earphone,
a small, flesh-colored star,
like a tiny miracle of hearing,
and fits it into place.
I see him plot black constellations
of figures and calculations
on the magazine's margins,
alternately squint and frown
as he fingers the knob of the tuner
searching for the one band
that will call out today's results.

There are whole cosmologies
in a single handicap,
a lifetime of two-dollar losing
in one pick of the Daily Double.

Maybe tonight is his night
for winning, his night
for beating the odds
of going deaf from a shell
at Anzio still echoing
in the cave of his inner ear,
his night for cashing in
the blue chips of shrapnel still grinding
at the thickening joints of his legs.

But no one calls
the horse's name, no one
says Shackles, Rebate, or Pouring Rain.
No one speaks a word.

–1982

BRUCE SPRINGSTEEN

(B. 1949)

During the 1980s, Springsteen was not only an enormously popular rock star—some of his albums sold over ten million copies and Born in the USA *eighteen million—but he became a political icon of the Reagan years. Reagan himself tried to coopt his songs by referring to him at a campaign stop in New Jersey, Springsteen's home state. The singer responded by suggesting that the president hadn't listened to his lyrics. Indeed, it is unlikely that conservatives, who knew only the title of "Born in the USA," actually heard the songs. For Springsteen was active in liberal causes, singing on behalf of Amnesty International, No Nukes, and the Christic Institute. More to the point, many of his most striking songs, including "Born in the USA," are bitter condemnations of the system that left Vietnam veterans homeless, and the "guy in the car" with no place to drive. In fact, the deindustrialization of America and its lacerating impact on ordinary working people, became his theme in those memorable eighties albums. As James Wolcott put it with only minor inaccuracy in a* Vanity Fair *article, "Silent factories are to him what church ruins were to the English Romantics, crumbling theatres of decay which serve as houses of lost faith."*

Springsteen was born and grew up in a declining area of New Jersey near the decayed resort, Asbury Park. His father held a variety of blue-collar jobs but was frequently unemployed; nor did he approve of Spring-

steen's musical passion. But his mother, who worked as a legal secretary, encouraged his playing, even when the family moved to California, and Springsteen and his guitar remained in the east. He formed a series of bands, playing in and around Asbury Park, in Greenwich Village, and even, with a group called "Steel Mill," in the legendary Fillmore West. Around 1971, Springsteen signed a multiple-album contract with Columbia records; it was only with the third of these albums, Born to Run *(1975), that the singer really hit his stride.*

The songs that commanded most attention were those, like "The River," which narrated the disillusion and decline of a young working-class couple—typical figures in those years of America's economic decline. Others expressed a sense of nihilism at a world grown out of control, at least from the perspective of the working people being downsized and made to feel superfluous.

GALVESTON BAY

Fifteen years Le Bing Son
Fought side by side with the Americans
In the mountains and deltas of Vietnam
In '75 Saigon fell and he left his command
And brought his family to the promised land

Seabrook Texas and the small towns in the Gulf of Mexico
It was delta country and reminded him of home
He worked as a machinist, put his money away
And bought a shrimp boat with his cousin
And together they harvested Galveston Bay

In the mornin' 'fore the sun come up
He'd kiss his sleepin' daughter
Steer out through the channel
And casts his nets into the water

Billy Sutter fought with Charlie Company
In the highlands of Quang Tri
He was wounded in the battle of Chu Lai
And shipped home in '68

There he married and worked the gulf fishing grounds
In a boat that'd been his father's
In the morning he'd kiss his sleeping son
And cast his nets into the water

Billy sat in front of his TV as the south fell
And the Communists rolled into Saigon
He and his friends watched as the refugees came

Settle on the same streets and worked the coast they grew up on
Soon in the bars around the harbor was talk
Of America for Americans
Someone said, "You want 'em out, you got to burn 'em out"
And brought in the Texas klan

One humid Texas night there were three shadows in the harbor
Come to burn the Vietnamese boats into the sea
In the fire's light shots rang out
Two Texans lay dead on the ground
Le stood with a pistol in his hand

A jury acquitted him in self defense
As before the judge he did stand
But as he walked down the courthouse steps
Billy said "My friend, you're a dead man"

One late summer night Le stood watch along the waterside
Billy stood in the shadows
His K-bar knife in his hand
And the moon slipped behind the clouds
Le lit a cigarette, the bay was as still as glass
As he walked by Billy stuck his knife into his pocket
Took a breath and let him pass

In the early darkness Billy rose up
Went into the kitchen for a drink of water
Kissed his sleeping wife
Headed into the channel
And casts his nets into the water
Of Galveston Bay

PHILIP LEVINE
(B. 1928)

"Make no mistake," Philip Levine writes in "Coming Close," "the place has a language." The place is an auto plant; the language what a man and a woman exchange in its venue, are able to exchange across the boundaries not just of sex, but of class and job category. The poem is from Levine's book, What Work Is *(1991), one of many in that volume and others that captures the qualities of industrial labor and of relationships between human beings in its domain.*

Like many of the poets who write about factory work, Levine is from Detroit. He has, however, gained unusual recognition for poems that remain sensitive both to the demands of heavy labor and to the nuances of human interactions. Among his sixteen books of poetry are 7 Years from Somewhere *(1979), which won the National Book Critics' Circle Award;* Ashes: Poems Old and New *(1980), which won that award and the first American Book Award for poetry; and* The Simple Truth *(1994), which won the Pulitzer Prize for poetry. Levine has also coedited and translated volumes by Gloria Fuentes and Jaime Sabines, edited* The Essential Keats *(1987), and published a collection of essays,* The Bread of Time: Toward an Autobiography *(1994).*

He has also been an important force in shaping the contemporary poetry scene, first as a teacher at the University of Michigan and at New York University, among other places, but also as a reader and supportive critic. In addition, he was for two years chair of the literature panel of the National Endowment for the Humanities. Levine's work never ignores the labor his people must perform, but neither is he willing to disregard the rest of human life, however compelling the demands of the assembly line. Thus he captures in subtle but approachable language more the tensions that arise out of work than the processes of labor as such.

You Can Have It

My brother comes home from work
and climbs the stairs to our room.
I can hear the bed groan and his shoes drop
one by one. You can have it, he says.

The moonlight streams in the window
and his unshaven face is whitened
like the face of the moon. He will sleep
long after noon and waken to find me gone.

Thirty years will pass before I remember
that moment when suddenly I knew each man
has one brother who dies when he sleeps
and sleeps when he rises to face this life,

and that together they are only one man
sharing a heart that always labors, hands
yellowed and cracked, a mouth that gasps
for breath and asks, Am I gonna make it?

All night at the ice plant he had fed
the chute its silvery blocks, and then I
stacked cases of orange soda for the children
of Kentucky, one gray box-car at a time

with always two more waiting. We were twenty
for such a short time and always in
the wrong clothes, crusted with dirt
and sweat. I think now we were never twenty.

In 1948 in the city of Detroit, founded
by de la Mothe Cadillac for the distant purpose
of Henry Ford, no one wakened or died,
no one walked the streets or stoked a furnace,

for there was no such year, and now
that year has fallen off all the old newspapers,
calendars, doctors' appointments, bonds,
wedding certificates, driver's licenses.

The city slept. The snow turned to ice.
The ice to standing pools or rivers
racing in the gutters. Then bright grass rose
between the thousands of cracked squares,

and that grass died. I give you back 1948.
I give you all the years from then
to the coming one. Give me back the moon
with its frail light falling across a face.

Give me back my young brother, hard
and furious, with wide shoulders and a curse
for God and burning eyes that look upon
all creation and say, You can have it.

WAKAKO YAMAUCHI
(B. 1924)

On at least two occasions, Yamauchi has transformed her short stories into
plays. That process suggests not only her commitment to the theater, but
the dramatic qualities of her stories. In a similar way, she has converted the
stories her mother told her about Japan into a variety of other forms:
poetry, stories, and painting, as is suggested by the title of one of her recent
volumes, Songs My Mother Taught Me (1994).

Yamauchi grew up in California's Imperial Valley, where her parents
were forced to move again and again by laws restricting Japanese ownership of land. At age seventeen, a high school senior, she and her family
were forced into the internment camp at Poston, Arizona, one of a number
to which the U.S. government sent people of Japanese origins after the outbreak of World War II. She was allowed to leave the camp after a year and
a half to take a job in a Chicago candy factory. She wrote about the camp

experience in 12-1-A (1993), a play that takes viewers into the Poston camp with a Japanese family trying to reconcile ideas of democracy to the tyrannical way they have been treated.

Her first play, And the Soul Shall Dance, *came out in 1974, two years after the story on which it is based. As has been the case with a number of her works, it draws on her own experiences, in this case living on a farm amidst racial hostility and the economic uncertainty of the Depression of the 1930s. Despite the discrimination she shared with other Japanese-Americans, and despite the oppressiveness of the camp experience, Yamauchi's work is neither gloomy nor bitter. Rather it offers a sense of the drive and inspiration her characters share with her.*

MAYBE

When I am out of sorts, I often drive to the outer edge of the city to calm myself. I love the outskirts. It reminds me of the land as it must have looked before we covered the earth with cement. I find there a feeling of the prairie where I was born. Sometimes when I see an old house with peeling paint squatting on a mound of dry weeds, the setting sun bleaching its west wall, I think I hear the children that have played there, perhaps now as old as myself—if they have survived the depression, three wars, sickness, and heartbreak. At this point I remember where I am in the scheme of things, smaller than a grain of sand and as dispensable. It comforts me.

One day on such a drive, I found the factory just outside of town. Here narrow roads burrow through low hills; and frame houses, shutters askew like unfocused eyes, along with rusting cars and oil drums, are enclosed by the chain-link fence that banks the city drain. The lots are oddly shaped; city planners had exercised eminent domain and sliced the properties at their convenience, creating instant prosperity to the owners (providing rabbit-skin coats and hand-tooled boots), maiming the lots for that brief prosperity (a tuft of fur caught in the chain links, a weathered boot lying with the flotsam in the weeds). A sign on the outer wall of the factory: HELP, succinct, desperate, still with a touch of humor, gave me courage to walk in. After all, I was no less in need, my alimony had dwindled to a trickle; after eight years, that's about par for course, my attorney said. Even after twenty-five years of marriage, he said. That's life. The owner himself, Chuck White, took me in like a lost member of a tribe. We're of the same generation.

I am embarrassed to tell you the name of the company; it's too presumptuous for the two stories of rotting wood and broken windows and air conditioners hanging off the walls. Those that still function spin out tails of spidery dust in the tepid air. But that's only in the offices, not for the majority of us.

I will call it Zodiac Prints. When I joined them, they were printing signs of the zodiac on T-shirts and cloth posters. I was hired as a quality-control person. They put me at the end of a long conveyor belt that slowly passes through several silk screens, each a different color, and a drying process. I check the colors, the print, and the material for flaws, and I stack and bundle the finished product. They don't say Zodiac till *I* say they say Zodiac.

Although I was the last hired, I was sent to the end of the belt largely because of Chuck White. White people (no pun intended) do not observe the difference between native Japanese and Japanese Americans. As I said, I was born in the southern California desert, but people are often amazed that I can speak English, and I guess Chuck White associates me with Japanese industry (Sony, Toyota, et cetera), and just for walking in and asking for a job, I went to the back of the line which in this case is the top of the bottom. This inability of white America to differentiate worked against thousands of us Japanese Americans in 1942 when we were all put in concentration camps, blamed for Japan's attack on Pearl Harbor. Since then there have been other harrowing moments—the save-the-whale issue, the slaughter of dolphins, and always during trade treaties over Japanese exports—each sending waves of guilt by association. On the extreme, some of us have been clubbed to death by our super-patriots, and we have always been admonished to go back where we came from.

Anyway, back at Zodiac, the story I hear is that Chuck White was having financial trouble and had taken steps toward declaring bankruptcy. He planned to drop out, wipe off the slate of debts, and start clean at another place under his wife's name—Zenobia. They say it isn't the first time Chuck did this, but the first with the new wife.

Preparations for the change had been made; a new site was selected, new business cards with Zenobia's name were printed, and Zenobia was coming in daily to get a working knowledge of the business. Then, suddenly the orders came pouring in and with it thousands of dollars. New people had to be hired. The factory started to hum again, and the move was postponed. This is where I came in.

They say that Zenobia—Colombian by birth, a ravishing overweight beauty at least twenty years Chuck White's junior (like my husband's new wife)—changed from a quiet housewife to a formidable boss as easily as she would put on a coat, wearing all the executive qualities, the harassed eyes, the no-nonsense walk, the imperial forefinger, and also a touch of paternal benevolence—the sodas and tacos on the days that we worked overtime. Most of the workers are from Mexico, Nicaragua, and Costa Rica. The sales staff is white, but they are often not at the factory.

Zenobia watches me when she thinks I'm not looking. I catch her reflection on the dirty glass panes, and when I turn to face her, she flashes her perfect teeth. She doesn't like me. Maybe I remind her of someone. Maybe she's amazed that I can speak English. China, she calls me. Maybe she thinks I'm a communist.

Most of the time, she's busy on the phone or is rushing off somewhere in her silver Mercedes. Probably to the bank. She wears Gloria Vanderbilt jeans and carries a Gucci bag and smells of expensive perfume. When Chuck White is out of town, she moves me from one floor to the other for unimportant reasons. Just to let me know how superfluous I am.

So it goes. I've had worse things happen to me, and nothing about this job causes me to lose sleep. Almost nothing. There's a certain confidence in knowing you're overqualified, and Zenobia does not diminish me. Besides, I like the second floor; the project is more interesting. They tie-dye there. Twenty people bend over paint troughs, dipping and squeezing shirts, skirts, and other things, and the items hang to dry on rows and rows of lines, dripping and making puddles of color on the worn floor.

There are three big German shepherd dogs in the factory. During the worst of his days (I'm told), Chuck White had to sell his Bel Air house, but Zenobia would not let him sell the dogs. So the dogs live in the ramshackle factory, and they follow Umberto, who feeds and cleans up after them, everywhere he goes—roaming the floors (they're not permitted outside), in and out of rooms, up and down the stairs, stumbled on and cursed at by the workers. When Umberto is not here, these monstrous animals lie disconsolately on the floor wherever their depression happens to drop them. Umberto calls them by name and rubs their monster heads, and they thump their powerful tails and slosh him with saliva. He's patient and gentle. He's twenty-four and quite handsome.

Everyone here who is from the other Americas is between seventeen and twenty-five. They all speak Spanish, some a little English, and they generally work quietly, obeying Zenobia or Rachel (the floorlady) without question or comment. In the late afternoons and on paydays, Jesus (El Savior) begins to sing and an excitement prevails, even though we groan and laugh at his comic straining for high notes. I am reminded of my own youth, after being released from camp, the period that I spent working in factories, looking over the boys, waiting for the end of the day, looking forward to my paycheck, mentally parceling out the money—to the layaway at Lerner's, for rent, food, for bus tokens. Fridays were just like these, with another Jesus singing and cutting up, with everyone waiting for the factory whistle so we could go on with our real lives. I've come full circle, back to a place that has remained unchanged in the changing times, in the age of Pac-Man and the computer. Maybe all displaced people go through a period of innocence before the desire to own, the ambition to be, propel us away from simple pleasures. The return is sweet with remembrance, along with a little sorrow—for the loss of innocence. But I'm older now, and none of the senses are so acute and no pain so unbearable. And yet . . .

On a coffee break, I walk to the low hills for a breath of fresh air. Reynaldo and Anabella sit on top of the knoll on a scrap of plastic. Reynaldo is in charge of the keys to the factory and is married to Anabella. She doesn't speak much English, so she always stays close to him, letting him transact the business of their lives. Faded pop cans lie in the dry grass.

"How romantic," I say to them.

"It is hot in the factory," Reynaldo says. Anabella whispers something.

"We are talking about our son," Reynaldo says.

Why, Anabella looks no more than seventeen. I tell him this.

"She is twenty-one, same as me," Reynaldo says. "We are married already five years. Our son is in Mexico still. Today is his birthday."

Walking down the hill, I am filled with their longing. I stop to look back at them. Anabella waves.

Umberto is not conscientious about cleaning the factory. The women's bathroom is dotted with dog droppings. I complain, and Umberto tells me not to use it.

"I cannot clean everything all the time and do the work also," he says. "The dogs, you know, they do it all the time. I cannot keep up. Go to the office toilet."

He tells me they pay him three dollars and thirty-five cents an hour—the minimum. He gets up at four to come to work; his bus fare is three dollars, and lunch from the catering truck almost always costs six dollars a day. He is so tired at the end of day, he cannot stay awake. He shakes his head. "I am still a young man," he says.

The reedy whistle of the catering truck rises above factory noises and a surge of people run to meet it. The chatter grows bright with food words: *tortillas, pollo, naranja.* My high-school Spanish is inadequate; I wish I knew what else is said. Umberto sits on the ground to eat, carefully placing the paper plate in the circle of his legs. I feel the sublime intimacy of the man and his food.

To get to the office bathroom, I must pass through Chuck White's office. He sits at a big desk looking over invoices in a pool of sunlight. The floor is carpeted, the walls are papered; the room is an oasis in the factory. He looks up briefly and smiles—almost an apology. "The other bathroom is filthy," I say. He nods and returns to his papers. No doubt he's heard of the fastidious Japanese.

Someone tried to bring some class to the bathroom and had painted the walls a dark green and installed a pair of fancy faucets in the sink. An electric hotplate on a crate destroys the ambiance, and there is a bottle of shampoo on the floor. The toilet here doesn't flush right either.

Umberto tells me that Reynaldo and Anabella live in the factory at night. I see no bed, no blankets, no clothes—only the hotplate and shampoo in the office bathroom. I think about the eerie loneliness of this huge factory at night, the three dogs groaning and snuffling and shuffling, the doors that hardly close, and Reynaldo and Anabella copulating on the production table with the smell of the dogs and the spoiling vegetable dyes and the summer moon shining on their skin. And in the morning I see them putting away the evidence of their living: the underwear, the socks, the toothbrushes, combs, and towels.

But Umberto says Zenobia knows about this. She lets them stay because they have nowhere else to go. Umberto himself shares rent with six other people. "I have no room for them," he says.

In winter, icy winds will blow through those broken windows and ill-fitting doors, and the production table will be cold and hard, I tell Umberto.

"That's winter," he shrugs.

Reynaldo makes a sandwich from a loaf of Weber's bread and pressed meat. He spreads the bread with a thin swipe of mayonnaise and eats this with a gusto that can come only from hunger or habit. Anabella buys fried chicken, frijoles, and tortillas from the truck and shares these with Reynaldo. She eats slowly and sensually, careful not to lose a morsel from the chicken bones. She eats a sandwich too. I make fun; I point to her stomach and ask, "How many months?" She holds up four fingers.

I have a feeling Zenobia likes the sales staff as little as she does me. They bring her extravagant gifts and she puts on a dazzling smile and turns away, quickly dropping the smile as though she hopes her hypocrisy would be discovered. But on her birthday she invites them all to a party—everyone except me. I'd already contributed five dollars toward her gift, and I had signed the birthday card.

She's happy all day, smiling and humming, but I pretend not to know what's up and try to look happy too. What do I care? If she has a conscience at all, she'll feel rotten when she sees my name on the card. I wish Rachel had let me do the shopping; I'd have fixed her good (I thought I'd given up feelings like that).

At the party they say Zenobia drinks too much and kisses all the young men. That's because she married an old man, Umberto says. Late in the evening she sniffs cocaine and turns up the music and wants to dance with all the guys. Chuck White serves the cake and goes to bed. Neighbors call to complain about the noise, and everyone gets nervous thinking about police and raids and such things. These are always on the top of an undocumented alien's mind, Umberto says. Zenobia doesn't care; she married a white man and holds a green card. Umberto says everyone in the factory except the sales staff is undocumented. Reynaldo comes to sit with us.

"Are you illegal too?" I ask.

Reynaldo nods. "Everybody is. In this factory, in all the restaurants around here, all these places," he waves his hands. "These places, they would not stand without us." He pokes my arm and laughs. "Hey, you want to marry me? I'll give you one thousand dollars," he says.

"What will we do with Anabella?" I say.

"After our divorce, I will marry her," he says.

"But I have children older than you," I say.

He moves away and calls back, "One thousand dollars, Florence." Anabella smiles at me.

Andrea stands at the bus stop with a plastic purse clasped to her breast. She is seventeen and the prettiest girl in the factory, but today she looks awful. It's before the lunch hour. "Is she sick?" I ask Umberto.

"Well, Chuck told her to go home," he says.

The story is, Zenobia was so anxious to get an order off, she told Andrea to remove the bands before time and dry the shirts. Andrea did this, but she put the shirts in the tumble dryer, and the wet dyes ran together and the whole order was ruined. Chuck White found the mess and fired Andrea. Even after he was told about Zenobia's instructions, he would not relent. "She should know better," he said and went to his office and closed the door.

Umberto taps his head. "She should know better," he says.

"Look how she holds her purse," I say.

"Well, she's sad," he says.

"Her mother will ask what happened, and she'll have to say she lost her job."

"Rachel will find another for her," Umberto says.

"What will happen if she doesn't?" I ask.

"Then I will find for her," he says.

Reynaldo punches my arm every time he passes by, mocking me softly, "One thousand dollars, Florence." Sometimes he catches my eye from across the room and mouths, "One thousand dollars."

I call a young single friend to ask if she would marry Reynaldo. She is divorced and always in need of money, but she tells me that immigration laws require a full three years of marriage before they will issue green cards. "That's longer than some real marriages last," my friend says. "One thousand dollars for three years is three hundred and thirty-three dollars a year," she says.

"And thirty-three cents," I add.

"I turned down ten thousand for the same service," she says. "And I could very well meet someone myself in three years. A real marriage, you know what I mean?"

I give Reynaldo the bad news. He looks hurt even though we only joke about it. I tell him my friend says three years is too long to be tied to a stranger.

"I just want a green card so I can bring my son here," he says. "My son was two years when we left him. He already forgot me, I think." Anabella turns her face away.

"I can't marry you, Reynaldo," I say.

"I know," he says. After a while he walks away.

I'm afraid I shall leave Zodiac soon. In the deceptive simplicity of the lives here, there is a quality I am unable to face. It's the underbelly of a smile. I know it well.

I remember our life in the Arizona camp—the first day our family entered that empty barracks room (our home for the next four years), my father squatted on the dusty floor, his head deep in his shoulders, and my mother unwrapped a roll of salami and sliced it for us. I wanted so much to cry, but my mother gripped my arm and gave me the meat. I turned to my father; he looked up and smiled. Two years later, the day I was to leave them and relocate to Chicago, my mother stood by the army truck that was to take us to the train in Parker. She had not wanted me to leave because my father was in the hospital with stomach ulcers. She did not touch me. The corners of her mouth wavered once, then turned up in a smile. And in the same tradition, I smiled when my husband told me he was marrying a young woman from Japan. "That's good," I said.

It did not seem so brave or so sad then. Maybe living it is easier than remembering or watching someone else living it. My son is in Mexico still, ha-ha; he will soon forget me.

Late in the afternoon Reynaldo comes back to me and pokes my arm. "Thank you for telling your friend to marry me," he says.

"I'm sorry it didn't work out," I say. I ask him if he crossed the border at Tijuana. My sister lives in National City, just north of the border. I remember those immigration roundups that show periodically on television nightly news: soft gray blurs running in the California twilight, crouching, routed out of bushes, herded into covered pickup trucks, their faces impassive.

"We crossed the river in Texas," he says.

"You swam the Rio Grande at night?" I ask.

Reynaldo nods. "Anabella, you know, she does not swim so I . . ." He crooks his left arm to make a circle for Anabella's head and with his right arm he makes swimming strokes and looks at me and smiles.

Maybe it does not seem so brave or so sad to him. Maybe I should spare myself the pain.

CHARLIE KING
(B. 1948)

Charlie King describes himself as "singer/songwriter/guitarist, some typing, no shorthand." The self-portrait captures both what he does and something of the irony, whimsy, and seriousness of his performances. He traces his roots to Mark Twain and Tom Lehrer, satirists with whom he has a good deal in common, as well as to singers like Phil Ochs, Malvina Reynolds, Tom Paxton and Pete Seeger. In his songs King celebrates the common decency of ordinary folk, even as he is lampooning the daily pieties and pomposities of American life and politics.

After graduating from Stonehill College, King lived and worked at a soup kitchen in New York. There he helped the United Farm Workers during their grape and lettuce boycotts, singing at rallies, picket lines, and fund raisers. He was a conscientious objector during the Vietnam war and did his alternative service at a Massachusetts hospital. He has since sung to support clerical and technical workers at Harvard and Yale Universities, as well as for auto workers, coal miners and meat packers. He serves as secretary-treasurer of Local 1000 of the North American Traveling Musicians Union, which he helped start.

King has issued ten albums, many of which consist of his own songs on topical issues. But he also sings and records traditional ballads from Ireland, Scotland, Australia, and Canada, as well as from the United States. One of his specialties is a performance called "Working People: A Musical History," that includes songs in a variety of styles from rock to folk, and from blues to bluegrass.

OUR LIFE IS MORE THAN OUR WORK

Look all around you, say, look all around you
See all there is just to be alive about
Look all around you at the people around you
See all there is just to being alive.

Chorus:
Oh, our life—is—more than our work
And our work—is—more than our jobs
You know that our life—is—more than our work
And our work—is—more than our jobs

Time clocks and bosses, investments and losses
How can we measure our life in numerals?
Time clocks and bosses, investments and losses
How can we measure our life in this way?

Think how our life could be, feel how our life could flow
If just for once we could get into letting go
Think how our life could be, feel how our life could flow
If just for once we could let ourselves go.

So, let go what holds you back, close your eyes, take a dive
We got a universe we got to keep alive
Let go what holds you back, close your eyes, take a dive
We got a universe fighting to live.

BRUCE SPRINGSTEEN
(B. 1949)

(For information about Springsteen, see the headnote above in this section.)

MY HOMETOWN

I was eight years old and running with a dime in my hand
Into the bus stop to pick up a paper for my old man
I'd sit on his lap in that big old Buick and steer as we drove through town
He'd tousle my hair and say son take a good look around

This is your hometown, this is your hometown
This is your hometown, this is your hometown

In '65 tension was running high at my high school
There was a lot of fights between the black and white
There was nothing you could do

Two cars at a light on a Saturday night in the back seat there was a gun
Words were passed in a shotgun blast
Troubled times had come to my hometown
My hometown, my hometown, my hometown

Now Main Street's whitewashed windows and vacant stores
Seems like there ain't nobody wants to come down here no more
They're closing down the textile mill across the railroad tracks
Foreman says these jobs are going boys and they ain't coming back to
Your hometown, your hometown, your hometown, your hometown

Last night me and Kate we laid in bed talking about getting out
Packing up our bags maybe heading south
I'm thirty-five we got a boy of our own now
Last night I sat him up behind the wheel and said son take a good look
    around
This is your hometown

PATRICIA DOBLER

In this poem Dobler focuses more on the spectacle of consumption as a central ingredient of class distinctions. (See entry in section I for biographical information.)

CONSUMERS, 1965

Suddenly they were all rich.
Pickups bloomed with trailer hitches,
outboard motors shone in the driveways.
They'd convoy to the lake, swim and grill steaks
until the men left for 4 to 12's.

Daily, the women had
something new to talk about,
but the chromed machines
purring in their kitchens
and the strangeness of old rooms
masked with stiff brocade

unnerved them; frowning, they fingered
drapes and carpets like curators.

They began to pack fat onto bellies and thighs
as if preparing for a long journey on foot
through a frozen country, a journey
they would have to take alone and without provision.

LAWRENCE KEARNEY
(B. 1948)

Kearney was born in England but came to the United States in time to earn a B.A. at the State University of New York Buffalo campus. Subsequently he achieved the M.F.A. at the University of Arizona in 1975. He taught for brief periods at Arizona and at Wayne State University in Detroit. He has held a number of significant fellowships, including awards from the Guggenheim Foundation and the National Endowment for the Humanities. His first book of poetry, Kingdom Come, *was published in 1980.* Streaming: 1981-1987 *was published in 1988. His poems have also appeared in a number of literary and general interest magazines, including* The Atlantic Monthly, The Massachusetts Review, The Paris Review, *and* The Chicago Review.

K MART

Mother is off to LADIES WEAR,
Father to HOME FURNISHINGS.
As usual, I'm with him.

Passing HARDWARE, he instructs me
in the merits of variable-speed
drills, the sham of saber saws,
the parable of human folly
embodied in third-rate drop-forged
hammers. I nod. I'm twelve. He's
teaching me to shop like a man.

AUTOMOTIVE, SPORTING GOODS
a foray into COSMETICS
for deodorant & shave cream—
the lights droning overhead
their rheumy, incessant gossip,
here, in the one place we talk.

When it's time to go, his lessons
lapse. He wanders off by himself,
whistling his special call for Mother:
two notes
so high & clear they rise
above the whole store—
that tired, adult head, the jowls
rich with ridicule, with affection, Father
floating there like some exotic bird—
calling again & again for his unseen lover
across the abyss of goods between them.

JANIS JOPLIN
(1943-1970)

Janis Joplin's time in the lights of rock stardom lasted a brief four years. Her first performance, with Big Brother and the Holding Company, took place in June of 1966. By October of 1970, she was dead. It was quite a ride, as she might have said.

Joplin grew up in Port Arthur, Texas, from whose drive-in movies, soda parlors, and Welcome Wagons she first ran away at age 17. That lasted only a month before she was sufficiently beaten down to return. Her next sojourn lasted five years, during which she hitchhiked across much of the country, briefly attended, or at least visited, colleges, and sang in a few bars and clubs. She came back to Port Arthur in 1965, strung out and spent, applied herself to study at Lamar State College, and tried to fit in. It was useless. An invitation to sing with Big Brother drew her back to the Haight in San Francisco; they were a smash hit at the Avalon ballroom in 1966. The following June, Joplin stopped the show at the Monterey International Pop Festival with her rendition of Big Mama Thornton's "Love Is Like a Ball and Chain." From that point, her career took off: she played in virtually every important festival and at every significant auditorium in the United States, her first real album with Big Brother, Cheap Thrills *(1968), hit the gold by selling over a million copies before its release date, and she received the kind of adulation that had been reserved for the Beatles and the Rolling Stones.*

She had the capacity, with her grainy, rasping, big voice, and her total absorption in her singing, to bring her audience into the ecstasy she seemed to enter as she moaned, jumped, shouted, sang, whispered, and gyrated around the stage. Her lyrics, like the song that follows, often had a sardonic edge, born, perhaps, of her view that America was, when you came down to it, one big Port Arthur.

MERCEDES-BENZ

O Lord, won't you buy me a Mercedes-Benz?
My friends all have Porsches I must make amends,
Worked hard all my lifetime, no help from my friends,
O Lord, won't you buy me a Mercedes-Benz?

O Lord, won't you buy me a color TV?
Dialing for Dollars is trying to find me.
I'll wait for delivery each day until 3,
O Lord, won't you buy me a color TV?

O Lord won't you buy me a night on the town?
I'm counting on you Lord, please don't let me down.
Prove that you love me & buy the next round.
O Lord won't you buy me a night on the town?

CHRISTIAN MCEWEN
(B. 1956)

McEwen, an essayist, novelist, and teacher, was born in London and grew up in Scotland. She has taught poetry, nature writing and the personal memoir in the New York City public schools as well as at the Eugene Lang College and the Parsons School of Design of New School University, and at Lesley College. She has edited three collections of writing, Naming the Waves: Contemporary Lesbian Poetry *(1988), with Sue O'Sullivan,* Out the Other Side: Contemporary Lesbian Writing *(1989), and, most recently,* Jo's Girls: Tomboy Tales of High Adventure, True Grit & Real Life *(1997). Her essays and poems have appeared in* Granta, The Village Voice *and* The Nation, *and she has been active with the theater group Roots and Branches Intergenerational Theater and with Teachers and Writers Collaborative. She has also made a documentary called* Tom Girls. *Among other kinds of work, she has served in half-way houses as a counselor and as a paramedical assistant in the Ban Noi Leprosy Mission of northeast Thailand.*

GROWING UP UPPER CLASS

Telling

These days I live in London, where I earn my living as a teacher of creative writing and as a reader for a feminist publishing firm. I belong, most obviously, to the fringes of the professional middle class. But as a child in that Scottish nursery, I grew up with a very different sense of my identity. As a child, I grew up upper class. . . .

Since then, as a teacher, I've grown used to breaking certain rules, to admitting, "Yes, my father was an alcoholic," to saying, "No, you're not the only one who's tried to kill herself. I've done that too." I have come out as a lesbian in a room of straight (and mainly hostile) London professionals. But I can count on my fingers the number of times I've said, "My father was a baronet." Even now it frightens me to write it down.

If I do write now about my background and my growing up, it is because I think there's information there and that is needed. Despite the flood of upper class memoirs, journals, anecdotes and collected letters, very little has appeared which tries to question such an upbringing from inside, either in its own terms or in relation to the rest of society.[1] Meanwhile, life in Britain continues to be dominated by the class system, to a degree perhaps unimaginable in other countries. People do not talk easily or honestly across class barriers, and the stereotypes remain extremely powerful. . . .

In the piece which follows, I will be using my family history as the basis for some more extended arguments. The people I'm describing here are real. Because I've loved them and been loved by them, they loom too close. It is hard to maintain a consistent perspective, to know when their behavior is peculiar to them, and when it is characteristically upper class. Inevitably there will be warps and failures in my telling. Inevitably too, some of what I write will touch off angry memories in other people. All I can say is that I welcome correspondence. As much as almost anything, I think, we need each other's stories.

Why Have We Not Met?

When I was born, in 1956, my father was working as barrister[2] at the Inner Temple, London. His father was a politician,[3] and had recently been made a baronet,[4] but Papa, as the second son, was not expected to inherit. He was, at twenty-nine, an upper middle class professional, with a starred First[5] at Cambridge to his credit, and the promise of a fine career ahead.

My mother, twenty-one when I was born, was herself an educated woman, though she had left Oxford after her first year in order to get married. Her parents were a writer[6] and an actress,[7] self-made professional people from Liverpool and County Donegal, and my father, with his connections among the landed gentry, was said to have married beneath him. "Why have we not met her?" asked Princess Margaret when she heard of their engagement.

They had not met because Britain is a highly stratified society, and the different layers don't necessarily mix. As a young bachelor, home from war in Germany, my father had led a glamorous social life, doing the rounds of the big country houses, staying up dancing till all hours of the morning. Six foot three in his stockinged feet, with his easy jokes, his charm and his enthusiasm, he is remembered as a golden boy whom everybody loved.

Mama, in the meantime, had been living much more quietly. During term time she was still at boarding-school, reading French and Italian, studying for her A' levels.[8] Life in her parents' flat centered round their work. Grandpa Laver was Keeper of Prints and Drawings at the Victoria and Albert Museum; he wrote his books in the evening while my grandmother was at the theater. Mama watched and listened, went to the occasional play. Photographs of the time show a tall shy girl with great hooded eyelids, and the poise and manner of a young Madonna. She already had her quota of admirers, but her social experience was small. There was little chance she would ever have crossed paths with Princess Margaret. . . .

My parents saw themselves as enlightened, open-minded. They would never have agreed that in some final way they believed themselves "better" than other people. Nonetheless, they both devoted a terrific amount of energy to the business of making distinctions: separating themselves off from the rest of the world, and then going on to elaborate why this separation should "naturally" be so. As a child, I learnt that we were "lucky" to be Catholics, because Catholicism was the "One True Faith." Papa had that starred First from Cambridge; he was "cleverer" than other people's fathers. Such things were valuable, not in and of themselves, but because they were better than something, or, all too often, someone else. I took these lessons thoroughly to heart. . . .

Inheritance: Papa

For the first ten years of their marriage, from 1954 to 1964, my parents lived in the south of England. They were originally based in London, where my father worked, but moved to Wiltshire in 1959, a year after my sister Kate was born. James arrived in 1960, followed by another daughter, Helena, in 1961. Meanwhile, Papa commuted every week to London. He continued to practice as a barrister, and did some literary work on the side: writing, not surprisingly, for Catholic and right-wing papers. He wrote a legal column for the *Spectator* with two friends of his, and reviewed books for the *Spectator*, the *Tablet*, and a Jesuit magazine called *The Month*. In 1961, following in the political footsteps of his father, he was appointed Tory candidate for East Edinburgh. But in 1962, his father died.

When Grandpa McEwen died, he left two houses: one on the east coast of Scotland, near Berwick-on-Tweed, and one on the west, not far from Girvan. The one on the east coast was called Marchmont, a large pink sandstone house set in four thousand acres of good arable land, with a river running through, and six or seven farms besides. The other, smaller house was called Bardrochat.

According to Grandpa's will, both Marchmont and Bardrochat went to his eldest son, Jamie, along with a third of the family money. The rest of the money was to be divided equally among the remaining six children. At the time, such a decision would not have been considered in any way unusual or unfair. This, after all, was the law of primogeniture. With Grandpa's death, Jamie had become the baronet. No-one questioned his right to the two properties, or to the funds needed to maintain them.

In writing his will, however, my grandfather had made one important proviso. Should Jamie elect to keep only one of the houses, the other was to be offered in turn to each member of the immediate family. If no-one could afford to run it, the house was to be sold, at which point the proceeds would be divided as before: one-third to Jamie, two-thirds to everybody else.

Jamie had come home to Marchmont after the Second War, wounded and heart-sick. The place still had painful memories for him. As soon as he got married, he moved to Bardrochat. It came as no surprise to anyone when he decided to stay on there, and to let Marchmont go.

But if Jamie didn't feel very strongly about Marchmont, the rest of the family certainly did. They had been children there, and they loved every inch of it: the ninety-plus rooms, the long avenue of beeches, the old walled garden with its espaliered apple-trees. Nobody wanted the house to be sold, least of all my father.

In the summer of 1964, two years after Grandpa's death, Papa moved his entire family up to Marchmont. It was, he claimed, a temporary arrangement. He did not have the money to keep up the house, and legally, therefore, no right to live there, which as a lawyer he knew very well. But a couple of years later, he approached Jamie directly, and persuaded him to sign over the estate.

What this meant in terms of family politics, I only know through hearsay. Clearly my aunts and uncles were not pleased. Jamie's wife, my Aunt Clare, was especially incensed. For a while she spoke of taking Papa to court. There were mutters of "asset-stripping," of "taking advantage." My grandmother's skills as intermediary were taxed to the utmost. But in the end, the row blew over. Family attention passed on to something else, and Papa was left to cope with what he'd done. . . .

What Were We Actually Living On?

When my parents first got married, my mother had a larger income than my father. Grandpa Laver gave her £250 a year, while Grandpa McEwen gave Papa only £200. This "only" was the point of the story, which showed the triumph of the literary professionals over the landed gentry, at the same time emphasising that as a young married couple my parents too had had to pinch and scrape. In comparison with their richer friends this certainly was true. But in the larger scale of things they could consider themselves lucky. £450 annual unearned income was a lot of money to most people.

As a child I could make no sense of these discrepancies. All I knew was that from 1964, when we first moved to Marchmont, the so-called "stately home" in the borders of Scotland, there was never what Papa thought of as "enough money." During the years that followed, he had a hundred schemes to "make things work," to "save the family fortunes." An old railway track lay right across the land, and some special grit had been used in its construction. Why shouldn't we dig up the railway line and sell the grit at enormous profit? I remember him standing in front of the library fire-place with a glass in his hand, vigorous, intent, expounding this scheme to the assembled company. Nothing came of it. Other schemes, like selling local game-birds to classy London restaurants (rushing them down on the night train from Berwick) looked promising for a few brief months and then collapsed.

What, my father asked, was he supposed to do? With the house to keep up and six children to educate (John had been born in 1965, and Isabella in 1968), money had to come from somewhere. Papa could have saved several thousand pounds a year by sending us to local schools, but that he never thought of as an option. Instead, he took out covenants with his sister and one of his younger brothers. Along with the interest from his stocks and shares, that provided some sort of basic income. The farms too brought in something, even though most of it had to be ploughed back into their upkeep. "What were the figures though?" I want to ask. "What were we actually living on?" But at this distance it is impossible to know. Papa ran his life and ours on a series of borrowings and overdrafts,[9] tied up with zigzags of red tape by the accountant in Edinburgh. Beyond the rhetoric and the funny stories, what remains clear is the pitch of his anxiety. "You must marry a White Russian," he used to say to Kate and me. "Then we can mend the Adam Bridge."

The Adam Bridge had been built two hundred years earlier, and shook whenever heavy traffic crossed it. Two or three balusters had fallen in the burn, and the sandstone was flaking off the sides. Even as a child, I knew we'd never mend the Adam

Bridge. At the same time, I didn't believe that it would ever quite collapse. I accepted its shakiness as I accepted Papa's anxieties: part of the language, part of the atmosphere, like the little jingle that he used to find so witty:

"That money talks, I don't deny:

I heard it once, it said, 'Goodbye.'"

The money "whistling" in my father's pocket (as my aunt once said), never took too long to say goodbye. Yet in its vanishing, it did sometimes transform itself into the most amazing things. There were family holidays in Greece for example, with a villa overlooking the Aegean, and a yacht freighted with champagne. There was a sleek new dark green Daimler. And once there was a racehorse called Bold Daimon, a chestnut gelding with a vicious temperament, bought, Papa told us, as a present for our mother.

There was no way that the stocks and shares could have paid for any of this. The Americans were the source of all these riches.

The Americans

It is difficult to describe the Americans without turning them into one of Papa's stories. "Take five or six millionaires, each with a wife or secretary in tow. Place them in a Scottish country house during the shooting season. Hire a butler from London, along with two matching footmen, and dress them up in ancient livery rescued from the attic. Import cooks and cleaning-women, game-keepers and parlour-maids as appropriate. Require everyone to know their place and keep to it. Swing back the velvet curtains and on with the show!"

A production, a performance, it was always that. Pheasant shooting six days of the week, with breakfast, lunch and tea at three-hour intervals, and in the evening, a full-scale dinner in the dining-room. If it was, as I once said, with childish pomposity, "a purely mercenary venture," at least the Americans got good value for their money. Old friends and neighbors were invited over, and there was always plenty of red wine and conversation. At least once during each visit, the street-sweeper from the local village would dress up in the kilt and full regalia. Starting from the far corner of the house he would walk towards the dining-room playing the bagpipes. As he reached the table, the whine and blast of sound struck conversation dead. Local people knew what they were in for and pretended to enjoy it. That, after all, was part of why they'd been invited. The Americans sat completely still, astonished.

Each "gun," each shooting American, paid my father £1,000 for the privilege. They came back year after year (from 1965 to 1976), and although they never stayed more than two weeks, their presence made a considerable difference to the family finances. It also meant, of course, a great deal of work and planning, especially for my mother. In many ways it was she who set the tone of the occasion, welcoming the guests as they arrived, and looking after the wives while the men were out shooting. As for Papa, he did all that was required of him. He master-minded the shoots, charmed the visitors, and played the laird as best as he knew how. But underneath it all, he wasn't happy. He claimed to prefer "low-ceilinged life," by which he meant, I think, the book-lined Chelsea houses of his friends. He missed those friends very much, and tended to romanticise their busy lives. "The best things in life are *cheap*," he said, citing kipper and scrambled eggs. It was as if, in taking on Marchmont, such modest pleasures had become forever unattainable.

In the Big House

We had moved to Scotland in the summer of 1964, when I was eight. I didn't want to go. I liked Wiltshire: our comfortable yellow-washed house with its solid black thatch, the governess I'd been to for the first few years, and after that the little convent-school in Salisbury. I liked the two-acre field at the side of the house, and the woods behind it, with the view of Stonehenge. Marchmont was different. That house belonged to Grandmama. For me, as the eldest, there was always the sense of treading in someone else's footsteps, trying to copy "the uncles" (my father and his five tall brothers), and somehow doing a very mediocre job of it. For a long time I felt inadequate and small. What I didn't know (and probably it was just as well) was that in social terms my stock was on the rise. In moving from Wiltshire to Scotland my family had gone up in the world. From then on we were landed gentry, established upper class.

That September, as soon as the holidays were over, I was sent to boarding school. This meant another convent, seventeen miles away, just across the border into England. For four years I was driven there every Sunday night by a dour chauffeur called Mr. Corcoran. He had big sad hands and a mutilated ear, and I used to sing to him to cheer us both up. The separations never got any easier. I started off each week tearful and subdued, and by the time I felt settled again, it was the weekend. My brothers and sisters had been at home all week. They were cheerful and belonged, while I was the difficult one, the stranger, fighting for the privilege of sitting between Papa and Mama at the tea-table: "It's my turn now. I'm only here two days."

Perhaps it was in reaction to those perpetual upheavals that I held on so hard to my (fairly idiosyncratic) view of class. I did not understand it as a system, though I remember Papa teaching me the Peerage, from dukes through marquises and earls all the way down to baronets and knights and commoners. My own sense of my class position was simply, "what we were": some idealized version of Papa's place in the world, with a touch of Mama's thrown in to make it "cultured," "sensitive," "exotic." Baffled by the move and by the new girls at school whose fathers were clerks and shop-keepers and farmers, I clung to the family, making of it some kind of sacred unassailable thing, source and fountain-head of our hidden "betterness." Because of Papa's First and Mama's beauty, because we were Catholic and spoke with the "right" accent, we were special, more than special; we were better, we were best.

This version of things sounds like a child's version, a child of five or six perhaps, younger than I was then. Most children defend their families against the rest of the world. But in my case, parental and family betterness was also ratified from outside. I was not the only one who looked up to my mother and did what I was told. The nannies and the servants did that too. Our house was "the Big House" to grownups as well as children.

Out in what we always called "the real world," nothing seemed very different. Papa had friends in London and Washington and New York. His name was in the newspapers and theirs were too. We saw them on the television, heard them on the radio. They all seemed to know each other, and everyone was a success or famous, or at least, "very interesting." Sir Alec Douglas-Home came over for a shoot. Terence

Stamp[10] appeared for the New Year with Jean Shrimpton[11] on his arm. Jim Dine[12] arrived in a Volkswagen bus with a troop of squealing children. One week the exiled King of Uganda came to stay; sometime later it was Princess Margaret.

Nowadays I am perplexed by all of this, as if it had happened to someone else. I know my life will never be quite the same again, and, in retrospect, I miss the glamour and excitement. But as a child, I took it very much for granted. My parents' friends might be interesting and important, but in our house they were simply visitors who didn't know their way from their own bedrooms to the dining-room for breakfast. ("Down the front stairs, through the saloon,[13] and it's straight ahead. Not that door, that's the library.") I soon forgot that we had ever lived anywhere else, in particular the "little house" in Wiltshire. I looked not back, but forwards, far into the future, despising grownups because they were already, irrecoverably, themselves. I would be different: a gardener, an acrobat, a writer, a traveller, a saint. I spent a lot of time constructing different versions, taking as base my parents' hopes and expectations, and building castle upon castle onto that. I would be clever because "we" always were. I'd be the kind of person Gavin was,[14] the kind that didn't have to keep clean all the time. I would be an animal person just like him, someone who lived on an island, someone who broke the rules. I'd have an interesting and exotic and morally irreproachable life. Once I'd cured my jealousy and bad temper, everyone would love me. And I'd be beautiful as well, like Mama.

When I look back, I marvel at my confidence. I really did believe that all those identities were there for the taking. At the same time I had no idea of how to go about acquiring them. I was not prepared for work or for the world. In the end, intellectual freedom was the thing I needed most, the chance to get some distance from my parents' house, and to question the assumptions I'd been taught.

People Like Us

What I know of upper class values, upper class attitudes and assumptions, I mostly learned through my father. Mama did her best to practice them, but Papa spelled them out. Words like "responsibility" and "right" (as in the "right thing to do") I still hear with his particular emphasis. Betterness brought responsibilities in its train, and these we should learn to accept. Grandpa McEwen had been an M.P. for example, not just because he liked the work, but because he had "taken on the responsibility" for the people of Berwick and Haddington. It was a classic case of "noblesse oblige." For the same reasons, Papa accepted a position as local Sheriff,[15] and acted as trustee for the estates of several friends. . . .

At thirteen, I'd been sent to yet another boarding school, this time down in Sussex, where my mother had once gone. I was mocked for my Scottishness ("Do you have running water up there in the Highlands?") and it took me a long time to make friends. "People like us" was a reassuring phrase. Papa and I spent several sets of holidays defining exactly what it should mean. We would be Catholics, we said, but not blindly, foolishly so. We would be upper class, but not in the haw-haw huntin', shootin', fishin' manner. We would be cultured and well-read, but not humorlessly pompous or academic. Above all, we promised, we would stand by each other. We would unite against the enemy.

Choices

By then, I saw this enemy as the upper class itself, personified in most of Papa's friends. On his good days, I knew it didn't matter. Papa triumphed over it. Either he defeated it on its own terms (somehow managing to be more moral, more educated and better bred than anyone else),[16] or he abandoned it altogether (he was the artist, the eccentric). But on bad days the walls of the drawing-room closed in, and I felt him torn apart by contradictory demands, unable to fulfill his "real" self because of the duties he had assumed as a landowner.

"Why did you take the house in the first place? Why don't you let it go?" Those were the obvious questions. But I already knew the answers. Papa was steeped in his parents' values: *duty, honor, loyalty, tradition.* He had taken on the house, he always said, "for the sake of the family." As an angry adolescent, I was up in arms for him. I saw the family as parasites and scroungers, dropping by for shooting parties and excursions, lunches, teas and suppers, while papa was left struggling with the debts.

This view, however, was always too much his to be entirely accurate. Papa was, after all, the second son. No-one had forced him to take on the house. On the contrary. By the early seventies most of the family would have been relieved to sell up. Undoubtedly they would have been grateful for the extra cash. But Papa would not admit that he could ever have done otherwise, or, indeed, that any choices still remained. As far as he was concerned, the house was nothing but a loss, a deadweight. "The place is going to the dogs," he always said.

What Papa didn't see (and what took me years to realize) was that there were real advantages in the life that he had chosen. As a member of the landed gentry and a baronet (after his brother's death in 1971),[17] he had a definite position in the world. He had an income from the covenants, the farms and stocks and shares and, whether or not he wanted it, he had some place in the community, simply as a result of living where he lived. These things meant power. If Papa had given up the house and land, he would have lost that power. This was a deeply alarming prospect, especially for a man as depressed as he often was. . . .

Nannies and Servants

My youngest sister was born in March, 1968, just a month before my twelfth birthday. From then on there were six of us at home, at least during the holidays, six of us in the nursery watching television, hunched on the fireguard and jammed together on the sofa; six of us piling into the back of the Dormobile, all of us dressed the same in Marks and Spencers[18] corduroys (pale brown) and bright red woolen jerseys.

Compared to the intensity of my talks with Papa, nursery life seemed casual and dull. I remember coming home from boarding school and just "hanging around." The nursery itself always seemed to slip into a kind of time-warp. Clothes were airing by the fire, the rocking-horse moved gently in the corner. The cuckoo-clock ticked *loud-soft-loud* just as it had done in Grandmama's day. . . .

For seven pounds a week apiece, plus board and lodging, the nanny and the nursery-maid took total care of all of us, and all our physical needs. They made the beds and cleaned the rooms and did the laundry; they gave us meals and did the washing-up. They were on call twenty-four hours a day. But despite this vast responsibility, they always remained accountable to my mother. Even now, I remember the atmosphere of the nursery when Mama entered it, the anxious eyes checking round to make sure that everything was in its place, and the "Yes, Lady McEwen," when she gave the orders.

Downstairs in the kitchen and the pantry, another version of this scene would be enacted. Mama would walk in on a tea or coffee break, and everyone would stop laughing and put their mugs back on the table. There'd be jokes about the number of biscuits that had been consumed, and that quiet waiting silence as she spoke. "Yes, Lady McEwen, yes—" when she was finished.

For all the talk about equality, it was clear to me even then that "servants weren't like us," and I capitalized upon it, cruelly, disobeying the nannies and teasing the other servants as I would never have dared to tease my mother's friends. Nor was I the only one. If the nannies did try to control us ("You'll wear that kilt tomorrow, James, because I say so—"), all of us were adept at appealing to our parents. ("I asked Mama and she says I don't have to.") We were proud of this, and thought we managed well, playing the two lots of grownups against each other, and manipulating them to get what we wanted. . . .

Not Good Enough

In relation to our daily life, that truth was always complicated and ambiguous. On the one hand, there's no doubt that we were privileged. We grew up with space around us, both physical and mental. Arriving home for the holidays, our time was marvellously our own. Everything was done for us: our meals cooked, beds made. We were each supposed to take care of our own pet animals (Katie's rats and ferrets, James' pigs, Helena's fox, my black labrador), but even then there was a back-up person in case we forgot. The house was ours, with its attics and its store-rooms and the long back corridor in which we bicycled up and down on rainy days. In every direction stretched "our" fields and "our" woods, with "our" burn and "our" river running through. We could make whatever use of these we wished: climbing trees and walking half the day, guddling for trout in the burn, and coming home to long hours of dressing-up or "rescue" (our particular version of hide-and-seek). As I grew older, I began to make up little plays which we'd perform, usually one every holiday. I spent an entire summer camping in the attic, reading Dante and Jane Austen, listening to Bach and trying to write a novel, while Katie sang and painted through the wall. There was time for this: time to investigate new things, to make experiments, and encouragement to do so.

The other side of such luxurious self-absorption was a terrifying ignorance and alienation. Despite the comings and goings of those glamorous visitors, our daily life was really very isolated. After we moved to Scotland, there were no streets to play on, no shops just down the road, no ordinary community to which we all belonged. At the time I experienced this as "lack of friends" and complained bitterly to my mother that the little ones were "too little" and I wanted children my own age I could play with. Mama did her best. Our uncles and aunts arrived, bringing with them their various offspring. Some of Papa's friends had children too, and they were asked to stay. But the principle behind this was never mentioned, "You can't play with the local kids. Your friends must be imported. You're better. They're not good enough for you."

Why couldn't we play with the local children? No-one asked. We scarcely knew we might have wanted to. We were afraid of them, just as our parents, I think, were afraid of theirs. Once again, this fear was never stated. On the whole it masqueraded as romanticism (Papa's warmth and admiration for the shepherd, for example), though at other times it showed itself in all its coldness and contempt. Every Sunday we gave a Catholic family a lift to the local church, and I remember Papa noting dryly how they smelt, the girls especially. I winced at this remark (myself fourteen, the age of the chief offender), but I know I didn't really question it. Papa was right. The working classes were dirty, stupid. Above all they weren't interesting, except in a caricatured, rustic sort of way. The ones round us had pretty accents (Scots were immeasurably better than Midlands, for example), and sometimes they said funny things which made you laugh. But they couldn't hold up their end of a conversation, and you had to be polite and not embarrass them. However much you might have wished things otherwise, that was just the way they are. . . .

Blame the Mother

An upper class woman is expected to be pretty and to get married. If she does some charity work on the side, well and good. She can do anything she pleases: write or paint, play music, take up gardening, so long as it does not interfere with her primary responsibility, her duty to her husband, house and children. I put "house" before "children" because the upper class woman does exactly that. She is a married woman and a hostess first, a mother second.

Until the age of twenty-nine, when we moved up to Scotland, Mama had no particular position to maintain. Thereafter, things were very different. Throughout my childhood and adolescence, Papa worked in his study, read and watched television in the sitting-room. It was Mama who did the rounds of the house every morning, checking the activities of the day with the nanny and nursery-maid, the cook and the cleaning-woman. She was the one who made us (literally) pull up our socks before we went into church, curtsey to the visitors, say "please" and "thank you." Because of this, as we grew older, she was the one who took the brunt of our rejection. "Don't let Mama down," was the line, and we let her down constantly, appearing in the drawing-room ragged and ill-kept, bridling at everything from the crystal chandeliers to the dining-room table laid for twenty-four. It was as if, in taking responsibility for so much, she had become inseparable from it. Quarrelling with the upper classes became quarrelling with her.

While these confrontations were taking place, I failed to understand them. All I knew was that when I looked at Mama, I saw no female future I could want. Kate and I did our best to construct one for ourselves, devouring everything from Simone de Beauvoir's *The Second Sex* to *The Sensuous Woman* by "J." But Mama lived in another world entirely. She seemed to us entirely submerged in those same duties, loyalties and traditions which tormented Papa. When she wasn't at home running the house, she was out on the road, driving to endless Red Cross Coffee Mornings, Benefit Concerts and Catholic Sales of Work. She was forever putting up posters, opening fêtes, and showing people round the house and gardens. Because, unlike Papa, her spirit never seemed to fail her, she was, as she said cheerfully, "always on the go."

I remember standing at the front of the house while Mama was opening a fête. Katie was beside me, and all through Mama's speech we joked and whispered to each other. People stared at us. "Her ladyship is speaking!" But we would not be hushed. That was Mama up there on the platform. This was our front drive. We had to make clear, if only to ourselves, that somehow we refused to be impressed.

Part of what was happening then, I think, was a claiming of the ordinary (our mother) over the saccharine-sweet, public version the loud-speakers were giving us. "I would like to thank Sir Robert and Lady McEwen for their great kindness this afternoon—" As we listened to those speeches we faced our parents' betterness head-on, and therefore our own difference and alienation. It was hard to take. But we talked through Mama's speech for other, more complicated reasons. However ordinary we tried to make her, the truth was she was very often on that platform, "doing her bit," as Papa said, bowing gracefully, accepting flowers. She was Lady McEwen, our father's wife, the lady of the house, and we resented it. *Why didn't she have time to spare for us?* . . .

Leaving Home

In 1974, when I was seventeen, I had nine months off between school and university. For three of those months I went to Thailand, and worked at a mission for people with leprosy. I put medical cards in order, made physiotherapy drawings, helped out at minor operations, distributed soap and baby-food and vitamins. When I arrived back in England, I had acute culture shock. I felt crazy, suicidal, desperately at odds with my complicated past, and quite unable to make sense of the new world of King's College, Cambridge.

Oxford and Cambridge have always been elitist universities, drawing most of their students from the English public school system,[19] and going on to supply the politicians and civil servants of the capital. The colleges themselves are run like mini-stately homes, each with its own ceremonies and traditions. With Marchmont and my father looming in the background, I might have been expected to fit right in. Instead, I reacted with a long campaign of downward mobility.

During those final years of the hippy era, downward mobility was a fashionable option. For many people it was an aesthetic and moral choice. In my case, it was also a financial one: Other people's parents subsidised their student grants, or gave them free board and lodging while they took a job during the holidays. My parents gave me £40 a quarter, barely enough for food, let alone for bus or train-fare up to Scotland. (Rent was always paid, something I took for granted.) I grew tense and frugal, stealing books on occasion, and buying most of my clothes in the city flea-market. I kept a pet snake during my first year, and I remember there was often a choice between buying a goldfish for the snake (he needed one a week), or a bowl of soup for me.

While I was living in this way, it all seemed real and necessary. It was connected in my mind with the absolute poverty I'd seen in Thailand, the extravagance of Western consumer society, and the sexual games I saw all round me and wanted to reject. What I didn't see was the convenience of such a theory to someone who was, after all, my father's daughter. It gave me an identity separate from his, which, of course, as eldest daughter (and not the heir), I somehow had to find.

Meanwhile I was at Cambridge, which I did not like. I worked hard. I had no idea how to play. As far as possible I passed as middle class, trying to understand what that meant as I went along. But I still believed that somehow round the corner an exotic life was waiting, and I held on tightly to the one strand of my betterness which I still valued. I was a poet, a writer, a misunderstood artist in the top floor garret of my ivory tower. . . .

I had got myself to Cambridge, and I had finished my degree. That in itself was something of an achievement. My mother had left Oxford early in order to get married. My aunt Kisty had not even been allowed to go to university. It was not supposed to be "necessary" for a woman. What good was a B.A. when it came to arranging flowers? Apart from the advantages of being able to keep up "an intelligent conversation" with her husband, the upper class wife had no need for further education.

Throughout my childhood and my growing up, this was the prevailing attitude. My parents were unusual in that they definitely encouraged me to go to university, and were delighted when I got in. All the same, neither of them had the faintest idea of what might be supposed to happen afterwards. Going to Cambridge had become an end in itself. They had no sense of it as the possible preparation for a future career. Papa's First belonged to the masculine world of professional achievement. My own studies were viewed very differently. I was "only a girl," after all. I was going to get married.

When I think about this now, I see how well it blended in with other upper class assumptions. Once again, as so often, energy and ambition were being sapped from below. "Yes indeed, why bother? Why even *try* to aim for anything?" Growing up upper class meant that we already were (owned, had access to) everything that ordinary people worked towards. As children we were constantly reminded just how lucky we were. We had a beautiful house to live in, wonderful parents, and were ourselves "beautiful, talented, intelligent." *In some very basic way this was enough.* Very little emphasis was given to developing our so-called skills and qualities—risking something to further an unknown goal. After all, the only goals that mattered were preservation, conservation, more of the same. Since this "same" was daily criticised (Papa hated the world he lived in, even while he hastened to defend it), the result was that we had next to no initiative. Our sense of what was possible was both stunted and blasé.

Built into my character as a layer of apathy and condescension, this heritage lives on. It is true, painfully and pitifully true, but it is not all of the truth. Even then, as a teenager and a young adult, I did everything I could think of to defend myself against it, coping with what I understood as upper class goals by turning my back on them as much as possible. For a long time I had only the negative versions of choice. "No, I don't want that—" I wanted something else, another life, another set of values. But I had no idea what that entailed. My rage at upper class hypocrisy left me critical and intense. I had very little money ("bourgeois ambition"), nor did I know how to acquire it (upper class ignorance and lack of practical skills). Underneath it all, I was enormously afraid.

Nonetheless, somewhere about this time, an important choice was beginning to be made. It took its impetus from a year I'd spent away from Cambridge, earning money and travelling around the States. On my return I applied for every scholarship within reach. I was lucky enough to win a Fulbright. Soon after, at the age of twenty-three, I moved to Berkeley. . . .

My father died of a heart-attack in May, 1980, towards the end of my first year in Berkeley. I went back to Scotland for the funeral. It was a strained and murky time. Despite everything, Papa had always been the center of the house. Now that he was dead, there was no center. "Papa was, Papa did, Papa used to say—" We had to learn to talk about him in the past tense. It was as if everything he believed in were slowly being dispersed.

Being Nice

Being nice meant manners ("please" and "thank you," "ladies first"), and an endless outpouring of hospitality. It meant interest (or the appearance of interest) on the part of the women, laughter and anecdotes on the part of the men. But it did not, perhaps could not, involve saying what you really thought. That, we were told firmly, was called tactlessness.

As a child I was often scolded for this so-called tactlessness. "Why does Roberta have linoleum on her floor when Mama has a carpet?" This was really a social question, "Why are some people richer than others?" But it was interpreted as personal criticism, and thus as an embarrassment. I was snubbed, and told to be quiet. The implication was that I would hurt Roberta's feelings.

It is obvious to me now that both niceness and betterness are maintained on a firm foundation of unasked questions. The pattern of exchange is laid down in childhood, and assiduously reinforced thereafter. People are kept separate from each other, even when they meet and talk and smile. There is small risk, small danger of intimacy. This is bad enough among the upper classes themselves. Across classes, its function becomes altogether more sinister.

Upper class betterness is built on centuries of other people's work. It is built on land and industry maintained by other people, income and profits got at their expense. Most of those involved are well aware of this, and the feelings (understandably) are strong. Guilt and fear and ignorance on the part of those in power, anger and resentment on the part of the workers, threaten to burst through at any minute. Under the circumstances, niceness is a very useful tool. It gives the upper classes some sort of camouflage to operate behind, at the same time as it aims to distract everyone else from what is actually going on. "Lord and Lady Bountiful are so generous, so polite . . ." If you continue to think along these lines, social privilege soon appears entirely natural.

Growing up as I did, such basic analysis was far beyond me. I did not see that niceness served a purpose. I only knew I did not like or trust it. I thought all nice people must be hypocrites. At the same time I blamed myself for not being able to be as nice as they were. There I was, filled to the brim with moods and jealousies, while they were always calm and self-contained. They might be fakes, I told myself, but I was evil.

This kind of logic left me muddled and unhappy, and blocked my thinking for a long time. Between Mama's composure and Papa's towering self-disgust there seemed no place of rest, no human ordinary. . . .

Behind the violence of that solution lies an extended argument about power. For all of us children, it was difficult to take power without assuming it, to claim it easily, as human beings, rather than asserting it as something due. Living in the States, I went through a long period of refusing power—at least as it might have reached me through the family. I took no money from them and I asked for no advice. I wanted to make my own way in the world. . . .

"What is your story? How were things for you?" In the past few years I've come to ask this more and more. I want to know what it felt like growing up in the suburbs, in the country, or the inner-city. I want to know what it means to be French or Russian, Nigerian or Icelandic or Chinese. What is difficult about it? What is wonderful? In what ways are we different from each other? Where are we the same?

Sometimes, as I write, I see the ruins of an enormous tower. Long ago, in biblical times, it was the Tower of Babel. Now the grass is growing up around the stones, the birds are singing, and the sun and moon shine together out of a cloudless sky. In the courtyard, or what used to be the courtyard, since it too is overgrown with grass, hundreds and thousands of people are massed together. Each one is telling stories in his or her own language, but there are never any problems with translation.

We sit together, and we tell our stories. And in that conversation, everything gets said. It gets said slowly and carefully, and it gets said loudly and extravagantly. It is desperate and angry, it is calm and full of hope. Action is born of it, and fear goes out the window. Everybody talks at once, and everybody listens.

Christian McEwen 1983–85

FOOTNOTES

[1]One notable exception is Ronald Fraser's *In Search of A Past* (Verso, 1984). See also Susanna J. Sturgis' "Class/Act: Beginning a Translation from Privilege" in *Out the Other Side*, edited by Christian McEwen and Sue O'Sullivan (Crossing Press, 1989).

[2]*Barrister:* A student of law, who, having been called to the bar, has the privilege of practising as an advocate in the superior courts of law. The formal title is barrister-at-law: the equivalent designation in Scotland is *advocate. (Oxford English Dictionary)*; hereafter, *O.E.D.*

[3]Conservative M.P. for Berwick and Haddington, Parliamentary Under Secretary of State for Scotland (1939–40) and Lord Commissioner of the Treasury (1942–44). He was made a baronet in 1953.

[4]*Baronet:* A titled order, the lowest that is hereditary, ranking next in line to baron, having precedence of all orders of knighthood, except that of the garter. A baronet is a commoner, the principle of the order being "to give rank, precedence and title without privilege." *(O.E.D.)*

[5]*First:* the best possible degree.

[6]James Laver: author of more than a hundred books, among them *Nostradamus, The Age of Optimism* and *A Concise History of Costume.*

[7]Veronica Turleigh: who worked with such "names" as Paul Schofield, Laurence Olivier and Alec Guinness, for example as Gertrude to Guinness' Hamlet in Guthrie's modern dress production in 1938.

[8]*A' Level:* examination at end of school course demanding an advanced knowledge of a school subject. *(O.E.D.)* Cf. *O' Level:* examination at end of school course requiring ordinary, i.e., less than A' level, knowledge of a school subject. *(O.E.D.)*

[9]*Overdraft:* overdrawing of bank account, amount by which sums drawn exceed credit balance. *(O.E.D.)* Thus, loosely, bank loans.

[10]Terence Stamp: film actor. See, for example, *Billy Budd, The Collector, Far From the Madding Crowd, Meetings With Remarkable Men, The Hit.*

[11]Jean Shrimpton: fashion model.

[12]Jim Dine: American painter.

[13]*Saloon:* this was a kind of hall or second drawing-room at the center of the house, the word is presumably a corruption of "salon."

[14]Gavin Maxwell: author and naturalist, some of whose books my father illustrated. See *Ring of Bright Water, Raven Seek Thy Brother.*

[15]*Sheriff:* the office is now mainly honorary, the specific duties attached to it varying in different towns.

[16]I should say here that Papa had an extraordinarily comparative and hierarchical turn of mind. He was almost unable to praise something in its own terms. "You're very good—but you're not as good as Mozart," he told Jonathan Miller (doctor, stage-director, writer and editor), a remark which astonished Jonathan. He had never supposed he was.

[17]My uncle Jamie died on the 2nd July 1972.

[18]Marks and Spencers is a British department store, roughly equivalent to Macy's.

[19]What the British call a public school is in American terms exactly the opposite. Eton College, for example, a well-known English public school, is very obviously the equivalent of an American private school.

MICHAEL M. LEWIS

Though he holds degrees from the London School of Economics and Princeton University, Lewis's knowledge about the rich and how they got that way comes from first-hand knowledge. In two years he moved from stock boy for a New York Art dealer, tour guide for teenage girls in Europe, and brokerage trainee to million-dollar bond trader for the Wall Street firm of Salomon Brothers, a set of experiences he wrote about in a book entitled Liar's Poker: Rising through the Wreckage on Wall Street *(1989). The book, often characterized as a real life* Bonfire of the Vanities, *is an amusing and sometimes acerbic account of the investment business and its cast of characters in the late 1980s. Lewis has continued to put his Street experience to use in writing about the wealthy and the practices of creating riches in today's America, as in his 1991 book,* The Money Culture, *and in his biography of a computer industry leader,* The New New Thing: A Silicon Valley Story *(1999). He has also written about American economic relations with Asia as well as American politics, particularly in his 1997 book,* Trail Fever: Spin Doctors, Rented Strangers, Thumb Wrestlers, Toe Suckers, Grizzly Bears, and Other Creatures on the Road to the White House.

THE RICH:
HOW THEY'RE DIFFERENT . . .
THAN THEY USED TO BE

Whatever Happened to the Leisure Class?

I've been loitering in the vicinity of rich people for nearly 15 years now, and in that time I have seen and heard a lot of strange things, but nothing as strange as what was related to me during a single brief encounter with the species in the summer of 1982. It was during a picnic in the Blue Ridge Mountains of North Carolina. I was minding my own business, more or less, when a middle-aged woman appeared and introduced herself as a close relation of Pierre du Pont 5th, with whom I had just graduated from Princeton University. After she asked what I intended to do with my life, and I replied that I had no idea, she explained to me how much more difficult things were for young Pierre. In a surprisingly aggressive tone she ticked off his many achievements: Pierre had graduated with honors, she said; Pierre had 23 job offers; Pierre was already putting in 14-hour days at some computer company; the company was paying Pierre nearly $30,000 a year. The list was long but somehow failed to include the fact most central to Pierre's existence: the du Pont family fortune, recently estimated by Forbes to be at least $10 billion, a large chunk of which he stands to inherit. Clearly, something was amiss. I had no trust fund (or job) and yet there I was having a picnic. Young Pierre was well on his way to inheriting millions, and yet there he was, a veritable human workhorse, enslaved to some dreary corporation for a pittance. The contrast was a clear confirmation of my own lassitude—but also, I think, a small sign of the shift taking place in the imaginations of the rich: just as new money once sought to obscure itself with the trappings of ancienne noblesse, old money was now shifting its focus to achievement. The antimarket snobbery, the pursuit of useless hobbies, the preference for filigreed personalities over human ramrods, the taste for understatement—all those qualities that had distinguished du Ponts for more than a century apparently had vanished. Old money was being buffeted not merely economically but culturally. It was uncomfortable in its own skin.

In his marvelous 1988 memoir, "Old Money," Nelson Aldrich revealed, among other things, the then-recent creation of a support group for troubled heirs. The Dough Nuts, as they dubbed themselves, felt ill at ease in the modem world. You could sympathize—after you heard the gruesome tales about the rich kids who wed to overcome their trust funds. One evening in 1989 a young Mellon found the decal on the back window of his BMW defaced. On top of "The Wharton School" someone had scrawled "Night School" in thick black letters. The villains, as it turned out, were a couple of full-time Wharton students. The worst part was that it was true. A Mellon was attending night school. Life was that harsh.

Making money, once regarded as the first in a series of steppingstones to the top of society, now was the only step that really mattered. Even as young Mellon wiped his sticker clean, the new ground rule—that you had to earn your way to the top of society—was being reinforced by several related trends:

   • Money is being made faster than ever before. In 1987 Warren Buffett was worth $2.1 billion and Bill Gates $1.25 billion; in eight years Buffett's wealth has more than quintupled to $12 billion and Gates is now worth $15 billion. One year Michael Eisner is an upper-middle-class American; the next he has exercised his Disney stock options and has $200 million in the bank, thus launching him onto the Forbes list of the 400 richest Americans. The speed with which wealth is now amassed gives it a magical, rabbit-from-the-hat quality. The rich man has performed a wonderful trick. We applaud him so loudly he wants to do it again.

   • The ultra-rich are growing richer faster than the very rich and the very rich are becoming richer faster than the merely rich. Between 1977 and 1989, the average income of the top 1 percent of American families rose from $323,942 to $576,553— even as the incomes of average families remained essentially flat. And the gains among the richest Americans have been even greater. In 1987 a net worth of $225 million landed you on the Forbes list; this year it took $340 million. The yawning and ever-changing gaps enhance the tendency of rich people to compare themselves mostly with other rich people. If the sale of CNN to Time Warner goes through, Ted Turner can gloat that he has gone from being a billion or so dollars behind to being a billion or so dollars ahead of Rupert Murdoch. (It's worth noting that Malcolm Forbes the elder poached the idea for his list, first published in 1982, from Mrs. Astor, of New York and Newport, who judged people by more than their money, and whose social adviser decreed that only 400 could fit into her ballroom comfortably. Fittingly the Forbes list has reduced the complex blue-blood social formula of the Astor 400 to simple, coldblooded accounting.)

• Partly because of the trend in the raw numbers, there has been an odd shift in the rich man's view of his social role. The source of all fortunes is, of course, profits. Rich men have always romanticized these. The robber barons—and indeed all American businessmen until about 15 years ago—arrogated to themselves the prestige of military leaders. Hence the phrase "captain of industry." Beginning in the 80's, however, the controlling metaphor of wealth accumulation changed. The modern rich man—and those who make huge sums still are, as a rule, men—is much less likely to imagine himself a military leader, or even a great sports hero. Such images are too sweaty and concrete for a group of people who, less and less, make things and, more and more, earn their money in such intangibles, or barely tangibles, as media, entertainment, investment, finance and computer software.

To the timeless and thorny question, "Daddy, how come you make a billion dollars?" the answer is no longer, "I am an iron-willed leader of men." The answer is, "I am an artist." All the prestige we accord the artist in his quest for originality and authenticity we now grant the businessman in his quest for profits. Saying Warren Buffett is limited because all he can think to do with his $12 billion is to turn it into $20 billion is like saying Picasso is limited because he couldn't think of anything else to do but paint. The rich man's "duty," such as it is, is not to society but to his art, and his art is making money.

"Much of old money's esthetic," Nelson Aldrich observed, "depends on the belief that membership in the class is a gift beyond achievement." But in a society less inclined than ever to credit any gift beyond achievement, the old-money esthetic appears increasingly ridiculous. Sensing this, rich people have been fashioning themselves a new esthetic—call it the esthetic of windfall gains. Herewith, its salient features:

Inconspicuous consumption: The flushing of fortunes down gilded toilets is a lost art. The rich will never entirely escape their acquisitions, of course. But there is nothing in the 1990's, for example, to compare with the consumption of the 1890's, when rich men habitually raised ballroomed palaces of Numidian marble and filled them with dozens of servants and hundreds of oil paintings and thousands of trinkets that made life bearable for the European aristocracy (plus a few luxuries never thought of in Europe, like linen beds for the horses). William K. Vanderbilt, a fairly typical Gilded Age specimen, spent the equivalent today of $365 million to build his Newport "summer cottage," Marble House. Even Andrew Carnegie, who wrote that "the duty of the man of wealth is first to set an example of modest, unostentatious living, shunning display and extravagance," owned 32,000 acres and a castle in Scotland, and a palace on Fifth Avenue.

The waste value of these homes was further enhanced by their intense discomfort. Next to their cavernous ballrooms, their dark gothic chambers, the chilly dripping of their ormolu-accented fountains, the Metropolitan Museum feels like a cozy place to curl up with a cup of tea. There were reasons the great Newport mansions were closed for nine months of the year and slept in only on weekends by the men who paid for them; the effective cost of sleeping in Marble House came to about $1 million a night, in current dollars. By comparison the $30 million and counting that Bill Gates is dropping on a suburban Seattle residence in which he intends actually to live, and which is often cited as proof of the wild-eyed extravagance of rich people, is a disgrace to the tradition. Gates's stock in Microsoft has been appreciating on average at a rate of $450 million a month. He could build himself a proper home. Why doesn't he?

The answer begins with the collapse in the appeal of European aristocracy. One important purpose of the Newport mansions was to create the illusion of dynasty, and thus to curry favor with old money in general and European old money in particular. As sugar cubes to attract the blue bloods, these places worked wonders. For example, in 1895, according to "To Marry an English Lord," a 1989 book on Anglomania, nine American girls from Newport society married peers of the British realm, most of whom the girls had first met at Newport summer parties. Try to imagine Ted Turner writing a check so that a daughter might marry an English Lord. It's far easier imagining an English Lord writing a fan letter to Ted Turner. Indeed, in the past 20 years one of the surest ways for an *Englishman* to become a Lord was to mimic this sort of quintessential American tycoon, and more or less buy the title. (Lord Hanson of Hanson Trust, Lord Weinstock of Britain's General Electric Company, Sir James Goldsmith, et al.)

But there is another reason still for the decline in conspicuous waste: anybody can do it! In 1895 big-ticket shopping was a competitive sport, like tennis, open to the few. In 1995, any of the more than 65,000 American families that declare an annual income of $1 million can play. A few years ago, American Express nicely illustrated the nature of this very modern problem. Its first charge card issued in 1958—the green card—was quickly taken up by the rich. It genuinely was exclusive, for a brief moment. Over time, however, the rich were joined by the not-so-rich, and then by the frankly middle class. The company responded by creating the gold card, but this, too, soon was lost to the chest-hair-and-gold-chain crowd. Gold segued into platinum and platinum into the mysterious black card until finally the American Express Company, perhaps sensing its own absurdity, threw in the towel, issued a down-market credit card, Optima, and toned down its noise about prestige.

What was true about a little plastic card is nearly as true even of expensive homes: too many people can afford them. As soon as some bauble acquires sufficient appeal it attracts so many buyers that it loses its cachet and becomes faintly risible. The end result is that the home with all its chattels has lost its grip on the social imagination of the very rich. The only people who behave consistently the way the middle class expect the rich to behave are the middle class. The Old World belief in *magnificenza*—in the hoary tradition of spending well that has shaped the landscape of Europe for 600 years—echoes clearly only in the Visa statements of the Jersey suburbs.

Rich people still afflicted by consumption neuroses are now more likely to obsess about what they do *not* buy: Warren Buffett, who is worth $12 billion, still lives with great self-consciousness in a house that cost $31,500 in 1958. Back when he was a multibillionaire, Michael Milken never bought anything for himself but more junk bonds. Bill Gates once explained that it did not matter to him if the stock price of Microsoft collapsed, because "I would still eat the same hamburgers." We should be thankful that he eats at all. The wealthier moguls in Hollywood have taken to lunching without food—just a plate of undressed arugula and a glass of Evian.

Conspicuous production: When a man becomes rich the best way for him to boost his status is not to give alms to the poor or to acquire a wall full of Roman sarcophagi but to become even richer. Like shopping, leisure has ceded its bragging rights to the middle class. This year's Forbes 400 list confirms that many very rich people also want to be seen to be doing nothing other than making even more money: "No hobbies. 'I work too hard.'" (Steven Anthony Ballmer. Software. $2.9 billion.) "'I don't do anything but work. I used to play golf. I made a hole in one once, so I quit.'" (Alpheus Lee Ellis. Banking. $490 million.) "'If you slow down, you really doom yourself.'" (Gordon Earle Moore. Computer chips. $2.8 billion.) Summing it all up: "'I love America. We've got the only system that works. It keeps everyone hustling.'" (John Richard Simplot. French fries. $2.2 billion.) In this crowd the legendary hours of Bill Gates (72 hours a week) and Michael Milken (at his Drexel desk by 3 A.M.) are unexceptional.

Here is where the American rich have turned for psychic income: production has replaced consumption at the core of the rich man's identity. Production, not consumption, is also the source of a rich man's publicity. Just as crowds once gathered in the streets to witness the unveiling of a new mansion, now the public, in search of revelation pores over the details of the latest giant deal cobbled together by moneycrats over a pitcher of ice water. The degradation of large corporations through highly publicized mergers or buyouts has replaced the degradation of the Rhode Island coastline through highly publicized construction. As a result, the modem tycoon can focus on what genuinely interests him without having to learn which fork to use, or how to spell Houdon.

But there is a trade-off. The rich man's identity is less diversified than ever before: he is distinguished only by his commercial acumen, as measured by his net worth. It is no coincidence that the one hobby many rich people allow themselves—owning a professional sports franchise—is dressed up as a successful business.

The need for constant financial success, actual or perceived, has spawned a new form of madness—the tycoon who is obsessed with his financial image. Warren Buffett, who one would think would have better things to do with his time, sees red when accused in print of underperforming the market averages. (I found out the hard way, by making the embarrassing mistake.) At least a few of the more extravagant corporate buyouts and takeovers of the past decade—RJR Nabisco, to name one—gathered steam for no better reason than that a rich man—Henry Kravis, in this case—wanted to call attention to his capacity to get richer.

The old-money concern with social reputation has been transformed into a new-money concern for commercial reputation. This extends far beyond the desire for more spending power. Buffett, for instance, probably wouldn't care very much if he lost half his pile in a market crash, as long as everyone else lost more than he did. But if he lagged the market for, say, five years running, even if his pile kept growing, he would suffer an identity crisis. The crowds would cease to turn up at his annual meetings, his old annual reports would go out of print, his hagiographers would turn sour and he'd lose his ability to merge giant corporations on his lunch breaks.

In the rich man's image-grooming the unrich play the role of willing accomplices. Up to the point of bankruptcy or incarceration we regard the rich man and his work as complex beyond our understanding. Beyond understanding, it is also beyond criticism. All highly public business decisions made by rich men are, at the time of the decision, not evaluated on their own terms but widely applauded as strokes of genius. The major business magazines exist in part to whip up this applause (while occasionally stomping on smaller fry to maintain journalistic credibility). When Warren Buffett buys into US Air or Salomon Brothers it's a sign that the firm is undervalued. When the Wait Disney Company agrees to buy Capital Cities/ABC, it is both bold and ingenious because the deal was dreamed up by Michael Eisner and Warren Buffett. This deal met with near-unanimous approval, though the only reason ever given for it was that last refuge of crackpots, "synergy." What this means, in fact, is that ABC, which already was able to buy as much from Disney as it wanted, will now be coerced into taking things it doesn't want. Already everyone has forgotten the disasters that befell Sony and Matsushita when, governed by the same logic, they bought Columbia and MCA.

The illusion of independence: The rich man is ever less entwined in the society that has made him wealthy. Unlike the captain of industry, the modem artist is a loner. His prestige does not depend much on giving away money (the ungiving Buffett is maybe the country's most-highly-thought-of rich man), or on marrying his daughter off well, or in draping his wife in furs and jewels. He derives status from his marriage only insofar as he monopolizes the childbearing years of a series of women much younger than himself. A timely divorce, for example, may actually raise his status in the eyes of his adoring public: his creative juices are flowing again! Thus the price for women's liberation was paid in part by the women at the top of society, who, with a couple of notable exceptions, now enjoy less control than ever over the lives of their husbands. The Gilded Age party in which the men were required to make fools of themselves for the amusement of the women—dining on horseback, dressing up as Roman orators—is a thing of the past. So, increasingly, is the giant trust fund. The rich man's conviction that achievement is all often outweighs his desire to see his children spend his money. On the rare occasions when Warren Buffett was willing to lend his kids money, he required them to sign loan agreements. The centi-millionaire Ronnie Chan has been quoted in Forbes saying, "I told my kids early on: you're not going to get a dime." This echoes sentiments heartfelt by many rich men today.

Not surprisingly, then, the rich man's empathy for the unrich has diminished. Or, since it was never very great, perhaps it is more true to say that the pretense of compassion for life's losers is no longer as fashionable as it once was. What we have lost in civility we have gained in honesty. Rich people used to shield themselves from the pleas of the unrich with social-class pretensions. Their chief defense these days is their keen sense of personal accomplishment. From this follows their righteous indignation toward the claims of the unrich: you can't give money to anyone you don't respect, and you can't respect anyone who doesn't make money.

The conundrum has led to an odd development: alms for the rich. When David Geffen buys and temporarily buries his friend Calvin Klein's junk bonds, or Ted Turner earmarks a $50 million tip for his friend Michael Milken as a way of thanking him for his role in Time Warner's planned purchase of Turner Broadcasting, we are witnessing a strange permutation of noblesse oblige. Rich men have always loved to impress other rich men, but these gestures seem fueled by something deeper than the desire to impress. They are a form of atonement. We have arrived at a point where the rich man disposes of his social responsibility by giving $50 million of other people's money to another rich man who has fallen on hard times. (According to Forbes, Milken is worth only about $500 million today, down from about $2 billion a few years ago.)

Cut loose from society the rich man can play his chosen role free of guilt and responsibility. He becomes that great figure of American mythology—the roaming frontiersman. These days the man who has made a fortune is likely to spend more on his means of transportation than on his home: the private jet is the possession that most distinguishes him from the rest of us. The jet facilitates his favorite male ritual—gathering in out-of-the-way places with other rich men. With his jet, he can go anywhere he wants when he wants and, more important, leave.

The old aristocratic conceit of place has given way to a glorious placelessness. There was a time when the next step for the man who made his fortune mining gold in Colorado was to build a house on Fifth Avenue and pretend he had always lived in it. The East offered the rich man his places—in Newport and Charleston and New York. Now he goes West, to the last nonplaces in America. He builds a ranch in the remote Wyoming desert or the Montana grasslands or the Colorado steppes—someplace far away from the society he has mastered. On his ranch he experiences Shane-like surges of rugged individualism—but without actually being alone. For other rich men have come before him, and other rich men are there to keep score of what he has made, and still other rich men are sure to follow—to reassure one another that they are, in fact, different.

RICHARD TODD

Todd is a staff writer for Worth *magazine. He has written for* The Atlantic *as well as for a variety of travel magazines. In addition to travel features about places as divergent as the Isle of Sark and the Lazy E L Ranch, he deals with political issues in a humorous and often pointed way. He has written commentary on the media as well as on the foibles and lifestyles of the wealthy, as in the article that follows.*

WHO ME, RICH?

I really may take money too seriously. A billionaire told me as much not long ago when he said that he thought we lived in a "classless society." His explanation was that all his friends had a lot less money than he did and yet drove the same cars, went to the same places, and so on. They were all comfortably well off—professors, artists, doctors—and what, really, did his extra money buy him? The conversation took sort of a droll turn when the billionaire's lawyer, a friend of mine, gently reminded him of his airplane, and I asked what kind it was. "It's a 727." Still, I had a glimpse of the world through his eyes, and it was a world in which money, after a point, seemed to have only a marginal utility. I myself dwell on money. I think a lot about what it does to people and how very much of it we seem to have in our country these days. I wonder about all these rich people.

Who are they?

The Remington, a condominium building, is the newest addition to the Bay Colony community in Naples, Florida, on the Gulf of Mexico. A brochure renders the approach to the place better than I could: "A gracious perimeter wall encloses the entire development; a meticulously manicured entry replete with stately palm trees and luxuriant floral plantings leads to a sentry gate." The Remington itself rises 21 stories from the edge of the water, across from some responsibly preserved "wetlands," a mangrove swamp. In its lobby the building offers another line of defense against something, a security guard behind a reception desk, and it also offers marble floors, heavy silk draperies, and a mélange of English and French reproduction antique furniture. It's a slightly disconcerting structure to find on a beach.

On the 16th floor an unfinished condominium awaits sale, a vast slab of cement 250 feet above the flat blue gulf. Its floor plan is in place: master bedroom overlooking the water, the requisite master-bath complex with its twin sinks and Jacuzzi, a suite of plumbing large enough to accommodate a water-polo team. (One wonders about these bathrooms. Properties like this sell chiefly to buyers of an age when the mirror becomes an inconstant friend at best, yet everyone seems to want an Olympic-sized bathroom.) Two guest bedrooms, a large kitchen and "dining area," a long living room, and a private utilities and delivery hall complete the ensemble. It is hard to imagine the life meant to be lived here, so high above the water, in this urban building sprouting from a mangrove swamp. I ask the price and am told, "This is one-point-six." If I'm interested I should hurry because the building is almost sold out. Everything in Bay Colony sells quickly. The real-estate agent explains, "We have very good product."

One-point-six seems like a lot of money to me, especially for a second home, and I have the idea that an expenditure like this ought to involve sketch pads and site selection and architects. Not to be heavy about it, but it will likely enough be the house you die in—at least if you die between Thanksgiving and Easter; no one dies here after April, because no one lives here then. But I'm wrong; buying is not a big deal. Plenty of people just take a weekend in Florida to have a look, they've heard of the Bay Colony and know it's "good product," and they call back from Dayton on Tuesday and say, "We'll take it."

Who are these people? Everyone seems to know, at least anecdotally, as in: "He's a lawyer, and she's a doctor" . . . "He made a lot of money in cell phones" . . . "He's a businessman, and she's old money from Cleveland." Around Naples the stereotype is that everyone is from the Midwest. But what is really behind the question "Who are they?" is a simple acknowledgment of wonder: There are so many of "them." So many rich people.

Yes and no. If a couple is buying a vacation-retirement condominium for $1.6 million, you can be reasonably sure of one thing: They are one-percenters. That is, they belong to the group you hear more and more about these days: the top 1 percent of the population, the 2.6 million people (about a million households) who now control some 36 percent of the nation's personal wealth, 16 percent of the total personal income, and over a third of the dividend and interest income.

It is a briefly amusing dinner-table game, as I've discovered in recent weeks, to ask people to guess how much money you'd need to be in the top 1 percent. "Let's see, how low would you have to go," mused a successful venture capitalist, revealing his certainty about his own rank. "I'd say about $25 million." Answers vary wildly, but not many guess low, and the median answer, in my unscientific study, is about $20 million. The correct answer is considerably less—between $2.5 and $3 million in net worth. As for income, according to the Internal Revenue Service, the top 1 percent of returns last year were those that listed adjusted gross incomes in excess of $200,000. (These are what you might call entry levels. The mean net worth of the 1 percent stands at about $7.6 million and the mean income at about $675,000.)

People reveal their surprise at these facts variously, but often enough they react with a pleased little downturned smile. "Oh. Well. Then I guess we qualify!" If you are surprised because it seems that not only you but many of the people you know qualify, then you, all unwittingly, are living the one-percenter's life.

Ordinary People

We commissioned Roper Starch Worldwide to conduct a survey of 500 members of the top 1 percent—people with at least $250,000 in income or $2.5 million in assets. Some of the results are highlighted in the following pages. Roper found the typical respondent to be:

A Republican (average age 52)	52%
Caucasian	92
Homeowner	96
With a postgraduate education	47
Who is employed as an executive or professional	66
Married	88
With children under the age of 18	52

Gradations

The top 1 percent of the richest nation in the history of the world ought to weigh in as a coherent elite of overweening wealth and power, and so it may—but it doesn't appear to feel that way to its members. The *Worth*-Roper Starch survey of the 1 percent found that 57 percent of respondents didn't consider themselves "rich" (and only a quarter thought themselves "upper class"), even though they have a median annual income of $330,000.

The United States has long prided itself on being a middle-class society, an admirable myth in many ways. Also a self-serving one, if you are trying to disguise your wealth. But there's a sense in which some one-percenters who resist the idea that they're rich are scarcely being disingenuous. It is quite possible to be earning around $200,000 a year and think of yourself as "in the middle." James Atlas, the literary critic and journalist, recently described in *The New Yorker* the plight of parents like him who are coping with the demands their children's New York private day schools put on them. "No wonder those of us caught in the middle—somewhere between the privileged and the working classes—care so much about which nursery school our kids attend." I don't know the Atlas-household income, but on the internal evidence of the piece (two kids in Manhattan private schools, each with a "huge tuition," for starters) what he is "in the middle" of could not be called American society. But you know what he means! Urban life is especially good at making the nominally rich feel somewhere in the middle, though a good suburb can do the job, too. "Once you buy a Mercedes station wagon," says a fellow who knows the meaning of debt, "you seem to set a chain of events in place." (The Mercedes drives a child to day camp, and a parent at day camp invites you sailing, and sailing introduces you to the yacht club and all these things you can surely afford if you can afford the Mercedes.) "Soon you are balancing on a high wire, with a long way to fall."

Part of the problem is the overhanging presence of those "privileged classes" who never need to stretch for anything. Highly publicized fortunes have their effect on the spirit. I mean not only the Buffett-Gates syndrome ($15 billion each and counting). There is also the incessant news of lesser lights. The new CEO salaries are posted this year: the median is $1.9 million. Lou Gerstner checks in at $10.5 million . . . Jack Welch at $33 million . . . John Reed of Citicorp at $46 million. . . Michael Eisner at $8.7 million, which may seem low for Michael, until you realize he has more than $180 million in stock options. The sports pages contain parallel tales, of Tiger's $60 million, of Rick Pitino's 70. And then there are stories about people who until that moment were utterly unknown and will quickly be again, except for one's dim awareness that they are out there somewhere in the night, skinny-dipping in money: "Three at Morgan Stanley received $10 million last year . . ." It has become a familiar story, but familiarity hasn't made it less significant—on the contrary, we have read so much about multimillion-dollar "compensation" that we think the people who receive these sums must now be beyond counting. (They aren't. According to the IRS, some 70,000 households filed tax returns reporting incomes in excess of $1 million in 1995. They represent about one 15th of the 1 percent.)

A rich man I know with a wry sense of humor had this to say about wealth: "All I know is that it seems to take another digit these days. There are lots of people around here" (we were talking in Florida) "who retired a few years ago with two or three million, thinking they were set. Now they feel poor. Of course, it costs $50,000 to join the golf club now."

When those on the bottom edge of privilege look upward, they have a long way to gaze. The distance from the bottom of the 1 percent to the top is, after all, far, far greater than the distance from the bottom of the 1 percent to the bottom of society. If you were to build a ladder of a hundred rungs, with each rung proportionally representing a percentile of wealth—well, the point is, you couldn't, because even if the bottom 99 rungs were fused into one, the ladder would stretch into the sky à la *Jack and the Beanstalk.*

The People Speak
U.S. Federal Income-Tax Rates

Years	Range of rates (%)	Taxable-income brackets*	
		Lowest: amount under	Highest: amount over
1913-15	1–7	$20,000	$500,000
1923	3–56	4,000	200,000
1932–33	4–63	4,000	1,000,000
1942–43	19–88	2,000	200,000
1954–63	20–91	2,000	200,000
1972–76	14–70	500	100,000
1983	0–50	3,400	109,400
1996	15–39.6	40,100	263,750

I observe my lawyer friend as he talks to his client the billionaire. The lawyer is a perfectly anonymous one-percenter, someone who, it's true, owns three houses (but two of them modest vacation places), two upmarket cars, whose children have been expensively educated—but not an ostentatiously rich man. The client has about $2 billion. I reflect on seeing them together: One has a thousand times more money than the other. Someone who has a thousand times less money than the lawyer would be worth about $2,000.

The Roper Starch survey reports an intriguing finding: that a surprising portion (about a third) of the 1 percent thinks the distribution of wealth in the country is "unfair." The result seems to suggest a blossoming of egalitarianism at the top, until one is informed that most of those holding this view are at the bottom of the 1 percent. Some of them (the "guilty rich," as the survey calls them) are looking downward in sympathy, but others are looking up in resentment. And not a few are doubtless looking both ways at once, with that collision of feeling well described by a woman of liberal sentiments: "I don't deserve what I have, and I need so much more."

I asked a young bond salesman recently what he thought would constitute not riches but security for himself "Well, I think if I had $10 million to put into tax-free municipals, with about a 6 percent yield, I could be sure I'd have enough to withstand inflation and so on." That is, an annual tax-free income of $600,000 and you can start to breathe easy, but not before.

When you travel in the world of the 1 percent, just as when you are immersed in a city, it becomes increasingly hard to remember that the rest of the world exists. It happens to the one-percenter, too. We live in a Pentium-chip society, a world of a billion social circuits, and you can, with the insulation of money, zip around the country and remain in the same comfortable place, a place of Four Seasons suites, helicopters, $500 dinner tabs. The rest of the world tends to fall away, through no fault of your own. It happens to everybody—your immediate surroundings loom larger and larger until everything else becomes just a dimly perceived backdrop.

Here are some remarks I have heard in recent weeks, all made by people I like, all of them musing about things that didn't seem to them very extraordinary. **A Palm Beach hostess on the cost of living in that town:** "It's outrageous. I sent the butler down for a case of wine the other day, and it cost $3,500—the same wine I'd paid $2,100 for a year ago." **A Boston businessman and his wife, talking about the small family foundation they had just established. Husband:** "It's just a few million dollars." **Wife:** "You know, we talk about millions the way we used to talk about hundreds of thousands. It sort of bothers me." **A CEO's widow:** "I've never had a worse case of withdrawal than I did when I had to give up that airplane." **A member of the "working rich":** "I can retire if I can figure out how to live on $200,000 a year."

Meanwhile, however dimly visible, the rest of the world is out there.

Holidays, not on ice	
Traveled abroad for business	40%
Traveled abroad for pleasure	58
Took a cruise	18
Went to a ski resort	38
Went to a beach or island resort	73
Attended a charity benefit	84

Shares

As a measure of the distance the 1 percent enjoys from society as a whole, consider some basic facts. The median household income is about $31,000, and median household net worth (including real estate and personal property) is about $51,000. About 60 percent of all American households have liquid assets of less than $10,000. These are the sorts of numbers one passes over in the newspaper, but it is worth considering them for a moment. For the 1 percent, $31,000 is an income so low that it is hard to imagine. (Asked in the Roper survey what they could "get by" on, the respondents said, on average, $80,000, but one wonders.) For many people, and not just one-percenters, $31,000 is a price tag, not a salary. It buys a low-end Land Rover, a year at Brown, a wedding, a dozen or so Prada dresses.

It has become a commonplace that the distribution of both wealth and income has become more lopsided in recent years, and the growing gap between rich and poor has become an almost ritualistic cause of concern. That wealth has accreted at the very top is beyond dispute, though interesting skirmishes are fought over the numbers.

Perhaps the most convincing account of the gilding of the 1 percent has been written by Edward N. Wolff, an economist at New York University, in his book *Top Heavy* and in subsequent research. Wolff notes a simple set of statistics that serves as a benchmark: Mean wealth in the country (now more than $212,000 per household) has risen steadily, but the median has dropped (to about $51,000). In other words, more money is going to fewer people. But these numbers don't reveal how the wealth is distributed. The details are quite impressive. Between 1983 and 1992 (the last year for which fully analyzed figures are available from the Federal Reserve Board's consumer-finances survey), virtually all gains in wealth went to the top 20 percent. (The next two-fifths stayed about even, and the bottom two-fifths actually got poorer in constant dollars.) Of those gains, almost two-thirds went to the 1 percent. The bottom 20 percent of the population has a negative net worth, and the bottom 60 percent accounts for about 7 percent of total net worth. Financial wealth (liquid assets) has grown even more for the 1 percent during recent years. By 1992, the 1 percent owned 46 percent of all household financial wealth in the country. (The top 20 percent controls an astonishing 92 percent of all financial wealth, leaving 8 percent of that particular pie for 80 percent of the people.)

What to make of these facts? For many, they spell the loss of something vital in our national life, the steady upward progress of the middle class. As he left his post in January as secretary of labor, Robert Reich put this argument eloquently: "In the America of my youth we were growing together. . . . The remarkable thing about the first three decades after World War II is that prosperity was widely shared. Most people in the top fifth of the income ladder saw their incomes double, and so did most people in the bottom. Today, all the rungs on the economic ladder are now farther apart than they were a generation ago and the space between them continues to widen."

It is the implication of Reich's remark that it doesn't really matter how much richer the rich get if everybody else is getting a little richer, too. We have staked a lot on the idea of opportunity, and it is remarkable how upward movement can sustain not only an individual but a society. Such was the magic—one is tempted to say the mass delusion—of the postwar years.

I have just had the curious experience of re-reading one of the most influential American books of the era, whose title embodied our self-concept, John Kenneth

Galbraith's *The Affluent Society*. According to Galbraith, by 1958 the age-old problem of production had been solved in America: Almost everyone had enough of
everything, or soon would, and our social mission was to turn to higher things—creating good schools, clean streets, improved housing. As late as 1966, it was possible for *Time* magazine to predict that "by 2000 machines will be producing so much
that everyone in the U.S. will, in effect, be independently wealthy." Galbraithism was
a classic case of mistaking the trend for the fact: Because wages for the poor and
middle class were rising, they would continue to do so. Indeed, we might as well
assume that we had arrived where we were headed. We were an affluent society.

(There were startlingly few dissenting voices to this view. Even Michael Harrington's landmark book, *The Other America*, discovered poverty as a nasty exception
to the general rule. No one paid much attention to the 1 percent either. In those days
they were anomalous or vestigial figures—East Coast snobs or Texas millionaires—
in a middle-class society. But it is interesting to note that in 1958, the year *The Affluent Society* appeared, the 1 percent controlled about 34 percent of personal net
worth, just a bit less than it does today.)

By 1973, median family income (in inflation-adjusted dollars) had ceased its long
sustained climb and began to stagnate. It is also true that by this time there had been
a dramatic shift in the percentage of wealth controlled by the 1 percent: from 34 percent to just 20 percent. But the cause of this was not primarily increases in income
at the lower end of the scale. There was another, far more important economic condition at work—"stagflation." The stock market was languishing, but many prices,
notably housing prices, were rising, as they had for decades. Few remember those
days with nostalgia, but it's possible that the middle class should think again. Many
a retirement nest egg was secured by the long upward march of real-estate values. It
turns out that over the decades a major factor in determining the relative wealth of
the top and the middle of society is the ratio of stock prices to housing prices. The
apparent leveling in the early 1970s had a lot to do with the inflated real-estate market combined with the depressed stock market, and much of the rise in inequality in
recent years is accounted for by the reversal of those conditions.

But the early 1970s were truly an exception in terms of the relative equality of
the classes. It is important not to forget that for more than 150 years, ever since the
full-fledged industrialization of the country, through boom and bust, under Republicans, Democrats, or Whigs, the 1 percent accounted for 25 percent or more of the
nation's personal wealth.

We notice the 1 percent now as it seems to leave everyone else behind, and it is
tempting to think we are living in another Gilded Age, when the 1 percent controlled
nearly half of the household wealth. We are about ten percentage points short of
this record, and on our current trajectory we would arrive there shortly after the
turn of the century. Now, as then, people are famous essentially for being rich, and
huge fortunes seem made out of thin air: The emblematic fortunes, Buffett-Gates,
just like Carnegie, Rockefeller, and Morgan before them, derive from technology or
financial wizardry. And now as then, money tends to trump all else.

Although individual fortunes may have been more spectacular in the Gilded Age,
as a group the rich have gotten richer. They have also, of course, gotten more
numerous.

The Mass Elite

I awake one morning in the Delano Hotel, in Miami Beach, and all around me see nothing but white: It is the style of the hotel. White floors and walls and furniture. The strange, austere bathroom, with no place to put anything, is all in white, too. I am thinking, in a kind of abstract way, about suicide. I don't mean that I really want to kill myself, just that the first image in my mind is of hurtling to the beach 14 stories below. It is only several hours later, when I tell a Miami friend where I'm staying, that I understand why. The Delano is high fashion, a creation of the brilliant designer-entrepreneur Ian Schrager. The rooms cost about $300 a night, and the white-jacketed doormen love to tell you which stars have just checked out. My friend is not impressed. "It's kind of like an asylum, isn't it?" she says. And that's it; that's why I was thinking about suicide: It just seemed the appropriate thing to do.

So many rich people, and the Delano is a cozy home for some of them, for guys in sandals and black T-shirts, their gray hair drawn into ponytails, women with proudly ungovernable frizzes, wearing black dresses from some Moroccan marketplace. Record producers, agents, hippies who got rich selling carrot juice. Whatever. One-percenters all.

So many rich people, and those who understand how to sell things to them realize it's not enough to target the affluent anymore. It is now a matter of niche-marketing to the rich. Ian Schrager understands perfectly. With the Delano, he has created an anti-hotel for people who disdain conventional luxury. It could not exist without the existence of the Ritz. (The ultimate Schrager experience will be called the Bellevue, and you will sleep in beautifully lacquered metal beds on wards, and muscular men will hose you down in shower rooms.) My problem with the Delano is, as they say, my problem: I am out of my niche. In Naples, my warm real-estate agent had tucked a breast into my arm and confided, "You're Naples people," and God help me, she may have been right.

The tent of the 1 percent is a big tent, and there is room for all sorts inside. One percent is a small part of anything, but absolute numbers count, and 2.6 million people take up a lot of space, especially when many of them can afford to maintain two or three houses.

If you have not yet gotten your solicitation for the new magazine *Golf Course Living,* that may be because you are known to be a yachtsman or you spend too much

Flights of Fancy

Members of the top 1% were asked what they'd bid for the following (spending money they really have):

	Mean bid	% who chose to bid
A place in heaven	$640,000	38%
True love	487,000	42
Great intellect	407,000	56
Talent	285,000	51
Eternal Youth	259,000	38
To be reunited with a lost love	206,000	27
Great beauty	83,000	35
To be president of the U.S.	55,000	16
Fame	15,000	23
Relationship with celebrity	4,000	16

time on international fly-fishing trips. The two and a half million richest Americans make up a diverse enough group so that, to one another, they do not look much alike—indeed, they give a fair amount of emotional energy to the distinctions among themselves. Not long ago, Martha's Vineyard and Nantucket were two bucolic little islands that in summer attracted a laid-back assortment of the Eastern rich. Today they are fiercely desirable ground, but different: Nantucket heavily corporate, the Vineyard more literary and liberal. In the eyes of anyone who has read Marx, these distinctions are ludicrous. In summer, the average net worth on either island is well into 1 percent range, yet residents of each have disdainful views of the other island. Each thinks the other is full of elitists.

In a lighthearted book a few years ago, called *Class*, Paul Fussell set out to delineate the social structure of the country, and—taking issue with the usual three-tier system—he proposed nine levels, from "bottom out-of-sight" to "top out-of-sight." Writing today, Fussell would, I expect, want to complicate things considerably. The old markers—school, parentage, accent, manners, taste—still count, but they are confounded by the new amounts of money involved. The waning of a cozy, homogeneous upper-class life only fuels people's acquisitive desires. A billionaire lights up the room in a way that the fairest-haired Groton old boy no longer can. At the end of the Palm Beach winter season, I met an old-money clubman who lamented that "many of the nicest people can no longer pay the dues."

We are witnessing, according to David Frum, a conservative thinker at the Manhattan Institute, "history's first mass upper class. . . . Nothing like this immense crowd of wealthy people," he says, "has been seen in the history of the planet." Frum's larger point is that this "mass upper class" is a triumph of American capitalism and that those who mock the new rich fail to see that they are viewing an economic miracle.

Perhaps in the end wealth is in the eyes of the beholder, but in the eyes of those who are earning and spending this new money, what appears to be happening is a constant upward redefinition of the middle class. Large numbers of people living in apparent luxury no longer seem so rarefied, and their presence stimulates restlessness and desire among a middle class that used to think of its own life as the norm. This is perhaps the real meaning of "the mass elite."

If the 1 percent cut a fairly wide swath, the top 10 percent are themselves disproportionately visible—and we are now talking about a truly substantial number of people, some 26 million of them. Many of the things the rich do at will—fly to Europe—the prosperous do less frequently. But the impression to the onlooker—the true middle class, which can't afford the trip—is of an awful lot of people who can fly to Europe.

Thus is ambition, upward-longing, stimulated. Seen from high atop Marketing Mountain, this is a truly glorious system, breeding constant, self-replenishing appetite. From the top of Philosophy Mountain the view is less happy—a land of continual discontent.

A rough narrative of the progress of American life, one that we all carry around in our heads, tells of the insistent democratizing of the society. In many ways it is true. Think of the class barriers that have fallen—barriers of accent, of dress, of all sorts of permissible behavior among people of different social stations. Society has grown less formal, less self-evidently hierarchical in the time that anyone now adult has been alive. Nobody is immune from being first-named by a stranger on the telephone, and the guy sitting next to you in business class may be wearing a T-shirt—

you may be wearing a T-shirt. Our richest man and our president are two guys who would just as soon have you call them "Bill." In these and countless other ways our society has become more egalitarian.

Yet a strange thing has happened to relations between the economic classes. As everyone aggressively asserts his equality, we lose the ability to talk about our inequality, that is, to identify our class interests. In the Gilded Age, benighted as it may have been, populist sentiment flourished. William Jennings Bryan wasn't going to be intimidated from giving his Cross of Gold speech by a rival's accusing him of fomenting class warfare. But that charge awaits any politician today who even speaks of raising taxes on the wealthy. As late as the 1940s it was possible to talk without irony of "soaking the rich"; today we are all, in effect, trickle-down economists.

In 1954, the highest marginal tax rate was 91 percent, for incomes over $200,000. Writing a few years later in that decade, Galbraith noted that a significant reduction in this rate was simply not politically supportable. Shortly after that John Kennedy began the long process of disassembling the progressive income tax that continues, with lurches back and forth, to this day. One can argue about the effectiveness of the high tax rates of mid-century, one can even accept that they served only to spawn loophole navigators, and yet one can still feel an odd wistfulness for this system—not for what it accomplished but for what it expressed in terms of society's sense of the seemliness of high incomes. With the depression still in mind, the tax code seemed to say that there was a social limit to inequalities of reward. And even if a dozen ways, like the notorious oil-depletion allowance, were found to circumvent the law, the law nonetheless surely had a restraining effect on what was paid. In 1954, a board could plausibly say to its president that compensation in excess of a million dollars was rather pointless, since the government was just going to take 91 percent. It seems reasonable to think that with similar rates in place we would now see fewer $8 million point guards and $12 million CEOs.

But maybe this argument is purely circular. Current law reflects popular ideas. Little enthusiasm appears to exist for higher taxes for the very rich.

Edward Wolff, the NYU economist, has advanced the notion of a wealth tax, modeled on similar taxes in some European countries, such as Switzerland. The tax would assess a small percentage, starting at 0.05 percent for household wealth between $100,000 and $200,000, graduating to a maximum of 0.3 percent for wealth above $1,000,000. At these painless levels (about two-thirds of American households would pay nothing; a family with a net worth of $500,000 would pay $1,000) it would raise $40 billion annually. Such a tax presents all sorts of practical problems (chiefly having to do with assessing wealth), but the real hurdles are political. Wolff says he found a supporter for his plan in Congress—Bernie Sanders, the former "socialist mayor" of Burlington, Vermont. It is hard to imagine that Trent Lott will get on board.

Why is there so little sense of resentment toward the imbalance of our society? Is it possible that we, or some significant part of us, may want a world of outlandish compensation at the top? Do we, in an important part of our heart, think the rich deserve their money?

The New Snobbery

Dining alone one evening at the folksily elegant Alexis Hotel in Seattle, I find myself becoming aware of a conversation at the table next to me. The tone reaches me before the words, and a glance at the participants reveals the essential dramatic situation. The players: a middle-aged couple and two boys, or young men. One is clearly their son, the other a friend of his. The friend is getting special, respectful attention from the parents. They are oddly deferential to him. It would seem odd even if the boy were not wearing a baseball cap during his $300 dinner. The son, discomfited, is cracking jokes. If you are old enough, you have probably acted each part in this play at one time or another.

I turn to the Pacific Coast creation on my plate: quail with a mango sauce—good restaurant. Words float over to my table. The young guest speaks of his new apartment, his new car, his travel, and finally of the company that provides all this: Microsoft. It is a little later, when the son has briefly left the table, that the parents ask the question they have clearly been dying to ask from the start: Do you get your stock options right away?

A perverse genius is built into our culture. At the small price of making ourselves a little bit insane, we maintain social order and make our economic engine work very well. The genius part is self-blame. In a land of opportunity—and who, looking around at the bizarre successes that sprout up everywhere, can deny that it is a land of opportunity?—if you are not rich it's your own fault.

If there is a consensus in our country about what constitutes fairness it would go under the currently fashionable name "meritocracy." This is the condition that supposedly results when the barriers to success that have marred our system—prejudice against race, religion, gender, reliance on old-boy networks—are removed. It is the triumph of innate worth, talent and intelligence, and, of course, their earnest little brother, hard work. In our sunnier moments, we congratulate ourselves on having gotten closer to this ideal state of things.

Meritocracy is the ideology of the technological West Coast, of Silicon Valley and the new Northwest. It is increasingly the ideology of all major corporations, as business becomes ever more "knowledge based," "information driven." It is the ideology of our colleges and universities, which ironically have only made the credential they offer that much more a dividing line between haves and have-nots. Never before have smart and rich been so nearly synonymous in the public imagination. (In Douglas Coupland's entertaining novel *Microserfs,* we learn that "in the Silicon Valley the IQ baseline (as at Microsoft) *starts* at 130, and bellcurves quickly, plateauing near 155, and only *then* does it decrease.") It is a belief in the power of meritocracy that allows a middle-aged couple to devalue the wisdom of a lifetime and defer to a kid in a baseball cap with a high IQ and stock options. And it's this ethic that helps the very rich to feel deserving.

The history of the word "meritocracy" deserves mention. Most words begin life simply and take on whatever ironic connotations they may acquire with use. With "meritocracy" it's just the opposite. The British sociologist Michael Young coined the term in 1958 in a spirit of mordant satire. First Americans, then the British, adopted it as a virtue. Young's book, *The Rise of the Meritocracy, 1870–2033,* depicts a dystopian world of the future in which society is in fact sorted out according to intelligence, level of schooling, and training. At length a rebellion occurs—but the bright and obtuse narrator goes to his death not able to understand why. What the rebels want, according to their "manifesto," is a world in which, "were we to evaluate people, not only according to their intelligence and their education, their occupation and their power, but according to their kindliness and their courage, their imagination and sensitivity, their sympathy and generosity, there could be no classes."

The book is forgotten; the word lives on, stripped of its irony. It seems that we move closer and closer to a market-economy world, in which people are judged—in which we judge ourselves—on a single axis.

The simplest way to describe the axis is, of course, money—the pursuit of which never seems to cease, not even at the top. Ted Turner's famous diatribe about billionaires afraid to slip down a notch on the Forbes 400 list plainly drew blood. Lawrence Ellison, head of Oracle, is notoriously rivalrous with Bill Gates. Asked what it is Ellison feels, exactly, toward Gates, a friend of Ellison's in the industry replies, "Well, I don't know that there's a word for it. I mean, how many times in history has somebody with $7 billion been unhappy because he doesn't have 18 billion?"

Something has changed about the way we think of money. It is hard to define, but to try to get at it, imagine a woman on a yawl at anchor in Pulpit Harbor, in Maine, on an August morning. Call her Phoebe.

She is having her morning coffee on deck, her legs stretched out on the cockpit cushions. Her beauty, which is considerable, suggests another era—her thin lips, her prominent nose—but she's just barely 40. She grew up on the Massachusetts coast, the 14th generation of her father's family to do so. He's a (now retired) classics professor, and the guardian of an old China-trade fortune, which did very well on his watch. Phoebe has had a Boston education, a Boston life: Winsor School, Harvard, Harvard Law, married at Trinity Church. Her biography qualifies her as one of that class many people claim does not exist: an American aristocrat.

There is one other fact about her: She left her law firm after just two years to work with (and bankroll) a little company founded by three guys from MIT. They now produce a cloying, but extremely successful, computer game for children. She has turned her $5 million trust fund into nearly $100 million, and the end is not yet.

How you think about this life suggests something about your attitudes toward money and class. Once, many people would have disapproved of Phoebe's turn to commerce: The point of having money was to free yourself for other things, a life of art, service, pleasure, perhaps work in a profession. Why should this elegant woman contribute to the national glut of junk? But this Jamesian view of life, which implies an upper class, even an unapologetic leisure class, has few current advocates. I think that for most of us now, Phoebe's new fortune enhances her, makes her more interesting, even redeems her. She "did it on her own."

The entrepreneurial virtues dominate our culture, and it is hard to resist them, hard even to see sometimes how completely they have permeated life. Indeed, even those most cosseted of people, CEOs, perhaps the most secure people in the history of the world, like to style themselves as "risk takers" and justify their pay accordingly. It is fashionable now among entrepreneurs to take the position that they will leave little or nothing to their children. This always seems kind of virtuous and bracing, until you realize they're really saying that they can imagine no higher calling for the next generation than doing it all over: making it again.

The American Dream

I was sitting at a Washington, D.C., dinner party in the middle of a conversation (a conversation I had initiated) about the rich. As is customary, everyone around the table was pretending that he or she wasn't rich. A nice woman to my left was lamenting the excesses of somebody and then of somebody else, and I was match-ing her, and we were just generally on the side of fairness. A fellow to her left, an entrepreneur, intervened with a burst of what I took to be candor.

"Let's face it," he said. "In this country the destructive behavior is done by the bottom 5 percent. The productive behavior comes from the top 5 percent. Every-body in the middle just eats the food." Stark and ghastly a vision as this may be, it had the virtue of explicitness, of saying something that one often senses at the top ranks of our country but seldom hears: a true abhorrence of the people in the mid-dle. The entrepreneur went on to say that in the end he couldn't take inequality very seriously because of the great saving grace of our society: mobility. The ability of the "productive" to rise to the top.

It is an argument, living where and as we do, that has to be taken seriously. *The Wall Street Journal* recently proclaimed THE AMERICAN DREAM LIVES above a piece about a longitudinal study of economic class over some 15 years. Between 1975 and 1991, the story said, almost 30 percent of those in the bottom fifth had risen to the top fifth. About half of the billionaires on the 1996 Forbes 400 list are there by virtue of money they have made, not inherited, and virtually all the very largest for-tunes are "first generation." (To be sure, many on the list came from comfortable upper-middle-class upbringings.)

This sort of data, and the rags-to-riches anecdotes we encounter almost daily, are seductive. It is important to remember that figures on income inequality are not static, that when you speak of the poor you are speaking about some people, any-way, who one day will be rich. Net worth typically rises over the course of a lifetime, but the median household net worth of those for whom the mobility game is over—people at retirement age—is just $92,000.

But debates like these—the American dream is dead; no, the American dream lives—leave something out. Why does one wince a bit at the very phrase—only because it has become such a cliché?

I did not fully know what I found so unsatisfying about this argument until I encountered a passage by the late Christopher Lasch, in his book *The Revolt of the Elites and the Betrayal of Democracy,* reminding me that, once, the American dream had meant something nobler, the belief that in a democratic society equality refers to more than opportunity. Lasch refers to the most important choice a democratic society has to make: "Whether to raise the general level of competence, energy, and devotion—'virtue,' as it was called in an older political tradition—or merely to pro-mote a broader recruitment of elites. Our society has clearly chosen the second course . . . generating social conditions in which ordinary people are not expected to know anything at all."

In many ways we live in a thrilling society. On a day in spring, I have lunch at a club in San Jose, California, with a man who embodies American opportunity—a Korean-born software entrepreneur just months from taking his fledgling com-pany public. He speaks of the hopeful engineers who came to the valley willing to work for stock options. It is another heartening story of wealth being created by intelligence, initiative, energy. Later, driving to San Francisco, I stop on a ridgetop and look out over Silicon Valley, the bright green hills torn by new construction—a sensuality in that sullied landscape, like a mussed silk blouse—and though the agents of change are technology and money, they seem here as irresistible as nature itself.

But the fragile idea that there is an equality based on worth that transcends net worth, the original American dream—what place does it have here? How much success, how many billionaires, how large and prosperous a "mass elite" can it survive? When it disappears entirely, we will all suffer equal loss—the 1 percent no less than the rest of us.

GREGORY MANTSIOS

Mantsios is director of worker education at Queens College, CUNY. His primary work has been in initiating and directing college degree programs for nontraditional students, particularly those from poor, working-class, and minority backgrounds. In this capacity, he was responsible for creating a campus-based degree program for working adults (LEAP), the Queens College Extension Center in mid-Manhattan, and the Queens College Labor Resource Center. He is also responsible for developing a new bachelor's degree program in Applied Social Science that is specifically designed to prepare students for public service and advocacy work.

Editor and contributor to A New Labor Movement for a New Century *(1998), he is also the founder and publisher of* New Labor Forum, *a national journal of ideas, analysis, and debate. His reviews and articles have appeared in the* New York Times, *professional journals, and college text anthologies.*

Mantsios holds a Ph.D. in sociology and has taught both sociology and labor studies at a number of institutions of higher education, including Queens College, Cornell University, Empire State College, William Paterson College, and Fairleigh Dickinson University. He also has a long history of community activism and volunteer service. He spent two years as a full-time volunteer for the ACTION program, led a community organizing project in New York, and participated in various community service projects. He has served as a trustee to the Michael Harrington Center, an advisor to the cable television channel of the City University of New York, and a board member of the New York Labor History Association, among other posts.

REWARDS AND OPPORTUNITIES: THE POLITICS AND ECONOMICS OF CLASS IN THE U.S. *

"[Class is] for European democracies or something else—it isn't for the United States of America. We are not going to be divided by class." George Bush, 1988[1]

Strange words from a man presiding over a nation with more than 32 million people living in poverty and one of the largest income gaps between rich and poor in

---

*The author wishes to thank Bill Clark for his assistance in preparing this selection.

the industrialized world.* Politicians long before and long after George Bush have made and will continue to make statements proclaiming our egalitarian values and denying the existence of class in America. But they are not alone: most Americans dislike talking about class. We minimize the extent of inequality, pretend that class differences do not really matter, and erase the word "class" from our vocabulary and from our mind. In one survey, designed to solicit respondents' class identification, 35% of all those questioned told interviewers they had never thought about their class identification before that very moment.[2]

"We are all middle-class" or so it would seem. Our national consciousness, as shaped in large part by the media and our political leadership, provides us with a picture of ourselves as a nation of prosperity and opportunity with an ever expanding middle-class life style. As a result, our class differences are muted and our collective character is homogenized.

Yet class divisions are real and arguably the most significant factor in determining both our very being in the world and the nature of the society we live in.

The Extent of Poverty in the U.S.

The official poverty line in 1990 was $12,675 for an urban family of four and $9,736 for a family of three. For years, critics have argued that the measurements used by the government woefully underestimate the extent of poverty in America.[3] Yet even by the government's conservative estimate, nearly one in eight Americans currently lives in poverty.

As deplorable as this is, the overall poverty rate for the nation effectively masks both the level of depravation and the extent of the problem within geographic areas and within specific populations. Three short years prior to George Bush's speech, the Physicians Task Force on Hunger in America declared that "Hunger is a problem of epidemic proportion across the nation." Upon completing their national field investigation of hunger and malnutrition, the team of twenty-two prominent physicians estimated that there were up to 20 million citizens hungry at least some period of time each month.

> Touring rural Mississippi the Task Force filed this report from one of the many such homes they visited:
>
> Inside the remnants of a house, alongside a dirt road in Greenwood, lived a family of thirteen people. Graciously welcomed by the mother and father, the doctors entered another world—a dwelling with no heat, no electricity, no windows, home for two parents, their children, and several nieces and nephews. Clothes were piled in the corner, the substitute location for closets which were missing; the two beds in the three-room house had no sheets, the torn mattresses covered by the bodies of three children who lay side by side. In the kitchen a small gas stove was the only appliance.
>
> No food was in the house. The babies had no milk; two were crying as several of the older children tried to console them. "These people are starving," the local

* The income gap in the United States, measured as a percentage of total income held by the wealthiest 20% of the population vs. the poorest 20% is approximately 11 to 1. The ratio in Great Britain is 7 to 1; in Japan, it is 4 to 1. (see "U.N. National Accounts Statistics", Statistical Papers, Series M no. 79. N.Y. U.N. 1985 pp 1-11.)

guide told the doctors. Twice a week she collected food from churches to bring to the family. . . . Only the flies which crawled on the face of the smallest child seemed to be well fed. The parents were not; they had not eaten for two days. The children had eaten some dried beans the previous evening.

from *Hunger in America: The Growing Epidemic,* the Physicians Task Force[4]

Nearly a quarter of the population of the state of Mississippi lives below the federal poverty level. Over a third of the population of Mississippi is so poor it qualifies for food stamps, although only 15% actually receive them.[5]

The face of poverty in Greenwood, Mississippi, is not much different than that in other parts of the deep south and beyond. Appalling conditions of poverty are facts of life in the foothills of Appalachia, the reservations of Native America, the barrios of the Southwest, the abandoned towns of the industrial belt, and the ghettoes of the nation's urban centers. There are more than 2 million poor people in New York City alone, a figure that exceeds the entire population of some nations.

Today, the poor include the very young and the elderly, the rural poor and the urban homeless: increasingly, the poor also include men and women who work full time. When we examine the incidence of poverty within particular segments of the population, the figures can be both shameful and sobering:

- more than one out of every five children in the U.S. (all races) lives below the poverty line[6]
- 39% of Hispanic children and 45% of Black children in the U.S. live below the poverty line[7]
- one in every four rural children is poor[8]
- if you are Black and 65 years of age or older, your chances of being poor are one in three[9]
- roughly 60% of all poor work at least part-time or in seasonal work[10]
- 2 million Americans worked full time throughout the year and were still poor[11]

Poverty statistics have either remained relatively constant over the years or have shown a marked increase in the incidence of poverty. The number of full-time workers below the poverty line, for example, increased by more than 50% from 1978 to 1986.[12]

The Level of Wealth

Business Week recently reported that the average salary for the CEO of the nation's top 1,000 companies was $841,000.[13] As high as this figure is, however, it fails to capture the level of compensation at the top of the corporate world. Short-term and long-term bonuses, stock options and stock awards can add significantly to annual compensation. Take the following examples:

- annual compensation in 1989, including short-term bonuses, for the Chief Executive Officer of UAL, came to $18.3 million; for the head of Reeboks, compensation came to $14.6 million (in what was not a particularly hot year in the sneaker business).[14]
- annual compensation, including short-term and long-term bonuses and stock

awards, for the head of Time Warner Inc. totaled $78.2 million; for the CEO of LIN Broadcasting, it came to a whooping $186 million.[15]

The distribution of income in the United States is outlined in Table 1.

TABLE 1
Income Inequality in the U.S.[16]

Income group (families)	Percent of income received
Lowest fifth	4.6
Second fifth	10.8
Middle fifth	16.8
Fourth fifth	24.0
Highest fifth	43.7
(Highest 5 percent)	(17.0)

By 1990, according to economist Robert Reich, the top fifth of the population took home more money than the other four-fifths put together.[17]

Wealth, rather than income, is a more accurate indicator of economic inequality. Accumulated wealth by individuals and families runs into the billions, with the U.S. now boasting at least 58 billionaires, many of them multi-billionaires. The distribution of wealth is far more skewed than the distribution of income. In 1986, the Joint Economic Committee of the U.S. Congress released a special report entitled "The Concentration of Wealth in the United States." Table 2 summarizes some of the findings.

TABLE 2
Distribution of Wealth in the U.S.[18]

Families	Percent of wealth owned
The richest 10%	71.7
(The top 1/2%)	(35.1)
Everyone else, or 90% of all families	28.2

It should be noted that because of the way the statistics were collected by the Congressional Committee, the figure for 90% of all other families includes half of the families who fall into the wealthiest quintile of the population. The "super rich," that is, the top one-half of one percent of the population, includes approximately 420,000 households with the average value of the wealth for each one of these households amounting to $8.9 million.[19]

Most people never see the opulence of the wealth, except in the fantasy world of television and the movies. Society pages in local newspapers, however, often provide a glimpse into the real life-style of the wealthy. A recent article in the *New York Times,* described the lifestyle of John and Patricia Kluge.

Mr. Kluge, chairman of the Metromedia Company, has an estimated worth of $5.2 billion. . . . The Kluges (pronounced Kloog-ee) have an apartment in Manhattan, an estate in the Virginia hunt country, and a horse farm in Scotland. . . .

They are known in Washington and New York social circles for opulent parties. Mr. Kluge had the ballroom of the Waldorf done up like the interior of a Viennese belle epoque palace for Mrs. Kluge's 49th birthday.

Her birthday parties for him have been more intimate, friends say. Typically these involve, only one or two other couples (once it was Frank and Barbara Sinatra) who take over L'Orangerie, a private dining room at Le Cirque that seats 100. The room was turned into an English garden for Mr. Kluge's 70th birthday, with dirt covering the carpet, flowering plants and trees. Hidden among the trees were nine violinists. The wine was a Chateau Lafite from 1914, the year of his birth. The birthday cake was in the shape of a $1 billion bill.[20]

The Plight of the Middle Class

The percentage of households with earnings at a middle-income level has been falling steadily.[21] The latest census figures show that the percentage of families with an annual income between $15,000 and $50,000 (approximately 50% and 200% of the median income) has fallen by nearly 10 percentage points since 1970.[22] While some of the households have moved upward and others have moved downward, what is clear is that the United States is experiencing a significant polarization in the distribution of income. The gap between rich and poor is wider and the share of income earned by middle-income Americans has fallen to the lowest level since the census bureau began keeping statistics in 1946. More and more individuals and families are finding themselves at one or the other end of the economic spectrum as the middle class steadily declines.

Furthermore, being in the middle class is no longer what it used to be. Once, middle class status carried the promise that one's standard of living would steadily improve over time. Yet 60% of Americans will have experienced virtually no income gain between 1980 and 1990. (Compare this to the income gains experienced by the wealthiest fifth of the population—up by 33%, and the wealthiest one percent of the population—up by 87%.)[23] One study showed that only one in five (males) will surpass the status, income, and prestige of their fathers.[24]

Nor does a middle class income any longer guarantee the comforts it once did. Home ownership, for example, has increasingly become out of reach for a growing number of citizens. During the last decade home ownership rates dropped from 44% to 36% among people in the 25–29 year old age group and from 61% to 53% among those in their thirties.[25]

The Rewards of Money

The distribution of income and wealth in the U.S. is grossly unequal and becomes increasingly more so with time. The rewards of money, however, go well beyond those of consumption patterns and life style. It is not simply that the wealthy live such opulent life styles, it is that class position determines one's life chances. Life chances include such far-reaching factors as life expectancy, level of education, occupational status, exposure to industrial hazards, incidence of crime victimization, rate of incarceration, etc. In short, class position can play a critically important role in determining how long you live, whether you have a healthy life, if you fail in school, or if you succeed at work.

The link between economic status and health is perhaps the most revealing and most disheartening. Health professionals and social scientists have shown that income is closely correlated to such factors as infant mortality, cancer, chronic disease, and death due to surgical and medical complications and "misadventures."[26]

The infant mortality rate is an example that invites international as well as racial and economic comparisons. At 10.6 infant deaths per 1,000 live births, the U.S. places nineteenth in the world—behind such countries as Spain, Singapore, and Hong Kong; a statistic that is in and of itself shameful for the wealthiest nation in the world. When infant mortality only among Blacks in the U.S. is considered, the rate rises to 18.2 and places the U.S. 28th in rank—behind Bulgaria and equal to Costa Rica. The infant mortality rate in poverty stricken areas, such as Hale County, Alabama, is three times the national rate and nearly twice that of the nation of Malaysia (whose GNP per capita is one tenth that of the U.S.).[27]

TABLE 3

Infant mortality rate per 1,000 births[28]

Total (national, all racial and ethnic groups)	10.6
Among Blacks only	18.2
In Hale County, Alabama	31.0

Analyses of the relationship between health and income are not always easy to come by. A recent study conducted in New York City, however, provided some important information. The study examined the difference in health status and delivery of health services among residents from different neighborhoods. The data provided allows for comparing incidents of health problems in neighborhoods where 40% or more of the population lives below the poverty line with those in other neighborhoods where less than 10% of the population lives below the poverty line. The study found that the incidence of health problems, in many categories, was several times as great in poorer neighborhoods. For example, death associated with vascular complications (from the heart or brain) occurred nearly twice as often in poor areas than in non-poor. Similarly, chances of being afflicted with bronchitis is 5 times as great in poor areas than in non-poor areas.[29] The study concluded, "The findings clearly indicate that certain segments of the population—poor, minority, and other disadvantaged groups—are especially vulnerable and bear a disproportionate share of preventable, and therefore unnecessary deaths and diseases."[30]*

The reasons for such a high correlation are many and varied: inadequate nutrition, exposure to occupational and environmental hazards, access to health-care facilities, quality of health services provided, ability to pay and therefore receive medical services, etc. Inadequate nutrition, for example, is associated with low birth weights and growth failure among low-income children and with chronic disease among the elderly poor. It has also been shown that the uninsured and those cov-

---

*It should be noted that the study was conducted in a major metropolitan area where hospitals and health-care facilities are in close proximity to the population, rich and poor. One might expect the discrepancies to be even greater in poor, rural areas where access to health care and medical attention is more problematic.

ered by Medicaid are far less likely to be given common hospital procedures than are patients with private medical coverage.

The relationship between income and health is similar to that of income and rate of incarceration. One in four young Black men, age 20 to 29, are either in jail or court supervised (i.e., on parole or probation). This figure surpasses the number of Black men enrolled in higher education. The figure also compares negatively to that for white men where 1 in 16 are incarcerated in the same age group.[31]

While it is often assumed that differences in rates of arrest and incarceration reflect differences in the incidents of crime, a recent study conducted in Pinellas County, Florida, found that most women prosecuted for using illegal drugs while pregnant have been poor members of racial minorities, even though drug use in pregnancy is equally prevalent in white middle class women. Researchers found that about 15% of both the white and the Black women used drugs, but that the Black women were 10 times as likely as whites to be reported to the authorities and poor women were more likely to be reported than middle class women. Sixty percent of the 133 women reported had incomes of less than $12,000 a year. Only 8% had incomes of more than $25,000 a year.

Differences in Opportunity

The opportunity for social and economic success are the hallmarks of the American Dream. The dream is rooted to two factors: education and jobs.

Our nation prides itself on its ability to provide unprecedented educational opportunities to its citizens. As well it should. It sends more of its young people to college than any other nation in the world. There are nearly 13 million Americans currently enrolled in colleges and universities around the country, a result of the tremendous expansion of higher education since World War II. The establishment of financial assistance for veterans and for the needy, and the growth of affordable public colleges all have had an important and positive effect on college enrollment. Most importantly from the point of view of a national consciousness, the swelling of college enrollments has affirmed our egalitarian values and convinced us that our educational system is just and democratic.

Our pride, however, is a false pride. For while we have made great strides in opening the doors of academe, the system of education in the United States leaves much to be desired and is anything but egalitarian.

More than a quarter of our adult population has not graduated from high school, nearly three quarters do not hold a college degree.[32] This is a record that does not bode well for the most industrialized and technologically advanced nation in the world. Perhaps more importantly, the level of educational achievement is largely class determined.

At least equal in importance to the amount of education received, is the quality of education. The quality of primary and secondary schools is largely dependent on geography and proximity to schools with adequate resources. Educational funding, and the tax base for it, are determined by residency and who can afford to live where. Schools in poorer districts are just not as likely to provide a high-quality education.

Student achievement in the classroom and on standardized tests is also class determined. Studies from the late 1970s showed a direct relation between SAT scores and family income. Grouping SAT scores into twelve categories from highest to lowest, researchers found that the mean family income decreased consistently from one group to the next as test scores declined. The study was done by examining the test results and family income of over 600,000 students![33] In other words, the higher the family income, the higher the test scores and vice versa.

Furthermore, for that segment of the population that does enter and complete a college education (approximately 18% of the population, including Associate degrees), the system is highly stratified. Precious few from poor and working class families have gained access to the elite colleges. For the most part, these have remained the bastion of the wealthy, leaving the less prestigious two year colleges almost exclusively the domain of the poor and the disadvantaged. The result is that colleges today are performing the same sorting function previously performed by high schools, where students are divided into vocational and academic tracks. The rate of participation in vocational programs at the college level is closely related to socioeconomic class, so that students from poorer backgrounds who do enroll in college are still being channeled into educational programs and institutions that are vocational in nature and that lead to less desirable occupations and futures.[34]*

The "junior" colleges, whose growth once promised to serve as a stepping stone for the disadvantaged and the underprepared to gain access to four year liberal arts colleges have been transformed into "community" colleges which provide vocational programs and terminal degrees in fields that narrow occupational options. The effect is to limit opportunity and to provide what some critics have referred to as a "cooling out function"—the managing of ambitions of the poor and working class who might otherwise take the American dream seriously.[35]

Some might argue that intelligence and drive are more significant than education in determining a young person's future. For example, a study by the Carnegie Foundation found that even when IQ test scores were the same, a young person's ability to obtain a job that will pay in the top 10% of the income structure is 27 times as great if he or she comes from a wealthy background.[36]

Culture, the Media, and Ideology

If the U.S. is so highly stratified and if economic class makes such a difference, why is it then, that we retain such illusions about an egalitarian society? In part, it is because for many of us it is simply more comfortable to deny the class nature of our society and the rigid boundaries such a society suggests: we would rather consider our economic predicament, whatever our class standing, to be temporary and anticipate a brighter future in what we prefer to believe is a fluid and open opportunity structure. In part, it is also because we are constantly bombarded with cultural messages from the media and other sources that tell us that class in America, if it exists at all, does not really matter.

Both in entertainment and in relating the news of the day, the media convey important, albeit contradictory messages: classes do not exist, the poor and the working class are morally inferior, America is a land of great social and economic mobility, class is irrelevant.

TV sitcoms and feature films have traditionally ignored class issues. There have been relatively few serious portrayals of the poor or the working class in the his-

---

* This does not deny the intrinsic value of vocational education, but points to the fact that poor and working class students are found in the sector of education that yields the smallest socioeconomic return.

tory of film and television. Television, in particular, presents a view of America where everyone is a professional and middle class: daddy, it seems, always goes to the office, not to the factory.[37] There are notable exceptions and these are of particular interest in that they usually present story lines that distort class realities even further.

Story lines about class do one of three things. First, they present and reinforce negative class stereotypes. The poor are presented as hapless or dangerous and the working class as dumb, reactionary, and bigoted. Those not members of the professional middle class are to be laughed at, despised, or feared.[38] Second, they portray instances of upward mobility and class fluidity. These include rags-to-riches stories, Pygmalion tales, and comic instances of downward mobility. Third, they stress that the people who think firm class lines exist come to discover that they are mistaken: everybody is really the same.[39] These are often rich girl/poor boy romances or their opposite.

Story lines about class make for good comedy, good romance, and in the last example, even good lessons in human relations. They also perform, however, a great disservice: "treating class differences totally inconsequential strengthens the national delusion that class power and position are insignificant".[40]

A Structural Perspective

Vast differences in wealth have serious consequences and are neither justifiable nor a result of individual and personal deficiencies. People are poor because they have no money and no power to acquire money. The wealthy are rich because they have both.

The distribution of income and wealth occurs because a society is structured and policies are implemented in such a way to either produce or alleviate inequalities. A society can choose to minimize the gaps in wealth and power between its most privileged and its most disenfranchised. Government can serve as the equalizer by providing mechanisms to redistribute wealth from the top to the bottom. The promise of government as the great equalizer has clearly failed in the U.S. and rather than redoubling the efforts to redistribute wealth, traditional redistributive mechanisms, such as the progressive income tax, have declined in use in recent years. The tax rate for the wealthiest segment of the population, for example, steadily declined in spite of, or perhaps because of, the increasing concentration of wealth and power at the top. In 1944 the top tax rate was 94%, after World War II it was reduced to 91%, in 1964 to 72%, in 1981 to 50%, in 1990 to 28% (for those with an annual income over $155,000). *

Nor is it the case that conditions of wealth simply coexist side-by-side with conditions of poverty. The point is not that there are rich and poor, but that some are rich precisely because others are poor, and that one's privilege is predicated on the other's disenfranchisement. If it were not for the element of exploitation, we might celebrate inequality as reflective of our nation's great diversity.

The great anti-poverty crusader, Michael Harrington, tells of the debate in Congress over Richard Nixon's Family Assistance Plan during the 1970s. If the government provided a minimum income to everyone, "Who," asked a southern legislator, "will iron my shirts and rake the yard?"[41]

---

* Ironically those with an annual income between $75,000 and $150,000 pay a higher rate of 33%.

The legislator bluntly stated the more complex truth: the privileged in our society require a class-structured social order in order to maintain and enhance their economic and political well-being. Industrial profits depend on cheap labor and on a pool of unemployed to keep workers in check. Real estate speculators and developers create and depend on slums for tax-evading investments. These are the injustices and irrationalities of our economic system.

What is worse is that inequalities perpetuate themselves. People with wealth are the ones who have the opportunity to accumulate more wealth.

The fortune of Warren Buffett is estimated to be approximately $4 billion dollars. He is one of 71 billionaires in the United States (their average holding is about $3 billion each).[42] Calculated below is the interest generated by Buffett's wealth at anl 8% return.

Interest generated by $4 billion, at 8% return
$10 each second
$600 each minute
$36,000 each hour
$864,000 each day
$6,048,000 each week
$320,000,000 each year ($320 million)

In other words, Mr. Buffett makes more money in two days of non-work than most people earn in a lifetime of work.

It is this ability to generate additional resources that most distinguishes the nation's upper class from the rest of society. It is not simply bank interest that generates more money, but income producing property: buildings, factories, natural resources; those assets Karl Marx referred to as the means of production. Today, unlike the early days of capitalism, these are owned either directly or indirectly through stocks. Economists estimate that for the super rich, the rate of return on such investments is approximately 30%.[43] Economists have also designed a device, called Net Financial Assets (NFA), to measure the level and concentration of income-producing property. While Net Worth (NW), a figure that considers all assets and debts, provides a picture of what kind of life-style is being supported, the NFA figure specifically excludes in its calculation ownership of homes and motor vehicles. By doing so, the NFA figure provides a more reliable measure of an individual's life chances and ability to accumulate future resources. A home or a car are not ordinarily converted to purchase other resources, such as a prep school or college education for one's children. Neither are these assets likely to be used to buy medical care, support political candidates, pursue justice in the courts, pay lobbyists to protect special interests, or finance a business or make other investments. Net financial assets include only those financial assets normally available for and used to generate income and wealth.[44] Stock ownership, for example, is a financial asset and is highly concentrated at the top, with the wealthiest 10% of the population owning over 89% of the corporate stocks.[45] Since home ownership is the major source of wealth for those who own a house, removing home equity as well as car ownership from the calculations has a significant impact on how we view the question of equity.

- The median net household income in the U. S. is $21,744, net worth in the U.S. is $32,609, and the median Net Financial Assets is $2,599.

- While the top 20% of American households earn over 43% of all income, that same 20% holds 67% of Net Worth, and nearly 90% of Net Financial Assets.
- The median income of the top one percent of the population is 22 times greater than that of the remaining 99%. The median Net Financial Assets of the top one percent is 237 times greater than the median of the other 99% of the population.[46]

The ability to generate wealth on the part of this class of owners is truly staggering. It contrasts sharply with the ability of those who rely on selling their labor power. For those with income under $25,000, wage and salary income from labor comprised 90% of their total income.

There is also an entrepreneurial middle class in America that includes farmers, shopkeepers, and others. The small entrepreneurs, however, are becoming increasingly marginal in America and their income-producing property hardly exempts them from laboring.

The wealthy usually work too: their property income, however, is substantial enough to enable them to live without working if they chose to do so.

People with wealth and financial assets have disproportionate power in society. First, they have control of the workplace in enterprises they own. They determine what is produced and how it is produced. Second, they have enormous control over the media and other institutions that influence ideology and how we think about things, including class. Third, they have far greater influence over the nations' political institutions than their numbers warrant. They have the ability to influence not only decisions affecting their particular business ventures, but the general political climate of the nation.

Spheres of Power and Oppression

When we look at society and try to determine what it is that keeps most people down—what holds them back from realizing their potential as healthy, creative, productive individuals—we find institutionally oppressive forces that are largely beyond their individual control. Class domination is one of these forces. People do not choose to be poor or working class; instead they are limited and confined by the opportunities afforded or denied them by a social system. The class structure in the United States is a function of its economic system—capitalism, a system that is based on private rather than public ownership and control of commercial enterprises and on the class division between those who own and control and those who do not. Under capitalism, these enterprises are governed by the need to produce a profit for the owners, rather than to fulfill collective needs.

Racial and gender domination are other such forces that hold people down. Although there are significant differences in the way capitalism, racism and sexism affect our lives, there are also a multitude of parallels. And although race, class, and gender act independently of each other, they are at the same time very much interrelated.

On the one hand, issues of race and gender oppression cut across class lines. Women experience the effects of sexism whether they are well-paid professionals or poorly paid clerks. As women, they face discrimination and male domination, as well as catcalls and stereotyping. Similarly, a Black man faces racial oppression whether he is an executive, an auto worker, or a tenant farmer. As a Black, he will be subjected to racial slurs and be denied opportunities because of his color.

Regardless of their class standing, women and members of minority races are confronted with oppressive forces precisely because of their gender, color, or both.

On the other hand, class oppression permeates other spheres of power and oppression, so that the oppression experienced by women and minorities is also differentiated along class lines. Although women and minorities find themselves in subordinate positions vis-à-vis white men, the particular issues they confront may be quite different depending on their position in the class structure. Inequalities in the class structure distinguish social functions and individual power, and these distinctions carry over to race and gender categories.

Power is incremental and class privileges can accrue to individual women and to individual members of a racial minority. At the same time, class-oppressed men, whether they are white or Black, have privileges afforded them as men in a sexist society. Similarly, class-oppressed whites, whether they are men or women, have privileges afforded them as whites in a racist society. Spheres of power and oppression divide us deeply in our society, and the schisms between us are often difficult to bridge.

Whereas power is incremental, oppression is cumulative, and those who are poor, Black, and female have all the forces of classism, racism, and sexism bearing down on them. This cumulative oppression is what is meant by the double and triple jeopardy of women and minorities.

Furthermore, oppression in one sphere is related to the likelihood of oppression in another. If you are Black and female, for example, you are much more likely to be poor and working class than you would be as a white male. Census figures show that the incidence of poverty and near-poverty (calculated as 125% of the poverty line) varies greatly by race and gender.

TABLE 4
Chances of Being Poor in America[47]

	White male & female	White female head	Black male & female	Black female head
Poverty	1 in 9	1 in 4	1 in 3	1 in 2
Near Poverty	1 in 6	1 in 3	1 in 2	2 in 3

In other words, being female and being nonwhite are attributes in our society that increase the chances of poverty and of lower-class standing. Racism and sexism compound the effects of classism in society.

Notes

1. Quoted in George Will, "A Case for Dukakis," in *The Washington Post*, November 13, 1988, p. A27.

2. Marian Irish and James Prothro, *The Politics of American Democracy*, Englewood Cliffs, N. J., Prentice-Hall, 1965, p. 2, 38.

3. See, for example, Patricia Ruggles, "The Poverty Line—Too Low for the 90's," in the *New York Times*, April 26, 1990, p. A31.

4. Physicians Task Force on Hunger in America, *Hunger in America: The Growing Epidemic*, Wesleyan University Press, 1985, p. 27.

5. Ibid.

6. Bureau of Census, "Statistical Abstract of the U.S. 1990," Department of Commerce, Washington, D.C., 1990, p. 460.

7. Ibid.

8. Ibid.

9. Ibid.

10. *U. S. News and World Report*, January 1, 1988, pp. 18-24.

11. Ibid.

12. Ibid.

13. *Business Week*, October 19, 1990, p. 11.

14. Ibid, p. 12.

15. *Business Week*, May 6, 1991, p. 90.

16. U. S. Department of Commerce, "Statistical Abstract of the U.S. 1988," Washington, D.C., 1988, p. 428.

17. Robert Reich, "Secession of the Successful," *New York Times*, January 20, 1991, p. M42.

18. Joint Economic Committee of the U.S. Congress, "The Concentration of Wealth in the United States," Washington, D.C., 1986, p. 24.

19. Richard Roper, *Persistent Poverty: The American Dream Turned Nightmare*, Plenum Press, 1991, p. 60.

20. *New York Times*, April 29, 1990, p. 48.

21. Chris Tilly, "U-Turn on Equality," *Dollars and Sense*, May 1986, p. 84.

22. Census, ibid, p. 450.

23. "And the Rich Get Richer," *Dollars and Sense*, October 1990, p. 5.

24. Richard DeLone, *Small Futures*, Harcourt Brace Jovanovich, 1978, pp. 14-19.

25. Roper, ibid, p. 32.

26. Melvin Krasner, *Poverty and Health in New York City*, United Hospital Fund of New York, 1989. See also, U. S. Dept of Health and Human Services, *Health Status of Minorities and Low Income Groups*, 1985; and Dana Hughes, Kay Johnson, Sara Rosenbaum, Elizabeth Butler, Janet Simons, *The Health of America's Children*, The Children's Defense Fund, 1988.

27. Physicians Task Force, ibid; Hughes, et al, ibid; and "World Development Report 1990, " World Bank, Oxford University Press, 1990, pp. 232-233.

28. Ibid.

29. Krasner, ibid, p. 134.

30. Ibid, p. 166.

31. *Washington Post*, February 27, 1990, p. A3, citing Marc Mauer, "Young Black Men and the Criminal Justice System: A Growing National Problem," The Sentencing Project January 1990.

32. The Chronicle of Higher Education, *The Almanac of Higher Education, 1989-1990*, The University of Chicago Press, 1989.

33. Richard DeLone, ibid, p. 102.

34. David Karen, "The Politics of Class, Race, and Gender," paper presented at Conference on "Class Bias in Higher Education," Queens College, Flushing N.Y., November 1990.

35. Steven Brint and Jerome Karabel, *Diverted Dream: Community Colleges and the Promise of Educational Opportunity in America, 1990-1985*, Oxford University Press, 1989.

36. Richard DeLone, ibid.

37. Barbara Ehrenreich, *Fear of Falling: The Inner Life of the Middle Class*, Pantheon, 1989, p. 140.

38. See Barbara Ehrenreich, ibid.

39. Benjamin DeMott, *The Imperial Middle: Why Americans Can't Think Straight About Class*, William Morrow, 1990.

40. DeMott, ibid.

41. Michael Harrington, *The New American Poverty*, Penguin, 1985, p. 3.

42. *Fortune Magazine*, September 10, 1990, p. 98; *Forbes*, October 21, 1991, pp. 145–160.

43. E. K. Hunt and Howard Sherman, *Economics*, Harper and Row, 1990, pp. 254–257.

44. Melvin Oliver and Thomas Shapiro, "Wealth of a Nation," *The American Journal of Economics and Sociology*, April 1990, p. 129.

45. The Joint Economic Committee, ibid.

46. Oliver, ibid, p. 129.

47. "Characteristics of the Population Below the Poverty Line: 1984," from Current Population Reports, Consumer Income Series P-60, No. 152, Washington, D.C., U.S. Department of Commerce, Bureau of the Census, June 1986, pp. 5–9.

ELIZABETH FAUE

Faue grew up in Minneapolis and went to the University of Minnesota for her B.A. in English. She also obtained a Ph.D. in history there. Her first book was a study of working-class activism in her hometown, Community of Suffering and Struggle: Women, Men and the Labor Movement in Minneapolis, 1915-1945. *She is completing a book on Eva McDonald Valesh and the political culture of American labor reform. She teaches labor and women's history at Wayne State University in Detroit and organizes the annual North American Labor History Conference.*

WHAT WORKING CLASS IS ABOUT

As a third-generation union member who worked her way through college and graduate school (even if I have finally "left" the ranks of the "working class"—and I don't believe that one leaves that experience behind), I can tell you that not all working-class men and women in the United States in the 1990s have forgotten or dismissed their working-class identities, roots, or politics. The "working class," as *Roger and Me* defined it, has shrunk only if you allow membership to be confined to the narrow grounds of belonging to a union like the UAW and working in a factory that builds Chevrolets or Fords. The great mass of people who could be defined as working-class today, because of their income, family, or occupational history, cultural context, and/or politics, do not share the *Roger and Me* experience. Union members, and people who identify with working-class/union politics, are found in public sector employment as service workers, clerks, and lower-level professionals; they are found in lower-wage, competitive manufacturing jobs—sometimes unionized, sometimes not—in Silicon Valley, in the "Rust Belt" building auto parts, and everywhere in the United States at places like Judy Toys; they work clerking and cashiering and filing in insurance and in banking and at colleges and universities, where their income rarely passes $20,000 a year, they dig ditches, do nonunion construction work and home repair; they are intermittent members of the labor force, because employment is seasonal or unsteady; they work in nursing homes and hospitals and elementary schools cleaning the floors, changing the sheets, distributing water containers, running cash registers, and handing out food. Some of them have strong family histories of unionization; some of them fear or resent unions; many of them wish they could belong to a union, if only because it might offer them better healthcare, a few more days of vacation a year, a better standard of living, the ability to help their children go to school, access to daycare, or simply less personal harassment on the job.

Being working class is not just about where you work or what union you belong to; it is about the experience of deprivation in a culture of plenty; the experience of having one's frontiers closed and expectations lowered in "the opportunity society"; it is about losing one's friends if one actually can take advantage of opportunity—or, at the very least, not being able to "bring them with you." It is about not being able to pay the bills for years on end and of being humiliated by bill-collectors who call you up and banks that harass you for checks that bounce, and it is about debts that mean that you cannot even plan or save for the future, whether the future is education for your children or a better retirement for yourself or a vacation away from your home. It is also about not having access to the information that might better enable you to handle your problems; it is about not knowing how to apply for college or get financial aid or about having anyone in the family to ask how to do these things; it is about feeling powerless in the face of government clerks and bank tellers and sales people and police and about not knowing your rights or how much leeway you have. It is about not having the self-esteem to know that McDonald's is only your first job and that you are free to quit; it is also sometimes about knowing you can't quit, because there is no time to find another job and about not having the money to move, because you spent the money you were saving for it on an expensive prescription. It is also about feeling that there is nothing you can do about it, because politicians and parties don't listen to working people and the union steward doesn't have a lot of leeway either. It is also about the camaraderie of those who share your circumstance, and it is about competition over the things that make up working-class life. It is about retired janitors who gather in a restaurant for breakfast to talk about their "investments" (made another million, they joke) and about retired hospital workers who still have lunch together or go to have their hair done together to keep their connection with each other alive. It is about parties at the office and on the block and about learning what possibilities there are in life, even if you don't have enough money.

These are the attributes of being working class (and not just about being poor) that most middle- and upper-class college students would have trouble understanding, because they have not experienced these things in their family lives. They often can afford to give up the job at McDonald's because there's a check that can be put in the mail. These are the things that show us that class is not something only linked to the production sector or industrial manufacturing, but that class is rooted in family, in neighborhood, in community, in both culture (a culture that truncates self-esteem and keeps people ignorant of options) and in income, and also in politics, even when workers differ about what party they support or if they like unions. And if working-class people do not universally share these attributes (they have self-esteem, they choose to work in certain jobs, or they belong to unions that occasionally listen), then that is another thing that we all have trouble grasping—that is, that the working class has a varied experience and nothing that can be boiled down to Flint, Michigan, alone.

"Between the Workers and the Owners": Class Conflict

The 1905 Preamble to the manifesto of the Industrial Workers of the World, the revolutionary international union movement, begins, "The working class and the employing class have nothing in common. There can be no peace so long as hunger and want are found among millions of working people and the few, who make up the employing class, have all the good things of life." That is among the most succinct, and absolute, statements of the idea of class conflict. That fundamental idea is embodied in many of the works in this section, from Florence Reece's famous song, "Which Side Are You On?," to Alice Wirth Gray's "He Was When He Died."

The most familiar forms of class conflict, movingly illustrated in Rebecca Harding Davis's "Life in the Iron-Mills" and hilariously exemplified in Steve Turner's *Night Shift in a Pickle Factory*, concern the hostilities between bosses and workers. But as William Faulkner's story "Barn Burning" and Carolina Pearl's autobiography demonstrate, the most intense forms of class conflict can occur outside the workplace in the daily interactions of the poor and weak with the wealthy and powerful. The familiar forms of such conflict are, of course, the strike, the demonstration, the revolution. Still, as works like Kenneth Patchen's "The Orange Bears" show, class conflict is manifest not just in the moments of intense crisis, but rather in the very dailiness of life, and especially in the lives of the less privileged and powerful, who do not have the margins of comfort provided by wealth to insulate them from the raw friction of class encounters. Class conflict is also the inner theme of statements of principle and position, like Carnegie's "The Gospel of Wealth" and London's "How I Became a Socialist," for these are basically arguments for particular values (of capitalism and socialism, respectively) and against others. Finally, as we suggested in the general introduction, class conflict may be less a matter of physical confrontation or the clash of principles so much as a battle of cultures and "structures of feeling" that differ far more radically than might at first seem to be the case. The question in any society, in fact, is the extent to which differences—as of race, gender, ethnicity, or class—can be balanced against the imperatives of unity.

REBECCA HARDING DAVIS

(1831-1910)

Davis, with Charlotte Perkins Gilman and Mary Wilkins Freeman, was the first of the "forgotten" nineteenth-century women writers to be rediscovered by the feminist movement of the 1960s and 1970s. She had been known, when she was known at all, as the mother of the popular journalist Richard Harding Davis; indeed, in many used bookstores, her works would occasionally be found among his. A few also knew her as the author of a powerful story, "Life in the Iron-Mills," the first American work to portray with anything like realism the lives of people laboring in the heavy industry of an industrializing United States. Among those who knew Davis's story was the author Tillie Olsen, who had found it in an 1861 copy of The Atlantic Monthly, *where it had first been published; it was through Olsen's efforts that the story regained the attention it so strongly deserved.*

The story is significant not only as an early example of realism and, with Melville's "The Tartarus of Maids," the first treatment of industrial workers and the resulting class conflict in American literature, but also because of what Olsen called Davis's "trespass vision," the ability to cross boundaries of class and gender to see deeply into lives so unlike one's own. The oldest daughter of a middle-class family of Wheeling, in what is now West Virginia, Rebecca Harding attended the nearby Washington Female Seminary in Pennsylvania, then returned home to contribute to the household and raising the younger children. She read extensively, but more important for her writing, observed the lives of the working people around her, from which she was so distanced. Her story, when it appeared out of nowhere on the desk of publisher James T. Fields, must have been startling indeed. Perhaps he asked, "Who is this unknown woman, and how is she able to see so deeply into another world?" At any rate, he quickly accepted the story and invited the thirty-year-old writer to come to Boston. There she met many of the leading literary lights of the time, including Nathaniel Hawthorne, whose stories she had long admired, and Fields's wife, Annie, with whom she formed a lifelong friendship.

Returning to Wheeling, Harding continued to write what Fields and others saw as somewhat too gloomy tales. Some she wrote primarily to make money for a growing family, especially after her marriage in 1863 to an admirer, L. Clarke Davis, and her move to Philadelphia. But others, including the novels, Margaret Howth *(1862),* Waiting for the Verdict *(1868),* Earthen Pitchers *(1873-1874), and* John Andross *(1874), have recently undergone a reassessment. They deal with such subjects as the problems of the emancipated slaves and, with political corruption, but above all with the predicament of women, whose capacities for creativity remain unused in a society bound up in patriarchal structures. Davis's stories and novels give them voice, directly or indirectly, as in Hugh Wolfe's apt phrase about his "Korl Woman" in "Life in the Iron-Mills," "She be hungry."*

LIFE IN THE IRON-MILLS

"Is this the end?
O Life, as futile, then, as frail!
What hope of answer or redress?"

A cloudy day: do you know what that is in a town of iron-works? The sky sank down before dawn, muddy, flat, immovable. The air is thick, clammy with the breath of crowded human beings. I open the window, and, looking out, can scarcely see through the rain the grocer's shop opposite, where a crowd of drunken Irishmen are puffing Lynchburg tobacco in their pipes. I can detect the scent through all the foul smells ranging loose in the air.

The idiosyncracy of this town is smoke. It rolls sullenly in slow folds from the great chimneys of the iron-foundries, and settles down in black, slimy pools on the muddy streets. Smoke on the wharves, smoke on the dingy boats, on the yellow river,—clinging in a coating of greasy soot to the house-front, the two faded poplars, the faces of the passers-by. The long train of mules, dragging masses of pig-iron through the narrow street, have a foul vapor hanging to their reeking sides. Here, inside, is a little broken figure of an angel pointing upward from the mantel-shelf; but even its wings are covered with smoke, clotted and black. Smoke everywhere! A dirty canary chirps desolately in a cage beside me. Its dream of green fields and sunshine is a very old dream—almost worn out, I think.

From the back-window I can see a narrow brick-yard sloping down to the river-side, strewed with rain-butts and tubs. The river, dull and tawny-colored, (la bella rivière!) drags itself sluggishly along, tired of the heavy weight of boats and coal-barges. What wonder? When I was a child, I used to fancy a look of weary, dumb appeal upon the face of the negro-like river slavishly bearing its burden day after day. Something of the same idle notion comes to me to-day, when from the street-window I look on the slow stream of human life creeping past, night and morning, to the great mills. Masses of men, with dull, besotted faces bent to the ground, sharpened here and there by pain or cunning; skin and muscle and flesh begrimed with smoke and ashes; stooping all night over boiling cauldrons of metal, laired by day in dens of drunkenness and infamy; breathing from infancy to death an air saturated with fog and grease and soot, vileness for soul and body. What do you make of a case like that, amateur psychologist? You call it an altogether serious thing to be alive: to these men it is a drunken jest, a joke,—horrible to angels perhaps, to them commonplace enough. My fancy about the river was an idle one: it is no type of such a life. What if it be stagnant and slimy here? It knows that beyond there waits for it odorous sunlight,—quaint old gardens, dusky with soft, green foliage of apple-trees, and flushing crimson with roses,—air, and fields, and mountains. The future of the Welsh puddler passing just now is not so pleasant. To be stowed away, after his grimy work is done, in a hole in the muddy graveyard, and after that,—not air, nor green fields, nor curious roses.

Can you see how foggy the day is? As I stand here, idly tapping the window-pane, and looking out through the rain at the dirty backyard and the coal-boats below, fragments of an old story float up before me,—a story of this old house into which I happened to come today. You may think it a tiresome story enough, as foggy as the day, sharpened by no sudden flashes of pain or pleasure.—I know: only the outline of a dull life, that long since, with thousands of dull lives like its own, was vainly lived and lost: thousands of them,—massed, vile, slimy lives, like those of the torpid lizards in yonder stagnant water butt.—Lost? There is a curious point for you to settle, my friend, who study psychology in a lazy, *dilettante* way. Stop a moment. I am going to be honest. This is what I want you to do. I want you to hide your disgust, take no heed to your clean clothes, and come right down with me,—here, into the thickest of the fog and mud and foul effluvia. I want you to hear this story. There is a secret down here, in this nightmare fog, that has lain dumb for centuries: I want to make it a real thing to you. You, Egoist, or Pantheist, or Arminian, busy in making straight paths for your feet on the hills, do not see it clearly,—this terrible question which men here have gone mad and died trying to answer. I dare not put this secret into words. I told you it was dumb. These men, going by with drunken faces and brains full of unawakened power, do not ask it of Society or of God. Their lives ask it; their deaths ask it. There is no reply. I will tell you plainly that I have a great hope; and I bring it to you to be tested. It is this: that this terrible dumb question is its own reply; that it is not the sentence of death we think it, but, from the very extremity of its darkness, the most solemn prophecy which the world has known of the Hope to come. I dare make my meaning no clearer, but will only tell my story. It will, perhaps, seem to you as foul and dark as this thick vapor about us, and as pregnant with death; but if your eyes are free as mine are to look deeper, no perfume-tinted dawn will be so fair with promise of the day that shall surely come.

My story is very simple,—only what I remember of the life of one of these men,—a furnace-tender in one of Kirby & John's rolling-mills,—Hugh Wolfe. You know the mills? They took the great order for the Lower Virginia railroads there last winter; run usually with about a thousand men. I cannot tell why I choose the half-forgotten story of this Wolfe more than that of myriads of these furnace-hands. Perhaps because there is a secret underlying sympathy between that story and this day with its impure fog and thwarted sunshine,—or perhaps simply for the reason that this house is the one where the Wolfes lived. There were the father and son,—both hands, as I said, in one of Kirby & John's mills for making railroad-iron,—and Deborah, their cousin, a picker in some of the cotton-mills. The house was rented then to half a dozen families. The Wolfes had two of the cellar-rooms. The old man, like many of the puddlers and feeders of the mills, was Welsh, had spent half of his life in the Cornish tin-mines. You may pick the Welsh emigrants, Cornish miners, out of the throng passing the windows, any day. They are a trifle more filthy; their muscles are not so brawny; they stoop more. When they are drunk, they neither yell, nor shout, nor stagger, but skulk along like beaten hounds. A pure, unmixed blood, I fancy: shows itself in the slight angular bodies and sharply-cut facial lines. It is nearly thirty years since the Wolfes lived here. Their lives were like those of their class: incessant labor, sleeping in kennel-like rooms, eating rank pork and molasses, drinking—God and the distillers only know what; with an occasional night in jail, to atone for some drunken excess. Is that all of their lives?—of the portion given to them and these their duplicates swarming the streets to-day?—nothing beneath?—all? So many a political reformer will tell you,—and many a private reformer too, who has gone among them with a heart tender with Christ's charity, and come out outraged, hardened.

One rainy night, about eleven o'clock, a crowd of half-clothed women stopped outside of the cellar-door. They were going home from the cotton-mill.

"Good-night, Deb," said one, a mulatto, steadying herself against the gas-post. She needed the post to steady her. So did more than one of them.

"Dah's a ball to Miss Potts' to-night. Ye'd best come."

"Inteet, Deb, if hur'll come, hur'll hef fun," said a shrill Welsh voice in the crowd.

Two or three dirty hands were thrust out to catch the gown of the woman, who was groping for the latch of the door.

"No."

"No? Where's Kit Small, then?"

"Begorra! on the spools. Alleys behint, though we helped her, we dud. An wid ye! Let Deb alone! It's ondacent frettin' a quite body. Be the powers, an' we'll have a night of it! there'll be lashin's o' drink,—the Vargent be blessed and praised for't!"

They went on, the mulatto inclining for a moment to show fight, and drag the woman Wolfe off with them; but, being pacified, she staggered away.

Deborah groped her way into the cellar, and, after considerable stumbling, kindled a match, and lighted a tallow dip, that sent a yellow glimmer over the room. It was low, damp,—the earthen floor covered with a green, slimy moss,—a fetid air smothering the breath. Old Wolfe lay asleep on a heap of straw, wrapped in a torn horse-blanket. He was a pale, meek little man, with a white face and red rabbit-eyes. The woman Deborah was like him; only her face was even more ghastly, her lips bluer, her eyes more watery. She wore a faded cotton gown and a slouching bonnet. When she walked, one could see that she was deformed, almost a hunchback. She trod softly, so as not to waken him, and went through into the room beyond. There she found by the half-extinguished fire an iron saucepan filled with cold boiled potatoes, which she put upon a broken chair with a pint-cup of ale. Placing the old candlestick beside this dainty repast, she untied her bonnet, which hung limp and wet over her face, and prepared to eat her supper. It was the first food that had touched her lips since morning. There was enough of it, however: there is not always. She was hungry,—one could see that easily enough,—and not drunk, as most of her companions would have been found at this hour. She did not drink, this woman,—her face told that, too,—nothing stronger than ale. Perhaps the weak, flaccid wretch had some stimulant in her pale life to keep her up,—some love or hope, it might be, or urgent need. When that stimulant was gone, she would take to whiskey. Man cannot live by work alone. While she was skinning the potatoes, and munching them, a noise behind her made her stop.

"Janey!" she called, lifting the candle and peering into the darkness. "Janey, are you there?"

A heap of rigged coats was heaved up, and the face of a young girl emerged, staring sleepily at the woman.

"Deborah," she said, at last, "I'm here the night."

"Yes, child. Hur's welcome," she said, quietly eating on.

The girl's face was haggard and sickly; her eyes were heavy with sleep and hunger: real Milesian eyes they were, dark, delicate blue, glooming out from black shadows with a pitiful fright.

"I was alone," she said, timidly.

"Where's the father?" asked Deborah, holding out a potato, which the girl greedily seized.

"He's beyant,—wid Haley,—in the stone house." (Did you ever hear the word *jail* from an Irish mouth?) "I came here. Hugh told me never to stay me-lone."

"Hugh?"

"Yes."

A vexed frown crossed her face. The girl saw it, and added quickly,—

"I have not seen Hugh the day, Deb. The old man says his watch lasts till the mornin'."

The woman sprang up, and hastily began to arrange some bread and flitch in a tin pail, and to pour her own measure of ale into a bottle. Tying on her bonnet, she blew out the candle.

"Lay ye down, Janey dear," she said, gently, covering her with the old rags. "Hur can eat the potatoes, if hur's hungry."

"Where are ye goin', Deb? The rain's sharp."

"To the mill, with Hugh's supper."

"Let him bide till th' morn. Sit ye down."

"No, no,"—sharply pushing her off. "The boy'll starve."

She hurried from the cellar, while the child wearily coiled herself up for sleep. The rain was falling heavily, as the woman, pail in hand, emerged from the mouth of the alley, and turned down the narrow street, that stretched out, long and black, miles before her. Here and there a flicker of gas lighted an uncertain space of muddy foot-walk and gutter; the long rows of houses, except an occasional lager-bier shop, were closed; now and then she met a band of mill-hands skulking to or from their work.

Not many even of the inhabitants of a manufacturing town know the vast machinery of system by which the bodies of workmen are governed, that goes unceasingly from year to year. The hands of each mill are divided into watches that relieve each other as regularly as the sentinels of an army. By night and day the work goes on, the unsleeping engines groan and shriek, the fiery pools of metal boil and surge. Only for a day in the week, a half-courtesy to public censure, the fires are partially veiled; but as soon as the clock strikes midnight, the great furnaces break forth with renewed fury, the clamor begins with fresh, breathless vigor, the engines sob and shriek like "gods in pain."

As Deborah hurried down through the heavy rain, the noise of these thousand engines sounded through the sleep and shadow of the city like far-off thunder. The mill to which she was going lay on the river, a mile below the city-limits. It was far, and she was weak, aching from standing twelve hours at the spools. Yet it was her almost nightly walk to take this man his supper, though at every square she sat down to rest, and she knew she should receive small word of thanks.

Perhaps, if she had possessed an artist's eye, the picturesque oddity of the scene might have made her step stagger less, and the path seem shorter; but to her the mills were only "summat deilish to look at by night."

The road leading to the mills had been quarried from the solid rock, which rose abrupt and bare on one side of the cinder-covered road, while the river, sluggish and black, crept past on the other. The mills for rolling iron are simply immense tent-like roofs, covering acres of ground, open on every side. Beneath these roofs Deborah looked in on a city of fires, that burned hot and fiercely in the night. Fire in every horrible form: pits of flame waving in the wind; liquid metal-flames writhing in tortuous streams through the sand; wide caldrons filled with boiling fire, over which bent ghastly wretches stirring the strange brewing; and through all, crowds of half-clad men, looking like revengeful ghosts in the red light, hurried, throwing masses of glittering fire. It was like a street in Hell. Even Deborah muttered, as she crept through, "'T looks like t' Devil's place!" It did,—in more ways than one.

She found the man she was looking for, at last, heaping coal on a furnace. He had not time to eat his supper; so she went behind the furnace, and waited. Only a few men were with him, and they noticed her only by a "Hyur comes t' hunchback, Wolfe."

Deborah was stupid with sleep; her back pained her sharply; and her teeth chattered with cold, with the rain that soaked her clothes and dripped from her at every step. She stood, however, patiently holding the pail, and waiting.

"Hout, woman! ye look like a drowned cat. Come near to the fire,"—said one of the men, approaching to scrape away the ashes.

She shook her head. Wolfe had forgotten her. He turned, hearing the man, and came closer.

"I did no' think; gi' me my supper, woman."

She watched him eat with a painful eagerness. With a woman's quick instinct, she saw that he was not hungry,—was eating to please her. Her pale, watery eyes began to gather a strange light.

"Is't good, Hugh? T'ale was a bit sour, I feared."

"No, good enough." He hesitated a moment. "Ye're tired, poor lass! Bide here till I go. Lay down there on that heap of ash, and go to sleep."

He threw her an old coat for a pillow, and turned to his work. The heap was the refuse of the burnt iron, and was not a hard bed; the half-smothered warmth, too, penetrated her limbs, dulling their pain and cold shiver.

Miserable enough she looked, lying there on the ashes like a limp, dirty rag,—yet not an unfitting figure to crown the scene of hopeless discomfort and veiled crime: more fitting, if one looked deeper into the heart of things,—at her thwarted woman's form, her colorless life, her waking stupor that smothered pain and hunger,—even more fit to be a type of her class. Deeper yet if one could look, was there nothing worth reading in this wet, faded thing, half-covered with ashes? no story of a soul filled with groping passionate love, heroic unselfishness, fierce jealousy? Of years of weary trying to please the one human being whom she loved, to gain one look of real heartkindness from him? If anything like this were hidden beneath the pale, bleared eyes, and dull, washed-out-looking face, no one had ever taken the trouble to read its faint signs: not the half-clothed furnace-tender, Wolfe, certainly. Yet he was kind to her: it was his nature to be kind, even to the very rats that swarmed in the cellar: kind to her in just that same way. She knew that. And it might be that very knowledge had given to her face its apathy and vacancy more than her low, torpid life. One sees that dead, vacant look steal sometimes over the rarest, finest of women's faces,—in the very midst, it may be, of their warmest summer's day; and then one can guess at the secret of intolerable solitude that lies hid beneath the delicate laces and brilliant smile. There was no warmth, no brilliancy, no summer for this woman; so the stupor and vacancy had time to gnaw into her face perpetually. She was young, too, though no one guessed it; so the gnawing was the fiercer.

She lay quiet in the dark corner, listening, through the monotonous din and uncertain glare of the works, to the dull plash of the rain in the far distance,—shrinking back whenever the man Wolfe happened to look towards her. She knew, in spite of all his kindness, that there was that in her face and form which made him loathe the sight of her. She felt by instinct, although she could not comprehend it, the finer nature of the man, which made him among his fellow-workmen something unique, set apart. She knew, that, down under all the vileness and coarseness of his life, there was a groping passion for whatever was beautiful and pure,—that his soul sickened with disgust at her deformity, even when his words were kindest. Through this dull consciousness, which never left her, came, like a sting, the recollection of the little Irish girl she had left in the cellar. The recollection struck through even her stupid intellect with a vivid glow of beauty and grace. Little Janey, timid, helpless, clinging to Hugh as her only friend: that was the sharp thought, the bitter thought, that drove into the glazed eyes a fierce light of pain. You laugh at it? Are pain and jealousy less savage realities down here in this place I am taking you to than in your own house or your own heart,—your heart, which they clutch at sometimes? The note is the same, I fancy, be the octave high or low.

If you could go into this mill where Deborah lay, and drag out from the hearts of these men the terrible tragedy of their lives, taking it as a symptom of the disease of their class, no ghost Horror would terrify you more. A reality of soul-starvation, of living death, that meets you every day under the besotted faces on the street,—I can paint nothing of this, only give you the outside outlines of a night, a crisis in the life of one man: whatever muddy depth of soul-history lies beneath you can read according to the eyes God has given you.

Wolfe, while Deborah watched him as a spaniel its master, bent over the furnace with his iron pole, unconscious of her scrutiny, only stopping to receive orders. Physically, Nature had promised the man but little. He had already lost the strength and instinct vigor of a man, his muscles were thin, his nerves weak, his face (a meek, woman's face) haggard, yellow with consumption. In the mill he was known as one of the girl men: "Molly Wolfe" was his *sobriquet*. He was never seen in the cockpit, did not own a terrier, drank but seldom; when he did, desperately. He fought sometimes, but was always thrashed, pommelled to a jelly. The man was game enough, when his blood was up: but he was no favorite in the mill; he had the taint of school-learning on him,—not to a dangerous extent, only a quarter or so in the free-school in fact, but enough to ruin him as a good hand in a fight.

For other reasons, too, he was not popular. Not one of themselves, they felt that, though outwardly as filthy and ash-covered; silent, with foreign thoughts and longings breaking out through his quietness in innumerable curious ways: this one, for instance. In the neighboring furnace-buildings lay great heaps of the refuse from the ore after the pig-metal is run. *Korl* we call it here: a light, porous substance, of a delicate, waxen, flesh-colored tinge. Out of the blocks of this korl, Wolfe, in his off-hours from the furnace, had a habit of chipping and moulding figures,—hideous, fantastic enough, but sometimes strangely beautiful: even the mill-men saw that, while they jeered at him. It was a curious fancy in the man, almost a passion. The few hours for rest he spent hewing and hacking with his blunt knife, never speaking, until his watch came again,—working at one figure for months, and, when it was finished, breaking it to pieces perhaps, in a fit of disappointment. A morbid, gloomy man, untaught, unled, left to feed his soul in grossness and crime, and hard, grinding labor.

I want you to come down and look at this Wolfe, standing there among the lowest of his kind, and see him just as he is, that you may judge him justly when you hear the story of this night. I want you to look back, as he does every day, at his birth in vice, his starved infancy; to remember the heavy years he has groped through as boy and man,—the slow, heavy years of constant, hot work. So long ago he began, that he thinks sometimes he has worked there for ages. There is no hope that it will ever end. Think that God put into this man's soul a fierce thirst for beauty,—to know it, to create it; to be—something, he knows not what,—other than he is. There are moments when a passing cloud, the sun glinting on the purple thistles, a kindly smile, a child's face, will rouse him to a passion of pain,—when his nature starts up with a mad cry of rage against God, man, whoever it is that has forced this vile, slimy life upon him. With all this groping, this mad desire, a great blind intellect stumbling through wrong, a loving poet's heart, the man was by habit only a coarse, vulgar laborer, familiar with sights and words you would blush to name. Be just: when I tell you about this night, see him as he is. Be just,—not like man's law, which seizes on one isolated fact, but like God's judging angel, whose clear, sad eye saw all the count-less cankering days of this man's life, all the countless nights, when, sick with starv-ing, his soul fainted in him, before it judged him for this night, the saddest of all.

I called this night the crisis of his life. If it was, it stole on him unawares. These great turning-days of life cast no shadow before, slip by unconsciously. Only a tri-fle, a little turn of the rudder, and the ship goes to heaven or hell.

Wolfe, while Deborah watched him, dug into the furnace of melting iron with his pole, dully thinking only how many rails the lump would yield. It was late,—nearly Sunday morning; another hour, and the heavy work would be done,—only the fur-naces to replenish and cover for the next day. The workmen were growing more noisy, shouting, as they had to do, to be heard over the deep clamor of the mills. Suddenly they grew less boisterous,—at the far end, entirely silent. Something unusual had happened. After a moment, the silence came nearer; the men stopped their jeers and drunken choruses. Deborah, stupidly lifting up her head, saw the cause of the quiet. A group of five or six men were slowly approaching, stopping to examine each furnace as they came. Visitors often came to see the mills after night: except by growing less noisy, the men took no notice of them. The furnace where Wolfe worked was near the bounds of the works; they halted there hot and tired: a walk over one of these great foundries is no trifling task. The woman, drawing out of sight, turned over to sleep. Wolfe, seeing them stop, suddenly roused from his indifferent stupor, and watched them keenly. He knew some of them: the overseer, Clarke,—a son of Kirby, one of the mill-owners,—and a Doctor May, one of the town-physicians. The other two were strangers. Wolfe came closer. He seized eagerly every chance that brought him into contact with this mysterious class that shone down on him perpetually with the glamour of another order of being. What made the difference between them? That was the mystery of his life. He had a vague notion that perhaps to-night he could find it out. One of the strangers sat down on a pile of bricks, and beckoned young Kirby to his side.

"This *is* hot, with a vengeance. A match, please?"—lighting his cigar. "But the walk is worth the trouble. If it were not that you must have heard it so often, Kirby, I would tell you that your works look like Dante's Inferno."

Kirby laughed.

"Yes. Yonder is Farinata himself in the burning tomb,"—pointing to some figure in the shimmering shadows.

"Judging from some of the faces of your men," said the other, "they bid fair to try the reality of Dante's vision, some day."

Young Kirby looked curiously around, as if seeing the faces of his hands for the first time.

"They're bad enough, that's true. A desperate set, I fancy. Eh, Clarke?"

The overseer did not hear him. He was talking of net profits just then,—giving, in fact, a schedule of the annual business of the firm to a sharp peering little Yan-kee, who jotted down notes on a paper laid on the crown of his hat: a reporter for one of the city-papers, getting up a series of reviews of the leading manufactories. The other gentlemen had accompanied them merely for amusement. They were silent until the notes were finished, drying their feet at the furnaces, and sheltering their faces from the intolerable heat. At last the overseer concluded with—

"I believe that is a pretty fair estimate, Captain."

"Here, some of you men!" said Kirby, "bring up those boards. We may as well sit down, gentlemen, until the rain is over. It cannot last much longer at this rate."

"Pig-metal,"—mumbled the reporter,—"um!—coal facilities,—um!—hands employed, twelve hundred,—bitumen,—um!—all right, I believe, Mr. Clarke;—sinking-fund—what did you say was your sinking-fund?"

"Twelve hundred hands?" said the stranger, the young man who had first spoken. "Do you control their votes, Kirby?"

"Control? No." The young man smiled complacently. "But my father brought seven hundred votes to the polls for his candidate last November. No force-work, you understand,—only a speech or two, a hint to form themselves into a society, and a bit of red and blue bunting to make them a flag. The Invincible Roughs,—I believe that is their name. I forget the motto: 'Our country's hope,' I think."

There was a laugh. The young man talking to Kirby sat with an amused light in his cool gray eye, surveying critically the half-clothed figures of the puddlers, and the slow swing of their brawny muscles. He was a stranger in the city,—spending a couple of months in the borders of a Slave State, to study the institutions of the South,—a brother-in-law of Kirby's,—Mitchell. He was an amateur gymnast,—hence his anatomical eye; a patron, in a *blasé* way, of the prize-ring; a man who sucked the essence out of a science or philosophy in an indifferent, gentlemanly way; who took Kant, Novalis, Humboldt, for what they were worth in his own scales; accepting all, despising nothing, in heaven, earth, or hell, but one-idead men; with a temper yielding and brilliant as summer water, until his Self was touched, when it was ice, though brilliant still. Such men are not rare in the States.

As he knocked the ashes from his cigar, Wolfe caught with a quick pleasure the contour of the white hand, the blood-glow of a red ring he wore. His voice, too, and that of Kirby's, touched him like music,—low, even, with chording cadences. About this man Mitchell hung the impalpable atmosphere belonging to the thorough-bred gentleman. Wolfe, scraping away the ashes beside him, was conscious of it, did obeisance to it with his artist sense, unconscious that he did so.

The rain did not cease. Clarke and the reporter left the mills; the others, comfortably seated near the furnace, lingered, smoking and talking in a desultory way. Greek would not have been more unintelligible to the furnace-tenders, whose presence they soon forgot entirely. Kirby drew out a newspaper from his pocket and read aloud some article, which they discussed eagerly. At every sentence, Wolfe listened more and more like a dumb, hopeless animal, with a duller, more stolid look creeping over his face, glancing now and then at Mitchell, marking acutely every smallest sign of refinement, then back to himself, seeing as in a mirror his filthy body, his more stained soul.

Never! He had no words for such a thought, but he knew now, in all the sharpness of the bitter certainty, that between them there was a great gulf never to be passed. Never!

The bell of the mills rang for midnight. Sunday morning had dawned. Whatever hidden message lay in the tolling bells floated past these men unknown. Yet it was there. Veiled in the solemn music ushering the risen Saviour was a key-note to solve the darkest secrets of a world gone wrong,—even this social riddle which the brain of the grimy puddler grappled with madly to-night.

The men began to withdraw the metal from the caldrons. The mills were deserted on Sundays, except by the hands who fed the fires, and those who had no lodgings and slept usually on the ash-heaps. The three strangers sat still during the next hour, watching the men cover the furnaces, laughing now and then at some jest of Kirby's.

"Do you know," said Mitchell, "I like this view of the works better than when the glare was fiercest? These heavy shadows and the amphitheatre of smothered fires are ghostly, unreal. One could fancy these red smouldering lights to be the half-shut eyes of wild beasts, and the spectral figures their victims in the den."

Kirby laughed. "You are fanciful. Come, let us get out of the den. The spectral figures, as you call them, are a little too real for me to fancy a close proximity in the darkness,—unarmed, too."

The others rose, buttoning their overcoats, and lighting cigars.

"Raining, still," said Doctor May, "and hard. Where did we leave the coach, Mitchell?"

"At the other side of the works.—Kirby, what's that?"

Mitchell started back, half-frightened, as, suddenly turning a corner, the white figure of a woman faced him in the darkness,—a woman, white, of giant proportions, crouching on the ground, her arms flung out in some wild gesture of warning.

"Stop! Make that fire burn there!" cried Kirby, stopping short.

The flame burst out, flashing the gaunt figure into bold relief.

Mitchell drew a long breath.

"I thought it was alive," he said, going up curiously.

The others followed.

"Not marble, eh?" asked Kirby, touching it.

One of the lower overseers stopped.

"Korl, Sir."

"Who did it?"

"Can't say. Some of the hands; chipped it out in off-hours."

"Chipped to some purpose, I should say. What a flesh-tint the stuff has! Do you see, Mitchell?"

"I see."

He had stepped aside where the light fell boldest on the figure, looking at it in silence. There was not one line of beauty or grace in it: a nude woman's form, muscular, grown coarse with labor, the powerful limbs instinct with some one poignant longing. One idea: there it was in the tense, rigid muscles, the clutching hands, the wild, eager face, like that of a starving wolf's. Kirby and Doctor May walked around it, critical, curious. Mitchell stood aloof, silent. The figure touched him strangely.

"Not badly done," said Doctor May. "Where did the fellow learn that sweep of the muscles in the arm and hand? Look at them! They are groping,—do you see?—clutching: the peculiar action of a man dying of thirst."

"They have ample facilities for studying anatomy," sneered Kirby, glancing at the half-naked figures.

"Look," continued the Doctor, "at this bony wrist, and the strained sinews of the instep! A working-woman,—the very type of her class,"

"God forbid!" muttered Mitchell.

"Why?" demanded May. "What does the fellow intend by the figure? I cannot catch the meaning."

"Ask him," said the other, dryly. "There he stands,"—pointing to Wolfe, who stood with a group of men, leaning on his ash-rake.

The Doctor beckoned him with the affable smile which kindhearted men put on, when talking to these people.

"Mr. Mitchell has picked you out as the man who did this,—I'm sure I don't know why. But what did you mean by it?"

"She be hungry."

Wolfe's eyes answered Mitchell, not the Doctor.

"Oh-h! But what a mistake you have made, my fine fellow! You have given no sign of starvation to the body. It is strong,—terribly strong. It has the mad, half-despairing gesture of drowning."

Wolfe stammered, glanced appealingly at Mitchell, who saw the soul of the thing, he knew. But the cool, probing eyes were turned on himself now,—mocking, cruel, relentless.

"Not hungry for meat," the furnace-tender said at last.

"What then? Whiskey?" jeered Kirby with a coarse laugh.

Wolfe was silent a moment, thinking.

"I dunno," he said, with a bewildered look. "It mebbe. Summat to make her live, I think,—like you. Whiskey ull do it, in a way."

The young man laughed again. Mitchell flashed a look of disgust somewhere,— not at Wolfe.

"May," he broke out impatiently, "are you blind? Look at that woman's face! It asks questions of God, and says 'I have a right to know.' Good God, how hungry it is!"

They looked a moment; then May turned to the mill-owner:—

"Have you many such hands as this? What are you going to do with them? Keep them at puddling iron?"

Kirby shrugged his shoulders. Mitchell's look had irritated him.

"*Ce n'est pas mon affaire.* I have no fancy for nursing infant geniuses. I suppose there are some stray gleams of mind and soul among these wretches. The Lord will take care of his own; or else they can work out their own salvation. I have heard you call our American system a ladder which any man can scale. Do you doubt it? Or perhaps you want to banish all social ladders, and put us all on a flat table-land,— eh, May?"

The Doctor looked vexed, puzzled. Some terrible problem lay hid in this woman's face, and troubled these men. Kirby waited for an answer, and, receiving none, went on, warming with his subject.

"I tell you, there's something wrong that no talk of '*Liberté*' or '*Egalité*' will do away. If I had the making of men, these men who do the lowest part of the world's work should be machines,—nothing more,—hands. It would be kindness. God help them! What are taste, reason, to creatures who must live such lives as that?" He pointed to Deborah, sleeping on the ash-heap. "So many nerves to sting them to pain. What if God had put your brain, with all its agony of touch, into your fingers, and bid you work and strike with that?"

"You think you could govern the world better?" laughed the Doctor.

"I do not think at all."

"That is true philosophy. Drift with the stream, because you cannot dive deep enough to find bottom, eh?"

"Exactly," rejoined Kirby. "I do not think. I wash my hands of all social prob-lems,—slavery, caste, white or black. My duty to my operatives has a narrow limit,— the pay-hour on Sâturday night. Outside of that, if they cut korl, or cut each other's throats, (the more popular amusement of the two,) I am not responsible."

The Doctor sighed,—a good honest sigh, from the depths of his stomach.

"God help us! Who is responsible?"

"Not I, I tell you," said Kirby, testily. "What has the man who pays them money to do with their souls' concerns, more than the grocer or butcher who takes it?"

"And yet," said Mitchell's cynical voice, "look at her! How hungry she is!"

Kirby tapped his boot with his cane. No one spoke. Only the dumb face of the rough image looking into their faces with the awful question, "What shall we do to be saved?" Only Wolfe's face, with its heavy weight of brain, its weak, uncertain mouth, its desperate eyes, out of which looked the soul of his class,—only Wolfe's face turned towards Kirby's. Mitchell laughed,—a cool, musical laugh.

"Money has spoken!" he said, seating himself lightly on a stone with the air of an amused spectator at a play. "Are you answered?"—turning to Wolfe his clear, magnetic face.

Bright and deep and cold as Arctic air, the soul of the man lay tranquil beneath. He looked at the furnace-tender as he had looked at a rare mosaic in the morning; only the man was the more amusing study of the two.

"Are you answered? Why, May, look at him! *'De profundis clamavi.'* Or, to quote in English, 'Hungry and thirsty, his soul faints in him.' And so Money sends back its answer into the depths through you, Kirby! Very clear the answer, too!—I think I remember reading the same words somewhere:—washing your hands in Eau de Cologne, and saying, 'I am innocent of the blood of this man. See ye to it!'"

Kirby flushed angrily.

"You quote Scripture freely."

"Do I not quote correctly? I think I remember another line, which may amend my meaning: 'Inasmuch as ye did it unto one of the least of these, ye did it unto me.' Deist? Bless you, man, I was raised on the milk of the Word. Now, Doctor, the pocket of the world having uttered its voice, what has the heart to say? You are a philanthropist, in a small way,—*n'est ce pas?* Here, boy, this gentleman can show you how to cut korl better,—or your destiny. Go on, May!"

"I think a mocking devil possesses you to-night," rejoined the Doctor, seriously.

He went to Wolfe and put his hand kindly on his arm. Something of a vague idea possessed the Doctor's brain that much good was to be done here by a friendly word or two: a latent genius to be warmed into life by a waited-for sunbeam. Here it was: he had brought it. So he went on complacently:—

"Do you know, boy, you have it in you to be a great sculptor, a great man?—do you understand?" (talking down to the capacity of his hearer: it is a way people have with children, and men like Wolfe,)—"to live a better, stronger life than I, or Mr. Kirby here? A man may make himself anything he chooses. God has given you stronger powers than many men,—me, for instance."

May stopped, heated, glowing with his own magnanimity. And it was magnanimous. The puddler had drunk in every word, looking through the Doctor's flurry, and generous heat, and self-approval, into his will, with those slow, absorbing eyes of his.

"Make yourself what you will. It is your right."

"I know," quietly. "Will you help me?"

Mitchell laughed again. The Doctor turned now, in a passion,—

"You know, Mitchell, I have not the means. You know, if I had, it is in my heart to take this boy and educate him for"——

"The glory of God, and the glory of John May."

May did not speak for a moment; then, controlled, he said,—

"Why should one be raised, when myriads are left? —I have not the money, boy," to Wolfe, shortly.

"Money?" He said it over slowly, as one repeats the guessed answer to a riddle, doubtfully. "That is it? Money?"

"Yes, money,—that is it," said Mitchell, rising, and drawing his furred coat about him. "You've found the cure for all the world's diseases.—Come, May, find your good-humor, and come home. This damp wind chills my very bones. Come and preach your Saint-Simonian doctrines to-morrow to Kirby's hands. Let them have a clear idea of the rights of the soul, and I'll venture next week they'll strike for higher wages. That will be the end of it."

"Will you send the coach-driver to this side of the mills?" asked Kirby, turning to Wolfe.

He spoke kindly: it was his habit to do so. Deborah, seeing the puddler go, crept after him. The three men waited outside. Doctor May walked up and down, chafed. Suddenly he stopped.

"Go back, Mitchell! You say the pocket and the heart of the world speak without meaning to these people. What has its head to say? Taste, culture, refinement? Go!"

Mitchell was leaning against a brick wall. He turned his head indolently, and looked into the mills. There hung about the place a thick, unclean odor. The slightest motion of his hand marked that he perceived it, and his insufferable disgust. That was all. May said nothing, only quickened his angry tramp.

"Besides," added Mitchell, giving a corollary to his answer, "it would be of no use. I am not one of them."

"You do not mean"—said May, facing him.

"Yes, I mean just that. Reform is born of need, not pity. No vital movement of the people's has worked down, for good or evil; fermented, instead, carried up the heaving, cloggy mass. Think back through history, and you will know it. What will this lowest deep—thieves, Magdalens, negroes—do with the light filtered through ponderous Church creeds, Baconian theories, Goethe schemes? Some day, out of their bitter need will be thrown up their own light-bringer,—their Jean Paul, their Cromwell, their Messiah."

"Bah!" was the Doctor's inward criticism. However, in practice, he adopted the theory; for, when, night and morning, afterwards, he prayed that power might be given these degraded souls to rise, he glowed at heart, recognizing an accomplished duty.

Wolfe and the woman had stood in the shadow of the works as the coach drove off. The Doctor had held out his hand in a frank, generous way, telling him to "take care of himself, and to remember it was his right to rise." Mitchell had simply touched his hat, as to an equal, with a quiet look of thorough recognition. Kirby had thrown Deborah some money, which she found and clutched eagerly enough. They were gone now, all of them. The man sat down on the cinder-road, looking up into the murky sky.

"'T be late, Hugh. Wunnot hur come?"

He shook his head doggedly, and the woman crouched out of his sight against the wall. Do you remember rare moments when a sudden light flashed over yourself, your world, God? when you stood on a mountain-peak, seeing your life as it might have been, as it is? one quick instant, when custom lost its force and every-day usage? when your friend, wife, brother, stood in a new light? your soul was bared, and the grave,—a fore-taste of the nakedness of the Judgment-Day? So it came before him, his life, that night. The slow tides of pain he had borne gathered themselves up and surged against his soul. His squalid daily life, the brutal coarseness eating into his brain, as the ashes into his skin: before, these things had been a dull aching into his consciousness; to-night, they were reality. He griped the filthy red shirt that clung, stiff with soot, about him, and tore it savagely from his arm. The flesh beneath was muddy with grease and ashes,—and the heart beneath that! And the soul? God knows.

Then flashed before his vivid poetic sense the man who had left him,—the pure face, the delicate, sinewy limbs, in harmony with all he knew of beauty or truth. In his cloudy fancy he had pictured a Something like this. He had found it in this Mitchell, even when he idly scoffed at his pain: a Man all-knowing, all-seeing, crowned by Nature, reigning,—the keen glance of his eye falling like a sceptre on other men. And yet his instinct taught him that he too——He! He looked at himself with sudden loathing, sick, wrung his hands with a cry, and then was silent. With all the phantoms of his heated, ignorant fancy, Wolfe had not been vague in his ambitions. They were practical, slowly built up before him out of his knowledge of what he could do. Through years he had day by day made this hope a real thing to himself,—a clear, projected figure of himself, as he might become.

Able to speak, to know what was best, to raise these men and women working at his side up with him: sometimes he forgot this defined hope in the frantic anguish to escape,—only to escape,—out of the wet, the pain, the ashes, somewhere, anywhere,—only for one moment of free air on a hill-side, to lie down and let his sick soul throb itself out in the sunshine. But to-night he panted for life. The savage strength of his nature was roused; his cry was fierce to God for justice.

"Look at me!" he said to Deborah, with a low, bitter laugh, striking his puny chest savagely. "What am I worth, Deb? Is it my fault that I am no better? My fault? My fault?"

He stopped, stung with a sudden remorse, seeing her hunchback shape writhing with sobs. For Deborah was crying thankless tears, according to the fashion of women.

"God forgi' me, woman! Things go harder wi' you nor me. It's a worse share."

He got up and helped her to rise; and they went doggedly down the muddy street, side by side.

"It's all wrong," he muttered, slowly,—"all wrong! I dunnot understan'. But it'll end some day."

"Come home, Hugh!" she said, coaxingly; for he had stopped, looking around bewildered.

"Home,—and back to the mill!" He went on saying this over to himself, as if he would mutter down every pain in this dull despair.

She followed him through the fog, her blue lips chattering with cold. They reached the cellar at last. Old Wolfe had been drinking since she went out, and had crept nearer the door. The girl Janey slept heavily in the corner. He went up to her, touching softly the worn white arm with his fingers. Some bitterer thought stung him, as he stood there. He wiped the drops from his forehead, and went into the room beyond, livid, trembling. A hope, trifling, perhaps, but very dear, had died just then out of the poor puddler's life, as he looked at the sleeping, innocent girl,— some plan for the future, in which she had borne a part. He gave it up that moment, then and forever. Only a trifle, perhaps, to us: his face grew a shade paler,—that was all. But, somehow, the man's soul, as God and the angels looked down on it, never was the same afterwards.

Deborah followed him into the inner room. She carried a candle, which she placed on the floor, closing the door after her. She had seen the look on his face, as he turned away: her own grew deadly. Yet, as she came up to him, her eyes glowed. He was seated on an old chest, quiet, holding his face in his hands.

"Hugh!" she said, softly.

He did not speak.

"Hugh, did hur hear what the man said,—him with the clear voice? Did hur hear? Money, money,—that it wud do all?"

He pushed her away,—gently, but he was worn out; her rasping tone fretted him.

"Hugh!"

The candle flared a pale yellow light over the cobwebbed brick walls, and the woman standing there. He looked at her. She was young, in deadly earnest; her faded eyes, and wet, ragged figure caught from their frantic eagerness a power akin to beauty.

"Hugh, it is true! Money ull do it! Oh, Hugh, boy, listen till me! He said it true! It is money!"

"I know. Go back! I do not want you here."

"Hugh, it is t' last time. I'll never worrit hur again."

There were tears in her voice now, but she choked them back.

"Hear till me only to-night! If one of t' witch people wud come, them we heard of t' home, and gif hur all hur wants, what then? Say, Hugh!"

"What do you mean?"

"I mean money."

Her whisper shrilled through his brain.

"If one of t' witch dwarfs wud come from t' lane moors to-night, and gif hur money, to go out,—out, I say,—out, lad, where t' sun shines, and t' heath grows, and t' ladies walk in silken gownds, and God stays all t' time,—where t' man lives that talked to us to-night,—Hugh knows,—Hugh could walk there like a king!"

He thought the woman mad, tried to check her, but she went on, fierce in her eager haste.

"If *I* were t' witch dwarf, if I had t' money, wud hur thank me? Wud hur take me out o' this place wid hur and Janey? I wud not come into the gran' house hur wud build, to vex hur wid t' hunch,—only at night, when t' shadows were dark, stand far off to see hur."

Mad? Yes! Are many of us mad in this way?

"Poor Deb! poor Deb!" he said, soothingly.

"It is here," she said, suddenly jerking into his hand a small roll. "I took it! I did it! Me, me!—not hur! I shall be hanged, I shall be burnt in hell, if anybody knows I took it! Out of his pocket, as he leaned against t' bricks. Hur knows?"

She thrust it into his hand, and then, her errand done, began to gather chips together to make a fire, choking down hysteric sobs.

"Has it come to this?"

That was all he said. The Welsh Wolfe blood was honest. The roll was a small green pocket-book containing one or two gold pieces, and a check for an incredible amount, as it seemed to the poor puddler. He laid it down, hiding his face again in his hands.

"Hugh, don't be angry wud me! It's only poor Deb,—hur knows?"

He took the long skinny fingers kindly in his.

"Angry? God help me, no! Let me sleep. I am tired."

He threw himself heavily down on the wooden bench, stunned with pain and weariness. She brought some old rags to cover him.

It was late on Sunday evening before he awoke. I tell God's truth, when I say he had then no thought of keeping this money. Deborah had hid it in his pocket. He found it there. She watched him eagerly, as he took it out.

"I must gif to him," he said, reading her face.

"Hur knows," she said with a bitter sigh of disappointment. "But it is hur right to keep it."

His right! The word struck him. Doctor May had used the same. He washed himself, and went out to find this man Mitchell. His right! Why did this chance word cling to him so obstinately? Do you hear the fierce devils whisper in his ear, as he went slowly down the darkening street?

The evening came on, slow and calm. He seated himself at the end of an alley leading into one of the larger streets. His brain was clear to-night, keen, intent, mastering. It would not start back, cowardly, from any hellish temptation, but meet it face to face. Therefore the great temptation of his life came to him veiled by no sophistry, but bold, defiant, owning its own vile name, trusting to one bold blow for victory.

He did not deceive himself. Theft! That was it. At first the word sickened him; then he grappled with it. Sitting there on a broken cartwheel, the fading day, the noisy groups, the church bells' tolling passed before him like a panoraina, while the sharp struggle went on within. This money! He took it out, and looked at it. If he gave it back, what then? He was going to be cool about it.

People going by to church saw only a sickly mill-boy watching them quietly at the alley's mouth. They did not know that he was mad, or they would not have gone by so quietly: mad with hunger; stretching out his hands to the world, that had given so much to them, for leave to live the life God meant him to live. His soul within him was smothering to death; he wanted so much, thought so much, and *knew*—nothing. There was nothing of which he was certain, except the mill and things there. Of God and heaven he had heard so little, that they were to him what fairy-land is to a child: something real, but not here; very far off. His brain, greedy, dwarfed, full of thwarted energy and unused powers, questioned these men and women going by, coldly, bitterly, that night. Was it not his right to live as they,—a pure life, a good, true-hearted life, full of beauty and kind words? He only wanted to know how to use the strength within him. His heart warmed, as he thought of it. He suffered himself to think of it longer. If he took the money?

Then he saw himself as he might be, strong, helpful, kindly. The night crept on, as this one image slowly evolved itself from the crowd of other thoughts and stood triumphant. He looked at it. As he might be! What wonder, if it blinded him to delirium,—the madness that underlies all revolution, all progress, and all fall?

You laugh at the shallow temptation? You see the error underlying its argument so clearly,—that to him a true life was one of full development rather than self-restraint? that he was deaf to the higher tone in a cry of voluntary suffering for truth's sake than in the fullest flow of spontaneous harmony? I do not plead his cause. I only want to show you the mote in my brother's eye: then you can see clearly to take it out.

The money,—there it lay on his knee, a little blotted slip of paper, nothing in itself; used to raise him out of the pit; something straight from God's hand. A thief! Well, what was it to be a thief? He met the question at last, face to face, wiping the clammy drops of sweat from his forehead. God made this money—the fresh air, too—for his children's use. He never made the difference between poor and rich. The Something who looked down on him that moment through the cool gray sky had a kindly face, he knew,—loved his children alike. Oh, he knew that!

There were times when the soft floods of color in the crimson and purple flames, or the clear depth of amber in the water below the bridge, had somehow given him a glimpse of another world than this,—of an infinite depth of beauty and of quiet somewhere,—somewhere,—a depth of quiet and rest and love. Looking up now, it became strangely real. The sun had sunk quite below the hills, but his last rays struck upward, touching the zenith. The fog had risen, and the town and river were steeped in its thick, gray, damp; but overhead, the sun-touched smoke-clouds opened like a cleft ocean,—shifting, rolling seas of crimson mist, waves of billowy silver veined with blood-scarlet, inner depths unfathomable of glancing light. Wolfe's artist-eye grew drunk with color. The gates of that other world! Fading, flashing before him now! What, in that world of Beauty, Content, and Right, were the petty laws, the mine and thine, of mill-owners and mill-hands?

A consciousness of power stirred within him. He stood up. A man,—he thought, stretching out his hands,—free to work, to live, to love! Free! His right! He folded the scrap of paper in his hand. As his nervous fingers took it in, limp and blotted, so his soul took in the mean temptation, lapped it in fancied rights, in dreams of improved existences, drifting and endless as the cloud-seas of color. Clutching it, as if the tightness of his hold would strengthen his sense of possession, he went aimlessly down the street. It was his watch at the mill. He need not go, need never go again, thank God!—shaking off the thought with unspeakable loathing.

Shall I go over the history of the hours of that night? how the man wandered from one to another of his old haunts, with a half-consciousness of bidding them farewell,—lanes and alleys and backyards where the mill-hands lodged,—noting, with a new eagerness, the filth and drunkenness, the pig-pens, the ash-heaps covered with potato-skins, the bloated, pimpled women at the doors,—with a new disgust, a new sense of sudden triumph, and, under all, a new, vague dread, unknown before, smothered down, kept under, but still there? It left him but once during the night, when, for the second time in his life, he entered a church. It was a sombre Gothic pile, where the stained light lost itself in far-retreating arches; built to meet the requirements and sympathies of a far other class than Wolfe's. Yet it touched, moved him uncontrollably. The distances, the shadows, the still, marble figures, the mass of silent kneeling worshippers, the mysterious music, thrilled, lifted his soul with a wonderful pain. Wolfe forgot himself, forgot the new life he was going to live, the mean terror gnawing underneath. The voice of the speaker strengthened the charm; it was clear, feeling, full, strong. An old man, who had lived much, suffered much; whose brain was keenly alive, dominant; whose heart was summer-warm with charity. He taught it to-night. He held up Humanity in its grand total; showed the great world-cancer to his people. Who could show it better? He was a Christian reformer; he had studied the age thoroughly; his outlook at man had been free, world-wide, over all time. His faith stood sublime upon the Rock of Ages; his fiery zeal guided vast schemes by which the gospel was to be preached to all nations. How did he preach it to-night? In burning, light-laden words he painted the incarnate Life, Love, the universal Man: words that became reality in the lives of these people,—that lived again in beautiful words and actions, trifling, but heroic. Sin, as he defined it, was a real foe to them; their trials, temptations, were his. His words passed far over the furnace-tender's grasp, toned to suit another class of culture; they sounded in his ears a very pleasant song in an unknown tongue. He meant to cure this world-cancer with a steady eye that had never glared with hunger, and a hand that neither poverty nor strychnine-whiskey had taught to shake. In this morbid, distorted heart of the Welsh puddler he had failed.

Wolfe rose at last, and turned from the church down the street. He looked up; the night had come on foggy, damp; the golden mists had vanished, and the sky lay dull and ash-colored. He wandered again aimlessly down the street, idly wondering what had become of the cloud-sea of crimson and scarlet. The trial-day of this man's life was over, and he had lost the victory. What followed was mere drifting circumstance,—a quicker walking over the path,—that was all. Do you want to hear the end of it? You wish me to make a tragic story out of it? Why, in the police-reports of the morning paper you can find a dozen such tragedies: hints of shipwrecks unlike any that ever befell on the high seas; hints that here a power was lost to heaven,—that there a soul went down where no tide can ebb or flow. Commonplace enough the hints are,—jocose sometimes, done up in rhyme.

Doctor May, a month after the night I have told you of, was reading to his wife at breakfast from this fourth column of the morning-paper: an unusual thing,— these police-reports not being, in general, choice reading for ladies; but it was only one item he read.

"Oh, my dear! You remember that man I told you of, that we saw at Kirby's mill?—that was arrested for robbing Mitchell? Here he is; just listen:—'Circuit Court. Judge Day. Hugh Wolfe, operative in Kirby & John's Loudon Mills. Charge, grand larceny. Sentence, nineteen years hard labor in penitentiary.'—Scoundrel! Serves him right! After all our kindness that night! Picking Mitchell's pocket at the very time!"

His wife said something about the ingratitude of that kind of people, and then they began to talk of something else.

Nineteen years! How easy that was to read! What a simple word for Judge Day to utter! Nineteen years! Half a lifetime!

Hugh Wolfe sat on the window-ledge of his cell, looking out. His ankles were ironed. Not usual in such cases; but he had made two desperate efforts to escape. "Well," as Haley, the jailer, said, "small blame to him! Nineteen years' imprisonment was not a pleasant thing to took forward to." Haley was very good-natured about it, though Wolfe had fought him savagely.

"When he was first caught," the jailer said afterwards, in telling the story, "before the trial, the fellow was cut down at once,—laid there on that pallet like a dead man, with his hands over his eyes. Never saw a man so cut down in my life. Time of the trial, too, came the queerest dodge of any customer I ever had. Would choose no lawyer. Judge gave him one, of course. Gibson it was. He tried to prove the fellow crazy; but it wouldn't go. Thing was plain as daylight: money found on him. 'Twas a hard sentence,—all the law allows; but it was for 'xample's sake. These mill-hands are gettin' onbearable. When the sentence was read, he just looked up, and said the money was his by rights, and that all the world had gone wrong. That night, after the trial, a gentleman came to see him here, name of Mitchell,—him as he stole from. Talked to him for an hour. Thought he came for curiosity, like. After he was gone, thought Wolfe was remarkable quiet, and went into his cell. Found him very low; bed all bloody. Doctor said he had been bleeding at the lungs. He was as weak as a cat; yet, if ye'll b'lieve me, he tried to get a-past me and get out. I just carried him like a baby, and threw him on the pallet. Three days after, he tried it again:

that time reached the wall. Lord help you! he fought like a tiger,—giv' some terrible blows. Fightin' for life, you see; for he can't live long, shut up in the stone crib down yonder. Got a death-cough now. 'T took two of us to bring him down that day; so I just put the irons on his feet. There he sits, in there. Goin' to-morrow, with a batch more of 'em. That woman, hunchback, tried with him,—you remember?—she's only got three years. 'Complice. But *she's* a woman, you know. He's been quiet ever since I put on irons: giv' up, I suppose. Looks white, sick-lookin'. It acts different on 'em, bein' sentenced. Most of 'em gets reckless, devilish-like. Some prays awful, and sings them vile songs of the mills, all in a breath. That woman, now, she's desper't'. Been beggin' to see Hugh, as she calls him, for three days. I'm a-goin' to let her in. She don't go with him. Here she is in this next cell. I'm a-goin' now to let her in."

He let her in. Wolfe did not see her. She crept into a corner of the cell, and stood watching him. He was scratching the iron bars of the window with a piece of tin which he had picked up, with an idle, uncertain, vacant stare, just as a child or idiot would do.

"Tryin' to get out, old boy?" laughed Haley. "Them irons will need a crowbar beside your tin, before you can open 'em."

Wolfe laughed, too, in a senseless way.

"I think I'll get out," he said.

"I believe his brain's touched," said Haley, when he came out.

The puddler scraped away with the tin for half an hour. Still Deborah did not speak. At last she ventured nearer, and touched his arm.

"Blood?" she said, looking at some spots on his coat with a shudder.

He looked up at her. "Why, Deb!" he said, smiling,—such a bright, boyish smile, that it went to poor Deborah's heart directly, and she sobbed and cried out loud.

"Oh, Hugh, lad! Hugh! dunnot look at me, when it wur my fault! To think I brought hur to it! And I loved hur so! Oh, lad, I dud!"

The confession, even in this wretch, came with the woman's blush through the sharp cry.

He did not seem to hear her,—scraping away diligently at the bars with the bit of tin.

Was he going mad? She peered closely into his face. Something she saw there made her draw suddenly back,—something which Haley had not seen, that lay beneath the pinched, vacant look it had caught since the trial, or the curious gray shadow that rested on it. That gray shadow,—yes, she knew what that meant. She had often seen it creeping over women's faces for months, who died at last of slow hunger or consumption. That meant death, distant, lingering: but this——Whatever it was the woman saw, or thought she saw, used as she was to crime and misery, seemed to make her sick with a new horror. Forgetting her fear of him, she caught his shoulders, and looked keenly, steadily, into his eyes.

"Hugh!" she cried, in a desperate whisper,—"oh, boy, not that! for God's sake, not *that!*"

The vacant laugh went off his face, and he answered her in a muttered word or two that drove her away. Yet the words were kindly enough. Sitting there on his pallet, she cried silently a hopeless sort of tears, but did not speak again. The man looked up furtively at her now and then. Whatever his own trouble was, her distress vexed him with a momentary sting.

It was market-day. The narrow window of the jail looked down directly on the carts and wagons drawn up in a long line, where they had unloaded. He could see, too, and hear distinctly the clink of money as it changed hands, the busy crowd of whites and blacks shoving, pushing one another, and the chaffering and swearing at the stalls. Somehow, the sound, more than anything else had done, wakened him up,—made the whole real to him. He was done with the world and the business of it. He let the tin fall, and looked out, pressing his face close to the rusty bars. How they crowded and pushed! And he,—he should never walk that pavement again! There came Neff Sanders, one of the feeders at the mill, with a basket on his arm. Sure enough, Neff was married the other week. He whistled, hoping he would look up; but he did not. He wondered if Neff remembered he was there,—if any of the boys thought of him up there, and thought that he never was to go down that old cinder-road again. Never again! He had not quite understood it before; but now he did. Not for days or years, but never!—that was it.

How clear the light fell on that stall in front of the market! and how like a picture it was, the dark-green heaps of corn, and the crimson beets, and golden melons! There was another with game: how the light flickered on that pheasant's breast, with the purplish blood dripping over the brown feathers! He could see the red shining of the drops, it was so near. In one minute he could be down there. It was just a step. So easy, as it seemed, so natural to go! Yet it could never be—not in all the thousands of years to come—that he should put his foot on that street again! He thought of himself with a sorrowful pity, as of some one else. There was a dog down in the market, walking after his master with such a stately, grave look!—only a dog, yet he could go backwards and forwards just as he pleased: he had good luck! Why, the very vilest cur, yelping there in the gutter, had not lived his life, had been free to act out whatever thought God had put into his brain; while he——No, he would not think of that! He tried to put the thought away, and to listen to a dispute between a countryman and a woman about some meat; but it would come back. He, what had he done to bear this?

Then came the sudden picture of what might have been, and now. He knew what it was to be in the penitentiary,—how it went with men there. He knew how in these long years he should slowly die, but not until soul and body had become corrupt and rotten,—how, when he came out, if he lived to come, even the lowest of the mill-hands would jeer him,—how his hands would be weak, and his brain senseless and stupid. He believed he was almost that now. He put his hand to his head, with a puzzled, weary look. It ached, his head, with thinking. He tried to quiet himself. It was only right, perhaps; he had done wrong. But was there right or wrong for such as he? What was right? And who had ever taught him? He thrust the whole matter away. A dark, cold quiet crept through his brain. It was all wrong; but let it be! It was nothing to him more than the others. Let it be!

The door grated, as Haley opened it.

"Come, my woman! Must lock up for t' night. Come, stir yerself!"

"Good-night, Deb," he said, carelessly.

She had not hoped he would say more; but the tired pain on her mouth just then was bitterer than death. She took his passive hand and kissed it.

"Hur'll never see Deb again!" she ventured, her lips growing colder and more bloodless.

What did she say that for? Did he not know it? Yet he would not be impatient with poor old Deb. She had trouble of her own, as well as he.

"No, never again," he said, trying to be cheerful.

She stood just a moment, looking at him. Do you laugh at her, standing there, with her hunchback, her rags, her bleared, withered face, and the great despised love tugging at her heart?

"Come, you!" called Haley, impatiently.

She did not move.

"Hugh!" she whispered.

It was to be her last word. What was it?

"Hugh, boy, not THAT!"

He did not answer. She wrung her hands, trying to be silent, looking in his face in an agony of entreaty. He smiled again, kindly.

"It is best, Deb. I cannot bear to be hurted any more."

"Hur knows," she said, humbly.

"Tell my father good-bye; and—and kiss little Janey."

She nodded, saying nothing, looked in his face again, and went out of the door. As she went, she staggered.

"Drinkin' to-day?" broke out Haley, pushing her before him. "Where the Devil did you get it? Here, in with ye!" and he shoved her into her cell, next to Wolfe's, and shut the door.

Along the wall of her cell there was a crack low down by the floor, through which she could see the light from Wolfe's. She had discovered it days before. She hurried in now, and, kneeling down by it, listened, hoping to hear some sound. Nothing but the rasping of the tin on the bars. He was at his old amusement again. Something in the noise jarred on her ear, for she shivered as she heard it. Hugh rasped away at the bars. A dull old bit of tin, not fit to cut korl with.

He looked out of the window again. People were leaving the market now. A tall mulatto girl, following her mistress, her basket on her head, crossed the street just below, and looked up. She was laughing; but, when she caught sight of the haggard face peering out through the bars, suddenly grew grave, and hurried by. A free, firm step, a clear-cut olive face, with a scarlet turban tied on one side, dark, shining eyes, and on the head the basket poised, filled with fruit and flowers, under which the scarlet turban and bright eyes looked out half-shadowed. The picture caught his eye. It was good to see a face like that. He would try to-morrow, and cut one like it. *To-morrow!* He threw down the tin, trembling, and covered his face with his hands. When he looked up again, the daylight was gone.

Deborah, crouching near by on the other side of the wall, heard no noise. He sat on the side of the low pallet, thinking. Whatever was the mystery which the woman had seen on his face, it came out now slowly, in the dark there, and became fixed,— a something never seen on his face before. The evening was darkening fast. The market had been over for an hour; the rumbling of the carts over the pavement grew more infrequent: he listened to each, as it passed, because he thought it was to be for the last time. For the same reason, it was, I suppose, that he strained his eyes to catch a glimpse of each passerby, wondering who they were, what kind of homes they were going' to, if they had children,—listening eagerly to every chance word in the street, as if—(God be merciful to the man! what strange fancy was this?)—as if he never should hear human voices again.

It was quite dark at last. The street was a lonely one. The last passenger, he thought, was gone. No,—there was a quick step: Joe Hill, lighting the lamps. Joe was a good old chap; never passed a fellow without some joke or other. He remembered once seeing the place where he lived with his wife. "Granny Hill" the boys called her. Bedridden she was; but so kind as Joe was to her! kept the room so clean!—and the old woman, when he was there, was laughing at "some of t' lad's foolishness." The step was far down the street; but he could see him place the ladder, run up, and light the gas. A longing seized him to be spoken to once more.

"Joe!" he called, out of the grating. "Good-bye, Joe!"

The old man stopped a moment, listening uncertainly; then hurried on. The prisoner thrust his hand out of the window, and called again, louder; but Joe was too far down the street. It was a little thing; but it hurt him,—this disappointment.

"Good-bye, Joe!" he called, sorrowfully enough.

"Be quiet!" said one of the jailers, passing the door, striking on it with his club.

Oh, that was the last, was it?

There was an inexpressible bitterness on his face, as he lay down on the bed, taking the bit of tin, which he had rasped to a tolerable degree of sharpness, in his hand,—to play with, it may be. He bared his arms, looking intently at their corded veins and sinews. Deborah, listening in the next cell, heard a slight clicking sound, often repeated. She shut her lips tightly, that she might not scream; the cold drops of sweat broke over her, in her dumb agony.

"Hur knows best," she muttered at last, fiercely clutching the boards where she lay.

If she could have seen Wolfe, there was nothing about him to frighten her. He lay quite still, his arms outstretched, looking at the pearly stream of moonlight coming into the window. I think in that one hour that came then he lived back over all the years that had gone before. I think that all the low, vile life, all his wrongs, all his starved hopes, came then, and stung him with a farewell poison that made him sick unto death. He made neither moan nor cry, only turned his worn face now and then to the pure light, that seemed so far off, as one that said, "How long, O Lord? how long?"

The hour was over at last. The moon, passing over her nightly path, slowly came nearer, and threw the light across his bed on his feet. He watched it steadily, as it crept up, inch by inch, slowly. It seemed to him to carry with it a great silence. He had been so hot and tired there always in the mills! The years had been so fierce and cruel! There was coming now quiet and coolness and sleep. His tense limbs relaxed, and settled in a calm languor. The blood ran fainter and slow from his heart. He did not think now with a savage anger of what might be and was not; he was conscious only of deep stillness creeping over him. At first he saw a sea of faces: the millmen,—women he had known, drunken and bloated,—Janeys timid and pitiful,—poor old Debs: then they floated together like a mist, and faded away, leaving only the clear, pearly moonlight.

Whether, as the pure light crept up the stretched-out figure, it brought with it calm and peace, who shall say? His dumb soul was alone with God in judgment. A Voice may have spoken for it from far-off Calvary, "Father, forgive them, for they know not what they do!" Who dare say? Fainter and fainter the heart rose and fell, slower and slower the moon floated from behind a cloud, until, when at last its full tide of white splendor swept over the cell, it seemed to wrap and fold into a deeper stillness the dead figure that never should move again. Silence deeper than the Night! Nothing that moved, save the black, nauseous stream of blood dripping slowly from the pallet to the floor!

There was outcry and crowd enough in the cell the next day. The coroner and his jury, the local editors, Kirby himself, and boys with their hands thrust knowingly into their pockets and heads on one side, jammed into the corners. Coming and going all day. Only one woman. She came late, and outstayed them all. A Quaker, or Friend as they call themselves. I think this woman was known by that name in heaven. A homely body, coarsely dressed in gray and white. Deborah (for Haley had let her in) took notice of her. She watched them all—sitting on the end of the pallet, holding his head in her arms—with the ferocity of a watch-dog, if any of them touched the body. There was no meekness, no sorrow, in her face; the stuff out of which murderers are made, instead. All the time Haley and the woman were laying straight the limbs and cleaning the cell, Deborah sat still, keenly watching the Quaker's face. Of all the crowd there that day, this woman alone had not spoken to her,—only once or twice had put some cordial to her lips. After they all were gone, the woman, in the same still, gentle way, brought a vase of wood-leaves and berries, and placed it by the pallet, then opened the narrow window. The fresh air blew in, and swept the woody fragrance over the dead face. Deborah looked up with a quick wonder.

"Did hur know my boy wud like it? Did hur know Hugh?"

"I know Hugh now."

The white fingers passed in a slow, pitiful way over the dead, worn face. There was a heavy shadow in the quiet eyes,

"Did hur know where they'll bury Hugh?" said Deborah in a shrill tone, catching her arm.

This had been the question hanging on her lips all day.

"In t' town-yard? Under t' mud and ash? T' lad'll smother, woman! He wur born on t' lane moor, where t' air is frick and strong. Take hur out, for God's sake, take hur out where t' air blows!"

The Quaker hesitated, but only for a moment. She put her strong arm around Deborah and led her to the window.

"Thee sees the hills, friend, over the river? Thee sees how the light lies warm there, and the winds of God blow all the day? I live there,—where the blue smoke is, by the trees. Look at me." She turned Deborah's face to her own, clear and earnest. "Thee will believe me? I will take Hugh and bury him there to-morrow."

Deborah did not doubt her. As the evening wore on, she leaned against the iron bars, looking at the hills that rose far off, through the thick sodden clouds, like a bright, unattainable calm. As she looked, a shadow of their solemn repose fell on her face: its fierce discontent faded into a pitiful, humble quiet. Slow, solemn tears gathered in her eyes: the poor weak eyes turned so hopelessly to the place where Hugh was to rest, the grave heights looking higher and brighter and more solemn than ever before. The Quaker watched her keenly. She came to her at last, and touched her arm.

"When thee comes back," she said, in a low, sorrowful tone, like one who speaks from a strong heart deeply moved with remorse or pity, "thee shall begin thy life again,—there on the hills. I came too late; but not for thee,—by God's help, it may be."

Not too late. Three years after, the Quaker began her work. I end my story here. At evening-time it was light. There is no need to tire you with the long years of sunshine, and fresh air, and slow, patient Christ-love, needed to make healthy and hopeful this impure body and soul. There is a homely pine house, on one of these hills, whose windows overlook broad, wooded slopes and clover-crimsoned meadows,—niched into the very place where the light is warmest, the air freest. It is the

Friends' meeting-house. Once a week they sit there, in their grave, earnest way, waiting for the Spirit of Love to speak, opening their simple hearts to receive His words. There is a woman, old, deformed, who takes a humble place among them: waiting like them: in her gray dress, her worn face, pure and meek, turned now and then to the sky. A woman much loved by these silent, restful people; more silent than they, more humble, more loving. Waiting: with her eyes turned to hills higher and purer than these on which she lives,—dim and far off now, but to be reached some day. There may be in her heart some latent hope to meet there the love denied her here,—that she shall find him whom she lost, and that then she will not be all-unworthy. Who blames her? Something is lost in the passage of every soul from one eternity to the other,—something pure and beautiful, which might have been and was not: a hope, a talent, a love, over which the soul mourns, like Esau deprived of his birthright. What blame to the meek Quaker, if she took her lost hope to make the hills of heaven more fair?

Nothing remains to tell that the poor Welsh puddler once lived, but this figure of the mill-woman cut in korl. I have it here in a corner of my library. I keep it hid behind a curtain,—it is such a rough, ungainly thing. Yet there are about it touches, grand sweeps of outline, that show a master's hand. Sometimes,—to-night, for instance,—the curtain is accidentally drawn back, and I see a bare arm stretched out imploringly in the darkness, and an eager, wolfish face watching mine: a wan, woful face, through which the spirit of the dead korl-cutter looks out, with its thwarted life, its mighty hunger, its unfinished work. Its pale, vague lips seem to tremble with a terrible question. "Is this the End?" they say,—"nothing beyond?—no more?" Why, you tell me you have seen that look in the eyes of dumb brutes,—horses dying under the lash. I know.

The deep of the night is passing while I write. The gas-light wakens from the shadows here and there the objects which lie scattered through the room: only faintly, though; for they belong to the open sunlight. As I glance at them, they each recall some task or pleasure of the coming day. A half-moulded child's head; Aphrodite; a bough of forest-leaves; music; work; homely fragments, in which lie the secrets of all eternal truth and beauty. Prophetic all! Only this dumb, woful face seems to belong to and end with the night. I turn to look at it. Has the power of its desperate need commanded the darkness away? While the room is yet steeped in heavy shadow, a cool, gray light suddenly touches its head like a blessing, and its groping arm points through the broken cloud to the far East, where, in the flickering, nebulous crimson, God has set the promise of the Dawn.

ANDREW CARNEGIE

(1835-1919)

One of the world's richest men in his time, Carnegie came from a Scottish family that, as he explains, had been well-off for two generations as skilled workmen, but that had been reduced to poverty by the changes brought about by the new factory system. The family emigrated to Pittsburgh, where father and son soon obtained jobs in the cotton mills and the mother worked binding shoes at home. Carnegie narrates his rags-to-riches rise as a natural progression based on hard work, a good basic self-education, and a refusal to complain, but in fact, he was helped by what he had learned early on, and also substantially by a fellow Scotsman, John Hay. His rapid rise also took place in an economy that was rapidly expanding, especially in railroading and iron manufacture, the businesses into which Carnegie entered. Early in the post–Civil War boom, he invested his substantial profits in the new steel industry and through shrewd investment in new sources of raw materials and a changing technology, and a ruthless labor policy, he accumulated enormous wealth and power.

Carnegie had always been interested in education as well as, in his family's tradition, doing good. He developed a significant rationale for charitable enterprise as an obligation and an opportunity for the wealthy. He formulated his ideas in The Gospel of Wealth *(1900), and he put his notions into practice by, among other things, supporting the creation of libraries in hundreds of towns and cities, building cultural centers, like Carnegie Hall in New York, underwriting scientific research, and, somewhat ingenuously, pursuing international peace. His book and his essays can be seen as recipes for the principled application of riches to social betterment, or as rationalizations that hide the exploitation of others necessarily attendant on the accumulation of great wealth. Perhaps they are both.*

from The Gospel of Wealth

Introduction:
How I Served My Apprenticeship

It is a great pleasure to tell how I served my apprenticeship as a business man. But there seems to be a question preceding this: Why did I become a business man? I am sure that I should never have selected a business career if I had been permitted to choose.

The eldest son of parents who were themselves poor, I had, fortunately, to begin to perform some useful work in the world while still very young in order to earn an honest livelihood, and was thus shown even in early boyhood that my duty was to assist my parents and, like them, become, as soon as possible, a bread-winner in the family. What I could get to do, not what I desired, was the question.

When I was born my father was a well-to-do master weaver in Dunfermline, Scotland. He owned no less than four damask-looms and employed apprentices. This was before the days of steam-factories for the manufacture of linen. A few large merchants took orders, and employed master weavers, such as my father, to weave the cloth, the merchants supplying the materials.

As the factory system developed hand-loom weaving naturally declined, and my father was one of the sufferers by the change. The first serious lesson of my life came to me one day when he had taken in the last of his work to the merchant, and returned to our little home greatly distressed because there was no more work for him to do. I was then just about ten years of age, but the lesson burned into my heart, and I resolved then that the wolf of poverty should be driven from our door some day, if I could do it.

The question of selling the old looms and starting for the United States came up in the family council, and I heard it discussed from day to day. It was finally resolved to take the plunge and join relatives already in Pittsburgh. I well remember that neither father nor mother thought the change would be otherwise than a great sacrifice for them, but that "it would be better for the two boys."

In after life, if you can look back as I do and wonder at the complete surrender of their own desires which parents make for the good of their children, you must reverence their memories with feelings akin to worship.

On arriving in Allegheny City (there were four of us: father, mother, my younger brother, and myself), my father entered a cotton factory. I soon followed, and served as the "bobbin-boy," and this is how I began my preparation for subsequent apprenticeship as a business man. I received one dollar and twenty cents a week, and was then just about twelve years old.

I cannot tell you how proud I was when I received my first week's own earnings. One dollar and twenty cents made by myself and given to me because I had been of some use in the world! No longer entirely dependent upon my parents, but at last admitted to the family partnership as a contributing member and able to help them! I think this makes a man out of a boy sooner than almost anything else, and a real man, too, if there be any germ of true manhood in him. It is everything to feel that you are useful.

I have had to deal with great sums. Many millions of dollars have since passed through my hands. But the genuine satisfaction I had from that one dollar and twenty cents outweighs any subsequent pleasure in money-getting. It was the direct reward of honest, manual labor; it represented a week of very hard work—so hard that, but for the aim and end which sanctified it, slavery might not be much too strong a term to describe it.

For a lad of twelve to rise and breakfast every morning, except the blessed Sunday morning, and go into the streets and find his way to the factory and begin to work while it was still dark outside, and not be released until after darkness came again in the evening, forty minutes' interval only being allowed at noon, was a terrible task.

But I was young and had my dreams, and something within always told me that this would not, could not, should not last—I should some day get into a better position. Besides this, I felt myself no longer a mere boy, but quite a little man, and this made me happy.

A change soon came, for a kind old Scotsman, who knew some of our relatives, made bobbins, and took me into his factory before I was thirteen. But here for a time it was even worse than in the cotton factory, because I was set to fire a boiler in the cellar, and actually to run the small steam-engine which drove the machinery. The firing of the boiler was all right, for fortunately we did not use coal, but the refuse wooden chips; and I always liked to work in wood. But the responsibility of keeping the water right and of running the engine, and the danger of my making a mistake and blowing the whole factory to pieces, caused too great a strain, and I often awoke and found myself sitting up in bed through the night, trying the steam-gauges. But I never told them at home that I was having a hard tussle. No, no! everything must be bright to them.

This was a point of honor, for every member of the family was working hard, except, of course, my little brother, who was then a child, and we were telling each other only all the bright things. Besides this, no man would whine and give up—he would die first.

There was no servant in our family, and several dollars per week were earned by the mother by binding shoes after her daily work was done! Father was also hard at work in the factory. And could I complain?

My kind employer, John Hay,—peace to his ashes!—soon relieved me of the undue strain, for he needed someone to make out bills and keep his accounts, and finding that I could write a plain school-boy hand and could "cipher," he made me his only clerk. But still I had to work hard upstairs in the factory, for the clerking took but little time.

You know how people moan about poverty as being a great evil, and it seems to be accepted that if people had only plenty of money and were rich, they would be happy and more useful, and get more out of life.

As a rule, there is more genuine satisfaction, a truer life, and more obtained from life in the humble cottages of the poor than in the palaces of the rich. I always pity the sons and daughters of the rich men, who are attended by servants, and have governesses at a later age, but am glad to remember that they do not know what they have missed.

They have kind fathers and mothers, too, and think that they enjoy the sweetness of these blessings to the fullest: but this they cannot do; for the poor boy who has in his father his constant companion, tutor, and model, and in his mother—holy name!—his nurse, teacher, guardian angel, saint, all in one, has a richer, more precious fortune in life than any rich man's son who is not so favored can possibly know, and compared with which all other fortunes count for little.

It is because I know how sweet and happy and pure the home of honest poverty is, how free from perplexing care, from social envies and emulations, how loving and how united its members may be in the common interest of supporting the family, that I sympathize with the rich man's boy and congratulate the poor man's boy; and it is for these reasons that from the ranks of the poor so many strong, eminent, self-reliant men have always sprung and always must spring.

If you will read the list of the immortals who "were not born to die," you will find that most of them have been born to the precious heritage of poverty.

It seems, nowadays, a matter of universal desire that poverty should be abolished. We should be quite willing to abolish luxury, but to abolish honest, industrious, self-denying poverty would be to destroy the soil upon which mankind produces the virtues which enable our race to reach a still higher civilization than it now possesses. . . .

The Problem of the Administration of Wealth

The problem of our age is the proper administration of wealth, that the ties of brotherhood may still bind together the rich and poor in harmonious relationship. The conditions of human life have not only been changed, but revolutionized, within the past few hundred years. In former days there was little difference between the dwelling, dress, food, and environment of the chief and those of his retainers. The Indians are to-day where civilized man then was. When visiting the Sioux, I was led to the wigwam of the chief. It was like the others in external appearance, and even within the difference was trifling between it and those of the poorest of the braves. The contrast between the palace of the millionaire and the cottage of the laborer with us today measures the change which has come with civilization. This change, however, is not to be deplored, but welcomed as highly beneficial. It is well, nay, essential, for the progress of the race that the houses of some should be homes for all that is highest and best in literature and the arts, and for all the refinements of civilization, rather than that none should be so. Much better this great irregularity than universal squalor. Without wealth there can be no Maecenas. The "good old times" were not good old times. Neither master nor servant was as well situated then as to-day. A relapse to old conditions would be disastrous to both— not the least so to him who serves—and would sweep away civilization with it. But whether the change be for good or ill, it is upon us, beyond our power to alter, and, therefore, to be accepted and made the best of. It is a waste of time to criticize the inevitable.

It is easy to see how the change has come. One illustration will serve for almost every phase of the cause. In the manufacture of products we have the whole story. It applies to all combinations of human industry, as stimulated and enlarged by the inventions of this scientific age. Formerly, articles were manufactured at the domestic hearth, or in small shops which formed part of the household. The master and his apprentices worked side by side, the latter living with the master, and therefore subject to the same conditions. When these apprentices rose to be masters, there was little or no change in their mode of life, and they, in turn, educated succeeding apprentices in the same routine. There was, substantially, social equality, and even political equality, for those engaged in industrial pursuits had then little or no voice in the State.

The inevitable result of such a mode of manufacture was crude articles at high prices. To-day the world obtains commodities of excellent quality at prices which even the preceding generation would have deemed incredible. In the commercial world similar causes have produced similar results, and the race is benefited thereby. The poor enjoy what the rich could not before afford. What were the luxuries have become the necessaries of life. The laborer has now more comforts than the farmer had a few generations ago. The farmer has more luxuries than the landlord had, and is more richly clad and better housed. The landlord has books and pictures rarer and appointments more artistic than the king could then obtain.

The price we pay for this salutary change is, no doubt, great. We assemble thousands of operatives in the factory, and in the mine, of whom the employer can know little or nothing, and to whom he is little better than a myth. All intercourse between them is at an end. Rigid castes are formed, and, as usual, mutual ignorance breeds mutual distrust. Each caste is without sympathy with the other, and ready to credit anything disparaging in regard to it. Under the law of competition, the employer of thousands is forced into the strictest economies, among which the rates paid to labor figure prominently, and often there is friction between the employer and the employed, between capital and labor, between rich and poor. Human society loses homogeneity.

The price which society pays for the law of competition, like the price it pays for cheap comforts and luxuries, is also great; but the advantages of this law are also greater still than its cost—for it is to this law that we owe our wonderful material development, which brings improved conditions in its train. But, whether the law be benign or not, we must say of it, as we say of the change in the conditions of men to which we have referred: It is here; we cannot evade it; no substitutes for it have been found; and while the law may be sometimes hard for the individual, it is best for the race, because it insures the survival of the fittest in every department. We accept and welcome, therefore, as conditions to which we must accommodate ourselves, great inequality of environment; the concentration of business, industrial and commercial, in the hands of a few; and the law of competition between these, as being not only beneficial, but essential to the future progress of the race. Having accepted these, it follows that there must be great scope for the exercise of special ability in the merchant and in the manufacturer who has to conduct affairs upon a great-scale. That this talent for organization and management is rare among men is proved by the fact that it invariably secures enormous rewards for its possessor, no matter where or under what laws or conditions. The experienced in affairs always rate the man whose services can be obtained as a partner as not only the first consideration, but such as render the question of his capital scarcely worth considering: for able men soon create capital; in the hands of those without the special talent required, capital soon takes wings. Such men become interested in firms or corporations using millions; and, estimating only simple interest to be made upon the capital invested, it is inevitable that their income must exceed their expenditure and that they must, therefore, accumulate wealth. Nor is there any middle ground which such men can occupy, because the great manufacturing or commercial concern which does not earn at least interest upon its capital soon becomes bankrupt. It must either go forward or fall behind; to stand still is impossible. It is a condition essential to its successful operation that it should be thus far profitable, and even that, in addition to interest on capital, it should make profit. It is a law, as certain as any of the others named, that men possessed of this peculiar talent for affairs, under the free play of economic forces must, of necessity, soon be in receipt of more revenue than can be judiciously expended upon themselves; and this law is as beneficial for the race as the others. . . .

This, then, is held to be the duty of the man of wealth: To set an example of modest, unostentatious living, shunning display or extravagance; to provide moderately for the legitimate wants of those dependent upon him; and, after doing so, to consider all surplus revenues which come to him simply as trust funds, which he is called upon to administer, and strictly bound as a matter of duty to administer in the manner which, in his judgment, is best calculated to produce the most beneficial results for the community—the man of wealth thus becoming the mere trustee and agent for his poorer brethren, bringing to their service his superior wisdom, experience, and ability to administer, doing for them better than they would or could do for themselves.

We are met here with the difficulty of determining what are moderate sums to leave to members of the family; what is modest, unostentatious living; what is the test of extravagance. There must be different standards for different conditions. The answer is that it is as impossible to name exact amounts or actions as it is to define good manners, good taste, or the rules of propriety; but, nevertheless, these are verities, well known, although indefinable. Public sentiment is quick to know and to feel what offends these. So in the case of wealth. The rule in regard to good taste in dress of men or women applies here. Whatever makes one conspicuous offends the canon. If any family be chiefly known for display, for extravagance in home, table, or equipage, for enormous sums ostentatiously spent in any form upon itself—if these be its chief distinctions, we have no difficulty in estimating its nature or culture. So likewise in regard to the use or abuse of its surplus wealth, or to generous, free-handed coöperation in good public uses, or to unabated efforts to accumulate and hoard to the last, or whether they administer or bequeath. The verdict rests with the best and most enlightened public sentiment. The community will surely judge, and its judgments will not often be wrong. . . .

There is room and need for all kinds of wise benefactions for the common weal. The man who builds a university, library, or laboratory performs no more useful work than he who elects to devote himself and his surplus means to the adornment of a park, the gathering together of a collection of pictures for the public, or the building of a memorial arch. These are all true laborers in the vineyard. The only point required by the gospel of wealth is that the surplus which accrues from time to time in the hands of a man should be administered by him in his own lifetime for that purpose which is seen by him, as trustee, to be best for the good of the people. To leave at death what he cannot take away, and place upon others the burden of the work which it was his own duty to perform, is to do nothing worthy. This requires no sacrifice, nor any sense of duty to his fellows.

Time was when the words concerning the rich man entering the kingdom of heaven were regarded as a hard saying. To-day, when all questions are probed to the bottom and the standards of faith receive the most liberal interpretations, the startling verse has been relegated to the rear, to await the next kindly revision as one of those things which cannot be quite understood, but which, meanwhile, it is carefully to be noted, are not to be understood literally. But is it so very improbable that the next stage of thought is to restore the doctrine in all its pristine purity and force, as being in perfect harmony with sound ideas upon the subject of wealth and poverty, the rich and the poor, and the contrasts everywhere seen and deplored? In Christ's day, it is evident, reformers were against the wealthy. It is none the less evident that we are fast recurring to that position to-day; and there will be nothing to surprise the student of sociological development if society should soon approve the text which has caused so much anxiety: "It is easier for the camel to enter the eye of a needle than for a rich man to enter the kingdom of heaven." Even if the needle were the small casement at the gates, the words betoken serious difficulty for the rich. It will be but a step for the theologian from the doctrine that he who dies rich dies disgraced, to that which brings upon the man punishment or deprivation hereafter.

The gospel of wealth but echoes Christ's words. It calls upon the millionaire to sell all that he hath and give it in the highest and best form to the poor by administering his estate himself for the good of his fellows, before he is called upon to lie down and rest upon the bosom of Mother Earth. So doing, he will approach his end no longer the ignoble hoarder of useless millions; poor, very poor indeed, in money, but rich, very rich, twenty times a millionaire still, in the affection, gratitude, and admiration of his fellow-men, and—sweeter far—soothed and sustained by the still, small voice within, which, whispering, tells him that, because he has lived, perhaps one small part of the great world has been bettered just a little. This much is sure: against such riches as these no bar will be found at the gates of Paradise.

JACK LONDON
(1876–1916)

In this entry, London offers a brief account of how a working-class kid became, through hard experience and observation, an active socialist intellectual. (See the entry for London in section I for biographical information.)

How I Became a Socialist

It is quite fair to say that I became a Socialist in a fashion somewhat similar to the way in which the Teutonic pagans became Christians—it was hammered into me. Not only was I not looking for Socialism at the time of my conversion, but I was fighting it. I was very young and callow, did not know much of anything, and though I had never even heard of a school called "Individualism," I sang the pæan of the strong with all my heart.

This was because I was strong myself. By strong I mean that I had good health and hard muscles, both of which possessions are easily accounted for. I had lived my childhood on California ranches, my boyhood hustling newspapers on the streets of a healthy Western city, and my youth on the ozone-laden waters of San Francisco Bay and the Pacific Ocean. I loved life in the open, and I toiled in the open, at the hardest kinds of work. Learning no trade, but drifting along from job to job, I looked on the world and called it good, every bit of it. Let me repeat, this optimism was because I was healthy and strong, bothered with neither aches nor weaknesses, never turned down by the boss because I did not look fit, able always to get a job at shovelling coal, sailorizing, or manual labor of some sort.

And because of all this, exulting in my young life, able to hold my own at work or fight, I was a rampant individualist. It was very natural. I was a winner. Wherefore I called the game, as I saw it played, or thought I saw it played, a very proper game for MEN. To be a MAN was to write man in large capitals on my heart. To adventure like a man, and fight like a man, and do a man's work (even for a boy's pay)—these were things that reached right in and gripped hold of me as no other thing could. And I looked ahead into long vistas of a hazy and interminable future, into which, playing what I conceived to be MAN'S game, I should continue to travel with unfailing health, without accidents, and with muscles ever vigorous. As I say, this future was interminable. I could see myself only raging through life without end like one of Nietzsche's *blond beasts,* lustfully roving and conquering by sheer superiority and strength.

As for the unfortunates, the sick, and ailing, and old, and maimed, I must confess I hardly thought of them at all, save that I vaguely felt that they, barring accidents, could be as good as I if they wanted to real hard, and could work just as well. Accidents? Well, they represented FATE, also spelled out in capitals, and there was no getting around FATE. Napoleon had had an accident at Waterloo, but that did not dampen my desire to be another and later Napoleon. Further, the optimism bred of a stomach which could digest scrap iron and a body which flourished on hardships did not permit me to consider accidents as even remotely related to my glorious personality.

I hope I have made it clear that I was proud to be one of Nature's strong-armed noblemen. The dignity of labor was to me the most impressive thing in the world.

Without having read Carlyle, or Kipling, I formulated a gospel of work which put theirs in the shade. Work was everything. It was sanctification and salvation. The pride I took in a hard day's work well done would be inconceivable to you. It is almost inconceivable to me as I look back upon it. I was as faithful a wage slave as ever capitalist exploited. To shirk or malinger on the man who paid me my wages was a sin, first, against myself, and second against him. I considered it a crime second only to treason and just about as bad.

In short, my joyous individualism was dominated by the orthodox bourgeois ethics. I read the bourgeois papers, listened to the bourgeois preachers, and shouted at the sonorous platitudes of the bourgeois politicians. And I doubt not, if other events had not changed my career, that I should have evolved into a professional strikebreaker, (one of President Eliot's American heroes), and had my head and my earning power irrevocably smashed by a club in the hands of some militant trades-unionist.

Just about this time, returning from a seven months' voyage before the mast, and just turned eighteen, I took it into my head to go tramping. On rods and blind baggages I fought my way from the open West, where men bucked big and the job hunted the man, to the congested labor centres of the East, where men were small potatoes and hunted the job for all they were worth. And on this new *blond-beast* adventure I found myself looking upon life from a new and totally different angle. I had dropped down from the proletariat into what sociologists love to call the "submerged tenth," and I was startled to discover the way in which that submerged tenth was recruited.

I found there all sorts of men, many of whom had once been as good as myself and just as *blond-beastly;* sailor-men, soldier-men, labor-men, all wrenched and distorted and twisted out of shape by toil and hardship and accident, and cast adrift by their masters like so many old horses. I battered on the drag and slammed back gates with them, or shivered with them in box cars and city parks, listening the while to life-histories which began under auspices as fair as mine, with digestions and bodies equal to and better than mine, and which ended there before my eyes in the shambles at the bottom of the Social Pit.

And as I listened my brain began to work. The woman of the streets and the man of the gutter drew very close to me. I saw the picture of the Social Pit as vividly as though it were a concrete thing, and at the bottom of the Pit I saw them, myself above them, not far, and hanging on to the slippery wall by main strength and sweat. And I confess a terror seized me. What when my strength failed? when I should be unable to work shoulder to shoulder with the strong men who were as yet babes unborn? And there and then I swore a great oath. It ran something like this: *All my days I have worked hard with my body, and according to the number of days I have worked, by just that much am I nearer the bottom of the Pit. I shall climb out of the Pit, but not by the muscles of my body shall I climb out. I shall do no more hard work, and may God strike me dead if I do another day's hard work with my body more than I absolutely have to do.* And I have been busy ever since running away from hard work.

Incidentally, while tramping some ten thousand miles through the United States and Canada, I strayed into Niagara Falls, was nabbed by a fee-hunting constable, denied the right to plead guilty or not guilty, sentenced out of hand to thirty days' imprisonment for having no fixed abode and no visible means of support, handcuffed and chained to a bunch of men similarly circumstanced, carted down country to Buffalo, registered at the Erie County Penitentiary, had my head clipped and my budding mustache shaved, was dressed in convict stripes, compulsorily vaccinated by a medical student who practised on such as we, made to march the lock-step, and put to work under the eyes of guards armed with Winchester rifles—all for adventuring in *blond-beastly* fashion. Concerning further details deponent sayeth not, though he may hint that some of his plethoric national patriotism simmered down and leaked out of the bottom of his soul somewhere—at least, since that experience he finds that he cares more for men and women and little children than for imaginary geographical lines.

To return to my conversion. I think it is apparent that my rampant individualism was pretty effectively hammered out of me, and something else as effectively hammered in. But, just as I had been an individualist without knowing it, I was now a Socialist without knowing it, withal, an unscientific one. I had been reborn, but not renamed, and I was running around to find out what manner of thing I was. I ran back to California and opened the books. I do not remember which ones I opened first. It is an unimportant detail anyway. I was already It, whatever It was, and by aid of the books I discovered that It was a Socialist. Since that day I have opened many books, but no economic argument, no lucid demonstration of the logic and inevitableness of Socialism affects me as profoundly and convincingly as I was affected on the day when I first saw the walls of the Social Pit rise around me and felt myself slipping down, down, into the shambles at the bottom.

EDWIN MARKHAM
(1852-1940)

Markham's "The Man With the Hoe" was undoubtedly, with Longfellow's "Hiawatha," Lowell's "Old Ironsides," Whittier's "Snowbound," and Emerson's "Concord Hymn," among the most popular of nineteenth-century poems. In the days and weeks after it first appeared on January 15, 1899, in the San Francisco Examiner, *Markham's poem was republished in over 10,000 newspapers and magazines, and translated into more than forty languages. But unlike those earlier popular successes, Markham's poem was, in its time, a controversial work: it was both proclaimed and denounced as advocating socialism. There were those who saw it as articulating the grievances of farmers and workers against the excessive power of banks, railroads, and capitalists. Others took it to express a "radical" solution to the troubles of an America that had just moved from being a majority rural to a majority urban nation, a country within which disparities of wealth were rapidly widening, a populace wherein the presumably inarticulate voice of the worker and the immigrant were little heard. But there were also those who perceived it as a dangerous call to unneeded and unwanted reforms. Markham himself saw it as "a poem of hope." Written after seeing Jean-François Millet's famous painting, the poem for Markham was an effort to capture what the painter had seized upon. Millet, Markham wrote, "had swept his canvas bare of everything that was merely pretty, and projected this startling figure before us in all its rugged and savage reality. . . . I saw in it the symbol of betrayed humanity."*

Read today, it is hard to understand just why the poem hit such sensitive nerves. In its elaborate language, learned metaphors, and narrowly reformist ideology, it seems, as it is, the expression of middle-class fear as well as middle-class desire for top-down solutions to prevailing social problems. However that might have been, the poem and its promotion by the Hearst newspapers in which it was first published established Markham's career. From that point until almost the end of his life, he became a fixture of poetry societies and reading circuits, as well as of the periodicals that spoke to, or at least helped create, mass culture. Few personalities of the time were as widely known as Markham, and few profited so systematically as he from his celebrity.

He had been born in the Oregon Territory to an extremely demanding mother, who moved to California with her youngest children when Edwin was four. There he was educated, learned to work a ranch, attended California College in Vacaville and San Jose Normal School, and taught and administered a number of schools. He also entered into a series of disastrous marriages and liaisons and in the 1880s began to earn money by writing poetry, published at first in local newspapers, then in nationally circulated magazines including The Century and Scribner's. He also for a period came under the influence of the leader, Thomas Lake Harris, of a utopian colony of the sort rather too often charged against California. The efforts of the Brotherhood of the New Life to reconcile vague ideals of equality, religious aspirations, and social reform would brand Markham's poetry—widely popular in its time but increasingly marginal in the formally experimental and intellectually ambiguous world of the inter-war period. A philosophy that claimed "two things—reverence for women and consecration to Social Solidarity" as the hope for political progress could not withstand the onslaught of modernism. Thus, while he may have been the most well known poet of his period among ordinary people, his reputation among critics and other writers declined almost to vanishing. "The Man with the Hoe" and, perhaps, his "Lincoln, the Man of the People" are of all his verse alone read today.

THE MAN WITH THE HOE

Bowed by the weight of centuries he leans
Upon his hoe and gazes on the ground,
The emptiness of ages in his face,
And on his back the burden of the world.
Who made him dead to rapture and despair,
A thing that grieves not and that never hopes,
Stolid and stunned, a brother to the ox?
Who loosened and let down this brutal jaw?
Whose was the hand that slanted back this brow?
Whose breath blew out the light within this brain?

Is this the Thing the Lord God made and gave
To have dominion over sea and land;
To trace the stars and search the heavens for power;
To feel the passion of Eternity?
Is this the dream He dreamed who shaped the suns
And marked their ways upon the ancient deep?
Down all the caverns of Hell to their last gulf
There is no shape more terrible than this—
More tongued with censure of the world's blind greed—
More filled with signs and portents for the soul—
More packt with danger to the universe.

What gulfs between him and the seraphim!
Slave of the wheel of labor, what to him
Are Plato and the swing of Pleiades?
What the long reaches of the peaks of song,
The rift of dawn, the reddening of the rose?
Through this dread shape the suffering ages look;
Time's tragedy is in that aching stoop;
Through this dread shape humanity betrayed,
Plundered, profaned, and disinherited,
Cries protest to the Judges of the World,
A protest that is also prophecy.

O masters, lords and rulers in all lands,
Is this the handiwork you give to God,
This monstrous thing distorted and soul-quenched?
How will you ever straighten up this shape;
Touch it again with immortality;
Give back the upward looking and the light;
Rebuild in it the music and the dream;
Make right the immemorial infamies,
Perfidious wrongs, immedicable woes?

O masters, lords and rulers in all lands,
How will the Future reckon with this Man?
How answer his brute question in that hour
When whirlwinds of rebellion shake all shores?
How will it be with kingdoms and with kings—
With those who shaped him to the thing he is—
When this dumb terror shall rise to judge the world
After the silence of the centuries?

JOE HILL
(B. ?-1915)

(For biographical information about Joe Hill, see the headnote in section I.)

THE PREACHER AND THE SLAVE

Long-haired preachers come out ev'ry night,
Try to tell you what's wrong and what's right,
But when asked about something to eat,
They will answer with voices so sweet:

CHORUS: You will eat (you will eat), bye and bye (bye and bye),
     In that glorious land in the sky (way up high).
     Work and pray (work and pray), live on hay (live on hay),
     You'll get pie in the sky when you die (that's a lie!).

And the starvation army they play,
And they sing and they clap and they pray,
Till they get all your coin on the drum—
Then they tell you when you're on the bum:

If you fight hard for children and wife—
Try to get something good in this life—
You're a sinner and bad man, they tell;
When you die you will sure go to Hell.

Working men of all countries, unite!
Side by side we for freedom will fight.
When the world and its wealth we have gained,
To the grafters we'll sing this refrain:

LAST CHORUS:
     You will eat (you will eat), bye and bye, (bye and bye),
     When you've learned how to cook and to fry (way up high).
     Chop some wood (chop some wood)—'twill do you good
      (do you good)
     And you'll eat in the sweet bye and bye (that's no lie!).

RALPH CHAPLIN

(1887–1961)

Chaplin was a painter and graphic artist as well as a songwriter, poet, journalist, organizer, and editor. All these talents he devoted to the labor movement in a variety of venues. He edited newspapers of the Industrial Workers of the World (the IWW or "Wobblies"), as well as more conventional union papers. He wrote and illustrated a famous pamphlet on the frame-up and killing of Wobbly activists at Centralia, Washington. He himself was among the Wobblies convicted under the Espionage Act for opposing U.S. participation in World War I and served some four years in federal prison before being pardoned. He maintained the anarchist principles at the heart of the IWW when others had embraced other forms of political conviction.

But his most lasting contribution has been the song "Solidarity Forever," which he wrote early in 1915. It emerged, he said, from his experiences helping organize miners in West Virginia during a major strike in the Kanawha Valley. He set his song, in the style of other Wobbly songwriters like Joe Hill, to a tune familiar to those who would sing it, in this case the Civil War marching song "John Brown's Body." The song rapidly caught on. In time, it became the most familiar of all American labor songs and, in effect, the unofficial anthem of the union movement in the United States.

SOLIDARITY FOREVER

When the union's inspiration through the workers' blood shall run,
There can be no power greater anywhere beneath the sun.
Yet what force on earth is weaker than the feeble strength of one?
But the union makes us strong.

CHORUS: Solidarity forever!
Solidarity forever!
Solidarity forever!
For the union makes us strong.

They have taken untold millions that they never toiled to earn,
But without our brain and muscle not a single wheel could turn.
We can break their haughty power, gain our freedom when we learn
That the union makes us strong.

In our hands is placed a power greater than their hoarded gold,
Greater than the might of armies magnified a thousand fold.
We can bring to birth a new world from the ashes of the old,
For the union makes us strong.

MARY HARRIS ("MOTHER") JONES
(1836?–1930)

Mary Harris was born in Ireland around 1836 and came to the United States with her father during the potato famine, in the early 1840s. She worked as a seamstress and as a schoolteacher, eventually marrying an iron molder, George Jones, with whom she had four children. Her husband and children died, like many working people, in the yellow fever epidemic in Memphis in 1867. She moved to Chicago, but her dressmaking shop was burned up during the great fire of 1871. Subsequently, she became active with the Knights of Labor and in the anti-Chinese agitation among working people of that period. Later, for almost forty years, she organized primarily among miners.

Grandmotherly in appearance and initial demeanor, she proved to be a militant and colorful organizer, who played important roles in a variety of miner strikes. Her tactics were designed to put the bosses and their hirelings on the defensive: in her seventies, she confronted mine guards and went to jail, she organized a march of child workers from textile mills to dramatize the evils of child labor, she led a campaign to free Mexican revolutionaries held in U.S. prisons. Her life became something of a legend, as is illustrated by the adoption of "Mother Jones" to name a muckraking magazine as well as various radical groups of the 1960s. But as this excerpt from Autobiography of Mother Jones *indicates, she saw herself not as a legendary figure, but as a practical agitator whose opposition to capitalism she was intent on translating into efforts to organize the working class.*

FROM THE AUTOBIOGRAPHY OF MOTHER JONES

The March of the Mill Children

In the spring of 1903 I went to Kensington, Pennsylvania, where seventy-five thousand textile workers were on strike. Of this number at least ten thousand were little children. The workers were striking for more pay and shorter hours. Every day little children came into Union Headquarters, some with their hands off, some with the thumb missing, some with their fingers off at the knuckle. They were stooped little things, round shouldered and skinny. Many of them were not over ten years of age, although the state law prohibited their working before they were twelve years of age.

The law was poorly enforced and the mothers of these children often swore falsely as to their children's age. In a single block in Kensington, fourteen women, mothers of twenty-two children all under twelve, explained it was a question of starvation or perjury. That the fathers had been killed or maimed at the mines.

I asked the newspaper men why they didn't publish the facts about child labor in Pennsylvania. They said they couldn't because the mill owners had stock in the papers.

"Well, I've got stock in these little children," said I, "and I'll arrange a little publicity."

We assembled a number of boys and girls one morning in Independence Park and from there we arranged to parade with banners to the court house where we would hold a meeting.

A great crowd gathered in the public square in front of the city hall. I put the little boys with their fingers off and hands crushed and maimed on a platform. I held up their mutilated hands and showed them to the crowd and made the statement that Philadelphia's mansions were built on the broken bones, the quivering hearts and drooping heads of these children. That their little lives went out to make wealth for others. That neither state or city officials paid any attention to these wrongs. That they did not care that these children were to be the future citizens of the nation.

The officials of the city hall were standing in the open windows. I held the little ones of the mills high up above the heads of the crowd and pointed to their puny arms and legs and hollow chests. They were light to lift.

I called upon the millionaire manufacturers to cease their moral murders, and I cried to the officials in the open windows opposite, "Some day the workers will take possession of your city hall, and when we do, no child will be sacrificed on the altar of profit."

The officials quickly closed the windows, just as they had closed their eyes and hearts.

The reporters quoted my statement that Philadelphia mansions were built on the broken bones and quivering hearts of children. The Philadelphia papers and the New York papers got into a squabble with each other over the question. The universities discussed it. Preachers began talking. That was what I wanted. Public attention on the subject of child labor.

The matter quieted down for a while and I concluded the people needed stirring up again. The Liberty Bell that a century ago rang out for freedom against tyranny was touring the country and crowds were coming to see it everywhere. That gave me an idea. These little children were striking for some of the freedom that childhood ought to have, and I decided that the children and I would go on a tour.

I asked some of the parents if they would let me have their little boys and girls for a week or ten days, promising to bring them back safe and sound. They consented. A man named Sweeny was marshal for our "army." A few men and women went with me to help with the children. They were on strike and I thought they might as well have a little recreation.

The children carried knapsacks on their backs in which was a knife and fork, a tin cup and plate. We took along a wash boiler in which to cook the food on the road. One little fellow had a drum and another had a fife. That was our band. We carried banners that said, "We want more schools and less hospitals." "We want time to play." "Prosperity is here. Where is ours?"

We started from Philadelphia where we held a great mass meeting. I decided to go with the children to see President Roosevelt to ask him to have Congress pass a law prohibiting the exploitation of childhood. I thought that President Roosevelt might see these mill children and compare them with his own little ones who were spending the summer on the seashore at Oyster Bay. I thought, too, out of politeness, we might call on Morgan in Wall Street who owned the mines where many of these children's fathers worked.

The children were very happy, having plenty to eat, taking baths in the brooks and rivers every day. I thought when the strike is over and they go back to the mills, they will never have another holiday like this. All along the line of march the farmers drove out to meet us with wagon loads of fruit and vegetables. Their wives brought the children clothes and money. The interurban trainmen would stop their trains and give us free rides.

Marshal Sweeny and I would go ahead to the towns and arrange sleeping quarters for the children, and secure meeting halls. As we marched on, it grew terribly hot. There was no rain and the roads were heavy with dust. From time to time we had to send some of the children back to their homes. They were too weak to stand the march.

We were on the outskirts of New Trenton, New Jersey, cooking our lunch in the wash boiler, when the conductor on the interurban car stopped and told us the police were coming down to notify us that we could not enter the town. There were mills in the town and the mill owners didn't like our coming.

I said, "All right, the police will be just in time for lunch."

Sure enough, the police came and we invited them to dine with us. They looked at the little gathering of children with their tin plates and cups around the wash boiler. They just smiled and spoke kindly to the children, and said nothing at all about not going into the city.

We went in, held our meeting, and it was the wives of the police who took the little children and cared for them that night, sending them back in the morning with a nice lunch rolled up in paper napkins.

Everywhere we had meetings, showing up with living children, the horrors of child labor.

At one town the mayor said we could not hold a meeting because he did not have sufficient police protection. "These little children have never known any sort of protection, your honor," I said, "and they are used to going without it. He let us have our meeting.

One night in Princeton, New Jersey, we slept in the big cool barn on Grover Cleveland's great estate. The heat became intense. There was much suffering in our ranks, for our little ones were not robust. The proprietor of the leading hotel sent for me. "Mother," he said, "order what you want and all you want for your army, and there's nothing to pay."

I called on the mayor of Princeton and asked for permission to speak opposite the campus of the University. I said I wanted to speak on higher education. The mayor gave me permission. A great crowd gathered, professors and students and the people; and I told them that the rich robbed these little children of any education of the lowest order that they might send their sons and daughters to places of higher education. That they used the hands and feet of little children that they might buy automobiles for their wives and police dogs for their daughters to talk French to. I said the mill owners take babies almost from the cradle. And I showed those professors children in our army who could scarely read or write because they were working ten hours a day in the silk mills of Pennsylvania.

"Here's a text book on economics," I said, pointing to a little chap, James Ashworth, who was ten years old and who was stooped over like an old man from carrying bundles of yarn that weighed seventy-five pounds. "He gets three dollars a week and his sister who is fourteen gets six dollars. They work in a carpet factory ten hours a day while the children of the rich are getting their higher education."

That night we camped on the banks of Stony Brook where years and years before the ragged Revolutionary Army camped, Washington's brave soldiers that made their fight for freedom.

From Jersey City we marched to Hoboken. I sent a committee over to the New York Chief of Police, Ebstein, asking for permission to march up Fourth Avenue to Madison Square where I wanted to hold a meeting. The chief refused and forbade our entrance to the city.

I went over myself to New York and saw Mayor Seth Low. The mayor was most courteous but he said he would have to support the police commissioner. I asked him what the reason was for refusing us entrance to the city and he said that we were not citizens of New York.

"Oh, I think we will clear that up, Mr. Mayor," I said. "Permit me to call your attention to an incident which took place in this nation just a year ago. A piece of rotten royalty came over here from Germany, called Prince Henry. The Congress of the United States voted $45,000 to fill that fellow's stomach for three weeks and to entertain him. His brother was getting $4,000,000 dividends out of the blood of the workers in this country. Was he a citizen of this land?"

"And it was reported, Mr. Mayor, that you and all the officials of Now York and the University Club entertained that chap." And I repeated, "Was he a citizen of New York?"

"No, Mother," said the mayor, "he was not."

"And a Chinaman called Lee Woo was also entertained by the officials of New York. Was he a citizen of New York?"

"No, Mother," "he was not."

"Did they ever create any wealth for our nation?"

"No, Mother, they did not," said he.

"Well, Mr. Mayor, these are the little citizens of the nation and they also produce its wealth. Aren't we entitled to enter your city?"

"Just wait," says he, and he called the commissioner of police over to his office.

Well, finally they decided to let the army come in. We marched up Fourth Avenue to Madison Square and police officers, captains, sergeants, roundsmen and reserves from three precincts accompanied us. But the police would not let us hold a meeting in Madison Square. They insisted that the meeting be held in Twentieth Street.

I pointed out to the captain that the single taxers were allowed to hold meetings in the square. "Yes," he said, "but they won't have twenty people and you might have twenty thousand."

We marched to Twentieth Street. I told an immense crowd of the horrors of child labor in the mills around the anthracite region and I showed them some of the children. I showed them Eddie Dunphy, a little fellow of twelve, whose job it was to sit all day on a high stool, handing in the right thread to another worker. Eleven hours a day he sat on the high stool with dangerous machinery all about him. All day long, winter and summer, spring and fall, for three dollars a week.

And then I showed them Gussie Rangnew, a little girl from whom all the childhood had gone. Her face was like an old woman's. Gussie packed stockings in a factory, eleven hours a day for a few cents a day.

We raised a lot of money for the strikers and hundreds of friends offered their homes to the little ones while we were in the city.

The next day we went to Coney Island at the invitation of Mr. Bóstick who owned the wild animal show. The children had a wonderful day such as they never had in all their lives. After the exhibition of the trained animals, Mr. Bostick let me speak to the audience. There was a back drop to the tiny stage of the Roman Colosseum with the audience painted in and two Roman emperors down in front with their thumbs down. Right in front of the emperors were the empty iron cages of the animals. I put my little children in the cages and they clung to the iron bars while I talked.

I told the crowd that the scene was typical of the aristocracy of employers with their thumbs down to the little ones of the mills and factories, and people sitting dumbly by.

"We want President Roosevelt to hear the wail of the children who never have a chance to go to school but work eleven and twelve hours a day in the textile mills of Pennsylvania; who weave the carpets that he and you walk upon; and the lace curtains in your windows, and the clothes of the people. Fifty years ago there was a cry against slavery and men gave up their lives to stop the selling of black children on the block. Today the white child is sold for two dollars a week to the manufacturers. Fifty years ago the black babies were sold C. O. D. Today the white baby is sold on the installment plan.

"In Georgia where children work day and night in the cotton mills they have just passed a bill to protect song birds. What about the little children from whom all song is gone?

"I shall ask the president in the name of the aching hearts of these little ones that he emancipate them from slavery. I will tell the president that the prosperity he boasts of is the prosperity of the rich wrung from the poor and the helpless.

"The trouble is that no one in Washington cares. I saw our legislators in one hour pass three bills for the relief of the railways but when labor cries for aid for the children they will not listen.

"I asked a man in prison once how he happened to be there and he said he had stolen a pair of shoes. I told him if he had stolen a railroad he would be a United States Senator.

"We are told that every American boy has the chance of being president. I tell you that these little boys in the iron cages would sell their chance any day for good square meals and a chance to play. These little toilers whom I have taken from the mills—deformed, dwarfed in body and soul, with nothing but toil before them—have never heard that they have a chance, the chance of every American male citizen, to become the president.

"You see those monkeys in those cages over there." I pointed to a side cage. "The professors are trying to teach them to talk. The monkeys are too wise for they fear that the manufacturers would buy them for slaves in their factories."

I saw a stylishly dressed young man down in the front of the audience. Several times he grinned. I stopped speaking and pointing to him I said, 'Stop your smiling, young man! Leave this place! Go home and beg the mother who bore you in pain, as the mothers of these little children bore them, go home and beg her to give you brains and a heart."

He rose and slunk out, followed by the eyes of the children in the cage. The people sat stone still and out in the rear a lion roared.

The next day we left Coney Island for Manhattan Beach to visit Senator Platt, who had made an appointment to see me at nine o'clock in the morning. The children got stuck in the sand banks and I had a time cleaning the sand off the littlest ones. So we started to walk on the railroad track. I was told it was private property and we had to get off. Finally a saloon keeper showed us a short cut into the sacred grounds of the hotel and suddenly the army appeared in the lobby. The little fellows played "Hail, hail, the gang's all here" on their fifes and drums, and Senator Platt when he saw the little army ran away through the back door to New York.

I asked the manager if he would give the children breakfast and charge it up to the Senator as we had an invitation to breakfast that morning with him. He gave us a private room and he gave those children such a breakfast as they had never had in all their lives. I had breakfast too, and a reporter from one of the Hearst papers and I charged it all up to Senator Platt.

We marched down to Oyster Bay but the president refused to see us and he would not answer my letters. But our march had done its work. We had drawn the attention of the nation to the crime of child labor. And while the strike of the textile workers in Kensington was lost and the children driven back to work, not long afterward the Pennsylvania legislature passed a child labor law that sent thousands of children home from the mills, and kept thousands of others from entering the factory until they were fourteen years of age.

WILLIAM RICHARD HEREFORD
(1871-1928)

After attending the Harvard Law School and being admitted to the bar in Kansas City, Hereford began to work as a journalist, both in the United States and in Europe. He became the editor of the European edition of the New York Herald *and later the Paris correspondent for the* New York World. *During his journalist years, he had written two novels with something of a protest character,* The Demagog *(1909), which traces how the powerful owner of a newspaper chain conducts an unscrupulous campaign for president, and* When Fools Rush In *(1913).*

After working for the Carnegie Endowment for International Peace in 1913, he became, during World War I, executive secretary for the American Ambulance Field Service and later an official with the Red Cross. He remained in Europe after the war, working primarily as a banker, though he continued to write, including some poems like the one that follows.

WELFARE SONG

Sing a song of "Welfare,"
    A pocket full of tricks
To soothe the weary worker
    When he groans or kicks.
If he asks for shorter hours
    Or for better pay,
Little stunts of "Welfare"
    Turn his thoughts away.

Sing a song of "Welfare,"
    Sound the horn and drum,
Anything to keep the mind
    Fixed on Kingdom Come.
"Welfare" loots your pocket
    While you dream and sing,
"Welfare" to your paycheck
    Doesn't do a thing.

Sing a song of "Welfare,"
    Forty 'leven kinds,
Elevate your morals,
    Cultivate your minds.
Kindergartens, nurses,
    Bathtubs, books, and flowers,
Anything but better pay
    Or shorter working hours.

SHOLEM ASCH
(1880-1957)

Asch has suffered the strange fate of a cosmopolitan writer who outgrows or defies the audience he has won. The fact that he is virtually unknown in "American" literature suggests, moreover, that work originally written in Yiddish does not really fit into whatever constitutes the American canon. Born in Kutno, a small town not far from Warsaw, he began as a teenager to write in Hebrew, somewhat to the scandal of his family. Eventually, influenced by the advice of Leib Peretz, a significant Yiddish writer in Warsaw, to which he had moved, Asch shifted to that tongue, much more the common language of ordinary, working Jews of Eastern Europe. His collection of sketches of small-town Jewish life, Dos Shtetl (The Village—1904), won him a wide readership among Eastern Europe's Jews, and he followed that success by a series of effective dramas. The most famous of these, God of Vengeance (1907), produced in Russia and Germany as well as in Poland, concerned a brothel-keeper and his daughter; it was denounced among both orthodox and progressive intellectual circles for its sexual frankness and presumably immoral subject matter.

    In 1908, Asch's work began to be published in the United States; six years later, after a sojourn in Paris, he and his family moved to New York. His vivid, funny novel of 1916, Mottke the Thief (1916), won him a wide audience among American Jews. So successful were his books that he was nominated for a Nobel Prize in 1933. But late in the thirties, he launched into a series of novels about Jesus and early Christianity, among them The Nazarene (1939) and The Apostle (1943). These won him a considerable Christian audience— indeed some were best-sellers—but were bitterly rejected by many among his Yiddish readership. It became virtually impossible for him to find a publisher; only the Marxist Morning Freiheit was willing to print his work and, as a consequence, he was called by Congressional witch-hunters of the Cold War period. It is not clear to what extent Asch was attacked for violating Jewish sol-

idarity at the moment of the Holocaust, or to what extent he became a victim of the desire of some during the Cold War to lower the public profile of what had earlier been a rich and deep working-class and leftist Yiddish culture. In any case, so heated did the criticism become that he left the New York area in 1951, first for Miami Beach, then for England, and finally for Israel.

Asch's is but one of many treatments in prose, verse, and drama of the Triangle Shirtwaist factory fire, a hideous sweatshop conflagration in which primarily Jewish and Italian women lost their lives, many by jumping from the windows. Investigators blamed the lack of proper safety precautions and mainly the fact that the fire doors had been locked shut, presumably to prevent the workers from taking breaks. The martyrdom of these young women, many in their teens and early twenties, nevertheless helped organize the textile industry in New York.

THE TRIANGLE FIRE

The shop where Mary found work was in a long, large cellar in the neighborhood of 34th Street and Second Avenue. The cellar opened on a large yard full of grain stores and warehouses for merchandise, with a cheap restaurant for the truckmen who worked in the vicinity. The cellar, formerly used as a laundry, was under the restaurant, and the stench of decayed food and greasy cooking permeated the cellar workroom. There was no ventilation; only a single window, always closed, which faced a blank wall, grimy with cobwebs. There was no daylight, except for the light that came in through the open door to the cellar together with the waves of heat of the summer and the cold blasts of the winter. The cellar was illuminated by electric bulbs which hung naked from the low ceiling, without covering of any kind. In the summer, when the heat scorched the walls of the warehouses, the fetid smell of meat, cheese, fish, and other foods kept in them would be borne into the workroom. Piles of garbage were strewn about the yard. Stray cats and bedraggled beggars dug into the garbage cans outside the restaurant kitchen and the warehouses.

Wagons laden with merchandise rattled in and out of the yard all day. The heavy creaking of truck wheels, the noise and shouts of the truckmen and porters poured in through the workroom door. Overhead, through the ceiling, came the noise of footsteps and the clatter of dishes from the restaurant above.

In this cellar Mendel Greenspan, the owner of the work-room, had placed a row of sewing machines purchased on time payments. The machines were so constructed that they could be operated by foot pedals or by electric power. For the present, until Greenspan had enough money to equip a real shop and get enough orders, they were operated by foot pedals.

Before the twelve machines, each of them set below a naked electric bulb hanging from the low ceiling, sat twelve girls—Irish, Jewish, Italian—of whom Mary was now one. In addition to the machines there were long tables at which sat seven or eight finishers, hand workers. These were all middle-aged Jews, with grizzled beards and orthodox ear curls. Two sad-faced youths stood at ironing boards, in the midst of clouds of vapor raised by the hot irons on damp cloth.

Greenspan was a man in his thirties, with a carefully trimmed beard, artfully cropped so as to avoid the impression that he was one of the modern "pagan" Jews addicted to the use of the razor; in the trim of his sidelocks there was even the slight suggestion of the ear curls. He wore a skullcap. He stood at the long table and from paper patterns cut piles of cheap printed fabrics to be made into dresses. His meek-eyed wife, about the same age as himself and wearing a smock, worked on a bundle of garments at the head of the row of sewing machines and kept an eye on the girls to see that they labored with proper diligence.

The Greenspans, with their two children and Mrs. Greenspan's mother, lived in the two rooms that shut off the front end of the factory, thus blocking off the only windows leading onto the street below the restaurant.

Greenspan and his wife hardly slept or ate. He worked at the bench himself, and even found jobs to do for his old mother-in-law, and his two children, for all their tender years. He was acquainted with some pious Jews who frequented the same synagogue on the East Side. He talked it into them that at his shop they would be able to gather for the afternoon prayers without interruption—and on his time, too; that they would be able to wear their cherished skullcaps, and even be able to chant from the sacred Psalms as they worked—something they certainly wouldn't be able to do in a union shop. In this way, he exploited their piety by working them long hours and paying them starvation wages. He hired young, inexperienced girls forced by the desperate poverty in their homes to help contribute to the family larder. He convinced the girls that the union shops wouldn't take them in, and that, to get into the union, they'd have to pay enormous initiation fees.

He worked side by side with them, his wife, too, at one of the machines, and speeded up their work by putting before them the example of his own industry. He got up at dawn to prepare the work for the hands, and he sat at the bench until late at night—he, his wife, and often his mother-in-law—to finish the work the hands hadn't completed during the long day. He begrudged himself a single minute's rest, hastily gulping the food his mother-in-law would set beside him at the cutting table. It was as though he were saying to his employees: "How can you have the heart to take off to eat your lunch in peace when I, the boss, work until I'm ready to drop!"

When Mary came to the factory early on Monday morning Greenspan welcomed her with a broad smile.

"You're a good girl," he said, "to help out your family. I know your mother; she worked for us. Homework. Come, sit down here. They'll show you how it goes."

He had his own system for breaking in green hands. He sat Mary between two experienced operators, old employees in the shop, who knew how to make the foot pedals fly. One of them sewed one edge of a dress and handed it over to Mary to complete the other side. The operations had to dovetail so that the dress could be handed over to the finishers to complete.

"You'll catch on! You'll learn! In the beginning it's a little bit hard. You'll get used to it," Greenspan said to the embarrassed girl who in her inexperience was not able to drive the pedal as fast as the other two.

Mary was swimming in perspiration; her cheeks flushed with embarrassment, and although she had been used to operating a sewing machine at home at a fair speed, now her limbs seemed to be made of lead. She began to make clumsy blunders; the thread came out of the needle time after time. But Greenspan was patient.

"Don't worry! You'll do it! You'll be all right!"

And she did do it. She managed to catch up with the fast tempo and keep abreast of the others.

"You see!" Greenspan said. "I told you you could do it! You're a smart girl."

Greenspan left her side and went back to the cutting table.

But no sooner had Greenspan left them than the two girls at either side of Mary began to slow down. Now it was Mary who was finished with her part of the garment first. She caught a wink from the bright black eyes of the girl who sat at her right, and heard the quiet whisper: "Take it easy!"

Mary caught on and answered with a smile from her own dark eyes.

Now she found the tempo of the machine much easier and as natural as her handling of it at home.

Her feet were getting tired and her hands weary. The heavy footsteps and clatter from the restaurant above the shop hammered into her head. Her throat was suffocating from the smell of the fumes of frying lard which came down from the restaurant kitchen. But she stuck to the work. Gradually she got used to the constant thump of footsteps and the kitchen smells. Then at last it was time for lunch.

The old Jews in the shop had their lunch indoors. The girls went out into the courtyard, where some of them found seats on the tailboard of a truck, and opened up the packages of sandwiches they had brought along with them.

For Mary's first day at the factory, Grandma McCarthy had prepared a corned beef sandwich, of meat she had managed to save from the Sunday meal, with a bit of lettuce and spread with mayonnaise, the way Mary liked it. She had also given her a nickel for a cup of coffee, but Mary preferred to invest it in some ice cream.

On the way out of the shop, the girl who had advised Mary to take it easy came over.

"This is your first day here, isn't it?" she said. "Where do you come from?"

"I live on 48th Street. We know the boss. He used to give my mother work to take home."

"You know that this isn't a union shop."

"I couldn't help myself. This is the first place I ever worked. My family needs my wages."

"My parents, too. My father's in the hospital for two months already. They say that he needs an operation. Something to do with his stomach. I looked for work in a union shop, but I couldn't find a job. Besides, you have to work on Saturday in a union shop, and my parents are orthodox; they wouldn't let me work on Saturday. They said it's better to work even for less wages as long as you don't have to work on the Sabbath. That's why I'm working here. I had no choice. It's only for a while, anyway. I know the boss is taking advantage of us. He uses green hands—old orthodox Jews and inexperienced girls. We ought to get the union to organize the place. What's your name?"

Mary told her.

"My name is Sarah Lifschitz. Look, Mary, we ought to stick together. I already talked to the other girls. Some are willing, but the others are afraid. Will you stick with us?"

"Sure."

"Fine, Mary! Gee, I'd like to have you for a friend."

"Why not?" Mary said. Their eyes met in a warm glance. They broke into spontaneous laughter.

Mary had been working at Greenspan's shop for about two months. She and Sarah Lifschitz had become close friends. One day, as the two girls sat together eating lunch, Sarah said:

"Listen to this, Mary. The Triangle Waist Company on Washington Place is looking for girls to work on blouses. It's easy work, one of the girls who works there told me, because this season's styles are simple, not much fancy stuff. It's not a union shop, but even if you're a union member you can get in—you just don't have to tell them. The pay's wonderful, ten or twelve dollars a week, if you work from half-past seven in the morning to six. With overtime some of the girls make fourteen dollars a week, even though they don't pay extra rates for overtime. It's a big shop, and the working conditions are pretty good. I'm going to try to get a job there; I wouldn't mind earning more money; they need it at home. What do you say? Do you want to come with me?"

"Twelve dollars a week!" Mary could hardly believe it. "And fourteen with overtime! Sure I'll go with you. I'm sick of this place, with all the smells of that darned restaurant. And I can't stand working with all those old men. I'd like to work among a lot of girls in a real shop for a change, even though it would take longer to get all the way down there. I get up early, anyway. I have to make breakfast for my father— my grandma hasn't been feeling well lately and my mother's supposed to stay in bed as much as she can. I could use a few extra dollars. The kids at home are in rags; my mother can't patch Jimmy's pants any more. I'd like to earn some extra money and get some new clothes for the kids as a surprise for Easter."

A few days later both girls went over to the Triangle firm on Washington Place to ask about jobs. When they satisfied the foreman that they were experienced hands and didn't belong to the union, he took them on.

That evening Mary came home radiant. At last she would be working in a real shop. Besides she would be earning at least six dollars a week more than she was getting at Greenspan's; with some overtime she might even make as much as fourteen dollars a week.

The Triangle firm was housed in a modern building, practically a skyscraper, situated on the edge of the enormous open square in the heart of the city. The factory took up several floors of the building. The offices, showrooms, and cutting rooms were on the lower floors. On the ninth floor about two hundred and thirty girls and a few men worked at sewing machines. Other hands worked on the eighth floor. The tenth floor housed the finishers, cleaners, and examiners. Besides a large number of men, cutters and pressers, Triangle employed more than seven hundred girls.

Entrance and exit to the ninth floor were furnished by two doors, one opposite the other. One of them, the one giving on the stairway on the Washington Square side, was always kept locked. The other door opened on the corridor and elevator leading to Greene Street. This door was constantly guarded by a watchman who looked the girls over each time they left the shop. His beady eyes were like exploring, impudent fingers, making sure that a girl didn't have a blouse or a stray piece of material concealed under her dress or coat. Nor did he hesitate to paw them for a more thorough inspection. There was no other way for the girls to enter or leave the shop except through the door guarded by the watchman.

March twenty-fifth fell on a Saturday. Through the wide windows overlooking Washington Place the afternoon sky was snowladen and gloomy. The ninth floor bustled with activity. Rows of girls sat at the sewing machines, the electric bulbs gleaming over their bowed heads. The work was going on at full speed; all the girls were hurrying to get through with the day's work so as to get home as early as possible. Although Saturday was a full working day, the girls were permitted to leave an hour earlier if the day's quota was disposed of. Saturday was payday, another inducement to hurry; everyone had plans for the evening, to go visiting, to go shopping, to go to the movies or to a dance.

Mary and Sarah sat at adjoining machines. As they worked they chatted of their evening plans. The electricity-driven leather belts of the machines clattered so noisily they were barely able to hear one another.

Sarah was in an elated mood. This week she had managed to earn, with overtime, all of fourteen dollars, an enormous sum. Besides, she was going to a dance in the evening; Jack Klein, who worked in the factory, had invited her. Her problem was what to wear, the new evening dress she had bought with her increased earnings at Triangle, or her black skirt and waist; the waist was a Triangle number; she might even have worked on it herself.

"Gee, Sarah," Mary commented, "I love those new waists with the ribbon at the collar that we're making now. But I guess it's really a question of how interested you are in Jack. Do you want to look gorgeous—or just attractive?"

"Well, naturally, a girl wants to look gorgeous when a fellow takes her out to a dance for the first time," Sarah replied.

"In that case you better wear your evening dress. A girl looks more—more important in an evening dress. That's what the fellows like."

As they talked above the whirr of the machines a sudden quiet fell on the shop; even the machines sounded subdued. Something seemed to be happening at the far end of the room. Sarah stood up to see what was going on. Mary scrambled up beside her. They could see nothing.

"What is it?" Mary asked in sudden alarm.

"I don't know," Sarah answered.

All at once they saw puffs of thick smoke coming up between the cracks of the floor boards near the door leading to the elevator. Forked flames of fire followed the smoke. All the fright in the world broke out in a chorus of hysterical screams.

"Fire! Fire! Fire!"

Panic swept through the room. There was the noise of running feet, the clatter of chairs and stools being thrown over. The two girls began to run with the rest.

The running mob pushed them toward the exit door on the Greene Street side. It was near the door leading to the elevator that the flames were licking through the planks of the floor. They remembered that no stairway descended from the corridor. The elevator was the only exit. They would be trapped in the corridor by the flames. The smoke and fire coming through the floor near the door terrified them. The crowd veered and dashed to the other side of the loft, where the door led to the stairway that went down to Washington Place. Mary and Sarah, holding each other by the hand, ran with the rest.

They stumbled over chairs and upended stools. They were blocked by hysterical girls who were too terrified to move. Sarah and Mary tried to drag some of them along with them. Here and there tongues of fire were coming up through the floor. Around the sewing machines the heaps of remnants of material and trimmings, silks, linings padded cotton, the oil-soaked rags which the girls used to clean the machines after oiling them, blazed into flame. The oil-soaked rags were the first to catch fire, setting alight the piles of cuttings and feeding the flames from one machine to the next. The grease-covered machines themselves began to blaze together with the piles of material on them. The fire grew in volume by the minute. It spread like a stream overflowing its banks. The waves of living flame licked at the skirts of the fleeing, screaming, trapped girls.

Barely had they escaped through the corridor of flame between the rows of machines when they were blocked by a wall of smoke which rose up from the large stacks of finished blouses. With the smoke came a suffocating odor. The smoke arose to the ceiling, where it hung like a cloud. They began to suffocate, gagging and choking. Her eyes blinded and her throat gasping, Sarah dragged Mary along. The door, when they reached it, was blocked with a mass of bodies. Hair loosed, clothing torn, the mob pulled and tore at each other in panicked attempts to get to the door. From the packed mass of bodies came a high-pitched keening, a hysterical yammering.

Those nearest the door were jammed against it, beating at it with their fists, tearing at it with their fingers, clawing at it with their nails. Some, in an ecstasy of terror, beat against it with their heads. The door did not budge.

The press around the door grew thicker. Sarah and Mary, midway in the mob, were held immovable and helpless in the tightly pressed crush of girls' bodies.

Some of the cooler heads among them tried to shout out advice to those nearest the door. Their shouts were lost in the hysterical shrieks of the terrified girls. Someone, more resourceful, managed to pass the metal head of a sewing machine over the struggling mob to the girls at the door. One of them began to beat the door frantically with the heavy metal head. The door did not yield.

The press of bodies was now an immovable mass. Sarah and Mary saw themselves hopelessly hemmed in. Sarah kept her senses. Unless they got out of the packed crowd around the door they were lost. She could see the tongues of flame coming closer and closer. With an energy born of desperation she grabbed Mary by the arm and began to drag her after her. With heads, shoulders, feet, and arms they managed to force their way through the mass of bodies and away from the door. Biting, scratching, tearing and clawing at arms, bodies, and legs, Sarah, half crawling, pulled Mary along after her, until they reached the outer edge of the crush.

Desperately Sarah looked around. Half of the floor was in flames, and the flames were coming toward them. The space near the windows which overlooked Washington Place was still untouched. In front of the windows frantic girls were weaving, clutching at the window sills, desperately trying to find some way of escape.

Near one of the windows the flames were coming closer. Here only a few girls were gathered. If there was any escape it would have to be through this window, the thought flashed through Sarah's mind. They would have to get through it before the flames reached it. She began to drag Mary toward the window. Mary showed no resistance. She was only half conscious. She let the other do what she willed.

The window was nailed down. It resisted all Sarah's efforts to open it. There was a small, jagged break in the pane, stained with blood about the edges; others had tried to shatter the glass. Sarah banged her clenched fist against the glass again and again and made the opening larger.

When the opening was big enough she put her head through. On the street below she could see crowds of people. She could see firemen holding safety nets to catch the girls who dropped from the openings in other windows. From the crowd came frantic shouts. The wails of the girls answered them. The firemen made unavailing attempts to raise too-short ladders to the upper floors. One girl after another dropped from the windows. Sarah looked to see if there was a ledge below the window which she might be able to reach with her toes. Outside the eighth floor window there was a small iron balcony. It might be possible to reach that, and from there to the balcony outside the seventh floor window, and so on down to safety.

She turned to Mary. "Quick, crawl through to the window ledge!"

"I'm afraid. . . ."

"Quick! Come on! Here, through the broken glass."

"I can't! I can't! What will I hold on to?"

"I'll hold your arms. Try to get your toes on the iron balcony down there. Look, the other girls are doing it."

"You go first, Sarah."

"No, I'm stronger than you. I'll be able to hold on to you. You're too weak to hold on to me. I'll come after you. Go ahead!"

The flames came closer. Urged on by Sarah and driven by the terrifying spectacle of the approaching tongues of flame, Mary scrambled onto the sill, and, with her back to the street, managed to get her legs through the hole in the window, holding on frantically to Sarah's shoulders. She gashed her knee on the jagged edges of the glass but never felt the pain. Holding tightly to Sarah, she groped for some projecting ledge to support her. Except for the balconies outside the line of windows below her, the wall fell sheer. But the balcony was too far down; she couldn't reach it. Sarah, holding Mary firmly by the arms, reached out of the window as far as she dared, trying to lower her as close as possible to the balcony. It was still too far to be reached.

Yells came up to Mary's ears from the street, but she could not understand what they were shouting. Only one thought possessed her, how to get a toehold on the iron balcony below. She still gripped Sarah's arms in an iron clutch. Sarah managed to shift her hold so as to grab Mary by both hands, thus lowering her body farther down. Mary strained to reach the balcony; still it was no use. Sarah strained even farther out of the window; she was now halfway out of the jagged opening. The sharp edges of the broken glass cut into her arms and chest. As Mary strained with her feet to find a hold, the jagged edges cut deeper and deeper into Sarah's flesh. She felt the edges going into her, but she felt no pain. There was only the one overwhelming urge—to lower Mary closer to the balcony. She strained farther out. Suddenly she felt a fierce wave of heat licking at her legs. The anguish was so intense, the instinct for self-preservation so compelling, that all thoughts of Mary disappeared from her mind. She couldn't withdraw her body into the room to face the enemy that was attacking her. But she knew what the enemy was. The flames were licking at her stockings. In another moment her dress would be on fire.

"Mama!" she screamed hysterically. Her body went farther out through the window. The broken edges of the jagged glass tore at her flesh.

With the tips of her toes Mary could feel the balcony under her feet. The faint hint of safety only served to heighten her terror. Through the mist of consciousness left to her Sarah saw that Mary could now find a footing. "Just a little more. Just a little more," she thought. She could feel herself moving farther forward. She could feel the flames licking up from her shoes, climbing her legs. Then she could feel nothing. If only she could lean out a little more, Mary would reach the balcony. She dare not let go of Mary's hands. She was no longer herself. She no longer existed. She had become a part of Mary. She was only an instrument to help her reach the balcony. . . . Now she could reach it. Sarah threw the upper half of her body violently forward. Mary felt below her feet the firm surface of the balcony. Her hands, suddenly released, clutched at the bare sides of the building. Above her, out of the shattered window, a flaming body fell, like a living torch, down to the street below.

Mary knew that flaming torch. She opened her mouth to shriek Sarah's name. In her pain and terror no sound came from her lips. Now the single thought of escape obsessed her. From the window outside of which she stood, a wave of blasting heat came to her from the roaring flames inside.

She threw a terrified glance to the street below. It was so far away that it seemed to her that it must be a distant, unattainable world. The area immediately below her was an empty expanse. The crowds had been herded away by lines of police; there were only the firemen and firefighting apparatus. She could see safety nets held out spread by groups of firemen. She could see bodies falling from the walls of the building with hair and clothing aflame. She could hear voices calling to her; she did not know what they were shouting. She looked around her at the other windows of the building. She could see girls crawling through the windows on hands and knees, trying frantically to hold on to the bare walls. Others seemed to be hanging in mid-air, their falling bodies caught by projecting cornices.

The second that she remained crouched on the balcony seemed like an eternity. Angry flames were shooting out through the window, licking at her. She was alone now; there was no Sarah holding on to her hands. Her consciousness and resourcefulness began to function; she would have to depend on her own initiative now. Driven more by fear of the flames that licked at her from the window than by any considered design, she held on to the iron rail of the balcony and let her body down. Her feet swung in the air; she hadn't looked first to see whether she could reach the landing below. She was afraid to let go of the rail. Her feet sought for a foothold; they found none; the wall was smooth and unbroken. Again and again her toes sought out a niche in the wall, but they found only a sheer surface. Her hands were getting weak, she would have to let go the iron rail; it was hot from the flames which were shooting farther and farther through the window. The palms of her hands burned. She could feel her fingers relaxing. She would let herself go, like the others, to fall into the safety net—or to crash onto the sidewalk.

She couldn't summon up the courage to let go. But she knew if she didn't let go herself, her fingers would slip from the rail and she would fall onto the sidewalk. She must jump. She must try to jump to the nets spread below. Her lips kept murmuring "Jesus, Christ, Jesus, Mary." She closed her eyes for a second. She saw before her the carved wooden figure of Jesus to which she prayed in the Italian church. She knelt before it and prayed her familiar prayer. "Sweet Jesus, save me." As her lips murmured the words her fingers let go their clutch on the iron balcony rail and her body fell.

She did not fall to the ground. Her dress caught on the iron bar of a sign extending outside the third floor window. In the second that she remained suspended, strong arms reached out of the window and pulled her in.

For three weeks Mary was kept at the hospital. By the end of that time her gashed knee had healed. Also her shattered nerves.

More than one hundred and fifty girls had lost their lives in the fire. They were buried at mass funerals; the Jewish girls in the Jewish cemeteries, the Christian girls in Christian cemeteries. The survivors soon began to search for work in other factories. The wave of excitement and anger that swept through the city and all through the country didn't last very long. A commission was appointed to investigate fire hazards in the state's garment factories. Some bills were introduced into the Assembly. There were heated debates; some measures were adopted, others were defeated. When it was all over, everything in the needle industries remained the same.

The McCarthy family had become accustomed to Mary's contributions to the household; now they found it impossible to manage on the reduced scale. Patrick McCarthy renewed his old, endless arguments. Although most of the victims were Jewish girls, only a few Gentile girls having been killed, McCarthy blamed the fire and everything about it on the Jews. He swore he would not allow Mary to go back to work, but he soon began to drown his troubles in drink—with the help of the rent money to which Mary had so substantially contributed in the weeks past. After she had been out of the hospital for about two weeks, the McCarthy larder was so empty that Mary had to go out looking for a job.

She found work in a factory whose owner assured her it was fireproof. McCarthy made a show of protesting, but, like the rest of the family, he knew well enough what Mary's earnings meant. Since she had been working he had been able to go more often to the rent money in the bowl in the cupboard with less pangs of conscience.

"Fire or no fire," Grandma McCarthy said, "the world has to go on about its business. Coal miners go back to the pit after a mine disaster."

They all had to agree with her.

One vivid vision remained in Mary's memory: Sarah's terrified eyes staring from below her flaming hair.

JOHN REED

(1887–1920)

Even Warren Beatty's Hollywood version of John Reed, the movie Reds, *could hardly romanticize more than the reality a life devoted at first to experiment and risk, but finally to serious radical politics on behalf of the most oppressed workers, peons, and serfs of the United States, Mexico, and Russia. Serious enough, indeed, that Reed sacrificed his robust health to the cause, died for it, and was buried as a revolutionary martyr in the wall of the Kremlin.*

Reed was a child of privilege: his grandparents' house in Portland, Oregon, was modeled on a French château and had tame deer wandering among the trees and gardens. Educated primarily at home, where he was a passionate reader, he also attended prep school in Morristown, New Jersey. At Harvard, he wrote for the Advocate *and the* Lampoon, *managed musical clubs, captained the water polo team, edited two college newspapers, and engaged in an awesome set of other activities from leading fight songs at football games to participating in an undergraduate insurgency against Harvard's eastern student aristocracy.*

Shortly after graduation, he settled in Greenwich Village, moving in Bohemian and radical circles, writing for the left-wing magazine Masses *and working for the* American Magazine, *engaging in love affairs, and becoming interested in the Industrial Workers of the World, the "Wobblies." With others, he visited the picket lines of the great Wobbly-led strike of silk workers in Paterson, New Jersey, where some twenty-five hundred workers had been arrested. Observing the picket line, Reed, too, was detained and spent four days in jail. There he learned from the primarily immigrant workers about the misery of their jobs and lives and determined to take a role in supporting them. Introduced at a strike meeting by Wobbly leader Big Bill Haywood, Reed led some twenty-three thousand strikers in a fight song. He then helped organize a moving pageant of the strikers' lives at Madison Square Garden, one of the more famous episodes in radical labor history.*

After a brief period of R&R in Europe, Reed was asked to report on the Mexican revolution for the Metropolitan *magazine, increasingly sympathetic to progressive causes, and for Pulitzer's New York World. In Mexico, he rode with Pancho Villa's guerrillas, ate and sang with them, faced bullets and desert hardships with them. He came to see their cause as his: they were underdogs, fighting for land and freedom against the same kind of forces he had come to hate in Paterson. He wrote about them passionately and energetically, trying to defend the Mexican revolution from its domestic opponents as well as from U.S. intervention. His book,* Insurgent Mexico *(1914), presented a new form of journalism: fervent, personal, committed. And while some mocked it as the enthusiasms of a playboy, it marked a new stage in Reed's development as a writer and as a political activist.*

With the outbreak of World War I, Reed was sent as a correspondent to Europe. His book, The War in Eastern Europe *(1916), lacked something of the personal involvement of his earlier work. But when the Russian revolution broke out, he hurried to St. Petersburg in time to observe the seizure of power by the Bolsheviks. There he watched events, joined in some, interviewed leaders, studied documents, and threw himself into what he recognized as a world-altering moment. Back in the United States, he rapidly wrote what has become a classic description of revolution,* Ten Days that Shook the World *(1919).*

Then he threw himself into the organization of what would become the American Communist party, struggling for what he believed to be the correct politics—that is, organizing workers along the industrial lines advocated by the IWW—to bring in a revolutionary future. He traveled back to Russia to pursue these politics and to contribute what he could to the ongoing revolutionary struggle there. Contracting typhus in Baku, where he had gone to speak at a conference, and exhausted by earlier efforts to support the Bolshevik cause, Reed died at age 33.

WAR IN PATERSON

There's war in Paterson, New Jersey. But it's a curious kind of war. All the violence is the work of one side—the mill owners. Their servants, the police, club unresisting men and women and ride down law-abiding crowds on horseback. Their paid mercenaries, the armed detectives, shoot and kill innocent people. Their newspapers, the Paterson *Press* and the Paterson *Call*, publish incendiary and crime-inciting appeals to mob violence against the strike leaders. Their tool, Recorder Carroll, deals out heavy sentences to peaceful pickets that the police net gathers up. They control absolutely the police, the press, the courts.

Opposing them are about twenty-five thousand striking silk workers, of whom perhaps ten thousand are active, and their weapon is the picket line. Let me tell you what I saw in Paterson and then you will say which side of this struggle is "anarchistic" and "contrary to American ideals."

At six o'clock in the morning a light rain was falling. Slate-gray and cold, the streets of Paterson were deserted. But soon came the cops—twenty of them—strolling along with their nightsticks under their arms. We went ahead of them toward the mill district. Now we began to see workmen going in the same direction, coat collars turned up, hands in their pockets. We came into a long street, one side of which was lined with silk mills, the other side with the wooden tenement houses. In every doorway, at every window of the houses clustered men and women, laughing and chatting as if after breakfast on a holiday. There seemed no sense of expectancy, no strain or feeling of fear. The sidewalks were almost empty, only over in front of the mills a few couples—there couldn't have been more than fifty—marched slowly up and down, dripping with the rain. Some were men, with here and there a man and woman together, or two young boys. As the warmer light of full day came the people drifted out of their houses and began to pace back and forth, gathering in little knots on the corners. They were quick with gesticulating hands, and low-voiced conversation. They looked often toward the corners of side streets.

Suddenly appeared a policeman, swinging his club. "Ah-h-h!" said the crowd softly.

Six men had taken shelter from the rain under the canopy of a saloon. "Come on! Get out of that!" yelled the policeman, advancing. The men quietly obeyed. "Get off this street! Go on home, now! Don't be standing here!" They gave way before him in silence, drifting back again when he turned away. Other policemen materialized, hustling, cursing, brutal, ineffectual. No one answered back. Nervous, bleary-eyed, unshaven, these officers were worn out with nine weeks incessant strike duty.

On the mill side of the street the picket line had grown to about four hundred. Several policemen shouldered roughly among them, looking for trouble. A workman appeared, with a tin pail, escorted by two detectives. "Boo! Boo!" shouted a few scattered voices. Two Italian boys leaned against the mill fence and shouted a merry Irish threat, "Scab! Come outa here I knock your head off!" A policeman grabbed the boys roughly by the shoulder. "Get to hell out of here!" he cried, jerking and pushing them violently to the corner, where he kicked them. Not a voice, not a movement from the crowd.

A little further along the street we saw a young woman with an umbrella, who had been picketing, suddenly confronted by a big policeman.

"What the hell are *you* doing here?" he roared. "God damn you, you go home!" and he jammed his club against her mouth. "I *no* go home!" she shrilled passionately, with blazing eyes. "You big stiff!"

Silently, steadfastly, solidly the picket line grew. In groups or in couples the strikers patrolled the sidewalk. There was no more laughing. They looked on with eyes full of hate. These were fiery Italians, and the police were the same brutal thugs that had beaten them and insulted them for nine weeks. I wondered how long they could stand it.

It began to rain heavily. I asked a man's permission to stand on the porch of his house. There was a policeman standing in front of it. His name, I afterwards discovered, was McCormack. I had to walk around him to mount the steps.

Suddenly he turned round, and shot at the owner: "Do all them fellows live in that house?" The man indicated the three other strikers and himself, and shook his head at me.

"Then you get to hell off of there!" said the cop, pointing his club at me.

"I have the permission of this gentleman to stand here," I said. "He owns this house."

"Never mind! Do what I tell you! Come off of there, and come off damn quick!"

"I'll do nothing of the sort."

With that he leaped up the steps, seized my arm, and violently jerked me to the sidewalk. Another cop took my arm and they gave me a shove.

"Now you get to hell off this street!" said Officer McCormack.

"I won't get off this street or any other street. If I'm breaking any law, you arrest me!"

Officer McCormack was dreadfully troubled by my request. He didn't want to arrest me, and said so with a great deal of profanity.

"I've *got* your number," said I sweetly. "Now will you tell me your name?"

"Yes," he bellowed, "an' I got *your* number! I'll arrest you." He took me by the arm and marched me up the street.

He was sorry he *had* arrested me. There was no charge he could lodge against me. I hadn't been doing anything. He felt he must make me say something that could be construed as a violation of the law. To which end he God-damned me harshly, loading me with abuse and obscenity, and threatened me with his night stick, saying, "You big——lug, I'd like to beat the hell out of you with this club."

I returned airy persiflage to his threats.

Other officers came to the rescue, two of them, and supplied fresh epithets. I soon found them repeating themselves, however, and told them so. "I had to come all the way to Paterson to put one over on a cop!" I said. Eureka! They had at last found a crime! When I was arraigned in the Recorder's Court that remark of mine was the charge against me!

Ushered into the patrol wagon, I was driven with much clanging of gongs along the picket line. Our passage was greeted with "Boos" and ironical cheers, and enthusiastic waving. At headquarters I was interrogated and lodged in the lockup. My cell was about four feet wide by seven feet long, at least a foot higher than a standing man's head, and it contained an iron bunk hung from the side-wall with chains, and an open toilet of disgusting dirtiness in the corner. A crowd of pickets had been jammed into the same lockup only three days before, *eight or nine in a cell,* and kept there without food or water for *twenty-two hours!* Among them a young girl of seventeen, who had led a procession right up to the police sergeant's nose and defied him to arrest them. In spite of the horrible discomfort, fatigue and thirst, these prisoners had *never let up cheering and singing* for a day and a night!

In about an hour the outside door clanged open, and in came about forty pickets in charge of the police, joking and laughing among themselves. They were hustled into the cells, two in each. Then pandemonium broke loose! With one accord the heavy iron beds were lifted and slammed thunderingly against the metal walls. It was like a cannon battery in action.

"Hooray for I.W.W.!" screamed a voice. And unanimously answered all the voices as one, "Hooray!"

"Hooray for Chief Bums!" (Chief of Police Bimson).

"Boo-o-o-!" roared forty pairs of lungs—a great boom of echoing sound that had more of hate in it than anything I ever heard.

"To hell with Mayor McBride!"

"Boo-o-o-!" It was an awful voice in that reverberant iron room, full of menace.

"Hooray for Haywood! One big Union! Hooray for strike! To hell with the police! Boo-o-o-o! Boo-o-o-o! Hooray!"

"Music! Music!" cried the Italians. Whereupon one voice went "Plunk-plunk! Plunk-plunk!" like a guitar, and another, a rich tenor, burst into the first verse of the

Italian-English song, written and composed by one of the strikers to be sung at the strike meetings. He came to the chorus:

> Do you like Miss Flynn?
> (Chorus) Yes! Yes! Yes! Yes!
> Do you like Mayor McBride?
> (Chorus) No! No! NO! NO!!!
> Hooray for I.W.W.!
> Hooray! Hooray!! Hooray!!!

"Bis! Bis!" shouted everybody, clapping hands, banging the beds up and down. An officer came in and attempted to quell the noise. He was met with "Boos" and jeers. Some one called for water. The policeman filled a tin cup and brought it to the cell door. A hand reached out swiftly and slapped it out of his fingers on the floor. "Scab! Thug!" they yelled. The policeman retreated. The noise continued.

The time approached for the opening of the Recorder's Court, but word had evidently been brought that there was no more room in the county jail, for suddenly the police appeared and began to open the cell doors. And so the strikers passed out, cheering wildly. I could hear them outside, marching back to the picket line with the mob which had waited for them at the jail gates.

And then I was taken before the court of Recorder Carroll. Mr. Carroll has the intelligent, cruel, merciless face of the ordinary police court magistrate. But he is worse than most police court magistrates. He sentences beggars to *six months' imprisonment* in the county jail without a chance to answer back. He also sends little children there, where they mingle with dopefiends, and tramps, and men with running sores upon their bodies—to the county jail, where the air is foul and insufficient to breathe, and the food is full of dead vermin, and grown men become insane.

Mr. Carroll read the charge against me. I was permitted to tell my story. Officer McCormack recited a clever *mélange* of lies that I am sure he himself could never have concocted. "John Reed," said the Recorder. "Twenty days." That was all.

And so it was that I went up to the county jail. In the outer office I was questioned again, searched for concealed weapons, and my money and valuables taken away. Then the great barred door swung open and I went down some steps into a vast room lined with three tiers of cells. About eighty prisoners strolled around, talked, smoked, and ate the food sent in to them by those outside. Of this eighty almost half were strikers. They were in their street clothes, held in prison under 500 dollar bail to await the action of the Grand Jury. Surrounded by a dense crowd of short, dark-faced men, Big Bill Haywood towered in the center of the room. His big hand made simple gestures as he explained something to them. His massive, rugged face, seamed and scarred like a mountain, and as calm, radiated strength. These strikers, one of many desperate little armies in the vanguard of the battle-line of labor, quickened and strengthened by Bill Haywood's face and voice, looked up at him lovingly, eloquently. Faces deadened and dulled with grinding routine in the sunless mills glowed with hope and understanding. Faces scarred and bruised from policemen's clubs grinned eagerly at the thought of going back on the picket line. And there were other faces, too—lined and sunken with the slow starvation of a nine weeks' poverty—shadowed with the sight of so much suffering, or the hopeless brutality of the police. But not one showed discouragement; not one a sign of faltering or of fear. As one little Italian said to me, with blazing eyes: "We all one big Union. I.W.W.—the word is pierced in the heart of the people!"

"Yes! Yes! right! I.W.W.! One big Union"—they murmured with soft, eager voices, crowding around.

I shook hands with Haywood.

"Boys," said Haywood, indicating me, "this man wants to *know* things. You tell him everything—"

They crowded around me, shaking my hand, smiling, welcoming me. "Too bad you get in jail," they said, sympathetically. "We tell you everything. You ask. We tell you. Yes. Yes. You good feller."

And they did. Most of them were still weak and exhausted from their terrible night before in the lockup. Some had been lined up against a wall, as they marched to and fro in front of the mills, and herded to jail on the charge of "unlawful assemblage!" Others had been clubbed into the patrol wagon on the charge of "rioting," as they stood at the track, on their way home from picketing, waiting for a train to pass! They were being held for the Grand Jury that indicted Haywood and Gurley Flynn. *Four of these jurymen were silk manufacturers, another the head of the local Edison company—which Haywood tried to organize for a strike—and not one for a workingman!*

"We not take bail," said another, shaking his head. "We stay here. Fill up the damn jail. Pretty soon no more room. Pretty soon can't arrest no more pickets!"

It was visitors' day. I went to the door to speak with a friend. Outside the reception room was full of women and children, carrying packages, and pasteboard boxes, and pails full of dainties and little comforts lovingly prepared, which meant hungry and ragged wives and babies, so that the men might be comfortable in jail. The place was full of the sound of moaning; tears ran down their work-roughened faces; the children looked up at their fathers' unshaven faces through the bars and tried to reach them with their hands. . . .

The keeper ordered me to the "convicted room," where I was pushed into a bath and compelled to put on regulation prison clothes. I shan't attempt to describe the horrors I saw in that room. Suffice it to say that forty-odd men lounged about a long corridor lined on one side with cells; that the only ventilation and light came from one small skylight up a funnel-shaped airshaft; that one man had syphilitic sores on his legs and was treated by the prison doctor with sugar-pills for "nervousness"; that a seventeen-year-old boy *who had never been sentenced* had remained in that corridor without ever seeing the sun for over *nine months*; that a cocaine fiend was getting his "dope" regularly from the inside, and that the background of this and much more was the monotonous and terrible shouting of a man who had lost his mind in that hell-hole and who walked among us.

There were about fourteen strikers in the "convicted" room—Italians, Lithuanians, Poles, Jews, one Frenchman and one "free-born" Englishman! That Englishman was a peach. He was the only Anglo-Saxon striker in prison except the leaders—and perhaps the only one who *had been* there for picketing. He had been sentenced for insulting a mill owner who came out of his mill and ordered him off the sidewalk. "Wait till I get out," he said to me. "If them damned English-speaking workers don't go on picket *I'll* put the curse o' Cromwell on 'em!"

Then there was a Pole—an aristocratic, sensitive chap, a member of the local strike committee, a born fighter. He was reading Bob Ingersoll's lectures, translating them to the others. Patting the book, he said with a slow smile: "Now I don't care if I stay in here one year. . . ."

With laughter, the strikers told me how the combined clergy of the city of Paterson had attempted from their pulpits to persuade them back to work—back to wage-slavery and the tender mercies of the mill owners on grounds of religion! They told me of that disgraceful and ridiculous conference between the clergy and the strike committee, with the clergy in the part of Judas. It was hard to believe that until I saw in the paper the sermon delivered the previous day at the Presbyterian Church by the Reverend William A. Littell. He had the impudence to flay the strike leaders and advise workmen to be respectful and obedient to their employers—to tell them that the saloons were the cause of their unhappiness—to proclaim the horrible depravity of Sabbath-breaking workmen and more rot of the same sort. And this while living men were fighting for their very existence and singing gloriously of the Brotherhood of Man! . . .

Then there was the strikebreaker. He was a fat man, with sunken, flabby cheeks, jailed by some mistake of the Recorder. So completely did the strikers ostracize him—rising and moving away when he sat by them, refusing to speak to him, absolutely ignoring his presence—that he was in a pitiable condition of loneliness.

"I've learned my lesson," he moaned. "I ain't never goin' to scab on workingmen no more!"

One young Italian came up to me with a newspaper and pointed to three items in turn. One was "American Federation of Labor hopes to break the strike next week," another, "Victor Berger says 'I am a member of the A. F. of L., and I have no love for the I.W.W. in Paterson,'" and the third, "Newark Socialists refuse to help the Paterson strikers."

"I no understand," he told me, looking up at me appealingly. "You tell me. I Socialist—I belong union—I strike with I.W.W. Socialist, he say, 'Workmen of the world, unite!' A. F. of L., he say, 'All workmen join together.' Both these organizations, he say, 'I am for the working class.' All right, I say, I am the working class. I unite, I strike. Then he say, 'No! You *cannot* strike.' What that? I no understand. You explain me."

But I could not explain. All I could say was that a good share of the Socialist Party and the American Federation of Labor have forgotten all about the class struggle, and seem to be playing a little game with capitalistic rules, called "Button, button, who's got the vote!"

When it came time for me to go out I said good-bye to all those gentle, alert, brave men, ennobled by something greater than themselves. *They* were the strike— not Bill Haywood, not Gurley Flynn, not any other individual. And if they should lose all their leaders other leaders would arise from the ranks, even as *they* rose, and the strike would go on! Think of it! Twelve years they have been losing strikes—twelve solid years of disappointments and incalculable suffering. They must not lose again! They cannot lose!

And as I passed out through the front room they crowded around me again, patting my sleeve and my hand, friendly, warm-hearted, trusting, eloquent. Haywood had gone out on bail.

"You go out," they said softly. "That's nice. Glad you go out. Pretty soon we go out. Then we go back on picket line."

-1913

MIKE GOLD

(1893-1967)

Mike Gold is probably known for two things: his novel, sometimes taken for autobiography, Jews Without Money *(1930), and his polemical writings, particularly about the relations between politics and literature. Regarding the latter, no American contributed more to the conception of "proletarian literature," the idea that revolutionary writing should, could, and would be produced by workers determined to give direct expression to their experiences and aspirations. He described the proletarian writer he saw, or hoped to see, emerging in America in these memorable and ambiguous terms:*

> *[He is] a wild youth of about twenty-two, the son of working-class parents, who himself works in the lumber camps, coal mines, steel mills, harvest fields and mountain camps of America. He is sensitive and impatient. He writes in jets of exasperated feeling and has no time to polish his work. He is violent and sentimental by turns. He lacks self-confidence but writes because he must—and because he has real talent.*

To be sure, Gold's is an extraordinarily masculinist and romantic conception both of the working class and of its writers, himself included. But as was usual with him, he is deeply engaged in a conflict with those, like Leon Trotsky, for example, who believed it was necessary for working people first to learn the traditional culture of bourgeois society before they might produce meaningful new art of their own. These were positions strongly held and powerfully argued in the first days of the Soviet Union and, reflexively, among 1920s leftists in the United States and elsewhere in Europe.

Jews Without Money *was seen as exemplifying precisely the virtues of "proletarian fiction" Gold had extolled. It does in certain respects. And appearing, as it did, just as the boom times of the 1920s collapsed into the Great Depression of the 1930s, it seemed to offer a model for the aspiring working-class writer who would become active in the John Reed Clubs organized by the Communist party in the early 1930s. But there are a couple of discrepancies. The novel narrates primarily the experiences of immigrant Jews of the turn-of-the-century period; it promotes rather more the virtues of the narrator's mother than those of a revolutionary proletariat. And while the origins of the narrator, Mickey, are portrayed as working class, Gold's own were not . . . precisely. He was actually the son of a small-time Jewish entrepreneur in New York's Lower East Side ghetto, who seldom made more than his workers. Moreover, Itzok Isaac Granich's (for that was what the writer had been named) initial argument with America had as much to do with his disappointment in never being able to pursue his education as with capitalism, per se.*

But no matter, by the time he was twenty-one, Irwin Granich, the Mike Gold to be, had discovered the bohemian radical scene of Greenwich Village and had begun writing columns for the Masses *magazine and plays for the Provincetown Theatre. Through the flush twenties, Gold edited and wrote for the San Francisco* Call *and for left-wing magazines like* The Liberator *and the*

New Masses, *wrote and produced plays on radical themes, and struggled to develop the nascent Communist party. With the financial crash of 1929, the success of* Jews Without Money, *the impact of his widely read attack on the politics and prose of Thornton Wilder, and the leadership role played by the Communist party in protesting the economic disaster of capitalism, Gold became a critical figure in left-wing literary circles. Beginning in 1933 and continuing for over thirty years, he wrote a daily column for the CP's newspaper,* The Daily Worker, *but never again a novel or play. His editor and biographer, Mike Folsom, suggested that through his columns, Gold made more enemies than any writer of his time. That may well be, but for his avid readers, even those who did not fully share his politics, he provided expression for their rage at injustice, their laughter at bourgeois pomposity, and their hopes for a transformed nation where, as Gold had written early in his career, "in every American factory there is a drama-group of the workers, [a time] when mechanics paint in their leisure, and farmers write sonnets. . . ."*

from Jews Without Money

The Soul of a Landlord

1

On the East Side people buy their groceries a pinch at a time; three cents' worth of sugar, five cents' worth of butter, everything in penny fractions. The good Jewish black bread that smells of harvest time, is sliced into a dozen parts and sold for pennies. But that winter even pennies were scarce.

There was a panic on Wall Street. Multitudes were without work; there were strikes, suicides, and food riots. The prostitutes roamed our street like wolves; never was there so much competition among them.

Life froze. The sun vanished from the deathly gray sky. The streets reeked with snow and slush. There were hundreds of evictions. I walked down a street between dripping tenement walls. The rotten slush ate through my shoes. The wind beat on my face. I saw a stack of furniture before a tenement: tables, chairs, a washtub packed with crockery and bedclothes, a broom, a dresser, a lamp.

The snow covered them. The snow fell, too, on a little Jew and his wife and three children. They huddled in a mournful group by their possessions. They had placed a saucer on one of the tables. An old woman with a market bag mumbled a prayer in passing. She dropped a penny in the saucer. Other people did the same. Each time the evicted family lowered its eyes in shame. They were not beggars, but "respectable" people. But if enough pennies fell in the saucer, they might have rent for a new home. This was the one hope left them.

Winter. Building a snow fort one morning, we boys dug out a litter of frozen kittens and their mother. The little ones were still blind. They had been born into it, but had never seen our world.

Other dogs and cats were frozen. Men and women, too, were found dead in hallways and on docks. Mary Sugar Bum met her end in an alley. She was found half-naked, clutching a whiskey bottle in her blue claw. This was her last "love" affair.

Horses slipped on the icy pavement, and quivered there for hours with broken legs, until a policeman arrived to shoot them.

The boys built a snow man. His eyes were two coals; his nose a potato. He wore a derby hat and smoked a corncob pipe. His arms were flung wide; in one of them he held a broom, in the other a newspaper. This Golem with his amazed eyes and idiotic grin amused us all for an afternoon.

The next morning we found him strangely altered. His eyes and nose had been torn out; his grin smashed, like a war victim's. Who had played this joke? The winter wind.

2

Mrs. Rosenbaum owned a grocery store on our street. She was a widow with four children, and lived in two rooms back of the store. She slaved from dawn until midnight; a big, clumsy woman with a chapped face and masses of untidy hair; always grumbling, groaning, gossiping about her ailments. Sometimes she was nervous and screamed at her children, and beat them. But she was a kind-hearted woman, and that winter suffered a great deal. Every one was very poor, and she was too good not to give them groceries on credit.

"I'm crazy to do it!" she grumbled in her icy store. "I'm a fool! But when a child comes for a loaf of bread, and I have the bread, and I know her family is starving, how can I refuse her? Yet I have my own children to think of! I am being ruined! The store is being emptied! I can't meet my bills!"

She was kind. Kindness is a form of suicide in a world based on the law of competition.

One day we watched the rewards of kindness. The sheriff's men arrived to seize Mrs. Rosenbaum's grocery. They tore down the shelves and fixtures, they carted off tubs of butter, drums of kerosene, sacks of rice, flour and potatoes.

Mrs. Rosenbaum stood by watching her own funeral. Her fat kind face was swollen with crying as with toothache. Her eyes blinked in bewilderment. Her children clung to her skirts and cried. Snow fell from the sky, a crowd muttered its sympathy, a policeman twirled his club.

What happened to her after that, I don't know. Maybe the Organized Charities helped her; or maybe she died. O golden dyspeptic God of America, you were in a bad mood that winter. We were poor, and you punished us harshly for this worst of sins.

3

My father lay in bed. His shattered feet ached in each bone. His painter's sickness came back on him; he suffered with lung and kidney pains.

He was always depressed. His only distraction was to read the Yiddish newspapers, and to make gloomy conversation at night over the suicides, the hungry families, the robberies, murders and catastrophes that newspapers record.

"It will come to an end!" said my father. "People are turning into wolves! They will soon eat each other! They will tear down the cities, and destroy the world in flames and blood!"

"Drink your tea," said my mother cheerfully, "God is still in the world. You will get better and work and laugh again. Let us not lose courage."

My father was fretful and nervous with an invalid's fears.

"But what if we are evicted, Katie?"

"We won't be evicted, not while I have my two hands and can work," said my mother.

"But I don't want you to work!" my father cried. "It breaks up our home!"

"It doesn't!" said my mother. "I have time and strength for everything."

4

At first my mother had feared going out to work in a cafeteria among Christians. But after a few days she settled easily into the life of the polyglot kitchen, and learned to fight, scold, and mother the Poles, Germans, Italians, Irish and Negroes who worked there. They liked her, and soon called her "Momma," which made her vain.

"You should hear how a big black dishwasher named Joe, how he comes to me to-day, and says, 'Momma, I'm going to quit. Every one is against me here because I am black,' he says. 'The whole world is against us black people.'"

"So I said to him, 'Joe, I am not against you. Don't be foolish, don't go out to be a bum again. The trouble with you here is you are lazy. If you would work harder the others would like you, too.' So he said, 'Momma, all right I'll stay,' So that's how it is in the restaurant. They call me Momma, even the black ones."

It was a large, high-priced cafeteria for businessmen on lower Broadway. My mother was a chef's helper, and peeled and scoured tons of vegetables for cooking. Her wages were seven dollars a week.

She woke at five, cooked our breakfast at home, then had to walk a mile to her job. She came home at five-thirty, and made supper, cleaned the house, was busy on her feet until bedtime. It hurt my father's masculine pride to see his wife working for wages. But my mother liked it all; she was proud of earning money, and she liked her fights in the restaurant.

My dear, tireless, little dark-faced mother! Why did she always have to fight? Why did she have to give my father a new variety of headache with accounts of her battles for "justice" in the cafeteria? The manager there was a fat blond Swede with a *Kaiserliche* mustache, and the manners of a Mussolini. All the workers feared this bull-necked tyrant, except my mother. She told him "what was what." When the meat was rotten, when the drains were clogged and smelly, or the dishwashers overworked, she told him so. She scolded him as if he were her child, and he listened meekly. The other workers fell into the habit of telling their complaints to my mother, and she would relay them to the Swedish manager.

"It's because he needs me," said my mother proudly. "That's why he lets me scold him. I am one of his best workers; he can depend on me in the rush. And he knows I am not like the other kitchen help; they work a day, or two; then quit, but I stay on. So he's afraid to fire me, and I tell him what is what."

It was one of those super-cafeterias, with flowers on the tables; a string orchestra during the lunch hour, and other trimmings. But my mother had no respect for it. She would never eat the lunch served there to the employees, but took along two cheese sandwiches from home.

"Your food is *Dreck,* it is fit only for pigs," she told the manager bluntly. And once she begged me to promise never to eat hamburger steak in a restaurant when I grew up.

"Swear it to me, Mikey!" she said. "Never, never eat hamburger!"

"I swear it, momma."

"Poison!" she went on passionately. "They don't care if they poison the people, so long as there's money in it. I've seen with my own eyes. If I could write English, I'd write a letter to all the newspapers."

"Mind your own business!" my father growled. "Such things are for Americans. It is their country and their hamburger steak."

5

Our tenement was nothing but a junk-heap of rotten lumber and brick. It was an old ship on its last voyage; in the battering winter storms, all its seams opened, and wind and snow came through.

The plaster was always falling down, the stairs were broken and dirty. Five times that winter the water pipes froze, and floods spurted from the plumbing, and dripped from the ceilings.

There was no drinking water in the tenement for days. The women had to put on their shawls and hunt in the street for water. Up and down the stairs they groaned, lugging pails of water. In December, when Mr. Zunzer the landlord called for rent, some of the neighbors told him he ought to fix the plumbing.

"Next week," he murmured into his scaly beard.

"Next week!" my mother sneered, after he had gone. "A dozen times he has told us that, the yellow-faced murderer! May the lice eat him next week! May his false teeth choke him to death next week!"

Some tenants set out hunting for other flats, but could find none. The cheap ones were always occupied, the better flats were too dear. Besides, it wasn't easy to move; it cost money, and it meant leaving one's old neighbors.

"The tenements are the same everywhere, the landlords the same," said a woman. "I have seen places to-day an Irisher wouldn't live in, and the rents are higher than here."

Toward the end of January, during a cataclysmic spell of snow, ice, and iron frost, the pipes burst again, and for weeks every one suffered for lack of water; the babies, old people, the sick ones. The neighbors were indignant. They gathered in the halls and held wild conversations. Mrs. Cracauer suggested that some one send in a complaint to the Board of Health. Mrs. Schuman said this was useless, the Board of Health belonged to Tammany Hall, and the landlord had a pull there.

Mrs. Tannenbaum exploded like a bomb of Jewish emotion. She was a worse agitator than my mother, a roly-poly hysterical hippopotamus with a piercing voice.

"Let's all move out together!" she shrieked. "Let's get axes and hack out the walls and smash the windows and then move out!"

"No," said my mother, "I know something better."

Then and now, on the East Side, there have been rent strikes of tenants against their landlords. East Side tenants, I am sure, have always been the most obstreper-ous that ever gave a landlord sleepless nights and indigestion. My mother suggested a rent strike. The neighbors agreed with enthusiasm. They chattered about it in the weeks that followed. One told the other how she would curse the landlord when he came, and refuse to pay the rent.

"I'll spit in his face," said Mrs. Tannenbaum, "and tell him to kiss my *tochess* for his rent. Then I'll slam the door on him. That's what I'll do."

There spread through our tenement that feeling of exhilarating tension which precedes a battle. One counted the days until the first of February, when the landlord called for rent. What would he do? What would he say?

The hour came. Mrs. Tannenbaum, the fat, wildeyed hippopotamus agitator, was the first tenant upon whose door the landlord knocked. She opened it meekly, paid the rent, and never spoke a word. Her husband had forbade her to make a fuss. He didn't want the bother of moving.

The next tenant, Mrs. Schuman across the hall, was so amazed at this treachery to the cause, that she paid her rent, too. Every one else paid; except my mother. She faced the landlord boldly, and said in a clear voice, for every one to hear:

"Fix first the plumbing, Mr. Zunzer, then I'll pay the rent."

Mr. Zunzer glared at her with his goggly eyes. For a minute he could not speak for rage. Then he yanked his red scrubby beard, and said:

"I'll throw you out! Mischief-maker, I know who you are! You're the one who has been starting the rent strike here!"

"Yes," said my mother coolly. "And you've scared the others into paying you, but you can't scare me."

"I can't?" sputtered the landlord. "I will show you. To-morrow I'll call the sheriff and throw your furniture on the street!"

"No!" said my mother. "First you will have to take me to court! I know what my rights are!"

"*Pfoo* on your rights!" said the landlord. "I can do anything I want in this district. I have a pull with Tammany Hall!"

My mother put her hands on her hips, and asked him quietly: "But with God have you a pull, Mr. Zunzer?"

Mr. Zunzer was startled by this sally. He tried to meet it with haughtiness.

"Don't talk to me of God," he said. "I am more often in the synagogue than you and your husband together. I give a dozen times more money there."

"Every one knows you have money," said my mother quietly, "even the Angel of Death. Some day he will come for *all* your money, Mr. Zunzer."

The landlord's face paled; he trembled. He tried to speak, but the words choked him. He looked queer, as if he were about to faint. Then he pulled himself together, and walked away. My mother slammed the door after him, and laughed heartily. She rushed to the window, and called across the airshaft to Mrs. Ashkenazi and other neighbors. They had been sitting at their windows, listening greedily to the quarrel.

"'Did you hear what hell I gave to that landlord? Didn't I give it to him good?"

"Madwoman!" my father called from the bedroom. "Where will we go when he puts us out to-morrow?"

"He won't put us out," said my mother confidently. "The landlord is scared of me, I could see it in his eyes."

My father sneered at her. Who ever heard of a landlord being scared of his tenant? But it was true this time; the landlord did not bother us again. He actually fixed the plumbing. He sent an agent to collect the rent. He was scared; my mother had made a lucky hit when she taunted him with the Angel of Death.

Mr. Zunzer was superstitious. His deepest fear was that burglars would break in some night and kill him and take his money. Dr. Solow told us the story one night:

6

"When Mr. Zunzer first came to America," Dr. Solow related, "he peddled neckties, shoelaces and collarbuttons from a tray. He was very poor. He slept on a mattress in a cobbler's damp cellar, and lived on herrings and dry bread. He starved and suffered for five years. That's how he got the yellow face you see on him.

"Every penny he could grab he saved like a miser. He tied the nickels and dimes in a bag which he hid in a crack under his mattress. He worried. Big rats ran across his face while he slept. They did not bother him a tenth as much as did thoughts of his money.

"Oh, how sacred was that money to him. It was money to bring his wife and children from Europe. He was hungry for them. He would cry at night thinking about them. The money was not money; it was his family, his peace, his happiness, his life and death.

"One night some one stole this money from under the mattress. It was the savings of three years. Mr. Zunzer almost went crazy. He was sick in a hospital for months. He refused to eat. He wanted to die. But he took heart and commenced saving again. In two years he was able to send for his wife and children.

"Happiness did not come with them. Mr. Zunzer had formed the habit of saving money. He was a miser. He grudged his wife and children every cent they needed. He gave them little to eat. His wife fell sick; he grudged her a doctor. She died. At the funeral he fought with the undertaker over the burial price. He was always thinking of money.

"His children grew up hating him for his miserly ways. One by one they left him. The eldest boy became a thief. The second boy joined the U.S. Army. The girl disappeared.

"Mr. Zunzer was left alone. He is rich now, he owns a pawnshop and several tenement houses. But he still lives on herring and dry bread, and saves pennies like a miser. It is a disease.

"He has fits," said Dr. Solow. "Every few months I am, called to him. He is rolling on the floor, he knocks his head against furniture, he cuts his face on falling dishes. He screams robbers are killing him, and stealing his money. I talk to him quietly. I give him a medicine. I light the gas, to show him there are no burglars. All night I talk to him as to a child.

"About ten years ago, a junkman he knew was murdered by thieves and robbed. Since then Mr. Zunzer has the fear the same thing will happen to him.

"'Listen,' I tell him, 'you must stop worrying about money. It is making you crazy, Mr. Zunzer.'

"He wrings his hands, he weeps, and says to me: 'Yes, Dr. Solow, it is making me crazy. But what can I do? It is in my blood, in my heart. Can I cut it out of me with a knife?'

"'No,' I answer him, 'there are other ways, Mr. Zunzer.'

"'What other ways?' he weeps. 'Shall I throw my money in the river? Shall I give it to the synagogue? What good would it do? How can one one live without money? And if other men fight for money, must one not fight, too? The whole world is sick with this disease, Dr. Solow, I am not the only one.'

"So what can I answer? He will die in one of his fits. His money will disappear down the sewer. Sometimes I am sorry for him; it's not altogether his fault. It *is* a world sickness. Even we who are not misers suffer from it. How happy the world would be without money! Yet what's to be done?"

My mother wagged her head mournfully through this tale of Mr. Zunzer's sickness. She said:

"The poor man! Maybe he needs another wife."

Ach, my mother! She could be sorry for any one, even a landlord.

<h2 style="text-align:center">7</h2>

Yet she fought the landlord again that winter. The rent was due, and by a coincidence my brother, my sister, my mother and I all needed shoes. We had worn the old ones until they were in shreds. It was impossible to patch them any longer. My mother decided to pawn the family's diamond ring—the one my father had bought in a prosperous period.

I went with my mother to Mr. Zunzer's pawnshop. In summer it had swinging wicker doors like a saloon. Now we entered through heavy curtained doors that shut out the daylight.

It was a grim, crowded little store smelling of camphor. There were some gloomy East Side people standing around. The walls were covered with strange objects: guitars, shovels, blankets, clocks; with lace curtains, underwear and crutches; all these miserable trophies of the defeat of the poor.

Everything worth more than a quarter was taken in pawn by Mr. Zunzer, from an old man's false teeth to a baby's diapers. People were sure to redeem these little necessities. If he made ten cents on a transaction he was satisfied, for there were hundreds of them. At the end of a week there was a big total.

It was said in the neighborhood he also bought stolen things from the young thieves and pickpockets.

We waited for our turn. An old Irish worker in overalls, with merry blue eyes and a rosy face, was trying to pawn some tools. He was drunk and pleaded that he be given a dollar. Mr. Zunzer gave him only half a dollar, and said, "Get the hell out." The white-haired Irishman jigged and sang as he left for the saloon.

A dingy little woman pawned a baby carriage. An old Jewish graybeard pawned his prayer book and praying shawl. A fat Polish woman with a blowsy, weepy face pawned an accordion. A young girl pawned some quilts; then our turn came.

The landlord wore a black alpaca coat in the pawnshop, and a skull cap. He crouched on a stool behind the counter. One saw only his scaly yellow face and bulging eyes; he was like an anxious spider. He picked up the ring my mother presented him, screwed a jeweler's glass into his eye, and studied it in the gaslight.

"Ten dollars," he said abruptly.

"I must have fifteen," said my mother.

"Ten dollars," said the landlord.

"No, fifteen," said my mother.

He looked up irritably and stared at her with his near-sighted eyes. He recognized her in the pawnshop gloom.

"You're my tenant, aren't you?" he asked, "the one that made all the trouble for me?"

"Yes," said my mother, "what of it?"

The landlord smiled bitterly.

"Nothing," he said, "but you are sure to come to a bad end."

"No worse end than yours," said my mother, "may the bananas grow in your throat!"

"Don't curse me in my own shop!" said the landlord. "I'll have you arrested. What do you want here?"

"I told you," said my mother, "I want fifteen dollars on this ring."

"It is worth only ten, " said the landlord.

"To me you must give fifteen," said my mother boldly.

The landlord paled. He looked at my mother fearfully. She knew his secret. My mother mystified and alarmed him with her boldness. He was accustomed to people who cowered.

He wrote out a ticket for the ring, gave my mother fifteen dollars. She crowed over her victory as we walked home. Next day she bought shoes for my brother, my sister Esther, and myself. Her own shoes she forgot to buy. That's the way she generally arranged things.

1930

TILLIE OLSEN
(B. 1912?)

This poem represents a more direct expression of Olsen's political objectives than some of her later work. (For biographical information, see the headnote on Olsen in section I.)

I WANT YOU WOMEN
UP NORTH TO KNOW

(Based on a Letter by Felipe Ibarro in New Masses, *Jan. 9th, 1934.)*

> i want you women up north to know
> how those dainty children's dresses you buy
>   at macy's, wanamakers, gimbels, marshall fields,
> are dyed in blood, are stitched in wasting flesh,
> down in San Antonio, "where sunshine spends the winter."
>
> I want you women up north to see
> the obsequious smile, the salesladies trill
>   "exquisite work, madame, exquisite pleats"
> vanish into a bloated face, ordering more dresses,
>   gouging the wages down,
> dissolve into maria, ambrosa, catalina,

stitching these dresses from dawn to night,
in blood, in wasting flesh.

Catalina Rodriguez, 24,
    body shrivelled to a child's at twelve,
catalina rodriguez, last stages of consumption,
    works for three dollars a week from dawn to midnight.
A fog of pain thickens over her skull, the parching heat
    breaks over her body.
and the bright red blood embroiders the floor of her room.
    White rain stitching the night, the bourgeois poet would say,
    white gulls of hands, darting, veering,
    white lightning, threading the clouds,
this is the exquisite dance of her hands over the cloth,
and her cough, gay, quick, staccato,
    like skeleton's bones clattering,
is appropriate accompaniment for the esthetic dance
    of her fingers,
and the tremolo, tremolo when the hands tremble with pain.
Three dollars a week,
two fifty-five,
seventy cents a week,
no wonder two thousands eight hundred ladies of joy
are spending the winter with the sun after he goes down—
for five cents (who said this was a rich man's world?) you can get
    all the lovin you want
"clap and syph aint much worse than sore fingers, blind eyes,
    and t.m."

Maria Vasquez, spinster,
for fifteen cents a dozen stitches garments for children she has
    never had,
Catalina Torres, mother of four,
to keep the starved body starving, embroiders from dawn to
    night.
Mother of four, what does she think of,
    as the needle pocked fingers shift over the silk—
    of the stubble-coarse rags that stretch on her own brood,
    and jut with the bony ridge that marks hunger's landscape
    of fat little prairie-roll bodies that will bulge in the
    silk she needles?
(Be not envious, Catalina Torres, look!
    on your own children's clothing, embroidery,
    more intricate than any thousand hands could fashion,
    there where the cloth is ravelled, or darned,
    designs, multitudinous, complex and handmade by Poverty
    herself.)

Ambrosa Espinoza trusts in god,
   "Todos es de dios, everything is from god,"
   through the dwindling night, the waxing day, she bolsters
   herself up with it—
but the pennies to keep god incarnate, from ambrosa,
and the pennies to keep the priest in wine, from ambrosa,
ambrosa clothes god and priest with hand-made children's
   dresses.

Her brother lies on an iron cot, all day and watches,
on a mattress of rags he lies.
For twenty-five years he worked for the railroad, then they laid
   him off.
   (racked days, searching for work; rebuffs; suspicious eyes of
   policemen.)
   goodbye ambrosa, mebbe in dallas I find work; desperate
     swing for a freight,
   surprised hands, clutching air, and the wheel goes over a
   leg,
   the railroad cuts it off, as it cut off twenty-five years of his
   life.)
She says that he prays and dreams of another world, as he lies
   there, a heaven (which he does not know was brought to
   earth in 1917 in Russia, by workers like him).
Women up north, I want you to know
when you finger the exquisite hand made dresses
what it means, this working from dawn to midnight,
on what strange feet the feverish dawn must come
   to maria, catalina, ambrosa,
how the malignant fingers twitching over the pallid faces jerk
   them to work,
and the sun and the fever mounts with the day—
   long plodding hours, the eyes burn like coals, heat jellies the
   flying fingers,
down comes the night like blindness.
   long hours more with the dim eye of the lamp, the breaking
   back,
   weariness crawls in the flesh like worms, gigantic like earth's
   in winter.
And for Catalina Rodriguez comes the night sweat and the blood
   embroidering the darkness.
   for Catalina Torres the pinched faces of four huddled
   children,
   the naked bodies of four bony children,
   the chant of their chorale of hunger.
And for twenty eight hundred ladies of joy the grotesque act
   gone over—
   the wink—the grimace—the "feeling like it baby?"

And for Maria Vasquez, spinster, emptiness, emptiness.
    flaming with dresses for children she can never fondle.
And for Ambrosa Espinoza—the skeleton body of her brother on
his mattress of rags, boring twin holes in the dark with his eyes
to the image of christ remembering a leg, and twenty-five years cut
off from his life by the railroad.

Women up north, I want you to know,
I tell you this can't last forever.

I swear it won't.

WILLIAM FAULKNER

(1897-1962)

Faulkner, one of America's rare Nobel Prize winners in literature, is not often thought about in terms of class conflict. His works are studied for their technical innovations, like his use of multiple narrative points of view (including that of an idiot in The Sound and the Fury*), or his sometimes baroque prose style, as in the opening sentence of* Light in August. *Or he is analyzed for his masterly evocation of family and racial relations and tangled histories in his gothic Southern invention, Yoknapatawpha County, the site of his most successful novels. Or he is read for his meditations on human desire, the complexities of time, the force of obligations, accepted or rejected, and the similar themes that make his novels intellectually compelling.*

But in fact, class conflict—within the distinctive frameworks mandated by the nineteenth- and twentieth-century South—are critical to many of his books. Nowhere more so than in the story that follows, "Barn Burning," for a significant part of Snopes's rage and his ways of giving it expression and scope have to do, as the title suggests, with differing relations to property.

Faulkner grew up where he came to live for most of his life, in Oxford, Mississippi, a somewhat unusual town by virtue of being the site of the University of Mississippi. That fact meant little to the young "Bill," as he was called, for he was bored by school and dropped out of high school and later out of the university. In between, however, he read widely, guided by a friend from Oxford, Phil Stone, who was enrolled at Yale. Faulkner enlisted in the Canadian Royal Air Force, but the Armistace ended any chance of combat. He wrote poetry in a neo-Romantic mode, a book of which, The Marble Faun, *he published in 1924. Moving to New Orleans, he fell in with the circle around Sherwood Anderson, came to know something about Freudian theories as well as about the modernist innovations of writers like Joyce and Eliot, wrote innovative sketches for local newspapers, and finally a first novel,* Soldier's Pay (1926). *Having returned from travel in Europe and published a second novel, Faulkner focused his imagination on what he knew well, a fictionalized version of his home area. And beginning in 1929 with* Sartoris, *he wrote and published with amazing rapidity the series of novels that established his reputation. These included* The Sound and the

Fury *(1929)*, As I Lay Dying *(1930)*, Light in August *(1932)*, Absalom, Absalom! *(1936)*, The Unvanquished *(1938)*, The Hamlet *(1940)*, *and* Go Down, Moses *(1942)*.

In between, however, he felt compelled to work as a scriptwriter in Hollywood in order to make money; for the same reason he wrote some potboilers and magazine fiction. One of these, the novel Sanctuary *(1931), was the only one in print in 1946, when his reputation was at a low ebb. But shortly thereafter, a process of rediscovery and appreciation of his enormous accomplishments began, a process that continues to the present day. Faulkner's success lies not only in his manner of suggesting in prose the complex workings of the minds of a huge cast of characters, but also his vivid dramatization of human conflicts in compelling stories.*

BARN BURNING

The store in which the Justice of the Peace's court was sitting smelled of cheese. The boy, crouched on his nail keg at the back of the crowded room, knew he smelled cheese, and more: from where he sat he could see the ranked shelves close-packed with the solid, squat, dynamic shapes of tin cans whose labels his stomach read, not from the lettering which meant nothing to his mind but from the scarlet devils and the silver curve of fish—this, the cheese which he knew he smelled and the hermetic meat which his intestines believed he smelled coming in intermittent gusts momentary and brief between the other constant one, the smell and sense just a little of fear because mostly of despair and grief, the old fierce pull of blood. He could see the table where the Justice sat and before which his father and his father's enemy (*our enemy* he thought in that despair; *ourn! mine and hisn both! He's my father!*) stood, but he could hear them, the two of them that is, because his father had said no word yet:

"But what proof have you, Mr. Harris?"

"I told you. The hog got into my corn. I caught it up and sent it back to him. He had no fence that would hold it. I told him so, warned him. The next time I put the hog in my pen. When he came to get it I gave him enough wire to patch up his pen. The next time I put the hog up and kept it. I rode down to his house and saw the wire I gave him still rolled on to the spool in his yard. I told him he could have the hog when he paid me a dollar pound fee. That evening a nigger came with the dollar and got the hog. He was a strange nigger. He said, 'He say to tell you wood and hay kin burn.' I said, 'What?' 'That whut he to tell you,' the nigger said. 'Wood and hay kin burn.' That night my barn burned. I got the stock out but I lost the barn."

"Where is the nigger? Have you got him?"

"He was a strange nigger, I tell you. I don't know what became of him."

"But that's not proof. Don't you see that's not proof?"

"Get that boy up here. He knows." For a moment the boy thought too that the man meant his older brother until Harris said, "Not him. The little one. The boy," and, crouching, small for his age, small and wiry like his father, in patched and faded jeans even too small for him, with straight, uncombed, brown hair and eyes gray and wild as storm scud, he saw the men between himself and the table part and become a lane of grim faces, at the end of which he saw the Justice, a shabby, collarless, graying man in spectacles, beckoning him. He felt no floor under his bare feet; he seemed to walk beneath the palpable weight of the grim turning faces. His father, stiff in his black Sunday coat donned not for the trial but for the moving, did not even look at him. *He aims for me to lie,* he thought, again with that frantic grief and despair. *And I will have to do hit.*

"What's your name, boy?" the Justice said.

"Colonel Sartoris Snopes," the boy whispered.

"Hey?" the Justice said. "Talk louder. Colonel Sartoris? I reckon anybody named for Colonel Sartoris in this country can't help but tell the truth, can they?" The boy said nothing. *Enemy! Enemy!* he thought; for a moment he could not even see, could not see that the Justice's face was kindly nor discern that his voice was troubled when he spoke to the man named Harris: "Do you want me to question this boy?" But he could hear, and during those subsequent long seconds while there was absolutely no sound in the crowded little room save that of quiet and intent breathing it was as if he had swung outward at the end of a grape vine, over a ravine, and at the top of the swing had been caught in a prolonged instant of mesmerized gravity, weightless in time.

"No!" Harris said violently, explosively. "Damnation! Send him out of here!" Now time, the fluid world, rushed beneath him again, the voices coming to him again through the smell of cheese and sealed meat, the fear and despair and the old grief of blood:

"This case is closed. I can't find against you, Snopes, but I can give you advice. Leave this country and don't come back to it."

His father spoke for the first time, his voice cold and harsh, level, without emphasis: "I aim to. I don't figure to stay in a country among people who . . ." he said something unprintable and vile, addressed to no one.

"That'll do," the Justice said. "Take your wagon and get out of this country before dark. Case dismissed."

His father turned, and he followed the stiff black coat, the wiry figure walking a little stiffly from where a Confederate provost's man's musket ball had taken him in the heel on a stolen horse thirty years ago, followed the two backs now, since his older brother had appeared from somewhere in the crowd, no taller than the father but thicker, chewing tobacco steadily, between the two lines of grim-faced men and out of the store and across the worn gallery and down the sagging steps and among the dogs and half-grown boys in the mild May dust, where as he passed a voice hissed:

"Barn burner!"

Again he could not see, whirling; there was a face in a red haze, moonlike, bigger than the full moon, the owner of it half again his size, he leaping in the red haze toward the face, feeling no blow, feeling no shock when his head struck the earth, scrabbling up and leaping again, feeling no blow this time either and tasting no blood, scrabbling up to see the other boy in full flight and himself already leaping into pursuit as his father's hand jerked him back, the harsh, cold voice speaking above him: "Go get in the wagon."

It stood in a grove of locusts and mulberries across the road. His two hulking sisters in their Sunday dresses and his mother and her sister in calico and sunbonnets were already in it, sitting on and among the sorry residue of the dozen and more movings which even the boy could remember—the battered stove, the broken beds and chairs, the clock inlaid with mother-of-pearl, which would not run, stopped at some fourteen minutes past two o'clock of a dead and forgotten day and time, which had been his mother's dowry. She was crying, though when she saw him she. drew her sleeve across her face and began to descend from the wagon. "Get back," the father said.

"He's hurt. I got to get some water and wash his . . ."

"Get back in the wagon," his father said. He got in too, over the tail-gate. His father mounted to the seat where the older brother already sat and struck the gaunt mules two savage blows with the peeled willow, but without heat. It was not even sadistic; it was exactly that same quality which in later years would cause his descendants to over-run the engine before putting a motor car into motion, striking and reining back in the same movement. The wagon went on, the store with its quiet crowd of grimly watching men dropped behind; a curve in the road hid it. *Forever* he thought. *Maybe he's done satisfied now, now that he has* . . . stopping himself, not to say it aloud even to himself. His mother's hand touched his shoulder.

"Does hit hurt?" she said.

"Naw," he said. "Hit don't hurt. Lemme be."

"Can't you wipe some of the blood off before hit dries?"

"I'll wash to-night," he said. "Lemme be, I tell you."

The wagon went on. He did not know where they were going. None of them ever did or ever asked, because it was always somewhere, always a house of sorts waiting for them a day or two days or even three days away. Likely his father had already arranged to make a crop on another farm before he . . . Again he had to stop himself. He (the father) always did. There was something about his wolflike independence and even courage when the advantage was at least neutral which impressed strangers, as if they got from his latent ravening ferocity not so much a sense of dependability as a feeling that his ferocious conviction in the rightness of his own actions would be of advantage to all whose interest lay with his.

That night they camped, in a grove of oaks and beeches where a spring ran. The nights were still cool and they had a fire against it, of a rail lifted from a nearby fence and cut into lengths—a small fire, neat, niggard almost, a shrewd fire; such fires were his father's habit and custom always, even in freezing weather. Older, the boy might have remarked this and wondered why not a big one; why should not a man who had not only seen the waste and extravagance of war, but who had in his blood an inherent voracious prodigality with material not his own, have burned everything in sight? Then he might have gone a step farther and thought that that was the reason: that niggard blaze was the living fruit of nights passed during those four years in the woods hiding from all men, blue or gray, with his strings of horses (captured horses, he called them). And older still, he might have divined the true reason: that the element of fire spoke to some deep mainspring of his father's being, as the element of steel or of powder spoke to other men, as the one weapon for the preservation of integrity, else breath were not worth the breathing, and hence to be regarded with respect and used with discretion.

But he did not think this now and he had seen those same niggard blazes all his life. He merely ate his supper beside it and was already half asleep over his iron plate when his father called him, and once more he followed the stiff back, the stiff and ruthless limp, up the slope and on to the starlit road where, turning, he could see his father against the stars but without face or depth—a shape black, flat, and bloodless as though cut from tin in the iron folds of the frockcoat which had not been made for him, the voice harsh like tin and without heat like tin:

"You were fixing to tell them. You would have told him." He didn't answer. His father struck him with the flat of his hand on the side of the head, hard but without heat, exactly as he had struck the two mules at the store; exactly as he would strike either of them with any stick in order to kill a horse fly, his voice still without heat or anger: "You're getting to be a man. You got to learn. You got to learn to stick to your own blood or you ain't going to have any blood to stick to you. Do you think either of them, any man there this morning, would? Don't you know all they wanted was a chance to get at me because they knew I had them beat? Eh?" Later, twenty years later, he was to tell himself, "If I had said they wanted only truth, justice, he would have hit me again." But now he said nothing. He was not crying. He just stood there. "Answer me," his father said.

"Yes," he whispered. His father turned.

"Get on to bed. We'll be there tomorrow."

Tomorrow they were there. In the early afternoon the wagon stopped before a paintless two-room house identical almost with the dozen others it had stopped before even in the boy's ten years, and again, as on the other dozen occasions, his mother and aunt got down and began to unload the wagon, although his two sisters and his father and brother had not moved.

"Likely hit ain't fitten for hawgs," one of the sisters said.

"Nevertheless, fit it will and you'll hog it and like it," his father said. "Get out of them chairs and help your Ma unload."

The two sisters got down, big, bovine, in a flutter of cheap ribbons; one of them drew from the jumbled wagon bed a battered lantern, the other a worn broom. His father handed the reins to the older son and began to climb stiffly over the wheel. "When they get unloaded, take the team to the barn and feed them." Then he said, and at first the boy thought he was still speaking to his brother: "Come with me."

"Me?" he said.

"Yes," his father, said. "You."

"Abner," his mother said. His father paused and looked back—the harsh level stare beneath the shaggy, graying, irascible brows.

"I reckon I'll have a word with the man that aims to begin to-morrow owning me body and soul for the next eight months."

They went back up the road. A week ago—or before last night, that is—he would have asked where they were going, but not now. His father had struck him before last night but never before had he paused afterward to explain why; it was as if the blow and the following calm, outrageous voice still rang, repercussed, divulging nothing to him save the terrible handicap of being young, the light weight of his few years, just heavy enough to prevent his soaring free of the world as it seemed to be ordered but not heavy enough to keep him footed solid in it, to resist it and try to change the course of its events.

Presently he could see the grove of oaks and cedars and the other flowering trees and shrubs where the house would be, though not the house yet. They walked beside a fence massed with honeysuckle and Cherokee roses and came to a gate swinging open between two brick pillars, and now, beyond a sweep of drive, he saw the house for the first time and at that instant he forgot his father and the terror and despair both, and even when he remembered his father again (who had not stopped) the terror and despair did not return. Because, for all the twelve movings, they had sojourned until now in a poor country, a land of small farms and fields and houses, and he had never seen a house like this before. *Hit's big as a courthouse* he thought quietly, with a surge of peace and joy whose reason he could not have thought into words, being too young for that: *They are safe from him. People whose lives are a part of this peace and dignity are beyond his touch, he no more to them than a buzzing wasp: capable of stinging for a little moment but that's all; the spell of this peace and dignity rendering even the barns and stable and cribs which belong to it impervious to the puny flames he might contrive . . .* this, the peace and joy, ebbing for an instant as he looked again at the stiff black back, the stiff and implacable limp of the figure which was not dwarfed by the house, for the reason that it had never looked big any-where and which now, against the serene columned backdrop, had more than ever that impervious quality of something cut ruthlessly from tin, depthless, as though, sidewise to the sun, it would cast no shadow. Watching him, the boy remarked the absolutely undeviating course which his father held and saw the stiff foot come squarely down in a pile of fresh droppings where a horse had stood in the drive and which his father could have avoided by a simple change of stride. But it ebbed only for a moment, though he could not have thought this into words either, walking on in the spell of the house, which he could ever want but without envy, without sor-row, certainly never with that ravening and jealous rage which unknown to him walked in the ironlike black coat before him: *Maybe he will feel it too. Maybe it will even change him now from what maybe he couldn't help but be.*

They crossed the portico. Now he could hear his father's stiff foot, as it came down on the boards with clocklike finality, a sound out of all proportion to the dis-placement of the body it bore and which was not dwarfed either by the white door before it, as though it had attained to a sort of vicious and ravening minimum not to be dwarfed by anything—the flat, wide, black hat, the formal coat of broadcloth which had once been black but which had now that friction-glazed greenish cast of the bodies of old house flies, the lifted sleeve which was too large, the lifted hand like a curled claw. The door opened so promptly that the boy knew the Negro must have been watching them all the time, an old man with neat grizzled hair, in a linen jacket, who stood barring the door with his body, saying, "Wipe yo foots, white man, fo you come in here. Major ain't home nohow."

"Get out of my way, nigger," his father said, without heat too, flinging the door back and the Negro also entering, his hat still on his head. And now the boy saw the prints of the stiff foot on the doorjamb and saw them appear on the pale rug behind the machinelike deliberation of the foot which seemed to bear (or transmit) twice the weight which the body compassed. The Negro was shouting "Miss Lula! Miss Lula!" somewhere behind them, then the boy, deluged as though by a warm wave by a suave turn of carpeted stair and a pendant glitter of chandeliers and a mute gleam of gold frames, heard the swift feet and saw her too, a lady—perhaps he had never seen her like before either—in a gray, smooth gown with lace at the throat and an apron tied at the waist and the sleeves turned back, wiping cake or biscuit dough from her hands with a towel as she came up the hall, looking not at his father at all but at the tracks on the blond rug with an expression of incredu-lous amazement.

"I tried," the Negro cried. "I tole him to . . ."

"Will you please go away?" she said in a shaking voice. "Major de Spain is not at home. Will you please go away?"

His father had not spoken again. He did not speak again. He did not even look at her. He just stood stiff in the center of the rug, in his hat, the shaggy iron-gray brows twitching slightly above the pebble-colored eyes as he appeared to examine the house with brief deliberation. Then with the same deliberation he turned; the boy watched him pivot on the good leg and saw the stiff foot drag round the arc of the turning, leaving a final long and fading smear. His father never looked at it, he never once looked down at the rug. The Negro held the door. It closed behind them, upon the hysteric and indistinguishable woman-wail. His father stopped at the top of the steps and scraped hsi booth clean on the edge of it. At the gate he stopped again. He stood for a moment, planted stiffly on the stiff foot, looking back at the house. "Pretty and white, ain't it?" he said. "That's sweat. Nigger sweat. Maybe it ain't white enough yet to suit him. Maybe he wants to mix some white sweat with it."

Two hours later the boy was chopping wood behind the house within which his mother and aunt and the two sisters (the mother and aunt, not the two girls, he knew that; even at this distance and muffled by walls the flat loud voices of the two girls emanated an incorrigible idle inertia) were setting up the stove to prepare a meal, when he heard the hooves and saw the linen-clad man on a fine sorrel mare, whom he recognized even before he saw the rolled rug in front of the Negro youth following on a fat bay carriage horse—a suffused, angry face vanishing, still at full gallop, beyond the corner of the house where his father and brother were sitting in the two tilted chairs; and a moment later, almost before he could have put the axe down, he heard the hooves again and watched the sorrel mare go back out of the yard, already galloping again. Then his father began to shout one of the sisters' names, who presently emerged backward from the kitchen door dragging the rolled rug along the ground by one end while the other sister walked behind it.

"If you ain't going to tote, go on and set up the wash pot," the first said.

"You, Sarty!" the second shouted. "Set up the wash pot!" His father appeared at the door, framed against that shabbiness, as he had been against that other bland perfection, impervious to either, the mother's anxious face at his shoulder.

"Go on," the father said. "Pick it up." The two sisters stooped, broad, lethargic; stooping, they presented an incredible expanse of pale cloth and a flutter of tawdry ribbons.

"If I thought enough of a rug to have to git hit all the way from France I would-n't keep hit where folks coming in would have to tromp on hit," the first said. They raised the rug.

"Abner," the mother said. "Let me do it."

"You go back and git dinner," his father said. "I'll tend to this."

From the woodpile through the rest of the afternoon the boy watched them, the rug spread flat in the dust beside the bubbling wash-pot, the two sisters stooping over it with that profound and lethargic reluctance, while the father stood over them in turn, implacable and grim, driving them though never raising his voice again. He could smell the harsh homemade lye they were using; he saw his mother come to the door once and look toward them with an expression not anxious now but very like despair; he saw his father turn, and he fell to with the axe and saw from the corner of his eye his father raise from the ground a flattish fragment of field stone and examine it and return to the pot, and this time his mother actually spoke: "Abner. Abner. Please don't. Please, Abner."

Then he was done too. It was dusk; the whippoorwills had already begun. He could smell coffee from the room where they would presently eat the cold food remaining from the mid-afternoon meal, though when he entered the house he realized they were having coffee again probably because there was a fire on the hearth, before which the rug now lay spread over the backs of the two chairs. The tracks of his father's foot were gone. Where they had been were now long, water-cloudy scoriations resembling the sporadic course of a lilliputian mowing machine.

It still hung there while they ate the cold food and then went to bed, scattered without order or claim up and down the two rooms, his mother in one bed, where his father would later lie, the older brother in the other, himself, the aunt, the two sisters on pallets on the floor. But his father was not in bed yet. The last thing the boy remembered was the depthless, harsh silhouette of the hat and coat bending over the rug and it seemed to him that he had not even closed his eyes when the silhouette was standing over him, the fire almost dead behind it, the stiff foot prodding him awake. "Catch up the mule," his father said.

When he returned with the mule his father was standing in the black door, the rolled rug over his shoulder. "Ain't you going to ride?" he said.

"No. Give me your foot."

He bent his knee into his father's hand, the wiry, surprising power flowed smoothly, rising, he rising with it, on to the mule's bare back (they had owned a saddle once; the boy could remember it though not when or where) and with the same effortlessness his father swung the rug up in front of him. Now in the starlight they retraced the afternoon's path, up the dusty road rife with honeysuckle, through the gate and up the black tunnel of the drive to the lightless house, where he sat on the mule and felt the rough warp of the rug drag across his thighs and vanish.

"Don't you want me to help?" he whispered. His father did not answer and now he heard again that stiff foot striking the hollow portico with that wooden and clock-like deliberation, that outrageous overstatement of the weight it carried. The rug, hunched, not flung (the boy could tell that even in the darkness) from his father's shoulder struck the angle of wall and floor with a sound unbelievably loud, thunderous, then the foot again, unhurried and enormous; a light came on in the house and the boy sat, tense, breathing steadily and quietly and just a little fast, though the foot itself did not increase its beat at all, descending the steps now; now the boy could see him.

"Don't you want to ride now?" he whispered. "We kin both ride now," the light within the house altering now, flaring up and sinking. *He's coming down the stairs now,* he thought. He had already ridden the mule up beside the horse block; presently his father was up behind him and he doubled the reins over and slashed the mule across the neck, but before the animal could begin to trot the hard, thin arm came round him, the hard, knotted hand jerking the mule back to a walk.

In the first red rays of the sun they were in the lot, putting plow gear on the mules. This time the sorrel mare was in the lot before he heard it at all, the rider collarless and even bareheaded, trembling, speaking in a shaking voice as the woman in the house had done, his father merely looking up once before stooping again to the hame he was buckling, so that the man on the mare spoke to his stooping back:

"You must realize you have ruined that rug. Wasn't there anybody here, any of your women . . ." he ceased, shaking, the boy watching him, the older brother leaning now in the stable door, chewing, blinking slowly and steadily at nothing apparently. "It cost a hundred dollars. But you never had a hundred dollars. You never will. So I'm going to charge you twenty bushels of corn against your crop. I'll add it in your contract and when you come to the commissary you can sign it. That won't keep Mrs. de Spain quiet but maybe it will teach you to wipe your feet off before you enter her house again."

Then he was gone. The boy looked at his father, who still had not spoken or even looked up again, who was now adjusting the logger-head in the hame.

"Pap," he said. His father looked at him—the inscrutable face, the shaggy brows beneath which the gray eyes glinted coldly. Suddenly the boy went toward him, fast, stopping as suddenly. "You done the best you could!" he cried. "If he wanted hit done different why didn't he wait and tell you how? He won't git no twenty bushels! He won't git none! We'll gether hit and hide hit! I kin watch . . ."

"Did you put the cutter back in that straight stock like I told you?"

"No, sir," he said.

"Then go do it."

That was Wednesday. During the rest of that week he worked steadily, at what was within his scope and some which was beyond it, with an industry that did not need to be driven nor even commanded twice; he had this from his mother, with the difference that some at least of what he did he liked to do, such as splitting wood with the half-size axe which his mother and aunt had earned; or saved money some-how, to present him with at Christmas. In company with the two older women (and on one afternoon, even one of the sisters), he built pens for the shoat and the cow which were a part of his father's contract with the landlord, and one afternoon, his father being absent, gone somewhere on one of the mules, he went to the field.

They were running a middle buster now, his brother holding the plow straight while he handled the reins, and walking beside the straining mule, the rich black soil shearing cool and damp against his bare ankles, he thought *Maybe this is the end of it. Maybe even that twenty bushels that seems hard to have to pay for just a rug will be a cheap price for him to stop forever and always from being what be used to be;* thinking, dreaming now, so that his brother had to speak sharply to him to mind the mule: *Maybe he even won't collect the twenty bushels. Maybe it will all add up and balance and vanish—corn, rug, fire; the terror and grief, the being pulled two ways like between two teams of horses—gone, done with for ever and ever.*

Then it was Saturday; he looked up from beneath the mule he was harnessing and saw his father in the black coat and hat. "Not that," his father said. "The wagon gear." And then, two hours later, sitting in the wagon bed behind his father and brother on the seat, the wagon accomplished a final curve, and he saw the weathered paintless store with its tattered tobacco- and patent-medicine posters and the tethered wagons and saddle animals below the gallery. He mounted the gnawed steps behind his father and brother, and there again was the lane of quiet, watching faces for the three of them to walk through. He saw the man in spectacles sitting at the plank table and he did not need to be told this was a Justice of the Peace; he sent one glare of fierce, exultant, partisan defiance. at the man in collar and cravat now, whom he had seen but twice before in his life; and that on a galloping horse, who now wore on his face an expression not of rage but of amazed unbelief which the boy could not have known was at the incredible circumstance of being sued by one of his own tenants, and came and stood against his father and cried at the Justice: "He ain't done it! He ain't burnt. . ."

"Go back to the wagon," his father said.

"Burnt?" the Justice said. "Do I understand this rug was burned too?"

"Does anybody here claim it was?" his father said. "Go back to the wagon." But he did not, he merely retreated to the rear of the room, crowded as that other had been, but not to sit down this time, instead, to stand pressing among the motion-less bodies, listening to the voices:

"And you claim twenty bushels of corn is too high for the damage you did to the rug?"

"He brought the rug to me and said he wanted the tracks washed out of it. I washed the tracks out and took the rug back to him."

"But you didn't carry the rug back to him in the same condition it was in before you made the tracks on it."

His father did not answer, and now for perhaps half a minute there was no sound at all save that of breathing, the faint, steady suspiration of complete and intent listening.

"You decline to answer that, Mr. Snopes?" Again his father did not answer. "I'm going to find against you, Mr. Snopes. I'm going to find that you were responsible for the injury to Major de Spain's rug and hold you liable for it. But twenty bushels of corn seems a little high for a man in your circumstances to have to pay. Major de Spain claims it cost a hundred dollars. October corn will be worth about fifty cents. I figure that if Major de Spain can stand a ninety-five dollar loss on something he paid cash for, you can stand a five-dollar loss you haven't earned yet. I hold you in damages to Major de Spain to the amount of ten bushels of corn over and above your contract with him, to be paid to him out of your crop at gathering time. Court adjourned."

It had taken no time hardly, the morning was but half begun. He thought they would return home and perhaps back to the field, since they were late, far behind all other farmers. But instead his father passed on behind the wagon, merely indicating with his hand for the older brother to follow with it, and crossed the road toward the blacksmith shop opposite, pressing on after his father, overtaking him, speaking, whispering up at the harsh, calm face beneath the weathered hat: "He won't git no ten bushels neither. He won't git one. We'll . . ." until his father glanced for an instant down at him, the face absolutely calm, the grizzled eyebrows tangled above the cold eyes, the voice almost pleasant, almost gentle:

"You think so? Well, we'll wait till October anyway."

The matter of the wagon—the setting of a spoke or two and the tightening of the tires—did not take long either, the business of the tires accomplished by driving the wagon into the spring branch behind the shop and letting it stand there, the mules nuzzling into the water from time to time, and the boy on the seat with the idle reins, looking up the slope and through the sooty tunnel of the shed where the slow hammer rang and where his father sat on an upended cypress bolt, easily, either talking or listening, still sitting there when the boy brought the dripping wagon up out of the branch and halted it before the door.

"Take them on to the shade and hitch," his father said. He did. so and returned. His father and the smith and a third man squatting on his heels inside the door were talking, about crops and animals; the boy, squatting too in the ammoniac dust and hoof-parings and scales of rust, heard his father tell a long and unhurried story out of the time before the birth of the older brother even when he had been a professional horsetrader. And then his father came up beside him where he stood before a tattered last year's circus poster on the other side of the store, gazing rapt and quiet at the scarlet horses, the incredible poisings and convolutions of tulle and tights and the painted leers of comedians, and said, "It's time to eat."

But not at home. Squatting beside his brother against the front wall, he watched his father emerge from the store and produce from a paper sack a segment of cheese and divide it carefully and deliberately into three with his pocket knife and produce crackers from the same sack. They all three squatted on the gallery and ate, slowly, without talking; then in the store again, they drank from a tin dipper tepid water smelling of the cedar bucket and of living beech trees. And still they did not go home. It was a horse lot this time, a tall rail fence upon and along which men stood and sat and out of which one by one horses were led, to be walked and trotted and then cantored back and forth along the road while the slow swapping and buying went on and the sun began to slant westward, they—the three of them—watching and listening, the older brother with his muddy eyes and his steady, inevitable tobacco, the father commenting now and then on certain of the animals, to no one in particular.

It was after sundown when they reached home. They ate supper by lamplight, then, sitting on the doorstep, the boy watched the night fully accomplish, listening to the whippoorwills and the frogs, when he heard his mother's voice: "Abner! No! No! Oh, God. Oh, God. Abner!" and he rose, whirled, and saw the altered light through the door where a candle stub now burned in a bottle neck on the table and his father, still in the halt and coat, at once formal and burlesque as though dressed carefully for some shabby and ceremonial violence, emptying the reservoir of the lamp back into the five-gallon kerosene can from which it had been filled, while the mother tugged at his arm until he shifted the lamp to the other hand and flung her back, not savagely or viciously, just hard, into the wall, her hands flung out against the wall for balance, her mouth open and in her face the same quality of hopeless despair as had been in her voice. Then his father saw him standing in the door. "Go to the barn and get that can of oil we were oiling the wagon with," he said. The boy did not move. Then he could speak.

"What . . ." he cried. "What are you . . ."

"Go get that oil," his father said. "Go."

Then he was moving, running, outside the house, toward the stable: this the old habit, the old blood which he had not been permitted to choose for himself, which had been bequeathed him willy nilly and which had run for so long (and who knew where, battening on what of outrage and savagery and lust) before it came to him. *I could keep on,* he thought. *I could run on and on and never look back, never need to see his face again. Only I can't. I can't,* the rusted can in his hand now, the liquid sploshing in it as he ran back to the house and into it, into the sound of his mother's weeping in the next room, and handed the can to his father.

"Ain't you going to even send a nigger?" he cried. "At least you sent a nigger before!"

This time his father didn't strike him. The hand came even faster than the blow had, the same hand which had set the can on the table with almost excruciating care flashing from the can toward him too quick for him to follow it, gripping him by the back of his shirt and on to tiptoe before he had seen it quit the can, the face stooping at him in breathless and frozen ferocity, the cold, dead voice speaking over him to the older brother who leaned against the table, chewing with that steady, curious, sidewise motion of cows:

"Empty the can into the big one and go on. I'll catch up with you."

"Better tie him up to the bedpost," the brother said.

"Do like I told you," the father said. Then the boy was moving, his bunched shirt and the hard, bony hand between his shoulder-blades, his toes just touching the floor, across the room and into the other one, past the sisters sitting with spread heavy thighs in the two chairs over the cold hearth, and to where his mother and aunt sat side by side on the bed, the aunt's arms about his mother's shoulders.

"Hold him," the father said. The aunt made a startled movement. "Not you," the father said. "Lennie. Take hold of him. I want to see you do it." His mother took him by the wrist. "You'll hold him better than that. If he gets loose don't you know what he is going to do? He will go up yonder." He jerked his head toward the road. "Maybe I'd better tie him." "I'll hold him," his mother whispered.

"See you do then." Then his father was gone, the stiff foot heavy and measured upon the boards, ceasing at last.

Then he began to struggle. His mother caught him in both arms, he jerking and wrenching at them. He would be stronger in the end, he knew that. But he had no time to wait for it. "Lemme go!" he cried. "I don't want to have to hit you!"

"Let him go!" the aunt said. "If he don't go, before God, I am going up there myself!"

"Don't you see I can't?" his mother cried. "Sarty! Sarty! No! No! Help me, Lizzie!"

Then he was free. His aunt grasped at him but it was too late. He whirled, running, his mother stumbled forward on to her knees behind him, crying to the nearer sister: "Catch him, Net! Catch him!" But that was too late too, the sister (the sisters were twins, born at the same time, yet either of them now gave the impression of being, encompassing as much living meat and volume and weight as any other two of the family) not yet having begun to rise from the chair, her head, face, alone merely turned, presenting to him in the flying instant an astonishing expanse of young female features untroubled by any surprise even, wearing only an expression of bovine interest. Then he was out of the room, out of the house, in the mild dust of the star-lit road and the heavy rifeness of honeysuckle, the pale ribbon unspooling with terrific slowness under his running feet, reaching the gate at last and turning in, running, his heart and lungs drumming, on up the drive toward the lighted house, the lighted door. He did not knock, he burst in, sobbing for breath, incapable for the moment of speech; he saw the astonished face of the Negro in the linen jacket without knowing when the Negro had appeared.

"De Spain!" he cried, panted. "Where's . . ." then he saw the white man too emerging from a white door down the hall. "Barn!" he cried. "Barn!"

"What?" the white man said. "Barn?"

"Yes!" the boy cried. "Barn!"

"Catch him!" the white man shouted.

But it was too late this time too. The Negro grasped his shirt, but the entire sleeve, rotten with washing, carried away, and he was out that door too and in the drive again, and had actually never ceased to run even while he was screaming into the white man's face.

Behind him the white man was shouting, "My horse! Fetch my horse!" and he thought for an instant of cutting across the park and climbing the fence into the road, but he did not know the park nor how high the vine-massed fence might be and he dared not risk it. So he ran on down the drive, blood and breath roaring; presently he was in the road again though he could not see it. He could not hear either: the galloping mare was almost upon him before he heard her, and even then he held his course, as if the very urgency of his wild grief and need must in a moment more find him wings, waiting until the ultimate instant to hurl himself aside and into the weed-choked roadside ditch, as the horse thundered past and on, for an instant in furious silhouette against the stars, the tranquil early summer night sky which, even before the shape of the horse and rider vanished, stained abruptly and violently upward: a long, swirling roar incredible and soundless, blotting the stars, and he springing up and into the road again, running again, knowing it was too late yet still running even after he heard the shot and, an instant later, two shots, pausing now without knowing he had ceased to run, crying "Pap! Pap!," running again before he knew he had begun to run, stumbling, tripping over something and scrabbling up again without ceasing to run, looking backward over his shoulder at the glare as he got up, running on among the invisible trees, panting, sobbing, "Father! Father!"

At midnight he was sitting on the crest of a hill. He did not know it was midnight and he did not know how far he had come. But there was no glare behind him now and he sat now, his back toward what he had called home for four days anyhow, his face toward the dark woods which he would enter when breath was strong again, small, shaking steadily in the chill darkness, hugging himself into the remainder of his thin, rotten shirt, the grief and despair now no longer terror and fear but just grief and despair. *Father. My father,* he thought. "He was brave!" he cried suddenly, aloud but not loud, no more than a whisper: "He was! He was in the war! He was in Colonel Sartoris' cav'ry!" not knowing that his father had gone to that war a private in the fine old European sense, wearing no uniform, admitting the authority of and giving fidelity to no man or army or flag, going to war as Malbrouck himself did: for booty—it meant nothing and less than nothing to him if it were enemy booty or his own.

The slow constellations wheeled on. It would be dawn and then sun-up after a while and he would be hungry. But that would be to-morrow and now he was only cold, and walking would cure that. His breathing was easier now and he decided to get up and go on, and then he found that he had been asleep because he knew it was almost dawn, the night almost over. He could tell that from the whippoorwills. They were everywhere now among the dark trees below him, constant and inflectioned and ceaseless, so that, as the instant for giving over to the day birds drew nearer and nearer, there was no interval at all between them. He got up. He was a little stiff, but walking would cure that too as it would the cold, and soon there would be the sun. He went on down the hill, toward the dark woods within which the liquid silver voices of the birds called unceasing   the rapid and urgent beating of the urgent and quiring heart of the late spring night. He did not look back.

–1938

CAROLINA PEARL

(B. 1941)

A pseudonym for Nina Pearl Williamson, Carolina Pearl was born in a tiny four-room wooden house, one of twelve children of South Carolina share-croppers. Unable to keep a job and subject to bouts of drunkenness, her father moved the family frequently; cornbread and cane patch syrup was often the only food in the latest shack. When she was sixteen and unsuccessful at school, Pearl moved in with relatives in Charleston and got a job at the jewelry counter at Ward's five-and-dime store. At eighteen, she married a sailor, with whom she moved to Norfolk. There, among other jobs, she dressed up in an elf suit and helped kids tell Santa what they wanted for Christmas. She worked her way up to saleslady, department manager, office worker, office manager, and later worked in a bank. But she had cut her own hair sinced she was fifteen and realized that hair styling was what she wanted to do, so she enrolled in the Virginia Beach Boulevard Beauty Academy.

Moving back to her hometown after her husband's retirement, she went to work in a Myrtle Beach beauty salon, owned her own for a time, and now continues in the "hair profession," apart from writing about her own life. The following selection is a part of that writing.

FROM SOUTHERN BITCH

We was sharecroppers. We mostly farmed for the Farradays who owned a bunch of big ole cotton and tobacco farms. We mostly raised more tobacco than anythin else. We had only one big patch of cotton and a corn field that we raised for feedin the mules, hogs and chickens, when we had some.

We coulda had a house all our own. One time a brother of Mr. Samuel Farraday, the one who owned most of the farms, offered Pa a house if he would straighten himself up and stay sober. I reckon Pa couldn't stop drinkin cause we don't have us no house.

Mr. Samuel has him a great big white house with a white fence that goes all the way around it. We past right by it everytime we goes to the Galivants Ferry general store. Pa calls it the Ferry. Next to the store runs the Big Pee Dee River. It looks big and scary to me. There's a bridge over it that goes to Marion county. Ma says we live in Horry county.

You kinda have to watch out how you said "Horry". Ma says that you don't pronounce the "H". You just say "Orry". Sometimes, we pronounce the "H" and say "Whorey" so we can have a good laugh.

Across the road sets this big red packhouse. I reckon its for packing things. Next to it was this funny lookin thing. There was this big ole long pole that the mule pulled round and round. Pa said folks take their sugar cane there and that thing makes syrup out of that cane for them. Not too far over from that big red packhouse is the ole wooden windmill. I spent most my time just settin there lookin at it when we go down to the Ferry. I loved that ole windmill.

Over on the other side of the general store is the corn mill. That's where folks take their corn. That big machine in there turns that corn into grits and cornmeal for makin corn dodgers and cornbread. You use that cornmeal to roll them fish in before you drop em in that iron skillet and fry em up good and brown. We mostly go to the Ferry on the mule and wagon.

Mr. Farraday has a bunch of pecan trees growin all around his house and along side the road that goes past it. Sometimes Ma stops so we could pick up the pecans that had fell in the road. We weren't allowed to touch none of them pecans on Mr. Farraday's land but, we could have everyone of them that fell in the road. If we could get there and pick them up before somebody else did.

One day when Ma stopped and was busy pickin up them pecans, I jumped outta that wagon and snuck over to that big white fence that went around that big ole house. I could see through one of the cracks in it. That was the first time I'd ever seen the yard. I was justa lookin and thinkin, "I bet heaven looks just like this." That house was pure white. I mean white all over. Not a speck of dirt on it. Big ole white posts holdin up the porch. It would take me and Jeanette both to reach around them things. I never seen so many big long windows and none of the glass was broke out of them either. Them windows was long as that wagon we was ridin in.

That yard was all covered with the greenest grass I'd ever seen. It was thicker than a rug. We didn't have no grass in our yard. We had to chop it up just as soon as it growed there.

There was a big bush of white gardinias on one side of that brick walkway and a big bush of pink flowers on the other side. Them two big ole magnolia trees was all covered in big white flowers. They was as big as dinner plates. There was some statues of angles sittin over to one side of that yard with a bunch of pretty flowers growin around them. Right where that brick walk turned to go around the side of that house was a statue of a little black boy holdin a fishing pole. He was wearin a little red cap.

"Carolina Pearl, get yourself back in this wagon." I'd forgot all about Ma and Jeanette. I'd just thought I'd died and gone to heaven.

I heard tell that Mr. Samuel and Ms. Ida has seventeen cats livin inside that house with them. I heard they have fancy pillows to sleep on and their own dishes to eat out of. They even feed them cats pink salmon.

I'm thinkin, "Shoot, we never get no pink salmons to eat, but them ole cats do."

Ma and Pa was both raised in Horry county. Most all their kin folks lives here too. Grandpa and grandma believes in keeping to your own family. I reckon that's why when Pa beats up on us or anythin was wrong, we couldn't tell nobody cause we had to keep it in the family.

Sometimes I'd lie in bed at night wantin a piece of ham or some meat so bad, cause I'd come to bed hungry. That was the times we had only cornbread and syrup to eat. I could just taste some ham. There would be some meat hangin in the smoke-house that we mostly got from helpin the neighbors kill hogs. It would be hangin there and the worms was in it so bad. We'd pick through them shoulders and hams till we'd find a piece that the worms hadn't eat.

Sunday seemed to be our day for a special meal. If we had anythin special to cook. If we had meat, it was mostly fish or chicken. We mostly had some kind of chicken on Sundays. It might be fried chicken or chicken and dumplins or chicken bog. Some folks called it chicken stirred in rice. Me and Jeanette called it chicken turd in rice cause Ma didn't waste any of that chicken when she cooked it in that rice.

Sometimes if we had any sugar, Ma would make up one of them seven layer bri-arberry jelly cakes. I love them to death. Grandma puts chocolate between them lay-ers of her cake. We don't hardly ever have chocolate at our house so Ma puts jelly in her cakes.

Sometimes, we have a big ole pan full of briarberry or blueberry dumplins. My most favorite cake in the whole wide world is coconut. Honey, I'd eat a brick if you was to put enough coconut on it. We hardly never get a coconut cake around here except at Christmas time.

Well, anyways, most of them chickens we have for Sunday dinner stays up under the house next to them cement blocks that's holdin up the house. I reckon that's about the coolist place them chickens can find when that ole sun gets hotter-n-blazes in the daytime. Them chickens find them a tree or the chicken coop to sleep in when it gets dark. Shoot, them chickens goes to bed way before it ever gets dark. I'm thinkin, I bet that's why grandma Estelle is always sayin that grandpa Herman goes to bed with the chickens cause grandpa's mostly always goin to bed before dark.

The cracks in the floor of this ole shotgun house is so big that we can feed the chickens right through them. You can just lay down on the floor and put your eye over that crack and see them chickens walkin all around on that ground underneath the house.

Mary Jane and D. M. likes to lay down there and drop food through them cracks so they can see them chickens pick it up. Sometimes, I can hear them just a laughin. They look so cute layin over there on the floor a liftin that foot up and down and a lookin through them cracks.

Sometimes, ole Duke will run round and round the house and keep them chickens up under it. Not one of them chickens will come out from under there until he stops runnin and goes over there and lays down somewhere.

Duke is our dog that Pa come home with one day. I think Pa musta betted somebody something for Duke cause Pa didn't have no money to buy a dog like that. He was trained in the army just like a man. He had a actual honorable military discharge. He could hunt Jap's and play dead. You'd just say "Japs, Duke, Japs," and he'd get down on his knees and crawl on that ground just like he was huntin Japs. You could say "dead, Duke, dead," and he'd fall down on that ground lookin deader than a door nail. You could walk right up to him and he wouldn't even budge. I don't thank he even breathed when he was playin dead. I like ole Duke, he's a pretty good ole dog.

Well, anyway, it's mine and Jeanette's job to catch them chickens for Sunday dinner then wring their necks and scauld em and pluck all the feathers off of them. I'm gettin pretty good at cuttin them up too.

When we wanted a chicken, all me and Jeanette would have to say was, "chicken, Duke, chicken." He'll run up underneath that house and run us out some of them chickens. Then me and Jeanette will have to spot us a chicken and run it down till we caught it. We mostly have two chickens for dinner.

I can't help it but almost ever time I'm chasin down one of them chickens now, I'm thinkin back to that Sunday when Duke had run us out some of them chickens.

Me and Jeanette spotted our chicken. We was runnin down our chicken this a way and that a way till we finally caught em. Well, my ole hen was kinda heavy, so I had to take both my hands to sling her round and round. There's an art to wringin that chicken's neck. You first have to grab it around the neck and sling it round and round. When you have it goin round pretty good, you have to give it a big ole yank so's to break it's neck.

Well, me and Jeanette always likes to make a bet about who could wring their chicken's neck first and their chicken would die first. After we yanked and popped their necks, we'd throw em on the ground and run a circle round em with our foot or a stick. The one who's chicken would die closest to the center of that circle was the winner. But, if your chicken touched the circle, then you was the loser.

Well, that Sunday, we wrung our chickens necks and throwed em down on the ground. Mine just kinda fluttered round a few times and kinda kicked a little bit and just lay there, you know. Well, Jeanette's kinda fluttered and fluttered and kinda scraped it's little foot one sided and got over there on the edge of the circle and I'm yellin, "oops, oops, you lost, you lost."

Then that chicken got to flutterin a little bit more, kinda got to raisin up sideways and started scootin on off on its side. And directly that old hen got up, took a couple of steps and fell over. It acted just like Pa when Pa was real drunk. That ole hen got up and staggered about ten more steps and fell over and then it got up and started flutterin here and flutterin there and a weavin here and a weavin there and then it took off runnin sideways past the smokehouse, past the hog pasture, and out through the dog fennels and on off into the woods. And do you know to this day we ain't never seen that hen since.

I had to help Jeanette catch her another chicken and we was laughin and laughin. But you know, we never did tell Ma and Pa about that. That had to be our secret.

Sometimes, I remember when we didn't even have no chickens up under the house and there was no hogs out there in the pens. That's when we'd eat alot of Ma's biscuits. We'd mostly have biscuits and rice or biscuits and cane patch syrup that Pa buys in that big ole can.

I remember a few years back when we lived in the clay hill house. We called it that cause all the dirt round it was that ole hard red clay. It just killed your feet when you walked round barefooted in it, specially out there in them fields.

D. M., my brother, next to the baby was born there. About the time he was born, Pa went off on a drunk for a spell. We didn't have nothin much to eat in the house. We'd even run out of flour and rice. All we had was some cornmeal and cane patch syrup. So, Ma cooked up some cornbread outta that cornmeal in that little thin iron skillet on top of the stove.

Ma took down that little glass pitcher with the metal top full of syrup. She tole us to pour some of that syrup in our plates and to break off pieces of that cornbread and sop that syrup with it.

Well, I ask you, have you ever tried to sop syrup with cornbread? It just tore all to pieces and we wound up eatin it with a spoon.

F L O R E N C E R E E C E

(1 9 0 0 – 1 9 8 6)

Florence Reece wrote her now-famous song, "Which Side Are You On?," during a miners' strike in "Bloody Harlan" County, Kentucky, in 1931. Her husband, Sam, was among the organizers of the miners, and he was often being hunted by gun thugs hired by the mine bosses and deputized by the sheriff, J. H. Blair. Thugs frequently came around searching for Sam and other union activists—beatings and killings were not at all unusual, and the miners gave as good as they got, whenever they could. One night when her husband had avoided the thugs by sneaking back to the house through a corn field, Mrs. Reece took an old wall calendar and wrote out the song. She set it, like many working-class poets, to an old Baptist hymn. It rapidly circulated as an effective organizing tool and was, subsequently, often adapted to other strike situations; for that reason, there are many versions of the song. In fact, during the civil rights movement of the 1960s, one verse was recast:

They say in Mississippi
No neutrals can be met,
You'll either be a freedom fighter
Or a thug for Ross Barnett.

As the song says, Florence Reece's father was a miner. He was killed in the mines by falling slate, loading a ton-and-a-half of coal for thirty cents. Florence was fourteen and Sam nineteen when they were married, a union that lasted 64 years until Sam's death in 1978. They raised ten children, every one "born at home," as Florence Reece put it. Sam first joined the miners' union in 1917, and he and Florence continued as activists in union and other progressive causes throughout much of their adult lives, mainly in Kentucky and in Tennessee. Florence Reece was one among a group of Kentucky women—Sarah Ogan Gunning and Aunt Molly Jackson were two others—whose songs helped inspire working people in times of desperate poverty and fierce and often bloody battles during the nearly half-century it took to unionize the Kentucky mines.

WHICH SIDE ARE YOU ON?

Come all you poor workers,
Good news to you I'll tell,
How the good old union
Has come in here to dwell.

(Chorus:)
Which side are you on?
Which side are you on?

We're starting our good battle,
We know we're sure to win,
Because we've got the gun thugs
A-lookin' very thin.

(Chorus:)
Which side are you on?
Which side are you on?

If you go to Harlan County,
There is no neutral there,
You'll either be a union man
Or a thug for J. H. Blair.

(Chorus:)
Which side are you on?
Which side are you on?

They say they have to guard us
To educate their child,
Their children live in luxury,
Our children almost wild.

(Chorus:)
Which side are you on?
Which side are you on?

With pistols and with rifles
They take away our bread,
And if you miners hinted it
They'll sock you on the head.

(Chorus:)
Which side are you on?
Which side are you on.?

Gentlemen, can you stand it?
Oh, tell me how you can?
Will you be a gun thug
Or will you be a man?

(Chorus:)
Which side are you on?
Which side are you on?

My daddy was a miner,
He's now in the air and sun,*
He'll be with you fellow workers
Till every battle's won.

(Chorus:)
Which side are you on?
Which side are you on?

KENNETH PATCHEN

(1911–1972)

Kenneth Patchen was born and brought up in the Mahoning Valley in Northeastern Ohio, once one of the primary steel-making areas of the world. The experience of the steel towns, the flashing, unearthly beauty of

---

*Blacklisted and without a job.

*the blast furnaces, the corruption of air, water, and men's lives, the eco-
nomic highs and desperate declines, influenced Patchen throughout a
remarkably productive life, during which he published more than forty
books. His finest poetry is balanced on that tricky edge expressed by the title
of one of his best-known collections,* Poems of Humor & Protest *(1954).
While much of his work protests against the violence and abuse human
beings impose on one another, he writes in a style marked by surreal fantasy and bitter playfulness, qualities illustrated by the selection here, "The
Orange Bears."*

*Patchen developed not only a unique poetic style but a distinctive tech-
nique for combining original paintings and drawings with written texts, as
in his "painted books," each volume of which featured an original cover
painting created by him. Some of his poems dart across the page, others
appear like blocks of prose, others are decorated with drawings reminiscent
sometimes of those of Paul Klee, sometimes of Krazy Kat. He can speak in
the voice of an angry working man, deploying at the same time thick and
funny literary allusions, as in his poem "Eve of St. Agony or the Middleclass
Was Sitting on Its Fat." Most of his work, in short, is innovative, quirky,
engaged.*

*Patchen's father worked in the mills (as did Patchen briefly) but in a
relatively well paying job; he supplemented his income by building
homes. But with the crash of 1929, the family's fortunes declined sharply.
Patchen was able to attend the experimental college at the University of
Wisconsin for a year on scholarship and then Commonwealth College for
some months. Between 1930 and 1933, he wandered over the United
States, taking odd jobs when they could be found, writing when he might.
His first published poem came out in the* New York Times *in 1932. Later
he worked in a rubber plant, on the WPA guides to New York and California, as a scriptwriter, and as an office worker for New Directions
Press. His first book,* Before the Brave *(1936), was published by Random
House, was very widely reviewed, and led to a Guggenheim fellowship.
But for many years Patchen's relationships with publishers were problematic: he could not find a publisher for his innovative work,* The Journal of Albion Moonlight, *so he and his wife brought it out themselves by
subscription (1941). In 1946, seven new books came out, issued by five
different publishers. Ultimately, he would become one of the mainstays of
New Directions Press, a major publisher for a number of the most innovative modernist writers. Having moved to the west coast for reasons of
health in 1956, Patchen also became one of the originators of the poetry
and jazz movement, reading with a variety of musical groups until back
injuries confined him to bed. But he continued to draw and write, now
including plays, despite intense pain, near paralysis, and only rare
moments of recognition.*

THE ORANGE BEARS

The Orange bears with soft friendly eyes
Who played with me when I was ten,
Christ, before I'd left home they'd had
Their paws smashed in the rolls, their backs

Seared by hot slag, their soft trusting
Bellies kicked in, their tongues ripped
Out, and I went down through the woods
To the smelly crick with Whitman
In the Haldeman-Julius edition,
And I just sat there worrying my thumbnail
Into the cover—What did he know about
Orange bears with their coats all stunk up with soft coal
And the National Guard coming over
From Wheeling to stand in front of the millgates
With drawn bayonets jeering at the strikers?

I remember you would put daisies
On the windowsill at night and in
The morning they'd be so covered with soot
You couldn't tell what they were anymore.

A hell of a fat chance my orange bears had!

MARY FELL
(B. 1947)

Born and raised in Worcester, Massachusetts, Mary Fell often evokes in her poems the working class environment and culture in which she grew up. "Picket Line in Autumn," for example, was written when she was in graduate school at the University of Massachusetts/Amherst, during an attempt to organize a nursing home there. She earned her M.F.A. at the University of Massachusetts in 1981 and began teaching writing the same year at Indiana University East, in Richmond, where she has been chair of English. In 1983, she published her master's thesis, a book-length poem entitled The Triangle Fire. *In the following year her first full book of poetry,* The Persistence of Memory, *came out in the Random House National Poetry series. She received an Indiana Arts Commission Master Artist Fellowship in 1985, and in 1991 she was poet-in-residence at Fort Juniper, the home of the late poet Robert Francis, in Amherst, Massachusetts. Recently she has had residencies at the Ragdale Foundation in Lake Forest, Illinois, and at the Mary Anderson Center for the Arts in Indiana.*

PICKET LINE IN AUTUMN

The face getting brown
as morning falls
just ripe out of the sky—

a change from last night's
cold, warm gloves and
frost poured into
these empty coffee cups—

you've never been so much
in the world as now,
spending all daylight
and all night too outdoors,
going in circles like the world does,
though sometimes it seems
standing still, getting nowhere—

except you know your tired feet
are turning the earth
and someday the sun
will give itself up to you,
the leaves surrender—
you know they will, if
you keep on walking long enough.

ALICE CHILDRESS

(B. 1920)

Born in Charleston, South Carolina, to poor and uneducated parents, Childress was raised in New York by her grandmother, Eliza Campbell. Unable to finish high school, she joined the American Negro Theater in 1940 and worked with the troupe as an actress, playwright, and activist until 1952. Her first play, Florence *(1949), focuses, like most of her later work, on a black woman struggling against racism and condescension. Her* Gold through Trees *(1952) was the first play by an African-American woman to be produced by a professional company. Her 1955* Trouble in Mind *deals with black actors contesting demands that they portray stereotypes rather than people; despite its then controversial themes, it played for ninety-one performances and won an Obie, the first awarded to a woman playwright. She is probably best known for her play* Wedding Band, *which deals directly with an interracial relationship between a black man and a white woman in 1918 South Carolina. Initially deemed too controversial for conventional theater companies, it was first produced at the University of Michigan in 1966; by 1973, however, the play had been adapted for television.*

During the 1940s, Childress often had to seek work as a domestic to supplement her meager theatrical earnings. She drew on these experiences to write a column, "Here's Mildred," for the Baltimore Afro-American *and for* Freedom. *Her satirical 1956 book,* Like One of the Family: Conversations from a Domestic's Life *(from which the following piece is derived), repre-*

sents a selection from those articles. One of her essays, "The Negro Woman in American Literature," published in 1966 in Freedomways, *anticipates many later works on the subject. But Childress not only attacked stereotypes and prejudice and promoted progressive politics in her writing: she was instrumental, despite the pressures of the Cold War of the 1950s, in winning union recognition and contracts for black stagehands and performers.*

Childress has also been active since 1971 writing and producing works for young adults. The best known of these, a novel, is A Hero Ain't Nothin' But a Sandwich *(1973), which she turned into a film in 1977, starring Cicely Tyson and Paul Winfield. With her husband, Nathan Woodward, a composer, Childress has also staged a number of original works that draw upon African-American historical and musical experiences.*

IN THE LAUNDRY ROOM

Marge . . . Sometimes it seems like the devil and all his imps are tryin' to wear your soul case out. . . . Sit down, Marge, and act like you got nothin' to do. . . . No, don't make no coffee, just sit. . . .

Today was laundry day and I took Mrs. M . . .'s clothes down to the basement to put them in the automatic machine. In a little while another houseworker comes down—a white woman. She dumps her clothes on the bench and since my bundle is already in the washer I go over to sit down on the bench and happen to brush against her dirty clothes. . . . Well sir! She gives me a kinda sickly grin and snatched her clothes away quick. . . .

Now, you know, Marge, that it was nothin' but the devil in her makin' her snatch that bundle away 'cause she thought I might give her folks gallopin' pellagra or somethin'. Well, honey, you know what the devil in me wanted to do! . . . You are right! . . . My hand was just itchin' to pop her in the mouth, but I remembered how my niece Jean has been tellin' me that *poppin'* people is not the way to solve problems. . . . So I calmed myself and said, "Sister, why did you snatch those things and look so flustered?" She turned red and says, "I was just makin' room for you." Still keepin' calm, I says, "You are a liar." . . . And then she hung her head.

"Sister," I said, "you are a houseworker and I am a houseworker—now will you favor me by answering some questions?" She nodded her head. . . . The first thing I asked her was how much she made for a week's work and, believe it or not, Marge, she earns less than I do and *that ain't easy.* . . . Then I asked her, "Does the woman you work for ask you in a *friendly* way to do extra things that ain't in the bargain and then later on get *demandin'* about it?" . . . She nods, yes. . . . "Tell me, young woman," I went on, "does she cram eight hours of work into five and call it *part time?*" . . . She nods yes again. . . .

Then, Marge, I added, "I am not your enemy, so don't get mad with me just because you ain't free! . . . Then she speaks up fast, "I am free!" . . . All right," I said. "How about me goin' over to your house tonight for supper?" . . . "Oh," she says, "I room with people and I don't think they . . ." I cut her off. . . . "If you're free," I said, "you can pick your own friends without fear."

Wait a minute, Marge, let me tell it now. . . . "How come," I asked her, "the folks I work for are willin' to have me put my hands all over their chopped meat patties and yet ask me to hang my coat in the kitchen closet instead of in the hall with theirs?" . . . By this time, Marge, she looked pure bewildered. . . . "Oh," she said, "it's all so mixed up I don't understand!"

"Well, it'll all get clearer as we go along," I said. . . . "Now when you got to plunge your hands in all them dirty clothes in order to put them in the machine . . . how come you can't see that it's a whole lot safer and makes more sense to put your hand in mine and be friends?" Well, Marge, she took my hand and said, "I want to be friends!"

I was so glad I hadn't popped her, Marge. The good Lord only knows how hard it is to do things the right way and make peace. . . . All right now, let's have the coffee, Marge.

STEVE TURNER

Steve Turner is the one writer in this collection about whom we have been able to find no information, apart from what he himself narrates in Night Shift in a Pickle Factory. *Perhaps, therefore, he can stand as a representative of the many unknown creators from the working classes who have, nevertheless, contributed meaningfully to the worlds of art and to the narration of class struggle. His story, like Lloyd Zimpel's* Foundry Foreman, Foundrymen, *was published by Singlejack Books, a now defunct publisher in San Pedro, California, who issued these and other titles in a 2½" x 4" format, modeled after the turn-of-the-century series issued by Haldeman-Julius, that was designed to fit in the shirt pocket of a working man.*

FROM NIGHT SHIFT IN A PICKLE FACTORY

Three-forty P.M. on a scorching August day: I'm following a hopper truck full of cucumbers into a driveway marked *Brogan Pickle Company. As* the big dual wheels ahead hit dirt surface, dust boils out like smoke, and it gets me before I can close the windows. My nose is choked. My sweat turns into a light covering of mud.

I'm off to a great start on my first shift at the pickle factory.

Stupidly, too, the first thing I'm going to have to do here is kill some time. Even though I've been held up behind a whole string of cucumber haulers—they're top-heavy and slow, and they're lumbering along everywhere now on the flat valley roads—I'm still early.

It is nerves rather than eagerness that has me here too soon. For several weeks I have been trying to avoid this moment. But my unemployment has run out, and my wife's income is losing ground fast at the stores and gasoline pumps. I haven't been able to find anything steady since the layoff at my mill and nothing to match the wage I was getting. And now the layoff seems to be turning into a shutdown: they're going to reopen in Taiwan.

So the same choice came to me as to all the other people out of work in the dying old factory towns here: either go along the river with the migrant crews, picking the tobacco and vegetables, or sign on at the pickle cannery. I've done both kinds of work before, and you can have either one for fertilizer as far as I'm concerned. But the bugs and heat are especially bad here in August. And I really don't have the right body for stoop labor anymore.

So, finally, this morning I went to the pickle factory office. The personnel people there let me know they were deeply bored by my arrival. Without even breaking off a phone conversation, the desk man handed me an application to fill out. But the paperwork was just a formality. Turnover is so high there that all they really wanted to know was could I understand the spoken word, and was I really alive or just faking it. I passed both tests. They hired me for the night shift: 4:00 P.M.–12:00 A.M., with two fifteen-minute breaks and a half-hour for dinner. Minimum wage plus ten cents' shift differential. Hot stuff. It's not a union shop. Not yet.

"Be here tonight," said the personnel manager, yawning between his sentences. "See Lucy downstairs for your assignment."

And here I am, early. But I can't hang around the parking lot any longer: people will think I'm a car thief. Also my lunch will decompose in the heat.

So I go on into the production area, where the day shift is still working. It is a big, busy place, actually many big busy places—work-rooms leading on to more work-rooms, all sporting a surprising number of conveyors and machines.

There are a lot of different packing lines. But looking at how the conveyors run, I begin to understand the layout of the place. The hopper trucks are unloading in bins outside, and belts bring the cucumbers in. Some go to slicing machines (I can see the pieces flying out) in a side bay. The rest are dropping into big, fork-liftable fiberglass carryalls called (I later learn) "totes," 4'x4'x4½' high. I can see overhead belts carrying cut pieces from the slicers to some of the packing lines. Forklifts are trucking totes of whole cucumbers around to the others.

Whether they start out cut or whole, however, the next steps for the cucumbers on each line look pretty much the same. Some combination of machines and people get the vegetables into jars or cans, add brine, put on tops, and send the product on toward what can only be pasteurizers: they're big, low cabinets puffing out steam and heat. (On the other side of the pasteurizers, I later learn, are the labelling machines and the warehouse where the boxes of finished product are stored).

All in all, I'm surprised. I had imagined something much less mechanized: hand-rolled barrels; ladles, paddles, troughs. Also missing are the old-world costumes that my wife claimed I would have to wear. Everyone has on white plastic aprons and head-deforming hairnets. Tired, sweaty people. Their glazed eyes scan me and then move on to the clock. Tufts of what look like cotton stick out of most ears, and I understand why as I move into the first room and noise engulfs me: the rattle of conveyors and *chuff-sigh of* a big pneumatic packing machine, and the whining hum of many motors, and a major roaring from a device that is vacuum-cleaning jars — which are themselves hustling and clinking on the conveyors like a million glass chickens.

Also bathing me now is the breath of the place, thickly humid and warm but not (hooray!) as pungent as I feared. There is vinegar in the air, indeed, but not enough to overcome the dull smell of cut cucumbers—which litter the floor everywhere, with water puddling and flowing around them. Water seems to be running, spraying, or dripping from all equipment. Looking below conveyors I see that everybody has soggy footwear and pants wet to the knees.

And I see glass: dense, sparkly scatterings of it blended here and there with the vegetable scrap and water in a horrible stew, thicker around my feet as I slog toward the production office. Can this really be the Great Shiny Kitchen where our nation's canned foods are made?

I check in. The young woman who clerks in the office tells me to shut the door quick: it's quiet in there, and also air conditioned (the air conditioner, of course, exhausts its heat out into the production area). She has a very appealing face, this clerk, and I find myself staring at her. But she does not exchange the glance. Instead, she hands me a time card, a hairnet, and an apron, and I have to go back into the heat and noise.

I join the growing night shift crowd punching in at the clock. It prints my card, *chungg,* and I find my slot in the rack and drop the card in. Time to start waiting again. Some of the others are conversing, but not with me. I'm lonely and self-conscious. I don't mind the apron, but really want not to put on the hairnet. Staring around, I notice a vending machine on the outside wall of the office which dispenses pressed cones of ear cotton. I have heard that this stuff doesn't really block dangerous noise. Also it dries out and scratches the ears. But I take some, better than nothing. At least it dims down the general level of sound.

Three supervisors arrive with clipboards. One is a woman about my size (not small) with a voice very large for her dolphin-like mouth. Her hair is coiled uniquely to a point on top of her head. It is Lucy, the line-crew boss, and at the end of her roll she calls my name. "Dill Spears line," she says. "And put on your hairnet."

We're off to see the Wizard.

* * *

It's my second night. I'm out of shape for this: stiff back, sore body, desperate knees. But I'm surviving. Our crew is making dill spears again, which are "fresh pack": they go in the jars as raw pieces, then brine is added (an intense, Day-Glo yellow fluid) and spices, and it's all cooked up in there by the pasteurizers. Instant pickle.

Fresh-pack pickles of various sorts are what the harvest expansion crew is mainly hired to produce. Out on the factory's back lot are many huge tanks used for the long-term fermenting of traditional "process" pickles, reeking away to make winter work for the year-round people on the day shift.

I have this information from the friendly Johnson T., military veteran like me, with whom I share the joy of poling the dipper. This task is the factory's answer to a little flaw in the mechanization. Once the cucumbers are on the conveyor, they go mighty fast. But getting them on there is a problem, because they are floating in a ten-foot by four-foot wood tub of rinsewater. Solution? A basketball-size net on a six-foot pole. Alternating every two hours, Johnson T. and I stand on a wobbly platform beside the tub and dip them out, 20 to 40 pounds per netful, and dump them in the hopper at the end of the conveyer. Dip and dump enough to keep a flow going that will bring—even with all the rejects culled out—four dozen jars' worth every minute through the spray washer to the packing machine, a dandy big robot that cuts off the ends of the pickles, slices and inserts them, two cucumbers into each pint jar. Watching all this shiny automation carry away my laboriously lifted netfuls, I am reminded of the old cartoon of the fancy car with its hood up, and instead of an engine inside it has a cage of squirrels with a treadmill.

Alternating on stints away from the dipper, Johnson T. and I work beside the two sorters, who are assigned to catch and discard rejects as the belt speeds the cucumbers past them. All injured or rotten ones, and those of wrong size or shape for mechanical packing efficiency must be snatched from the conveyor (both hands are needed for fairly constant grabbing) and flipped into a "tote." When the tote is full of rejects, a forklift comes and shunts it aside, puts another in its place, and trucks the full one away to dump into the vats of stock used for relish.

The sorting job is not as hard as dipping, but just standing there and doing it really gets to the knees. Also it is a total wet pants job: the conveyor has an open-mesh belt, so all the rinsewater from the cucumbers, and the drain-off from the spray washer runs right down on us as we work. A simple splash-guard at the work zone would help a lot and probably a lot of people have asked for one, but that's the sort of thing the management here doesn't install. Sometimes we get cardboard boxes from where the glass is unpacked, flatten them out and hang them from the conveyor rails to deflect the constant shower. They soon sog through. By the end of the shift we are usually too tired to care.

I find solace in the memory of another cannery where I worked years before. They were running a 10-hour day shift and a 12-hour night shift, packing peas. I was stacking the finished product there instead of sorting, and glad for it. Sorters had to search an endless fast moving stream of shelled peas to find—and pinch out—bad ones, gravel, poison belladonnas and other undesirables. They weren't wet all the time like at Brogan's, but they were worse off. Periodically they went pea-happy and began smashing the stock. I haven't eaten canned peas since.

* * *

I'm feeling more fit on my third night, which is good because this evening we experience our first High Management Official (HIMO). He appears with a small flotilla of subordinates, all wearing hard hats and no aprons. This makes us feel even sillier with our heads misshapen by the hairnets. I am poling the dipper. Johnson T. is sorting. The line is really rolling. The HIMO peers into the reject tote, grabs out a little cucumber, and holds it up for Johnson T. to see.

"What criteria are you using to discard this pickle?" the front office man asks. (Inside the factory, cucumbers tend to be called pickles whether they are yet or not.)

Yes, the HIMO wants Johnson T. to explain to him the fate of this one of tens of thousands of cucumbers we will handle tonight. Johnson T. immediately understands that this is a military situation. He snaps to attention. "Sir," he shouts, "criteria for pickle discarding, sir." Hands of the other two sorters accelerate desperately in the sudden overload created by the absence of Johnson T's.

"None under four inches, sir," yells Johnson T. "None too fat to go through the measuring ring. None too whopping large, sir, nor the sick nor broken." The HIMO's eyes begin to glaze over. Johnston T. snatches up and brandishes a huge, J-shaped mutant from the passing swarm. "None too curvy, sir," he shouts, "none too bent!"

"This one is more than four inches," hisses the HIMO. He holds it against the length-measure tape on the sidewall of the conveyor, and it is four-and-one-half inches long. Johnson T. gestures silently to the fast mass passage on the belt, inviting HIMO to demonstrate his rare binocular skill in action. The other sorters are keeping careful poker faces but have begun doing exaggerated slumps and acting out other signs of despair.

"Just keep a sharp eye," says the HIMO, returning the reject to the tote as he leaves. Johnson T. salutes his departure with the mutant, and goes back to work. I have had to keep on dipping throughout the exchange, but stop now to applaud.

Later I start to laugh from the recollection. By break time I realize that I am finished with my new-guy adjustment. Like most, if not all the others, I am no longer upset about being unable to do the job right at the speed they run the line.

* * *

It's the fourth night now, and I'm beginning to feel at home. At dinner break, Johnson T. and I join Carl and Alfred on the tarmac outside the big doors to the parking lot. We are the veterans group, relative elders among the 70-or-so others on the shift. More than half of those others are women, and many of both sexes are high-school or college students. They are eating bag lunches like us, sitting on the pavement or on nearby cars—the lunch-rooms inside are hot and dreary. After eating, some drift off deeper among the cars to smoke dope (how can they stand to slow the time down here?). The rest of us relax, enjoying the nice sunset.

Introductions come slowly because everyone's relationships to the place and to each other are temporary and casual. We'll all be laid off as soon as the crop is packed. So most conversations occur without an exchange of names. In my mind, however, I give people identities: Mandrake, Blondie, Egyptian Eyes, Fulminator.

Motormouth is a quality inspector who dispenses a more-or-less continuous breaktime monologue of Grossnesses Of Our Work, and he is at it again tonight.

"It's not so sweet in there now," says Motormouth to anyone in earshot, "but a couple of years ago it was a lot worse, under the old management. I had an old guy tell me that back then, when they came in in the mornings, the brine in the tanks would have a layer of dead cockroaches floating on it. It's full of sugar. So that was the first thing they'd do, scoop the bugs off. Now they got plastic covers for the tanks."

Appropriate retching sounds are heard among Motormouth's listeners. Gap-tooth the forklift driver speaks up: "There's still roaches in there. We caught a big Virginia roach in there, about yea long [fingers indicating two inches]. Put him in a jar with some brine so he could eat. Come back Monday, though, he was dead."

"Oh, there's still roaches in there, all right," says Motormouth. "Hell, they fog the place every night with insecticide, but doesn't kill them all. Matter of fact, they fog so thick that one morning the whole crew walked out."

"What kind of insecticide?" someone says.

"Don't know," Motormouth says. "The barrels are blank, no labels, nothing, and the foreman won't tell me. But it stinks bad. And they aren't too particular about washing it off the equipment, either." He pauses to take a bite of a sandwich, then goes right on talking, "Speaking of stinks, though," he says, "have you seen the cabbages? You want to see something bad, you got to see the cabbages they keep for the relish. You got to smell *them,* if you want a treat."

So a bunch of us go with Motormouth to see the cabbages, off in a back bay, in big vats like the one we dip from on the spears line but with plastic tarpaulin covers. Motormouth lifts a cover slightly and out comes a puff of powerful vapor. Inside are heaps of cabbages, pickling in something pretty strong. They look like they have a skin disease. I move close enough to see that the odd color is in fact not decay, and to determine that the odor is fermentatious rather than rotten. But the stomach helplessly boggles at the thought of consuming this ugly stuff.

"It looks bad," Motormouth says, "but it's okay to eat. Besides, there's worse than this going into the relish with the cucumber scrap from those totes." Motormouth is ready to go on with the monologue, but a larger sound drowns him out: the reverberating bellows of Lucy the Line Boss, calling us back to work.

* * *

The next night, Johnson T. informs me that there are several people on our shift who are "mental." They have been sent here (apparently) for jobs as a therapy for adjusting them to the workaday world. He points out three. Over on line number one (the main, fast packing line), one of them is assigned to inspect jars as they move toward a packing machine. She is poised under a bright light to look for cracks and chips as the glass streams by, 148 jars per minute, shoulder to shoulder, each one sparkling the same series of refractions as it passes. Great therapy. Mercifully, the job seems to hypnotize those who do it.

The most surprising thing about Johnson T.'s list of the mind-blown among us is its shortness. What about Fulminator, who yells out great wolf cries while operating the line one brine injector? Also Knife Woman, on our own dill spears line, who is either cracked or cracking up. She has very bright eyes and chews gum and grins on a fairly steady basis (which strengthens her resemblance to Harpo Marx). She also twitches and jitters a lot. During shut downs and other odd breaks on the spears line, when the supervisors are distracted, Knife Woman comes to our rinse tub and takes out cucumbers, one at a time, wrings them like chicken necks and throws them over her shoulder onto the floor.

Johnson T. argues that Knife Woman's work explains this behavior. Equipped with a long paring knife, she receives the jars as they come from the brine filler. The dripping ends of spears stuffed in for final tight packing (the work of the eight hand-packers who finish up what the machine begins) stick up out of the jars' necks. Knife Woman slices these off flush with the rim, 48 jars in a minute, as they head for the capper. The lopped-off, yellow-stained pieces fall down to pile up under the conveyor, forming a mound that spreads slowly over her foot mat, then over her feet.

She also has responsibility for the start-up and shut-down switches, pairs of red and green buttons on an obscure panel, mounted absurdly high above the conveyor. When the shut-down order comes (as it does, unpredictably, when glass or machines break), Knife Woman must charge up out of her moosh pile onto the bottom strut of the conveyor trestle, and smear at the buttons with her stretched, gooey fingers until she has stopped the machinery. As she lurches up toward the controls, she often utters a kind of yipping, frantic cry. I never could figure out why, so one time when she came over to our tub to strangle some pickles I asked her about it.

"Revenge," she said, and gave a sort of giggle. Then she stared at me, chewing gum and grinning. I couldn't think of anything more to say. I know that at dinner and the rest of the breaks she talks and hangs around as normally as anyone else. But when the line starts she just seems to go into another gear.

I concede that Johnson T. is right.

* * *

Tonight our crew (about one third of the people on the shift) moves to another packing line, one that I hadn't noticed, off in a decrepit, nowhere room. And as Lucy describes the new work, I feel reality slipping away. We are going to spend the next eight hours squeezing pickles.

These are *real* pickles—aged, fermented, "process" whole dills, which are going into five gallon white plastic pails for hotels and restaurants. Half of us are lined up along the conveyor to handle the stock. We are given sheets of mimeographed paper which display the outlines of three sizes of pickles—large, medium and small. The pails are lined up on the other side of the conveyor from us in sets of three, one for each size. Others in the crew are assigned to the weighing, brining, sealing, labelling and stacking of the filled pails. There is also a big holding tub and a dip-net, but Lucy has selected a new worker to do the dipping tonight.

The pace is much slower than on the spear line. But the resulting relaxation is more than made up for by the disgusting and ludicrous nature of the work. Only firm, solid pickles may be packed, says Lucy, and to test the firmness we must give each candidate a full-hand clench. The unacceptables collapse under this pressure, squirting their rank fluids down the squeezer's arm. The mushed pulp of the failures goes back on the conveyor, headed (where else?) for relish stock. Those that pass the test are chucked into the pails.

At first there is confusion, as people try to compare the pickles in their hands to the size outlines on the paper sheets. But the result is that the sheets are soon soaked through with pickle juice, and become useless. People begin tossing the pickles into whichever pail they feel like aiming for. Lucy makes a point of coming by every few minutes to quell the outbreaks of long-range tossing, basketball-type hook shots and other unapproved packing techniques that we begin to indulge in.

But even Lucy knows that horsing around a little is necessary relief from this crummy job. The odor is strong, and so is the noise: an overhead conveyor moving fresh stock to another line sends down a keen whine along with a steady, slow rain of rinsewater. And of course the physical sensations are lousy. No one tells us to wear gloves, so, most of us are barehanded, printing the outbound pickles with our puckering fingers. Bandaids for two cuts I got cleaning up glass on the spear lines are soon gone. The iodine beneath them then washes slowly away.

Hygiene is not dominant on the other side of the conveyor either. The brine for filling the pails of pickles is in an open tub, and is dipped out with a spare packing pail. There is no clean place to set the pail between dippings except to float it in the brine. Sometimes it gets set on the muddy floor by accident, and then goes back in the brine.

And labelling contributes some unauthorized crud to the pails, too. The labels are stencilled on with an ink-brush, and hand-held, card-paper stencils. These stencils have worn down so small that labellers' hands unavoidably get inked up along with the code letters. Then the inky hands have to get new pails out of the supply stack, which requires a firm grip on the inside of the fresh pails' rims. Result: frequent marking of pail interiors with big black thumbprints of stencil ink. Quality control supervisors come up periodically and complain about these prints. Finally one of them yells, "Would you eat something that came out of this [ink smeared] pail?"

"Would you eat shit?" shouts Mandrake, who is dipping out brine. But Blondie, who is labelling, simply says "Get me a better stencil if you want them clean."

Quality Control goes away. New stencils are apparently beyond the fiscal reach of the factory owners.

* * *

Another night of squeezing. Or could this be a dream? . . .

* * *

The speedup rate set last night is still on: it is the new rate. Our wages, of course, remain the same. At dinner break, the veterans group makes its first reprisal. We are at Oxie's, a bar about three minutes' walk from the factory (featuring air conditioning and free popcorn)—Alfred Carl, Johnson T. and I, sharing a table as we have lately come to do. Others in the shift crew are at other tables. There is a general air of lament and exhaustion in the room.

A moment of crucial realization comes as the clock moves to 8:20, seven minutes before we have to leave if we want to punch in on time. We are staring at an empty beer pitcher and feeling still thirsty. Carl suddenly says, "What happens if we just don't go back on time? They can dock us, but I bet they wouldn't fire us all."

"Couldn't even start the line," Alfred says. "We got the briner, the capper, and the pasteurizer all right here. Right?"

Carl then points out that he is assigned as backup to all three machines. We think about it for a moment. Then Johnson T. turns and yells, "Hey, at the bar—send us another pitcher."

It is the best beer I will drink all year. We sit beaming self-consciously as the rest of the crew droops out to go back. And to break the nervousness that swells up in the suddenly empty room, Johnson T. leans back and talks, continuing his tales of Frank the Frag, fabled trooper on Nam who would blow up any commander for his friends.

In this first effort, we hold out for only five minutes past clock-in time. But the supervisors look at us angrily, warily as we come in. They know something is up, and we confirm it on several nights thereafter. We push the limit a little more each time, feeling for the point where discipline will begin to come down.

I seem to be the most mathematically inclined among us, so I work out the figures that we set our sights against: the speedup is adding (under ideal conditions) about 300 cases per shift. But every minute we keep the line from moving knocks out seven cases from the night's potential. We add on more minutes, subtract more units of seven cases. Finally we reach a record of 11 minutes. It is a fine night: one-quarter of the speedup has been offset by our delay.

"We keep this up," Carl says, "and they're going to come after us. There's going to be a searchlight in the window, and Lucy out there on a bullhorn yelling 'Come out! We know you are in there!'"

"Lucy don't need a bullhorn," says Alfred, and we drink to that.

But it is Ted, the night production overseer, who we meet as we head back through the dark alleys to work. He has indeed come to get us.

"Ted!" says Johnson T., spying the anxious Boss. "Whatcha say, man? Want to come on back for a beer with us?"

"Very funny," says Ted. "Let's just get back to work, shall we?" But he makes no threats. As we have guessed by now, the number of people quitting (the speedup, plus knowledge that the layoff is coming close) has left management unwilling to fire us unless we really do something drastic.

"Ah, Ted," says Johnson T., "what's a few pickles between friends?"

We laugh. Ted tries to smile. He is pulling steadily ahead of us, looking back over his shoulder, obviously using all his brain power to try to wish us along faster as we amble through the night toward the noise, the heat, the smell, the machines.

* * *

Mathematical analysis, once begun, seems hard to stop. This time I have multiplied store prices for pickles times the production totals on the wall. At the first break I am able to reveal that our line is making an average $4,500 per hour in product value—while our total wages for the same period, including an estimate for supervisors, come to about $100. The sense of a bad ripoff festers in the gap between.

"But you got to count for glass and pickles, and like that," says Motormouth,

Hell, give them $2,000 an hour for that, I say, and they still make $25,000 extra from this crew every shift. The slower work on the other lines yields less, but there are three crews minimum working both shifts while the harvest lasts. Take out all the rest of the overhead, there's still a big bundle left for the owners to play with. Our work pays for everything in the end, but it pays us least of all.

There is a short silence. Then Mandrake says, "Ain't that some shit?"

"Cream's gonna rise unless you homogenize," someone says.

We sit there with the sweat cooling, watching the evening come on.

"It's not right, this way of doing things," Alfred says. And I think by this point everyone on the shift would second that, even though there are different opinions about what ought to happen instead. It's just that there isn't anyone among us who doesn't resent how the factory is operated so fast and sloppy, because there's no way to respect what we're doing and what we're making.

In fact, most people here like it best when things don't work right and production goes to hell, and I'm right along with them. And that's a crummy way to waste your working time.

We're told there is a union organizing now among the full-timers on the day shift, and that ought to balance the situation up a little, maybe a lot. We don't know: the organizers are leaving us seasonals alone, since we won't be around for the long battle the permanent people are going to have with this management. We can feel good for the day shift while we feel bad for ourselves.

But not liking the place hasn't meant disliking the experience. I'm still getting the good feeling of linked-up strength when I trade glances with Johnson T. at the next machine, or when I just take a moment to look up and down the line when we're going at full speed. Our crew is operating a great deal of fast running metal that can't do anything without us. We're turning out the goods, and that's an importance that ties us together. We're in a situation that offers some very satisfying moments of kinship of spirit: in the zoo, for instance, when the women slashed back at the line that was swamping them. In Arletta's artwork (and goodbye again, Arletta), and Mandrake's refusal to kowtow. And in the gratification we felt in the veterans' group for even that minor resistance to the speedup.

Unfortunately, however, the good people and the good moments here aren't quite enough to make up for all that is unlikable—at least not when the final layoff is drawing so near. I'm fed up with the place, in fact, and with the end-of-season layoff just days away I've begun to think of cashing in early just for the satisfaction of quitting. I figure I have less than no chance to get a day shift job, let alone a permanent spot — even if I wanted one. And the unemployment money I'd get by waiting for the layoff is hardly worth waiting in line for anyway (minimum wage!).

And so it is that an incident with Lucy becomes one straw too many for me to bear.

It is the dog hours of the shift, after the second break, and I am sitting down on an overturned bucket. The packing machine is stopped for something minor. It will be back on soon: Lucy is diddling with it. Everyone is waiting, not enough of a delay to start cleaning the floor.

The machine starts. Jars come out as Lucy returns control to the operator. I remain sitting because it takes about one minute for the jars to get down to me, and a minute's a extra sitting is important when you spend the night on your feet.

But Lucy sees me resting there, with the line already moving, and her resentment over the dinner-break delay tactics and who knows what else boil right out. She jerks her thumb at me and screams, "UP!"

"What?" I say, honestly disbelieving she can have said that to me in that way.

"Up!" she shouts again, and again her thumb jerks. "UP FOR THE JARS!"

I should have risen then and walked out of the factory. But I didn't. I merely sat, staring at her enraged eyes, until the jars arrived at the briner. Then I got up, switched on, and finished the shift.

But when I punched out, I wrote a big note on my card: *Mail my check, I quit.* I said my goodbyes as we all split for our cars. And you won't find me packing pickles up at Brogan's anymore.

THEODORE ROETHKE

(1908-1963)

One of America's great poets, Roethke came from a family in which the authoritative father ran a large commercial greenhouse in Saginaw, Michigan. His father's force and the opportunities offered by the flower business to observe nature with care and intensity influenced Roethke's poetry throughout his life. Roethke attended the University of Michigan, then did graduate work there and at Harvard. He began teaching in 1931 at Lafayette College in Easton, PA, and after a number of moves, came to the University of Washington in Seattle in 1947, where he remained until his death. In outer form, Roethke's life was that of a longterm professor. But in actual fact, neither his poetry nor his life were in any way academic.

Personally, the poet suffered from a serious alcohol problem, probably manic-depression, and other interpersonal difficulties. He spent a number of periods in treatment facilities and mental institutions. His poetry is enormously varied in terms of the rhythms he deploys within what are often—though not always—intensely regular forms, illustrated even in the very brief "Pickle Belt" (printed here primarily as a pendant to Night Shift in a Pickle Factory*). The poem also displays his ability to capture vividly and sympathetically the personalities of the varied cast of characters about whom he writes. Many of his poems also use highly symbolic, even surrealistic details drawn from his close scrutiny of natural phenomena as well as of human idiosyncrasies. The care with which he developed both formal properties and imagery took time, and Roethke was ten years in completing his first poetry collection,* Open House *(1941). He continued publishing steadily but slowly, some ten books in all, to increasing acclaim. His* Collected Poems *of 1954 won the Pulitzer Prize, one of many such awards accumulated by him over his career.*

PICKLE BELT

The fruit rolled by all day.
They prayed the cogs would creep;
They thought about Saturday pay,
And Sunday sleep.

Whatever he smelled was good:
The fruit and flesh smells mixed.
There beside him she stood,—
And he, perplexed;

He, in his shrunken britches,
Eyes rimmed with pickle dust,
Prickling with all the itches
Of sixteen-year-old lust.

ALICE WIRTH GRAY

(B. 1934)

Alice Wirth Gray's father was an urban sociologist and her mother a social worker who routinely took her young daughter places very few middle-class female children ever saw in the 1930s and 1940s: for instance, the Dwight State Prison for Women, where she went on assignment from Governor Adlai Stevenson to investigate reports of abuse by the prison staff. As the administrator of the Federal Writers' Project during the Depression in Chicago, Gray's mother gave Richard Wright his first literary job and they became lifetime friends. Langston Hughes was the young Gray's first poetry teacher when he was poet-in-residence at her school (in 1948 or 1949). These experiences account, Gray believes, for poems like "He Was When He Died."

Cleveland State University Poetry Center published her first book, What the Poor Eat, *in 1993. It was a finalist for the PEN/West award for poetry that year. Her poems have also been published in* The Atlantic, The American Scholar, *and* Poetry, *among other magazines. She has also had a dozen short stories published: one of them won an Illinois Arts Council Literary Award. Gray attended six or seven schools (law, architecture, English) but finally got her B.A. and M.A. in English from the University of California/Berkeley. She has resided in Berkeley since then.*

HE WAS WHEN HE DIED

The dead man was "an unemployed
mattress factory worker."
                              –San Francisco Chronicle
                              June 28, 1981

Not president of Inland Steel
or the International Monetary Fund.
Not engaged in price-fixing
or planning the Hudson River Valley
breeder reactor. He was not breeding
racehorses. He did not suffer
from dental caries at the time
of his death. He did not meet death
in the arms of an art historian.
Not under indictment by the IRS
nor under investigation by the SEC.
When he died, it was not the first time
he was absent from the annual encampment
at the Bohemian Grove. Nor was he
stuffing ticking at the mattress factory.

At the time of his death he was not
concerned with a faltering professional
practice, nor did he leave an unfinished
painting of water lilies. Fantastic swirls
of red and blue tatoo did not cover
84% of his body. He died,
not at the mattress factory
where he didn't work. He died
not doing so many things,
it's clear his life was thickly textured,
deep. Uncommonly rich.

Mornings he breakfasted at the Bulky Burger,
one egg on a corn muffin and two links.
Being unemployed at the mattress factory,
he couldn't afford it, but he ate
with no sense of guilt, revealing his complex
understanding of free will. No need
to pity him: he was not a member
of an oppressed minority,
not on a disability pension,
not long out of love, no sort of scapegoat,
not working at the Sleeprite factory
on Cowan Road or the Simmons factory
on Fairway Drive or the Sealy Company
on 7th Street in Richmond or even
at any mattress factory where he
ever had worked. He was, at the time
of his death, not

BOB DYLAN

(B. 1941)

Born Robert Allen Zimmerman, Dylan grew up in Duluth and then Hibbing, Minnesota. His father owned an appliance store and was sufficiently well-to-do to enable his son to learn to play piano and guitar. Dylan entered the University of Minnesota in 1959, but he was more interested in playing folk music in Minneapolis's Dinkytown than in hitting the books. In 1961, he moved to New York, where he became a regular at hoots, parties, and other folk events. He met Woody Guthrie, who encouraged him to write his own songs. In the fall of 1961, his career was forwarded by a favorable review in the New York Times; shortly thereafter, he was signed to a contract by Columbia Records.

Initially he produced nothing remarkable, but in the spring of 1962 he wrote his first major song, "Blowin' in the Wind," which was popularized in a recording by Peter, Paul, and Mary. Other hits—"A Hard Rain's a-Gonna Fall," "Only a Pawn in Their Game," "Master of War," "Don't Think Twice, It's All Right"—followed shortly, most of them gathered in albums The Freewheelin' Bob Dylan *(1963),* The Times They Are a-Changin' *(1964), and* Another Side of Bob Dylan *(1964). Many of the songs caught the sense of outrage and long-ing of the New Left political movement, then gathering strength among young people north and south. Dylan's phrases seemed to express the demand for equal rights, the rage at the war on Vietnam, the anomie of students at complacent, self-serving universities. In fact, a line from one of his songs, "Subterranean Homesick Blues" (1965), provided the name, Weathermen, for the underground offshoot of Students for a Democratic Society: "You don't need a weatherman to tell which way the wind blows."*

In 1965 Dylan moved away from his earlier folk idiom toward rock-'n'-roll, adopting an electric rather than an acoustic guitar. Some fans were out-raged, but many of the same thematic elements of protest and yearning appeared in his first album in the new style, Bringing It All Back Home *(1965). In fact, it could be said that Dylan helped bring protest music from the relatively restricted venues of folk to the wider stage provided by rock-'n'-roll, then in the ascendent. "Maggie's Farm," which follows, dates from that era, as do some of his biggest hits, like "Desolation Row" and "Like a Rolling Stone." After 1966, when Dylan was apparently injured in a motorcycle acci-dent, the singer's career has had a number of ups and downs. Undoubtedly, he no longer expressed the sentiments of a generation of young people. On the other hand, he anticipated the move of pop music into country rock and capitalized on that process. He remains active as a singer and songwriter, interesting to younger generations, but appealing most of all to those who grew up politically with phrases like "it's hard rain a-gonna fall" and "the executioner's face is always well hidden" in their ears.*

I Ain't Gonna Work
on Maggie's Farm

I ain't gonna work on Maggie's Farm no more
No, I ain't gonna work on Maggie's Farm no more,
Well I wake in the morning
Fold my hands and pray for rain,
I got a head full of ideas
That are drivin' me insane
It's a shame the way she makes me scrub the floor
I ain't gonna work on Maggie's Farm no more.

I ain't gonna work for Maggie's brother no more
No, I ain't gonna work for Maggie's brother no more
Well he hands you a nickel
He hands you a dime
He asks with a grin
If you're havin' a good time
Then he fines you every time you slam the door
I ain't gonna work for Maggie's brother no more.

I ain't gonna work for Maggie's pa no more
No, I ain't gonna work for Maggie's pa no more
Well he puts his cigar
Out in your face just for kicks
His bedroom window
It is made out of bricks
The National Guard stands around his door
Ah, I ain't gonna work for Maggie's pa no more.

I ain't gonna work for Maggie's ma no more
No, I ain't gonna work for Maggie's ma no more
Well she talks to all the servants
About man and God and law
Everybody says she's the brains behind pa
She's sixty-eight, but she says she's twenty-four
I ain't gonna work for Maggie's ma no more.

I ain't gonna work on Maggie's farm no more
I ain't gonna work on Maggie's farm no more
Well, I try my best
To be just like I am
But everybody wants you
To be just like them
They sing while you slave
And I just get bored
I ain't gonna work on Maggie's farm no more.

SUSAN EISENBERG

(B. 1950)

Susan Eisenberg is a master electrician, activist, and poet—a remarkable combination in itself. She first apprenticed with Local 103 of the International Brotherhood of Electrical Workers in 1978; since then she moved up to journeyman and then master. Meantime, her poems began to appear, first in magazines like Prairie Schooner *and* Willow Springs, *then as books:* It's a Good Thing I'm Not Macho *in 1984 and* Pioneering: Poems from the Construction Site *(1998).*

She has been an active force in organizing women in the trades. She published a book based on interviews with thirty women who work as carpenters, electricians, ironworkers, painters, and plumbers in We'll Call You If We Need You: Experiences of Women Working Construction *(1998). The book was a part of the twentieth-anniversary celebration of President Carter's efforts to increase job opportunities for women on federally aided contracts. She has also been a frequent speaker on the subject of women in nontraditional trades and on what has to be done to increase women's share of such work.*

SUBWAY CONVERSATIONS

Sometimes I try to pick out the job hunters
riding the morning train:

> that one, the way her eyes hunch down
> her smile slightly frayed but
> carefully pressed
>
> or him, sizing up the rest of us, one by one
> guessing paychecks and perks
> checking hands for calluses
> faces for a fatal flaw—certain
> he would be brighter and faster at
> whatever it is we do.

Churchsilent, morning and evening
—unless a boombox or prophet sings out—
we pass this time together
alone, seating ourselves so even our clothing
avoids touch
inhaling each other's perfumes, chemical solvents, sweat.

If once workboots talked with white flats
and leather suitcases understood
the sly jokes between the faded gray jacket

and the ones who always carry some shopping
home with them and if the toolbox
stopped worrying whether the manicured hands
really *do* make more money—
     computing in for overtime   subtracting for
     no sick days or paid holidays—or just
dress and talk like they do . . .

If we spoke together on the train home
about more than
        Heat won't be on 'til summer or
        Watch your bag . . .
If I told you *We can re-direct this train*
I wait for your signal watching you each day
Would you hear me? Must I shout
or whisper? Explain for me why, in America

if I see a cleaning woman and a carpenter and a
teacher salesman secretary lawyer nurse's aide
grasping arms in one unified embrace I know

it must always be a commercial for
hand cream or
an airline that's going bankrupt.

DAVID IGNATOW
(B. 1914)

*For much of his life, David Ignatow worked, like his father before him, as a
New York businessman, despite his ambivalence, if not hatred, of that life.
Indeed, many of his poems attack the money-grubbing of business culture
and the outlooks of people like "The Boss" of the poem that follows; others
present insane businessmen as speakers and America as a crazed surreal
machine gone out of control. One poem from the mid-1960s describes the
spectacle of a man being skinned alive on television, a parable for Ignatow
of America in that brutal time. His characters speak American vernacular,
which the poet deploys with deceptive ease.*

    *Ignatow's poems, while never trendy, have changed in relation to pub-
lic events: his poems of the 1930s reflected the Depression, those of the
1940s, a world at war, those of the 1960s, the debacle of Vietnam. But this
more public verse is set against poems that express Ignatow's personal relationships, his emotions about the work into which he felt forced, his playful
sexuality, his empathy with the oppressed, but his coincident sense of isolation from his fellow creatures.*

    *Ignatow had little recognition as a significant poet until he was almost
fifty; indeed, he did not publish his first book until he was forty-four (*Poems,

*1958). Then, in the 1960s, Wesleyan University Press published three of his
books,* Say Pardon *(1961),* Figures of the Human *(1964), and* Rescue the
Dead *(1968). During this period, Ignatow won Guggenheim and Rockefeller
fellowships, the 1977 Bollingen Prize, and other awards. He taught at a
number of universities, becoming an adjunct faculty member at Columbia's
School of the Arts and in 1969 poet-in-residence at the York College of City
University of New York.*

THE BOSS

who hoarded among the monthly bank statements
nude photos,
the drawer locked,
the key in his pocket,
still could complain
of the stupidity of his help—
their incompetency,
their secretiveness;
he could sense it
in their guarded snickers
when he criticized;
who could walk the shop
in possession as he walked,
stoop-shouldered, careless
how he went, sagging;
it was his shop
and his machinery
and his steel cabinet
where the photos lay.

YSAYE MARIE BARNWELL

*Barnwell has sung with the a capella quintet Sweet Honey in the Rock since
1979. She has composed many songs for the group, including "Breaths,"
"On Children," and the one that follows. She has also written music for*
Sesame Street, *for the Women's Philharmonic of San Francisco, and for a
production of the Tennessee Repertory Theater on the life of Dr. Martin
Luther King, Jr. Barnwell conducts vocal workshops based on African-
American singing traditions and has published an instructional guide with
cassettes to teach those traditions. She has also written a book for children,*
No Mirrors in My Nana's House *(1998).*

*Barnwell studied violin for many years, as well as vocal music. She holds
a doctorate in speech pathology and a post-doctoral degree in public health.*

In addition to her work as singer, composer, actress, she has administered projects on health, computers, and the arts, particularly in the Washington, D.C., area.

MORE THAN A PAYCHECK

We bring more than a paycheck to our loved ones and families;
We bring more than a paycheck to our loved ones and families.

I wanted more pay, but what I've got today
Is more than I bargained for when I walked through your door.
I bring home asbestosis, silicosis, brown lung, black lung disease;
And radiation hits the children before they've really been conceived.

Well now, workers lend an ear, 'cause it's important that you know
With every job there is the fear that disease will take its toll.
If not disease, then injury may befall your lot,
And if not injury, then stress is gonna tie you up in knots.

So we bring home more than a paycheck to our loved ones and families;
We bring more than a paycheck to our loved ones and families.

SUE DORO
(B. 1937)

For thirteen years, Doro worked as the only female machinist on the Milwaukee Road Railway, and also as a maintenance machinist in the Allis Chalmers tractor shop in Milwaukee. When the railroad was bought up and closed down, and Doro's job had disappeared, she moved to California to become executive director of Tradeswomen, Inc., a national organization providing advocacy and support for women in nontraditional (for women) blue-collar jobs. She then went to work for the U.S. Department of Labor monitoring compliance with affirmative action regulations. Along the road, she and her husband have had five children.

Meantime, she had begun to publish poetry. Her first book, Of Birds and Factories, *came out in 1983.* Heart, Home & Hard Hats: the Non-traditional Work and Words of a Woman Machinist and Mother *was published in 1986. Her most recent book,* Blue Collar Goodbyes *(1993), looks at the painful experiences connected to the ending of the railroad and, in effect, Doro's life in Wisconsin as a machinist. "Subject to Change," a prose poem which follows, captures one episode in that saga of downsizing and corporate indifference.*

SUBJECT TO CHANGE

Hump Day, Wednesday, midafternoon, and it's another meeting in the Milwaukee Road back shop. Nothing there but empty aisles since bankruptcy court erased jobs clear as a Sunday A.M. parking lot. No machinery screams, roars, and squeals. No bright orange and black locomotives balanced over maintenance pits. No overhead crane cabs swaying and clacking on their rails. The only sounds bounding off cracked cement walls are the murmurs of our own voices mingling with flapping whirs and coos of pigeons in the wooden beams high above us.

And here we stand, hands in overalled pockets, curious eyes counting numbers against another layoff clock. Green, red, blue, and gold hard hats dot the crowd, depending on each individual shop craft. They are the only colors of life from a pigeon's-eye view. The work-dirty hats are askew, tilted purposefully at disrespectful angles to greet management "reps" when they arrive.

Near as we can tell, there's about 150 of us gathered under the unpatched roof of this century-old building. And we're all waiting. The building itself, ancient history to the bankruptcy judge, is scheduled for demolition in the coming months. The employees, futures less reliable, shift from one steel-toed boot to another, centered in this particular moment of waiting.

We have lost count of these assemblies. They're not worth getting out of work to attend. We'd rather be back at the machines, producing something tangible.

And here come the company men down the aisle. Six of them in business suits topped off by spotless white hard hats, like a row of snowballs in summer. I automatically shiver. The guy next to me stuffs his hands in his pockets. We watch these men with the nervous anticipation of patients waiting in a surgeon's office. And yet we know they won't know all the answers. They aren't the owners, or even the ones who sit at the board meetings. We know it. They know it. They have a job as long as we do. Their faces are strained. Smiles forced. They stop several feet away from the first row of blue collar employees as if there were an invisible line drawn in the concrete floor.

Slanted afternoon sun rays arc from broken ceiling windows to spotlight the scene. Particles of dust and pigeon feathers are pushed up/down in drafts of air blowing in through the overhead doorway. The movie-screen-wide doors gape open to view the end of Wisconsin summer in the Menomonee River industrial valley. Brown clumps of weeds toss in the breeze. Idle forklift trucks grip empty pallets in their teeth. Stacks of miscellaneous diesel engine parts are tagged in metal bins waiting for some place to go. A wrecking ball dangling from a tractor crane cable is not swayed by the wind.

A snowball coughs. Another wipes his glasses on a handkerchief, white as the papers he caresses protectively under his arm. The meeting begins. The sounds of their voices swirl in the air with pigeon dirt. What tiny hope we might have had is lost in phrases like: "maybe next month . . . could be travel package . . . some layoffs . . . can't be sure how many . . . some relocation . . . can't be sure when . . . but of course it's all subject to change." Meaningless sentences bombard our hard hats like bird shit. A pigeon flies out the door.

"Are there any questions?" asks a snowball.

"Sure," comes an anonymous wisecrack from the captured audience, "but you won't give us any straight answers."

And it's another meeting to leave, feeling helpless as the tumbling weeds rolling 'cross the train tracks. We are unusually quiet as we make our way back to finish our shift. The bankruptcy court decree has completed another one of its duties. Produced a perfunctory meeting, directed by a right-wing Illinois judge who has known contacts with organized crime. Our intelligence has been insulted. We are victims of a criminal act. Pieces of reality left behind.

Positive that we are the only things left alive in this dying valley, we begin to shout, push, shove each other like school kids outside at a fire drill. We are a blue-jeaned parade without a crowd in the reviewing stand. Anger pulls our boots to kick at passing weeds. Rocks take to the air, ricocheting off side-tracked box cars. Blushes of adrenaline that raged in our veins at the meeting surface to explode in a sort of crazed humor.

Eddie takes a baseball pitcher's stance, and flings a rusty bolt at a tin shed. Then he says, "Just might make a car paymerit this month." (They sent him two late notices.) "Course," he pauses with a sarcastic grin, "it's subject to change."

Earl winks, immediately playing along, "Tonight for sure, I'm goin' right home after work." He clears his throat dramatically, "Then again, it *could be* subject to change."

We laugh together. It feels good.

I throw a large gray rock at a puddle several yards away. It lands on its mark with a good splash and I yell, "Hey! I hear there's five new machinists coming tomorrow. All women! But maybe that's subject to change too!"

And we march along, releasing frustration with each step. Our procession shrinks in size as people enter buildings along the way. The wheel shop gang is the last to reach its destination. We experience a communal surge of relief to be back on familiar ground and away from the sight of a wrecking ball. Inside, the machines have been waiting. Patient green monsters with sleeping jaws. We walk the last few steps to our separate work areas, then, one at a time, awaken each monster with the vengeance of dictators. The air compressor blasts. Cranes clatter. Engine lathes, boring-bars, mills, drills, and forklifts rumble and growl, till the football-field-sized factory is a comforting roar, loud enough to silence the sound of our futures, subject to change.

ED OCHESTER

(B. 1939)

One of Ed Ochester's most recent books (1988) was titled Changing the Name to Ochester. *The reference is to his grandfather William Olchevski, who came to the United States in the nineteenth century, settling in Brooklyn, beginning a family, and then abandoning it. Ochester was, as a consequence, cut off from his Polish roots until, in his twenties, he actively sought to discover them. He had received his B.A. from Cornell in 1961 and his master's degree from Harvard in 1962. He came to the University of Pittsburgh to teach, where he teaches poetry in the English department and serves as editor of the University of Pittsburgh Press poetry series, one of the most important publishing venues for working-class writers.*

Ochester's first book, Dancing on the Edge of Knives, *came out in 1973. Subsequently, he has published nine more volumes, including* The End of the Ice Age *(1977),* Miracle Mile *(1984), and* Weehawken Ferry *(1985). He was a winner of the Pushcart Prize, as well as of fellowships from the National Endowment for the Arts and the Pennsylvania Council on the Arts. He has also been elected for two terms as president of the Associated Writing Programs.*

THE WORLD WE DREAMED OF

the factories shimmer
in the pure hum of machines

a watchman slumps toward sleep
on his balustrade

we play on the choked wealth
of production through the golden corridors
of afternoons

ore from Patagonia and Durban
pours down the chutes
by itself

this is what we have dreamed of:
to be rich and not be ashamed,
to watch our daughters dance alone
down fields of the world empty
as far as our eyes can see

BILLY JOEL
(B. 1949)

Born in the Bronx, William Martin Joel grew up in Levittown, the planned village of tract houses in Hicksville, Long Island, that became a synonym for suburban ticky-tacky and anomie. Like many kids growing up in the fifties, he got involved with street gangs, some drugs, and the usual suburban hell-raising. After trying out boxing for a while, Joel returned to the piano, which he had begun studying at age four. In the mid-sixties he organized or played in a series of bands, none of which were particularly successful, though Joel developed something of a local reputation as a keyboard side-man. His first album, Cold Spring Harbor, *was released in 1971, after which he moved to the west coast, where he played piano under the name Bill Martin. That experience led to the release in 1973 of "Piano Man," which sold over a million copies and became his signature title and nickname.*

His first big hit album was The Stranger *(1977); one of the songs in it, "Just the Way You Are," won the Song of the Year Grammy for 1978. Since then, he has been a prominent figure on the rock and pop music scenes, winning numerous awards, being granted honorary college degrees, and being elected to the Rock & Roll Hall of Fame in 1999. A number of his albums have sold upwards of five million copies. "Allentown" was part of his 1982 album,* The Nylon Curtain.

ALLENTOWN

Well we're living here in Allentown
And they're closing all the factories down
Out in Bethlehem they're killing time
Filling out forms
Standing in line
Well our fathers fought the Second World War
Spent their weekends on the Jersey Shore
Met our mothers in the USO
Asked them to dance
Danced with them slow
And we're living here in Allentown
But the restlessness was handed down
And it's getting very hard to stay
Well we're waiting here in Allentown
For the Pennsylvania we never found
For the promises our teachers gave
If we worked hard
If we behaved
So the graduations hang on the wall
But they never really helped us at all
No they never taught us what was real
Iron and coke
And chromium steel
And we're waiting here in Allentown
But they've taken all the coal from the ground
And the union people crawled away
Every child has a pretty good shot
To get at least as far as their old man got
But something happened on the way to that place
They threw an American flag in our place
Well I'm living here in Allentown
And it's hard to keep a good man down
But I won't be getting very hard to stay
And we're living here in Allentown

MICHAEL WINERIP

Winerip is a staff writer for the New York Times Magazine. *He has written about historical subjects, including the Holocaust and immigration. He has specialized in issues relating to mental illness. His publications include a book on group homes for the mentally ill,* 9 Highland Road: Sane Living for the Mentally Ill *(1995).*

THE BLUE-COLLAR MILLIONAIRE

There are fortunes to be made running
a cleaning company — as long as your low-wage employees
don't keep quitting on you.

As a teen-ager growing up on Long Island in the 1970's, Robert Bertuglia Jr. used to get bored fast. "Toys, cars, girls—I'd go through one after another," he says. He barely graduated from Copiague High—"Basically I cheated my way through." But what he loved, what he gave up the beach for, skipped school for, quit sports for, what filled his free time and made his mind race, what never, ever bored him was work. "I picked up my first lawn mower at 15," he says in a way that makes you envision Mickey Mantle reaching for his first Louisville Slugger. He started on neighbors' lawns. Then his mother, a waitress, began driving him around town, the power mower sticking out of the trunk of their Chevy. He took $250 from his earnings and bought a '58 Studebaker pickup to haul the mower. While still in high school he hired his first workers and began doing landscaping for businesses, too.

When he realized that the lawn of practically every office building he wanted to cut had the same sign out front—"Property of Racanelli Realty"—he paid a visit to the large real-estate developer's headquarters. On a Monday at 9 A.M., dressed in a clean T-shirt, the teen-ager introduced himself to the receptionist. "I'm here to discuss landscaping," he said. She told him the Racanelli brothers would be tied up all day. "I'll wait," he replied. Around 4, he overheard her say, "Marty, this kid's still in the lobby."

Marty and Nick Racanelli were curious. "I told them I wanted to do the landscaping maintenance on all their buildings," said Bertuglia. They laughed but gave him one building, as a lark. Then more. He was still living at home, and there were days his corporate clients phoned and his mother said, "He's outside playing football, who's calling?" A few years later when the Racanellis were having trouble with their cleaner, they asked Bertuglia to try. "I said, 'What do I know about cleaning?'" he recalls. "Marty says, 'What's to know?'" He was 22, had eight people working for him and after cutting grass all day, he cleaned the building himself at night. "Money wasn't the issue," he says. "I needed to see if it was something I could expand."

The year 1981 was a golden time to start a cleaning company. The Reagan revolution was fresh under way; the air-traffic controllers' union had just been broken. Businesses and municipalities were looking to cut costs by laying off in-house union crews and outsourcing work to companies like Bertuglia's that paid cleaners pennies above minimum wage. One of his first big contracts was the Nassau County court complex. "They wanted to get rid of—I don't want to use 'get rid of'—*phase out* the union cleaners," says Bertuglia. "We were low bidder."

And so began the rise of Robert Bertuglia Jr. Today Laro Service Systems is one of the largest privately owned building-service companies in New York, with 1,800 workers and $50 million in annual revenue. It is the company that cleans the Port Authority Bus Terminal in Manhattan, the international terminal at Kennedy airport and Orlando airport; most famously, it is the company the Giuliani administration hired in 1995 to do the unloading at Fulton fish market, after organized-crime-related operators had been kicked out and were threatening bloody murder and there was so much fear, no one except Laro would bid the job.

Cleaning is, as they say, "24-7"—24 hours a day, 7 days a week, and those are nearly the hours Bertuglia kept for two decades. His first retail store was a Marshall's in 1983. Bertuglia, his brother-in-law and Lou Vacca Jr., now the Laro vice president, cleaned it themselves. "We'd never done a retail store," says Vacca. "Robert sold them a bill of goods to get us the job. . . . We'd been working all day, and did this at night—we were so tired, Robert slept on the floor for three hours." That led to getting all the Marshall's stores on the Island, then Caldor, Kmart, J.C. Penney.

Often they bid low just to win a prestigious job, the goal being to grow. "It wasn't so much the money," says Bertuglia, "it was the action." They won the contract to clean Ellis Island, then the Statue of Liberty. Bertuglia was figuring it out as he went, and there were times in the 1980's when he didn't meet his payroll. His car was repossessed, his phone shut off. He didn't pay his Federal taxes, and only after his brother-in-law Jimmy Latham and his neighbor Bobby Vetter took second mortgages on their homes to lend him money did he pay off the tax liens. And still he pushed growth. "You couldn't let down," he said. "Another company could always take it away." He'd sleep four hours. "I came home, ate and slept, that was it. My wife was with the kids. I didn't see my son growing up. I spent time, but not quality time. I was always thinking about the next job, the next problem, who was yelling at me on the phone." On weekend outings, he'd take his three kids to see buildings Laro was cleaning.

By 1990, he was making real money and decided to move from the ranch house he'd bought for $36,500 a decade earlier. He picked a 6,000-square-foot house for $650,000 on the water in a gated community in Islip, then spent $600,000 renovating. He could have lived anywhere, but he picked that gated community because the first millionaire businessman he'd ever met, the developer Martin Racanelli, lived there. "After we moved in, Marty invited me over to his house for drinks—cocktails—and congratulated me," Bertuglia says. "It was a great moment, yeah. I used to do that man's lawn! I didn't feel like the head porter any more. I'd become a company. I was in a million-dollar house in a million-dollar neighborhood—I had doctors and lawyers for friends, for constituents, as they say."

But he didn't get to savor it. "About the time I finished renovating, I moved out," he said. "I'd worked so much, it contributed to my divorce."

If ever there was a metaphor for America's booming economy, it is Laro Service Systems. There's great money to be made for the people at the top and good money for the 200 middle-level managers—many with only high-school degrees. They are part of a new class of service-industry entrepreneurs, the blue-collar rich. In 1982, at the start of the Reagan revolution, there were 29,000 self-employed Americans making more than $100,000 in industries like cleaning, landscaping, food preparation, warehousing; today there are 80,000 (with both years calculated in 1996 dollars). Since 1980, membership in the Building Service Contractors Association has tripled, to 3,000 companies. Competition is fierce; it is capitalism at its rawest. Laro managers live in a world where victory goes to the lowest bidder and where the standard cleaning contract has a 30-day termination clause, meaning at any time your company can get knifed in the back and dumped onto the street. "How do you do it cheaper?" asked Vacca, the vice president, who makes $80,000 a year. "You take it out of the labor."

In February, Laro beat out 10 bidders to win a $17 million contract at Orlando airport. Laro had a month to hire 280 workers in a state where it had never done a job. A team of Long Island managers was rushed to Orlando and spent weeks working out of a motel. Even after the April start-up there was no rest—their pay scale was so low, they had 25 cleaners quitting every day and were constantly hunting replacements. "I worked three straight days with no sleep, I slept six hours in five days," Vacca said.

Laro's hard-charging management style is good news for taxpayers. The company's bid to clean the Port Authority terminal was a million dollars less than the union contractor's it beat out.

Laro is good news for profit-hungry publicly held companies looking to push up stock prices by cutting costs. In the midst of this economic boom, Kmart, J.C. Penney and Bell Atlantic have all demanded that Laro cut its rates—or they'd find another company. And Laro did.

Laro is good news for the public. Commuters say that the Port Authority Bus Terminal has never been cleaner. Deputy Mayor Randy Mastro, who considers eliminating the Mafia from Fulton fish market one of Giuliani's great feats, gets rhapsodic about Laro, making Bertuglia sound like Errol Flynn, a "true hero" who "stepped into the breach." But even Ken Fisher, a Democratic city councilman and no fan of the Mayor, says there's been great savings because of Laro.

About the only people Laro has not been good for is cleaners—who account for 1,500 of Laro's 1,800 employees and typically earn $5.80 to $7 an hour. They are economically worse off than cleaners of a generation ago. In 1980, says Michael Baratz of the Service Employees International, union janitors in big cities earned $10 an hour. But developers had overbuilt and went hunting ways to slash costs. Building owners defied the union and by the mid-80's, the heavily minority work force was earning minimum wage in many places. They have never recovered. After a decadelong union campaign in Los Angeles, dubbed Justice for Janitors, owners signed a union pact in 1995—for $6.80 an hour.

Even in New York City, a union stronghold, where members in service workers' locals average $32,000 a year, labor's might has been eroded. Membership has fallen from 70,000 to 52,000 in recent years as companies like Laro make inroads. The union used to wreak havoc by striking, but a walkout in 1996 was far less effective as Laro and other cleaners provided 15,000 replacement workers. "That strike was good," said Bertuglia. "We picked up two new buildings out of that—I hope they strike again."

Bertuglia went head to head over the bus-terminal contract with the legendary president of New York's service workers, Gus Bevona (the city's highest-paid union leader, with a salary of more than $400,000). In January 1996, Laro took over the terminal, planning to cut the work force 30 percent. Union cleaners put on new Laro uniforms, and on the third day staged a surprise early-morning walkout. Bertuglia was ready. "A union guy inside tipped me," he said. "At 4 A.M. I got beeped." He had interviewed 400 replacement workers and had their phone numbers. By 4:30 A.M. the secretaries were at their desks in Bay Shore. "The girls in the office made the phone calls," says Bertuglia. "By 9 we were up and running." The bus terminal is now a non-union job. Since 1996, two pickets holding signs saying Laro is unfair have stood daily outside the Eighth Avenue entrance, squeezed between a police barricade and a wall, invisible.

These last years, says Bertuglia, more companies are demanding contract reopeners that reduce cleaning rates. "Everyone's making money but they want to make more," he says. "Bell Atlantic brought us in last September at 165 locations—they've asked for two reductions since." Profit margins are thin; Bertuglia says from Laro's $50 million in revenues, he expects a profit of 1.5 percent.

Some days Vacca feels as if his head is caught in a mop ringer. Laro's sales force works on commission and bids low to win jobs; then Vacca must figure out ways to squeeze the cleaners. When Laro was taking jobs from union workers, it was easy to reduce labor costs. But these days, bidding against other nonunion companies or replacing low-paid in-house crews at retail stores, it's like wringing blood from a stone. One morning Vacca raced into a Wal-Mart to drop off a bid to replace the in-house crew. How does Laro clean Wal-Mart cheaper than Wal-Mart? "I'll get as many part-timers as I can," Vacca said. "I don't have to pay the benefits, vacation, holidays."

There are places where you cannot skimp. Laro was hired by Schiphol, a Dutch company, to clean Kennedy airport's international terminal. Schiphol has an office on the terminal's second floor. Laro assigned its best janitor, Nelson Cardona, a Colombian immigrant, to spend his entire eight-hour shift in the second-floor men's room. "This is the bathroom Schiphol executives use," said Mike Conlon, Laro's Kennedy manager. "A strategic location. You should hear them rave about this bathroom. They love Nelson; he owns this bathroom." Indeed, I saw something I'd never seen in a restroom when I walked in—Cardona, dressed in Laro blue, was sponge-mopping the walls.

When Cardona (who speaks little English) is asked how he likes Laro, he says, Better than the previous cleaner. "They paid me $5.80. Now I make $7." Laro's Conlon added, "When we saw how good Nelson was, we upped him to the top rate—didn't want to lose him."

After getting the Kennedy contract last year, Bertuglia wanted to show some gratitude to his new cleaners. At Thanksgiving he sent a truck full of turkeys to the airport. "We've made a couple of bucks, no question about it," Bertuglia says. "A lot of these guys work for $5, $6 an hour—to get a 20-pound turkey from the boss is something special."

Not that special. Turnover does not stop. "Every day we lose people," Vacca says. "People leave for a quarter here, a nickel there. We have a lot take jobs picking crops on farms—they get food, a bed, $7 an hour."

"When I started in the early 80's," says Vacca, "we got white males to work, guys you could converse with—Americans, or whatever you call white guys. Now you can't speak to these guys—they don't speak English."

Last winter, at a building-service contractors' convention in Cancun, Mexico, a buyout specialist from Consolidation Capital pitched Bertuglia over drinks. "I was tempted—for a minute," says Bertuglia, Laro's sole owner who says he'd net $20 million by selling. "What am I going to do? I'm 42. I'll go nuts if I retire." Bertuglia has eased up the last few years. He sees his children more—two have jobs at Laro, as does his father, who'd been a school-bus driver and handyman. The family has Sunday dinners at the condo Bertuglia bought his parents. Winter weekends, Bertuglia, his 30-year-old fiancée and his children caravan to his Vermont ski house. He has taken up golf. One recent Monday he skipped work to play in a Lion's Club charity tournament.

It is the 35-year-old Vacca, the vice president, who is living the 24-7 life now. In many ways, Vacca is a junior Bertuglia; Vacca also barely made it through high school and started cleaning at 15. He admires Bertuglia—he made him the godfather of his firstborn. "It means a lot when Robert recognizes something I did," Vacca said. Last year Bertuglia promoted him. "I never thought I'd be a V. P.," Vacca said. "I'm not really book smart." Vacca moved from a blue-collar Valley Stream neighborhood to a house twice the size in West Islip. "It's more of an upper-class people," he said. The vice presidency is different from what Vacca expected. "I envisioned a V. P. looks over reports and sits on top of a podium and no one sees him." Truth is, now Vacca is 24-7-52—he can't even take a vacation. "Robert would let me have a week—I don't have time." Since the promotion, his family income has actually decreased; the job is so demanding that his wife gave up a manager's position at a bank and took a part-time job to be with their two pre-schoolers more. "Hopefully I'll get some increases or incentives," Vacca said. "I've never asked Robert for a raise. He takes care of me."

Vacca's wife, Christina, thought being vice president would mean more family time. "I thought he'd paid his dues and worked his butt off, now he'd be able to sit back," she said. "It's worse." She still hasn't got over his being gone a month for the Orlando job, and so neither has he. Each night he'd call, and he could hear the edge in his wife's voice, and then she'd put his 3-year-old daughter on, who'd start crying, asking when Daddy would be home. "I sort of was beginning to hate his job," his wife said. "He's not like a doctor, but it's always 24-7. It's hard on all of us. I've aged somewhat. I look in the mirror, I see how tired I am."

I met Vacca at an Edwards Supermarket at 6:30 A.M. to ride with him to Stewart Airport in Newburgh, N.Y., where Laro had just taken over the cleaning contract. "I couldn't sleep," he said. "So I got up at 4:30 and checked out our crews at the Merrick and Freeport Edwardses. I walk in, I saw guys running around—'The boss is here! The boss is here!'"

Stewart Airport was having a ribbon cutting for its newly renovated main terminal. Vacca knew the place would be thick with politicians and wanted to make sure there would be no cleaning slip-ups. Laro's Kennedy supervisor, Mike Conlon, had been working 20-hour days all week, covering both airports.

"A big event like this," Vacca said on the drive up, "the V. P. shows—I know it'll mean a lot to Mike." The first thing Vacca asked Conlon was "How's the men's room?"

"Look," said Conlon, leading him in. You could have run a neonatal clinic in the toilets. Conlon led Vacca to the urinals. At the bottom of each was a deodorizing tab that said "Laro," with the company's 800 number.

"These are new!" Vacca said.

"First thing I did," Conlon said. He showed Vacca the terminal's trouble spots, like the Jet Set Deli. The floor was uneven. "Every table slants," Conlon said. "Everyone spills. They step in it and they walk out into the terminal."

"This is a bad situation," Vacca said.

"Tell me about it," Conlon said. "At this point I can't remember the last time I slept. I slept six hours in three days. Me and Louie, we're the king of that. Right Lou?"

Vice President Vacca stuck his hand in a trash basket. "Wrong size bag in here," he said.

"I'll get that," Conlon said.

Conlon introduced Vacca to Marie Baxter, the head cleaner. She had worn a special dress for the ribbon cutting and was nervous about whether the airport would meet the Laro vice president's standards. Several times she had asked Conlon, "What do you think he'll say?"

As it turns out, Vacca was impressed. "This place looks 100 percent better," Vacca said.

"It'd mean a lot to Marie to hear that from you, Lou," said Conlon, who told Vacca that they never would have finished in time for the grand opening without Baxter. "Marie's been unbelievable," Conlon said. "She worked 60 hours this week, on her hands and knees. I'm going to put her in for 50."

"That's fair," Vacca said.

JIM GOGOLAK
(B. 1953)

Gogolak is a welder with twenty-seven years of experience at Ispat Inland, a Chicago-based integrated steel mill. He now works in the trucking department and is an active member of Local 1010, United Steel Workers of America, serving as assistant griever. He has been a departmental union representative for eight years and writes regularly for the union newspaper.

Gogolak holds a bachelor of science degree in labor studies from Indiana University. He began attending college when his work schedule was cut back to four days during the economic downturn of the eighties. He majored in labor studies because he hoped to help improve the situation of workers in the plant where he works.

He writes: "I almost feel guilty taking credit for what I write in the union paper. I simply listen to what fellow workers are saying to determine what they are thinking and feeling. Then I put it on paper in such a way as to make a point while expressing the gut-level feelings of people on the shop floor. It's not what I am thinking; it's what we are thinking."

INLAND AND THE TITANIC:
A COMPARISON

The other day, someone from management asked me why the tone of the articles in the union paper seemed to be getting more "adversarial." Every department has it's own problems, but I believe this gentleman meant the question in a general way, so I'll give you a general answer based on a familiar cliche.

Whenever management wants us to be more cooperative and less adversarial, they say, "We'd better cooperate, because we're all in the same boat." The implication is that we share a common fate linked to the success or failure of the company.

I agree to a point. If a boat sinks, we're all in the water. Inland, however, is more like a huge ship. That complicates things a little. To illustrate, I'll use an extended metaphor based on the current hit movie Titanic. (It's worth the price to see it on the big screen, even if you aren't interested in the point I'm trying to make.)

All the passengers on the Titanic were most assuredly on the same ship. But, some of the passengers were traveling first class; others had simpler accommodations; some were in steerage. Even without the tragic accident, it would have been a far more pleasant trip for some than for others.

The people in steerage were working class folks, while the first class passengers were rich management people. The poor were simply along for the ride. But the "upper crust" people were there to prove a point, make a show, and revel in the glory of this fabulous new ocean liner. It also became obvious that some of them felt their lives were inherently more valuable than the lives of those of lesser station.

Due to poor planning, bad management decisions, and plain crummy luck, the Titanic hit an iceberg. That shouldn't have been so bad, because it took a long time to sink. But one of the bad management decisions was to have only enough lifeboats for half the people of the ship.

Management kept the seriousness of the situation secret for as long as possible while taking care of the rich folks (who happened to be family and friends) first. Steerage passengers were held behind locked gates as long as possible so they didn't hamper the evacuation of the "more worthy" passengers.

Can you imagine the frustration of the poor working class passengers when they realized the ship was indeed sinking? All the while, the people who had made the decisions that caused this dilemma were loading family and friends onto lifeboats.

In all fairness, some of the management people responsible for this tragedy showed a recognition of their culpability and did the honorable thing by going down with the ship. Others, however, showed their lack of character by sneaking into the lifeboats. One guy, the fiancee of the female romantic lead, was so slimy that when he escaped with his life, the audience murmured in anger. Later, when the narrator revealed that this slimeball eventually lost his fortune and blew his brains out, the audience expressed righteous contempt. (Coincidentally, this guy was a steel executive.)

The lesson to be learned is that all of us on the ship called "Inland" don't necessarily share a common fate. Trite cliches spouted by management simply divert attention from the real issues; they don't address them. Those of us who had no say in the design of the boat, the specific course it took, the speed at which it traveled, and its response to catastrophic events in a treacherous environment must accept a fate largely dictated by those in charge. "Who gets the lifeboats?" may now be as valid a question as "How do we save the ship?"

We've had reports of ice in the water. We've got our doubts about the soundness of the ship, the course it's taking, and the character of its owners, captain, and crew. We've heard rumblings, and the people in charge are whispering secrets to each other, but not making us privy to their plans. We've passed the USX iceberg and the Greenway iceberg still looms on the horizon. We sense danger on the cold, unfriendly waters.

Can you feel the frustration of those of us in steerage? Can you hear our indignation and outrage at the arrogance of people who have reserved lifeboats (golden parachutes) and are asking us to cooperate by standing silently behind the gates while the more worthy people are loaded into the lifeboats?

Is the tone of the union paper the result of irritation with a handful of arrogant bosses in each particular area? Or is it the result of a general frustration with a situation workers feel powerless to change? You be the judge. Do you smell ice?

[I'd like to thank the people who made Titanic for a fine movie. Thanks, also, to Sam Reipas for the book *Exit with Excellence*, which helped me to relate the movie to our situation at Inland.]

CLASSIC OR CLASSY:

ART AND CLASS

How does—does?—class shape art? Writers on the left, such as Mike Gold and the Chinese revolutionary leader Mao Tse-tung, argue that "great" art is always defined by the class position of the artist and his or her objectives in creating art. Others, however, see in artistic creation a way of transcending matters of class, as well as of gender or race. These positions are by no means of merely historical interest: they have continued to inform the debates about culture and politics of the 1980s and the discussions of aesthetics and ideas of beauty of the 1990s. Where, after all, do we locate beauty—in the painting hung upon a museum wall or in the march of spliced cables across the landscape bringing power and illumination to peoples' everyday lives? In the dancer's pirouette or in the welder's intense blue flame—or somehow in both?

Besides that, out of what is art created? Miners, marches, machinery—to mention the subjects of three works ("Johannesburg Mines," "I Was Marching," and "Heavy Machinery") in this section? The articulation of actual labor—its anguish, dignity, and triumph—has been halting and relatively rare in literary texts until recent years. And it is certainly true that the demands of artistic creation tend to draw the creators away from other forms of work. Still, as Sterling Brown's "Ma Rainey" illustrates, poets and singers can and do draw upon popular traditions and the experiences of ordinary people to fashion art.

Finally, too, this section deals with the functions of art. There are those, of course, who would insist that "beauty is its own excuse for being," that creation, not function, is the artist's proper domain. But precisely because art has power—the power to reveal, to move, to persuade—there have always been efforts to use, indeed to control, its production. "May's Poem" by Jim Daniels suggests another way in which art can function by honoring the everyday lives of everyday people. The works in this section will not provide definitive answers to the questions of beauty and function, but they embody many of the most critical debates about these issues raised by approaching them through the lens of class.

MATTHEW ARNOLD

(1822-1888)

Arnold was one of the most important poets, critics, and educators of Victorian England, indeed of western Europe during the nineteenth century. He combined a profound knowledge of the Western classical tradition, gained at Winchester, Rugby, and Balliol College, Oxford, with an understanding of the fundamental changes underway in British society and culture. The problem for him, one that he explored in poetry and prose, as well as in the educational reforms he advanced, was how to sustain the values of that tradition when it was no longer the possession of a small but dominant elite. As a "middle class" grew in numbers, wealth, and influence, the question became, as he saw it, how they might be acculturated to carry out their responsibilities as educated citizens and perhaps as leaders in an inevitably more democratic nation. His essays in Culture and Anarchy *(1872) effectively offer a program for inducting the newly rising classes into the realms of the "best that has been thought and said."*

But poems like "Dover Beach" (from his volume New Poems, *1867) embody his doubt about the outcome of this experiment in culture. The world, he writes, "Hath really neither joy, nor love, nor light,/Nor certitude, nor peace, nor help for pain." Again, in "Stanzas from the Grand Chartreuse," he speaks of*

> *Wandering between two worlds, one dead,*
> *The other powerless to be born,*
> *With nowhere yet to rest my head,*
> *Like these, on earth I wait forlorn.*

Arnold served from 1851 until 1886 as a "lay" inspector of schools. In that capacity, he frequently visited the continent to observe the development of education in other European nations and proposed a variety of reforms for implementation in English schools. At the same time, between 1857 and 1867, he was professor of poetry at Oxford, writing and lecturing about classical texts, about Celtic literature, and about applying to biblical texts the approaches of literary criticism. His influence has extended well into the twentieth century in the social and cultural criticism of, for example, a writer like Lionel Trilling and others concerned to sustain ideas of a Western tradition not only of culture but of social and political values.

In the sections from Culture and Anarchy *that follow, Arnold argues that culture transcends class interests and that the objectives of culture, "sweetness and light," cannot be achieved within the frameworks offered by the three traditional classes of nineteenth-century British society. His approach may usefully be contrasted with that of Mao Tse-tung, who sees culture as one among the many fields upon which class interests are sharply contested.*

FROM CULTURE AND ANARCHY

The pursuit of perfection, then, is the pursuit of sweetness and light. He who works for sweetness and light, works to make reason and the will of God prevail. He who works for machinery, he who works for hatred, works only for confusion. Culture looks beyond machinery, culture hates hatred; culture has one great passion, the passion for sweetness and light. It has one even yet greater!—the passion for making them *prevail.* It is not satisfied till we *all* come to a perfect man; it knows that the sweetness and light of the few must be imperfect until the raw and unkindled masses of humanity are touched with sweetness and light. If I have not shrunk from saying that we must work for sweetness and light, so neither have I shrunk from saying that we must have a broad basis, must have sweetness and light for as many as possible. Again and again I have insisted how those are the happy moments of humanity, how those are the marking epochs of a people's life, how those are the flowering times for literature and art and all the creative power of genius, when there is a *national* glow of life and thought, when the whole of society is in the fullest measure permeated by thought, sensible to beauty, intelligent and alive. Only it must be *real* thought and *real* beauty; *real* sweetness and *real* light. Plenty of people will try to give the masses, as they call them, an intellectual food prepared and adapted in the way they think proper for the actual condition of the masses. The ordinary popular literature is an example of this way of working on the masses. Plenty of people will try to indoctrinate the masses with the set of ideas and judgments constituting the creed of their own profession or party. Our religious and political organizations give an example of this way of working on the masses. I condemn neither way; but culture works differently. It does not try to teach down to the level of inferior classes; it does not try to win them for this or that sect of its own, with ready-made judgments and watchwords. It seeks to do away with classes; to make the best that has been thought and known in the world current everywhere; to make all men live in an atmosphere of sweetness and light, where they may use ideas, as it uses them itself, freely,—nourished, and not bound by them.

This is the *social idea;* and the men of culture are the true apostles of equality. The great men of culture are those who have had a passion for diffusing, for making prevail, for carrying from one end of society to the other, the best knowledge, the best ideas of their time; who have laboured to divest knowledge of all that was harsh, uncouth, difficult, abstract, professional, exclusive; to humanise it, to make it efficient outside the clique of the cultivated and learned, yet still remaining the *best* knowledge and thought of the time, and a true source, therefore, of sweetness and light. Such a man was Abelard in the Middle Ages, in spite of all his imperfections; and thence the boundless emotion and enthusiasm which Abelard excited. Such were Lessing and Herder in Germany, at the end of the last century; and their services to Germany were in this way inestimably precious. Generations will pass, and literary monuments will accumulate, and works far more perfect than the works of Lessing and Herder will be produced in Germany; and yet the names of these two men will fill a German with a reverence and enthusiasm such as the names of the most gifted masters will hardly awaken. And why? Because they *humanised* knowledge; because they broadened the basis of life and intelligence; because they worked powerfully to diffuse sweetness and light, to make reason and the will of God prevail. With Saint Augustine they said: "Let us not leave thee alone to make in the secret of thy knowledge, as thou didst before the creation of the firmament, the division of light from darkness; let the children of thy spirit, placed in their firmament, make their light shine upon the earth, mark the division of night and day, and announce the revolution of the times; for the old order is passed, and the new arises; the night is spent, the day is come forth; and thou shalt crown the year with thy blessing, when thou shalt send forth labourers into thy harvest sown by other hands than theirs; when thou shalt send forth new labourers to new seed-times, whereof the harvest shall be not yet."

II. Doing as One Likes

I have been trying to show that culture is, or ought to be, the study and pursuit of perfection; and that of perfection is pursued by culture, beauty and intelligence, or, in other words, sweetness and light, are the main characters. Bid hitherto I have been insisting chiefly on beauty, or sweetness, as a character of perfection. To complete rightly my design, it evidently remains to speak also of intelligence, or light, as a character of perfection.

First, however, I ought perhaps to notice that, both here and on the other side of the Atlantic, all sorts of objections are raised against the "religion of culture," as the objectors mockingly call it, which I am supposed to be promulgating. It is said to be a religion proposing parmaceti, or some scented salve or other, as a cure for human miseries; a religion breathing a spirit of cultivated inaction, making its believer refuse to lend a hand at uprooting the definite evils on all sides of us, and filling him with antipathy against the reforms and reformers which try to extirpate them. In general, it is summed up as being not practical, or,—as some critics familiarly put it,—all moonshine. That Alcibiades, the editor of the *Morning Star*, taunts me, as its promulgator, with living out of the world and knowing nothing of life and men. That great austere toiler, the editor of the *Daily Telegraph,* upbraids me,—but kindly, and more in sorrow than in anger,—for trifling with aesthetics and poetical fancies, while he himself, in that arsenal of his in Fleet Street, is bearing the burden and heat of the day. An intelligent American newspaper, the *Nation*, says that it is very easy to sit in one's study and find fault with the course of modem society, but the thing is to propose practical improvements for it. While, finally, Mr. Frederic Harrison, in a very good-tempered and witty satire, which makes me quite understand his having apparently achieved such a conquest of my young Prussian friend, Arminius, at last gets moved to an almost stern moral impatience, to behold, as he says, "Death, sin, cruelty stalk among us, filling their maws with innocence and youth," and me, in the midst of the general tribulation, handing out my pouncet-box.

It is impossible that all these remonstrances and reproofs should not affect me, and I shall try my very best, in completing my design and in speaking of light as one of the characters of perfection, and of culture as giving us light, to profit by the objections I have heard and read, and to drive at practice as much as I can, by showing the communications and passages into practical life from the doctrine which I am inculcating.

It is said that a man with my theories of sweetness and light is full of antipathy against the rougher or coarser movements going on around him, that he will not lend a hand to the humble operation of uprooting evil by their means, and that therefore the believers in action grow impatient with him. But what if rough and coarse action, ill-calculated action, action with insufficient light, is, and has for a long time been, our bane? What if our urgent want now is, not to act at any price, but rather to lay in a stock of light for our difficulties? In that case, to refuse to lend a hand to the rougher and coarser movements going on round us, to make the primary need, both for oneself and others, to consist in enlightening ourselves and qualifying ourselves to act less at random, is surely the best and in real truth the most practical line our endeavours can take. So that if I can show what my opponents call rough or coarse action, but what I would rather call random and ill-regulated action,—action with insufficient light, action pursued because we like to be doing something and doing it as we please, and do not like the trouble of thinking and the severe constraint of any kind of rule,—if I can show this to be, at the present moment, a practical mischief and dangerous to us, then I have found a practical use for light in correcting this state of things, and have only to exemplify how, in cases which fall under everybody's observation, it may deal with it.

When I began to speak of culture, I insisted on our bondage to machinery, on our proneness to value machinery as an end in itself, without looking beyond it to the end for which alone, in truth, it is valuable. Freedom, I said, was one of those things which we thus worshipped in itself, without enough regarding the ends for which freedom is to be desired. In our common notions and talk about freedom, we eminently show our idolatry of machinery. Our prevalent notion is,—and I quoted a number of instances to prove it,—that it is a most happy and important thing for a man merely to be able to do as he likes. On what he is to do when he is thus free to do as he likes, we do not lay so much stress. Our familiar praise of the British Constitution under which we live, is that it is a system of checks,—a system which stops and paralyses any power in interfering with the free action of individuals. To this effect Mr. Bright, who loves to walk in the old ways of the Constitution, said forcibly in one of his great speeches, what many other people are every day saying less forcibly, that the central idea of English life and politics is *the assertion of personal liberty.* Evidently this is so; but evidently, also, as feudalism, which with its ideas and habits of subordination was for many centuries silently behind the British Constitution, dies out, and we are left with nothing but our system of checks, and our notion of its being the great right and happiness of an Englishman to do as far as possible what he likes, we are in danger of drifting towards anarchy. We have not the notion, so familiar on the Continent and to antiquity, of *the State,*—the nation in its collective and corporate character, entrusted with stringent powers for the general advantage, and controlling individual wills in the name of an interest wider than that of individuals. We say, what is very true, that this notion is often made instrumental to tyranny; we say that a State is in reality made up of the individuals who compose it, and that every individual is the best judge of his own interests. Our leading class is an aristocracy, and no aristocracy likes the notion of a State-authority greater than itself, with a stringent administrative machinery superseding the decorative inutilities of lord-lieutenancy, deputy-lieutenancy, and the *posse comitatus*, which are all in its own hands. Our middle class, the great representative of trade and Dissent, with its maxims of every man for himself in business, every man for himself in religion, dreads a powerful administration which might somehow interfere with it; and besides, it has its own decorative inutilities of vestrymanship and guardianship, which are to this class what lord-lieutenancy and the county magistracy are to the aristocratic class, and a stringent administration might either take these functions out of its hands, or prevent its exercising them in its own comfortable, independent manner, as at present.

Then as to our working class. This class, pressed constantly by the hard daily compulsion of material wants, is naturally the very centre and stronghold of our national idea, that it is man's ideal right and felicity to do as he likes.

. . . For a long time, as I have said, the strong feudal habits of subordination and deference continued to tell upon the working class. The modern spirit has now almost entirely dissolved those habits, and the anarchical tendency of our worship of freedom in and for itself, of our superstitious faith, as I say, in machinery, is becoming very manifest. More and more, because of this our blind faith in machinery, because of our want of light to enable us to look beyond machinery to the end for which machinery is valuable, this and that man, and this and that body of men, all over the country, are beginning to assert and put in practice an Englishman's right to do what he likes; his right to march where he likes, meet where he likes, enter where he likes, hoot as he likes, threaten as he likes, smash as he likes. All this, I say, tends to anarchy. . . .

Having, I say, at the bottom of our English hearts a very strong belief in freedom, and a very weak belief in right reason, we are soon silenced when a man pleads the prime right to do as he likes, because this is the prime right for ourselves too; and even if we attempt now and then to mumble something about reason, yet we have ourselves thought so little about this and so much about liberty, that we are in conscience forced, when our brother Philistine with whom we are meddling turns boldly round upon us and asks: *Have you any light?*—to shake our heads ruefully, and to let him go his own way after all.

There are many things to be said on behalf of this exclusive attention of ours to liberty, and of the relaxed habits of government which it has engendered. It is very easy to mistake or to exaggerate the sort of anarchy from which we are in danger through them. . . .

Now, if culture, which simply means trying to perfect oneself, and one's mind as part of oneself, brings us light, and if light shows us that there is nothing so very blessed in merely doing as one likes, that the worship of the mere freedom to do as one likes is worship of machinery, that the really blessed thing is to like what right reason ordains, and to follow her authority, then we have got a practical benefit out of culture. We have got a much wanted principle, a principle of authority, to counteract the tendency to anarchy which seems to be threatening us.

But how to organise this authority, or to what hands to entrust the wielding of it? How to get your *State,* summing up the right reason of the community, and giving effect to it, as circumstances may require, with vigour? And here I think I see my enemies waiting for me with a hungry joy in their eyes. But I shall elude them.

The *State,* the power most representing the right reason of the nation, and most worthy, therefore, of ruling,—of exercising, when circumstances require it, authority over us all,—is for Mr. Carlyle the aristocracy. For Mr. Lowe, it is the middle class with its incomparable Parliament. For the Reform League, it is the working class, the class with "the brightest powers of sympathy and readiest powers of action." Now culture, with its disinterested pursuit of perfection, culture, simply trying to see things as they are in order to seize on the best and to make it prevail, is surely well fitted to help us to judge rightly, by all the aids of observing, reading, and thinking, the qualifications and titles to our confidence of these three candidates for authority, and can thus render us a practical service of no mean value.

So when Mr. Carlyle, a man of genius to whom we have all at one time or other been indebted for refreshment and stimulus, says we should give rule to the aristocracy, mainly because of its dignity and politeness, surely culture is useful in reminding us, that in our idea of perfection the characters of beauty and intelligence are both of them present, and sweetness and light, the two noblest of things, are united. Allowing, therefore, with Mr. Carlyle, the aristocratic class to possess sweetness, culture insists on the necessity of light also, and shows us that aristocracies, being by the very nature of things inaccessible to ideas, unapt to see how the world is going, must be somewhat wanting in light, and must therefore be, at a moment when light is our great requisite, inadequate to our needs. Aristocracies, those children of the established fact, are for epochs of concentration. In epochs of expansion, epochs such as that in which we now live, epochs when always the warning voice is again heard: *Now is the judgment of this world,*—in such epochs aristocracies with their natural clinging to the established fact, their want of sense for the flux of things, for the inevitable transitoriness of all human institutions, are bewildered and helpless. Their serenity, their high spirit, their power of haughty resistance,—the great qualities of an aristocracy, and the secret of its distinguished manners and dignity,—these very qualities, in an epoch of expansion, turn against their possessors. Again and again I have said how the refinement of an aristocracy may be precious and educative to a raw nation as a kind of shadow of true refinement; how its serenity and dignified freedom from petty cares may serve as a useful foil to set off the vulgarity and hideousness of that type of life which a hard middle class tends to establish, and to help people to see this vulgarity and hideousness in their true colours. But the true grace and serenity is that of which Greece and Greek art suggest the admirable ideals of perfection,—a serenity which comes from having made order among ideas and harmonised them; whereas the serenity of aristocracies, at least the peculiar serenity of aristocracies of Teutonic origin, appears to come from their never having had any ideas to trouble them. And so, in a time of expansion like the present, a time for ideas, one gets perhaps, in regarding an aristocracy, even more than the idea of serenity, the idea of futility and sterility. . . .

Now this satisfaction of our middle-class member of Parliament with the mental state of the middle class was truly representative, and makes good his claim to stand as the beautiful and virtuous mean of that class. But it is obviously at variance with our definition of culture, or the pursuit of light and perfection, which made light and perfection consist, not in resting and being, but in growing and becoming, in a perpetual advance in beauty and wisdom. So the middle class is by its essence, as one may say, by its incomparable self-satisfaction decisively expressed through its beautiful and virtuous mean, self-excluded from wielding an authority of which light is to be the very soul. . . .

This distrust of themselves as an adequate centre of authority does not mark the working class, as was shown by their readiness the other day in Hyde Park to take upon themselves all the functions of government. But this comes from the working class being, as I have often said, still an embryo, of which no one can yet quite foresee the final development; and from its not having the same experience and self-knowledge as the aristocratic and middle classes. Honesty it no doubt has, just like the other classes of Englishmen, but honesty in an inchoate and untrained state; and meanwhile its powers of action, which are, as Mr. Frederic Harrison says, exceedingly ready, easily run away with it. That it cannot at present have a sufficiency of light which comes by culture,—that is, by reading, observing, and thinking,— is clear from the very nature of its condition. . . . I conclude, therefore,—what indeed, few of those who do me the honour to read this disquisition are likely to dispute, that we can as little find in the working class as in the aristocratic or in the middle class our much-wanted source of authority, as culture suggests it to us.

Well, then, what if we tried to rise above the idea of class to the idea of the whole community, *the State,* and to find our centre of light and authority there? Every one of us has the idea of country, as a sentiment; hardly any one of us has the idea of *the State,* as a working power. And why? Because we habitually live in our ordinary selves, which do not carry us beyond the ideas and wishes of the class to which we happen to belong. And we are all afraid of giving to the State too much power, because we only conceive of the State as something equivalent to the class in occupation of the executive government, and are afraid of that class abusing power to its own purposes. If we strengthen the State with the aristocratic class in occupation of the executive government, we imagine we are delivering ourselves up captive to the ideas and wishes of our fierce aristocratical baronet; if with the middle class in occupation of the executive government, to those of our truculent middle-class Dissenting minister; if with the working class, to those of its notorious tribune, Mr. Bradlaugh. And with much justice; owing to the exaggerated notion which we English, as I have said, entertain of the right and blessedness of the mere doing as one likes, of the affirming oneself, and oneself just as it is. People of the aristocratic class want to affirm their ordinary selves, their likings and dislikings; people of the middle class the same, people of the working class the same. By our every day selves, however, we are separate, personal, at war; we are only safe from one another's tyranny when no one has any power; and this safety, in its turn, cannot save us from anarchy. And when, therefore, anarchy presents itself as a danger to us, we know not where to turn.

But by our *best self* we are united, impersonal, at harmony. We are in no peril from giving authority to this, because it is the truest friend we all of us can have; and when anarchy is a danger to us, to this authority we may turn with sure trust. Well, and this is the very self which culture, or the study of perfection, seeks to develop in us; at the expense of our old untransformed self, taking pleasure only in doing what it likes or is used to do, and exposing us to the risk of clashing with every one else who is doing the same! So that our poor culture, which is flouted as so unpractical, leads us to the very ideas capable of meeting the great want of our present embarrassed times! We want an authority, and we find nothing but jealous classes, checks, and a deadlock; culture suggests the idea of *the State.* We find no basis for a firm State-power in our ordinary selves; culture suggests one to us in our *best self.*

It cannot but acutely try a tender conscience to be accused, in a practical country like ours, of keeping aloof from the work and hope of a multitude of earnest-hearted men, and of merely toying with poetry and aesthetics. So it is with no little sense of relief that I find myself thus in the position of one who makes a contribution in aid of the practical necessities of our times. The great thing, it will be observed, is to find our *best self,* and to seek to affirm nothing but that; not,—as we English with our over-value for merely being free and busy have been so accustomed to do,—resting satisfied with a self which comes uppermost long before our best self, and affirming that with blind energy. In short,—to go back yet once more to Bishop Wilson,—of these two excellent rules of Bishop Wilson's for a man's guidance: "Firstly, never go against the best light you have; secondly, take care that your light be not darkness," we English have followed with praiseworthy zeal the first rule, but we have not given so much heed to the second. We have gone manfully according to the best light we have; but we have not taken enough care that this should be really the best light possible for us, that it should not be darkness. And, our honesty being very great, conscience has whispered to us that the light we were following, our ordinary self, was, indeed, perhaps, only an inferior self, only darkness; and that it would not do to impose this seriously on all the world.

But our best self inspires faith, and is capable of affording a serious principle of authority. For example. We are on our way to what the late Duke of Wellington, with his strong sagacity, foresaw and admirably described as "a revolution by due course of law." This is undoubtedly,—if we are still to live and grow, and this famous nation is not to stagnate and dwindle away on the one hand, or, on the other, to perish miserably in mere anarchy and confusion,—what we are on the way to. Great changes there must be, for a revolution cannot accomplish itself without great changes; yet order there must be, for without order a revolution cannot accomplish itself by due course of law. So whatever brings risk of tumult and disorder, multitudinous processions in the streets of our crowded towns, multitudinous meetings in their public places and parks,—demonstrations perfectly unnecessary in the present course of our affairs,—our best self, or right reason, plainly enjoins us to set our faces against. It enjoins us to encourage and uphold the occupants of the executive power, whoever they may be, in firmly prohibiting them. But it does this clearly and resolutely, and is thus a real principle of authority, because it does it with a free conscience; because in thus provisionally strengthening the executive power, it knows that it is not doing this merely to enable our aristocratical baronet to affirm himself as against our working-men's tribune, or our middle class Dissenter to affirm himself as against both. It knows that it is establishing *the State*, or organ of our collective best self, of our national right reason. And it has the testimony of conscience that it is stablishing the State on behalf of whatever great changes are needed, just as much as on behalf of order; stablishing it to deal just as stringently, when the time comes, with our baronet's aristocratical prejudices, or with the fanaticism of our middle-class Dissenter, as it deals with Mr. Bradlaugh's street-processions.

RAYMOND WILLIAMS

(1921–1988)

Williams has been among the two or three most influential creators of cultural studies and of New Left literary thought. His books Culture and Society *(1958), an excerpt from which follows, and* The Long Revolution *(1966) placed the project of a socialist transformation of British society into the historical context of changes both in the production of culture and in its functions. He conceived culture not in terms of a few great works of art, supposed to embody what was best in human history and thought, created by fewer extraordinary artists and fully appreciated mainly by a limited number of initiates. Rather, he saw culture as a variety of forms of expression and organization by which men and women of every class articulate and devise means to realize their hopes and desires, as well as to voice their pain, confusion, and, often, anger. The culture of the British working class, for example, might, he wrote, better be understood in the pattern of Council houses and unions than in formal poetry or literary fictions. Williams's* work helped bring a new respect for and appreciation of the creative forms developed by working-class people.

Williams was himself the son of a Welsh railway signalman, and was educated in grammar school and at Cambridge. He was elected a fellow of Jesus College, Cambridge, and served there as professor of drama from 1974 to 1983. He wrote a number of critical books about drama, including Modern Tragedy (1966) and Drama from Ibsen to Brecht (1968). He was also the author of five novels, most focused on Welsh life. A longterm activist, he authored the New Left May Day Manifesto in 1968 as well as Marxism and Literature (1977), and the widely used Keywords: A Vocabulary of Culture and Society (1976), with its crisp but politically charged definitions of the terms in which social and cultural debates have been carried out in the twentieth century.

FROM CULTURE AND SOCIETY: 1780–1950

From "Introduction"

In the last decades of the eighteenth century, and in the first half of the nineteenth century, a number of words, which are now of capital importance, came for the first time into common English use, or, where they had already been generally used in the language, acquired new and important meanings. There is in fact a general pattern of change in these words, and this can be used as a special kind of map by which it is possible to look again at those wider changes in life and thought to which the changes in language evidently refer.

Five words are the key points from which this map can be drawn. They are *industry, democracy, class, art* and *culture*. The importance of these words, in our modern structure of meanings, is obvious. The changes in their use, at this critical period, bear witness to a general change in our characteristic ways of thinking about our common life: about our social, political and economic institutions; about the purposes which these institutions are designed to embody; and about the relations to these institutions and purposes of our activities in learning, education and the arts.

The first important word is *industry,* and the period in which its use changes is the period which we now call the Industrial Revolution. *Industry,* before this period, was a name for a particular human attribute, which could be paraphrased as 'skill, assiduity, perseverance, diligence'. This use of *industry* of course survives. But, in the last decades of the eighteenth century, *industry* came also to mean something else; it became a collective word for our manufacturing and productive institutions, and for their general activities. Adam Smith, in *The Wealth of Nations* (1776), is one of the first writers to use the word in this way, and from his time the development of this use is assured. *Industry,* with a capital letter, is thought of as a thing in itself—an institution, a body of activities—rather than simply a human attribute. *Industrious,* which described persons, is joined, in the nineteenth century, by *industrial,* which describes the institutions. The rapid growth in importance of these institutions is seen as creating a new system, which in the 1830s is first called *Industrialism.* In part, this is the acknowledgement of a series of very important technical changes, and of their transforming effect on methods of production. It is also, however, an acknowledgement of the effect of these changes on society as a whole, which is similarly transformed. The phrase *Industrial Revolution* amply confirms this, for the phrase, first used by French writers in the 1820s, and gradually adopted, in the course of the century, by English writers, is modelled explicitly on an analogy with the French Revolution of 1789. As that had transformed France, so this has transformed England; the means of change are different, but the change is comparable in kind: it has produced, by a pattern of change, a new society.

The second important word is *democracy,* which had been known, from the Greek, as a term for 'government by the people', but which only came into common English use at the time of the American and French Revolutions. Weekley, in *Words Ancient and Modern,* writes:

> It was not until the French Revolution that *democracy* ceased to be a mere literary word, and became part of the political vocabulary.

In this he is substantially right. Certainly, it is in reference to America and France that the examples begin to multiply, at the end of the eighteenth century, and it is worth noting that the great majority of these examples show the word being used unfavourably: in close relation with the hated *Jacobinism,* or with the familiar *mob-rule.* England may have been (the word has so many modern definitions) a democracy since Magna Carta, or since the Commonwealth, or since 1688, but it certainly did not call itself one. *Democrats,* at the end of the eighteenth and the beginning of the nineteenth centuries, were seen, commonly, as dangerous and subversive mob agitators. Just as *industry* and its derived words record what we now call the Industrial Revolution, so *democracy* and *democrat,* in their entry into ordinary speech, record the effects, in England, of the American and French Revolutions, and a crucial phase of the struggle, at home, for what we would now call democratic representation.

Industry, to indicate an institution, begins in about 1776; *democracy,* as a practical word, can be dated from about the same time. The third word, *class,* can be dated, in its most important modern sense, from about 1772. Before this, the ordinary use of *class,* in English, was to refer to a division or group in schools and colleges: 'the usual Classes in Logick and Philosophy'. It is only at the end of the eighteenth century that the modern structure of *class,* in its social sense, begins to be built up. First comes *lower classes,* to join *lower orders,* which appears earlier in the eighteenth century. Then, in the 1790s, we get *higher classes; middle classes* and *middling classes* follow at once; *working classes* in about 1815; *upper classes* in the 1820s. *Class prejudice, class legislation, class consciousness, class conflict* and *class war* follow in the course of the nineteenth century. The *upper middle classes* are first heard of in the 1890s; the *lower middle class* in our own century.

It is obvious, of course, that this spectacular history of the new use of *class* does not indicate the *beginning* of social divisions in England. But it indicates, quite clearly, a change in the character of these divisions, and it records, equally clearly, a change in attitudes towards them. *Class* is a more indefinite word than *rank,* and this was probably one of the reasons for its introduction. The structure then built on it is in nineteenth-century terms: in terms, that is to say, of the changed social structure, and the changed social feelings, of an England which was passing through the Industrial Revolution, and which was at a crucial phase in the development of political democracy.

The fourth word, *art*, is remarkably similar, in its pattern of change, to *industry*. From its original sense of a human attribute, a 'skill', it had come, by the period with which we are concerned, to be a kind of institution, a set body of activities of a certain kind. An *art* had formerly been any human skill; but *Art*, now, signified a particular group of skills, the 'imaginative' or 'creative' arts. *Artist* had meant a skilled person, as had *artisan*; but *artist* now referred to these selected skills alone. Further, and most significantly, *Art* came to stand for a special kind of truth, 'imaginative truth', and *artist* for a special kind of person, as the words *artistic* and *artistical*, to describe human beings, new in the 1840s, show. A new name, *aesthetics*, was found to describe the judgement of art, and this, in its turn, produced a name for a special kind of person—*aesthete*. *The arts*—literature, music, painting, sculpture, theatre—were grouped together, in this new phrase, as having something essentially in common which distinguished them from other human skills. The same separation as had grown up between *artist* and *artisan* grew up between *artist* and *craftsman. Genius*, from meaning 'a characteristic disposition', came to mean 'exalted ability', and a distinction was made between it and *talent*. As *art* had produced *artist* in the new sense, and *aesthetics aesthete*, so this produced *a genius*, to indicate a special kind of person. These changes, which belong in time to the period of the other changes discussed, form a record of a remarkable change in ideas of the nature and purpose of art, and of its relations to other human activities and to society as a whole.

The fifth word, *culture*, similarly changes, in the same critical period. Before this period, it had meant, primarily, the 'tending of natural growth', and then, by analogy, a process of human training. But this latter use, which had usually been a culture *of* something, was changed, in the nineteenth century, to *culture* as such, a thing in itself. It came to mean, first, 'a general state or habit of the mind,' having close relations with the idea of human perfection. Second, it came to mean 'the general state of intellectual development, in a society as a whole'. Third, it came to mean 'the general body of the arts'. Fourth, later in the century, it came to mean 'a whole way of life, material, intellectual and spiritual'. It came also, as we know, to be a word which often provoked either hostility or embarrassment.

The development of *culture* is perhaps the most striking among all the words named. It might be said, indeed, that the questions now concentrated in the meanings of the word *culture* are questions directly raised by the great historical changes which the changes in *industry, democracy* and *class*, in their own way, represent, and to which the changes in *art* are a closely related response. The development of the word *culture* is a record of a number of important and continuing reactions to these changes in our social, economic political life, and may be seen, in itself, as a special kind of map by means of which the nature of the changes can be explored.

I have stated, briefly, the fact of the changes in these important words. As a background to them I must also draw attention to a number of other words which are either new, or acquired new meanings, in this decisive period. Among the new words, for example, there are *ideology, intellectual, rationalism, scientist, humanitarian, utilitarian, romanticism, atomistic; bureaucracy, capitalism, collectivism, commercialism, communism, doctrinaire, equalitarian, liberalism, masses, mediaeval* and *mediaevalism, operative* (noun), *primitivism, proletariat* (a new word for 'mob'), *socialism, unemployment; cranks, highbrow, isms* and *pretentious*. Among words which then acquired their now normal modern meanings are *business* (=trade), *common* (=vulgar), *earnest* (derisive), *Education* and *educational, getting-on, handmade, idealist* (=visionary), *Progress, rank-and-file* (other than military), *reformer* and reformism, revolutionary and revolutionize, salary (as opposed to 'wages'), Science (=natural and physical sciences), speculator (financial), solidarity, strike and suburban (as a description of attitudes). The field which these changes cover is again a field of general change, introducing many elements which we now point to as distinctively modern in situation and feeling. It is the relations within this general pattern of change which it will be my particular task to describe.

The word which more than any other comprises these relations is culture, with all its complexity of idea and reference. My overall purpose in the book is to describe and analyse this complex, and to give an account of its historical formation. Because of its very range of reference, it is necessary, however, to set the enquiry from the beginning on a wide basis. I had originally intended to keep very closely to culture itself, but, the more closely I examined it, the more widely my terms of reference had to be set. For what I see in the history of this word, in its structure of meanings, is a wide and general movement in thought and feeling. I shall hope to show this movement in detail. In summary, I wish to show the emergence of culture as an abstraction and an absolute: an emergence which, in a very complex way, merges two general responses—first, the recognition of the practical separation of certain moral and intellectual activities from the driven impetus of a new kind of society; second, the emphasis of these activities, as a court of human appeal, to be set over the processes of practical social judgement and yet to offer itself as a mitigating and rallying alternative. But, in both these senses, culture was not a response to the new methods of production, the new Industry, alone. It was concerned, beyond these, with the new kinds of personal and social relationship: again, both as a recognition of practical separation and as an emphasis of alternatives. The idea of culture would be simpler if it had been a response to industrialism alone, but it was also, quite evidently, a response to the new political and social developments, to Democracy. Again, in relation to this, it is a complex and radical response to the new problems of social class. Further, while these responses define bearings, in a given external area that was surveyed, there is also, in the formation of the meanings of culture, an evident reference back to an area of personal and apparently private experience, which was notably to affect the meaning and practice of art. These are the first stages of the formulation of the idea of culture, but its historical development is at least as important. For the recognition of a separate body of moral and intellectual activities, and the offering of a court of human appeal, which comprise the early meanings of the word, are joined, and in themselves changed, by the growing assertion of a whole way of life, not only as a scale of integrity, but a mode of interpreting all our common experience, and, in this new interpretation, changing it. Where culture meant a state or habit of the mind, or the body of intellectual and moral activities, it means now, also, a whole way of life. This development, like each of the original meanings and the relations between them, is not accidental, but general and deeply significant. . . .

from "Conclusion": Culture and Which Way of Life?

We live in a transitional society, and the idea of culture, too often, has been identified with one or other of the forces which the transition contains. Culture is the product of the old leisured classes who seek now to defend it against new and destructive forces. Culture is the inheritance of the new rising class, which contains the humanity of the future; this class seeks, now, to free it from its restrictions. We say things like this to each other, and glower. The one good thing, it seems, is that all the contending parties are keen enough on culture to want to be identified with it. But then, we are none of us referees in this; we are all in the game, and playing in one or other direction.

I want to say something about the idea of 'working-class culture', because this seems to me to be a key issue in our own time, and one in which there is a considerable element of misunderstanding. I have indicated already that we cannot fairly or usefully describe the bulk of the material produced by the new means of communication as 'working-class culture'. For neither is it by any means produced exclusively for this class, nor, in any important degree, is it produced by them. To this negative definition we must add another: that 'working-class culture,' in our society, is not to be understood as the small amount of 'proletarian' writing and art which exists. The appearance of such work has been useful, not only in its more self-conscious forms, but also in such material as the post-Industrial ballads, which were worth collecting. We need to be aware of this work, but it is to be seen as a valuable dissident element rather than as a culture. The traditional popular culture of England was, if not annihilated, at least fragmented and weakened by the dislocations of the Industrial Revolution. What is left, with what in the new conditions has been newly made, is small in quantity and narrow in range. It exacts respect, but it is in no sense an alternative culture.

This very point of an alternative is extremely difficult, in terms of theory. If the major part of our culture, in the sense of intellectual and imaginative work, is to be called, as the Marxists call it, bourgeois, it is natural to look for an alternative culture, and to call it proletarian. Yet it is very doubtful whether 'bourgeois culture' is a useful term. The body of intellectual and imaginative work which each generation receives as its traditional culture is always, and necessarily, something more than the product of a single class. It is not only that a considerable part of it will have survived from much earlier periods than the immediately pre-existing form of society; so that, for instance, literature, philosophy and other work surviving from before, say, 1600, cannot be taken as 'bourgeois'. It is also that, even within a society in which a particular class is dominant, it is evidently possible both for members of other classes to contribute to the common stock, and for such contributions to be unaffected by or in opposition to the ideas and values of the dominant class. The area of a culture, it would seem, is usually proportionate to the area of a language rather than to the area of a class. It is true that a dominant class can to a large extent control the transmission and distribution of the whole common inheritance; such control, where it exists, needs to be noted as a fact about that class. It is true also that a tradition is always selective, and that there will always be a tendency for this process of selection to be related to and even governed by the interests of the class that is dominant. These factors make it likely that there will be qualitative changes in the traditional culture when there is a shift of class power, even before a newly ascendant class makes its own contributions. Points of this kind need to be stressed, but the particular stress given by describing our existent culture as bourgeois culture is in several ways misleading. It can, for example, seriously mislead those who would now consider themselves as belonging to the dominant class. If they are encouraged, even by their opponents, to think of the existing culture (in the narrow sense) as their particular product and legacy, they will deceive themselves and others. For they will be encouraged to argue that, if their class position goes, the culture goes too; that standards depend on the restriction of a culture to the class which, since it has produced it, alone understands it. On the other hand, those who believe themselves to be representatives of a new rising class will, if they accept the proposition of 'bourgeois culture', either be tempted to neglect a common human inheritance, or, more intelligently, be perplexed as to how, and how much of, this bourgeois culture is to be taken over. The categories are crude and mechanical in either position. Men who share a common language share the inheritance of an intellectual and literary tradition which is necessarily and constantly revalued with every shift in experience. The manufacture of an artificial 'working-class culture', in opposition to this common tradition, is merely foolish. A society in which the working class had become dominant would, of course, produce new valuations and new contributions. But the process would be extremely complex, because of the complexity of the inheritance, and nothing is now to be gained by diminishing this complexity to a crude diagram.

The contrast between a minority and a popular culture cannot be absolute. It is not even a matter of levels, for such a term implies distinct and discontinuous stages, and this is by no means always the case. In Russian society in the nineteenth century one finds perhaps the clearest example of a discontinuous culture within recent history; this is marked, it should be noted, by a substantial degree of rejection of even the common language by the ruling minority. But in English society there has never been this degree of separation, since English emerged as the common language. There has been marked unevenness of distribution, amounting at times to virtual exclusion of the majority, and there has been some unevenness of contribution, although in no period has this approached the restriction of contribution to members of any one class. Further, since the beginning of the nineteenth century it has been difficult for any observer to feel that the care of intellectual and imaginative work could be safely entrusted to, or identified with, any existing social or economic class. It was in relation to this situation that the very idea of culture was, as we have seen, developed.

The most difficult task confronting us, in any period where there is a marked shift of social power, is the complicated process of revaluation of the inherited tradition. The common language, because in itself it is so crucial to this matter, provides an excellent instance. It is clearly of vital importance to a culture that its common language should not decline in strength, richness and flexibility; that it should, further, be adequate to express new experience, and to clarify change. But a language like English is still evolving, and great harm can be done to it by the imposition of crude categories of class. It is obvious that since the development, in the nineteenth century, of the new definition of 'standard English', particular uses of the common language have been taken and abused for the purposes of class distinction. Yet the dialect which is normally equated with standard English has no necessary superiority over other dialects. Certain of the grammatical clarifications have a common importance, but not all even of these. On the other hand, certain selected sounds have been given a cardinal authority which derives from no known law of language, but simply from the fact that they are habitually made by persons who, for other reasons, possess social and economic influence. The conversion of this kind of arbitrary selection into a criterion of 'good' or 'correct' or 'pure' English is merely a subterfuge. Modern communications make for the growth of uniformity, but the necessary selection and clarification have been conducted, on the whole, on grounds quite irrelevant to language. It is still thought, for instance, that a double negative ('I don't want none') is *incorrect* English, although millions of English-speaking persons use it regularly: not, indeed, as a misunderstanding of the rule, which they might be thought too ignorant to apprehend; but as the continuation of a habit which has been in the language continuously since Chaucer. The broad 'a', in such words as 'class', is now taken as the mark of an 'educated person', although till the eighteenth century it was mainly a rustic habit, and as such despised. Or 'ain't', which in the eighteenth century was often a mark of breeding, is now supposed to be a mark of vulgarity: in both cases, the valuation is the merest chance. The extraordinary smugness about aspirates, vowel-sounds, the choice of this or that synonym ('couch' 'sofa'), which has for so long been a normal element of middle-class humour, is, after all, not a concern for good English, but parochialism. (The current controversy about what are called 'U' and 'non-U' speech habits clearly illustrates this; it is an aspect, not of major social differences, but of the long difficulty of drawing the lines between the upper and lower sections of the *middle* class.) Yet, while this is true, the matter is complicated by the fact that in a society where a particular class and hence a particular use of the common language is dominant a large part of the literature, carrying as it does a body of vital common experience, will be attracted to the dominant language mode. At the same time, a national literature, as English has never ceased to be, will, while containing this relation, contain also elements of the whole culture and language. If we are to understand the process of a selective tradition, we shall not think of exclusive areas of culture but of degrees of shifting attachment and intersection, which a crude theory either of class or of standards is incompetent to interpret.

A culture can never be reduced to its artifacts while it is being lived. Yet the temptation to attend only to external evidence is always strong. It is argued, for instance, that the working class is becoming 'bourgeois', because it is dressing like the middle class, living in semi-detached houses, acquiring cars and washing-machines and television sets. But it is not 'bourgeois' to possess objects of utility, nor to enjoy a high material standard of living. The working class does not become bourgeois by owning the new products, any more than the bourgeois ceases to be bourgeois as the objects he owns change in kind. Those who regret such a development among members of the working class are the victims of a prejudice. An admiration of the 'simple poor' is no new thing, but it has rarely been found, except as a desperate rationalization, among the poor themselves. It is the product either of satiety or of a judgement that the material advantages are purchased at too high a human cost. The first ground must be left to those who are sated; the second, which is more important, is capable of a false transference. If the advantages were 'bourgeois' because they rested on economic exploitation, they do not continue to be 'bourgeois' if they can be assured without such exploitation or by its diminution. The worker's envy of the middle-class man is not a desire to be that man, but to have the same kind of possessions. We all like to think of ourselves as a standard, and I can see that it is genuinely difficult for the English middle class to suppose that the working class is not desperately anxious to become just like itself. I am afraid this must be unlearned. The great majority of English working people want only the middle-class material standard and for the rest want to go on being themselves. One should not be too quick to call this vulgar materialism. It is wholly reasonable to want the means of life in such abundance as is possible. This is the materialism of material provision, to which we are all, quite rightly, attentive. The working people, who have felt themselves long deprived of such means in any adequacy, intend to get them and to keep them if they can. It would need more evidence than this to show that they are becoming vulgar materialists, or that they are becoming 'bourgeois'.

The question then, perhaps, is whether there is any meaning left in 'bourgeois'? Is there any point, indeed, in continuing to think in class terms at all? Is not industrialism, by its own momentum, producing a culture that is best described as classless? Such questions, today, command a significant measure of assent, but again, while drawing support from the crudities of certain kinds of class interpretation, they rest, essentially, on an external attitude alike to culture and to class. If we think of culture, as it is important to do, in terms of a body of intellectual and imaginative work, we can see that with the extension of education the distribution of this culture is becoming more even, and, at the same time, new work is being addressed to a public wider than a single class. Yet a culture is not only a body of intellectual and imaginative work; it is also and essentially a whole way of life. The basis of a distinction between bourgeois and working-class culture is only secondarily in the field of intellectual and imaginative work, and even here it is complicated, as we have seen, by the common elements resting on a common language. The primary distinction is to be sought in the whole way of life, and here, again, we must not confine ourselves to such evidence as housing, dress and modes of leisure. Industrial production tends to produce uniformity in such matters, but the vital distinction lies at a different level. The crucial distinguishing element in English life since the Industrial Revolution is not language, not dress, not leisure—for these indeed will tend to uniformity. The crucial distinction is between alternative ideas of the nature of social relationship.

'Bourgeois' is a significant term because it marks that version of social relationship which we usually call individualism: that is to say, an idea of society as a neutral area within which each individual is free to pursue his own development and his own advantage as a natural right. The course of recent history is marked by a long fighting retreat from this idea in its purest form, and the latest defenders would seem to the earliest to have lost almost the entire field. Yet the interpretation is still dominant: the exertion of social power is thought necessary only in so far as it will protect individuals in this basic right to set their own course. The classical formula of the retreat is that, in certain defined ways, no individual has a right to harm others. But, characteristically, this harm has been primarily interpreted in relation to the individual pursuit—no individual has a right to prevent others from doing *this kind of thing.*

The reforming bourgeois modification of this version of society is the idea of service, to which I shall return. But both this idea and the individualist idea can be sharply contrasted with the idea that we properly associate with the working class: an idea which, whether it is called communism, socialism or cooperation, regards society neither as neutral nor as protective, but as the positive means for all kinds of development, including individual development. Development and advantage are not individually but commonly interpreted. The provision of the means of life will, alike in production and distribution, be collective and mutual. Improvement is sought, not in the opportunity to escape from one's class, or to make a career, but in the general and controlled advance of all. The human fund is regarded as in all respects common, and freedom of access to it as a right constituted by one's humanity; yet such access, in whatever kind, is common or it is nothing. Not the individual, but the whole society, will move.

The distinction between these versions of society has been blurred by two factors: the idea of service, which is the great achievement of the Victorian middle class, and is deeply inherited by its successors; and the complication of the working-class idea by the fact that England's position as an imperial power has tended to limit the sense of community to national (and, in the context, imperialist) lines. Further, the versions are blurred by a misunderstanding of the nature of class. The contending ideas, and the actions which follow from them, are the property of that part of a group of people, similarly circumstanced, which has become conscious of its position and of its own attitude to this position. Class feeling is a mode, rather than a uniform possession of all the individuals who might, objectively, be assigned to that class. When we speak, for instance, of a working-class idea, we do not mean that all working people possess it, or even approve of it. We mean, rather, that this is the essential idea embodied in the organizations and institutions which that class creates: the working-class movement as a tendency, rather than all working-class people as individuals. It is foolish to interpret individuals in rigid class terms, because class is a collective mode and not a person. At the same time, in the interpretation of ideas and institutions, we can speak properly in class terms. It depends, at any time, on which kind of fact we are considering. To dismiss an individual because of his class, or to judge a relationship with him solely in class terms, is to reduce humanity to an abstraction. But, also, to pretend that there are no collective modes is to deny the plain facts.

We may now see what is properly meant by 'working-culture'. It is not proletarian art, or council houses, or a particular use of languages; it is, rather, the basic collective idea, and the institutions, manners, habits of thought and intentions which proceed from this. Bourgeois culture, similarly, is the basic individualist idea and the institutions, manners, habits of thought and intentions which proceed from that. In our culture as a whole, there is both a constant interaction between these ways of life and an area which can properly be described as common to or underlying both. The working class, because of its position, has not, since the Industrial Revolution, produced a culture in the narrower sense. The culture which it has produced, and which it is important to recognize, is the collective democratic institution, whether in the trade unions, the cooperative movement or a political party. Working-class culture, in the stage through which it has been passing, is primarily social (in that it has created institutions) rather than individual (in particular intellectual or imaginative work). When it is considered in context, it can be seen as a very remarkable creative achievement. . . .

The Idea of Community

The development of the idea of culture has, throughout, been a criticism of what has been called the bourgeois idea of society. The contributors to its meaning have started from widely different positions, and have reached widely various attachments and loyalties. But they have been alike in this, that they have been unable to think of society as a merely neutral area, or as an abstract regulating mechanism. The stress has fallen on the positive function of society, on the fact that the values of individual men are rooted in society, and on the need to think and feel in these common terms. This was, indeed, a profound and necessary response to the disintegrating pressures which were faced.

Yet, according to their different positions, the idea of community, on which all in general agree, has been differently felt and defined. In our own day we have two major interpretations, alike opposed to bourgeois liberalism, but equally, in practice, opposed to each other. These are the idea of service, and the idea of solidarity. These have in the main been developed by the middle class and the working class respectively. From Coleridge to Tawney the idea of function, and thence of service to the community, has been most valuably stressed, in opposition to the individualist claim. The stress has been confirmed by the generations of training which substantiate the ethical practice of our professions, and of our public and civil service. As against the practice of *laissez-faire*, and of self-service, this has been a major achievement which has done much for the peace and welfare of our society. Yet the working-class ethic, of solidarity, has also been a major achievement, and it is the difference of this from the idea of service which must now be stressed. . . .

The idea of service, ultimately, is no substitute for the idea of active mutual responsibility, which is the other version of community. Few men can give the best of themselves as servants; it is the reduction of man to a function. Further, the servant, if he is to be a good servant, can never really question the order of things; his sense of authority is too strong. Yet the existing order is in fact subject to almost overwhelming pressures. The break through into what together we want to make of our lives, will need qualities which the idea of service not only fails to provide, but, in its limitation of our minds, actively harms.

The idea of service to the community has been offered to the working class as an interpretation of solidarity, but it has not, in the circumstances, been fully accepted, for it is, to them, inferior in feeling. Another alternative to solidarity which has had some effect is the idea of individual opportunity—of the ladder. It has been one of the forms of service to provide such a ladder, in industry, in education and elsewhere. And many working-class leaders, men in fact who have used the ladder, have been dazzled by this alternative to solidarity. Yet the ladder is a perfect symbol of the bourgeois idea of society, because, while undoubtedly it offers the opportunity to climb, it is a device which can only be used individually: you go up the ladder alone. This kind of individual climbing is of course the bourgeois model: a man should be allowed to better himself. The social conscience, which produced the idea of service, argued that no greater benefit could be conferred on the working people than that this ladder should be extended to them. The actual process of reform, in so far as it has not been governed by working-class pressure, has been, in large part, the giving of increasing opportunity to climb. Many indeed have scrambled up, and gone off to play on the other side; many have tried to climb and failed. Judged in each particular case, it seems obviously right that a working man, or the child of a working-class family, should be enabled to fit himself for a different kind of work, corresponding to his ability. Because of this, the ladder idea has produced a real conflict of values within the working class itself. My own view is that the ladder version of society is objectionable in two related respects: first, that it weakens the principle of common betterment, which ought to be an absolute value; second, that it sweetens the poison of hierarchy, in particular by offering the hierarchy of merit as a thing different in kind from the hierarchy of money or of birth. On the educational ladder, the boy who has gone from a council school to Oxford or Cambridge is of course glad that he has gone, and he sees no need to apologize for it, in either direction. But he cannot then be expected to agree that such an opportunity constitutes a sufficient educational reform. A few voices, softened by the climb, may be found to say this, which they are clearly expected to say. Yet, if he has come from any conscious part of the working class, such a boy will take leave to doubt the proffered version. The education was worth the effort, but he sees no reason why it should be interpreted as a ladder. For the ladder, with all its extra-educational implications, is merely an image of a particular version of society; if he rejects the version, he will reject the image. Take the ladder image away, and interest is returned to what is, for him, its proper object: to the making of a common educational provision; to the work for equity in material distribution; to the process of shaping a tradition, a community of experience, which is always a selective organization of past and present, and which he has been given particular opportunities to understand. The ladder, which is a substitute for all these things, must be understood in all its implications; and it is important that the growing number who have had the ladder stamped on their brows should interpret it to themselves and to their own people, whom, as a class, it could greatly harm. For in the end, on any reckoning, the ladder will never do; it is the product of a divided society, and will fall with it.

EMILY DICKINSON
(1830-1886)

Emily Dickinson lived out practically all her life in and around the family home in Amherst, Massachusetts. She wrote over 1200 poems, almost all of which display extraordinary invention, wit, originality, and passion. Once upon a time, critics saw these two statements as somehow contradictory and strove mightily to explain how someone whose life appeared so constrained, and a woman at that, could achieve the conceptual reach and linguistic brilliance of Dickinson's poetry. The supposed contradiction existed not in Dickinson's life or art but in the conceptual frameworks brought to bear on them. For within the boundaries she established for herself, Dickinson experienced not only the full range of emotions her poems capture, but the intense contradictions of nineteenth-century America.

Take the issue of publication, for example. Only about a dozen of Dickinson's poems were put into print during her life, none with her cooperation. But that does not mean that she was indifferent to publication or ultimately to her standing as a poet. In fact, she "published" large numbers of her poems . . . in ways amenable to herself—as letters, gifts, friendship offerings. And she collected and organized her work in carefully prepared fascicles that she stitched together by hand into little manuscript books. Further, her poem attacking publication as the "Auction/Of the Mind of Man—" displays in its language and imagery an acute sensitivity about and hostility toward the rise of bourgeois business culture in mid-century America. It may be that she regarded publication as a surrender not only of her precious privacy, but of her own and her family's gentry class status, which was actually eroding. However that might be, it is clear that Dickinson did not stand apart from the flux of events in America, though she never wrote directly about them.

She did write quite directly about pain, the distance of God ("an Eclipse"), the frightening yet compelling natural world ("a Stranger"), the desire for and loss of love. That last she seems to have experienced intensely, especially in relation to her sister-in-law, Susan Dickinson, who lived next door and with whom she maintained to the end of her life an ardent connection—whether sexual or not remains unclear. Part of the irony of the gradual emergence of Dickinson's importance as a poet has had to do with the many false assumptions about her as a person that recent scholarship has had to explode in order to approach the power and originality of her verse without prejudice and misconception.

PUBLICATION—IS THE AUCTION

Publication—is the Auction
Of the Mind of Man—
Poverty—be justifying
For so foul a thing

Possibly—but We—would rather
From Our Garret go
White—Unto the White Creator—
Than invest—Our Snow—

Thought belong to Him who gave it—
Then—to Him Who bear
It's Corporeal illustration—Sell
The Royal Air—

In the Parcel—Be the Merchant
Of the Heavenly Grace—
But reduce no Human Spirit
To Disgrace of Price—

WILLA CATHER
(1873-1947)

Probably no one has written with more complexity of feeling about the great American middle west than Cather. Though she was born in Virginia, she moved with her family when she was nine to a farm in Nebraska and two years later to the thriving town of Red Cloud, where her father opened a real estate business. These became the scenes for most of her successful novels (she published thirteen) and many of her stories. Hers was not the provincial and narrow-minded west that characters in F. Scott Fitzgerald's books rushed to leave or about which Sinclair Lewis raised many a knowing laugh. Provinciality and narrowness there were among Cather's people, of course, together with the cultural deprivation and isolation so feelingly portrayed in the story that follows, "A Wagner Matinee." But there were also the virtues of loyalty to certain largely European traditions, of a sense of community, and above all, determination.

That last was a quality in which Cather herself excelled. From early in life, for example, she hated skirts and crinolines, the frippery of traditional female styles; rejecting disapproval, she cut her hair short, dressed in a masculine way, and began signing herself William Cather, M.D. She was the only graduate of her high school class to go to college, the University of Nebraska, where she planned to study science. But when a professor had one of her essays published in the local newspaper, she turned to writing, producing more than three hundred pieces in two years. After graduation, she wrote, edited, and later taught in Pittsburgh before moving to New York in 1903 to assume a key editorial position with the muckraking McClure's Magazine. *But she was never fully committed to* McClure's *reformist program, and she continued to write fiction throughout the nine years she served as editor. A volume of stories,* The Troll Garden, *came out in 1905. Then in 1912, her first novel,* Alexander's Bridge, *was published and she left the magazine to devote herself full time to her own writing. Many of her finest books emerged in the next decade,* O Pioneers! *(1913),* The Song of the Lark *(1915),* My Antonía *(1918), and* A Lost Lady *(1923), which was made into a silent movie two years later and redone in 1934 with Barbara Stanwyck as star. With* One of Ours *(1922), she won the Pulitzer Prize.*

Always reticent about her personal life, Cather nevertheless drew heavily for her fiction on the world she had experienced as a girl and young woman. It was a world of immigrants, farmers, and small-town working folk trying to wrest a livelihood from a difficult environment and yet maintain not only a set of strong values, but a sense of beauty and aspiration in their everyday lives.

A WAGNER MATINEE

I received one morning a letter, written in pale ink on glassy, blue-lined note-paper, and bearing the postmark of a little Nebraska village. This communication, worn and rubbed, looking as if it had been carried for some days in a coat pocket that was none too clean, was from my uncle Howard, and informed me that his wife had been left a small legacy by a bachelor relative, and that it would be necessary for her to go to Boston to attend to the settling of the estate. He requested me to meet her at the station and render her whatever services might be necessary. On examining the date indicated as that of her arrival, I found it to be no later than tomorrow. He had characteristically delayed writing until, had I been away from home for a day, I must have missed my aunt altogether.

The name of my Aunt Georgiana opened before me a gulf of recollection so wide and deep that, as the letter dropped from my hand, I felt suddenly a stranger to all the present conditions of my existence, wholly ill at ease and out of place amid the familiar surroundings of my study. I became in short, the gangling farmer-boy my aunt had known, scourged with chilblains and bashfulness, my hands cracked and sore from the corn husking. I sat again before her parlour organ, fumbling the scales with my stiff, red fingers, while she, beside me, made canvas mittens for the huskers.

The next morning, after preparing my landlady for the visitor, I set out for the station. When the train arrived I had some difficulty in finding my aunt. She was the last of the passengers to alight, and it was not until I got her into the carriage that she seemed really to recognize me. She had come all the way in a day coach; her linen duster had become black with soot and her black bonnet grey with dust during the journey. When we arrived at my boarding-house the landlady put her to bed at once and I did not see her again until the next morning.

Whatever shock Mrs. Springer experienced at my aunt's appearance, she considerately concealed. As for myself, I saw my aunt's battered figure with that feeling of awe and respect with which we behold explorers who have left their ears and fingers north of Franz-Joseph-Land, or their health somewhere along the Upper Congo. My Aunt Georgiana had been a music teacher at the Boston Conservatory, somewhere back in the latter sixties. One summer, while visiting in the little village among the Green Mountains where her ancestors had dwelt for generations, she had kindled the callow fancy of my uncle, Howard Carpenter, then an idle, shiftless boy of twenty-one. When she returned to her duties in Boston, Howard followed her, and the upshot of this infatuation was that she eloped with him, eluding the reproaches of her family and the criticism of her friends by going with him to the Nebraska frontier. Carpenter, who, of course, had no money, took up a homestead in Red Willow County, fifty miles from the railroad. There they had measured off their land themselves, driving across the prairie in a wagon, to the wheel of which they had tied a red cotton handkerchief, and counting its revolutions. They built a dug-out in the red hillside, one of those cave dwellings whose inmates so often reverted to primitive conditions. Their water they got from the lagoons where the buffalo drank, and their slender stock of provisions was always at the mercy of bands of roving Indians. For thirty years my aunt had not been farther than fifty miles from the homestead.

I owed this woman most of the good that ever came my way in my boyhood, and had a reverential affection for her. During the years when I was riding herd for my uncle, my aunt, after cooking the three meals—the first of which was ready at six o'clock in the morning—and putting the six children to bed, would often stand until midnight at her ironing-board, with me at the kitchen table beside her, hearing me recite Latin declensions and conjugations, gently shaking me when my drowsy head sank down over a page of irregular verbs. It was to her, at her ironing or mending, that I read my first Shakepere, and her old textbook on mythology was the first that ever came into my empty hands. She taught me my scales and exercises on the little parlour organ which her husband had bought her after fifteen years during which she had not so much as seen a musical instrument. She would sit beside me by the hour, darning and counting, while I struggled with the "Joyous Farmer." She seldom talked to me about music, and I understood why. Once when I had been doggedly beating out some easy passages from an old score of *Euryanthe* I had found among her music books, she came up to me and, putting her hands over my eyes, gently drew my head back upon her shoulder, saying tremulously, "Don't love it so well, Clark, or it may be taken from you."

When my aunt appeared on the morning after her arrival in Boston, she was still in a semi-somnanbulant state. She seemed not to realize that she was in the city where she had spent her youth, the place longed for hungrily half a lifetime. She had been so wretchedly trainsick throughout the journey that she had no recollection of anything but her discomfort, and to all intents and purposes, there were but a few hours of nightmare between the farm in Red Willow County and my study on New-bury Street. I had planned a little pleasure for her that afternoon, to repay her for some of the glorious moments she had given me when we used to milk together in the straw-thatched cowshed and she, because I was more than usually tired, or because her husband had spoken sharply to me, would tell me of the splendid per-formance of the *Huguenots* she had seen in Paris, in her youth.

At two o'clock the Symphony Orchestra was to give a Wagner program, and I intended to take my aunt; though, as I conversed with her, I grew doubtful about her enjoyment of it. I suggested our visiting the Conservatory and the Common before lunch, but she seemed altogether too timid to wish to venture out. She ques-tioned me absently about various changes in the city, but she was chiefly concerned that she had forgotten to leave instructions about feeding half-skimmed milk to a certain weakling calf, "old Maggie's calf, you know, Clark," she explained, evidently having forgotten how long I had been away. She was further troubled because she had neglected to tell her daughter about the freshly-opened kit of mackerel in the cellar, which would spoil if it were not used directly.

I asked her whether she had ever heard any of the Wagnerian operas, and found that she had not, though she was perfectly familiar with their respective situations, and once possessed the piano score of The Flying Dutchman. I began to think it would be best to get her back to Red Willow County without waking her, and regret-ted having suggested the concert.

From the time we entered the concert hall, however, she was a trifle less passive and inert, and for the first time seemed to perceive her surroundings. I had left some trepidation lest she might become aware of her queer, country clothes, or might experience some painful embarrassment at stepping suddenly into the world to which she had been dead for a quarter of a century. But, again, I found how super-ficially I had judged her. She sat looking about her with eyes as impersonal, almost as stony, as those with which the granite Rameses in a museum watches the froth and fret that ebbs and flows about his pedestal. I have seen this same aloofness in old miners who drift into the Brown hotel at Denver, their pockets full of bullion, their linen soiled, their haggard faces unshaven; standing in the thronged corridors as solitary as though they were still in a frozen camp on the Yukon.

The matinee audience was made up chiefly of women. One lost the contour of faces and figures, indeed any affect of line whatever, and there was only the colour of bodices past counting, the shimmer of fabrics soft and firm, silky and sheer; red, mauve, pink, blue, lilac, purple, ecru, rose, yellow, cream, and white, all the colours that an impressionist finds in a sunlit landscape, with here and there the dead shadow of a frock coat. My Aunt Georgiana regarded them as though they had been so many daubs of tube-paint on a palette.

When the musicians came out and took their places, she gave a little stir of antic-ipation, and looked with quickening interest down over the rail at that invariable grouping, perhaps the first wholly familiar thing that had greeted her eye since she had left old Maggie and her weakling calf. I could feel how all those details sank into her soul, for I had not forgotten how they had sunk into mine when I came fresh from ploughing forever and forever between green aisles of corn, where, as in a treadmill, one might walk from daybreak to dusk without perceiving a shadow of change. The clean profiles of the musicians, the gloss of their linen, the dull black of their coats, the beloved shapes of the instruments, the patches of yellow light on the smooth, varnished bellies of the 'cellos and the bass viols in the rear, the restless, wind-tossed forest of fiddle necks and bows—I recalled how, in the first orchestra I ever heard, those long bow-strokes seemed to draw the heart out of me, as a conjurer's stick reels out yards of paper ribbon from a hat.

The first number was the *Tännhauser* overture. When the horns drew out the first strain of the Pilgrim's chorus, Aunt Georgiana clutched my coat sleeve. Then it was I first realized that for her this broke a silence of thirty years. With the battle between the two motives, with the frenzy of the Venusberg theme and its ripping of strings, there came to me an overwhelming sense of the waste and wear we are so powerless to combat; and I saw again the tall, naked house on the prairie, black and grim as a wooden fortress; the black pond where I had learned to swim, its margin pitted with sun-dried cattle tracks; the rain gullied clay banks about the naked house, the four dwarf ash seedlings where the dish-cloths were always hung to dry before the kitchen door. The world there was the flat world of the ancients; to the east, a cornfield that stretched to daybreak; to the west, a corral that reached to sunset; between, the conquests of peace, dearer-bought than those of war.

The overture closed, my aunt released my coat sleeve, but she said nothing. She sat staring dully at the orchestra. What, I wondered, did she get from it? She had been a good pianist in her day, I knew, and her musical education had been broader than that of most music teachers of a quarter of a century ago. She had often told me of Mozart's operas and Meyerbeer's, and I could remember hearing her sing, years ago, certain melodies of Verdi. When I had fallen ill with a fever in her house she used to sit by my cot in the evening—when the cool, night wind blew in through the faded mosquito netting tacked over the window and I lay watching a certain bright star that burned red above the cornfield—and sing "Home to our mountains, O, let us return!" in a way fit to break the heart of a Vermont boy near dead of homesickness already.

I watched her closely through the prelude to *Tristan and Isolde,* trying vainly to conjecture what that seething turmoil of strings and winds might mean to her, but she sat mutely staring at the violin bows that drove obliquely downward, like the pelting streaks of rain in a summer shower. Had this music any message for her? Had she enough left to at all comprehend this power which had kindled the world since she had left it? I was in a fever of curiosity, but Aunt Georgiana sat silent upon her peak in Darien. She preserved this utter immobility throughout the number from *The Flying Dutchman,* though her fingers worked mechanically upon her black dress, as if, of themselves, they were recalling the piano score they had once played. Poor hands! They had been stretched and twisted into mere tentacles to hold and lift and knead with;—on one of them a thin, worn band that had once been a wedding ring. As I pressed and gently quieted one of those groping hands, I remembered with quivering eyelids their services for me in other days.

Soon after the tenor began the "Prize Song," I heard a quick drawn breath and turned to my aunt. Her eyes were closed, but the tears were glistening on her cheeks, and I think, in a moment, more they were in my eyes as well. It never really died, then—the soul which can suffer so excruciatingly and so interminably; it withers to the outward eye only; like that strange moss which can lie on a dusty shelf half a century and yet, if placed in water, grows green again. She wept so throughout the development and elaboration of the melody.

During the intermission before the second half, I questioned my aunt and found that the "Prize Song" was not new to her. Some years before there had drifted to the farm in Red Willow County a young German, a tramp cowpuncher, who had sung in the chorus at Bayreuth when he was a boy, along with the other peasant boys and girls. Of a Sunday morning he used to sit on his gingham-sheeted bed in the hands' bedroom which opened off the kitchen, cleaning the leather of his boots and saddle, singing the "Prize Song," while my aunt went about her work in the kitchen. She had hovered over him until she had prevailed upon him to join the country church, though his sole fitness for this step, in so far as I could gather, lay in his boyish face and his possession of this divine melody. Shortly afterward, he had gone to town on the Fourth of July, been drunk for several days, lost his money at a faro table, ridden a saddled Texas steer on a bet, and disappeared with a fractured collar-bone. All this my aunt told me huskily, wanderingly, as though she were talking in the weak lapses of illness.

"Well, we have come to better things than the old *Trovatore* at any rate, Aunt Georgie?" I queried, with a well meant effort at jocularity.

Her lip quivered and she hastily put her handkerchief up to her mouth. From behind it she murmured, "And you have been hearing this ever since you left me, Clark?" Her question was the gentlest and saddest of reproaches.

The second half of the program consisted of four numbers from the *Ring*, and closed with Siegfried's funeral march. My aunt wept quietly, but almost continuously, as a shallow vessel overflows in a rain-storm. From time to time her dim eyes looked up at the lights, burning softly under their dull glass globes.

The deluge of sound poured on and on; I never knew what she found in the shining current of it; I never knew how far it bore her, or past what happy islands. From the trembling of her face I could well believe that before the last number she had been carried out where the myriad graves are, into the grey, nameless burying grounds of the sea; or into some world of death vaster yet, where, from the beginning of the world, hope has lain down with hope and dream with dream and, renouncing, slept.

The concert was over; the people filed out of the hall chattering and laughing, glad to relax and find the living level again, but my kinswoman made no effort to rise. The harpist slipped the green felt cover over his instrument; the flute-players shook the water from their mouthpieces; the men of the orchestra went out one by one, leaving the stage to the chairs and music stands, empty as a winter cornfield.

I spoke to my aunt. She burst into tears and sobbed pleadingly. "I don't want to go, Clark, I don't want to go!"

I understood. For her, just outside the concert hall, lay the black pond with the cattle-tracked bluffs; the tall, unpainted house, with weather-curled boards, naked as a tower; the crook-backed ash seedlings where the dishcloths hung to dry; the gaunt, moulting turkeys picking up refuse about the kitchen door.

MIKE GOLD

(1893–1967)

Gold's story here captures some of the conflicts between a young Jewish man, who wants nothing more than to enter the precincts of "culture," and his boss, his peers, and his parents, whose understanding of life has nar-

rowed to the necessities of making a living. It was an experience familiar to Gold, less from his own upbringing than from those of many of his peers. (For biographical information on Gold, see the headnote in section III.)

THE PASSWORD TO
THOUGHT—TO CULTURE

The factory of Shinster and Neuheim, Makers of the Hytone Brand Ladies' Cloaks and Suits, rushed along busily in its usual channels that sweet May afternoon; the machines racing and roaring; the workers gripped by their tasks; the whole dark loft filled with a furious mechanical life, hot and throbbing as the pulse of an aeroplane.

Outside the sunlight lay in bright patterns on the dusty streets and buildings, illuminating for two or three hours more the city crowds moving to and fro on their ever-mysterious errands. But the factory was filling with darkness, and the hundred silent figures at the sewing machines bent even lower to their work, as if there were some mighty matter for study before them, needing a sterner and tenser notice as the day deepened into twilight.

The pressers, at their boards at one end of the long loft, thumped with their irons, and surrounded themselves with hissing steam like a fog. The motors roared and screamed, and one of the basters, a little Italian girl, sang in a high voice a sad, beautiful love song of her native province in Italy. It ran through the confusion of the loft like a trickle of silver, but now and again its fragile beauty was drowned by the larger, prosaic voice of Mr. Neuheim, the junior partner, as he bustled about and shouted commands to one or another of his workers.

"Chaim, come here and take this bundle to Abe's machine!" he would shout in Yiddish, and a very old, white-bearded Jew came patiently and slowly, and took the huge bundle of cloaks on his brittle shoulders, and delivered them to the operator.

"Hurry up on this Flachsman job, boys!" Mr. Neuheim would say, rubbing his hands, as he stood behind one of the operators, and a few of them in the vicinity would frown slightly and murmur some inaudible answer from between closed lips.

Mr. Neuheim, a short, flabby man with a bald head and reddish moustache that was turning white, was the practical tailor of the firm and stayed in the factory and looked after production. His partner had been a salesman when they joined their poverty and ambition not many years ago, and there looked after the selling and business end now. Mr. Neuheim liked this arrangement, for he had sat at the bench for years, and still liked the smell of steam and the feel of cloth, the putting together of "garments." Best of all, he liked to run things, to manage, to bustle, and to have other tailors under him, dependent on his word.

He trudged about the factory all day like a minor Napoleon, and wherever he went there was a tightening of nerves, an increased activity of fingers, and a sullenness as if his every word were an insult. He was a good manager, and kept things moving. His very presence was like a lash lightly flicked at the backs of the workers. They did not like him, but they responded when they felt him near.

Mr. Neuheim trotted about more strenuously than usual on this afternoon. There was a big order to be delivered the next morning, and he was making sure that it would be on time. He sped from his basters to his pressers, from his pressers to his opera-tors, a black, unlighted cigar in his mouth, a flush of worry on his gross, round face.

"Where are those fifty suits in the 36 size of the Flachsman lot?" he suddenly demanded of the white-bearded factory porter.

"I brought them to David an hour ago, Mr. Neuheim," Chaim said, looking at him with meek eyes.

"Good. Then they'll be sure to get off tonight," said the Boss, scowling like a busy general. "Good."

He thought a moment, and then hurried on his short legs through the piles of unfinished clothing till he came to the door that led from the factory to the ship-ping room. There was a glass panel in the upper part of the door, and Mr. Neuheim stopped and looked through it before entering.

What he saw made him take the cigar out of his mouth, swear, and then open the door with a violent kick that almost tore it from its hinges.

"My God!" he cried fervently, "what is this, anyways?"

His shipping clerk, David Brandt, a Jewish youth of about twenty-three, was seated on the table near the open window, staring dreamily at the grey masses of building opposite, that now were flashing with a thousand fires in the sun. He was hugging his knees, and beside him on the table lay an open green-covered book that he had evidently put aside for a moment.

David Brandt was a well-built youth, with good shoulders and chest, a body that would have been handsome had he not carried it like a sloven; tense brown eyes, and a lean face with hungry, high Slavic features. He was shabbily dressed, almost downright dirty in his carelessness of shirt and clothes, and he stood up hastily as the Boss spoke and ran his fingers nervously through a shock of wild black hair.

Mr. Neuheim strode over to him, picked up the book, and read the title.

"Ruskin's Sea-same and Lilies!" he pronounced contemptuously. "My God, boy, is this what we're payin' you good money for? What are you here for anyway, to work or to stuff yourself with fairy tales? Tell me!" he demanded.

"To work," David answered reluctantly, his eyes fixed on the floor.

"Then work, in God's name, work! This ain't a public library, ye know, or a city college for young shipping clerks to come to for a free education! What sort of a book is this, anyway?" he asked staring again at the title. "What's a sea-same, any-way?"

"It's a sort of password," David stammered, a crimson wave of blood creeping over his dark face.

"A password to what?" the Boss demanded, looking at him sternly, with the air of a judge determined upon the whole truth and nothing but the truth. "Is it some-thing like the Free Masons?"

David floundered guiltily. "It's used only in a sort of symbolical sense here," he explained. "Sesame was used as a password by Ali Baba in the story, when he wanted to get into the robbers' cave, but here it means the password to thought—to culture."

"To thought—to culture!" Mr. Neuheim mimicked grandiosely, putting in imagi-nary monocle to his eye, and walking a few mincing steps up and down the room. "And I suppose, Mr. Brandt, while you was learning the password to Thought and to Culture—ahem!"—he put an incredible sneer into these two unfortunate words—"you forgot all about such little things like that Flachsman lot! Look at it, it's still laying around, and Chaim brought it in an hour ago! My God, boy, this can't go on, ye know! I been watching you for the past two months, and I'll tell you frankly, you ain't got your mind on business! I didn't know what it was before, but I see how it's this Thought"—he sneered again—"and this Culture. Cut it out, see? If ye want to read, do it outside the factory, and read something that'll bring you in dividends—good American reading."

"Yes."

"What do ye want with thought and culture, anyway?" the Boss cried, waving his cigar like an orator. "Me and Mr. Shinster was worse off than you once; we started from the bottom; and look where we got to without sea-sames or lilies! You're wasting your good time, boy."

David looked at the plump little Jew, with his glittering bald head, his flabby face, and his perfectly rounded stomach that was like some fleshly monument to years of champagne suppers, auto rides, chorus girl debauches, and all the other splendid rewards of success in the New York garment trade.

"Do you ever read Shakespeare?" Mr. Neuheim said more tolerantly, as he lit his cigar.

"Yes."

"Well, ye know in his Choolyus Caesar, this man Caesar says: Let me have men about me that are fat, and that don't think; that is, don't think outside of business, ye understand. Well, that's my advice to you, my boy, especially if ye want to hold your job and got any ambition. The last feller that held your job was made a salesman on the road after five years, and the same chances are open to you. Now let's see whether you're smart or not. I like you personally, but you gotta change your ways. Now let's see you use common sense after this—not Thought and Culture."

He laughed a broad, gurgling, self-satisfied laugh, and passed into the factory again, where the machines were warring, and the little Italian girl singing, and the pressers were sending up their strange, white fog of steam.

David spat viciously at the door that closed behind him.

He worked fiercely all that afternoon, in a state of trembling indignation; his hands shook, and his forehead perspired with the heat of the internal fires that consumed him. He was debating over and over again the problem of thought and culture with Mr. Neuheim, and his eyes would flash as he made some striking and noble point, and withered the fat little Boss with his scorn.

Six o'clock came at last; the factory motors were shut off, and died away with a last lingering scream. The operators and pressers and basters became men and women again. They rose stiffly from their seats, and talked and laughed, and dressed themselves and hurried away from the factory as from a prison.

The rage that sustained David died with the iron-throated wailing of the whistles that floated over the city, unyoking so many thousands of weary shoulders.

A curious haze came upon him then. He walked home weakly, as if in a debilitating dream. He hardly felt the scarlet sky above the roofs, the twilight beginning to fall upon the city like a purple doom, the air rich with spring. Mighty streams were flowing through the factory district, human working masses silent and preoccupied after the day's duties, and David slipped into these broad currents without thought, and followed them automatically.

He lived in a tenement on Forsythe Street, on the East Side, and the tides all flowed in that direction; down Broadway, through Grand Street and Prince Street and other streets running east and west and across the dark, bellowing Bowery. Then they spread again and filtered and poured out into the myriad crisscrossing streets where stand the tenements row after row, like numberless barracks built for the conscripts of labor.

It was a Friday night, the eve of the East Side's Sabbath, and Mrs. Brandt, David's little dark, round-backed mother, was blessing the candles when he entered. She had a white kerchief over her hair, and her brown eyes, deep and eager in her wrinkled face as David's own, shone with a pious joy as she read the pre-Sabbath ritual from an old "Sidar" that had come with her from Russia. She looked at David's clouded face anxiously for a moment, but did not interrupt her prayers to greet him when he came in. David did not greet her either, but limp and nerveless went directly to his room and flung himself upon the bed.

There he lay for a few minutes in the darkness. He heard the sounds of life rising from the many windows on the airshaft; the clatter of dishes and knives, the crying of babies, voices lifted in talk. He heard his mother move about; she had evidently finished her prayers, and was coming to his room. Some strange weakness suddenly assailed him; as she knocked at the door, David began weeping; quietly, reasonlessly, like a lonely child.

"David?" his mother inquired, waiting at the threshold. There was no answer, and she called his name again.

"David!"

David answered this time.

"I'm all right, mommer," he said, his voice muffled by the pillows.

"Supper'll be ready in five or ten minutes," Mrs. Brandt said. "Better come out now and wash yourself. And David. . . ."

"Yes?"

"David darling," she whispered, opening the door a little, "you should not do like you did tonight. You should always go and kiss your papa the first thing when you come home. You don't know how bad it makes him feel when you don't do that. He cries over it, and it makes him sicker. He's very sick now; the doctor said today your popper is worse than he's ever seen him. Be good, David, and go speak to him."

"Yes, mommer," David said wearily.

He washed at the sink, and ate the Friday night supper of stuffed fish, noodle soup, boiled chicken and tea. His mother chattered to him all the while, but David listened in that haze that had come on him at the end of the factory day, and answered her vaguely. When he had finished eating he continued sitting at the supper table, and was only aroused when she again suggested that he go in to see his father.

The elder Brandt was a sad, pale, wasted little Jew who had spent fourteen years in the sweatshops of America, and now, at the age of forty-five, was ready to die.

He had entered the factories a hopeful immigrant, with youthful, rosy cheeks that he had brought from Russia, and a marvelous faith in the miracle of the Promised Land that had come from there, too. The sweatshops had soon robbed him of that youthful bloom, however; then they had eaten slowly, like a beast in a cave gnawing for days at a carcass, his lungs, his stomach, his heart, all his vital organs, one by one.

The doctor came to see him twice a week, and wondered each time how he managed to live on. He lay in the bed, propped up high against the pillows, a *Vorwaerts* clutched in his weary hand.

His face, wax-yellow and transparent with disease, was the face of a humble Jewish worker, mild and suffering, but altogether dead now except for the two feverish eyes. He lay exhausted and limp, his whole attitude that of a figure noted down in the books of Death.

David's father was sucked dry, and there was only one spark of life and youth remaining in him—incredibly enough—his faith in the miracles of the Promised Land.

He put down the newspaper and looked up with a timid smile as David entered the room. David came over and kissed him, and he sat on a chair beside his father's bed.

"Well, David, boy, did you have a hard day in the shop today?" the sick man began in a weak voice, fingering his straggly beard and trying to appear cheerful.

"Yes," David answered dully.

"Are you getting on good there?" Mr. Brandt continued, in his poor, hopeful quaver.

"Yes."

"And did you ask the boss yet about that raise he promised you two months ago?"

"No," said David, vacantly, staring with lustreless eyes at the floor.

Mr. Brandt looked apprehensive, as if he had made an error in asking the question. He stroked the feather-bed quilt under which he lay imprisoned, and stole little anxious glances at David's brooding face, as if to implore it for the tiniest bit of attention and pity. Another difficult question hesitated on his lips.

"Davie, dear," he said at last, "why don't you come in to see you popper any more when you get home from work?"

"It's because I'm tired, I guess," David answered.

"No, it ain't that, Davidka. You know it ain't. You used to come in regular and tell me all the news. Do you hate your popper now, David?"

"No, why should I?"

"I don't know. God knows I've done all I could for you; I worked night and day for long years in the shop, thinking only of you, of my little son. I wanted better things for you than what you've got, I couldn't help myself; I was always only a working-man. Some men have luck; and they are able to give their children college educations and such things. But I've always been a *shlemozel*; but you must try to get more out of life than I have found."

"Yes."

"David, don't hate me so; you hardly want to speak to me. Look at me."

David turned his eyes toward his father, but he saw him only dimly, and heard in the same dim way the feeble, high voice uttering the familiar lamentations. In the flickering gaslight his father seemed like some ghostly, unreal shadow in a dream.

"David, you hate me because I'm sick and you have to support me along with your mother. I know; I know! don't think I don't see it all! But it's not my fault, is it, Davie, and I've only been sick a year, and who knows, maybe soon I will be able to take my place in the shop again, and earn my own bread, as I did for so many years before."

"Don't, popper, for God's sake, don't talk about it!" David spoke sharply.

"All right, I won't. All right. Excuse me."

They sat in silence, and then David moved uneasily, as if to go. Mr. Brandt reached over and took his hand in his own moist, trembling one, and held it there.

"Davie," he said, "Davie, dear, tell me why you didn't come tonight. I must know."

"I was tired popper, I told you."

"But why were you tired?"

"I had a fight in the shop."

"A fight? With whom?"

"With the boss—with Mr. Neuheim."

"With the boss? God in heaven, are you crazy? Are you going to lose your job again? What is wrong with you? You have never stuck to one job more than six months. Can't you do like other boys, and stick to a job and make a man of yourself?"

"Let me alone!" David cried in sudden rage, rushing from the room. "For God's sake, let me alone!"

III

With both elbows on the sill, and with his face in his hands, David sat at the air-shaft window again during the next half hour. His mind whirled with formless ideas, like the rout of autumn leaves before a wind. His head throbbed, and again a haze had fallen upon him, a stupor painful as that of a man with a great wound.

The airshaft was still clamorous with the hymn of life that filled it night and day. Babies were squalling, women were berating their children, men were talking in rapid Yiddish, there was rattling of plates and knives, and the shrieking of a clothes line pulley like a knife through it all. The aircraft was dark; and overhead, in the little patch of sky, three stars shown down. Pungent spring odors mingled with the smell of rubbish in the courtyard below.

David's mother moved about carefully as she took away the supper dishes. She knew David's moods, and went on tiptoe, and let him sit there until she had cleaned up in the kitchen. He heard vaguely the sound of her labors, and then she came and laid her rough hand, still red and damp from the dish water, on his shoulder.

"What's the matter, Davie?" she asked, tenderly. "What are you worrying about?"

"Nothing."

"Why did you fight with your popper? You know he's sick, and that you mustn't mind what he says. Why did you do it?"

"I don't know."

"You must be nice to him now; he feels it terribly because he's sick, and that you have to support him. Do you worry because you have to support us?"

"I don't know."

"It won't last forever, Davie boy. Something must happen—there must come a change. God can't be so bad as all that. Is that what worries you?"

David's eyes grew melancholy and his head sunk more deeply between his cupped hands.

"Life isn't worth living; that's what's the trouble mommer," he said. "I feel empty and black inside, and I've got nothing to live for."

"That's foolishness," his mother said warmly. "Everyone lives, and most people have even more troubles than us. If there are so many poor, we can be poor, too. What do you think God put us here for anyway? A healthy young boy like you saying he's got nothing to live for! It's a disgrace!"

"Mommer," David said, passionately, "can you tell me why you live? Why do you yourself live? Give me one good reason!"

"Me? Are you asking me this question?" David's mother exclaimed, in a voice in which there was surprise mixed with a certain delight that her usually silent boy was admitting her on an equality to such intimacies.

She wrinkled her brow. It was the first time, probably, in her work-bound, busy life that she had thought on such a theme, and she put her finger on her lip in a characteristic gesture and meditated for a minute.

"Well, Davie," she said slowly, "I will tell you why your Popper and I have gone on struggling and living. It is because we loved you, and because we wanted to see you grow up healthy and strong and happy, with a family of your own around you in your old age. That's the real reason."

"But supposing I don't want to grow up," Davie cried. "Supposing you raised a failure in me. Supposing I'm sick of this world. Supposing I die before I raise a family. . . ."

"That's all foolishness. Don't talk that way."

"But supposing. . . ."

"I won't suppose anything."

"Very well," said David. "You live for me. But tell me, mommer, what do people who have no children live for? What does the whole human race live for? Do you know? Who knows anyone that knows?"

Mrs. Brandt thought again. Then she dismissed the whole subject with a wave of her hand.

"Those are just foolish questions, like a child's," she said. "They remind me of the time when you were a little boy, and cried for days because I would not buy you an automobile, or a lion we saw in Central Park, or some such thing. Why should we have to know why we live? We live because we live, Davie dear. You will have to learn that some day, and not from books, either. I don't know what's the matter with those books, anyway; they make you sick, David."

"No, it's life makes me sick—this dirty life!"

"You're a fool! You must stop reading books, and you must stop sitting here every night, like an old graybeard. You must go out more and enjoy yourself."

"I have no friends."

"Make them! What a funny, changeable boy you are! Two or three years ago we could never keep you at home nights, you were so wild. You did nothing but go about till early morning with your friends—and fine friends they were too, poolroom loafers, gamblers, pimps, all the East Side filth. Now you read those books that settlement lady gave you; and I don't know which is worse. Go out; put on your hat and coat and go!"

"Where?"

"Anywhere! The East Side is big, and lots of things are going on! Find them!"

"But I want to read!"

"You won't! I won't let you! I should drop dead if I let you!"

David stared wrathfully at her for a moment, stung into anger by her presumptuous meddling into affairs beyond her world of illiteracy and hope. He was about to speak sharply to her, but changed his mind with a weary shrug of his shoulders. He put on his hat and coat and wandered aimlessly into the East Side night, not in obedience to his mother, but because it was easier than to sit here under the impending flow of her nightly exhortations.

LANGSTON HUGHES
(1902–1967)

Few twentieth-century artists produced as diverse and influential a body of work as Langston Hughes. He published at least twelve volumes of poetry, a novel, collections of stories, two autobiographies, dramas, historical writings, newspaper columns, and literary and cultural criticism. He edited important anthologies of African-American folklore, poetry, and stories. He was a significant figure not only in the Harlem of the New Negro Renaissance of the 1920s, but for decades after. He was active in left-wing cultural circles and an important contributor to progressive journals for over thirty years. All the same, Hughes's recognition by the literary establishment was slow in coming.

Born in Joplin, Missouri, he grew up in Lawrence, Kansas, a city with a long tradition of black militance, in Cleveland, Ohio, and in other cities to which his mother moved in search of work. His family was prominent and active: the first husband of his grandmother had been one of John Brown's raiders killed at Harper's Ferry, and his great uncle John Mercer Langston, a noted abolitionist, became the first black to serve in the U.S. Congress. Hughes's father, James Hughes, studied to be a lawyer but was denied permission to enter the bar by the all-white examining board in Oklahoma; afterward, he left his family and the United States to settle in Mexico, where he became wealthy as a businessman. Though he spent some time in Mexico with his father, Hughes was mainly raised by his grandmother. After teaching English in Mexico for a year, he attended Columbia University, working in a variety of jobs and integrating himself into the life of Harlem, including that of the gay black community. In 1923, he shipped out as a sailor on a boat for Africa, and later traveled to the Netherlands and, for a time, lived in Paris, consorting with writers of the Négritude movement. On his return to the United States, he worked as a busboy in Washington, in which job he was supposed to have been "discovered" as a poet by Vachel Lindsay. In fact, by that time, he had begun to publish poetry in prominent places like the NAACP's journal, The Crisis, as well as in the Amsterdam News.

Hughes's first book of poems, The Weary Blues, came out in 1926; Fine Clothes to the Jew followed in 1927. By then, Hughes had established himself in Harlem, publishing stories and poems, traveling across the country to read them, especially in the South, collecting folklore and working with Zora Neale Hurston on a play, Mule Bone, and writing a novel, Not without Laughter (1930). He visited Europe and the Soviet Union in 1932 as a part of a black film group, later traveling to China, Korea, and Japan, where he was briefly detained as a suspected Communist spy. In fact, during the thirties, Hughes wrote and published a significant number of poems and stories with politically progressive themes, like Scottsboro Limited (1932) and one of the poems that follows, "Johannesburg Mines," and he remained active in a variety of left-wing causes. He lived in besieged Madrid, covering the Spanish Civil War for the Baltimore Afro-American newspaper. And he continued to write poems, stories, plays (seven during the late thirties), autobiography (e.g., The Big Sea—1940), and books for children (with Arna Bontemps), as well as journalism. In 1943 he began the "Simple" columns for the Chicago Defender, stories told by Jesse B. Semple, an ordinary guy from Harlem trying to get by. The stories were enormously popular and were collected in a series of volumes, including Simple Speaks His Mind (1950), Simple Takes a Wife (1953), and Simple Stakes a Claim (1957). During this time, Hughes also edited, with Arna Bontemps, the influential anthology The Poetry of the Negro, 1746–1949; translated the work of Frederico Garcia Lorca, Nicolas Guillen, and Haitian writer Jacques Romain; and published his first book-length poem, Montage of a Dream Deferred (1951).

But it was hardly the case that Hughes moved from triumph to triumph. Early in his career he had been attacked by Negro critics for concentrating on the lives of down-home black people, like the pianist of "Weary Blues," rather than those who supposedly "uplifted" the race. And white critics criticized him for his supposed simplicity. During the thirties he was picketed and his readings heckled by right-wingers. The FBI had long been keeping tabs on him. And, during the Cold War, Life magazine attacked him together with Albert Einstein, Paul Robeson, and Leonard Bernstein as "commie dupes." Finally, in 1953, Senator Joseph McCarthy subpoenaed him to appear before his witchhunting committee. Moreover, Hughes has been subject to a great deal of speculation regarding his sexuality, which seemed directed primarily to working-class black men. In spite of, or perhaps because of, the controversy, Hughes has emerged as one of the most significant literary figures of the twentieth century, a person whose career for formal variety, international influence, and sheer accomplishment matches that of any artist of our time.

JOHANNESBURG MINES

In the Johannesburg mines
There are 240,000 natives working.

What kind of poem
Would you make out of that?

240,000 natives working
In the Johannesburg mines.

THE WEARY BLUES

Droning a drowsy syncopated tune,
Rocking back and forth to a mellow croon,
    I heard a Negro play.
Down on Lenox Avenue the other night
By the pale dull pallor of an old gas light
    He did a lazy sway . . .
    He did a lazy sway . . .
To the tune o' those Weary Blues.
With his ebony hands on each ivory key
He made that poor piano moan with melody.
    O Blues!
Swaying to and fro on his rickety stool
He played that sad raggy tune like a musical fool.
    Sweet Blues!
Coming from a black man's soul.
    O Blues!
In a deep song voice with a melancholy tone

I heard that Negro sing, that old piano moan—
    "Ain't got nobody in all this world,
    Ain't got nobody but ma self.
    I's gwine to quit ma frownin'
    And put ma troubles on the shelf."
Thump, thump, thump, went his foot on the floor.
He played a few chords then he sang some more—
    "I got the Weary Blues
    And I can't be satisfied.
    Got the Weary Blues
    And can't be satisfied—
    I ain't happy no mo'
    And I wish that I had died."
And far into the night he crooned that tune.
    The stars went out and so did the moon.
    The singer stopped playing and went to bed
    While the Weary Blues echoed through his head.
    He slept like a rock or a man that's dead.

STERLING BROWN

(1901-1989)

Ma Rainey was not, of course, Sterling Brown's creation. A significant singer in her own right, she also represented a moment in the transition of the blues from a rural to an urban form. But for Brown, she meant a great deal more, for in this poem he embodies in her a powerful theory of the role of the African-American creative artist. Her subjects emerge from the experiences of ordinary black people, their tragedies, such as the great Mississippi floods, and their everyday ordeals, like those of the "lonesome road." Her formal roots are in their music, their language, the cadences of their speech and laughter. Her relation to them is not the remoteness of the precious academic poet; rather, she follows some of the people outside to share in their tears. Brown's was not a conventional theory nor one easily arrived at, for there were many who thought that a man of his background and talents ought to be writing not about the folk and certainly not in dialect, but about "upstanding" people who spoke "proper" English.

He was himself the product of the black middle class of Washington, D.C., his father a well-known pastor and active promoter of social betterment. Graduating from Williams College in 1922, Brown won a Clark Fellowship to study for his master's degree, which he obtained from Harvard the following year. He then went south, to Lynchburg, Virginia, where he taught at the Virginia Seminary and College for three years and, by his own account, spent a good deal more time learning from the local black folks he met at night outside the seminary's gates. They furnished him with the originals of many of his literary portraits, but they also provided him with rich insights about African-American culture and art.

These he would embody not only in poems like "Ma Rainey," but in his years of teaching at Howard University and in a series of pivotal articles and books. The first of these was perhaps his groundbreaking 1933 essay on "Negro Characters as Seen by White Authors." This was followed by two major surveys of the field, Negro Poetry and Drama *(1938) and* The Negro in American Fiction *(1938). Incensed at the omission of black writers from the supposedly comprehensive volume called* The American Caravan, *Brown, with Arthur P. Davis and Ulysses Lee, compiled an influential anthology,* The Negro Caravan, *in 1941. Brown also served as editor on Negro affairs for the Federal Writers' Project and as a key researcher for the study that would lead to Gunner Myrdal's* An American Dilemma *(1944). But most of all, he developed in his critical writings, and illustrated in his poetry, an idea of the flexibility and range of the everyday speech of black people that has remained an important source of inspiration to poets and teachers to this day.*

MA RAINEY

I
When Ma Rainey
Comes to town,
Folks from anyplace
Miles aroun',
From Cape Girardeau,
Poplar Bluff,
Flocks in to hear
Ma do her stuff;
Comes flivverin' in,
Or ridin' mules,
Or packed in trains,
Picknickin' fools. . . .
That's what it's like,
Fo' miles on down,
To New Orleans delta
An' Mobile town,
When Ma hits
Anywheres aroun'.

II
Dey comes to hear Ma Rainey from de little river settlements,
From blackbottom cornrows and from lumber camps;
Dey stumble in de hall, jes a-laughin' an' a-cacklin',
Cheerin' lak roarin' water, lak wind in river swamps.

An' some jokers keeps deir laughs a-goin' in de crowded aisles,
An' some folks sits dere waitin' wid deir aches an' miseries,
Till Ma comes out before dem, a-smilin' gold-toofed smiles
An' Long Boy ripples minors on de black an' yellow keys.

III

O Ma Rainey,
Sing yo' song;
Now you's back
Whah you belong,
Git way inside us,
Keep us strong. . . .
O Ma Rainey,
Li'l an' low;
Sing us 'bout de hard luck
Roun' our do';
Sing us 'bout de lonesome road
We mus' go. . . .

IV

I talked to a fellow, an' the fellow say,
"She jes' catch hold of us, somekindaway.
She sang Backwater Blues one day:
    'It rained fo' days an' de skies was dark as night,
    Trouble taken place in de lowlands at night.

    'Thundered an' lightened an' the storm begin to roll
    Thousan's of people ain't got no place to go.

    'Den I went an' stood upon some high ol' lonesome hill,
    An' looked down on the place where I used to live.'

An' den de folks, dey natchally bowed dey heads an' cried,
Bowed dey heavy heads, shet dey moufs up tight an' cried,
An' Ma lef' de stage, an' followed some de folks outside."

Dere wasn't much more de fellow say:
She jes' gits hold of us dataway.

F. SCOTT FITZGERALD
(1896-1940)

Fitzgerald's name summons all the clichéd images of the "jazz age": "flaming youth," full-length beaver coats, night-long parties, the romance of New York seen from the Queensboro bridge at dusk. These images were rooted in the experiences of real people—some, some few and fortunate, young and rich and, for a time, happy. But it was Fitzgerald's great virtue as a writer not to be taken in by the very romance he so powerfully evoked. Rather, his books capture the evanescence of these images, the ambiguities, even downright viciousness that lurked just under the surface of privilege.

He knew these ambiguities and contradictions in his own life. His father's people could be traced back to the writer of the "Star Spangled Banner," Francis Scott Key, but they had slid down the economic scale, to be rescued by the climbing immigrant family from which his mother came. Few courtships could have been more romantic than that of the Alabama belle, Zelda Sayre, and the dashing young World War I lieutenant, Scott Fitzgerald; few marriages became more notorious for conflict and mutually inflicted pain. No writing career began with greater success and notoriety than Fitzgerald's after he published his first book, This Side of Paradise *(1920); but few men had to work harder at potboiler stories and silly movie scripts to sustain not only a certain style of life but the opportunities to do the kind of work Fitzgerald had accomplished in novels like* The Great Gatsby *(1925) and in stories like "May Day" and "The Diamond as Big as the Ritz."*

Many of Fitzgerald's works, such as "Babylon Revisited" and Tender Is the Night *(1934), powerfully register the meanings of privilege dissipated, hope shriveled, and at the end, Frost's words, "what to make of a diminished thing." If Fitzgerald seems at first to be a devotee of glamour, what he finally displays in his fiction is rather the nakedness of class.*

THE DIAMOND AS BIG AS THE RITZ

John T. Unger came from a family that had been well known in Hades—a small town on the Mississippi River—for several generations. John's father had held the amateur golf championship through many a heated contest; Mrs. Unger was known "from hot-box to hot-bed," as the local phrase went, for her political addresses; and young John T. Unger, who had just turned sixteen, had danced all the latest dances from New York before he put on long trousers. And now, for a certain time, he was to be away from home. That respect for a New England education which is the bane of all provincial places, which drains them yearly of their most promising young men, had seized upon his parents. Nothing would suit them but that he should go to St. Midas' School near Boston—Hades was too small to hold their darling and gifted son.

Now in Hades—as you know if you ever have been there—the names of the more fashionable preparatory schools and colleges mean very little. The inhabitants have been so long out of the world that, though they make a show of keeping up to date in dress and manners and literature, they depend to a great extent on hearsay, and a function that in Hades would be considered elaborate would doubtless be hailed by a Chicago beef-princess as "perhaps a little tacky."

John T. Unger was on the eve of departure. Mrs. Unger, with maternal fatuity, packed his trunks full of linen suits and electric fans, and Mr. Unger presented his son with an asbestos pocket-book stuffed with money.

"Remember, you are always welcome here," he said. "You can be sure, boy, that we'll keep the home fires burning."

"I know," answered John huskily.

"Don't forget who you are and where you come from," continued his father proudly, "and you can do nothing to harm you. You are an Unger—from Hades."

So the old man and the young shook hands and John walked away with tears streaming from his eyes. Ten minutes later he had passed outside the city limits, and he stopped to glance back for the last time. Over the gates the old-fashioned

Victorian motto seemed strangely attractive to him. His father had tried time and time again to have it changed to something with a little more push and verve about it, such as "Hades—Your Opportunity," or else a plain "Welcome" sign set over a hearty handshake pricked out in electric lights. The old motto was a little depressing, Mr. Unger had thought—but now. . . .

So John took his look and then set his face resolutely toward his destination. And, as he turned away, the lights of Hades against the sky seemed full of a warm and passionate beauty.

St. Midas' School is half an hour from Boston in a Rolls-Pierce motor-car. The actual distance will never be known, for no one, except John T. Unger, had ever arrived there save in a Rolls-Pierce and probably no one ever will again. St. Midas' is the most expensive and the most exclusive boys' preparatory school in the world.

John's first two years there passed pleasantly. The fathers of all the boys were money-kings and John spent his summers visiting at fashionable resorts. While he was very fond of all the boys he visited, their fathers struck him as being much of a piece, and in his boyish way he often wondered at their exceeding sameness. When he told them where his home was they would ask jovially, "Pretty hot down there?" and John would muster a faint smile and answer, "It certainly is." His response would have been heartier had they not all made this joke—at best varying it with, "Is it hot enough for you down there?" which he hated just as much.

In the middle of his second year at school, a quiet, handsome boy named Percy Washington had been put in John's form. The newcomer was pleasant in his manner and exceedingly well dressed even for St. Midas', but for some reason he kept aloof from the other boys. The only person with whom he was intimate was John T. Unger, but even to John he was entirely uncommunicative concerning his home or his family. That he was wealthy went without saying, but beyond a few such deductions John knew little of his friend, so it promised rich confectionery for his curiosity when Percy invited him to spend the summer at his home "in the West." He accepted, without hesitation.

It was only when they were in the train that Percy became, for the first time, rather communicative. One day while they were eating lunch in the dining-car and discussing the imperfect characters of several of the boys at school, Percy suddenly changed his tone and made an abrupt remark.

"My father," he said, "is by far the richest man in the world."

"Oh," said John, politely. He could think of no answer to make to this confidence. He considered "That's very nice," but it sounded hollow and was on the point of saying, "Really?" but refrained since it would seem to question Percy's statement. And such an astounding statement could scarcely be questioned.

"By far the richest," repeated Percy.

"I was reading in the *World Almanac*," began John, "that there was one man in America with an income of over five million a year and four men with incomes of over three million a year, and—"

"Oh, they're nothing," Percy's mouth was a half-moon of scorn. "Catch-penny capitalists, financial small-fry, petty merchants and money-lenders. My father could buy them out and not know he'd done it."

"But how does he—"

"Why haven't they put down *his* income tax? Because he doesn't pay any. At least he pays a little one—but he doesn't pay any on his real income."

"He must be very rich," said John simply. "I'm glad. I like very rich people."

"The richer a fella is, the better I like him." There was a look of passionate frankness upon his dark face. "I visited the Schnlitzer-Murphys last Easter. Vivian Schnlitzer-Murphy had rubies as big as hen's eggs, and sapphires that were like globes with lights inside them—"

"I love jewels," agreed Percy enthusiastically. "Of course I wouldn't want any one at school to know about it, but I've got quite a collection myself. I used to collect them instead of stamps."

"And diamonds," continued John eagerly. "The Schnlitzer-Murphys had diamonds as big as walnuts—"

"That's nothing." Percy had leaned forward and dropped his voice to a low whisper. "That's nothing at all. My father has a diamond bigger than the Ritz-Carlton Hotel."

II

The Montana sunset lay between two mountains like a gigantic bruise from which dark arteries spread themselves over a poisoned sky. An immense distance under the sky crouched the village of Fish, minute, dismal, and forgotten. There were twelve men, so it was said, in the village of Fish, twelve sombre and inexplicable souls who sucked a lean milk from the almost literally bare rock upon which a mysterious populatory force had begotten them. They had become a race apart, these twelve men of Fish, like some species developed by an early whim of nature, which on second thought had abandoned them to struggle and extermination.

Out of the blue-black bruise in the distance crept a long line of moving lights upon the desolation of the land, and the twelve men of Fish gathered like ghosts at the shanty depot to watch the passing of the seven o'clock train, the Transcontinental Express from Chicago. Six times or so a year the Transcontinental Express, through some inconceivable jurisdiction, stopped at the village of Fish, and when this occurred a figure or so would disembark, mount into a buggy that always appeared from out of the dusk, and drive off toward the bruised sunset. The observation of this pointless and preposterous phenomenon had become a sort of cult among the men of Fish. To observe, that was all; there remained in them none of the vital quality of illusion which would make them wonder or speculate, else a religion might have grown up around these mysterious visitations. But the men of Fish were beyond all religion—the barest and most savage tenets of even Christianity could gain no foothold on that barren rock—so there was no altar, no priest, no sacrifice; only each night at seven the silent concourse by the shanty depot, a congregation who lifted up a prayer of dim, anaemic wonder.

On this June night, the Great Brakeman, whom, had they deified any one, they might well have chosen as their celestial protagonist, had ordained that the seven o'clock train should leave its human (or inhuman) deposit at Fish. At two minutes after seven Percy Washington and John T. Unger disembarked, hurried past the spellbound, the agape, the fearsome eyes of the twelve men of Fish, mounted into a buggy which had obviously appeared from nowhere, and drove away.

After half an hour, when the twilight had coagulated into dark, the silent negro who was driving the buggy hailed an opaque body somewhere ahead of them in the gloom. In response to his cry, it turned upon them a luminous disk which regarded them like a malignant eye out of the unfathomable night. As they came closer, John saw that it was the tail-light of an immense automobile, larger and more magnificent than any he had ever seen. Its body was of gleaming metal richer than nickel and lighter than silver, and the hubs of the wheels were studded with irridescent geometric figures of green and yellow—John did not dare to guess whether they were glass or jewel.

Two negroes, dressed in glittering livery such as one sees in pictures of royal processions in London, were standing at attention beside the car and as the two young men dismounted from the buggy they were greeted in some language which the guest could not understand, but which seemed to be an extreme form of the Southern negro's dialect.

"Get in," said Percy to his friend, as their trunks were tossed to the ebony roof of the limousine. "Sorry we had to bring you this far in that buggy, but of course it wouldn't do for the people on the train or those Godforsaken fellas in Fish to see this automobile."

"Gosh! What a car!!" This ejaculation was provoked by its interior. John saw that the upholstery consisted of a thousand minute and exquisite tapestries of silk, woven with jewels and embroideries, and set upon a background of cloth of gold. The two armchair seats in which the boys luxuriated were covered with stuff that resembled duvetyn, but seemed woven in numberless colors of the ends of ostrich feathers.

"What a car!" cried John again, in amazement.

"This thing?" Percy laughed. "Why, it's just an old junk we use for a station wagon."

By this time they were gliding along through the darkness toward the break between the two mountains.

"We'll be there in an hour and a half," said Percy, looking at the clock. "I may as well tell you it's not going to be like anything you ever saw before."

If the car was any indication of what John would see, he was prepared to be astonished indeed. The simple piety prevalent in Hades has the earnest worship of and respect for riches as the first article of its creed—had John felt otherwise than radiantly humble before them, his parents would have turned away in horror at the blasphemy.

They had now reached and were entering the break between the two mountains and almost immediately the way became much rougher.

"If the moon shone down here, you'd see that we're in a big gulch," said Percy, trying to peer out of the window. He spoke a few words into the mouthpiece and immediately the footman turned on a searchlight and swept the hillsides with an immense beam.

"Rocky, you see. An ordinary car would be knocked to pieces in half an hour. In fact, it'd take a tank to navigate it unless you knew the way. You notice we're going uphill now."

They were obviously ascending, and within a few minutes the car was crossing a high rise, where they caught a glimpse of a pale moon newly risen in the distance. The car stopped suddenly and several figures took shape out of the dark beside it—these were negroes also. Again the two young men were saluted in the same dimly recognizable dialect; then the negroes set to work and four immense cables dangling from overhead were attached with hooks to the hubs of the great jeweled wheels. At a resounding "Hey-yah!" John felt the car being lifted slowly from the ground—up and up—clear of the tallest rocks on both sides—then higher, until he could see a wavy, moonlit valley stretched out before him in sharp contrast to the quagmire of rocks that they had just left. Only on one side was there still rock—and then suddenly there was no rock beside them or anywhere around.

It was apparent that they had surmounted some immense knifeblade of stone, projecting perpendicularly into the air. In a moment they were going down again, and finally with a soft bump they were landed upon the smooth earth.

"The worst is over," said Percy, squinting out the window. "It's only five miles from here, and our own road—tapestry brick—all the way. This belongs to us. This is where the United States ends, father says."

"Are we in Canada?"

"We are not. We're in the middle of the Montana Rockies. But you are now on the only five square miles of land in the country that's never been surveyed."

"Why hasn't it? Did they forget it?"

"No," said Percy, grinning, "they tried to do it three times. The first time my grandfather corrupted a whole department of the State survey; the second time he had the official maps of the United States tinkered with—that held them for fifteen years. The last time was harder. My father fixed it so that their compasses were in the strongest magnetic field ever artificially set up. He had a whole set of surveying instruments made with a slight defection that would allow for this territory not to appear, and he substituted them for the ones that were to be used. Then he had a river deflected and he had what looked like a village built up on its banks—so that they'd see it, and think it was a town ten miles farther up the valley. There's only one thing my father's afraid of," he concluded, "only one thing in the world that could be used to find us out."

"What's that?"

Percy sank his voice to a whisper.

"Aeroplanes," he breathed. "We've got half a dozen anti-aircraft guns and we've arranged it so far—but there've been a few deaths and a great many prisoners. Not that we mind *that,* you know, father and I, but it upsets mother and the girls, and there's always the chance that some time we won't be able to arrange it."

Shreds and tatters of chinchilla, courtesy clouds in the green moon's heaven, were passing the green moon like precious Eastern stuffs paraded for the inspection of some Tartar Khan. It seemed to John that it was day, and that he was looking at some lads sailing above him in the air, showering down tracts and patent medicine circulars, with their messages of hope for despairing, rockbound hamlets. It seemed to him that he could see them look down out of the clouds and stare—and stare at whatever there was to stare at in this place whither he was bound—What then? Were they induced to land by some insidious device there to be immured far from patent medicines and from tracts until the judgment day—or, should they fail to fall into the trap, did a quick puff of smoke and the sharp round of a splitting shell bring them drooping to earth—and "upset" Percy's mother and sisters. John shook his head and the wraith of a hollow laugh issued silently from his parted lips. What desperate transaction lay hidden here? What a moral expedient of a bizarre Croesus? What terrible and golden mystery? . . .

The chinchilla clouds had drifted past now and outside the Montana night was bright as day. The tapestry brick of the road was smooth to the tread of the great tires as they rounded a still, moonlit lake; they passed into darkness for a moment, a pine grove, pungent and cool, then they came out into a broad avenue of lawn and John's exclamation of pleasure was simultaneous with Percy's taciturn "We're home."

Full in the light of the stars, an exquisite château rose from the borders of the lake, climbed in marble radiance half the height of an adjoining mountain, then melted in grace, in perfect symmetry, in translucent feminine languor, into the massed darkness of a forest of pine. The many towers, the slender tracery of the sloping parapets, the chiselled wonder of a thousand yellow windows with their oblongs and hectagons and triangles of golden light, the shattered softness of the intersecting planes of star-shine and blue shade, all trembled on John's spirit like a chord of music. On one of the towers, the tallest, the blackest at its base, an arrangement of exterior lights at the top made a sort of floating faiyland—and as John gazed up in warm enchantment the faint acciaccare sound of violins drifted down in a rococo harmony that was like nothing he had ever heard before. Then in a moment the car stopped before wide, high marble steps, around which the night air was fragrant with a host of flowers. At the top of the steps two great doors swung silently open and amber light flooded out upon the darkness, silhouetting the figure of an exquisite lady with black, high-piled hair, who held out her arms toward them.

"Mother," Percy was saying, "this is my friend, John Unger, from Hades."

Afterward John remembered that first night as a daze of many colors, of quick sensory impressions, of music soft as a voice in love, and of the beauty of things, lights and shadows, and motions and faces. There was a white-haired man who stood drinking a many-hued cordial from a crystal thimble set on a golden stem. There was a girl with a flowery face, dressed like Titania with braided sapphires in her hair. There was a room where the solid, soft gold of the walls yielded to the pressure of his hand, and a room that was like a platonic conception of the ultimate prison—ceiling, floor, and all, it was lined with an unbroken mass of diamonds, diamonds of every size and shape, until, lit with tall violet lamps in the corners, it dazzled the eyes with a whiteness that could be compared only with itself, beyond human wish or dream.

Through a maze of these rooms the two boys wandered. Sometimes the floor under their feet would flame in brilliant patterns from lighting below, patterns of barbaric clashing colors, of pastel delicacy, of sheer whiteness, or of subtle and intricate mosaic, surely from some mosque on the Adriatic Sea. Sometimes beneath layers of thick crystal he would see blue or green water swirling, inhabited by vivid fish and growths of rainbow foliage. Then they would be treading on furs of every texture and color or along corridors of palest ivory, unbroken as though carved complete from the gigantic tusks of dinosaurs extinct before the age of man. . . .

Then a hazily remembered transition, and they were at dinner—where each plate was of two almost imperceptible layers of solid diamond between which was curiously worked a filigree of emerald design, a shaving sliced from green air. Music, plangent and unobtrusive, drifted down through far corridors—his chair, feathered and curved insidiously to his back, seemed to engulf and overpower him as he drank his first glass of port. He tried drowsily to answer a question that had been asked him, but the honeyed luxury that clasped his body added to the illusion of sleep—jewels, fabrics, wines, and metals blurred before his eyes into a sweet mist. . . .

"Yes," he replied with a polite effort, "it certainly is hot enough for me down there."

He managed to add a ghostly laugh; then, without movement, without resistance, he seemed to float off and away, leaving an iced dessert that was pink as a dream. . . . He fell asleep.

When he awoke he knew that several hours had passed. He was in a great quiet room with ebony walls and a dull illumination that was too faint, too subtle, to be called a light. His young host was standing over him.

"You fell asleep at dinner," Percy was saying. "I nearly did, too—it was such a treat to be comfortable again after this year of school. Servants undressed and bathed you while you were sleeping."

"Is this a bed or a cloud?" sighed John. "Percy, Percy—before you go? I want to apologize."

"For what?"

"For doubting you when you said you had a diamond as big as the Ritz-Carlton Hotel."

Percy smiled.

"I thought you didn't believe me. It's that mountain, you know."

"What mountain?"

"The mountain the château rests on. It's not very big for a mountain. But except about fifty feet of sod and gravel on top it's solid diamond. One diamond, one cubic mile without a flaw. Aren't you listening? Say—"

But John T. Unger had again fallen asleep.

III

Morning. As he awoke he perceived drowsily that the room had at the same moment become dense with sunlight. The ebony panels of one wall had slid aside on a sort of track, leaving his chamber half open to the day. A large negro in a white uniform stood beside his bed.

"Good-evening," muttered John, summoning his brains from the wild places.

"Good-morning, sir. Are you ready for your bath, sir? Oh, don't get up—I'll put you in, if you'll just unbutton your pajamas—there. Thank you, sir."

John lay quietly as his pajamas were removed—he was amused and delighted; he expected to be lifted like a child by this black Gargantua who was tending him, but nothing of the sort happened; instead he felt the bed tilt up slowly on its side— he began to roll, startled at first, in the direction of the wall, but when he reached the wall its drapery gave way, and sliding two yards farther down a fleecy incline he plumped gently into water the same temperature as his body.

He looked about him. The runway or rollway on which he had arrived had folded gently back into place. He had been projected into another chamber and was sitting in a sunken bath with his head just above the level of the floor. All about him, lining the walls of the room and the sides and bottom of the bath itself, was a blue aquarium, and gazing through the crystal surface on which he sat, he could see fish swimming among amber lights and even gliding without curiosity past his outstretched toes, which were separated from them only by the thickness of the crystal. From overhead, sunlight came down through sea-green glass.

"I suppose, sir, that you'd like hot rosewater and soapsuds this morning, sir— and perhaps cold salt water to finish."

The negro was standing beside him.

"Yes," agreed John, smiling inanely, "as you please." Any idea of ordering this bath according to his own meagre standards of living would have been priggish and not a little wicked.

The negro pressed a button and a warm rain began to fall, apparently from overhead, but really, so John discovered after a moment, from a fountain arrangement near by. The water turned to a pale rose color and jets of liquid soap spurted into it from four miniature walrus heads at the corners of the bath. In a moment a dozen little paddle-wheels, fixed to the sides, had churned the mixture into a radiant rainbow of pink foam which enveloped him softly with its delicious lightness, and burst in shining, rosy bubbles here and there about him.

"Shall I turn on the moving-picture machine, sir?" suggested the negro deferentially. "There's a good one-reel comedy in this machine to-day, or I can put in a serious piece in a moment, if you prefer it."

"No, thanks," answered John, politely but firmly. He was enjoying his bath too much to desire any distraction. But distraction came. In a moment he was listening intently to the sound of flutes from just outside, flutes dripping a melody that was like a waterfall, cool and green as the room itself, accompanying a frothy piccolo, in play more fragile than the lace of suds that covered and charmed him.

After a cold salt-water bracer and a cold fresh finish, he stepped out into a fleecy robe, and upon a couch covered with the same material he was rubbed with oil, alcohol, and spice. Later he sat in a voluptuous chair while he was shaved and his hair was trimmed.

"Mr. Percy is waiting in your sitting-room," said the negro, when these operations were finished. "My name is Gygsum, Mr. Unger, sir. I am to see to Mr. Unger every morning."

John walked out into the brisk sunshine of his living-room, where he found breakfast waiting for him and Percy, gorgeous in white kid knickerbockers, smoking in an easy chair.

IV

This is a story of the Washington family as Percy sketched it for John during breakfast.

The father of the present Mr. Washington had been a Virginian, a direct descendant of George Washington, and Lord Baltimore. At the close of the Civil War he was a twenty-five-year-old Colonel with a played-out plantation and about a thousand dollars in gold.

Fitz-Norman Culpepper Washington, for that was the young Colonel's name, decided to present the Virginia estate to his younger brother and go West. He selected two dozen of the most faithful blacks, who, of course, worshipped him, and bought twenty-five tickets to the West, where he intended to take out land in their names and start a sheep and cattle ranch.

When he had been in Montana for less than a month and things were going very poorly indeed, he stumbled on his great discovery. He had lost his way when riding in the hills, and after a day without food he began to grow hungry. As he was without his rifle, he was forced to pursue a squirrel, and in the course of the pursuit he noticed that it was carrying something shiny in its mouth. Just before it vanished into its hole—for Providence did not intend that this squirrel should alleviate his hunger—it dropped its burden. Sitting down to consider the situation Fitz-Norman's eye was caught by a gleam in the grass beside him. In ten seconds he had completely lost his appetite and gained one hundred thousand dollars. The squirrel, which had refused with annoying persistence to become food, had made him a present of a large and perfect diamond.

Late that night he found his way to camp and twelve hours later all the males among his darkies were back by the squirrel hole digging furiously at the side of the mountain. He told them he had discovered a rhinestone mine, and, as only one of two of them had ever seen even a small diamond before, they believed him, without question. When the magnitude of his discovery became apparent to him, he found himself in a quandary. The mountain was a diamond—it was literally nothing else but solid diamond. He filled four saddle bags full of glittering samples and started on horseback for St. Paul. There he managed to dispose of half a dozen small stones—when he tried a larger one a storekeeper fainted and Fitz-Norman was arrested as a public disturber. He escaped from jail and caught the train for New York, where he sold a few medium-sized diamonds and received in exchange about two hundred thousand dollars in gold. But he did not dare to produce any exceptional gems—in fact, he left New York just in time. Tremendous excitement had been created in jewelry circles, not so much by the size of his diamonds as by their appearance in the city from mysterious sources. Wild rumors became current that a diamond mine had been discovered in the Catskills, on the Jersey coast, on Long Island, beneath Washington Square. Excursion trains, packed with men carrying picks and shovels began to leave New York hourly, bound for various neighboring El Dorados. But by that time young Fitz-Norman was on his way back to Montana.

By the end of a fortnight he had estimated that the diamond in the mountain was approximately equal in quantity to all the rest of the diamonds known to exist in the world. There was no valuing it by any regular computation, however, for it was *one solid diamond*—and if it were offered for sale not only would the bottom fall out of the market, but also, if the value should vary with its size in the usual arithmetical progression, there would not be enough gold in the world to buy a tenth part of it. And what could any one do with a diamond that size?

It was an amazing predicament. He was, in one sense, the richest man that ever lived—and yet was he worth anything at all? If his secret should transpire there was no telling to what measures the Government might resort in order to prevent a panic, in gold as well as in jewels. They might take over the claim immediately and institute a monopoly.

There was no alternative—he must market his mountain in secret. He sent South for his younger brother and put him in charge of his colored following—darkies who had never realized that slavery was abolished. To make sure of this, he read them a proclamation that he had composed, which announced that General Forrest had reorganized the shattered Southern armies and defeated the North in one pitched battle. The negroes believed him implicitly. They passed a vote declaring it a good thing and held revival services immediately.

Fitz-Norman himself set out for foreign parts with one hundred thousand dollars and two trunks filled with rough diamonds of all sizes. He sailed for Russia in a Chinese junk and six months after his departure from Montana he was in St. Petersburg. He took obscure lodgings and called immediately upon the court jeweller, announcing that he had a diamond for the Czar. He remained in St. Petersburg for two weeks, in constant danger of being murdered, living from lodging to lodging, and afraid to visit his trunks more than three or four times during the whole fortnight.

On his promise to return in a year with larger and finer stones, he was allowed to leave for India. Before he left, however, the Court Treasurers had deposited to his credit, in American banks, the sum of fifteen million dollars—under four different aliases.

He returned to America in 1868, having been gone a little over two years. He had visited the capitals of twenty-two countries and talked with five emperors, eleven kings, three princes, a shah, a khan, and a sultan. At that time Fitz-Norman estimated his own wealth at one billion dollars. One fact worked consistently against the disclosure of his secret. No one of his larger diamonds remained in the public eye for a week before being invested with a history of enough fatalities, amours, revolutions, and wars to have occupied it from the days of the first Babylonian Empire.

From 1870 until his death in 1900, the history of Fitz-Norman Washington was a long epic in gold. There were side issues, of course—he evaded the surveys, he married a Virginia lady, by whom he had a single son, and he was compelled, due to a series of unfortunate complications, to murder his brother, whose unfortunate habit of drinking himself into an indiscreet stupor had several times endangered their safety. But very few other murders stained these happy years of progress and expansion.

Just before he died he changed his policy, and with all but a few million dollars of his outside wealth bought up rare minerals in bulk, which he deposited in the safety vaults of banks all over the world, marked as bric-à-brac. His son, Braddock Tarleton Washington, followed this policy on an even more tensive scale. The minerals were converted into the rarest of all elements—radium—so that the equivalent of a billion dollars in gold could be placed in a receptacle no bigger than a cigar box.

When Fitz-Norman had been dead three years his son, Braddock, decided that the business had gone far enough. The amount of wealth that he and his father had taken out of the mountain was beyond all exact computation. He kept a note-book in cipher in which he set down the approximate quantity of radium in each of the thousand banks he patronized, and recorded the alias under which it was held. Then he did a very simple thing—he sealed up the mine.

He sealed up the mine. What had been taken out of it would support all the Washingtons yet to be born in unparalleled luxury for generations. His one care must be the protection of his secret, lest in the possible panic attendant on its discovery he should be reduced with all the property-holders in the world to utter poverty.

This was the family among whom John T. Unger was staying. This was the story he heard in his silver-walled living-room the morning after his arrival.

V

After breakfast, John found his way out the great marble entrance, and looked curiously at the scene before him. The whole valley, from the diamond mountain to the steep granite cliff five miles away, still gave off a breath of golden haze which hovered idly above the fine sweep of lawns and lakes and gardens. Here and there clusters of elms made delicate groves of shade, contrasting strangely with the tough masses of pine forest that held the hills in a grip of dark-blue green. Even as John looked he saw three fawns in single file patter out from one clump about a half mile away and disappear with awkward gayety into the black-ribbed half-light of another. John would not have been surprised to see a goat-foot piping his way among the trees or to catch a glimpse of pink nymph-skin and flying yellow hair between the greenest of the green leaves.

In some such cool hope he descended the marble steps, disturbing faintly the sleep of two silky Russian wolfhounds at the bottom, and set off along a walk of white and blue brick that seemed to lead in no particular direction.

He was enjoying himself as much as he was able. It is youth's felicity as well as its insufficiency that it can never live in the present, but must always be measuring up the day against its own radiantly imagined future—flowers and gold, girls and stars, they are only prefigurations and prophecies of that incomparable, unattainable young dream.

John rounded a soft corner where the massed rosebushes filled the air with heavy scent, and struck off across a park toward a patch of moss under some trees. He had never lain upon moss, and he wanted to see whether it was really soft enough to justify the use of its name as an adjective. Then he saw a girl coming toward him over the grass. She was the most beautiful person he had ever seen.

She was dressed in a white little gown that came just below her knees, and a wreath of mignonettes clasped with blue slices of sapphire bound up her hair. Her pink bare feet scattered the dew before them as she came. She was younger than John—not more than sixteen.

"Hello," she cried softly, "I'm Kismine."

She was much more than that to John already. He advanced toward her scarcely moving as he drew near lest he should tread on her bare toes.

"You haven't met me," said her soft voice. Her blue eyes added, "Oh, but you've missed a great deal!" . . . "You met my sister, Jasmine, last night, I was sick with lettuce poisoning," went on her soft voice, and her eyes continued, "and when I'm sick I'm sweet—and when I'm well."

"You have made an enormous impression on me," said John's eyes, "and I'm not so slow myself"—"How do you do?" said his voice. "I hope you're better this morning."—"You darling," added his eyes tremulously.

John observed that they had been walking along the path. On her suggestion they sat down together upon the moss, the softness of which he failed to determine.

He was critical about women. A single defect—a thick ankle, a hoarse voice, a glass eye—was enough to make him utterly indifferent. And here for the first time in his life he was beside a girl who seemed to him the incarnation of physical perfection.

"Are you from the East?" asked Kismine with charming interest.

"No," answered John simply. "I'm from Hades."

Either she had never heard of Hades, or she could think of no pleasant comment to make upon it, for she did not discuss it further.

"I'm going East to school this fall," she said. "D'you think I'll make it? I'm going to New York to Miss Bulge's. It's very strict, but you see over the weekends I'm going to live at home with the family in our New York house, because father heard that the girls had to go walking two by two."

"Your father wants you to be proud," observed John.

"We are," she answered, her eyes shining with dignity. "None of us has ever been punished. Father said we never should be. Once when my sister Jasmine was a little girl she pushed him down-stairs and he just got up and limped away.

"Mother was—well, a little startled," continued Kismine, "when she heard that you were from—from where you *are* from, you know. She said that when she was a young girl—but then, you see, she's a Spaniard and old-fashioned."

"Do you spend much time out here?" asked John, to conceal the fact that he was somewhat hurt by this remark. It seemed an unkind allusion to his provincialism.

"Percy and Jasmine and I are here every summer, but next summer Jasmine is going to Newport. She's coming out in London a year from this fall. She'll be presented at court."

"Do you know," began John hesitantly, "you're much more sophisticated than I thought you were when I first saw you?"

"Oh, no, I'm not," she exclaimed hurriedly. "Oh, I wouldn't think of being. I think that sophisticated young people are *terribly* common, don't you? I'm not at all, really. If you say I am, I'm going to cry."

She was so distressed that her lip was trembling. John was impelled to protest: "I didn't mean that; I only said it to tease you."

"Because I wouldn't mind if I *were,*" she persisted, "but I'm *not.* I'm very innocent and girlish. I never smoke, or drink, or read anything except poetry. I know scarcely any mathematics or chemistry. I dress *very* simply—in fact, I scarcely dress at all. I think sophisticated is the last thing you can say about me. I believe that girls ought to enjoy their youths in a wholesome way."

"I do too," said John heartily.

Kismine was cheerful again. She smiled at him, and a still-born tear dripped from the corner of one blue eye.

"I like you," she whispered, intimately. "Are you going to spend all your time with Percy while you're here, or will you be nice to me? Just think—I'm absolutely fresh ground. I've never had a boy in love with me in all my life. I've never been allowed even to see boys alone —except Percy. I came all the way out here into this grove hoping to run into you, where the family wouldn't be around."

Deeply flattered, John bowed from the hips as he had been taught at dancing school in Hades.

"We'd better go now," said Kismine sweetly. "I have to be with mother at eleven. You haven't asked me to kiss you once. I thought boys always did that nowadays."

John drew himself up proudly.

"Some of them do," he answered, "but not me. Girls don't do that sort of thing-in Hades."

Side by side they walked back toward the house.

VI

John stood facing Mr. Braddock Washington in the full sunlight. The elder man was about forty with a proud, vacuous face, intelligent eyes, and a robust figure. In the mornings he smelt of horses—the best horses. He carried a plain walking-stick of gray birch with a single large opal for a grip. He and Percy were showing John around.

"The slaves' quarters are there." His walking-stick indicated a cloister of marble on their left that ran in graceful Gothic along the side of the mountain. "In my youth I was distracted for a while from the business of life by a period of absurd idealism. During that time they lived in luxury. For instance, I equipped every one of their rooms with a tile bath."

"I suppose," ventured John, with an ingratiating laugh, "that they used the bathtubs to keep coal in. Mr. Schnlitzer-Murphy told me that once he—"

"The opinions of Mr. Schnlitzer-Murphy are of little importance, I should imagine," interrupted Braddock Washington, coldly. "My slaves did not keep coal in their bathtubs. They had orders to bathe every day, and they did. If they hadn't I might have ordered a sulphuric acid shampoo. I discontinued the baths for quite another reason. Several of them caught cold and died. Water is not good for certain races—except as a beverage."

John laughed, and then decided to nod his head in sober agreement. Braddock Washington made him uncomfortable.

"All these negroes are descendants of the ones my father brought North with him. There are about two hundred and fifty now. You notice that they've lived so long apart from the world that their original dialect has become an almost indistinguishable patois. We bring a few of them up to speak English—my secretary and two or three of the house servants.

"This is the golf course," he continued, as they strolled along the velvet winter grass. "It's all a green, you see—no fairway, no rough, no hazards."

He smiled pleasantly at John.

"Many men in the cage, father?" asked Percy suddenly.

Braddock Washington stumbled, and let forth an involuntary curse.

"One less than there should be," he ejaculated darkly—and then added after a moment, "We've had difficulties."

"Mother was telling me," exclaimed Percy, "that Italian teacher—"

"A ghastly error," said Braddock Washington angrily. "But of course there's a good chance that we may have got him. Perhaps he fell somewhere in the woods or stumbled over a cliff. And then there's always the probability that if he did get away his story wouldn't be believed. Nevertheless, I've had two dozen men looking for him in different towns around here."

"And no luck?"

"Some. Fourteen of them reported to my agent that they'd each killed a man answering to that description, but of course it was probably only the reward they were after—"

He broke off. They had come to a large cavity in the earth about the circumference of a merry-go-round and covered by a strong iron grating. Braddock Washington beckoned to John, and pointed his cane down through the grating. John stepped to the edge and gazed. Immediately his ears were assailed by a wild clamor from below.

"Come on down to Hell!"

"Hello, kiddo, how's the air up there?"

"Hey! Throw us a rope!"

"Got an old doughnut, Buddy, or a couple of second-hand sandwiches?"

"Say, fella, if you'll push down that guy you're with, we'll show you a quick disappearance scene."

"Paste him one for me, will you?"

It was too dark to see clearly into the pit below, but John could tell from the coarse optimism and rugged vitality of the remarks and voices that they proceeded from middle-class Americans of the more spirited type. Then Mr. Washington put out his cane and touched a button in the grass, and the scene below sprang into light.

"These are some adventurous mariners who had the misfortune to discover El Dorado," he remarked.

Below them there had appeared a large hollow in the earth shaped like the interior of a bowl. The sides were steep and apparently of polished glass, and on its slightly concave surface stood about two dozen men clad in the half costume, half uniform, of aviators. Their upturned faces, lit with wrath, with malice, with despair, with cynical humor, were covered by long growths of beard, but with the exception of a few who had pined perceptibly away, they seemed to be a well-fed, healthy lot.

Braddock Washington drew a garden chair to the edge of the pit and sat down.

"Well, how are you, boys?" he inquired genially.

A chorus of execration in which all joined except a few too dispirited to cry out, rose up into the sunny air, but Braddock Washington heard it with unruffled composure. When its last echo had died away he spoke again.

"Have you thought up a way out of your difficulty?"

From here and there among them a remark floated up.

"We decided to stay here for love!"

"Bring us up there and we'll find us a way!"

Braddock Washington waited until they were again quiet. Then he said:

"I've told you the situation. I don't want you here. I wish to heaven I'd never seen you. Your own curiosity got you here, and any time that you can think of a way out which protects me and my interests I'll be glad to consider it. But so long as you confine your efforts to digging tunnels—yes, I know about the new one you've started—you won't get very far. This isn't as hard on you as you make it out, with all your howling for the loved ones at home. If you were the type who worried much about the loved ones at home, you'd never have taken up aviation."

A tall man moved apart from the others, and held up his hand to call his captor's attention to what he was about to say.

"Let me ask you a few questions!" he cried. "You pretend to be a fair-minded man."

"How absurd. How could a man of *my* position be fair-minded toward you? You might as well speak of a Spaniard being fair-minded toward a piece of steak."

At this harsh observation the faces of the two dozen steaks fell, but the tall man continued:

"All right!" he cried. "We've argued this out before. You're not a humanitarian and you're not fair-minded, but you're human—at least you say you are—and you ought to be able to put yourself in our place for long enough to think how—how—how—"

"How what?" demanded Washington, coldly.

"—how unnecessary——"

"Not to me."

"Well,—how cruel——"

"We've covered that. Cruelty doesn't exist where self-preservation is involved. You've been soldiers: you know that. Try another."

"Well, then, how stupid."

"There," admitted Washington, "I grant you that. But try to think of an alternative. I've offered to have all or any of you painlessly executed if you wish. I've offered to have your wives, sweethearts, children, and mothers kidnapped and brought out here. I'll enlarge your place down there and feed and clothe you the rest of your lives. If there was some method of producing permanent amnesia I'd have all of you operated on and released immediately, somewhere outside of my preserves. But that's as far as my ideas go."

"How about trusting us not to peach on you?" cried some one.

"You don't proffer that suggestion seriously," said Washington, with an expression of scorn. "I did take out one man to teach my daughter Italian. Last week he got away."

A wild yell of jubilation went up suddenly from two dozen throats and a pandemonium of joy ensued. The prisoners clog-danced and cheered and yodled and wrestled with one another in a sudden uprush of animal spirits. They even ran up the glass sides of the bowl as far as they could, and slid back to the bottom upon the natural cushions of their bodies. The tall man started a song in which they all joined——

> *"Oh, we'll hang the kaiser*
> *On a sour apple tree——"*

Braddock Washington sat in inscrutable silence until the song was over.

"You see," he remarked, when he could gain a modicum of attention. "I bear you no ill-will. I like to see you enjoying yourselves. That's why I didn't tell you the whole story at once. The man—what was his name? Critchtichiello?—was shot by some of my agents in fourteen different places."

Not guessing that the places referred to were cities, the tumult of rejoicing subsided immediately.

"Nevertheless," cried Washington with a touch of anger, "he tried to run away. Do you expect me to take chances with any of you after an experience like that?"

Again a series of ejaculations went up.

"Sure!"

"Would your daughter like to learn Chinese?"

"Hey, I can speak Italian! My mother was a wop."

"Maybe she'd like t'learna speak N'Yawk!"

"If she's the little one with the big blue eyes I can teach her a lot of things better than Italian."

"I know some Irish songs—and I could hammer brass once't."

Mr. Washington reached forward suddenly with his cane and pushed the button in the grass so that the picture below went out instantly, and there remained only that great dark mouth covered dismally with the black teeth of the grating.

"Hey!" called a single voice from below, "you ain't goin' away without givin' us your blessing?"

But Mr. Washington, followed by the two boys, was already strolling on toward the ninth hole of the golf course, as though the pit and its contents were no more than a hazard over which his facile iron bad triumphed with ease.

VII

July under the lee of the diamond mountain was a month of blanket nights and of warm, glowing days. John and Kismine were in love. He did not know that the little gold football (inscribed with the legend *Pro deo et patria et St. Mida*) which he had given her rested on a platinum chain next to her bosom. But it did. And she for her part was not aware that a large sapphire which had dropped one day from her simple coiffure was stowed away tenderly in John's jewel box.

Late one afternoon when the ruby and ermine music room was quiet, they spent an hour there together. He held her hand and she gave him such a look that he whispered her name aloud. She bent toward him—then hesitated.

"Did you say 'Kismine'?" she asked softly, "or——"

She had wanted to be sure. She thought she might have misunderstood.

Neither of them had ever kissed before, but in the course of an hour it seemed to make little difference.

The afternoon drifted away. That night when a last breath of music drifted down from the highest tower, they each lay awake, happily dreaming over the separate minutes of the day. They had decided to be married as soon as possible.

VIII

Every day Mr. Washington and the two young men went hunting or fishing in the deep forests or played golf around the somnolent course—games which John diplomatically allowed his host to win—or swam in the mountain coolness of the lake. John found Mr. Washington a somewhat exacting personality—utterly uninterested in any ideas or opinions except his own. Mrs. Washington was aloof and reserved at all times. She was apparently indifferent to her two daughters, and entirely absorbed in her son Percy, with whom she held interminable conversations in rapid Spanish at dinner.

Jasmine, the elder daughter, resembled Kismine in appearance—except that she was somewhat bow-legged, and terminated in large hands and feet—but was utterly unlike her in temperament. Her favorite books had to do with poor girls who kept house for widowed fathers. John learned from Kismine that Jasmine had never recovered from the shock and disappointment caused her by the termination of the World War, just as she was about to start for Europe as a canteen expert. She had even pined away for a time, and Braddock Washington had taken steps to promote a new war in the Balkans—but she had seen a photograph of some wounded Serbian soldiers and lost interest in the whole proceedings. But Percy and Kismine seemed to have inherited the arrogant attitude in all its harsh magnificence from their father. A chaste and consistent selfishness ran like a pattern through their every idea.

John was enchanted by the wonders of the château and the valley. Braddock Washington, so Percy told him, had caused to be kidnapped a landscape gardener, an architect, a designer of stage settings, and a French decadent poet left over from the last century. He had put his entire force of negroes at their disposal, guaranteed to supply them with any materials that the world could offer, and left them to work out some ideas of their own. But one by one they had shown their uselessness. The decadent poet had at once begun bewailing his separation from the boulevards in spring—he made some vague remarks about spices, apes, and ivories, but said nothing that was of any practical value. The stage designer on his part wanted to make the whole valley a series of tricks and sensational effects—a state of things that the Washingtons would soon have grown tired of. And as for the architect and the landscape gardener, they thought only in terms of convention. They must make this like this and that like that.

But they had, at least, solved the problem of what was to be done with them—they all went mad early one morning after spending the night in a single room trying to agree upon the location of a fountain, and were now confined comfortably in an insane asylum at Westport, Connecticut.

"But," inquired John curiously, "who did plan all your wonderful reception rooms and halls, and approaches and bathrooms—?"

"Well," answered Percy, "I blush to tell you, but it was a moving-picture fella. He was the only man we found who was used to playing with an unlimited amount of money, though he did tuck his napkin in his collar and couldn't read or write."

As August drew to a close John began to regret that he must soon go back to school. He and Kismine had decided to elope the following June.

"It would be nicer to be married here," Kismine confessed, "but of course I could never get father's permission to marry you at all. Next to that I'd rather elope. It's terrible for wealthy people to be married in America at present—they always have to send out bulletins to the press saying that they're going to be married in remnants, when what they mean is just a peck of old second-hand pearls and some used lace worn once by the Empress Eugénie."

"I know," agreed John fervently. "When I was visiting the Schnlitzer-Murphys, the eldest daughter, Gwendolyn, married a man whose father owns half of West Virginia. She wrote home saying what a tough struggle she was carrying on on his salary as a bank clerk—and then she ended up by saying that 'Thank God, I have four good maids anyhow, and that helps a little.'"

"It's absurd," commented Kismine. "Think of the millions and millions of people in the world, laborers and all, who get along with only two maids."

One afternoon late in August a chance remark of Kismine's changed the face of the entire situation, and threw John into a state of terror.

They were in their favorite grove, and between kisses John was indulging in some romantic forebodings which he fancied added poignancy to their relations.

"Sometimes I think we'll never marry," he said sadly. "You're too wealthy, too magnificent. No one as rich as you are can be like other girls. I should marry the daughter of some well-to-do wholesale hardware man from Omaha or Sioux City, and be content with her half-million."

"I knew the daughter of a wholesale hardware man once," remarked Kismine. "I don't think you'd have been contented with her. She was a friend of my sister's. She visited here."

"Oh, then you've had other guests?" exclaimed John in surprise.

Kismine seemed to regret her words.

"Oh, yes," she said hurriedly, "we've had a few."

"But aren't you—wasn't your father afraid they'd talk outside?"

"Oh, to some extent, to some extent," she answered. "Let's talk about something pleasanter."

But John's curiosity was aroused.

"Something pleasanter!" he demanded. "What's unpleasant about that? Weren't they nice girls?"

To his great surprise Kismine began to weep.

"Yes—th—that's the—the whole t-trouble. I grew qu-quite attached to some of them. So did Jasmine, but she kept inv-viting them anyway. I couldn't understand it."

A dark suspicion was born in John's heart.

"Do you mean that they *told*, and your father had them removed?"

"Worse than that," she muttered brokenly. "Father took no chances—and Jasmine kept writing them to come, and they had such a good time!"

She was overcome by a paroxysm of grief.

Stunned with the horror of this revelation, John sat there open-mouthed, feeling the nerves of his body twitter like so many sparrows perched upon his spinal column.

"Now, I've told you, and I shouldn't have," she said, calming suddenly and drying her dark blue eyes.

"Do you mean to say that your father had them *murdered* before they left?"

She nodded.

"In August usually—or early in September. It's only natural for us to get all the pleasure out of them that we can first."

"How abominable! How—why, I must be going crazy! Did you really admit that——"

"I did," interrupted Kismine, shrugging her shoulders. "We can't very well imprison them like those aviators, where they'd be a continual reproach to us every day. And it's always been made easier for Jasmine and me, because father had it done sooner than we expected. In that way we avoided any farewell scene——"

"So you murdered them! Uh!" cried John.

"It was done very nicely. They were drugged while they were asleep and their families were always told that they died of scarlet fever in Butte."

"But—I fail to understand why you kept on inviting them!"

"I didn't," burst out Kismine. "I never invited one. Jasmine did. And they always had a very good time. She'd give them the nicest presents toward the last. I shall probably have visitors too—I'll harden up to it. We can't let such an inevitable thing as death stand in the way of enjoying life while we have it. Think how lonesome it'd be out here if we never had any one. Why, father and mother have sacrificed some of their best friends just as we have."

"And so," cried John accusingly, "and so you were letting me make love to you and pretending to return it, and talking about marriage, all the time knowing perfectly well that I'd never get out of here alive——"

"No," she protested passionately. "Not any more. I did at first. You were here. I couldn't help that, and I thought your last days might as well be pleasant for both of us. But then I fell in love with you, and I'm honestly sorry you're going to—going to be put away—though I'd rather you'd be put away than ever kiss another girl."

"Oh, you would, would you?" cried John ferociously.

"Much rather. Besides, I've always heard that a girl can have more fun with a man whom she knows she can never marry. Oh, why did I tell you? I've probably spoiled your whole good time now, and we were really enjoying things when you didn't know it. I knew it would make things sort of depressing for you."

"Oh, you did, did you?" John's voice trembled with anger. "I've heard about enough of this. If you haven't any more pride and decency than to have an affair with a fellow that you know isn't much better than a corpse, I don't want to have any more to do with you."

"You're not a corpse!" she protested in horror. "You're not a corpse! I won't have you saying that I kissed a corpse!"

"I said nothing of the sort!"

"You did! You said I kissed a corpse!"

"I didn't!"

Their voices had risen, but upon a sudden interruption they both subsided into immediate silence. Footsteps were coming along the path in their direction, and a moment later the rose bushes were parted displaying Braddock Washington, whose intelligent eyes set in his good-looking vacuous face were peering in at them.

"Who kissed a corpse?" he demanded in obvious disapproval.

"Nobody," answered Kismine quickly. "We were just joking."

"What are you two doing here, anyhow?" he demanded gruffly. "Kismine, you ought to be—to be reading or playing golf with your sister. Go read! Go play golf! Don't let me find you here when I come back!"

Then he bowed at John and went up the path.

"See?" said Kismine crossly, when he was out of hearing. "You've spoiled it all. We can never meet any more. He won't let me meet you. He'd have you poisoned if he thought we were in love."

"We're not, any more!" cried John fiercely, "so he can set his mind at rest upon that. Moreover, don't fool yourself that I'm going to stay around here. Inside of six hours I'll be over those mountains, if I have to gnaw a passage through them, and on my way East."

They had both got to their feet, and at this remark Kismine came close and put her arm through his.

"I'm going, too."

"You must be crazy——"

"Of course I'm going," she interrupted impatiently.

"You most certainly are not. You——"

"Very well," she said quietly, "we'll catch up with father now and talk it over with him."

Defeated, John mustered a sickly smile.

"Very well, dearest," he agreed, with pale and unconvincing affection, "we'll go together."

His love for her returned and settled placidly on his heart. She was his—she would go with him to share his dangers. He put his arms about her and kissed her fervently. After all she loved him; she had saved him, in fact.

Discussing the matter they walked slowly back toward the château. They decided that since Braddock Washington had seen them together they had best depart the next night. Nevertheless, John's lips were unusually dry at dinner, and he nervously emptied a great spoonful of peacock soup into his left lung. He had to be carried into the tourquoise and sable card-room and pounded on the back by one of the under-butlers, which Percy considered a great joke.

IX

Long after midnight John's body gave a nervous jerk, and he sat suddenly upright, staring into the veils of somnolence that draped the room. Through the squares of blue darkness that were his open windows, he had heard a faint far-away sound that died upon a bed of wind before identifying itself on his memory, clouded with uneasy dreams. But the sharp noise that had succeeded it was nearer, was just outside the room—the click of a turned knob, a footstep, a whisper, he could not tell; a hard lump gathered in the pit of his stomach, and his whole body ached in the moment that he strained agonizingly to hear. Then one of the veils seemed to dissolve, and he saw a vague figure standing by the door, a figure only faintly limned and blocked in upon the darkness, mingled so with the folds of the drapery as to seem distorted, like a reflection seen in a dirty pane of glass.

With a sudden movement of fright or resolution John pressed the button by his bedside, and the next moment he was sitting in the green sunken bath of the adjoining room, waked into alertness by the shock of the cold water which half filled it.

He sprang out, and, his wet pajamas scattering a heavy trickle of water behind him, ran for the aquamarine door which he knew led out onto the ivory landing of the second floor. The door opened noiselessly. A single crimson lamp burning in a great dome above lit the magnificent sweep of the carved stairways with a poignant beauty. For a moment John hesitated, appalled by the silent splendor massed about him, seeming to envelop in its gigantic folds and contours the solitary drenched little figure shivering upon the ivory landing. Then simultaneously two things happened. The door of his own sitting-room swung open, precipitating three naked negroes into the hall—and, as John swayed in wild terror toward the stairway, another door slid back in the wall on the other side of the corridor, and John saw Braddock Washington standing in the lighted lift, wearing a fur coat and a pair of riding boots which reached to his knees and displayed, above, the glow of his rose-colored pajamas.

On the instant the three negroes—John had never seen any of them before, and it flashed through his mind that they must be the professional executioners—paused in their movement toward John, and turned expectantly to the man in the lift, who burst out with an imperious command:

"Get in here! All three of you! Quick as hell!"

Then, within the instant, the three negroes darted into the cage, the oblong of light was blotted out as the lift door slid shut, and John was again alone in the hall. He slumped weakly down against an ivory stair.

It was apparent that something portentous had occurred, something which, for the moment at least, had postponed his own petty disaster. What was it? Had the negroes risen in revolt? Had the aviators forced aside the iron bars of the grating? Or had the men of Fish stumbled blindly through the hills and gazed with bleak, joyless eyes upon the gaudy valley? John did not know. He heard a faint whir of air as the lift whizzed up again, and then, a moment later, as it descended. It was probable that Percy was hurrying to his father's assistance, and it occurred to John that this was his opportunity to join Kismine and plan an immediate escape. He waited until the lift had been silent for several minutes; shivering a little with the night cool that whipped in through his wet pajamas, he returned to his room and dressed himself quickly. Then he mounted a long flight of stairs and turned down the corridor carpeted with Russian sable which led to Kismine's suite.

The door of her sitting-room was open and the lamps were lighted. Kismine, in an angora kimono, stood near the window of the room in a listening attitude, and as John entered noiselessly, she turned toward him.

"Oh, it's you!" she whispered, crossing the room to him. "Did you hear them?"

"I heard your father's slaves in my——"

"No," she interrupted excitedly. "Aeroplanes!"

"Aeroplanes? Perhaps that was the sound that woke me."

"There're at least a dozen. I saw one a few moments ago dead against the moon. The guard back by the cliff fired his rifle and that's what roused father. We're going to open on them right away."

"Are they here on purpose?"

"Yes, it's that Italian who got away——"

Simultaneously with her last word, a succession of sharp cracks tumbled in through the open window. Kismine uttered a little cry, took a penny with fumbling fingers from a box on her dresser, and ran to one of the electric lights. In an instant the entire château was in darkness—she had blown out the fuse.

"Come on!" she cried to him. "We'll go up to the roof garden, and watch it from there!"

Drawing a cape about her, she took his hand, and they found their way out the door. It was only a step to the tower lift, and as she pressed the button that shot them upward he put his arms around her in the darkness and kissed her mouth. Romance had come to John Unger at last. A minute later they had stepped out upon the star-white platform. Above, under the misty moon, sliding in and out of the patches of cloud that eddied below it, floated a dozen darkwinged bodies in a constant circling course. From here and there in the valley flashes of fire leaped toward them, followed by sharp detonations. Kismine clapped her hands with pleasure, which a moment later, turned to dismay as the aeroplanes at some prearranged signal, began to release their bombs and the whole of the valley became a panorama of deep reverberate sound and lurid light.

Before long the aim of the attackers became concentrated upon the points where the anti-aircraft guns were situated, and one of them was almost immediately reduced to a giant cinder to lie smouldering in a park of rose bushes.

"Kismine," begged John, "you'll be glad when I tell you that this attack came on the eve of my murder. If I hadn't heard that guard shoot off his gun back by the pass I should now be stone dead."

"I can't hear you!" cried Kismine, intent on the scene before her. "You'll have to talk louder!"

"I simply said," shouted John, "that we'd better get out before they begin to shell the château!"

Suddenly the whole portico of the negro quarters cracked asunder, a geyser of flame shot up from under the colonnades, and great fragments of jagged marble were hurled as far as the borders of the lake.

"There go fifty thousand dollars' worth of slaves," cried Kismine, "at prewar prices. So few Americans have any respect for property."

John renewed his efforts to compel her to leave. The aim of the aeroplanes was becoming more precise minute by minute, and only two of the anti-aircraft guns were still retaliating. It was obvious that the garrison, encircled with fire, could not hold out much longer.

"Come on!" cried John, pulling Kismine's arm, "we've got to go. Do you realize that those aviators will kill you without question if they find you?"

She consented reluctantly.

"We'll have to wake Jasmine!" she said, as they hurried toward the lift. Then she added in a sort of childish delight: "We'll be poor, won't we? Like people in books. And I'll be an orphan and utterly free. Free and poor! What fun!" She stopped and raised her lips to him in a delighted kiss.

"It's impossible to be both together," said John grimly. "People have found that out. And I should choose to be free as preferable of the two. As an extra caution you'd better dump the contents of your jewel box into your pockets."

Ten minutes later the two girls met John in the dark corridor and they descended to the main floor of the château. Passing for the last time through the magnificence of the splendid halls, they stood for a moment out on the terrace, watching the burning negro quarters and the flaming embers of two planes which had fallen on the other side of the lake. A solitary gun was still keeping up a sturdy popping, and the attackers seemed timorous about descending lower, but sent their thunderous fireworks in a circle around it, until any chance shot might annihilate its Ethiopian crew.

John and the two sisters passed down the marble steps, turned sharply to the left, and began to ascend a narrow path that wound like a garter about the diamond mountain. Kismine knew a heavily wooded spot half-way up where they could lie concealed and yet be able to observe the wild night in the valley—finally to make an escape, when it should be necessary, along a secret path laid in a rocky gully.

X

It was three o'clock when they attained their destination. The obliging and phlegmatic Jasmine fell off to sleep immediately, leaning against the trunk of a large tree, while John and Kismine sat, his arm around her, and watched the desperate ebb and flow of the dying battle among the ruins of a vista that had been a garden spot that morning. Shortly after four o'clock the last remaining gun gave out a clanging sound and went out of action in a swift tongue of red smoke. Though the moon was down, they saw that the flying bodies were circling closer to the earth. When the planes had made certain that the beleaguered possessed no further resources, they would land and the dark and glittering reign of the Washingtons would be over.

With the cessation of the firing the valley grew quiet. The embers of the two aeroplanes glowed like the eyes of some monster crouching in the grass. The château stood dark and silent, beautiful without light as it had been beautiful in the sun, while the woody rattles of Nemesis filled the air above with a growing and receding complaint. Then John perceived that Kismine, like her sister, had fallen sound asleep.

It was long after four when he became aware of footsteps along the path they had lately followed, and he waited in breathless silence until the persons to whom they belonged had passed the vantage-point he occupied. There was a faint stir in the air now that was not of human origin, and the dew was cold; he knew that the dawn would break soon. John waited until the steps had gone a safe distance up the mountain and were inaudible. Then he followed. About half-way to the steep summit the trees fell away and a hard saddle of rock spread itself over the diamond beneath. Just before he reached this point he slowed down his pace, warned by an animal sense that there was life just ahead of him. Coming to a high boulder, he lifted his head gradually above its edge. His curiosity was rewarded; this is what he saw:

Braddock Washington was standing there motionless, silhouetted against the gray sky without sound or sign of life. As the dawn came up out of the east, lending a cold green color to the earth, it brought the solitary figure into insignificant contrast with the new day.

While John watched, his host remained for a few moments absorbed in some inscrutable contemplation; then he signalled to the two negroes who crouched at his feet to lift the burden which lay between them. As they struggled upright, the first yellow beam of the sun struck through the innumerable prisms of an immense and exquisitely chiselled diamond—and a white radiance was kindled that glowed upon the air like a fragment of the morning star. The bearers staggered beneath its weight for a moment—then their rippling muscles caught and hardened under the wet shine of the skins and the three figures were again motionless in their defiant impotency before the heavens.

After a while the white man lifted his head and slowly raised his arms in a gesture of attention, as one who would call a great crowd to hear—but there was no crowd, only the vast silence of the mountain and the sky, broken by faint bird voices down among the trees. The figure on the saddle of rock began to speak ponderously and with an inextinguishable pride.

"You out there—" he cried in a trembling voice. "You—there—!" He paused, his arms still uplifted, his head held attentively as though he were expecting an answer.

John strained his eyes to see whether there might be men coming down the mountain, but the mountain was bare of human life. There was only sky and a mocking flute of wind along the tree-tops. Could Washington be praying? For a moment John wondered. Then the illusion passed—there was something in the man's whole attitude antithetical to prayer.

"Oh, you above there!"

The voice was become strong and confident. This was no forlorn supplication. If anything, there was in it a quality of monstrous condescension.

"You there—"

Words, too quickly uttered to be understood, flowing one into the other. . . . John listened breathlessly, catching a phrase here and there, while the voice broke off, resumed, broke off again—now strong and argumentative, now colored with a slow, puzzled impatience. Then a conviction commenced to dawn on the single listener, and as realization crept over him a spray of quick blood rushed through his arteries. Braddock Washington was offering a bribe to God!

That was it—there was no doubt. The diamond in the arms of his slaves was some advance sample, a promise of more to follow.

That, John perceived after a time, was the thread running through his sentences. Prometheus Enriched was calling to witness forgotten sacrifices, forgotten rituals, prayers obsolete before the birth of Christ. For a while his discourse took the form of reminding God of this gift or that which Divinity had deigned to accept from men—great churches if he would rescue cities from the plague, gifts of myrrh and gold, of human lives and beautiful women and captive armies, of children and queens, of beasts of the forest and field, sheep and goats, harvests and cities, whole conquered lands that had been offered up in lust or blood for His appeasal, buying a meed's worth of alleviation from the Divine wrath—and now he, Braddock Washington, Emperor of Diamonds, king and priest of the age of gold, arbiter of splendor and luxury, would offer up a treasure such as princes before him had never dreamed of, offer it up not in suppliance, but in pride.

He would give to God, he continued, getting down to specifications, the greatest diamond in the world. This diamond would be cut with many more thousand facets than there were leaves on a tree, and yet the whole diamond would be shaped with the perfection of a stone no bigger than a fly. Many men would work upon it for many years. It would be set in a great dome of beaten gold, wonderfully carved and equipped with gates of opal and crusted sapphire. In the middle would be hollowed out a chapel presided over by an altar of iridescent, decomposing, ever-changing radium which would burn out the eyes of any worshipper who lifted up his head from prayer—and on this altar there would be slain for the amusement of the Divine Benefactor any victim He should choose, even though it should be the greatest and most powerful man alive.

In return he asked only a simple thing, a thing that for God would be absurdly easy—only that matters should be as they were yesterday at this hour and that they should so remain. So very simple! Let but the heavens open, swallowing these men and their aeroplanes—and then close again. Let him have his slaves once more, restored to life and well.

There was no one else with whom he had ever needed to treat or bargain.

He doubted only whether he had made his bribe big enough. God had His price, of course. God was made in man's image, so it had been said: He must have His price. And the price would be rare—no cathedral whose building consumed many years, no pyramid constructed by ten thousand workmen, would be like this cathedral, this pyramid.

He paused here. That was his proposition. Everything would be up to specifications and there was nothing vulgar in his assertion that it would be cheap at the price. He implied that Providence could take it or leave it.

As he approached the end his sentences became broken, became short and uncertain, and his body seemed tense, seemed strained to catch the slightest pressure or whisper of life in the spaces around him. His hair had turned gradually white as he talked, and now he lifted his head high to the heavens like a prophet of old—magnificently mad.

Then, as John stared in giddy fascination, it seemed to him that a curious phenomenon took place somewhere around him. It was as though the sky had darkened for an instant, as though there had been a sudden murmur in a gust of wind, a sound of far-away trumpets, a sighing like the rustle of a great silken robe—for a time the whole of nature round about partook of this darkness: the birds' song ceased; the trees were still, and far over the mountain there was a mutter of dull, menacing thunder.

That was all. The wind died along the tall grasses of the valley. The dawn and the day resumed their place in a time, and the risen sun sent hot waves of yellow mist that made its path bright before it. The leaves laughed in the sun, and their laughter shook the trees until each bough was like a girl's school in fairyland. God had refused to accept the bribe.

For another moment John watched the triumph of the day. Then, turning, he saw a flutter of brown down by the lake, then another flutter, then another, like the dance of golden angels alighting from the clouds. The aeroplanes had come to earth.

John slid off the boulder and ran down the side of the mountain to the clump of trees, where the two girls were awake and waiting for him. Kismine sprang to her feet, the jewels in her pockets jingling, a question on her parted lips, but instinct told John that there was no time for words. They must get off the mountain without losing a moment. He seized a hand of each, and in silence they threaded the tree-trunks, washed with light now and with the rising mist. Behind them from the valley came no sound at all, except the complaint of the peacocks far away and the pleasant undertone of morning.

When they had gone about half a mile, they avoided the park land and entered a narrow path that led over the next rise of ground. At the highest point of this they paused and turned around. Their eyes rested upon the mountainside they had just left—oppressed by some dark sense of tragic impendency.

Clear against the sky a broken, white-haired man was slowly descending the steep slope, followed by two gigantic and emotionless negroes, who carried a burden between them which still flashed and glittered in the sun. Half-way down two other figures joined them—John could see that they were Mrs. Washington and her son, upon whose arm she leaned. The aviators had clambered from their machines to the sweeping lawn in front of the chateau, and with rifles in hand were starting up the diamond mountain in skirmishing formation.

But the little group of five which had formed farther up and was engrossing all the watchers' attention had stopped upon a ledge of rock. The negroes stooped and pulled up what appeared to be a trap-door in the side of the mountain. Into this they all disappeared, the white-haired man first, then his wife and son, finally the two negroes, the glittering tips of whose jeweled head-dresses caught the sun for a moment before the trap-door descended and engulfed them all.

Kismine clutched John's arm.

"Oh," she cried wildly, "where are they going? What are they going to do?"

"It must be some underground way of escape—"

A little scream from the two girls interrupted his sentence.

"Don't you see?" sobbed Kismine hysterically. "The mountain is wired!"

Even as she spoke John put up his hands to shield his sight. Before their eyes the whole surface of the mountain had changed suddenly to a dazzling burning yellow, which showed up through the jacket of turf as light shows through a human hand. For a moment the intolerable glow continued, and then like an extinguished filament it disappeared, revealing a black waste from which blue smoke arose slowly, carrying off with it what remained of vegetation and of human flesh. Of the aviators there was left neither blood nor bone—they were consumed as completely as the five souls who had gone inside.

Simultaneously, and with an immense concussion, the château literally threw itself into the air, bursting into flaming fragments as it rose, and then tumbling back upon itself in a smoking pile that lay projecting half into the water of the lake. There was no fire—what smoke there was drifted off mingling with the sunshine, and for a few minutes longer a powdery dust of marble drifted from the great featureless pile that had once been the house of jewels. There was no more sound and the three people were alone in the valley.

XI

At sunset John and his two companions reached the high cliff which had marked the boundaries of the Washingtons' dominion, and looking back found the valley tranquil and lovely in the dusk. They sat down to finish the food which Jasmine had brought with her in a basket.

"There!" she said, as she spread the table-cloth and put the sandwiches in a neat pile upon it. "Don't they look tempting? I always think that food tastes better outdoors."

"With that remark," remarked Kismine, "Jasmine enters the middle class."

"Now," said John eagerly, "turn out your pocket and let's see what jewels you brought along. If you made a good selection we three ought to live comfortably all the rest of our lives."

Obediently Kismine put her hand in her pocket and tossed two handfuls of glittering stones before him.

"Not so bad," cried John, enthusiastically. "They aren't very big, but—Hello!" His expression changed as he held one of them up to the declining sun. "Why, these aren't diamonds! There's something the matter!"

"By golly!" exclaimed Kismine, with a startled look. "What an idiot I am!"

"Why, these are rhinestones!" cried John.

"I know." She broke into a laugh. "I opened the wrong drawer. They belonged on the dress of a girl who visited Jasmine. I got her to give them to me in exchange for diamonds. I'd never seen anything but precious stones before."

"And this is what you brought?"

"I'm afraid so." She fingered the brilliants wistfully. "I think I like these better. I'm a little tired of diamonds."

"Very well," said John gloomily. "We'll have to live in Hades. And you will grow old telling incredulous women that you got the wrong drawer. Unfortunately your father's bank-books were consumed with him."

"Well, what's the matter with Hades?"

"If I come home with a wife at my age my father is just as liable as not to cut me off with a hot coal, as they say down there."

Jasmine spoke up.

"I love washing," she said quietly. "I have always washed my own handkerchiefs. I'll take in laundry and support you both."

"Do they have washwomen in Hades?" asked Kismine innocently.

"Of course," answered John. "It's just like anywhere else."

"I thought—perhaps it was too hot to wear any clothes."

John laughed.

"Just try it!" he suggested. "They'll run you out before you're half started."

"Will father be there?" she asked.

John turned to her in astonishment.

"Your father is dead," he replied somberly. "Why should he go to Hades? You have it confused with another place that was abolished long ago."

After supper they folded up the table-cloth and spread their blankets for the night.

"What a dream it was," Kismine sighed, gazing up at the stars. "How strange it seems to be here with one dress and a penniless fiancé!"

"Under the stars," she repeated. "I never noticed the stars before. I always thought of them as great big diamonds that belonged to some one. Now they frighten me. They make me feel that it was all a dream, all my youth."

"It *was* a dream," said John quietly. "Everybody's youth is a dream, a form of chemical madness."

"How pleasant then to be insane!"

"So I'm told," said John gloomily. "I don't know any longer. At any rate, let us love for a while, for a year or so, you and me. That's a form of divine drunkenness that we can all try. There are only diamonds in the whole world, diamonds and perhaps the shabby gift of disillusion. Well, I have that last and I will make the usual nothing of it." He shivered. "Turn up your coat collar, little girl, the night's full of chill and you'll get pneumonia. His was a great sin who first invented consciousness. Let us lose it for a few hours."

So wrapping himself in his blanket he fell off to sleep.

MERIDEL LeSUEUR

(1900–1996)

For most of her ninety-six years, Meridel LeSueur was, first, an agitator, then a writer and journalist. She saw no contradiction in these two vocations. On the contrary, for her, writing was—as the selection that follows, "I Was March-ing," documents—a powerful form of agitation, and the one through which she could best do her political work. But if one were to look to her writing for the simplicity and one-dimensional character of propaganda, one would be deceived. In fact, in novels like The Girl *(1978—but mostly written forty years earlier) and* I Hear Men Talking *(1983), LeSueur deploys a rich narrative vocabulary derived from modernist experimentation with consciousness, cinematic techniques of montage, and the realism of thirties proletarian fiction.*

She was familiar with them all. The daughter of midwestern socialists, LeSueur grew up in Kansas and Minnesota knowing many of the leading radical figures of her day. She never finished high school, worked as an actress both in New York and in the Hollywood of the silent films, campaigned to save Sacco and Vanzetti, joined the Communist Party, and performed the dual role of journalist and participant. In 1927, burned out by the failure of the Sacco and Vanzetti defense, she decided to have a child, against the preferences of her comrades. She wrote about the experience in an extraordinary story, "Annunciation" (1935), in which she poses an understanding of revolution not just as the transfer of economic or political power, but as an organic transformation of people's lives.

During the Depression, she wrote for journals of opinion about the impact of poverty and hopelessness, of evictions and drought, of unemployment and strikes, on men and women across America. She was one of the few to bring into focus the often-hidden poverty of women. In fact, The Girl *is drawn from stories the women she lived and shared with had told her.* Salute to Spring *(1940) collected some of her best journalism and fiction and seemed to establish her reputation. But during the Cold War, she was harassed as a leftist, publishers feared taking on her work, and she turned to writing biographies for children at least in part to keep bread on the table. With the renewal of a progressive political movement in the 1960s, and particularly with the emergence of a new feminism, LeSueur was rediscovered, earlier work was reissued or published for the first time, and she undertook a number of fictional experiments that reflected her commitments to Native American rights and to the values she saw as characteristic of Indian communities. And she never stopped agitating for justice.*

I WAS MARCHING

Minneapolis, 1934

I have never been in a strike before. It is like looking at something that is happening for the first time and there are no thoughts and no words yet accrued to it. If you come from the middle class, words are likely to mean more than an event. You are likely to think about a thing, and the happening will be the size of a pin point and the words around the happening very large, distorting it queerly. It's a case of "Remembrance of Things Past." When you are in the event, you are likely to have a distinctly individualistic attitude, to be only partly there, and to care more for the happening afterwards than when it is happening. That is why it is hard for a person like myself and others to be in a strike.

Besides, in American life, you hear things happening in a far and muffled way. One thing is said and another happens. Our merchant society has been built upon a huge hypocrisy, a cut-throat competition which sets one man against another and at the same time an ideology mouthing such words as "Humanity," "Truth," the "Golden Rule," and such. Now in a crisis the word falls away and the skeleton of that action shows in terrific movement.

For two days I heard of the strike. I went by their headquarters, I walked by on the opposite side of the street and saw the dark old building that had been a garage and lean, dark young faces leaning from the upstairs windows. I had to go down there often. I looked in. I saw the huge black interior and live coals of living men moving restlessly and orderly, their eyes gleaming from their sweaty faces.

I saw cars leaving filled with grimy men, pickets going to the line, engines roaring out. I stayed close to the door, watching. I didn't go in. I was afraid they would put me out. After all, I could remain a spectator. A man wearing a polo hat kept going around with a large camera taking pictures.

I am putting down exactly how I felt, because I believe others of my class feel the same as I did. I believe it stands for an important psychic change that must take place in all. I saw many artists, writers, professionals, even business men and women standing across the street, too, and I saw in their faces the same longings, the same fears.

The truth is I was afraid. Not of the physical danger at all, but an awful fright of mixing, of losing myself, of being unknown and lost. I felt inferior. I felt no one would know me there, that all I had been trained to excel in would go unnoticed. I can't describe what I felt, but perhaps it will come near it to say that I felt I excelled in competing with others and I knew instantly that these people were NOT competing at all, that they were acting in a strange, powerful trance of movement *together.* And I was filled with longing to act with them and with fear that I could not. I felt I was born out of every kind of life, thrown up alone, looking at other lonely people, a condition I had been in the habit of defending with various attitudes of cynicism, preciosity, defiance, and hatred.

Looking at that dark and lively building, massed with men, I knew my feelings to be those belonging to disruption, chaos, and disintegration and I felt their direct and awful movement, mute and powerful, drawing them into a close and glowing cohesion like a powerful conflagration in the midst of the city. And it filled me with fear and awe and at the same time hope. I knew this action to be prophetic and indicative of future actions and I wanted to be part of it.

Our life seems to be marked with a curious and muffled violence over America, but this action has always been in the dark, men and women dying obscurely, poor and poverty-marked lives, but now from city to city runs this violence, into the open, and colossal happenings stand bare before our eyes, the street churning suddenly upon the pivot of mad violence, whole men suddenly spouting blood and running like living sieves, another holding a dangling arm shot squarely off, a tall youngster, running, tripping over his intestines, and one block away, in the burning sun, gay women shopping and a window dresser trying to decide whether to put green or red voile on a manikin.

In these terrible happenings you cannot be neutral now. No one can be neutral in the face of bullets.

The next day, with sweat breaking out on my body, I walked past the three guards at the door. They said, "Let the women in. We need women." And I knew it was no joke.

At first I could not see into the dark building. I felt many men coming and going, cars driving through. I had an awful impulse to go into the office which I passed, and offer to do some special work. I saw a sign which said "Get your button." I saw they all had buttons with the date and the number of the union local. I didn't get a button. I wanted to be anonymous.

There seemed to be a current, running down the wooden stairs, toward the front of the building, into the street, that was massed with people, and back again. I followed the current up the old stairs packed closely with hot men and women. As I was going up I could look down and see the lower floor, the cars drawing up to await picket call, the hospital roped off on one side.

Upstairs men sat bolt upright in chairs asleep, their bodies flung in attitudes of peculiar violence of fatigue. A woman nursed her baby. Two young girls slept together on a cot, dressed in overalls. The voice of the loudspeaker filled the room. The immense heat pressed down from the flat ceiling. I stood up against the wall for an hour. No one paid any attention to me. The commissary was in back and the women came out sometimes and sat down, fanning themselves with their aprons and listening to the news over the loudspeaker. A huge man seemed hung on a tiny folding chair. Occasionally someone tiptoed over and brushed the flies off his face. His great head fell over and the sweat poured regularly from his forehead like a spring. I wondered why they took such care of him. They all looked at him tenderly as he slept. I learned later he was a leader on the picket line and had the scalps of more cops to his name than any other.

Three windows flanked the front. I walked over to the windows. A red-headed woman with a button saying "Unemployed Council" was looking out. I looked out with her. A thick crowd stood in the heat below listening to the strike bulletin. We could look right into the windows of the smart club across the street. We could see people peering out of the windows half hidden.

I kept feeling they would put me out. No one paid any attention. The woman said without looking at me, nodding to the palatial house, "It sure is good to see the enemy plain like that." "Yes," I said. I saw that the club was surrounded by a steel picket fence higher than a man. "They know what they put that there fence there for," she said. "Yes," I said. "Well," she said, "I've got to get back to the kitchen. Is it ever hot!" The thermometer said ninety-nine. The sweat ran off us, burning our skins. "The boys'll be coming in," she said, "for their noon feed." She had a scarred face. "Boy, will it be a mad house!" "Do you need any help?" I said eagerly. "Boy," she said, "some of us have been pouring coffee since two o'clock this morning, steady without no let-up." She started to go. She didn't pay any special attention to me as an individual. She didn't seem to be thinking of me, she didn't seem to see me. I watched her go. I felt rebuffed, hurt. Then I saw instantly she didn't see me because she saw only what she was doing. I ran after her.

I found the kitchen organized like a factory. Nobody asks my name. I am given a large butcher's apron. I realize I have never before worked anonymously. At first I feel strange and then I feel good. The forewoman sets me to washing tin cups. There are not enough cups. We have to wash fast and rinse them and set them up quickly for buttermilk and coffee as the line thickens and the men wait. A little shortish man who is a professional dishwasher is supervising. I feel I won't be able to wash tin cups, but when no one pays any attention except to see that there are enough cups I feel better.

The line grows heavy. The men are coming in from the picket line. Each woman has one thing to do. There is no confusion. I soon learn I am not supposed to help pour the buttermilk. I am not supposed to serve sandwiches. I am supposed to wash tin cups. I suddenly look around and realize all these women are from factories. I know they have learned this organization and specialization in the factory. I look at the round shoulders of the woman cutting bread next to me and I feel I know her.

The cups are brought back, washed and put on the counter again. The sweat pours down our faces, but you forget about it.

Then I am changed and put to pouring coffee. At first I look at the men's faces and then I don't look any more. It seems I am pouring coffee for the same tense dirty sweating face, the same body, the same blue shirt and overalls. Hours go by, the heat is terrific. I am not tired. I am not hot. I am pouring coffee. I am swung into the most intense and natural organization I have ever felt. I know everything that is going on. These things become of great matter to me.

Eyes looking, hands raising a thousand cups, throats burning, eyes bloodshot from lack of sleep, the body dilated to catch every sound over the whole city. Buttermilk? Coffee?

"Is your man here?" the woman cutting sandwiches asks me.

"No," I say, then I lie for some reason, peering around as if looking eagerly for someone, "I don't see him now."

But I was pouring coffee for living men.

For a long time, about one o'clock, it seemed like something was about to happen. Women seemed to be pouring into headquarters to be near their men. You could hear only lies over the radio. And lies in the papers. Nobody knew precisely what was happening, but everyone thought something would happen in a few hours. You could feel the men being poured out of the hall onto the picket line. Every few minutes cars left and more drew up and were filled. The voice of the loudspeaker was accelerated, calling for men, calling for picket cars.

I could hear the men talking about the arbitration board, the truce that was supposed to be maintained while the board sat with the Governor. They listened to every word over the loudspeaker. A terrible communal excitement ran through the hall like a fire through a forest. I could hardly breathe. I seemed to have no body at all except the body of this excitement. I felt that what had happened before had not been a real movement, these false words and actions had taken place on the periphery. The real action was about to show, the real intention.

We kept on pouring thousands of cups of coffee, feeding thousands of men.

The chef with a woman tattooed on his arm was just dishing the last of the stew. It was about two o'clock. The commissary was about empty. We went into the front hall. It was drained of men. The chairs were empty. The voice of the announcer was excited. "The men are massed at the market," he said. "Something is going to happen." I sat down beside a woman who was holding her hands tightly together, leaning forward listening, her eyes bright and dilated. I had never seen her before. She took my hands. She pulled me toward her. She was crying. "It's awful," she said. "Something awful is going to happen. They've taken both my children away from me and now something is going to happen to all those men." I held her hands. She had a green ribbon around her hair.

The action seemed reversed. The cars were coming back. The announcer cried, "This is murder." Cars were coming in. I don't know how we got to the stairs. Everyone seemed to be converging at a menaced point. I saw below the crowd stirring, uncoiling. I saw them taking men out of cars and putting them on the hospital cots, on the floor. At first I felt frightened, the close black area of the barn, the blood, the heavy moment, the sense of myself lost, gone. But I couldn't have turned away now. A woman clung to my hand. I was pressed against the body of another. If you are to understand anything you must understand it in the muscular event, in actions we have not been trained for. Something broke all my surfaces in something that was beyond horror and I was dabbing alcohol on the gaping wounds that buckshot makes, hanging open like crying mouths. Buckshot wounds splay in the body and then swell like a blow. Ness, who died, had thirty-eight slugs in his body, in the chest and in the back.

The picket cars kept coming in. Some men have walked back from the market, holding their own blood in. They move in a great explosion, and the newness of the movement makes it seem like something under ether, moving terrifically toward a culmination.

From all over the city workers are coming. They gather outside in two great half-circles, cut in two to let the ambulances in. A traffic cop is still directing traffic at the corner and the crowd cannot stand to see him. "We'll give you just two seconds to beat it," they tell him. He goes away quickly. A striker takes over the street.

Men, women, and children are massing outside, a living circle close packed for protection. From the tall office building business men are looking down on the black swarm thickening, coagulating into what action they cannot tell.

We have living blood on our skirts.

That night at eight o'clock a mass-meeting was called of all labor. It was to be in a parking lot two blocks from headquarters. All the women gather at the front of the building with collection cans, ready to march to the meeting. I have not been home. It never occurs to me to leave. The twilight is eerie and the men are saying that the chief of police is going to attack the meeting and raid headquarters. The smell of blood hangs in the hot, still air. Rumors strike at the taut nerves. The dusk looks ghastly with what might be in the next half hour.

"If you have any children," a woman said to me, "you better not go." I looked at the desperate women's faces, the broken feet, the torn and hanging pelvis, the worn and lovely bodies of women who persist under such desperate labors. I shivered, though it was 96° and the sun had been down a good hour.

The parking lot was already full of people when we got there and men swarmed the adjoining roofs. An elegant café stood across the street with water sprinkling from its roof and splendidly dressed men and women stood on the steps as if looking at a show.

The platform was the bullet-riddled truck of the afternoon's fray. We had been told to stand close to this platform, so we did, making the center of a wide massed circle that stretched as far as we could see. We seemed buried like minerals in a mass, packed body to body. I felt again that peculiar heavy silence in which there is the real form of the happening. My eyes burn. I can hardly see. I seem to be standing like an animal in ambush. I have the brightest, most physical feeling with every sense sharpened peculiarly. The movements, the masses that I see and feel I have never known before. I only partly know what I am seeing, feeling, but I feel it is the real body and gesture of a future vitality. I see that there is a bright clot of women drawn close to a bullet-riddled truck. I am one of them, yet I don't feel myself at all. It is curious, I feel most alive and yet for the first time in my life I do not feel myself as separate. I realize then that all my previous feelings have been based on feeling myself separate and distinct from others and now I sense sharply faces, bodies, closeness, and my own fear is not my own alone, nor my hope.

The strikers keep moving up cars. We keep moving back together to let cars pass and form between us and a brick building that flanks the parking lot. They are connecting the loudspeaker, testing it. Yes, they are moving up lots of cars, through the crowd and lining them closely side by side. There must be ten thousand people now, heat rising from them. They are standing silent, watching the platform, watching the cars being brought up. The silence seems terrific like a great form moving of itself. This is real movement issuing from the close reality of mass feeling. This is the first real rhythmic movement I have ever seen. My heart hammers terrifically. My hands are swollen and hot. No one is producing this movement. It is a movement upon which all are moving softly, rhythmically, terribly.

No matter how many times I looked at what was happening I hardly knew what I saw. I looked and I saw time and time again that there were men standing close to us, around us, and then suddenly I knew that there was a living chain of men standing shoulder to shoulder, forming a circle around the group of women. They stood shoulder to shoulder slightly moving like a thick vine from the pressure behind, but standing tightly woven like a living wall, moving gently.

I saw that the cars were now lined one close fitted to the other with strikers sitting on the roofs and closely packed on the running boards. They could see far over the crowd, "What are they doing that for?" I said. No one answered. The wide dilated eyes of the women were like my own. No one seemed to be answering questions now. They simply spoke, cried out, moved together now.

The last car drove in slowly, the crowd letting them through without command or instruction. "A little closer," someone said. "Be sure they are close." Men sprang up to direct whatever action was needed and then subsided again and no one had noticed who it was. They stepped forward to direct a needed action and then fell anonymously back again.

We all watched carefully the placing of the cars. Sometimes we looked at each other. I didn't understand that look. I felt uneasy. It was as if something escaped me. And then suddenly, on my very body, I knew what they were doing, as if it had been communicated to me from a thousand eyes, a thousand silent throats, as if it had been shouted in the loudest voice.

THEY WERE BUILDING A BARRICADE.

Two men died from that day's shooting. Men lined up to give one of them a blood transfusion, but he died. Black Friday men called the murderous day. Night and day workers held their children up to see the body of Ness who died. Tuesday, the day of the funeral, one thousand more militia were massed downtown.

It was still over ninety in the shade. I went to the funeral parlors and thousands of men and women were massed there waiting in the terrific sun. One block of women and children were standing two hours waiting. I went over and stood near them. I didn't know whether I could march. I didn't like marching in parades. Besides, I felt they might not want me.

I stood aside not knowing if I could march. I couldn't see how they would ever organize it anyway. No one seemed to be doing much.

At three-forty some command went down the ranks. I said foolishly at the last minute, "I don't belong to the auxiliary—could I march?" Three women drew me in. "We want all to march," they said gently. "Come with us."

The giant mass uncoiled like a serpent and straightened out ahead and to my amazement on a lift of road I could see six blocks of massed men, four abreast, with bare heads, moving straight on and as they moved, uncoiled the mass behind and pulled it after them. I felt myself walking, accelerating my speed with the others as the line stretched, pulled taut, then held its rhythm.

Not a cop was in sight. The cortege moved through the stop-and-go signs, it seemed to lift of its own dramatic rhythm, coming from the intention of every person there. We were moving spontaneously in a movement, natural, hardy, and miraculous.

We passed through six blocks of tenements, through a sea of grim faces, and there was not a sound. There was the curious shuffle of thousands of feet, without drum or bugle, in ominous silence, a march not heavy as the military, but very light, exactly with the heart beat.

I was marching with a million hands, movements, faces, and my own movement was repeating again and again, making a new movement from these many gestures, the walking, falling back, the open mouth crying, the nostrils stretched apart, the raised hand, the blow falling, and the outstretched hand drawing me in.

I felt my legs straighten. I felt my feet join in that strange shuffle of thousands of bodies moving with direction, of thousands of feet, and my own breath with the gigantic breath. As if an electric charge had passed through me, my hair stood on end. I was marching.

MAO TSE-TUNG
(1893-1976)

Mao was the primary leader of the Chinese communist forces that swept to victory in 1949 to end the civil war that had racked the country since the 1920s. But Mao was, besides being a brilliant revolutionary tactician and theorist, also a poet and a cultural critic, deeply interested in how literature and other forms of cultural work might be enlisted in the revolutionary cause. In 1942, during the height of the war with Japan and in the midst of the simultaneous struggle against the Chinese Nationalist forces, the Communist party summoned many of its cultural workers to a meeting in Yenan province, which it controlled, to consider the roles of culture in revolution. Mao addressed the gathering twice, to set its charge and to focus its deliberations. The excerpts that follow are from these talks.

Mao's position is perhaps the clearest exposition of one wing of thought on the relationship of politics and literature. Put simply, it amounts to placing politics in command. Politics commands, he argues, not because people wish to have it that way. Rather, culture is shaped by the material conditions under which it is produced and consumed. A bourgeois-dominated society will produce bourgeois art; and working-class art will emerge only from the conditions established by the struggle of the proletariat to achieve power. Of course, it turns out to be more complicated, since part of the point of Mao's remarks and of the conference were to win the allegiance of artists and other cultural workers, whatever their origins and present status, to the cause of the revolution. Still, his ideas about the relationship of popularization and raising standards, of the functions of art, and of the roles of artists in political struggles remain provocative.

Mao's remarks—indeed many of his comments gathered reverentially in the Little Red Book *popular worldwide during the 1960s—were influential, especially among younger people of that moment of upheaval. And while his "Talks at the Yenan Forum" may now seem one-dimensional, they*

*express clearly one view, that of a committed Communist leader, in the
debates over the relationship of class to art. Furthermore, they help illumi-
nate why it was that Mao, having led a successful political revolution in
China, then fostered a violent "cultural revolution" in the late 1960s and
early 1970s that challenged the authority of many within the revolutionary
leadership and led to the incarceration, and in some cases the death, of
many Chinese. For Mao, as these "Talks" suggest, culture was not a marginal product of a small group of intellectuals; rather, the term described
the central ways in which people looked at and understood the world. A
political revolution without an equivalent transformation in culture was
bound to slide back into older attitudes, hierarchies, and policies. The "Talks
at the Yenan Forum on Literature and Art" can thus in certain respects be
seen as predicting later events that were to shake the world's largest country and that reverberate there to this day.*

FROM TALKS AT THE YENAN FORUM ON LITERATURE AND ART

Comrades! You have been invited to this forum today to exchange ideas and examine the relationship between work in the literary and artistic fields and revolutionary work in general. Our aim is to ensure that revolutionary literature and art follow the correct path of development and provide better help to other revolutionary
work in facilitating the overthrow of our national enemy and the accomplishment
of the task of national liberation.

In our struggle for the liberation of the Chinese people there are various fronts,
among which there are the fronts of the pen and of the gun, the cultural and the
military fronts. To defeat the enemy we must rely primarily on the army with guns.
But this army alone is not enough; we must also have a cultural army, which is
absolutely indispensable for uniting our own ranks and defeating the enemy. Since
the May 4th Movement[1] such a cultural army has taken shape in China, and it has
helped the Chinese revolution, gradually reduced the domain of China's feudal culture and of the comprador culture which serves imperialist aggression, and weakened their influence. To oppose the new culture the Chinese reactionaries can now
only "pit quantity against quality". In other words, reactionaries have money, and
though they can produce nothing good, they can go all out and produce in quantity.
Literature and art have been an important and successful part of the cultural front
since the May 4th Movement. During the ten years' civil war, the revolutionary literature and art movement grew greatly. That movement and the revolutionary war
both headed in the same general direction, but these two fraternal armies were not
linked together in their practical work because the reactionaries had cut them off
from each other. It is very good that since the outbreak of the War of Resistance
Against Japan, more and more revolutionary writers and artists have been coming
to Yenan and our other anti-Japanese base areas. But it does not necessarily follow
that, having come to the base areas, they have already integrated themselves completely with the masses of the people here. The two must be completely integrated
if we are to push ahead with our revolutionary work. The purpose of our meeting

today is precisely to ensure that literature and art fit well into the whole revolutionary machine as a component part, that they operate as powerful weapons for
uniting and educating the people and for attacking and destroying the enemy, and
that they help the people fight the enemy with one heart and one mind. What are
the problems that must be solved to achieve this objective? I think they are the
problems of the class stand of the writers and artists, their attitude, their audience,
their work and their study.

The problem of class stand. Our stand is that of the proletariat and of the masses.
For members of the Communist Party, this means keeping to the stand of the Party,
keeping to Party spirit and Party policy. Are there any of our literary and art workers
who are still mistaken or not clear in their understanding of this problem? I think
there are. Many of our comrades have frequently departed from the correct stand.

The problem of attitude. From one's stand there follow specific attitudes towards
specific matters. For instance, is one to extol or to expose? This is a question of attitude. Which attitude is wanted? I would say both. The question is, whom are you
dealing with? There are three kinds of persons, the enemy, our allies in the united
front and our own people; the last are the masses and their vanguard. We need to
adopt a different attitude towards each of the three. With regard to the enemy, that
is, Japanese imperialism and all the other enemies of the people, the task of revolutionary writers and artists is to expose their duplicity and cruelty and at the same
time to point out the inevitability of their defeat, so as to encourage the anti-Japanese army and people to fight staunchly with one heart and one mind for their overthrow. With regard to our different allies in the united front, our attitude should be
one of both alliance and criticism, and there should be different kinds of alliance and
different kinds of criticism. We support them in their resistance to Japan and praise
them for any achievement. But if they are not active in the War of Resistance, we
should criticize them. If anyone opposes the Communist Party and the people and
keeps moving down the path of reaction, we will firmly oppose him. As for the
masses of the people, their toil and their struggle, their army and their Party, we
should certainly praise them. The people, too, have their shortcomings. Among the
proletariat many retain petty-bourgeois ideas, while both the peasants and the urban
petty bourgeoisie have backward ideas; these are burdens hampering them in their
struggle. We should be patient and spend a long time in educating them and helping
them to get these loads off their backs and combat their own shortcomings and
errors, so that they can advance with great strides. They have remoulded themselves
in struggle or are doing so, and our literature and art should depict this process. As
long as they do not persist in their errors, we should not dwell on their negative side
and consequently make the mistake of ridiculing them or, worse still, of being hostile to them. Our writings should help them to unite, to make progress, to press
ahead with one heart and one mind, to discard what is backward and develop what
is revolutionary, and should certainly not do the opposite.

The problem of audience, *i.e.,* the people for whom our works of literature and
art are produced. In the Shensi-Kansu-Ningsia Border Region[2] and the anti-Japanese
base areas of northern and central China, this problem differs from that in the
Kuomintang areas, and differs still more from that in Shanghai before the War of
Resistance. In the Shanghai period, the audience for works of revolutionary literature and art consisted mainly of a section of the students, office workers and shop
assistants. After the outbreak of the War of Resistance the audience in the Kuomintang areas became somewhat wider, but it still consisted mainly of the same kind

of people because the government there prevented the workers, peasants and soldiers from having access to revolutionary literature and art. In our base areas the situation is entirely different. Here the audience for works of literature and art consists of workers, peasants, soldiers and revolutionary cadres. There are students in the base areas, too, but they are different from students of the old type; they are either former or future cadres. The cadres of all types, fighters in the army, workers in the factories and peasants in the villages all want to read books and newspapers once they become literate, and those who are illiterate want to see plays and operas, look at drawings and paintings, sing songs and hear music; they are the audience for our works of literature and art. Take the cadres alone. Do not think they are few; they far outnumber the readers of any book published in the Kuomintang areas. There, an edition usually runs to only 2,000 copies, and even three editions add up to only 6,000; but as for the cadres in the base areas, in Yenan alone there are more than 10,000 who read books. Many of them, moreover, are tempered revolutionaries of long standing, who have come from all parts of the country and will go out to work in different places, so it is very important to do educational work among them. Our literary and art workers must do a good job in this respect.

Since the audience for our literature and art consists of workers, peasants and soldiers and of their cadres, the problem arises of understanding them and knowing them well. A great deal of work has to be done in order to understand them and know them well, to understand and know well all the different kinds of people and phenomena in the Party and government organizations, in the villages and factories and in the Eighth Route and New Fourth Armies. Our writers and artists have their literary and art work to do, but their primary task is to understand people and know them well. In this regard, how have matters stood with our writers and artists? I would say they have been lacking in knowledge and understanding; they have been like "a hero with no place to display his prowess". What does lacking in knowledge mean? Not knowing people well. The writers and artists do not have a good knowledge either of those whom they describe or of their audience; indeed they may hardly know them at all. They do not know the workers or peasants or soldiers well, and do not know the cadres well either. What does lacking in understanding mean? Not understanding the language, that is, not being familiar with the rich, lively language of the masses. Since many writers and artists stand aloof from the masses and lead empty lives, naturally they are unfamiliar with the language of the people. Accordingly, their works are not only insipid in language but often contain nondescript expressions of their own coining which run counter to popular usage. Many comrades like to talk about "a mass style". But what does it really mean? It means that the thoughts and feelings of our writers and artists should be fused with those of the masses of workers, peasants and soldiers. To achieve this fusion, they should conscientiously learn the language of the masses. How can you talk of literary and artistic creation if you find the very language of the masses largely incomprehensible? By "a hero with no place to display his prowess", we mean that your collection of great truths is not appreciated by the masses. The more you put on the airs of a veteran before the masses and play the "hero", the more you try to peddle such stuff to the masses, the less likely they are to accept it. If you want the masses to understand you, if you want to be one with the masses, you must make up your mind to undergo a long and even painful process of tempering. Here I might mention the experience of how my own feelings changed. I began life as a student and at school acquired the ways of a student; I then used to feel it undignified to do even a little manual labour, such as carrying my own luggage in the presence of my fellow students, who were incapable of carrying anything, either on their shoulders or in their hands. At that time I felt that intellectuals were the only clean people in the world, while in comparison workers and peasants were dirty. I did not mind wearing the clothes of other intellectuals, believing them clean, but I would not put on clothes belonging to a worker or peasant, believing them dirty. But after I became a revolutionary and lived with workers and peasants and with soldiers of the revolutionary army, I gradually came to know them well, and they gradually came to know me well too. It was then, and only then, that I fundamentally changed the bourgeois and petty-bourgeois feelings implanted in me in the bourgeois schools. I came to feel that compared with the workers and peasants the unremoulded intellectuals were not clean and that, in the last analysis, the workers and peasants were the cleanest people and, even though their hands were soiled and their feet smeared with cow-dung, they were really cleaner than the bourgeois and petty-bourgeois intellectuals. That is what is meant by a change in feelings, a change from one class to another. If our writers and artists who come from the intelligentsia want their works to be well received by the masses, they must change and remould their thinking and their feelings. Without such a change, without such remoulding, they can do nothing well and will be misfits.

The last problem is study, by which I mean the study of Marxism-Leninism and of society. Anyone who considers himself a revolutionary Marxist writer, and especially any writer who is a member of the Communist Party, must have a knowledge of Marxism-Leninism. At present, however, some comrades are lacking in the basic concepts of Marxism. For instance, it is a basic Marxist concept that being determines consciousness, that the objective realities of class struggle and national struggle determine our thoughts and feelings. But some of our comrades turn this upside down and maintain that everything ought to start from "love". Now as for love, in a class society there can be only class love; but these comrades are seeking a love transcending classes, love in the abstract and also freedom in the abstract, truth in the abstract, human nature in the abstract, etc. This shows that they have been very deeply influenced by the bourgeoisie. They should thoroughly rid themselves of this influence and modestly study Marxism-Leninism. It is right for writers and artists to study literary and artistic creation, but the science of Marxism-Leninism must be studied by all revolutionaries, writers and artists not excepted. Writers and artists should study society, that is to say, should study the various classes in society, their mutual relations and respective conditions, their physiognomy and their psychology. Only when we grasp all this clearly can we have a literature and art that is rich in content and correct in orientation.

I am merely raising these problems today by way of introduction; I hope all of you will express your views on these and other relevant problems.

Conclusion

May 23, 1942

Comrades! Our forum has had three meetings this month. In the pursuit of truth we have carried on spirited debates in which scores of Party and non-Party comrades have spoken, laying bare the issues and making them more concrete. This, I believe, will very much benefit the whole literary and artistic movement.

In discussing a problem, we should start from reality and not from definitions. We would be following a wrong method if we first looked up definitions of literature and art in textbooks and then used them to determine the guiding principles for the present-day literary and artistic movement and to judge the different opinions and controversies that arise today. We are Marxists, and Marxism teaches that in our approach to a problem we should start from objective facts, not from abstract definitions, and that we should derive our guiding principles, policies and measures from an analysis of these facts. We should do the same in our present discussion of literary and artistic work.

What are the facts at present? The facts are: the War of Resistance Against Japan which China has been fighting for five years; the world-wide anti-fascist war; the vacillations of China's big landlord class and big bourgeoisie in the War of Resistance and their policy of high-handed oppression of the people; the revolutionary movement in literature and art since the May 4th Movement—its great contributions to the revolution during the last twenty-three years and its many shortcomings; the anti-Japanese democratic base areas of the Eighth Route and New Fourth Armies and the integration of large numbers of writers and artists with these armies and with the workers and peasants in these areas; the difference in both environment and tasks between the writers and artists in the base areas and those in the Kuomintang areas; and the controversial issues concerning literature and art which have arisen in Yenan and the other anti-Japanese base areas. These are the actual, undeniable facts in the light of which we have to consider our problems.

What then is the crux of the matter? In my opinion, it consists fundamentally of the problems of working for the masses and how to work for the masses. Unless these two problems are solved, or solved properly, our writers and artists will be ill-adapted to their environment and their tasks and will come up against a series of difficulties from without and within. My concluding remarks will centre on these two problems and also touch upon some related ones.

I

The first problem is: literature and art for whom?

This problem was solved long ago by Marxists, especially by Lenin. As far back as 1905 Lenin pointed out emphatically that our literature and art should "serve . . . the millions and tens of millions of working people".[3] For comrades engaged in literary and artistic work in the anti-Japanese base areas it might seem that this problem is already solved and needs no further discussion. Actually, that is not the case. Many comrades have not found a clear solution. Consequently their sentiments, their works, their actions and their views on the guiding principles for literature and art have inevitably been more or less at variance with the needs of the masses and of the practical struggle. Of course, among the numerous men of culture, writers, artists and other literary and artistic workers engaged in the great struggle for liberation together with the Communist Party and the Eighth Route and New Fourth Armies, a few may be careerists who are with us only temporarily, but the overwhelming majority are working energetically for the common cause. By relying on these comrades, we have achieved a great deal in our literature, drama, music and fine arts. Many of these writers and artists have begun their work since the outbreak of the War of Resistance; many others did much revolutionary work before the war, endured many hardships and influenced broad masses of the people by their activities and works. Why do we say, then, that even among these comrades there are some who have not reached a clear solution of the problem of whom literature and art are for? Is it conceivable that there are still some who maintain that revolutionary literature and art are not for the masses of the people but for the exploiters and oppressors?

Indeed literature and art exist which are for the exploiters and oppressors. Literature and art for the landlord class are feudal literature and art. Such were the literature and art of the ruling class in China's feudal era. To this day such literature and art still have considerable influence in China. Literature and art for the bourgeoisie are bourgeois literature and art. People like Liang Shih-chiu,[4] whom Lu Hsun criticized, talk about literature and art as transcending classes, but in fact they uphold bourgeois literature and art and oppose proletarian literature and art. Then literature and art exist which serve the imperialists—for example, the works of Chou Tso-jen, Chang Tzu-ping[5] and their like—which we call traitor literature and art. With us, literature and art are for the people, not for any of the above groups. We have said that China's new culture at the present stage is an anti-imperialist, anti-feudal culture of the masses of the people under the leadership of the proletariat. Today, anything that is truly of the masses must necessarily be led by the proletariat. Whatever is under the leadership of the bourgeoisie cannot possibly be of the masses. Naturally, the same applies to the new literature and art which are part of the new culture. We should take over the rich legacy and the good traditions in literature and art that have been handed down from past ages in China and foreign countries, but the aim must still be to serve the masses of the people. Nor do we refuse to utilize the literary and artistic forms of the past, but in our hands these old forms, remoulded and infused with new content, also become something revolutionary in the service of the people.

Who, then, are the masses of the people? The broadest sections of the people, constituting more than 90 per cent of our total population, are the workers, peasants, soldiers and urban petty bourgeoisie. Therefore, our literature and art are first for the workers, the class that leads the revolution. Secondly, they are for the peasants, the most numerous and most steadfast of our allies in the revolution. Thirdly, they are for the armed workers and peasants, namely, the Eighth Route and New Fourth Armies and the other armed units of the people, which are the main forces of the revolutionary war. Fourthly, they are for the labouring masses of the urban petty bourgeoisie and for the petty-bourgeois intellectuals, both of whom are also our allies in the revolution and capable of long-term co-operation with us. These four kinds of people constitute the overwhelming majority of the Chinese nation, the broadest masses of the people.

Our literature and art should be for the four kinds of people we have enumerated. To serve them, we must take the class stand of the proletariat and not that of the petty bourgeoisie. Today, writers who cling to an individualist, petty-bourgeois stand cannot truly serve the masses of revolutionary workers, peasants and soldiers. Their interest is mainly focused on the small number of petty-bourgeois intellectuals. This is the crucial reason why some of our comrades cannot correctly solve the problem of "for whom?" In saying this I am not referring to theory. In theory, or in words, no one in our ranks regards the masses of workers, peasants and soldiers as less important than the petty-bourgeois intellectuals. I am referring to practice, to action. In practice, in action, do they regard petty-bourgeois intellectuals as more important than workers, peasants and soldiers? I think they do. Many comrades concern themselves with studying the petty-bourgeois intellectuals and analysing their psychology, and they concentrate on portraying these intellectuals and excusing or defending their shortcomings, instead of guiding the intellectuals to join with them in getting closer to the masses of workers, peasants and soldiers, taking part in the practical struggles of the masses, portraying and educating the masses. Coming from the petty bourgeoisie and being themselves intellectuals, many comrades seek friends only among intellectuals and concentrate on studying and describing them. Such study and description are proper if done from a proletarian position. But that is not what they do, or not what they do fully. They take the petty-bourgeois stand and produce works that are the self-expression of the petty bourgeoisie, as can be seen in quite a number of literary and artistic products. Often they show heartfelt sympathy for intellectuals of petty-bourgeois origin, to the extent of sympathizing with or even praising their shortcomings. On the other hand, these comrades seldom come into contact with the masses of workers, peasants and soldiers, do not understand or study them, do not have intimate friends among them and are not good at portraying them; when they do depict them, the clothes are the clothes of working people but the faces are those of petty-bourgeois intellectuals. In certain respects they are fond of the workers, peasants and soldiers and the cadres stemming from them; but there are times when they do not like them and there are some respects in which they do not like them: they do not like their feelings or their manner or their nascent literature and art (the wall newspapers, murals, folk songs, folk tales, etc.). At times they are fond of these things too, but that is when they are hunting for novelty, for something with which to embellish their own works, or even for certain backward features. At other times they openly despise these things and are partial to what belongs to the petty-bourgeois intellectuals or even to the bourgeoisie. These comrades have their feet planted on the side of the petty-bourgeois intellectuals; or, to put it more elegantly, their innermost soul is still a kingdom of the petty-bourgeois intelligentsia. Thus they have not yet solved, or not yet clearly solved, the problem of "for whom?" This applies not only to newcomers to Yenan; even among comrades who have been to the front and worked for a number of years in our base areas and in the Eighth Route and New Fourth Armies, many have not completely solved this problem. It requires a long period of time, at least eight or ten years, to solve it thoroughly. But however long it takes, solve it we must and solve it unequivocally and thoroughly. Our literary and art workers must accomplish this task and shift their stand; they must gradually move their feet over to the side of the workers, peasants and soldiers, to the side of the proletariat, through the process of going into their very midst and into the thick of practical struggles and through the process of studying Marxism and society. Only in this way can we have a literature and art that are truly for the workers, peasants and soldiers, a truly proletarian literature and art. . . .

II

Having settled the problem of whom to serve, we come to the next problem, how to serve. To put it in the words of some of our comrades: should we devote ourselves to raising standards, or should we devote ourselves to popularization?

In the past, some comrades, to a certain or even a serious extent, belittled and neglected popularization and laid undue stress on raising standards. Stress should be laid on raising standards, but to do so one-sidedly and exclusively, to do so excessively, is a mistake. The lack of a clear solution to the problem of "for whom?", which I referred to earlier, also manifests itself in this connection. As these comrades are not clear on the problem of "for whom?", they have no correct criteria for the "raising of standards" and the "popularization" they speak of, and are naturally still less able to find the correct relationship between the two. Since our literature and art are basically for the workers, peasants and soldiers, "popularization" means to popularize among the workers, peasants and soldiers, and "raising standards" means to advance from their present level. What should we popularize among them? Popularize what is needed and can be readily accepted by the feudal landlord class? Popularize what is needed and can be readily accepted by the bourgeoisie? Popularize what is needed and can be readily accepted by the petty-bourgeois intellectuals? No, none of these will do. We must popularize only what is needed and can be readily accepted by the workers, peasants and soldiers themselves. Consequently, prior to the task of educating the workers, peasants and soldiers, there is the task of learning from them. This is even more true of raising standards. There must be a basis from which to raise. Take a bucket of water, for instance; where is it to be raised from if not from the ground? From mid-air? From what basis, then, are literature and art to be raised? From the basis of the feudal classes? From the basis of the bourgeoisie? From the basis of the petty-bourgeois intellectuals? No, not from any of these; only from the basis of the masses of workers, peasants and soldiers. Nor does this mean raising the workers, peasants and soldiers to the "heights" of the feudal classes, the bourgeoisie or the petty-bourgeois intellectuals; it means raising the level of literature and art in the direction in which the workers, peasants and soldiers are themselves advancing, in the direction in which the proletariat is advancing. Here again the task of learning from the workers, peasants and soldiers comes in. Only by starting from the workers, peasants and soldiers can we have a correct understanding of popularization and of the raising of standards and find the proper relationship between the two.

In the last analysis, what is the source of all literature and art? Works of literature and art, as ideological forms, are products of the reflection in the human brain of the life of a given society. Revolutionary literature and art are the products of the reflection of the life of the people in the brains of revolutionary writers and artists. The life of the people is always a mine of the raw materials for literature and art, materials in their natural form, materials that are crude, but most vital, rich and fundamental; they make all literature and art seem pallid by comparison; they provide literature and art with an inexhaustible source, their only source. They are the only source, for there can be no other. Some may ask, is there not another source in books, in the literature and art of ancient times and of foreign countries? In fact, the literary and artistic works of the past are not a source but a stream; they were created by our predecessors and the foreigners out of the literary and artistic raw materials they found in the life of the people of their time and place. We must take over all the fine things in our literary and artistic heritage, critically assimilate whatever is beneficial, and use them as examples when we create works out of the literary and artistic raw materials in the life of the people of our own time and place. It makes a difference whether or not we have such examples, the difference between crudeness and refinement, between roughness and polish, between a low and a high level, and between slower and faster work. Therefore, we must on no account reject the legacies of the ancients and the foreigners or refuse to learn from them, even though they are the works of the feudal or bourgeois classes. But taking over legacies and using them as examples must never replace our own creative work; nothing can do that. Uncritical transplantation or copying from the ancients and the foreigners is the most sterile and harmful dogmatism in literature and art. China's revolutionary writers and artists, writers and artists of promise, must go among the masses; they must for a long period of time unreservedly and whole-heartedly go among the masses of workers, peasants and soldiers, go into the heat of the struggle, go to the only source, the broadest and richest source, in order to observe, experience, study and analyse all the different kinds of people, all the classes, all the masses, all the vivid patterns of life and struggle, all the raw materials of literature and art. Only then can they proceed to creative work. Otherwise, you will have nothing to work with and you will be nothing but a phoney writer or artist, the kind that Lu Hsun in his will so earnestly cautioned his son never to become.[6]

Although man's social life is the only source of literature and art and is incomparably livelier and richer in content, the people are not satisfied with life alone and demand literature and art as well. Why? Because, while both are beautiful, life as reflected in works of literature and art can and ought to be on a higher plane, more intense, more concentrated, more typical, nearer the ideal, and therefore more universal than actual everyday life. Revolutionary literature and art should create a variety of characters out of real life and help the masses to propel history forward. For example, there is suffering from hunger, cold and oppression on the one hand, and exploitation and oppression of man by man on the other. These facts exist everywhere and people look upon them as commonplace. Writers and artists concentrate such everyday phenomena, typify the contradictions and struggles within them and produce works which awaken the masses, fire them with enthusiasm and impel them to unite and struggle to transform their environment. Without such literature and art, this task could not be fulfilled, or at least not so effectively and speedily.

What is meant by popularizing and by raising standards in works of literature and art? What is the relationship between these two tasks? Popular works are simpler and plainer, and therefore more readily accepted by the broad masses of the people today. Works of a higher quality, being more polished, are more difficult to produce and in general do not circulate so easily and quickly among the masses at present. The problem facing the workers, peasants and soldiers is this: they are now engaged in a bitter and bloody struggle with the enemy but are illiterate and uneducated as a result of long years of rule by the feudal and bourgeois classes, and therefore they are eagerly demanding enlightenment, education and works of literature and art which meet their urgent needs and which are easy to absorb, in order to heighten their enthusiasm in struggle and confidence in victory, strengthen their unity and fight the enemy with one heart and one mind. For them the prime need is not "more flowers on the brocade" but "fuel in snowy weather". In present conditions, therefore, popularization is the more pressing task. It is wrong to belittle or neglect popularization.

Nevertheless, no hard and fast line can be drawn between popularization and the raising of standards. Not only is it possible to popularize some works of higher quality even now, but the cultural level of the broad masses is steadily rising. If popularization remains at the same level for ever, with the same stuff being supplied month after month and year after year, always the same "Little Cowherd"[7] and the same "man, hand, mouth, knife, cow, goat",[8] will not the educators and those being educated be six of one and half a dozen of the other? What would be the sense of such popularization? The people demand popularization and, following that, higher standards; they demand higher standards month by month and year by year. Here popularization means popularizing for the people and raising of standards means raising the level for the people. And such raising is not from mid-air, or behind closed doors, but is actually based on popularization. It is determined by and at the same time guides popularization. . . .

Now that we have settled the problem of the relationship between the raising of standards and popularization, that of the relationship between the specialists and the popularizers can also be settled. Our specialists are not only for the cadres, but also, and indeed chiefly, for the masses. Our specialists in literature should pay attention to the wall newspapers of the masses and to the reportage written in the army and the villages. Our specialists in drama should pay attention to the small troupes in the army and the villages. Our specialists in music should pay attention to the songs of the masses. Our specialists in the fine arts should pay attention to the fine arts of the masses. All these comrades should make close contact with comrades engaged in the work of popularizing literature and art among the masses. On the one hand, they should help and guide the popularizers, and on the other, they should learn from these comrades and, through them, draw nourishment from the masses to replenish and enrich themselves so that their specialities do not become "ivory towers", detached from the masses and from reality and devoid of content or life. We should esteem the specialists, for they are very valuable to our cause. But we should tell them that no revolutionary writer or artist can do any meaningful work unless he is closely linked with the masses, gives expression to their thoughts and feelings and serves them as a loyal spokesman. Only by speaking for the masses can he educate them and only by being their pupil can he be their teacher. If he regards himself as their master, as an aristocrat who lords it over the "lower orders", then, no matter how talented he may be, he will not be needed by the masses and his work will have no future. . . .

A thing is good only when it brings real benefit to the masses of the people. Your work may be as good as "The Spring Snow", but if for the time being it caters only to the few and the masses are still singing the "Song of the Rustic Poor",[9] you will get nowhere by simply scolding them instead of trying to raise their level. The question now is to bring about a unity between "The Spring Snow" and the "Song of the Rustic Poor", between higher standards and popularization. Without such a unity, the highest art of any expert cannot help being utilitarian in the narrowest sense; you may call this art "pure and lofty" but that is merely your own name for it which the masses will not endorse.

Once we have solved the problems of fundamental policy, of serving the workers, peasants and soldiers and of how to serve them, such other problems as whether to write about the bright or the dark side of life and the problem of unity will also be solved. If everyone agrees on the fundamental policy, it should be adhered to by all our workers, all our schools, publications and organizations in the field of literature and art and in all our literary and artistic activities. It is wrong to depart from this policy and anything at variance with it must be duly corrected. . . .

III

In the world today all culture, all literature and art belong to definite classes and are geared to definite political lines. There is in fact no such thing as art for art's sake, art that stands above classes or art that is detached from or independent of

politics. Proletarian literature and art are part of the whole proletarian revolutionary cause; they are, as Lenin said, cogs and wheels in the whole revolutionary
machine. Therefore, Party work in literature and art occupies a definite and assigned
position in Party revolutionary work as a whole and is subordinated to the revolutionary tasks set by the Party in a given revolutionary period. . . . We do not favour
overstressing the importance of literature and art, but neither do we favour under-
estimating their importance. Literature and art are subordinate to politics, but in
their turn exert a great influence on politics. Revolutionary literature and art are
part of the whole revolutionary cause, they are cogs and wheels in it, and though in
comparison with certain other and more important parts they may be less significant and less urgent and may occupy a secondary position, nevertheless, they are
indispensable cogs and wheels in the whole machine, an indispensable part of the
entire revolutionary cause. If we had no literature and art even in the broadest and
most ordinary sense, we could not carry on the revolutionary movement and win
victory. Failure to recognize this is wrong. Furthermore, when we say that literature
and art are subordinate to politics, we mean class politics, the politics of the
masses, not the politics of a few so-called statesmen. Politics, whether revolutionary or counter-revolutionary, is the struggle of class against class, not the activity
of a few individuals. The revolutionary struggle on the ideological and artistic fronts
must be subordinate to the political struggle because only through politics can the
needs of the class and the masses find expression in concentrated form. Revolutionary statesmen, the political specialists who know the science or art of revolutionary politics, are simply the leaders of millions upon millions of statesmen—the
masses. Their task is to collect the opinions of these mass statesmen, sift and refine
them, and return them to the masses, who then take them and put them into practice. They are therefore not the kind of aristocratic "statesmen" who work behind
closed doors and fancy they have a monopoly of wisdom. Herein lies the difference
in principle between proletarian statesmen and decadent bourgeois statesmen. This
is precisely why there can be complete unity between the political character of our
literary and artistic works and their truthfulness. It would be wrong to fail to realize this and to debase the politics and the statesmen of the proletariat. . . .

IV

There is the political criterion and there is the artistic criterion; what is the relationship between the two? Politics cannot be equated with art, nor can a general
world outlook be equated with a method of artistic creation and criticism. We deny
not only that there is an abstract and absolutely unchangeable political criterion,
but also that there is an abstract and absolutely unchangeable artistic criterion; each
class in every class society has its own political and artistic criteria. But all classes
in all class societies invariably put the political criterion first and the artistic criterion second. The bourgeoisie always shuts out proletarian literature and art, however great their artistic merit. The proletariat must similarly distinguish among the
literary and art works of past ages and determine its attitude towards them only
after examining their attitude to the people and whether or not they had any progressive significance historically. Some works which politically are downright reactionary may have a certain artistic quality. The more reactionary their content and
the higher their artistic quality, the more poisonous they are to the people, and the
more necessary it is to reject them. A common characteristic of the literature and

art of all exploiting classes in their period of decline is the contradiction between their reactionary political content and their artistic form. What we demand is the unity of politics and art, the unity of content and form, the unity of revolutionary political content and the highest possible perfection of artistic form. Works of art which lack artistic quality have no force, however progressive they are politically. Therefore, we oppose both the tendency to produce works of art with a wrong political viewpoint and the tendency towards the "poster and slogan style" which is correct in political viewpoint but lacking in artistic power. On questions of literature and art we must carry on a struggle on two fronts. . . .

"The fundamental point of departure for literature and art is love, love of humanity." Now love may serve as a point of departure, but there is a more basic one. Love as an idea is a product of objective practice. Fundamentally, we do not start from ideas but from objective practice. Our writers and artists who come from the ranks of the intellectuals love the proletariat because society has made them feel that they and the proletariat share a common fate. We hate Japanese imperialism because Japanese imperialism oppresses us. There is absolutely no such thing in the world as love or hatred without reason or cause. As for the so-called love of humanity, there has been no such all-inclusive love since humanity was divided into classes. All the ruling classes of the past were fond of advocating it, and so were many so-called sages and wise men, but nobody has ever really practised it, because it is impossible in class society. There will be genuine love of humanity—after classes are eliminated all over the world. Classes have split society into many antagonistic groupings; there will be love of all humanity when classes are eliminated, but not now. We cannot love enemies, we cannot love social evils, our aim is to destroy them. This is common sense; can it be that some of our writers and artists still do not understand this?

"Literary and artistic works have always laid equal stress on the bright and the dark, half and half." This statement contains many muddled ideas. It is not true that literature and art have always done this. Many petty-bourgeois writers have never discovered the bright side. Their works only expose the dark and are known as the "literature of exposure." Some of their works simply specialize in preaching pessimism and world-weariness. On the other hand, Soviet literature in the period of socialist construction portrays mainly the bright. It, too, describes shortcomings in work and portrays negative characters, but this only serves as a contrast to bring out the brightness of the whole picture and is not on a so-called half-and-half basis. The writers and artists of the bourgeoisie in its period of reaction depict the revolutionary masses as mobs and themselves as saints, thus reversing the bright and the dark. Only truly revolutionary writers and artists can correctly solve the problem of whether to extol or to expose. All the dark forces harming the masses of the people must be exposed and all the revolutionary struggles of the masses of the people must be extolled; this is the fundamental task of revolutionary writers and artists.

"The task of literature and art has always been to expose." This assertion, like the previous one, arises from ignorance of the science of history. Literature and art, as we have shown, have never been devoted solely to exposure. For revolutionary writers and artists the targets for exposure can never be the masses, but only the aggressors, exploiters and oppressors and the evil influence they have on the people. The masses too have shortcomings, which should be overcome by criticism and self-criticism within the people's own ranks, and such criticism and self-criticism is also one of the most important tasks of literature and art. But this should not be regarded as any sort of "exposure of the people". As for the people, the question is basically one of education and of raising their level. . . .

"It is not a question of stand; my class stand is correct, my intentions are good and I understand all right, but I am not good at expressing myself and so the effect turns out bad." I have already spoken about the dialectical materialist view of motive and effect. Now I want to ask, is not the question of effect one of stand? A person who acts solely by motive and does not inquire what effect his action will have is like a doctor who merely writes prescriptions but does not care how many patients die of them. Or take a political party which merely makes declarations but does not care whether they are carried out. It may well be asked, is this a correct stand? And is the intention here good? Of course, mistakes may occur even though the effect has been taken into account beforehand, but is the intention good when one continues in the same old rut after facts have proved that the effect is bad? In judging a party or a doctor, we must look at practice, at the effect. The same applies in judging a writer. A person with truly good intentions must take the effect into account, sum up experience and study the methods or, in creative work, study the technique of expression. A person with truly good intentions must criticize the shortcomings and mistakes in his own work with the utmost candour and resolve to correct them. This is precisely why Communists employ the method of self-criticism. This alone is the correct stand. Only in this process of serious and responsible practice is it possible gradually to understand what the correct stand is and gradually obtain a good grasp of it. If one does not move in this direction in practice, if there is simply the complacent assertion that one "understands all right", then in fact one has not understood at all.

"To call on us to study Marxism is to repeat the mistake of the dialectical materialist creative method, which will harm the creative mood." To study Marxism means to apply the dialectical materialist and historical materialist viewpoint in our observation of the world, of society and of literature and art; it does not mean writing philosophical lectures into our works of literature and art. Marxism embraces but cannot replace realism in literary and artistic creation, just as it embraces but cannot replace the atomic and electronic theories in physics. Empty, dry dogmatic formulas do indeed destroy the creative mood; not only that, they first destroy Marxism. Dogmatic "Marxism" is not Marxism, it is anti-Marxism. Then does not Marxism destroy the creative mood? Yes, it does. It definitely destroys creative moods that are feudal, bourgeois, petty-bourgeois, liberalistic, individualist, nihilist, art-for-art's sake, aristocratic, decadent or pessimistic, and every other creative mood that is alien to the masses of the people and to the proletariat. So far as proletarian writers and artists are concerned, should not these kinds of creative moods be destroyed? I think they should; they should be utterly destroyed. And while they are being destroyed, something new can be constructed. . . .

NOTES

[1]The May 4th Movement was an anti-imperialist and anti-feudal revolutionary movement which began on May 4. 1919. In the first half of that year, the victors of World War I, *i.e.*, Britain, France, the United States, Japan, Italy and other imperialist countries, met in Paris to divide the spoils and decided that Japan should take over all the privileges previously enjoyed by Germany in Shantung Province, China. The students of Peking were

the first to show determined opposition to this scheme, holding rallies and demonstrations on May 4. The Northern warlord government arrested more than thirty students in an effort to suppress this opposition. In protest, the students of Peking went on strike and large numbers of students in other parts of the country responded. On June 3 the Northern warlord government started arresting students in Peking en masse, and within two days about a thousand were taken into custody. This aroused still greater indignation throughout the country. From June 5 onwards, the workers of Shanghai and many other cities went on strike and the merchants in these places shut their shops. Thus, what was at first a patriotic movement consisting mainly of intellectuals rapidly developed into a national patriotic movement embracing the proletariat, the urban petty bourgeoisie and the bourgeoisie. And along with the growth of this patriotic movement, the new cultural movement which had begun before May 4 as a movement against feudalism and for the promotion of science and democracy, grew into a vigorous and powerful revolutionary cultural movement whose main current was the propagation of Marxism-Leninism.

[2]The Shensi-Kansu-Ningsia Border Region was the revolutionary base area which was gradually built up after 1931 through revolutionary guerrilla warfare in northern Shensi. When the Central Red Army arrived in northern Shensi after the Long March, it became the seat of the Central Committee of the Chinese Communist Party and the central base area of the revolution. The Shensi-Kansu-Ningsia Red Area was changed into the Shensi-Kansu-Ningsia Border Region after the formation of the Anti-Japanese National United Front in 1937. Nearly thirty counties, i.e., Yenan, Fuhsien, Kanchuan, Yenchuan, Yenchang, Anting (now Tzechang), Ansai, Chihtan, Chingpien, Shenmu, Fuku, Tingpien, Hsunyi, Chunhua, Huanhsien, Chingyang, Hoshui, Chenyuan, Ninghsien, Chengning, Yenchih, Suiteh, Chingchien, Wupao, Michih, Chiahsien, etc., were under its jurisdiction.

[3]See V. I. Lenin, "Party Organisation and Party Literature", in which he described the characteristics of proletarian literature as follows:

It will be a free literature, because the idea of socialism and sympathy with the working people, and not greed or careerism, will bring ever new forces to its ranks. It will be a free literature, because it will serve, not some satiated heroine, not the bored "upper ten thousand" suffering from fatty degeneration, but the millions and tens of millions of working people — the flower of the country, its strength and its future. It will be a free literature, enriching the last word in the revolutionary thought of mankind with the experience and living work of the socialist proletariat, bringing about permanent interaction between the experience of the past (scientific socialism, the completion of the development of socialism from its primitive, utopian forms) and the experience of the present (the present struggle of the worker comrades). (Collected Works, Eng. ed., FLPH, Moscow, 1961, Vol. X, PP. 48–49.)

[4]Liang Shih-chiu, a member of the counter-revolutionary National Socialist Party, for a long time propagated reactionary American bourgeois ideas on literature and art. He stubbornly opposed the revolution and reviled revolutionary literature and art.

[5]Chou Tso-jen and Chang Tzu-ping capitulated to the Japanese aggressors after the Japanese occupied Peking and Shanghai in 1937.

[6]See Lu Hsun's essay, "Death", in the "Addenda", The Last Collection of Essays Written in a Garret in the Quasi-Concession, Complete Works, Chin. ed., 1958, Vol. VI.

[7]The "Little Cowherd" is a popular Chinese folk operetta with only two people acting in it, a cowherd and a village girl, who sing a question and answer duet. In the early days of the War of Resistance Against Japan, this form was used, with new words, for anti-Japanese propaganda and for a time found great favour with the public.

[8]The Chinese characters for these six words are written simply, with only a few strokes, and were usually included in the first lessons in old primers.

[9]"The Spring Snow" and the "Song of the Rustic Poor" were songs of the Kingdom of Chu in the 3rd century B.C. The music of the first was on a higher level than that of the second. As the story is told in "Sung Yu's Reply to the King of Chu" in Prince Chao Ming's *Anthology of Prose and Poetry*, when someone sang "The Spring Snow" in the Chu capital, only a few dozen people joined in, but when the "Song of the Rustic Poor" was sung, thousands did so.

HAROLD ROME
(B. 1908)

Rome came from a well-to-do family in Hartford, Connecticut, where his father was a fuel company executive. He attended Trinity College and Yale, where he first studied law, and then architecture, in which he received an MFA in 1934. All through his undergraduate and graduate days, he had helped support himself by playing piano and composing music for dance bands and ballets. Having graduated with an architecture degree in the middle of the Great Depression, he found little demand for his training and so went to work in the Lescaze design studio. But he continued to write songs, one of which attracted the well-known performer, Gypsy Rose Lee, who helped him to sell it and thus pushed him one further step toward Broadway. In 1935 he was employed at the Adirondack summer home of the Group Theater, Green Mansions. Over three summers, he helped write and produce nine original musicals, containing some ninety songs.

He was also introduced to Louis Schaffer, who was then beginning to develop plans for a musical to be put on at the Labor Stage Theater by the Union Players of the International Ladies Garment Workers' Union. Rome was invited to write material for that production, Pins and Needles *(1937), and ended up writing almost all the lyrics and music for that first production and the subsequent revivals. Performed by amateurs and semi-professionals from the needle trades,* Pins and Needles *proved not only to further labor's cause in a light-hearted way but to be a hit with people from every walk of life and economic stratum.*

Rome continued to write tuneful and often politically pointed songs during and after World War II. He arranged and put into English Dmitri Shostakovich's United Nations "Hymn," and wrote the music and lyrics for hits like "This Is the Army, Mr. Jones," Fanny *(1954), and* I Can Get It for You Wholesale *(1962).*

SING ME A SONG WITH SOCIAL SIGNIFICANCE

I'm tired of moon gons, of star and of June songs,
They simply make me nap.
And ditties romantic drive me nearly frantic,
I think they're all full of pap.
History's making, nations are quaking,
Why sing of stars above?
For while we are waiting, father time's creating
New things to be singing of. . .

Sing me a song with social significance,
All other tunes are taboo.
I want a ditty with heat in it,
Appealing with feeling and meat in it.
Sing me a song with social significance,
Or you can sing till you're blue,
Let meaning shine from every line
Or I won't love you.

Sing me of wars, sing me of breadlines,
Tell me of front page news,
Sing me of strikes and last minute headlines,
Dress your observations in syncopation.

Sing me a song with social significance,
There's nothing else that will do.
It must get hot with what is what
Or I won't love you.

Sing me a song with social significance,
All other tunes are taboo,
I want a song that's satirical,
And putting the mere into miracle.
Sing me a song with social significance,
Or you can sing till you're blue,
It must be packed with social fact
Or I won't love you.

Sing me of crime and conferences martial,
Tell me of mills and of mines,
Sing me of courts that aren't impartial,
What's to be done with 'em? Tell me in rhythm.

Sing me a song with social significance,
There's nothing else that will do.
It must be dense with common sense
Or I won't love you.

CARLOS BULOSAN

(1913-1956)

Like many working people from the Philippines, Bulosan came to the United States (in 1930) to escape the intense poverty that colonization had produced in his country. The Philippine Islands had first been occupied by Spain and then, following the Spanish-American war in 1898, by the United States after a brutal campaign between 1899 and 1902 to put down an independent Philippine republic. His father had been a small farmer, but had been forced by debt into peonage. Young Carlos was recruited as an agricultural labor by a contractor who held out before jobless Filipino youth dreams of material success in America. Filipinos were in demand in part because Chinese and Japanese workers had been excluded from the United States though the fields and canneries of the west still needed a supply of "cheap labor." Landing in Seattle, Bulosan's contract—in effect, he himself—was sold for five dollars to a salmon cannery. He labored there and up and down the west coast through much of the Great Depression of the 1930s, helping to organize a union of fish cannery workers and writing for the union newspapers. In 1936, he came down with tuberculosis and, undergoing three operations for lung lesions, was confined to a TB hospital until 1938. The TB hospital was his Harvard, for there he had the opportunity for the first time to read widely, at the rate often of a book a day, in American and other English-language literatures.

With the advent of World War II, and the importance of the Philippines in that struggle, Bulosan's writing took on a certain vogue. His work was published in the Saturday Evening Post, The New Yorker, Harper's Bazaar, *and other widely read magazines. And his somewhat fictionalized autobiography,* America Is in the Heart *(1946), was widely circulated. For a time, he could command a thousand dollars for an article. Fundamentally, however, Bulosan's outlook was that of a working-class radical; he commented that while Americans read his book,* Laughter of My Father *(1940) as humor, he wrote it out of rage. And as the Cold War increasingly stifled radical and to some extent immigrant culture, Bulosan's stock plunged. He died in Seattle, largely forgotten until the revival of interest during the 1970s in writing by Asian Americans.*

THE AMERICANO FROM LUZON

Crispin Balison was picking peas one morning when he suddenly stopped working and flung his can down the hill. I was on the other side of the field with a crew of ten men when I heard the noise of the can rolling down the hillside. It finally landed with a bang on the highway below. I thought Crispin was fighting a snake that had crawled under the vines from the blistering sun. But when I saw him standing silently in the bright sunlight and looking toward the blue ocean, I smiled and concluded that he was homesick for the Philippines.

I resumed my work. The vines were heavy, and I knew that if I worked faster I would be able to buy a new pair of corduroy pants. I was about to go to my sack with the full can when I saw Crispin walking toward me. I waited for him. Then together we walked to the empty sack.

Crispin held the mouth of the sack open. I poured the peas. I looked at him sur-reptitiously and went back to my unfinished row. I sat down slowly and looked back at him, hoping that he would return to his work. But he sat by the sack with his chin in his hands, looking sadly toward the calm spring ocean. Then I walked back to him and sat silently beside him, waiting for him to tell me what was bothering him. When he did not say anything, I began to worry. His mother had written to me the other day about him, and although I never met her it was my lot to watch over him.

"Well, Crispin," I began "I think we will have a successful season this time. Last year the rains did not come and the vines were stunted by the strong heat of the sun. But you can see for yourself that this spring the vines are heavy with fruit. It means that we will earn more than in any of the other years."

"I'm not thinking of the money side of it," Crispin answered, throwing a handful of peas into the sack. "I have been thinking there at the end of my long row, and what I thought is this: Why should I work in the blistering sun or torrential rain when I have done just that all my life in the Islands? That is what I have been think-ing down there in the long row of unpicked peas, while watching the wide span of the blue ocean and listening to the silence around me."

There was something to what he had said. I had never thought of it before. I had been in the new land many years now, but it had never occurred to me that I should question the type of my occupation. I had also worked all my life in the fields like him.

"Well, Crispin," I said kindly, "if you are not in the mood to work this morning, I would advise you to lie under the tree and think some more. We will manage to fin-ish this field with the crew we have got today."

"It's not that at all," he said. "But I will take your sound advice. I will lie down in the cool shade of the tree and think long thoughts about this day and other days to come."

He got up slowly and walked toward the tree. But as he walked away, I felt some-how that it was just the beginning of Crispin's long walk away from me, away from our happy crew of young men who followed the crops and the seasons, away from the pea fields, and the green hills that were almost like home.

I went back to work considering Crispin's disturbing question. All my life, I knew, I had been looking for a new avenue through which I could follow, and dis-cover the life of the new land. And as I stopped working to look at the distant moun-tains for a moment, I felt that somewhere there was a road that would lead some of us to a day of certitude and fulfillment.

When we drove back to our little house that late afternoon, I noticed that Crispin was very silent. He was sitting in the back seat with his chin in his hands. His eyes were far away. The other members of our crew kept him undisturbed, talking loudly and boisterously like most boys do when they are away from home.

Crispin was the first to jump out of the car when we reached our house. He was also the first to sit at the dinner table, eating slowly and very little at a time. Then he returned silently to his room and shut the door and paced up and down the floor all night long.

We had no work the following morning. Crispin came to my room and woke me up. I went to the small window and looked out. There was a slight fog in the air. It had rained in the middle of the night, when I was sound asleep, drops of water were still shimmering on the leaves of the pepper trees. There were paddies in the yard and the road that led to town was clean and glistening in the faint morning sun.

"Let's walk to town," Crispin said.

I looked at him. There was something new in his face. Evidently he had arrived at a concrete resolution. I went to the bathroom and cleaned myself. At the breakfast table, Crispin was not as quiet as the night before. He ate like one of us now, as though he were in a great hurry to accomplish something.

After breakfast we walked to town. He stopped in front of a bookshop, reading the titles with his lips. He also stopped by the theater. Then he urged me to go to the public library with him. He went inside without forcing me to accompany him. I sat on the cement steps outside and watched the blackbirds hopping on the trimmed lawn, picking little worms and tiny seeds with their small beaks.

When Crispin came out I saw that his pockets were full of books. He was reading some notes that he had scribbled on a piece of cheap paper. There was a glow of discovery in his face. He stuffed the papers in his hat and walked silently beside me.

We had walked three blocks when he stopped suddenly to read his notes again. Then he took me across the street to a small printing shop, where the day's edition was being prepared. Crispin looked through the glass wall with great interest. He was rolling on his heels. His nose was pressed flat against the glass. Then he put his arm in mine and we walked to our house.

I left him there because he entered his room right away and closed the door. I went to the poolroom two blocks away where most of the farmhands congregated when there was no work. I shot a game of pool and lost. I watched the card players for a while, hoping there would be no fight. When dinner time came, I walked home.

Crispin was still in his room, pacing up and down. I went to my room after dinner and lay down on my bed. I wanted to sleep early because we would resume our work in the morning. But in the middle of the night, when I had finally worried myself to sleep, Crispin came bursting into my room.

"It's done!" he shouted.

"What is done?" I asked in a frightened voice. I jumped from the bed and grabbed his shoulders. My mind was running through the channels of tragedy. I asked again, "What is done, Crispin?"

"I have finally decided to become an Americano," he said expansively. "That's what is done!"

"How would you go about it?" I asked, thinking of his brown face and flat nose. "How would you accomplish that miraculous act?"

"It is simple," Crispin said decidedly. "It is very simple indeed. Did that printing shop in town interest you today?"

"I saw it," I said. "But it did not interest me at all. What would I do with a printing shop?"

Then, majestically, grandly, Crispin spoke: "I will be a newspaperman."

There was a royal note of finality in his voice. And as I looked at him in the half-light, I seemed to see that he was actually growing in stature. He was no longer the small puny Crispin Balison that I had met at the bus station a week before. He was no longer the small and frightened immigrant that had talked in a faltering English that day. He was now an Americano. Now he had the liveliness and eagerness to discover things like an Americano.

"But you went only as far as the fourth grade in your village," I said in half reprimand and half condescension. "I think it takes a better education than you have to be a newspaperman."

"Have you seen those books I took from the library?" Crispin asked.

"I saw two books," I said. "But I did not read the titles."

"Two books are enough," he said confidently. "One book is about the racket and the other is about a man who started it. I will be the editor and publisher, all in one throw. Never mind the grammar. That will come later."

"You are right, Crispin," I said, humoring him, thinking that in a day or two he would forget the idea. "We Filipinos are not particular about the grammar."

"I'm not thinking only of the Filipinos," he answered proudly. "I'm an Americano now, you see. I'm thinking of the whole country."

That was how Crispin Balison started. He had a big dream. But I did not know then how far he would reach it. I did not know until later how a big dream could stir a man's life and break fragments of happiness in its wake. I did not know that a big dream could be utterly cruel and tremendously kind also. I did not know that Crispin, because he had come from a small village of semiprimitive farmers, would some day escape from his obscure beginning and start a heritage for his people in the new land.

I did not go to work the following morning. I helped him make an improvised table and a chair in the backyard. We found discarded boards in the toolshed and painted them. Then we carried the table and chair to the back of the poolroom two blocks away and put up this sign on the wall:

PHILIPPINE TIMES

CRISPIN BALISON
Editor & Publisher

For some days afterward, when I was busy picking peas with the rest of our crew, I thought of Crispin sitting at his office with only a simple table and a chair. He did not even have a typewriter. But he had piled up some yellow sheets of paper on one side of the table and old newspapers on the other side. There was a big bottle of ink in front of him and a rusty pen in his hand. There were several pencils in his breast pocket.

When I went to see him one afternoon, I noticed that he had started smoking cigars. He got up quickly and reached for my hand. He was smiling broadly.

"Can I do something for you?" he asked eagerly. He spoke as though he were a businessman about to put over a big deal. "Can I interest you in the first edition of my paper?"

The pool players stopped chalking their cues and listened to him. The gamblers put down their cards and looked toward us, lighting their cigars and spitting nonchalantly on the bare floor. Even the bystanders stopped daydreaming and became attentive. Outside in the street, where I saw the slanting shadow of a tree, the passersby stopped to listen for a moment. Crispin's voice boomed in the room and echoed on the walls, refracting to the wide door and shooting out into the street. There was something fanatical in the way he spoke, but his words rang with great sincerity.

"Well, Crispin," I said quietly, "I kind of wondered how you were getting along. I had not been able to see you because we are very busy in the fields. But the season will soon be over."

"Fine, fine, fine!" Crispin said, biting the end of his cigar. And although he did not really smoke, he kept puffing and chewing at it. "Sit down and I will show you what I have done."

There was a pile of galley proofs on the table. He shoved them to me. I rapidly glanced at them, not comprehending the mechanics of his profession.

"Is this not a great first issue?" he asked, throwing away his cigar and lighting another which he had extracted from a row of ten in his vest pocket. "Have a cigar?"

I did not smoke, but I accepted his offer. He leaned over the table and lighted my cigar. I puffed at it, watching the continuous flow of heavy smoke issuing from his cigar. While I was looking at the proofs, he was constantly jumping to his feet and walking around the table. Once he stopped in the middle of the floor at my back and stood there silently for a long time. I had that strange fear when someone is watching me at my back, so I turned around and asked him for another light. He shook himself from his thoughts and scratched a match. The blue flame leaped into my cigar, and I turned back to the proofs. I was still apprehensive of him.

Crispin sat in his chair and put his feet on the table. I glanced up quickly and saw his beaming brown face between his shoes. I saw the continuous, flow of smoke from his cigar. I saw the air of satisfaction radiating all about him.

"Didn't I tell you this is a good racket?" he said at last. And slapping a hand on a pile of paper, he shouted: "Look at all this business? Now I can make you my general manager!"

I wanted to say something, but the cigar fell from my mouth. I bent down to pick it up, but Crispin jumped to his feet and offered me another.

"Never mind it, partner," he said convincingly. "Here is a fresh one. And you'd better run to the house and change your dirty working clothes. Newspapermen do not dress like that at all. Let's live like Americanos in the new country."

I accepted the cigar and Crispin lighted it. Then I sat more comfortably, puffing vigorously at the cigar, watching the continuous flow of heavy smoke coming from it.

RUBE GOLDBERG
(1883-1970)

Goldberg, named by his parents Reuben Lucius, was one of the most widely read and successful newspaper cartoonists in history. His cartoon series Mike and Ike—They Look Alike, The Weekly Meeting of the Tuesday Women's Club, *and* Boob McNutt *ran in newspapers throughout the United States beginning in 1916 and continuing into the 1950s. But he is probably best known for the zany inventions of his Professor Lucifer Gorgonzola Butts, elaborate and often hilarious drawings of constructions designed to accomplish absurdly simple everyday tasks. They came to be known as Rube Goldberg inventions.*

His ability to design them was probably rooted, in part, in his training as an engineer. His father, a banker, real estate promoter, police and fire com-missioner in San Francisco, wished him to take a position in the city engi-neering department. He did—for a while. But Rube liked to draw, was good at it, and soon turned to sports cartooning for the San Francisco Chronicle *in 1905. After that, he rapidly moved upward in the newspaper game, relo-cating to New York to work for the Hearst paper, the* Evening Journal. *By the end of World War I, he was making over a million dollars a year through the syndication of his cartoons. In 1938, he became the political cartoonist for the* New York Sun. *He won a Pulitzer Prize for his 1947 cartoon showing a family atop an atomic bomb teetering between "world control" and "world*

destruction." Apart from cartoons, he wrote a number of comic stories and
a few movie scripts. Not radical in his politics—he was active with the artists'
committee supporting Republican Thomas Dewey for president in 1948—he
still loved to poke fun at the pomposity of bourgeois America, one of his
main attractions to his huge audience. That satiric streak endeared him as
well to Soviet intelligentsia and writers, one of whom included the story that
follows in a collection of socially conscious pieces by American authors—a
paradox Goldberg would probably have found delicious.

ART FOR HEART'S SAKE

"Here, take your pineapple juice," gently persuaded Koppel, the male nurse.

"Nope!" grunted Collis P. Ellsworth.

"But it's good for you, sir."

"Nope!"

"It's doctor's orders."

"Nope!"

Koppel heard the front door bell and was glad to leave the room. He found Doctor Caswell in the hall downstairs. "I can't do a thing with him," he told the doctor. "He won't take his pineapple juice. He doesn't want me to read to him. He hates the radio. He doesn't like anything!"

Doctor Caswell received the information with his usual professional calm. He had done some constructive thinking since his last visit. This was no ordinary case. The old gentleman was in pretty good shape for a man of seventy six. But he had to be kept from buying things. He had suffered his last heart attack after his disastrous purchase of that jerkwater railroad out in Iowa. The one before that came from the excitement engendered by the disintegration of The Happy Package chain of grocery stores which he had acquired at a fabulous price. All of his purchases of recent years had to be liquidated at a great sacrifice both to his health and his pocketbook.

Collis P. Ellsworth sat in a huge over-upholstered chair by the window. He looked around as Doctor Caswell inquired, "Well, how's the young man today?"

"Umph!" grunted the figure in the chair in a tone like a rasping cough with all the implications of a sneer.

"I hear you haven't been obeying orders," the doctor chided.

"Who's giving me orders at my time of life?"

The doctor drew up a chair and sat down close to the old man. "I've got a proposition for you," he said quietly.

Old Ellsworth looked suspiciously over his spectacles. "What is it, more medicine, more automobile rides, more balderdash to keep me away from the office?"

"How'd you like to take up art?" The doctor had his stethoscope ready in case the abruptness of the suggestion proved too much for the patient's heart.

But the old gentleman's answer was a vigorous "Rot!"

"I don't mean seriously," said the doctor, relieved that disaster had been averted. "Just fool around with chalk and crayons. It'll be fun."

"Bosh!"

"All right." The doctor stood up. "I just suggested it, that's all."

Collis P. sucked his gums and his wrinkled chin bobbed up and down. "Where'd you get this crazy idea, anyway?"

"Well, it's only a suggestion—"

"But, Caswell, how do I start playing with the chalk—that is, if I'm foolish enough to start?"

"I've thought of that, too. I can get a student from one of the art schools to come here once a week and show you. If you don't like it after a little while you can throw him out."

Doctor Caswell went to his friend, Judson Livingston, head of the Atlantic Art Institute, and explained the situation. Livingston had just the young man—Frank Swain, eighteen years old and a promising student. He needed the money. Ran an elevator at night to pay tuition. How much would he get? Five dollars a visit. Fine.

Next afternoon young Swain was shown into the big living room. Collis P. Ellsworth looked at him appraisingly.

"Sir, I'm not an artist yet," answered the young man.

"Umph!"

Swain arranged some paper and crayons on the table. "Let's try and draw that vase over there on the mantelpiece," he suggested.

"Try it, Mister Ellsworth, please."

"Umph!" The old man took a piece of crayon in a shaky hand and made a scrawl. He made another scrawl and connected the two with a couple of crude lines. "There it is, young man," he snapped with a grunt of satisfaction. "Such foolishness. Poppycock!" Frank Swain was patient. He needed the five dollars. "If you want to draw you will have to look at what you're drawing, sir."

Old Ellsworth squinted and looked. "By gum, it's kinda pretty. I never noticed it before."

Koppel came in with the pronouncement that his patient had done enough for the first lesson.

"Oh, it's pineapple juice again," Ellsworth mumbled. Swain left.

When the art student came the following week there was a drawing on the table that had a slight resemblance to the vase. The wrinkles deepened at the corners of the old gentleman's eyes as he asked elfishly, "Well, what do you think of it?"

"Not bad, sir," answered Swain. "But it's a bit lopsided."

"By gum," Old Ellsworth chuckled, "I see. The halves don't match." He added a few lines with a palsied hand and colored the open spaces blue like a child playing with a picture book. Then he looked towards the door. "Listen, young man," he whispered, "I want to ask you something before old pineapple juice comes back."

"Yes, sir," responded Swain respectively.

"I was thinking could you spare the time to come twice a week or perhaps three times?"

"Sure, Mister Ellsworth."

"Good. Let's make it Monday, Wednesday and Friday. Four o'clock."

Koppel entered and was flabbergasted when his patient took his pineapple juice without a whimper.

As the weeks went by Swain's visits grew more frequent. He brought the old man a box of water colors and some tubes of oils.

When Doctor Caswell called Ellsworth would talk about the graceful lines of the andirons. He would dwell on the rich variety of color in a bowl of fruit. He proudly displayed the variegated smears of paint on his heavy silk dressing gown. He would not allow his valet to send it to the cleaner's. He wanted to show the doctor how hard he'd been working.

The treatment was working perfectly. No more trips downtown to become involved in purchases of enterprises of doubtful solvency. No more crazy commercial gyrations to tax the strength of a lumbering old heart. Art was a complete cure for acute financial deterioration.

The doctor thought it safe to allow Ellsworth to visit the Metropolitan, the Museum of Modern Art and other exhibits with Swain. An entirely new world opened up its charming mysteries. The old man displayed an insatiable curiosity about the galleries and the painters who exhibited in them. How were the galleries run? Who selected the canvases for the exhibitions? An idea was forming in his brain.

When the late Spring sun began to cloak the fields and gardens with color Ellsworth executed a god-awful smudge which he called, "Trees Dressed in White." Then he made a startling announcement. He was going to exhibit it in the Summer show at the Lathrop Gallery!

For the Summer show at Lathrop Gallery was the biggest art exhibit of the year in quality, if not in size. The lifetime dream of every mature artist in the United States was a Lathrop prize. Upon this distinguished group Ellsworth was going to foist his "Trees Dressed in White," which resembled a gob of salad dressing thrown violently up against the side of a house!

"If the papers get hold of this, Mister Ellsworth will become a laughing-stock. We've got to sop him," groaned Koppel.

"No," admonished the doctor. "We can't interfere with him now and take a chance of spoiling all the good work that we've accomplished."

To the utter astonishment of all three—and especially Swain—"Trees Dressed in White" was accepted for the Lathrop show. Not ony was Mister Ellsworth crazy, thought Koppel, but the Lathrop Gallery was crazy, too.

Fortunately, the painting was hung in an inconspicuous place where it could not excite any noticeable comment. Young Swain sneaked into the gallery one afternoon and blushed to the top of his ears when he saw "Trees Dressed in White," a loud, raucous splash on the wall. As two giggling students stopped before the strange anomaly Swain fled in terror. He could not bear to hear what they had to say.

During the course of the exhibition the old man kept on taking his lessons, seldom mentioning his entry in the exhibit. He was unusually cheerful. Every time Swain entered the room he found Ellsworth chuckling. Maybe Koppel was right. The old man was crazy. But it seemed equally strange that the Lathrop committee should encourage his insanity by accepting his picture.

Two days before the close of the exhibition a special messenger brought a long official-looking envelope to Mister Ellsworth while Swain, Koppel and the doctor were in the room. "Read it to me," requested the old man. "My eyes are tired from painting."

> It gives the Lathrop Gallery pleasure to announce that the First Landscape Prize of $1,000 has been awarded to Collis P. Ellsworth for his painting, "Trees Dressed in White."

Swain and Koppel uttered a series of inarticulate gurgles. Doctor Caswell, exercising his professional selfcontrol with a supreme effort, said "Congratulations, Mister Ellsworth. Fine, fine . . . See, see . . . Of course, I didn't expect such great news. But, but—well, now, you'll have to admit that art is much more satisfying than business."

"Art's nothing," snapped the old man. "I bought the Lathrop Gallery last month."

MAGGIE ANDERSON
(B. 1948)

Anderson was born in New York but returned to West Virginia, where her parents had come from, when she was thirteen. Both her parents were teachers, but most of the men and some of the women in her father's family worked for the Baltimore & Ohio Railroad.

Anderson received her B.A. and M.A. from West Virginia University, where she has also taught. She has been an artist-in-residence at West Virginia schools and a visiting poet at a number of colleges and universities, including Pittsburgh, Penn State, and Hamilton. She now teaches at Kent State University. Her volumes of poetry include The Great Horned Owl *(1979),* Years That Answer *(1980), and* Cold Comfort *(1986).*

MINING CAMP RESIDENTS, WEST VIRGINIA, JULY, 1935

They had to seize something in the face of the camera.
The woman's hand touches her throat as if feeling
for a necklace that isn't there. The man buries one hand
in his overall pocket, loops the other through a strap,
and the child twirls a strand of her hair as she hunkers
in the dirt at their feet. Maybe Evans asked them to stand
in that little group in the doorway, a perfect triangle
of people in the morning sun. Perhaps he asked them
to hold their arms that way, or bend their heads. It was
his composition after all. And they did what he said.

FRANK O'HARA
(1926-1966)

In writing why he is "Not a Painter," O'Hara actually reflected the fact that he was very much a part of the post–World War II New York avant-garde art scene within which the painters of the abstract expressionist school flourished. O'Hara had come to New York in 1951 after completing Harvard on the GI Bill and obtaining a master's degree at the University of Michigan. He had served as a sonarman on a destroyer during the latter part of the war, having enlisted after completing high school in Grafton, Massachusetts. Moving to New York enabled him to escape the repressive background in which he had been raised, and allowed him to live openly as a gay man. But more importantly, perhaps, it placed him in the midst of a flourishing artistic movement that included poets John Ashberry and Kenneth Koch, and painters like Willem de Kooning and Jackson Pollock.

In New York, he got a job at the front desk of the Museum of Modern Art and began writing articles for Art News, at which he worked for a period of time. His initial book, A City Winter and Other Poems, containing two drawings by Larry Rivers, was published by the Tibor de Nagy gallery in 1952, the first in a series of small volumes containing the work of poets and painters. O'Hara also became an active participant in public panels on art and poetry sponsored by the Club, an artists' group. His first large book, Meditations in an Emergency, came out in 1957, and in 1960 both Second Avenue and Odes. Between 1957 and 1960 he collaborated with Rivers on a series of twelve lithographs, Stones, which were created by working directly on the stones from which the lithographs were struck. O'Hara gained national attention when he was featured in the important 1960 anthology, The New American Poetry, 1945–1960, edited by Donald Allen; the book helped bring to the attention of a wider readership the innovative poets of New York, Black Mountain, San Francisco, and in other centers where avant garde, nonacademic verse was being written.

Two more of O'Hara's books of poetry came out before his life was cut short when he was hit and killed by a vehicle on the Fire Island beach. Three more collections were issued posthumously. While he was part of an art scene whose productions were often difficult and abstract, O'Hara's own work is frequently direct and approachable.

WHY I AM NOT A PAINTER

I am not a painter, I am a poet.
Why? I think I would rather be
a painter, but I am not. Well,

for instance, Mike Goldberg
is starting a painting. I drop in.
"Sit down and have a drink" he
says. I drink; we drink. I look
up. "You have SARDINES in it."
"Yes, it needed something there."
"Oh." I go and the days go by
and I drop in again. The painting
is going on, and I go, and the days
go by. I drop in. The painting is
finished. "Where's SARDINES?"
All that's left is just
letters, "It was too much," Mike says.

But me? One day I am thinking of
a color: orange. I write a line
about orange. Pretty soon it is a
whole page of words, not lines.

Then another page. There should be
so much more, not of orange, of
words, of how terrible orange is
and life. Days go by. It is even in
prose, I am a real poet. My poem
is finished and I haven't mentioned
orange yet. It's twelve poems, I call
it ORANGES. And one day in a gallery
I see Mike's painting, called SARDINES.

–1971

KATE DANIELS

(B. 1953)

Daniels has published poetry in many journals, including The Massachusetts Review, Virginia Quarterly Review, *and* Poetry Now. *She was co-
founder and editor of* Poetry East. *Her 1983 book,* The White Wave, *won the
Agnes Lynch Starrett prize and became part of the Pitt poetry series. Her
second book of poetry was entitled* The Niobe Poems, *and her most recent
book is* Four Testimonies: Poems *(1998). She has also co-edited a collection
of essays on the work of Robert Bly (1982), and edited a selection of poems
of Muriel Rukeyser (1992). She has taught at the University of Virginia and
now teaches writing at Louisiana State University.*

SELF-PORTRAIT WITH POLITICS

At the dinner table, my brother says something
Republican he knows I will hate.
He has said it only for me, hoping
I will rise to the argument as I usually do
so he can call me "communist"
and accuse me of terrible things—not loving
the family, hating the country, unsatisfied
with my life. I feel my fingers tighten
on my fork and ask for more creamed potatoes
to give me time to think.

He's right: It's true I am not satisfied
with life. Each time I come home
my brother hates me more for the life
of the mind I have chosen to live.
He works in a factory and can never understand
why I am paid a salary for teaching poetry

just as I can never understand his factory job
where everyone loves or hates the boss like god.
He was so intelligent as a child
his teachers were scared of him.
He did everything well and fast
and then shot rubberbands at the girls' legs
and metal lunchboxes lined up neatly beneath the desks.
Since then, something happened I don't know about.
Now he drives a forklift every day.
He moves things in boxes from one place
to another place. I have never worked
in a factory and can only imagine
the tedium, the thousand escapes
the bright mind must make.

But tonight I will not fight again.
I just nod and swallow and in spite
of everything remember my brother as a child.
When I was six and he was five, I taught him everything
I learned in school each day while we waited for dinner.
I remember his face—smiling always,
the round, brown eyes, and how his lower lip
seemed always wet and ready to kiss.
I remember for a long time his goal in life
was to be a dog, how we were forced
to scratch his head, the pathetic sound
of his human bark. Now he glowers
and acts like a tyrant and cannot eat
and thinks I think
I am superior to him.

The others ignore him as they usually do:
My mother with her bristly hair.
My father just wanting to get back to the TV.
My husband rolling his eyes in a warning at me.

It has taken a long time to get a politics
I can live with in a world that gave me
poetry and my brother an assembly line.
I accept my brother for what he is
and believe in the beauty of work
but also know the reality of waste,
the good minds ground down through circumstance
and loss. I mourn the loss of all I think
he could have been, and this is what he feels,
I guess, and cannot face and hates me
for reminding him of what is gone and wasted
and won't come back.

For once, it's too sad to know all this.
So I give my brother back his responsibility
or blandly blame it all on sociology,
and imagine sadly how it could have been different,
how it will be different for the son I'll bear.
And how I hope in thirty years he'll touch
his sister as they touched as children
and let nothing come between the blood they share.

TODD JAILER

(B. 1956)

Jailer grew up in New Jersey and attended the University of Pittsburgh, from which he graduated in 1978. He worked for the Pittsburgh electric company for 5 years before moving to Boston to become part of the South End Press collective from 1984 to 1989. He then went to El Salvador and worked with the Salvadoran Association of Art and Cultural Workers between 1990 and 1996 to help establish Editorial Sombrero Azul. He is currently publications coordinator at the Hesperian Foundation (Berkeley, CA), producing materials directed toward community health and empowerment. His poems have been published in various magazines and anthologies including Working Classics *and* Paper Work. *His articles have appeared in* Z Magazine *and, in Spanish, in various newspapers and books in El Salvador. His experiences working at the electric company are reflected in his first book of poems, appropriately titled* Power and Light.

THE AESTHETICS OF LINE WORK

We spend all afternoon hanging
the 3-phase bank of transformers.
Notice the flat futuristic curve
of the common neutral, the perfectly
straight 1/ought copper risers
in parallel, the unobtrusive
bulge of the taped connectors.
The lineman squints, hands on
hips, "I'm gonna bring the wife
and kids around to see this
on Sunday," he says, only half
joking.

ROBERT LOUTHAN
(B. 1951)

Louthan was born in Brooklyn and earned a bachelor's degree at Empire State College, a branch of the State University of New York specializing in individualized instruction for nontraditional students. He subsequently took an M.F.A. at Goddard. His books include Shrunken Planets *(1980) and* Living in Code *(1984). His poems have appeared, among other places, in* American Poetry Review, Hudson Review, Paris Review, *and* Partisan Review.

HEAVY MACHINERY

What is poetry for? To tell the man
who has just driven home
too fast from his job at the factory
that what he wants is out of this world,
that the descending sun and materializing moon
weren't installed in his windshield but beyond it,
that his eyes can't fly, that their fluttering lids
are certainly wings but atrophied,
and a steering wheel is the only orbit
he'll ever own? Oh yes. But it should also
give him something consoling to say to the guys
tomorrow at break: no matter how delicate the stars may look
the cosmos is heavy machinery, and much harder to operate
than the kind they work and curse.
And it should tell him the rest: the future
features bedtime, and to go to sleep is to remove
and unfold and let go
of the mind, the levitating blanket.

TOM WAYMAN
(B. 1945)

Probably no writer is more identified with the poetry of work than Wayman. His own writing aside, he has edited three collections of work poems, Beaton Abbot's Got the Contract *(1974),* A Government Job at Last *(1976), and* Going for Coffee *(1981). In addition, he has written two collections of critical essays on the subject,* Inside Job: Essays on the New Work Writing *(1983) and* A Country Not Considered: Canada, Culture, Work *(1993). Much of his own poetry focuses on work, as is illustrated by the title of his third* volume, Free Time: Industrial Poems *(1977). Many of his poems are straightforward narratives about what people do for a living, anecdotes about how their work shapes their lives, and analyses of the ways in which capitalism constrains human possibility.*

Wayman is familiar with forms of industrial labor from personal and family experience. His father, a chemist by training, worked as a technician in a mill in Prince Rupert, British Columbia, before resettling in Vancouver, which has remained Wayman's base. Wayman himself worked construction after obtaining degrees from the University of British Columbia and the University of California/Irvine. He taught at Colorado State University in the late sixties, where he was active in the anti-Vietnam War movement and in other radical causes, joining the Industrial Workers of the World, and writing poems that, among other things, attacked the presence of Dow Chemical recruiters on campus. Wayman has also taught at Wayne State University, the University of Windsor, the Kootenay School of Writing, the University of Alberta in Edmonton, and Simon Fraser University.

Much of his writing is unabashedly political: some of his best work (in the 1975 book and cassette, Money and Rain: Tom Wayman Live!*) is a sequence dedicated to the Chilean government of Salvador Allende, overthrown by general and later dictator Augusto Pinochet with the support of the American CIA. But while Wayman's poetry deals with serious issues, it often does so with a comic touch. He invents a persona, "Wayman," who makes his way through sometimes hilarious misadventures on and off the job, and whose comments, humorous, self-pitying, enraged, express a range of responses to the oppressions of contemporary life. Wayman has collected many of these comic poems in the wonderfully titled* The Nobel Prize Acceptance Speech *(1981) and these and other poems in a selection,* Did I Miss Anything? Selected Poems *(1993).*

THE COUNTRY OF EVERYDAY:
LITERARY CRITICISM

"He was in a hurry," Wood said, "the young foreman
only 26, down on his knees at the base of
the heavy lamppost, impatient to push it back on the block.
He was yelling at the rest of us to give him a hand
and didn't see the top of the pole, as it
swayed over and touched the powerline.

"I was looking right at him. There was a flash
and he just folded over onto his side and
turned black: his ears melted.
There were two holes burned in the pavement
where his knees were. Somebody started giving him
mouth-to-mouth and I said *Forget it. I mean, he's dead.*"

And there are poets who can enter in
to the heart of a door, and discover the rat inside us
that must be kept caged in the head because it is perfectly sane.

There are poets who claim to know what it's like
to have a crucifix wedged in the throat
unable to swallow, and how the knot of the stomach
turns into a bowl of fire.

But around and ahead of them
is the housewife endlessly washing
linoleum, sheets, fruit dishes, her hands
and the face of a child. And there is the girl who stands
in the cannery line twelve hours in season
to cut out the tips of the fish.
For the paper they tear out to write on
is pulled from the weeks of working graveyard
and all the weariness of millwork, the fatigue
of keeping it going, the urge to reclaim the body
for the hours not working or sleeping
when the body ends too tired for much but a beer and a laugh.

Beside every dazzling image, each line
desperate to search the unconscious
are the thousand hours someone is spending
watching ordinary television.
For every poet who considers the rhythm
of the word "dark" and the word "darkness"
a crew is balancing high on the grid
of a new warehouse roof, gingerly taking the first load of lumber
hauled thirty feet up to them.

For every hour someone reads critical articles
Swede is drunk in a bar again
describing how he caught his sleeve once in the winch of an oil rig
whirling him round till his ribs broke.
And for every rejection of a manuscript
a young apprentice is riding up on the crane
to work his first day on high steel.
"Left my fingerprints in the metal
when I had to grab a beam to get off," he says.
And Ed Shaw stands looking down into the hold
where a cable sprang loose lifting a pallet
and lashed across the dock, just touching one of the crew
whose body they are starting to bring up from the water.

When the poet goes out for a walk in the dusk
listening to his feet on the concrete, pondering
all of the adjectives for rain, he is walking on work
of another kind, and on lives that wear down like cement.

Somewhere a man is saying, "Worked twenty years for the City
but I'm retired now."
Sitting alone in a room, in the poorhouse of a pension
he has never read a modern poem.

HELENA MARÍA VIRAMONTES
(B. 1954)

*Viramontes has become one of the most powerful chroniclers of the lives of
Latina/o people in the barrios of increasingly international cities like Los
Angeles. She is herself a product of a working-class family of Mexican immigrants, who settled in East L.A., where she was born, raised, and educated.
She was coordinator of the L.A. Latino Writer's Association as well as literary
editor of* Xhisme Arte *magazine. She obtained an M.F.A. from the University
of California/Irvine and now teaches at Cornell University. Her first volume,*
The Moths and Other Stories *(1985), tracks the often-wrenching experiences
of women coming of age or trying to sustain their humanity within the
frameworks of oppressed immigrant communities. Her story "The Cariboo
Cafe" has become a modern classic, drawing readers into the physical and
psychological horrors destroying the lives both of working-class Anglos and
of refugees from the death squads of Central American military regimes.*

*"Miss Clairol," a story of 1987, is one of her pieces that deals from a
feminist perspective with the troubled relationships between young Latinas
and the Anglo-American culture that negates and marginalizes them. She
has written critically about the kinds of stories she is attempting to create,
as in "Nopalitos: The Making of Fiction" (1989) and in* Chicana Creativity
and Criticism: Charting New Frontiers in American Literature *(1988),
which she co-edited with María Herrera-Sobek. She is a frequent reader and
lecturer both in the United States and particularly in Spanish-speaking
countries. Her most recent collections are* Paris Rats in E.L.A. *(1993), and*
Under the Feet of Jesus *(1995).*

MISS CLAIROL

Arlene and Champ walk to Kmart. The store is full of bins mounted with bargain
buys from T-shirts to rubber sandals. They go to aisle 23, Cosmetics. Arlene, wearing bell-bottom jeans two sizes too small, can't bend down to the Miss Clairol boxes,
asks Champ.

—Which one, *amá?* —asks Champ, chewing her thumb nail.

—Shit, *mija,* I dunno. —Arlene smacks her gum, contemplating the decision. —
Maybe I need a change, *tú sabes.* What do you think? —She holds up a few blond
strands with black roots. Arlene has burned the softness of her hair with peroxide; her
hair is stiff, breaks at the ends, and she needs plenty of Aqua Net hairspray to tease

and tame her ratted hair, then folds it back into a high lump behind her head. For the last few months she has been a platinum "Light Ash" blonde, before that a Miss Clairol "Flame" redhead, before that Champ couldn't even identify the color—somewhere between orange and brown, a "Sun Bronze." The only way Champ knows her mother's true hair color is by her roots, which, like death, inevitably rise to the truth.

—I hate it, *tú sabes,* when I can't decide. —Arlene is wearing a pink, strapless tube top. Her stomach spills over the hiphugger jeans. Spits the gum onto the floor. —Fuck it. —And Champ follows her to the rows of nail polish, next to the Maybelline rack of makeup, across the false eyelashes that look like insects on display in clear, plastic boxes. Arlene pulls out a particular color of nail polish, looks at the bottom of the bottle for the price, puts it back, gets another. She has a tattoo of purple XXX's on her left finger like a ring. She finally settles for a purple-blackish color, Ripe Plum, that Champ thinks looks like the color of Frankenstein's nails. She looks at her own stubby nails, chewed and gnawed.

Walking over to the eye shadows, Arlene slowly slinks out another stick of gum from her back pocket, unwraps and crumbles the wrapper into a little ball, lets it drop on the floor. Smacks the gum.

—Grandpa Ham used to make chains with these gum wrappers —she says, toe-ing the wrapper on the floor with her rubber sandals, her toes dotted with old nail polish. —He started one, *tú sabes,* that went from room to room. That was before he went nuts —she says, looking at the price of magenta eye shadow. —¿*Sabes qué?* What do you think? —lifting the eye shadow to Champ.

—I dunno know —responds Champ, shrugging her shoulders the way she always does when she is listening to something else, her own heartbeat, what Gregorio said on the phone yesterday, shrugs her shoulders when Miss Smith says, OFELIA, answer my question. She is too busy thinking of things people otherwise dismiss like paren-theses, but stick to her like gum, like a hole on a shirt, like a tattoo, and sometimes she wishes she weren't born with such adhesiveness. The chain went from room to room, round and round like a web, she remembers. That was before he went nuts.

—Champ. You listening? Or in la-la land again? —Arlene has her arms akimbo on a fold of flesh, pissed.

—I said, I dunno know—Champ whines back, still looking at the wrapper on the floor.

—Well you better learn, *tú sabes,* and fast too. Now think, will this color go good with Pancha's blue dress? —Pancha is Arlene's *comadre.* Since Arlene has a special date tonight, she lent Arlene her royal blue dress that she keeps in a plastic bag at the end of her closet. The dress is made of chiffon, with satinlike material under-lining, so that when Arlene first tried it on and strutted about, it crinkled sounds of elegance. The dress fits too tight. Her plump arms squeeze through, her hips breathe in and hold their breath, the seams do all they can to keep the body con-tained. But Arlene doesn't care as long as it sounds right.

—I think it will —Champ says, and Arlene is very pleased.

—Think so? So do I, *mija.*

They walk out the double doors and Champ never remembers her mother paying.

It is four in the afternoon, but already Arlene is preparing for the date. She scrubs the tub, Art Labo on the radio, drops crystals of Jean Naté into the running water, lemon scent rises with the steam. The bathroom door ajar, she removes her top and her breasts flop and sag, pushes her jeans down with some difficulty, kicks them off, and steps in the tub.

—*Mija. MIJA* —she yells. —*Mija,* give me a few bobby pins. —She is worried about her hair frizzing and so wants to pin it up.

Her mother's voice is faint because Champ is in the closet. There are piles of clothes on the floor, hangers thrown askew and tangled, shoes all piled up or thrown on the top shelf. Champ is looking for her mother's special dress. Pancha says every girl has one at the end of her closet.

—Goddamn it, Champ.

Amidst the dirty laundry, the black hole of the closet, she finds nothing.

—NOW.

—Alright, ALRIGHT. Cheeze *amá,* stop yelling —says Champ, and goes in the steamy bathroom, checks the drawers, hairbrushes jump out, rollers, strands of hair, rummages through bars of soap, combs, eye shadows, finds nothing; pulls open another drawer, powder, empty bottles of oil, manicure scissors, Kotex, dye instructions crinkled and botched, finally, a few bobby pins.

After Arlene pins up her hair, she asks Champ, —*¿Sabes qué?* Should I wear my hair up? Do I look good with it up? — Champ is sitting on the toilet.

—Yea, *amá, you* look real pretty.

—Thanks, *mija* —says Arlene. —*¿Sabes qué?* When you get older I'll show you how you can look just as pretty —and she puts her head back, relaxes, like the Calgon commercials.

Champ lies on her stomach, TV on to some variety show with pogo-stick dancers dressed in outfits of stretchy material and glitter. She is wearing one of Gregorio's white T-shirts, the ones he washes and bleaches himself so that the whiteness is impeccable. It drapes over her deflated ten-year-old body like a dress. She is busy cutting out Miss Breck models from the stacks of old magazines Pancha found in the back of her mother's garage. Champ collects the array of honey-colored-haired women, puts them in a shoe box with all her other special things.

Arlene is in the bathroom, wrapped in a towel. She has painted her eyebrows so that the two are arched and even, penciled thin and high. The magenta shades her eyelids. The towel slips, reveals one nipple blind from a cigarette burn, a date to forget. She rewraps the towel, likes her reflection, turns to her profile for additional inspection. She feels good, turns up the radio to . . . your love. For your loveeeee, I will do anything, I will do anything, forrr your love. For your kiss . . .

Champ looks on. From the open bathroom door, she can see Arlene, anticipation burning like a cigarette from her lips, sliding her shoulders to the ahhhh ahhhhh, and pouting her lips until the song ends. And Champ likes her mother that way.

Arlene carefully stretches black eyeliner, like a fallen question mark, outlines each eye. The work is delicate, her hand trembles cautiously, stops the process to review the face with each line. Arlene the mirror is not Arlene the face who has worn too many relationships, gotten too little sleep. The last touch is the chalky, beige lipstick.

By the time she is finished, her ashtray is full of cigarette butts, Champ's variety show is over, and Jackie Gleason's dancing girls come on to make kaleidoscope patterns with their long legs and arms. Gregorio is still not home, and Champ goes over to the window, checks the houses, the streets, corners, roams the sky with her eyes.

Arlene sits on the toilet, stretches up her nylons, clips them to her girdle. She feels good thinking about the way he will unsnap her nylons, and she will unroll them slowly, point her toes when she does.

Champ opens a can of Campbell soup, finds a perfect pot in the middle of a stack of dishes, pulls it out to the threatening rumbling of the tower. She washes it out, pours the contents of the red can, turns the knob. After it boils, she puts the pan on the sink for it to cool down. She searches for a spoon.

Arlene is romantic. When Champ begins her period, she will tell her things that only women can know. She will tell her about the first time she made love with a boy, her awkwardness and shyness forcing them to go under the house, where the cool, refined soil made a soft mattress. How she closed her eyes and wondered what to expect, or how the penis was the softest skin she had ever felt against her, how it tickled her, searched for a place to connect. She was eleven and his name was Harry.

She will not tell Champ that her first fuck was a guy named Puppet who ejaculated prematurely, at the sight of her apricot vagina, so plump and fuzzy. —*Pendejo* —she said —you got it all over me. —She rubbed the gooey substance off her legs, her belly, in disgust. Ran home to tell Rat and Pancha, her mouth open with laughter.

Arlene powder-puffs under her arms, between her breasts, tilts a bottle of Love Cries perfume and dabs behind her ears, neck and breasts for those tight caressing songs which permit them to grind their bodies together until she can feel a bulge in his pants and she knows she's in for the night.

Jackie Gleason is a bartender in a saloon. He wears a black bow tie, a white apron, and is polishing a glass. Champ is watching him, sitting in the radius of the gray light, eating her soup from the pot.

Arlene is a romantic. She will dance until Pancha's dress turns a different color, dance until her hair becomes undone, her hips jiggering and quaking beneath a new pair of hosiery, her mascara shadowing under her eyes from the perspiration of the ritual dance, spinning herself into Miss Clairol, and stopping only when it is time to return to the sewing factory, time to wait out the next date, time to change hair color. Time to remember or to forget.

Champ sees Arlene from the window. She can almost hear Arlene's nylons rubbing against one another, hear the crinkling sound of satin when she gets in the blue and white shark-finned Dodge. Champ yells goodbye. It all sounds so right to Arlene, who is too busy cranking up the window to hear her daughter.

SUE DORO

(B. 1937)

In this prose poem Doro, with a good deal of humor, traces the tensions between literary and factory work. (For biographical information about Doro, see the headnote in Section III.)

THE CULTURAL WORKER

The poem waited for her outside the wheel shop door in the Menomonee Valley train yard. Waited, as if it were one of the countless raw cast-iron train wheels propped upright against the factory wall in the moonlight. Train wheels in long, neat rows leaning like round rusty-brown, 500-pound dominoes. Train wheels waiting to be machined.

So too, the poem waited. It had been waiting for her to finish work since 3:30 that afternoon. Now it was midnight. Soon she would step out of second shift into the dark of the going home night.

Hours ago in the early evening, the summer sun hung low and rosy over side-tracked freight cars in the yard. The poem had gone to look in the window nearest the machine the woman was operating that night. The poem thought that the sunset would surely get her attention. But then it saw her leaning across the table of a boring-mill machine, measuring inside the hub of a freight car wheel with her micrometer. She was straining on tiptoes to reach across the machine's table to the wheel's freshly cut center, and the poem could see she was too busy to be thinking poem words, so it did what it knew how to do.

It waited.

Measuring minutes against the sun's shadows on the dirty cream-colored brick wall, it waited. When five o'clock break time arrived, it waited and watched through a different window as the woman ate half her sandwich sitting at the lunch table by the men's locker room. She was sharing a newspaper and conversation with some of her coworkers. She kept on talking as she reached under the table to feed a bit of cheese to a dusty yellow, scrawny factory cat that grabbed the scrap of food in its mouth and bolted away.

The woman was the only female in the shop, and there were nights when she was lonely for the company of other women. But tonight the poem saw she was having a good time, laughing and joking with her work "buddies."

It was an hour and a half later when the poem checked in again. The woman was standing at the same machine working on a different wheel, listening intently to a short leathery-faced man with a chin full of gray quarter-inch whiskers. He wore a work-scratched green hard hat low over his dark eyes. His hands hung at his sides, glistening with soiled brown train bearing grease. In one hand he held a red-handled putty knife used to scrape lard-like gobs of grease off old train bearings. In his other hand, by their cuffs, he grasped a pair of oily black rubber gloves. The ring finger was missing on that hand. A cigarette bobbed up and down in his lips as he spoke, its ashes dusting the man's brown shirt every so often. The poem moved in closer to hear the conversation above the roar and clatter of the machine. It could catch only a few of the man's mumbling phrases: "love her . . . the kids don't talk . . . need more time." The woman was concentrating on the man's hesitant sentences with one eye on the boring-mill's cutting tool, ready to slap the stop button and flip the lever that pulled the cutting bar out of the wheel's center.

The poem went back to wait at the door until dinner break.

In summer, it was still light at eight o'clock in the evening when the break whistle blew, and the poem knew that the woman would go outside to relax on the long bench against the building. Most of the other second shifters would travel up the hill to the tavern, so she was generally alone. Some evenings after eating the rest of her saved sandwich, she'd take a stroll along the railroad tracks heading under the nearby freeway.

The walk was quiet and calming except for the faint rumble of cars far overhead. And if she walked a little further, the traffic noise faded completely. There was a small stream at that end of the valley, and a hill where she'd sit and gaze at the water, listening to it ripple over rocks and chunks of cement. Wildflowers grew along the riverbanks. In springtime there were baby asparagus plants and tiny green onions hidden in the tall, waving grass. Once when she brought a spray of yellow daisies back to the shop, one of the guys found and washed a mayonnaise jar to use as a vase. The flowers lit up the tool bench by the window, and everyone that passed by that night stopped to smell the daisies or to comment on the display. She was pleasantly surprised and happy that not one man teased her about it.

Other evenings found the woman writing in her journal. But tonight there was neither a walk nor journal writing happening at dinner break, and she wasn't alone. When the poem came around the corner of the building, it saw her leaning forward on the bench, holding a small open book and flipping through its pages. She referred to certain passages by tapping the index finger of her right hand on the page while she and a group of seven or eight men seemed to be talking at the same time: "contract . . . bargaining . . . Chicago . . . layoffs in July . . . four guys fired . . . bankruptcy . . . they can't . . . it's illegal . . . they'll try." The poem decided it was fruitless to try to get into her head. Then the sound of a factory whistle pierced the air, and moments later a foreman appeared in the doorway motioning everyone back to work.

The sun was beginning to slide down behind the freeway overpass. The poem stayed outside.

At ten o'clock the poem looked in the window by the woman again. She was staring out into the deep blackness of the night without even noticing the poem. Her eyes were taking in moonlight silhouettes of axles, train wheels, and oil drums. She watched three crows gliding like slow motion, velvet shadows in front of a glowing pink yard light—one of the many fifty-foot-tall globes illuminating the train yard. A shop-cat scampered over a discarded train bearing lying in the grass at the base of the pole. A warm west wind brushed the woman's cheek. She sniffed the air, smiling a little, and the poem thought for a moment that she was thinking poem thoughts. She wasn't. She was simply relieved that the night smelled of sweet Menomonee Valley city wilderness thanks to the west wind, instead of the stockyards to the east of the wheel shop.

"A few more wheels," she commented aloud to no one in particular, and then turned away from the window. Thoughts of home and her sleeping family filled her with a flash of emotion—God, how she missed them on night shift. She shrugged her shoulders, shivering at the same time, like a cat shaking off water. Then she attacked the unfinished wheel in the machine with the frenzy of someone who wished to believe her own speed could control the clock.

And finally it was minutes away from midnight. A full moon waited high over the factory roof like a white ball with a golden ring, outshining any stars. Pink lights cast shadows on the path next to the tracks. The entire train yard was a watercolored wash of pink and black. The poem waited with the moon, holding its breath.

The woman was usually the first ready to leave because her locker was in the bathroom of the foreman's office near the door. On other nights she waited to walk to the parking lot with the guys; however, tonight felt different to her as she stepped out ahead of the whistle.

She was short, but her shadow was ten feet tall. She carried a paper sack of dirty work clothes. The poem was with her like another shadow, walking quickly. The farther away she got from the building, the taller her shadow grew, from the yard lights and the moon on her shoulders. Little rocks and pebbles at her feet crunched under her shoes. Each pebble had its own rosy shadow, like pink moon rocks under her feet. She smiled to herself, relishing the moment.

A cat meowed from the path ahead, scurrying away from the woman's flying feet. Stopping abruptly, the cat turned its head to stare back at her, its yellow eyes frozen in black midair. Then it disappeared under a parked freight car.

Night birds called in the distance.

Now her shadow split in two, growing taller, taller, taller. Racing past more pink lights. Stepping nimbly across one, two, three sets of train tracks. Passing flatbed cars stacked with unmachined axles and rows of wheels. Past lines of mounted wheel and axle sets waiting to be shipped out.

A lone crow cawed at her from a telephone wire. Something stirred in her brain. Some disjointed words seemed to come together. She laughed aloud, and the crow cawed again, leaving its perch to soar over her head into the blackness beyond the realm of pink lights. For a fleeting second she saw its dark wings gleam with a blush of pink. Then suddenly the woman threw back her head and shouted up into the pink and black sky. "HEY. . . I'm a midnight rider. A cat's eye glider. I'm a second shift mother goin' home!"

She laughed again. Surprised and delighted, the poem jumped *inside her* like a fetus kicking in the ninth month. She hurried along, faster now, running the last few yards past the guard shanty.

Finally, she was at her car in the parking lot. She plopped her dirty work clothes on the car hood to pull her keys out of her pocket. She unlocked the door, opened it, and flung the sack into the backseat. Jumping in, she started the car, revved its engine, put the car in gear, and aimed the old '68 Ford out of the lot. She saw the other workers, just then crossing the tracks, waving at her, and she beeped her car horn a couple times in response.

Now she would have time for herself. A smile, glorious as a weekend, spread across her face. She felt the uneasy urgency she'd buried deep inside all night leave her in a great, earthmoving sigh as she drove through the open gate and turned up the road to the ramp leading from the valley.

And a poem was born, comfortable as a well-fitting work shoe, satisfying as the end of the work day. The poem. The woman. The mother. The machinist. All became one. And she sang to the hum of her car:

> *I'm a midnight rider*
> *A cat's eye glider*
> *A second shift mother goin' home.*
>
> *I'm a moon rock walker*
> *A pink bird stalker*
> *A short tall shadow headin' home.*

I'm a cool old river
A seasoned survivor
I'm a factory workin' poet goin' home.

MICHAEL L. JOHNSON

Johnson teaches English at the University of Kansas. He has written or edited a number of books on the West and about education. The former include Violence and Grace: Poems About the American West *(1993) and* New Westers: The West in Contemporary American Culture *(1996). With G. Douglas Atkins and Nancy R. Comley, he has edited* Writing and Reading Differently: Deconstruction and the Teaching of Composition and Literature *(1985), and he has written a book on critical pedagogy and other educational issues in the United States* Education on the Wild Side: Learning for the Twenty-First Century *(1993). He also has been writing about growing up in the midwest.*

COWBOY POEM

This poem rises before dawn;
guzzles strong coffee; gobbles eggs
over easy with bacon, grits,
biscuits, and red-eye gravy; then
begins its day of lonely work:
riding the line on the mind's ranch,
keeping the words under its charge
on home range, pulling them from bogs,
tending to their various ills,
protecting them from predators.

This poem in the saddle goes
dashing, rolls its own smokes, sometimes
may need to take its guns to town.

This poem has an evening sip
of whiskey, ponders the long view,
sleeps in a shack under clear stars.

This poem has a quick and wry
sense of humor, gets the job done,
dallies its rope, dallies its tongue.

JIM DANIELS

(B. 1956)

(For biographical information about Daniels, see the headnote in Section II.)

MAY'S POEM

"I want to write a poem
about something beautiful,"
I tell May, the cook.
On my break from the grill
I stand against the open kitchen door
getting stoned.

"That shit make you stupid."
May wrinkles her forehead
in waves of disapproval.

"I don't need to be smart
to work here."
The grease sticks to my skin
a slimy reminder
of what my future holds.

"I thought you was gonna be
a writer. What about that
beautiful poem?"

I take a long hit
and pinch out the joint.
"You'll end up no good
like my boy Gerald."

"May, I'm gonna make you
a beautiful poem." I say
and I turn and grab her
and hug her to me
pick her up
and twirl her in circles
our sweaty uniforms sticking
together, her large breasts
heaving in my face
as she laughs and laughs
and the waitresses all come back

and the dishwasher who never smiles
makes a noise that could be
half a laugh.

But she's heavy
and I have to put her down.
The manager stands there:
"Play time's over. Break's over."
Everyone walks away
goes back to work.

This isn't my beautiful poem, I know.
My poem would have no manager
no end to breaks.
My poem would have made her lighter.
My poem would have never put her down.

ELMO MONDRAGON

*Mondragon grew up in a small village near Taos, New Mexico. Though he
has written extensively and frequently read his work, he has published little.*

WHY I AM A POET

My craft is the emotions. The ship I build
Is intended for starry nights and open water.
Nights where barefoot sailors stand and wonder
How will it end? Will we ever see the earth again?
The drift beneath our feet carries us to our deaths
And to blossom teeming shores beautiful beyond our imagination.
It is the work of my hands.
Carpenter hands my father gave me
Call to every piece of work
To the fruit and labor of this earth:
Here, rest here, in my palms.
Each strike, every flail, a tenderness.
I will build, will strike and shape
Will nudge and nestle to their peak
The startled doves of your emotion.
I will take your breath away.

Appendix

WRITING ABOUT
LITERATURE AND
CULTURE

This section of the book focuses on the relationship between critical thinking and effective writing. It provides an important linkage between the kinds of critical reading and interpretation skills and the necessary role that writing plays for thinking about literature and social issues.

It offers ideas, guidelines, strategies, and working principles for writing about literature. This appendix will accompany all the books in the Longman Literature and Culture series *(Literature and the Environment: A Reader on Nature and Culture; Literature, Culture, and Class: A Thematic Anthology; Literature, Race, and Ethnicity: Contested American Identities; Literature and Gender: Thinking Critically Through Fiction, Poetry, and Drama)*, a series devoted to reading and thinking critically in ways that promote exploration and discovery. Writing about literature furthers these goals of critical analysis.

What I have attempted to do is focus on innovative approaches that will help you better analyze and understand the exciting and perhaps somewhat unfamiliar territory of writing about literature. I will begin by describing good writing—that is, writing that stays in the mind and positively influences readers. Next, I will offer some principles that underlie successful academic writing generally and critical work in literature classes more specifically. After that, I will discuss what it means to read for meaning, suggest how to get ready for class discussions, and then move to a consideration of the writing process with a particular focus on purpose, audience, drafting, and revising. Since one of the chief difficulties many writers face is "the blank page syndrome," I particularly address the problem of getting started on a writing project. The next section examines the various elements that comprise an essay, its various components. I then move to a brief consideration of the computer, with a particular focus on both word processing and electronic researching. Finally,

I offer a brief guide to research, with a listing of some of the most common biblio-graphic entries according to the Modern Language Association format.

WHAT IS GOOD WRITING?

Let's begin with some general principles that apply to all good academic writing. Many students equate academic writing with boredom, stuffiness, and abstraction. From their perspective, only academics write—and read—academic writing, which most others find dull, dry, and abstract. Now there is no doubt that writing of this kind exists, but most of it is not good writing, academic or otherwise.

Good writing has energy, clarity, and a liveliness of mind. It creates satisfaction by enlightening and persuading. It asks writers to place themselves at risk since they are making their ideas public. It changes minds because it illuminates its subject in a new light. It explores ideas thoughtfully, drawing upon research and other forms of evidence to persuade the reader.

Good writing has economy: it offers a thoughtful, efficient route toward increased understanding. No reader likes to read an essay that digresses or uses 35 words to state a 15-word idea. You may be assigned an essay with a required length, for exam-ple "Write a 2500-word essay that argues for a specific environmental policy to pre-serve western wilderness." Such essays can be challenging since students sometimes think they have to pad them to get the necessary words. This procedure is ill advised; no essay profits from repetition or flabby style. In this situation, the only choice is to do more reading, researching, and analyzing—subjects I will consider shortly.

Good writing leaves the author with a sense of accomplishment and satisfaction. Writing a passing essay may be easy, but unless writers are engaged in the hard struggle with the text and with their writing process, they are unlikely to experience a meaningful sense of accomplishment. Take your internal pulse after you complete an essay. Do you like it? Do you feel that it succeeds? Are you glad to have written it? Are you aware of your struggles, frustrations, and accomplishments? If you can answer "yes" to these questions, you stand a good chance of success. Good writing reveals insights that are often as surprising to the writer as they are to the reader. Good writing packs a punch. It stays in the memory. It makes a difference.

Although there is no single formula for good writing, certain general truths apply. First, writers need to capture their excitement, passion, and intellectual com-mitment. If a writer lacks those qualities—that is, writes simply to get done or to fill blank pages—the writing almost always is lackluster. Many times, writers get stuck and cannot complete a good draft, or work for hours and then throw up their hands in despair. If they possess an emotional and intellectual desire to produce a good piece of work, however, half the battle is won. They will try again, revise, seek the help of a teacher or tutor, research the subject more extensively, experiment, and otherwise redouble their effort. Most writers do not produce good first drafts, but if they care about the writing, they find ways to make it into something worth reading.

Good writing thus requires both time and effort. Even a short assignment ("Write a 500-word essay that explores why you think America is—or is not—a classless society") makes significant demands on any writer: time and effort to think, read, reflect, procrastinate, get started and get nowhere, draft, revise, edit, proofread. Few writers, be they students or professionals, can dash off two or three quick pages and achieve satisfying results.

Good writing generally exhibits active and descriptive verbs that perform "work" for the writer. Thus, instead of stating "John McPhee is a good writer and is my favorite author," try "John McPhee writes well and remains my favorite author" or "John McPhee is my favorite author because he writes so well" or "John McPhee, my favorite author, writes so well that reading one of his books is like seeing a movie" or some other version. Note the differences among these sentences: the ways that verbs get changed, altering sentence structure and meaning as well. Lackluster writing can often be traced to overdependence on the verb "to be" in its various forms: "am," "is," "are," "was," "were," "be," "been." If your writing is flat, examine it for overuse of the various "to be" verbs and try to find meaningful, accurate replacements.

Good writing conveys new information to readers. At first glance, this seems to pose a problem: after all, how can you write something "new" about literature when your instructor knows so much more? Although instructors do possess considerable knowledge, they by no means know everything about an essay, story, poem, drama, author, or subject. In fact, their love of literature can make them easy to write for, since they enjoy learning more. The key is to convey new information: an interpretation supported by quotes, analysis, and research; a historical exploration of a work or author; an argument about the meaning or significance of a literary subject; a personal assessment of why or how a literary work affects you; a well-documented research paper; and so on. Instructors respond positively to student work that teaches them something, that changes their interpretations, adds to their knowledge, or improves their appreciation. When students accomplish one or more of those objectives, they produce "good writing."

READING FOR MEANING

To be able to write, you—like any good writer—must find something to say. Too often, students receive an assignment and produce a quick and visceral response (sometimes just before class). One important key to succeeding in a literature class is to learn how to engage in sustained inquiry—that is, learning how to read for meaning and asking questions that lead toward improved understanding. Most literary works are sufficiently complex that at first they often frustrate readers. Success in this class will depend on learning how to read well.

Typically, we read to gain information. That is why we read many textbooks, newspapers, magazines, instructions, and the like. The kind of reading required in an English literature or composition course, however, requires a different set of strategies. Although most of us first read a story, essay, poem, or drama to find out what happens—that is, to gain some information and knowledge of how the "story" will end—the primary intent of literature is not simply to provide readers with information or a plot. Rather, its purpose is to give pleasure, to offer multiple possibilities for interpretation, to surprise, to shock, to amaze, to alter the reader's thinking. Works such as the ones in this book offer *more* than information, and figuring out that "more" takes effort, time, and critical analysis.

Here are some practical strategies and suggestions for how to get the most out of the selections in this anthology:

Sound Reading Strategies

1. Read when your concentration is at its peak. Many people do their reading when they are tired or distracted. They read at work or during television commercials. This is fine if you are skimming for information or pleasure—reading a newspaper, magazine, or the comic page, for example—but the selections in this book demand concentration. You need to read when you are focused and full of energy, alert and clear eyed.

2. Read for pleasure first. During your first time through a text, read for enjoyment. Every author in this book intends to give you pleasure—to make you enjoy exploring and analyzing ideas, language, form, structure, style, arguments.

3. Read actively, not passively. As you read, stop occasionally and imagine what will happen on the next page or in the next section; such a process helps to involve you in the ebb and flow of the text. Stop, occasionally, to write down your prediction, your emerging interpretation, your view of why you think the author wrote this work, what its strengths and weaknesses are. Compare your responses to those of your classmates.

4. Reread. Read the first time for pleasure; read the second time for increased understanding. Most of the selections in this anthology present complicated ideas in complicated ways; the reader's job is to figure out what the selection means beyond the obvious. How does the writer make her/his points? What kinds of similes, metaphors, and other figurative language does the writer use? Are there contradictions and paradoxes? What choices does the writer make—and why? Are the writer's arguments convincing and well supported? These kinds of questions often can only be answered through rereading.

5. Take notes. Underline passages that are memorable, surprising, confusing, provocative—that provoke a personal response. Opposite each underlined passage, write a marginal comment explaining why you underlined the passage, such as:

   "what is she saying here?"
   "why does he stumble—symbolic?"
   "empty purse—are they also empty emotionally?"
   "this desert is real but it is also symbolic of her despair"
   "who benefited from the slave trade?"
   "I can feel the author's love of his family here" etc.

   These comments along with the underlinings point the way toward a good, critical essay. Most importantly, they provide a written record of thoughts and impressions, some of which you may otherwise lose.

6. Discuss. Although reading is a solitary activity, understanding improves when students share interpretations. All readers bring their own experiences

to a text, their own strengths, weaknesses, experiences, insights, and blind spots. Perhaps the most important aspect of discussion is learning how to listen, comprehend, and respond thoughtfully. Listening is a parallel activity to reading; it requires us to be attentive and to work hard at understanding someone else's point of view.

GETTING READY FOR CLASS DISCUSSION

Class discussion is almost always a crucial and fundamental element of a literature or composition class. Most of us both enjoy and learn better when we engage in focused, thoughtful discussion with our peers. Aside from reading and rereading the assignment, certain other habits and practices can improve the quality of class conversation. What follows are some suggestions and strategies for preparing yourself to discuss literature in this class and the others you might take.

- Bring your textbook and notes to class. This may seem like obvious common-sense advice, but surprisingly many students do not follow it. It is especially important to have the text handy when enrolled in a class that focuses on literature, because frequently in discussion students need to quote from the assigned text in order to provide support for a comment or clarify an interpretation. Since many students (and faculty, for that matter) write marginal notes in the text as they read, they have an additional reason for wanting the book handy—namely, for ready reference.

- Do not read any out-of-class assignments in class. One of the fastest ways to sour instructors is if they observe you reading the assignment at your desk rather than participating in class activities. Bring your text, have it ready, but use it only for reference or clarification, unless instructed otherwise.

- Take notes. Both lecture and class discussion often produce creative and surprising insights. They trigger important questions that can lead directly to an essay or term paper. When that happens, it is crucial to write them down so that they can be remembered and reconsidered. Some faculty have been known to stop discussion in the middle of class in order to take hurried notes on something that was said. Students should do the same. Aside from having a record of useful comments, taking notes has the added benefit of focusing one's attention more on the discussion, thus keeping the mind from wandering off while others speak.

- Listen carefully. One of the best ways to improve listening is to write down a brief, succinct summary of what someone has said once he or she has finished. This technique is, of course, a form of note-taking. As others in the class speak, good listeners work hard to understand what they are saying and how it improves understanding of the text.

- In a class that centers on literature, discussion usually does not center on factual material ("In what year did Frederick Douglass first publish his autobiography?" "Who was Mother Jones?"). That kind of information, which is very important in terms of knowledge and mastery, is usually presented in a short lecture by the instructor or is something you are expected to learn through reading and outside research. Rather, most class discussions emphasize interpretation, analysis, and argumentation ("Consider the concept of family in Gwendolyn Brooks's poem, 'Mother.'" "What images and associations of the city does Tom Wolfe invoke in 'O Rotten Gotham'—and what effect do they have on you as a reader?"). Meaningful class discussion requires not only offering an interpretation or analysis, but providing support if others in the class disagree. When class discussion goes well, it is usually because reasonable and thoughtful readers express differing interpretations and explanations equally supported by careful textual analysis.

- Be ready to explain yourself. The key to illuminating discussions is not just offering an opinion about a work of literature; it is possessing the knowledge and information to explain it. To do this, a reader should constantly be asking "why?" and then discovering the answer. For example, if a poem makes you feel exalted, it is important to know why and then pinpoint the language, ideas, and arguments that produce this result. Responses to literature are created through a combination of author intent, literary form and structure, social and historical contexts, the reader's personal history, and other factors. Thoughtful class participants learn how to explain themselves and their interpretations.

- Let others speak. When only the instructor or a few students dominate discussion, class soon becomes a bore. Although many instructors like to present short lectures in order to provide information efficiently, class discussion can only succeed if everyone limits his or her time and no one dominates. If you find yourself talking too much or too often, learn to love silence. Quite often, reticent students will begin to speak and participate if the "natural talkers" in the class restrain themselves.

- Be succinct. Students and teachers alike zone out when someone makes the same point repeatedly. Once you say it, don't repeat it. To say the same thing again and again is boring and repetitious—even redundant—even when there is slight variation. Like this paragraph.

- Focus. As you read an assignment, you may discover an interpretation or come up with questions. If so, write them out and bring them with you to class. Many instructors will welcome such written comments and provide class time for discussing them.

- Change the perspective from which you read and interpret the assignment. Put yourself in the place of the author: try to think why she wrote it, what she intended, why she made specific choices. Insert yourself in the role of a character or even that of a reviewer or critic. Write down your comments for use in class.

- Remember that not all interpretations or analyses are equally persuasive or insightful, but that does not mean they lack value, at least to the individual who offers them. This does not mean that anything goes; rather, that interpretation and analysis is a negotiation involving the reader, the author, the text, the class, historical circumstance, and the world of literary criticism. One of the major purposes of class discussion is to provide students and instructors with a rich and reasonable forum in which to test their hypotheses and participate in a collaborative give-and-take about meaning and understanding.

THE WRITING PROCESS

Preliminary Steps

Different writers write differently, and all writers must strive to find the composing process that best suits their needs. Professional writers demonstrate the diversity of composing processes. John McPhee, for example, plans extensively and creates an elaborate structure for his essays and books. This planning process can be extremely laborious, but once he develops the structure (which might take days, weeks, or longer), it provides a framework for the actual writing (and rewriting) that follows. When Jamaica Kincaid writes, she often spends a great deal of time deliberating and choosing. She might write down just one word in an hour, but once that word is on paper she knows it is the right one and seldom if ever changes it. Richard Selzer writes out of a sense almost of compulsion. He pours out many pages of prose every day longhand in his notebooks, only a small fraction of which ever makes its way to print. None of these writers would choose to follow the composing process of any other; what they do works for them.

The pages that follow offer a variety of approaches to writing, not all of which are likely to work for any one student. Even the order is somewhat arbitrary; my "Step One" might be someone else's "Step Four." What all writers must do is experiment, particularly if they are having trouble writing or are not achieving desired results. Although there is no one right way to write, there are wrong ways that can get someone stuck and frustrated. All writers, however, can alter their ways of composing and make the process more efficient and productive; it just takes time, practice, and the will to change.

Step One: Establish a Sense of Purpose

Frequently, instructors establish an outcome for their students in the assignment itself. For example:

> Analyze the metaphors that Barry Lopez uses to describe wilderness in his essay "The Stone Horse." In your essay, be sure to cite at least three metaphors and discuss their appropriateness to his themes of tenderness and fragility.

This instructor wants students to analyze Lopez's use of metaphors and offer reasons why they are—or are not—appropriate to two major themes in his work. Some students might prefer to write personal responses, but however satisfying to the writer, they are unlikely to fulfill the instructor's purpose (and will probably receive a poor grade).

Some instructors assign essays that allow more individual choice:

> Respond to Tillie Olsen's "I Stand Here Ironing." Can you relate your own experiences as either a parent or a child to this fictional monologue? In your essay, be sure and discuss who this speaker is—that is, describe in your own terms the speaker's values, feelings, and sense of self. Your essay should be at least 600 words, typed, and should include quotations from the story to support your interpretation.

This assignment asks students to present a written response, without specifying content. Students can write a personal reflection or an impersonal analysis, but they must analyze the speaker of the story in an essay of at least 600 typed words and include appropriate supporting quotations.

Whatever the assignment, students need to establish their own sense of purpose and commitment to their readers. Otherwise the writing becomes perfunctory.

Step Two: Analyze Your Audience's Expectations

Although audiences can vary, in most cases you will write essays that will be read by your instructor. My focus will thus be on writing for the teacher. Knowing that an essay is intended for an instructor does not necessarily help you successfully address this audience. What is more important is that your work satisfy the instructor's expectations. How can you accomplish this? Here are some suggestions.

- Study the assignment carefully and make sure that you understand what the instructor is asking you to do. Look for key words and phrases, especially those that are underlined or in boldface. Most assignments clearly state the instructor's expectations.
- Stuck? Then visit your instructor. A short conversation with an instructor can both clarify the situation and bolster confidence.
- Determine whether your instructor wants your essay to be a demonstration of knowledge (a synthesis of class discussion, an informed discussion of the ways a particular theory applies to a particular set of readings); a factual presentation (historical, biographical, a report); an interpretation (what a work means, why a student believes the meaning of the text to be "X"); an appreciation (why this work is so powerful and enduring); or something else. Asking detailed questions about expectations either in class or during an instructor's office hours is essential.
- Consider the assignment a form of conversation, of dialogue with the instructor. An essay offers each student an opportunity to have the instructor's exclusive attention. Successful essays engage readers because they bring a writer and reader together; they are a medium for the exchange of ideas.
- Try to state something new. Think of your audience as someone who is willing to try out your ideas and be surprised and informed by what you have to say. Instructors enjoy having their understanding and appreciation of a literary work enhanced because of something a student has written.
- Avoid plot summary. Because they want to learn something when they read student essays, most instructors do not like plot summary. When writing, assume that the reader already has read the work you are discussing. Plot summary is usually a surefire way to bore a reader—and write a pedestrian essay in the process.

Step Three: Draw On Your Resources

Student Resource List:

- conversations with other students in the class or others who have an interest in the topic

- the local Writing Center, where tutors can help you think through your subject, goals, possibilities, frustrations, structure, focus, and all the other aspects of writing
- the instructor, who is one of the best resources for getting comfortable with a topic and figuring out the best way to proceed
- the library research database, where you can look up primary material (that is, other works that the author has written, historical materials composed at the same time as the subject you are writing about) or secondary sources (books and articles written about your subject)
- electronic conversations over the Internet
- Web pages, which can be particularly helpful if you are researching a contemporary subject

Step Four: Start Early

The time to start writing an essay is immediately after an instructor hands out an assignment. The worst case scenario is to delay the writing until the day before it is due. To put it bluntly, this is a prescription for disaster.

Good ideas need to simmer. They need to be reflected upon, revised, researched, and explored. This takes time. Delay often results in ill-conceived work. Waiting too long to start can create a host of problems for writers, including: disliking what one has written but not having the time to change it; discovering that essential research materials are missing, stolen, or otherwise out of circulation; getting sick or stuck; or even deciding that one's argument no longer makes sense. There is no reason to have to create a panic situation every time a writing assignment is given.

Instead, good writers start early. That way, if something goes wrong, as it inevitably does in some situations, there is time to make adjustments.

Step Five: Share

Most professional writers share their work as they write: they produce a page or two, bring that work home, and read it to someone they trust to give an honest response. Students need to share their writing as well, and many instructors will create that possibility by setting up a rough draft workshop in the classroom or by reading drafts. Many times, an outside reader (not a roommate, spouse, or parent) can best tell a writer when an essay is making sense, where more support is needed, where the work is gaining or losing focus. Such readings can make a huge difference in the success of an essay; almost always, they provide a valuable road map for revision. Take advantage of this opportunity; it can make a world of difference.

Step Six: Revise

Virtually all successful writers spend the great majority of their time not drafting but revising, not writing but rewriting. In general, writing an essay is messy: It demands that writers explore a variety of ideas, go off on various tangents, explore various research sources, find appropriate examples and quotations, etc. As you write at this early stage, it is important not to spend much time editing and revising. Writing at this drafting stage should lead you forward; editing and revising are activities that require you constantly to look backward.

Only after you have finally produced a significant mass of words and ideas is it time to start pulling your essay together. This is revision: refocusing, deleting the unnecessary and repetitious, finding additional examples, cutting and pasting (using the computer, I hope), refining the essay so that it achieves its purpose. Sometimes revision means substantially changing the original; sometimes it means throwing out everything but two or three sentences! Whatever form it takes, revision is almost always the key to producing successful final essays.

Step Seven: Work Appropriately

At different points in the writing process, some kinds of attention are appropriate and others ill-advised. It is important to recognize that a first or second draft of an essay is just that: a draft. It is likely to have a variety of problems with focus, word usage, syntax, support, and other elements. Early in the composing process, writers need to concentrate on global issues: organization, development, finding examples, crafting the overall shape and scope of the essay. There is no sense editing and correcting sentences that may not make it into the final version. It makes no sense spell checking, correcting subject-verb agreement, or clarifying every phrase in the first draft. Instead, experienced writers focus on big ticket items such as building coherence or developing a cogent argument.

Only after a reasonably good draft has been achieved should you edit line by line for usage, correctness, and word choice. Correcting and editing are very important functions, but they should occur only when the writing is close to being finished.

GETTING STARTED

Many writers have trouble getting started; they defer the writing, often until too late. Then they do a poor job, excusing themselves because they ran out of time. Sometimes they sit down to write, but run out of steam after a few paragraphs: the essay lacks focus; everything written down seems dumb or obvious; the essay is too general and vague; the room is too hot; the paper is too white; the pencils are too sharp or not sharp enough. Almost all writers, even professional authors who make their living selling what they produce, have trouble at times getting started. John McPhee, who has written over twenty nonfiction books on sports, geology, wilderness, and many other topics, had so much trouble getting started early in his career that he would go into his office and tie himself into his chair with his bathrobe sash to force himself to get words down on paper. Although tying yourself to your chair may be an excellent technique, here are some less drastic strategies that can help.

Keep a reading log. Marginal notation is an excellent strategy, but many students want their notes and commentary collected in one place rather than distributed in the white space of various textbooks. They use a reading log, which is a written record of their interpretations, questions, and concerns. Your instructor may assign you to keep such a log or journal because it has proven to be so helpful to many students. To be successful, a log must be used consistently, at least three entries per week. When an essay is assigned, a reading log can become a great resource, since it is a repository of ideas and personal responses.

A typical entry might look like the following:

"The Horse"

I loved this poem. The horse is described as being so fluid, so full of power. But I don't understand why its hooves flash "blood red" in the last stanza. Why blood? Nor am I clear as to why it is "eternally riderless." After all, it is the "horseman's desire."

Rhythm. There's a kind of klop/klop rhythm to the lines, especially the last line of each stanza. Or am I imagining it?

Is this in some kind of form—like a sonnet? It isn't 14 lines, so that's not right—but I wonder if this is some form I should know (ask instructor) . . .

I'd love to write about the ways that this horse stands for freedom. Am I reading that into the poem? I don't think so. Freedom is mentioned in line 4 and once again in lines 15 and 26. That has to mean something, I think. . . .

As you can see, this is mostly a response that describes the feelings of the writer—as well as her ideas, confusions, and maybe even a possible essay topic. Even if this student does not choose to write about "The Horse," she is engaging in the kind of close and active reading that will help her throughout this course and beyond.

Write a letter, not an essay. Most writers find it much easier to write a personal letter than an essay. The reasons are fairly obvious: they know and like their audience; the letter is informal; they are used to writing in this format; they can usually find a congenial style for themselves; etc. Some students write their essay as a letter addressed to a friend or close relative, explaining why it is important to write about this story or poem, or why they are uncomfortable and then what it is they would like to say about this topic in an essay. Even though the letter is a fiction, writing it can be a great way to make that initial leap into the topic.

Create writing rituals. Like any sustained activity, writing can be hard to start unless it becomes part of another set of actions. In order to wash the car, for example, a person might gather together clean cloths, fill a pail with soapy water, park the car at the curb, and bring out the garden hose. Washing the car becomes an inevitable result of those preparations.

Writing benefits from the same kinds of ritualized activities. One writer gathers her research materials, reads them over several times, cleans off her desk, turns on her computer, and makes some notes about how she will structure her writing for the day. Other writers have other actions they must perform to write: they make a fresh pot of coffee, put on a certain baseball cap, take a dessert out of the freezer and leave it as a reward for a certain amount of writing (of course, the latter ritual can produce both pages and pounds). A friend of mine takes his laptop every weekday morning to a local coffeehouse, finds a quiet table, and writes for two hours; somehow he finds that ritual more productive than coming into the office where he gets distracted by mail, phone calls, and personal visits from me.

Productive writers discover or create rituals that get them in the mood for writing, that lead them toward pen and paper or the computer. Once you have devised such rituals, they can lead you toward writing.

Use index cards or some easily organizable form of note-taking. Many writers keep track of different ideas, quotations, references, and other pertinent information by listing each as a single entry so that they all can be stored and rearranged. Copying quotations and taping them on cards is one handy technique; another is using the computer to create and organize files, which then can be easily printed out during the drafting process. Each card should include not only a quotation or idea but also source information about where it was found.

Write before writing. Professor Donald Murray, a well-known writer and teacher, advocated that students "write before writing"—and this is excellent advice. How do you do that? One of the best strategies is to purchase a small notebook that fits handily in purse or pocket. As you read, think, and research about your assignments, write down ideas, insights, fragments, potential topics, words, quotations, and snatches of relevant conversations. Use the material in that notebook to jump-start your essay.

Try freewriting. Other writers use the technique of freewriting or quick writing to get started. First, of course, they have to do the necessary reading, rereading, and research. Once they possess some knowledge and ideas, they write nonstop for 10 or more minutes, not worrying about spelling, correctness, transitions, or even coherence. The purpose is to get ideas and sentences on paper; once that is done, the writer organizes, cuts and pastes, develops some ideas and discards others. Freewriting is an excellent way to write before writing, especially since it is low stress and produces a lot of words. Some writers begin their writing process this way, and then use successive and more focused freewritings to create later and longer drafts of an essay. Freewriting usually cannot be used to write a final draft, but with practice, this technique can help a writer get quite far along in the drafting process.

The Elements of a Successful Essay

Although there are many different kinds of essays, most of the good ones share certain features.

1. **A main point.** Most successful essays drive toward a central conclusion or major insight. It really does not matter if the essay is an appreciation, a critique, an argument, or a close reading: it collects around a main point like iron filings around a magnet. For example, let's say I am writing about William Stafford's poem "Traveling Through the Dark." After multiple readings, two entries in my reading log, and one freewriting, I begin to glimpse what makes this poem moving and powerful to me. I write a "discovery" draft, toward the end of which I compose the following sentence that defines my main point and thus becomes my thesis:

    "Traveling Through the Dark" is therefore a powerful poem that holds a central contradiction: it is a celebration of life that describes the poet's act of destroying the life of an innocent fawn. I think it reveals the speaker as tender and compassionate, perhaps in contrast to the unnamed, unseen other driver who first hit the doe.

    This is enough of a start for an essay because it is making a significant point that I can now develop over the course of an essay.

Please note: Not every writer knows the main point when first starting an essay. Oftentimes, writers discover their main point during the composing process. Thus good writers do not worry if they begin to write without a main point; if they are completing the assignment and still do not know their main point, however, that usually means real trouble.

2. **Specificity.** A successful essay examines a work of literature by analyzing a particular theme, meaning, image, use of language, argument, or interpretation. Too often, beginning writers attempt general and grandiose themes or generalized statements; they try to write, for example, about "the genius of Edward Abbey" or "That Perfect Poetic Form: The Ballad." Although there is much that can be said about both topics, they are too vague as stated to be covered in a short essay; indeed, they are more appropriate for entire books. An essay needs to examine more specific topics: *What Edward Abbey means by 'the Hoboken mystique' in his essay "Manhattan Twilight, Hoboken Night"* or *A Bittersweet Play of Voices in Langston Hughes's "Ballad of the Landlord."* An essay on either of these more focused topics is more likely to succeed.

3. **Complexity.** Good essays lock in on a complex subject and develop it thoughtfully. In general, this means that an essay must pursue a subject that is not superficially obvious to the most casual reader. To look for insights beyond the obvious, a writer must examine a work of literature for contradictions and paradox. Many literary authors use contradiction and paradox to put a spin on their creations. Theodore Roethke's "My Papa's Waltz," for example, is a poem that can be read simultaneously as a loving tribute and as a cry for help. Which interpretation is correct? Most critics would say that the poem can and should be read both ways at once, that it represents the complex and contradictory feelings a young boy has toward his father.

To achieve complexity, then, writers must be willing to explore seeming contradiction and not be afraid to take risks; they must be willing to explore questions that have no right answer. For example, to return to "Traveling Through the Dark," a student might at first compose the following focus sentence:

"Traveling Through the Dark" is a terrific poem because it is about a man in the wilderness.

This statement, though perhaps true, does not offer a writer any real purchase on a topic worth writing about. It is not very specific and does not offer a complex view of the poem. Why is the poem terrific? What is meant by "terrific"? Is every poem about a man and wilderness terrific? Other than finding a lot of different ways to repeat this main point, there is not much that can be said that would fill more than a page or so of text. This topic does not allow a very complicated or insightful essay to be written. After some struggle, this writer reformulates her main point as follows:

"Traveling Through the Dark" is about literal and figurative darkness, about the darkness of night and the darkness of death.

This statement is more specific, and it offers a thoughtful and complex interpretation of "darkness," an important image in this poem. The statement may need to be refined further, but it offers a useful starting point.

4. **Examples and illustrations.** Almost always, successful essays incorporate many examples, illustrative quotations, and statements that prove the point(s) that the writer is making. In English Studies, most successful essays put forward assertions that then have to be proven and supported. They move from the general to the specific and back again, weaving the particular constantly into the fabric of the overall argument. Clearly one of the most important ways to achieve this end is to use quotations, examples, and particular citations for support. Just as an economist uses statistics, a writer of essays about literature must nail down insights with an appropriate use of specific quotation. Quotes from the primary text (the actual work of literature being studied) or from secondary texts (criticism, history, biography, etc.) illustrate the points being made and persuade readers that the author knows what she is talking about. They also can inspire a writer to dig deeper into the meaning of a work of literature.

5. **Coherence.** All readers have formal expectations when they read. Although different in various cultures, these formal expectations guide readers and help them to understand what the writer is doing. They allow readers to anticipate where the writer is headed, a very important dimension to successful interaction between readers and writers. Typically, in United States higher education, successful essays have a beginning, middle, and end in some formal sense. They exhibit logical transitions between the various parts of the essay. They provide the reader with a sense of wholeness and completion. Typically, a formal essay will:

- articulate a main point
- illustrate and exemplify that main point through several pages that develop and explore the theme of the essay through the use of analysis, appropriate quotation, assertions, insights
- conclude by offering possibilities for additional exploration, returning to the image or argument presented at the beginning of the essay, summarizing and extending what has already been stated, or otherwise creating a sense of completion

6. **Style.** Instructors generally enjoy reading essays that express the voice, personal commitment, and investment of the writer—what we typically call "style." Style cannot be located in any one element; rather, it consists of a writer's individual perspective, phrasing, word choice, sentence construction, creation of paragraphs, organization, even formatting (font, type size, illustrations, spacing, etc.).

One of the most important aspects of style is word and sentence variety. Successful writing keeps readers interested not just because of ideas, examples, and coherence, but also because of language use that pleases, surprises, and delights. Here is an example of a passage that has a lot of repetition and not much sentence variety:

Theodore Roethke's "My Papa's Waltz" is a powerful poem. It is a poem that draws its power from its theme of love and fear. The poem is written from the point of view of a young boy. The title of the poem . . .

This passage is likely to bore a reader because the sentences all have a similar subject-verb structure, use many of the same words, and express little sense of style. It is acceptable to write such sentences in a first draft, but once a writer starts moving toward the final draft, an improved version that achieves much more sentence variation is needed:

A powerful poem, Theodore Roethke's "My Papa's Waltz" expresses the love— and fear—that a young boy feels for his father. As is made clear from the title of the poem . . .

This revised version consolidates the sentences, cuts out the repetition of words ("is," "power," "of"), and expresses more vividly the stylistic personality of the writer. Successful writers create word and sentence variety in order to enhance their style.

Another key aspect to creating a successful style is not to overreach. That is, one of the worst decisions a writer can make is to refer constantly to a thesaurus while writing or to otherwise insert words and phrases that "sound good" because they are long, Latinate, or unfamiliar. A thesaurus is an excellent tool to rediscover a synonym that has slipped out of memory, but you should not use it to replace a familiar word with one you do not know. For example, a writer might state that he has "a great deal of empathy for a character's situation." But with the help of a thesaurus, he might revise that sentence to read that he has "a surfeit of vicarious emotion for a character's locale." Although brimming with excellent words, the second sentence makes little sense and sounds as though its author is living in the wrong century. It is far better to use words you know and can control.

7. **Correctness.** Correctness is easy to define but difficult to achieve: It consists of getting everything right. English instructors in particular urge their students to aim for correctness as part of what they do; after all, they are the educational caretakers of sentence structure, research format, spelling, grammar, and diction. Many writers have a difficult time achieving correctness on their own; they need the help of an outside reader (such as a tutor) to help them see error patterns or other areas where their essay needs to be edited and refashioned into standard academic English.

One of the best ways to get help with correctness is to go to the course instructor, who can provide professional help. Another good strategy is to buy a good handbook and then use it. Most handbooks have sections on grammar, usage, computers, footnoting, and other writing considerations. If a student possesses the motivation and knowledge to use such a handbook, it can be a great resource.

Here is a brief checklist that can help determine if an essay is ready to be handed in.

THE WRITER'S CHECKLIST

____ Essay has a title.

____ Writer's name is included on all the pages.

____ Spelling has been checked.

____ Footnotes are in proper form as determined by instructor.

____ Sentence structure has been checked, especially for fragments, run-on sentences, and comma splices (to obtain definitions of these terms, consult a handbook, or see instructor or Writing Center tutor).

____ Essay has been typed or completed on a word processor.

____ Pages are numbered.

____ Print is double-spaced with one-inch margins around all four borders.

____ Essay has been read carefully by a Writing Center tutor or some other informed and attentive reader.

____ Essay has been read carefully by the author at least one day after "finishing" it.

____ Quotation marks, semicolons, and colons are used properly and consistently (again, consult a handbook, or see instructor or Writing Center tutor).

____ Essay includes sufficient supporting material, such as quotations, examples, and narrative summaries.

A NOTE ABOUT USING COMPUTERS FOR WRITING AND RESEARCH

Another important resource is a computer. Students who know keyboarding and are familiar with word processing programs (such as Word or WordPerfect) have a strong advantage over those students who use less versatile technologies. Word processors allow writers to produce words relatively quickly and then revise them more easily. What with the "copy" and "cut and paste" functions on a computer, basic revision becomes easy, as long as the writer has a good sense of the essay's structure, purpose, and overall organization. A good word processing program can make a lot of editing easy, from spell-checking to formatting headers, footnotes, and page numbers.

Any writer who uses a computer to write an essay must *BACK THAT ESSAY UP CONTINUOUSLY* on a floppy disk during the entire writing process; too many tragedies occur when computers stall or otherwise eat up hours of work. Few events are more frustrating to a writer, especially one under deadline, than to write three or four effective paragraphs and then suddenly find that the computer has stalled or that the word processing program has crashed. The only remedy is to SAVE the writing to a floppy disk continuously during composing.

Once an essay is on disk, a good word processing program can make a lot of work easier, such as:

- adding and deleting sentences, paragraphs, ideas
- moving words and whole passages for improved focus and clarity
- revising passages until they are focused and coherent

- checking spelling (but be careful of misused words that are spelled correctly)
- making final copy look more presentable by formatting an essay in terms of margins, spacing, typeface, and related elements
- printing out rough drafts

Most writers who use computers agree that essays in progress should not just exist in virtual space, on screen. For one thing, a computer screen can hold only a small portion of the essay, even if it is single-spaced, making it hard to see how the different parts of the essay connect with one another. For another, many writers have a difficult time seeing errors or lapses on screen; somehow, the monitor display makes all writing look professionally presentable. Thus most writers find that they have to print out successive drafts of their essays; indeed, some of them revise the essay on paper the old-fashioned way, with pen, pencil, or scissors and paste, and then translate those revisions to the text via computer. Whatever revision method a writer chooses, printing drafts of the essay on paper is almost always a good idea.

Engaging in research on the World Wide Web via computer is much less beneficial, at least as of this writing, but it can be fun and it offers a dazzling array of images, texts, ideas, opinions, and information. To view material on the Web, users have to use a browser, the two chief competitors being Netscape's Navigator and Microsoft's Internet Explorer. The term "browser" is perfect for what these software programs do: They allow users to browse through an extraordinary array of verbal, audio, and visual presentations, from restaurant reviews and music CD catalogs to mapping programs and hobbyist bulletin boards. The materials available through the Web are seemingly infinite, but most of them are aimed toward the casual and commercial user.

The Web is much less useful to the student engaged in specific and narrow research on an author. Few long textual works have been scanned electronically, although there are sites that allow a user to access some classic works of literature, as well as dictionaries, thesauruses, handbooks, and the like. If a reader is looking for scholarly articles, however, the first and best resource is still the library. The library's electronic databases, including the Wilson Periodical Index, the PMLA Index, ERIC, and the Humanities Index, to name just a few, are extraordinarily rich electronic treasure-troves.

Starting one's research with the computer by accessing either library databases, the Internet, or the Web is an excellent way to initiate a project. Using search engines and search commands, a writer can build a useful bibliography of names, articles, and periodicals; the next step is to make use of the library stacks and spend some time reading the scholarship the old-fashioned way, in books, magazines, and journals. The mode of doing scholarship may change, but it is unlikely that the print medium will be replaced by the digitized computer file, if only because it is easier both to read longer texts on paper and to write marginal notes about them. The other great advantage that books have is that they are not battery operated and do not have to be plugged in, a real plus when on the bus or at the beach.

REFERENCE AND CITATION

One of the most frustrating moments in writing a research essay is discovering that you cannot find where a crucial quotation comes from. Almost always, it seems, that quotation is the I-beam on which the entire essay hangs, and no matter where you look, it has totally disappeared from sight. You vaguely remember that it came from an article but that's all, and now you need to know author, title, periodical, year and date of publication, and page number. So you spend an hour searching desperately through books, note cards, legal pads, computer files, bookshelves, desktops, briefcases, and wastebaskets while methodically beating your head against the nearest hard object.

There is no surefire way to prevent this from happening, other than careful researching. Each time you find a quotation or important item of source material, write it down, including essential information such as author, title, and page number; that way, you will almost always be able to find it again if you need to cite it. Thus every note card or piece of paper with a quotation should have a brief reference on it indicating where it came from. In addition, using either a copying machine, a word processor, or the old-fashioned pen and paper method, make sure you have all the necessary bibliographic material that you need to write a "Works Cited" page, something that I will discuss shortly. This means creating a separate file or folder where you keep full bibliographic information on all your sources. Researched essays require students to perform three related actions: to quote sources, to provide appropriate references for those sources, and then to indicate on a Works Cited page where those quotations can be found. Let's take these steps in order.

Quoting Sources

Whenever you are indebted to an author for a specific quotation, specific information, or a particular insight or idea, it is necessary to give that author credit through quotation and citation. This means that you have to know the difference between the knowledge gained through research and "common knowledge," which is what most people are expected to know. For example, if you were writing an essay about Amy Tan and you indicated that she is a popular contemporary author, such a statement would not need to be footnoted since it is common knowledge. If, however, you stated that she was born in 1952 in Oakland, California, and that both her parents are from China, you would need to indicate that you learned that information from, say, *Contemporary Authors*, since it is not general knowledge. Deciding what information you need to reference and what is common knowledge is a judgment call, one that your instructor can help you to determine. Remember, however, that if you are deeply indebted to an author for information or an interpretation, you need to state that in a footnote or a parenthetical citation.

The two primary ways of quoting material are through direct quotation and paraphrase. Direct quotation consists of putting specific words, phrases, or sentences within quotation marks followed by a parenthetical citation. For example:

```
In her autobiographical talk-story "White Tigers," Maxine Hong

Kingston writes: "My American life has been such a disappointment"

(45).
```

Note that the quotation from Kingston's essay/story appears in quotation marks and that it is followed by a parenthetical page citation so that the reader can turn to p. 45 in the cited book and find the quotation. The particular edition from which this quotation is taken will appear on the Works Cited page that appears at the end of every research essay. Whenever directly quoting an author or work, this kind of format is needed.

Indirect quotation is a bit trickier, in that it requires writers to decide whether the passage or idea that they are using is derived from a specific text or is common knowledge. If the idea or information is derived from a specific text, then it needs to be cited. For example:

> Many of us attribute great and even mystical powers to our mothers. This is certainly the case with Maxine Hong Kingston who endows her mother with supernatural powers within a world of ghosts and dark spirits as illustrated in "Shaman" (<u>The Woman Warrior</u> 57-109).

Even though the writer is not quoting directly from the book, this statement is derived from a reading of Kingston's story "Shaman," and therefore a citation is required. Whether the writer paraphrases an interpretation, summarizes the writer's life, or condenses several articles into a two- or three-sentence review, if the idea derives from a book or article, parenthetical citation is required.

Using Footnotes and Parenthetical Citation

Many of the newer word processors have a footnote feature which will organize, number, and format your footnotes. This is a useful aid, especially since footnotes are often hard to format. Unfortunately, many contemporary research essays (at least in English classes) do not require formal footnoting. About the only occasion when students are required to use them is if they need to comment on a statement or source and do not wish to put that comment in the main body of the essay, or if the essay is quoting from just one source and thus it is easier to cite it in a footnote than an entire page at the end of the essay. Check with your instructor to see if footnoting will be required.

The more common form of citation used today is parenthetical; that is, the citation is inserted between two parentheses as demonstrated in the quotations from *The Woman Warrior*. Parenthetical citation is advocated by the Modern Language Association, since it is efficient for both writers and readers. Footnotes drag a reader's eye down to the bottom of the page and break the flow of the text; parenthetical citations maintain the flow of the essay while providing necessary information about sources, page numbers, and research. Moreover, it is much easier for writers to use parenthetical citation since they do not have to worry about numbering their references in sequence and fitting them onto the page.

Parenthetical citation is formatted in slightly different ways, depending on whether the quotation appears within your sentence or as a block that is separated from your own writing. Note the differences below:

One of the more important genres that have recently received
critical and popular attention are the narratives of slaves. One
of the earliest and most influential collections of those
narratives is <u>The Classic Slave Narratives</u> edited by Henry Louis
Gates. Gates makes a good case for why these texts were created:

> The black slave narrators sought to indict both those who
> enslaved them and the metaphysical system drawn upon to justify
> their enslavement. They did so using the most enduring weapon at
> their disposal, the printing press. (ix)

Thus what we can see in the narratives is an account of the life
they led as slaves, an account which by virtue of its own telling
condemns the system of values that supports slavery for the sake
of economic gain.

Note certain key conventions: Because the quotation is two or more sentences long, it gets set off in a block. Because it is set off, it does not need quotation marks around it. The page from which the quotation is taken appears at the very end within parentheses, after any end punctuation.

Here is a different version of the same student essay. In this case, the author is using only a part of the Gates quotation and is thus using internal parenthetical citation. It is called "internal" because the citation occurs within the student's own sentences:

One of the more important genres that have recently received
critical and popular attention are the narratives of slaves. One
of the earliest and most influential collections of those
narratives is <u>The Classic Slave Narratives</u> edited by Henry Louis
Gates. Gates makes a good case for why these texts were created,
since he believes that the authors "sought to indict both those
who enslaved them and the metaphysical system drawn upon to
justify their enslavement" (ix). By that Gates means that what we
can see in the narratives is an account of the life they led as
slaves, an account which by virtue of its own telling condemns the
system of values that supports slavery for the sake of economic
gain.

Note the differences: Here the quotation is short, being less than a full sentence; thus it can be easily integrated into the student author's own paragraph. The page number still is cited, but now—since the citation occurs within the student's own sentence, it must be followed by a period since it ends a sentence.

Here is one more example of internal parenthetical citation:

> In his Introduction to <u>The Classic Slave Narratives</u>, Henry Louis Gates writes that the slaves wanted to be "free and literate" (ix) and that is why they told their powerful and terrible stories. I agree, but only in part: I think we have to be equally aware that the slaves told these stories as a profound way of coming to terms with an experience that virtually defies language.

This internal parenthetical citation immediately follows the quotation it references, and no punctuation marks surround it since they would interfere with the grammar of the sentence.

Internal parenthetical citation provides necessary reference information with as little obstruction as possible. Thus it does not include abbreviations such as "p." for page or "2nd ed." for second edition; all the necessary bibliographic information goes onto the Works Cited page so that the reader can locate your sources. If you are citing a poem, your instructor will likely want your parenthetical reference to include line numbers; if citing a play, you will need to include act, scene, and line so that your instructor can find the quotation easily. Such inclusions follow the rule of thumb for parenthetical references: Include only the information a reader will need to find the quotation easily, neither more nor less.

Providing Full References: The Works Cited Page

Once you have filled in all the appropriate parenthetical citations, it is time to complete the project by writing a "Works Cited" page. Just as its name suggests, the Works Cited page is a bibliographic list that allows the reader to track down the specific books, articles, magazines, films, and other resources you cite in your essay.

No short guide can provide a complete list of proper forms; indeed, the Modern Language Association, to name just one such group, publishes an entire book devoted to forms and formats for references and bibliographies (see Joseph Gibaldi and Walter S. Achtert, *MLA Handbook for Writers of Research Papers*, 4th ed. [New York: MLA, 1995]). What I will include here is a brief listing of the more common forms for books, articles, periodicals, short works of literature, film, TV, and newspapers. These forms should provide proper formatting for most of the research sources that you will use.

Titles on the "Works Cited" page should be arranged alphabetically according to the first initial of the author's or editor's last name. You need only include the texts you actually cite; if for some reason you want to include every book or article that you read while researching your essay, even if you did not use all of them, title your page "List of Works Consulted," but first check with your instructor. You can use the model entries in the pages that follow to put your entries in the correct format. The entries do not correspond to real authors or real books or articles (for the most part), but the form (and explanations) should prove useful.

One last suggestion: even when an essay has proper references and a full "Works Cited" page, it is often helpful to the reader if the author opens with an Acknowledgments page. You can find a model in many scholarly books: the author begins her book by thanking those people who have helped in the formation of ideas, the reading of drafts, the revision of sentences. If your instructor allows it, writing an Acknowledgments page that leads off your essay can help establish the context for the essay that you have produced, and it is an excellent way of saying thank you to those students, staff members, and faculty who have helped you produce it, from conception to final draft.

SAMPLE CITATIONS FOR "WORKS CITED" FROM AN ESSAY ON LITERATURE AND CULTURE

A single book by a single author:

Auteur, Robin. <u>Literature and Culture</u>. New York: Knopf, 1997.

Note the order: author's name (last name first); then the title of the book, underlined, except for the final period. Then the place of publication, followed by a colon (if the city is not well known, include the state abbreviation as well. If the title page lists several cities, give only the first, as in Portsmouth, N.H. or Fargo, N.D.). Then the name of the publisher, followed by a comma. And then the year of publication.

A single book by two or more authors:

Auteur, Robin, and Chang Lee. <u>Literature and Culture</u>. Columbus, Ohio:

    Ohio State UP, 1949.

The first author appears with last name first, then the second author follows with first name first. If the book has more than three authors, give the name of the first author only (last name first) and follow it with "et al." (Latin for "and others"). The phrase "University Press" is abbreviated as "UP" for the sake of efficiency.

A book in several volumes:

Auteur, Robin, et al., eds. <u>Literature and Culture</u>. 4th ed. 3 vols.

    Chicago: Gilead UP, 1998.

Note that "eds." here means "editors" and not "edited by." The abbreviation "eds." always means "editors," whereas "ed." can mean either "editor" or "edited by," depending on its context.

Auteur, Robin. <u>Literature and Culture</u>. 11 vols. Ed. Chang Lee.

    Columbia, S.C.: Wellman, 1955.

You will need to indicate the total number of volumes after the title. If you have used more than one volume, you can indicate which one as follows: (3:30), which means you are referring to page 30 of volume 3. If you have used only one volume of a multivolume work, in your entry in Works Cited indicate the volume number right after the period following the date, i.e., "Wellman, 1955. Vol. 2." You need only include the page reference in your parenthetical citations since readers will know all examples come from volume 2 when they consult the Works Cited page.

A book with a separate title in a set of volumes:

Auteur, Robin. <u>Literature and Culture</u>. Vol. 1 of <u>Encyclopedia of</u>

    <u>Literature and Culture</u>. New York: Balloon, 1994.

Auteur, Robin. <u>Literature and Culture</u>. Ed. Chang Lee. Vol. 113 of <u>The</u>

    <u>Literature and Culture Reader</u>. Princeton: Princeton UP, 1988.

A revised edition of a book:

Auteur, Robin. <u>Literature and Culture</u>. Rev. ed. Hamburg, Germany:

    Berlin UP, 1974.

Auteur, Robin. <u>Literature and Culture</u>. Ed. Chang Lee. 5th ed. Norfolk:

    Harcourt, 1997.

A reprint of an earlier edition:

Auteur, Robin. <u>Literature and Culture</u>. 1911. Ellis, Iowa: Central UP,

    1993.

Note that the author is citing the original date (1911) but indicates that the writer is using the Iowa Central University Press reprint published in 1993.

An edited book other than an anthology:

Auteur, Robin. <u>Literature and Culture</u>. Ed. Chang Lee. 4 vols.

    Cambridge, MA: Harvard UP, 1969.

An anthology:

<u>Literature and Culture</u>. Ed. Robin Auteur. 12 vols. Monrovia, La.:

    Literature and Culture Books, 1918.

Or:

Auteur, Robin, ed. <u>Literature and Culture</u>. 12 vols. Monrovia, La.:

    Literature and Culture Books, 1918.

Note that you have two choices: You can list it either by title or by editor.

A work by one author in a multivolume anthology:

Auteur, Robin. "Critical Studies." Literature and Culture. Ed. Chang

    Lee. 5th ed. 3 vols. New York: Farrar, 1997. 3:145-98.

This entry indicates that you are citing Auteur's essay, entitled "Critical Studies," which appears in volume 3 of a five-volume anthology entitled *Literature and Culture,* edited by Chang Lee. Note that the page numbers of Auteur's complete essay are cited.

A work in an anthology that includes a number of authors:

Auteur, Robin. "Critical Studies." Literature and Culture. Ed. Chang

    Lee. Fargo, N.D.: Houghton, 1888. 243-76.

Start by listing the author and the title of the work you are citing, not the title of the anthology or the name of the editor. The entry ends by citing the pages of the selection you are citing. Note that the title of the short work you are citing is in quotation marks; if it is a long work (book length), the title is underlined. If the work is translated, after the period that follows the title, write "Trans." and give the name of the translator, followed by a period and then the name of the anthology.

Citing other works in the same anthology:

Auteur, Robin. Literature and Culture. Lee 301-46.

To avoid repetition, under each author's name (in the appropriate alphabetical order), list the author, the title of the work, then a period, one space, and the name of the editor of the anthology, followed by the page numbers for the selection.

Two or more works by the same author:

Auteur, Robin. Critical Studies. Boulder, Colo.: U of Harriman P,

    1948.

---. Literature and Culture. Seattle: Jacob H. Library, 1955.

Note that the works are given in alphabetical order on the Works Cited page, so that *Critical Studies* comes before *Literature and Culture.* In the second listing, the author's name is represented by three dashes followed by a period. If the author is the translator or editor of a volume, the three dashes are followed by a comma, then a space, then the appropriate abbreviation (trans. or ed.), then (one space after the period) the title.

The Bible:

The HarperCollins Study Bible. Wayne A. Meeks, Gen. ed. New York:

    HarperCollins, 1989.

Note: If using the King James version, do not list the Bible in your Works Cited page, since it is familiar and available. In your essay, cite chapter and verse parenthetically as follows: (Isaiah 52.7-12 or Gen. 19.1-11).

A translated book:

```
Auteur, Robin. Literature and Culture. Trans. Chang Lee. New York:

    Culture Studies Press, 1990.
```

Note that "Trans." can mean "translated by" (just as "ed." can mean "edited by"). It is also the abbreviation for "translator."

An introduction, foreword, afterword, or other editorial apparatus:

```
Auteur, Robin. Introduction. Literature and Culture. By Chang Lee. New

    York: Epicurean, 1990, vii-x.
```

Use this form if you are specifically referring to the Introduction, Foreword, Afterword, etc. Otherwise, list the work under the name of the book's author. Words such as *Preface, Introduction, Afterword,* and *Conclusion* are capitalized in the entry but are neither enclosed within quotation marks nor underlined.

A book review:

```
Auteur, Robin. Rev. of Literature and Culture. Ed. Chang Lee. Critical

    Studies 104 (1991): 1-48.
```

This is a citation for a review of a book entitled *Literature and Culture.* The review, which does not have a title, was published in a journal entitled *Critical Studies.*

```
Auteur, Robin. "One Writer's View." Rev. of Literature and Culture.

    Ed. Chang Lee. Critical Studies 104 (1991): 1-48.
```

This is a citation for a review which has a title.

```
"One Writer's View." Rev. of Literature and Culture. Ed. Chang Lee.

    Critical Studies 104 (1991): 1-48.
```

This is an anonymous review of *Literature and Culture.* Place it on your "Works Cited" page under the first word of the review's title; if the review lacks a title, begin your entry with "Rev. of" and then alphabetize it under the title of the work being reviewed.

An encyclopedia:

```
Auteur, Robin. "Literature and Culture." Encyclopaedia Britannica. 1984

    ed.
```

This is how you cite a signed article; note that the article is from the 1984 edition of the *Encyclopaedia.*

"Literature and Culture." <u>Encyclopaedia Britannica</u>. 1984 ed.

This is how you would cite the same article if it were unsigned.

An article in a scholarly journal that numbers its pages consecutively from one issue to the other through the year:

Auteur, Robin. "Literature and Culture." <u>Critical Studies</u> 33 (1992):

   231-59.

Auteur's article appeared in the journal, *Critical Studies*, in 1992; the volume number was 33 and it appeared on pages 231 through 259. Even though each of the four issues of *Critical Studies* published in 1992 has a separate number, you do not need to indicate the issue number since the pages are numbered continuously throughout the year.

An article in a scholarly journal that begins each issue during the year with page one:

Auteur, Robin. "Literature and Culture." <u>Critical Studies</u> 12.2 (1993):

   9-21.

Note that you now must provide the volume number followed by a period and then the issue number, with no spaces in between.

An article in a weekly, biweekly, or monthly publication:

Auteur, Robin. "Literature and Culture." <u>Critical Studies</u> 30 Mar. 1945:

   1-12.

If you are citing from a very well known weekly, such as *Newsweek* or *The New Yorker*, you can omit the volume and issue numbers.

An article in a newspaper:

Auteur, Robin. "Literature and Culture." <u>Critical Studies Times</u> 17 Mar.

   1947, sec. 6: 9+.

Because newspapers often have a number of sections, you should include a section number before the page number so that your reader can find the article easily. Auteur's article begins on page 9 of section 6 and continues on to a later page.

A personal interview:

Lee, Chang. Personal interview. 26 Apr. 1974.

Auteur, Robin. Telephone interview. 14 Feb. 1983.

Note that the interviews are *with* Chang Lee and Robin Auteur, not *by* Chang Lee or Robin Auteur.

A lecture:

Lee, Chang. "Literature and Culture." University of Wisconsin-

    Milwaukee. 31 Oct. 1995.

A television or radio program:

Literature and Culture. Public Television, Charlotte, N.C. 3 Feb. 1996.

A film or videotape:

Literature and Culture. Dir. Chang Lee. MGM, 1948.

A recording:

Auteur, Robin. "Literature and Culture." Chang Lee Reads Personal

    Favorites from Around the World. Harmony, HAR 4853C, 1988.

A performance:

Literature. By Chang Lee. Dir. Robin Auteur. Urban Theatre of the

    Arts, Urban, Wisconsin. 4 July 1912.

A file from the World Wide Web:

Auteur, Robin. "Literature and Culture." Critical Studies.

    http://www.litcult.wor .vvv.ecp.tlc/text/rmudts/ittip.html (18 May

    1995).

Note that the citation includes the author's name (if available), the name of the article, the name (underlined) of the entire text from which the article was taken (if available), the URL (Uniform Resource Locator), followed immediately by the date that you visited the site.

At this point, you may have decided that you have had enough of citations. If the particular form you are looking for does not appear in this list, consult the *MLA Handbook for Writers of Research Papers* or some other more extensive reference book. The basic principle of citation is that you should be absolutely clear about essential research information in the most concise format possible.

FINAL WORDS

Much more could be said about writing essays about literature and culture, but perhaps the most important goal for such essays is that they provide a sense of satisfaction to both the writer and the reader. Writing an essay invites analysis, research, discovery, and satisfaction. The exciting and provocative reading selections in this book create many possible topics to engage writers on the voyage ahead.

CREDITS

FOR FURTHER
STUDY

The most useful bibliography of books and other materials on class is located on the web site of the Center for Working-Class Studies at Youngstown State University. The URL is <http://www.as.ysu.edu/~cwcs/BIB.html>. Within that site, see particularly Eric Schocket's bibliography of working-class novels and stories. The Center for Working-Class Studies site also contains a list of museums dealing with labor and working-class issues; the URL is <http://www.as.ysu.edu/~cwcs/museums .html>. For films in which the issue of class is prominent, see the list compiled by Bottom Dog Press; the URL is <http://members.aol.com/lsmithdog/bottomdog/ CHRONFIL.htm>.

The following are books and articles we have found useful and interesting in the study of class issues. This list does *not* include the books from which we have reprinted sections in this collection, like Carolyn Steedman's *Landscapes for a Good Woman* or Raymond Williams's *Culture and Society*, nor does it include works by Karl Marx, much of whose writing is important to the study of class issues.

Arnesen, Eric, Julie Greene, and Bruce Laurie, Eds. *Labor Histories: Class, Politics, and the Working Class Experience.* Urbana: U of Illinois P, 1998.

Aronowitz, Stanley. *Working Class Hero.* New York: Pilgrim P, 1983.

Aronowitz, Stanley. *False Promises: The Shaping of American Working Class Consciousness,* 2nd ed. Durham, NC: London: Duke UP, 1992 (1973).

Berberoglu, Berch. *The Legacy of Empire: Economic Decline and Class Polarization in the United States.* New York: Praeger, 1992.

Bluestone, Barry, and Bennett Harrison. *The De-Industrialization of America.* New York: Basic Books, 1982.

Booker, M. Keith. *Film and the American Left: a Research Guide.* Westport, CT: Greenwood Press, 1999.

Braverman, Harry. *Labor and Monopoly Capital: The Degradation of Labor in the Twentieth Century.* New York: Monthly Review Press, 1974.

Brecher, Jeremy. *Strike!* Boston: South End Press, 1998.

Brody, David. *Steelworkers in America: The Nonunion Era.* Cambridge: Harvard U P, 1960.

Bromell, Nicholas Knowles. *By the Sweat of the Brow: Literature and Labor in Antebellum America.* Chicago: U of Chicago P, 1993.

Buhle, Paul. *From the Knights of Labor to the New World Order: Essays on Labor and Culture.* New York: Garland, 1997.

Coiner, Constance. *Better Red: the Writing and Resistance of Tillie Olsen and Meridel Le Sueur.* New York: Oxford U P, 1995.

Coles, Nicholas and Peter Oresick. *For a Living: The Poetry of Work.* Urbana: University of Illinois Press, 1995.

Crompton, Rosemary. *Class and Stratification: an Introduction to Current Debates,* 2nd ed. Cambridge, U.K.: Polity Press; Malden, MA: Blackwell, 1998.

DeMott, Benjamin. *The Imperial Middle: Why Americans Can't Think Straight About Class.* New York: William Morrow and Co., 1990.

Dews, C.L. Barney and Carolyn Leste Law, eds. *This Fine Place So Far from Home: Voices of Academics from The Working Class.* Philadelphia: Temple University Press, 1995.

Ehrenreich, Barbara. *Fear of Falling: The Inner Life of the Middle Class.* New York: Harper Collins, 1989.

Eisler, Benita. *Class Act: America's Last Dirty Secret.* New York: Franklin Watts, 1983.

Ellis, Jacqueline. *Silent Witnesses: Representations of Working-class Women in the United States.* Bowling Green, OH: Bowling Green State University Popular Press, 1998.

Engels, Friedrich. *The Condition of the Working Class in England,* edited with an introduction and notes by David McLellan. Oxford; New York: Oxford University Press, 1999.

Finn, Patrick J. *Literacy with an Attitude : Educating Working-class Children in Their Own Self-interest.* Albany: State University of New York Press, 1999.

Foley, Barbara. *Radical Representations: Politics and Form in U.S. Proletarian Fiction, 1929-1941.* Durham: Duke UP, 1993.

Foner, Philip S. and Ronald L. Lewis, eds. *The Black Worker: a Documentary History from Colonial Times to the Present, 8 vols.* Philadelphia: Temple U P, 1978-1984.

Foner, Philip S. *History of the Labor Movement in the United States.* 10 vols. New York: International Publishers, 1947-1982.

Fowke, Edith and Joe Glazer, eds. *Songs of Work and Protest.* New York: Dover [1960], 1973.

Giddens, Anthony and David Held. *Classes, Power, and Conflict: Classical and Contemporary Debates.* Berkeley: U of California P, 1982.

Gutman, Herbert G. *Power and Culture: Essays on the American Working Class.* Ira Berlin, ed. New York: Pantheon Books, 1987.

Halker, Clark D. *For Democracy, Workers, and God: Labor Song-poems and Labor Protest, 1865-95.* Urbana: U of Illinois P, 1991.

Hall, John R., ed. *Reworking Class.* Ithaca, NY: Cornell U P, 1997.

Hapke, Laura. *Tales of the Working Girl: Wage-earning Women in American Literature, 1890-1925.* New York: Twayne Publishers, 1992.

Herreshoff, David Sprague. *Labor into Art : the Theme of Work in Nineteenth-century American Literature.* Detroit, MI: Wayne State U P, 1991.

Hille, Waldemar, ed. *The People's Song Book.* New York: Oak Publications, 1948.

Hobsbawm, Eric. *Workers.* New York: Pantheon Books, 1984.

Jackman, Mary R. and Robert W. Jackman. *Class Awareness in the United States.* Berkeley: U of California P, 1983.

Jones, Jacqueline. *Labor of Love, Labor of Sorrow: Black Women Workers and the Family from Slavery to the Present.* New York: Vintage Books, 1985.

Joyce, Patrick, ed. *Class.* Oxford; New York: Oxford U.P., 1995.

Karen, David. "The Politics of Class, Race, and Gender: Access to Higher Education in the United States, 1960-1986." *American Journal of Education* (February 1991): 208-233.

Katznelson, Ira and Margaret Weir. *Schooling for All: Class, Race, and the Decline of the Democratic Ideal.* New York: Basic Books, 1985.

Katznelson, Ira and Artistide R. Zolberg, eds. *Working-Class Formation: Nineteenth-Century Patterns in Western Europe and the United States.* Princeton: Princeton University Press, 1986.

Kelley, Robin D.G. *Race Rebels: Culture, Politics, and the Black Working Class.* New York: Free Press, 1994.

Kessler-Harris, Alice. *Out To Work: A History of Wage Earning Women in the United States.* New York: Oxford University Press, 1982.

Kloby, Jerry. "The Growing Divide: Class Polarization in the 1980's." *Monthly Review* 4 (September 1987): 1-3.

Lauter, Paul, "Working-Class Women's Literature—An Introduction to Study." *Women in Print, I,* J. Hartman and E. Messer-Davidow, eds. New York: Modern Language Association, 1982. Reprinted in *Politics of Education: Essays from **Radical Teacher**.* Albany: SUNY Press, 1990, pp. 110-139.

Lens, Sydney. *The Labor Wars: From the Molly Maguires to the Sitdown Strikes.* New York: Anchor Books, 1973.

Linkon, Sherry. *Teaching Working Class.* Amherst: U of Massachusetts P, 1999.

McNall, Scott G., Rhonda F. Levine, and Rick Fantasia, eds. *Bringing Class Back In: Contemporary and Historical Perspectives.* Boulder, Colorado: Westview Press, 1991.

Nekola, Charlotte and Paula Rabinowitz, eds. *Writing Red: An Anthology of American Women Writers, 1930-1940.* New York: Feminist Press at the City U of New York, 1987.

Nelson, Cary. *Repression and Recovery: Modern American Poetry and the Politics of Cultural Memory, 1910-1945.* Madison: U of Wisconsin P, 1989.

Newman, Katherine S. *Falling from Grace: The Experience of Downward Mobility in the American Middle Class.* New York: Free Press, 1988.

Olsen, Tillie. *Silences.* New York: Delacorte Press/Seymour Lawrence, 1978

Oresick, Peter and Nicholas Coles, eds. *Working Classics: Poems on Industrial Life.* Urbana: U of Illinois P, 1990.

Penelope, Julia, ed. *Out Of the Class Closet: Lesbians Speak.* Freedom, CA: The Crossing Press, 1994.

Rosengarten, Theodore. *All God's Dangers; The Life of Nate Shaw.* New York: Knopf, 1975.

Ross, Steven J. *Working-Class Hollywood: Silent Film and the Shaping of Class in America.* Princeton, N.J.: Princeton U P, 1998.

Rubin, Lilian B. *Worlds of Pain: Life in the Working Class Family.* New York: Basic Books, 1976.

Rytina, Joan H., William H. Form, and John Pease. "Income and Stratification Ideology: Beliefs about the American Opportunity Structure." *American Journal of Sociology*, 75 (January 1970): 702–716.

Sayles, John. *Thinking in Pictures: The Making of the Movie "Matewan."* New York: Houghton Mifflin, 1987.

Sennett, Richard. *The Corrosion of Character: the Personal Consequences of Work in the New Capitalism.* New York: W.W. Norton, 1998.

Sennett, Richard and Jonathan Cobb. *The Hidden Injuries of Class.* New York: Knopf/Vintage Books, 1972.

Sinclair, Upton, ed. *The Cry for Justice; an Anthology of the Literature of Social Protest.* New ed., rev. and ed. with the cooperation of Edward Sagarin and Albert Teichner. New York, L. Stuart [1915], 1963.

Terkel, Studs. *Working: People Talk about What They Do All Day and How They Feel about What They Do.* New York: Pantheon Books, 1972.

Vanneman, Reeve and Lynn Weber Cannon. *The American Perception of Class.* Philadelphia: Temple U P, 1987.

Wolf, Robert, ed. *An American Mosaic: Prose and Poetry by Everyday Folk.* Illustrated by Bonnie Koloc. New York: Oxford U P, 1999.

Wood, Ellen Meiksins. *The Retreat from Class: a New "True" Socialism.* London: Verso, 1986.

Wright, Erik Olin. *Classes.* London: Verso, 1985.

Wright, Erik Olin. *Class Counts: Comparative Studies in Class Analysis.* Cambridge; New York: Cambridge U P, 1997.

Zandy, Janet, ed. *Calling Home: Working-Class Women's Writings: An Anthology.* New Brunswick; London: Rutgers UP, 1990.

Zandy, Janet, ed. *Liberating Memory: Our Work and Our Working-Class Consciousness.* New Brunswick; London: Rutgers UP, 1994.

Zaniello, Tom. *Working Stiffs, Union Maids, Reds, and Riffraff: An Organized Guide to Films About Labor.* Ithaca,NY: Cornell U P, 1996.

Index of Authors and Titles